EU

CEFTA

TAFTA

SAPTA

SADC

ATPA

MERCOSUR

OPERATIONS MANAGEMENT

Focusing on Quality and Competitiveness

Roberta S. Russell

Professor
Virginia Polytechnic Institute and State University

Bernard W. Taylor III

R. B. Pamplin Professor
Virginia Polytechnic Institute and State University

Prentice Hall, Inc.
Upper Saddle River, New Jersey 07458

Library of Congress Cataloging in Publication Data

Russell, Roberta S.
     Operations management : focusing on quality and competitiveness /
Roberta S. Russell, Bernard W. Taylor III. —2nd ed.
        p. cm.
        Rev. ed. of: Production and operations management. c1995.
        Includes bibliographical references and index.
        ISBN 0-13-849936-5
        1. Production management.   2. Quality control.   I. Taylor, Bernard W.
II. Russell, Roberta S.   Production and operations management.
TS155.R755   1998
658.5—DC21   97-650
                                                        CIP
                                                        Rev.

Acquisitions Editor: Tom Tucker
Development Editor: Michael Elia
Assistant Editor: Audrey Regan
Marketing Manager: Patrick Lynch
Editor-in-Chief: Natalie Anderson
Director of Development: Steve Deitmer
Production Editor: Susan Rifkin
Production Coordinator: Cindy Spreder
Managing Editor: Katherine Evancie
Senior Manufacturing Supervisor: Paul Smolenski
Manufacturing Manager: Vincent Scelta
Senior Designer: Suzanne Behnke
Interior Design: Gerri Davis
Cover Design: Suzanne Behnke
Cover Art: Boris Lyubner/SIS
Composition/Interior Art: University Graphics

©1998, 1995 by Prentice Hall, Inc.
A Simon & Schuster Company
Upper Saddle River, N.J. 07458

Printed in the United States of America
10   9   8   7   6   5   4   3   2   1

ISBN 0-13-849936-5

Prentice Hall International (UK) Limited, London
Prentice Hall of Australia Pty. Limited, Sydney
Prentice Hall of Canada Inc., Toronto
Prentice Hall Hispanoamericana, S.A., Mexico
Prentice Hall of India Private Limited, New Delhi
Prentice Hall of Japan, Inc., Tokyo
Simon & Schuster Asia Pte. Ltd., Singapore
Editora Prentice Hall do Brasil, Ltda., Rio de Janeiro

To my family
Tom, Travis, and Amy

To my parents
Jean V. Taylor and Bernard W. Taylor, Jr.
with love and appreciation.

ABOUT THE AUTHORS

Bernard Taylor and Roberta Russell

Bernard W. Taylor, III, is the R. B. Pamplin Professor of Management Science and Head of the Department of Management Science and Information Technology in the Pamplin College of Business at Virginia Polytechnic Institute and State University. He received the Ph.D. and M.B.A. from the University of Georgia and B.I.E. from the Georgia Institute of Technology. He is the author of the book *Introduction to Management Science* (5th ed.) and co-author of *Management Science* (4th ed.), both published by Prentice-Hall. Dr. Taylor has published over eighty articles in such journals as *Operations Research, Management Science, Decision Sciences, IIE Transactions, Journal of the Operational Research Society, Computers and Operations Research, Omega,* and the *International Journal of Production Research* among others. His paper in *Decision Sciences* (with P. Y. Huang and L. P. Rees) on the Japanese kanban production system received the Stanley T. Hardy Award for its contribution to the field of production and operations management. He has served as President of the Decision Sciences Institute (DSI) as well as Associate Program Chair, Council Member, Vice President, Treasurer, and as the Editor of *Decision Line,* the newsletter of DSI. He is a Fellow of DSI and a recipient of their Distinguished Service Award. He is a former President, Vice-President, and Program Chair of the Southeast Decision Sciences Institute and a recipient of their Distinguished Service Award. He teaches management science and production and operations management courses at both the undergraduate and graduate level.

He has received the University Certificate of Teaching Excellence on four occasions, the R. B. Pamplin College of Business Certificate of Teaching Excellence Award, and the R. B. Pamplin College of Business Ph.D. Teaching Excellence Award at Virginia Tech.

Roberta S. Russell is Professor of Management Science and Information Technology. She received the Ph.D. from Virginia Polytechnic Institute and State University, an M.B.A. from Old Dominion University, and a B.S. degree from Virginia Polytechnic Institute and State University. Dr. Russell's primary research and teaching interests are in the areas of production and operations management, service operations management, simulation, and quality. She has published in *Decision Sciences, IIE Transactions, The International Journal of Production Research, Material Flow, Business Horizons, Computers, Environment and Urban Systems, Computers and Operations Research* and others. She is also co-author of the Prentice-Hall text, *Service Operations Management.* Dr. Russell is a member of DSI, TIMS, ASQC, and IIE, and a certified fellow of APICS. She is Past President of the Southwest Virginia Chapter of APICS and has held numerous offices in Southeast DSI. She has received the R. B. Pamplin College of Business Certificate of Teaching Excellence, the University Certificate of Teaching Excellence, and the MBA Association's Outstanding Professor Award. She is also listed in Outstanding Young Women of America and is a recipient of the Virginia Tech Outstanding Young Alumna Award.

Brief Contents

Contents

9 *Supply Chain Management*   *369*

9 SUPPLEMENT
Operational Decision-Making Tools: The Transportation Method   *415*

PART III

OPERATING PRODUCTIVE SYSTEMS   435

10 Forecasting   437

11 Capacity Planning and Aggregate Production Planning   499

11 SUPPLEMENT
Operational Decision-Making Tools: Linear Programming   535

Preface

We originally embarked on this project to create a textbook in operations management with several objectives in mind. First, we wanted the text to be eminently readable for the student—clear, concise, and organized. We also wanted to include lots of features and examples to make the topics interesting. Next, we wanted the concepts we describe to be logical and easy to understand. We wanted to make efficient use of the English language to avoid drowning straightforward topics in a sea of verbiage or a blizzard of mathematical notation. And most important, we wanted the student to feel excited about operations management because we live in an exciting time with many new, unique, and interesting changes occurring in manufacturing and service operations around the world.

We like to think that we accomplished these objectives to a large degree in our first edition, but there is always room for improvement in a project like this, so much of this second edition focuses on how to better achieve these objectives and achieve new ones.

MAJOR TEXT THEMES

We have sought to make our textbook contemporary and comprehensive. There are many new and important changes taking place in operations management today, and we want to make sure that they are conspicuously integrated with the more traditional topics in OM. That's why we focus a lot of our attention on *quality* and *competitiveness*, and their implications for *strategy*, as consistent themes throughout the text. We do not believe that quality is simply a recent trend, but rather a pervasive philosophy that impacts on and influences all the other topics and functions in operations management. Quality has become an especially important part of a company's overall strategy to compete in today's global market. For many companies, their total quality management program (TQM) is the engine that drives their strategic plan.

Operations managers make decisions in functional areas such as product and service design, facility layout and location, planning and scheduling, and supply chain management based on how effectively these decisions fit together in a strategic design to achieve the firm's goals. The chapters in this text are organized around functional topics, some new and some traditional. However, in each case we attempt to show how these topics are connected to the common themes of quality and competitiveness, and then are connected to each other in terms of strategy.

Quality

We cover our two primary topics related to quality, Quality Management and Statistical Quality Control, in Chapters 3 and 4, respectively. We put these topics together because in most companies they are so closely interrelated in an overall total quality management program that it is hard to consider one separate from the other. We introduce them early in the text so that the student can see how the functional topics in subsequent chapters are affected by, and affect, quality management. For example, in Chapter 5 on Product and Service Design our discussion focuses on Improving the Design Process through well-recognized TQM processes, and, in Chapter 10 on Forecasting we discuss how forecasting is related to TQM in a company's strategic design process.

Competitiveness

Although most firms express their goals in terms of customer satisfaction or level of quality, their underlying objective is to beat out their competitors. One way in which companies can gain a competitive edge is by deploying the basic functions of operations management in a more effective manner than their rivals. In each chapter we give numerous examples of how companies deploy specific operations functions in a way that has provided them with a competitive edge and made them successful. We begin our discussion of competitiveness in Chapter 1 and continue throughout the text with "Competitive Edge" boxes describing how successful companies have gained a competitive edge through operations.

Strategy

A company's battle plan for achieving a competitive edge is its strategy. The success of a strategic plan is determined by how well a company coordinates all of its internal functions, including operations, and brings them to bear on its goals. Throughout the text we try to show how the functions and processes described in each chapter fit into a company's strategic plan. The importance of strategy in operations management is emphasized by our creation of a new Chapter 2—Operations Strategy—and its placement up front in the text. In each subsequent chapter we emphasize the need for considering the overall strategic implications of particular operating decisions. For example, in Chapter 3 on Quality Management we discuss the "strategic implications of TQM," in Chapter 9 on Supply Chain Management we emphasize that "supply chain design is a strategic issue," and in Chapter 11 we discuss "capacity planning as a long-term strategic decision."

Services and Manufacturing

We have attempted to strike a balance between manufacturing and service operations in our text. Traditionally operations management was thought of almost exclusively in a manufacturing context, and OM texts frequently reflect this bias. However, in the United States and other highly industrialized nations, there has been a perceptible shift in the economy toward service industries and away from manufacturing. Thus, managing service operations has become equally as important as managing manufacturing operations. In many cases, operations management techniques and processes are indistinguishable between service and manufacturing. However, in many other instances, service operations present unique situations and problems that require focused attention and unique solutions. We have tried to reflect the uniqueness of service operations in our text by providing numerous examples that address service situations, and by providing focused discussions on service operations when there is a clear distinction between operations in a service environment and in a manufacturing environment. For example, in Chapter 3 on Quality Management we specifically address the unique conditions of "TQM in service companies"; in Chapter 5 on Product and Service Design; we emphasize the differences in design considerations between manufacturing and services; and in Chapter 11, we discuss "aggregate planning in services."

Quantitative versus Qualitative Processes

We have also attempted to strike a balance between the quantitative aspects of operations management and the qualitative (or behavioral) aspects. Too often in the past, OM texts have presented themselves as a loose compilation of different quantitative techniques applied to various functional topics. In the contemporary world of operations management, the quantitative and technological aspects are probably more important than ever. However, the ability to manage people and resources effectively, to motivate, organize, control, evaluate, and particularly to adapt to change, have become critical to competing in today's international markets. Thus, throughout this text we seek to explain and demonstrate how the successful operations manager manages, and when quantitative techniques and technology are applicable, how they are used to help manage and make decisions.

LEARNING FEATURES

We have introduced many features in our text which we hope will help sustain and accelerate the student's learning of the material. Some of these features remain from the first edition while others are new to this edition. In the following sections we summarize the various learning features that appear in the text.

Text Organization

One of our most important objectives is to have a well-organized text that flows smoothly, follows a logical progression of topics, and places the different functions of operations management in their proper perspectives. We have organized this new edition of our text into three groupings. The first four chapters focus on *The Strategy of Productive Systems*. These chapters seek to place operations management in a proper perspective and emphasize the importance of strategy and quality for competing in today's highly competitive global marketplace. Chapters 5 through 10 comprise a group we refer to as *Designing Productive Systems*, while Chapters 11 through 17 focus on *Operating Productive Systems*. Thus a logical flow is created from strategically establishing the operating environment and defining a quality program, to designing the operations function to meet the company's strategic goals, and finally to producing the product or service that will achieve the strategic goals and enable a company to compete in a global market.

New Chapters in This Edition

In an effort to keep our book current and abreast of contemporary trends in operations management we have altered several chapters, some to the extent that they appear for the first time in this edition. Chapter 1 contains more information on globalization and competitiveness. Chapter 2 on Operations Strategy is new and emphasizes the importance of making strategic choices consistent with operational capabilities, as well as looking at the strategic issues associated with individual topics in OM. The coverage of policy deployment has been increased and topics such as core competencies, core rigidities, and competency-based strategies have been added. Chapter 5 on Product and Service Design has been streamlined with tightened discussions of Quality Function Deployment and Taguchi methods of design. Chapter 6 on Process Planning and Technology Decisions has been enhanced with new sections on process re-engineering and information technology. Chapter 8 provides a broader, more comprehensive view of human resource management within the operations function than the chapter on job design from the previous edition. Chapter 9 on Supply Chain Management attempts to pull together the related components of this increasingly important topic by looking at its strategic design, while retaining some of the topics from the previous edition on location and transportation. In Chapter 11 we expanded coverage of capacity planning to include strategies for capacity expansion and for determining the best over-all level of productive resources for a firm.

"The Competitive Edge" Application Boxes

These boxes are located in every chapter in the text. They describe how a company, organization, or agency uses the particular management technique or function being discussed in the chapter to compete in a global environment. There are more than 60 of these boxes throughout the text and they encompass a broad range of service and manufacturing operations, foreign and domestic.

Chapter Introductory Applications

Each chapter begins with a description relating the subject of the chapter to an actual application in a company. These applications are provided first to give the reader a realistic perspective of the topic before embarking on its discussion.

Photos

The text includes a variety of color photographs that enhance and complement the presentation of the written textual material. These photos accompany the introductory application that starts off each chapter, as well as various other points of interest within the body of the chapters. Each photo is accompanied by an extensive descriptive caption that complements the text material.

Operational Decision-Making Tools Supplements

The text includes four quantitative chapter supplements that address some of the more traditional and mathematically rigorous quantitative techniques used in operations management: *decision analysis, linear programming, transportation solution methods,* and *simulation.* These topics have been segregated from the normal chapters because in many instances students already will have studied them in a separate quantitative methods course. In addition, their study can be time-consuming and often the instructor will prefer not to take time from the coverage of other important OM topics.

Marginal Notes

Notes that are included in the margins serve the same basic function as notes that students themselves might write in the margin. They highlight certain topics to make it easier for the student to locate them, they summarize topics and important points, and they provide brief definitions of key terms and concepts.

Examples

Examples are liberally inserted throughout the text, primarily to demonstrate quantitative techniques and to make them easier to understand. The examples illustrate how the results of the quantitative technique may be used to help the manager make decisions. The examples are organized into a problem statement and solution format. We also make frequent use of real world applications, often citing the experiences of companies as they relate to individual topics.

POM for Windows Computer Software

This text features illustrations from a computer software package, *POM for Windows*. A disk is packaged with each *instructor's* complimentary copy of this text. *POM for Windows* is very user-friendly software that solves problems in all the decision-making areas of operations management. It is easy to understand and use, requiring virtually no preliminary instruction except for the "help" screens that can be accessed directly from the program. *POM for Windows* is used frequently in the text to show how to solve example problems on the computer. This software can be packaged—at a reasonable additional cost to students—with each copy of the text. If you wish to order this software with the text, please be sure to order ISBN **0-13-667965-X,** as this will ensure that you get the software at a discounted price. For further details, contact your Prentice Hall sales representative or phone Prentice Hall at 1-800-526-0485.

Excel Spreadsheets

Although *POM for Windows* can be used to solve almost any quantitative problem in the text, we also solve many of the quantitative examples in the text with the Microsoft Excel spreadsheet program. Spreadsheets have become an increasingly popular and convenient means for solving operational problems. However, while we generally outline the basic steps for setting up a spreadsheet and solving a problem with Excel, some basic, fundamental knowledge of the Excel program is usually required.

Web Sites and Home Page

Throughout the text **WWW** icons in the margins (as shown at right) identify companies and topics that can be accessed on the internet through our text home page located at *http://www.prenhall.com/russell*. If you are interested in accessing one of the highlighted web sites simply go to the appropriate text chapter on our home page and scroll down to the web site identified by the icon in the margin of the text and click on it. In addition to the web site links provided for each chapter, students will be able to access Internet exercises, virtual factory tours, chapter lectures, interactive chapter quizzes, and sample student projects. Faculty members will be able to access sample course outlines, annotated lecture slides, alternate examples, projects and special assignments, and in-depth background material not included in the text.

www.prenhall.com/russell

Lands' End Boxes and Videos

In ten of the chapters we illustrate various subjects and topics with brief descriptions of operations at Lands' End, the national catalogue retailer. These boxes are similar to "The Competitive Edge" boxes used throughout the text. Taken together, they have the advantage of describing operations across the breadth of an entire company and since it is a service company, they are particularly insightful. Seven of the Land's End boxes are accompanied by video programs that accompany the text.

Summary of Key Formulas

Following the summary at the end of each chapter is a "Summary of Key Formulas" that provides a list of the most important formulas derived in the presentation of any quantitative techniques introduced in the chapter. These enable the students to turn to a specific location to refresh their memories about a formula without having to search through the chapter. The formulas are also provided electronically in the faculty section of the web page for easy reproduction for exams.

Summary of Key Terms

Following the "Summary of Key Formulas" at the end of each chapter is a "Summary of Key Terms." It provides a list of the most important terms for the chapter and their definitions. This list enables the students to refresh their memories about an important term without having to search through the chapter or marginal notes.

Solved Example Problems

At the end of each chapter just prior to the homework questions and problems, there is a section with solved examples that serve as a guide for doing the homework problems. These examples are solved in a detailed, step-by-step fashion.

Supplemental Items

The text is accompanied by a number of supplemental items that the instructor may wish to use in the course. These supplements include a set of videos that complement the textual presentation of material in a number of locations throughout the text. The videos include: *Competitiveness and Continuous Improvement at Xerox, Teams and Employee Involvement at Hewlett-Packard, Statistical Process Control at Kurt Manufacturing, Process Strategy and Selection, Flexible Manufacturing Systems, Operations Strategy at Whirlpool, Product Design and Supplier Partnerships at Motorola, Service Quality and Service Design at Marriott, A Plant Tour of Winnebago Industries,* and seven installments of *On Location at Lands' End.*

The locations where these videos might be used, and a description of each video, is provided on the web site and in the *Instructor's Manual.*

The *Instructor's Manual* contains a wealth of information to help the instructor prepare and deliver a dynamic introductory course in operations management, including sample course syllabi, chapter outlines, teaching notes for the instructor, PowerPoint lecture slides, alternate examples to those examples provided in the text, in-class exercises, projects and special assignments.

Also included with this text is a *Solutions Manual* detailing answers to end-of-chapter questions, homework problems, and case problems; and an extensive *Text Bank.*

Acknowledgments

The writing and revision of a textbook, like any large project, requires the help and creative energy of many people and this is certainly not the exception. We especially appreciate the confidence, support, help, and friendship of our editor, Tom Tucker. We also thank the various support personnel at Prentice Hall including Diane Peirano, Susan Rifkin, Mike Elia, and numerous other people who work behind the scenes and whom we never saw or talked to. We are indebted to the reviewers of the second edition including: Scott A. Dellana, East Carolina University; Thomas Foster, Jr., Boise State University; Lawrence D. Fredenhall, Clemson University; Richard W. Garrett, University of Indiana; Linguo Gong, Louisiana State University; Robert Handfield, Michigan State University; Ray M. Hayes, California Polytechnic State University at San Luis Obispo; John Haywood-Farmer, University of Western Ontario; James K. Higginson, Wilfred Laurier University; Steve Lawrence, University of Colorado; Terry Nels Lee, Brigham Young University; J. R. Minifie, Southwest Texas State University; Michael J. Pesch, St. Cloud State University; Paul H. Randolph, Texas Tech University, and Edward W. Watson, Louisiana State University. They contributed numerous suggestions, comments, and ideas that dramatically improved and changed our first edition. We offer our sincere thanks to these colleagues and hope that they can take some satisfaction in their contribution to our final product. We wish to thank our students who have class-tested, critiqued, and contributed to the first edition and this revision from a consumer's point of view. We are especially grateful to Tracy McCoy at Virginia Tech for her unstinting help, hard work, and patience.

R.S.R.
B.T.T.

THE STRATEGY OF PRODUCTIVE SYSTEMS

1

Introduction to Operations and Competitiveness

Getting to Know Lands' End

www.prenhall.com/russell

Lands' End, the well-known direct retailer, was founded by Gary Comer in 1963 in Chicago. Initially, the company supplied sailboat hardware and equipment by mail. In the early 1970s, catalogs also featured a sampling of outerwear and casual clothing. In 1977, the company decided to focus its efforts on selling clothing and soft luggage. By 1979, Lands' End had moved to Dodgeville, Wisconsin, expanded the clothing selection in its catalog, and had begun to recruit personnel experienced in the areas of fabrics and clothing manufacturing.

Since then, the company has been a leader in the integration of consumer advertising techniques with mail-order practices. In 1981, Lands' End began a national advertising campaign to describe its business philosophy and expand its reputation for quality, value, and service. The Lands' End philosophy is outlined in its "Principles of Doing Business" that appear below.

Lands' End catalogs are known for descriptive product narratives that tell customers everything they could want to know about a garment and its construction. The company's toll-free phone lines for sales and customer service are open 24 hours a day, 364 days a year. Over 1,000 phone lines handle about 50,000 calls each day—almost 100,000 calls daily in the weeks prior to Christmas. Eighty-five percent of all orders are placed by phone.

In-stock orders leave Lands' End's Dodgeville distribution center (a structure the size of 16 football fields) the day after they are received. Standard delivery is two business days anywhere within the continental United States. Lands' End works directly with some of the best fabric mills and manufacturers in the world. Garments are produced to Lands' End's own quality specifications, not to less stringent industry-wide specifications.

Lands' End, headquartered in Dodgeville, Wisconsin, is the largest specialty catalogue company in the United States. The company's products include casual and tailored clothing for men, women, and children, shoes and accessories, soft luggage, and items for bed and bath. Fast, efficient operations allows Lands' End to offer convenient at-home shopping of quality merchandise at competitive prices. We'll examine operations management at Lands' End in special boxes throughout this text.

Lands' End became a public company in 1986, trading on the New York Stock Exchange under the ticker symbol, *LE*. In 1994, its sales surpassed those of L.L. Bean, making it the leading specialty-catalogue company in the United States. In addition to its booming U.S. business, the company now does business in 75 countries, with facilities or special licensing agreements in Canada, the United Kingdom, Japan, and Germany.

Lands' End
Principles of Doing Business

Principle 1: We do everything we can to make our products better. We improve material, and add back features and construction details that others have taken out over the years. We never reduce the quality of a product to make it cheaper.

Principle 2: We price our products fairly and honestly. We do not, have not, and will not participate in the common retailing practice of inflating mark-ups to set up a future phony "sale."

Principle 3: We accept any return, for any reason, at any time. Our products are guaranteed. No fine print. No arguments. We mean exactly what we say: GUARANTEED, PERIOD.

Principle 4: We ship items in stock the day after we receive the order. At the height of the last Christmas season, the longest time an order was in the house was 36 hours, excepting monograms, which took another 12 hours.

Principle 5: We believe that what is best for our customer is best for all of us. Everyone here understands that concept. Our sales and service people are trained to know our products and to be friendly and helpful. They are urged to take all the time necessary to take care of you. We even pay for your call, for whatever reason you call.

Principle 6: We are able to sell at lower prices because we have eliminated middlemen; because we don't buy branded merchandise with high protected mark-ups; and because we have placed our contracts with manufacturers who have proved that they are cost conscious and efficient.

Principle 7: We are able to sell at lower prices because we operate efficiently. Our people are hard-working, intelligent, and share in the success of the company.

Principle 8: We are able to sell at lower prices because we support no fancy emporiums with their high overhead. Our main location is in the middle of a 40-acre cornfield in rural Wisconsin.

Traditionally, **operations** has been defined as a transformation process. As shown in Figure 1.1, inputs (such as material, machines, labor, management, and capital) are transformed into outputs (goods and services). Requirements and feedback from customers are used to adjust factors in the transformation process, which may in turn alter inputs. In operations management, we try to ensure that the transformation process is performed efficiently and that the output is of greater *value* than the sum of the inputs. Thus, the role of operations is to create value. Any activities that do not add value during the transformation process are superfluous and should be eliminated.

Operations: a function or system *that* transforms inputs into outputs of greater value.

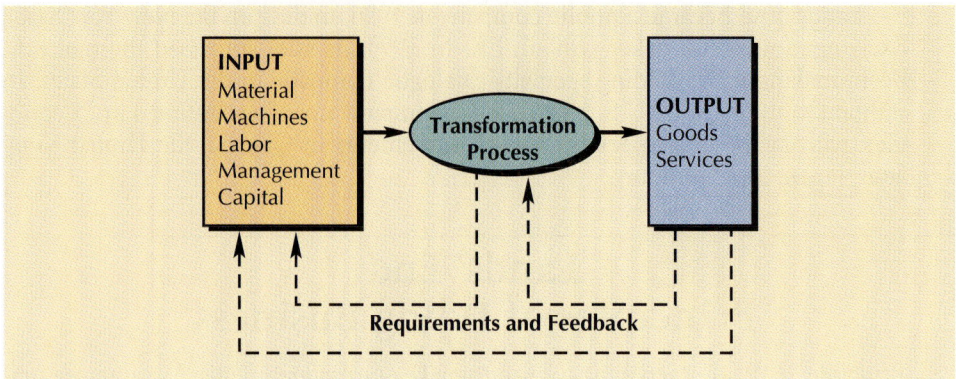

FIGURE 1.1   Operations as a Transformation Process

The input-transformation-output process is characteristic of a wide variety of operating systems. In an automobile factory, sheet steel is formed into different shapes, painted and finished, and then assembled with thousands of component parts to produce a working automobile. In an aluminum factory, various grades of bauxite are mixed, heated, and cast into ingots of different sizes. In a hospital, patients are restored into healthier individuals through special care, meals, medication, lab work, and surgical procedures. Obviously, "operations" can take many different forms. The transformation process can be

physical,   as in manufacturing operations,
locational,   as in transportation or warehouse operations,
exchange,   as in retail operations,
physiological,   as in health care,
psychological,   as in entertainment, or
informational,   as in communications.

The Operations Function

Activities in operations management (OM) include organizing work, selecting processes, arranging layouts, locating facilities, designing jobs, measuring performance, controlling quality, scheduling work, managing inventory, and planning production. Operations managers deal with people, technology, and deadlines. These managers need good technical, conceptual, and behavioral skills. Their activities are closely intertwined with other functional areas of a firm.

As shown in Figure 1.2, the three primary functions of a firm are marketing, fi-

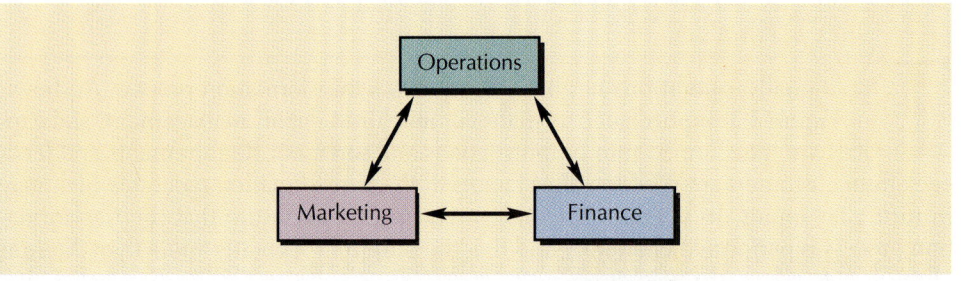

FIGURE 1.2   Operations as One of the Three Basic Functions of a Firm

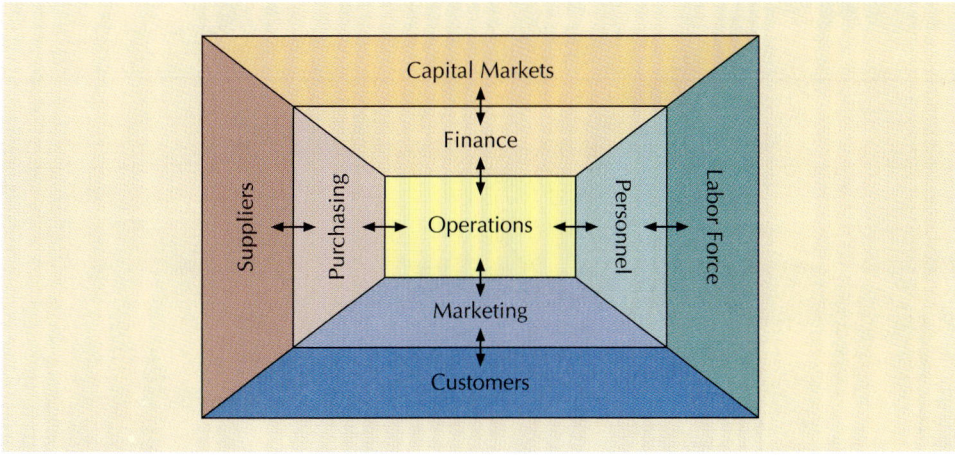

FIGURE 1.3 Operations as the Technical Core

nance, and operations. *Marketing* establishes the demand for goods or services, *finance* provides the capital, and *operations* actually makes the goods or provides the service. Of the three functions, operations typically employs the greatest number of people and requires the largest investment in assets. For these reasons, management of the operations function has often been viewed as an opportunity to improve a firm's efficiency and reduce costs. But operations can also be an avenue to increase sales, gain market share, and eliminate the competition!

Operations can also be viewed as the *technical core* of an organization. In this scenario, depicted in Figure 1.3, operations is the central function of an organization. The organization exists to produce goods and services. All other functions exist to support the operations function. Operations interacts with *marketing* to receive estimates of customer demand and customer feedback on problems; with *finance* for capital investments, budgets, and stockholder requirements; with *personnel* to train, hire, and fire workers; and with *purchasing* to order needed materials for production. The operations function is purposely isolated from contact with outside influences, such as customers and financial markets, so that a stable environment for top efficiency can be created and maintained. However, this isolation can be dangerous, as we learned in the 1970s and 1980s. Operations managers do more than efficiently convert inputs to outputs. As part of a management team, they need direct access to internal and external customers to be responsive to their needs.

> Operations can be viewed as the technical core.

To understand better the role of operations and the operations manager, let's examine some historical events in OM.

A Brief History of Operations Management

Although history is full of amazing production feats—the pyramids of Egypt, the Great Wall of China, the roads and aqueducts of Rome—the widespread production of consumer goods—and thus, operations management—did not begin until the Industrial Revolution in the 1700s. Prior to that time, skilled craftspersons and their apprentices fashioned goods for individual customers from studios in their own homes. Every piece was unique, hand-fitted, and made entirely by one person. Then, the invention of an improved steam engine by James Watt and the availability of coal and iron ore set into motion a series of industrial inventions that revolutionized the way

Operating a large amusement park, such as Disney's Epcot Center, is every bit as complicated as manufacturing an aircraft carrier. Thousands of activities must be coordinated on a daily basis. Equipment must be well-maintained, workers well-trained, and shelves well-stocked, while keeping costs down. On top of this, services typically deal with more customers (each with their own service expectations) more frequently than manufacturers, and handle more unexpected occurrences. Maybe that's why GM, Xerox, IBM, and other manufacturers routinely benchmark Disney operations.

www.prenhall.com/russell

work was performed. Great mechanical-powered machines replaced the laborer as the primary factor of production and brought workers to a central location to perform tasks under the direction of an "overseer" in a place called a "factory." The revolution first took hold in textile mills, grain mills, metalworking, and machine-making facilities.

Around the same time, Adam Smith's *Wealth of Nations* (1776) proposed the *division of labor*, in which the production process was broken down into a series of small tasks, each performed by a different worker. The specialization of the worker on limited, repetitive tasks allowed him or her to become very proficient at those tasks and further encouraged the development of specialized machinery.

From the Industrial Revolution to the Quality Revolution

The introduction of *interchangeable parts* by Eli Whitney (1790s) allowed the manufacture of firearms, clocks, watches, sewing machines, and other goods to shift from customized one-at-a-time production to volume production of standardized parts. This meant the factory needed a system of measurements and inspection, a standard method of production, and supervisors to check the quality of the worker's production.

Advances in technology continued through the 1800s. Cost accounting and other control systems were developed, but management theory and practice were virtually nonexistent.

In the early 1900s an enterprising laborer (and later chief engineer) at Midvale Steel Works named Frederick W. Taylor approached the management of work as a science. Based on observation, measurement, and analysis, he identified the best method for performing each job. Once determined, the methods were standardized for all workers and economic incentives were established to encourage workers to follow the standards. Taylor's philosophy became known as *scientific management*. His ideas were embraced and extended by efficiency experts Frank and Lillian Gilbreth, and Henry Gantt, among others. One of Taylor's biggest advocates was Henry Ford.

Henry Ford applied scientific management to the production of the Model T in 1913 and reduced the time required to assemble a car from a high of 728 hours to $1\frac{1}{2}$ hours. A Model T chassis moved slowly down a conveyor belt with six workers walking along beside it, picking up parts from carefully spaced piles on the floor and fitting them to the chassis.[1] The short assembly time per car allowed the Model T to be produced in high volumes, or "en masse," yielding the name **mass production.**

American manufacturers became adept at mass production over the next fifty years and easily dominated manufacturing worldwide. The human relations movement of the 1930s, led by Elton Mayo and the Hawthorne studies, introduced the idea that worker motivation, as well as the technical aspects of work, affected productivity. Theories of motivation were developed by Herzberg, Maslow, McGregor, and others. Quantitative models and techniques spawned by the operations research groups of World War II continued to develop and were applied successfully to manufacturing. Com-

Mass production is high-volume production of a standardized product for a mass market.

TABLE 1.1 Some Historical Events in Operations Management

Era	Events/Concepts	Dates	Originator
Industrial Revolution	Steam engine	1769	James Watt
	Division of labor	1776	Adam Smith
	Interchangeable parts	1790	Eli Whitney
Scientific Management	Principles of scientific management	1911	Frederick W. Taylor
	Time and motion studies	1911	Frank and Lillian Gilbreth
	Activity scheduling chart	1912	Henry Gantt
	Moving assembly line	1913	Henry Ford
Human Relations	Hawthorne studies	1930	Elton Mayo
	Motivation theories	1940s,	Abraham Maslow
		1950s,	Frederick Herzberg
		1960s	Douglas McGregor
Management Science	Linear programming	1947	George Dantzig
	Digital computer	1951	Remington Rand
	Simulation, waiting line theory, decision theory, PERT/CPM	1950s, 1960s	Operations research groups
Quality Revolution	Lean production, JIT (just-in-time)	1970s, 1980s	Taiichi Ohno (Toyota)
	TQM (total quality management)	1980s, 1990s	W. Edwards Deming, Joseph Juran, and others
Information Age	CIM (computer-integrated manufacturing)	1980s, 1990s	Numerous individuals and companies
	EDI, EFT	1970s	
	World Wide Web	1990	Tim Berners-Lee
Globalization	Worldwide markets and operations	1990s	Numerous companies and nations

---

[1] David Halberstam, *The Reckoning* (New York: William Morrow, 1986), pp. 79–81.

puters and automation led still another upsurge in technological advancements applied to operations. These events are summarized in Table 1.1.

From the Industrial Revolution through the 1960s, the United States was the world's greatest producer of goods and services, as well as the major source of managerial and technical expertise. Looking back, 1960 was probably the peak for American manufacturing. From then on, industry by industry, U.S. manufacturing superiority was challenged by lower costs and higher quality from foreign manufacturers, led by Japan.

In the 1970s, U.S. productivity rose an average of only 1.3 percent per year, and in the 1980s, barely 0.2 percent (with many years negative), while foreign competitors boasted increases of 4 percent and 5 percent per year. Several studies published during those years confirmed what the consumer already knew—U.S.-made products of that era were inferior and could not compete on the world market. Table 1.2 compares the product performance of U.S. versus Japanese automobiles, semiconductors, air conditioners, and color televisions of the 1970s and 1980s.

TABLE 1.2   A Comparison of American and Japanese Products in the 1970s and 1980s

Quality of Automobiles	TGWs (things gone wrong) in First 8 Months per 100 cars	
Chrysler	285	
GM	256	
Ford	214	
Japanese (avg.)	132	
Toyota	55	
Quality of Semiconductors	**U.S. Companies**	**Japanese Companies**
Defective on delivery	16%	0%
Failure after 1000 hours	14%	1%
Quality of Room Air Conditioners	**U.S. Companies**	**Japanese Companies**
Fabrication defects	4.4%	<0.1%
Assembly line defects	63.5%	0.9%
Service calls	10.5%	0.6%
Warranty cost (as % of sales)	2.2%	0.6%
Quality of Color TVs	**U.S. Companies**	**Japanese Companies**
Assembly line defects per set	1.4	0.01
Service calls per set	1.0	0.09

SOURCES: National Academy of Engineering, *The Competitive Status of the U.S. Auto Industry* (Washington, D.C.: National Academy Press, 1982), pp. 90–108; A. L. Robinson, "Perilous Times for U.S. Microcircuit Makers," *Science* (May 9, 1980), pp. 582–86; D. Garvin, "Quality on the Line," *Harvard Business Review* (September–October 1983), pp. 64–75; I. Magaziner and R. Reich, *Minding America's Business* (New York: Harcourt Brace Jovanovich, 1982), p. 176; M. Porter, *Cases in Competitive Strategy* (New York: Free Press, 1983), p. 511.

Early rationalizations that the Japanese success in manufacturing was a cultural phenomenon were disproved by the successes of Japanese-owned plants in the United States. A prime example is the Matsushita purchase from Motorola of a failing Quasar television plant in Chicago. Part of the purchase contract specified that Matsushita had to retain the entire hourly work force of 1,000 persons. After only two years, with the identical workers, half the management staff, and little or no capital investment, Matsushita doubled production, cut assembly repairs from 130 percent to 6 percent, and reduced warranty costs from $16 million a year to $2 million a year. You can bet Motorola took notice. (Today Motorola is one of the success stories of American manufacturing.)

How did this come about? How did a country that dominated manufacturing for most of the twentieth century suddenly become no good at it? Quite simply, U.S. companies weren't paying attention. They thought mass production had solved the "problem" of production, so they delegated the function of manufacturing to technical specialists (usually engineers) who ignored changes in the consumer environment and the strategic impact of operations.

Mass production can produce large volumes of goods quickly, but it cannot adapt very well to changes in demand. Todays' consumer market is characterized by product proliferation, shortened product lifecycles, shortened product development times, changes in technology, more customized products, and segmented markets. Mass production does not "fit" that type of environment. Japanese manufacturers changed the rules of production with an adaptation of mass production known as *lean production*. Lean production prizes flexibility (rather than efficiency) and quality (rather than quantity). The "total quality" fervor has since spread across the globe and is the focus of operations in many successful global enterprises.

Misfit between the market and production.

But lest we think that *lean production* is the new solution to the "problem" of production, we should emphasize that world-class companies have achieved their status by recognizing the *strategic importance* of operations and adapting operating systems to changes in the environment. This awareness is especially important today as continuing advances in information technology have further increased competition, rejuvenating old firms and bringing many new ones to the forefront. Technology, together with changing political and economic conditions, have prompted an era of industrial *globalization* in which companies compete worldwide for both market access and production resources.

Let's examine globalization and competitiveness from an operations perspective.

Globalization

The Global 500,[2] comprising the most successful companies worldwide, is not dominated by any one country. For 1995, Japan's Mitsubishi Corporation posted the highest revenue, the Netherland's Royal Dutch/Shell continued as the world's most profitable company, Canada's Seagram's had the highest return on revenues, and America's Intel the highest return on assets. Six of the top ten biggest companies were Japanese, but U.S. firms were more profitable, and so were companies in less developed countries. Shell attributes its success to operations in 120 countries (more than any of its competitors) and a strong presence in East Asia. Overreliance on home markets was a common characteristic of firms at the bottom of the 500, in particular, domestic-bound Japanese and French firms. The most successful companies in the Global 500 were

www.prenhall.com/russell

No one country dominates the Global 500.

---

[2] Published annually by *Fortune.* The data in this section comes from the August 5, 1996 issue.

www.prenhall.com/russell

In the 1980s, as a competitive response to comparable but cheaper products from foreign manufacturers, Motorola began assembling products offshore in Singapore, Puerto Rico, and the South Pacific. Production costs were lower, but the speed of production was insufficient to meet customer demands. Motorola decided to change manufacturing strategies and create a state-of-the-art production facility onshore for its paging products. Within eighteen months of the decision, the so-called Bandit project (because it borrowed the best technology) successfully completed the design of a new production system that was fast and cost competitive. The photo above shows part of the carefully designed assembly line. Pagers that used to take three weeks to manufacture took two hours on the new line. Further improvements reduced the leadtime for customized pagers to less than ninety minutes from order placement to order shipment. It is no surprise that Motorola currently dominates the pager market.

www.prenhall.com/russell

able to use the best and lowest price inputs in the world to access markets around the globe. Worldwide market access also insulates companies against economic downturns in individual countries.

Companies "go global" to take advantage of favorable costs (usually labor rates) in foreign countries and to access foreign markets. Figure 1.4 shows the hourly wage rates in U.S. dollars for production workers in six countries from 1975 to 1995. U.S. labor rates have remained remarkably stable, while the labor rates of Japan, Germany, and the European Union have increased. Currently, wage rates are 25 percent higher in Japan and 60 percent higher in Germany, than in the United States. Labor rates in Mexico and in the newly industrialized economies (NIEs) of Asia remained at low levels—$1.51 an hour in Mexico and $.52 an hour in Sri Lanka, for example. This data certainly supports the trend toward foreign investments in Mexico and in the Pacific Rim.

A study of fifteen industries shows that U.S. firms are more "global" than firms in Europe or Asia, producing more than twice as much outside U.S. borders than inside. Ironically, more than 60 percent of American manufacturing investment has occurred in countries with labor rates comparable to U.S. labor rates. It appears that many U.S. companies are more interested in accessing new customers, technologies, or skills, rather than capitalizing on cheap labor.

Trade barriers are falling.

Falling trade barriers and changing markets are fueling the trend toward globalization. Fourteen major trade agreements were enacted in the 1990s. Figure 1.5 on page 14 shows their effect on U.S. imports and exports.

THE COMPETITIVE EDGE

Whirlpool's Global Strategy

www.prenhall.com/russell

Whirlpool's globalization strategy has doubled revenues and transformed it from a sleepy Rust Belt manufacturer into an aggressive international competitor. Faced with a maturing home market, Whirlpool decided to enter foreign markets rather than diversify into furniture or garden products. Now Whirlpool makes appliances in 12 countries and sells them in 140. Thirty-eight percent of its revenue comes from abroad. Whirlpool is number one in North and Latin America, and trails only Electrolux and Bosch-Siemens in Europe. Its 1 percent market share in Asia is the largest of any Western appliance maker.

But start-up costs have been high and demand in Europe weak. Whirlpool's profit margins are down from 8 percent to 5 percent, and its stock price is lower than three years ago. Four joint ventures with the Chinese in one year may have been too much. Will Whirlpool's strategy succeed? Only time will tell. Maytag sold its European operations at a loss of $135 million, and its stock rose 20 percent.

SOURCE: Bill Vlasic and Zachary Schiller, "Did Whirlpool Spin too Far too Fast?" *Business Week* (June 24, 1996): 133–36.

The U.S. market is a healthy contributor to international trade, accounting for 24 percent of Honda's revenue, 81 percent of Seagram's, 65 percent of Delaize's (a grocery chain from Belgium), and 34 percent of Bridgestone's. But the newly expanding economies of East Asia, Latin America, and Eastern Europe constitute the major growth opportunities in international trade. Competition in those markets is fierce, and local production helps solidify trade. In 1995, nearly 60 percent of large capital investments in new facilities ($200 million or more each) took place in the Asia-Pacific region.[3]

www.prenhall.com/russell

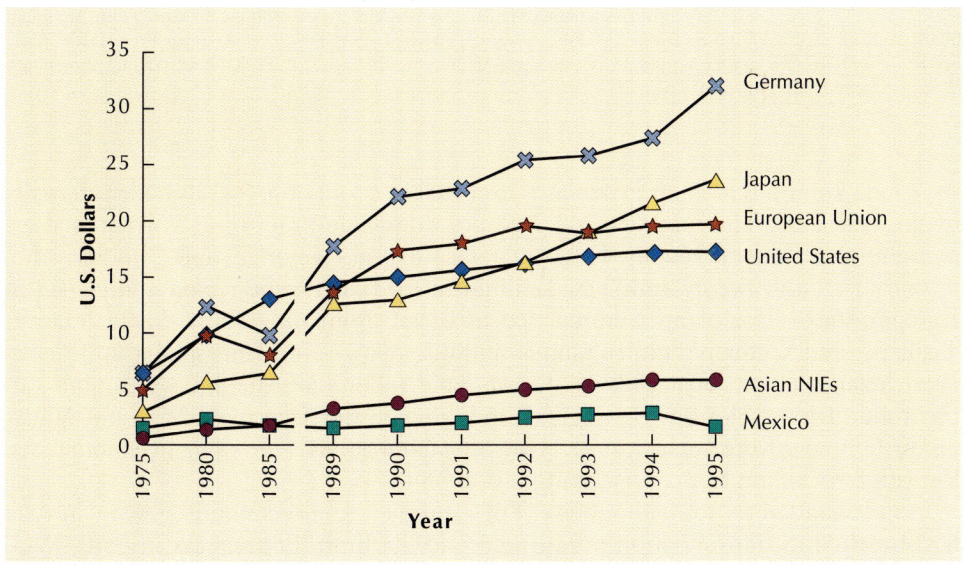

FIGURE 1.4 A Comparison of Hourly Wage Rates
SOURCE: U.S. Department of Labor, Bureau of Labor Statistics, *International Comparisons of Manufacturing Productivity and Unit Labor Cost Trends* (July 17, 1996).

---

[3] The data in this section come from Audrey Pennington, "Global Facilities Go Gangbusters," *Site Selection* 41, no. 1 (February 1996): 156–59.

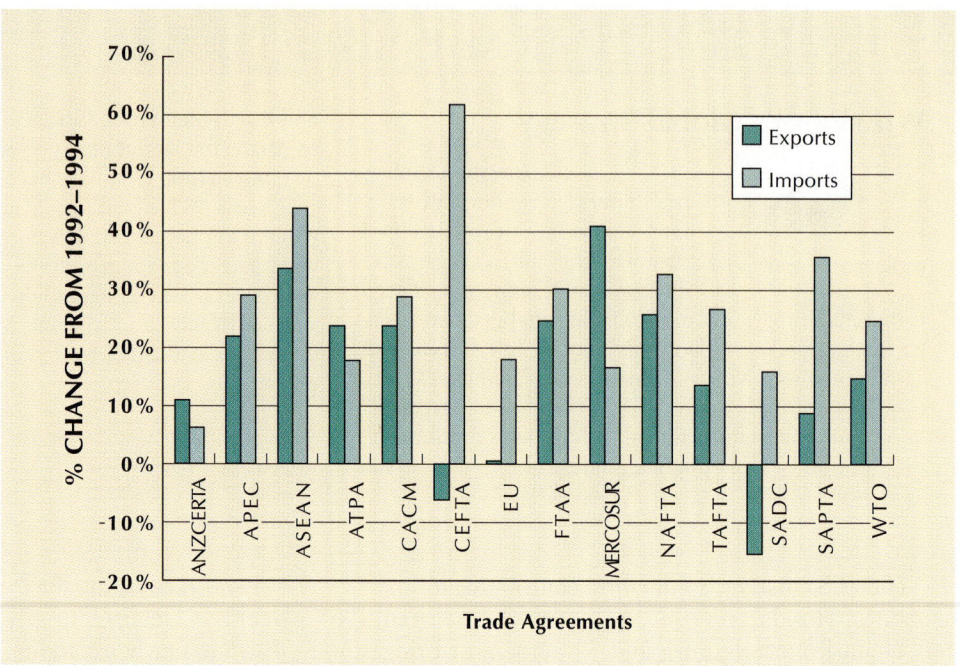

FIGURE 1.5   The Impact of Trade Agreements on U.S. Imports and Exports

SOURCE: U.S. Bureau of Census, Merchandise Trade Series, as given in Justin Zubrod and Mary Beth Barron, "Trade Pacts Fuel a Transformation in the Rules of Global Logistics," *Transportation and Distribution* (April 1996): 62.

Note: ANZCERTA—Australia New Zealand Closer Economic Relations Trade Agreement; APEC—Asian Pacific Economic Cooperation; ASEAN—Association of Southeast Asian Nations; ATPA—Andean Trade Preference Act; CACM—Central America Common Market; CEFTA—Central Europe Free Trade Agreement; EU—European Union; FTAA—Free Trade Area of the Americas; MERCOSUR—Mercado Commun del Sur (Latin American trade treaties); NAFTA—North American Free Trade Agreement; TAFTA—TransAtlantic Free Trade Area; SADC—Southern African Development Community; SAPTA—South Asian Area Preferential Trading Agreement; WTO—World Trade Organization

Global companies produce, as well as sell, around the world.	Asia, long known as a major exporter, is expected to conduct half of its trade internally by the year 2000. The most active companies worldwide in terms of international expansion were General Motors, Ford, General Electric, Motorola, and Chrysler, who, in one year, built twenty-three new facilities in the Asia-Pacific region and eleven in Europe. Automobile plants were opened in Brazil, Romania, China, Spain, France, Thailand, and Vietnam. Semiconductor and microprocessor plants sprang up in England, Ireland, Israel, Japan, China, Taiwan, and Indonesia. The toy, watch, and garment industries of Hong Kong migrated to China, as did Taiwanese Nike and Adidas production, and Korean electronics. Tiny Singapore gained "developed economy" status with $4.8 billion in manufacturing investments.
Globalization can be risky.	Globalization is not without risk. For example, rapid economic growth in Asia has stretched its transportation infrastructure to the limit. Bottlenecks in ports, road, and rail, delay products from reaching their market. The markets themselves are highly fragmented with distinct languages, customs, trade barriers, and levels of development. In addition, distribution channels within regions are unorganized and inefficient. That means operations must be customized to each country and logistics carefully planned. In Latin America and the Eastern European countries, stability of the governments and poor economic conditions continue to inhibit increased trade and localized operations.

The arrival of the global marketplace has dramatically increased international trade and the logistics operations to support it. Shown here is Singapore's global port where 16 million containers are processed annually from ship to rail car or tractor trailer for distribution. Its geographic location, highly skilled workforce, advanced telecommunications systems, and excellent financial services make Singapore an ideal hub for international business.

Competitiveness

A global marketplace means more customers and more intense competition. Competitiveness can be viewed from a national, industry, or firm perspective.

In the broadest terms, we speak of competitiveness in reference to other *countries* rather than to other companies. That's because competitiveness affects the economic success of a nation and the quality of life for its citizens. **Competitiveness** is "the degree to which a nation, can, under demanding and rapidly changing market conditions, produce goods and services that meet the test of international markets while simultaneously maintaining or expanding the real incomes of its citizens."[4] We measure a nation's competitiveness by its gross national product (GNP), import/export ratio, and increases in productivity.

Competitiveness: the degree to which a nation can produce goods and services that meet the test of international markets while simultaneously maintaining or expanding the real incomes of its citizens.

Productivity as a Measure of Competitiveness

Productivity, the most common measure of competitiveness, is calculated by dividing units of output by units of input.

Productivity: the ratio of output to input.

$$\text{Productivity} = \frac{\text{output}}{\text{input}}$$

Productivity increases when firms:

1. Become *more efficient*: output increases with little or no increase in input,
2. *Downsize*: output remains the same and input is reduced,
3. *Expand*: both output and input grow with output growing more rapidly,
4. *Retrench*: both output and input decrease, with input decreasing faster, or
5. Achieve *breakthroughs*: output increases while input decreases.

---

[4] *Report of the President's Commission on Industrial Competitiveness*, chaired by John A. Young, President and CEO, Hewlett-Packard, 1985.

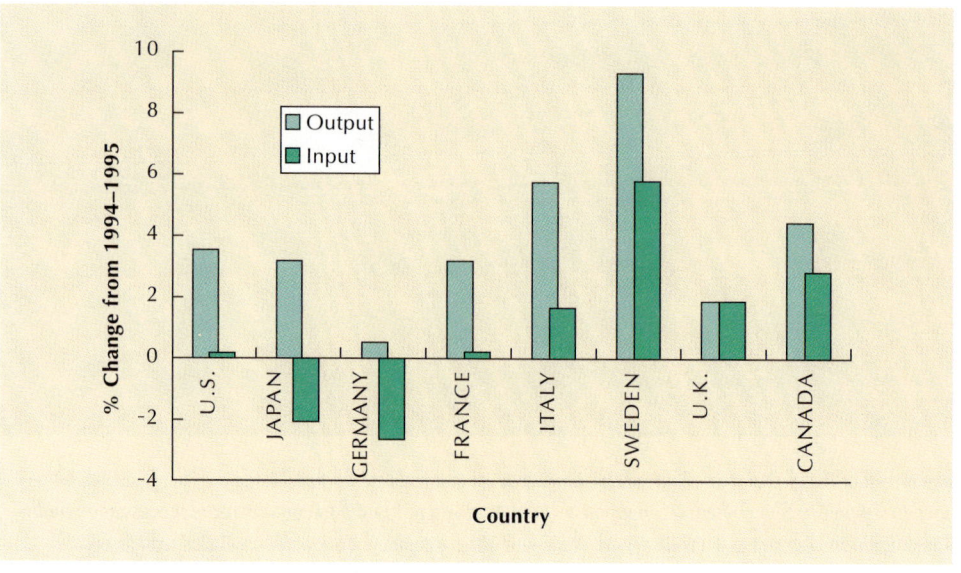

FIGURE 1.6 Changes in Input and Output

SOURCE: U.S. Department of Labor, Bureau of Labor Statistics, *International Comparisons of Manufacturing Productivity and Unit Labor Cost Trends* (July 17, 1996).

www.prenhall.com/russell

Several of these scenarios occurred from 1994 to 1995 as shown in Figure 1.6. U.S. and French manufacturers became more *efficient*, German and Japanese firms achieved *breakthroughs,* and the remaining economies (with the exception of the United Kingdom) *expanded.*

Figure 1.7 shows percent changes in productivity[5] for each year from 1990 to 1995 for the United States, Germany, and Japan. From the graph we can see that while U.S. performance was encouraging in the early 1990s, by 1995 the competitive battle between the United States, Germany, and Japan was once again in full swing. The lesson? The world is a very competitive place and maintaining competitiveness is a tough job.

Competitive Industries

Competition within industries is more intense when the firms are relatively equal in size and resources, products and services are standardized, and industry growth is either slow (so that one company gains at the expense of another) or exponential (so that gaining a foothold in the market is a strategic imperative). Industry competitiveness can be measured by the number of major players in the industry, average market share, and average profit margin. Probably most competitive industry worldwide is pharmaceuticals, where the largest manufacturer holds a mere 4.7 percent market share. Price wars, relentless advertising (such as nightly phone calls from long-distance carriers), frequency of new product or service introductions, and purchasing incentives (extended

---

[5] The most commonly used input in productivity calculations is *labor hours.* Although labor is the only factor of production explicitly considered, comparisons of productivity *over time* implicitly reflect the joint effects of other factors, including technology, capital investment, capacity utilization, energy use, and managerial skills. For this reason, productivity statistics provided in government reports typically measure *changes* in productivity from month to month, quarter to quarter, year to year, or over a number of years.

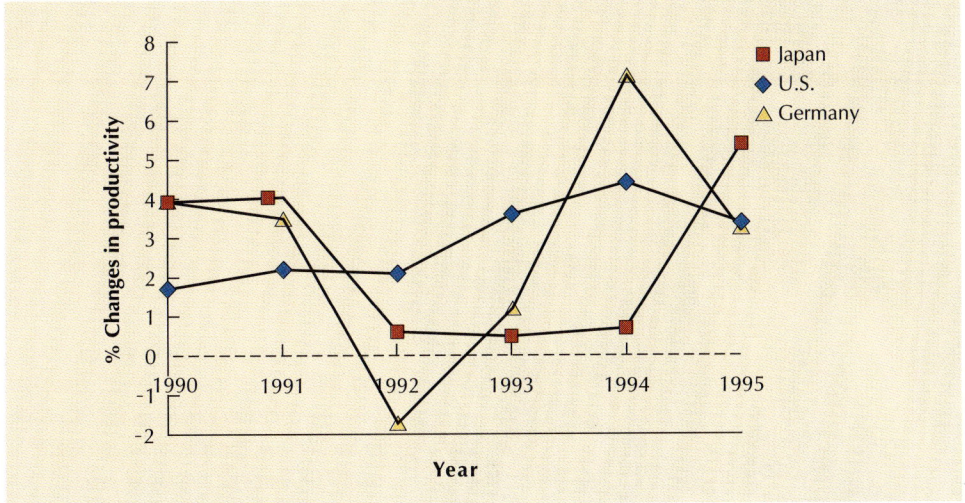

FIGURE 1.7 Productivity in the 1990s

SOURCE: U.S. Department of Labor, Bureau of Labor Statistics, *International Comparisons of Manufacturing Productivity and Unit Labor Cost Trends* (July 17, 1996).

warranties, financial packages, switching bonuses, etc.) provide additional evidence of competition within industries.

In some industries, competition is limited because it is difficult for new firms to enter the industry. Many of the **barriers to entry**—economies of scale, capital requirements, access to supply and distribution channels, and learning curves—are operations-oriented. Let's explore them in more detail.

1. *Economies of scale.* In many industries, as the number of units produced increases, the cost of producing each individual unit decreases, which is known as **economies of scale.** New companies entering such an industry may not have the demand to support large volumes of production, and thus, their unit cost would be higher.

2. *Capital investment.* Large initial investments in facilities, equipment, and training may be required to become a "player" in some industries. For example, opening a new hospital requires an enormous investment in facilities, equipment, and professional personnel; whereas, a day-care center may operate out of an existing home with only minimal equipment, training, and licensing requirements.

3. *Access to supply and distribution channels.* Existing firms within an industry have established supply and distribution channels that may be difficult for new firms to replicate. Examples: Toys 'Я Us dominates its suppliers. Wal-Mart's information and distribution systems provide a strong competitive advantage. VISA will not allow its member banks to do business with American Express.

4. *Learning curves.* Lack of experience can be a barrier to entry in an industry with significant learning curves. For example, U.S. firms dominate the aerospace industry because of their experience and expertise in airplane design and construction. However, this may not always be the case, as component manufacturers in Korea and Japan are gaining valuable experience as suppliers to aerospace firms. Shipbuilders claim a 10-percent learning curve (and corre-

Barriers to entry make it difficult for new firms to enter an industry.

Economies of scale: as the number of units produced increases, the cost of producing each individual unit decreases.

Federal Express began operations in 1973 with a fleet of eight small aircraft. Five years later, the company employed 10,000 people to handle 35,000 daily deliveries. Today, over 90,000 FedEx employees process 1.5 million shipments daily, all of which must be tracked, sorted, and delivered in a short amount of time. The SuperTracker, shown here, is a hand-held computer used for scanning a shipment's bar code every time a package changes hands between pickup and delivery. It provides valuable input data for locating the root causes or problems and calculating the company's 12-component Service Quality Indicator (SQI).

sponding cost advantage) for each similar vessel built. Hospitals performing heart transplants exhibit an amazing 79 percent learning curve.[6]

Competitive Firms

Measures of a firm's competitiveness include market share, earnings per share, revenue growth, and profit margins. A firm is competitive if it performs *at least as well* as its rivals. However, being as good (or as bad) as the competition is not an inspiring goal. It puts the firm in a defensive stance and ensures second-rate status.

Leading the competition—breaking new ground—is more difficult and risky than being a follower, but it is also more exciting, more energizing, and more instructive. That's why in this text we provide examples of firms that consistently go beyond the competition—with a competitive edge. Look for application boxes in each chapter and learn how a variety of organizations have found **The Competitive Edge!**

www.prenhall.com/russell

Issues and Trends in Operations

Operations is a field that is rapidly changing and growing in importance. Current issues and future trends in operations include:

---

[6] David Smith and Jan Larson, "The Impact of Learning on Cost: The Case of Heart Transplantation," *Hospital and Health Services Administration* (Spring 1989): 85–97. Learning curves are discussed in more detail in Chapter 8.

THE COMPETITIVE EDGE

FedEx Uses Technology Wisely

www.prenhall.com/russell

Service companies seldom come to mind as examples of high-tech operations, but Federal Express was built on advanced technology. Their hub-and-spokes transportation system has been copied by every major airline in the world. Manufacturers often benchmark against FedEx's specially designed package-sortation system that processes 1 million packages in less than three hours. FedEx also has one of the most sophisticated computer information systems in the world. The COSMOS network can receive information from transfer terminals in delivery vans and in customer facilities and from hand-held computers called SuperTrackers. They use the information to track customer orders, adjust delivery routes, determine load factors and docking sequences for aircraft, schedule maintenance activities, and maintain a sufficient inventory of service parts.

Customers can access much of this information electronically over the Internet. They can also print mailing labels, schedule pickups, and follow every move their package makes from pickup to delivery. FedEx even designs and operates inventory management systems, distribution centers, and specialized web pages that link its customers' customers directly to FedEx pickups and deliveries. Clearly, FedEx's use of technology has given the company a competitive edge.

1. *Intense competition.* The intensity of worldwide competition will continue to increase. Global restructuring and the emergence of newly industrialized economies have opened new markets worldwide. As world markets grow, so do potential customers, as well as the number and quality of competitors.

2. *Global markets, global sourcing, and global financing.* Few companies will be able to survive by competing in the domestic market alone. Companies need to learn about foreign societies, understand foreign customers, build networks, and forge partnerships. Production will take place wherever in the world it can be done the cheapest. Access to capital markets will be worldwide.

3. *Importance of strategy.* Companies will need long-term global strategies to survive in the marketplace. Vertically integrated partnerships, partnerships with other companies in the same industry, partnerships with educational institutions, and partnerships with government will be needed to strengthen competitive positions. A new type of capitalism based on strategic alliances and cooperative specialization within industries may become a necessity.

4. *Product variety and customization.* An increasing variety of products and services will be offered, in many cases, customized for individuals. This means the expected life of products will continue to decrease, and product and service innovations will hit the market at an increasing rate.

5. *More services.* Eighty percent of jobs in the United States are provided by the service sector. Many corporations we think of as successful manufacturing firms, such as GM, GE, IBM, and Westinghouse, actually generate more than half of their income from services. For both manufacturing and service firms, *customer service* is a competitive battleground that will continue to intensify.

6. *Emphasis on quality.* The quality of products and services will continue to improve as customer expectations of quality grow. Zero defects will be the norm. Quality that delights the customer and provides a competitive advantage will be the goal.

7. *Flexibility.* The most successful production systems will be the most flexible. Flexibility will be measured by the ability to adjust to changes in product design, changes in product mix, changes in the volume of demand, and changes in process technology.

8. *Advances in technology.* Technology will continue to advance at a rapid rate, particularly in the areas of advanced materials (metal-based composites, polymer-based

Future trends–more, better, cheaper, faster, anywhere, anytime.

www.prenhall.com/russell

THE COMPETITIVE EDGE

Malden Mills' Greatest Asset— Its People

A five-alarm fire destroys your textile factory in Massachusetts where costs are high. Do you retire and pocket the insurance money? Do you use the opportunity to relocate to the Sunbelt or overseas? Not if you're Aaron Feuerstein, the 70-year-old owner of Malden Mills. You rebuild on the same site, and you pay full wages to your 1,000 employees until production can be restarted—that's a $15 million payout for months of idle labor. Crazy, you say? Feuerstein calls it good business.

"Why would I chase cheap labor [or alienate my workers] when I might run the risk of losing the advantage I've got, which is superior quality?" says Feuerstein. The key to continued success is to create unsurpassed *value* "with superior products, service, teamwork, productivity and cooperation with the buyer." To do that,

you need capable, experienced textile designers, engineers, and workers.

It's Malden's workers that give the company its competitive edge. Employee retention at Malden Mills is above 95 percent—so is customer retention. The correlation between loyal customers and loyal employees is no coincidence. In the 1980s, when the market for its major product—artificial furs—collapsed, it was employees in R&D and production who saved the company by inventing a new fabric called *Polartec*. L. L. Bean, Lands' End, Patagonia, North Face, and Eddie Bauer buy as much of the fabric as Malden can supply.

At the European trade show this fall (one year after the fire), Malden introduced a new line of fabric based on Polartec—for upholstery. Maybe those workers weren't complete couch potatoes after all.

SOURCE: Thomas Teal, "Not a Fool, Not a Saint," *Fortune* (November 11, 1996): 201–4.

---

composites, high-tech ceramics, and smart materials), advanced machining (EDM, lasers, electron beams, plasma flame cutting, flexible tooling and fixturing), intelligent sensors, smart robots, biotechnology, digital imaging, artificial intelligence, superconductors, and supercomputing.

Needed: Brainpower

9. *Worker involvement*. The empowerment of the work force has had a significant impact on operations in the past decade. This trend will continue in the future as the ability to create, absorb, and utilize *knowledge* will hold the key to success. Countries that perform the best in the world market will have the best R&D, the best education system, the brightest people, and the savvy to use those assets to their fullest.

10. *Environment and ethical concerns*. Companies and industries will increasingly consider the environmental impact of the design, manufacture, distribution, use, and disposal of their products and services. The impetus for environmental responsibility will shift from government regulations to customer requirements. As companies compete and produce across national borders, corporate ethics and social responsibility will be dictated more by customer expectations and corporate culture than by legalities in the host country.

www.prenhall.com/russell

Primary Topics in Operations Management

There are many issues, concepts, and techniques associated with the field of operations management (OM). This text is designed as an introductory survey course in OM that covers many different topics. In the following sections, we provide a brief overview of the primary topics in operations management. They are presented in the order in which operational decisions are made within a firm. It is not a coincidence that the chapters in this text are organized in a similar fashion.

Deploying Strategy

Strategy is only as good as the results it produces. Good results require that the corporate vision and strategic plan be converted into a series of consistent, achievable action plans to be deployed throughout the organization. Operations strategy must be consistent with corporate strategy and may provide the distinctive competence on which a firm competes. This topic appears in the text as *operations strategy*.

Chapter 2: Maintaining an operations strategy to support the firm's competitive advantage.

Assuring Quality

Quality drives operational decisions. The level of quality a company seeks to achieve is a strategic decision that eventually determines how a product is made or a service is delivered. Designing products and services, designing and planning the production process, locating and developing the production facility, designing jobs and work activities, and planning and scheduling the flow of products throughout the system are all areas of operations management that are increasingly dominated by quality. For this reason, the first two topics presented after the initial discussion of strategy are *quality management* and *statistical quality control*.

Chapters 3 and 4: Focusing on quality in operational decision making.

Designing Products and Services

The traditional starting point in the production process is designing the product or service. Decisions related to design include converting customer requirements to product or service characteristics, determining the desired level of quality, selecting materials, and evaluating the resulting production costs. This topic is covered in the text as *product and service design*.

Chapter 5: Designing quality into the product or service.

Planning the Production Process

Once the product or service has been designed, the physical process that will produce the product or deliver the service must be constructed. Plans are developed for acquiring materials, determining the types of job skills, equipment, and technology required, and managing the process. This topic is referred to as *process planning and technology decisions*.

Chapter 6: Developing the physical process to implement the design.

Laying Out the Facility

The production process that has been designed must be physically housed in a facility and laid out in an effective manner so that the product can be produced or service delivered as efficiently as possible. Decision making focuses on how to arrange different parts of the production or delivery process in the facility in order to ensure a smooth flow and minimal cycle time. The title of this area of operations management is *facility layout*.

Chapter 7: Setting up the process so that it works smoothly and efficiently.

Designing Jobs and Work

A primary component of the production process is the work performed by people, alone, together, or with machines and equipment. *Human resources management* is the area of Operations Management concerned with making sure that jobs meet the requirements of the production process in the most efficient and effective manner possible.

Chapter 8: Designing jobs and work to produce quality products.

Managing the Supply Chain

Chapter 9: Locating the business, selecting suppliers, and managing the supply chain.

Once the production process and facility have been designed, decisions must be made regarding where to locate the facility in relation to customers and suppliers, and how to manage the supply chain. A *supply chain* encompasses all the facilities, functions, and activities involved in producing and delivering a product or service, from the suppliers (and their suppliers) to the customer (and their customers).

Forecasting Demand for Products and Services

Chapter 10: Predicting demand–how much to produce and when to produce it.

Once the physical facility and production process are in place to produce a product or deliver a service, a host of planning decisions are required to determine how much to produce and when to produce it. These decisions are based on customer demand. *Forecasting* involves using a number of different methods and quantitative techniques to provide accurate estimates of demand, which are subsequently used to make production decisions.

Production Planning and Scheduling

Chapters 11, 12, 13, 14, 15, 16, and 17: Planning and scheduling production to meet demand.

Once management has determined how much product or service is needed to meet the demand, production schedules that involve a myriad of decisions are developed. These decisions include how much material or how many parts to order, when material or parts should be ordered, how many workers to hire, and how these workers should be scheduled on jobs and machines. Decisions must also be made to ensure the amount of inventory available at each stage of the production process is sufficient to avoid unnecessary delays, and the amount of final inventory is sufficient to meet customer demand. For service operations, the number of servers required to serve customers in a timely manner must be established. Production planning represents a major area of decision making in operations management and includes the topics of *capacity and aggregate production planning, inventory management, material requirements planning, scheduling, just-in-time systems, service improvement,* and *project planning.*

Organization and Purpose of This Book

In organizing this text, we envisioned three phases to the learning process: understanding the strategic impact of productive systems, designing productive systems, and operating productive systems. The chapters included in each phase are outlined on the next page.

Chapters 1 through 4 introduce the concepts and skills needed throughout the course and relate them to the competitive *strategy* of the firm. Chapters 5 through 9 relate to the *design* of productive systems, and Chapters 10 through 17 relate primarily to the *operation* of productive systems.

The purpose of this text is threefold:

1. *To ensure that business students are "operations literate."* Regardless of your major or career aspiration, as a business student, you will need to understand the basic issues, capabilities, and limitations of the operations function. Especially relevant are issues related to quality, strategy, and competitiveness.

2. *To instill in students a respect for operations.* By the conclusion of this course,

The Strategy of Productive Systems	Designing Productive Systems	Operating Productive Systems
1 Introduction to Operations and Competitiveness	5 Product and Service Design	10 Forecasting
2 Operations Strategy	6 Process Planning and Technology Decisions	11 Capacity and Aggregate Production Planning
3 Quality Management	7 Facility Layout	12 Inventory Management
4 Statistical Quality Control	8 Human Resources in Operations Management	13 Material Requirements Planning
	9 Supply Chain and Logistics Management	14 Scheduling
		15 Just-In-Time Systems
		16 Waiting Line Models for Service Improvement
		17 Project Management

you should be able to describe the impact of operations on other functions within a firm as well as on the competitive position of the firm.

3. *To encourage students to apply the concepts and methods they learn in this course.* The ability to conceptualize how systems are interrelated, to organize activities effectively, to analyze processes critically, to make decisions based on data, and to push for continual improvement can revolutionize jobs, industries, and society.

Summary

Operations can be viewed as a transformation process that converts inputs into outputs of greater value. Operations is also a basic function of a firm and the technical core of an organization. Operations management involves deploying strategy, assuring quality, designing products and services, planning the production process, laying out the facility, designing jobs and work, managing the supply chain, forecasting demand for products and services, and production planning and scheduling.

From the Industrial Revolution through the 1960s, the United States was the world's greatest producer of goods and services as well as the major source of managerial and technical expertise. In the 1970s and 1980s, America experienced competitive problems due to strategic weaknesses and inattentiveness to operations. Today, while no single country dominates the global marketplace, the United States does compete successfully, and operations plays a major role in maintaining competitiveness.

Current issues and trends in operations include intense competition in global markets; an emphasis on strategy, quality, and flexibility; advances in technology and worker involvement; more services and product variety; and environmental and ethical concerns.

Summary of Key Terms

barriers to entry: factors such as economies of scale, capital investment, access to supply and distribution channels, and learning curves that make it difficult for a new firm to enter an industry.

competitiveness: the degree to which a nation can produce goods and services that meet the test of international markets while simultaneously maintaining or expanding the real incomes of its citizens.

economies of scale: an advantage that accrues from high-volume production; as the number of units produced increases, the cost of producing each individual unit decreases.

mass production: the high-volume production of a standardized product for a mass market.

operations: a function or system that transforms inputs into outputs of greater value.

productivity: the ratio of output to input.

Questions

1-1. What activities are involved in the operations function?

1-2. What constitutes "operations" at (a) a bank, (b) a retail store, (c) a hospital, and (d) a cable TV company?

1-3. Briefly describe how operations have been affected as we have moved from the Industrial Revolution to the current era of globalization.

1-4. Why did the United States experience competitive problems in the 1970s and 1980s?

1-5. Think about the operations function at Lands' End. What is involved in the transformation process? How does the company "add value" for its customers?

1-6. Examine Lands' End's eight principles for doing business. What image is the company trying to portray? What specific activities support the image?

www.prenhall.com/russell

1-7. Gather information on Lands' End's competitors, L. L. Bean and Eddie Bauer. Are there any obvious differences in their competitive strategies?

1-8. Discuss four common barriers that firms may experience as they try to enter a new industry.

1-9. Describe the global activities of General Motors, Ford, General Electric, Motorola, and Chrysler. How many foreign plants do they have? Where are they located? How much of their business is foreign? Are any global strategies evident?

1-10. What countries constitute the newly industrialized economies of Asia? Compare the industrial progress of these countries.

1-11. Compare foreign investment in Europe and South America.

1-12. Identify the parent corporation and country of origin of the following firms or products: Food Lion, Burger King, Arrow shirts, Firestone tires, Godiva chocolate, and MGM movies.

1-13. Determine the home country and percent of sales outside the home country for the following firms: Nestlé, Philips, IBM, Honda, Siemens, Avon, Bayer, and Unilever.

www.prenhall.com/russell

1-14. Make a list of the top 10 companies in the Fortune 500 from five, ten, and twenty years ago. Compare them to this year's list. Comment on the companies that remained on the list and those that are newcomers.

1-15. Update the statistics on productivity given in the chapter. Do you see any new trends? Who do you think will be the leader in the twenty-first century?

1-16. Examine this year's <u>Global 500</u> by industry. Which industries are the most competitive? Which industries are the least competitive? Are some industries dominated by certain countries? Which industries are the most profitable?

1-17. Choose an industry on which you will be the class "expert" for the duration of this course. Write an initial profile of major players, customers, structure, and competitive issues.

1-18. How is competitiveness measured for a country? An industry? A firm?

1-19. What are your expectations regarding this course? What are your instructor's expectations? Reach consensus on four major goals for the course.

1-20. List several issues and trends in operations for the future. What actions do you recommend to prepare for the future challenges?

www.prenhall.com/russell

CASE PROBLEM

What Does It Take to Compete?

Rubatex Corporation manufactures rubber and foam products for a variety of products, including artificial turf, hosing and insulation, hockey helmet liners, scuba diving suits, Thighmasters, sports sandals, and mouse pads. The company was purchased last year by an investment firm called American Industrial Partners (AIP) that has so far earned only a 1 percent return on its investment. Obviously, the company is having problems. Its sales are up but earnings down. In the first three months of this year, the company lost $2 million on $68 million in sales. Understandably, AIP wants to know why and is demanding aggressive action.

Employees at the Bedford, Virginia, plant say they know something's wrong. The plant is hot and dirty and crumbling, and they are working harder to produce items of poorer quality. Fewer than seven out of ten orders are shipped on time, and 2 percent of sales are returned as defective. Built in 1924, the plant sprawls over 14 buildings, with only the offices and lunchroom air conditioned. Equipment is old and outdated, much of it purchased in the 1940s. The 800 to 2000 workers at the Bedford plant are paid an average of $11.50 an hour, far above the minimum wage average for the area. In the mill room, workers get a twenty-minute lunch break and two ten-minute breaks each eight-hour shift. They spend their day lifting and loading heavy bags of compounds into mixers and working with rubber stock that can reach temperatures of 300 degrees or more. At the end of the day, workers leave covered with chemical dust from the mixing compounds. The company says exposure to the chemical poses no cancer or health risks. The workers aren't so sure.

Recently, in an effort to increase productivity, workers in the mill area were asked to increase the amount of rubber made in a single batch and decrease the bake time. Batches that used to take thirty minutes to cook were scheduled for fifteen minutes, and fifteen-minute batches were reduced to twelve minutes or less. Paradoxically, even though the workers were running about a third more batches than before, they produced less usable rubber.

Labor–management relations are not good. Management says it pays the workers well and expects top notch performance. If productivity does not increase soon, AIP will be forced to lay off about a third of the Rubatex work force and may eventually close down the Bedford plant. Cost estimates to update the plant exceed $6 million. AIP does not want to authorize additional investment in plant and equipment until worker commitment to improved productivity is assured. Rubatex management vows to engineer a turnaround. They have set goals for the plant to increase sales by 30 percent.

What should Rubatex do to remain competitive?

SOURCE: Material for this case was taken from Jeff Sturgeon, "Rubatex Building Road to Recovery," and Richard Foster, "Old Plant Takes Toll on Workers, Morale," *Roanoke Times and World News* July 21, 1996.

References

Blackburn, J., ed. *Time-Based Competition: The Next Battle-ground in American Manufacturing.* Homewood, Ill.: Irwin, 1991.

Clark, Kim. "Competing Through Manufacturing and the New Manufacturing Paradigm: Is Manufacturing Strategy Passé?" *Production and Operations Management* 5, no. 1 (spring 1996): 42–58.

Dertouzos, Michael, Richard Lester, and Robert Solow. *Made in America.* Cambridge, Mass.: MIT Press, 1989.

Ferdows, K., and A. DeMeyer. "Lasting Improvements in Manufacturing Performance." *Journal of Operations Management* 9, no. 2 (1990): 168–84.

Garvin, David. *Operations Strategy: Text and Cases.* Englewood Cliffs, N.J.: Prentice Hall, 1992.

Hayes, Robert H., Gary P. Pisano, and David M. Upton. *Strategic Operations: Competing Through Capabilities.* New York: Free Press, 1996.

Hayes, Robert, and Steven Wheelwright. *Restoring Our Competitive Edge: Competing Through Manufacturing.* New York: John Wiley, 1984.

Hoerr, John. *And the Wolf Finally Came: The Decline of the American Steel Industry.* Pittsburgh, Penn.: University of Pittsburgh Press, 1988.

Holland, Max. *When the Machine Stopped: A Cautionary Tale from Industrial America.* Boston, Mass.: Harvard Business School Press, 1988.

Manufacturing Studies Board. *Towards a New Era in Manufacturing: The Need for a National Vision.* Washington, D.C.: National Academy Press, 1986.

Peters, Tom. *Thriving on Chaos.* New York: Alfred A. Knopf, 1987.

Porter, Michael. *Competitive Advantage.* New York: Free Press, 1985.

Skinner, Wickham. *Manufacturing: The Formidable Competitive Weapon.* New York: John Wiley, 1985.

Skinner, Wickham. "Three Yards and a Cloud of Dust: Industrial Management at Century End." *Production and Operations Management* 5, no. 1 (Spring 1996): 15–24.

Thurow, Lester. *Head to Head: The Coming Economic Battle Among Japan, Europe, and America.* New York: William Morrow, 1992.

Womack, James, Daniel Jones, and Daniel Roos. *The Machine that Changed the World.* New York: Macmillan, 1990.

2

Operations Strategy

So You Have a Mission Statement . . . Now What?

Visioning is big in corporate America. Everyone from IBM to the Little League team has mission statements, visions, philosophies, and core values. Mission statements started appearing in the 1980s when corporations faced the issues of diversity, empowerment, globalization, environmental responsibility, total quality, teamwork, and customer focus—and they've rapidly multiplied since. Let's look at a few examples.[1]

Some mission statements clarify what business a company is in—for Levi Strauss it's *"branded casual apparel"*; for Intel it's supplying *"building blocks to the computing industry"*; for Lowe's it's helping *"customers build, improve, and enjoy their homes"*; for Binney & Smith (Crayola) it's *"colorful visual expression"*; and for Currency Doubleday it's *"ideas that link business with life's meaning."*

Other mission statements reflect the character of the company—Southwest Airlines delivers its service *"with a sense of warmth, friendliness, individual pride, and Company Spirit"*; Ben and Jerry's creates *"a new corporate concept of linked prosperity"* that includes a social mission; Hanna Andersson wants to *"enhance the richly textured experience of family and community"*; and Ritz Carlton proclaims *"we are ladies and gentlemen serving ladies and gentlemen."*

Still others are short and focused—Motorola: *"Total Customer Satisfaction,"* and Delta Air Lines: *"Worldwide Airline of Choice."*

Finally, some mission statements signal a radical change in the way the company does business—General Electric: *"Boundaryless . . . Speed . . . Stretch."*

www.prenhall.com/russell

Source: Dilbert reprinted by permission of United Feature Syndicate, Inc.

---

[1] The examples are taken from Patricia Jones and Larry Kahaner, *Say It and Live It: The 50 Corporate Mission Statements That Hit the Mark* (New York: Currency Doubleday, 1995).

Mission statements are the "constitution" for an organization, the corporate directive. But they aren't any good, as <u>Dilbert</u> implies, unless they can be converted into action. And that's what this chapter is all about—converting strategy into results.

Strategy Formulation

Strategy is a common vision that unites an organization, provides consistency in decisions, and keeps the organization moving in the right direction. Strategy formulation consists of four basic steps:

Strategy provides direction.

1. *Defining a primary task*. The **primary task** represents the purpose of a firm—what the firm is in the business of doing. It also determines the competitive arena. As such, the primary task should not be defined too narrowly. For example, <u>Norfolk Southern</u> Railways is in the business of transportation, not railroads. Paramount is in the business of communication, not making movies. Disney goes one step further—its primary task is not entertainment, it's making people happy! The primary task is usually expressed in a firm's *mission* statement. The mission may be accompanied by a *vision* statement that describes what the organization sees itself becoming.

Primary task: What is the firm in the business of doing?

2. *Assessing core competencies*. **Core competency** is what a firm does better than anyone else. Also known as *distinctive competence* or *competitive advantage*, it can be defined only in comparison with competitors. A firm's core competence can be exceptional service, higher quality, faster delivery, or lower cost. It can be superior performance, better reliability, more features, more variety, or simply being most convenient. One company may strive to be first to the market with innovative designs, whereas another may look for success arriving later but with better quality.

Core competency: What does the firm do better than anyone else?

To be successful, companies must identify and capitalize on what sets them apart from other firms—their core competencies. Distinctive competence is not static; it is not something a firm either has or doesn't have. Competencies are dynamic, they can be developed, nurtured, and enhanced. They can also become obsolete! In a later section, we will examine how to develop and fully utilize core competencies.

3. *Determining order winners and order qualifiers*. A firm is in trouble if the things it does best are not important to the customer. That's why it's essential to look toward the customers to determine what influences their purchase decision.

Order qualifiers are characteristics of a product or service that qualify it to be considered for purchase by a customer. An **order winner** is the characteristic of a product or service that wins orders in the marketplace—the final factor in the purchasing decision. For example, when purchasing a CD player, customers may determine a price range (order qualifier) and then choose the product with the most features (order winner) within that price range. Or they may have a set of features in mind (order qualifiers) and then select the least expensive CD player (order winner) that has all the required features.

Order qualifiers: What qualifies an item to be considered for purchase?

Order winner: What wins the order?

Order winners and order qualifiers can evolve over time, just as competencies can be gained and lost. Japanese automakers initially competed on price but had to assure certain levels of quality before the U.S. consumer would consider their product. Over time, the consumer was willing to pay a higher price (within reason) for the assurance of a superior-quality Japanese car. Price became a qualifier, but quality won the orders. Today, high quality, as a standard of the automotive industry, has become an order qualifier and innovative design wins the orders.

It is important for a firm to meet the order qualifiers and excel on the order winner. Ideally, a firm's distinctive competence should match the market's order winner.

If it does not, perhaps a segment of the market could be targeted that more closely matches the firm's expertise. Or the firm could begin developing additional competencies that are more in tune with market needs.

Positioning: How will the firm compete?

4. *Positioning the firm.* No firm can be all things to all people. **Positioning** involves making choices—choosing one or two important things to concentrate on and doing them extremely well. A firm's positioning strategy defines how it will compete in the marketplace. An effective positioning strategy considers the strengths and weaknesses of the organization, the needs of the marketplace, and the position of competitors.[2]

Let's look at companies who have positioned themselves to compete on cost, quality, flexibility, and speed.

Competing on Cost

Competing on cost: Eliminate all waste.

Companies that compete on cost relentlessly pursue the elimination of all waste. In the past, companies in this category produced standardized products for large markets. They improved yield by stabilizing the production process, tightening productivity standards, and investing in automation. Today, the entire cost structure is examined for reduction potential, not just direct labor costs. High-volume production and automation may or may not provide the most cost-effective alternative.

www.prenhall.com/russell

Take the example of Lincoln Electric, a manufacturer that has reduced costs by $10 million a year for the past 10 years. One example of cost-cutting measures: Air currents from ducts behind a waterfall draw paint that has missed its mark during the painting process and carry it into a filtering system so that it can be reused. Skilled machine operators, working on a strict piece-rate system, earn around $80,000 a year. They make their own tools, maintain and repair the equipment themselves, and check their own quality. Called "million-dollar men," these workers have saved the company millions of dollars that would have been spent on automated equipment.

www.prenhall.com/russell

Southwest Airlines' strategy of low cost and controlled growth is supported by carefully designed service, efficient operations, and committed personnel. Southwest uses only one type of airplane, the Boeing 737, to facilitate crew changes and to streamline training, record-keeping, maintenance, and inventory costs. Turnaround time between flights is 15 minutes. Since its flights are limited to short routes (about an hour), all flights are direct. That means no baggage transfers and no meals to be served. There are no assigned seats and no printed boarding passes for flights. Passengers show their ID at the gate, are checked off the reservation list and issued plastic boarding passes that the airline can use again and again. Southwest saves $30 million annually in travel agent commissions by requiring customers to call the airline directly to book flights. The airline carefully selects employees and reinforces its commitment with a model profit sharing plan. The result? Southwest boasts the lowest cost per passenger mile and the highest number of passengers per employee in the industry, as well as the most on-time arrivals and the fewest number of mishandled baggage complaints.

Companies that compete successfully on cost realize that low cost cannot be sustained as a competitive advantage if increases in productivity are obtained solely by short-term cost reductions. A long-term productivity "portfolio" is required that trades off current expenditures for future reductions in operating cost. The portfolio consists of investments in updated facilities and equipment, programs and systems to streamline

---

[2] These factors can be depicted in a SWOT matrix which lists the current strengths (S) and weaknesses (W) internal to the company, and the opportunities (O) and threats (T) external to the company.

operations, and training and development that enhances the skills and capabilities of people.

Competing on Quality

Most companies approach quality in a defensive or reactive mode; quality is confined to minimizing defect rates or conforming to design specifications. To compete on quality, companies must view quality as an opportunity to please the customer, not just a way to avoid problems or reduce rework costs. Table 1.2's quality comparisons of several U.S. and Japanese products clearly showed that quality can provide a competitive advantage.

David Garvin, a Harvard quality expert, cites the following tenets for companies that compete on quality:

1. Quality is defined from the customer's point of view.
2. Quality is linked with profitability on both the market and cost sides.
3. Quality is viewed as a competitive weapon.
4. Quality is built into the strategic planning process.
5. Quality receives organizationwide commitment.

Competing on quality:
Please the customer.

THE COMPETITIVE EDGE

Wal-Mart Brings It All Together

www.prenhall.com/russell

Wal-Mart has a corporate strategy not unlike most retailers—its goal is to provide customers access to quality goods at competitive prices. The key to Wal-Mart's phenomenal success is the vigor with which it has pursued its goal and the support structure it has built. To Wal-Mart "access" means providing the right goods when and where the customers want them. This requires a sophisticated logistics infrastructure and decentralized stocking decisions by store managers.

Wal-Mart ships goods from warehouses to stores in less than 48 hours. Store shelves are replenished twice a week, in contrast to the industry average of every 2 weeks. The company has 19 distribution centers and nearly 2000 company-owned trucks. Wal-Mart's private satellite communication system sends point-of-sales data directly to its 4000 vendors. The satellite system also serves as a video link connecting individual stores to corporate headquarters and to each other. Store managers frequently hold conferences to exchange information on what is and isn't selling and which promotions are working. Each store manager decides how to stock his or her store. The job of senior management is to create an environment in which the managers can learn from the market and from each other. Store managers are provided with detailed in-

formation about customer behavior. Within the store, 36 separate merchandising departments (compared to K-mart's 5) are run by employees trained to be attuned to the customer and provide input to stocking decisions.

Wal-Mart practices an interesting logistics technique known as *cross-docking*. In this system, goods delivered to Wal-Mart warehouses are selected, repacked, and dispatched to stores without ever sitting in inventory. Goods cross from one loading dock to another in 48 hours or less. Cross-docking allows Wal-Mart to order merchandise in full truckloads from suppliers and save on freight charges, but it is a difficult system to manage. Information must flow smoothly and quickly between the stores, distribution centers, and suppliers. The satellite communications network connected to data-collection cash registers and knowledgeable store managers support the information requirements.

Wal-Mart's strategy, supported by its operations (i.e., information system, logistics/inventory replenishment system, and decentralization), has enabled the company to locate equally successful stores in the rural South and urban North and to expand into new retail sectors, such as pharmacies, warehouse clubs, and superstores.

SOURCE: Based on George Stalk, Philip Evans, and Lawrence Shulman, "Competing on Capabilities: The New Rules of Corporate Strategy," *Harvard Business Review* (March–April 1992): 57–69.

www.prenhall.com/russell

An annual survey by the American Society for Quality Control (ASQC) provides some insight into consumer preferences for quality. A recent survey found that Americans were willing to spend 33 percent more for a better-quality car, 50 percent more for a better-quality dishwasher, 65 percent more for a better TV, 70 percent more for a better sofa, and more than twice as much for a better pair of shoes. It is important to understand the customer's attitude toward and expectations of quality.

The pursuit of the quality advantage can be quite tough in today's competitive environment. For example, Corning Glass discovered in the early 1980s that its 2 percent defect rate was no longer acceptable, since its Japanese competitors achieved a 0.04 percent defect rate. After several years of hard work, Corning was pleased with its remarkable 0.02 percent defect rate until it examined its competitors' newly achieved 0.00008 percent defective—about as close to zero defects as you can get!

Competing on Flexibility

Flexibility is the ability to adjust to changes in product mix, production volume, or design.

Marketing always wants more variety to offer its customers. Manufacturing resists this trend because variety upsets the stability (and efficiency) of a production system and increases costs. The ability of manufacturing to respond to variation has opened up a new level of competition. **Flexibility** has become a competitive weapon. It includes the ability to produce a wide variety of products, to introduce new products and modify existing products quickly, and to respond to customer needs.

An example of the strategic importance of flexibility is provided by the so-called H-Y war in Japan in the early 1980s, when Yamaha challenged Honda's dominance of the motorcycle market. Before the challenge, both companies offered about 60 different models of motorcycles. Within 18 months, Honda had introduced and retired 113 models. Yamaha was able to introduce only 37 new models in that time frame. Honda's new models had four-valve engines, direct drive, and other innovations. Compared to a Honda, a Yamaha motorcycle was perceived as old and outdated. Two years later, with its complete field inventory rendered obsolete, Yamaha conceded defeat. Honda "won" the war with innovation and variety. Its key to achieving market dominance was flexibility through superior methods for developing, manufacturing and introducing new products.

Technology can also provide the tools for flexibility. Handmade shoes begin with custom-sculpted models, called *lasts*, that can cost hundreds of dollars and take ten to twenty hours to construct. The entire shoemaking process takes about eight months and is very expensive. At Custom Foot shoe store, a customer's feet are scanned electronically to capture twelve different three-dimensional measurements. The measurements are sent to a factory in Italy where a library of 3,000 computerized "lasts" can be modified digitally instead of manually, then milled by a machine out of plastic. Custom shoes are mailed to the customer's home within a month, and since the shoe store carries no inventory, the prices are comparable to off-the-shelf shoes.

The National Bicycle Industrial Company fits bicycles to exact customer measurements. Bicycle manufacturers typically offer customers a choice between 20 or 30 different models. National offers 11,231,862 variations and delivers within 2 weeks at costs only 10 percent above standard models. Computerized design and computer-controlled machinery allow customized products to be essentially mass produced. The popular term for this phenomenon is *mass customization*.

Competing on Speed

Speed has become a new source of competitive advantage. Service organizations such as McDonald's, LensCrafters, and Federal Express have always competed on speed. Citicorp advertises a fifteen-minute mortgage approval, L. L. Bean ships orders the day

Andersen Windows of Bayport, Minnesota, is a $1 billion private company skilled at meeting the demands of individual customers with efficient operations. Retail store customers worldwide can design their own windows by computer, then send their creations to Andersen's Minnesota factory for delivery within a month's time.

they are received, and Wal-Mart replenishes its stock twice a week instead of the industry average of every two weeks. Now manufacturers are discovering the advantages of *time-based competition.* In the garment industry, Saks Fifth Avenue has terminals from the French national Videotex system that link retailers to manufacturers abroad. Tailors in New York send suit measurements via satellite to France, where a laser cuts the cloth and tailors begin their work. The suit is completed and shipped back to New York within four days. That's about the same amount of time required for alterations in most clothing stores. The standard for custom-made suits is ten weeks.

In five days, Hewlett-Packard can produce electronic testing equipment that used to take four weeks to produce. General Electric has reduced the time of manufacture for circuit-breaker boxes from three weeks to three days and the manufacture of dishwashers from six days to eighteen hours. Motorola now needs sixty minutes to build to order and ship pagers that used to take three weeks! Reductions in the time required to get new products to the market is also improving. For the past decade Japanese automakers have held a two-year advantage in new product development. Now U.S. automakers have closed that gap.

Competing on speed: Fast moves, fast adaptations, and tight linkages.

Competing on speed—the "hustle strategy"—requires a new type of organization characterized by fast moves, fast adaptations, and tight linkages.[3] Decision making is pushed down the organization as levels of management are collapsed and work is performed in cross-functional teams. Change is embraced and risk taking encouraged. Close contact is maintained with both suppliers and customers.

Forming alliances is one of the most effective avenues for competing on speed. The best example is the textile industry's quick response (QR) initiative, designed to improve the flow of information, standardize recording systems, and reduce turnaround times along the entire supply chain from fiber to textiles to apparel to retailing. Automotive,

www.prenhall.com/russell

---

[3] See Chapter C-4 in Tom Peters, *Thriving on Chaos* (New York: Alfred A. Knopf, 1987).

THE COMPETITIVE EDGE

Andersen Windows Gets Flexible

www.prenhall.com/russell

Andersen Windows, like most manufacturers, used to produce a limited range of standard products in large volumes. As customers demanded more uniqueness, Andersen introduced more and more options to their standard windows—so many, in fact, that the number of products offered grew from 28,000 to 86,000. Thick catalogs allowed customers to combine thousands of options into truly unique windows. However, a price quote took several hours to calculate, required a working knowledge of trigonometry, and was as long as 15 pages. With this degree of complexity, the rate of error in the finished product was also high (one in five truckloads shipped had at least one error), and Andersen's reputation as a quality manufacturer was threatened.

In 1992, Andersen introduced an electronic version of its catalog that salespeople can use to add, change, and strip away features until the customer is pleased with the design. The computer then checks the window specs for structural soundness, generates a price quote, and transmits the order to an Andersen factory. At the factory, standard parts from inventory are used to assemble custom products, and bar codes keep track of the customer order as it moves through assembly. In five years, demand for Andersen windows has tripled, the number of different products offered has topped 188,000, and errors are down to one per 200 truckloads. Flexibility has provided Andersen Windows with a competitive edge.

SOURCE: Justin Martin, "Are You as Good as You Think You Are?" *Fortune* (September 30, 1996): 142–4.

www.prenhall.com/russell

electronics, and equipment manufacturers encourage similar alliances within their respective industries with an initiative called agile manufacturing.

Competency-Based Strategies

Traditional strategic planning first looks external to the company at competitors, markets, and trends in order to identify strategic opportunities, then develops the internal capabilities to capitalize on those opportunities. The trouble with this approach today is that by the time new capabilities are developed, the opportunities may have passed and the strategies become obsolete. The increased number of buyouts, mergers, and joint ventures in the past decade is proof of fact that, in the short term, the only way a firm can build competencies is to buy them.

Build capabilities.

Today's leading companies focus more on building basic internal capabilities than on achieving specific marketing or financial goals. They develop the competencies first, then look for opportunities to use the competencies. This proactive approach to strategy positions the firm to take advantage of opportunities created by changes in markets, technologies, and the competitive environment. To use this approach companies must learn how to develop and exploit core competencies. These issues are explored in the next two sections.

Developing Core Competencies

Core competencies are the essential capabilities that create a firm's sustainable competitive advantage. They have usually been built up over time and cannot be easily imitated. Core competencies are forward looking; they are the stepping stones to new opportunities. We have learned from IBM and others that a large market share (even 90 percent) today does not guarantee a large market share tomorrow. Customers, markets, products and technologies change too rapidly. For this reason, products and technologies are seldom core competencies. The advantage they provide is short-lived—other companies can readily purchase, emulate, or improve upon products and technologies. Core competencies are more likely to be based on experience, knowledge, and know-how.

Consider Chaparral Steel, the tenth largest steel producer in the United States, a mini-mill of fewer than 1,000 workers, that, nevertheless, has set world productivity records several times and is the first American steel company to receive a Japanese Industrial Quality Certification.[4] Chaparral management allows its competitors to tour its plants at will because "they can't take [what we do best] home with them." Although Chaparral is known for its low cost and high technology, its core competency is not technology, but *the ability to transform technology rapidly into new products and processes*. By the time its competitor has copied its current technology, Chaparral is confident its people will have moved on to something else. Similarly, Hewlett-Packard's core competency is not its knowledge of measurement, communications, and computation, but the ability to create products and services that *synergize* these three skills.

In today's changing business environment, many companies are struggling to identify appropriate core competencies. Harvard professor Dorothy Leonard-Barton has identified four activities that encourage the development of effective core competencies (see Figure 2.1): (1) shared problem solving, (2) integrating new technologies and methodologies, (3) experimenting, and (4) importing knowledge.

To see how these activities encourage the development of core competencies, let's look at the Chaparral example. At Chaparral Steel, problem solving is the responsibility of every individual. There are no staff positions with resident experts to consult, and there

www.prenhall.com/russell

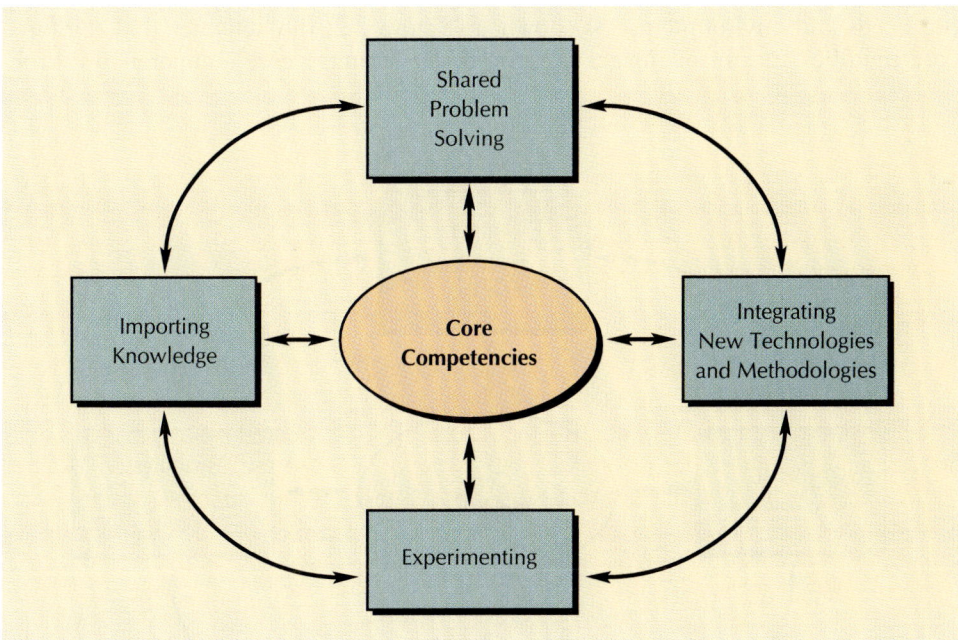

FIGURE 2.1   Activities Leading to Core Competencies
SOURCE: Adapted from Dorothy Leonard-Barton, *Wellsprings of Knowledge: Building and Sustaining the Sources of Knowledge* (Boston: Harvard Business School Press, 1995), p. 9.

---

[4] The discussion of Chaparral Steel and core competencies is adapted from Dorothy Leonard-Barton, *Wellsprings of Knowledge: Building and Sustaining the Sources of Knowledge* (Boston: Harvard Business School Press, 1995), Chapters 1 and 2.

are only two levels of management. As a result, 90 percent of all problems are fixed in the field. Machine operators check their own quality, production workers do maintenance tasks, everyone is a salesperson, and ideas come from every segment of the company.

Chaparral works on integrating new technologies and methodologies. Production processes are constantly being improved, purchased equipment is routinely enhanced, and process improvements are enacted immediately. All engineers and technicians must work on the production line, and work is structured so that knowledge is shared. For example, when a shift supervisor is absent, one of her workers takes over the position and another shift supervisor is called in to assume the worker's normal duties (and to coach the worker as needed in his new role).

Experimentation and individual initiative are encouraged at Chaparral Steel. CEO Gordon Forward says, "We figured if we could tap the egos of everyone in the company, we could move mountains." The company practices *creative destruction*—tearing down what works now to find what might work better—and considers riskless projects worthless.

Knowledge is also imported from outside the organization. Chaparral constantly benchmarks and scans the environment for ideas. The firm works with the world's best suppliers and pushes them to innovate. Chaparral sponsors considerable outside research and believes that "there is no value in *recreating* something—only in building on the best existing knowledge."

In this type of organization, core competencies can evolve with the times. Core competencies that are not being updated or enhanced can easily become *core rigidities*.

Core rigidities para-
lyze a company.

Core rigidities paralyze a company and prevent it from changing to meet emerging needs and environments. As shown in Figure 2.2, the activities that reinforce core rigidities are mirror images of those that encourage core competencies. Prob-

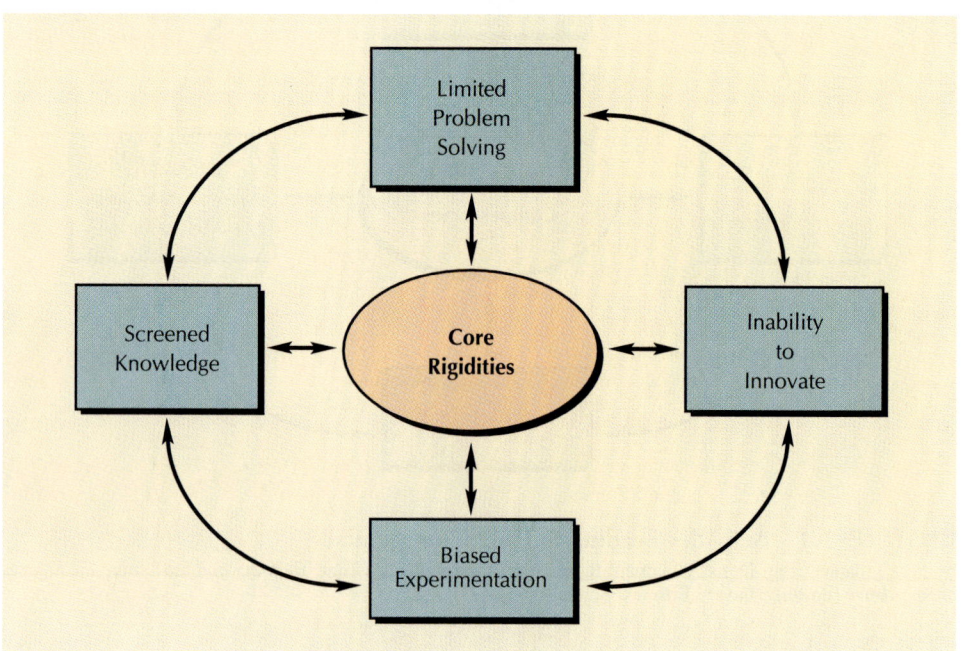

FIGURE 2.2 Activities That Reinforce Core Rigidities
SOURCE: Adapted from Dorothy Leonard-Barton, *Wellsprings of Knowledge: Building and Sustaining the Sources of Innovation* (Boston: Harvard Business School Press, 1995), p. 36.

lem solving is limited, the company finds it difficult to implement new technologies and methodologies, experimentation is biased, and knowledge from the outside is screened with existing paradigms that reject radically different ideas. Examples of companies that ignored the obvious: Sears failed to recognize Wal-Mart as its competitor; IBM saw itself as unbeatable; and GM was slow to react to changing customer needs. Why did this happen? Management consultant Michael Hammer says that Wal-Mart didn't open new stores under the cloak of darkness when Sears executives were asleep; Apple didn't disguise its PCs as toasters to fool the Big Blue; nor did Nissan and Honda put Chrysler and Ford nameplates on their cars to confuse GM scouts. The market leaders were so sure of their strengths and inevitable success that they never bothered to look at the changes taking place around them. Their core competencies had indeed become core rigidities that shielded them from changing, learning, and evolving.

Exploiting Core Competencies

Many firms fail to capitalize on their existing competencies or to use them as a springboard to new competencies. Companies can further develop and exploit their core competencies by:[5]

- *Enhancing the value a competency provides to customers.* As a starting point, companies should determine which processes, products, and services matter most to their customers and work to improve the competencies related to them. This may lead to new opportunities.[6] For example, Goodyear no longer just delivers tires to Navistar's warehouse. It operates the tire warehouse for Navistar and mounts and balances the tires on Navistar's trucks. Similarly, Federal Express for years has maintained inventory levels of small parts and critical supplies for its major customers.

www.prenhall.com/russell

- *Transforming an internal competence into a salable item.* American Airlines markets its SABRE reservation system to airlines and travel agents, and its maintenance system to other airlines. Trigon of Massachusetts sells its telemarketing services; L. L. Bean markets its customer service process; and Xerox, Westinghouse, AT&T, and others have spun off firms to market their quality-improvement processes.

- *Applying competencies in a creative way to new products and services.* Circuit City, the retail electronics store, excelled in managing inventory levels and handling customer credit applications. The company discovered that these competencies were also critical to success in the used-car business. Circuit City's subsidiary, CarMax, is now a hugely successful used-car business that is setting new standards of performance in that industry. H&R Block used its expertise in recruiting and managing short-term employees during tax season to create a competitive advantage in the field of temporary services.

Capitalize on core competencies: enhance, transform, apply, create

- *Creating new ways of working and finding new markets.* John Deere, a farm equipment manufacturer, developed competencies in financial services so that it could provide its retail dealer network with insurance. The company later sold these processes to automobile dealers, boat dealers, and recreational dealers.

---

[5] The examples in this section come from Michael Hammer, *Beyond Reengineering* (New York: HarperCollins, 1996).

[6] Similarly, a company can identify which processes, products, and services have marginal impact on its customers, and for which they have no particular expertise. These processes are candidates for outsourcing.

Circuit City, the retail electronics store, applied its competencies in high-tech selling techniques, managing large inventories, and handling customer credit applications, to an entirely new line of business—used-cars. A Circuit City subsidiary, called CarMax: The Auto Superstore offers a huge selection of quality used cars (from 500 to 1,500 at each location), lots of information for the customer in an electronic format, and one-price, no-haggle sales. Customers enter their requirements for a vehicle into sales kiosks on the lot, from area shopping malls, or from the Internet. In seconds, the system reviews the inventory of cars available and directs the customer to the appropriate sales lot and car location, where the car can be inspected and taken for a test drive. Fixed prices speed the selling process, as do electronic loan approvals on the spot. CarMax's new concept for selling cars has revolutionized the used car business and also brought out scores of competitors. Car dealerships across the country have instituted no-haggle pricing, and Blockbuster Video's AutoNation USA has replicated the CarMax concept. Armed with purchases of two rental car companies and new-car dealerships, AutoNation has a ready source of used cars. In the meantime, CarMax has centralized its reconditioning centers, freeing up repair facilities in its superstores to service cars. Servicing cars is a dealer's biggest source of profitability, and CarMax hopes top notch servicing will attract customers and build customer loyalty.

From Strategy to Results

"The difficulty is not in knowing what to do. It's doing it," said Kodak's CEO, George Fisher.[7] How often do elaborate strategic plans in fancy binders lay in the bottom file drawer until the next planning cycle rolls around? Unfortunately, quite often. Implementing strategy can be more difficult than formulating strategy. Strategies unveiled with much fanfare may never be followed because they are hard to understand, too general, or unrealistic. Strategies that aim for results five years or so down the road mean very little to the worker who is evaluated on his or her daily performance. Different departments or functional areas in a firm may interpret the same strategy in different ways. If their efforts are not coordinated, the results can be disastrous.

---

[7] Hammer, *Beyond Reengineering*, p. 193.

THE COMPETITIVE EDGE

Bendix Uses Its Expertise to Open New Markets

Does your car have antilock brakes? Most do these days, but there was a time when the market for antilock brakes was limited to luxury vehicles. That's because the part was too heavy and too expensive. Through market research, Bendix Automotive Services, a subsidiary of Allied-Signal, discovered that the market for antilock brakes could be increased 500 percent to 1,000 percent if their weight and cost could be cut in half.

So Bendix engineers, production managers, and accountants got together and pooled their expertise to design a product with 70 percent fewer parts that takes half as much time to produce and costs 60 percent less. And that opened up a huge new market.

SOURCE: David Carr, Kevin Dougherty, Henry Johansson, Robert King, and David Moran, *Breakpoint Business Process Redesign* (Arlington, Va.: Coopers & Lybrand, 1992), pp. 6–7, 20.

Consider Schlitz Brewing Company whose strategy called for reduced costs and increased efficiency. Operations achieved its goals by dramatically shortening its brewing cycle—and, in the process, lost six out of every ten customers when the clarity and taste of the beer suffered. The efficiency move that was to make the company the most profitable in its industry, instead caused its stock value to plummet from $69 per share to $5 per share.

Companies struggling to align day-to-day decisions with corporate strategy have found success with a planning system known in Japan as *hoshin kanri,* and in the United States as policy deployment, or hoshin planning. *Hoshin kanri* is roughly translated from Japanese as "shining metal pointing direction"—a compass. That's what Harvard professor Robert Hayes suggests we need from strategy:

> When you are lost on a highway, a roadmap is very useful; but when you are lost in a swamp whose topography is constantly changing, a roadmap is of little help. A simple *compass*—which indicates the general direction to be taken and allows you to use your own ingenuity in overcoming various difficulties—is much more valuable.[8]

www.prenhall.com/russell

Policy Deployment

Policy deployment tries to focus everyone in an organization on common goals and priorities by translating corporate strategy into measurable objectives throughout the various functions and levels of the organization. As a result, everyone in the organization should understand the strategic plan, be able to derive several goals from the plan, and determine how each goal ties into their own daily activities.

Figure 2.3 outlines the strategic planning hierarchy. Senior management, with input and participation from different levels of the organization, develops a corporate strategic plan in concurrence with the firm's mission and vision, customer requirements (*voice of the customer*), and business conditions (*voice of the business*). The strategic plan focuses on the gap between the firm's vision and its current position. It identifies and prioritizes what needs to be done to close the gap, and provides direction for formulating strategies in the functional areas of the firm such as marketing, operations, and finance.

Policy deployment translates corporate strategy into measurable objectives.

---

[8] Robert Hayes, "Strategic Planning—Forward in Reverse," *Harvard Business Review* (May–June 1985): 111–19.

www.prenhall.com/russell

Is your company pointed in one direction? AT&T uses the analogy of migrating geese to explain the concept of policy deployment. Naturalists believe the instinctive V-formation allows the geese to follow one leader and migrate in a cohesive unit toward their destination. Policy deployment does the same thing—it enables business leaders to mobilize the organization toward a common destination, aligning all employees behind a common goal and a collective wisdom.

Suppose the corporate strategic plan called for a reduction of 30 percent in the length of the business cycle. Senior management from each functional area would gather together to assess how their activities contribute to the business cycle, confer on the feasibility of reducing the cycle by 30 percent, and agree upon their particular role in achieving the reduction. Marketing might decide that creating strategic alliances with its distributors would

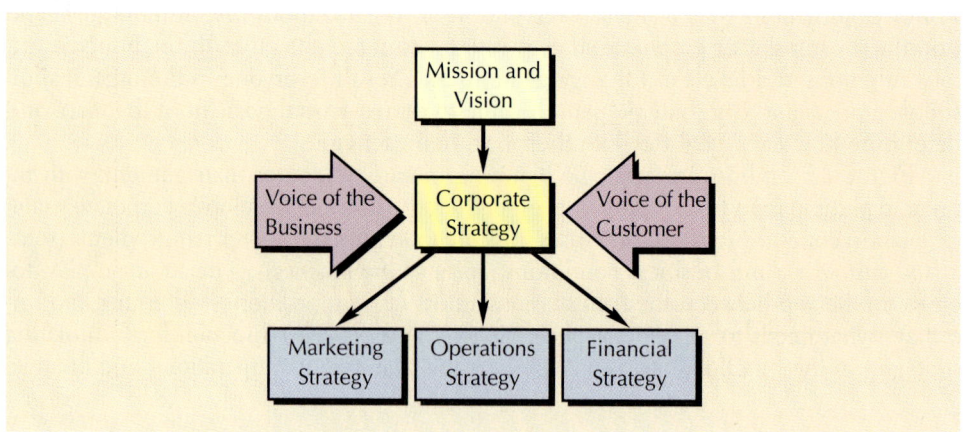

FIGURE 2.3   Strategic Planning

shorten the average time to release a new product. Operations might try to reduce its purchasing and production cycles by reducing its supplier base, certifying suppliers, and implementing a just-in-time (JIT) system. Finance might decide to eliminate unnecessary approval loops for expenditures, begin pre-qualifying sales prospects, and explore the use of electronic funds transfer (EFT) in conjunction with operations' JIT strategy.

The process for forming objectives would continue in a similar manner down the organization with the *means* of achieving objectives for one level of management becoming the *target* or objectives for the next level. The outcome of the process is a cascade of action plans (or **hoshins**) aligned to complete each functional objective which will, in turn, combine to achieve the strategic plan.

Hoshins: the action plans generated from the policy deployment process.

Figure 2.4 shows the derivation of an action plan for employee Gladys Wray at

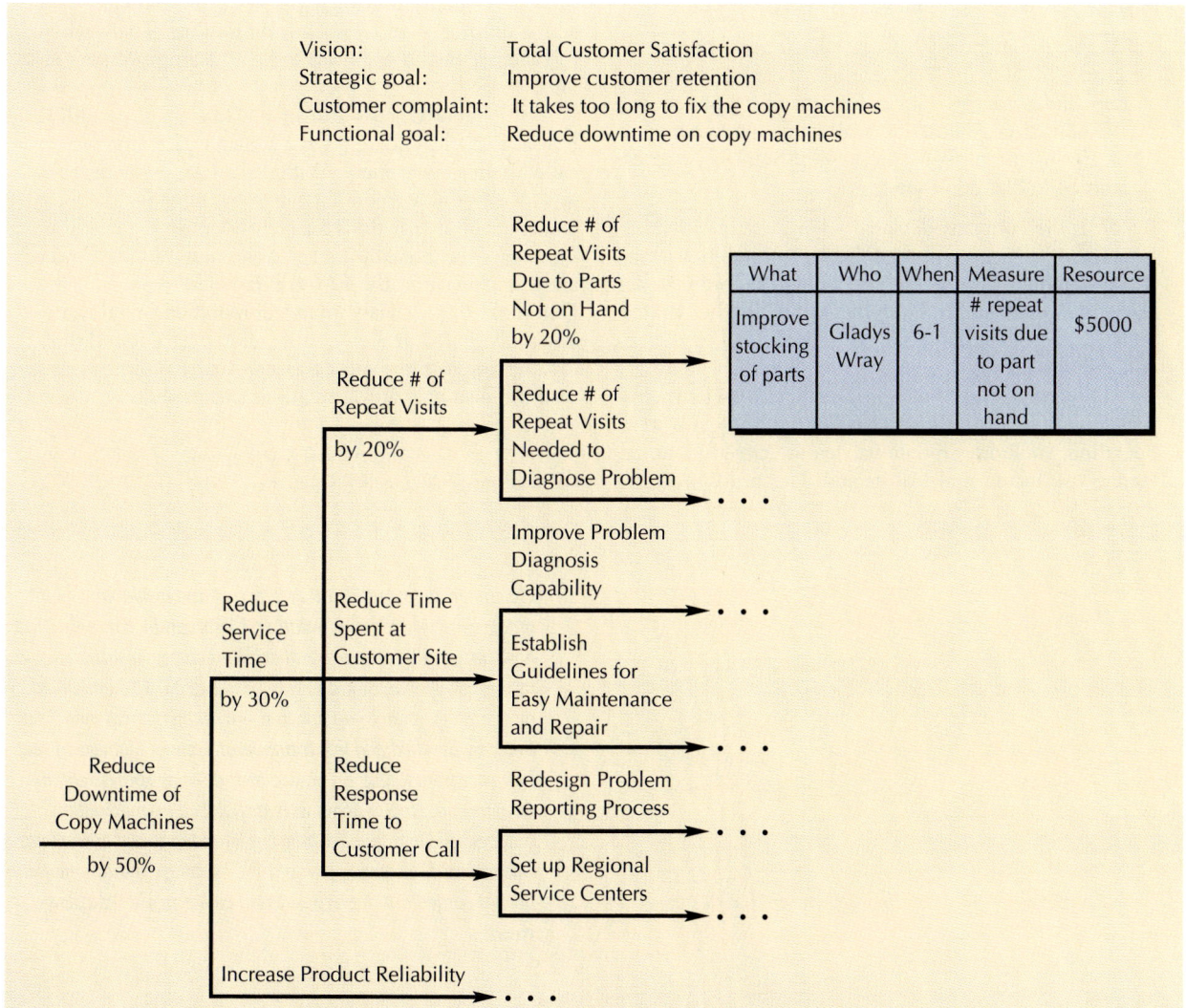

FIGURE 2.4   Action Plan for CopyPlus Office Supplies
SOURCE: Adapted from AT&T Quality Steering Committee, *Policy Deployment*, Indianapolis: AT&T Technical Publications Center, 1992.

THE COMPETITIVE EDGE

Strategy Gives Direction to FPL's Quality Initiatives

In the 1970s, public utilities were hit hard by severe oil shortages, high energy costs, higher customer dissatisfaction, and huge capital expenditures. In the state of Florida, with a rapidly increasing population and few resources, Florida Power and Light (FPL) was fighting for its survival. FPL's CEO described his company's attitude toward quality as follows:

www.prenhall.com/russell

> We were concerned with keeping rejects down, instead of quality up. We were busy keeping imperfection under control, rather than trying for perfection. We sometimes burnt the toast and then scraped it clean, instead of fixing the toaster. Some of us even learned to like burnt toast.

By 1981, the company declared all-out war on anything less than total quality and published an ambitious mission statement: "During the next decade, we want to become the best-managed electric utility in the United States and an excellent company overall, and to be recognized as such."

The company set out in earnest with 10 quality improvement teams. Within 5 years, over 1400 teams were operating, including functional teams, cross-functional teams, task teams, and lead teams. The teams were required to follow a systematic process for quality improvement that emphasized "management by fact." The 5-year experience established teams as the primary vehicle for improvement at FPL and institutionalized top management's role in supporting quality. However, there were problems.

Employees were no longer anxious to volunteer for teams, middle management was disenfranchised, teams generated more recommendations than management could process, and they seemed to be going in too many directions at once. Although the teams met with much success on their individual projects, the company as a whole did not seem to be moving forward. That's when FPL began looking for a way to focus its improvement efforts.

FPL followed the lead of the top Japanese utility, Kansai Electric, and adopted a strategic planning system called *policy deployment*. With policy deployment, FPL was able to link corporate goals with individual actions, and concentrate its efforts on a few key objectives. Within four years the breakthroughs came, and Florida Power and Light became the first non-Japanese winner of the Deming Prize. Today, many corporations worldwide, originally stalled in their quality efforts, have found strategy the key to their success. Keep that in mind as you read the next chapter on quality management.

SOURCE: John Hudiberg, *Winning with Quality: The FPL Story* (White Plains, N.Y.: Quality Resources, 1991).

Customers define utility quality by cost and availability. Utility outages are a function of weather. Costs can be controlled, but how can a utility control weather? With customer satisfaction as its overriding goal, Florida Power and Light (FPL) embarked on a strategic plan to do just that—a mathematical model on tree growth scheduled tree trimmers at optimal intervals to keep branches from falling on power lines, de-icing sprays kept lines from freezing, repair crews were dispatched in anticipation of outages, and a gradual conversion to underground power lines was initiated. These are part of FPL's strategic improvement initiatives carried out through a system called policy deployment.

CopyPlus Office Supplies. For simplicity, only the top branch of the tree diagram is completed.

Now that we've seen how corporate strategies provide the framework for functional strategies, let's look at the issues involved in formulating a consistent strategy within the operations function.

Operations Strategy

Operations can play two roles in corporate strategy—it can provide *support* for the overall strategy of a firm, and it can serve as a firm's *distinctive competence*. It is important that operations strategy be internally consistent, as well as consistent with the firm's overall strategy. Strategic decisions in operations involve products and services, processes and technology, capacity and facilities, human resources, quality, sourcing, and operating systems. As shown in Figure 2.5, all these decisions should "fit" like pieces in a puzzle. Let's briefly discuss what is involved in each set of decisions.

Products and Services

The kinds of products and services offered by a company drive operations strategy. Products and services can be classified as make-to-order, make-to-stock, or assemble-to-order. **Make-to-order** products and services are designed, produced, and delivered to customer specifications in response to customer orders.[9] Examples include wedding invitations, custom-built homes, custom-tailored clothes, charter airline flights, component parts, and most professional services (such as medical, legal, and financial services). Critical operations issues relate to satisfying the customer (since each customer wants something different) and minimizing the time required to complete the order.

Make-to-stock products and services are designed and produced for "standard" customers in anticipation of demand. Shelves are pre-stocked with the items, and customers choose from among the products or services that are available for purchase. Examples include ready-to-wear apparel, books, televisions, airline flights, spec homes, and standard vacation packages. Critical operations issues are forecasting future demand and maintaining inventory levels that meet customer service goals.

Assemble-to-order products and services are produced in standard modules to which

> **Make-to-order** products and services are made to customer specifications after an order has been received.
> **Make-to-stock** products and services are made in anticipation of demand.

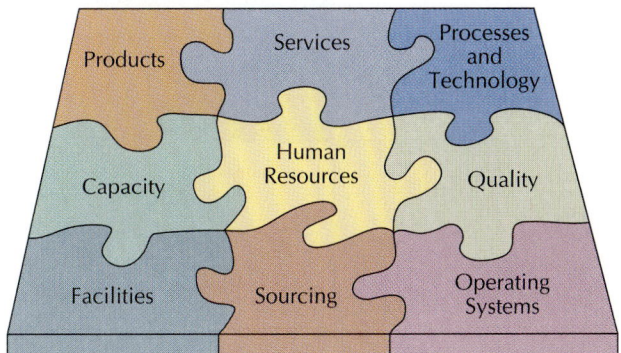

FIGURE 2.5 **Operations Strategy**

---

[9] Some companies refer to products that are designed in response to the customer as *engineered-to-order*, and those that are built and delivered in response to the customer as *made-to-order*.

Assemble-to-order products and services add options according to customer specifications.

options are added according to customer specifications. Thus, components are made-to-stock, then assembled-to-order after the customer order has been received. Examples include computer systems, corporate training, and industrial equipment. The operations function is concerned with minimizing the inventory level of standard components, as well as the delivery time of the finished product.

Processes and Technology

Processes can be classified into *projects, batch production, mass production,* and *continuous production* as shown in Figure 2.6. A **project** takes a long time to complete, involves a large investment of funds and resources, and produces one item at a time to customer order. Examples include construction projects, shipbuilding, new-product development, and aircraft manufacturing.

A project is a one-at-a-time production of a product to customer order.

Batch production systems process many different jobs at the same time in groups (or batches).

Batch production processes many different jobs through the production system at the same time in groups or batches. Products are made to customer order, volume (in terms of customer order size) is low, and demand fluctuates. Examples of batch production include machine shops, printers, bakeries, education, and furniture making.

Mass production produces large volumes of a standard product for a mass market.

Mass production produces large volumes of a standard product for a mass market. Product demand is stable, and product volume is high. Goods that are mass-produced include automobiles, televisions, personal computers, fast food, and most consumer goods.

Continuous production is used for very high-volume commodity products.

Continuous production is used for *very* high-volume commodity products that are *very* standardized. The system is *highly* automated and is typically in operation continuously 24 hours a day. Refined oil, treated water, paints, chemicals, and foodstuffs are produced by continuous production.

The process chosen to create the product or service must be consistent with product and service characteristics. The most important product characteristics (in terms of

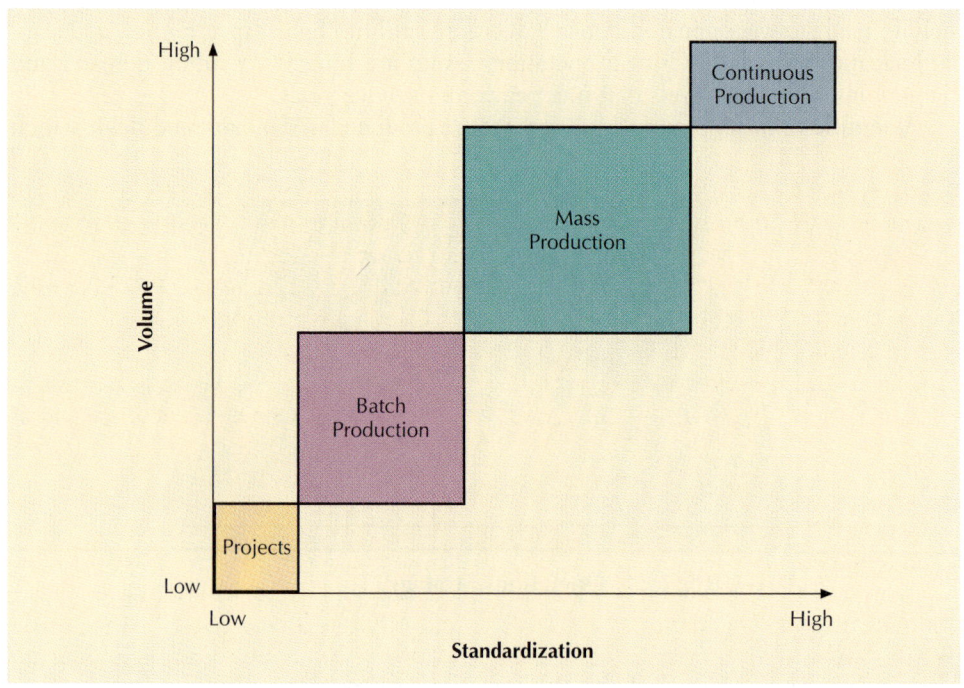

FIGURE 2.6 A Product-Process Matrix

process choice) are degree of *standardization* and *demand volume.* Figure 2.6 shows a product-process matrix which matches product characteristics with process choice.

The best process strategy is found on the diagonal of the matrix. Companies or products that are off the diagonal have either made poor process choices or have found a means to execute a competitive advantage. For example, technological advancements in flexible automation allow Motorola to mass-produce customized pagers. Volvo and Rolls Royce occupy a special market niche by producing cars in a crafted, customized fashion. Examples of poor process choice include Texas Instrument's attempt to produce consumer products for mass markets by the same process that had been successful in the production of scientific products for specialized markets and Corning's production of low-volume consumer items, such as range covers, with the same continuous process used for other items formed from glass.

It is important to obtain a good product-process match.

Capacity and Facilities

Strategic issues in terms of capacity and facilities begin with determining how much capacity should be provided—to meet all demand, to meet average demand, or to meet some established level of demand? Should capacity be provided in large chunks or in small increments? Does the company prefer to handle excess demand with overtime, extra shifts, or subcontracting? At what point should workers be hired or fired? At what point should new facilities be built?

What is the best size for a facility? Should demand be met with a few large facilities or with several smaller ones? Should a facility focus on serving certain geographic regions, product lines, or customers? Should the entire product be made (or service provided) in one facility, or should the process be broken down and placed in a series of facilities? Where should facilities be located—near markets, near raw materials, or near labor sources?

If globalization is part of the firm's strategy, should items be made, as well as sold, in foreign countries? If so, what kind of relationship is needed with manufacturers in the foreign country—licensing agreement, joint venture, partnership, alliance, merger? What legal and cultural issues might arise? Who should manage these facilities? How should they be operated?

Human Resources

Strategic issues in human resources involve determining the skill levels and degree of autonomy required to operate the productive system, outlining training requirements and selection criteria, and setting up policies on performance evaluations, compensation, and incentives. Will workers be salaried, paid an hourly rate or paid a piece rate? Will profit sharing be allowed, and if so, on what criteria? Will workers perform individual tasks or work in teams? Will they have supervisors or work in self-managed work groups? How many levels of management will be required? Will extensive worker training be necessary? Should the work force be cross-trained? What efforts will be made in terms of retention?

Quality

Quality permeates virtually every strategic decision. What is the target level of quality for our products and services? How will it be measured? How will employees be involved with quality? What types of training are necessary? What will be the responsibilities of the quality department? What types of systems will be set up to ensure quality? How will quality awareness be maintained? How will quality efforts be evaluated? How will customer perceptions of quality be determined? How will decisions in other functional areas affect quality?

Competing at Lands' End

Doing Business in the Global Arena

International sales are not new to Lands' End (LE).

www.prenhall.com/russell

The company first started servicing Canadian customers through its regular U.S. mailings in 1987. But overseas expansion presented new challenges and opportunities for the midwestern retailer.

It was agreed from the start that no international venture would compromise the values that had made Lands' End successful—its culture, its principles, its customer focus, how it treats its employees, its way of doing business. But how would those values mix with foreign business cultures?

Lands' End's first overseas foray was to the United Kingdom in 1991. A pound-denominated catalog was developed by LE copywriters in Dodgeville, Wisconsin. Phone operators in London handled calls on a contractual basis, and distribution was managed jointly through the Dodgeville facility and a contract U.K. facility. The venture was a success, but there were a few problems.

First, the British ad agencies didn't like the copy specs for the newspaper inserts—large photos, detailed descriptions of products, testimonials, even some company history. They argued that it was silly and a waste of money. But Lands' End prevailed, and the ads were well-received.

Second, the American English of the catalog confused British customers. LE corrected the obvious problems in the next issue, and hired a U.K. executive with mail-order experience to direct all British marketing and merchandising initiatives thereafter. Within two years, Lands' End had leased a 60,000-square-foot telephone and distribution center near London, and hired its own creative staff to write copy especially for its British customers.

Japan was next. Again, Lands' End had difficulty getting local authorities to go along with its style of newspaper inserts. But LE stood firm.

"Our catalogue and ads are our store," explained VP of international operations, Frank Buettner. "So we have to make sure that the photography is big, bright, and beautiful—it must capture the tone, the texture, and the essence of what the product is like. Further, the ads must describe how the product is made, why our product has an edge over the competition, and even the occasions at which the garment might be worn."

As was the case in Britain, the newspaper ads were well-received by customers. Then came the biggest challenge—*the guarantee*. No one believed it. Interest in the American company and its unusual guarantee led to a nationwide press conference carried on all three networks. The Japanese media asked to examine a number of actual returns so that they could verify the guarantee. The shipment that came from the United States included monogrammed items, items that were soiled and torn, and items that were years old. True to the guarantee, all the customers had received a full refund, no questions asked.

With that, Japanese consumers were convinced they could trust Lands' End. Now it was time for Lands' End to trust the Japanese consumer. Unlike in the United States where checks and credit cards are used to pay for an order before it is received, Japanese customers order an item, receive it, try it on, and if they like it, send in payment. While this approach was unusual for LE, the company complied with the Japanese way of doing business. And so far Lands' End has had very few problems!

Sourcing

A firm that sells the product, assembles the product, makes all the parts, and extracts the raw material is completely **vertically integrated.** But most companies cannot (or do not want to) make all of the parts that go into a product. A major strategic decision, then, is how much of the work should be done outside the firm. The decision involves questions of dependence, competency-building, and proprietary knowledge, as well as cost.

On what basis should particular items be made in-house? When should items be outsourced? How should suppliers be selected? What type of relationship should be maintained with suppliers—arm's length, controlling, partnership, alliance? What is expected from our suppliers? How many suppliers should be used? How can the quality and dependability of suppliers be assured? How can suppliers be encouraged to work together?

> **Vertical integration** is the degree to which a firm produces the parts that go into its products.

Operating Systems

Operating systems execute strategic decisions on a day-to-day basis, so it is important that they be designed to support how the firm competes in the marketplace. The information technology system must be able to support both customer and worker demands for rapid access, storage, and retrieval of information. Planning and control systems must be set up with timely feedback loops and consistent decision-making criteria. Inventory levels, scheduling priorities, and reward systems should align with strategic goals.

Strategy, at both the corporate and functional levels, involves setting direction into an uncertain future. Decision making under these conditions can be scary at best. Fortunately, there are quantitative tools available for making decisions under uncertain conditions. The supplement to this chapter reviews several of them for us.

Summary

There is no one best way to design a product, make a product, manage operations, or serve customers. The "best way" depends on a firm's objectives, resources, competencies, and context (products and customers). Firms choose to compete in different ways. A firm's *strategy* defines how it will compete in the marketplace—its own best way.

Strategy formulation involves (1) defining the primary task, (2) assessing core competence, (3) determining order winners and order qualifiers, and (4) positioning the firm. The secret to effective strategy? Excel on the order winners, meet the order qualifiers, capitalize on core competencies, and maintain focus.

Corporate strategy drives functional strategy. Functional strategies must be consistent with and supportive of corporate strategy. Strategic decisions in the operations function involve products and services, processes and technology, capacity and facilities, human resources, quality, sourcing, and operating systems. *Policy deployment* is a planning system that helps align day-to-day operating decisions with the company's overall strategy.

Summary of Key Terms

assemble-to-order: products or services created in standard modules to which options are added according to customer specifications.

batch production: a type of process that produces a variety of jobs in groups or batches.

continuous production: a type of process used to produce very high volume commodity products.

core competencies: the essential capabilities that create a firm's sustainable competitive advantage.

core rigidities: outdated capabilities that prevent a firm from attaining a sustainable competitive advantage.

flexibility: in operations, the ability to adjust to changes in product mix, production volume, or product or process design.

hoshins: the action plans generated from the policy deployment process.

make-to-order: products or services made to customer specifications after an order has been received.

make-to-stock: products or services created in anticipation of demand.

mass production: a type of process that produces large volumes of a standard product or service for a mass market.

order qualifiers: the characteristics of a product or service that qualify it to be considered for purchase.

order winner: the characteristic of a product or service that wins orders in the marketplace.

positioning: determining how a firm will compete in the marketplace.

policy deployment: a planning system for converting strategy to measurable objectives throughout all levels of an organization.

primary task: the task that is most central to the operation of a firm; it defines the business that a firm is in and is often expressed in a mission statement.

project: a type of process that creates a product or service one-at-a-time to customer order.

strategy: a common vision that unites an organization, provides consistency in decisions, and keeps the organization moving in the right direction.

vertical integration: the degree to which a firm produces the parts that go into a product.

vision: what an organization sees itself becoming and how it intends to get there.

Questions

2-1. List and explain the four steps of strategy formulation.

2-2. What is the difference between an order winner and an order qualifier?

2-3. Discuss the requirements from an operations perspective of competing on
(a) Quality; (b) Cost; (c) Flexibility; (d) Speed; (e) Dependability; (f) Service
Give examples of manufacturing or service firms that successfully compete on each of the criteria listed.

2-4. What role should operations play in corporate strategy?

2-5. Explain the concept of core competencies in your own words. Provide examples of a core competence for a bank, a retail store, and an auto manufacturer with which you are familiar.

2-6. Do you have a core competence? Make a list of the core competencies you will need to successfully compete in the job market. Design a strategy for developing the competencies that you do not have and capitalizing on the competencies that you do have.

2-7. What activities encourage the development of effective core competencies? What activities maintain core rigidities?

2-8. How do core competencies become core rigidities? Give three examples of outdated competencies at your school or business that are now rigidities.

2-9. Our thinking process, limited by the paradigms under which we operate, can become very rigid. Try these out-of-box thinking exercises:

a. Where does the letter Z belong in this pattern, above or below the line? Why?

$$\overline{\text{BCD} \quad \text{G} \quad \text{J} \qquad \text{OPQRS} \quad \text{U}}$$
$$\text{A} \qquad \text{EF} \quad \text{HI} \quad \text{KLMN} \qquad \text{T} \quad \text{VWXY}$$

b. What letter comes next in the following pattern? Why?

OTTFF

c. Connect the nine dots below with four straight lines. Do not lift your pencil.

2-10. Why do companies need policy deployment? What does it do?

2-11. Gather mission or vision statements from five different companies. (These are usually printed in annual reports, posted in a place of business, or accessible from the company web site.) What do they tell you about the organizations? Is their mission or vision reflected in the way they do business?

2-12. How can competencies help in formulating strategy? Give three examples of competency-based strategies.

2-13. Name several strategic decisions that involve the operations function.

2-14. Explain the difference between make-to-stock, make-to-order, and assemble-to-order products and services. Give an example of each.

2-15. What are the four basic types of processes? How do they differ? Give an example of each.

2-16. What two product characteristics have the most influence on process choice?

2-17. How does the product-process matrix relate to operations strategy?

2-18. Examine the annual reports of a company of your choosing over a number of years. Use quotes from the reports to describe the company's overall strategy and its specific goals each year.

CASE PROBLEM

Whither an MBA at Strutledge?

Strutledge is a small private liberal arts school located within 50 miles of a major urban area in the southeast United States. As with most institutions of higher education, Strutledge's costs are rising, and its enrollments are decreasing. In an effort to expand its student base, build valuable ties with area businesses, and simply survive, the Board of Regents is considering establishing an MBA program.

Currently, no undergraduate degree is given in business, although business courses are taught. The dean of the school visualizes the MBA as an interdisciplinary program emphasizing problem solving, communication, and global awareness. Faculty expertise would be supplemented by instructors from local industry. The use of local faculty would better connect the university with the business community and provide opportunities for employment of the program's graduates.

In terms of competition, a major state-funded university that offers an MBA is located in the

(Continued)

adjacent urban area. Strutledge hopes that state budget cutbacks and perceptions of overcrowded classrooms and overworked professors at public institutions will open the door for a new entrant into the market. The Board of Regents also feels that the school's small size will allow Strutledge to tailor the MBA program more closely to area business needs.

Several members of the Board are concerned about recent reports of the dwindling value of an MBA and are wondering if a better niche could be found with another graduate degree, perhaps a master of science in business or something in the education or health-care field.

1. What action would you recommend to the Board of Regents?

2. How should Strutledge go about making a strategic decision such as this?

CASE PROBLEM

Weighing Options at the Weight Club

The Weight Club started out as a student organization of 25 individuals who gathered together to discuss fitness goals and lift weights in the campus gym. When budget cutbacks cut gym hours and equipment availability, the students began to look elsewhere for a facility they could organize and control as they wished. They found an empty store in a small, dying mall in town, rented it for next to nothing, asked its members to pay dues, and began sponsoring weight-lifting contests to raise money for equipment. Off-campus now, they could recruit members from the town as well as the university. Their members had many talents, and they began sponsoring cheerleading training and other specialized training programs for athletes.

Growth of the student-run organization was phenomenal. Within six years the club had over 4,000 members from inside and outside of the university community. The facility itself extended over three additional storefronts in the now bustling mall, housing over fifty pieces of aerobic equipment, two complete sets of Nautilus equipment for circuit training, an entire floor of free weights, a separate room for heavy weights, and a large exercise room for a full range of aerobic, step, funk, slide, and stretch and tone classes. Graduate students found the facility an excellent source of subjects for projects ranging from nutrition to exercise to lifestyle changes (after heart attacks, for instance). Members were often able to take advantage of these additional services "free of charge."

The Weight Club clientele began to change as more non-university students joined (from moms in the morning hours to teenagers after school and business persons after work). This diversity brought with it numerous requests for additional services such as child care, personal trainers, children's classes, massages, swimming and running facilities, locker rooms and showers, food and drink, sportswear, gymnastics, hotel and corporate memberships, meetings, and sponsored events.

Currently, all members pay the same $25 monthly usage fee with no other membership fees or assessments for additional services (like exercise classes). The staff consists predominantly of student members, many of whom have financed their way through school by working at The Weight Club. The organization has remained nonprofit and is run by a founding member of the original weight club, who will finally graduate this year. Two other founding members have already graduated but work full time in the area and help administer the club whenever they can, serving as an informal "board of directors." In general, this arrangement has worked well, although there are no accurate membership records, control over the money is loose, decisions are made by whoever is behind the desk at the time, and there is no long-range planning.

The Weight Club has no significant competition. The three remaining "administrators" wonder if they need to make any changes.

References

AT&T Quality Steering Committee. *Policy Deployment: Setting the Direction for Change.* Indianapolis: AT&T Technical Publications Center, 1992.

Byrne, John. "Strategic Planning—It's Back!" *Business Week* (August 26, 1996): 46–53.

Carr, David, Kevin Dougherty, Henry Johansson, Robert King, and David Moran. *Breakpoint Business Process Redesign.* Arlington, Va.: Coopers & Lybrand, 1992.

Hammer, Michael. *Beyond Reengineering.* New York: Harper-Collins, 1996.

Hayes, Robert H., and Gary P. Pisano. "Manufacturing Strategy: At the Intersection of Two Paradigm Shifts." *Production and Operations Management* 5, no. 1 (spring 1996): 25–41.

Hayes, Robert H., Gary P. Pisano, and David M. Upton. *Strategic Operations: Competing Through Capabilities.* New York: Free Press, 1996.

Hill, Terry. *Manufacturing Strategy: Text and Cases.* Homewood, Ill.: Irwin, 1993.

Jones, Patricia, and Larry Kahaner. *Say It and Live It: The 50 Corporate Mission Statements That Hit the Mark.* New York: Currency Doubleday, 1995.

King, Bob. *Hoshin Planning: The Developmental Approach.* Springfield, Mass.: GOAL/QPC, 1989.

Leonard-Barton, Dorothy. *Wellsprings of Knowledge: Building and Sustaining the Sources of Innovation.* Boston: Harvard Business School Press, 1995.

Peters, Tom. *Liberation Management.* New York: Alfred A. Knopf, 1992.

Porter, Michael. "What Is Strategy?" *Harvard Business Review* (November–December 1996): 61–106.

Shiba, Shoji, Alan Graham, and David Walden. *A New American TQM: Four Practical Revolutions in Management.* Boston: Center for Quality Management, 1993.

Wheelwright, Steven, and H. Kent Bowen. "The Challenge of Manufacturing Advantage." *Production and Operations Management* 5, no. 1 (spring 1996): 59–77.

2

Operational Decision-Making Tools: Decision Analysis

A t the operational level hundreds of decisions are made in order to achieve local outcomes that contribute to the achievement of the company's overall strategic goal. These local outcomes are usually not measured directly in terms of profit, but instead are measured in terms of quality, cost-effectiveness, efficiency, productivity, and so forth. Achieving good results for local outcomes is an important objective for individual operational units and individual operations managers. However, all these decisions are interrelated and must be coordinated for the purpose of attaining the overall company goals. Decision making is analogous to a great stage play or opera, in which all the actors, the costumes, the props, the music, the orchestra, and the script must be choreographed and staged by the director, the stage managers, the author, and the conductor so that everything comes together for the performance.

For many topics in operations management, there are quantitative models and techniques available that help managers make decisions. Some techniques simply provide information that the operations manager might use to help come to a decision; other techniques recommend a decision to the manager. Some techniques are specific to a particular aspect of operations management; others are more generic and can be applied to a variety of decision-making categories. These different models and techniques are the "tools" of the operations manager. Simply having these tools does not make someone an effective operations manager, just as owning a saw and a hammer does not make someone a carpenter. An operations manager must know how to use decision-making tools. How these tools are used in the decision-making process is an important and necessary part of the study of operations management. In this supplement and others throughout the text, we examine several different aspects of operational decision making.

Quantitative methods are the tools of the operations manager.

Decision Analysis

In this supplement we demonstrate a quantitative technique called **decision analysis** for decision-making situations where uncertainty exists. Decision analysis is a generic technique that can be applied to a number of different types of operational decision-making areas.

Decision analysis is a set of quantitative decision-making techniques for decision situations in which uncertainty exists.

Many decision-making situations occur under conditions of *uncertainty*. For example, the demand for a product may not be 100 units next week but may vary between 0 and 200 units, depending on the state of the market which is uncertain. Decision analysis is a set of quantitative decision-making techniques to aid the decision maker in dealing with a decision situation in which there is uncertainty. However, the usefulness of decision analysis for decision making is also a beneficial topic to study because it reflects a structured, systematic approach to decision making that many decision makers follow intuitively without ever consciously thinking about it. Decision analysis represents not only a collection of decision-making techniques but also an analysis of logic underlying decision making.

Decision-Making Without Probabilities

A decision-making situation includes several components—the decisions themselves and the events that may occur in the future, known as *states of nature*. Future states of nature may be high demand or low demand for a product or good economic conditions or bad economic conditions. At the time a decision is made, the decision maker is uncertain which state of nature will occur in the future and has no control over these states of nature.

TABLE S2.1   Payoff Table

	STATES OF NATURE	
Decision	a	b
1	Payoff 1a	Payoff 1b
2	Payoff 2a	Payoff 2b

When probabilities can be assigned to the occurrence of states of nature in the future, the situation is referred to as *decision making under risk.* When probabilities cannot be assigned to the occurrence of future events, the situation is called *decision making under uncertainty.* We discuss this latter case next.

To facilitate the analysis of decision situations, they are organized into **payoff tables.** A payoff table is a means of organizing and illustrating the payoffs from the different decisions, given the various states of nature, and has the general form shown in Table S2.1.

Each decision, 1 or 2, in Table S2.1 will result in an outcome, or **payoff**, for each state of nature that will occur in the future. Payoffs are typically expressed in terms of profit, revenues, or cost (although they may be expressed in terms of a variety of quantities). For example, if decision 1 is to expand a production facility and state of nature *a* is good economic conditions, payoff 1a could be $100,000 in profit.

Once the decision situation has been organized into a payoff table, several criteria are available to reflect how the decision maker arrives at a decision, including maximax, maximin, minimax regret, Hurwicz, and equal likelihood. These criteria reflect different degrees of decision-maker conservatism or liberalism. On occasion they result in the same decision; however, they often yield different results. These decision-making criteria are demonstrated by the following example.

> A **payoff table** is a method for organizing and illustrating the payoffs from different decisions given various states of nature.
>
> A **payoff** is the outcome of the decision.
>
> Decision-making criteria

EXAMPLE S2.1

Decision-Making Criteria Under Uncertainty

The Southern Textile Company is contemplating the future of one of its plants located in South Carolina. Three alternative decisions are being considered: (1) Expand the plant and produce lightweight, durable materials for possible sales to the military, a market with little foreign competition; (2) maintain the status quo at the plant, continuing production of textile goods that are subject to heavy foreign competition; or (3) sell the plant now. If one of the first two alternatives is chosen, the plant will still be sold at the end of the year. The amount of profit that could be earned by selling the plant in a year depends on foreign market conditions, including the status of a trade embargo bill in Congress. The following payoff table describes this decision situation.

	STATES OF NATURE	
Decision	Good Foreign Competitive Conditions	Poor Foreign Competitive Conditions
Expand	$ 800,000	$ 500,000
Maintain status quo	1,300,000	−150,000
Sell now	320,000	320,000

Determine the best decision using each of the decision criteria.

(Continued)

1. Maximax
2. Maximin
3. Minimax regret
4. Hurwicz
5. Equal likelihood

SOLUTION:

1. Maximax

The decision is selected that will result in the maximum of the maximum payoffs. This is how this criterion derives its name—the maximum of the maxima. The **maximax criterion** is very optimistic. The decision maker assumes that the most favorable state of nature for each decision alternative will occur. Thus, for this example, the company would optimistically assume that good competitive conditions will prevail in the future, resulting in the following maximum payoffs and decisions:

The **maximax criterion** is a decision criterion that results in the maximum of the maximum payoffs.

Expand:	$ 800,000	
Status quo:	1,300,000	← Maximum
Sell:	320,000	

Decision: Maintain status quo

2. Maximin

The **maximin criterion** is pessimistic. With the maximin criterion, the decision maker selects the decision that will reflect the *maximum* of the *minimum* payoffs. For each decision alternative, the decision maker assumes that the minimum payoff will occur; of these, the maximum is selected as follows:

The **maximin criterion** is a decision criterion that results in the maximum of the minimum payoffs.

Expand:	$500,000	← Maximum
Status quo:	−150,000	
Sell:	320,000	

Decision: Expand

3. Minimax Regret

The decision maker attempts to avoid *regret* by selecting the decision alternative that minimizes the maximum regret. A decision maker first selects the maximum payoff under each state of nature; then all other payoffs under the respective states of nature are subtracted from these amounts, as follows:

The **minimax regret criterion** is a decision criterion that results in the minimum of the maximum regrets for each alternative.

Good Competitive Conditions	*Poor Competitive Conditions*
$1,300,000 − 800,000 = 500,000	$500,000 − 500,000 = 0
1,300,000 − 1,300,000 = 0	500,000 − (−150,000) = 650,000
1,300,000 − 320,000 = 980,000	500,000 − 320,000 = 180,000

These values represent the regret for each decision that would be experienced by the decision maker if a decision were made that resulted in less than the maximum payoff. The maximum regret for *each decision* must be determined, and the decision corresponding to the minimum of these regret values is selected as follows:

Regret Value

Expand:	$500,000 ← Minimum
Status quo:	650,000
Sell:	980,000

Decision: Expand

4. Hurwicz

A compromise between the maximax and maximin criteria. The decision maker is neither totally optimistic (as the maximax criterion assumes) nor totally pessimistic (as the maximin criterion assumes). With the **Hurwicz criterion,** the decision payoffs are weighted by a **coefficient of optimism,** a measure of the decision maker's optimism. The coefficient of optimism, defined as α, is between 0 and 1 (i.e., $0 < \alpha < 1.0$). If $\alpha = 1.0$, then the decision maker is completely optimistic, and if $\alpha = 0$, the decision maker is completely pessimistic. (Given this definition, $1 - \alpha$ is the *coefficient of pessimism.*) For each decision alternative, the maximum payoff is multiplied by α and the minimum payoff is multiplied by $1 - \alpha$. For our investment example, if α equals 0.3 (i.e., the company is slightly pessimistic) and $1 - \alpha = 0.7$, the following decision will result:

Expand:	$ 800,000(0.3) + 500,000(0.7) = $590,000 ← Maximum
Status quo:	1,300,000(0.3) − 150,000(0.7) = 285,000
Sell:	320,000(0.3) + 320,000(0.7) = 320,000

Decision: Expand

The **Hurwicz criterion** is a decision criterion in which the decision payoffs are weighted by a coefficient of optimism, α.

The **coefficient of optimism (α)** is a measure of a decision maker's optimism, from 0 (completely pessimistic) to 1 (completely optimistic).

5. Equal Likelihood

The **equal likelihood** (or **LaPlace**) **criterion** weights each state of nature equally, thus assuming that the states of nature are equally likely to occur. Since there are two states of nature in our example, we assign a weight of 0.50 to each one. Next, we multiply these weights by each payoff for each decision and select the alternative with the maximum of these weighted values.

Expand:	$ 800,000(0.50) + 500,000(0.50) = $650,000 ← Maximum
Status quo:	1,300,000(0.50) − 150,000(0.50) = 575,000
Sell:	320,000(0.50) + 320,000(0.50) = 320,000

Decision: Expand

The **equal likelihood (La Place) criterion** is a decision criterion in which each state of nature is weighted equally.

The decision to expand the plant was designated most often by four of the five decision criteria. The decision to sell was never indicated by any criterion. This is because the payoffs for expansion, under either set of future economic conditions, are always better than the payoffs for selling. Given any situation with these two alternatives, the decision to expand will always be made over the decision to sell. The sell decision alternative could have been eliminated from consideration under each of our criteria. The alternative of selling is said to be *dominated* by the alternative of expanding. In general, dominated decision alternatives can be removed from the payoff table and not considered when the various decision-making criteria are applied, which reduces the complexity of the decision analysis.

Different decision criteria often result in a mix of decisions. The criteria used and the resulting decisions depend on the decision maker. For example, the extremely optimistic decision maker might disregard the preceding results and make the decision to maintain the status quo, because the maximax criterion reflects his or her personal decision-making philosophy.

Decision-Making with Probabilities

Risk involves assigning probabilities to state of nature.

For the decision-making criteria we just used we assumed no available information regarding the probability of the states of nature. However, it is often possible for the decision maker to know enough about the future states of nature to assign probabilities that each will occur, which is decision making under conditions of *risk*. The most widely used decision-making criterion under risk is **expected value**, computed by multiplying each outcome by the probability of its occurrence and then summing these products according to the following formula:

The **expected value** is a weighted average of decision outcomes in which each future state of nature is assigned a probability of occurrence.

$$EV(x) = \sum_{i=1}^{n} p(x_i)x_i$$

where

$$x_i = \text{outcome } i$$
$$p(x_i) = \text{probability of outcome } i.$$

**EXAMPLE
S2.2**

Expected Value

Assume that it is now possible for the Southern Textile Company to estimate a probability of 0.70 that good foreign competitive conditions will exist and a probability of 0.30 that poor conditions will exist in the future. Determine the best decision using expected value.

SOLUTION:

The expected values for each decision alternative are computed as follows.

$$EV(\text{expand}) = \$800,000(0.70) + 500,000(0.30) = \$710,000$$
$$EV(\text{status quo}) = 1,300,000(0.70) - 150,000(0.30) = 865,000 \leftarrow \text{Maximum}$$
$$EV(\text{sell}) = 320,000(0.70) + 320,000(0.30) = 320,000$$

The decision according to this criterion is to maintain the status quo, since it has the highest expected value.

Expected Value of Perfect Information

Occasionally additional information is available, or can be purchased, regarding future events, enabling the decision maker to make a better decision. For example, a company could hire an economic forecaster to determine more accurately the economic conditions that will occur in the future. However, it would be foolish to pay more for this information than it stands to gain in extra profit from having the information. The information has some maximum value that is the limit of what the decision maker would be willing to spend. This value of information can be computed as an expected value—hence its name, the **expected value of perfect information (EVPI)**.

To compute the expected value of perfect information, first look at the decisions

Expected value of perfect information (EVPI) is the maximum value of perfect information to the decision maker.

under each state of nature. If information that assured us which state of nature was going to occur (i.e., perfect information) could be obtained, the best decision for that state of nature could be selected. For example, in the textile company example, if the company executives knew for sure that good competitive conditions would prevail, they would maintain the status quo. If they knew for sure that poor competitive conditions will occur, then they would expand.

The probabilities of each state of nature (i.e., 0.70 and 0.30) indicate that good competitive conditions will prevail 70 percent of the time and poor competitive conditions will prevail 30 percent of the time (if this decision situation is repeated many times). In other words, even though perfect information enables the investor to make the right decision, each state of nature will occur only a certain portion of the time. Thus, each of the decision outcomes obtained using perfect information must be weighted by its respective probability:

$$\$1,300,000(0.70) + (500,000)(0.30) = \$1,060,000$$

The amount of $1,060,000 is the expected value of the decision *given perfect information*, not the expected value of perfect information. The expected value of perfect information is the maximum amount that would be paid to gain information that would result in a decision better than the one made *without perfect information*. Recall that the expected-value decision without perfect information was to maintain status quo and the expected value was $865,000.

The expected value of perfect information is computed by subtracting the expected value without perfect information from the expected value given perfect information:

> EVPI = expected value given perfect information − expected value without perfect information.

For our example, the EVPI is computed as,

$$\text{EVPI} = \$1,060,000 - 865,000 = \$195,000$$

The expected value of perfect information, $195,000, is the maximum amount that the investor would pay to purchase perfect information from some other source, such as an economic forecaster. Of course, perfect information is rare and is usually unobtainable. Typically, the decision maker would be willing to pay some smaller amount, depending on how accurate (i.e., close to perfection) the information is believed to be.

Sequential Decision Trees

A payoff table is limited to a single decision situation. If a decision requires a series of decisions, a payoff table cannot be created, and a **sequential decision tree** must be used. We demonstrate the use of a decision tree in the following example.

A **sequential decision tree** is a graphical method for analyzing decision situations that require a sequence of decisions over time.

> **EXAMPLE S2.3**
>
> *A Sequential Decision Tree*

The Southern Textile Company is considering two alternatives: to expand its existing production operation to manufacture a new line of lightweight material; or to purchase land to construct a new facility on in the future. Each of these decisions has outcomes based on product market growth in the future that result in another set of decisions (during a ten-year planning horizon), as shown in the following figure of a sequential decision tree. In this figure the square nodes represent decisions and the circle nodes reflect different states of nature and their probabilities.

The first decision facing the company is whether to expand or buy land. If the com-

(Continued)

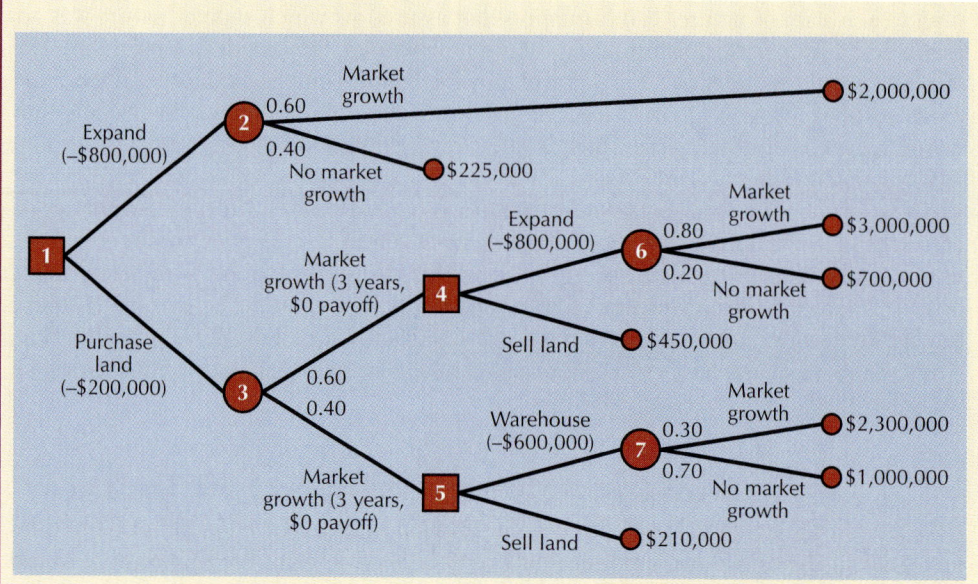

pany expands, two states of nature are possible. Either the market will grow (with a probability of 0.60) or it will not grow (with a probability of 0.40). Either state of nature will result in a payoff. On the other hand, if the company chooses to purchase land, three years in the future another decision will have to be made regarding the development of the land.

At decision node 1, the decision choices are to expand or to purchase land. Notice that the costs of the ventures ($800,000 and $200,000, respectively) are shown in parentheses. If the plant is expanded, two states of nature are possible at probability node 2: The market will grow, with a probability of 0.60, or it will not grow or will decline, with a probability of 0.40. If the market grows, the company will achieve a payoff of $2,000,000 over a ten-year period. However, if no growth occurs, a payoff of only $225,000 will result.

If the decision is to purchase land, two states of nature are possible at probability node 3. These two states of nature and their probabilities are identical to those at node 2; however, the payoffs are different. If market growth occurs for a three-year period, no payoff will occur, but the company will make another decision at node 4 regarding development of the land. At that point, either the plant will be expanded at a cost of $800,000 or the land will be sold, with a payoff of $450,000. The decision situation at node 4 can occur only if market growth occurs first. If no market growth occurs at node 3, there is no payoff, and another decision situation becomes necessary at node 5: A warehouse can be constructed at a cost of $600,000 or the land can be sold for $210,000. (Notice that the sale of the land results in less profit if there is no market growth than if there is growth.)

If the decision at decision node 4 is to expand, two states of nature are possible; the market may grow, with a probability of 0.80, or it may not grow, with a probability of 0.20. The probability of market growth is higher (and the probability of no growth is lower) than before because there has already been growth for the first three years, as shown by the branch from node 3 to node 4. The payoffs for these two states of nature at the end of the ten-year period are $3,000,000 and $700,000.

If the company decides to build a warehouse at node 5, then two states of nature can occur. Market growth can occur, with a probability of 0.30 and an eventual payoff, of $2,300,000, or no growth can occur, with a probability of 0.70 and a payoff of $1,000,000. The probability of market growth is low (i.e., 0.30) because there has already been no market growth, as shown by the branch from node 3 to node 5.

SOLUTION:

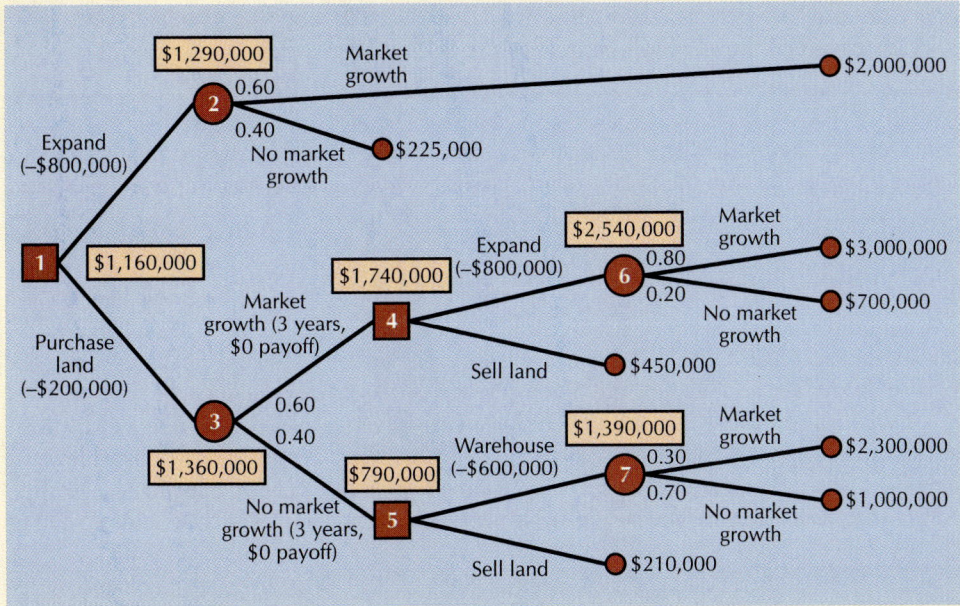

We start the decision analysis process at the end of the decision tree and work backward toward a decision at node 1.

First, we must compute the expected values at nodes 6 and 7.

EV(node 6) = 0.80($3,000,000) + 0.20($700,000) = $2,540,000
EV(node 7) = 0.30($2,300,000) + 0.70($1,000,000) = $1,390,000

These expected values (as well as all other nodal values) are shown in boxes in the figure above.

At decision nodes 4 and 5, a decision must be made. As with a normal payoff table, the decision is made that results in the greatest expected value. At node 4 the choice is between two values: $1,740,000, the value derived by subtracting the cost of expanding ($800,000) from the expected payoff of $2,540,000, and $450,000, the expected value of selling the land computed with a probability of 1.0. The decision is to expand, and the value at node 4 is $1,740,000.

The same process is repeated at node 5. The decisions at node 5 result in payoffs of $790,000 (i.e., $1,390,000 − 600,000 = $790,000) and $210,000. Since the value $790,000 is higher, the decision is to build a warehouse.

Next the expected values at nodes 2 and 3 are computed.

EV(node 2) = 0.60($2,000,000) + 0.40($225,000) = $1,290,000
EV(node 3) = 0.60($1,740,000) + 0.40($790,000) = $1,360,000

(Continued)

(Note that the expected value for node 3 is computed from the decision values previously determined at nodes 4 and 5.)

Now the final decision at node 1 must be made. As before, we select the decision with the greatest expected value after the cost of each decision is subtracted.

Expand: $1,290,000 - 800,000 = $490,000

Land: $1,360,000 - 200,000 = $1,160,000

Since the highest *net* expected value is $1,160,000, the decision is to purchase land, and the payoff of the decision is $1,160,000.

Decision trees allow the decision maker to see the logic of decision making by providing a picture of the decision process. Decision trees can be used for problems more complex than this example without too much difficulty.

Decision Analysis with POM for Windows and Excel

Throughout this text we will demonstrate how to solve quantitative models using the computer with POM for Windows, a software package by Howard J. Weiss published by Prentice Hall, and, Excel, the Microsoft spreadsheet package.

POM for Windows is a user-friendly, menu-driven package and requires little instruction. POM for Windows can solve the decision analysis problems in Examples S2.1 and S2.2, as well as the decision tree problem in Example S2.3. Following in Exhibits S2.1, S2.2, and S2.3 are the solution output screens for Examples S2.1 and S2.2. The

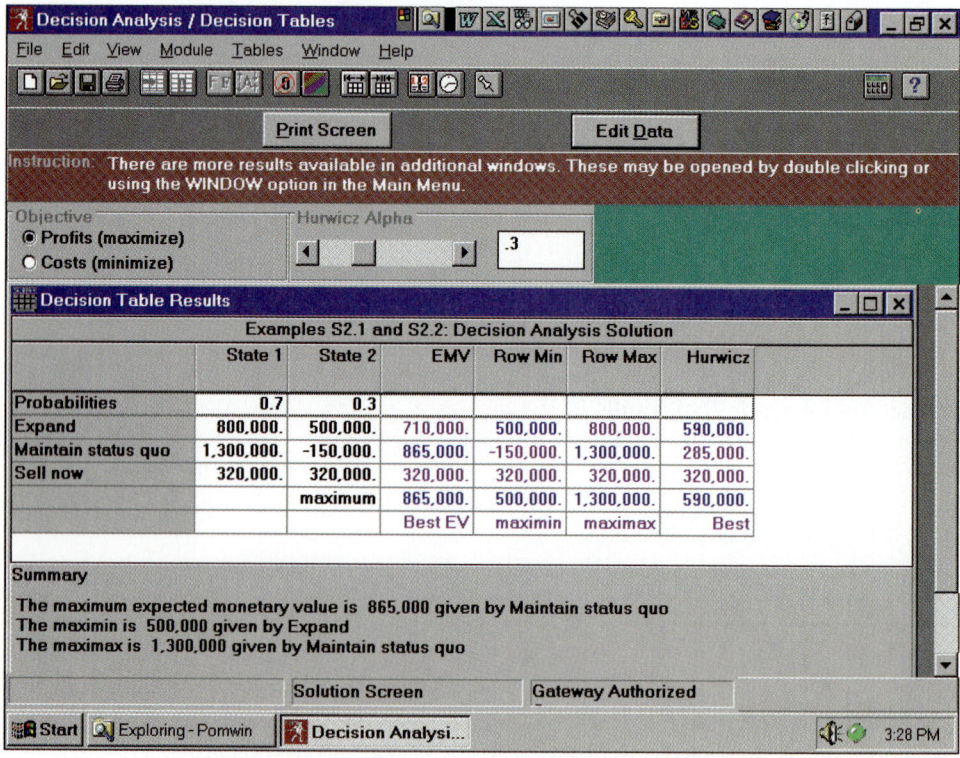

EXHIBIT S2.1

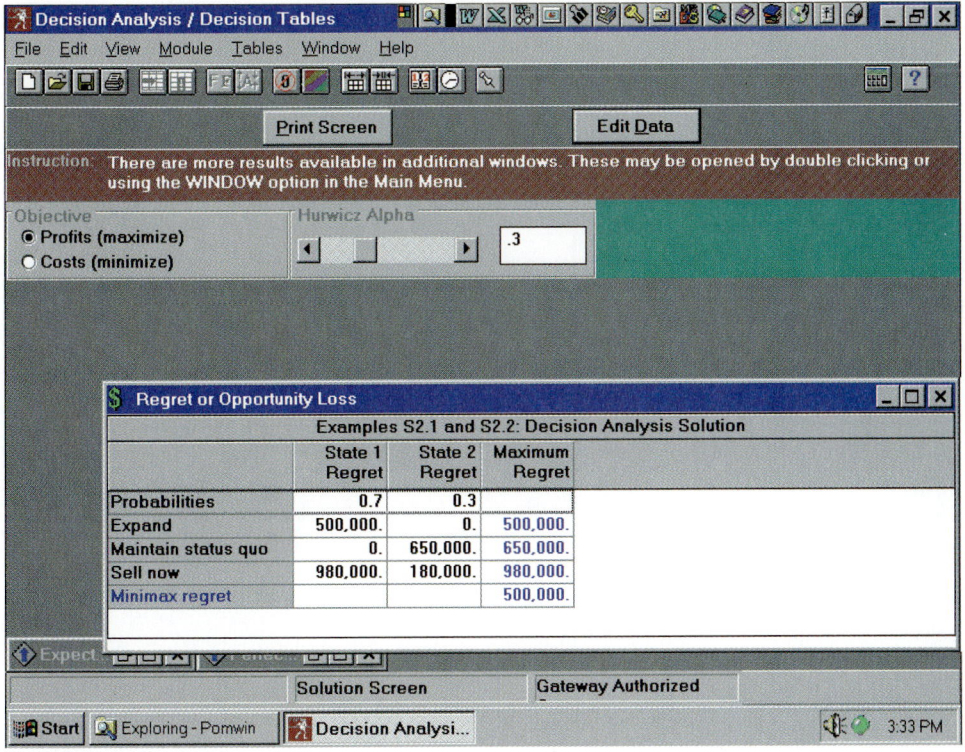

EXHIBIT S2.2

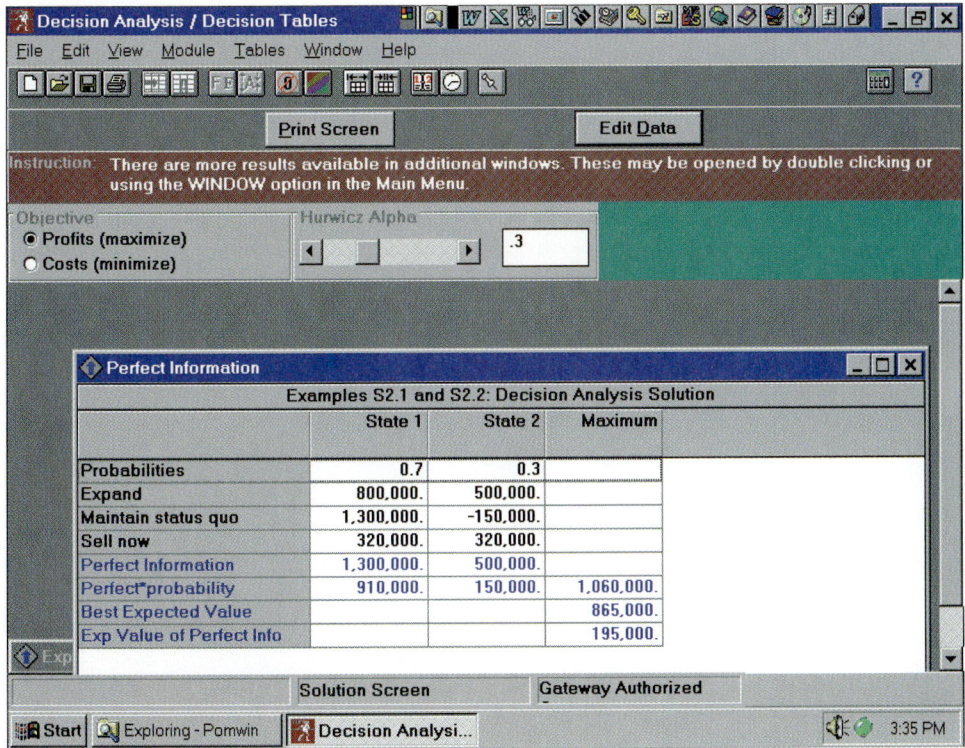

EXHIBIT S2.3

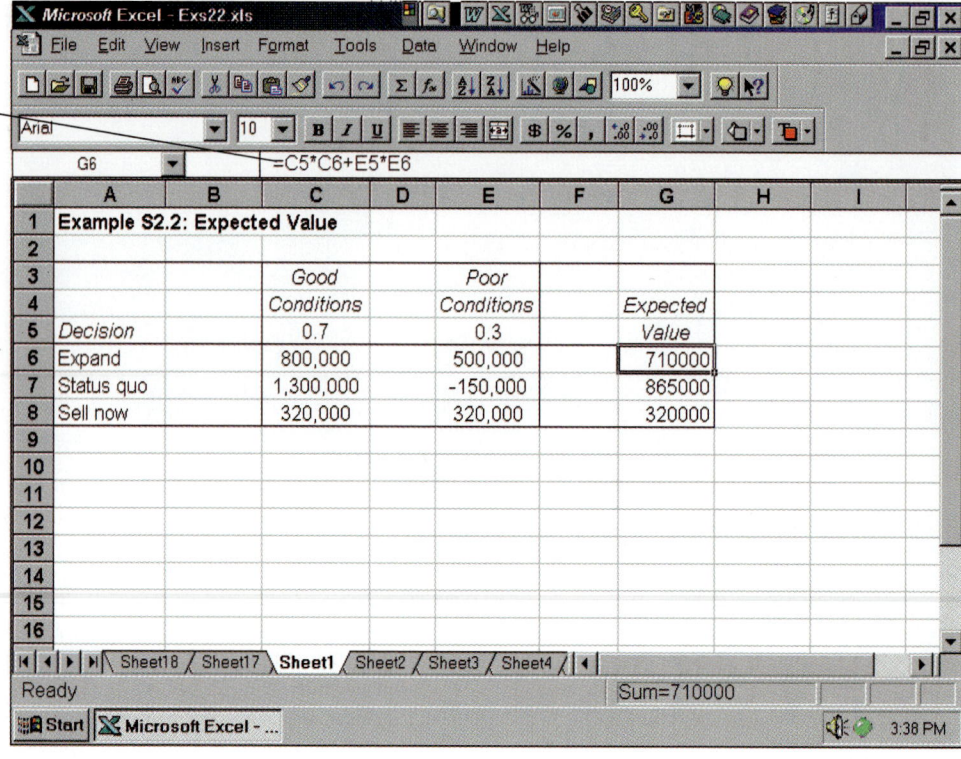

Formula for expected value computed in cell G6

EXHIBIT S2.4

first screen includes the maximax, minimax, Hurwicz, and expected value solutions. The second screen shows the minimax regret solution. The third screen shows the expected value of perfect information of our example.

We will also be using Excel spreadsheets to demonstrate how to solve quantitative operational problems throughout this text. In Exhibit S2.4, the Excel worksheet screen for the determination of the expected values in Example S2.2 is shown. Note that the expected values contained in cells G6, G7, and G8 were computed using the expected value formulas embedded in these cells. For example, the formula for cell G6 is shown on the formula bar on the Excel screen.

Summary

In this supplement we have provided a general overview of decision analysis. To a limited extent we have also shown the logic of such operational decisions throughout the organization are interrelated to achieve strategic goals.

Summary of Key Formulas

Expected Value

$$EV(x) = \sum_{i=1}^{n} p(x_i)x_i$$

Expected Value of Perfect Information

EVPI = expected value given perfect information − expected value without perfect information.

Summary of Key Terms

coefficient of optimism (α): a measure of a decision maker's optimism, from 0 (completely pessimistic) to 1 (completely optimistic), used in the Hurwicz decision criterion.

decision analysis: a set of quantitative decision-making techniques to aid the decision maker in dealing with decision situations in which uncertainty exists.

equal likelihood (La Place) criterion: a decision criterion in which each state of nature is weighted equally.

expected value: a weighted average of decision outcomes in which each future state of nature is assigned a probability of occurrence.

expected value of perfect information: the maximum value that a decision maker would be willing to pay for perfect information about future states of nature.

Hurwicz criterion: a decision criterion in which the decision payoffs are weighted by a coefficient of optimism, α.

maximax criterion: a decision criterion that results in the maximum of the maximum payoffs.

maximin criterion: a decision criterion that results in the maximum of the minimum payoffs.

minimax regret criterion: a decision criterion that results in the minimum of the maximum regrets for each alternative.

payoff table: a means of organizing and illustrating the payoffs from different decisions given various states of nature.

sequential decision tree: a graphical method for analyzing decision situations that require a sequence of decisions over time.

Solved Problem

Consider the following payoff table for three product decisions (A, B, and C) and three future market conditions (payoffs = $ millions).

	MARKET CONDITIONS		
DECISION	1	2	3
A	$1.0	$2.0	$0.5
B	0.8	1.2	0.9
C	0.7	0.9	1.7

Determine the best decision using the following decision criteria.

1. Maximax
2. Maximin

Solution:

Step 1. Maximax criterion

Maximum payoffs	
A	$2.0 ← Maximum
B	1.2
C	1.7

Decision: Product A

Step 2. Maximin criteria

Minimum payoffs	
A	0.5
B	0.8 ← Maximum
C	0.7

Decision: Product B

Problems

S2-1. Microcomp is a U.S.-based manufacturer of personal computers. It is planning to build a new manufacturing and distribution facility in either South Korea, China, Taiwan, the Philippines, or Mexico. It will take approximately five years to build the necessary infra-structure (roads, etc.), construct the new facility, and put it into operation. The eventual cost of the facility will differ between countries and will even vary within countries depending on the financial, labor, and political climate, including monetary exchange rates. The company has estimated the facility cost (in $ millions) in each country under three different future economic/political climates as follows.

	Economic/Political Climate		
Country	Decline	Same	Improve
South Korea	21.7	19.1	15.2
China	19.0	18.5	17.6
Taiwan	19.2	17.1	14.9
Philippines	22.5	16.8	13.8
Mexico	25.0	21.2	12.5

Determine the best decision using the following decision criteria.

a. Minimin
b. Minimax
c. Hurwicz ($\alpha = .40$)
d. Equal likelihood

S2-2. Place-Plus, a real estate development firm, is considering several alternative development projects. These include building and leasing an office park, purchasing a parcel of land and building and office building to rent, buying and leasing a warehouse, building a strip shopping center, and building and selling condominiums. The financial success of these projects depends on interest rate movement in the next five years. The various development projects and their five-year financial return ($ millions) given that interest rates will decline, remain stable, or increase are shown in the following payoff table.

Project	Interest Rates		
	Decline	Stable	Increase
Office park	0.5	1.7	4.5
Office building	1.5	1.9	2.4
Warehouse	1.7	1.4	1.0
Shopping center	0.7	2.4	3.6
Condominiums	3.2	1.5	0.6

Determine the best investment using the following decision criteria.

a. Maximax
b. Maximin
c. Equal likelihood
d. Hurwicz ($\alpha = .3$)

S2-3. Ann Tyler has come into an inheritance from her grandparents. She is attempting to decide between several investment alternatives. The return after one year is primarily dependent on the interest rate during the next year. The rate is currently 7 percent, and she anticipates it will stay the same or go up or down by at most 2 points. The various investment alternatives plus their returns ($10,000) given the interest rate changes are shown in the following table.

INVESTMENTS	INTEREST RATES				
	5%	6%	7%	8%	9%
Money market fund	2	3.1	4	4.3	5
Stock growth fund	−3	−2	2.5	4	6
Bond fund	6	5	3	3	2
Government fund	4	3.6	3.2	3	2.8
Risk fund	−9	−4.5	1.2	8.3	14.7
Savings bonds	3	3	3.2	3.4	3.5

Determine the best investment using the following decision criteria.

a. Maximax
b. Maximin
c. Minimax regret
d. Equal likelihood
e. Hurwicz ($\alpha = 0.7$)
f. Assume that Ann Tyler, with the help of a financial newsletter and some library research, has been able to assign probabilities to each of the possible interest rates during the next year as follows:

Interest Rate	5%	6%	7%	8%	9%
Probability	0.2	0.3	0.3	0.1	0.1

Using expected value, determine her best investment decision.

S2-4. The Tech football coaching staff has six basic plays it runs every game. Tech has an upcoming game against State on Saturday and the coaches know State employs five different defenses. The coaches have estimated the number of yards Tech will gain with each play against each defense, as shown in the following payoff table.

	DEFENSE				
PLAY	54	63	Wide Tackle	Nickel	Blitz
Off tackle	3	−2	9	7	−1
Option	−1	8	−2	9	12
Toss sweep	6	16	−5	3	14
Draw	−2	4	3	10	−3
Pass	8	20	12	−7	−8
Screen	−5	−2	8	3	16

a. If the coaches employ an offensive game plan, they will use the maximax criterion. What will their best play be?

b. If the coaches employ a defensive plan, they will use the maximin criterion. What will their best play be?

c. What will their best play be if State is equally likely to use any of its defenses?

d. The Tech coaches have reviewed game films and have determined the following probabilities that State will use each of its defenses.

Defense	54	63	Wide Tackle	Nickel	Blitz
Probability	0.40	0.10	0.20	0.20	0.10

Using expected value, rank Tech's plays from best to worst. During the actual game, Tech has a third down and 10 yards to go and the coaches are 60 percent certain State will blitz, with a 10 percent chance of any of the other four defenses. What play should Tech run, and is it likely Tech will make the first down?

S2-5. The Miramar Company is going to introduce one of three new products: a widget, a hummer, or a nimnot. The market conditions (favorable, stable, or unfavorable) will determine the profit or loss the company realizes, as shown in the following payoff table.

	MARKET CONDITIONS		
PRODUCT	Favorable 0.2	Stable 0.7	Unfavorable 0.1
Widget	$120,000	$70,000	−$30,000
Hummer	60,000	40,000	20,000
Nimnot	35,000	30,000	30,000

a. Compute the expected value for each decision and select the best one.

b. Determine how much the firm would be willing to pay to a market research firm to gain better information about future market conditions.

c. Assume that probabilities cannot be assigned to future market conditions, and determine the best decision using the maximax, maximin, minimax regret, and equal likelihood criteria.

S2-6. The Steak and Chop Butcher Shop purchases steak from a local meatpacking house. The meat is purchased on Monday at $2.00 per pound, and the shop sells the steak for $3.00 per pound. Any steak left over at the end of the week is sold to a local zoo for $0.50 per pound. The possible demands for steak and the probability for each are as follows.

Demand (lb)	Probability
20	0.10
21	0.20
22	0.30
23	0.30
24	0.10
	1.00

   a. The shop must decide how much steak to order in a week. Construct a payoff table for this decision situation and determine the amount of steak that should be ordered using expected value.
   b. Assuming that probabilities cannot be assigned to the demand values, what would the best decision be using the maximax and maximin criteria?

S2-7. The manager of the greeting card section of Mazey's department store is considering her order for a particular line of holiday cards. The cost of each box of cards is $3; each box will be sold for $5 during the holiday season. After the holiday season, the cards will be sold for $2 a box. The card section manager believes that all leftover cards can be sold at that price. The estimated demand during the holiday season for the cards, with associated probabilities, is as follows:

Demand (boxes)	Probability
25	0.10
26	0.15
27	0.30
28	0.20
29	0.15
30	0.10

   a. Develop the payoff table for this decision situation and compute the expected value for each alternative and identify the best decision.
   b. Compute the expected value of perfect information.

S2-8. The Americo Oil Company is considering making a bid for a shale oil development contract to be awarded by the federal government. The company has decided to bid $110 million. The company estimates that it has a 60-percent chance of winning the contract with this bid. If the firm wins the contract, it can choose one of three methods for getting the oil from the shale. It can develop a new method for oil extraction, use an existing (inefficient) process, or subcontract the processing out to a number of smaller companies once the shale has been excavated. The results from these alternatives are given as follows.

Develop New Process		
Outcomes	Probability	Profit (millions)
Great success	0.30	$600
Moderate success	0.60	300
Failure	0.10	−100
Use Present Process		
Outcomes	Probability	Profit (millions)
Great success	0.50	$300
Moderate success	0.30	200
Failure	0.20	−40
Subcontract		
Outcomes	Probability	Profit (millions)
Moderate success	1.00	$250

Retain existing transformer.

The cost of preparing the contract proposal is $2,000,000. If the company does not make a bid, it will invest in an alternative venture with a guaranteed profit of $30 million. Construct a sequential decision tree for this decision situation and determine whether the company should make a bid.

C A S E   P R O B L E M

Transformer Replacement at Mountain States Electric Service

Mountain States Electric Service is an electrical utility company serving several states in the Rocky Mountain region. It is considering replacing some of its equipment at a generating substation and is attempting to decide whether it should replace an older, existing PCB transformer. (PCB is a toxic chemical known formally as polychlorinated biphenyl.) Even though the PCB generator meets all current regulations, if an incident occurred, such as a fire, and PCB contamination caused harm either to neighboring businesses or farms or to the environment, the company would be liable for damages. Recent court cases have shown that simply meeting utility regulations does not relieve a utility of liability if an incident causes harm to others. Also, courts have been awarding large damages to individuals and businesses harmed by hazardous incidents.

If the utility replaces the PCB transformer, no PCB incidents will occur and the only cost will be the cost of the transformer, $85,000. Alternatively, if the company decides to keep the existing PCB transformer, then management estimates there is a 50–50 chance of their being a high likelihood of an incident or a low likelihood of an incident. For the case where there is a high likelihood that an incident will occur, there is a .004 probability that a fire will occur sometime during the remaining life of the transformer and a .996 probability that no fire will occur. If a fire occurs, there is a .20 probability that it will be bad and the utility will incur a very high cost of approximately $90 million for the cleanup, whereas there is a .80 probability that the fire will be minor and a cleanup can be accomplished at a low cost of approximately $8 million. If no fire occurs, then no cleanup costs will occur. For the case where there is a low likelihood of an incident occurring, there is a .001 probability that a fire will occur during the life of the existing transformer and a .999 probability that a fire will not occur. If a fire does occur, then the same probabilities exist for the incidence of high and low cleanup costs, as well as the same cleanup costs, as indicated for the previous case. Similarly, if no fire occurs, there is no cleanup cost.

Perform a decision tree analysis of this problem for Mountain States Electric Service and indicate the recommended solution. Is this the decision you believe the company should make? Explain your reasons.[1]

[1] This case was adapted from W. Balson, J. Welsh, and D. Wilson, "Using Decision Analysis and Risk Analysis to Manage Utility Environmental Risk," *Interfaces* 22, no. 6 (November–December 1992): 126–39.

References

Davis, G. B. *Management Information Systems: Conceptual Foundations, Structure and Development.* New York: McGraw-Hill, 1974.

Edelman, F. "Managers, Computer Systems, and Productivity." *Interfaces* 12, no. 5 (October 1982): 35–46; reprinted from *MIS Quarterly* 5, no. 3 (September 1981).

Holloway, C. A. *Decision Making Under Uncertainty.* Englewood Cliffs, N.J.: Prentice Hall, 1979.

Howard, R. A. "An Assessment of Decision Analysis." *Operations Research,* 28, no. 1 (January–February 1980): 4–27.

Keeney, R. L. "Decision Analysis: An Overview." *Operations Research,* 30, no. 5 (September–October 1982): 803–38.

Luce, R. D., and H. Raiffa. *Games and Decisions.* New York: John Wiley, 1957.

Sprague, R. H., and H. J. Watson. "MIS Concepts." *Journal of Systems Management* (January and February 1985).

Turban, E. *Decision Support and Expert Systems.* New York: Macmillan, 1988.

Von Neumann, J., and O. Morgenstern. *Theory of Games and Economic Behavior,* 3d ed. Princeton, N.J.: Princeton University Press, 1953.

Williams, J. D. *The Complete Strategist,* rev. ed. New York: McGraw-Hill, 1966.

3

Quality Management

Total Customer Satisfaction at Motorola

www.prenhall.com/russell

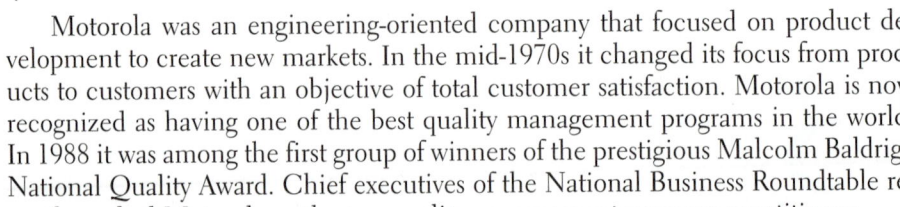

Motorola began in the late 1920s as a small manufacturer of car radios (hence the name *Motorola*). It has grown to a corporation with over 132,000 employees at 50 factories around the world, manufacturing such products as semiconductors, integrated circuits, paging systems, cellular telephones, computers, and satellite communications systems.

Motorola was an engineering-oriented company that focused on product development to create new markets. In the mid-1970s it changed its focus from products to customers with an objective of total customer satisfaction. Motorola is now recognized as having one of the best quality management programs in the world. In 1988 it was among the first group of winners of the prestigious Malcolm Baldrige National Quality Award. Chief executives of the National Business Roundtable recently ranked Motorola as the top quality management program practitioner.

Motorola's Six Sigma symbol represents its commitment to producing quality products and customer satisfaction. Technically, six sigma performance is a level of statistical variation in product quality that translates to only a little over 3 defects for every million parts produced, or virtually no defects. The six sigma performance program is part of the Motorola Corporate Quality Council (MCQC) which was established to coordinate and manage Motorola's corporate-wide quality program. Motorola's goal from this program has been to instill a commitment to absolute quality performance and total customer satisfaction throughout all areas of the company from purchasing to engineering and design to manufacturing to sales. Its MCQC program and its goal of six sigma performance enabled Motorola, Inc. to be among the first U.S. companies to receive the coveted Malcolm Baldrige National Quality Award from the U.S. Department of Commerce in 1988. Total quality management (TQM) with zero defects has been adopted by numerous companies that hope to survive in today's highly competitive global business environment.

Motorola has two quality-improvement goals to achieve total customer satisfaction. One goal is to reduce defects—where a defect is any failure to meet customer requirements in any of its products or services. Its current goal of "six sigma" quality means no more than 3.4 defects per million products or services. Its goal by the year 2000 is 2 defects per *billion* products or services, with an ultimate goal of zero defects. Its other goal is to reduce cycle time—the time from the point a customer places an order until it is delivered—by 50 percent each year.

Motorola continuously looks for ways to improve quality throughout its organization at all levels. For example, each employee has at least 40 hours of training that includes basic statistical quality control concepts; its goal is 160 hours of training per employee by the year 2000. Every task in every process in the company is measured by the employees who perform these tasks to identify defects and errors and to reduce cycle time. Every department at Motorola has a "participative management" team of eight to twelve employees who set local quality goals to achieve corporate goals. Small teams from its corporate quality council visit each of the company's divisions each year to conduct a quality audit, and teams from each sector in Motorola participate in company-wide quality competitions. Motorola teaches its suppliers its own quality management techniques and has its suppliers rate its production process and offer suggestions for quality improvement. Sales representatives at Motorola have the authority to replace defective products up to six years after their purchase.

Motorola's quality management program has been a success according to any measure. From 1988 to 1994 Motorola's employee productivity increased 100 percent (an annual rate of over 12 percent). From 1993 to 1994 its sales increased 31 percent and its stock rose 49 percent. By the mid-1990s it was selling more cellular phones in Japan than Japanese manufacturers. In 1994 alone the company estimated that it had saved several billion dollars because of its focus on quality improvement. The quality management program at Motorola is a standard or "benchmark" for companies around the world to try to emulate.[1]

W e emphasize quality throughout this text in the context of all operational functions. In today's international business environment, quality cannot be underestimated or overlooked by any firm, regardless of its size or assets. Business leaders and CEOs cite quality as the most important factor in the long-term profitability and success of their firms.

In our everyday life we are exposed to quality in a variety of forms, from product advertising with slogans like "Putting Quality on the Road" (General Motors) and "Quality Is Job 1" (Ford) to everyday phrases such as "quality of life" and "quality time."

Why has quality become so important to businesses and consumers around the world? Following World War II, when the consumption of goods and services expanded dramatically in the United States, quality was not a big concern to consumers or producers. Consumers purchasing U.S. goods and services assumed they were getting the best products available; that they were of good quality was accepted without question. "Made in Japan" stamped on inferior Japanese products was a term of derision. This

[1] K. Bemowski, "Motorola's Fountain of Youth," *Quality Progress* 28, no. 10 (October 1995): 29–31; and E. Pena, "Motorola's Secret to Quality Control," *Quality Progress* 23, no. 10 (October 1990): 43–45.

Globalization and foreign competition began to change the business environment in the 1970s.

began to change during the 1970s due mainly to foreign competition, especially from Japan, in markets for manufactured goods and electronic products. Consumers began to have more choices and more information to help them make these choices. This resulted in higher expectations for products and services. Consumers found that they could demand—and expect to receive—high-quality products that were reliable and priced affordably and competitively. In this new environment of increased competition from foreign companies, quality not only allows for product discrimination, it also has become a marketing weapon.

Quality was not the sole reason for the initial Japanese success in the U.S. market. High-quality products from foreign firms such as Rolls Royce and Mercedes Benz automobiles and Hasselblad cameras had been available in the United States for years but had not altered consumers' preferences or perceptions. However, these products were expensive; Japanese products were not. The Japanese were uniquely able to establish the concept of *value*—the combination of price plus quality—and change their product-design philosophy such that the cost of achieving better quality was not prohibitive.

The key to foreign competition—producing quality products at competitive prices.

How were Japanese firms able, in such a short time, to change their image from producers of inferior quality products to producers of high-quality products? There are many reasons; some were the result of chance and opportunity. A gasoline shortage in the mid-1970s awakened consumers to the high gas mileage of their cars at about the same time the Honda Accord was being introduced in the United States, making Americans aware of high performance standards in Japanese cars. The growing media attention to consumer issues, particularly quality (exemplified by publications such as *Consumer Reports*), consumer advocates such as Ralph Nader, and various consumer affairs' reports on radio and television provided information not previously available about the quality of products. However, the most important factor in changing consumer perspectives was that foreign competitors, especially the Japanese, were able to produce goods equal or superior in quality to U.S. goods at a very competitive price; through word of mouth, effective marketing, and circumstances, the U.S. consumer became quality and value conscious.

The Japanese achieved enhanced product quality by adapting many of the principles of quality management originally developed in the United States, combined with their own management philosophies. As a competitive reaction, American firms have focused attention on quality as possibly the most important factor in their long-term profitability and survival.

In this chapter we discuss some of the more popular aspects of quality management as they apply to business organizations.

The Meaning of Quality

What is quality in the eye of the beholder?

Asked "What is quality?" one of our students replied "getting what you pay for." Another student added that to her, quality was "getting *more* than you paid for!" The *Oxford American Dictionary* defines quality as "a degree or level of excellence." The "official" definition of quality by the American National Standards Institute (ANSI) and the American Society for Quality Control (ASQC) is "the totality of features and characteristics of a product or service that bears on its ability to satisfy given needs." Obviously quality can be defined in many ways, depending on who is defining it and to what product or service it is related. In this section we attempt to gain a perspective on what quality means to consumers and different people within a business organization.

www.prenhall.com/russell

Quality from the Consumer's Perspective

A business organization produces goods and services to meet its customers' needs. Quality is rapidly becoming a major factor in a customer's choice of products and service. Customers now perceive that certain companies produce better-quality products than others, and they buy accordingly. That means a firm must consider how the consumer defines quality. The consumer can be a manufacturer purchasing raw materials or parts, a store owner or retailer purchasing products to sell, or someone who purchases retail products or services. W. Edwards Deming, author and consultant on quality, says that "The consumer is the most important part of the production line. Quality should be aimed at the needs of the consumer, present and future." From this perspective, product and service quality is determined by what the consumer wants and is willing to pay for. Since consumers have different product needs, they will have different quality expectations. This results in a commonly used definition of quality as a service's or product's *fitness for its intended use*, or **fitness for use**; how well does it do what the consumer or user thinks it is supposed to do and wants it to do?

Products and services are designed with intentional differences in quality to meet the different wants and needs of individual consumers. A Mercedes and a Ford truck are equally "fit for use," in the sense that they both provide automobile transportation for the consumer, and each may meet the quality standards of its individual purchaser. However, the two products have obviously been designed differently for different types of consumers. This is commonly referred to as the **quality of design**—the degree to which quality characteristics are designed into the product. Although designed for the same use, the Mercedes and Ford differ in their performance, features, size, and various other quality characteristics.

The *dimensions of quality* primarily for manufactured products a consumer looks for in a product include the following.[2]

1. *Performance:* The basic operating characteristics of a product; for example, how well a car handles or its gas mileage.
2. *Features:* The "extra" items added to the basic features, such as a stereo CD or a leather interior in a car.
3. *Reliability:* The probability that a product will operate properly within an expected time frame; that is, a TV will work without repair for about seven years.
4. *Conformance:* The degree to which a product meets preestablished standards.
5. *Durability:* How long the product lasts; its life span before replacement. A pair of L.L. Bean boots, with care, might be expected to last a lifetime.
6. *Serviceability:* The ease of getting repairs, the speed of repairs, and the courtesy and competence of the repair person.
7. *Aesthetics:* How a product looks, feels, sounds, smells, or tastes.
8. *Safety:* Assurance that the customer will not suffer injury or harm from a product; an especially important consideration for automobiles.
9. *Other perceptions:* Subjective perceptions based on brand name, advertising, and the like.

These quality characteristics are weighed by the customer relative to the cost of the product. In general, consumers will pay for the level of quality they can afford. If they

Fitness for use is how well the product or service does what it is supposed to.

Quality of design involves designing quality characteristics into a product or service.

Dimensions of quality for which a consumer looks

---

[2] Adapted from D. A. Garvin, "What Does Quality Really Mean?" *Sloan Management Review* 26, no. 1 (1984): 25–43.

A Mercedes 560 SL and a Ford F-150 pick-up truck are equally "fit for use," but with different design dimensions for different customer markets that result in significantly different purchase prices. The Mercedes costs about twice as much as the Ford pick-up, however, the Ford purchaser uses a different set of quality characteristics for evaluation than the Mercedes purchaser and has a different set of quality expectations. Both vehicles can be of high quality depending on how they meet these customer expectations for quality. For example, a customer would expect the Mercedes to handle more smoothly on the highway and in traffic than a Ford pick-up truck; if it didn't the customer would think its quality was poor. However, because the Ford doesn't handle as well as the Mercedes in these conditions does not mean that it's of poor quality; the Ford owners' expectations for handling are different.

feel they are getting what they paid for, then they tend to be satisfied with the quality of the product.

Dimensions of service quality.

The dimensions of quality for a service differ somewhat from those of a manufactured product. Service quality is more directly related to time, and the interaction between employees and the customer. Evans and Lindsay[3] identify the following dimensions of service quality.

1. *Time and timeliness:* How long a customer must wait for service, and if it is completed on time. For example, is an overnight package delivered overnight?

2. *Completeness:* Is everything the customer asked for provided? For example, is a mail order from a catalog company complete when delivered?

3. *Courtesy:* How customers are treated by employees. For example, are catalog phone operators at Land's End nice and are their voices pleasant?

4. *Consistency:* Is the same level of service provided to each customer each time? Is your newspaper delivered on time every morning?

5. *Accessibility and convenience:* How easy it is to obtain the service. For example, when you call Lands' End or L.L. Bean does the service representative answer quickly?

6. *Accuracy:* Is the service performed right every time? Is your bank or credit card statement correct every month?

7. *Responsiveness:* How well the company reacts to unusual situations, which can happen frequently in a service company. For example, how well a telephone operator at L.L. Bean is able to respond to a customer's questions about a catalog item not fully described in the catalog.

---

[3] J. R. Evans and W. M. Lindsay, *The Management and Control of Quality*, 3d ed. (St. Paul, Minn.: West, 1996).

L.L. Bean's first product was the Maine Hunting Shoe, developed in 1912 by company founder, Leon Leonwood Bean, a Maine outdoorsman. Tired of wet, sore feet from the heavy leather boots of his day, L.L. Bean invented a new boot that combined lightweight leather tops with waterproof rubber bottoms. He initially sold 100 pairs to fellow sportsmen through the mail, but 90 pairs were sent back when the stitching gave way. However, true to his word L.L. Bean returned their money and started over with an improved boot. In years to come L.L. Bean operated his business according to the following belief: "Sell good merchandise at a reasonable profit, treat your customers like human beings, and they will always come back for more." L.L. Bean also guarantees their products to "give 100% satisfaction in every way." If they don't L.L. Bean will replace the item or refund the purchase price "at any time." In 1994 they replaced over 27,000 pairs of worn out rubber bottoms on its hunting shoe, and it remains one of L.L. Bean's most popular products. Since its inception L.L. Bean has remained committed to its founder's dedication to product quality and customer service that has given it a global reputation for quality.

All the product and service characteristics mentioned above must be considered in the design process to meet the consumer's expectations for quality. This requires that a company accurately assess what the consumer wants and needs. Consumer research to determine what kind of products are desired and the level of quality expected is a big part of a company's quality management program. Once consumer needs and wants have been determined by marketing, they are incorporated into the design of the product, and it is up to operations to ensure that the design is properly implemented, resulting in products and services consumers want and having quality they expect.

Quality from the Producer's Perspective

Now we need to look at quality the way a producer or service provider sees it. We already know that product development is a function of the quality characteristics (i.e., the product's fitness for use) the consumer wants, needs, and can afford. Product or service design results in design specifications that, hopefully, will achieve the desired quality. However, once the product design has been determined, the producer perceives quality to be how effectively the production process is able to conform to the specifications required by the design referred to as the **quality of conformance**. What this

Quality of conformance is making sure the product or service is produced according to design.

means is quality during production focuses on making sure that the product meets the specifications required by the design.

Examples of the quality of conformance: If new tires do not conform to specifications, they wobble. If a hotel room is not clean when a guest checks in, the hotel is not functioning according to the specifications of its design; it is a faulty service. From this producer's perspective, good-quality products conform to specifications—they are well made; poor-quality products are not made well—they do not conform to specifications.

Achieving quality of conformance depends on a number of factors including the design of the production process (distinct from product design), the performance level of machinery equipment and technology, the materials used, the training and supervision of employees, and the degree to which statistical quality control techniques are used. When equipment fails or is maladjusted, when employees make mistakes, when material and parts are defective, and when supervision is lax, design specifications are generally not met. Key personnel in achieving conformance to specifications include the engineering staff, supervisors and managers, as well as employees.

An important consideration from the consumer's perspective of product quality is product or service price. From the producer's perspective an important consideration is achieving quality of conformance at an acceptable cost. Product cost is also an important design specification. If products or services cannot be produced at a cost that results in a competitive price, then the final product will not have acceptable value—the price is more than the consumer is willing to pay given the product's quality characteristics. Thus, the quality characteristics included in the product design must be balanced against production costs.

We approached quality from two perspectives, the consumer's and the producer's. These two perspectives are dependent on each other as shown in Figure 3.1. Although product design is customer-motivated, it cannot be achieved without the coordination and participation of the production process. When a product is designed without considering how it will be produced, it may be impossible for the production process to meet design specifications or so costly to do so that the product or service must be priced prohibitively high.

Achieving quality of conformance involves design, materials and equipment, training, supervision, and control.

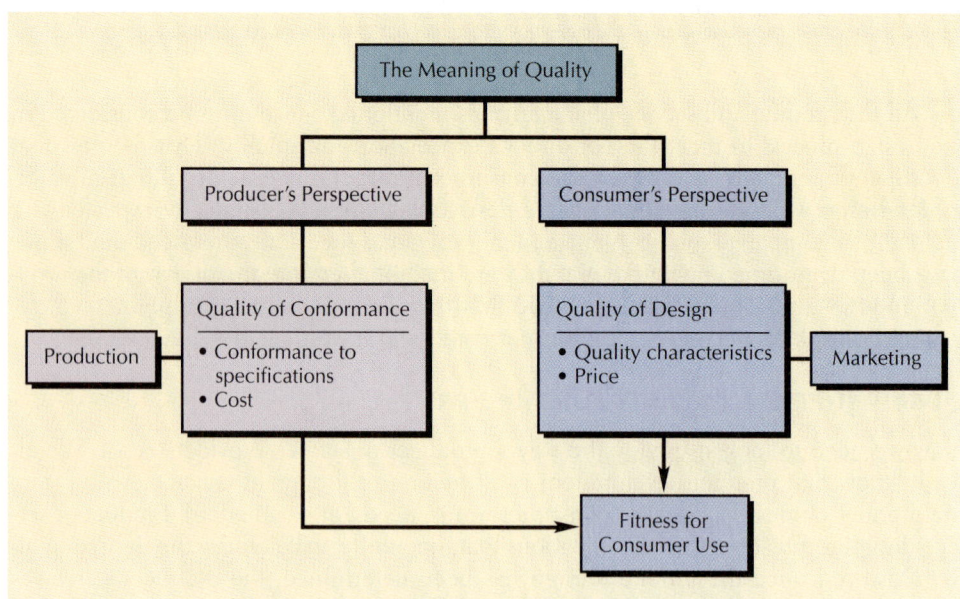

FIGURE 3.1 The Meaning of Quality

Figure 3.1 depicts the meaning of quality from the producer's and consumer's perspectives. The final determination of quality is fitness for use, which is the consumer's view of quality. It is the consumer who makes the final judgment regarding quality, and so it is the consumer's view that must dominate.

Competing at Lands' End

Giving high quality customer service: A focal point at Lands' End

A friendly phone staff is a key to customer services at

www.prenhall.com/russell

Lands' End. The number one priority for a sales representative at Lands' End is that he or she be friendly—and love to talk. Lands' End customer sales representatives are explicitly instructed that they are there not to sell, but to provide service. Director of Customer Service, Joan Conlin, explains that "our customer sales representatives are there to help customers accomplish what they called for—to meet a customer's need; they are not there to market other products . . . their job is to listen and respond to customer needs; it's service, not sales."

Vice President of Human Resources, Kelly Ritchie, notes that Lands' End employees are given an "incredible amount of responsibility. Right down to our front line sales reps, everybody has the authority to make whatever decision is necessary to please the customer. . . In every employee at every level, we try to instill the idea that they must do whatever is needed to meet a customer's need."

New hires at Lands' End are given 80 hours of training on all the company's basic products and core items, even fabrics, so they will have a basic understanding of what Lands' End sells. They are given training in proper politeness and how they are expected to operate when assisting customers. New employees are also given training on the computer system and a model phone system that replicates the actual system. As a result of this training most new customer service representatives feel very comfort-

able when they start taking real orders. Nevertheless, a trainer sits behind them for a few days to answer questions. Even when the formal training ends, an assist button can summon a supervisor able to answer questions. Operators can also call on specialty shoppers when a customer needs special assistance, and if an after-order problem arises they can call customer service.

Service representatives are assessed on a continuing basis. Supervisors listen to at least four calls for each service representative each month, they fill out monitoring forms for these calls and provide feedback to the representative. Monitoring is done at random and the representative does not know when it is occurring.

The speed with which a call is answered is one indicator of customer service quality. The Lands' End goal is to answer 90 percent of calls within 20 seconds of its being placed. The average answering speed is 5 seconds—maybe two rings—and most callers don't even hear a ring. An automatic call-distribution system in each of their phone centers allows Lands' End to monitor each center and shift more calls to any of the centers when the need arises. Call duration (talk-time) is also monitored. The company especially watches the high end to make sure there is not a system problem or that operators aren't becoming too chatty—something that customers do not like either.

Lands' End takes customer comments very seriously. Positive and negative customer phone comments to sales representatives are logged and, on a monthly basis, looked at by every department in the company. In 1995, for example, 10,000 comments were logged.

Total Quality Management

To make sure that products and services have the quality they have been designed for, a commitment to quality throughout the organization is required. This approach to the management of quality throughout the entire organization has evolved into what is referred to as total quality management, or TQM.

The Evolution of Total Quality Management

A handful of prominent individuals have had a dramatic impact on the rise of quality awareness in the United States, Japan, and other countries. These individuals include Walter Shewhart, W. Edwards Deming, Joseph Juran, and Philip Crosby.

Walter Shewhart was an employee of Bell Telephone Laboratories during the 1920s where he developed the technical tools that formed the beginning of statistical quality control. These tools became the foundation of the modern quality management movement in Japan and later in the United States. Shewhart helped start a quality revolution at AT&T and later became known as the father of statistical quality control.

Shewhart and his colleagues introduced the term **quality assurance** for their program to improve quality at Bell Telephone Laboratories using statistical quality control methods. For almost five decades these technical methods formed the foundation of quality assurance. However, it was one of Shewhart's disciples, W. Edwards Deming, who changed the focus of quality assurance from the technical aspects to more of a managerial philosophy. Today quality assurance refers to a commitment to quality throughout the organization.

W. Edwards Deming

W. Edwards Deming met Walter Shewhart in 1927 while working at the Department of Agriculture in Washington. Deming often visited Shewhart at his home in New Jersey on weekends to discuss statistics. In 1940 Deming moved to the Census Bureau, where he introduced the use of statistical process control to monitor the mammoth operation of key punching data from census questionnaires onto millions of punch cards. During World War II Deming worked on military-related problems, and beginning in 1942 he developed a national program of eight- and ten-day courses to teach statistical quality control techniques to executives and engineers of companies that were suppliers to the military during the war. Over 10,000 engineers were trained in Shewhart's statistical process control techniques. Many of them formed study groups that eventually developed into the American Society for Quality Control. By the end of World War II, Deming had an international reputation, and by the late 1940s he was consulting in Japan.

In 1950 Deming began teaching statistical quality control to Japanese companies. As a consultant to Japanese industries and as a teacher, he was able to convince them of the benefits of statistical quality control. He is a major figure in the Japanese quality movement, and in Japan he is frequently referred to as the father of quality control.

Deming's approach to quality management advocates continuous improvement of the production process to achieve conformance to specifications and reduce variability. He identifies two primary sources of process improvement: eliminating common causes of quality problems, such as poor product design and insufficient employee training, and eliminating special causes, such as specific equipment or an operator. Deming emphasizes the use of statistical quality control techniques to reduce variability in the production process. He dismisses the extensive use of final product inspection as coming too late to reduce product defects. Primary responsibility for quality improvement is em-

www.prenhall.com/russell

Shewhart developed statistical control charts.

Quality assurance is a commitment to quality throughout the organization.

www.prenhall.com/russell

W. E. Deming was a protégé of Walter Shewhart in the 1920s.

In the 1950s W. E. Deming began teaching quality control in Japan.

ployees' and management's—not the quality manager's or a technician's. He promotes extensive employee involvement in the quality improvement program, and he recommends training for workers in quality control techniques and methods.

Deming's overall philosophy for achieving improvement is embodied in his fourteen points, summarized as follows.

1. Create a constancy of purpose toward product improvement to achieve long-term organizational goals.

2. Adopt a philosophy of preventing poor-quality products instead of acceptable levels of poor quality as necessary to compete internationally.

3. Eliminate the need for inspection to achieve quality by relying instead on statistical quality control to improve product and process design.

4. Select a few suppliers or vendors based on quality commitment rather than competitive prices.

5. Constantly improve the production process by focusing on the two primary sources of quality problems, the system and workers, thus increasing productivity and reducing costs.

6. Institute worker training that focuses on the prevention of quality problems and the use of statistical quality control techniques.

7. Instill leadership among supervisors to help workers perform better.

8. Encourage employee involvement by eliminating the fear of reprisal for asking questions or identifying quality problems.

9. Eliminate barriers between departments, and promote cooperation and a team approach for working together.

10. Eliminate slogans and numerical targets that urge workers to achieve higher performance levels without first showing them how to do it.

11. Eliminate numerical quotas that employees attempt to meet at any cost without regard for quality.

12. Enhance worker pride, artisanry and self-esteem by improving supervision and the production process so that workers can perform to their capabilities.

13. Institute vigorous education and training programs in methods of quality improvement throughout the organization, from top management down, so that continuous improvement can occur.

14. Develop a commitment from top management to implement the previous thirteen points.

Deming is also credited for development of the *Deming Wheel*, or *plan-do-check-act (PDCA) cycle*, although it was originally formulated by Walter Shewhart and renamed by the Japanese. The Deming Wheel is a four-stage process for continuous quality improvement that complements Deming's fourteen points. This process is shown in Figure 3.2 and the stages of the process are described as follows.

The *Deming Wheel*—plan, do, check, act.

1. *Plan.* In this first stage of the Deming Wheel, a process or situation is studied, identifying problems and planning how to solve them. This is where customer expectations are determined and goals to measure quality improvement are established.

2. *Do.* In this stage, the plan is implemented on a test basis, improvement is measured, and the results documented.

3. *Study.* This stage was originally called the "check" stage, which is why the

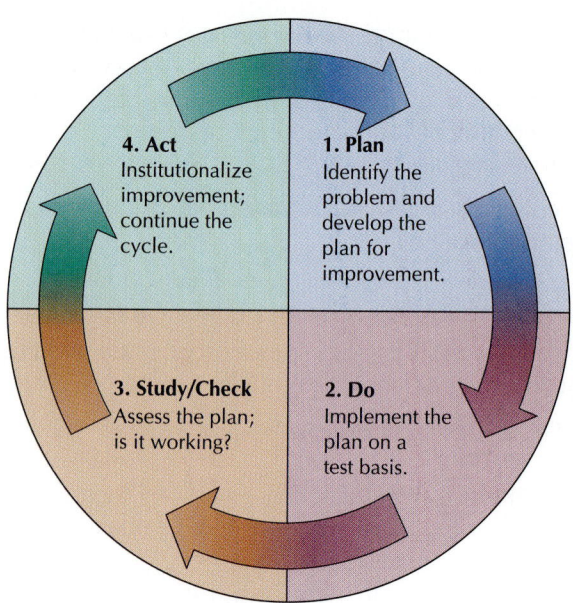

FIGURE 3.2   The Deming Wheel (PDCA Cycle)

cycle is called plan-do-check-act. Deming changed this to "study" in 1990 to reflect a more thorough analysis of the plan than a simple check. In this stage, the plan is assessed to see if it is achieving the goals established in stage 1, and to see if any new problems have developed.

4. *Act.* In the final stage, the plan is implemented and the quality improvement is made part of the normal operation. The process then returns to stage 1 to start the cycle over again to identify new quality problems and develop plans to solve them—the *continuous improvement* of a committed quality management program.

Joseph M. Juran, Philip Crosby, and Armand V. Feigenbaum

www.prenhall.com/russell

Juran included quality in the strategic planning process.

Joseph Juran, an author and consultant on quality, followed W. E. Deming to Japan in 1954, where he taught courses on the management of quality. Previously he had worked in the quality program at Western Electric. Like Deming, he has been a major contributor to the Japanese movement in quality improvement.

Juran focused on *strategic quality planning*—determining the product quality level and designing the production process to achieve the quality characteristics of the product. Strategic planning for quality is conducted within an annual quality program. Management sets goals and priorities, assesses the results of previous plans, and coordinates quality objectives with other company goals. He also emphasizes *quality improvement* by focusing on chronic quality problems and securing a "break-through" solution. Juran believes that at any time there should be hundreds (or perhaps even thousands) of quality improvement projects going on everywhere in the company where improvement is possible.

Crosby identified the cost of poor quality.

Another leader in quality management is Philip Crosby, whose 1979 book, *Quality Is Free*, emphasized that the costs of poor quality (including lost labor and equipment time due to scrap, downtime, and lost sales) far outweigh the cost of preventing poor quality, something not generally recognized in the United States at that time.

In the 1980s Armand V. Feigenbaum introduced **total quality control** to reflect a total commitment of effort from management and employees throughout an organization to improve on quality. Total quality control needs strong leadership from top management to improve quality and make it a continual process. The Japanese adopted this concept, referring to it as *company-wide quality control*. They believe that all employees at all levels of the organization, led by top management, are responsible for *continuous quality improvement*.

In recent years the term *TQM* has become popular. It embodies the same basic principles as quality assurance, total quality control, and company-wide quality control. TQM emphasizes top management's role in leading a total quality effort on which all employees at all levels must focus. All employees are responsible for continuous quality improvement, and quality is the focal part of all organizational functions. TQM also emphasizes that quality is a strategic issue. The organization must decide what the customer wants in terms of quality and then use strategic planning encompassing all functional areas to achieve goals for quality. From this perspective, quality is the most important company issue.

Total quality control is a company-wide, systems approach to quality.

Principles of Total Quality Management

Although companies use different terms to refer to their approach to quality, they mean pretty much the same thing and embody many of the same concepts: strategic goals, total commitment, continuous improvement, comprehensive focus, employee responsibility, job training, and so forth. Total quality management represents a set of management principles that focus on quality improvement as the driving force in all functional areas and at all levels in a company. These principles are:

1. The *customer* defines quality, and the customer's needs are the top priority.
2. Top management must provide the *leadership* for quality.
3. Quality is a *strategic* issue.
4. Quality is the responsibility of all *employees* at all levels of the organization.
5. All functions of the company must focus on *continuous quality improvement* to achieve strategic goals.
6. Quality problems are solved through *cooperation* among employees and management.
7. Problem solving and continuous quality improvement use *statistical quality control* methods.
8. *Training and education* of all employees are the basis for continuous quality improvement.

TQM—customer-oriented, leadership, strategic planning, employee responsibility, continuous improvement, cooperation, statistical methods, training and education.

TQM Throughout the Organization

Let's take a quick look at the impact of quality management on the various functions that make up the production process. *Marketing, sales*, and *research* have direct contact with the consumer. Marketing is typically responsible for the consumer research that determines the quality characteristics that consumers want and need, and the price they are willing to pay for it. Marketing also informs the consumer about the quality characteristics of a product through advertising and promotion. Sales provides feedback information through its interaction with the consumer, which is a determinant of product design. Research and development will explore new ideas for products and be actively involved in product innovation.

Marketing and R&D define what the consumer wants.

Engineering creates a design to meet customer expectations.

Engineering translates the product quality characteristics determined by marketing and top management into a product design, including technical specifications, material and parts requirements, equipment requirements, workplace and job design, and operator training and skills. Overdesigning the product is a drain on the company's resources and can erode profits, whereas underdesigned products will generally not meet the customer's quality expectations. Genichi Taguchi, the Japanese quality expert, estimates that poor product design is the cause of as much as 80 percent of all defective items. It is much cheaper and easier to make changes at the design stage than at the production stage, so companies need to focus on quality at all stages of the design process.

Purchasing acquires high-quality parts and materials.

Purchasing must make sure that the parts and materials required by the product design are of high quality. Quality of the final product will only be as good as the quality of the materials used to make it. Purchasing must select vendors who share the company's commitment to quality and who maintain their own quality management program for providing high-quality service, materials, and parts. In TQM a partnership exists between supplier and customer in which the supplier is expected to manage its own quality so the customer will not have to inspect incoming materials and parts. In a competitive global environment this means American suppliers must adopt TQM to do business with companies around the world.

Personnel hires employees with required skills and provides training.

Personnel is responsible for hiring employees that have the required abilities and skills, and training them for specific job tasks. Employees not well trained in their tasks will probably contribute to poor quality or service. Personnel also has responsibility for educating employees about quality and ways to achieve quality in their tasks. TQM requires that all employees throughout the organization be responsible for quality. Employees, collectively and individually, must not only perform their tasks according to design specifications but also be responsible for identifying poor quality or problems that may lead to poor quality and taking action to correct these problems. Performance appraisal under TQM focuses more on quality improvement and group and company achievement than on individual job performance.

Management maintains a smooth flow through the production or service process.

Management at all levels must implement the product design according to quality specifications, controlling labor, materials, and equipment. Failure to manage effectively can result in employee errors, equipment breakdown, bottlenecks, interrupted service, and the like, which contribute to poor quality.

Shipping prevents product damage.

Packing, storing, and *shipping* make sure that high-quality products are not damaged en route to the customer. Packaging methods and materials, storage facilities and procedures, and shipping modes must ensure that final products are protected and that customers receive them on time.

After the sale, quality service is as important as a quality product.

After-sale support (or customer service) has the responsibility of providing the customer with good instructions for the product's installation and use, with personal assistance if required. If the product fails to function properly, the company is responsible for repair or replacement. This is of major importance in TQM, since it represents a direct point of contact with the customer.

To have a successful TQM program, each of these areas in a business—as well as all other organizational support groups—must be committed to quality. However, this commitment must begin at the top and spread down through the organization. A successful TQM program must be planned, established, and initiated by top management and implemented by the various functions and employees in the organization. Although it is popular to say that quality is everyone's responsibility in a company, TQM generally requires a total commitment from top management to monitor and maintain quality throughout the organization.

THE COMPETITIVE EDGE

TQM at Kurt Manufacturing

Kurt Manufacturing Company, based in Minneapolis, is a midsize supplier of precision machine parts. It operates six plants and has 1,100 employees. To remain competitive in international markets, Kurt adopted a commitment to continuous improvement through total quality management principles and practices. Kurt's TQM program eliminates quality and production problems by systematic, continuous improvement of its processes. Kurt's top management estimates that in the United States probably 15 to 25 percent of labor is spent producing scrap or rework. Profit in Kurt's market is typically between 3 and 10 percent. Thus, it must eliminate scrap and rework to survive, and survival is based on TQM.

A goal of top management is for customers to be loyal to Kurt. They want customers to see Kurt as a company committed to total quality. This is achieved by understanding what their customers want and responding to their needs and problems. In Kurt's TQM approach, even though it is a manufacturing firm, the personnel interact with customers as if it were a service company. This means they focus on the whole job transaction, from the sale to responsiveness to the problems and unique needs of the customers after the part has been delivered. It is Kurt's belief that it will still not be perceived as a total quality company if its service side is not in order.

Many of Kurt's customers have reduced their suppliers, some from as many as 3,000 to about 150. Kurt Manufacturing has survived these cuts because of its commitment to TQM.

Source: Based on *Total Quality Management*, a video produced by the Society of Manufacturing Engineers (SME) and distributed by Prentice Hall, 1993.

Strategic Implications of TQM

A *strategy* is a set of decisions a company makes that establishes a plan to achieve its long-term goals. A company's success in implementing its strategy, or strategic plan, through its operations is a key to its long-term competitiveness. In today's global business environment, since a company competes on quality, it is likely the most important aspect of its strategic plan. For some companies, their strategic plan is embodied in their quality management program or, at the very least, quality is a key part of a company's strategic plan. In this section we will look at the relationship between strategy and TQM in those companies in which quality is the driving force.

Companies where quality drives their competitive strategy have certain common characteristics. They have a clear *strategic goal, vision,* or *mission* that focuses on customer satisfaction through quality. Ford's slogan that "Quality Is Job 1," Motorola's company objective of "Total Customer Satisfaction," and AT&T Universal Card Services headquarters inscription, "Customers are the center of our universe," all reflect their commitment to customer satisfaction and quality as part of their overall strategy or vision.

High goals for quality are characteristic of the strategic plans for these companies. Motorola's six sigma goal of 3.4 defects per million products is a policy of virtually no defective items. AT&T Consumer Communication Services, which provides long-distance services to 80 million residential customers, has the goal of providing a perfect connection every time.

Strategic planning also includes a set of programs, or *operational plans and policies,* to achieve the company's goals. Establishing goals without telling employees how to achieve them will be fruitless. In a quality management program goals and objectives are established at all levels, and the means and resources for achieving these goals are provided to employees and managers. This may include new or improved processes, employee training, and quality tools and techniques.

Quality is a key component of strategic planning.

Strategic plans should include a high goal for quality.

Strategic quality planning includes *a mechanism for feedback* to adjust, update, and make corrections in the strategic plan. Original quality goals may prove to be so easily attained that employees become complacent, or so impossible that employees become frustrated. Goals need to be continuously reevaluated and revised. The strategic plan also needs to be capable of quickly reflecting changing technology and market changes.

Strong leadership is a key to successfully integrating quality into a company's strategic plan. Robert Galvin, the former CEO of Motorola, often made quality the first item on the agenda at his staff meetings. David Kearns, the president of Xerox, was the driving force behind the development of his company's quality strategy that resulted in the 1989 Baldrige Award for Xerox's Leadership Through Quality program. However, strong leadership is not only about making the decision that quality will be an important component of a company's strategy; it is also about creating a company environment that is conducive to quality management. Such an environment actively involves manage-

> Strong leadership is a key to a successful strategic plan and achieving goals for quality.

THE COMPETITIVE EDGE

Strategy, Leadership, and Quality at Blue Cross/Blue Shield of Ohio

During the past decade the $1 trillion health-care industry has been in a state of crisis. Hospitals, health-care providers, and insurance companies have had to reassess their uncertain future. Blue Cross/Blue Shield of Ohio (BCBSO), a $1.7 billion mutual health-care insurer, undertook a series of far-reaching changes to better position itself to cope with its future.

In 1987 BCBSO lost $99 million. The company then established a strategic plan to achieve financial stability and sales growth, and drastically improve service performance. The strategic plan required BCBSO to establish well-defined goals, commit top management to achieve the goals, develop an incentive system to support the goals, unify management at all levels, and develop plans to carry out the changes the plan required. Employees who previously were outside the planning process found themselves directly involved, which excited them because they were able to see how their department and themselves fit into the overall plan and convinced them the planning process was worthwhile.

The strategic plan was a total quality program. Initially the program consisted of the traditional approach to quality improvement—educational programs on statistical quality control techniques, flowcharting techniques, and quick 90-day goals. It also included a "seize the day" philosophy that encouraged employees to address opportunities for improvement whenever they were identified. For example, a customer service representative decided to record the reasons for customer calls to see if a pattern existed, and discovered that a confusing code on the explanation-of-benefits statement generated a large number of help calls. The representative suggested altering the codes, an improvement that resulted in a 35% reduction in customer calls. In addition, extensive process improvement was conducted in the information technology area resulting in the development of three new major information systems at a cost of $35 million.

However, in 1991, when the strategic initiative seemed to be stalling, a Malcolm Baldrige National Quality Award examiner was hired to review the quality management program and recommend new initiatives. The examiner recommended that the company make the CEO's role more visible, reformulate steering committees with employees at every level, and target the Baldrige Award as a goal. Participation in the Baldrige Award process rejuvenated the quality management program and renewed employee enthusiasm. New goals included daily performance management in customer satisfaction, process improvement, and individual development. The strategic planning process and the quality management program was successful because of strong leadership at the top. Executive teams were willing to take the initiative to sustain the strategic plan even when it appeared it might falter.

In 1993, Blue Cross/Blue Shield of Ohio achieved $68 million in income and had enrolled 130,000 new members since the start of its strategic plan in 1987. It had reduced the time to turnaround claims from approximately four weeks to five to six calendar days, and increased the accuracy of claims processing, reducing numerous costly errors to achieve over 98% accuracy. Its overall rank among BC/BS plans rose from 72 out of 73 in 1987 to 4th out of 73 in 1993.

SOURCE: S. J. Smith, "Blue Cross/Blue Shield of Ohio: A Profile in Change," *Quality Progress* 28, no. 10 (October 1995): 87–90.

ment and employees in the strategic planning process, promotes teamwork between and among managers and employees, makes employees responsible for quality, and encourages managers and employees to take risks and talk openly about quality. It also rewards employees for quality improvement. If this type of environment is not created, then the company's quality strategy is not likely to be successful.

TQM in Service Companies

TQM evolved out of applications in manufacturing companies such as Toyota, IBM, and Motorola. In the 1990s service companies began to realize that they could benefit from quality management. This is important since the service sector is the largest segment of the U.S. economy employing almost three times as many people as manufacturing industries.

Service organizations and manufacturing companies both convert inputs into outputs—products or services—through a productive process. Both manufacturing and services use the same kinds of inputs—resources such as physical facilities, capital, materials, equipment, and people. In some instances the processes and products are similar. For example, both Ford and McDonald's product a tangible, physical product (cars and hamburgers) assembled from component parts. However, in pure service industries such as law, hotels, entertainment, communication, engineering, education, clubs, real estate, banks, retail, health care, and airlines, the processes are less similar and the products are not as tangible. The "products" provided by these organizations are not typically a physical item that can be held or stored. The customer of a manufacturer tends to interact only at the output end of the production process. The customer of a service often interacts directly with the production process, consuming services like legal advice, a classroom lecture, or an airline flight as they are being produced. Services tend to be customized and provided at the convenience of the customer; for example, doctors prescribe individually to patients. In addition, services are labor intensive while manufacturing is more capital intensive. Thus, human contact and its ramifications are an important part of the process of producing services.

> Services and manufacturing companies have similar inputs but different processes and outputs.

Manufactured products are physical items; they can be observed, held, felt, stored, and used again. If a manufactured item is defective, the defect can be felt or seen, and counted or measured. The improvement (or deterioration) in a product's quality can be measured. To implement a TQM program for a product, goals are established, and success or failure is measured against these goals.

> Services tend to be labor intensive.

It's not the same for service. A service cannot be held, felt, stored, and used again. A service output is not usually tangible; thus, it is not as easy to measure service defects. The dimensions of quality for manufactured items include such things as performance, features, reliability, conformance, and durability that can be quantitatively measured. The dimensions of service quality include timeliness, courtesy, consistency, accuracy, convenience, responsiveness, and completeness—all hard to measure beyond a subjective assessment by the customer. This does not mean that the potential for poor quality is any less in services. Each day thousands of travelers check into and out of Ritz Carlton Hotels, UPS handles and delivers millions of packages, and VISA processes millions of credit transactions worldwide. However, it is more difficult to assess defects in service and thus more difficult to measure customer satisfaction.

> Service defects are not always easy to measure since service output is not usually a tangible, physical item.

Service organizations must often rely on talking directly with customers in the form of surveys or interviews—both subjective responses—to measure the attributes of quality. Timeliness, or how quickly a service is provided, is an important dimension of service quality, and it is not difficult to measure. The difficulty is determining what is

> Timeliness is an important dimension of service quality.

Avis's well-known company slogan that it introduced in 1962, "We try harder," reflects its total commitment to customer satisfaction and quality management. Avis recognizes that its primary means of increasing market share is to constantly improve customer service. Avis's Worldwide Reservation Center handles over 23 million calls and 6.5 million reservations annually with a state-of-the-art information system that lets agents service most customers with little or no delay. Avis's Employee Participation Group (EPG) program enables employees to work with management to improve communications and develop quality improvement strategies that will improve the workplace environment, employee performance and increase job satisfaction. Employees are empowered to use their own initiative to assist customers in order to increase customer satisfaction. Employee training is extensive and Avis has been referred to as one of the "100 best companies to work for in America." Avis queries all customers when they return their car to monitor trends and customer satisfaction. The company also calls 1500 customers each month to get a detailed assessment of customer satisfaction in each of their nine service delivery areas. Avis, an employee-owned company, is recognized as a leader in quality management. Baldrige Award examiners visiting the company noted that "Customer-relationship management is a major strength of the company," and that "there is substantial evidence of a high level of customer satisfaction."

"quick" service and what is "slow" service. How long must a caller wait to place a phone catalog order before it is considered poor service?

Despite these differences, the definition of quality that we developed earlier in this chapter and the basic principles of TQM can apply equally well to services as to manufacturing. Quality service can be defined as "how well the service does what the customer thinks it is supposed to do." This is essentially the same fitness for use definition we developed earlier in this chapter. However, the differences between providing services and manufacturing products makes the management of service quality a challenging process.

Quality management in services must focus on employee performance related to intangible, difficult-to-measure quality dimensions. The most important of these quality dimensions is how quickly, correctly, and pleasantly employees are able to provide service. That is why service companies such as Federal Express, Lands' End, Avis, Disney, and Ritz Carlton Hotels have well-developed quality management programs that

> The principles of TQM apply equally well to services and manufacturing.

Competing at Lands' End

"Guaranteed. Period." The team approach to quality improvement at Lands' End

To back up their unique guarantee of customer satisfaction, "Guaranteed.Period." Lands' End addresses product development and improvement through a team approach. For example, the Adult Sleepwear and Slippers team, headed by merchandiser, Kelli Larke, includes an inventory manager to make sure sufficient quantities are ordered to meet customer needs; a quality-assurance specialist to make sure the products *exceed* customer expectations; a copywriter responsible for catalog presentations of products; an art director to make sure product features come across clearly in photography; and, a team-support member who provides assistance for all team members. A team like this frequently meets in a meeting area, but they also share a unique work area that includes individual workstations in a generally open area with no walls that facilitates communication between team members.

Quality problems are typically brought to the team's attention from the customer returns area or directly from customer comments. In one case, customer returns brought a pair of pajamas to the attention of Priscilla, the team's quality assurance specialist. The customer commented on the return slip that there was a problem with color bleeding after the pajamas had been washed a few times. Priscilla sent the pajamas to the lab and it was discovered that the piping on the garment bled into the fabric when washed with cold water. This set in motion activity by the team leader, Kelli, and other team members. Priscilla contacted the vendor who produces the pajamas for Lands' End and they immediately begin work on correcting the problem. Kelli alerts Dave, the inventory manager, so that he can begin determining the effect on stocking if they pull all the pajamas they currently have out of stock if it proves necessary. Ellen and Kelli begin discussing the need to provide more visible washing instructions on the pajamas to alert the customer to the cold water problem. The team approach enables Lands' End to move quickly with clear lines of communication to address quality problems and maintain customer satisfaction.

focus on employee performance, behavior, and training. These companies design their TQM programs to treat employees well, as if they were customers. Federal Express's slogan is "People, Service, Profits," and its treatment of employees, including its no lay-off policy, is viewed as a TQM model or **benchmark** that other companies try to copy. Disneyland's 12,000 park employees are treated as "cast members," and Disney's mission is to keep cast members happy so they will make customers happy.

McDonald's has a reputation for high-quality service resulting from its application of established TQM principles. Its food preparation process has been simplified into small autonomous units just as a manufacturing firm might do. It provides fresh food promptly on demand, which is essentially an inventory situation. Restaurant managers meet with customer groups on a regular basis and use questionnaires to identify quality "defects" in its operation. It monitors all phases of its process continuously from purchasing to restrooms to restaurant decor and maintenance in a total quality approach. It empowers all employees to make spot decisions to dispose of unfresh food or to speed

A **benchmark** is a "best" level of quality achievement in one company that other companies seek to achieve.

www.prenhall.com/russell

McDonald's is the largest food service retailer in the world with over 18,000 locations in 91 countries including the McDonald's shown here in Tokyo. System-wide sales for McDonald's was almost $30 billion in 1995. McDonald's goal is to dominate the global food service industry by setting performance standards for customer satisfaction, convenience, and value. Fast-food restaurants are generally recognized as having high quality standards in terms of cleanliness and service, and McDonald's is recognized as a quality leader in the industry. All phases of the food preparation and delivery process are closely monitored for quality. Food items are expected to be of the highest quality and fresh, and employees are expected to be well-trained, efficient, knowledgeable, helpful, and friendly. Restaurant managers meet with customer groups and use customer questionnaires to monitor quality and identify weaknessess and areas of improvement, and food items are sampled (tasted) on a regular basis to insure quality. Employee training emphasizes the customer first and the method of doing a job second and employees are trained to do different jobs so they can fill in as needed to maintain quick service. Employees have the freedom to make decisions such as replacing food items for customers in order to insure customer satisfaction. McDonald's embodies a commitment to total quality management as organized, pervasive and focused as any manufacturing company.

service. The McDonald's work force is flexible so that changes in customer traffic and demand can be met promptly by moving employees to different tasks. Food is sampled regularly for taste and freshness. Extensive use is made of information technology for scheduling, cash register operation, food inventory, cooking procedures, and food assembly processes—all with the objective of faster service. All of these quality improvement procedures are standard and similar to quality improvement techniques that could be found in a manufacturing firm.

THE COMPETITIVE EDGE

Quality Management at Kentucky Fried Chicken

Kentucky Fried Chicken (KFC) Corporation, USA, includes 2,000 company-owned and 3,000 franchised restaurants with annual sales exceeding $3 billion from over 600 million customers. The fast-food restaurant industry is very competitive. Quick, high-quality service is essential to maintain and increase market share. KFC measures quality at its restaurants using two programs: a quality, service, and cleanliness (QSC) program for evaluating service from a customer's perspective; and an operations facility review (OFR) program for measuring process implementation relative to specifications. To measure its performance against other companies, KFC uses customer and market surveys. In the QSC program, independent "mystery shoppers" are hired to evaluate each restaurant twice a month. In the OFR program, KFC uses in-house specially trained evaluators.

Declining profit margin in its South Central (Oklahoma and Texas) division resulted in a major quality improvement project whose objective was to improve service time for the drive-through window (DTW) operations at four test restaurants. Speed is the most important dimension of service quality in this type of operation. The quality project team set a goal to reduce service speed at drive-in windows from over two minutes per customer to 60 seconds—considered an unrealistic goal by KFC management. The team set short-term, incremental goals of 10-second reductions in service time until the one minute goal was realized. These short-run achievable goals helped keep employees from getting discouraged. Large, visible timers were placed at each identifiable step in the order process to help employees see if they were taking too long. It was discovered that there are three primary service components at a drive-through window: time at the menu board, travel time from the menu once an order has been placed to the service window, and time at the window waiting for the order and paying for it. Observations showed that 58% of total customer time was at the window so the team concentrated on this area. Employees were provided with notebooks to identify causes for delays whenever customer service was not completed within the target time as shown by the timers. Causes of slow service were identified in the process including headset problems, being out of menu items, and poor equipment layout. Changes in the drive-in window process included improved equipment layout to eliminate wasted motion (such as putting food items and food packing in more convenient locations), streamlined menus eliminating slow-moving items, even-dollar tax-inclusive pricing to speed the payment process, more extensive use of headsets, clearer signs for customers to read easily, more rigorous employee training, and, most important, the continued use of the timers as a constant reminder that customers were waiting. Within 10 months the 60-second service goal was achieved at the test restaurants—and profit margin increased from 5 to 9 percent, customer orders increased by almost 30 percent, sales volume increased by 17.5 percent, and labor productivity measured as drive-in window transactions per labor hour increased by 12.3 percent. In the past two years over 1,300 franchised KFC restaurants have adopted all or part of the test team's quality-improvement program for drive-through window operations.

SOURCE: U. M. Apte and C. Reynolds, "Quality Management at Kentucky Fried Chicken," *Interfaces* 25, no. 3 (1995): 6–21.

Service industries like fast-food restaurants, airlines, entertainment, and hotel lodging are extremely competitive. Companies in these and similar industries lose more customers because either their customer service is poor or their competitors are providing better service, than for any other reason, including price.

The Cost of Quality

Quality costs fall into two categories, the cost of achieving good quality, also known as the *cost of quality assurance*, and the cost associated with poor-quality products, also referred to as the *cost of not conforming* to specifications.

The Cost of Achieving Good Quality

The costs of a quality management program are *prevention costs* and *appraisal costs*. **Prevention costs** are the costs of trying to prevent poor-quality products from reaching

Prevention costs are costs incurred during product design.

the customer. Prevention reflects the quality philosophy of "do it right the first time," the ultimate goal of a quality management program. Examples of prevention costs include the following:

The costs of preventing poor quality include planning, design, process, training, and information costs.

Quality planning costs: The costs of developing and implementing the quality management program.

Product design costs: The costs of designing products with quality characteristics.

Process costs: The costs expended to make sure the productive process conforms to quality specifications.

Training costs: The costs of developing and putting on quality training programs for employees and management.

Information costs: The costs of acquiring and maintaining (typically on computers) data related to quality, and the development and analysis of reports on quality performance.

Appraisal costs are costs of measuring, testing, and analyzing.

Costs of measuring quality include inspection, testing, equipment, and operator costs.

Appraisal costs are the costs of measuring, testing, and analyzing materials, parts, products, and the productive process to ensure that product quality specifications are being met. Examples of appraisal costs include the following:

Inspection and testing: The costs of testing and inspecting materials, parts, and the product at various stages and at the end of the process.

Test equipment costs: The costs of maintaining equipment used in testing the quality characteristics of products.

Operator costs: The cost of the time spent by operators to gather data for testing product quality, to make equipment adjustments to maintain quality, and to stop work to assess quality.

In a service organization appraisal costs tend to be higher than in a manufacturing company and, therefore, are a greater proportion of total quality costs. Quality in services is related primarily to the interaction between an employee and a customer, which makes the cost of appraising quality more difficult. Quality appraisal in a manufacturing operation can take place almost exclusively in-house; appraisal of service quality usually requires customer interviews, surveys, questionnaires, and the like.

The Cost of Poor Quality

Costs associated with poor quality are also referred to as the cost of nonconformance, or failure costs. The cost of failures is the difference between what it actually costs to produce a product or deliver a service and what it would cost if there were no failures. This is generally the largest quality cost category in a company, frequently accounting for 70 percent to 90 percent of total quality costs. This is where the greatest cost improvement is possible.

The cost of poor quality can be categorized as *internal failure costs* or *external failure costs*. **Internal failure costs** are incurred when poor-quality products are discovered before they are delivered to the customer. Examples of internal failure costs include the following:

Internal failure costs include scrap, rework, process failure, downtime, and price reductions.

Scrap costs: The costs of poor-quality products that must be discarded, including labor, material, and indirect costs.

Rework costs: The costs of fixing defective products to conform to quality specifications.

Process failure costs: The costs of determining why the production process is producing poor-quality products.

Process downtime costs: The costs of shutting down the productive process to fix the problem.

Price-downgrading costs: The costs of discounting poor-quality products—that is, selling products as "seconds."

External failure costs are incurred after the customer has received a poor-quality product and are primarily related to customer service. Examples of external failure costs include the following:

Customer complaint costs: The costs of investigating and satisfactorily responding to a customer complaint resulting from a poor-quality product.

Product return costs: The costs of handling and replacing poor-quality products returned by the customer.

Warranty claims costs: The costs of complying with product warranties.

Product liability costs: The litigation costs resulting from product liability and customer injury.

Lost sales costs: The costs incurred because customers are dissatisfied with poor-quality products and do not make additional purchases.

Internal failure costs tend to be low for a service while external failure costs can be quite high. A service organization has little opportunity to examine and correct a defective internal process, usually a employee-customer interaction, before it actually happens. At that point it becomes an external failure. External failures typically result in an increase in service time or inconvenience for the customer. Examples of external failures include a customer waiting to place a catalog phone order; a catalog order that arrives with the wrong item, requiring the customer to repackage and send it back; an error in a charge card billing statement, requiring the customer to make phone calls or write letters to correct it; not sending a customer's orders or statements to the correct address; or an overnight mail package that does not arrive overnight.

> **External failure costs** include complaints, returns, warranty claims, liability, and lost sales.

Measuring and Reporting Quality Costs

Collecting data on quality costs can be difficult. The costs of lost sales, of responding to customer complaints, of process downtime, of operator testing, of quality information, and of quality planning and product design, are all costs that may be difficult to measure. These costs must be estimated by management. Training costs, inspection and testing costs, scrap costs, the cost of product downgrading, product return costs, warranty claims, and liability costs can usually be measured. Many of these costs are collected as part of normal accounting procedures.

Management wants quality costs reported in a manner that can be easily interpreted and is meaningful. One format for reporting quality costs are with **index numbers,** or **indices**. Index numbers are ratios that measure quality costs relative to some base value, such as the ratio of quality costs to total sales revenue or the ratio of quality costs to units of final product. These index numbers are used to compare quality management efforts between time periods or between departments or functions. Index numbers themselves do not provide very much information about the effectiveness of a quality management program. They usually will not show directly that a company is producing good- or poor-quality products. These measures are informative only when they are compared to some standard or other index. Some common index measures are:

> **Index numbers** are ratios that measure quality costs against a base value.

Labor index: The ratio of quality cost to direct labor hours; it has the advantage of being easily computed (from accounting records) and easily understood, but it is **not**

> The **labor index** is the ratio of quality cost to labor hours.

always effective for long-term comparative analysis when technological advances reduce labor usage.

The cost index is the ratio of quality cost to manufacturing cost.

Cost index: The ratio of quality cost to manufacturing cost (direct and indirect cost); it is easy to compute from accounting records and is not affected by technological change.

The sales index is the ratio of quality cost to sales.

Sales index: The ratio of quality cost to sales; it is easily computed, but it can be distorted by changes in selling price and costs.

The production index is the ratio of quality cost to units of final product.

Production index: The ratio of quality cost to units of final product; it is easy to compute from accounting records but is not effective if a number of different products exist.

The following example illustrates several of these index numbers.

EXAMPLE 3.1

An Evaluation of Quality Costs and Quality Index Numbers

The H&S Motor Company produces small motors (3 hp, etc.) for use in lawnmowers and garden equipment. The company instituted a quality management program in 1994 and has recorded the following quality cost data and accounting measures for four years.

	YEAR			
	1994	*1995*	*1996*	*1997*
Quality Costs				
Prevention	$ 27,000	41,500	74,600	112,300
Appraisal	155,000	122,500	113,400	107,000
Internal failure	386,400	469,200	347,800	219,100
External failure	242,000	196,000	103,500	106,000
Total	$810,400	829,200	639,300	544,400
Accounting Measures				
Sales	$4,360,000	4,450,000	5,050,000	5,190,000
Manufacturing costs	1,760,000	1,810,000	1,880,000	1,890,000

The company wants to assess its quality assurance program and develop quality index numbers using sales and manufacturing cost bases for the four-year period.

SOLUTION:

The H&S Company experienced many of the typical outcomes when its quality assurance program was instituted. Approximately 78 percent of H&S's total quality costs are a result of internal and external failures, not unlike many companies. Failure costs frequently contribute 50 to 90 percent of overall quality costs. The typical reaction to high failure costs is to increase product monitoring and inspection to eliminate poor-quality products resulting in high appraisal costs. This appeared to be the strategy employed by H&S when its quality management program was initiated in 1994. In 1995 H&S was able to identify more defective items, resulting in an apparent increase in internal failure costs and lower external failure costs (as fewer defective products reached the customer).

During 1994 and 1995 prevention costs were modest. However, prevention is critical in reducing both internal and external failures. By instituting quality, training programs, redesigning the production process, and planning how to build in product quality, companies are able to reduce poor-quality products within the production process and prevent them from reaching the customer. This was the case at H&S, because prevention costs increased by more than 400 percent during the four-year period. Since fewer poor-quality products are being made, less monitoring and inspection is necessary, and appraisal costs thus decline. Internal and external failure costs are also reduced because of a reduction in defective products. In general, an increase in expenditures for prevention will result in a decrease in all other quality-cost categories. It is also not uncommon for a quality management program to isolate one or two specific quality problems that, when prevented, have a large impact on overall quality cost reduction. Quality problems are not usually evenly distributed throughout the product process; a few isolated problems tend to result in the majority of poor-quality products.

The H&S Company also desired to develop index numbers using quality costs as a proportion of sales and manufacturing costs, generally two of the more popular quality indexes. The general formula for these index numbers is

$$\text{Quality index} = \frac{\text{total quality costs}}{\text{base}}(100)$$

For example, the index number for 1994 sales is

$$\text{Quality cost per sale} = \frac{\$810,400(100)}{4,360,000}$$
$$= 18.58$$

The quality index numbers for sales and manufacturing costs for the four-year period are given in the following table.

Year	Quality Sales Index	Quality Manufacturing Cost Index
1994	18.58	46.04
1995	18.63	45.18
1996	12.66	34.00
1997	10.49	28.80

These index numbers alone provide little insight into the effectiveness of the quality management program; however, as a standard to make comparisons over time they can be useful. The H&S Company quality index numbers reflect dramatically improved quality during the four-year period. Quality costs as a proportion of both sales and manufacturing costs improved significantly. Quality index numbers do not provide information that will enable the company to diagnose and correct quality problems in the production process. They are useful in showing trends in product quality over time and reflecting the impact of product quality relative to accounting measures with which managers are usually familiar.

The Quality-Cost Relationship

In Example 3.1 we showed that when the sum of prevention and appraisal costs increased, internal and external failure costs decreased. Recall that prevention and appraisal costs are costs of achieving good quality, and internal and external failure costs are the costs of poor quality. In general, when the cost of achieving good quality increases, the cost of poor quality declines.

U.S. and foreign companies committed to TQM believe that the increase in sales and market share resulting from increased consumer confidence in the quality of their products offsets the higher costs of achieving good quality. Further, as a company focuses on improved quality, the cost of achieving good quality will be less because of the innovations in technologies, processes, and work methods that will result from the quality-improvement effort. These companies frequently seek to achieve 100 percent quality and *zero defects*.

The Japanese first recognized that the costs of poor quality had been traditionally underestimated. These costs did not take into account the customer losses that can be attributed to a reputation for poor quality. Costs of poor quality were hard to quantify, so they were ignored. The Japanese viewed the cost associated with a reputation for poor quality to be quite high. The traditional quality-cost relationship does not reflect the total impact of an effective quality management program on a company's performance. A General Accounting Office report on companies that were Baldrige (Quality) Award finalists has shown that corporate-wide quality-improvement programs result in higher worker motivation, improved employee relations, increased productivity, higher customer satisfaction, and increased market share and profitability.[4]

Another reason for Japanese success has been their commitment to achieving quality at minimum cost. One way they have done this is to focus more on improving the capabilities and training of employees, getting them more involved in preventing poor quality and focusing less on "engineering" solutions. The Japanese have also concentrated on improving quality at the new product development stage instead of trying to build in quality during the production process for products already developed. This tends to reduce appraisal costs. Finally, the Japanese recognized that if they provided higher-quality products, they could charge higher prices. The traditional view of quality costs implied that a "satisfactory" quality level was optimal because higher levels of quality would require prices higher than the customer would be willing to pay to offset the higher costs. The Japanese showed that this was not the case; in fact, they created a market for higher quality, for which consumers were willing to pay.

The Bottom Line—Profitability

Quality improvement, as initiated by Japanese companies, was not intended to improve profitability but to gain customer focus and be more competitive. Quality management was considered to be a longer-term commitment than simply short-run cost savings and profits. However, quality management has been around now for over a decade, and researchers have begun to look at it to see if it has been profitable.

Some research studies suggest that quality management does not contribute to the "bottom line." A recent survey of 5,000 U.S. firms showed that only a third of the companies' bottom lines benefited from TQM. A similar study of 100 British companies showed an 80 percent failure rate of TQM based on profitability as a measure of success. However, such results must be observed cautiously. Many companies in these surveys implemented TQM programs without the total commitment required for their success. These studies also take a short-run view of success, failing to recognize that TQM typically results in a decline in profitability in the short run with the promise of greater financial rewards in the long run.

[4] Robert E. Cole, "The Quality Revolution," *Production and Operations Management* 1, no. 1 (1992): 118–20.

It is more informative to observe how companies that have demonstrated a stronger, long-term commitment to TQM have fared. A recent survey of 26 Japanese Deming Quality Prize–winning companies committed to TQM showed that all gained higher-than-average results for different financial performance indicators. Several surveys of Baldrige Award winners in the United States have consistently shown that their financial performance exceeds industry averages. Researchers at PIMS Associates, Inc., a subsidiary of the Strategic Planning Institute, have found that quality "is an important determinant of business profitability," and that "quality is positively and significantly related to a higher return on investment" among 1,200 companies it studied.[5] In his book *Quality Is Free*, quality pioneer Philip Crosby states that, "Quality is not only free, it is an honest-to-everything profit maker. . . ."[6] Gary L. Tooker, CEO and vice chairman of Motorola, in response to the question, "Is there a link between quality and profitability?" responded that, "We've saved several billion dollars over the last year because of our focus on quality improvement and the six sigma initiative. . . . there is no doubt about the fact that it has enhanced our bottom line."[7]

This is only the tip of a mountain of conclusive evidence that *in the long run* quality improvement and profitability are closely related. As quality improves, the costs associated with poor quality decline. Quality improvements result in increased productivity. As the quality of a company's products or services improve, it becomes more competitive and its market share increases. Customers' perception of a company's products as being of high quality and its competitive posture enables the company to charge higher prices. Taken together, these things result in higher long-run profitability.

The Effect of Quality Management on Productivity

In the previous section we saw how an effective quality management program can help to reduce quality-related costs and improve market share and profitability. Quality management can also improve productivity—the number of units produced from available resources.

Productivity

Productivity is a measure of a company's effectiveness in converting inputs into outputs. It is broadly defined as,

$$\text{Productivity} = \frac{\text{output}}{\text{input}}$$

An output is the final product from a service or production process, such as an automobile, a hamburger, a sale, or a catalog order. Inputs are the parts, material, labor, capital, and so on that go into the productive process. Productivity measures, depending on the outputs and inputs used, are labor productivity (output per labor-hour) and machine productivity (output per machine-hour).

Improving quality by reducing defects will increase good output and reduce inputs. In fact, virtually all aspects of quality improvement have a favorable impact on different measures of productivity. Improving product design and production processes, im-

Productivity is the ratio of output to input.

Quality impact on productivity: Fewer defects increase output and quality improvement reduces inputs.

[5] James R. Evans and William M. Lindsay, *The Management and Control of Quality*, 3d ed. (St. Paul, Minn.: West, 1996), p. 18.

[6] Philip Crosby, *Quality Is Free* (New York: McGraw-Hill, 1979).

[7] K. Bemowski, "Motorola's Fountain of Youth, *Quality Progress* 28, no. 10 (October 1995): 29–31.

proving the quality of materials and parts, and improving job designs and work activity will all increase productivity.

Measuring Product Yield and Productivity

Yield is a measure of productivity.

Product **yield** is a measure of output used as an indicator of productivity. It can be computed for the entire production process (or for one stage in the process) as follows:

$$\text{Yield} = (\text{total input})\ (\%\ \text{good units}) + (\text{total input})\ (1 - \%\ \text{good units})\ (\%\ \text{reworked})$$

or

$$Y = (I)\ (\%G) + (I)\ (1 - \%G)\ (\%R)$$

where

I = planned number units of product started in the production process

$\%G$ = percentage of good units produced

$\%R$ = percentage of defective units that are successfully reworked

In this formula, yield is the sum of the percentage of products started in the process (or at a stage) that will turn out to be good quality plus the percentage of the defective (rejected) products that are reworked. Any increase in the percentage of good products through improved quality will increase product yield.

Improved quality increases product yield.

EXAMPLE 3.2

Computing Product Yield

The H&S Motor Company starts production for a particular type of motor with a steel motor housing. The production process begins with 100 motors each day. The percentage of good motors produced each day averages 80 percent and the percentage of poor-quality motors that can be reworked is 50 percent. The company wants to know the daily product yield and the effect on productivity if the daily percentage of good-quality motors is increased to 90 percent.

SOLUTION:

$$\text{Yield} = (I)\ (\%G) + (I)\ (1 - \%G)\ (\%R)$$
$$Y = 100\ (0.80) + 100\ (1 - 0.80)\ (0.50)$$
$$= 90\ \text{motors}$$

If product quality is increased to 90 percent good motors, the yield will be:

$$Y = 100\ (0.90) + 100\ (1 - 0.90)(0.50)$$
$$= 95\ \text{motors}$$

A 10 percentage-point increase in quality products results in a 5.5 percent increase in productivity output.

Now we will expand our discussion of productivity to include product manufacturing cost. The manufacturing cost per (good) product is computed by dividing the sum of total direct manufacturing cost and total cost for all reworked units by the yield, as follows.

Product cost = (direct manufacturing cost per unit)(input) + (rework cost per unit)(reworked units) / yield

or

$$\text{Product cost} = \frac{(K_d)(I) + (K_r)(R)}{Y}$$

where

K_d = direct manufacturing cost per unit
I = input
K_r = rework cost per unit
R = reworked units
Y = yield

EXAMPLE
3.3

Computing Product Cost Per Unit

The H&S Motor Company has a direct manufacturing cost per unit of $30, and motors that are of inferior quality can be reworked for $12 per unit. From Example 3.2, 100 motors are produced daily, 80 percent (on average) are of good quality and 20 percent are defective. Of the defective motors, half can be reworked to yield good-quality products. Through its quality management program, the company has discovered a problem in its production process that, when corrected (at a minimum cost), will increase the good-quality products to 90 percent. The company wants to assess the impact on the direct cost per unit of improvement in product quality.

SOLUTION:

The original manufacturing cost per motor is

$$\text{Product cost} = \frac{(K_d)(I) + (K_r)(R)}{Y}$$

$$\text{Product cost} = \frac{(\$30)(100) + (\$12)(10)}{90 \text{ motors}}$$

$$= \$34.67 \text{ per motor}$$

The manufacturing cost per motor with the quality improvement is

$$\text{Product cost} = \frac{(\$30)(100) + (\$12)(5)}{95 \text{ motors}}$$

$$\text{Product cost} = \$32.21 \text{ per motor}$$

The improvement in the production process as a result of the quality management program will result in a decrease of $2.46 per unit, or 7.1 percent, in direct manufacturing cost per unit as well as a 5.5 percent increase in product yield (computed in Example 3.2) with a minimal investment in labor, plant, or equipment.

In Examples 3.2 and 3.3 we determined productivity measures for a single production process. However, it is more likely that product quality would be monitored throughout the production process at various stages. Each stage would result in a portion of good-quality, "work-in-process" products. For a production process with n stages, the yield, Y (without reworking), is,

$$Y = (I)\,(\%g_1)\,(\%g_2)\cdots(\%g_n)$$

where

I = input of items to the production process that will result in finished products

g_i = good-quality, work-in-process products at stage i

EXAMPLE 3.4

Computing Product Yield for a Multistage Process

At the H&S Motor Company, motors are produced in a four-stage process. Motors are inspected following each stage with percentage yields (on average) of good quality in-process units as follows.

Stage	Average Percentage Good Quality
1	0.93
2	0.95
3	0.97
4	0.92

The company wants to know the daily product yield for product input of 100 units per day. Further, it would like to know how many input units it would have to start with each day to result in a final daily yield of 100 good quality units.

SOLUTION:

$$Y = (I)\,(\%g_1)\,(\%g_2)\,(\%g_3)\,(\%g_4)$$
$$= (100)\,(0.93)\,(0.95)\,(0.97)\,(0.92)$$
$$Y = 78.8 \text{ motors}$$

Thus, the production process has a daily good-quality product yield of 78.8 motors.

To determine the product input that would be required to achieve a product yield of 100 motors, I is treated as a decision variable when Y equals 100:

$$I = \frac{Y}{(\%g_1)(\%g_2)(\%g_3)(\%g_4)}$$

$$I = \frac{100}{(0.93)(0.95)(0.97)(0.92)}$$

$$= 126.8 \text{ motors}$$

To achieve output of 100 good-quality motors, the production process must start with approximately 127 motors.

The Quality-Productivity Ratio

Another measure of the effect of quality on productivity[8] combines the concepts of quality index numbers and product yield. Called the **quality-productivity ratio** (QPR),[8] it is computed as follows:

$$QPR = \frac{\text{good-quality units}}{(\text{input})(\text{processing cost}) + (\text{defective units})(\text{rework cost})} (100)$$

The **quality-productivity ratio** is a productivity index that includes productivity and quality costs.

This is actually a quality index number that includes productivity and quality costs. The QPR increases if either processing cost or rework costs or both decrease. It increases if more good-quality units are produced relative to total product input (i.e., the number of units that begin the production process).

EXAMPLE
3·5

Computing the Quality-Productivity Ratio (QPR)

The H&S Motor Company produces small motors at a processing cost of $30 per unit. Defective motors can be reworked at a cost of $12 each. The company produces 100 motors per day and averages 80 percent good-quality motors, resulting in 20 percent defects, 50% of which can be reworked prior to shipping to customers. The company wants to examine the effects of (1) increasing the production rate to 200 motors per day; (2) reducing the processing cost to $26 and the rework cost to $10; (3) increasing through quality improvement the product yield of good-quality products to 95 percent; and (4) the combination of 2 and 3.

SOLUTION:

The QPR for the base case is computed as follows.

$$QPR = \frac{80 + 10}{(100)(\$30) + (10)(\$12)} (100)$$

$$= 2.89$$

Case 1. Increase input to production capacity of 200 units.

$$QPR = \frac{160 + 20}{(200)(\$30) + (20)(\$12)} (100)$$

$$= 2.89$$

Increasing production capacity alone has no effect on the QPR; it remains the same as the base case.

Case 2. Reduce processing cost to $26 and rework cost to $10.

$$QPR = \frac{80 + 10}{(100)(\$26) + (10)(\$10)} (100)$$

$$= 3.33$$

These cost decreases caused the QPR to increase.

(Continued)

[8] E. E. Adam, J. E. Hershauer, and W. A. Ruch, *Productivity and Quality: Measurement as a Basis of Improvement*, 2d ed. (Columbia, Mo.: Research Center, College of Business and Public Administration, University of Missouri, 1986).

Case 3. Increase initial good-quality units to 95 percent.

$$QPR = \frac{95 + 2.5}{(100)(\$30) + (2.5)(\$12)} (100)$$

$$= 3.22$$

Again, the QPR increases as product quality improves.

Case 4. Decrease costs and increase initial good-quality units.

$$QPR = \frac{95 + 2.5}{(100)(\$26) + (2.5)(\$10)} (100)$$

$$= 3.71$$

The largest increase in the QPR results from decreasing costs and increasing initial good-quality product through improved quality.

Indirect Productivity Gains

We have shown how quality improvement can have a direct impact on productivity. However, we focused on the effect of fewer defective items, less scrap, and less rework on productivity. There are also quality improvements that indirectly increase productivity. For example, the increased output achieved from process improvements can result in increased productivity. In general, any quality improvements or improved designs that enhance the workplace, remove congestion, and work to smooth out and speed up the productive process increase output, which improves productivity. A recent study has shown that the indirect productivity gains from quality improvements may

THE COMPETITIVE EDGE

Increased Productivity at ITT

ITT Electro-Optical Products Division in Roanoke, Virginia, is a designer, developer, and producer of image-intensification devices used in night-vision products, such as helicopter pilot's goggles, aviator's night-vision imaging systems, and night goggles. Manufacturing the image intensifier is a complex operation, requiring over 400 different processes and 200 different chemicals, which combines the technologies of electronics, fiber optics, chemistry, optics, and semiconductors, among others. As a result, manufacturing yields are only 10 to 40 percent throughout the night-vision industry. In 1986 the company implemented a total quality management program that included continuous process improvement, statistical process control, and employee involvement, including the use of cause-and-effect diagrams. In 1985, prior to the initiation of the TQM program, the company av-

eraged a manufacturing yield of 35 percent, which increased to 75 percent by 1989 with the quality improvement program. In 1985 the company delivered only 500 image-intensifier tubes, but in 1990 deliveries exceeded 29,000 tubes, and during this same period, production capacity increased from 1,000 tubes to 35,000 tubes annually. As a result of this success (unique in the night-vision industry), the ITT Electro-Optical Products Division received the 1990 U.S. Senate Productivity Award for Virginia Medallion and became the first and only Virginia company to be invited by the U.S. Army to apply for certification in its Contractor Performance Certification Program.

SOURCE: Based on J. E. Kempster, "ITT Electro-Optical Products Division Roanoke, Virginia," *Quality and Productivity Management* 9, no. 2 (1991): 37–46.

outweigh the direct ones by a factor of two or three.[9] If companies focus on the usual productivity measures they may underestimate the extent of productivity gains that can be achieved from quality improvement.

Quality Improvement and the Role of Employees

To achieve high quality, it is absolutely necessary that management and employees cooperate and that each have an equally strong commitment to quality. Cooperation and commitment are not possible when management "dictates" quality to employees. Cooperation in a quality management program is achieved when employees are allowed to participate in the quality management process—that is, when they are given a voice.

When employees are directly involved in the quality management process it is referred to as **participative problem solving.** Employee participation in identifying and solving quality problems has been shown to be effective in improving quality, increasing employee satisfaction and morale, improving job skills, reducing job turnover and absenteeism, and increasing productivity.

In **participative problem solving,** employees are directly involved in the quality management process.

Mickey Mouse is not just a costumed character at the various Disney parks in the United States and abroad; he is a host who represents all the other costumed host and hostesses to Disney's thousands of "guests" each day. Every employee at a Disney park from janitors to Mickey has undergone extensive training to provide quality service to Disney's guests.

---

[9] C. D. Ittner, "An Examination of the Indirect Productivity Gains from Quality Improvement," *Production and Operations Management* 3, no. 3 (summer 1994): 153–70.

Participative problem solving is usually within an *employee-involvement* (EI) program, with a team approach. We will look at some of these programs for involving employees in quality management, beginning with the most popular, *quality circles.*

Quality Circles

A **quality circle** is a group of workers and supervisors from the same area who address production problems.

Quality circles, called quality control circles in Japan, when they originated during the 1960s, were introduced in the United States in the 1970s. A **quality circle** is a small, voluntary group of employees and their supervisor(s), comprising a team of about eight to ten members from the same work area or department. The supervisor is typically the circle moderator, promoting group discussion but not directing the group or making decisions; decisions result from group consensus. A circle meets about once a week during company time in a room designated especially for that purpose, where the team works on problems and projects of their own choice. These problems may not always relate to quality issues; instead, they focus on productivity, costs, safety, or other work-related issues in the circle's area. Quality circles follow an established procedure for identifying, analyzing, and solving quality-related (or other) problems. Figure 3.3 is a graphical representation of the quality circle process.

A group technique for identifying and solving problems is *brainstorming* to generate ideas. Free expression is encouraged, and criticism is not allowed. Only after brainstorming is completed are ideas evaluated.

Quality circle members are trained to conduct meetings and address problems as a group, as well as to collect data and analyze problems. When needed, outside technical and managerial assistance is available to the circle. The circle sometimes includes an advisor, who provides guidance but is not a team member.

Quality circles were developed by Kaoru Ishikawa in Japan in the 1960s.

Quality circles have been very successful in Japan. Their development has been credited to Dr. Kaoru Ishikawa of the University of Tokyo, who adapted many of the approaches to quality promoted by W. Edwards Deming and Joseph Juran. It is estimated that approximately 10 million Japanese workers and supervisors have participated

---

THE COMPETITIVE EDGE

Employee Quality Awareness at Disneyland

For 36 years Disneyland (of California) has maintained a reputation of exceptional quality. It has achieved this valued reputation by focusing on customer satisfaction and by an almost fanatical attention to detail. Employees, or "cast members," are especially important in the Disney quality effort. Disneyland has more than 12,000 cast members in more than 400 different roles (not simply jobs). Each cast member is considered to be a host or hostess to the park's guests (not just customers). Disney hiring and training programs are thorough and extensive, emphasizing the nature of the business, the Disney product, and how the employee's role contributes to the product. Training includes basic communication skills for interacting with other cast members and park guests. Focus groups of cast members meet regularly to assess the effectiveness of training programs, and cast members are regularly surveyed on issues such as training, wages, and management, from which action plans are developed. All Disneyland cast members have a strong quality awareness perspective and participate in routine maintenance. Cast members can point out any problem or item that needs attention. All cast members, from janitors to stage performers, learn that their jobs are important to overall quality and performance. The mission of Disneyland cast members is to create happiness, and this mission has been accomplished because Disney management attempts to make them happy.

SOURCE: Based on B. Stratton, "How Disneyland Works," *Quality Progress* 24, no. 7 (1991): 17–30.

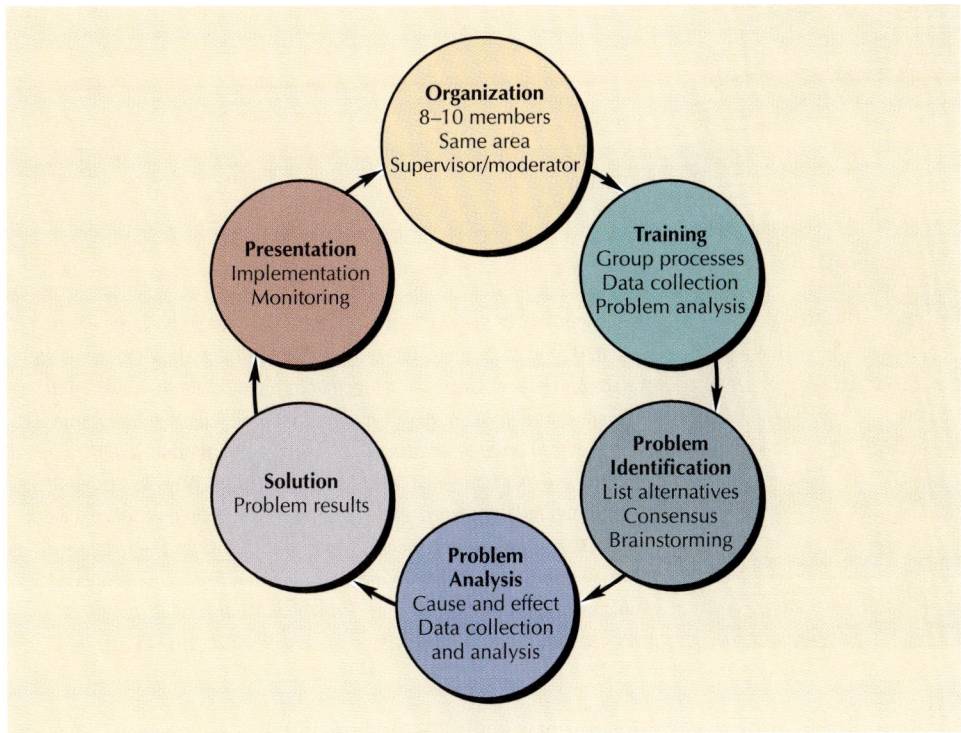

FIGURE 3.3 The Quality Circle Process

in quality circles, and several million projects have been undertaken, with an average return of several thousand dollars each since their inception in the 1960s.

The popularity of quality circles achieved in Japan has not been duplicated in the United States. The Japanese seem to have a cultural affinity for group participation that U.S. employees and supervisors do not always share. U.S. managers have been reluctant to share any of their functional responsibilities with employees. They view the analysis and solution of problems as a part of their own job domain that is not delegated. In addition, workers sometimes perceive themselves in an adversarial role with management and have not felt a responsibility to help managers improve quality performance.

Despite these obstacles, some U.S. firms such as Lockheed, Westinghouse, Ford, Coors, and General Electric, among others, have established successful quality circle programs.

A survey by the International Association of Quality Circles showed that the most effective quality circle programs were in larger, nonmanufacturing organizations with older, more established programs. The average net savings contributed by each circle member was estimated to be about $1,000.

A number of U.S. companies have adopted quality circle programs.

Employee Suggestions

The simple suggestion box is an example of a way to include employees in quality improvement as individuals, not as part of a group. A key to any type of employee suggestion program is a strong commitment and reinforcement from management at all levels. Equally important, operators must be sufficiently trained to identify quality problems so that they can make good suggestions. The suggestion box alone is not sufficient to achieve active employee involvement in quality management. A structured program

Quality circles like this one at a General Electric assembly plant are part of many TQM programs. They provide an organized format for allowing workers and supervisors to work together as a team to solve operational problems and improve quality. Quality circles originated in Japan were they have been popular and successful. They were introduced in the United States, where they have been less popular but generally no less successful. Normally a circle consists of eight to ten members who meet once a week to address problems and projects of their own choosing. They frequently make use of various techniques and tools for identifying causes of quality problems including brainstorming, Pareto charts, fish bone diagrams, process control charts, scatter diagrams, check sheets, and histograms.

is required that provides a convenient means for making quality suggestions, a commitment from management, and a reward structure. However, some companies view suggestion boxes as a hindrance to quality improvement because they inhibit direct communication between employees and management. Nevertheless, many U.S. companies and organizations have achieved some degree of employee involvement through suggestion programs for a number of years; in lieu of group participative programs, they are an effective alternative.

Identifying Quality Problems and Causes

Seven quality control tools for identifying quality problems and their causes.

Some of the most popular techniques for identifying the causes of quality problems are Pareto charts, flowcharts, check sheets, histograms, scatter diagrams, process control charts, and cause-and-effect diagrams. These well-known tools are sometimes known as the "magnificent seven" or the "seven QC tools." We discuss each in the following sections, and they are summarized in Figure 3.4.

Pareto Analysis

Pareto analysis: Most quality problems result from a few causes.

Pareto analysis is a method of identifying the causes of poor quality. It was devised in the early 1950s by the quality expert Joseph Juran. He named this method after a nineteenth century Italian economist, Vilfredo Pareto, who determined that a small percentage of the people accounted for most of the wealth. Pareto analysis is based on Juran's finding that most quality problems and costs result from only a few causes. For example, he discovered in a textile mill that almost 75 percent of all defective cloth was caused by only a few weavers, and in a paper mill he studied, more than 60 percent of the cost of poor quality was attributable to a single category of defects. Correcting the few major causes of most of the quality problems will result in the greatest cost impact.

Pareto analysis can be applied by tallying the number of defects for each of the different possible causes of poor quality in a product or service and then developing a fre-

FIGURE 3.4 The Seven Quality Control Tools

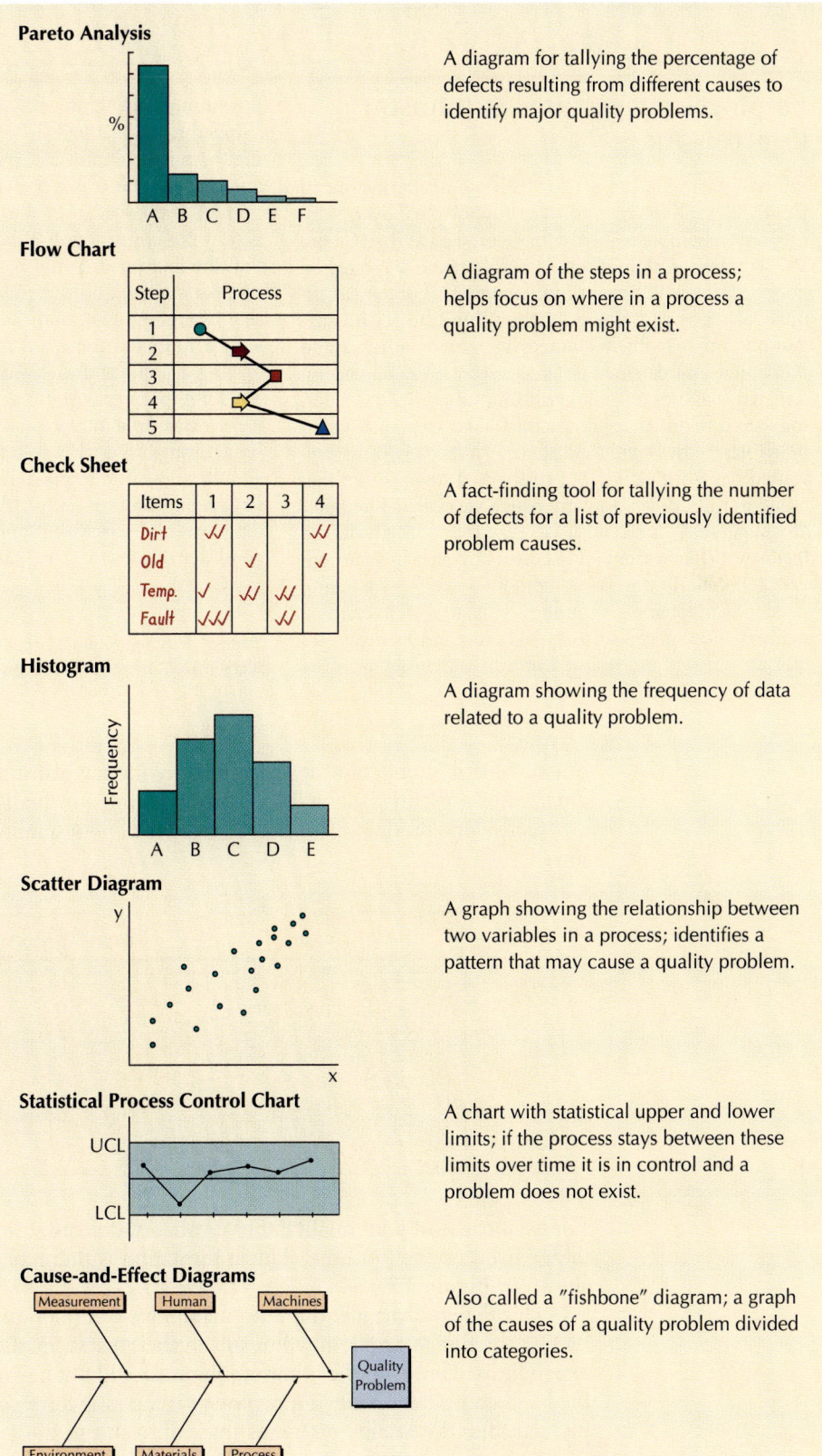

Pareto Analysis

A diagram for tallying the percentage of defects resulting from different causes to identify major quality problems.

Flow Chart

A diagram of the steps in a process; helps focus on where in a process a quality problem might exist.

Check Sheet

A fact-finding tool for tallying the number of defects for a list of previously identified problem causes.

Histogram

A diagram showing the frequency of data related to a quality problem.

Scatter Diagram

A graph showing the relationship between two variables in a process; identifies a pattern that may cause a quality problem.

Statistical Process Control Chart

A chart with statistical upper and lower limits; if the process stays between these limits over time it is in control and a problem does not exist.

Cause-and-Effect Diagrams

Also called a "fishbone" diagram; a graph of the causes of a quality problem divided into categories.

THE COMPETITIVE EDGE

Employee Suggestions at Johnson Controls Inc.

Johnson Controls Inc.'s FoaMech auto-parts factory in Georgetown, Kentucky, is a key supplier to Toyota Motors' auto-assembly plant also in Georgetown. In 1995 the 230 employees at Johnson Controls made 631 suggestions, 221 of which were implemented. Workers, as individuals or as part of teams, who submit successful suggestions improve their chances for group bonuses and individual awards such as large-screen TVs. In one instance a machine operator, who was also a team leader, found it difficult to locate maintenance specialists when machines on her team went down. The factory noise prevented her from yelling out so she had to leave her machine to track down a maintenance specialist. The operator suggested an electronic display located high on the factor wall like an outfield scoreboard on which an operator could illuminate a light if his or her machine needed maintenance or supplies. This suggestion enabled maintenance specialists to quickly respond to machines that were down and resulted in a reduction in machine

downtime from 9% to 2%. In a second case, the factory shipped foam seat pads to a seat-assembly plant by stuffing them into plastic bags, putting the bags in large boxes and carrying them by forklift to the loading dock for transport. A team leader in the packaging department suggested the construction of large metal carts with shelves that the foam pads could be stacked on then wheeled to the loading dock, loaded onto trailers, trucked to the car-seat assembly plant, and then returned. The returnable carts eliminated the need for thousands of plastic bags costing $1 apiece and saved the company an estimated $304,000 per year. Another team, noticing that workers were discarding many usable items like gloves, hoses, brass fittings, and wires as trash as they left work, made a simple suggestion to place receptacles near the plant exits for employees to empty their pockets into. The company was able to save thousands of dollars by recovering good items from the receptacles.

SOURCE: R. Rose, "Kentucky Plant Workers Are Cranking Out Good Ideas," *Wall Street Journal*, August 13, 1996, pp. B1, B6.

quency distribution from the data. This frequency distribution, referred to as a *Pareto diagram*, is a useful visual aid for focusing on major quality problems.

Consider a product for which the causes of poor quality have been identified as follows.

Cause	Number of Defects	Percentage
Poor design	80	64%
Wrong part dimensions	16	13
Defective parts	12	10
Incorrect machine calibration	7	6
Operator errors	4	3
Defective material	3	2
Surface abrasions	3	2
	125	100

For each cause of poor quality, the number of defects attributed to that cause has been tallied over a period of time. This information is then converted into the Pareto chart shown in Figure 3.5.

This Pareto chart identifies the major cause of poor quality to be poor design. Correcting the design problem will result in the greatest quality cost savings with the least expenditure. However, the other problems should not be ignored. TQM teaches us that total and continual quality improvement is the long-term goal. The Pareto diagram simply identifies the quality problems that will result in the greatest immediate impact in quality improvement.

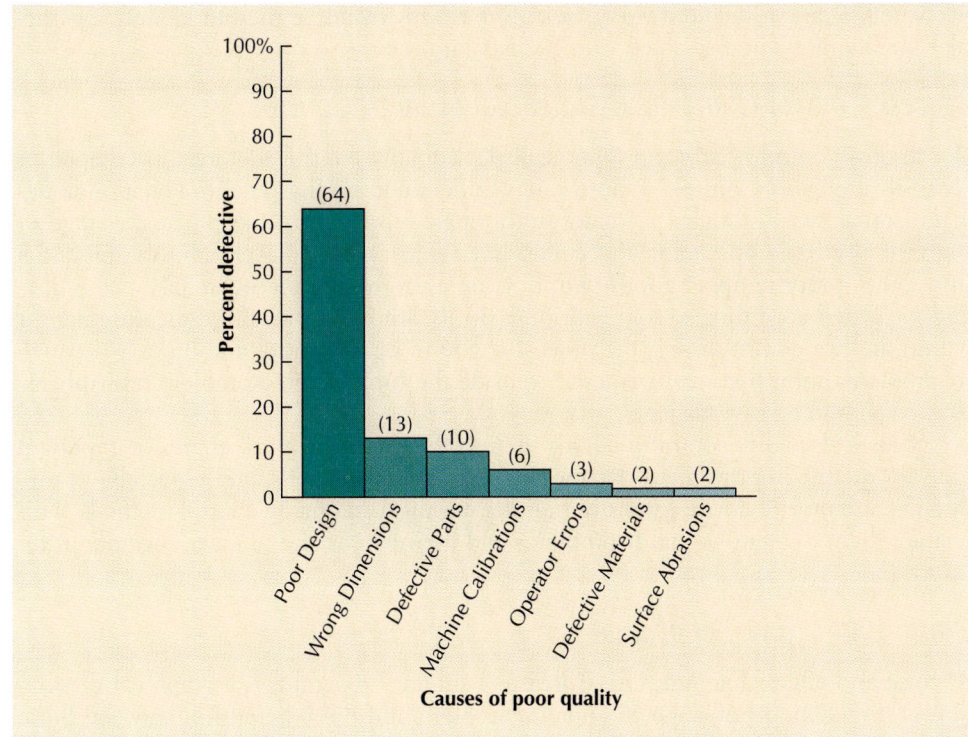

FIGURE 3.5 Pareto Chart

Flowcharts

A *flowchart* or process flowchart is a diagram of the steps in a job, operation, or process. It enables everyone involved in identifying and solving quality problems to have a clear picture of how a specific operation works and a common frame of reference. This helps focus on where problems might occur and if the process itself needs fixing. Development of the flowchart can help identify quality problems by helping the problem solvers better understand the process. Flowcharts are described in greater detail in Chapter 6 ("Process Planning and Technology Decisions") and Chapter 8 ("Human Resources in Operations Management").

A *flowchart* is a diagram of a job operation or process.

Check Sheets and Histograms

Check sheets are frequently used in conjunction with histograms, as well as with Pareto diagrams. A *check sheet* is a fact-finding tool used to collect data about quality problems. A typical check sheet for quality defects tallies the number of defects for a variety of previously identified problem causes. When the check sheet is completed, the total tally of defects for each cause can be used to create a *histogram* or a Pareto chart.

A *check sheet* is a list of causes of quality problems with the number of defects resulting from each cause used to develop a bar chart called a *histogram*.

Scatter Diagrams

Scatter diagrams graphically show the relationship between two variables, such as the brittleness of a piece of material and the temperature at which it is baked. One temperature reading should result in a specific degree of brittleness representing one point on the diagram. Many such points on the diagram visually show a pattern between the

A *scatter diagram* is a graph showing how two process variables relate to each other.

two variables and a relationship or lack of one. This could be used to identify a particular quality problem associated with the baking process.

Process Control Charts and Statistical Quality Control

Process control involves monitoring a production process using statistical quality control methods.

We discuss control charts and other statistical quality control methods in Chapter 4, "Statistical Quality Control." For now, it is sufficient to say that a control chart includes a horizontal line through the middle of a chart representing the process average or norm. It also has a line below this center line representing a lower control limit and a line above it for the upper control limit. Samples from the process are taken over time and measured according to some attribute. In its simplest form, if the measurement is within the two control limits, the process is said to be in control and there is no quality problem, but if the measurement is outside the limits, then a problem probably exists and should be investigated.

Statistical quality control methods such as the process control chart are important tools for quality improvement. Japanese employees at all levels, and especially in production, are provided with extensive training in statistical quality control methods. This enables them to identify quality problems and their causes and to make suggestions for improvement.

Cause-and-Effect Diagrams

A **cause-and-effect diagram**, or fishbone diagram, is a chart showing the different categories of problem causes.

A **cause-and-effect diagram**, also called a "fishbone" diagram, is a graphical description of the elements of a specific quality problem and the relationship between those elements. It is used to identify the causes of a quality problem so it can be corrected. Cause-and-effect diagrams are usually developed as part of participative problem solving to help a team of employees, supervisors, and managers identify causes of quality problems. This tool is a normal part of the problem-solving activity of quality circles in Japanese companies; however, in the United States it is often used separately, outside the quality circle program.

Figure 3.6 illustrates the general structure of the cause-and-effect diagram. The "effect" box at the end of the diagram is the quality problem that needs correction. A center line connects the effect box to the major categories of possible problem causes, displayed as branches off of the center line. The box at the end of each branch (or fishbone) describes the cause category. The diagram starts out in this form with only the major categories at the end of each branch. Individual causes associated with each category are attached as separate lines along the length of the branch during the brainstorming process. Sometimes the causes are rank-ordered along the branches in order to identify those that are most likely to impact on the problem. The cause-and-effect diagram is a means for thinking through a problem and recording the possible causes in an organized and easily interpretable manner. The causes listed along the branches under each category in Figure 3.6 are generic, but for a specific quality problem with an actual product, the causes would be product- and problem-specific.

Quality Awards and the Competitive Spirit

The Baldrige Award, Deming Prize, and other award competitions have given American firms the impetus to commit to quality management programs because they appeal to the American competitive spirit. The Baldrige Award in America has become a valuable and coveted prize to American companies eager to benefit from the aura and reputation for quality that awaits the winners. It has also provided a widely used set of guidelines to help companies implement an effective quality management program.

www.prenhall.com/russell

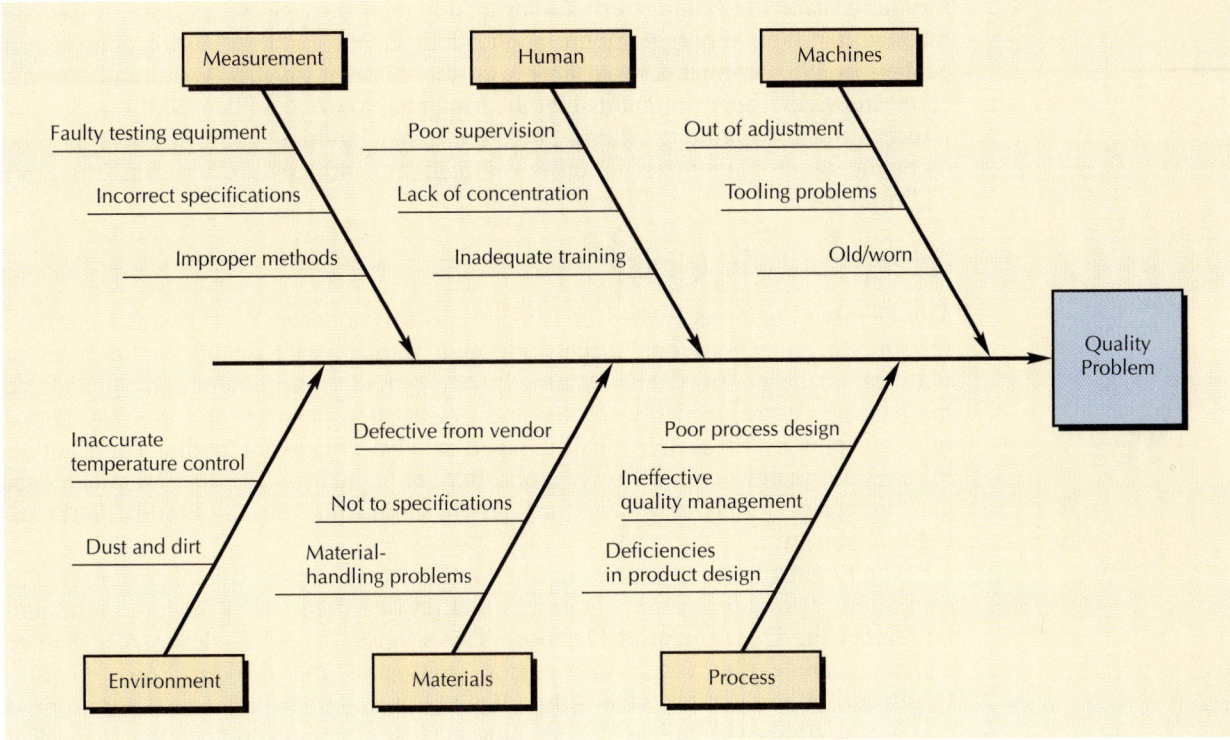

FIGURE 3.6   A General Cause-and-Effect Diagram

The Malcolm Baldrige Award

The Malcolm Baldrige National Quality Award is given annually to one or two companies in each of four categories: manufacturing, services, small businesses (with less than 500 full-time employees), and universities and hospitals. It was created by law in 1987 (named after former Secretary of Commerce Malcolm Baldrige, who died in 1987) to (1) stimulate U.S. companies to improve quality, (2) establish criteria for businesses to use to evaluate their individual quality improvement efforts, (3) set as examples those companies that were successful in improving quality, and (4) help other U.S. organizations learn how to manage quality by disseminating information about the award winners' programs.

The award criteria focus on the soundness of the approach to quality improvement, the overall quality management program as it is implemented throughout the organization, and customer satisfaction. The seven major categories of criteria over which companies are examined are leadership, information and analysis, strategic quality planning, human resource utilization, quality assurance of products and service, quality results, and customer satisfaction.

The Baldrige Award competition has had a marked influence on those companies who have been finalists and winners. They have achieved higher productivity, better employee relations, increased market share, greater customer relations, and higher profitability. The Baldrige Award has also had a major influence on U.S. companies by promoting the need for quality improvement. Thousands of U.S. companies request applications from the government each year to obtain a copy of the award guidelines and criteria for internal use in establishing quality management programs. Many compa-

The Baldrige Award was created in 1987 to stimulate growth of quality management in the United States.

nies have made the Baldrige criteria for quality their own. Some companies have demanded that their suppliers submit applications for the Baldrige Award. Since its inception in 1987, companies that have won the Baldrige Quality Award and have become known as leaders in quality include Motorola, Xerox, Cadillac, Milliken, Federal Express, and IBM, among others. These and other Baldrige Award winners have become models or benchmarks for other companies to emulate in establishing their own TQM programs.

Other Awards for Quality

The Deming Prize was created in 1957 in Japan in honor of W. Edwards Deming to recognize organizations that "successfully apply companywide quality control based on statistical quality control." The Deming Prize is extremely prominent in Japan and, like the Baldrige Award, is highly coveted and sought after. Japanese and overseas companies can apply as well as individuals in Japan who have made outstanding contributions in statistical quality control theory, application, or popularity. The first American company to receive the Deming Prize for Overseas Companies was the Florida Power and Light Company.

The President's Award was established in 1988 to recognize federal government organizations with 500 or more employees that provide products or services to the public (except the Department of Defense). Two winners are selected annually. Past recipients include the Naval Air Systems Command and the Air Force Logistics Command. A companion prize is the Quality Improvement Prototype Award for federal organizations with at least 100 employees. Past recipients include the Equal Employment Opportunity Commission, the Norfolk Naval Shipyard, the IRS Federal Tax Deposit System, and the VA Kansas City Medical Center.

The Award for Excellence in Productivity Improvement has been provided annually since 1980 by the Institute of Industrial Engineers (IIE) to recognize companies that have achieved a competitive advantage through productivity and quality programs. The four award categories include small and large companies, manufacturing and service companies. Past winners include Anheuser-Busch, Inc., Chrysler Corporation, Black and Decker Corporate Management, Norfolk Naval Shipyard, Ford Motor Company, and Texas Instruments (Johnson City, Tennessee).

The George M. Low trophy, NASA's Quality and Excellence Award, is awarded annually to NASA contractors, subcontractors, and suppliers demonstrating excellence in quality and productivity for three or more years. Past recipients include Thiokol Corporation and Grumman Corporation.

The European Quality Award is a European version of the Baldrige Award awarded by the European Foundation for Quality Management. The 1994 winner of this award was Design to Distribution, a British electronics firm.

ISO 9000

www.prenhall.com/russell

ISO: the International Organization for Standardization.

The International Organization for Standardization (ISO), headquartered in Geneva, Switzerland, has as its members the national standards organizations for more than ninety countries. The ISO member for the United States is the American National Standards Institute, ANSI. The purpose of ISO is to facilitate global consensus agreements on international quality standards. It has resulted in a system for certifying suppliers to make sure they meet internationally accepted standards for quality management. It is a nongovernment organization and is not a part of the United Nations.

During the 1970s it was generally acknowledged that the word *quality* had different meanings within and between industries and countries and around the world. In 1979 the ISO member representing the United Kingdom, the British Standard Institute (BSI), recognizing the need for standardization for quality management and assurance, submitted a formal proposal to ISO to develop international standards for quality assurance techniques and practices. Using standards that already existed in the United Kingdom and Canada as a basis, ISO established generic quality standards primarily for manufacturing firms that could be used worldwide.

ISO 9000 is a procedure for the international quality certification of suppliers.

The ISO 9000 series of quality management and assurance standards, was first published in 1978. ISO 9000, the first standard in the series, titled *Quality Management and Quality Assurance Standards for Selection and Use*, is a guide for using four other standards.

ISO 9001, *Quality Systems—Model for Quality Assurance in Design/Development, Production, Installation, and Servicing*, applies to suppliers who have responsibility for the design and development, production, installation, and servicing of a product. It includes a set of requirements for the suppliers' quality management program, beginning with top management responsibility and providing objective criteria to verify that key elements in the total quality management approach are present. It defines requirements for product handling, storage, packaging, and delivery and includes requirements for conducting internal quality audits to verify the effectiveness of the quality management system.

ISO 9000 standards certify that suppliers have a quality management system system that meets criteria; they do not certify products.

ISO 9002, *Quality Systems—Model for Quality Assurance in Production and Installation*, is similar to ISO 9001 except that it is limited to suppliers that only produce and install a product and do not design, develop, or service the product.

ISO 9003, *Quality Systems—Model for Quality Assurance in Final Inspection and Test*, is limited to guidelines for final inspection and testing because of the relative simplicity of the product. This standard shifts responsibility for quality to the supplier so the customer is assured of the level of quality when the product is received.

ISO 9004, *Quality Management and Quality System Elements—Guidelines*, provides guidelines for developing and implementing the quality management programs required in ISO 9001, 9002, and 9003. These guidelines and suggestions help management develop an effective quality management program so that their companies can be qualified to meet ISO 9001, 9002, and 9003 requirements. The ISO 9000 standards can generally be applied to the service sector by making such simple modifications as substituting terms; for example, *process* for *production* and *service* for *product*.

Implications of ISO 9000 for U.S. Companies

Originally, ISO 9000 was adopted by the twelve countries of the European Community (EC)—Belgium, Denmark, France, Germany, Greece, Ireland, Italy, Luxembourg, the Netherlands, Portugal, Spain, and the United Kingdom. The governments of the EC countries adopted ISO 9000 as a uniform quality standard for cross-border transactions within the EC and for international transactions. The EC was soon joined by the countries of the European Free Trade Association (EFTA), including Austria, Finland, Iceland, Liechtenstein, Norway, Sweden, and Switzerland. In addition Australia, Japan, and many other Pacific Rim countries plus South America and Africa have adopted ISO 9000.

These countries (especially those in the EC) are specifically acknowledging that they prefer suppliers with ISO 9000 certification. To remain competitive in international markets, U.S. companies must comply with the standards in the ISO 9000 series. Some products in the EC, for example, are "regulated" to the extent that the products must be certified to be in ISO 9000 compliance by an EC-recognized accreditation

Many overseas companies will not do business with a supplier unless it has ISO 9000 certification.

registrar. Most of these products have health and safety considerations. However, companies have discovered that to remain competitive and satisfy customer preferences, their products must be in compliance with ISO 9000 requirements even if these products are not specifically regulated.

The United States exports more than $100 billion annually to the European Community market, most of it to France, Germany, Italy, Spain, and the United Kingdom. Over half of these exports is impacted in some way by ISO 9000 standards.

Companies are also being pressured within the United States to comply with ISO 9000 by more and more customers. For example, the United States Department of Defense, and specifically the Department of the Navy, has adopted ISO 9000, as have such private companies as Du Pont, 3M, and AT&T. They recognize the value of these standards for helping to assure top-quality products and services, and require that their suppliers comply with ISO 9000.

ISO 9000 Accreditation

In ISO 9000 an accredited registrar, for a fee, assesses a company's quality program and determines if it is in compliance with ISO 9000 standards. If the company's quality program is in compliance, the registrar issues it a certificate and registers that certificate in a book that is widely distributed.

In the EC registration system, the third-party assessors of quality are referred to as

Registered Quality System

Issued To:
IMPACT FORGE
2805 Norcross Drive
Columbus, Indiana, U.S.A.

ISO 9002:1994/QS-9000:1995
Manufacture of carbon/alloy steel forgings for use in
automotive and truck applications

ISO 9002:1994
Manufacture of carbon/alloy steel forgings for use in automotive,
truck, refrigeration and other industrial applications

TRA Certification hereby declares that this facility has been audited in accordance with the requirements of ISO 9002:1994 and QS 9000:1995, Appendix B "Code of Practice" and meets the accreditation criteria as defined in the Certification Scheme operated by the TRA Certification Division of T. R. Arnold & Associates, Inc., Elkhart, Indiana, U.S.A.

CERTIFICATE #09603   ISSUED: 14 June 1996

SCOPE: S.I.C. 3462   EXPIRES: 14 June 1999

Authorized By: _____
Thomas R. Arnold, President

Thousands of businesses have improved their operations by fully implementing a quality system based on the international standards known as ISO 9001 and ISO 9002. Almost all of those companies have in turn gained recognition for their achievement by undergoing an assessment of that quality system by an independent third party, known as a quality system registrar. When the company has met all the requirements of the standards then the registrar will certify/register them. This status is represented by a certificate, such as this one for Impact Forge of Columbus, Indiana. The automotive industry is beginning to practice an enhancement of the ISO standards known as QS 9000. This certificate includes that designation.

notified bodies; that is, the twelve EC governments *notify* one another as to which organization in their country is the officially designated government-approved quality assessor. The notified bodies ultimately certify a company with a European Conformity (CE) mark. The CE mark must be on any product exported from the United States that is ISO 9000–regulated. It is illegal to sell a regulated product in a store in the EC without the CE mark. For a supplier in the United States to export regulated products to an EC country, it must be accredited by European registrars—notified bodies within the EC. However, more and more EC companies are requiring ISO 9000 certification for suppliers of products that fall in the unregulated categories, and eventually all products exported to the EC will probably require certification.

It is also important that U.S. companies obtain accreditation with a notified body that has widespread positive recognition in the EC so that they will have broad access to markets in the EC. In Germany and the United Kingdom, there appears to be preference for ISO registrars located within that country; in other countries such as the Netherlands, France, and Spain there seems to be less prejudice over where certification is obtained.

Because the third-party quality registration system has become accepted in the EC, and so many countries trade with EC countries, third-party registration has become im-

THE COMPETITIVE EDGE

The AT&T Quality Registrar

The AT&T Quality Registrar was one of the first accredited by the RAB in the United States. Because of its extensive experience in working with the quality systems of its own suppliers and its experience with ISO 9000 standards, AT&T was to provide a great deal of knowledge to the development of the U.S. registration system. As a result, AT&T formed its own quality registrar and went through the RAB accreditation process in order to assist in the actual development of the process as it went through it. The AT&T quality registrar was accredited in 1991 and began to register companies in the United States. They could concentrate on a broad range of product areas because AT&T suppliers historically included many varied products, such as electronic components, textile products, printing products, chemicals and plastics, rubber products, and fabricated metal products.

The ISO 9000 registration process employed by AT&T has nine steps. First, an application form is submitted by the supplier. This form includes a four-page questionnaire that provides general information about the company, including the type of product it makes, its locations, and so on. Next, the company is provided with a "Quality Manual Desk Audit" in order to determine the current extent to which the company is complying with ISO 9000 standards. This step is followed by a preliminary audit, which may last from one to several days. The next step is a full audit which typically requires two auditors and takes approximately three days. In this audit the auditors go through the whole facility to see if the company complies with ISO 9000 standards; the company is given verbal feedback immediately and a written report in a few weeks. The auditing team does not make the actual registration decision, but it presents a report to a registration board, which either approves or rejects the auditors' recommendation. The question the board members ask is, "If we were the customer, would we want this company to provide us with products or service?" If the board approves the company, it provides the company with a certificate and the right to use AT&T's mark and the RAB mark in its advertising and correspondence. However, the mark cannot be used on a product. The company receives a semiannual follow-up audit and a full audit every three years. Formal recognition of registration by the AT&T Quality Registrar has met with some resistance in the European Community. However, AT&T works with the supplier's European customers, explaining its registration process and credentials in order to obtain informal recognition with that particular company. AT&T provides the supplier with whatever support is needed to prove to a European customer that it and the RAB are credible accreditation bodies. As the AT&T quality registrar and other U.S. registrars successfully convince more and more EC companies of their credibility, U.S. suppliers will find it easier to move products into and within EC markets.

SOURCE: Based on "The AT&T Quality Registrar," *Profile of ISO 9000* (Needham Heights, Mass.: Allyn and Bacon, 1992) pp. 67–74.

portant in the rest of the world, particularly the United States. However, it has not been as easy for the United States to develop a registration system because of the separation between government and business that exists in the United States but not in most EC countries.

The U.S. member of the ISO, the American National Standards Institute (ANSI), designated the American Society for Quality Control (ASQC), as the sponsoring organization for ISO 9000 in the U.S. ASQC and ANSI created the Registrar Accreditation Board (RAB) to act as the third-party registrar in the United States.

In 1992 RAB developed an auditing system for the registration of supplier companies and accreditation of registrars based on the ISO standards. A registrar is an organization that conducts audits by individual auditors. Auditors are skilled in quality systems and the manufacturing and service environments in which an audit will be performed. The registrar develops an audit team of one or more auditors to evaluate a company's quality program and then report back to the registrar. An organization that wants to become a registrar must be accredited by RAB. Once RAB accredits a registrar, the registrar can then authorize its registered suppliers to use the RAB certificate in advertising, indicating compliance with ISO 9000.

Summary

In our discussion of quality management in this chapter, certain consistencies or commonalities have surfaced. The most important perspective of quality is the customer's; products and services must be designed to meet customer expectations and needs for quality. A total commitment to quality is necessary throughout an organization for it to be successful in improving and managing product quality. This commitment must start at the top and filter down through all levels of the organization and across all areas and departments. Employees need to be active participants in the quality-improvement process and must feel a responsibility for quality. Employees must feel free to make suggestions to improve product quality without fear of reprisal, and a systematic procedure is necessary to involve workers and solicit their input. Improving product quality is cost-effective; the cost of poor quality greatly exceeds the cost of attaining good quality. Quality can be improved with the effective use of statistical quality control methods. In fact, the use of statistical quality control has been a pervasive part of our discussions on quality management, and it has been identified as an important part of any quality management program. In the following chapter we concentrate on statistical quality control methods and principles.

A total commitment to quality is required throughout an organization.

Summary of Key Formulas

Quality Index Numbers

$$\text{Quality index} = \frac{\text{total quality costs}}{\text{base}} (100)$$

Product Yield

$$Y = (I)\,(\%G) + (I)\,(1 - \%G)\,(\%R)$$

Manufacturing Cost per Product

$$\text{Product cost} = \frac{(K_d)(I) + (K_r)(R)}{Y}$$

Multistage Product Yield

$$Y = (I)\,(\%g_1)\cdots(\%g_2)$$

Quality-Productivity Ratio

$$QPR = \frac{\text{good-quality units}}{(\text{input})(\text{processing cost}) + (\text{defective units})(\text{rework cost})} (100)$$

Summary of Key Terms

appraisal costs: costs of measuring, testing, and analyzing materials, parts, products, and the productive process to make sure they conform to design specifications.

benchmark: a level of quality achievement established by one company that other companies seek to achieve, i.e., a goal.

cause-and-effect diagram: a graphical description of the elements of a specific quality problem.

cost index: the ratio of quality cost to manufacturing cost.

external failure costs: costs of poor quality incurred after the product gets to the customer; that is, customer service, lost sales, and so on.

fitness for use: a measure of how well a product or service does what the consumer thinks it is supposed to do and wants it to do.

index numbers: ratios that measure quality costs relative to some base accounting values such as sales or product units.

internal failure costs: costs of poor-quality products discovered during the production process; that is, scrap, rework, and the like.

labor index: the ratio of quality cost to direct labor hours.

Pareto analysis: a method for identifying the causes of poor quality, which usually shows that most quality problems result from only a few causes.

participative problem solving: involving employees directly in the quality management process to identify and solve problems.

prevention costs: costs incurred during product design and manufacturing that prevent nonconformance to specifications.

production index: the ratio of quality cost to final product units.

productivity: a measure of effectiveness in converting resources into products, generally computed as output divided by input.

quality assurance: the management of quality throughout the organization.

quality circles: a small, voluntary group (team) of workers and supervisors formed to address quality problems in their area.

quality of conformance: the degree to which the product or service meets the specifications required by design during the production process.

quality of design: the degree to which quality characteristics are designed into a product or service.

quality-productivity ratio: a productivity index that includes productivity and quality costs.

sales index: the ratio of quality cost to sales.

total quality control: a total, companywide systems approach to quality developed by Armand V. Feigenbaum.

total quality management (TQM): the management of quality throughout the organization at all management levels and across all areas.

yield: a measure of productivity; the sum of good quality and reworked units.

Solved Problems

1. Product Yield

A manufacturing company has a weekly product input of 1,700 units. The average percentage of good-quality products is 83 percent. Of the poor-quality products, 60 percent can be reworked and sold as good-quality products. Determine the weekly product yield and the product yield if the good-product quality is increased to 92 percent.

Solution:

Step 1. Compute yield according to the formula:

$$Y = (I) (\%G) + (I) (1 - \%G) (\%R)$$
$$Y = (1,700) (0.83) + (1,700) (0.17) (0.60)$$
$$= 1,584.4 \text{ units}$$

Step 2. Increase %G to 92 percent:

$$Y = (1,700) (0.92) + (1,700) (0.08) (0.60)$$
$$= 1,645.6 \text{ units}$$

2. Quality-Productivity Ratio

A retail telephone catalog company takes catalog orders from customers and then sends the completed orders to the warehouses to be filled. An operator processes an average of 45 orders per day. The cost of processing an order is $1.15, and it costs $0.65 to correct an order that has been filled out incorrectly by the operator. An operator averages 7 percent bad orders per day, all of which are reworked prior to filling the customer order. Determine the quality-productivity ratio for an operator.

Solution:

Compute the quality-productivity ratio according to the formulas,

$$QPR = \frac{\text{good-quality units}}{(\text{input})(\text{processing cost}) + (\text{defective units})(\text{rework cost})} (100)$$

$$QPR = \frac{45}{(45)(\$1.15) + (3.15)(\$0.65)} (100)$$

$$= 83.65$$

Questions

3-1. How does the consumer's perspective of quality differ from the producer's?

3-2. Briefly describe the *dimensions of quality,* for which a consumer looks in a product, and apply them to a specific product.

3-3. How does *quality of design* differ from *quality of conformance?*

3-4. How do the marketing and sales areas impact on product quality in a total quality management system? Purchasing?

3-5. Define the two major categories of quality cost and how they relate to each other.

3-6. What is the difference between internal and external failure costs?

3-7. A defense contractor manufactures rifles for the military. The military has exacting quality standards that the contractor must meet. The military is very pleased with the quality of the products provided by the contractor and rarely has to return products or has reason for complaint. However, the contractor is experiencing extremely high quality-related costs. Speculate on the reasons for the contractor's high quality-related costs.

3-8. Consider your school (university or college) as a production system in which the final product is a graduate. For this system:
   a. Define quality from the producer's and customer's perspectives.
   b. Develop a fitness-for-use description for final product quality.
   c. Give examples of the cost of poor quality (internal and external failure costs) and the cost of quality assurance (prevention and appraisal) costs.
   d. Describe how quality circles might be implemented in a university setting. Do you think they would be effective?

3-9. Explain how the Japanese perspective on the cost of quality originally differed from the traditional American perspective.

3-10. Describe the differences between the American and Japanese business environments and cultures that make it difficult for American companies to duplicate successfully Japan's quality management programs such as quality circles.

3-11. Describe how a quality assurance program might impact the different organizational functions for a fast-food business (such as McDonald's or Burger King).

3-12. Discuss how a quality management program can affect productivity.

3-13. The Aurora Electronics Company has been receiving a lot of customer complaints and returns of a front-loading VCR that it manufactures. When a videotape is pushed into the loading mechanism, it can stick inside with the door open; the recorder cannot run, and it is difficult to get the tape out. Consumers will try to pull the tape out with their fingers or pry the tape out with an object such as a knife, pencil, or screwdriver, frequently damaging the VCR, tearing up the tape cartridge, or hurting themselves. What are the different costs of poor quality and costs of quality assurance that might be associated with this quality problem?

3-14. What are the different quality characteristics you (as a consumer) would expect to find in the following three products: a VCR, a pizza, running shoes?

3-15. AMERICARD, a national credit card company, has a toll-free, 24-hour customer service number. Describe the input for this system function and the final product. What quality-related costs might be associated with this function, and how might a quality management program impact on this area?

3-16. A number of quality management philosophies hold that prevention costs are the most critical quality-related costs. Explain the logic behind this premise.

3-17. Why is it important for companies to measure and report quality costs?

3-18. What traits of quality management are generally consistent among most current quality philosophies and trends?

3-19. Describe the primary contribution to quality management of each of the following: W. E. Deming, Joseph Juran, Phillip Crosby, Armand Feigenbaum, and, Kaoru Ishikawa.

3-20. Describe the impact that the creation of the Malcolm Baldrige Award had on quality improvement in the United States.

3-21. Write a one- to two-page summary of an article from *Quality Progress, Quality*

Forum, Quality and Productivity Management, or *Quality Review* about quality management in a company or organization.

3-22. Many more companies probably fail at implementing quality management programs than succeed. Discuss the reasons why a quality management program might fail.

3-23. Select a service company or organization and discuss the dimensions of quality that a customer might evaluate it on.

3-24. Select two competing service companies that you are familiar with or can visit, such as fast-food restaurants, banks, or retail stores, and compare how they interact with customers in terms of quality.

3-25. Develop a hypothetical improvement program for the class in which you are using this text. Include goals for quality improvement and ways to measure success.

3-26. Identify a company or organization from which you have received poor-quality products or services, describe the nature of the defects, and suggest ways in which you might improve quality.

3-27. Identify a company or organization from which you have received high-quality products and describe the characteristics which make it high quality.

3-28. Explain why strategic planning might benefit from a TQM program.

3-29. Why has ISO 9000 become so important to U.S. firms who do business overseas?

3-30. Research several companies that have won the Malcolm Baldrige Award in the library, and describe any common characteristics that the quality management programs in these companies have.

Problems

3-1. Backwoods American, Inc., produces expensive water-repellant, down-lined parkas. The company implemented a total quality management program in 1993. Following are quality-related accounting data that have been accumulated for the past five-year period, or one year prior to the program's start.

	YEAR				
	1992	*1993*	*1994*	*1995*	*1996*
Quality Costs (000s)					
Prevention	$ 3.2	10.7	28.3	42.6	50.0
Appraisal	26.3	29.2	30.6	24.1	19.6
Internal failure	39.1	51.3	48.4	35.9	32.1
External failure	118.6	110.5	105.2	91.3	65.2
Accounting Measures (000s)					
Sales	$2,700.6	2,690.1	2,705.3	2,810.2	2,880.7
Manufacturing cost	420.9	423.4	424.7	436.1	435.5

a. Compute the company's total failure costs as a percentage of total quality costs for each of the five years. Does there appear to be a trend to this result? If so, speculate on what might have caused the trend.

b. Compute prevention costs and appraisal costs, each as a percentage of total costs, during each of the five years. Speculate on what the company's quality strategy appears to be.

c. Compute quality-sales indices and quality-cost indices for each of the five years. Is it possible to assess the effectiveness of the company's quality management program from these index values?

d. List several examples of each quality-related cost—that is, prevention, appraisal, and internal and external failure—that might result from the production of parkas.

3-2. The Backwoods American company in Problem 3-1 produces approximately 20,000 parkas annually. The quality management program the company implemented was able to improve the average percentage of good parkas produced by 2 percent each year, beginning with 83 percent good-quality parkas in 1992. Only about 20 percent of poor-quality parkas can be reworked.

a. Compute the product yield for each of the five years.

b. Using a rework cost of $12 per parka, determine the manufacturing cost per good parka for each of the five years. What do these results imply about the company's quality management program?

3-3. The Colonial House Furniture Company manufactures two-drawer oak file cabinets that are sold unassembled through catalogs. The company initiates production of 150 cabinet packages each week. The percentage of good-quality cabinets averages 83 percent per week, and the percentage of poor-quality cabinets that can be reworked is 60 percent.

a. Determine the weekly product yield of file cabinets.

b. If the company desires a product yield of 145 units per week, what increase in the percentage good-quality products must result?

3-4. In Problem 3-3, if the direct manufacturing cost for cabinets is $27 and the rework cost is $8, compute the manufacturing cost per good product. Determine the manufacturing cost per product if the percentage of good-quality file cabinets is increased from 83 percent to 90 percent.

3-5. The Omega Shoe Company manufactures a number of different styles of athletic shoes. Its biggest seller is the X-Pacer running shoe. In 1994 Omega implemented a quality management program. The company's shoe production for the past three years and manufacturing costs are as follows.

	YEAR		
	1994	*1995*	*1996*
Units produced/input	32,000	34,600	35,500
Manufacturing cost	$278,000	291,000	305,000
Percent good quality	78%	83%	90%

Only one quarter of the defective shoes can be reworked, at a cost of $2.00 a piece. Compute the manufacturing cost per good product for each of the three years and indicate the annual percentage of increase or decrease resulting from the quality management program.

3-6. The Colonial House Furniture Company manufactures four-drawer oak filing cabinets in six stages. In the first stage, the boards forming the walls of the cabinet are cut; in the second stage the front drawer panels are woodworked; in the third stage the boards are sanded and finished; in the fourth stage the boards are cleaned, stained, and painted with a clear finish; in the fifth stage the hardware for pulls, runners, and fittings is installed; and in the final stage the cabinets are assembled. Inspection occurs at each stage of the process, and the average percentages of good-quality units are as follows,

Stage	Average Percentage Good Quality
1	87%
2	91%
3	94%
4	93%
5	93%
6	96%

The cabinets are produced in weekly production runs with a product input for 300 units.
a. Determine the weekly product yield of good-quality cabinets.
b. What would weekly product input have to be in order to achieve a final weekly product yield of 300 cabinets?

3-7. In Problem 3-6, the Colonial House Furniture Company has investigated the manufacturing process to identify potential improvements that would improve quality. The company has identified four alternatives, each costing $15,000, as follows.

Alternative	Quality Improvement
1	Stage 1: 93%
2	Stage 2: 96%, Stage 4: 97%
3	Stage 5: 97%, Stage 6: 98%
4	Stage 2: 97%

a. Which alternative would result in the greatest increase in product yield?
b. Which alternative would be the most cost effective?

3-8. The Backwoods American company operates a telephone order system for a catalog of its outdoor clothing products. The catalog orders are processed in three stages. In the first stage the telephone operator enters the order into the computer; in the second stage the items are secured and batched in the warehouse; and in the final stage the ordered products are packaged. Errors can be made in orders at any of these stages, and the average percentage of errors that occurs at each stage are as follows.

Stage	% Errors
1	12%
2	8%
3	4%

If an average of 320 telephone orders are processed each day, how many errorless orders will result?

3-9. The total processing cost for producing the X-Pacer running shoe in Problem 3-5 is $18. The Omega Shoe Company starts production of 650 pairs of the shoes weekly, and the average weekly yield is 90 percent, with 10 percent defective shoes. One quarter of the defective shoes can be reworked at a cost of $3.75.
a. Compute the quality-productivity ratio (QPR).
b. Compute the QPR if the production rate is increased to 800 pairs of shoes per week.
c. Compute the QPR if the processing cost is reduced to $16.50 and the rework cost to $3.20.
d. Compute the QPR if the product yield is increased to 93 percent good quality.

3-10. Airphone, Inc. manufactures cellular telephones at a processing cost of $47 per unit. The company produces an average of 250 phones per week and has a yield of 87 percent good-quality phones, resulting in 13 percent defective phones, all of which can be re-worked. The cost of reworking a defective telephone is $16.

a. Compute the quality-productivity ratio (QPR).

b. Compute the QPR if the company increased the production rate to 320 phones per week while reducing the processing cost to $42, reducing the rework cost to $12, and increasing the product yield of good-quality telephones to 94 percent.

3-11. Burger Doodle is a fast-food restaurant that processes an average of 680 food orders each day. The average cost of each order is $6.15. Four percent of the orders are incorrect and only 10 percent of the defective orders can be corrected with additional food items at an average cost of $1.75. The remaining defective orders have to be thrown out.

a. Compute the average product cost.

b. In order to reduce the number of wrong orders, Burger Doodle is going to invest in a computerized ordering and cash register system. The cost of the system will increase the average order cost by $.05 and will reduce defective orders to 1 percent. What is the annual net cost effect of this quality-improvement initiative?

c. What other indirect effects on quality might be realized by the new computerized order system?

3-12. Compute the quality-productivity ratio (QPR) for the Burder Doodle restaurant in parts (a) and (b) in Problem 3-11.

CASE PROBLEM

Designing a Quality Management Program for the Internet at D4Q

Design for Quality (D4Q) is a consulting firm that specializes in the design and implementation of quality management programs for service companies and organizations. It has had success designing quality programs for retail stores and catalog order services. Recently D4Q was approached by a catalog order company, BookTek Media, Inc., with the offer of a job. BookTek sells books, CDs, cassettes, and videos through its mail-order catalog operation. BookTek has decided to expand its service to the Internet. BookTek is experienced in catalog telephone sales and has a successful quality management program in place. Thus the company is confident that it can process orders and make deliveries on time with virtually no errors.

A key characteristic of BookTek's quality management program is the company's helpful, courteous, and informative phone representatives. These operators can answer virtually any customer question about BookTek products with the help of an information system. Their demeanor toward customers is constantly monitored and graded. Their telephone system is so quick that customers rarely have to wait

for a representative to assist them. However, the Internet ordering system BookTek is planning virtually eliminates direct human contact with the customer. Since there will be no human contact, BookTek is concerned about how it will be able to make customers feel that they are receiving high-quality service. Further, the company is unsure how its employees can monitor and evaluate the service to know if the customer thinks it is good or poor. The primary concern is how to make customers feel good about the company in such an impersonal, segregated environment. At this point BookTek is unconcerned with costs; management simply wants to develop the highest quality, and friendliest web site possible.

D4Q indicated that it would like to take on the job, but while it is familiar with BookTek's type of catalog order system, it is relatively unfamiliar with the Internet and how things are ordered on the Internet. It suggested that its first order of business might be to investigate what other companies were doing on the Internet.

Help D4Q develop a quality management plan for BookTek. Include in your plan the quality dimensions and characteristics of an Internet ordering system, suggestions for achieving customer satisfaction, ways to measure defective service, and how to evaluate the success of the order system in terms of quality.

TQM at State University

As a result of several years of severe cuts to its operating budget by the state legislature, the administration at State University has raised tuition annually for the past five years. Five years ago an education at State was a bargain for both in-state and out-of-state students; now it is one of the more expensive state universities. An immediate repercussion has been a decline in applications for admission. Since a portion of state funding is tied to enrollments, State has kept its enrollments up at a constant level by going deeper into its pool of applications, taking some less qualified students.

The increase in the cost of a State degree has also caused legislators, parents, and students to be more conscious of the value of a State education—that is, the value parents and students are receiving for their money. This increased scrutiny has been fueled by numerous media reports about the decreased emphasis on teaching in universities, low teaching loads by faculty, and the large number of courses taught by graduate students. This, in turn, has led the state legislature committee on higher education to call for an "outcomes assessment program" to determine how well State University is achieving its mission of producing high-quality graduates.

On top of those problems, a substantial increase in the college-age population is expected in the next decade, resulting from a "baby boom" during the early 1980s. Key members of the state legislature have told the university administration that they will be expected to absorb their share of the additional students during the next decade. However, because

of the budget situation, they should not expect any funding increases for additional facilities, classrooms, dormitory rooms, or faculty. In effect, they will be expected to do more with their existing resources. State already faces a classroom deficit, and faculty have teaching loads above the average of its peer institutions. Legislators are fond of citing a study that shows that if the university simply gets all the students to graduate within a four-year period or reduces the number of hours required for graduation, they can accommodate the extra students they will be expected to accommodate.

This entire scenario has made the university president, Fred McMahan, consider retirement. He has summarized the problems to his administration staff as "having to do more, better, with less." One of the first things he did to address these problems was to set up a number of task forces made up of faculty and administrators to brainstorm a variety of topics. Among the topics and problems these task forces addressed were quality in education, educational success, graduation rates, success rates in courses (i.e., the percentage of students passing), teaching, the time to graduation, faculty issues, student issues, facilities, class scheduling, admissions, and classroom space.

Several of the task forces included faculty from engineering and business. These individuals noted that many of the problems the university faced would benefit from the principles and practices of a total quality management (TQM) approach. This recommendation appealed to Fred McMahan and the academic vice president, Anne Baker.

Discuss in general terms how TQM philosophy and practices might be instituted at State University.

CASE PROBLEM

Product Yield at Continental Luggage Company

The Continental Luggage Company manufactures several different styles of soft- and hardcover luggage, briefcases, hanging bags, and purses. Their best-selling item is a line of hardcover luggage called the "Trotter." It is produced in a basic five-stage assembly process that can accommodate several different outer coverings and colors. The assembly process includes constructing a heavy-duty plastic and metal frame, attaching the outer covering, joining the top and bottom and attaching the hinge mechanism, attaching the latches, lock, and handle, and doing the finishing work, including the luggage lining.

The market for luggage is extremely competitive, and product quality is a very important component in product sales and market share. Customers normally expect luggage to be able to withstand rough handling, while at the same time retaining its shape and an attractive appearance and protecting the clothing and personal items inside the bag. They also prefer the bag to be lightweight and not cumbersome. Furthermore, customers expect the latches and locks to work properly over an extended period of time. Another key factor in sales is that the luggage must be stylish and visually appealing.

Because of the importance of quality, company management has established a process control procedure that includes inspection at each stage of the five major stages of the assembly process. The following table shows the percentage of good-quality units yielded at each stage of the assembly process and the percentage of bad units that can be reworked, on average.

Assembly Stage	Average Percentage Good Quality	Average Percentage Reworked
1	0.94	0.23
2	0.96	0.91
3	0.95	0.67
4	0.97	0.89
5	0.98	0.72

The first stage of the process is construction of the frame, and it is very difficult to rework the frame if an item is defective, which is reflected in the low percentage of reworked items.

Five hundred new pieces of luggage of a particular style and color are initiated through the assembly process each week. The company would like to know the weekly product yield and the number of input units that would be required to achieve a weekly yield of 500 units. Further, the company would like to know the impact on product yield (given 500 initial starting units) if a quality-improvement program was introduced that would increase the average percentage of good-quality units at each stage by 1 percent.

References

Crosby, P. B. *Quality Is Free.* New York: McGraw-Hill, 1979.

Deming, W. E. *Out of the Crisis.* Cambridge, Mass.: MIT Center for Advanced Engineering Study, 1986.

Evans, J. R., and W. M. Lindsay. *The Management and Control of Quality,* 3d ed. St. Paul, Minn.: West, 1996.

Feigenbaum, A. V. *Total Quality Control,* 3d ed. New York: McGraw-Hill, 1983.

Garvin, D. A. *Managing Quality.* New York: Free Press/Macmillan, 1988.

Ishikawa, K. *Guide to Quality Control,* 2d ed. White Plains, N.Y.: Kraus International Publications, 1986.

Juran, J. M. *Juran of Planning for Quality.* New York: Free Press/Macmillan, 1988.

Juran, J. M., and F. M. Gryna, Jr. *Quality Planning and Analysis,* 2d ed. New York: McGraw-Hill, 1980.

Montgomery, D. C. *Introduction to Statistical Quality Control,* 2d ed. New York: John Wiley, 1991.

Profile of ISO 9000. Needham Heights, Mass.: Allyn and Bacon, 1992.

Taguchi, G. *Introduction to Quality Engineering.* Tokyo: Asian Productivity Organization, 1986.

4

Statistical Quality Control

Statistical Process Control at Kurt Manufacturing

Kurt Manufacturing Company, based in Minneapolis, is a mid-size supplier of precision machine parts. It operates six plants with approximately 1,100 employees. To remain competitive in international markets Kurt has adopted a commitment to continuous quality improvement through TQM. One key tool Kurt uses in its TQM program is statistical process control (SPC). All Kurt employees at all six plants—from janitors to top managers—received 30 hours of basic training in SPC from 20 employees within Kurt, who were taught SPC methods. Kurt wrote its own SPC manual using data from the plant floor for examples.

SPC is used by machine operators to monitor their process by measuring variability, reliability, repeatability, and predictability for their machines. Training stresses that SPC is a tool for operators to use in monitoring manufacturing processes and making quality improvement, not just for the sake of documentation. Operators control their own processes, and SPC charts are kept by the operator directly on the shop floor. When SPC charts show a process to be out of control, operators are taught to investigate the process to see what caused it to be out of control. If a process is out of control, operators have the right and responsibility to shut down and make corrections.

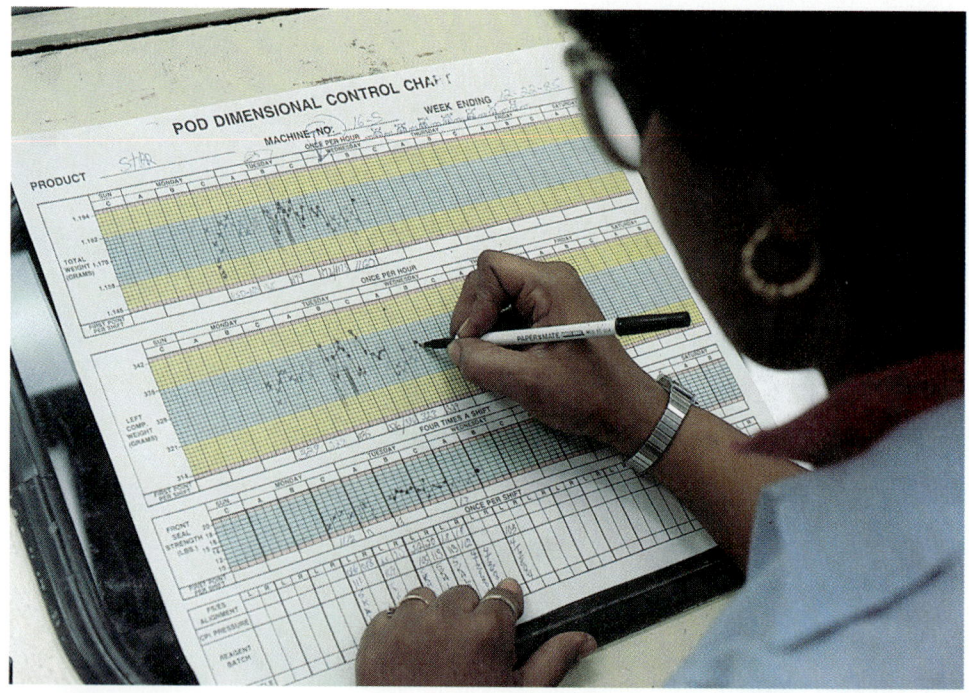

A statistical control chart like this one is a graph to monitor a production process. Samples are taken from the process periodically and the observations plotted on the graph. If an observation is outside of the upper or lower limits on the graph, it may indicate that something is wrong in the process; that is, it is not in control, which may cause defective or poor-quality items. By monitoring the production process with a control chart, the worker and management can detect problems quickly and prevent poor-quality items from passing on through the remainder of the process, and ending up as defective products that must be thrown away or re-worked, thus wasting time and resources. Control charts have become one of the most important statistical tools in TQM for continuous quality improvement. Training in statistical process control for all workers and managers is now a fundamental educational activity at most companies that have adopted TQM.

A number of Kurt's customers have reduced their suppliers from as many as 3,000 to around 150. In most cases Kurt Manufacturing has survived these cuts because of its commitment to TQM principles and continuous quality improvement.[1]

A fter World War II, W. E. Deming, the quality expert and consultant, was invited to Japan by the Japanese government to give a series of lectures on improving product reliability. This was probably the single most important event that started the Japanese toward a global quality revolution. These lectures were based on statistical quality control, and they became a cornerstone of the Japanese commitment to quality management.

A major topic in statistical quality control is *statistical process control* (SPC). **Statistical process control (SPC)** is a statistical procedure using control charts to see if any part of a production process is not functioning properly and could cause poor quality. In TQM operators use SPC to inspect and measure the production process to see if it is varying from what it is supposed to be doing. If there is unusual or undesirable variability, the process is corrected so that defects will not occur. In this way statistical process control is used to prevent poor quality before it occurs. It is such an important part of quality management in Japan that nearly all workers at all levels in Japanese companies are given extensive and continual training in SPC. Conversely, in the United States one reason cited for past failure to achieve high quality is the lack of comprehensive training for employees in SPC methods. U.S. companies that have been successful in adopting TQM train all their employees in SPC methods and make extensive use of SPC for continuous process improvement.

> **Statistical process control (SPC)** involves monitoring the production process to prevent poor quality.

> Employee training in SPC is a fundamental principle of TQM.

Another topic in statistical quality control, **acceptance sampling,** involves inspecting a sample of product input (i.e., raw materials or parts) and/or the final product and comparing it to a quality standard. If the sample fails the comparison, or test, then that implies poor quality, and the entire group of items from which the sample was taken is rejected. This traditional approach to quality control conflicts with the philosophy of TQM because it assumes that some degree of poor quality will occur and that it is acceptable. TQM seeks ultimately to have zero defects and 100 percent quality. Acceptance sampling identifies defective items after the product is already finished, whereas TQM preaches the prevention of defects altogether. To disciples of TQM, acceptance sampling is simply a means of identifying products to throw away or rework. It does nothing to prevent poor quality and to ensure good quality in the future. Nevertheless, acceptance sampling is still used by firms that have not adopted TQM. There may come a time when TQM becomes so pervasive that acceptance sampling will be used not at all or to a very limited extent. However, that time has not yet arrived, and until it does acceptance sampling still is a topic that requires some attention.

> **Acceptance sampling** involves taking a random sample to determine if a lot is acceptable.

Statistical Process Control

Process control is achieved by taking periodic **samples** from the process and plotting these sample points on a chart, to see if the process is within statistical control limits. If a sample point is outside the limits, the process may be out of control, and the cause is sought so the problem can be corrected. If the sample is within the control limits, the process continues without interference but with continued monitoring. In

> A **sample** is a subset of the items produced to use for inspection.

---

[1] *Total Quality Management*, video produced by the Society of Manufacturing Engineers (SME) and distributed by Allyn and Bacon, 1993.

this way, SPC prevents quality problems by correcting the process before it starts producing defects.

No production process produces exactly identical items, one after the other. All processes contain a certain amount of variability that makes some variation between units inevitable. There are two reasons why a production process might vary. The first is the inherent random variability of the process, which depends on the equipment and machinery, engineering, the operator, and the system used for measurement. This kind of variability is a result of natural occurrences. The other reason for variability is unique or special causes that are identifiable and can be corrected. These causes tend to be nonrandom and, if left unattended, will cause poor quality. These might include equipment that is out of adjustment, defective materials, changes in parts of materials, broken machinery or equipment, operator fatigue or poor work methods, or errors due to lack of training.

> All processes have variability—random and nonrandom (identifiable, correctable).

SPC in TQM

In TQM operators use SPC to see if their process is in control—working properly. This requires that companies provide SPC training on a continuing basis that stresses that SPC is a tool for operators to use to monitor their part of the production process *for the purpose of making improvements*. Through the use of statistical process control, employees are made responsible for quality in their area; to identify problems and either correct them or seek help in correcting them. By continually monitoring the production process and making improvements, the operator contributes to the TQM goal of continuous improvement and no defects.

> SPC is a tool for identifying problems in order to make improvements.

The first step in correcting the problem is identifying the causes. In Chapter 3 we described several quality control tools used for identifying causes of problems, including brainstorming, Pareto charts, histograms, check sheets, quality circles, and fishbone (cause-and-effect) diagrams.

When an operator is unable to correct a problem, the supervisor is typically notified who might initiate group problem solving. This group may be a quality circle, or it may be less formal including other operators, engineers, quality experts, and the supervisor. This group would brainstorm the problem to seek out possible causes. They might use a fishbone diagram to assist in identifying problem causes. Sometimes experiments are conducted under controlled conditions to isolate the cause of a problem.

Quality Measures: Attributes and Variables

The quality of a product can be evaluated using either an *attribute* of the product or a *variable measure*. An **attribute** is a product characteristic such as color, surface texture, or perhaps smell or taste. Attributes can be evaluated quickly with a discrete response such as good or bad, acceptable or not, or yes or no. Even if quality specifications are complex and extensive, a simple attribute test might be used to determine if a product is or is not defective. For example, an operator might test a light bulb by simply turning it on and seeing if it lights. If it does not, it can be examined to find out the exact technical cause for failure, but for SPC purposes, the fact that it is defective has been determined.

> An **attribute** is a product characteristic that can be evaluated with a discrete response (good/bad, yes/no).

A **variable measure** is a product characteristic that is measured on a continuous scale such as length, weight, temperature, or time. For example, the amount of liquid detergent in a plastic container can be measured to see if it conforms to the company's product specifications. Or the time it takes to serve a customer at McDonald's can be measured to see if it is quick enough. Since a variable evaluation is the result of some form of measurement, it is sometimes referred to as a *quantitative* classification method.

> A **variable measure** is a product characteristic that can be measured (weight, length).

THE COMPETITIVE EDGE

Statistical Process Control at ITT

ITT Electro-Optical Products Division in Roanoke, Virginia, designs, develops, and produces night-vision image-intensification devices for use in such products as helicopter pilot's goggles. Manufacturing these devices is extremely complex, requiring more than 400 processes, 200 chemicals, and the combination of such technologies as fiber optics, electronics, chemistry, and semiconductors. In 1986 the company implemented a TQM program that increased manufacturing yield from 35 percent to more than 75 percent by 1989. One reason was the use of statistical process control methods for sampling and statistical analysis of the process output. Statistical process control methods were used to reduce variation in raw material, subassembly purchases, internal processing, and assembly operations that affected final product quality. All senior managers and supervisors were trained in the use of statistical process control techniques by the ITT Statistical Program Group.

SOURCE: Based on J. E. Kempster, "ITT Electro-Optical Products Division, Roanoke, Virginia," *Quality and Productivity Management*, 9, no. 2 (1991): 37–46.

An attribute evaluation is sometimes referred to as a *qualitative* classification, since the response is not measured. Because it is a measurement, a variable classification typically provides more information about the product—the weight of a product is more informative than simply saying the product is good or bad.

SPC Applied to Services

Control charts have historically been used to monitor the quality of manufacturing processes. However, SPC is just as useful for monitoring quality in services. The difference is the nature of the "defect" being measured and monitored. Using Motorola's definition—*a failure to meet customer requirements in any product or service*—a defect can be an empty soap dispenser in a restroom or an error with a phone catalog order, as well as a blemish on a piece of cloth or a faulty plug on a VCR. Control charts for service processes tend to use quality characteristics and measurements such as time and customer satisfaction (determined by surveys, questionnaires, or inspections). Follow-

A service defect is a failure to meet customer requirements.

This Goodyear employee is using a dial caliper to measure variations in tire tread in a tire mold. The dial caliper is a mechanical device, or gauge, in which movable contacts touch the object to be measured and, using a gear train, translate the dimensions to the dial where it can be read by the operator. Measurements from a gauge like this are accurate to within 0.001 inch. Digital gauges, that perform the same function electronically, are more accurate than a mechanical gauge. Measuring instruments like the dial caliper are used by operators to take sample measurements during the inspection process for use with a process control chart.

ing is a list of several different services and the quality characteristics for each that can be measured and monitored with control charts.

Hospitals: Timeliness and quickness of care, staff responses to requests, accuracy of lab tests, cleanliness, courtesy, accuracy of paperwork, speed of admittance and check-outs.

Grocery stores: Waiting time to check out, frequency of out-of-stock items, quality of food items, cleanliness, customer complaints, check-out register errors.

Airlines: Flight delays, lost luggage and luggage handling, waiting time at ticket counters and check-in, agent and flight attendant courtesy, passenger cabin cleanliness and maintenance.

Fast-food restaurants: Waiting time for service, customer complaints, cleanliness, food quality, order accuracy, employee courtesy.

Catalog-order companies: Order accuracy, operator knowledge and courtesy, packaging, delivery time, phone order waiting time.

Insurance companies: Billing accuracy, timeliness of claims processing, agent availability and response time.

Control Charts

A **control chart** is a graph that establishes the control limits of a process.

Control limits are the upper and lower bands of a control chart.

Types of charts: attributes, *p* and *c*, variables, $\bar{x}$ and *R*.

Control charts are graphs that visually show if a sample is within statistical **control limits.** They have two basic purposes, to establish the control limits for a process and then to monitor the process to indicate when it is out of control. Control charts exist for attributes and variables; within each category there are several different types of control charts. We will present four commonly used control charts, two in each category: *p*-charts and *c*-charts for attributes and *mean* (*x*) and *range* (*R*) control charts for variables. Even though these control charts differ in how they measure process control, they all have certain similar characteristics. They all look alike, with a line through the center of a graph that indicates the process average and lines above and below the center line that represent the upper and lower limits of the process, as shown in Figure 4.1.

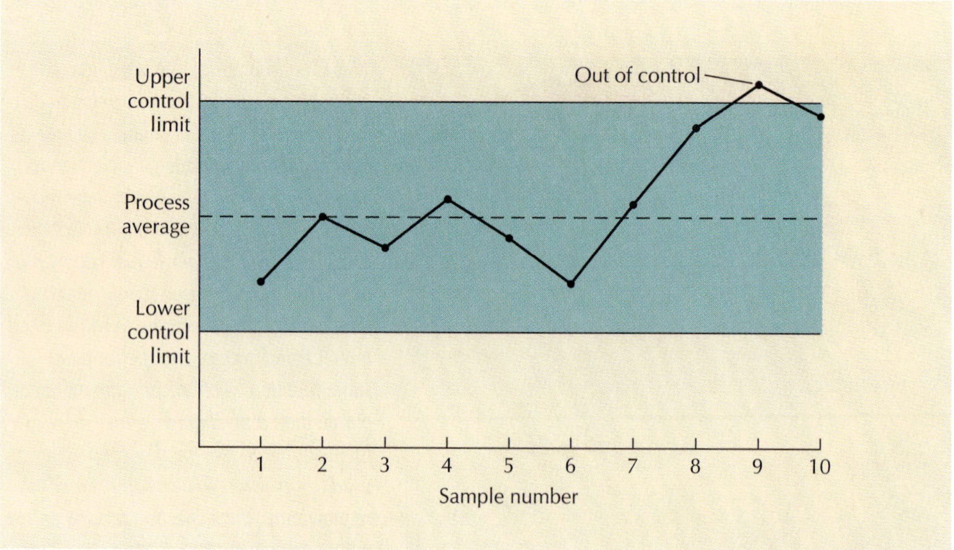

FIGURE 4.1   Process Control Chart

Competing At Lands' End

Assuring product quality and service at Lands' End

www.prenhall.com/russell

Service companies like Lands' End do not typically have the opportunity to use statistical process control charts directly, but they do employ other traditional quality control procedures to ensure product and service quality. As merchandise is received from vendors at the distribution center a certain percentage is inspected internally by quality-assurance inspectors. Each inspector is given a specific flaw or problem to look for—for example, loose threads on a button or a turtleneck collar that is too tight to pull over someone's head. If inspectors begin to find problems they can inspect every item in the order or send the entire order back to the vendor. In all cases, inspectors chart their findings, which are then reported to both vendors and Lands' End quality-assurance specialists.

Quality-assurance specialists also perform in-depth statistical analyses on a category basis of returns that come back. These specialists look for statistical trends that indicate a potential or existing problem with a particular category of merchandise or with a particular vendor. For example, customer comments about returned Rugby shirts indicated a problem with bleeding after washing. Analysis by a quality-assurance specialist and lab work found that customers were washing the shirts with cold water that created the bleeding problem. This alerted Lands' End to the fact that cold water washing could result in a bleeding problem. They resolved the problem by attaching large hang tags with washing instructions to the shirts. In another instance, a customer returned a shirt because "it didn't look right after being sent to the laundry." The quality-assurance specialist logged this comment and sent the item on to the vendor with the customer's comment. In another case, a shirt was returned with a tiny hole in the sleeve, a flaw that the quality-assurance specialist identified as a defect in wearing and this item was sent to the vendor for analysis.

On the customer service side, Lands' End supervisors monitor at least four phone calls for each customer-sales representative each month and complete monitoring forms related to those calls. Lands' End also employs a program called SOS—Strengthening Operator Skills—a peer monitoring process in which operators monitor each other. A group of six operators meets in a monitoring room and one volunteers to go out to a designated phone station and take calls. The operators in the monitoring room can hear both the operator and customer conducting business, and see on a large screen the computer screens the representative is accessing as the actual order is being input. General guidelines and a detailed checklist for phone orders are provided to the observers. After feedback is shared with volunteer number one, each of the other members of the peer group takes a turn and receives feedback.

Each time a sample is taken, the mathematical average of the sample is plotted as a point on the control chart as shown in Figure 4.1. A process is generally considered to be in control if, for example,

1. There are no sample points outside the control limits.
2. Most points are near the process average (i.e., the center line), without too many close to the control limits.

3. Approximately equal numbers of sample points occur above and below the center line.
4. The points appear to be randomly distributed around the center line (i.e., no discernible pattern).

If any of these conditions are violated, the process may be *out of control*. The reason must be determined, and if the cause is not random, the problem must be corrected.

Sample 9 in Figure 4.1 is above the upper control limit, suggesting the process is out of control. The cause is not likely to be random since the sample points have been moving toward the upper limit, so management should attempt to find out what is wrong with the process and bring it back in control. Although the other samples display some degree of variation from the process average, they are usually considered to be caused by normal, random variability in the process and are thus in control. However, it is possible for sample observations to be within the control limits and the process to be out of control anyway, if the observations display a discernible, abnormal pattern of movement. We discuss such patterns in a later section.

Theoretically, a process control chart should be based only on sample observations from when the process is in control so that the control chart reflects a true benchmark for an in-control process. However, it is not known whether the process is in control or not until the control chart is initially constructed. Therefore, when a control chart is first developed and the process is found to be out of control, if nonrandom causes are the reason the out-of-control observations (and any others influenced by the nonrandom causes) should be discarded. A new center line and control limits should then be determined from the remaining observations. This "corrected" control chart is then used to monitor the process. It may not be possible to discover the cause(s) for the out-of-control sample observations. In this case a new set of samples is taken, and a completely new control chart constructed. Or it may be decided to simply use the initial control chart assuming that it accurately reflects the process variation.

> A sample point can be within the control limits and the process still be out of control.

> The development of a control chart

Control Charts for Attributes

> A *p*-chart uses the proportion defective in a sample.

> A *c*-chart uses the number of defective items in a sample.

The quality measures used in *attribute control charts* are discrete values reflecting a simple decision criterion such as good or bad. A *p*-chart uses the proportion defective items in a sample as the sample statistic; a *c*-chart uses the actual number of defective items in a sample. A *p*-chart can be used when it is possible to distinguish between defective and nondefective items and to state the number of defectives as a percentage of the whole. In some processes, the proportion defective cannot be determined. For example, when counting the number of blemishes on a roll of upholstery material (at periodic intervals), it is not possible to compute a proportion. In this case a c-chart is required.

p-Chart

With a *p*-chart a sample is taken periodically from the production process, and the proportion of defective items in the sample is determined to see if the proportion falls within the control limits on the chart. Although a *p*-chart employs a discrete attribute measure (i.e., number of defective items) and thus is not continuous, it is assumed that as the sample size gets larger, the normal distribution can be used to approximate the distribution of the proportion defective. This enables us to use the following formulas based on the normal distribution to compute the upper control limit (UCL) and lower control limit (LCL) of a *p*-chart.

$$UCL = \bar{p} + z\sigma_p$$
$$LCL = \bar{p} - z\sigma_p$$

[handwritten: $\bar{p}$ = average % defective in sample
n = sample size]

where

z = the number of standard deviations from the process average

p = the sample proportion defective; an estimate of the process average

σ_p = the standard deviation of the sample proportion

The sample standard deviation is computed as

$$\sigma_p = \sqrt{\frac{\bar{p}(1 - \bar{p})}{n}}$$

where *n* is the sample size.

In the control limit formulas for *p*-charts (and other control charts), *z* is occasionally equal to 2.00 but most frequently is 3.00. A *z* value of 2.00 corresponds to an overall normal probability of 95 percent and *z* = 3.00 corresponds to a normal probability of 99.74 percent.

The normal distribution in Figure 4.2 shows the probabilities corresponding to *z* values equal to 2.00 and 3.00 standard deviations (σ).

The smaller the value of *z*, the more narrow the control limits are and the more sensitive the chart is to changes in the production process. Control charts using *z* = 2.00 are often referred to as having "2-sigma" (2σ) limits (referring to two standard deviations), whereas *z* = 3.00 means "3-sigma" (3σ) limits.

Sigma limits are the number of standard deviations.

Management usually selects *z* = 3.00 because if the process is in control it wants a high probability that the sample values will fall within the control limits. In other words, with wider limits management is less likely to (erroneously) conclude that the process is out of control when points outside the control limits are due to normal, random variations. Alternatively, wider limits make it harder to detect changes in the process that are not random and have an assignable cause. A process might change because of a nonrandom, assignable cause and be detectable with the narrower limits but not with the wider limits. However, companies traditionally use the wider control limits.

The following example demonstrates how a *p*-chart is constructed.

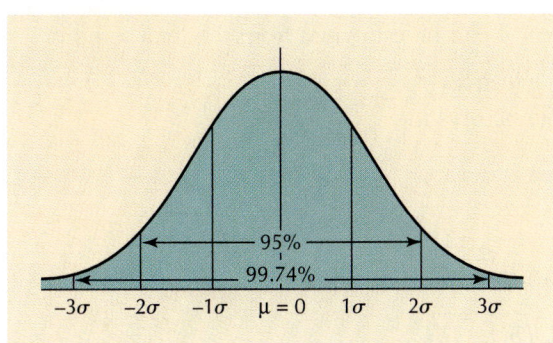

FIGURE 4.2 The Normal Distribution

EXAMPLE
4.1

*Construction of
a p-chart*

The Western Jeans Company produces denim jeans. The company wants to establish a *p*-chart to monitor the production process and maintain high quality. Western believes that approximately 99.74 percent of the variability in the production process (corresponding to 3-sigma limits, or $z = 3.00$) is random and thus should be within control limits, whereas .26 percent of the process variability is not random and suggests that the process is out of control.

The company has taken 20 samples (one per day for 20 days), each containing 100 pairs of jeans ($n = 100$), and inspected them for defects, the results of which are as follows.

Sample	Number of Defectives	Proportion Defective
1	6	.06
2	0	.00
3	4	.04
4	10	.10
5	6	.06
6	4	.04
7	12	.12
8	10	.10
9	8	.08
10	10	.10
11	12	.12
12	10	.10
13	14	.14
14	8	.08
15	6	.06
16	16	.16
17	12	.12
18	14	.14
19	20	.20
20	18	.18
	200	

The proportion defective for the population is not known. The company wants to construct a *p*-chart to determine when the production process might be out of control.

SOLUTION:

Since p is not known, it can be estimated from the total sample:

$$\bar{p} = \frac{\text{total defectives}}{\text{total sample observations}}$$

$$= \frac{200}{20(100)}$$

$$= 0.10$$

The control limits are computed as follows.

$$\text{UCL} = \bar{p} + z \sqrt{\frac{\bar{p}(1 - \bar{p})}{n}}$$

$$= 0.10 + 3.00 \sqrt{\frac{0.10(1 - 0.10)}{100}} = 0.190$$

$$\text{LCL} = \bar{p} - z \sqrt{\frac{\bar{p}(1 - \bar{p})}{n}}$$

$$= 0.10 - 3.00 \sqrt{\frac{0.10(1 - 0.10)}{100}} = 0.010$$

The *p*-chart, including sample points, is shown in the following figure.

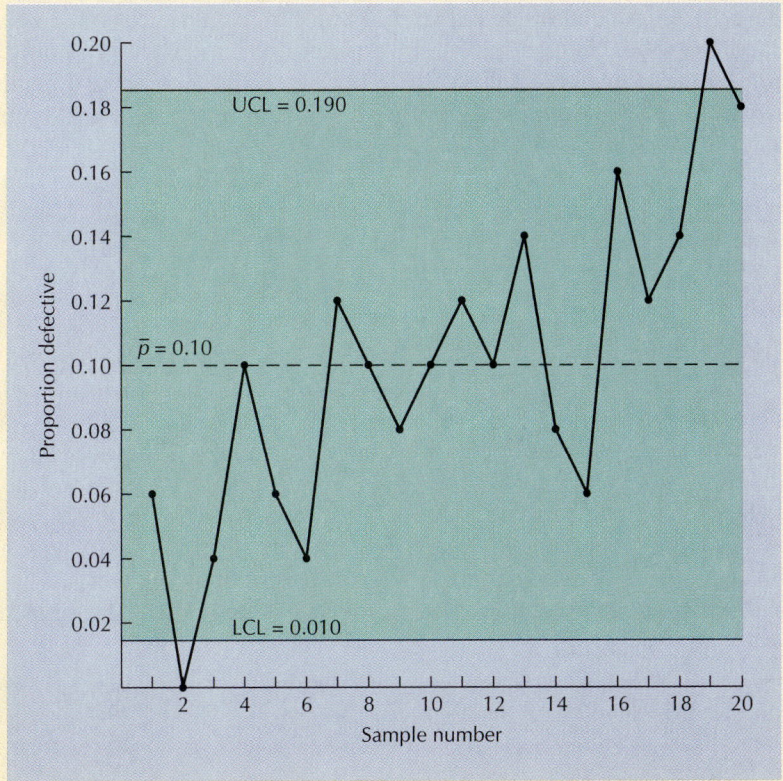

The process was below the lower control limits for sample 2 (i.e., during day 2). Although this could be perceived as a "good" result since it means there were very few defects, it might also suggest that something was wrong with the inspection process during that week that should be checked out. If there is no problem with the inspection process, then management would want to know what caused the quality of the process to improve. Perhaps "better" denim material from a new supplier that week or a different operator was working.

The process was above the upper limit during day 19. This suggests that the process may not be in control and the cause should be investigated. The cause could be defective or maladjusted machinery or a problem with an operator, defective materials (i.e., denim cloth), or a number of other correctable problems. In fact, there is an up-

(Continued)

ward trend in the number of defectives throughout the 20-day test period. The process was consistently moving toward an out-of-control situation. This trend represents a pattern in the observations, which suggests a nonrandom cause. If this was the actual control chart used to monitor the process (and not the initial chart), it is likely this pattern would have indicated an out-of-control situation before day 19, which would have alerted the operator to make corrections. Patterns are discussed in a separate section later in this chapter.

This initial control chart shows two out-of-control observations and a distinct pattern of increasing defects. Management would probably want to discard this set of samples and develop a new center line and control limits from a different set of sample values after the process has been corrected. If the pattern had not existed and only the two out-of-control observations were present, these two observations could be discarded, and a control chart could be developed from the remaining sample values, if the problem is corrected.

Once a control chart is established based solely on natural, random variation in the process, it is used to monitor the process. Samples are taken periodically, and the observations are checked on the control chart to see if the process is in control.

c-Chart

A *c*-chart is used when it is not possible to compute a proportion defective and the actual number of defects must be used. For example, when automobiles are inspected, the number of blemishes (i.e., defects) in the paint job can be counted for each car, but a proportion cannot be computed, since the total number of possible blemishes is not known.

Since the number of defects per sample is assumed to derive from some extremely large population, the probability of a single defect is very small. As with the *p*-chart, the normal distribution can be used to approximate the distribution of defects. The process average for the *c*-chart is the sample mean number of defects, $\bar{c}$, computed by dividing

THE COMPETITIVE EDGE

Process Control Charts at P*I*E Nationwide

P*I*E Nationwide, formed by the merger of Ryder Truck Lines and Pacific Intermountain Express, is the nation's fourth-largest trucking company. Part of the company's "Blueprint for Quality" program is the extensive use of statistical process control charts. A *p*-chart was initially used to monitor the proportion of daily defective freight bills. This resulted in a reduction in the error rate in freight bills from 10 percent per day to 0.8 percent within one year, and the subsequent reduction in inspection time increased productivity by 30 percent. Although the freight bill-rating process was in control, the company continued to evaluate the causes of the remaining errors. Using a *p*-chart for the proportion of bill of lading defects, the company found that 63 percent of the bills of lading P*I*E received from its customers contained errors. Many of the errors were corrected by employees (at a rework cost of $1.83 per error); however, some errors were not corrected, causing eventual service problems. Eventual correction of the process dropped the error rate from 63 percent to 8 percent, and savings at a single trucking terminal were greater than $38,000.

SOURCE: Based on C. Dondero, "SPC Hits the Road," *Quality Progress* 24, no. 1 (1991): 43–44.

the total number of defects by the number of samples. The sample standard deviation, σ_c, is $\sqrt{\bar{c}}$. The following formulas for the control limits are used:

$$UCL = \bar{c} + z\sigma_c$$
$$LCL = \bar{c} - z\sigma_c$$

$$\sigma_c = \sqrt{\bar{c}}$$

EXAMPLE
4.2

*Construction of
a c-chart*

Barrett Mills in North Carolina produces denim cloth used by manufacturers (such as the Western Jeans Company) to make jeans. The denim cloth is woven from thread on a weaving machine, and the thread occasionally breaks and is repaired by the operator, sometimes causing blemishes (called "picks"). The operator inspects rolls of denim on a daily basis as they come off the loom and counts the number of blemishes. Following are the results from inspecting fifteen rolls of denim during a three-week period.

Sample	Number of Defects
1	12
2	8
3	16
4	14
5	10
6	11
7	9
8	14
9	13
10	15
11	12
12	10
13	14
14	17
15	15
	190

The company believes that approximately 99 percent of the defects (corresponding to 3-sigma limits) are caused by natural, random variations in the weaving process, with 1 percent caused by nonrandom variability. They want to construct a *c*-chart to monitor the weaving process.

SOLUTION:

Since *c*, the population process average, is not known, the sample estimate, $\bar{c}$, can be used instead:

$$\bar{c} = \frac{190}{15} = 12.67$$

The control limits are computed using $z = 3.00$, as follows.

$$UCL = \bar{c} + z \sqrt{\bar{c}} = 12.67 + 3 (\sqrt{12.67}) = 23.35$$
$$LCL = \bar{c} - z \sqrt{\bar{c}} = 12.67 - 3 (\sqrt{12.67}) = 1.99$$

The resulting *c*-chart, with the sample points, is shown in the following figure on the next page.

(Continued)

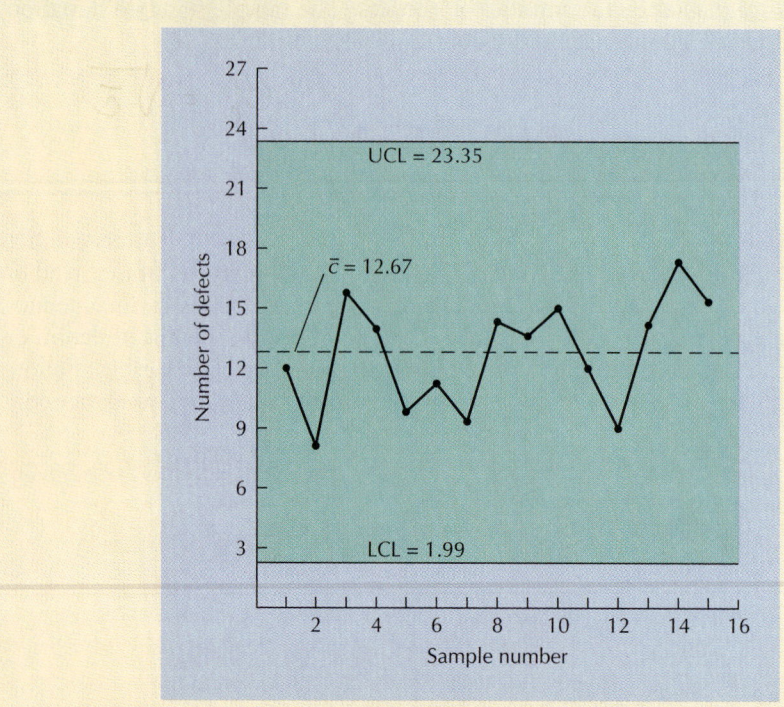

All the sample observations are within the control limits, suggesting that the weaving process is in control. This chart would be considered reliable to monitor the weaving process in the future.

Control Charts for Variables

An **R-chart** uses the amount of dispersion in a sample.

A **mean ($\bar{x}$-)chart** uses the process average of a sample.

The **range** is the difference between the smallest and largest values in a sample.

Variable control charts are for continuous variables that can be measured, such as weight or volume. Two commonly used variable control charts are the range chart, or *R*-chart, and the mean chart, or $\bar{x}$-chart. A **range (R-) chart** reflects the amount of dispersion present in each sample; a **mean ($\bar{x}$-) chart** indicates how sample results relate to the process average or mean. These charts are normally used together to determine if a process is in control.

Range (R-)Chart

In an *R*-chart, the **range** is the difference between the smallest and largest values in a sample. This range reflects the process variability instead of the tendency toward a mean value. The formulas for determining control limits are,

$$\text{UCL} = D_4\overline{R} \qquad \text{LCL} = D_3\overline{R}$$

$\overline{R}$ is the average range (and center line) for the samples,

$$\overline{R} = \frac{\Sigma R}{k}$$

where

$$R = \text{range of each sample}$$
$$k = \text{number of samples}$$

A conveyor of potato chips at a Frito-Lay plant. Periodically samples of chips will be taken from the conveyor and tested for salt content, thickness, crispness, and other product variables. The sample results will be plotted on a control chart to see if the production process is in control. If not, it will be corrected before a large number of defective chips are produced thereby preventing costly waste.

D_3 and D_4 are table values for determining control limits that have been developed based on range values rather than standard deviations. Table 4.1 includes values for D_3

TABLE 4.1   Factors for Determining Control Limits for $\bar{x}$- and R-Charts

Sample Size n	Factor for x-Chart A_2	Factors for R-Chart D_3	D_4
2	1.88	0	3.27
3	1.02	0	2.57
4	0.73	0	2.28
5	0.58	0	2.11
6	0.48	0	2.00
7	0.42	0.08	1.92
8	0.37	0.14	1.86
9	0.34	0.18	1.82
10	0.31	0.22	1.78
11	0.29	0.26	1.74
12	0.27	0.28	1.72
13	0.25	0.31	1.69
14	0.24	0.33	1.67
15	0.22	0.35	1.65
16	0.21	0.36	1.64
17	0.20	0.38	1.62
18	0.19	0.39	1.61
19	0.19	0.40	1.60
20	0.18	0.41	1.59
21	0.17	0.43	1.58
22	0.17	0.43	1.57
23	0.16	0.44	1.56
24	0.16	0.45	1.55
25	0.15	0.46	1.54

and D_4 for sample sizes up to 25. These tables are available in many texts on operations management and quality control. They provide control limits comparable to three standard deviations for different sample sizes.

EXAMPLE

4 · 3

Constructing an R-Chart

The Goliath Tool Company produces slip-ring bearings which look like flat doughnuts or washers. They fit around shafts or rods, such as drive shafts in machinery or motors. In the production process for a particular slip-ring bearing the employees have taken 10 samples (during a 10-day period) of 5 slip-ring bearings (i.e., $n = 5$). The individual observations from each sample are shown as follows

	OBSERVATIONS (SLIP-RING DIAMETER, *cm*)						
SAMPLE *k*	*1*	*2*	*3*	*4*	*5*	$\bar{x}$	*R*
1	5.02	5.01	4.94	4.99	4.96	4.98	0.08
2	5.01	5.03	5.07	4.95	4.96	5.00	0.12
3	4.99	5.00	4.93	4.92	4.99	4.97	0.08
4	5.03	4.91	5.01	4.98	4.89	4.96	0.14
5	4.95	4.92	5.03	5.05	5.01	4.99	0.13
6	4.97	5.06	5.06	4.96	5.03	5.01	0.10
7	5.05	5.01	5.10	4.96	4.99	5.02	0.14
8	5.09	5.10	5.00	4.99	5.08	5.05	0.11
9	5.14	5.10	4.99	5.08	5.09	5.08	0.15
10	5.01	4.98	5.08	5.07	4.99	5.03	0.10
						50.09	1.15

The company wants to develop an *R*-chart to monitor the process variability.

SOLUTION:

$\overline{R}$ is computed by first determining the range for each sample by computing the difference between the highest and lowest values shown in the last column in our table

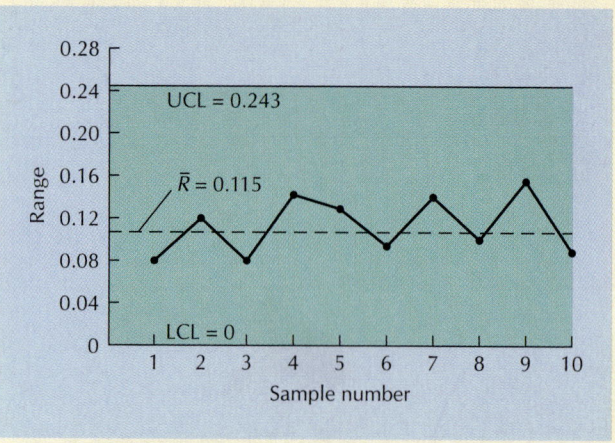

of sample observations. These ranges are summed and then divided by the number of samples, k, as follows:

$$\overline{R} = \frac{\Sigma R}{k} = \frac{1.15}{10} = 0.115$$

$D_3 = 0$ and $D_4 = 2.11$ from Table 4.1 for $n = 5$. Thus, the control limits are,

$$\text{UCL} = D_4\overline{R} = 2.11\,(0.115) = 0.243$$
$$\text{LCL} = D_3\overline{R} = 0\,(0.115) = 0$$

These limits define the R-chart shown in the following figure. It indicates that the process seems to be in control; the variability observed is a result of natural random occurrences.

Mean ($\overline{x}$-)Chart

For an $\overline{x}$-chart, the mean of each sample is computed and plotted on the chart; the points are the sample means. Each sample mean is a value of $\overline{x}$. The samples tend to be small, usually around 4 or 5. The center line of the chart is the overall process average, the sum of the averages of n samples,

$$\overline{\overline{x}} = \frac{\overline{x}_1 + \overline{x}_2 + \cdots \overline{x}_n}{n}$$

When an $\overline{x}$-chart is used in conjunction with an R-chart, the following formulas for control limits are used:

Control limits when $\overline{x}$- and R-charts are used together

$$\text{UCL} = \overline{\overline{x}} + A_2\overline{R}$$
$$\text{LCL} = \overline{\overline{x}} - A_2\overline{R}$$

where $\overline{\overline{x}}$ is the average of the sample means and $\overline{R}$ is the average range value. A_2 is a tabular value like D_3 and D_4 that is used to establish the control limits. Values of A_2 are included in Table 4.1. They were developed specifically for determining the control limits for $\overline{x}$-charts and are comparable to 3-standard deviation (3σ) limits.

Since the formulas for the control limits of the $\overline{x}$-chart use the average range values, $\overline{R}$, the R-chart must be constructed before the $\overline{x}$-chart.

EXAMPLE 4.4

An $\overline{x}$-Chart and $\overline{R}$-Chart Used Together

The Goliath Tool Company desires to develop an $\overline{x}$-chart to be used in conjunction with the R-chart developed in Example 4.3.

SOLUTION:

The data provided in Example 4.3 for the samples allow us to compute $\overline{\overline{x}}$ as follows:

$$\overline{\overline{x}} = \frac{\Sigma \overline{x}}{10} = \frac{50.09}{10} = 5.01 \text{ cm}$$

Using the value of $A_2 = 0.58$ for $n = 5$ from Table 4.1 and $\overline{R} = 0.115$ from Example 4.3, the control limits are computed as

$$\text{UCL} = \overline{\overline{x}} + A_2\overline{R}$$

(Continued)

$$= 5.01 + (0.58)(0.115) = 5.08$$
$$\text{LCL} = \bar{\bar{x}} - A_2\bar{R}$$
$$= 5.0 - (0.58)(0.115) = 4.94$$

The $\bar{x}$-chart defined by these control limits is shown in the following figure. Notice that the process is out of control for sample 9; in fact, samples 4 to 9 show an upward trend. This would suggest the process variability is subject to nonrandom causes and should be investigated.

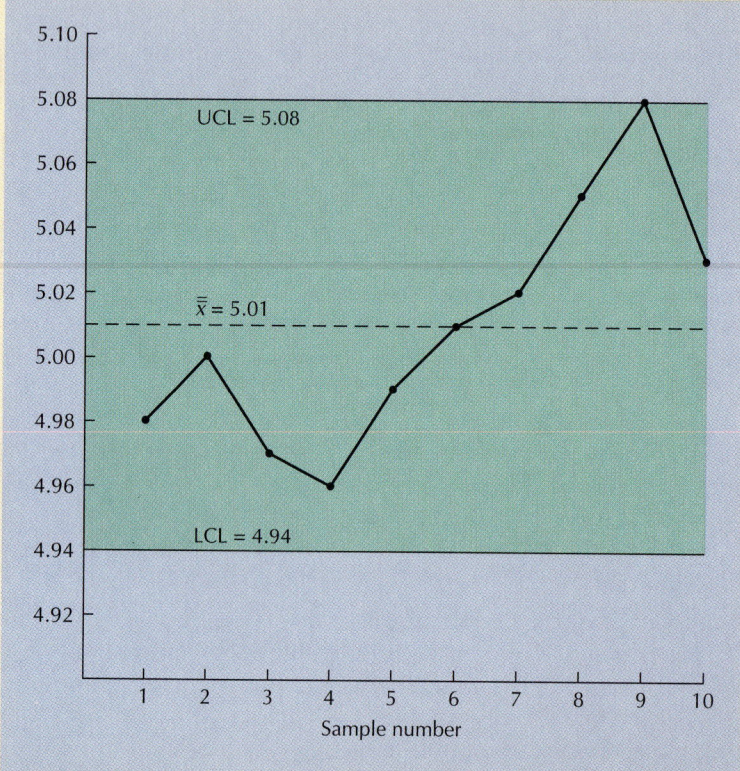

This example illustrates the need to employ the R-chart and the $\bar{x}$-chart together. The R-chart in Example 4.3 suggested that the process was in control, and none of the ranges for the samples were close to the control limits. However, the $\bar{x}$-chart suggests that the process is not in control. In fact, the ranges for samples 8 and 10 were relatively narrow, whereas the means of both samples were relatively high. The use of both charts together provided a more complete picture of the overall process variability.

Using $\bar{x}$- and R-Charts Together

Both the process average and variability must be in control.

The $\bar{x}$-chart is used with the R-chart under the premise that both the process average and variability must be in control for the process to be in control. This is logical. The two charts measure the process differently. It is possible for samples to have very narrow ranges, suggesting little process variability, but the sample averages might be beyond the control limits.

For example, consider two samples with the first having low and high values of 4.95 and 5.05 centimeters, and the second having low and high values of 5.10 and 5.20 centimeters. The range of both is 0.10 cm but $\bar{x}$ for the first is 5.00 centimeters and $\bar{x}$ for the second is 5.15 centimeters. The two sample ranges might indicate the process is in control and $\bar{x} = 5.00$ might be okay, but $\bar{x} = 5.15$ could be outside the control limit.

Conversely, it is possible for the sample averages to be in control, but the ranges might be very large. For example, two samples could both have $\bar{x} = 5.00$ centimeters, but sample 1 could have a range between 4.95 and 5.05 ($R = 0.10$ centimeter) and sample 2 could have a range between 4.80 and 5.20 ($R = 0.40$ centimeter). Sample 2 suggests the process is out of control.

It is also possible for an *R*-chart to exhibit a distinct downward trend in the range values, indicating that the ranges are getting narrower and there is less variation. This would be reflected on the $\bar{x}$-chart by mean values closer to the center line. Although this occurrence does not indicate that the process is out of control, it does suggest that some nonrandom cause is reducing process variation. This cause needs to be investigated to see if it is sustainable. If so, new control limits would need to be developed.

Sometimes an $\bar{x}$-chart is used alone to see if a process is improving. For example, in the "Competitive Edge" box for Kentucky Fried Chicken, an $\bar{x}$-chart is used to see if average service times at a drive-through window are continuing to decline over time toward a specific goal.

In other situations a company may have studied and collected data for a process for a long period of time and already know what the mean and standard deviation of the process is and all they want to do is monitor the process average by taking periodic samples. In this case it would be appropriate to use just the mean chart and the following formulas for establishing control limits,

$$\text{UCL} = \bar{\bar{x}} + z\sigma_{\bar{x}} \qquad \text{LCL} = \bar{\bar{x}} - z\sigma_{\bar{x}}$$

THE COMPETITIVE EDGE

Using Control Charts at Kentucky Fried Chicken

www.prenhall.com/russell

Kentucky Fried Chicken (KFC) Corporation, USA, is a fast-food chain consisting of 2,000 company-owned restaurants and over 3,000 franchised restaurants with annual sales of over $3 billion. Quality of service and especially speed of service at its drive-through window operations are critical in retaining customers and increasing its market share in the very competitive fast-food industry. As part of a quality-improvement project in KFC's South Central (Texas and Oklahoma) division, a project team established a goal of reducing customer time at a drive-through window from over two minutes down to 60 seconds. This reduction was to be achieved in 10-

second increments until the overall goal was realized. Large, visible electronic timers were used at each of four test restaurants to time window service and identify problem areas. Each week tapes from these timers were sent to the project leader who used this data to construct $\bar{x}$- and *R*-control charts. Since the project goal was to gradually reduce service time (in 10-second increments), the system was not stable. The $\bar{x}$-chart showed if the average weekly sample service times continued to go down toward to 60-second goal. The *R*-chart plotted the average of the range between the longest and shortest window times in a sample, and was used for the traditional purpose to insure that the variability of the system was under control and not increasing.

SOURCE: U. M. Apte and C. Reynolds, "Quality Management at Kentucky Fried Chicken," *Interfaces*, 25, no. 3 (1995): 6–21.

The sample standard deviation, $\sigma_{\bar{x}}$, is computed as

$$\sigma_{\bar{x}} = \frac{\sigma}{\sqrt{n}}$$

EXAMPLE 4·5

Constructing a Mean Chart

The Goliath Tool Company has studied its process for manufacturing slip-ring bearings and determined that the bearings have a mean diameter of 5 centimeters and a standard deviation of 0.04 centimeters. The company wants to develop a mean chart for this production process that will include 99.74 percent (i.e., three standard deviations) of the process variability using samples of size 20.

SOLUTION:
The control limits are computed as follows:

$$\text{UCL} = \bar{\bar{x}} + z\left(\frac{\sigma}{\sqrt{n}}\right) = 5 + (3)\left(\frac{0.04}{\sqrt{20}}\right) = 5.027 \text{ cm}$$

$$\text{LCL} = \bar{\bar{x}} - z\left(\frac{\sigma}{\sqrt{n}}\right) = 5 - (3)\left(\frac{0.04}{\sqrt{20}}\right) = 4.973 \text{ cm}$$

If a sample is taken and the sample mean falls outside of these control limits, it suggests that the process is out of control, so the cause is probably nonrandom and should be investigated.

Control Chart Patterns

A pattern can indicate an out-of-control process even if sample values are within control limits.

Even though a control chart may indicate that a process is in control, it is possible the sample variations within the control limits are not random. If the sample values display a consistent pattern, even within the control limits, it suggests that this pattern has a nonrandom cause that might warrant investigation. We expect the sample values to "bounce around" above and below the center line, reflecting the natural, random variation in the process that will be present. However, if the sample values are consistently above (or below) the center line for an extended number of samples or if they move

THE COMPETITIVE EDGE

Using x̄-Charts at Frito-Lay

www.prenhall.com/russell

Since the Frito-Lay Company implemented statistical process control, it has experienced a 50 percent improvement in the variability of bags of potato chips. As an example, the company uses x̄-charts to monitor and control salt content, an important taste feature in Ruffles potato chips. Three batches of finished Ruffles are obtained every 15 minutes. Each batch is ground up,

weighed, dissolved in distilled water, and filtered into a beaker. The salt content of this liquid is determined using an electronic salt analyzer. The salt content of the three batches is averaged to get a sample mean, which is plotted on an x̄-chart with a center line (target) salt content of 1.6 percent.

SOURCE: Based on "Against All Odds, Statistical Quality Control," COMAP Program 3, Annenberg/CPB Project, 1988. Allyn and Bacon.

consistently up or down, there is probably a reason for this behavior; that is, it is not random. Examples of nonrandom patterns are shown in Figure 4.3.

A pattern in a control chart is characterized by a sequence of sample observations that display the same characteristics—also called a **run.** One type of pattern is a sequence of observations either above or below the center line. For example, three values above the center line followed by two values below the line represent two runs of a pattern. Another type of pattern is a sequence of sample values that consistently go up or go down within the control limits. Several tests are available to determine if a pattern is nonrandom or random.

One type of **pattern test** divides the control chart into three "zones" on each side of the center line, where each zone is one standard deviation wide. These are often referred to as 1-sigma, 2-sigma, and 3-sigma limits. The pattern of sample observations in these zones is then used to determine if any nonrandom patterns exist. Recall that the formula for computing an $\bar{x}$-chart uses A_2 from Table 4.1, which assumes 3-standard deviation control limits (or 3-sigma limits). Thus, to compute the dividing lines between

A **run** is a sequence of sample values that display the same characteristic.

A **pattern test** determines if the observations within the limits of a control chart display a nonrandom pattern.

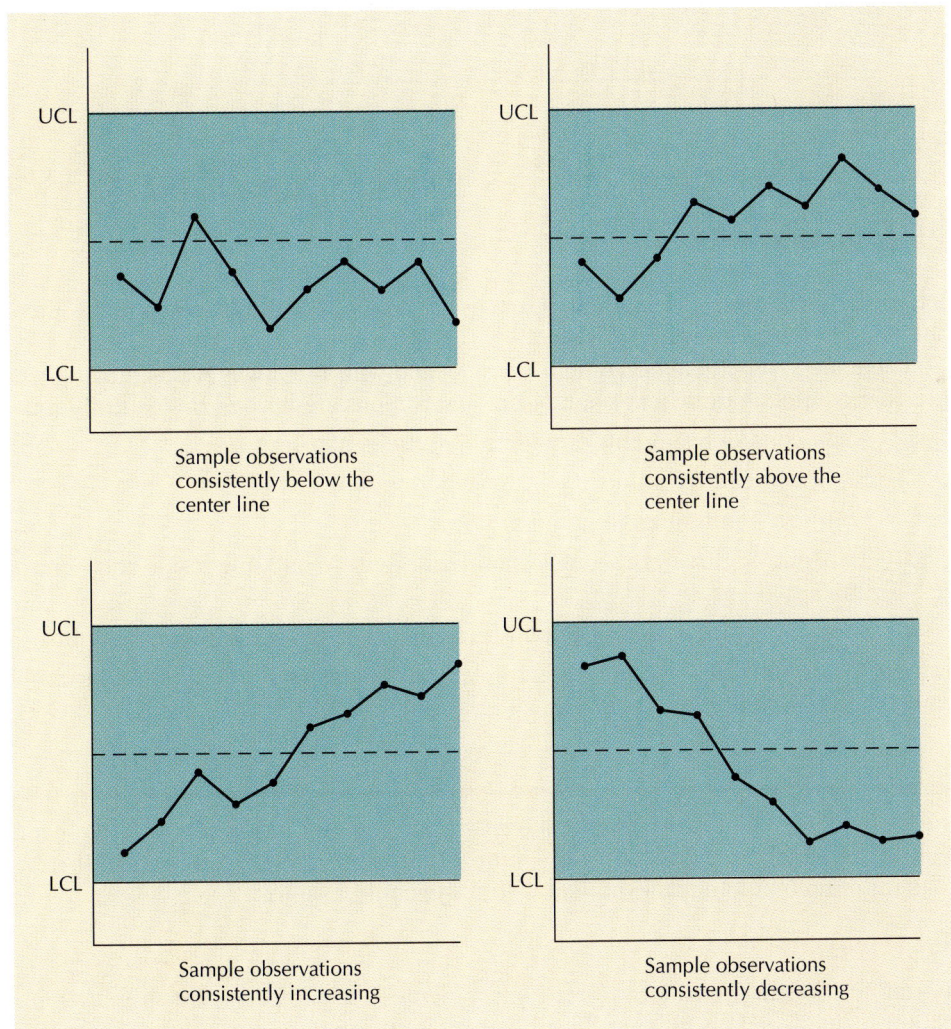

Sample observations
consistently below the
center line

Sample observations
consistently above the
center line

Sample observations
consistently increasing

Sample observations
consistently decreasing

FIGURE 4.3   **Control Chart Patterns**

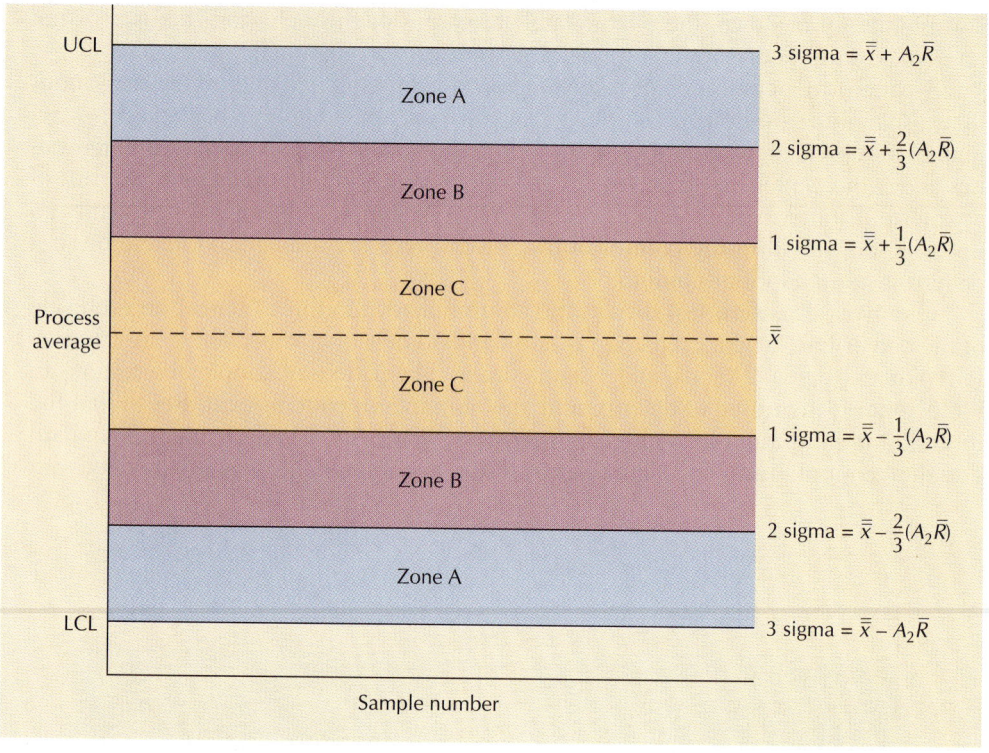

FIGURE 4.4   Zones for Pattern Tests

each of the three zones for an $\bar{x}$-chart, we use $^1/_3$ A_2. The formulas to compute these zone boundaries are shown in Figure 4.4.

Guidelines for identifying patterns

There are several general guidelines associated with the zones for identifying patterns in a control chart, where none of the observations are beyond the control limits:

1. Eight consecutive points on one side of the center line
2. Eight consecutive points up or down across zones
3. Fourteen points alternating up or down
4. Two out of three consecutive points in zone A but still inside the control limits
5. Four out of five consecutive points in zone B or beyond the 1-sigma limits

If any of these guidelines apply to the sample observations in a control chart, it would imply that a nonrandom pattern exists and the cause should be investigated.

EXAMPLE 4.6	The Goliath Tool Company $\bar{x}$-chart shown in Example 4.4 indicates that the process might not be in control. The company wants to perform a pattern test to see if there is a pattern of nonrandomness exhibited within the control limits.

Performing a Pattern Test

SOLUTION:

In order to perform the pattern test, we must identify the runs that exist in the sample data for Example 4.4, as follows. Recall that $\bar{x} = 5.01$ cm.

Sample	$\bar{x}$	Above/Below	Up/Down	Zone
1	4.98	B	—	B
2	5.00	B	U	C
3	4.97	B	D	A
4	4.96	B	D	A
5	4.99	B	U	C
6	5.01	—	U	C
7	5.02	A	U	C
8	5.05	A	U	B
9	5.08	A	U	A
10	5.03	A	D	B

The only pattern rule violated is that two out of three consecutive points (samples 3 and 4) are in zone A. Thus, the variation within the control limits may not be totally random. In this case the process should be checked.

Sample Size Determination

In our examples of control charts, sample sizes varied significantly. For p-charts and c-charts, we used sample sizes in the hundreds, whereas for $\bar{x}$- and R-charts we used samples of four or five. In general, larger sample sizes are needed for attribute charts because more observations are required to develop a usable quality measure. A population proportion defective of only 5 percent requires 5 defective items from a sample of 100. But, a sample of 10 does not even permit a result with 5 percent defective items. Variable control charts require smaller sample sizes because each sample observation provides usable information—for example, weight, length, or volume. After only a few sample observations (as few as two), it is possible to compute a range or a sample average that reflects the sample characteristics. It is desirable to take as few sample observations as possible, because they require the operator's time to take them.

Some companies use sample sizes of just two. They inspect only the first and last items in a production lot under the premise that if neither is out of control, then the process is in control. This requires the production of small lots (which are characteristic of some Japanese companies), so that the process will not be out of control for too long before a problem is discovered.

Size may not be the only consideration in sampling. It may also be important that the samples come from a homogeneous source so that if the process is out of control, the cause can be accurately determined. If production takes place on either one of two machines (or two sets of machines), mixing the sample observations between them makes it difficult to ascertain which operator or machine caused the problem. If the production process encompasses more than one shift, mixing the sample observation between shifts may make it more difficult to discover which shift caused the process to move out of control.

Design Tolerances and Process Capability

Control limits are occasionally mistaken for tolerances, however, they are quite different things. Control limits provide a means for determining natural variation in a production process. They are statistical results based on sampling. **Tolerances** are design or engineering specifications reflecting customer requirements for a product. They are

Attribute charts require larger sample sizes; variable charts require smaller samples.

Attribute –
50 – 100 parts
in a sample
Variable
2 – 10 parts
in a sample

Tolerances are design specifications reflecting product requirements.

not statistically determined and are not a direct result of the production process. Tolerances are externally imposed; control limits are determined internally. It is possible for a process to be in control according to control charts, yet not meet product tolerances. To avoid such a situation, the process must be evaluated to see if it can meet product specifications before the process is initiated and control charts are established. This is one of the principles of TQM (Chapter 3)—products must be designed so that they will meet reasonable and cost-effective standards.

Another use of control charts not mentioned is to determine *process capability*. **Process capability** is the range of natural variation in a process, essentially what we have been measuring with control charts. It is sometimes also referred to as the *natural tolerances* of a process. It is used by product designers and engineers to determine how well a process will fall within design specifications. In other words, charts can be used for process capability to determine if an existing process is capable of meeting the specifications for a newly designed product. Design specifications, sometimes referred to as specification limits, or *design tolerances*, have no statistical relationship to the natural limits of the control chart.

If the natural variation of an existing process is greater than the specification limits of a newly designed product, the process is not capable of meeting these specification limits. This situation will result in a large proportion of defective parts or products. If the limits of a control chart measuring natural variation exceed the specification limits or designed tolerances of a product, the process cannot produce the product according to specifications. The variation that will occur naturally, at random, is greater than the designed variation. This situation is depicted graphically in Figure 4.5(a).

Parts that are within the control limits but outside the design specification can be scrapped or reworked. This can be very costly and wasteful, and it conflicts with the basic principles of TQM. Alternatives include developing a new process or redesigning the product. However, these solutions can also be costly. As such it is important that

> **Process capability** is the range of natural variability in a process—what we measure with control charts.

> If the natural variability in a process exceeds tolerances, the process cannot meet design specifications.

THE COMPETITIVE EDGE

Design Tolerances at Harley-Davidson Company

www.prenhall.com/russell

Harley-Davidson is the only manufacturer of motorcycles in the United States. Once at the brink of going out of business, it is now a successful company known for high quality. It has achieved this comeback by combining the classic styling and traditional features of its motorcycles with advanced engineering technology and a commitment to continuous improvement. Harley-Davidson's manufacturing process incorporates computer-integrated manufacturing (CIM) techniques with state-of-the-art computerized numerical control (CNC) machining stations. These CNC stations are capable of performing dozens of machining operations and provide the operator with computerized data for statistical process control.

Harley-Davidson uses a statistical operator control (SOC) quality-improvement program to reduce parts variability to only a fraction of design tolerances. SOC ensures precise tolerances during each manufacturing step and predicts out-of-control components before they occur. Statistical operator control is especially important when dealing with complex components such as transmission gears.

The tolerances for Harley-Davidson cam gears are extremely close, and the machinery is especially complex. CNC machinery allows the manufacturing of gear centers time after time with tolerances as close as 0.0005 inch. Statistical operator control ensures the quality necessary to turn the famous Harley-Davidson Evolution engine shift after shift, mile after mile, year after year.

SOURCE: Based on *Harley-Davidson, Building Better Motorcycles the American Way*, video, Allyn and Bacon, 1991.

process capability studies be done during product design, and before contracts for new parts or products are entered into.

Figure 4.5(b) shows the situation where the natural control limits and specification limits are the same. This will result in a small number of defective items, the few that will fall outside the natural control limits due to random causes. For many companies, this is a reasonable quality goal. If the process distribution is normally distributed and the natural control limits are three standard deviations from the process average—that is, they are 3-sigma limits—then the probability between the limits is 0.9973. This is the probability of a good item. This means the area, or probability, outside the limits is 0.0027, which translates to 2.7 defects per thousand or 2,700 defects out of one million items. According to strict TQM philosophy, this is not an appropriate quality goal. As Evans and Lindsay point out in the book *The Management and Control of Quality*, this level of quality corresponding to 3-sigma limits is comparable to "at least 20,000 wrong drug prescriptions each year, more than 15,000 babies accidentally dropped by

In TQM, 3-sigma limits do not provide good quality.

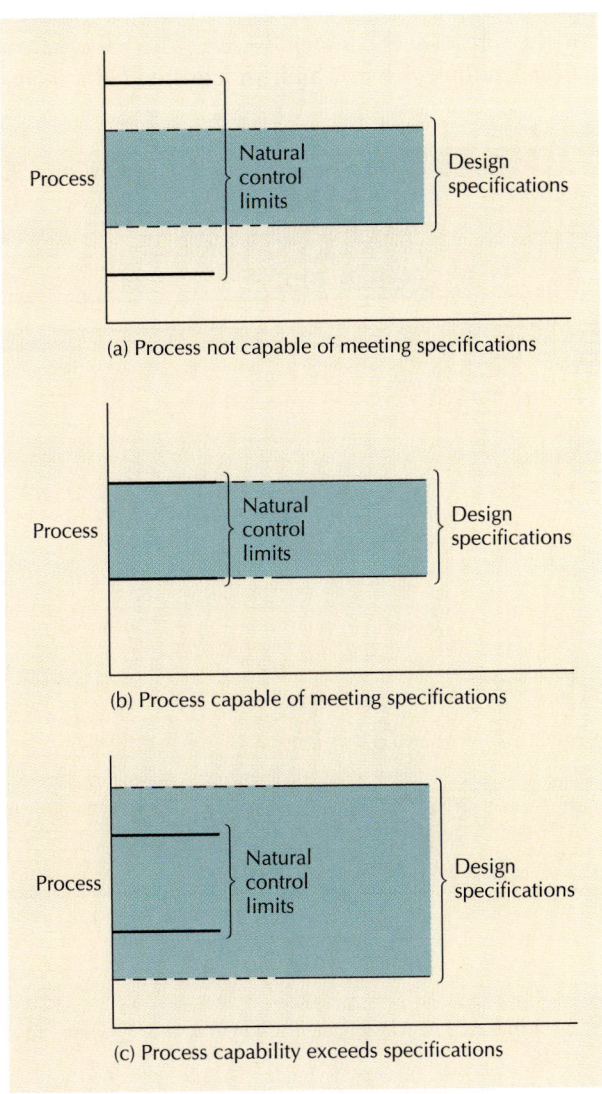

(a) Process not capable of meeting specifications

(b) Process capable of meeting specifications

(c) Process capability exceeds specifications

FIGURE 4.5   **Process Capability**

nurses and doctors each year, 500 incorrect surgical operations each week, and 2,000 lost pieces of mail each hour."[2]

As a result, a number of companies have adopted "6-sigma" quality. This represents product design specifications that are twice as large as the natural variations reflected in 3-sigma control limits. This type of situation, where the design specifications exceed the natural control limits, is shown graphically in Figure 4.5(c). Six-sigma limits correspond to 3.4 defective parts per million (very close to zero defects) instead of the 2.7 defective parts per thousand with 3-sigma limits. In fact, under Japanese leadership, the number of defective parts per million, or PPM, has become the international measure of quality, supplementing the old measure of a percentage of defective items.

> In 6-sigma quality, we have 3.4 defective PPM, or zero defects.

SPC with Excel and POM for Windows

A number of computer software and spreadsheet packages are available that perform statistical quality control analysis, including the development of process control charts. We will first demonstrate how to develop a statistical process control chart on the computer using the spreadsheet package, Excel.[3] The Excel spreadsheet in Exhibit 4.1 shows the data for Example 4.1 in which we constructed a *p*-chart to monitor the

Click on "Insert" then "Chart" to construct control chart

Sample Proportion defective

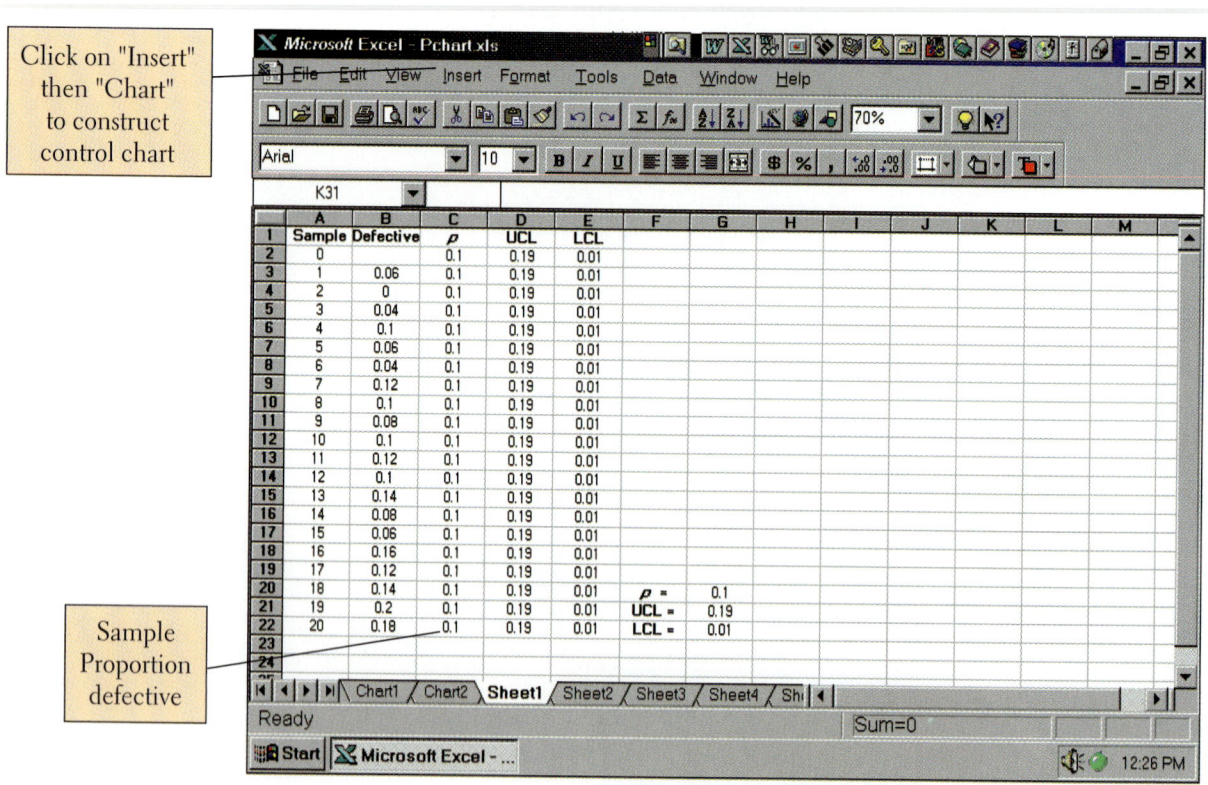

EXHIBIT 4.1

[2] J. R. Evans, and W. M. Lindsay, *The Management and Control of Quality*, 3d ed. (Minneapolis, Minn.: West, 1993), p. 602.

[3] The steps provided to develop a control chart may vary depending on the version of Excel being used.

production process for denim jeans at the Western Jeans Company. The values for UCL and LCL have been computed using formulas embedded in cells G21 and G22. To construct our control chart it is necessary to enter the values for the control chart mean ($\overline{p}$) and upper and lower control limits (UCL and LCL) in columns D and E for all 20 sample points. This will provide the data points to construct UCL and LCL lines on the control chart.

First, cover all cell values in columns A through E with the mouse and then click on "Insert" on the toolbar at the top of the worksheet. From the Insert window, click on "Chart," which will invoke a window for constructing a chart. Select the range of cells to include in constructing the chart (in this case, all the cells shown above). Click on "Next," which provides a menu of different chart types. Select "line" chart and go to the next window, which provides a menu for selecting the chart format. Select the format that connects the data points with a line and go to the next window, which shows the chart. Make sure you set the columns for the x-axis on "1," which should provide you with a facsimile of the control chart. The next window allows the axis to be labeled, and clicking on "Finish" brings up a full-screen version of the control chart. To clean up the chart, you can double click on the upper and lower control limit lines and the center line to invoke a window in which you can change the line intensity and color, and remove the data markers. To label the control limits lines, you can invoke the "Text Box" window from the toolbar. The resulting *p*-chart for Example 4.1 is shown in Exhibit 4.2.

POM for Windows[4] by Howard J. Weiss, published by Prentice Hall, is a software

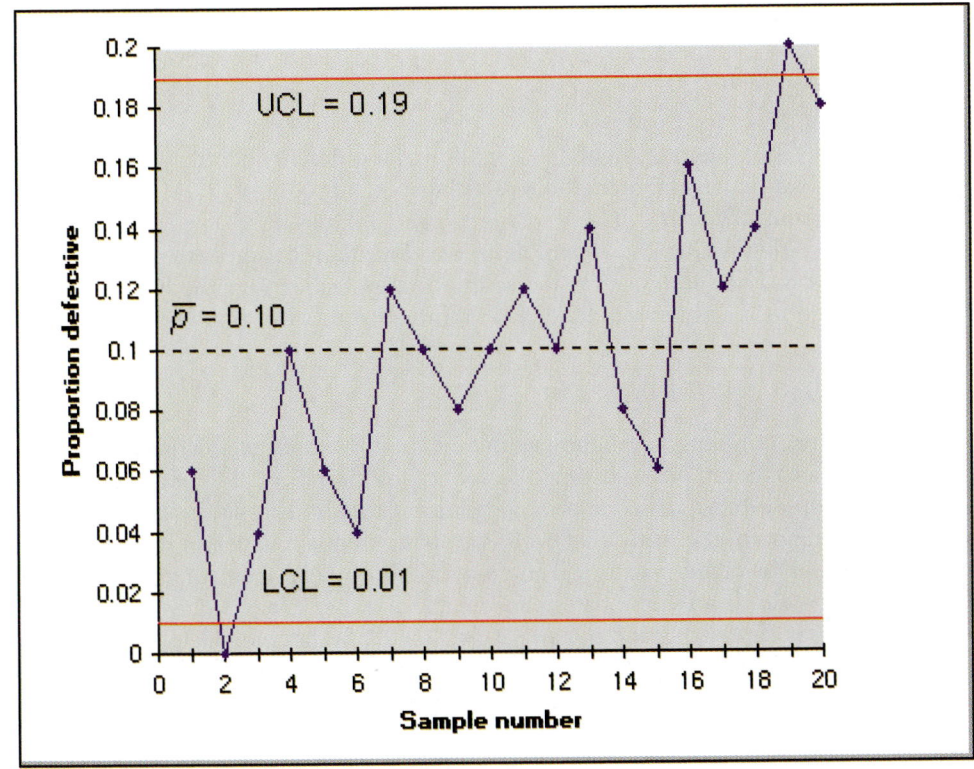

EXHIBIT 4.2

---

[4] Howard J. Weiss, *POM for Windows* (Upper Saddle River, N.J.: Prentice Hall, 1996).

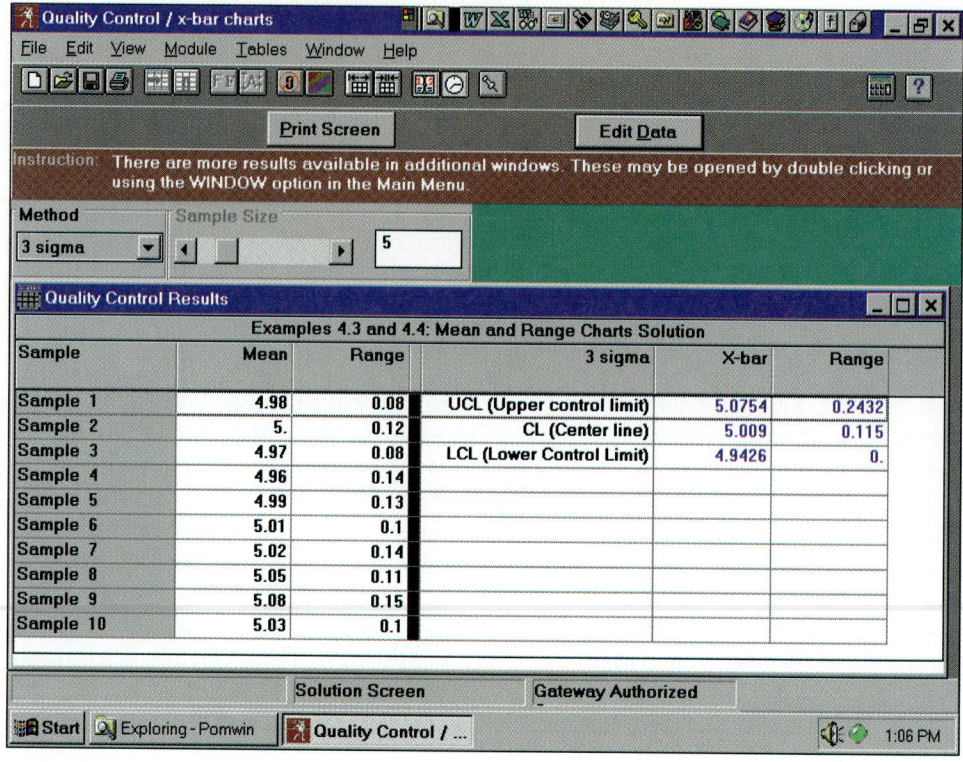

EXHIBIT 4.3

package for operations management. It has modules for different quantitative techniques used in operations management including statistical quality control. POM for Windows is used throughout this text.

POM for Windows has the capability to develop statistical process control charts for $\bar{p}$, $\bar{c}$, $\bar{x}$, and R. Exhibit 4.3 shows the solution output screen for the R-chart and $\bar{x}$-chart developed in Examples 4.3 and 4.4. Exhibit 4.4 shows the graph of the $\bar{x}$-chart.

Acceptance Sampling

In acceptance sampling, a random sample of the units produced is inspected, and the quality of this sample is assumed to reflect the overall quality of all items or a particular group of items, called a *lot*. Acceptance sampling is a statistical method, so if a sample is random, it ensures that each item has an equal chance of being selected and inspected. This enables statistical inferences to be made about the population—the lot—as a whole. If a sample has an acceptable number or percentage of defective items, the lot is accepted, but if it has an unacceptable number of defects, it is rejected.

Acceptance sampling is a historical approach to quality control based on the premise that some acceptable number of defective items will result from the production process. The producer and customer agree on the number of acceptable defects, normally measured as a percentage. However, the notion of a producer or customer agreeing to any defects at all is anathema to the adherents of TQM. The goal of companies that have adopted TQM is to achieve zero defects.

TQM companies do not even report the number of defective parts in terms of a percentage because the fraction of defective items they expect to produce is so small

Acceptance sampling is accepting or rejecting a production lot based on the number of defects in a sample.

Acceptance sampling is not consistent with the philosophy of TQM and zero defects.

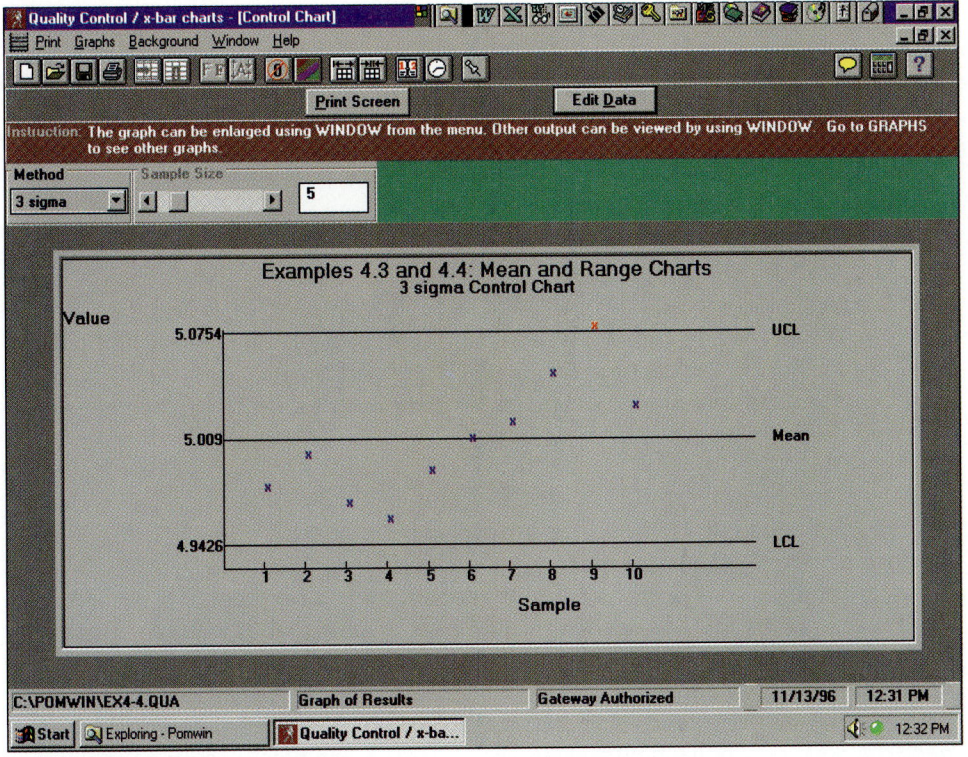

EXHIBIT 4.4

that a percentage is meaningless. As we noted previously, the international measure for reporting defects has become defective parts per million, or PPM.[5] For example, a defect rate of 2 percent, used in acceptance sampling, was once considered a high-quality standard: 20,000 defective parts per million! This is a totally unacceptable level of quality for TQM companies continuously trying to achieve zero defects. Three or four defects per million would be a more acceptable level of quality for these companies.

TQM companies measure defects as PPM, not percent.

Nevertheless, acceptance sampling is still used as a statistical quality control method by many companies who either have not yet adopted TQM or are required by customer demands or government regulations to use acceptance sampling. Since this method still has wide application, it is necessary for it to be studied.

When a sample is taken and inspected for quality, the items in the sample are being checked to see if they conform to some predetermined specification. A **sampling plan** establishes the guidelines for taking a sample and the criteria for making a decision regarding the quality of the lot from which was taken. The simplest form of sampling plan is a single-sample attribute plan.

A **sampling plan** provides the guidelines for accepting a lot.

Single-Sample Attribute Plan

A single-sample attribute plan has as its basis an attribute that can be evaluated with a simple, discrete decision, such as defective or not defective or good or bad. The plan includes the following elements:

Elements of a sampling plan—N, n, c, d

---

[5] B. B. Flynn, "Managing for Quality in the U.S. and in Japan," *Interfaces* 22, no. 5 (1992): 69–80.

N = the lot size

n = the sample size (selected randomly)

c = the acceptable number of defective items in a sample

d = the actual number of defective items in a sample

A single sample of size n is selected randomly from a larger lot, and each of the n items is inspected. If the sample contains $d \leq c$ defective items, the entire lot is accepted; if $d > c$, the lot is rejected.

Management must decide the values of these components that will result in the most effective sampling plan, as well as determine what constitutes an effective plan. These are design considerations. The design of a sampling plan includes both the structural components (n, the decision criteria, etc.) and performance measures. These performance measures include the *producer's* and *consumer's risks*, the *acceptable quality level*, and the *lot tolerance percent defective*.

Producer's and Consumer's Risks.

When a sample is drawn from a production lot and the items in the sample are inspected, management hopes that if the actual number of defective items exceeds the predetermined acceptable number of defective items ($d > c$) and the entire lot is rejected, then the sample results have accurately portrayed the quality of the entire lot. Management would hate to think that the sample results were not indicative of the overall quality of the lot and a lot that was actually acceptable was erroneously rejected and wasted. Conversely, management hopes that an actual bad lot of items is not erroneously accepted if $d \leq c$. An effective sampling plan attempts to minimize the possibility of wrongly rejecting good items or wrongly accepting bad items.

*The **AQL** is an acceptable proportion of defects in a lot to the consumer.*

When an acceptance-sampling plan is designed, management specifies a quality standard commonly referred to as the **acceptable quality level,** or **AQL.** The AQL reflects the consumer's willingness to accept lots with a small proportion of defective items. The AQL is the fraction of defective items in a lot that is deemed acceptable. For example, the AQL might be two defective items in a lot of 500, or 0.004. The AQL may be determined by management to be the level that is generally acceptable in the marketplace and will not result in a loss of customers. Or, it may be dictated by an individual customer as the quality level it will accept. In other words, the AQL is negotiated.

Producer's risk is the probability of rejecting a lot that has an AQL.

The probability of rejecting a production lot that has an acceptable quality level is referred to as the **producer's risk,** commonly designated by the Greek symbol α. In statistical jargon, α is the probability of committing a type I error.

*The **LTPD** is the maximum number of defective items a consumer will accept in a lot.*

Consumer's risk is the probability of accepting a lot in which the fraction of defective items exceeds LTPD.

α—producer's risk and β—consumer's risk

There will be instances in which the sample will not accurately reflect the quality of a lot and a lot that does not meet the AQL will pass on to the customer. Although the customer expects to receive some of these lots, there is a limit to the number of defective items the customer will accept. This upper limit is known as the **lot tolerance percent defective,** or **LTPD** (LTPD is also generally negotiated between the producer and consumer). The probability of accepting a lot in which the fraction of defective items exceeds the LTPD is referred to as the **consumer's risk,** designated by the Greek symbol β. In statistical jargon, β is the probability of committing a type II error.

In general, the customer would like for the quality of a lot to be as good or better than the AQL but willing to accept some lots with quality levels no worse than the LTPD. Frequently, sampling plans are designed with the producer's risk (α) about 5 percent and the consumer's risk (β) around 10 percent. Be careful not to confuse α with the AQL or β with the LTPD. If α equals 5 percent and β equals 10 percent, then management expects to reject lots that are as good or better than the AQL about 5 percent of the time, whereas the customer expects to accept lots that exceed the LTPD about 10 percent of the time.

The Operating Characteristic Curve

The performance measures we described in the previous section for a sampling plan can be represented graphically with an **operating characteristic curve (OC).** The OC curve measures the probability of accepting a lot for different quality (proportion defective) levels given a specific sample size (*n*) and acceptance level (*c*). Management can use such a graph to determine if their sampling plan meets the performance measures they have established for AQL, LTPD, *α*, and *β*. Thus, the OC curve indicates to management how effective the sampling plan is in distinguishing (more commonly known as *discriminating*) between good and bad lots. The shape of a typical OC curve for a single-sample plan is shown in Figure 4.6.

In Figure 4.6 the percentage defective in a lot is shown along the horizontal axis whereas the probability of accepting a lot is measured along the vertical axis. The exact shape and location of the curve is defined by the sample size (*n*) and acceptance level (*c*) for the sampling plan.

In Figure 4.6, if a lot has 3 percent defective items, the probability of accepting the lot (based on the sampling plan defined by the OC curve) is 0.95. If management defines the AQL as 3 percent, then the probability that an acceptable lot will be rejected (*α*) is 1 minus the probability of accepting a lot or $1 - 0.95 = 0.05$. If management is willing to accept lots with a percentage defective up to 15 percent (i.e., the LTPD), this

An **OC curve** is a graph that shows the probability of accepting a lot for different quality levels with a specific sampling plan.

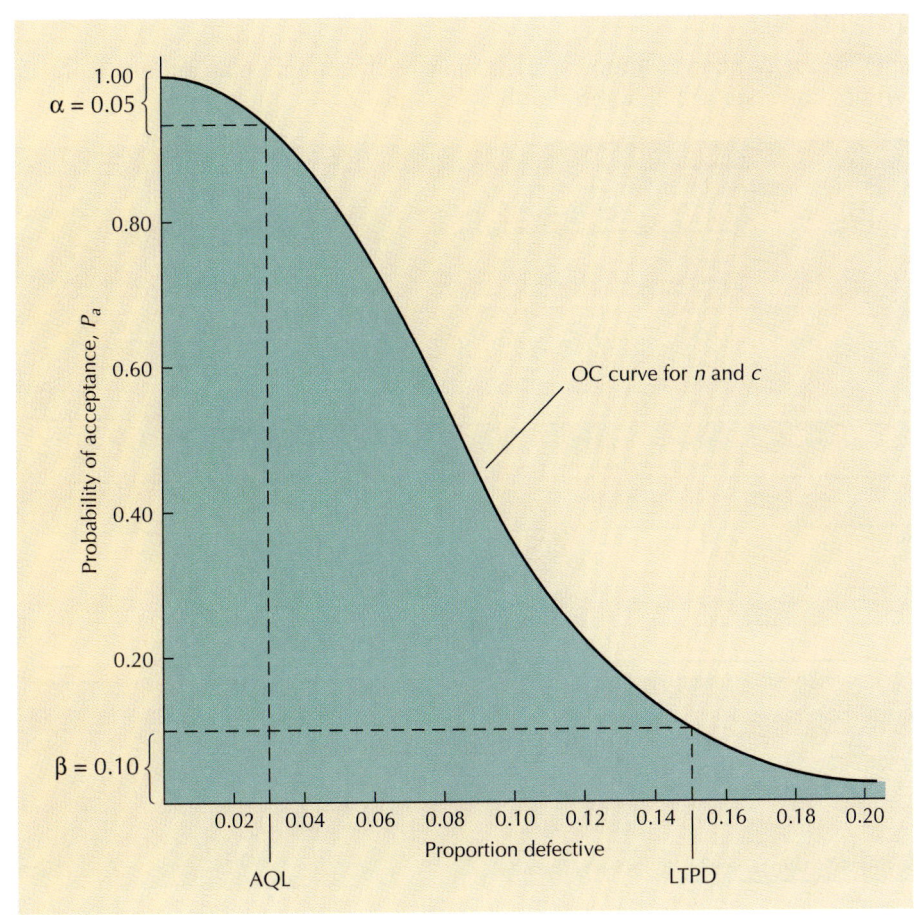

FIGURE 4.6 An Operating Characteristic Curve

corresponds to a probability that the lot will be accepted (β) of 0.10. A frequently used set of performance measures is $\alpha = 0.05$ and $\beta = 0.10$.

Developing a Sampling Plan with POM for Windows

Developing a sampling plan manually requires a tedious trial-and-error approach using statistical analysis. n and c are progressively changed until an approximate sampling plan is obtained that meets the specified performance measures. A more practical alternative is to use a computer software package like POM for Windows, that includes a module for acceptance sampling and the development of an OC curve. The following example demonstrates the use of POM for Windows to develop a sampling plan.

EXAMPLE 4·7

Developing a Sampling Plan and Operating Characteristic Curve

The Anderson Bottle and China (ABC) Company produces a style of solid-colored blue china exclusively for a large department store chain. The china includes a number of different items that are sold in open stock in the stores, including coffee mugs. Mugs are produced in lots of 10,000. Performance measures for the quality of mugs sent to the stores call for a producer's risk (α) of 0.05 with an AQL of 1 percent defective and a consumer's risk (β) of 0.10 with a LTPD of 5 percent defective. The ABC Company wants to know what size sample, n, to take and what the acceptance number, c, should be to achieve the performance measures called for in the sampling plan.

SOLUTION:

The POM for Windows solution screens showing the sample plan and operating characteristics curve are as follows in Exhibits 4.5 and 4.6.

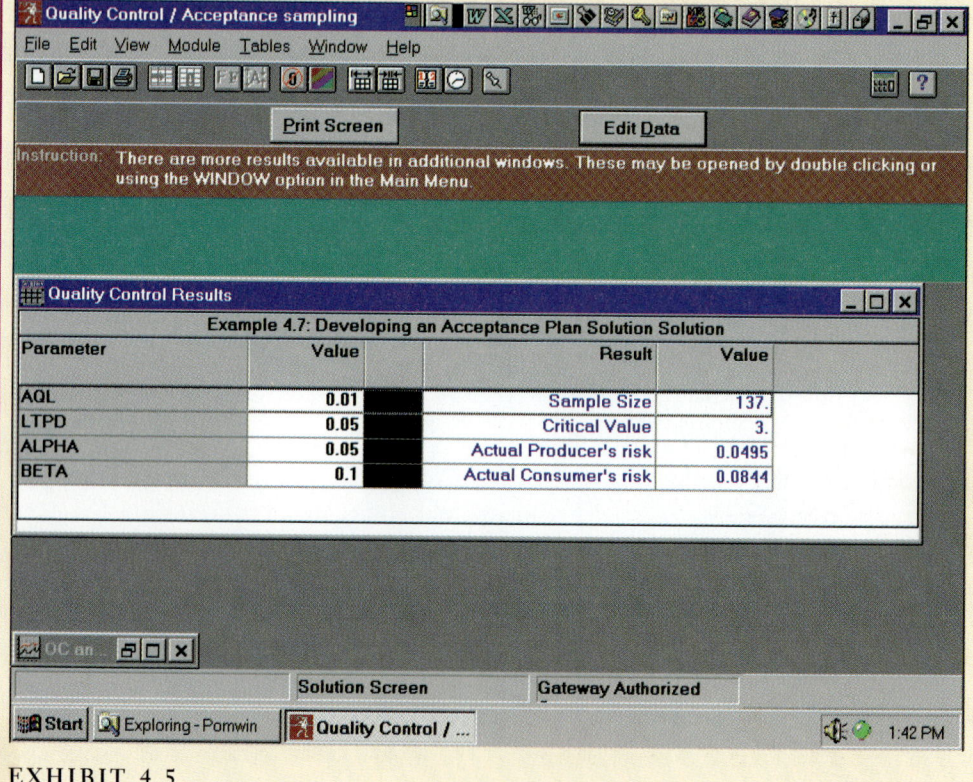

EXHIBIT 4.5

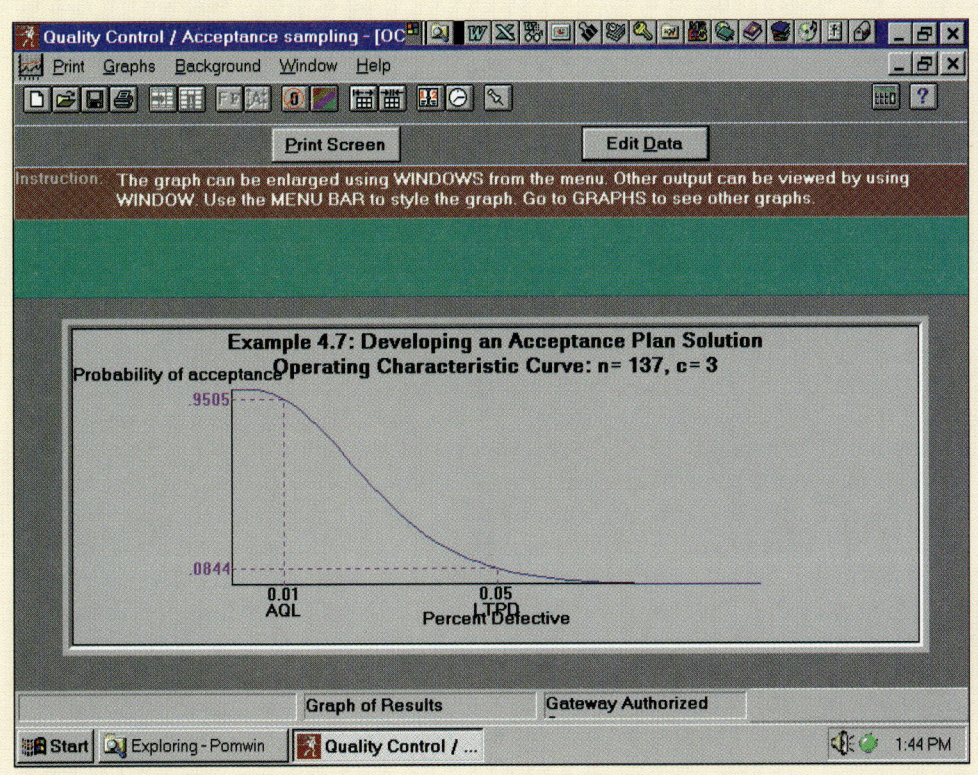

EXHIBIT 4.6

Sampling plans generally are estimates, and it is not always possible to develop a sampling plan with the exact parameters that were specified in advance. For example, notice in the solution screen that the actual consumer's risk (β) is .0844 instead of 0.10 as specified.

This sampling plan means the ABC Company will inspect samples of 137 mugs before they are sent to the store. If there are 3 or less defective mugs in the sample, the company will accept the production lot and send it on to the customer, but if the number of defects is greater than 3 the entire lot will be rejected. With this sampling plan either the company or the customer or both have decided that a proportion of 1 percent defective mugs (AQL) is acceptable. However, the customer has agreed to accept lots with up to 5 percent defects (LTPD). In other words, the customer would like for the quality of a lot to be contain no worse than 1 percent defects, but it is willing to accept some lots with no worse than 5 percent defects. The probability that a lot might be rejected given that it actually has an acceptable quality level of 1 percent or less is .0495, the actual producer's risk. The probability that a lot may be accepted given that it has more than 5 percent defects (the LTPD) is .0844, the actual consumer's risk.

Average Outgoing Quality

The shape of the operating characteristic curve shows that lots with a low percentage of defects have a high probability of being accepted, and lots with a high percentage of defects have a low probability of being accepted, as one would expect. For example, us-

Average outgoing quality (AOQ) is the expected number of defective items that will pass on to the customer with a sampling plan.

ing the OC curve for the sampling plan developed using POM for Windows in Exhibit 4.6 ($n = 137$, $c \leq 3$) for a percentage of defects = 0.01, the probability the lot will be accepted is approximately 0.95, whereas for 0.08, the probability of accepting a lot is very small. However, all lots, whether they are accepted or not, will pass on some defective items to the customer. The **average outgoing quality (AOQ)** is a measure of the expected number of defective items that will pass on to the customer with the sampling plan selected.

When a lot is rejected as a result of the sampling plan, it is assumed that it will be subjected to a complete inspection, and all defective items will be replaced with good ones. Also, even when a lot is accepted, the defective items found in the sample will be replaced. Thus, some portion of all the defective items contained in all the lots produced will be replaced before they are passed on to the customer. The remaining defective items that make their way to the customer are contained in lots that are accepted.

POM for Windows will also display the AOQ curve. The computer-generated curve corresponding to Exhibits 4.5 and 4.6 is shown in Exhibit 4.7.

The maximum point on the curve is referred to as the *average outgoing quality limit* (AOQL). For our example, the AOQL is approximately 1.4 percent defective when the actual proportion defective of the lot is 2 percent. This is the worst level of outgoing quality that management can expect on average, and if this level is acceptable, then the sampling plan is deemed acceptable. Notice that as the percentage of defects increases and the quality of the lots deteriorate, the AOQ improves. This occurs because as the quality of the lots becomes poorer, it is more likely that bad lots will be identified and rejected, and any defective items in these lots will be replaced with good ones.

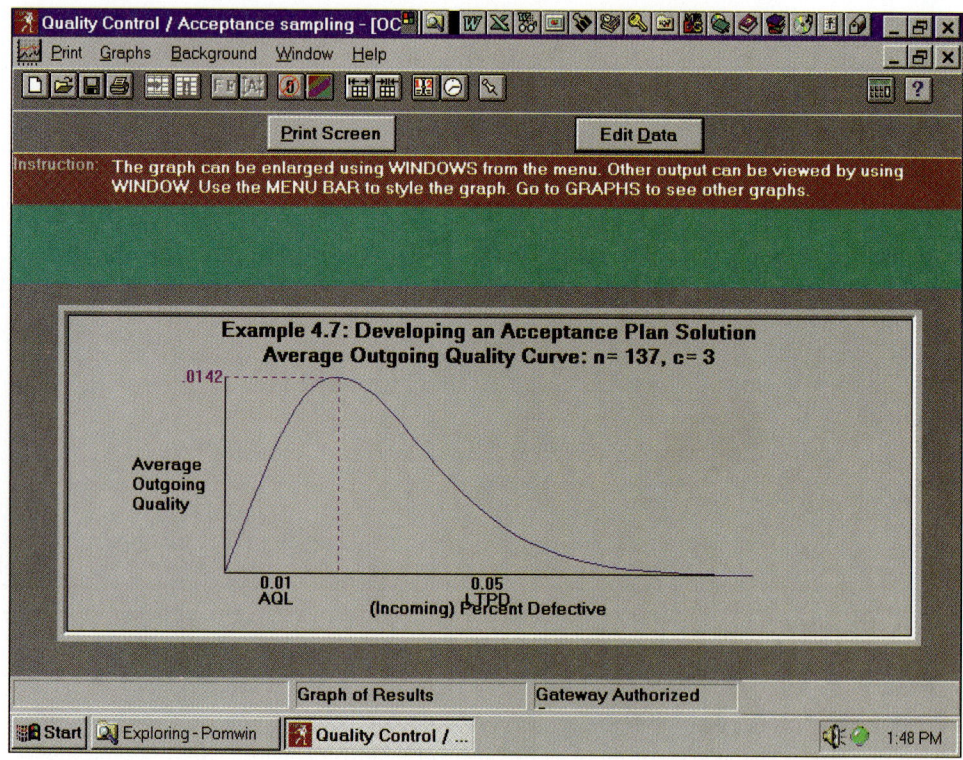

EXHIBIT 4.7

Double- and Multiple-Sampling Plans

In a *double-sampling plan*, a small sample is taken first; if the quality is very good, the lot is accepted, and if the sample is very poor, the lot is rejected. However, if the initial sample is inconclusive, a second sample is taken and the lot is either accepted or rejected based on the combined results of the two samples. The objective of such a sampling procedure is to save costs relative to a single-sampling plan. For very good or very bad lots, the smaller, less expensive sample will suffice and a larger, more expensive sample is avoided.

Double-sampling plans are less costly than single-sampling plans.

A *multiple-sampling plan*, also referred to as a sequential-sampling plan, generally employs the smallest sample size of any of the sampling plans we have discussed. In its most extreme form, individual items are inspected sequentially, and the decision to accept or reject a lot is based on the cumulative number of defective items. A multiple-sampling plan can result in small samples and, consequently, can be the least expensive of the sampling plans.

A *multiple-sampling plan* uses the smallest sample size of any sampling plan.

The steps of a multiple-sampling plan are similar to those for a double-sampling plan. An initial sample (which can be as small as one unit) is taken. If the number of defective items is less than or equal to a lower limit, the lot is accepted, whereas if it exceeds a specified upper limit, the lot is rejected. If the number of defective items falls in between the two limits, a second sample is obtained. The cumulative number of defects is then compared to an increased set of upper and lower limits, and the decision rule used in the first sample is applied. If the lot is neither accepted or rejected with the second sample, a third sample is taken, with the acceptance/rejection limits revised upward. These steps are repeated for subsequent samples until the lot is either accepted or rejected.

Choosing between single-, double-, or multiple-sampling plans is an economic decision. When the cost of obtaining a sample is very high compared to the inspection cost, a single-sampling plan is preferred. For example, if a petroleum company is analyzing soil samples from various locales around the globe, it is probably more economical to take a single, large sample in Brazil than to return for additional samples if the initial sample is inconclusive. Alternatively, if the cost of sampling is low relative to inspection costs, a double- or multiple-sampling play may be preferred. For example, if a winery is sampling bottles of wine, it may be more economical to use a sequential sampling plan, tasting individual bottles, than to test a large single sample containing a number of bottles, since each bottle sampled is, in effect, destroyed. In most cases where quality control requires destructive testing, the inspection costs are high compared to sampling costs.

Summary

Statistical process control is the main quantitative tool used in TQM. Companies that have adopted TQM provide extensive training in SPC methods for all employees at all levels. Japanese companies have provided such training for many years, whereas U.S. companies have only recently embraced the need for this type of comprehensive training. One of the reasons U.S. companies have cited for not training their workers in SPC methods was their general lack of mathematical knowledge and skills. However, U.S. companies are now beginning to follow the Japanese trend in upgrading hiring standards for employees and giving them more responsibility for controlling their own work activity. In this environment employees recognize the need for SPC for accomplishing a major part of their job, product quality. It is not surprising that when workers are provided with adequate training and understand what is expected of them, they have little difficulty using statistical process control methods.

Summary of Key Formulas

Control Limits for p-Charts

$$UCL = \bar{p} + z \sqrt{\frac{\bar{p}(1 - \bar{p})}{n}}$$

$$LCL = \bar{p} - z \sqrt{\frac{\bar{p}(1 - \bar{p})}{n}}$$

Control Limits for c-Charts

$$UCL = \bar{c} + z \sqrt{\bar{c}}$$

$$LCL = \bar{c} - z \sqrt{\bar{c}}$$

Control Limits for R-Charts

$$UCL = D_4\bar{R}$$

$$LCL = D_3\bar{R}$$

[handwritten] $\bar{R} = \dfrac{\text{difference between top + bottom of range}}{\text{\# of samples}}$

Control Limits for x̄-Charts

$$UCL = \bar{\bar{x}} + A_2\bar{R}$$

$$LCL = \bar{\bar{x}} - A_2\bar{R}$$

[handwritten] $\bar{\bar{x}}$ = average of samples in each range then average of averages

or

[handwritten] $\bar{R} =$

$$UCL = \bar{\bar{x}} + z\left(\frac{\sigma}{\sqrt{n}}\right)$$

$$LCL = \bar{\bar{x}} - z\left(\frac{\sigma}{\sqrt{n}}\right)$$

Summary of Key Terms

acceptable quality level (AQL): the fraction of defective items deemed acceptable in a lot.

acceptance sampling: a statistical procedure for taking a random sample in order to determine whether or not a lot should be accepted or rejected.

attribute: a product characteristic that can be evaluated with a discrete response such as yes or no, good or bad.

average outgoing quality (AOQ): the expected number of defective items that will pass on to the customer with a sampling plan.

c-chart: a control chart based on the number of defects in a sample.

consumer's risk (β): the probability of accepting a lot in which the fraction of defective items exceeds the most (LTPD) the consumer is willing to accept.

control chart: a graph that visually shows if a sample is within statistical limits for defective items.

control limits: the upper and lower bands of a control chart.

lot tolerance percent defective (LTPD): the maximum percentage defective items in a lot that the consumer will knowingly accept.

mean (x̄-) chart: a control chart based on the means of the samples taken.

operating characteristic (OC) curve: a graph that measures the probability of accepting a lot for different proportions of defective items.

p-chart: a control chart based on the proportion defective of the samples taken.

pattern test: a statistical test to determine if the observations within the limits of a control chart display a nonrandom pattern.

process capability: the capability of a process to accommodate design specifications of a product.

producer's risk (α): the probability of rejecting a lot that has an acceptable quality level (AQL).

range: the difference between the smallest and largest values in a sample.

range (R-) chart: a control chart based on the range (from the highest to the lowest values) of the samples taken.

run: a sequence of sample values that display the same tendency in a control chart.

sample: a portion of the items produced used for inspection.

sampling plan: the guidelines for taking a sample including the AQL, LTPD, n, and c.

statistical process control (SPC): a statistical procedure for monitoring the quality of the production process using control charts.

tolerances: product design specifications required by the customer.

variable measure: a product characteristic that can be measured, such as weight or length.

Solved Problems

1. p-Charts

Twenty samples of $n = 200$ were taken by an operator at a workstation in a production process. The number of defective items in each sample were recorded as follows.

Sample	Number of Defectives	p	Sample	Number of Defectives	p
1	12	0.060	11	16	0.080
2	18	0.090	12	15	0.075
3	10	0.050	13	13	0.065
4	15	0.075	14	16	0.080
5	16	0.080	15	18	0.090
6	19	0.095	16	17	0.085
7	17	0.085	17	18	0.090
8	12	0.060	18	20	0.100
9	11	0.055	19	21	0.105
10	14	0.070	20	22	0.110

Management wants to develop a *p*-chart using 3-sigma limits. Set up the *p*-chart and plot the observations to determine if the process was out of control at any point.

Solution:

Step 1. Compute $\bar{p}$:

$$\bar{p} = \frac{\text{total number of defectives}}{\text{total number of observations}} = \frac{320}{(20)(200)} = 0.08$$

Step 2. Determine the control limits:

$$\text{UCL} = \bar{p} + z \sqrt{\frac{\bar{p}(1 - p)}{n}} = 0.08 + (3.00)(0.019) = 0.137$$

$$\text{LCL} = \bar{p} - z \sqrt{\frac{\bar{p}(1 - p)}{n}} = 0.08 - (3.00)(0.019) = 0.023$$

Step 3. Construct the $\bar{p}$-chart with $\bar{p} = 0.08$, UCL = 0.137, and LCL = 0.023. The process does not appear to be out of control.

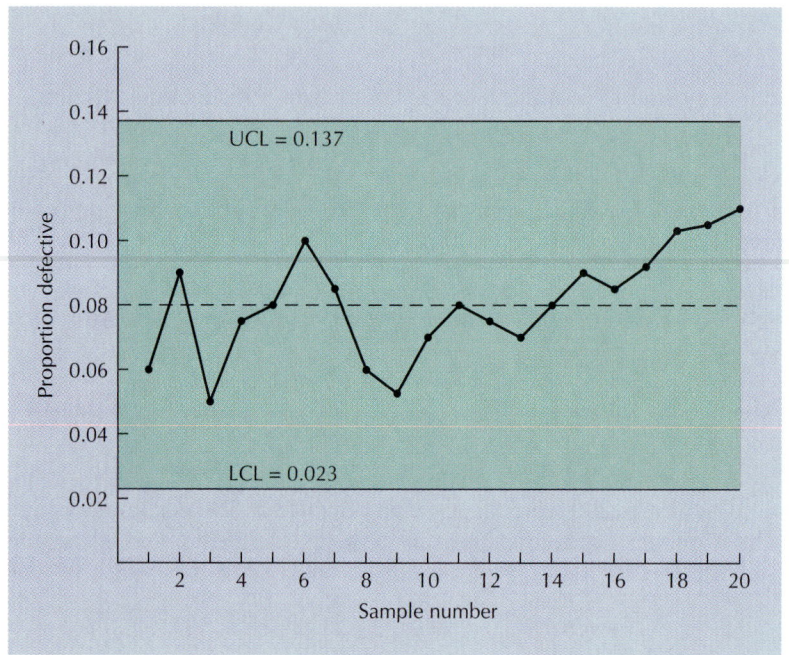

2. Pattern Tests

In the preceding problem, even though the control chart indicates that the process is in control, management wants to use pattern tests to further determine if the process is in control.

Solution:

Step 1. Determine the "up-and-down" and "above-and-below" runs and zone observations. Construct the zone boundaries on the control chart as follows.

Sample	Above/Below $\bar{p} = 0.08$	Up/Down	Zone	Sample	Above/Below $\bar{p} = 0.08$	Up/Down	Zone
1	B	—	B	11	A	U	C
2	A	U	C	12	B	D	C
3	B	D	B	13	B	D	C
4	B	U	C	14	A	U	C
5	A	U	C	15	A	U	C

(Continued)

Sample	Above/Below $\bar{p} = 0.08$	Up/Down	Zone	Sample	Above/Below $\bar{p} = 0.08$	Up/Down	Zone
6	A	U	B	16	A	D	C
7	A	D	C	17	A	U	C
8	B	D	B	18	A	U	B
9	B	D	B	19	A	U	B
10	B	U	C	20	A	U	B

(*Note:* Ties are broken in favor of A and U.)

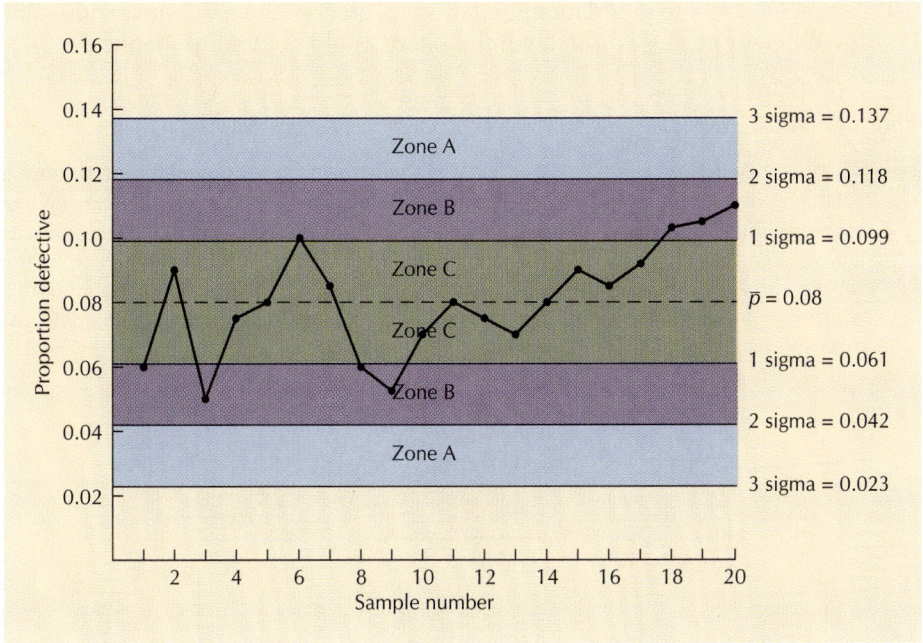

None of the pattern rules are violated, which suggests that no nonrandom patterns exist and that the process is in control.

Questions

4-1. What is the difference between acceptance sampling and process control?

4-2. Explain the difference between attribute control charts and variable control charts.

4-3. How are mean ($\bar{x}$-) and range (R-) charts used together?

4-4. Why are sample sizes for attributes necessarily larger than sample sizes for variables?

4-5. How is the sample size determined in a single-sample attribute plan?

4-6. What is the purpose of a pattern test?

4-7. What determines the width of the control limits in a process chart?

4-8. How does the acceptable quality level (AQL) relate to producer's risk (α) and the lot tolerance percent defective (LTPD) relate to consumer's risk (β)?

4-9. Under what circumstances should a c-chart be used instead of a p-chart?

4-10. What is the difference between tolerances and control limits?

4-11. Explain the difference between single-, double-, and multiple-sampling plans.

4-12. Why have companies traditionally used control charts with 3-sigma limits instead of 2-sigma limits?

4-13. Why is the traditional view of quality control reflected in the use of acceptance sampling unacceptable to adherents of TQM?

4-14. Under what circumstances is the total inspection of final products necessary?

4-15. Select three service companies or organizations you are familiar with and indicate how process control charts could be used in each.

4-16. Visit a local fast-food restaurant, retail store, grocery store, or bank, and identify the different processes which control charts could be used to monitor.

Problems

4-1. The Great North Woods Clothing Company sells specialty outdoor clothing through its catalog. A quality problem that generates customer complaints occurs when a warehouse employee fills an order with the wrong items. The company has decided to implement a process control plan by inspecting the ordered items after they have been obtained from the warehouse and before they have been packaged. The company has taken 30 samples (during a 30-day period), each for 100 orders, and recorded the number of "defective" orders in each sample, as follows.

Sample	Number of Defectives	Sample	Number of Defectives
1	12	16	6
2	14	17	3
3	10	18	7
4	16	19	10
5	18	20	14
6	19	21	18
7	14	22	22
8	20	23	26
9	18	24	20
10	17	25	24
11	9	26	18
12	11	27	19
13	14	28	20
14	12	29	17
15	7	30	18

Construct a p-chart for the company that describes 99.74 percent (3σ) of the random variation in the process, and indicate if the process seems to be out of control at any time.

4-2. The Road King Tire Company in Birmingham wants to monitor the quality of the tires it manufactures in its production process. Each day the company quality control manager takes a sample of 100 tires, tests them, and determines the number of defective tires. The results of 20 samples have been recorded as follows.

Sample	Number of Defectives	Sample	Number of Defectives
1	14	11	18
2	12	12	10
3	9	13	19
4	10	14	20
5	11	15	17
6	7	16	18
7	8	17	18
8	14	18	22
9	16	19	24
10	17	20	23

$$\bar{p} = \frac{\text{total defectives}}{\text{total sample}}$$

Construct a p-chart for this process using 2σ limits, and describe the variation in the process.

4-3. The Commonwealth Banking Corporation issues a national credit card through its various bank branches in five southeastern states. The bank credit card business is highly competitive and interest rates do not vary substantially, so the company decided to attempt to retain its customers by improving customer service through a reduction in billing errors. The credit card division monitored its billing department process by taking daily samples of 200 customer bills for 30 days and checking their accuracy. The sample results are as follows.

Sample	Number of Defectives	Sample	Number of Defectives	Sample	Number of Defectives
1	7	11	9	21	13
2	12	12	6	22	9
3	9	13	3	23	10
4	6	14	2	24	12
5	5	15	8	25	15
6	8	16	10	26	14
7	10	17	12	27	16
8	11	18	14	28	12
9	14	19	16	29	15
10	10	20	15	30	14

Develop a p-chart for the billing process using 3σ control limits and indicate if the process is out of control.

4-4. In the assembly process for automobile engines, at one stage in the process a gasket is placed between the two sections of the engine block before they are joined. If the gasket is damaged (bent, crimped, etc.), oil can leak from the cylinder chambers and foul the spark plugs, in which case the entire engine has to be disassembled and a new gasket inserted. The company wants to develop a p-chart with 2σ limits to monitor the quality of the gaskets prior to the assembly stage. Historically, 2 percent of the gaskets have been defective, and management does not want the upper control limit to exceed 3 percent defective. What sample size will be required to achieve this control chart?

4-5. The Great Northwoods Clothing Company is a mail-order company that processes thousands of mail and telephone orders each week. They have a customer service number to handle customer order problems, inquiries, and complaints. The company wants to monitor the number of customer calls that can be classified as complaints. The total number of complaint calls the customer service department has received for each of the last 30 weekdays are shown as follows.

Day	Complaint Calls	Day	Complaint Calls	Day	Complaint Calls
1	27	11	26	21	31
2	15	12	42	22	14
3	38	13	40	23	18
4	41	14	35	24	26
5	19	15	25	25	27
6	23	16	19	26	35
7	21	17	12	27	20
8	16	18	17	28	12
9	33	19	18	29	16
10	35	20	26	30	15

a. Construct a *c*-chart for this process with 3σ control limits, and indicate if the process was out of control at any time.

b. What nonrandom (i.e., assignable) causes might result in the process being out of control?

4-6. One of the stages in the process of making denim cloth at the Southern Mills Company is to spin cotton yarn onto spindles for subsequent use in the weaving process. Occasionally the yarn breaks during the spinning process, and an operator ties it back together. Some number of breaks is considered normal; however, too many breaks may mean that the yarn is of poor quality. In order to monitor this process, the quality control manager randomly selects a spinning machine each hour and checks the number of breaks during a 15-minute period. Following is a summary of the observations for the past 20 hours.

Sample	Number of Breaks	Sample	Number of Breaks
1	3	11	3
2	2	12	4
3	4	13	6
4	1	14	7
5	5	15	8
6	3	16	6
7	2	17	5
8	4	18	7
9	0	19	8
10	2	20	6

Construct a *c*-chart using 3σ limits for this process and indicate if the process was out of control at any time.

4-7. The Xecko Film Company manufactures color photographic film. The film is produced in large rolls of various lengths before it is cut and packaged as the smaller rolls purchased in retail stores. The company wants to monitor the quality of these rolls of film using a *c*-chart. Twenty-four rolls have been inspected at random, and the numbers of defects per roll are as follows.

Roll	Number of Defects	Roll	Number of Defects	Roll	Number of Defects
1	12	9	8	17	7
2	8	10	6	18	11
3	5	11	15	19	9
4	7	12	10	20	13
5	14	13	12	21	17
6	9	14	13	22	16
7	10	15	9	23	12
8	11	16	8	24	14

Construct a c-chart with 2σ limits for this process and indicate if the process was out of control at any time.

4-8. The Stryker Baseball Bat Company manufactures wooden and aluminum baseball bats at its plant in New England. Wooden bats produced for the mass market are turned on a lathe, where a piece of wood is shaped into a bat with a handle and barrel. The bat is cut to its specified length and then finished in subsequent processes. Once bats are cut to length, it is difficult to rework them into a different style, so it is important to catch defects before this step. As such, bats are inspected at this stage of the process. A specific style of wooden bat has a mean barrel circumference of 9 inches at its thickest point with a standard deviation of 0.6 inches. (The process variability is assumed to be normally distributed.)

a. Construct a mean control chart for this process for 3σ limits and a sample size of 10 bats.
b. Three samples are taken, and they have average bat diameters of 9.05 inches, 9.10 inches, and 9.08 inches. Is the process in control?
c. What effect will increasing the sample size to 20 bats have on the control charts? Will the conclusions reached in part (b) change for this sample size?

4-9. A machine at the Pacific Fruit Company fills boxes with raisins. The labeled weight of the boxes is 10 ounces. The company wants to construct an R-chart to monitor the filling process and make sure the box weights are in control. The quality control department for the company sampled five boxes every two hours for three consecutive working days. The sample observations are as follows.

Sample	Box Weights (oz)					Sample	Box Weights (oz)				
1	9.06	9.13	8.97	8.85	8.46	7	9.00	9.21	9.05	9.23	8.78
2	8.52	8.61	9.09	9.21	8.95	8	9.15	9.20	9.23	9.15	9.06
3	9.35	8.95	9.20	9.03	8.42	9	8.98	8.90	8.81	9.05	9.13
4	9.17	9.21	9.05	9.01	9.53	10	9.03	9.10	9.26	9.46	8.47
5	9.21	8.87	8.71	9.05	9.35	11	9.53	9.02	9.11	8.88	8.92
6	8.74	8.35	8.50	9.06	8.89	12	8.95	9.10	9.00	9.06	8.95

a. Construct an R-chart from these data with 3σ control limits, and plot the sample range values.
b. What does the R-chart suggest about the process variability?

4-10. The City Square Grocery and Meat Market has a large meat locker in which a constant temperature of approximately 40°F should be maintained. The market manager has decided to construct an R-chart to monitor the temperature inside the locker. The manager had one of the market employees take sample temperature readings randomly five times each day for 20 days in order to gather data for the control chart. Following are the temperature sample observations.

Sample	Temperature (°F)					Sample	Temperature (°F)				
1	46.3	48.1	42.5	43.1	39.6	11	42.6	43.5	35.4	36.1	38.2
2	41.2	40.5	37.8	36.5	42.3	12	40.5	40.4	39.1	37.2	41.6
3	40.1	41.3	34.5	33.2	36.7	13	45.3	42.0	43.1	44.7	39.5
4	42.3	44.1	39.5	37.7	38.6	14	36.4	37.5	36.2	38.9	40.1
5	35.2	38.1	40.5	39.1	42.3	15	40.5	34.3	36.2	35.1	36.8
6	40.6	41.7	38.6	43.5	44.6	16	39.5	38.2	37.6	34.1	38.7
7	33.2	38.6	41.5	40.7	43.1	17	37.6	40.6	40.3	39.7	41.2
8	41.8	40.0	41.6	40.7	39.3	18	41.0	34.3	39.1	45.2	43.7
9	42.4	41.6	40.8	40.9	42.3	19	40.9	42.3	37.6	35.4	34.8
10	44.7	36.5	37.3	35.3	41.1	20	37.6	39.2	39.3	41.2	37.6

a. Construct an R-chart based on these data using 3σ limits, and plot the 20 sample range values.

b. Does it appear that the temperature is in control according to the criteria establishment by management?

4-11. The Oceanside Apparel Company manufactures expensive, polo-style men's and women's short-sleeve knit shirts at its plant in Jamaica. The production process requires that material be cut into large patterned squares by operators, which are then sewn together at another stage of the process. If the squares are not of a correct length, the final shirt will be either too large or too small. In order to monitor the cutting process, management takes a sample of four squares of cloth every other hour and measures the length. The length of a cloth square should be 36 inches, and historically, the company has found the length to vary across an acceptable average range of 2 inches.

a. Construct an R-chart for the cutting process using 3σ limits.

b. The company has taken ten additional samples with the following results.

Sample	Measurements (in.)			
1	37.3	36.5	38.2	36.1
2	33.4	35.8	37.9	36.2
3	32.1	34.8	39.1	35.3
4	36.1	37.2	36.7	34.2
5	35.1	38.6	37.2	33.6
6	33.4	34.5	36.7	32.4
7	38.1	39.2	35.3	32.7
8	35.4	36.2	36.3	34.3
9	37.1	39.4	38.1	36.2
10	32.1	34.0	35.6	36.1

Plot the new sample data on the control chart constructed in part (a) and comment on the process variability.

4-12. For the sample data provided in Problem 4-9, construct an $\bar{x}$-chart in conjunction with the R-chart, plot the sample observations, and, using both $\bar{x}$- and R-charts, comment on the process control.

4-13. For the sample data provided in Problem 4-10, construct an $\bar{x}$-chart in conjunction with the R-chart, plot the sample observations, and, using both $\bar{x}$- and R-charts, comment on the process control.

4-14. Using the process information provided in Problem 4-11, construct an $\bar{x}$-chart in conjunction with the R-chart, plot the sample observations provided in part (b), and, using both the $\bar{x}$- and R-charts, comment on the process control.

4-15. Use pattern tests to determine if the sample observations used in the $\bar{x}$-chart in Problem 4-12 reflect any nonrandom patterns.

4-16. Use pattern tests to determine if the sample observations in Problem 4-5 reflect any nonrandom patterns.

4-17. Use pattern tests to determine if the sample observations in Problem 4-10 reflect any non-random patterns.

4-18. Use pattern tests to determine if the sample observations used in the $\bar{x}$-chart in Problem 4-13 reflect any nonrandom patterns.

4-19. Use pattern tests to determine if the sample observations used in the $\bar{p}$-chart in Problem 4-1 reflect any nonrandom patterns.

4-20. Dave's Restaurant is a chain that employs independent evaluators to visit its restaurants as customers and assess the quality of the service by filling out a questionnaire. The company evaluates restaurants in two categories, products (the food) and service (promptness, order accuracy, courtesy, friendliness, etc.). The evaluator considers not only his or her order experiences but also observations throughout the restaurant. Following are the results of an evaluator's 20 visits to one particular restaurant during a month showing the number of "defects" noted in the service category.

Sample	Number of Defects	Sample	Number of Defects
1	4	11	9
2	6	12	4
3	10	13	3
4	3	14	4
5	6	15	13
6	7	16	9
7	8	17	10
8	5	18	11
9	2	19	15
10	5	20	12

Construct a control chart for this restaurant using 3σ limits to monitor quality service and indicate if the process is in control.

4-21. The National Bank of Whitesville is concerned with complaints from customers about its drive-through window operation. Customers complain that it sometimes takes too long to be served and since there are often cars in front and back of a customer, they cannot leave if the service is taking a long time. To correct this problem the bank installed an intercom system so the drive-through window teller can call for assistance if the line backs up or a customer has an unusually long transaction. The bank's objective is an average customer's waiting and service time of approximately three minutes. The bank's operations manager wants to monitor the new drive-through window system with SPC. The manager has timed five customers' waiting and service times at random for twelve days as follows.

Sample	Observation Times (min)				
	1	2	3	4	5
1	3.05	6.27	1.35	2.56	1.05
2	7.21	1.50	2.66	3.45	3.78
3	3.12	5.11	1.37	5.20	2.65
4	2.96	3.81	4.15	5.01	2.15
5	3.25	3.11	1.63	1.29	3.74
6	2.47	2.98	2.15	1.88	4.95
7	6.05	2.03	3.17	3.18	2.34
8	1.87	2.65	1.98	2.74	3.63
9	3.33	4.15	8.06	2.98	3.05
10	2.61	2.15	3.80	3.05	3.16
11	3.52	5.66	1.18	3.45	2.07
12	3.18	7.73	2.06	1.15	3.11

Develop an $\bar{x}$-chart to be used in conjunction with an *R*-chart to monitor this drive-through window process and indicate if the process is in control using this chart.

4.22 The Great Outdoors Clothing Company is a mail-order catalog operation. Whenever a customer returns an item for a refund, credit, or exchange, he or she is asked to complete a return form. For each item returned the customer is asked to insert a code indicating the reason for the return. The company does not consider the returns related to style, size, or "feel" of the material to be a defect. However, it does consider returns because the item "was not as described in the catalog," "didn't look like what was in the catalog," or "the color was different than shown in the catalog," to be defects in the catalog. The company has randomly checked 100 customer return forms for 20 days and collected the following data for catalog defects.

Sample	Number of Catalog Defects	Sample	Number of Catalog Defects
1	18	11	54
2	26	12	37
3	43	13	26
4	27	14	29
5	14	15	37
6	36	16	65
7	42	17	54
8	28	18	31
9	61	19	28
10	37	20	25

Construct a control chart using 3σ limits to monitor catalog defects and indicate if the process is in control. Use pattern tests to verify an in-control situation.

4-23. The dean of the College of Business at State University wants to monitor the quality of the work performed by the college's secretarial staff. Each completed assignment is returned to the faculty with a check sheet on which the faculty member is asked to list the errors made on the assignment. The assistant dean has randomly collected the following set of observations from 20 three-day work periods.

Sample	Number of Errors	Sample	Number of Errors
1	17	11	12
2	9	12	17
3	12	13	16
4	15	14	23
5	26	15	24
6	11	16	18
7	18	17	14
8	15	18	12
9	21	19	20
10	10	20	16

Construct a process control chart for secretarial work quality using 3σ limits and determine if the process was out of control at any point. Use pattern tests to determine if any nonrandom patterns exist.

4-24. Martha's Wonderful Cookie Company makes a special super chocolate-chip peanut butter cookie. The company would like the cookies to average approximately eight chocolate chips apiece. Too few or too many chips distorts the desired cookie taste. Twenty samples of five cookies each during a week have been taken and the chocolate chips counted. The sample observations are as follows.

Sample	Chips per Cookie					Sample	Chips per Cookie				
1	7	6	9	8	5	11	5	5	9	8	8
2	7	7	8	8	10	12	6	8	8	5	9
3	5	5	7	6	8	13	7	3	7	8	8
4	4	5	9	9	7	14	6	9	9	8	8
5	8	8	5	10	8	15	10	8	7	8	6
6	7	6	9	8	4	16	5	6	9	9	7
7	9	8	10	8	8	17	6	10	10	7	3
8	7	6	5	4	5	18	11	4	6	8	8
9	9	10	8	9	7	19	9	5	5	7	7
10	11	9	9	10	6	20	8	8	6	7	3

Construct an $\bar{x}$-chart in conjunction with an R-chart using 3σ limits for this data and comment on the cookie production process.

4-25. Thirty patients who check out of the White Creek County Regional Hospital each week are asked to complete a questionnaire about hospital service. Since patients don't feel well when they are in the hospital, they typically are very critical of the service. The number of patients who indicated dissatisfaction of any kind with the service for each 30-patient sample for a 16-week period as follows.

Sample	Number of Dissatisfied Patients	Sample	Number of Dissatisfied Patients
1	6	9	6
2	3	10	6
3	10	11	5
4	7	12	3
5	2	13	2
6	9	14	8
7	11	15	12
8	7	16	8

Construct a control chart to monitor customer satisfaction at the hospital using 3σ limits and determine if the process is in control.

4-26. An important aspect of customer service and satisfaction at the Big Country theme park is the maintenance of the rest rooms throughout the park. Customers expect the rest rooms to be clean; odorless; well-stocked with soap, paper towels, and toilet paper; and to have a comfortable temperature. In order to maintain quality, park quality control inspectors randomly inspect rest rooms daily (during the day and evening) and record the number of defects (incidences of poor maintenance). The goal of park management is approximately 10 defects per inspection period. Following is a summary of the observations taken by these inspectors for 20 consecutive inspection periods.

Sample	Number of Defects	Sample	Number of Defects
1	7	11	14
2	14	12	10
3	6	13	11
4	9	14	12
5	12	15	9
6	3	16	13
7	11	17	7
8	7	18	15
9	7	19	11
10	8	20	16

Construct the appropriate control chart for this maintenance process using 3σ limits and indicate if the process was out of control at any time. If the process is in control, use pattern tests to determine if any nonrandom patterns exist.

4.27. The Great Outdoors Clothing Company, a mail-order catalog operation, contracts with the Federal Parcel Service to deliver all of its orders to customers. As such, Great Outdoors considers Federal Parcel to be part of its TQM program. Great Outdoors tells customers it will deliver their order (if the items are in stock) within three business days anywhere in the continental United States. Such a commitment requires Great Outdoors to process orders rapidly and Federal Parcel to pick them up and deliver them rapidly. Great Outdoors has tracked the delivery time for five randomly selected orders for twelve samples during a two-week period as follows.

Sample	Delivery Time (days)					Sample	Delivery Time (days)				
1	2	3	3	4	3	7	2	3	3	2	1
2	5	3	6	2	1	8	1	1	3	1	2
3	4	3	3	2	2	9	6	3	3	3	3
4	6	1	5	3	3	10	6	7	5	5	6
5	2	4	1	4	4	11	6	1	1	3	2
6	5	1	3	3	3	12	5	5	3	1	3

Construct an $\bar{x}$-chart in conjunction with an R-chart using 3σ limits for the delivery process and comment on the process in terms of the company's objective.

4.28. The Great Lakes Company, a grocery store chain, purchases apples from a produce distributor in Virginia. The grocery company has an agreement with the distributor that it desires shipments of 10,000 apples with no more than 2 percent defectives (i.e., severely blemished apples), although it will accept shipments with up to a maximum of 8 percent defective. The probability of rejecting a good lot is set at 0.05 whereas the probability of accepting a bad quality lot is 0.10.

a. Determine a sampling plan that will approximately achieve these quality performance criteria, and the operating characteristics curve.

b. Determine the average outgoing quality limit for this plan.

4.29. The Academic House Publishing Company sends out the textbooks it publishes to an independent book binder. When the bound books come back, they are inspected for defective bindings (warped boards, ripples, cuts, poor adhesion, etc.). The publishing company has an acceptable quality level of 4 percent defectives but will tolerate lots of up to

10 percent defective. What (approximate) sample size and acceptance level would result in a probability of 0.05 that a good lot will be rejected and a probability of 0.10 that a bad lot will be accepted?

4.30. The Metro Packaging Company in Richmond produces clear plastic bottles for the Kooler Cola Company, a soft-drink manufacturer. Metro inspects each lot of 5,000 bottles before they are shipped to the Kooler Company. The soft-drink company has specified an acceptable quality level of 0.06 and a lot tolerance percent defective of 0.12. Metro currently has a sampling plan with $n = 150$ and $c \leq 4$. The two companies have recently agreed that the sampling plan should have a producer's risk of 0.05 and a consumer's risk of 0.10. Will the current sampling plan used by Metro achieve these levels of α and β?

CASE PROBLEM

Quality Control at Rainwater Brewery

Bob Raines and Megan Waters own and operate the Rainwater Brewery, a micro-brewery that grew out of their shared hobby of making home-brew. The brewery is located in Whitesville, the home of State University where Bob and Megan went to college.

Whitesville has a number of bars and restaurants that are patronized by students at State and the local resident population. In fact, Whitesville has the highest per capita beer consumption in the state. In setting up their small brewery, Bob and Megan decided that they would target their sales toward individuals who would pick up their orders directly from the brewery and toward restaurants and bars, where they would deliver orders on a daily or weekly basis.

The brewery process essentially occurs in three stages. First, the mixture is cooked in a vat according to a recipe; then it is placed in a stainless-steel container, where it is fermented for several weeks. During the fermentation process the specific gravity, temperature, and pH need to be monitored on a daily basis. The specific gravity starts out at about 1.006 to 1.008 and decreases to around 1.002, and the temperature must be between 50° and 60°F. After the brew ferments, it is filtered into another stain-

less-steel pressurized container, where it is carbonated and the beer ages for about a week (with the temperature monitored), after which it is bottled and is ready for distribution. Megan and Bob brew a batch of beer each day, which will result in about 1,000 bottles for distribution after the approximately three-week fermentation and aging process.

In the process of setting up their brewery, Megan and Bob agreed they had already developed a proven product with a taste that was appealing, so the most important factor in the success of their new venture would be maintaining high quality. Thus, they spent a lot of time discussing what kind of quality control techniques they should employ. They agreed that the chance of brewing a "bad," or "spoiled," batch of beer was extremely remote, plus they really could not financially afford to reject a whole batch of 1,000 bottles of beer if the taste or color was a little "off" the norm. So they felt as if they needed to focus more on process control methods to identify quality problems that would enable them to adjust their equipment, recipe, or process parameters rather than to use some type of acceptance sampling plan.

Describe the different quality control methods that Rainwater Brewery might use to ensure good-quality beer and how these methods might fit into an overall TQM program.

Quality Control at Grass, Unlimited

Mark Sumansky owns and manages the Grass, Unlimited, lawn-care service in Middleton. His customers include individual homeowners and businesses that subscribe to his service during the winter months for lawn care beginning in the spring and ending in the fall with leaf raking and disposal. Thus, when he begins his service in April he generally has a full list of customers and does not take on additional customers unless he has an opening. However, if he loses a customer anytime after the first of June, it is difficult to find new customers, since most people make lawn-service arrangements for the entire summer.

Mark employs five crews, with between three to five workers each, to cut grass during the spring and summer months. A crew normally works 10-hour days and can average cutting about 25 normal-size lawns of less than a half-acre each day. A crew will normally have one heavy-duty, wide-cut riding mower, a regular power mower, and trimming equipment. When a crew descends on a lawn, the normal procedure is for one person to mow the main part of the lawn with the riding mower, one or two people to trim, and one person to use the smaller mower to cut areas the riding mower cannot reach. Crews move very fast, and they can often cut a lawn in 15 minutes.

Unfortunately, although speed is an essential component in the profitability of Grass, Unlimited, it can also contribute to quality problems. In his or her haste, a mower might cut flowers, shrubs, or border plants, nick and scrape trees, "skin" spots on the lawn creating bare spots, trim too close, scrape house paint, cut or disfigure house trim, and destroy toys and lawn furniture, among other things. When these problems occur on a too-frequent basis, a customer cancels service, and Mark has a difficult time getting a replacement customer. In addition, he gets most of his subscriptions based on word-of-mouth recommendations and retention of previous customers who are satisfied with his service. As such, quality is a very important factor in his business.

In order to improve the quality of his lawn-care service, Mark has decided to use a process control chart to monitor defects. He has hired Lisa Anderson to follow the teams and check lawns for defects after the mowers have left. A defect is any abnormal or abusive condition created by the crew, including those items just mentioned. It is not possible for Lisa to inspect the more than 100 lawns the service cuts daily, so she randomly picks a sample of 20 lawns each day and counts the number of defects she sees at each lawn. She also makes a note of each defect, so that if there is a problem, the cause can easily be determined. In most cases the defects are caused by haste, but some defects can be caused by faulty equipment or by a crew member using a poor technique or not being attentive.

Over a three-day period Lisa accumulated the following data on defects.

DAY 1		DAY 2		DAY 3	
Sample	Number of Defects	Sample	Number of Defects	Sample	Number of Defects
1	6	1	2	1	5
2	4	2	5	2	5
3	5	3	1	3	3
4	9	4	4	4	2
5	3	5	5	5	6
6	8	6	3	6	5
7	6	7	2	7	4
8	1	8	2	8	3
9	5	9	2	9	2
10	6	10	6	10	2
11	4	11	4	11	2
12	7	12	3	12	4
13	6	13	8	13	1
14	5	14	5	14	5
15	8	15	6	15	9
16	3	16	3	16	4
17	5	17	4	17	4
18	4	18	3	18	4
19	3	19	3	19	1
20	2	20	4	20	3

Develop a process control chart for Grass, Unlimited, to monitor the quality of its lawn service using 2σ limits. Describe any other quality control or quality management procedures you think Grass, Unlimited, might employ to improve the quality of its service.

C A S E   P R O B L E M

Improving Service Time at Dave's Burgers

Dave's Burgers is a fast-food restaurant franchise in Georgia, South Carolina, and North Carolina. Recently Dave's Burgers has followed the lead of larger franchise restaurants like Burger King, McDonald's, and Wendy's and constructed drive-through windows at all its locations. However, instead of making Dave's Burgers more competitive, the drive-through windows have been a source of continual problems, and it has lost market share to its larger competitors in almost all locations. To identify and correct the problems top management has selected three of its restaurants (one in each state) as test sites and has implemented a TQM program at each of them. A quality team made up of employees, managers, and a quality specialist from company headquarters, at the Charlotte, North Carolina, test restaurant using traditional TQM methods like Pareto charts, check sheets, fishbone diagrams, and process flowcharts, have determined that the primary problem is slow, erratic service at the drive-through window. Studies showed that from the time a customer arrived at the window to the time the order is received averages 2.6 minutes. To be competitive management believes service time should be reduced to at least 2.0 minutes and ideally 1.5 minutes.

The Charlotte Dave's Burgers franchise implemented a number of production process changes to improve service time at the drive-through window. It provided all employees with more training across all restaurant functions, improved the headset system, improved the equipment layout, developed clearer signs for customers, streamlined the menu, and initiated even-dollar (tax inclusive) pricing to speed the payment process. Most importantly the restaurant installed large, visible electronic timers that showed how long a customer was at the window. This not only allowed the quality team to measure service speed but also provided employees with a constant reminder that a customer was waiting.

These quality improvements were implemented over several months and their effect was immediate. Service speed was obviously reduced and market share at the Charlotte restaurant increased by 5 percent. To maintain quality service, make sure the service time remained fast, and continue to improve service, the quality team decided to use a statistical process control chart on a continuing basis. They collected six service time observations daily over a fifteen-day period, as follows.

	Observations of Service Time (min)					
Sample	1	2	3	4	5	6
1	1.62	1.54	1.38	1.75	2.50	1.32
2	1.25	1.96	1.55	1.66	1.38	2.01
3	1.85	1.01	0.95	1.79	1.66	1.94
4	3.10	1.18	1.25	1.45	1.09	2.11
5	1.95	0.76	1.34	2.12	1.45	1.03
6	0.88	2.50	1.07	1.50	1.33	1.62
7	1.55	1.41	1.95	1.14	1.86	1.02
8	2.78	1.56	1.87	2.03	0.79	1.14
9	1.31	1.05	0.94	1.53	1.71	1.15
10	1.67	1.85	2.03	1.12	1.50	1.36
11	0.95	1.73	1.12	1.67	2.05	1.42
12	3.21	4.16	1.67	1.75	2.87	3.76
13	1.65	1.78	2.63	1.05	1.21	2.09
14	2.36	3.55	1.92	1.45	3.64	2.30
15	1.07	0.96	1.13	2.05	0.91	1.66

Construct a control chart to monitor the service at the drive-through window. Determine if your control chart can be implemented on a continuing basis or if additional observations need to be collected. Explain why the chart you developed can or cannot be used. Also discuss what other statistical process control charts might be used by Dave's Burgers in its overall quality management program.

References

Charbonneau, H. C., and G. L. Webster. *Industrial Quality Control.* Englewood Cliffs, N.J.: Prentice Hall, 1978.

Dodge, H. F., and H. G. Romig. *Sampling Inspection Tables—Single and Double Sampling*, 2d ed. New York: John Wiley, 1959.

Duncan, A. J. *Quality Control and Industrial Statistics*, 4th ed. Homewood, Ill.: Irwin, 1974.

Evans, James R., and William M. Lindsay. *The Management and Control of Quality*, 3d ed. St. Paul, Minn.: West, 1993.

Fetter, R. B. *The Quality Control System.* Homewood, Ill.: Irwin, 1967.

Grant, E. L., and R. S. Leavenworth. *Statistical Quality Control*, 5th ed. New York: McGraw-Hill, 1980.

Montgomery, D. C. *Introduction to Statistical Quality Control*, 2d ed. New York: John Wiley, 1991.

II

DESIGNING PRODUCTIVE SYSTEMS

PART OUTLINE

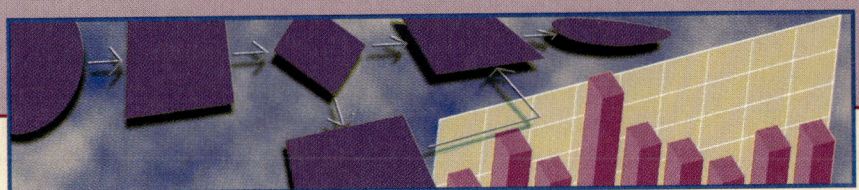

5

Product and Service Design

Ford Engages in Long-Distance Design[1]

www.prenhall.com/russell

Ford Motor Company has consolidated its European, North American, and Asian design operations into a single international network. Design sites on the network include Dearborn, Michigan; Dunton, England; Cologne, Germany; Turin, Italy; Valencia, California; Hiroshima, Japan; and Melbourne, Australia. The sites are connected via satellite links, undersea cables, and land lines purchased from telecommunications carriers.

Using a sophisticated CAD system and imaging software, a 3-D drawing of a new-car design can be sent from Dearborn to Dunton, where colleagues at each site can look at the design simultaneously and discuss changes. The image can be enlarged, shrunk, rotated, run through tests, modified, and then sent on to a computerized milling machine in Turin, where a clay or plastic foam model can be produced in a few hours.

What's the advantage of such a system? Getting input from suppliers, manufacturers, and customers—wherever they might be—means fewer repeated efforts by designers and better-quality designs. Forty percent of the development costs of a new car are spent modifying the design after production has begun. Ford hopes the worldwide network will cut down on the number of changes in a new car's initial design and shorten the design cycle to two years or less.

A design engineer styles a new Taurus via computer at Ford's design facility in Dearborn, Michigan. The 3-D design is projected on full-size screens for managers around the world to review and give fast feedback. After initial approval, the design is sent electronically to a milling machine in Turin, Italy, where a plastic foam model is created.

---

[1] Based on J. Halpert, "One Car, Worldwide, with Strings Pulled from Michigan," *New York Times,* August 29, 1993.

The purpose of any organization is to provide products or services to its customers. An organization can gain a competitive edge through designs that bring new ideas to the market quickly, do a better job of satisfying customer needs, or are easier to manufacture, use, and repair than existing products and services.

Design can provide a competitive edge.

Product design specifies which materials are to be used, determines dimensions and tolerances, defines the appearance of the product, and sets standards for performance.

Service design specifies what physical items, sensual benefits, and psychological benefits the customer is to receive from the service.

Design has a tremendous impact on the quality of a product or service. For example: What if the design does not meet customer needs or the design is difficult or costly to make? What if the design process takes so much time that a competitor is able to introduce new products, services, or features before we can? What if, in rushing to be first to the market, our design is flawed? An effective design process:

- Matches product or service characteristics with customer requirements,
- Ensures that customer requirements are met in the simplest and least costly manner,
- Reduces the time required to design a new product or service, and
- Minimizes the revisions necessary to make a design workable.

Strategy and Design

Design is a critical process for a firm. Strategically, it defines a firm's customers, as well as its competitors. It capitalizes on a firm's core competencies and determines what new competencies need to be developed. It is also the most obvious driver of change—new products and services often define new markets and require new processes.

New products can rejuvenate an organization, even an industry. Ford's Taurus, GM's Saturn, and Chrysler's minivan saved the American automobile industry. Motorola's Bandit pager, HP's DeskJet printer, and Kodak's FunSaver camera turned their corporations around. But the benefits from a newly designed product or service are more than increased revenues and market share. The design process itself is beneficial because it encourages companies to look outside their boundaries, bring in new ideas, challenge conventional thinking, and experiment. Product and service design provide a natural venue for learning, breaking down barriers, working in teams, and integrating across functions.

www.prenhall.com/russell

In this chapter we examine the design process with an eye toward ensuring quality in products and services, and enhancing strategic capabilities. The impact of technology on design and the differences between product and service design are also discussed.

The Design Process

The design process cuts across functional departments, requiring input, coordination, and action from marketing, engineering, and production. The process begins with ideas. Ideas for new products or improvements to existing products can be generated from many sources, including a company's own R&D department, customer complaints or suggestions, marketing research, suppliers, salespersons in the field, factory workers, actions by competitors, and new technological developments. Figure 5.1(a) shows customers generating ideas for a *product concept* that is sent to the marketing de-

Stages:
Idea
generation

Feasibility
Study
Preliminary
design
Final design

Process
Planning

partment. If the proposed product meets market and economic expectations, *performance specifications* for the product are developed and sent to the company's design engineers to be developed into preliminary technical specifications and then detailed *design specifications.* The design specifications are sent to the manufacturing engineers, who develop specific requirements for equipment, tooling, and fixtures. These *manufacturing specifications* are passed on to production personnel on the factory floor, where production of the new product can be scheduled.

When the steps of the design process are performed sequentially, physical and mental "walls" tend to build up between functional areas and departments. When this happens, the output from one design stage is "thrown over the wall" to the next stage, with little discussion or feedback. A more enlightened view of product and service design brings representatives from the various functions and departments *together* to work on the design concurrently, as shown in Figure 5.1(b).

Figure 5.2 outlines the design process from idea generation to manufacture. Let's examine each step in more detail.

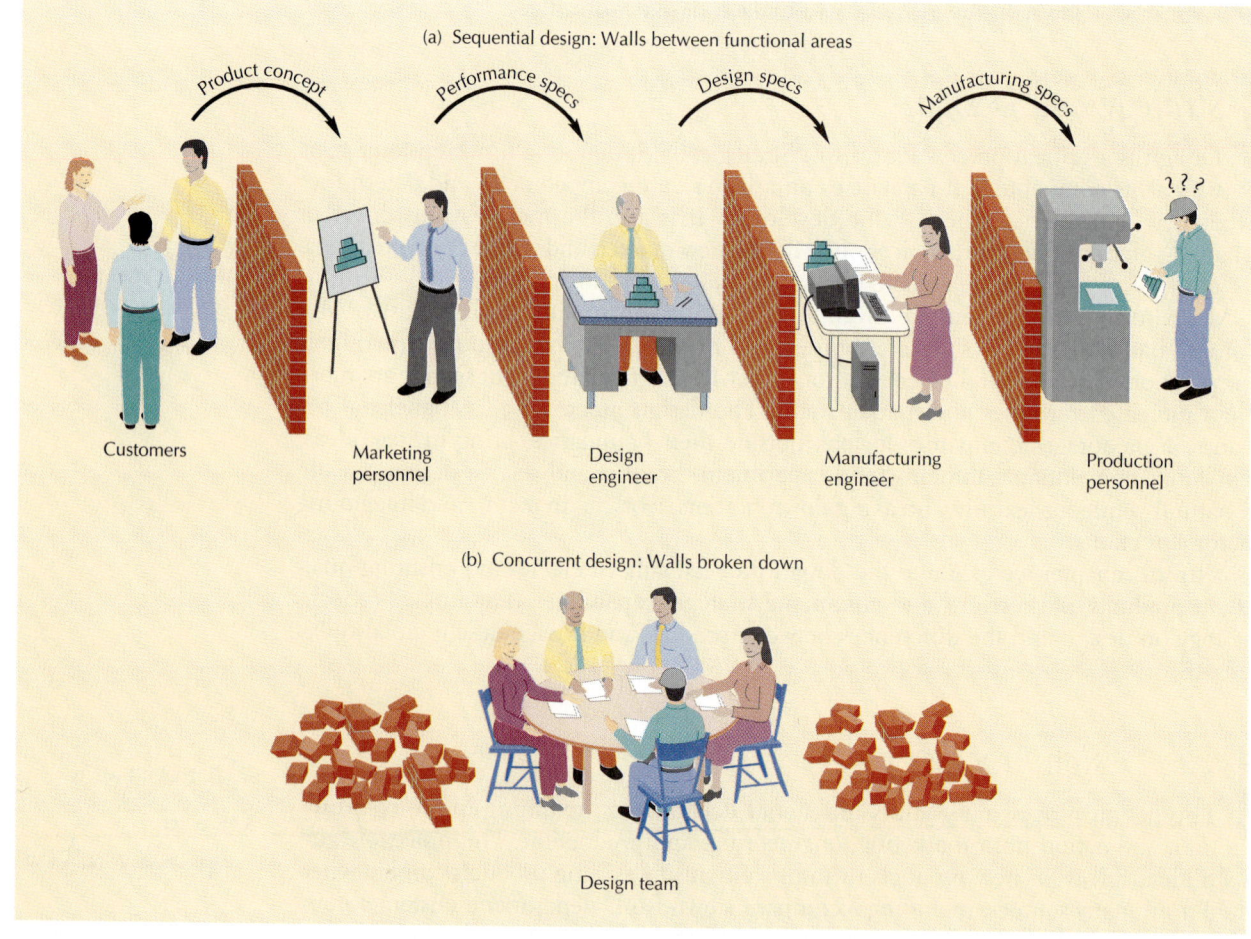

FIGURE 5.1 **Breaking Down the Barriers to Effective Design**

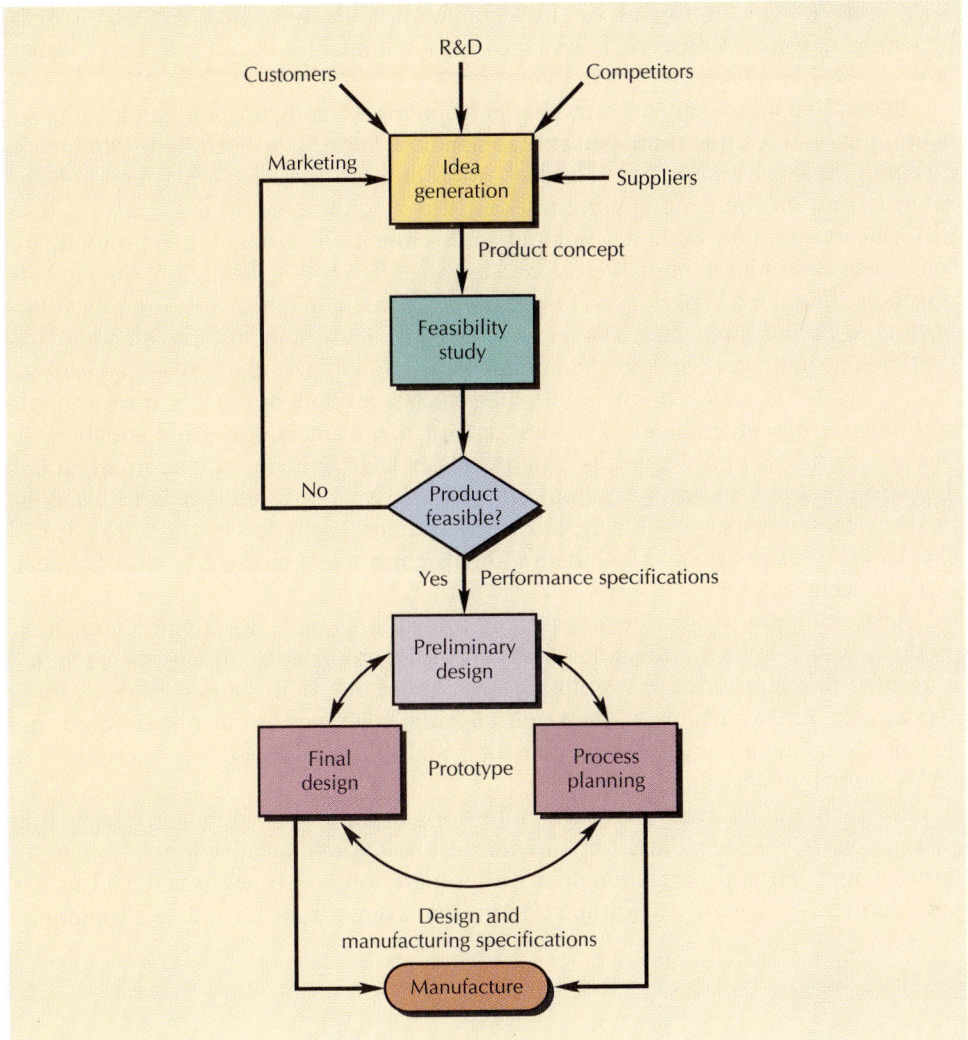

FIGURE 5.2 **The Design Process**

Idea Generation

Product innovation comes from understanding the customer and actively identifying customer needs. There are a variety of ways to garner customer input. Would-be customers as well as existing customers should be surveyed. The toughest and more exacting customers provide the most useful information. Customer surveys can be followed up with smaller focus groups or individual customer interviews. Field testing is imperative and should be done as soon as possible.

Anyone who comes in contact with a company's product or customers is a potential source of new product ideas. A formal channel for inputting ideas from suppliers, distributors, salespersons, and workers should be established—and used. Companies also need to use the information that is readily available to them through trade journals, government reports, and the news media, as well as a careful analysis of their own successes and failures.

Ideas come from many sources, including customers, competitors, and R&D.

Competitors are also a source of ideas for new products or services. Perceptual maps, benchmarking, and reverse engineering can help companies learn from their competitors.

A **perceptual map** is a visual method of comparing customer perceptions of different products or services.

Perceptual maps compare customer perceptions of a company's products with competitor products. Consider the perceptual map of breakfast cereals in terms of taste and nutrition shown in Figure 5.3. The lack of an entry in the good-taste, high-nutrition category suggests there are opportunities for this kind of cereal in the market. This is why Cheerios introduced honey-nut and apple-cinnamon versions while promoting its "oat" base. Fruit bits and nuts were added to wheat flakes to make them more tasty and nutritious. Shredded Wheat opted for more taste by reducing its size and adding a sugar frosting or berry filling. Rice Krispies, on the other hand, sought to challenge Cocoa Puffs in the "more tasty" market quadrant with marshmallow and fruit-flavored versions.

Benchmarking is comparing a product or process against the best-in-class product.

Benchmarking refers to finding the best-in-class product or process, measuring the performance of your product or process against it, and making recommendations for improvement based on the results. The benchmarked company may be in an entirely different line of business. For example, American Express is well-known for its ability to get customers to pay up quickly; Disney World, for its employee commitment; Federal Express, for its speed; McDonald's, for its consistency; and Xerox, for its benchmarking techniques.

www.prenhall.com/russell

Reverse engineering refers to carefully dismantling a competitor's product to improve your own product.

Reverse engineering refers to carefully dismantling and inspecting a competitor's product to look for design features that can be incorporated into your own product. Ford used this approach successfully in its design of the Taurus automobile, assessing 400 features of competitor products and copying, adapting, or enhancing more than 300 of them, including Audi's accelerator pedal, Toyota's fuel-gauge accuracy, and BMW's tire and jack storage.

For many products and services, following consumer or competitor leads is not enough; customers are attracted by superior technology and creative ideas. In these industries, research and development is the primary source of new product ideas. Expenditures for R&D can be enormous ($2 million a day at Kodak!) and investment risky

www.prenhall.com/russell

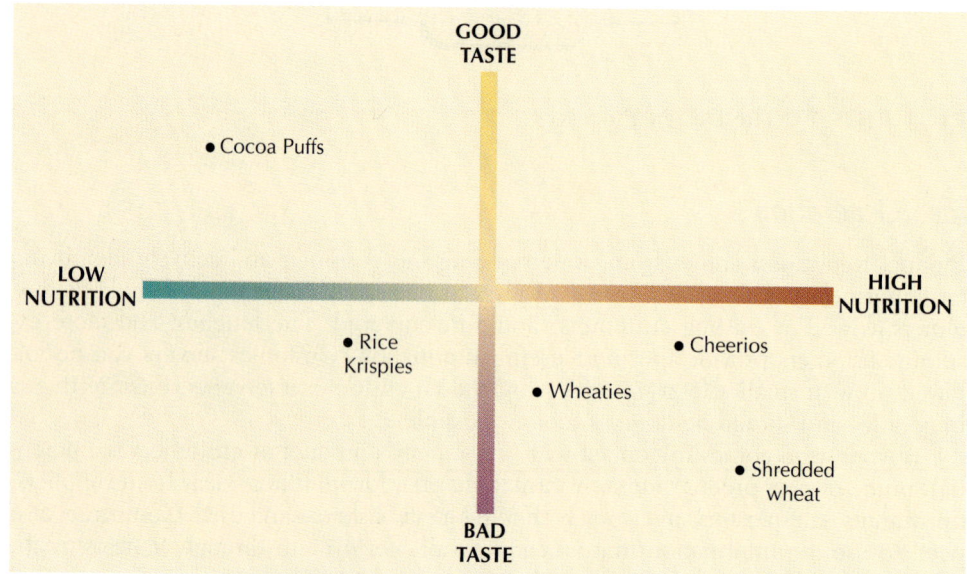

FIGURE 5.3   A Perceptual Map of Breakfast Cereals

Competing at Lands' End

Planning the coming home division

Home textiles represents a new direction for

www.prenhall.com/russell

Lands' End. The company decided to enter the new market when it noticed a decline in the quality of mill output. In the 1980s, a dozen textile mills were consolidated into three major ones, whose focus was keeping the mills busy. Volume and efficiency were emphasized at the expense of quality. With expertise in both textiles and cut-and-sew, Lands' End saw its chance to provide high quality home textiles that would exceed customer expectations.

The Coming Home (CH) division was created and given the task of creating a better sheet. CH management held focus groups with potential customers and analyzed the entire sheet market. What they came up with was a sheet with a totally unique *design*—12 inch deep pockets, six inches longer in length, and elastic that extends around the entire sheet with a 2-to-1 stretch ratio. Then they began looking for a mill that could *produce* a sheet of exceptional quality. They found one in Switzerland. The mill had never made sheets, but their operations were impressive. So their technical people and Lands' End product people worked together, testing two or three different runs of various weaves. They settled on a Swiss sateen. It took a year and a half to bring the new sheet to market, but the results were worth it. You've probably seen copies of the design in LE competitor catalogues.

Of course, Lands' End isn't about to stand still. Their next new product venture in the Coming Home division was window treatments. Why? Look at how the market for drapes is divided—*ready-made*, *made-to-measure*, and *custom-made*. Ready-mades are cheap and of lesser quality, but always available. Made-to-measure are better quality, but take four to six weeks for delivery. Custom-made are the best quality, but require an interior decorator and can take six months to a year to deliver. Lands' End found its niche by offering top quality window treatments in virtually any size or dimension delivered in a matter of days. And to replace the interior decorator—a catalogue full of ideas, along with step-by-step instructions and an on-line "window expert."

(only one in every twenty ideas ever becomes a product and only one of every ten new products is successful). In addition, ideas generated by R&D may follow a long path to commercialization.

Feasibility Study

Marketing takes the ideas that are generated and the customer needs that are identified from the first stage of the design process and formulates alternative product concepts. The promising concepts undergo a feasibility study that includes several types of analyses, beginning with a *market analysis*. Most companies have staffs of market researchers who can design and evaluate customer surveys, interviews, focus groups, or market tests. The market analysis assesses whether there's enough demand for the proposed product to invest in developing it further.

A feasibility study consists of a *market analysis,* an *economic analysis,* and a *technical/strategic analysis.*

If the demand potential exists, then there's an *economic analysis* that looks at estimates of production and development costs and compares them to estimated sales volume. A price range for the products that is compatible with the market segment and image of the new product is discussed. Quantitative techniques such as cost/benefit analysis, decision theory, net present value, or internal rate of return are commonly used to evaluate the profit potential of the project. The data used in the analysis are far from certain. Estimates of risk in the new product venture and the company's attitude toward risk are also considered.

Finally, there are *technical and strategic analyses* that answer such questions as: Does the new product require new technology? Is the risk or capital investment excessive? Does the company have sufficient labor and management skills to support the required technology? Is sufficient capacity available for production? Does the new product provide a competitive advantage for the company? Does it draw on corporate strengths? Is it compatible with the core business of the firm?

Performance specifications are written for product concepts that pass the feasibility study and are approved for development. *Performance specifications* describe the function of the product—that is, what the product should do to satisfy customer needs.

Preliminary Design

Preliminary design involves testing and revising a prototype.

Design engineers take the general performance specifications and translate them into technical specifications. The process involves creating a *preliminary design:* building a prototype, testing the prototype, revising the design, retesting, and so on, until a viable design is determined. Design incorporates both form and function.

Form design refers to how the product will look.

Form design refers to the physical appearance of a product—its shape, color, size, and style. Aesthetics such as image, market appeal, and personal identification are also part of form design. In many cases, functional design must be adjusted to make the product look or feel right. For example, the form design of Mazda's Miata sports car went further than looks—the exhaust had to have a certain "sound," the gearshift lever a certain "feel," and the seat and window arrangement the proper dimensions to encourage passengers to ride with their elbows out.

Functional design is concerned with how the product will perform.

Functional design is concerned with how the product performs. It seeks to meet the performance specifications of fitness for use by the customer. Two performance characteristics considered during this phase of design are *reliability* and *maintainability*.

Reliability is the probability that a product will perform its intended function for a specified period of time.

Reliability is the probability that a given part or product will perform its intended function for a specified length of time under normal conditions of use. You may be familiar with reliability information from product warranties. A hair dryer might be guaranteed to function (i.e., blow air with a certain force at a certain temperature) for one year under normal conditions of use (defined to be 300 hours of operation). A car warranty might extend for three years or 50,000 miles. Normal conditions of use would include regularly scheduled oil changes and other minor maintenance activities. A missed oil change or mileage in excess of 50,000 miles in a three-year period would not be considered "normal" and would nullify the warranty.

A product or system's reliability is a function of the reliabilities of its component parts and how the parts are arranged. If all parts must function for the product or system to operate, then the system reliability is the *product* of the component part reliabilities. For example, if two component parts are required and they each have a reliability of 0.90, the reliability of the system is $0.90 \times 0.90 = 0.81$, or 81 percent. The system can be visualized as a *series* of components as follows:

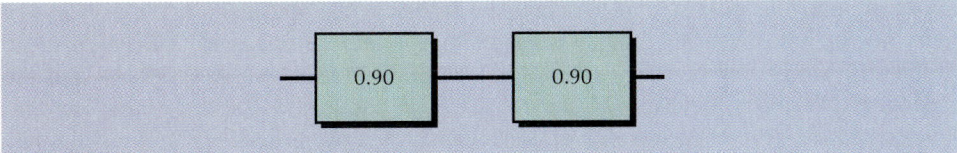

Note that the system reliability of 0.81 is considerably less than the component reliabilities of 0.90. As the number of serial components increases, system reliability will continue to deteriorate. This makes a good argument for simple designs with fewer components!

Failure of some components in a system is more critical than others—the brakes on a car, for instance. To increase the reliability of individual parts (and thus the system as a whole), *redundant* parts can be built in to back up a failure. Providing emergency brakes for a car is an example. Consider the following redundant design with R_1 representing the reliability of the original component and R_2 the reliability of the backup component.

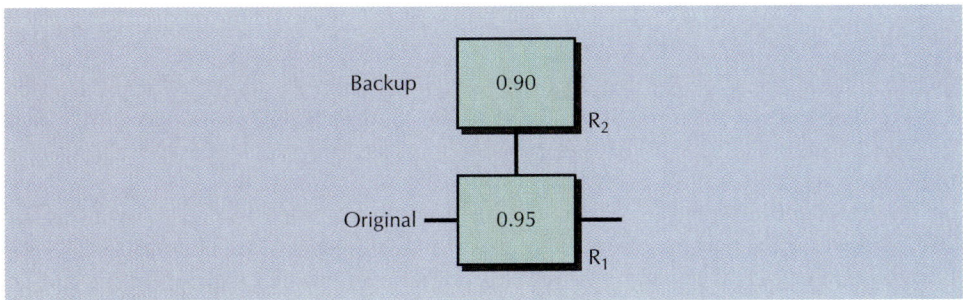

These components are said to operate in *parallel*. If the original component fails (a 5 percent chance), the backup component will automatically kick in to take its place—but only 90 percent of the time. Thus, the reliability of the system is the 0.95 reliability of the original component *plus* the 0.90 reliability of the backup component, which is called in $(1 - 0.95)$ of the time, or $R_1 + R_2(1 - R_1) = 0.95 + 0.90(1 - 0.95) = 0.995$.

Reliability can be improved by simplifying product design, improving the reliability of individual components, or adding redundant components. Products that are easier to manufacture or assemble, are well maintained, and have users who are trained in proper use have higher reliability.

Maintainability refers to the ease and/or cost with which a product is maintained or repaired. Products can be made easier to maintain by assembling them in modules, like computers, so that entire control panels, cards, or disk drives can be replaced when they malfunction. The location of critical parts or parts subject to failure affects the ease of disassembly and, thus, repair. Instructions that teach consumers how to anticipate malfunctions and correct them themselves can be included with the product. Specifying regular maintenance schedules is part of maintainability, as is proper planning for the availability of critical replacement parts.

Maintainability refers to the ease of repair.

Final Design and Process Planning

Final design produces detailed drawings and specifications for the new product after the preliminary design has been tested and trial production has taken place. *Process planning* converts designs into workable instructions for manufacture, selects and orders necessary equipment and tooling, decides which components will be made in-house and which will be purchased from a supplier, prepares job descriptions and procedures for workers, determines the order of operations and assembly, and programs automated machines. We discuss process planning in more detail in the next chapter.

Referring to Figure 5.2, notice the circular flow from preliminary design to process planning to final design, and back around again, if necessary. This reflects the design-build-test-produce emphasis of concurrent design (which is analogous to Deming's plan-do-check-act cycle). Portions of the new product are designed in preliminary form, then a prototype is built and tested with other parts of the design. If the tests are successful, a trial process is run to simulate manufacture under actual factory conditions. Adjustments are made as needed before the final design is agreed upon. In this way, the *design specifications* for the new product have considered how the product is to be produced, and the *manufacturing specifications* more closely reflect the intent of the design. Hopefully, this will mean less revisions in the design as the product is manufactured. Design changes are a major source of delay and cost overruns in the product development process.

Improving the Design Process

Many companies, known for creativity and innovation in product design, are slow and ineffective at getting new products to the market. Problems in converting ideas to finished products may be caused by poor manufacturing practices, but more than likely they are the result of poor design.

Design decisions affect sales strategies, efficiency of manufacture, speed of repair, and product cost. The impact on product cost is significant. It has been estimated that from 60 percent to 80 percent of the cost to produce a product is fixed during the design process—*before* manufacturing has had a chance to see the design. Manufacturing requests for changes in product design are not well received because of the high cost of changes and because an adjustment in one part may cause an adjustment in other parts, "unraveling" the entire product design.

Changes in design, known as engineering change orders (ECOs), increase dramatically in cost as the product is closer to production. For example, a major design change for an electronics product might cost $1,000 during the design phase, $100,000 during the planning stage for manufacture, and $10,000,000 during final production! With these cost differentials in mind, examine Figure 5.4, which shows two scenarios for the distribution of design changes. Clearly, company 1 has a competitive advantage in product development costs. What is not so obvious is its quality advantage. For company 1, a stable design allows manufacturing personnel to "get used to" and become skilled at producing the new product, thereby making fewer mistakes.

Improving the design process to remain competitive in the world market involves completely restructuring the decision-making process and the participants in that process. The series of *walls* between functional areas portrayed in Figure 5.1 must be broken down and replaced with new alliances and modes of interaction. This feat can be accomplished by:

1. Establishing multifunctional *design teams*,
2. Making product and process design decision *concurrently* rather than sequentially,
3. Designing for *manufacture* and *assembly*,
4. Designing for the *environment*,

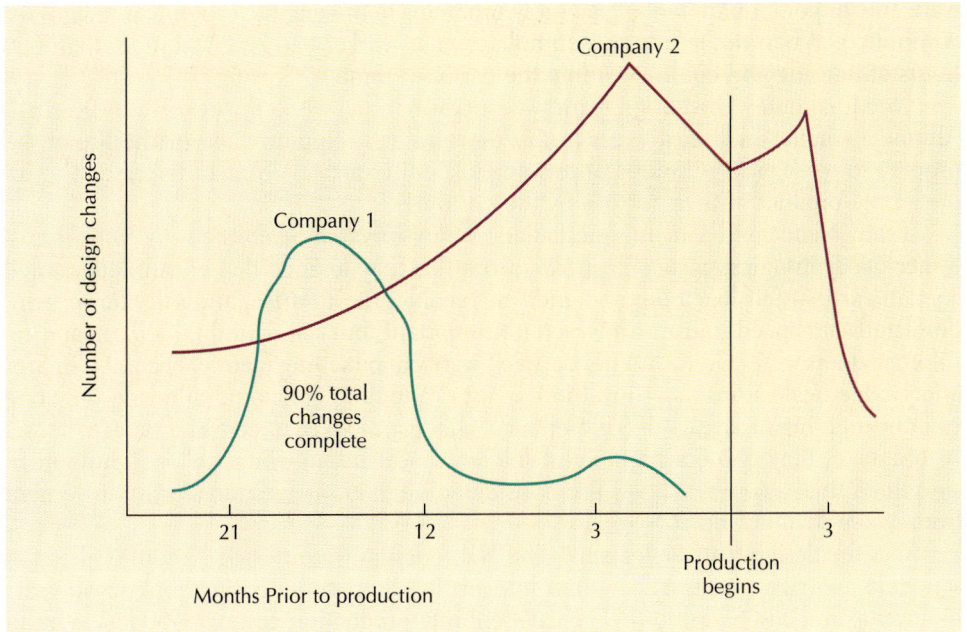

FIGURE 5.4   Distribution of Design Changes for Two Companies

5. Measuring *design quality*,
6. Utilizing *quality function deployment*, and
7. Designing for *robustness*.

We discuss each of these in the following sections.

Design Teams

The team approach to product design has proved to be successful worldwide. Full-time participants from marketing, manufacturing, and engineering are essential to effective product design. Customers, dealers, suppliers, lawyers, accountants, and others are also useful team members. A recent study of new product launchings in high-technology firms concluded that the critical factor between success and failure was the involvement and interaction of the "create, make, and market" functions from the beginning of the design project. Ford Motor Company has been a leader in the team approach to product design in the automotive industry and in U.S. industry. Team design of the Taurus automobile beat all previous development efforts by coming in well before schedule and $400 million under budget. Other automobile manufacturers followed suit.

Team Viper allowed Chrysler to bring the Viper sports car from concept to full production in less than three years and $2 million under budget. Working in a team was a cultural change for Chrysler engineers. The team (ranging from 20 to 85 members) met in one large room of a refurbished warehouse. Walls were literally torn down to encourage team members to communicate and work together.

Requests for bids on Viper parts were released to vendors with only functional dimensions. Vendors were given a Team Viper list and expected to contact team members directly if they ran into any problems. Four assembly line workers, called craftpersons, were trained at each manufacturing station of a mock assembly line set up in the design facility. By field-testing each work station as it was developed, the workers

Design-build teams find success in U.S. industry.

www.prenhall.com/russell

were able to point out potential assembly problems to the engineers before a design was committed. When the testing was complete, each worker had received more than 600 hours of training and could assemble the car from scratch.

One final note: The design team was not dismantled when the design was finished. Although smaller in size, it exists to this day and will remain intact for the life of the product to work on continuous improvements, either for ease of manufacture or to increase the product's fitness for use by the customer.

Team Neon used a technique called *quality function deployment* to convert customer needs into design specifications. From this they learned that consumers wanted a small car that felt like a big one and was reliable, fun to drive, and safe. Power windows and four-speed transmission weren't important, but standard dual airbags and reinforced doors were. Costs (but not corners) were cut by selling identical cars at Chrysler and Dodge dealerships (a $10 million savings in tooling costs) and allowing only one exterior molding (a savings of $50 per car). The team looked at cost in a broader sense. In one case, they chose a higher-cost folddown seat because it saved $1.1 million in simplified final assembly. They also considered all 4,000 suggestions for improvement from assembly line workers.

Was the design team successful? The Neon design was finished 3 months ahead of schedule and right on its $1.3 billion budget (in comparison, Saturn took seven years to develop and cost $5 billion). The car went into production costing $500 less to build than any competing subcompact.

Competing at Lands' End

From a functional to a team approach

Prior to 1994, product development at Lands' End was separated into five different departments—*creative ideas, merchandising, quality, inventory, and design*—which were located on separate floors of the main building. Communication was difficult and the product development process was far too time-consuming. A task force decided that cross-functional teams would alleviate a lot of the problems. But how many teams were needed and how should they be formed?

The task force visited several vendors and respected companies to gain another perspective on the product development process (and to benchmark). The result? Teams were set up for major product categories, such as adult sleepwear. The teams were permanent—once team members were assigned, they were no longer shared with other teams. Each team consisted of a *merchandiser*, an *inventory manager*, a *quality assurance specialist*, a *copywriter*, an *artist*, and a *support person*. The members co-located and shared a workspace where team meetings, vendor appointments, and product-fit sessions could be held.

Since the teams have been operational, the average time to bring new products to market has decreased significantly, and less design changes are necessary. Teams helped people do their jobs better, improved communications, and sparked creativity—and besides, as LE employees will tell you—"they're just more fun."

Concurrent Design

Concurrent design helps improve the quality of early design decisions and thereby reduces the length and cost of the design process. Product-design decisions are extended to process decisions whenever possible. In this manner, one stage of design is not completely finished before another stage begins.

One example of concurrent design is suppliers who complete the detailed design for the parts they will supply. A study of product development in automobile manufacturing revealed that Japanese firms prepare an engineering design for only 30 percent of their parts (suppliers do the rest), whereas American firms design 81 percent of their component parts. In the traditional design process, U.S. manufacturers determine component design in detail, down to the fraction of an inch, including the specific material to be used. Detailed engineering drawings are made, and only then are suppliers called in to submit their bids. Japanese manufacturers, on the other hand, provide general performance specifications to their component suppliers, such as these:

> Design a set of brakes that can stop a 2,200-pound car from 60 miles per hour in 200 feet ten times in succession without fading. The brakes should fit into a space 6 inches × 8 inches × 10 inches at the end of each axle and be delivered to the assembly plant for $40 a set.[2]

The supplier is asked to prepare a prototype for testing. Detailed design decisions are left up to the supplier, as a member of the design team who is the expert in that area. This approach saves considerable development time and resources.

The role of design engineer is both expanded and curtailed in the concurrent design process. Design engineers are no longer *totally* responsible for the design of the product. At the same time, they are responsible for more than what was traditionally considered "design." Their responsibilities extend to the manufacture and continuous improvement of the product as well.

In many cases, design engineers do not have a good understanding of the capabilities or limitations of their company's manufacturing facilities. Increased contact with manufacturing can sensitize them to the realities of making a product. Simply consulting manufacturing personnel early in the design process about critical factors or constraints can improve the quality of product design. This is where most companies begin their efforts in changing the corporate culture from a separated design function to one that is integrated with operations. IBM called their efforts in this area EMI—*early manufacturing involvement*. Initially, one manufacturing engineer was assigned to each product-development group. Later, more engineering staff were reassigned and physically relocated. In at least one instance, new design facilities were built within walking distance of where manufacturing occurred. The increased communication between design and manufacturing so improved the quality of the final product that IBM quickly threw out the term EMI and adopted CMI—*continuous manufacturing involvement*.

One more difference between sequential design and concurrent design is the manner in which prices are set and costs are determined. In the traditional process, the feasibility study includes some estimate of price to be charged to the customer, but that selling price is not firmed up until the end of the design process, when all the product costs are accumulated, a profit margin is attached, and it is determined whether the original price estimate and the resulting figure are close. This is a *cost-plus* approach. If there are

Concurrent design makes suppliers part of the design team.

Design engineers should be knowledgeable about manufacturing.

www.prenhall.com/russell

Concurrent design uses price-minus rather than cost-plus pricing.

---

[2] Womack, J.P., D.T. Jones, and D. Roos, *The Machine that Changed the World*, NY: Macmillan, (1990): 157, 60.

discrepancies, either the product is sold at the new price, a new feasibility study is made, or the designers go back and try to cut costs. Remember that design decisions are interrelated; the further back in the process you go, the more expensive are the changes.

Concurrent design uses a *price-minus* system. A selling price (that will give some advantage in the marketplace) is determined before design details are developed. Then a *target cost* of production is set and evaluated at every stage of product and process design. Techniques such as value analysis (which we discuss later) are used to keep costs in line.

Even with concurrent design, product design and development can be a long and tedious process. Because concurrent design requires that more tasks be performed in parallel, the scheduling of those tasks is even more complex than ever. Project-scheduling techniques, such as PERT/CPM discussed in Chapter 17, are being used to coordinate the myriad of interconnected decisions that constitute concurrent design.

Design for Manufacture

Design for manufacture involves designing a product so that it can be produced easily and economically.

Design for manufacture (DFM) describes designing a product so it can be produced easily and economically. DFM views product design as the first step in manufacturing a product. DFM identifies product-design characteristics that are easy to manufacture, focuses on the design of component parts that are easy to fabricate and assemble, and integrates product design with process planning. DFM ensures that manufacturing concerns are systematically incorporated into the design process. When successful, DFM not only improves the quality of product design but also reduces the time and cost of both product design and manufacture.

DFM guidelines are statements of good design practice.

DFM guidelines are statements of good design practice that can lead to good—but not necessarily optimum—designs. Examples include the following:

1. Minimize the number of parts.
2. Develop a modular design.
3. Design parts for many uses.
4. Avoid separate fasteners.
5. Eliminate adjustments.
6. Make assembly easy and foolproof. If possible, design for top-down assembly.
7. Design for minimal handling and proper presentation.
8. Avoid tools.
9. Minimize subassemblies.
10. Use standard parts when possible.
11. Simplify operations.
12. Design for efficient and adequate testing and replacement of parts.
13. Use repeatable, well-understood processes.
14. Analyze failures.
15. Rigorously assess value.

Let's see how these guidelines can be applied.

Consider the assembly shown in part (a) of Figure 5.5. It consists of 24 parts (lots of fasteners) and takes 84 seconds to assemble. The design is typical, in that the parts are common and cheap and nuts and bolts are used as fasteners. It does not appear to be complex, unless the assembly task is automated. For a robot to assemble this item, the method of fastening needs to be revised.

The design shown in Figure 5.5(b) has been simplified by molding the base as one

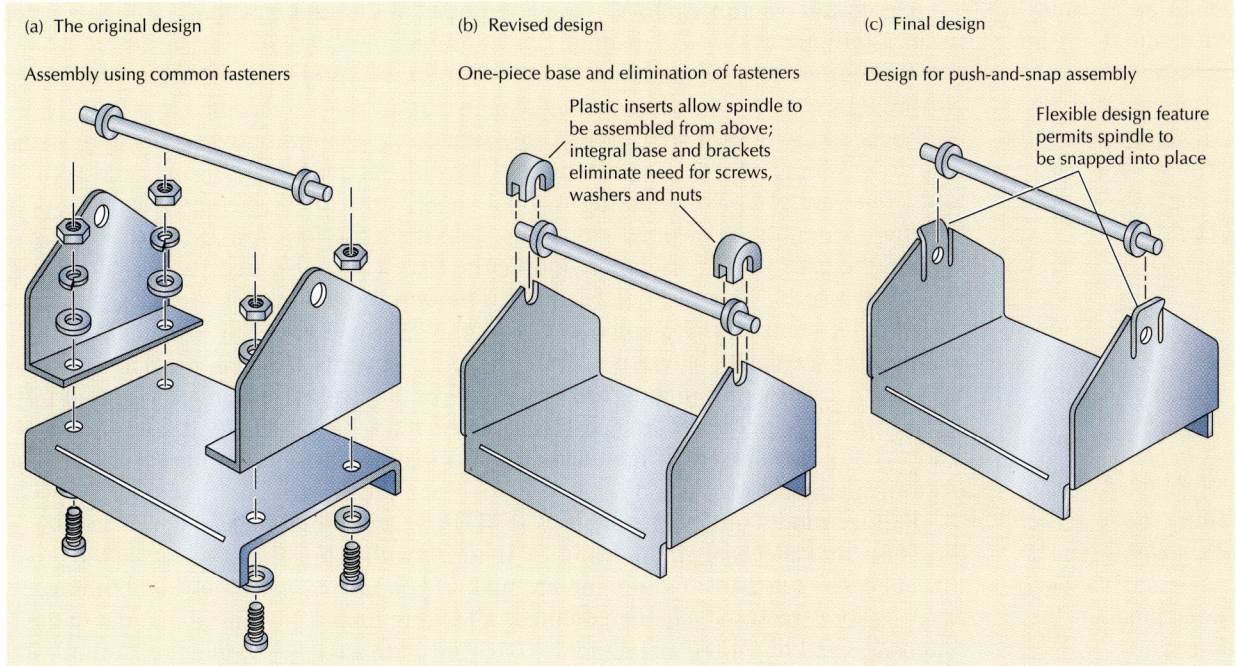

(a) The original design

Assembly using common fasteners

(b) Revised design

One-piece base and elimination of fasteners

Plastic inserts allow spindle to be assembled from above; integral base and brackets eliminate need for screws, washers and nuts

(c) Final design

Design for push-and-snap assembly

Flexible design feature permits spindle to be snapped into place

FIGURE 5.5   Design Simplification
SOURCE: Adapted from G. Boothroyd and P. Dewhurst, "Product Design . . . Key to Successful Robotic Assembly," *Assembly Engineering* (September 1986): 90–93.

piece and eliminating the fasteners. Plastic inserts snap over the spindle to hold it into place. The number of parts has been reduced to four, and the assembly time has been cut to 12 seconds. This represents a significant gain in productivity, from 43 assemblies per hour to 300 assemblies per hour.

Figure 5.5(c) shows an even simpler design consisting of only two parts, a base and spindle. The spindle is made of flexible material, allowing a quick, one-motion assembly: Snap the spindle downward into place. Now the assembly task seems too simple for a robot. Indeed, many manufacturers have followed this process in rediscovering the virtues of **simplification**—in redesigning a product for automation, they have found that automation isn't necessary!

Using standard parts in a product or throughout many products saves design time, tooling costs, and production worries. **Standardization** makes possible the interchangeability of parts among products, resulting in higher-volume production and purchasing, lower investment in inventory, easier purchasing and material handling, fewer quality inspections, and fewer difficulties in production. Some products, such as light bulbs, batteries, and VCR tapes, benefit from being totally standardized. For others, such as Snapple beverages, being different is a competitive advantage. The question becomes how to gain the cost benefits of standardization without losing the market advantage of variety and uniqueness.

One solution is **modular design.** Modular design consists of combining standardized building blocks, or *modules*, in a variety of ways to create unique finished products. Modular design is common in the electronics industry and the automobile industry. Even Campbell's Soup Company practices modular design by producing large volumes of four basic broths (beef, chicken, tomato, and seafood bisque) and then adding special ingredients to produce 125 varieties of final soup products.

Simplification reduces the number of parts, assemblies, or options in a product.

With **standardization,** commonly available and interchangeable parts are used.

Modular design combines standardized building blocks or modules to create unique finished products.

Design for assembly is a procedure for reducing the number of parts in an assembly, evaluating methods for assembly, and determining an assembly sequence.

Design for assembly (DFA) is a set of procedures for reducing the number of parts in an assembly, evaluating methods for assembly, and determining an assembly sequence. DFA was developed by Professors Boothroyd and Dewhurst at the University of Massachusetts. It provides a catalog of generic part shapes classified by means of assembly, along with estimates of assembly times. For example, some parts are assembled by pushing; others, by pushing and twisting or pushing, twisting, and tilting. Guidelines are given for choosing manual versus automated assembly, avoiding part tangling or nesting in feeding operations, achieving the fewest number of reorientations of the parts during assembly, finding the fewest assembly steps, and determining the most foolproof sequence of assembly. The best sequence of assembly differs considerably for manual versus automated assembly. Manual assembly is concerned with maintaining a balance between operations on the assembly line; automated assembly is concerned with minimizing the reorientation of parts for assembly. Common assembly mistakes include hiding parts that later need to be inspected, disassembling already assembled parts to fit new parts in, and making it difficult to access parts that need maintenance or repair.

Failure mode and effects analysis is a systematic method of analyzing product failures.

Failure mode and effects analysis (FMEA) is a systematic approach to analyzing the causes and effects of product failures. It begins with listing the functions of the product and each of its parts. Failure modes, such as fatigue, leakage, buckling, binding, or excessive force required, are then defined. All failure modes are ranked in order of their seriousness and likelihood of failure. Failures are addressed one by one (beginning with

THE COMPETITIVE EDGE

Simplification and Standardization Save Money

Workers and engineers at Ford's Chicago and Atlanta plants formed plant vehicle teams to suggest ways to trim the cost of the 1997 Taurus. Design changes were approved on the spot, eliminating months of phone calls, electronic mail, and meetings. Their changes were minor—use recycled plastic for splash shields ($0.45 savings), redesign door hinge pins ($2 savings), put an integrated bracket on the air conditioner's accumulator bottle ($4 savings), use plastic moldings for the moon roof instead of metal ($7.85 savings), and so forth—totaling $180 per vehicle or $73 million per year!

Ford also saved money, reduced its inventory, and eased the transition to new vehicles by using the same parts on different models. Switching from eighteen different air filters to five saved $0.45 per vehicle or $3 million per year. Reducing types of carpet from nine to three saved $1.25 per vehicle or $9 million annually. Standardizing on one out of fourteen cigarette lighters and one trunk carpet instead of seven saved $1.16 per car or $5 million annually. That's a total savings of $17 million per year.

Of course, Ford competitors are cost-cutting their designs, too. The 1997 Camry sold for $1,500 less than the older version, Honda's new model Accord is priced 20% lower, and Nissan's Infiniti costs 10.5% less. And at the same time, standard features such as air bags and ultraviolet protection glass have been added. Toyota is known for enlisting the help of its suppliers in reducing cost—challenging a supplier to make seats for $20 instead of $30, for example—but few would have expected Chrysler to work so well with its suppliers in reducing costs. The SCORE program (for supplier cost reduction effort) asks vendors to identify cost-cutting opportunities equal to 5% of its annual billings to Chrysler. To prevent capricious cost-cutting that may affect quality, ideas are submitted to Chrysler for approval. So far 16,000 ideas have been received for a total savings of $2.5 billion. Chrysler's supplier base has been cut by 36% in the past five years and will be cut an additional 25% by the year 2000. An important factor in survival is a supplier's SCORE savings.

SOURCES: Oscar Suris, "How Ford Cut Costs on Its 1997 Taurus, Little by Little," *Wall Street Journal*, July 18, 1996; Karen Schwartz, "Small Changes Save Companies Big Bucks," *Roanoke Times*, March 23, 1996; and Justin Martin, "Are You as Good as You Think You Are?" *Fortune* (September 30, 1996): 145–46.

TABLE 5.1 Failure Mode and Effects Analysis for Potato Chips

Failure Mode	Cause of Failure	Effect of Failure	Corrective Action
Stale	Low moisture content, expired shelf life, poor packaging	Tastes bad, won't crunch, thrown out, lost sales	Add moisture, cure longer, better package seal, shorter shelf life
Broken	Too thin, too brittle, rough handling, rough use, poor packaging	Can't dip, poor display, injures mouth, choking, perceived as old, lost sales	Change recipe, change process, change packaging
Too salty	Outdated recipe, process not in control, uneven distribution of salt	Eat less, drink more, health hazard, lost sales	Experiment with recipe, experiment with process, introduce low-salt version

the most catastrophic), causes are hypothesized, and design changes are made to reduce the chance of failure. The objective of FMEA is to anticipate failures and prevent them from occurring. Table 5.1 shows a partial FMEA for potato chips.

FMEA prioritizes failures and attempts to eliminate their causes but **fault tree analysis (FTA)** emphasizes the *interrelationship* among failures. FTA lists failures and their causes in a tree format using two hatlike symbols, one with a straight line on the bottom representing *and* and one with a curved line on the bottom for *or*. Figure 5.6 shows a partial FTA for a food manufacturer who has a problem with potato chip breakage. In this analysis, potato chips break because they are too thin *or* because they are too brittle. The options for fixing the problem of too-thin chips—increasing thickness or reducing size—are undesirable, as indicated by the Xs. The problem of too-brittle chips can be alleviated by adding more moisture *or* having fewer ridges *or* adjusting the frying procedure. We choose to adjust the frying procedure, which leads to the question of how hot the oil should be *and* how long to fry the chip. Once these values are determined, the issue of too-brittle chips (and thus chip breakage) is solved, as indicated.

Value analysis (VA; also known as value engineering) was developed by General Electric in 1947 to eliminate unnecessary features and functions in product designs. It has reemerged as a technique for use by multifunctional design teams. The design team defines the essential functions of a component, assembly, or product using two words, a noun and a verb. For example, the function of a container might be described as *holds fluid*. Then the team assigns a value to each function and determines the cost of providing the function. With that information, a ratio of value to cost can be calculated for each item. The team attempts to improve the ratio by either reducing the cost of the item or increasing its worth. Every material, every part, and every operation is subjected to such questions as:

1. Can we do without it?
2. Does it do more than is required?
3. Does it cost more than it is worth?
4. Can something else do a better job?

Fault tree analysis is a visual method for analyzing the interrelationships among failures.

www.prenhall.com/russell

Value analysis helps eliminate unnecessary features and functions.

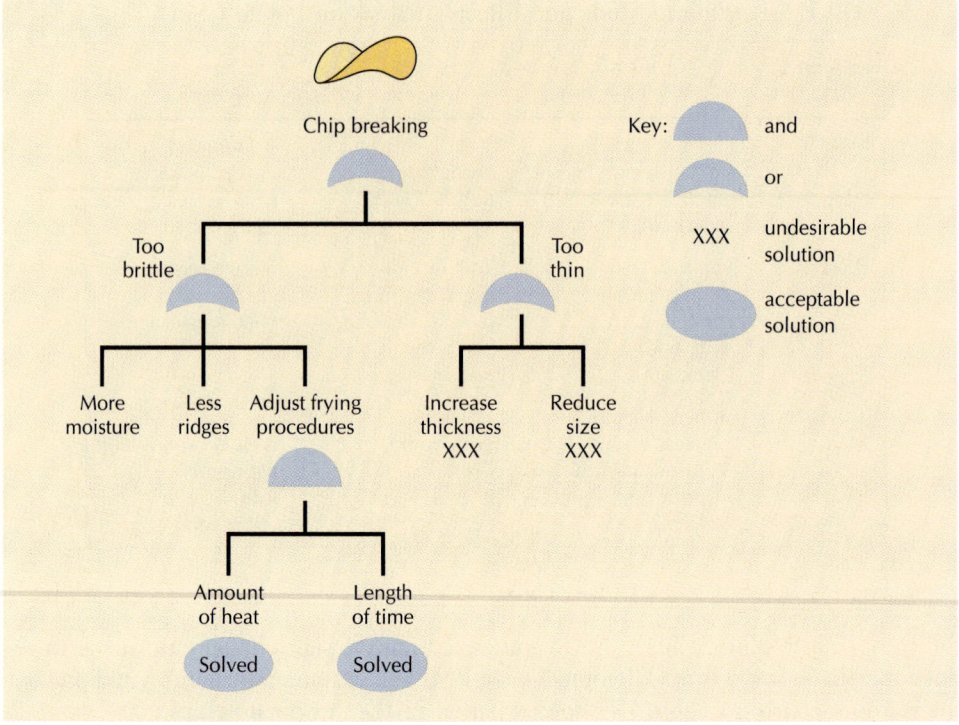

FIGURE 5.6   **Partial Fault Tree Analysis for Potato Chips**

5. Can it be made by a less costly method? With less costly tooling? With less costly material?

6. Can it be made cheaper, better, or faster by someone else?

Design for Environment

Each year Americans dispose of 350 million home and office appliances (50 million of them hair dryers) and more than 10 million PCs. At the current rate of discard, it's not hard to visualize city dumps filled with old refrigerators and computers. These types of images have prompted government and industry to consider the environmental impact of product and service design.

Design for environment (DFE) involves designing products from recycled material, using materials or components that can be recycled, designing a product so that it is easier to repair than discard, and minimizing unnecessary packaging. It also includes minimizing material and energy usage during manufacture, consumption, and disposal.

Governments worldwide are holding companies responsible for their products, even after the product's useful life has ended. A 1994 German law mandates the collection, recycling, and safe disposal of personal computers and household appliances, including stereos and video appliances, television sets, washing machines, dishwashers, and refrigerators. Some manufacturers pay a tax for recycling; others include the cost of disposal in a product's price. The Netherlands recently announced that a color TV set would be considered chemical waste and should be treated as such. Seven U.S. states now have "take-back" laws that require the return and recycling of batteries. Japan is developing energy-consumption limits for information technology products as well as

Design for environment involves minimizing material and energy usage during manufacture, consumption, and disposal.

THE COMPETITIVE EDGE

Green Design Can Be Profitable

Companies getting a head start on probable environmental legislation have discovered some surprising benefits. For example, McDonald's and Chrysler are saving millions of dollars through a waste audit process that concentrates on reducing the amount of waste generated in  the first place. McDonald's permanently eliminated 40 percent of its garbage costs. Similarly, a

www.prenhall.com/russell Chrysler Jeep plant eliminated 70 percent of the trash it used to send to landfills. Xerox's program to recycle copier parts (cartridges, power supplies, motors, paper-transport systems, printed wiring boards, and metal rollers), called *design for reassembly*,

saves the company more than $200 million annually. The process involves disassembling a machine, replacing worn-out parts with new, remanufactured, or used components, cleaning the machine, and then testing it to make sure it meets the same quality and reliability standards as a newly manufactured machine. Xerox's goal is zero waste. Whether consumers will buy (or pay full price for) refurbished products is yet to be seen. In addition, before large numbers of companies begin remanufacture efforts, several consumer-protection and government procurement laws would have to be changed.

SOURCE: John Holusha, "Who Foots the Bill for Recycling?" *New York times*, April 25, 1993.

---

business enterprises. The European Community currently has a policy for green labeling, and ISO standards for environmental attributes are now available.

www.prenhall.com/russell

Factors such as product life, recoverable value, ease of service, and disposal cost affect decisions on disposal, continued use, and recycling. Many products are discarded because they are difficult or expensive to repair. Materials from discarded products may not be recycled for a similar reason—the product is difficult to disassemble. Thus, guidelines for ease of assembly should also include disassembly guidelines.

Measures of Design Quality

Managers and designers need to monitor the *long-term quality* of a design which depends, in large part, on how easy or difficult it is to produce. Traditionally, product design is evaluated in terms of the cost of materials and the adherence to performance specifications provided by marketing. After a design is released to manufacturing, the responsibility of producing the product to design specifications is assigned to manufacturing. A more useful evaluation of design quality would include such measures as[3]:

1. Number of component parts and product options
2. Percentage of standard parts
3. Use of existing manufacturing processes
4. Cost of first production run
5. Cost of engineering changes during the first six months
6. First-year cost of field service and repair
7. Total product cost
8. Total product sales
9. Sustainable development

Long-term measures of design quality are needed.

---

[3] Adapted from D. A. Waliszewski, "The JIT Starter Kit for Design Engineering," *Conference Proceedings of the American Production and Control Society* (1986): 358–60.

Recycling plants such as this one have helped to reduce waste and protect the environment. But if waste is to be dramatically reduced, producers must start considering issues of recycling and disposal at the product design phase. Aids to green design include Volvo's environmental load units which guide material selection, Siemens' ecobalance system which examines both environmental and economic design requirements, DFE software that rates the environmental desirability of designs, and recycling indexes which determine the time that can be profitably spent on disassembly.

The first three measures of design quality refer to the simplicity of design. A design with a small number of parts, one with a large percentage of standard parts, and one that uses existing processes already familiar to manufacturing, is cheaper and easier to produce.

The cost of the first production run measures how realistic the initial design is—that is, how well the design matches production capabilities. At the conclusion of the first production run, a design is certified to be "producible," but changes in the design can still be requested by manufacturing that would make the product easier or cheaper to produce. Fewer engineering changes in the first six months of production indicate a more thorough and better quality design.

The cost of field service and repair is a measure of design quality that originates from the customer. It takes into consideration both the frequency and severity of product failure. Product recalls, warranty requests, and liabilities are included in this category.

Total product cost includes not only the cost of materials but also manufacturing costs (such as cost of assembly and investment in new equipment or processes) and development costs (such as cost of design revisions). One of the best examples of seemingly innocuous parts that significantly affect total product cost is screws and bolts. Although screws and bolts cost only pennies apiece, the assembly requirements of aligning the parts, inserting and tightening the screw, and threading the bolt can account for 75 percent of the cost of assembly. For its electronic cash registers, NCR estimates that over the lifetime of a product, each screw contributes $12,500 toward total product cost.[4]

Total product sales indicate the marketability of the product design and the initial level of customer satisfaction.

Sustainable development is defined as "a form of development or progress that meets the needs of the present without compromising the ability of future generations to meet their own needs."[5] This item reflects the importance of "greenness" in design quality.

Quality Function Deployment

Making design decisions *concurrently* rather than *sequentially* requires superior coordination among the parties involved. Consider the design of a new car. Even for the best Japanese manufacturers, the design of an automobile can take several years and involve hundreds of design engineers. The task of coordinating the design decisions of that many individuals can be difficult.

Imagine that two engineers are working on two different components of a car sunroof simultaneously but separately.[6] The "insulation and sealing" engineer develops a new seal that will keep out rain, even during a blinding rainstorm. The "handles, knobs, and levers" engineer is working on a simpler lever that will make the roof easier to open. The new lever is tested and works well with the old seal. Neither engineer is aware of the activities of the other. As it turns out, the combination of heavier roof (due to the increased insulation) and lighter lever means that the driver can no longer open the sunroof with one hand, thereby violating a quality characteristic *expected* by the consumer. It is to be hoped that the problem will be detected in prototype testing before the car is put into production. At that point, one or both components will need to be *redesigned*. Otherwise, cars already produced will need to be *reworked* and cars already sold, will have to be *recalled*. None of these alternatives is pleasant; they all involve considerable cost.

This likely would not happen if engineers worked in teams and shared information. But there is no guarantee that all decisions would be coordinated. A formal method is needed for making sure that everyone working on a design project knows the design objectives and is aware of the interrelationships of the various parts of the design. Similar communications are needed between the customer and marketing, between marketing and engineering, between engineering and production, and between production and the worker. In broader terms, then, a structured process is needed that will translate the *voice of the customer* to technical requirements at every stage of design and manufacture. Such a process is called **quality function deployment (QFD)**.

QFD uses a series of matrix diagrams (also called quality tables) that resemble connected houses. The first matrix, dubbed *the house of quality*, converts customer requirements into product design characteristics. As shown in Figure 5.7, the house of quality has six sections: a customer requirements section, a competitive assessment section, a product characteristics section, a relationship matrix, a trade-off matrix, and a technical assessment/target values section. Let's see how these sections interrelate by examining the detailed house of quality shown in Figure 5.8 for the redesign of a household steam iron.

www.prenhall.com/russell

Quality function deployment (QFD)
translates the voice of the customer into technical design requirements.

---

[4] O. Port, "The Best-Engineered Part Is No Part at All," *Business Week* (May 8, 1989): 150.

[5] Diana Bendz, "Green Products for Green Profits," *IEEE Spectrum* (September 1993): 63–66.

[6] Adapted from Bob King, *Better Designs in Half the Time*, Methuen, MA: GOAL/QPC (1989): 1.1–1.3.

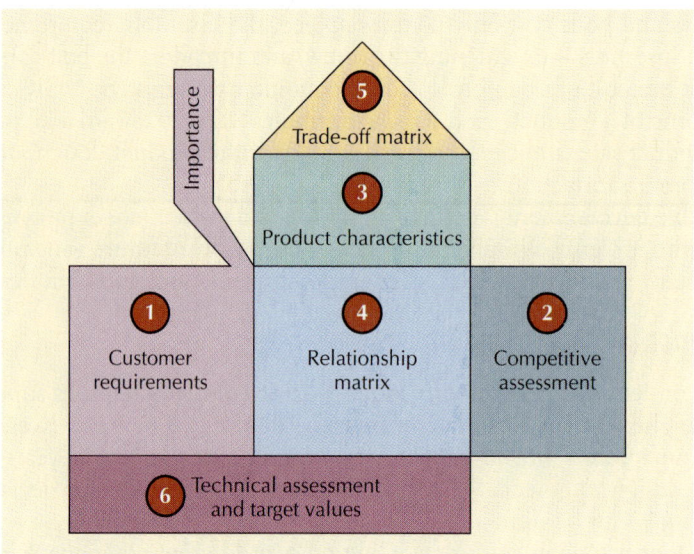

FIGURE 5.7   **Outline of the House of Quality**

1. *Customer requirements.* Customer requirements drive the entire QFD process. This section lists, in customer terminology, the attributes of the product that are important to the customer (as revealed by market research). These attributes can get quite lengthy, so they are grouped into bundles (e.g., irons well, easy and safe to use) by consensus of the design team or by more formal nonparametric statistics techniques (such as factor analysis or cluster analysis). The smokestack of the house shows the importance customers attach to each attribute on a scale of 1 to 10. Larger numbers denote greater importance.

2. *Competitive assessment.* On the right side of the house is a perceptual map in which customers rate the performance of our product, X, against competing products, A and B, for each customer requirement. Larger numbers represent better performance. This information is used to determine which customer needs will yield a competitive advantage and should be pursued. In this example, our iron already excels in the customer requirements of "presses quickly," "removes wrinkles," "provides enough steam," and "doesn't break when dropped," so we do not need to improve those factors. However, we are rated poorly on "doesn't stick," "doesn't spot," "heats quickly," "quick cool-down," and "not too heavy." Also, we could gain some competitive advantage with an iron that "doesn't scorch fabric" and "doesn't burn when touched," since products A, B, and X have similar ratings and there is room for improvement.

3. *Product characteristics.* Product characteristics, expressed in engineering terms, are located on the top floor of the house ("energy needed to press," "friction against cloth," etc.). These characteristics are bundled just like the customer attributes, except that the terminology reflects more of an engineering orientation ("force," "dimensions and material," etc.).

The objective measures toward the bottom of the house provide the technical data to support or refute customer perceptions. For example, customers rated our iron poorly on "quick cool-down." Quick cool-down is measured by the "time required to go from 450° to 100°." Our iron takes 600 seconds to cool down, while A and B take 500 and 300 seconds, respectively. The customer is correct, our iron does take longer to cool down than our competitors'.

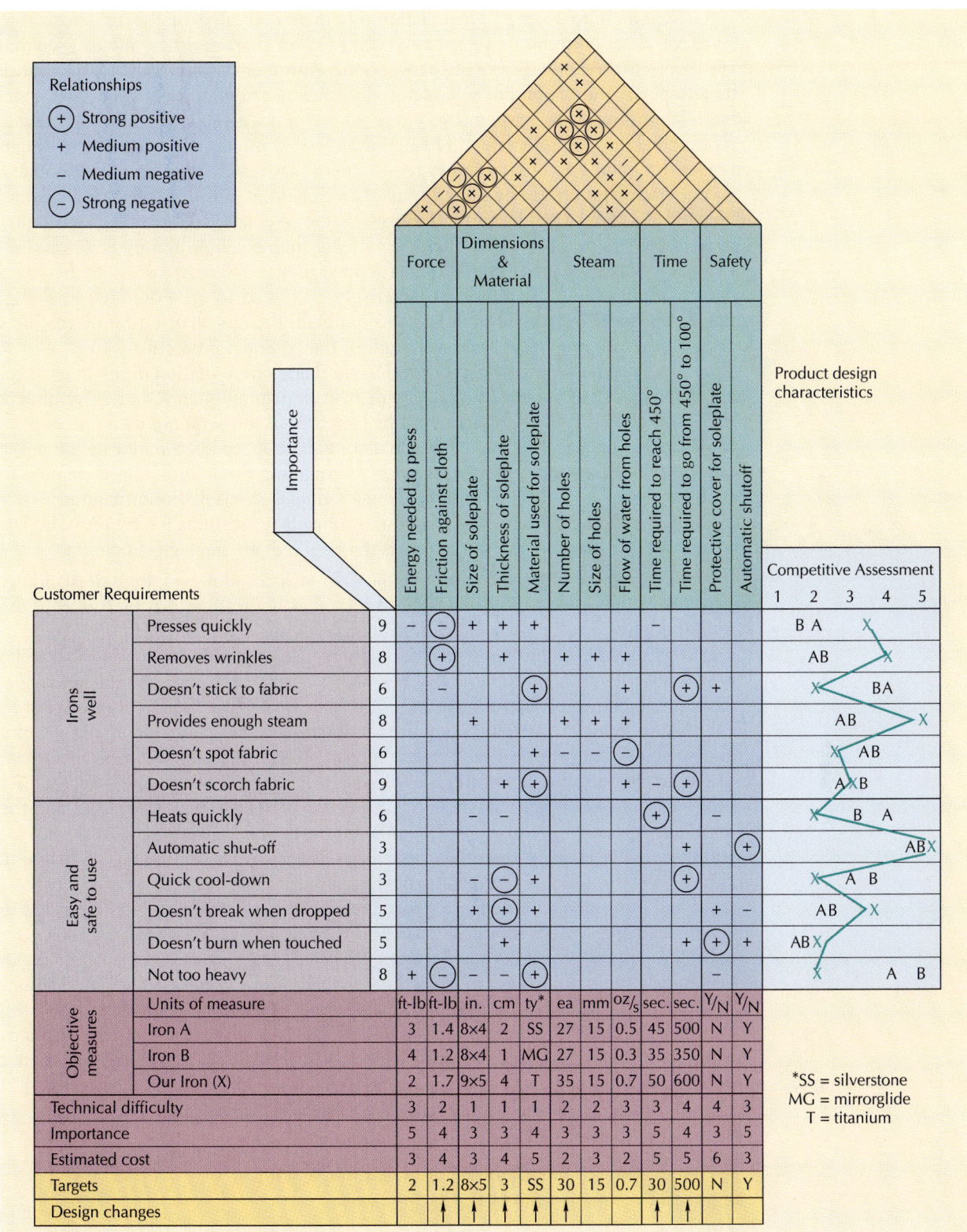

FIGURE 5.8   The House of Quality for a Steam Iron

4.   *Relationship matrix.* The relationship matrix, located in the middle of the house, correlates customer requirements with product characteristics. We can see that a strong positive relationship exists between the customer requirement "doesn't break when dropped" and the product characteristic "thickness of soleplate," but a strong negative relationship exists between the requirement "quick cool-down" and the characteristic "thickness of soleplate." This information is useful in coordinating design changes in response to one customer requirement that may be in conflict with others.

5.   *Trade-off matrix.* The trade-off matrix looks at the impact of changing product characteristics. For example, if the thickness of the soleplate is increased, the time required to heat up and cool down the iron will also increase, but the iron will press better ("energy needed to press" goes down, "friction against cloth" increases) and the steam will flow more evenly. All these characteristics will need to be monitored as design changes are made in soleplate thickness to maintain them at their desired level. This is not an easy task, but at least we are aware of the potential problems.

6.   *Technical assessments and design targets.* The bottom portion of the house contains various factors important to management in determining target values for design, such as cost, difficulty, and importance. The target row is the *output* of the house—measurable values of product characteristics that are to be achieved in the new design of the steam iron. These values are determined by considering the information contained in the house of quality, but they are not calculated directly from that information.

Compare the target values to the current objective measures for iron X. The last row indicates with arrows the design characteristics that are targeted for change.

The house of quality is the most popular QFD matrix. However, to understand the full power of QFD, we need to consider three other houses that can be linked to the house of quality (see Figure 5.9). In our example, suppose we decide to meet the customer requirement of "heats quickly" by reducing the thickness of the soleplate. The second house, *parts deployment*, examines which component parts are affected by reducing the thickness of the soleplate. Obviously, the soleplate itself is affected, but so are the fasteners used to attach the soleplate to the iron, as well as the depth of the holes and connectors that provide steam. These new part characteristics then become inputs to the third house, *process planning*. To change the thickness of the soleplate, the dies used by the metal-stamping machine to produce the plates will have to change, and the stamping machine will require adjustments. Given these changes, a fourth house, *operating requirements*, prescribes how the fixtures and gauges for the stamping machine will be set, what additional training the operator of the machine needs, and how process control and preventive maintenance procedures need to be adjusted. Nothing is left to chance—all bases are covered from customer to design to manufacturing.

In comparison with traditional design approaches, QFD forces management to spend more time defining the new product changes and examining the ramifications of those changes. More time spent in the early stages of design means less time is required later to revise the design and make it work. This reallocation of time shortens the design process considerably. Some experts suggest that QFD can produce better product designs in *half* the time as conventional design processes. In summary, QFD is a communications and planning tool that

QFD is a communications and planning tool.

■ Promotes better understanding of customer demands;

■ Promotes better understanding of design interactions;

■ Involves manufacturing in the design process;

■ Breaks down barriers between functions and departments;

■ Focuses the design effort;

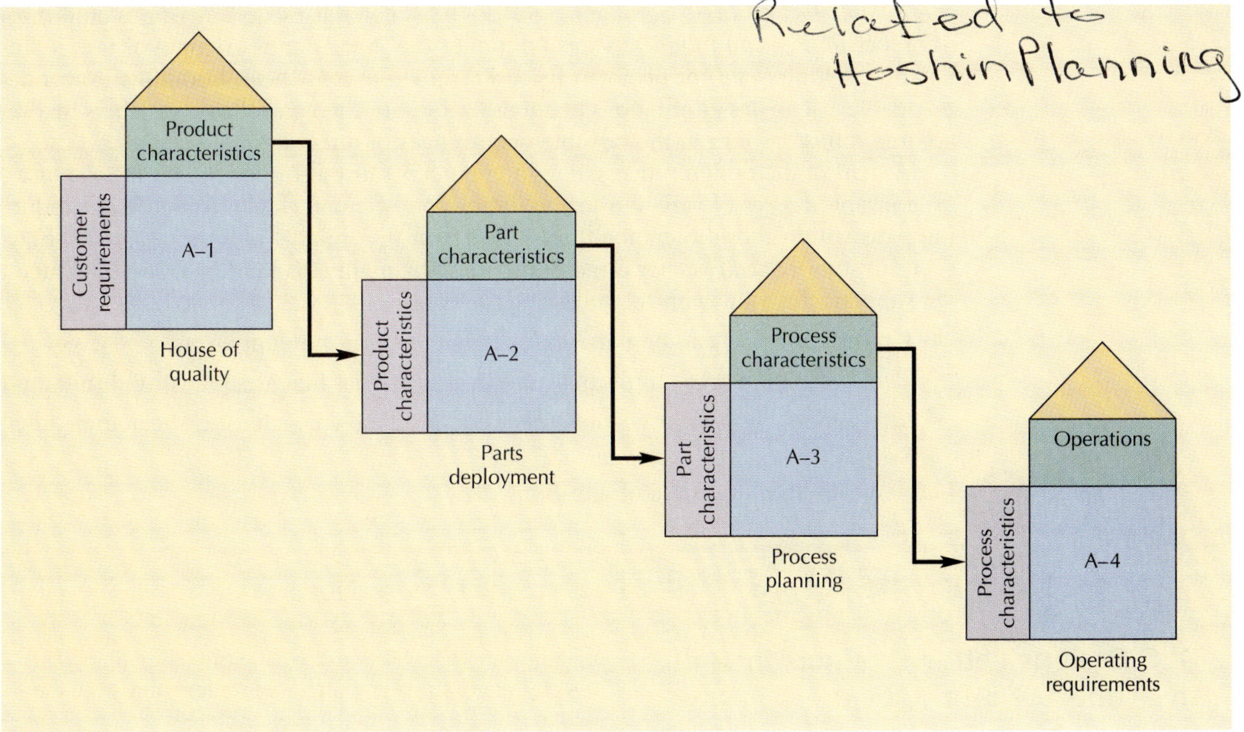

Related to Hoshin Planning -

FIGURE 5.9   A Series of Connected QFD Houses

- Fosters teamwork;
- Improves documentation of the design and development process;
- Provides a database for future designs;
- Increases customer satisfaction;
- Reduces the number of engineering changes;
- Brings new designs to the market faster; and
- Reduces the cost of design and manufacture.

Design for Robustness

A product can fail because it was manufactured wrong in the factory—*quality of conformance*—or because it was designed incorrectly—*quality of design*. Quality control techniques such as statistical process control (SPC) concentrate on quality of conformance. Genichi Taguchi, a Japanese industrialist and statistician, suggests that product failure is primarily a function of design quality.

Consumers subject products to an extreme range of operating conditions and still expect them to function normally. The steering and brakes of a car, for example, should continue to perform their function even on wet, winding roads or when the tires are not inflated properly. A product designed to withstand variations in environmental and operating conditions is said to be *robust* or possess *robust quality*. Taguchi believes that superior quality is derived from products that are more robust and that robust products come from **robust design.**

The conditions that cause a product to operate poorly (called *noise*) can be separated into controllable and uncontrollable factors. From a designer's point of view, the

Superior quality is derived from a robust design.

www.prenhall.com/russell

Robust design yields a product or service designed to withstand variations.

controllable factors are design parameters such as material used, dimensions, and form of processing. *Uncontrollable factors* are under the user's control (length of use, maintenance, settings, etc.) or occur in the user's environment (heat, humidity, excess demand, etc.). The designer's job is to choose values for the controllable variables that react in a robust fashion to the possible occurrences of uncontrollable factors.

As part of the design process, design engineers must also specify certain *tolerances*, or allowable ranges of variation in the dimension of a part. It is assumed that producing parts within those tolerance limits will result in a quality product. Taguchi, however, suggests that *consistency* is more important to quality than being within tolerances. He supports this view with the following observations:

- Consistent errors can be more easily corrected than random errors,
- *Parts* within tolerance limits may produce *assemblies* that are not within limits, and
- Consumers have a strong preference for product characteristics near their ideal values.

Let's examine each of these observations.

THE COMPETITIVE EDGE

DEC Designs Better Products in Half the Time at Half the Cost

www.prenhall.com/russell

When DEC decided to enter the workstation market in the late 1980s, it expected its world-class manufacturing operations to help it win considerable market share. After a disappointing performance, the company realized that "the best products don't count if they don't show up on time," and they began to examine their process for designing new products. Successful application of three techniques—quality function deployment, design for manufacture, and Taguchi methods—significantly improved the design process and enabled DEC's new workstations to hit the market in less than half the time, cut product costs in half while increasing customer options by fourfold, and capture twice the market share.

QFD was used as a conduit to drive the "voice of the customer" through design requirements, part characteristics, process control characteristics, and operating instructions. QFD readjusted the design team's approach by forcing team members to listen to the customer, reducing many misconceptions and unproductive debates within the team, encouraging greater competitive awareness, and focusing the team on design target values instead of acceptable limits. More than 100 QFD studies have since been conducted, resulting in a 75 percent reduction in the time spent on the concept phase of design, a 40 percent reduction in the total engineering changes needed to get the product to market, and a 25 percent re-duction in product features (mainly by designing what the customer wanted, rather than overdesigning what the design team *believed* the customer wanted).

Applying design for manufacture concepts resulted in a reduction in the number of parts, shorter assembly times, simpler production control, less inventory, and fewer operations and material costs. Specifically, the number of parts was cut in half (for a 40 percent cost savings), the number of assembly operations was reduced by 33 percent, and the assembly time was reduced by 65 percent—all this when the design cycle time was shortened by more than 70 percent.

Better quality used to mean tighter specifications and tolerances, but that's not necessarily the case with Taguchi methods. After a limited number of analyses à la Taguchi, an optimum set of parameter values can be determined for maximum design robustness. At DEC these more robust designs reduced rework by 60 percent, increased machine utilization by 44 percent, reduced the cost of quality by 25 percent, and increased the operational life of the product by 50 percent.

DEC continues to improve its product development process to achieve earlier-to-market and less-cost-to-market goals. The company measures the success of its design process by its accuracy of cost and time predictions, the number of engineering changes required, "ramp-up" time, the number of phase reworks, and break-even time.

SOURCE: Based on Keith Nichols, "Better, Cheaper, Faster Products—by Design," *Journal of Engineering Design* 3, no. 3 (1992): 217–28.

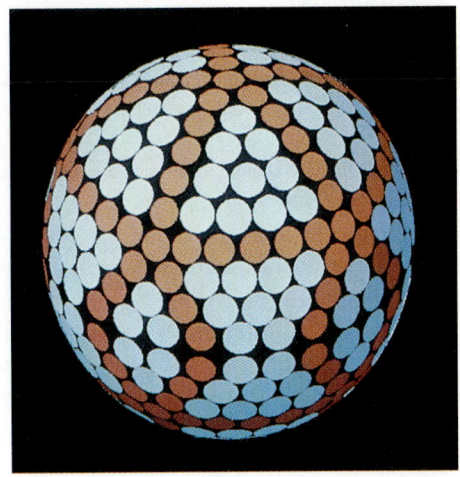

Computer-aided design (CAD) is used to design everything from pencils to submarines. Some of our everyday products are more difficult to design than you may think. Potato chips with ridges, the top of a soda can, a two-liter bottle of soft drink, a car door, and golf balls are examples of simple products that require the sophistication of CAD for effective design and testing. Shown here are two examples of dimple design on Titleist golf balls. The number, size, and patterns of dimples on a golf ball can affect the distance, trajectory, and accuracy of play. The advent of CAD has allowed many more designs to be tested. Today, over 200 different dimple patterns are used by golf-ball manufacturers. Golf clubs and golf courses are also designed with CAD.

Consistent mistakes are easier to correct. Consider the professor who always starts class five minutes late. Students can adjust their arrival patterns to coincide with the professor's, or the professor's clock can be set ahead by five minutes. But if the professor sometimes starts class a few minutes early, sometimes on time, and other times ten minutes late, the students are more apt to be frustrated, and the professor's behavior will be more difficult to change.

Consistency is especially important for assembled products. The assembly of two parts that are near opposite tolerance limits may result in *tolerance stack-ups* and poor quality. For example, a button diameter that is small (near to the lower tolerance limit) combined with a buttonhole that is large (near to its upper tolerance limit) results in a button that won't stay fastened. Although it is beyond the scope of this text, Taguchi advises how to set tolerance limits so that tolerance stack-up can be avoided.

Manufacturing tolerances define what is acceptable or unacceptable quality. Parts or products measured outside tolerance limits are considered defective and are either reworked or discarded. Parts or products within the limits are considered "good." Taguchi asserts that although all the parts or products within tolerances may be acceptable, they are not all of the same quality. Consider a student who earns an average grade of 60 in a course. He or she will pass, whereas a student who earns an average grade of 59 will fail. A student with a 95 average will also pass the course. Taguchi would claim that there is negligible difference between the quality of the students with averages of 59 and 60, even though one was "rejected" and the other was not. There is, however, a great deal of difference in the quality of the student with an average of 60 and the student with an average of 95. Further, a professor in a subsequent class or a prospective employer will be able to detect the difference in quality and will overwhelmingly prefer the student who passed the course with a 95 average.

Consistency is important to quality.

Technology in Design

New products for more segmented markets have proliferated over the past decade. Changes in product design are more frequent and product life cycles are shorter. Hewlett-Packard derives more than 50 percent of its sales from products developed within the past three years. IBM estimates the average life of its new product offerings is about six months. Sony has introduced more than 160 different models of its Walkman over the past ten years. The ability to get new products to the market quickly has revolutionized the competitive environment and changed the nature of manufacturing.

Part of the impetus for the deluge of new products is the advancement of technology available for designing products. It begins with computer-aided design (CAD) and includes related technologies such as computer-aided engineering (CAE), and computer-aided manufacturing (CAM).

Computer-Aided Design

CAD assists in the creation, modification, and analysis of a design.

Computer-aided design (CAD) is a software system that uses computer graphics to assist in the creation, modification, and analysis of a design. CAD can be used for geometric modeling, automated drafting and documentation, engineering analysis, and design analysis. *Geometric modeling* uses basic lines, curves, and shapes to generate the geometry and topology of a part. The part may appear as a wire mesh image or as a shaded, solid model. Once an object has been input into the system, it can be displayed and manipulated in a variety of ways. The design can be rotated for a front, side, or top view, separated into different parts, enlarged for closer inspection, or shrunk back so that another feature can be highlighted. The CAD database created from the geometric design includes not only the dimensions of the product but also tolerance information and material specifications. Libraries of designs can be accessed so that designers can modify existing designs instead of building new ones from scratch.

Circuit boards contain dozens of layers that must connect in the

www.prenhall.com/russell

right places. CAD allows this designer from Solectron to examine one layer of the board at a time and test the accuracy of the design. Since most circuit boards are populated with automated equipment (usually robots), the CAD design also serves as an important input to programming automation or CAM. Today's CAD/CAM systems can handle designs with over 250 layers.

Automated drafting produces engineering drawings directly from the CAD database. More advanced documentation merges text and graphics to produce assembly drawings, bills of material, instruction manuals and reports, parts catalogs, and sales brochures. Figure 5.10 shows a series of CAD drawings and an engineering analysis of an imaginary product.

Although the ability to combine, copy, translate, scale, and rotate designs or portions of designs is impressive, CAD is more than a drafter's version of a word processor. Its real power is derived from the ability to electronically link design with other automated systems. Engineering analysis, when performed at a computer terminal with a CAD system, is called **computer-aided engineering (CAE)**. CAE retrieves the description and geometry of a part from a CAD database and subjects it to testing and analysis on the computer screen without physically building a prototype. CAE can maximize the storage space in a car trunk, detect whether plastic parts are cooling evenly, and determine how much stress will cause a bridge to crack. With CAE, design teams can watch a car bump along a rough road, the pistons of an engine move up and down, or a golf ball soar through the air. In the field of chemistry, reactions of chemicals can be analyzed on a computer screen. And, in medicine, the effects of new drugs can be tested on computer-generated DNA molecules. Aerodynamic CAD/CAE software can replace expensive wind tunnels. *Cyberman*, a computer mannequin, tests the ergonomics of a design by examining arm reach, pedal position, and steering-column angle for Chrysler cars.

The ultimate design-to-manufacture connection is a CAD/CAM system. CAM is the acronym for *computer-aided manufacturing*. It basically refers to control of the manufacturing process by computers. CAD/CAM involves the automatic conversion of CAD design data into processing instructions for computer-controlled equipment and the subsequent manufacture of the part as it was designed. This integration of design and manufacture can save enormous amounts of time, ensure that parts and products are produced *precisely* as intended, and facilitate revisions in design or customized production.

CAE tests and analyzes designs on the computer screen.

www.prenhall.com/russell

CAD/CAM is the ultimate design-to-manufacture connection.

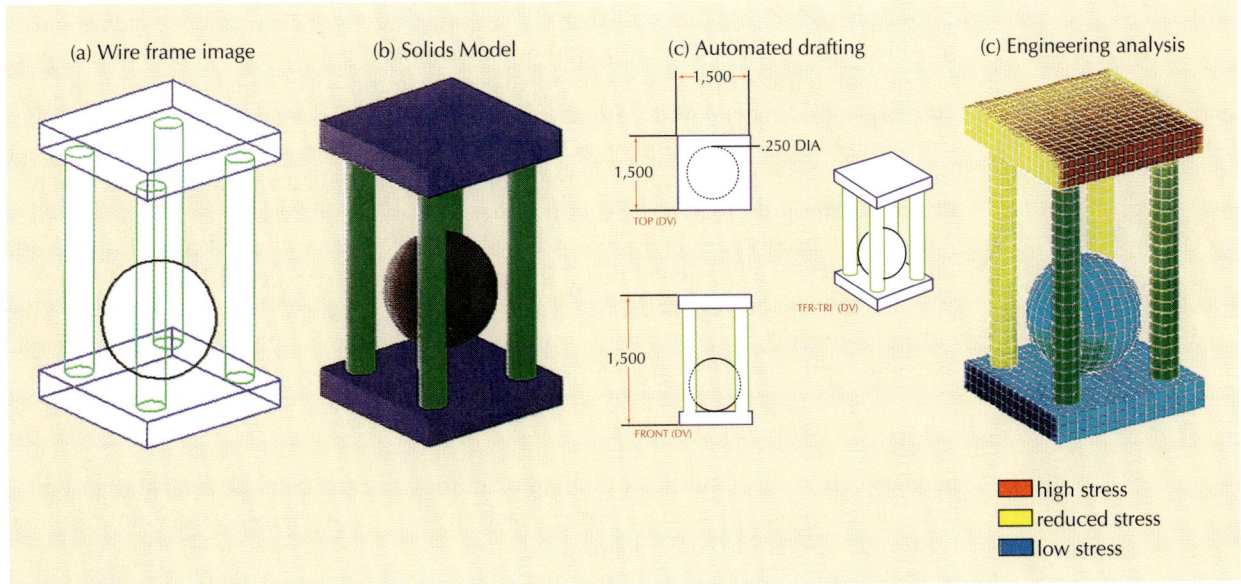

FIGURE 5.10 **A CAD Example**

Benefits of CAD   CAD radically reduces the leadtime for new product introduction. CAD's time advantage is not being able to *draw* lines faster, but being able to *find* them faster. The drafting of an original design by computer is not significantly faster than drafting by hand, but revising and adapting existing designs is almost twelve times faster. The ability to sort, classify, and retrieve similar designs facilitates standardization of parts, prompts ideas, and eliminates building a design from scratch.

CAD-generated products can be introduced faster to the market because they can be tested quicker. CAE systems interacting with CAD databases can test the functioning of a design so thoroughly that a prototype may never be built. Costly mistakes in design or production can be avoided because materials, parts fit, and conditions of use can be tested on the screen. Time to manufacture can also be reduced with CAD-initiated designs of molds, dies, and processing instructions. Documentation of CAD designs allows the information to be printed out in various forms for multiple users— as a parts list, sales catalog, or assembly instructions.

Besides the time savings, CAD and its related technologies have also improved the *quality* of designs and the products manufactured from them. The communications capabilities of CAD may be more important than its processing capabilities in terms of design quality. CAD systems enhance communication and promote innovation in multifunctional design teams by providing a visual, interactive focus for discussion. Watching a vehicle strain its wheels over mud and ice prompts ideas on product design and customer use better than stacks of consumer surveys or engineering reports. New ideas can be suggested and tested immediately, allowing more alternatives to be evaluated. To facilitate discussion or clarify a design, CAD data can be sent electronically between designer and supplier or viewed simultaneously on computer screens by different designers in physically separated locations. Prototypes can be tested more thoroughly with CAD/CAE. More prototypes can be tested as well. CAD improves every stage of product design and is especially useful as a means of integrating design and manufacture.

CAD produces better designs faster.

www.prenhall.com/russell

Service Design

Services that are allowed to just "happen" rarely meet customer needs. The service provider is left to figure out what the customer wants and how the service should be provided without sufficient support from management, policies and procedures, or physical surroundings. World-class services that come to mind—McDonald's, Nordstrom, Federal Express, Disney World—are all characterized by impeccable design. McDonald's plans every action of its employees (including forty-nine steps to making perfect french fries); Nordstrom creates a pleasurable shopping environment with well-stocked shelves, live music, fresh flowers in the dressing rooms, and legendary salespersons; Federal Express designs every stage of the delivery process for efficiency and speed; and Disney World in Japan was so well designed that it impressed even the zero-defect Japanese.

Can services be designed in the same manner as products? If we substitute the word *service* for *product*, and *delivery* for *manufacture* in Figure 5.2, the design process would *look* much the same, but there are some important differences. Let's examine them.

Services need to be carefully designed.

www.prenhall.com/russell

Characteristics of Services

Services can be distinguished from manufacturing by the eight characteristics listed below. Although not all services possess each of these characteristics, they do exhibit at least some of them to some degree.

1. *Services are intangible.* It is difficult to design something you cannot see, touch, store on a shelf, or try on for size. Services are *experienced*, and that experience may be

Eight characteristics distinguish services from manufacturing.

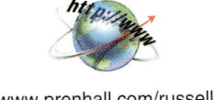

www.prenhall.com/russell

Within three years of entering the crowded credit card market, <u>AT&T Universal Card Services (UCS)</u> emerged second out of 6,000 competitors and became the proud recipient of a Malcolm Baldrige National Quality Award. In a market that others viewed as saturated, Paul Kahn, CEO of UCS, saw unmet customer needs and "room in the business to give something back to the customer." He set out to become a major contender in the marketplace by startling customers with service that went far beyond what they had come to expect. The "product" design included a variable interest rate linked to the prime rate; no annual fee for life; an unconditional service guarantee ($10 for every mistake or inconvenience); customer service available 24 hours a day, 7 days a week; commitment to act as the customer's advocate in billing disputes; a combination credit card/calling card with 10 percent discount on calls; a standard card with the same features as gold cards; and rapid application approval (completed over the phone in less than 4 minutes). Kahn read the public correctly—the innovative design delighted the customer and attracted one million accounts in just 78 days.

different for each individual customer. Designing a service involves describing what the customer is supposed to "experience," which can be a difficult task. Designers begin by compiling information on the way people think, feel, and behave (called *psychographics*).

Because of its intangibility, consumers perceive a service more risky to purchase than a product. Cues (such as physical surroundings, server's demeanor, service guarantees, etc.) need to be included in service design to help form or reinforce accurate perceptions of the service experience and reduce the consumer's risk.

The quality of a service experience depends largely on the customer's service *expectations*. Expectations can differ according to a customer's knowledge, experience, and self-confidence. The medical profession has done a masterful job of conditioning patients to be told little, accept what happens to them on faith, and not to be disappointed when medical problems are not corrected. Medical personnel who exceed these expectations, even by a small margin, are perceived as delivering outstanding service.[7]

[7] J. L. Heskett, W. E. Sasser, and C. Hart, *Service Breakthroughs: Changing the Rules of the Game* (New York: Free Press, 1990), p. 7.

Customers also have different expectations of different types of service providers. You probably expect more from a department store than a discount store, or from a car dealer's service center than an independent repair shop. Understanding the customer and his or her expectations is essential in designing good service.

2. *Service output is variable.* This is true because of the various service providers employed and the variety of customers they serve, each with his or her own special needs. Even though customer demands vary, the service experience is expected to remain consistent. According to a recent survey, reliability and consistency are the most important measures of service quality to the customer.[8] Service design, then, must strive for predictability or robustness. Examples of services known for their consistency include McDonald's, Holiday Inn, and ServiceMaster. Extensive employee training, set operating procedures, and standardized materials, equipment, and physical environments are used by these companies to increase consistency.

3. *Services have high customer contact.* The service "encounter" between service provider and customer *is* the service in many cases. Making sure the encounter is a positive one is part of service design. This involves giving the service provider the skills and authority necessary to complete a customer transaction successfully. Studies show a direct link between service provider motivation and customer satisfaction. Moreover, service providers are motivated primarily not by compensation but rather by concurrence with the firm's "service concept" and being able to perform their job competently.[9]

High customer contact can interfere with the efficiency of a service and make it difficult to control its quality (i.e., there is no opportunity for testing and rework). However, direct contact with customers can also be an advantage for services. Observing customers experiencing a service generates new service ideas and facilitates feedback for improvements to existing services.

4. *Services are perishable.* Since services can't be saved until later, the timing and location of delivery are important. Service design should define not only *what* is to be delivered but also *where* and *when.*

5. *Consumers do not separate the service from the delivery of the service.* That means service design and process design must occur concurrently. (This is one area in which services have an advantage over manufacturing—it has taken manufacturing a number of years to realize the benefits of concurrent design.) In addition to deciding "what, where, and when," service design also specifies *how* the service should be provided. "How" decisions include the degree of customer participation in the service process, which tasks should be done in the presence of the customer (called front-room activities) and which should be done out of the customer's sight (back-room activities), the role and authority of the service provider in delivering the service, and the balance of "touch" versus "tech" (i.e., how automated the service should be).

6. *Services tend to be decentralized and geographically dispersed.* Many service employees are on their own to make decisions. Although this can present problems, careful service design will help employees deal successfully with contingencies. Multiple service outlets can be a plus in terms of rapid prototyping. New ideas can be field-tested with a minimum disturbance to operations. McDonald's considers each of its outlets a "laboratory" for new ideas.

7. *Services are consumed more often than products,* so there are more opportuni-

---

[8] L. Berry, A. Parasuraman, and V. Zeithaml, "The Service Quality Puzzle," *Business Horizons* (September–October 1988): 37.

[9] Heskett, Sasser, and Hart, *Service Breakthroughs,* p. 15.

ties to succeed or fail with the customer. Jan Carlzon of SAS Airlines calls these opportunities "moments of truth." In a sense, the service environment lends itself more readily to continuous improvement than does the manufacturing environment.

8. *Services can be easily emulated.* Competitors can copy new or improved services quickly. New ideas are constantly needed to stay ahead of the competition. As a result, new service introductions and service improvements occur even more rapidly than new product introductions.

The Service Concept

Service design is more comprehensive and occurs more often than product design. The process of generating a design, however, can be quite similar. Service design begins with a service concept and ends with design specifications to communicate the concept.

The service concept involves creating a **service package**, or *bundle*, that meets certain customer needs. The package consists of a mixture of physical items, sensual benefits, and psychological benefits.[10] For a restaurant the physical items consist of the facility, food, drinks, tableware, napkins, and other touchable commodities. The sensual benefits include the taste and aroma of the food and the sights and sounds of the people. Psychological benefits could be rest and relaxation, comfort, status, or a sense of well-being.

A **service package** includes physical items, sensual benefits, and psychological benefits.

The key to effective service design is to recognize and define *all* the components of a service package—none of the components should be left to chance. Finding the appropriate mix of physical items and sensual and psychological benefits and designing them to be consistent with each other is also important. A fast-food restaurant promises nourishment with speed. The customer is served quickly and is expected to consume the food quickly. Thus, the tables, chairs, and booths are not designed to be comfortable, nor does their arrangement encourage lengthy or personal conversations. The service package is consistent. This is not the case for an upscale restaurant located in a renovated train station. The food is excellent, but it is difficult to enjoy a full-course meal sitting on wooden benches in a drafty facility, where conversations echo and tables shake when the trains pass by. In the hospitality industry, Mariott Corporation is known for its careful design of specialty hotels. From its Courtyard Mariott to Fairfield Inn to residential centers, each facility "fits" its clientele with a well-researched service concept.

www.prenhall.com/russell

Sometimes services are successful because their service concept fills a previously unoccupied niche or differs from the generally accepted mode of operation. For example, ClubMed perfected the "packaged vacation" concept for a carefree vacation experience. Citicorp offers 15-minute mortgage approvals through online computer networks with real estate offices, credit bureaus, and builder's offices, and an expert system loan-application adviser. Shouldice Hospital performs only inguinal hernia operations, for which its doctors are very experienced and its facilities carefully designed. Local anesthesia is used; patients walk into and out of the operating room under their own power; and telephones, televisions, and dining facilities are located in a communal area some distance from patient rooms. As a result, patients quickly become ambulatory, are discharged within hours (compared to normal week-long stays), and pay one-third less for their operations.

---

[10] The concept of a service package and its contents comes from W. E. Sasser, R. P. Olsen, and D. Wyckoff, *Management of Service Operations* (Boston: Allyn and Bacon, 1978), pp. 8–10.

Performance, Design, and Delivery Specifications

From the service concept, *performance specifications* are determined to meet customer requirements (in general and for specific customers). The performance specifications are then converted into *design specifications* and, finally, into *service delivery specifications* (in lieu of manufacturing specifications).

Performance, design, and delivery specifications allow a service to be replicated at different locations and times.

In services, the design process incorporates both service design and delivery. Design specifications must describe the service in sufficient detail for the desired service experience to be replicated for different individuals at numerous locations. The specifications typically consist of drawings, physical models, and narrative descriptions of the service package. Employee training or guidelines for service providers may also be included. Finally, service delivery specifications outline the steps required in the work process.

A well-designed service system is:[11]

- *Consistent* with the strategic focus of the firm—if the firm competes on speed, then every element of the service process should encourage speed.
- *User friendly*: Clear signs and directions, understandable forms, logical steps in the process, and accessible service providers.
- *Robust*: Able to cope with surges in demand, resource shortages, and varying customer expectations.
- *Easy to sustain*: Workers are given manageable tasks and the technology is supportive and reliable.
- *Effectively linked* between front office and back office activities.
- *Cost-effective*: No wasted time or resources, or appearance of inefficiency.
- *Visible to the customer*: Customers should clearly see the value of the service provided.

Summary

New products enhance a company's image, invigorate employees, and help a firm to grow and prosper. Product design and development, however, can be long and tedious, especially with a serial design process. Concurrent design combines product and process decisions, utilizes design teams and design for manufacture concepts, and calls for changes in the role of design engineers. Methods for improving the quality of design include monitoring long-term design quality, quality function deployment, and Taguchi methods for robust design.

Technology, in the form of CAD, CAE, and CAD/CAM, allows better-quality products to be designed, revised, tested, and produced with record speed.

Service design is more comprehensive than product design because the customer considers service delivery as part of the service itself. Thus, service design includes such factors as physical surroundings and the role of the service provider as well.

Designs define what goods or services are to be provided to the customer. We must now decide *how* to provide them. The next chapter describes the decisions involved in planning the production process.

---

[11] These characteristics are adapted from R. Chase and N. Aquilano, *Production and Operations Management* (Chicago: Irwin, 1995), p. 123.

Summary of Key Terms

benchmarking: finding the best-in-class product or process, measuring one's performance against it, and making recommendations for improvements based on the results.

computer-aided design (CAD): a software system that uses computer graphics to assist in the creation, modification, and analysis of a design.

computer-aided engineering (CAE): engineering analysis performed at a computer terminal with information from a CAD database.

concurrent design: a new approach to design that involves the simultaneous design of products and processes by design teams.

design for assembly (DFA): a set of procedures for reducing the number of parts in an assembly, evaluating methods of assembly, and determining an assembly sequence.

design for environment (DFE): designing a product from material that can be recycled or easily repaired rather than discarded.

design for manufacture (DFM): designing a product so that it can be produced easily and economically.

DFM guidelines: statements of good design practice.

failure mode and effects analysis (FMEA): a systematic approach for analyzing the causes and effects of product failures.

fault tree analysis (FTA): a visual method for analyzing the interrelationships among failures.

form design: the phase of product design concerned with how the product looks.

functional design: the phase of product design concerned with how the product performs.

maintainability: the ease with which a product is maintained or repaired.

modular design: combining standardized building blocks or modules in a variety of ways to create unique finished products.

perceptual map: a visual method for comparing customer perceptions of different products or services.

quality function deployment (QFD): a structured process that translates the voice of the customer into technical design requirements.

reliability: the probability that a given part or product will perform its intended function for a specified period of time under normal conditions of use.

reverse engineering: carefully dismantling and inspecting a competitor's product to look for design features that can be incorporated into your own product.

robust design: the design of a product or a service that can withstand variations in environmental and operating conditions.

service package: the mixture of physical items, sensual benefits, and psychological benefits provided to the customer.

simplification: reducing the number of parts, assemblies, or options in a product.

standardization: using commonly available parts that are interchangeable among products.

value analysis (VA): an analytical approach for eliminating unnecessary design features and functions.

Solved Problem

Jack McPhee, a production supervisor for McCormick, Inc., is committed to the company's new quality effort. Part of the program encourages making product components in-house to ensure higher quality levels and instill worker pride. The system seems to be working well. One assembly, which requires a reliability of 0.95, is normally purchased from a local supplier. Now it is being assembled in-house from three parts that each boast reliabilities of 0.96. However, customer complaints have risen in the last 12 months since McCormick started doing its own assembly work. Can you explain why? What can be done to correct the situation?

Solution:

The reliability of an assembly is the product of the reliabilities of its components. Thus, for the in-house assembly, the reliability is

$$0.96 \times 0.96 \times 0.96 = 0.8847$$

which is considerably less than the purchased assembly's reliability of 0.95. No wonder the customers are complaining.

To correct the situation, Jack could start purchasing the assembly again, redesign the product so that the number of components is reduced, increase the reliabilities of the individual components, or build in redundant components. To match an assembly reliability of 0.95, the individual reliabilities would need to be 0.983 for three components or 0.975 for two components.

The same effect could be achieved with the following backup system:

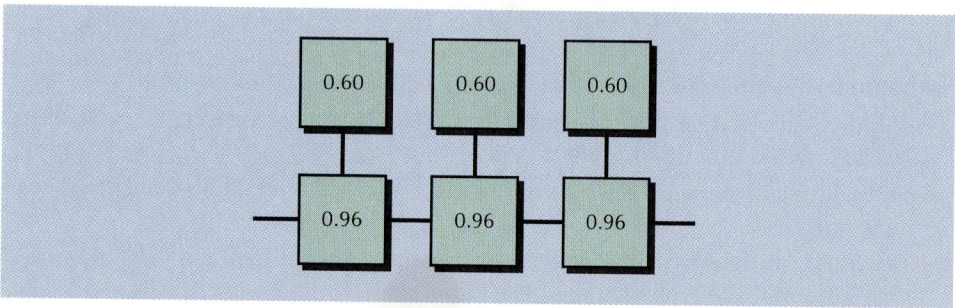

$$[0.96 + (0.04)(0.60)] \times [0.96 + (0.04)(0.60)] \times [0.96 + (0.04)(0.60)]$$
$$= 0.984 \times 0.984 \times 0.984 = 0.95$$

There are many possible answers to this question. Jack's decision will depend on the difficulty and cost of implementing the options you suggest.

Questions

5-1. Look around your classroom and make a list of items that impede your ability to learn. Classify them as problems in *quality of design* or *quality of conformance*.

5-2. How can organizations gain a competitive edge with product or service design?

5-3. Describe the strategic significance of design.

5-4. Differentiate between performance specifications, design specifications, and manufacturing specifications.

5-5. Discuss several methods for generating new product ideas.

5-6. Construct a perceptual map for the following products or services: (a) business schools in your state or region, (b) spreadsheet packages, and (c) video rental stores. Label the axes with the dimensions you feel are most relevant. Explain how perceptual maps are used.

5-7. Describe benchmarking and reverse engineering.

5-8. Find out if your university benchmarks itself against other universities. If so, write a summary of the characteristics that are considered, the measures that are used, and the results. Do the data support your views as a customer?

5-9. What kinds of analyses are conducted in a feasibility study for new products?

5-10. Discuss the objectives of form design and functional design.

5-11. Define reliability. Define maintainability. How are reliability and maintainability related?

5-12. Explain how simplification and standardization can improve designs.

5-13. How does modular design differ from standardization?

5-14. What types of decisions are involved in process planning?

5-15. How does the role of the design engineer change under concurrent design?

5-16. In what ways should design quality be measured?

5-17. What does design for manufacture entail? List several techniques that can facilitate the DFM process.

5-18. What does design for environment (DFE) involve?

5-19. Describe the objectives of failure mode and effects analysis, fault tree analysis, and value analysis.

5-20. Prepare a fault tree analysis for a project, computer assignment, or writing assignment you have recently completed.

5-21. How can design teams improve the quality of design?

5-22. Discuss the concept of concurrent design. What are the advantages of this approach?

5-23. Discuss the concept of robust design.

5-24. What is the purpose of quality function deployment (QFD)? How does it accomplish that purpose?

5-25. How has technology changed the manner in which products are designed?

5-26. Discuss the benefits of CAD.

5-27. List eight characteristics of services and explain how each characteristic impacts the design process.

5-28. How do product and service designs differ?

5-29. Describe the service package for (a) a bank, (b) an airline, and (c) a lawn service.

5-30. Generate as many ideas as you can for additional services or improvements in service delivery for (a) automated banking, (b) higher education, and (c) health care.

Problems

5-1. Use the following instructions to construct and test a prototype paper airplane. Are the instructions clear? How would you improve the design of the airplane or the manner in which the design is communicated?

- Begin with an $8\frac{1}{2}$-inch by 11-inch sheet of paper.
- Fold the paper together lengthwise to make a center line.
- Open the paper and fold the top corners to the center line.

- Fold the two top sides to the center line.
- Fold the airplane in half.
- Fold back the wings to meet the center line.
- Hold the plane by the center line and let it fly.

5-2. An alternate airplane design is given here. Follow the assembly instructions and test the airplane. Are the instructions clear? Compare the performance of this airplane design with the one described in Problem 5-1. Which plane was easier to construct? How would you improve the design of this plane or the manner in which the design is communicated?

- Begin with an $8^1/_2$-inch by 11-inch sheet of paper.
- Fold it lengthwise in alternating directions. The folds should be about 1 inch wide.
- Hold the top of the folded paper in one hand and fan out the back portion with the other hand.
- Make a small fold in the nose of the plane to hold it together, and let it fly.

5-3. You are a member of a group of engineers, production managers, financial analysts and marketing representatives. Your company has decided to produce a new product, the revolutionary triangular porthole, and each of you has been chosen to contribute your special knowledge and skills toward the product's design. You are given the following information about the new product:

- A triangular porthole consists of three sides with an empty area in the middle.
- The porthole must be able to stand on each side.
- The triangle formed must be isosceles. The sides should be straight and taut.
- The area in the middle should be large enough to enable an average size hand to pass through.
- Each side must be composed of the same material, with top sides facing out.

You have access to the following materials: index cards, construction paper, stapler with staples, tape, paper clips, ruler, and scissors.

The results of your deliberations should include a list of materials to be used, a diagram of the product at different stages of assembly (with dimensions and other specifications marked), and a sample triangular porthole. Your design must take into account how the product will look, how it will perform, and how it will be produced. Remember to consider such factors as market appeal, quality level, cost, reliability, maintainability, simplification, and standardization.

5-4. A broadcasting station has five major subsystems that must all be operational before a show can go on the air. If each subsystem has the same reliability, what reliability would be required to be 95 percent certain of broadcast success? 98 percent certain? 99 percent certain?

5-5. Competition for a new generation of computers is so intense that MicroTech has funded three separate design teams to create the new systems. Due to varying capabilities of the team members, it is estimated that team A has a 95 percent probability of coming up with an acceptable design before the competition, team B has an 85 percent chance, and team C has a 75 percent chance. What is the probability that MicroTech will beat the competition with its new computers?

5-6. MagTech assembles tape players from four major components arranged as follows:

$A + B(1-A) = X$

$X + C(1-X) =$ reliability

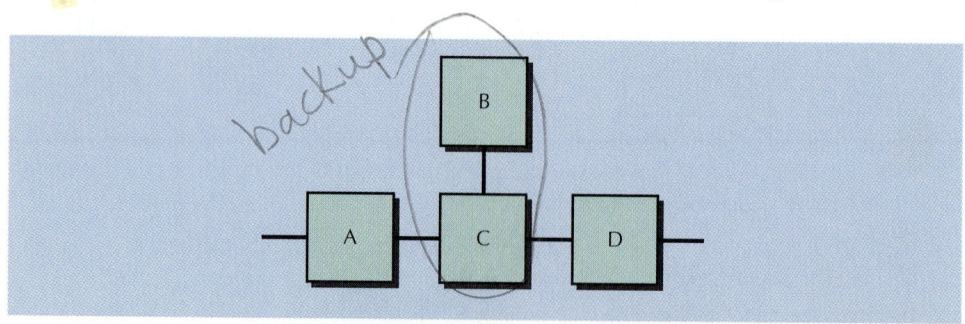

The components can be purchased from three different vendors, who have supplied the following reliability data:

	VENDOR		
Component	*1*	*2*	*3*
A	0.94	0.95	0.92
B	0.86	0.80	0.90
C	0.90	0.93	0.95
D	0.93	0.95	0.95

$A + C(1-B) + D$

a. If MagTech has decided to use only one vendor to supply all four components, which vendor should be selected?
b. Would your decision change if all the components were assembled in series?

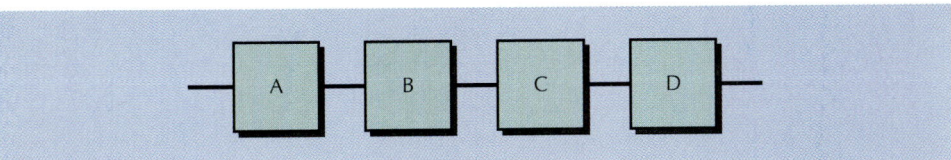

5-7. Glen Evans is an emergency medical technician for a local rescue team and is routinely called upon to render emergency care to citizens facing crisis situations. Although Glen has received extensive training, he also relies heavily on his equipment for support. During a normal call, Glen uses five essential pieces of equipment, whose individual reliabilities are 0.98, 0.975, 0.99, 0.96, and 0.995, respectively.
  a. Glen claims his equipment has a maximum probability of failure of 4 percent. Is he correct?
  b. What can be done to increase the reliability of Glen's equipment to 96 percent?

- add back-up equipment

5-8. Lisa Garrett has been a shift scheduler at a local fast-food chain for the past three years. Although the restaurant's patronage is relatively stable, employee attendance is not. For the most part, the restaurant employs students from a nearby high school. Experience has taught Lisa that both the age of the employee and the season of the year affect the reliability of employee attendance. During the school year, seniors are the most responsible and report to work 97 percent of the time, whereas juniors report only 95 percent of the time, and sophomores report 90 percent of the time. After graduation, however, students' thoughts turn to fun and freedom, and everyone's attendance drops to 90 percent.
  a. If a shift consists of two seniors, one junior, and one sophomore, what is the probability that Lisa will have to operate without a full shift during the school year? During the summer months?
  b. Suppose, during the summer months, Lisa can find a replacement worker 95 percent of the time. However, during the school years she is successful only 87 percent of the time. How does the employee reliability change during the summer months? During the school year?

5-9. A recent survey of college students yielded the following reasons for frequenting local nightspots:
  ■ Meet current friends and hang out with your crowd
  ■ Meet new people
  ■ Music format played
  ■ Drink prices

- ■ "Unwind" and drink
- ■ Dance
- ■ Promotions/giveaways/contests
- ■ Something to do when nothing else is happening

Use this information and your own insight to build a house of quality for a nightspot in your area.

5-10. The PlayBetter Golf Company has experienced a steady decline in sales of golf bags over the past five years. The basic golf bag design has not changed over that time period, and PlayBetter's CEO, Jack Palmer, has decided that the time has come for a customer-focused overhaul of the product. Jack read about a new design methodology called QFD in one of his professional magazines (it was used to design golf balls), and he commissioned a customer survey to provide data for the design process.

Customers considered the following requirements essential for any golf bag they would purchase and rated Playbetter's bag (X) against two competitor bags (A and B) on those requirements.

Customer Requirements	Competitive Assessment
	1 2 3 4 5
Lightweight	B A X
Comfortable carrying strap	X B A
Stands upright	X B A
Sturdy handle	X B A
Easy to remove/replace clubs	X B A
Easy to identify clubs	X B A
Protects clubs	B X A
Plenty of compartments	B X A
Place for towel	B A X
Place for scorecard/pencil	X B A
Easy to clean	X B A
Attractive	X A B

Construct a house of quality for golf bags. Then write a brief report to Mr. Palmer recommending revisions to the current golf bag design and explaining how those recommendations were determined.

5-11. Lean and Mean (L&M), a weight-reduction company, is considering entering the frozen-dinner market with a line of pricey, nutritious, low-calorie frozen dinners. Market research has shown that consumers want low-fat, low-cholesterol, low-calorie dinners that are good for you. They also want the dinners to taste good, fill them up, and contain both meat and vegetables, and dessert. In addition, the dinners should be reasonably priced, easy and fast to prepare, and come in a variety of entrées.

Help Lean and Mean find its competitive niche by constructing a house of quality. Choose three similar products currently on the market and assume that the most expensive product will most closely resemble L&M's new offering. What product design characteristics would you recommend for L&M? Why?

5-12. Create a house of quality for word processing software. Include the following customer attribute bundles: ease of use, cost, desired capabilities, and software interface. The customer requirements should be a "wish list" stated in nontechnical terms.

5-13. Students often complain that the requirements of assignments or projects are unclear. From the student's perspective, whoever can guess what the professor wants wins the highest grade. Thus, grades appear to be assigned somewhat arbitrarily. If you have ever felt that way, here is your chance to clarify that next project or assignment.

Construct a house of quality for a paper or project. View the professor as the customer. For the perceptual map, have your professor compare one of your papers with typical A, B, or C papers. When you have completed the exercise, give your opinion on the usefulness of QFD for this application.

5-14. Create a QFD example from your own experience. Describe the product or service to be designed and then complete a house of quality using representative data. Explain the entries in the house and how target values were reached. Also, describe how other houses might flow from the initial house you built. Finally, relate how QFD improves the design process for the example you chose.

CASE PROBLEM

Not That Color!

Casey Jones takes pride in his meticulous yard and sparkling house. Last year he added a large deck, and the year before he planted a grove of apple trees. "This summer I'll paint the house," he decided. That was before downsizing at work increased his workload and sent him out of town for weeks at a time.

Casey contracted the painting job to a reputable house repair service with these specific instructions:

Paint the exterior of the house gray with white trim. Get rid of mildew stains on the north side of the house and use a type of paint that is resistant to peeling and fading from the sun. Com-

plete the work as soon as possible for an amount not to exceed $2,500.

He returned three weeks later from a business trip to find the house painted North Carolina blue, the north side of the house noticeably darker than the rest, the window frames unpainted, splotches of paint on his lawn, and a bill for $2,750.

Taking the time to design a service carefully (often with direct customer participation) helps to prevent disagreements between customer and service provider and results in higher levels of customer satisfaction. How could Casey and his subcontractor have better designed the house painting service? Write separate performance, delivery, and design specifications for Casey's job.

CASE PROBLEM

Sure, the Highway May Be Intelligent, but What Can It Do for ME?

Amy Russell was still arranging her overheads as the planning commission filed into the room. She hated project-review time, but it was only once a year. Af-

ter everyone was seated, she began her presentation in a clear, strong voice.

"Let me begin by summarizing the significance and focus of the intelligent highway project. Highways are one of America's great assets. They give us the freedom to live, work, and play as we choose. However, they also present problems in the form of traffic congestion, safety, and air quality. 'Let's build more roads' is not the answer to these problems

(Continued)

given current budget constraints, land and fuel scarcities, and environmental restrictions. Fortunately, advancements in computer capabilities and accessibility, coupled with the information explosion, have provided new avenues for applying advanced technology to highways and transportation in general. The intelligent highway project is divided into five technology groups: (1) advanced traffic only management systems (ATMS), (2) advanced traveler information systems (ATIS), (3) advanced public transportation systems (APTS), (4) commercial vehicle operations (CVO), and (5) advanced vehicle control systems (AVCS). These technology groups provide the . . .”

“Now, hold on Amy,” interrupted a listener. “I know these acronyms and technology wonders make sense to you—you’re an engineer. But what do they mean to us as drivers on the highway, I mean to us as customers?”

“That’s a good question, Earl,” countered Amy. Thankful for a recent seminar on customer focus, she continued, “What uses would you and the other members of the commission make of an intelligent highway?” Blank stares answered her.

“Let me put it another way—what *information* would help you in your highway travels and what delays in driving would you like to eliminate?”

“I’d like to know the best route to take on my vacation,” said Eliza Boone.

“As a commuter, I’d like information on traffic conditions and weather conditions up ahead and some guidance on what alternate route I could take to avoid delays,” Hubert Banks commented.

“I’m a salesperson, so I travel alot. When I’m sent to a new city on business, I’d like to know how to get around,” volunteered Felipe Guzman.

To that, Stuart Schwartz added, “I’m a professional truck driver, and I hate to stop at those highway checkpoints. I figure it costs me about $1,000 for every 15 minutes I wait, and I can’t see any use for it. It’s just harassment. Can anything be done about that?”

“This might sound picky,” Mary Higgins thought aloud, “but I can’t understand what takes so long at those tollbooths downtown. The congestion adds 30 minutes to my drive to work. Isn’t there a better way than physically taking coins from drivers?”

After recording the group’s comments on a spare transparency, Amy faced the group. “Let me convert what you’ve said into what we call *user services.* Eliza, I’d call your request *pretrip planning.* Hubert and Felipe, you need *route guidance.*”

“Stuart, we can help you out with *commercial vehicle preclearance,* and, Mary, what you’d like is an *electronic payment system.* I also see four categories of customers here,” Amy continued somewhat excited by her discovery, “tourists, commuters, business travelers, and professional travelers.”

“Don’t forget a miscellaneous group,” Earl added.

“Okay, we’ll add miscellaneous travelers,” Amy sighed. “Now let me describe in nontechnical terms some alternate means of delivering the available technologies and get you to help me match up needs with appropriately designed services. I see two basic categories of service delivery: automated information with or without selection capability and personalized information delivered by service providers. Does that make sense?” queried Amy.

The group nodded and began to work.

Amy wondered what her boss was going to think about her spontaneous session with the commission.

How does the commission’s approach to designing intelligent highways differ from Amy’s approach? Do you think Amy will be able to bring back useful information to her boss?

For each of the five customer types identified, make a more complete list of their information needs. (This will serve as the basis for performance specifications for the intelligent highway service.) Then, for each type of service delivery, suggest alternate designs that would meet the performance specifications. (These are the start of design specifications for the intelligent highway service.)

References

Bedworth, D., M. Henderson, and P. Wolfe. *Computer-Integrated Design and Manufacturing.* New York: McGraw-Hill, 1991.

Berry, L., A. Parasuraman, and V. Zeithaml. “The Service Quality Puzzle.” *Business Horizons* (September–October 1988): 35–43.

Blackburn, J. (ed.) *Time-Based Competition: The Next Battleground.* Homewood, Ill.: Irwin, 1991.

Bowen, H. K., K. Clark, C. Holloway, *The Perpetual Enterprise Machine.* New York: Oxford University Press, 1994.

Collier, D. A. *The Service/Quality Solution*. New York: Irwin, 1994.

Ealey, L. *Quality by Design: Taguchi Methods and U.S. Industry*. Dearborn, Mich.: ASI Press, 1988.

Garvin, D. *Managing Quality*. New York: Macmillan, 1988.

Hauser, J. R. and D. Clausing. "The House of Quality." *Harvard Business Review* (May–June 1988): 63–73.

Heskett, J. L., W. E. Sasser, and C. Hart. *Service Breakthroughs: Changing the Rules of the Game*. New York: Macmillan, 1990.

Jacobson, G., and J. Hillkirk. *Xerox: American Samurai*. New York: Macmillan, 1986, pp. 178–79.

Kanter, R. M. *When Elephants Learn to Dance*. New York: Simon & Schuster, 1989.

King, B. *Better Designs in Half the Time*. Methuen, Mass.: GOAL/QPC, 1989.

Leonard-Barton, Dorothy. *Wellsprings of Knowledge: Building and Sustaining the Sources of Innovation*. Boston: Harvard Business School Press, 1995.

Nevens, J., D. Whitney, T. DeFazio, A. Edsall, R. Gustavson, R. Metzinger, and W. Dvorak. *Concurrent Design of Products and Processes: A Strategy for the Next Generation in Manufacturing*. New York: McGraw-Hill, 1989.

Peters, Tom. *Liberation Management*. New York: Alfred A. Knopf, 1992.

Port, O. "Back to the Basics." *Business Week Special Report on Innovation in America* (June 16, 1989): 15.

Schiller, Z. "Make It Simple." *Business Week* (September 9, 1996): 96–104.

Sprow, E. *Manufacturing Engineering* "Chrysler's Concurrent Engineering Challenge," (April 1992): 35–42.

Business Week "Chrysler's Neon, Is This the Small Car Detroit Couldn't Build?" (May 3, 1993): 116–26.

Stoll, H. "Design for Manufacture." *Manufacturing Engineering* (January 1988): 67–73.

Sullivan, L. P. "Quality Function Deployment." *Quality Progress* 19, no. 6 (1986): 39.

Taguchi, G., and D. Clausing. "Robust Quality." *Harvard Business Review* (January–February 1990): 65–75.

Whitney, D. "Manufacturing by Design." *Harvard Business Review* (July–August 1988): 83–91.

Womack, J. P., D. T. Jones, and D. Roos. *The Machine that Changed The World*. New York: Macmillan, 1990, pp. 118–19.

6

Process Planning and Technology Decisions

Allen-Bradley's Factory Showcase

www.prenhall.com/russell

Automation is <u>Allen-Bradley's</u> business. And its world contactor facility is its showcase. The "factory within a factory" covers 45,000 square feet on the eighth floor of Allen-Bradley's Milwaukee headquarters. Production is completely automated on an assembly line that's self-contained; no human hands touch the product from when it enters the line until exit.

The line produces contactors, a device for opening and closing electrical circuits. Each contactor contains about 76 parts, 22 of which are unique to a particular option. Production is initiated by laser markings on the contactor's base which call up a preprogrammed assembly sequence for over 900 contactor variations. The initial investment of $15 million has been returned several fold in profits from product sales, as well as in the promotion of Allen-Bradley control systems that operate the line.

One part of process planning is determining the degree of automation for a production system. This photo shows Allen-Bradley's automated assembly line for producing electrical contactors. Notice the warning lights overhead that signal equipment problems. The role of workers in this system is to schedule work, program the machines, and monitor their operation.

Processes are the essence of operations management. They transform inputs into outputs. More than products or technologies, the ability to *do* things well—*processes*—constitutes a firm's competitive advantage.

Process strategy is an organization's overall approach for physically producing goods and services.

Process strategy is an organization's overall approach for physically producing goods and services. Process decisions should reflect how the firm has chosen to compete in the marketplace, reinforce product decisions, and facilitate the achievement of corporate goals. A firm's process strategy will defines its:

- *Capital intensity:* The mix of capital (i.e., equipment, automation) and labor resources used in the productive process,
- *Process flexibility:* The ease with which resources can be adjusted in response to changes in demand, technology, products or services, and resource availability,

- *Vertical integration*: The extent to which the firm will produce the inputs and control the outputs of each stage of the productive process, and
- *Customer involvement*: The role of the customer in the productive process.

Types of Processes

We introduced four types of processes in Chapter 2—*projects, batch production, mass production*, and *continuous production*. Let's look at them more closely here and explore the implications of process choice for a firm.

Projects

Projects represent one-of-a-kind production for an individual customer. They tend to involve large sums of money and last a considerable length of time. For those reasons, customers are few and customer involvement intense. Customers are heavily involved in the design of the product and may also specify how certain processes are to be carried out. In some cases, the customer will have representatives on site to observe the production process, or send in inspectors to certify quality at critical stages of project development.

Most companies do not have the resources (or time) to complete all the work on a project themselves, so subcontracting is common. The production process, as well as the final product, are basically designed anew for each customer order. Thus, the process is very flexible. And given the lengthy duration of a project, changes in customer preferences, technology, and costs cause frequent adjustments in product and process design. Managing these *engineering change orders* (ECO) is a major concern in project management. Another concern is keeping track of all the activities that are taking place and making sure they are completed correctly and on time, so as not to delay other activities.

Cutting edge technology, project teams, and close customer contact make project work exciting. But projects can also be risky with their large investment in resources, huge swings in resource requirements (as new projects begin and old ones end), limited learning curve, and dependence on a small customer base.

Examples of projects include constructing a building, airplane, or ship, planning a rock concert, or developing a new product. Projects are managed very differently from other types of processes. We discuss project management in detail in Chapter 17.

A **project** is the one-of-a-kind production of a product to customer order.

www.prenhall.com/russell

Batch Production

Making products one-at-a-time and treating their production as a project can be time consuming and cost-prohibitive. Most products can be made more quickly and more efficiently in volume. A production system which processes items in small groups or *batches* is called batch production. **Batch production** is characterized by fluctuating demand, short production runs of a wide variety of products, and small to moderate quantities of any given product made to customer order.

Most of the operations in batch production involve fabrication (e.g., machining) rather than assembly. Jobs are sent through the system based on their processing requirements, so that those jobs requiring lathe work are sent to one location, those requiring painting to another, and so forth. A job may be routed through many different machine centers before it is completed. If you were to track the flow of a particular customer order through the system, you would see a lot of stopping and starting as jobs queue at different machines, waiting to be processed. Work on a particular product is not continuous; it is *intermittent*.

Batch production systems are also known as *job shops*. Examples include machine shops, printers, bakeries, education, and furniture making. Advantages of this type of

Batch production systems process many different jobs through the system in groups (or batches).

www.prenhall.com/russell

The construction of an aircraft carrier is an enormous project. The U.S. NIMITZ, shown in the first photo, accommodates a crew of more than 6,000 people and a full-load displacement of 91,000 tons. Each of the ship's four propellers weighs over 66,000 pounds. A single link in the anchor chain weighs 360 pounds. The carrier also houses two nuclear reactors enabling it to operate for 13 years without refueling. Modular construction, in which a ship is built in huge subassemblies or modules, has cut the production time of carriers and other ships in half. This is accomplished by outfitting several modules at one time, then adding them to the hull. Extensive use of CAD/CAM, precise tolerances, and careful quality control ensure that the modules fit together perfectly.

The second photo shows an "island house" being lifted onto the deck of a carrier at <u>Newport News Shipbuilding</u>. *The island house is the aircraft carrier's control center and contains the bridge and flight operations.*

The third photo shows a huge gantry crane putting a completed module (or appropriately named, superlift) into place. Superlifts, such as the one shown, weigh as much as 900 tons and are added to the hull almost weekly for the three years it takes to bring a ship from keel laying to launch.

These photos are examples of batch production, where items are processed in groups or batches to customer order. In the photo on the left, a skilled worker shapes, fits and glues wooden strips to a guitar frame by hand. In the photo on the upper right, a college professor instructs a classroom of students. In the photo on the lower right, computer-controlled lathes monitored by machine operators produce the crates of parts shown in the foreground. In each case, workers and machines are general purpose and flexible enough to adjust their processes to a variety of customer requests.

system are its flexibility, the customization of output, and the reputation for quality that customization implies. Disadvantages include high per-unit costs, frequent changes in product mix, complex scheduling problems, variations in capacity requirements, and lengthy job completion times.

Mass Production

Mass production is used by producers who need to create more standardized products in larger quantities than batch production can economically handle. Products are made-to-stock for a mass market, demand is stable, and volume is high. Because of the stability and size of demand, the production system can afford to dedicate equipment to the production of a particular product. Thus, this type of system tends to be capital-intensive and highly repetitive, with specialized equipment and limited labor skills.

Mass production is usually associated with *flow lines* or *assembly lines*. *Flow* describes how a product moves through the system from one workstation to the next in order of the processing requirements for that particular product. (Batch production cannot be set up in this way because the processing requirements are different for each customer order.) *Assembly line* describes the way mass production is typically arranged—most of the operations are assembly-oriented and are performed in a line. Goods that are mass-produced include <u>automobiles</u>, televisions, personal computers, fast food, and most consumer goods.

Mass production produces large volumes of a standard product for a mass market.

www.prenhall.com/russell

The high volume of mass production allows the production system to be arranged in a line according to the processing requirements of a particular product. Since most of the operations performed involve the assembling of components, this arrangement is known as an assembly line. *The photo on the left shows robots welding metal bodies of minivans as they move down an assembly line. The photo on the right shows computers going through final inspection on a clean room assembly line.*

Advantages of mass production are its efficiency, low per-unit cost, ease of manufacture and control, and speed. Disadvantages include the high cost of equipment, underutilization of human resources, the difficulties of adapting to changes in demand, technology, or product design, and the lack of responsiveness to individual customer requests.

Continuous Production

Continuous processes are used for very high-volume commodity products that are very standardized. The system is highly automated (the worker's role is to monitor the equipment) and is typically in operation continuously twenty-four hours a day. The output is also continuous, not discrete—meaning individual units are measured, rather than counted. Steel, paper, paints, chemicals, and foodstuffs are produced by continuous production. Companies that operate in this fashion are referred to as *process industries.*

Advantages of this type of system are its efficiency, ease of control, and enormous capacity. Disadvantages include the large investment in plant and equipment, the limited variety of items that can be processed, the inability to adapt to volume changes, the cost of correcting errors in production, and the difficulties of keeping pace with new technology.

Table 6.1 on page 234 summarizes our discussion of types of processes. As we move from proj-ects to continuous production, demand volume increases; products become more standardized; systems become more capital intensive, more automated, and less flexible; and customers become less involved.

Process choice depends on a firm's strategy, the type of products, type of customers, volume of demand, and organizational capabilities. The degree of automation is one aspect of process choice that can be quantified based on cost factors and demand volume. Break-even analysis, presented in the next section, is a commonly used quantitative technique.

Process Selection with Break-Even Analysis

There are several quantitative techniques available for selecting a process. One that bases its decision on the cost trade-offs associated with demand volume is **break-even analysis.** The components of break-even analysis are volume, cost, revenue, and profit.

Continuous processes are used for very high-volume commodity products.

www.prenhall.com/russell

Break-even analysis examines the cost trade-offs associated with demand volume.

Continuous processes are used for very high volume, commodity products whose output is measured rather than counted. The production system is capital intensive, highly automated (with workers who monitor the equipment rather than perform the work) and is typically operated 24 hours a day. The photo on the left shows a worker in a control booth of a chemical manufacturer. On the computer screen is a simulation of the mixing tank operations that can be seen in the factory. In the photo on the right, a paper manufacturer produces a continuous sheet of paper from wood pulp slurry which is mixed, pressed, dried and wound onto reels. Later, winders will cut the paper into customer-size rolls for wrapping and labeling. Production per day exceeds 1,700 tons of paper.

Volume is the level of production, usually expressed as the number of units produced and sold. We assume that the number of units produced can be sold.

Cost is divided into two categories, *fixed* or *variable*. *Fixed costs* remain constant regardless of the number of units produced, such as plant and equipment and other elements of overhead. *Variable costs* vary with the volume of units produced, such as labor and material. The total cost of a process is the sum of its fixed cost and its total variable cost (defined as volume times per unit variable cost).

Revenue on a per-unit basis is simply the price at which an item is sold. *Total revenue* is price times volume sold. *Profit* is the difference between total revenue and total cost. These components can be expressed mathematically as follows:

$$\text{Total cost} = \text{total fixed cost} + \text{total variable cost}$$
$$\text{TC} = c_f + vc_v$$
$$\text{Total revenue} = \text{volume} \times \text{price}$$
$$\text{TR} = vp$$
$$\text{Total profit} = \text{total revenue} - \text{total cost}$$
$$\text{Z} = \text{TR} - \text{TC}$$
$$= vp - (c_f + vc_v)$$

where

c_f = fixed cost

v = volume (i.e., number of units)

c_v = variable cost per unit

p = price per unit

TABLE 6.1   Types of Processes

	Project	*Batch Production*	*Mass Production*	*Continuous Production*
Type of product	Unique	Made-to-order (customized)	Made-to-stock (standardized)	Commodity
Type of customer	One-at-a-time	Few individual customers	Mass market	Mass market
Product demand	Infrequent	Fluctuates	Stable	Very stable
Demand volume	Very low	Low to medium	High	Very high
No. of different products	Infinite variety	Many, varied	Few	Very few
Production system	Long-term project	Intermittent, job shops	Flow lines, assembly lines,	Process industry
Production equipment	Varied	General-purpose	Special-purpose	Highly automated
Primary type of work	Specialized contracts	Fabrication	Assembly	Mixing, treating, refining
Worker skills	Experts, craftspersons	Wide range of skills	Limited range of skills	Equipment monitors
Advantages	Custom work, latest technology	Flexibility, quality	Efficiency, speed, low cost	Highly efficient, large capacity, ease of control
Disadvantages	Nonrepetitive, small customer base, expensive	Costly, slow, difficult to manage	Capital investment; lack of responsiveness	Difficult to change, far-reaching errors, limited variety
Examples	Construction, shipbuilding, aircraft	Machine shops, print shops, bakeries, education	Automobiles, televisions, computers, fast food	Paint, chemicals, foodstuffs

In selecting a process, it is useful to know at what volume of sales and production we can expect to earn a profit. We want to make sure that the cost of producing a product does not exceed the revenue we will receive from the sale of the product. By equating total revenue with total cost and solving for v, we can find the volume at which profit is zero. This is called the *break-even point*. At any volume above the break-even point, we will make a profit. A mathematical formula for the break-even point can be determined as follows:

$$TR = TC$$
$$vp = (c_f + vc_v)$$
$$vp - vc_v = c_f$$
$$v(p - c_v) = c_f$$
$$v = \frac{c_f}{p - c_v}$$

EXAMPLE
6.1

Break-Even Analysis

Several graduate students at Whitewater University formed a company called the New River Rafting Company to produce rubber rafts. The initial investment in plant and equipment is estimated to be $2,000. Labor and material cost is approximately $5 per raft. If the rafts can be sold at a price of $10 each, what volume of demand would be necessary to break even?

SOLUTION:

Given,

$$\text{Fixed cost} = c_f = \$2,000$$
$$\text{Variable cost} = c_v = \$5 \text{ per raft}$$
$$\text{Price} = \$10 \text{ per raft}$$

Then, the break-even point is

$$v = \frac{c_f}{p - c_v} = \frac{2,000}{10 - 5} = 400 \text{ rafts}$$

The solution is shown graphically in the following figure. The *x*-axis represents production or demand volume and the *y*-axis represents dollars of revenue, cost, or profit. The total revenue line extends from the origin, with a slope equal to the unit price of a raft. The total cost line intersects the *y*-axis at a level corresponding to the fixed cost of the process and has a slope equal to the per-unit variable cost. The intersection of these two lines is the break-even point. If demand is less than the break-even point, the company will operate at a loss. But if demand exceeds the break-even point, the company will be profitable. The company needs to sell more than 400 rafts to make a profit. Exhibit 6.1 shows the Excel solution for this problem.

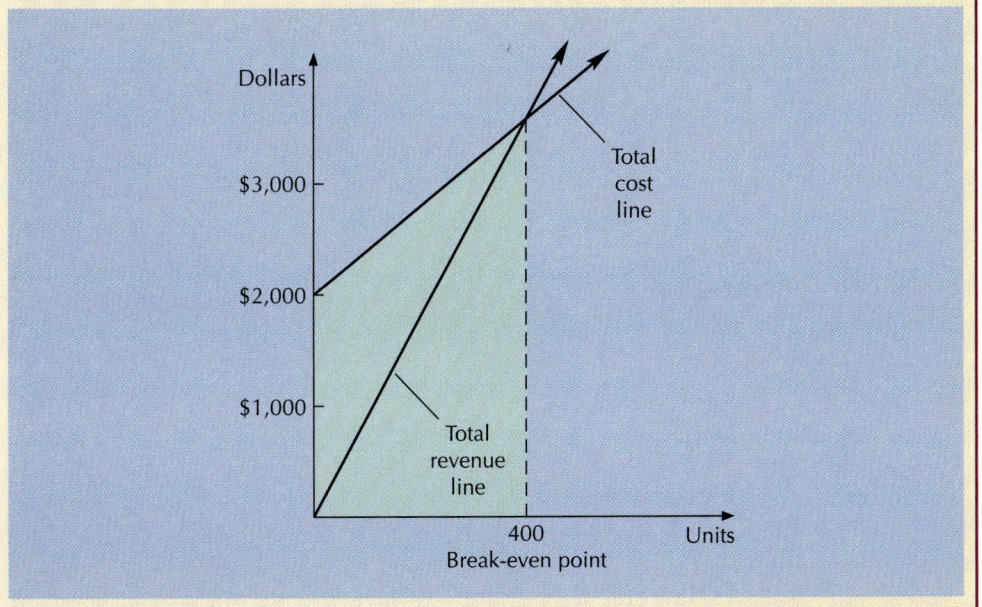

Formula for break even point

Number of rafts that must be sold to break even.

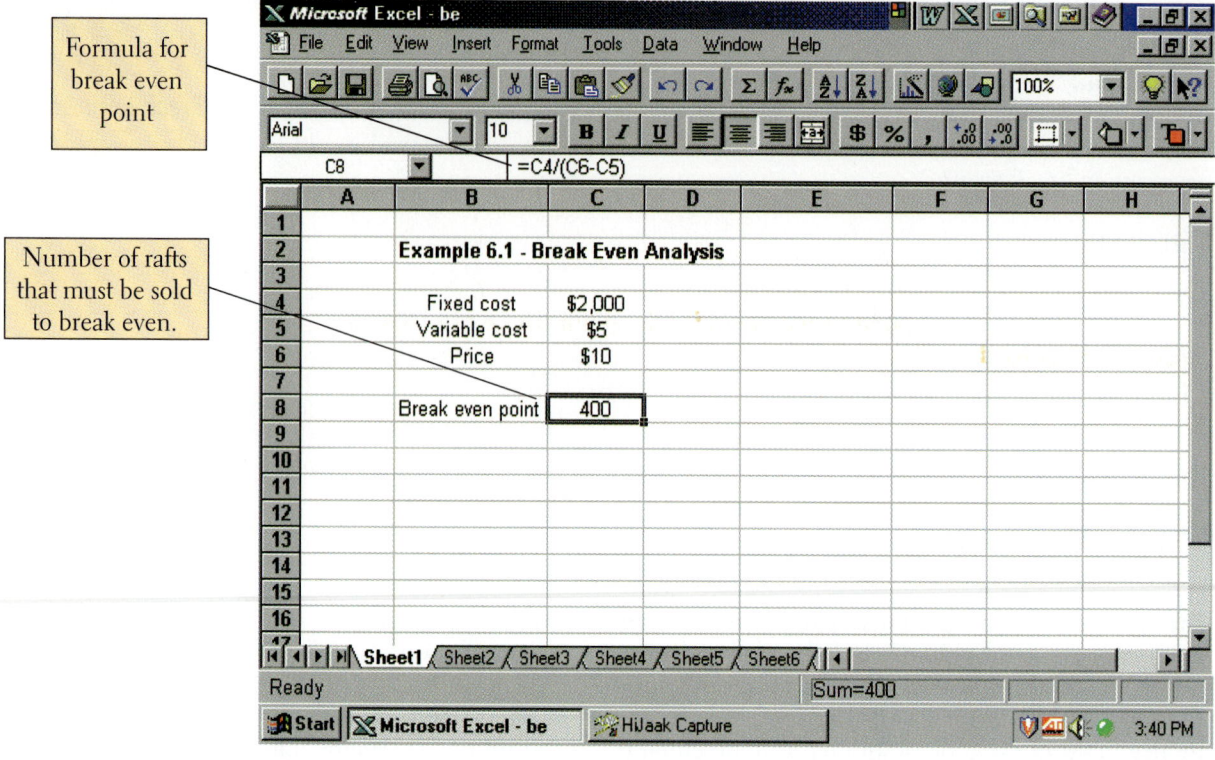

EXHIBIT 6.1

Break-even analysis can be used for evaluating alternative processes.

Break-even analysis is especially useful when evaluating different degrees of automation. More-automated processes have higher fixed costs but lower variable costs. The "best" process depends on the anticipated volume of demand for the product and the trade-offs between fixed and variable costs. Let's see how break-even analysis can guide the selection of a process among several alternatives.

EXAMPLE 6.2

Process Selection

The students from the New River Rafting Company believe demand for their product will far exceed the break-even point in Example 6.1. They are now contemplating a larger initial investment of $10,000 for more-automated equipment that would reduce the variable cost of manufacture to $2 per raft.

a. What is the break-even point for this new process?

b. Compare the process described in Example 6.1 with the process proposed here. For what volume of demand should each process be chosen?

SOLUTION:

a. The break-even point for the new process is

$$v = \frac{10,000}{10 - 2} = 1,250 \text{ rafts}$$

b. Let's label the process in Example 6.1, process A and the new process proposed here, process B. In comparing them, we note that the break-even point for process B of 1,250 rafts is larger than the break-even point for process A of 400 rafts. We can conclude that if demand is less than 400 units, the students should not go into business. In addition, if demand is greater than 400 units but less than 1,250 units, process A should be selected. But what if demand is above 1,250? Let's graph the problem to find a trade-off between the two processes. (Because the rafts will be sold for $10 apiece regardless of which process is used to manufacture them, we do not need to graph a total revenue line.)

The total cost lines for process A and process B intersect at 2,667 units. The intersection point is called the *point of indifference*—the point where the costs of the two processes are equal. If we look above the point of indifference, the total cost line for process B is lower than for process A. Below the point of indifference, the total cost line for process A is lower than process B.

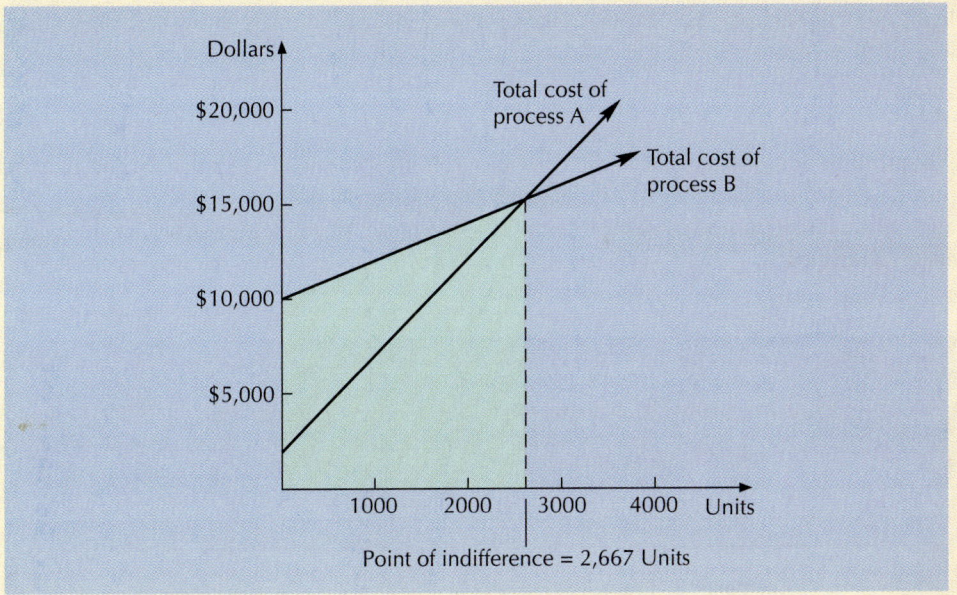

The solution procedure for process selection consists of four steps:

1. Formulate a total cost equation for each process considered.
2. Calculate the *point of indifference* between two alternatives by equating the total cost of each alternative and solving for *v*, the demand volume.
3. Above the point of indifference, choose the alternative with the lowest *variable cost*.
4. Below the point of indifference, choose the alternative with the lowest *fixed cost*.

For this example, the point of indifference is:

Process A   *Process B*

$$\$2,000 + \$5v = \$10,000 + \$2v$$
$$\$3v = \$8,000$$
$$v = 2,667 \text{ rafts}$$

(Continued)

If the demand for rafts is exactly 2,667 units, we can choose either process A or process B. If demand is less than 2,667 rafts, the alternative with the lowest fixed cost, process A, should be chosen. If demand is greater than 2,667 rafts, the alternative with the lowest variable cost, process B, is preferred. Exhibit 6.2 shows the Excel solution for this problem.

Process Planning

Process planning converts designs into workable instructions for manufacture.

Process planning determines *how* a product will be produced or a service provided. It decides which components will be made in-house and which will be purchased from a supplier, selects processes and specific equipment (purchasing new equipment, if necessary), and develops and documents the specifications for manufacture and delivery. In this section, we discuss make-or-buy decisions, specific equipment selection, and process plans.

Make-or-Buy Decisions

Components of a product may be purchased from a supplier or produced in-house.

Not all the components that make up a product are produced in-house. Some may be purchased from a supplier. The decision concerning which items will be purchased and which items will be made is refered to as *sourcing*, *vertical integration*, or the *make-or-buy decision*.

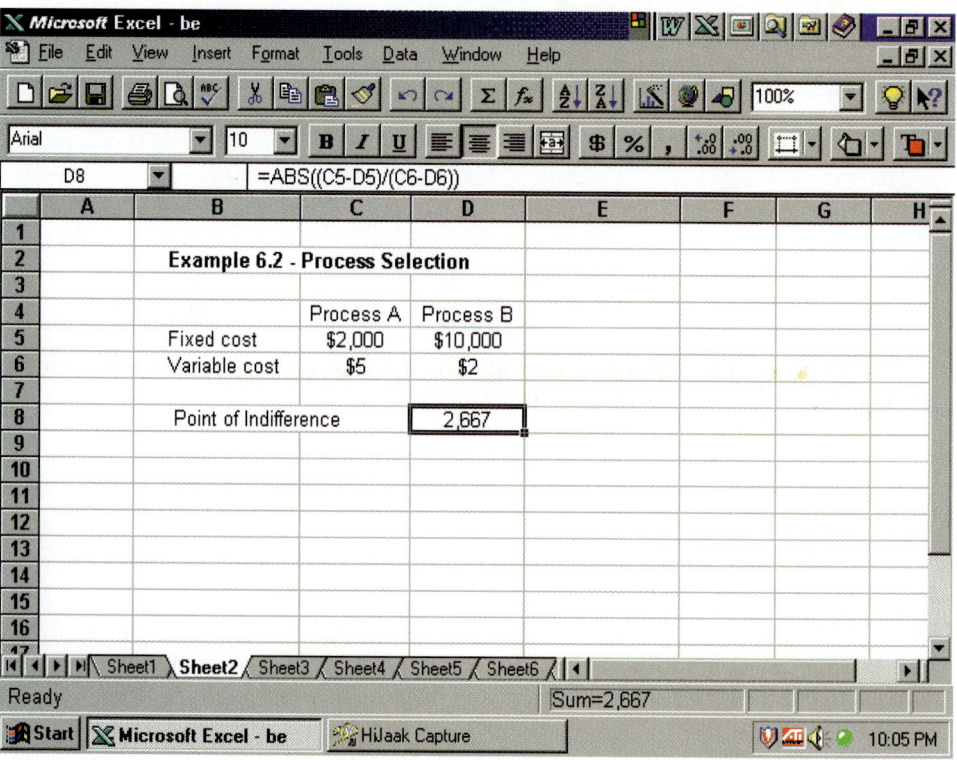

EXHIBIT 6.2 Process Selection

The make-or-buy decision rests on an evaluation of the following factors:

1. *Cost.* Would it be cheaper to make the item or buy it? To perform the service in-house or subcontract it out? This is the primary consideration in most make-or-buy decisions. Although the cost of *buying* the item is relatively straightforward (i.e., the purchase price), the cost of *making* the item includes overhead allocations that may not accurately reflect the cost of manufacture. In addition, there are situations in which a company may decide to buy an item rather than make it (or vice versa) when, from a cost standpoint, it would be cheaper to do otherwise. The remaining factors in this list represent noneconomic factors that can influence or dominate the economic considerations.

2. *Capacity.* Companies that are operating at less than full capacity usually make components rather than buy them, especially if maintaining a level work force is important. Sometimes the available capacity is not sufficient to make all the components, so choices have to be made. The stability of demand is also important. Typically, it is better to produce in-house those parts or products with steady demand that consume a set capacity, whereas those whose demand patterns are uncertain or volatile are usually subcontracted.

3. *Quality.* The capability to provide quality parts consistently is an important consideration in the make-or-buy decision. In general, it is easier to control the quality of items produced in your own factory. However, standardization of parts, supplier certification, and supplier involvement in design can improve the quality of supplied parts. Poor manufacturing practices in the 1970s forced many U.S. companies in the 1980s to purchase major components from foreign competitors to meet customer quality expectations. This led to the creation of "hollow" corporations that farmed out every task except putting the final label on.

4. *Speed.* Sometimes components are purchased because a supplier can provide goods sooner than the manufacturer. The smaller supplier is often more flexible, too, and can adapt quickly to design and technology changes. Of course, speed is useful only if it's reliable.

5. *Reliability.* Suppliers need to be reliable in both the quality and the timing of what they supply. Unexpected delays in shipments or partially filled orders because of quality rejects can wreak havoc with the manufacturing system. Many companies today are requiring their suppliers to meet certain quality and delivery standards to be certified as an approved supplier. ISO 9000 is the European Community's quality certification program. Those foreign companies that are not certified simply may not trade in Europe. Other companies assess huge penalties for unreliable supply. Chrysler, for example, fines its suppliers $30,000 for each *hour* an order is late.

6. *Expertise.* Companies that are especially good at making or designing certain items may want to keep control over their production. Coca-Cola would not want to release its formula to a supplier, even if there were guarantees of secrecy. Although automakers might outsource many of their component parts, they need proprietary control over major components such as engines, transmissions, and electronic guidance systems. Japanese, Taiwanese, and Korean firms are currently learning American expertise in aircraft design and manufacture by serving as suppliers of component parts. The decision of whether or not to share your expertise with a supplier for economic gains is a difficult one.

Companies that control the production of virtually all of their component parts, including the source of raw materials, are said to be *vertically integrated.* This strategy was popular for many years when companies did not want to be dependent on others for their livelihood. Today, buying components and raw materials from vendors is more common, but relationships with vendors have been strengthened. <u>Supplier partnerships</u>

www.prenhall.com/russell

are valuable assets in gaining a competitive edge. Chapter 9, "Supply Chain Management," discusses the importance of supplier relationships from a global perspective.

Specific Equipment Selection

www.prenhall.com/russell

After it is decided that a part will be produced or service provided in-house, specific equipment decisions can be made. Alternatives include using, replacing, or upgrading existing equipment, adding additional capacity, or purchasing new equipment. Any alternative that involves an outlay of funds is considered a *capital investment*. Capital investments involve the commitment of funds in the present with an expectation of returns over some future time period. The expenditures are usually large and can have a significant effect on the future profitability of a firm. These decisions are carefully analyzed and typically require top management approval.

The most effective quantitative techniques for capital investment consider the time value of money as well as the risks associated with benefits that will not accrue until the future. These techniques, known collectively as capital budgeting techniques, include payback period, net present value, and internal rate of return. Detailed descriptions can be found in any basic finance text.

Although capital budgeting techniques are beyond the scope of this text, we do need to comment on several factors that are often overlooked in a financial analysis of equipment purchases:

Several factors are often overlooked in the financial justification of new equipment.

1. *Purchase cost.* The initial investment in equipment consists of more than its basic purchase price. The cost of special tools and fixtures, installation, and engineering or programming adjustments (i.e., debugging) can represent a significant additional investment. This is especially true of automated equipment. For example, it is common for the cost of robot installation and added-on accessories to exceed the purchase price of the robot.

2. *Operating costs.* The annual cost of operating a machine includes direct labor, indirect labor (e.g., for programming, setups, material handling, or training), power and utilities, supplies, tooling, property taxes and insurance, and maintenance. In many cases indirect labor is underestimated, as are maintenance and tooling costs. To assess more accurately the requirements of the new equipment, it is useful to consider, step by step, how the machine will be operated, started, stopped, loaded, unloaded, changed over to produce another product, maintained, repaired, cleaned up, speeded up, and slowed down and what resources (i.e., labor, material, or equipment) will be needed for each step.

3. *Annual savings.* Most new equipment is justified based on direct labor savings. However, other savings can actually be more important. For example, a more efficient process may be able to use less material and require less machine time or fewer repairs, so that downtime is reduced. A process that produces a better-quality product can result in fewer inspections and less scrap and rework. Finally, new processes (especially those that are automated) may significantly reduce safety costs, in terms of compliance with required regulations, as well as fines or compensation for safety violations.

4. *Revenue enhancement.* Increases in revenue due to equipment upgrades or new-equipment purchases are often ignored in financial analysis because they are difficult to predict. New equipment can expand capacity and, assuming more units can be sold, increase revenue. Improvements in product quality, price reductions due to decreased costs, and more rapid or dependable delivery can increase market share and, thus, revenue. Flexibility of equipment can also be important in adapting to the changing needs of the customer. These are strategic advantages that have long-term implications. Unfortunately, most quantitative analyses are oriented toward short-term measures of performance.

5. *Replacement analysis.* As existing equipment ages, it may become slower, less reliable, and obsolete. The decision to replace old equipment with state-of-the-art equip-

THE COMPETITIVE EDGE

Hewlett-Packard Rereads the Numbers with Activity-Based Costing

What happens when manufacturing, marketing, and design come up with vastly different costs for producing the same product? Most companies argue it out, and the most powerful entity wins. The Roseville Networks Division of Hewlett-Packard decided, instead, to completely overhaul the cost accounting system and determine more accurate sources of information. Management formed a "Simple Six" task force (made up of representatives from manufacturing, design, procurement, accounting, sales, and information systems) to identify exactly what factors drove cost for their division's products. Direct materials remained a valid contributor to product cost, but not direct labor (on which, by the way, they were spending 30 minutes a day tracking). Accounting for less than 2 percent of product cost, direct labor was the first category eliminated by the Simple Six (it was lumped into overhead). Of course, a different manner of allocating overhead then had to be determined. First, two major categories, procurement and production overhead, were designated.

Costing procurement overhead was relatively easy; it varied by the number of pieces in each order. Costing production overhead took more analysis. In the end, eight separate measures of production overhead were determined. The activities at the beginning of the process and during soldering were costed by the number of boards processed. The cost of insertions varied by the number of insertions per board and the type of insertion (axial, dip, manual, or backload). Finally, the cost of testing and rework was allocated by the amount of time spent in each process.

Activity-based costing, the new system, is more complicated than the old formula of direct materials, direct labor, and overhead, but HP says it gives the company a solid base on which to make intelligent and informed manufacturing, marketing, and design decisions.

www.prenhall.com/russell

SOURCE: Based on Debbie Berlant, Reese Browning, and George Foster, "How Hewlett-Packard Gets Numbers It Can Trust," *Harvard Business Review* (January–February 1990): 178–83.

---

ment depends in large measure on the competitive environment. If a major competitor upgrades to a newer technology that improves quality, cost, or flexibility and you do not, your ability to compete will be severely damaged. Deciding when to invest in new equipment can be tricky.

A hidden cost in replacement analysis is the opportunity cost of not investing in new equipment when upcoming technology will make the equipment obsolete. Part of the analysis should include estimates of salvage value reductions, operating cost inferiority, quality inferiority, and flexibility inferiority as compared with state-of-the-art technology. Salvage value, similar to the trade-in value of an automobile, decreases every year a company waits to replace equipment. In some industries, technology changes so rapidly that a replacement decision also involves determining whether this generation of equipment should be purchased or if it would be better to wait for the next generation. Replacement analysis maps out different schedules for equipment purchases over a five- to ten-year period and selects a replacement cycle that will minimize cost.

6. *Risk and uncertainty.* Investment in new equipment, especially if it represents an untested technology, can be risky. Estimates of equipment capabilities, length of life, and operating cost may be uncertain. Because of the risk involved, financial analysts tend to assign higher hurdle rates (i.e., required rates of return) to technology investments, making it difficult to gain approval for them. Management's general lack of understanding of new technology and its potential impact does not help the situation.

7. *Piecemeal analysis.* Investment in equipment and technology is expensive. Rarely can a company afford to automate an entire plant all at once. This has led to the proposal and evaluation of equipment purchases in a piecemeal fashion. Frequently, pieces of technology don't fit into the existing system and fail to deliver the expected returns. There is a synergistic benefit to a well-designed technology plan that is too often ignored.

Process Plans

The entire set of documents that details manufacturing specifications is called a *process plan.*

The set of documents that details manufacturing and delivery specifications is called a *process plan.* Process plans may include:

- *Blueprints:* Detailed drawings of product design;
- A *bill of material:* A list of the materials and parts that go into a product;
- An *assembly diagram:* An illustration showing how various parts combine to form the final product, as given in Figure 6.1;

Bill of Material

No.	Part No.	Part name
1	51292	Outlet End
2	51284	Handle
3	52043	Switch & Insulator
4	51576	Electric Cord
5	51265	Rear Housing
6	51268	Motor Mounting Plate
7	51495	Motor Ass'y & Fan Spacer
8	51270	Screw & Lock Washer Ass'y
9	51273	Stationary Fan

No.	Part No.	Part name
10	51488	Rotary Fan & Spacer Ass'y
11	51281	Front Fan Cover
12	51272	Forward Housing
13	51286	Air Filter
14	52388	Reusable Bag
15	51288	Inlet End Ass'y
16	51642	Upholstery Tool
17	52074	Crevice Tool
18	50815	Dusting Tool
19	57432	Packaging Material

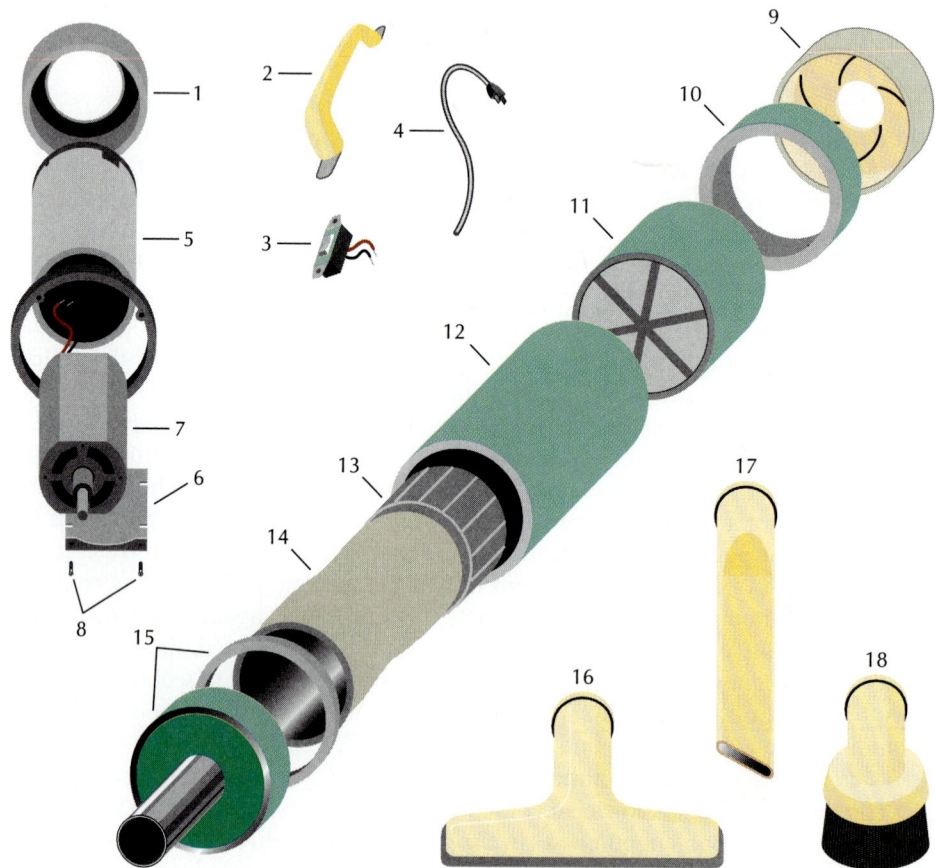

FIGURE 6.1   A Bill of Material and Assembly Diagram for the Hand-Vac

- An ***assembly chart*** or *product structure diagram:* A schematic diagram that shows the relationship of each component part to its parent assembly, the grouping of parts that make up a subassembly, and the overall sequence of assembly, as given in Figure 6.2;

- An ***operations process chart:*** A list of the operations to be performed in fabricating a part, along with the time required to complete each operation, special tools, fixtures, and gauges needed, and how the machine is to be set up and operated as given in Figure 6.3; and

- A *routing sheet:* An ordered list of machines or workstations which shows where a part is to be sent for its next operation.

Assembly charts show how a product is to be assembled.

Operations process charts show how a product is to be fabricated.

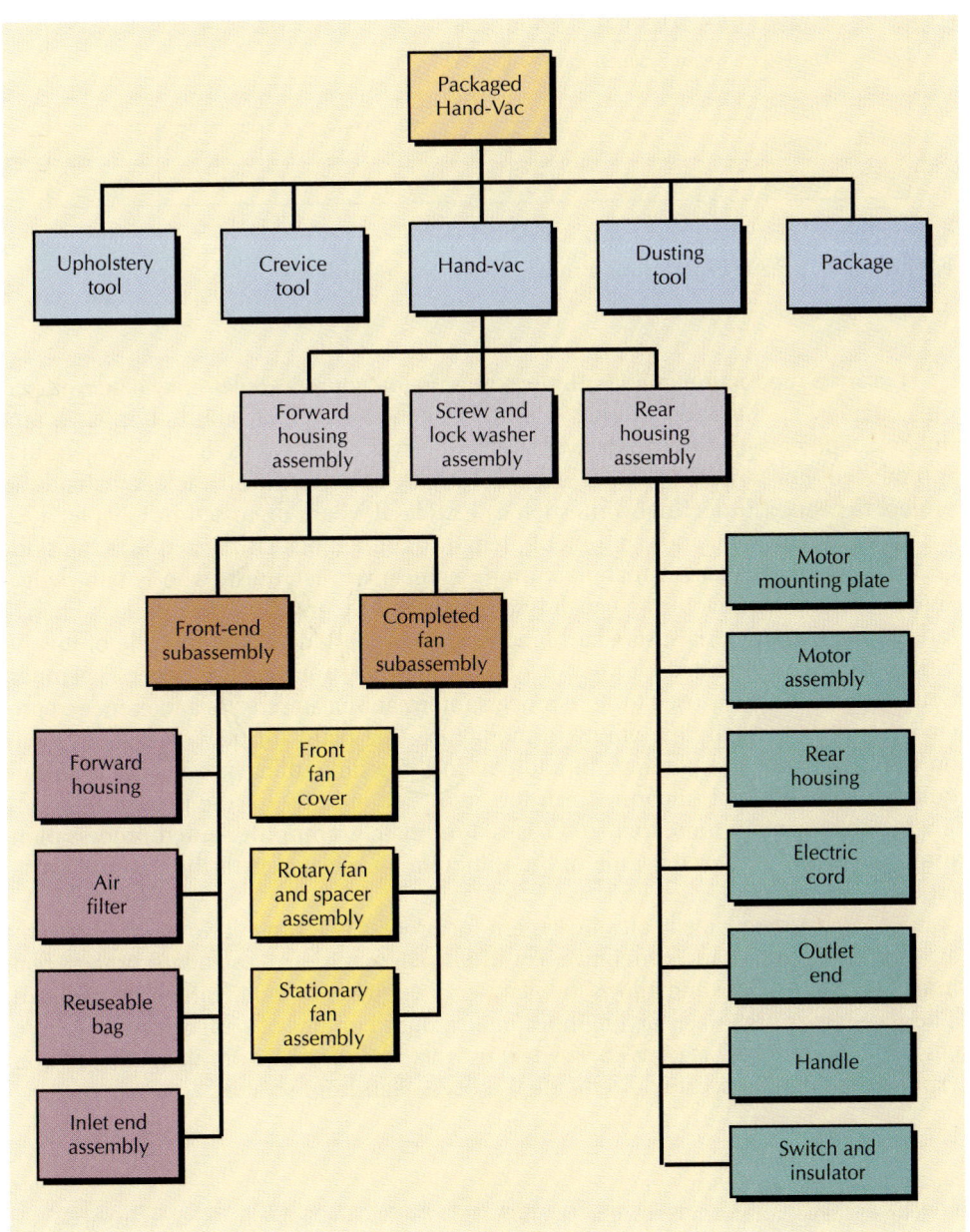

FIGURE 6.2 **A Product Structure Diagram for the Hand-Vac**

Part name	Table leg				
Part No.	2410				
Usage	Table				
Assembly No.	437				

Oper. No.	Description	Dept.	Machine	Time	Tools
10	Saw to rough length	041			
20	Plane to size	043			
30	Saw to finished length	041			
40	Measure dimensions	051			
50	Sand	052			

FIGURE 6.3   An Operations Process Chart for a Table Leg

For mass production and continuous production, a process plan may be developed only once, when the assembly line is set up or the process plant is built. For batch production, a process plan must be developed for every job that enters the shop or part that is produced. For projects, process plans are usually associated with each activity in the project network. (Project networks such as PERT/CPM are discussed in Chapter 17.)

Process planning can be a difficult, lengthy, and tedious task. It requires the skills of an individual (usually a manufacturing engineer or machinist) who is knowledgeable about the manufacturing capabilities of the factory, machine and process characteristics, tooling, materials, standard practices, and cost trade-offs. Very little of this information is documented; it may exist only in the mind of the process planner. Sometimes, workbooks used to store process information can serve as a reference to previous plans, but usually the ability to modify existing plans for new parts relies solely on the memory of the planner. In addition to these difficulties, process plans can be quite lengthy. It is not uncommon in the aerospace industry for the process plan of a single part to contain more than 100 pages. Fortunately, **computer-aided process planning (CAPP)** can alleviate some of the difficulties associated with the manual preparation of process plans.

CAPP is a specialized software system for process planning. Two types of systems are common, variant and generative. A *variant system* retrieves a standard process plan from a CAPP database and allows the planner or engineer to modify it for the new part. The database is organized by *group technology* into families of parts with similar processing requirements.[1] A *generative system* uses a knowledge base of rules gathered from expert machinists to create an individual process plan from scratch.

CAPP is a specialized software system for process planning.

www.prenhall.com/russell

---

[1] Group technology can also be used to organize CAD databases into families of parts based on shape and other physical features related to design, but CAD and CAPP part families are not necessarily the same.

Process Analysis

Process analysis is the systematic examination of all aspects of a process to improve its operation—make it faster, more efficient, less costly, or more responsive to the customer. A basic tool of process analysis is the process flowchart.

Process flowcharts look at the manufacture of a product or delivery of a service from a broad perspective. The chart uses five standard symbols, shown in Figure 6.4, to describe the process:

    ○ for operations,

    □ for inspections,

    ⇨ for transportation,

    D for delay, and

    ▽ for storage.

Process flowcharts highlight nonproductive activities.

The details of each process are not necessary for this chart; however, the time required to perform each process and the distance between processes are often included. By incorporating nonproductive activities (inspection, transportation, delay, storage), as well as productive activities (operations), process flowcharts may be used to analyze the efficiency of a series of processes, and suggest improvements. They also provide a standardized method for documenting the steps in a process and can be used as a training tool. Automated versions of these charts are available that will superimpose the charts on floor plans of facilities. In this fashion, bottlenecks can be identified and layouts can be adjusted. Process flowcharts are used in both manufacturing and service operations. They are the basic tool for reengineering and are also used in job design.

Date: 9-30-98   Location: Graves Mountain
Analyst: TLR   Process: Applesauce

Step	Operation	Transport	Inspect	Delay	Storage	Description of process	Time (min)	Distance (feet)
1	●	⇨	□	D	▽	Unload apples from truck	20	
2	○	⇨	□	D	▽	Move to inspection station		100 ft
3	○	⇨	■	D	▽	Weigh, inspect, sort	30	
4	○	⇨	□	D	▽	Move to storage		50 ft
5	○	⇨	□	D	▽	Wait until needed	360	
6	○	⇨	□	D	▽	Move to peeler		20 ft
7	●	⇨	□	D	▽	Apples peeled and cored	15	
8	○	⇨	□	D	▽	Soak in water until needed	20	
9	●	⇨	□	D	▽	Place on conveyor	5	
10	○	⇨	□	D	▽	Move to mixing area		20 ft
11	○	⇨	■	D	▽	Weigh, inspect, sort	30	
		Page 1 of 3				Total	480	190 ft

FIGURE 6.4   **A Process Flowchart of Apple Processing**

These workers at a Union Carbide Chemical plant are displaying a process map they developed to analyze an existing process. The flow chart is not neat and tidy, but it does offer some obvious candidates for improvement. U.S. workers and managers in both industry and government are examining their processes in an attempt to reengineer work for high quality, less waste, and speedier operation.

Process Reengineering

Processes are *designed* in response to new facilities, new products, new technologies, new markets, or new customer expectations. Processes should be *improved* on a continuous basis. When continual improvement efforts have been exhausted and performance expectations still cannot be reached with an existing process, it is time to completely redesign or *reengineer* the process. Figure 6.5 outlines the **reengineering** process.

Reengineering is the total redesign of a process.

Goals and Specifications   The initial step establishes the goals and specifications for process performance. Data from the existing process are used as a baseline to which benchmarking data on best industry practices, customer requirements data, and strategic directives are compared. Analyzing the gap between current and desired performance helps to determine whether or not the process needs to be redesigned. If reengineering is necessary, a reengineering project team is chartered and provided with the preliminary analysis and resulting goals and specifications for process performance. While the goals for a process may be specific, the specifications are not (or else the creativity of the group is hampered). It is important that the project team be convinced that total redesign of the process is absolutely necessary to achieve the performance objectives.

High-Level Process Map   A useful tool in beginning the redesign of a process is a *high-level process map*. Pared to its simplest form, a high-level map contains only the essential building blocks of a process. As shown in Figure 6.6, it is prepared by focusing on the performance goal—stated in customer terms—and working backward through the desired output, subprocesses, and initial input requirements. Design principles, such as performing subprocesses in parallel whenever possible, help to structure the map efficiently. Table 6.2 on page 248 lists several additional design principles recommended for reengineering. Innovative ideas can challenge the conventional ordering of sub-

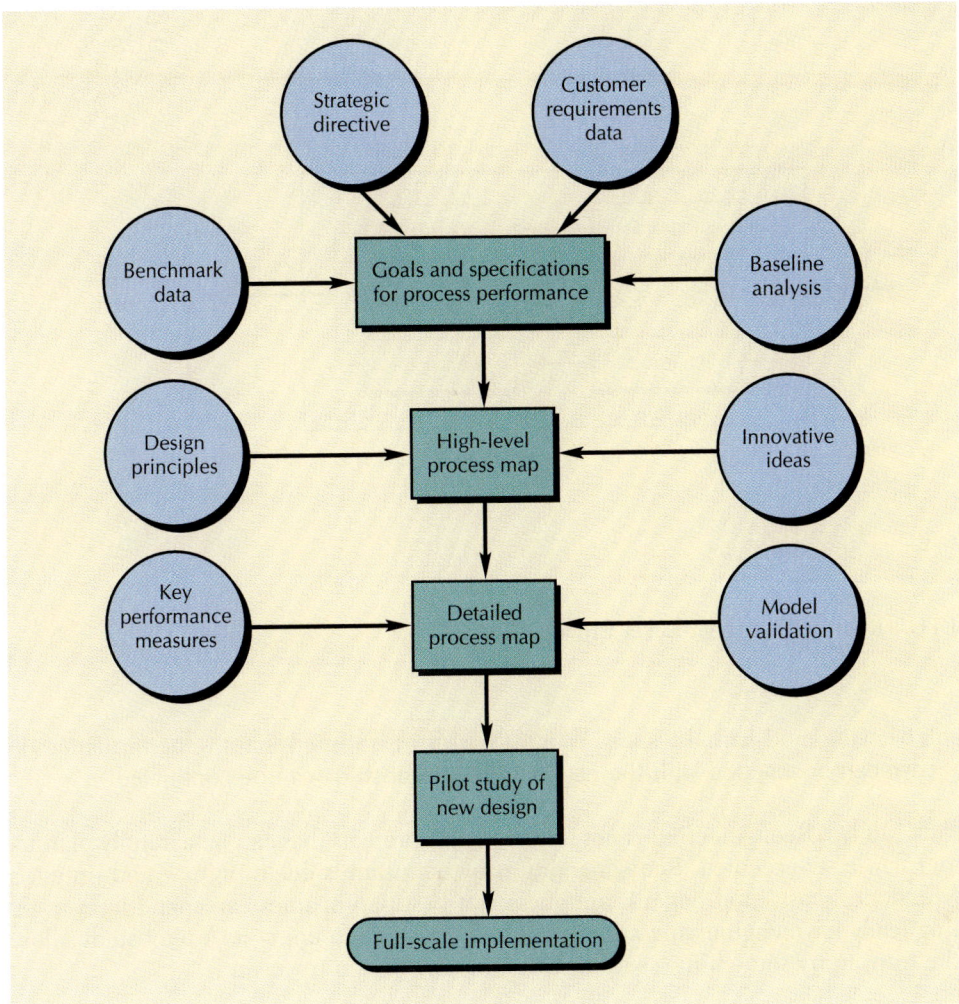

FIGURE 6.5 **The Reengineering Process**

processes, or the need for a subprocess. Table 6.3 on page 249 presents various techniques to prompt innovative thinking.

While reengineering means redesigning the process from scratch using a clean sheet approach, it does not mean that the existing process should be ignored. The existing process should be studied long enough to understand "what" the process is and "why" it is performed. Exactly "how" it is performed is less relevant because the how will change dramatically during the course of the project.

Detailed Process Map After the general concept of redesign is agreed upon, a detailed map is prepared for each subprocess or block in the high-level map. Blocks are added only if an activity can contribute to the output goal. The existence of each block or activity is challenged: Does it add value for the customer? Does it have to be done? Could it be done quicker, easier, or sooner? Could someone else do it better?

A detailed map guides decisions on allocation of resources and work methods. To guarantee that the detailed map will produce the desired results, key performance measures are determined and set in place. The model is also validated through simulation,

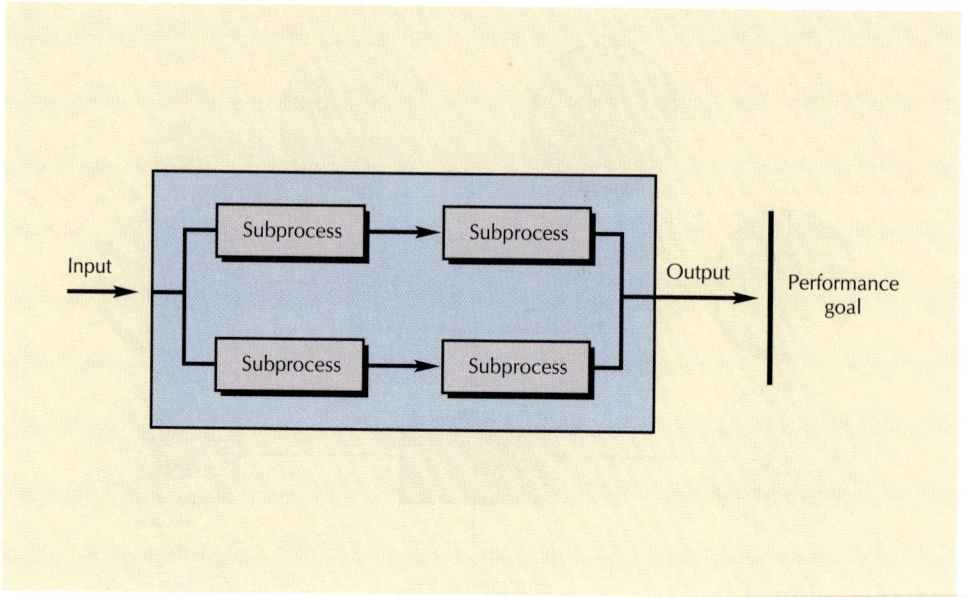

FIGURE 6.6   A High-Level Process Map

interviewing, and partial testing. When the team is satisfied that the performance objective can be reached with the new design, a pilot study can be conducted.

Pilot Study   Reengineering is not like the other projects that can be carefully planned and flawlessly executed. Reengineering is by definition something new and untested. Milestones, costs, and benefits are guesses at best. Companies can spend forever getting ready for reengineering and never getting around to doing it. A pilot study allows the team to try something, see if it works, modify it, and try again.

TABLE 6.2   Design Principles for Reengineering

1. Organize around outcomes, not tasks.
   The ultimate outcome is what satisfies a customer need.
2. Capture information once, at the source.
   Eliminate unnecessary information exchange, data redundancy, and rekeying.
   Gather relevant, accurate information that you need, but no more.
3. Centralize geographically dispersed resources through information technology.
   Eliminate multiple external contact points. Share information.
4. Link parallel subprocesses instead of integrating their results as a separate step.
   Build in feedback mechanisms to minimize the need for checkpoints and control.
5. Design the process so that work is done right the first time.
   Eliminate checking, reworking, and other nonvalue added subprocesses.
6. Remove complexity, exceptions, authorizations, and special cases.
   Put decision points where the work is performed.
7. Identify information and technology levers.
   Use technology to automate existing processes and enable new ones.

SOURCE: Adapted from Michael Hammer, "Reengineering Work: Don't Automate, Obliterate," *Harvard Business Review* (July–August 1990).

TABLE 6.3   Techniques for Generating Innovative Ideas

www.prenhall.com/russell

- Vary the entry point to a problem
  (in trying to untangle fishing lines, it's best to start from the fish, not the poles!)
- Draw analogies
  (a previous solution to an old problem might work)
- Change your perspective
  (think like a customer; bring in persons who have no knowledge of the process)
- Try inverse brainstorming
  (what would *increase* cost? *displease* the customer?)
- Chain forward as far as possible
  (if I solve this problem, what is the next problem?)
- Use attribute brainstorming
  (how would this process operate if . . . our workers were mobile and flexible? there were no monetary constraints? we had perfect knowledge?)

SOURCE: Adapted from AT&T Quality Steering Committee, *Reengineering Handbook* (Indianapolis: AT&T Technical Publications Center, 1991).

Implementation   After a successful pilot study, full-scale implementation can begin. Since reengineering involves radical change, the transition period between introducing the changed process and the incorporation of the new process into day-to-day operations can be lengthy and difficult. The redesigned process may involve changing the way executives manage, the way employees think about their work, or how workers interact. The transition needs to be managed with a special concern for the "people" aspects of change. The reengineering process is complete when the transition has been weathered and the new process consistently reaches its objective.

Technology Decisions

Technology decisions involve large sums of money and can have a tremendous impact on the cost, speed, quality, and flexibility of operations. More importantly, they define the future capabilities of a firm and set the stage for competitive interactions. Thus, it is dangerous to delegate technology decisions to technical experts or financial analysts. A manager's ability to ask questions and understand the basic thrust of proposed technology is invaluable in making wise technology choices. For that reason, in the next few sections we describe advances in information technology and manufacturing technology, and provide general guidelines on technology adoption.

www.prenhall.com/russell

Information Technology

Most organizations employ some form of computer-based technology to accumulate, organize, and distribute information for decision-making purposes. Information technology is also used to communicate with customers, suppliers, and employees internally and in remote locations. Types of information systems include management information systems, decision support systems, expert systems, and artificial intelligence. Advanced communications systems include electronic data interchange, electronic funds transfer, the Internet and intranets, wireless communication, and automatic identification systems. We discuss each of these briefly in the following sections.

www.prenhall.com/russell

Management Information Systems

A **management information system** (also known as **MIS**) is a system specifically designed to channel large quantities and numerous types of information through an organization. Data are collected, organized, processed, and made conveniently accessible to the manager to assist in making decisions and carrying out routine functions.

One component of an MIS is the *database*, an organized collection of numerical information. Prices, production output, cost data, inventory level, numbers of orders, available resources, capacities, and labor rates are examples of pieces of information that form a database. An efficient and effective database will have relevant, high-quality, well-organized information.

The computer in an MIS processes data and generates information for use by different units in an organization. Much of this information is in the form of reports that are posted according to a predetermined schedule. Examples include manpower and sales reports generated on a weekly or monthly basis, monthly inventory reports, load summary reports, input/output reports, shipping schedules, available-to-promise reports, and customer satisfaction reports. Such reports typically do not reflect any form of operations analysis but simply summarize and organize data so that it is useful and easily interpreted. They often include both current and historical information and are presented in graphical form. MIS reports enable the company to communicate information to various units, coordinate decision making, and maintain control.

Decision Support Systems

A **decision support system** (DSS) is an information system with which a manager interacts through an iterative process to reach a decision. A DSS frequently integrates a quantitative model within its framework. Decision support systems are used for pinpointing oil and gas deposits, spotting fraud on tax returns, scheduling workers, choosing test markets, and devising distribution networks.

The general framework of a decision support system is illustrated in Figure 6.7. The blocks designated as *data, computer system,* and *information,* along with the various information flows to *management* comprise an MIS. The added components that form a DSS are the *decision-making capabilities,* the *quantitative techniques,* and the interactive capabilities (i.e., the *what-if analysis*).

Expert Systems

A DSS assists decision makers in making decisions. In comparison, an **expert system** recommends a decision based on expert knowledge. An expert system includes a knowledge base, which contains an expert's knowledge on a particular type of problem, and a mechanism for reasoning that allows inferences to be made from the knowledge base.

Expert systems can be viewed as computerized "consultants" for decision making that use a collection of facts, knowledge, and rules to diagnose problems and suggest solutions. Expert systems have been applied in credit and loan approval, production scheduling, process control, design for manufacturing, repair services, and maintenance activities.

Artificial Intelligence

Artificial intelligence (AI) attempts to replicate human thought processes with computers to diagnose and solve problems. Expert systems can be viewed as one type of artificial intelligence. Other types of AI are neural networks, genetic algorithms, and fuzzy logic.

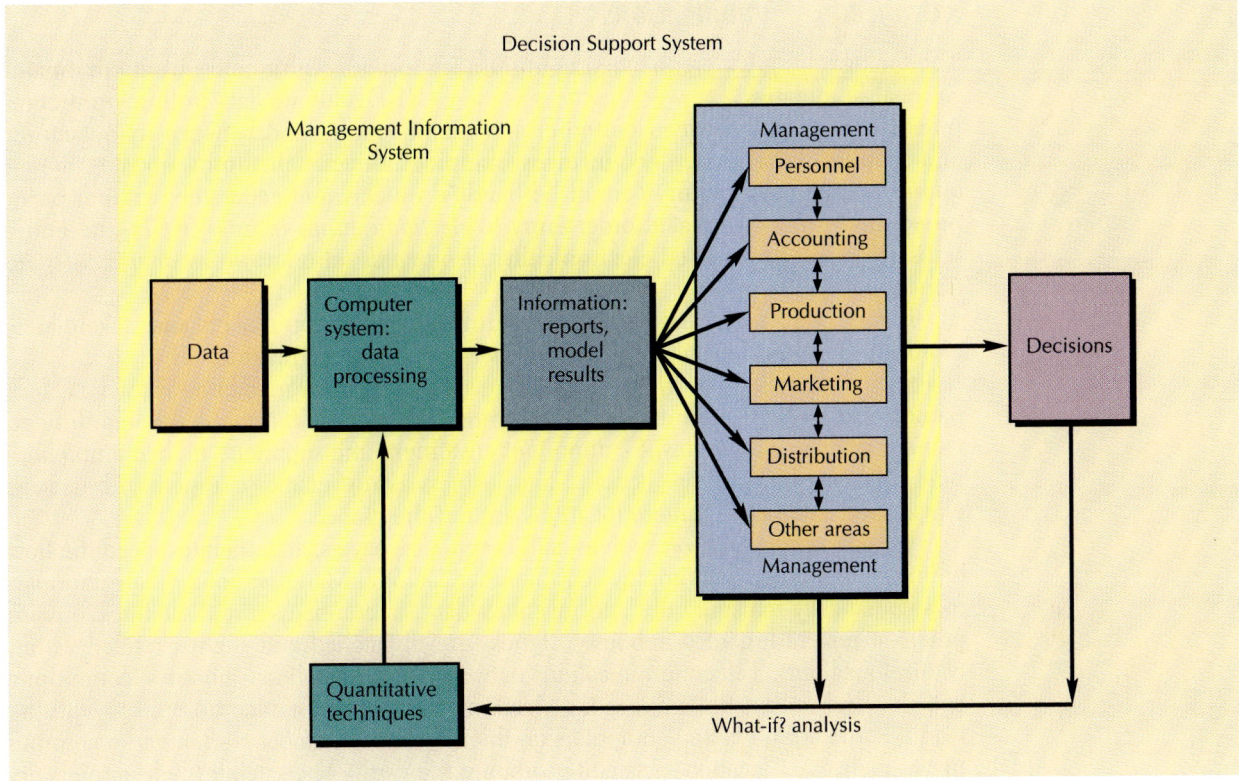

FIGURE 6.7 **A Decision Support System**

Artificial *neural networks* emulate the processing capabilities of the human brain with its thousands of interconnected neurons. In the human brain, stimuli flow from neuron to neuron along multiple paths instantaneously. The strength of the connections between neurons increases with the frequency of stimulation. An artificial network operates in the same manner. It "learns," as do humans, by repeated stimuli along certain neural paths.

Neural networks are good at searching large databases for hidden patterns or trends. The networks have been applied successfully to motion detection, DNA sequencing, character and voice recognition, financial risk assessment, speech generation, image compression, and stock market predictions. Neural networks are also an integral part of many robotic vision systems.

Genetic algorithms are patterned after the *adaptation* capabilities of biological systems. They use an iterative procedure to generate possible solutions, then narrow them down to an acceptable solution. Genetic algorithms are especially useful for dynamic process control and complex design decisions.

Fuzzy logic makes decisions based on incomplete information by simulating the ability of the human mind to deal with *ambiguity*. It is used in conjunction with automatic sensors for regulating anti-lock brakes, autofocus cameras, autosensor microwaves, and environmental controls for office buildings. GE has designed a "smart" washing machine that uses fuzzy logic to automatically determine the water temperature, amount of detergent, and the length of wash needed for a particular load of clothes.

Advanced Communications

www.prenhall.com/russell

Technology has greatly enhanced communication both within and outside of organizational boundaries. *Electronic data interchange* (EDI) allows data to flow from computer to computer, between customer and manufacturer, and between manufacturer and supplier. Purchase orders, invoices, shipping notices, scheduling updates, design approval, and order inquiry can all be handled quickly and accurately without paper processing. From automated order entry to *electronic funds transfer (EFT)*, the entire transaction can be handled electronically. *Debit cards* (also known as *smart cards*) are transforming retailing.

E-mail both inside and outside of a firm brings decision makers and stakeholders closer, and improves the quality and speed of decision making. The information superhighway, called the *Internet*, has dramatically changed marketing venues as companies have low-cost instant access to customers worldwide. *Intranets*, although limited to a company's own employees, important customers, and suppliers, are becoming popular. *Distance learning* has become big business as universities compete to broadcast classes over satellite to remote locations around the globe.

Wireless communication such as cellular phones, pagers, and satellites speed the flow of timely information and improve customer service. Wal-Mart uses point-of-sale terminals to automatically transmit sales and inventory data via company-owned satellites to computers at replenishment warehouses. Trucks are dispatched and shelves refilled within twenty-four hours. Telecommunications networks between schools, libraries, community colleges, and universities are creating electronic villages that can communicate with the world. Farmers with laptop computers on their tractors use *global positioning* to communicate their exact location to satellites orbiting the earth. The satellites help farmers determine precise amounts of herbicides, pesticides, and nutrients to be applied for a particular plot of land. The same satellites help motorists find their way on unfamiliar highways.

Teleconferencing and *telecommuting* can cut costs and increase worker productivity, allowing work to be performed almost anywhere. Xerox and other large corporations are following the lead of smaller businesses in setting up virtual offices in employee homes. Images of handwritten addresses from northern Virginia's Merryfield postal center are sent electronically 500 miles away to a preprocessing center in Salem, Virginia, where labor and land are cheaper. Within seconds, the proper ZIP code typed in at the Salem center is physically affixed to the letter at the Merrifield site. Electronic processing of insurance claims at remote sites is also common—more U.S. claims are processed in Ireland than anywhere else!

Bar coding automatically identifies parts and products, communicating information quickly to processing machines, material handling devices, and costing agents (such as a grocery store checkout). Bar coding also facilitates the collection and organization of data in such areas as sales, production, inventory, and quality control.

Virtual reality is a visual form of communication in which the user experiences animation as an active participant.

www.prenhall.com/russell

Virtual reality is a visual form of communication in which the user experiences animation as an active participant. With specialized gloves and helmet that contain fiber optic sensors, the user enters into a three-dimensional simulated world that reacts to his or her movement. More advanced systems use a CAVE environment in which 3-D images are projected on the walls, floor, and a 15-foot-high ceiling. The user can manipulate images with a wand similar to a PC's mouse. This technology has been used in the architectural design of buildings, where the client can walk through the design, look out a window, and tour the second floor. Creative uses include medical researchers, who enter themselves into a simulated human body to *experience* the clogging of arteries and other maladies as a method of prompting ideas for solving the problems.

Competing at Lands' End

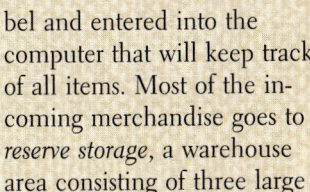

Getting the product out to the customer

www.prenhall.com/russell

Lands' End is one of the few companies that makes and keeps its promise to deliver a product two business days after receipt of the order, or three days if an item is hemmed or monogrammed. It achieves this promise through sophisticated technology including warehouses and super computers. The receiving to shipping process is diagrammed in the flowchart shown below.

Items are delivered by trucks from vendors to the *receiving* area where they are given a bar code la-

bel and entered into the computer that will keep track of all items. Most of the incoming merchandise goes to *reserve storage*, a warehouse area consisting of three large rooms, eight stories high. Boxes with items are put in an empty space by special cranes, and their bar codes are scanned so the computer knows where the boxes are located. Some of the incoming items are used to stock *active bins* to fill orders that need to go out that day. The computer prints out orders that must be filled and the bar codes of incoming items are scanned to "pick out" those items needed to fill orders. When a bin is getting low, the computer

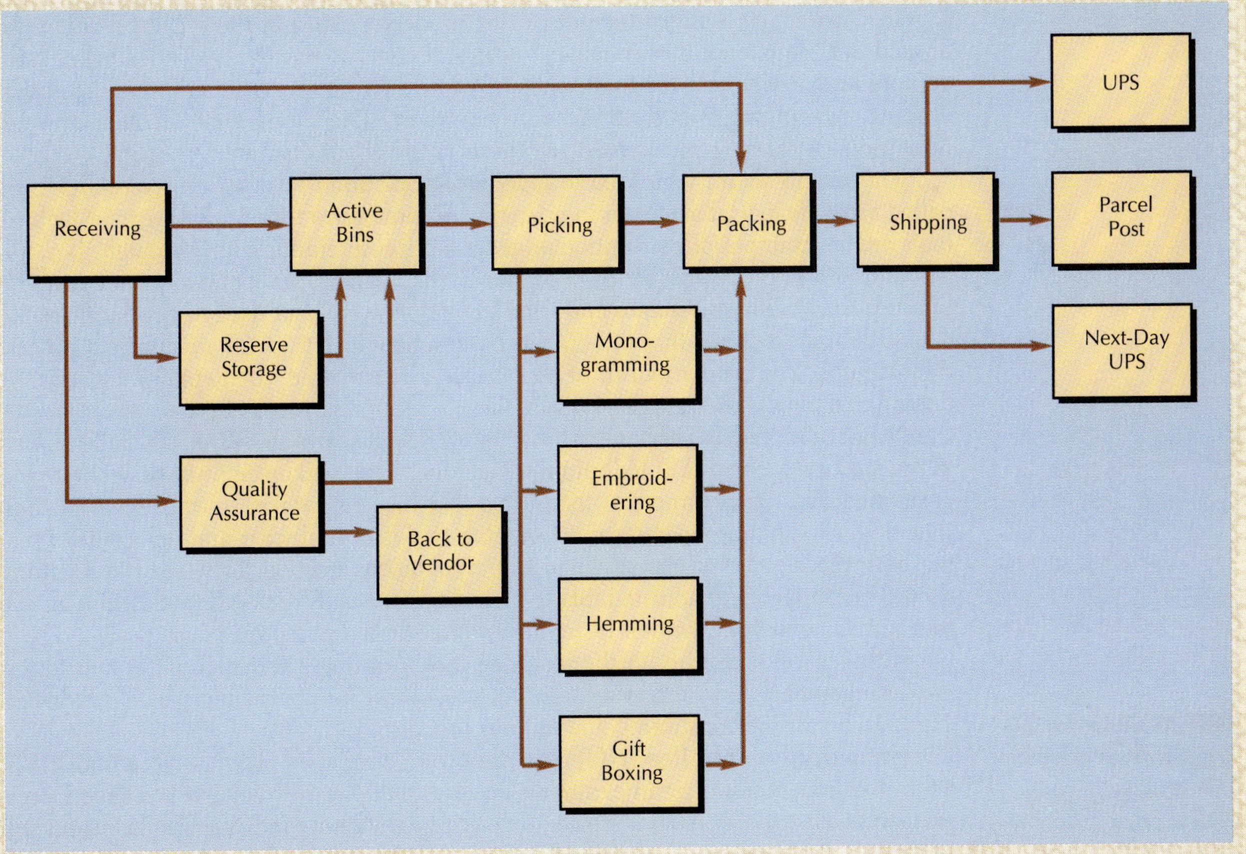

```
Receiving ──┬──────────────► Active Bins ──► Picking ──┬──► Packing ──► Shipping ──┬──► UPS
            │                    ▲                      │         ▲                │
            │                    │                      │         │                ├──► Parcel Post
            ├──► Reserve Storage ─┘                     │         │                │
            │                    ▲                      ├──► Mono-gramming          └──► Next-Day UPS
            │                    │                      │
            └──► Quality         │                      ├──► Embroid-ering
                 Assurance ──► Back to Vendor           │
                                                        ├──► Hemming
                                                        │
                                                        └──► Gift Boxing
```

(Continued)

knows to send more of that item from reserve storage. Once active bins are replenished, order-fillers pick items from the bins using order tickets printed the night before. Order-fillers are able to move down aisles taking items from active bins to fill orders without backtracking because the computer has printed the order tickets in sequence. Individual order-fillers are capable of picking several hundred items per hour and in a five-hour period 93,000 pieces of merchandise are picked.

The order-filler places a pressure sensitive "pick" ticket on each item and places the items in a cart; once the cart is full it is emptied onto a conveyor that takes the items to *packing*. As items enter the packing area they are placed on trays with the bar code up. As items move along the conveyor a scan-

ner reads the bar code on the item pick ticket. When the tray arrives at the proper packing station to be combined with the rest of the order, the tray tips the item into a packing bin. All the items for an order end up in the same bin. Packers then pack the items into boxes or mailing bags, making sure the items are correct according to packing lists. Packers are able to package 75 to 100 orders per hour. Packers catch 99.9 percent of all order-filling errors made up to this point. Packaged orders are moved by conveyor to shipping sorters where bar code scanners route the package to the appropriate shipper—UPS, Parcel Post or next-day UPS. Most packages are shipped by UPS. Private trucking firms are contracted to deliver packages to UPS hubs throughout the country.

Manufacturing Technology

There are many kinds of manufacturing processes. Most of them can be differentiated by the material they process. Plastic and ceramic parts are extruded or molded, composite material is layered, and metal parts are formed by casting, forging, and machining. Machining processes are very common. They represent an old and well-understood technology performed at various levels of automation.

The machines on which basic machining operations are performed, collectively called *machine tools*, have been in existence in some form for over 200 years. Machine tools are an example of conventional, general-purpose equipment. Although they can be dedicated to processing items of the same shape and size repetitively, they can also produce many different shapes and sizes by changing the *tool* used to cut the material. This flexibility requires that the operator know how to set up the machine to process the material. The proper tool must be selected and installed, the depth of cut must be determined, and a mechanism must be developed for stopping the tool when the desired cut is achieved. The operator must set the speed at which the tool operates as well as the rate at which work is fed into the machine. The workpiece must be secured and positioned with jigs, clamps, or fixtures so that the cut is taken in the exact location specified. Finally, the operator must be able to detect tool wear and determine when the tool needs to be replaced, when more coolant is needed, or when the machine should be stopped and adjusted. Skilled machinists usually make these decisions based on experience with no written instructions other than a blueprint of the designed part. Often this involves setting up the machine tool, running a few pieces through to test the arrangement, and then adjusting the setup until an acceptable part is produced. This can be a time-consuming and tedious process.

NC machines are machines whose motion is numerically controlled by instructions on a punched tape.

Numerically controlled (NC) machines were developed at MIT in the mid-1950s. With NC machines, machine motion is controlled by instructions contained on a punched tape. Operators do not have to determine machine settings, but they must still select and install the tools, and load and unload the machine. It is also the operator's job to monitor the operation of the machine tool to make sure the tape has been programmed properly and is in good condition, and to listen for signs of excessive tool wear.

The addition of an automatic tool changer (ATC) to an NC machine significantly increases the machine's flexibility, while reducing setup time and operator requirements. The punched tape not only guides the machine's operation, it also selects the right tool from a bank of 20 to 100 available tools and changes it within seconds.

Advances in computer technology since the mid-1970s have replaced the punched tape of NC machines with software instructions stored in the memory of a computer. These **computer numerical controlled (CNC)** machine tools are equipped with a screen and keyboard for writing and editing NC programs at the machine. This facilitates the access, editing, and loading of operating instructions and also encourages the collection of processing information and the control of processing quality. For example, records of tool use can be used to predict tool wear and generate replacement schedules before a substandard part is produced.

> **CNC machines** are NC machines controlled by software instructions in the memory of a computer.

The control of several NC machines by a larger single computer is referred to as **direct numerical control (DNC)**. DNC can also refer to distributed numerical control, in which each machine tool has its own microcomputer and the systems are linked to a central controlling computer. DNC machine tools can be of different types and can be programmed to carry out different tasks. When an automated material handling system is installed to link these machine tools together physically, a *flexible manufacturing system (FMS)* results.

> **DNC machines** are several NC machines under direct or distributed numerical control of a single computer.

Automated Material Handling

Conveyors are probably the type of <u>material-handling system</u> most associated with manufacturing. Today's conveyor systems are much different than the belt or chain conveyors of Henry Ford's era. Modern conveyor systems are both fast and flexible. They can move in both directions; "read" parts or packages via bar codes that direct them to specific locations; and move on the floor, overhead, or underground.

www.prenhall.com/russell

An *automated guided vehicle (AGV)* is a driverless truck that follows a path of rails, wires, or a special painted tape on the floor. Now available are AGVs radio-controlled by computer. A fleet of AGVs can be directed by computer to any location on the factory floor from any location. AGVs come in different shapes and sizes and can transport a variety of containers and pallets of material. Some AGVs even have microprocessor-based intelligence to handle unanticipated events. AGVs are considered the most flexible type of material handling system.

> Conveyors, AGVs, and ASRS are examples of automated material handling.

Automated storage and retrieval systems (ASRS) are basically automated warehouses, although their size has been considerably reduced in recent years. Parts stored in bins are retrieved by automated equipment and delivered to different collection and distribution points. The bins are stored in a carousel-type storage system that rotates to make the desired bin accessible for the "picking." A computer keeps track of how many items are stored in which bins and controls the system that selects the desired bin. Older ASRSs were large, some extending several stories beyond the factory floor. Newer, smaller ASRSs tend to use minibins and are located within easy reach of the assembly area. ASRSs provide space-efficient, fast, and accurate storing and retrieving of material.

Flexible Manufacturing Systems

A **flexible manufacturing system (FMS)** consists of numerous programmable machine tools connected by an automated material handling system and controlled by a common computer network. It is different from traditional automation which is fixed or

> An **FMS** consists of numerous programmable machine tools connected by an automated material handling system.

Workers stand on a movable cart to install a car engine on Ford*'s assembly line in Wayne, Michigan. The car chassis for an Escort arrives to the work station on an overhead monorail conveyor. The engine is "pumped up" to the correct height and placed in position. Material handling equipment such as this helps workers perform their jobs safely and easily.*

"hard wired" for a specific task. *Fixed automation* is very efficient and can produce in very high volumes—but it is not flexible. Only one type or model of product can be produced on most automated production lines, and a change in product design would require extensive changes in the line and its equipment.

An FMS combines flexibility with efficiency. Tools change automatically from large storage carousels at each machine that hold 100 or more tools. The material handling system (usually conveyors or automated guided vehicles) carries workpieces on pallets, which can be locked into a machine for processing. Pallets are transferred between the conveyor and machine automatically. Computer software keeps track of the routing and processing requirements for each pallet. Pallets communicate with the computer controller by way of bar codes or radio signals. Parts can be transferred between *any* two machines in *any* routing sequence. With a variety of programmable machine tools and large tool banks, an FMS can theoretically produce thousands of different items.

The efficiency of an FMS is derived from reductions in setup and queue times. Setup activities take place *before* the part reaches the machine. A machine is presented only with parts and tools that are ready for immediate processing. Queuing areas at each machine hold pallets that are ready to move in the moment the machine finishes with the previous piece. The pallet also serves as a work platform, so no time is lost transferring the workpiece from pallet to machine or positioning and fixturing the part. Advanced FMSs may contain a second material handling system, whose job consists of replacing old tools with new ones and, when possible, taking worn tools away to be sharpened or repaired. The machines in an advanced FMS, such as five-axis CNC *machining centers*, simultaneously perform up to five operations on a workpiece that would normally require a series of operations on individual milling machines, drill presses, and other machine tools.

Figure 6.8 is a schematic diagram of Ingersol-Rand's FMS in Roanoke, Virginia. Installed in the early 1970s, it was one of the first flexible manufacturing systems in the United States and is still in operation today. Originally designed to manufacture parts for hoists and winches, it currently produces rock drill bits for oil exploration. The system was flexible enough to adapt when the company went into an entirely new line of business. Flexible automation has become more important in today's manufacturing environment of rapidly changing and customized products. IBM's manufacturing facility for laptop PCs in Austin, Texas, can assemble any electronic product that will fit in the 2-foot by 2-foot by 14-inch cube that serves as a pallet and workspace for the system.

www.prenhall.com/russell

Robotics

Robots are manipulators that can be programmed to move workpieces or tools along a specified path. Contrary to popular images in science fiction, industrial robots show little resemblance to humans and provide only a fraction of the dexterity, flexibility, and intelligence of human beings. Robots do not necessarily perform a job faster than human workers, but they can tolerate hostile environments, work longer hours, and do the job more consistently. The first applications of robots were for unpleasant, hazardous, or monotonous jobs, such as loading and unloading die-casting machines (where it is very hot), welding, and spray painting. Currently, robots are used for a wide range of applications, including material handling, machining, assembly, and inspection. Applications are shifting from simple to complex operations. In the 1980s, almost 50 percent of robots sold were used for welding and painting operations. Now robots are purchased more for assembly and inspection.

> **Robots** are programmable manipulators.

www.prenhall.com/russell

The use of robots has been both exciting and disappointing. Robots perform over 98 percent of the welding for Ford Taurus, drill 550 holes in 3 hours (versus 24 hours' worth of manual drilling) for General Dynamic's F-16 fighter planes, install disk drives in personal computers, snap keys onto electronic keyboards, and assemble circuit boards with a feather-light touch. However, widespread adoption of robotics in the United States has been limited to larger industries. The automobile industry alone accounts for over half of the robots in use in this country. One reason for the slow diffusion of robotic technology may be the ineffective integration of robots into existing design and manufacturing systems or the failure to adapt those systems to the unique requirements of automation. The next section addresses the issues involved in integrating manufacturing technologies.

Computer-Integrated Manufacturing

CNC machines, DNC machines, FMSs, robots, and automated material handling systems are part of the collection of technologies referred to as **computer-aided manufacturing (CAM)**. The integration of these and other technologies is called **computer-integrated manufacturing (CIM)**. CIM is often perceived as the ultimate in automated processing—the lights-out factory of the future with no human interference. But a more accurate description of CIM is the use of computer technology to tie together the de-

> **CAM** is the use of programmable automation in manufacturing a product.

www.prenhall.com/russell

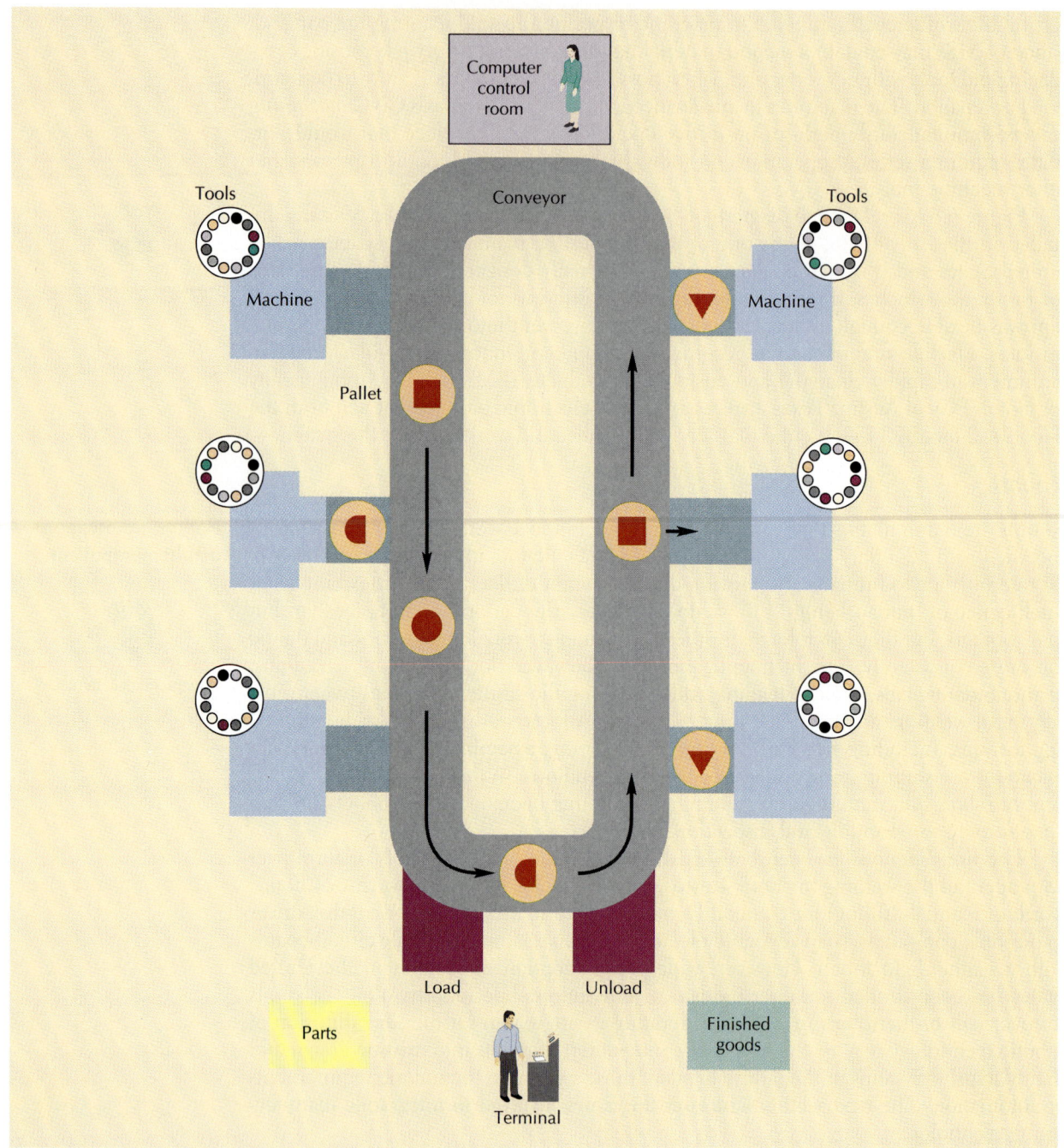

FIGURE 6.8 A Flexible Manufacturing System

CIM is the total integration of design, manufacture, and delivery through the use of computer technology. sign, production, marketing, and delivery of a product into a totally integrated system. Thus, CIM is a *strategy* for organizing and controlling a factory rather than specific technology that can be purchased.

CIM's job is to develop linkages between people, machines, databases, and decisions. The major components of CIM are shown in Figure 6.9. Each CIM component represents a different type of linkage.

THE COMPETITIVE EDGE

Fidelity Hones Its Mail Operations

www.prenhall.com/russell

Fidelity Investments, the nation's largest mutual fund company and a leader in personal investing, beats its rivals with technology, attention to detail, and hard work. Most financial services view tasks such as mail processing as back-room operations and run them with low-tech, labor-intensive equipment like forklifts. Fidelity claims efficient mail processing is essential to retaining its customers and has built a state-of-the art printing and mailing facility to back up its claim.

The 256,000-square-foot facility in Covington, Kentucky, employs 2,000 people and processes 140 million pieces of mail each year—more than double the output of the second largest mutual fund mailing facility. Fidelity borrowed the best material handling practices from man-

ufacturing—robots deftly assembly 3,000 different kits of material, and conveyor belts with rotating carousels haul material down long corridors. To ensure crisp folds and smooth toner application, paper spends 48 hours in a climate-controlled room at 70 degrees Fahrenheit and 45% humidity.

Fidelity promises a one-day turnaround on requested material. Each day's requests are sent electronically to the Covington facility where the material is automatically pulled from stock and stuffed into envelopes. Downloaded names and addresses are ink jet onto the cover, and metered postage is applied. Optical readers scan the ZIP code and sort the mail into different trays. Postal service trucks arrive to take the mail directly to the airport— 90% of the mail never sees the inside of a post office.

SOURCE: James Hirsch, "A High-Tech System for Sending the Mail Unfolds at Fidelity," *Wall Street Journal*, March 25, 1996.

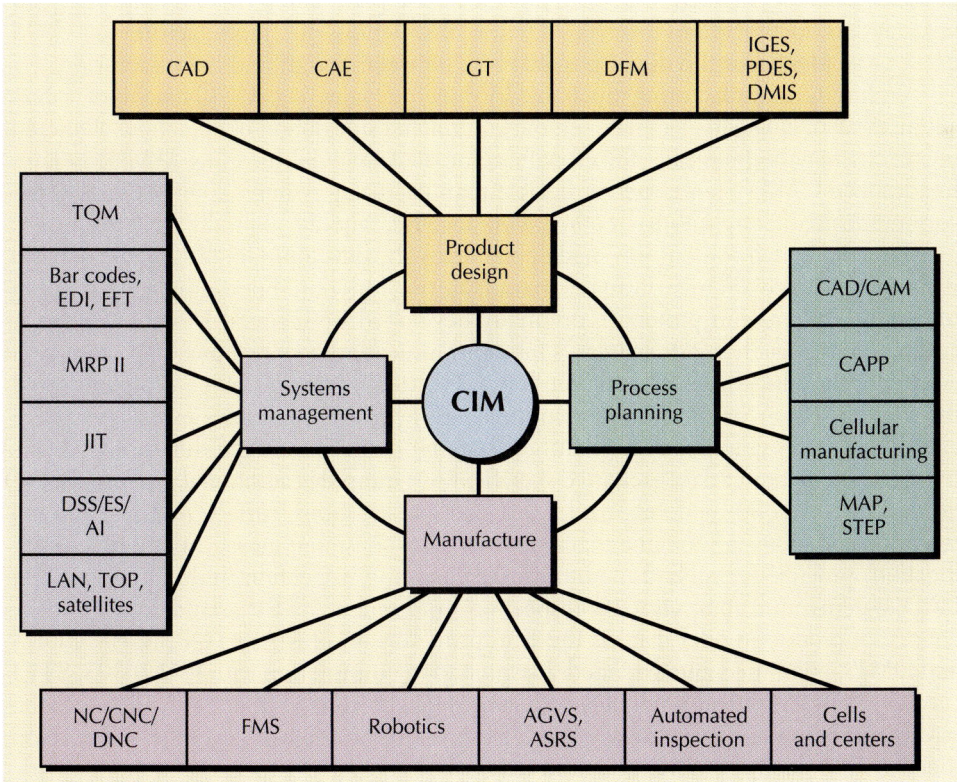

FIGURE 6.9   Components of CIM

THE COMPETITIVE EDGE

Cook Specialty Co. Overhauls Its Manufacturing Strategy with CIM

Cook Specialty Co. is a small manufacturer of precision metal parts. As its customers began to trim their supplier base, Cook looked for a competitive edge that would keep the company in business. Instead of just making products from customer-supplied blueprints, Cook needed to help its customers *design* products, too. "We don't really have a product line," says Cook's president, Tom Panzarella. "What we have is expertise in engineering and manufacturing."

To make the transformation to a custom manufacturer, Cook invested heavily in a technology called CIM (for computer-integrated manufacturing). With CIM, Cook can swap CAD parts drawings with customers and send instructions for finalized designs to CNC machines for exact manufacture. Robots can handle welding and other repetitive tasks. Quality can be assured with the digital probe of coordinate measurement machines.

Employees, working with minimal supervision in manufacturing cells around the plant, have access to 30 computer terminals. The terminals provide customer information online and enable operators to trade notes on the status of jobs. "The idea, says Panzarella, "is to bring the voice of the customer right onto the floor where the people running the jobs can hear it directly. Around here, CIM stands for *communication in manufacturing*."

SOURCE: Brian McWilliams, "Reengineering the Small Factory," *Inc. Technology* (March 19, 1996): 44–47.

Group technology is the grouping of parts into families.

www.prenhall.com/russell

CAD can physically link different design components together to create new or modified designs and communicate electronically to other systems. **Group technology (GT)** classifies existing designs so that new designs can incorporate the expertise of earlier designs. CAE (computer-aided engineering) links the functional design of the product to the CAD-generated form design. CAPP (computer-aided process planning) converts design specifications from CAD into instructions for manufacture for CAM. CAD/CAM describes the direct physical link between design and manufacturing.

Within the manufacturing function, CAM technologies (e.g., CNC machines, robots, automatic tool changers) facilitate remote control and integration of operations. Different operations may be physically linked with automated material handling (AMH) systems. In advanced CAM systems, such as flexible manufacturing systems, automated machines communicate directly with each other, work together, and are centrally controlled.

The CIM environment was made possible by the development of shared databases, standards, and networking within the manufacturing function. For example, MAP (manufacturing automation protocol), originally developed by General Motors to solve its automation headaches, sets standards for communication between pieces of automated equipment produced by different vendors. TOP (technical and office protocol) serves the same function in an office environment. IGES (initial graphics exchange specification) translates graphics data (mainly wireframe models) between different CAD systems. PDES (product data exchange specification) translates additional aspects of CAD design, such as solid modeling data, tolerance specifications, surface finishes, and material specifications in the same manner. DMIS (dimensional measuring interface specification) provides a standard medium for exchanging inspection information between CAD systems and computerized inspection equipment. STEP (standard for the exchange of product model data) is the European version of MAP, TOP, IGES, PDES, and DMIS, combined and extended. Developed in conjunction with ISO 10303, STEP can represent all critical product specifications (such as shape, material, tolerances, behavior, function, and structure); consider the entire product life cycle (from development to manufacture through use and disposal); and specify process sequences for specific production systems (such as automobiles, shipbuilding, architectural engineering, or plant engineering).

In the process of manufacturing a product, materials need to be ordered, workers scheduled, demand forecasted, customer orders received and entered into the manufacturing system, production planned, progress reports issued, costs and quality documented, and customers billed. Computerized manufacturing control systems developed to collect, store, and display this information are an integral part of CIM. Manufacturing resources planning (MRP II), discussed in Chapter 13, is an example of such a system.

Just-in-time (JIT) and total quality management (TQM) systems require the collection, sharing, and exchange of information outside of the manufacturing organization. CIM accomplishes this with automatic identification systems (bar codes), electronic data interchange (EDI), electronic funds transfer (EFT), electronic mail (e-mail), and satellite communications.

Guidelines for Technology Adoption

Technology is not a panacea for regaining competitiveness, nor should it be overlooked as a source of competitive advantage. Decisions on technology should consider:

- *Technology readiness.* Automation does not have the ability to grant exceptions, tweak a process, or modify a design. Poorly designed products and inefficient processes are often revealed when automation is introduced. This can be a learning experience (albeit an expensive one) for management.

- *Technology design.* Automation's advantage comes not from its ability to mimic humans, but from the ability to do things that humans cannot do. For example, people have difficulty returning a hand or tool to exactly the same spot (poor repeatability), but they have very good sensors that can be used to search for the correct spot. Machines, on the other hand, have good repeatability, so sophisticated sensors are not needed. Manual assembly of high-tech products is almost obsolete due to the ability of robots to perform the task with higher quality, uniformity, and cleanliness.

  Successful technologies look for the best way to perform a task and are not constrained by the limitations of the human body. Current experimentation with free-moving robots is patterned after insect movement, not human movement.

- *Technology selection.* The level of automation selected must match the requirements of the manufacturing system, the product being produced, and the competitive environment. Human-directed work is preferable in situations where sensing, judgment, or intelligence is required or in environments that change so frequently that the expense of programming automated equipment would be uneconomical. Specific guidelines can be found in the literature for when to use different types of manufacturing technologies. This makes the task of technology selection appear straightforward. However, even in those cases when it is a simple task to select a technology appropriate for the current product market, the market may change over the life of the technology. For example, if a formerly diverse market becomes large and homogeneous, flexible manufacturing may add undue cost to production. Similarly, if a focused market becomes more diverse, fixed automation will not be able to meet the varied demand requirements.

- *Technology integration.* Technology is so expensive that many firms can afford to automate only incrementally. Without a strategy for automation, it is difficult to ensure that the individual systems purchased can be integrated. GM, at one point, had 40,000 pieces of automated equipment, only 15 percent of which could communicate with each other or use the same database. Technology in the future is sure to become more powerful, more flexible, easier to use, more intelligent, and better integrated.

> Technology *readiness, design, selection,* and *integration* should be considered before adopting new technology.

www.prenhall.com/russell

www.prenhall.com/russell

Summary

Three important issues in process design are types of processes, process planning, and technology decisions.

The type of process selected depends primarily on demand volume and degree of product standardization. *Projects* are produced one-at-a-time to customer order. *Batch production* is used to process a variety of low-volume jobs. *Mass production* produces large volumes of a standard product for a mass market. *Continuous processes* are used for very high-volume commodity products.

Process planning consists of converting product designs into workable instructions for manufacture. These instructions may include the sequence of assembly, sequence of operations, machine assignments, tooling, machine settings, machine operating parameters, inspection criteria, operating procedures, and processing details. They often appear in the form of assembly charts, flow process charts, operations process charts, and manufacturing specifications. On a broader scale, process planning may involve decisions such as process selection, equipment purchases, and whether to make or buy product components.

Today, technological advances account for more than half of our nation's per capita growth. Technology is advancing so rapidly, managers find it difficult to keep abreast of the changes. Fortunately, they do not have to be *experts* in technology to make wise technology choices, but they must be *comfortable* with technology.

Decision support systems (DSS), expert systems, and artificial intelligence (AI) help managers make decisions based on data, knowledge, and experience. CAD/CAM, robotics, FMS, and CIM are examples of manufacturing technology available to managers.

Summary of Key Terms

artificial intelligence: a computer system that attempts to replicate human thought processes to diagnose and solve problems.

assembly chart: a schematic diagram of a product that shows the relationship of component parts to parent assemblies, the groupings of parts that make up a subassembly, and the overall sequence of assembly.

batch production: the low-volume production of customized products.

bill of material: a document that lists the materials and parts that go into a product.

break-even analysis: a technique that determines the volume of demand needed to be profitable; it takes into account the trade-off between fixed and variable costs.

CNC machines: NC machines that are controlled by software instructions stored in the memory of a computer.

computer-aided manufacturing (CAM): the use of programmable automation in the manufacture of a product.

computer-aided process planning (CAPP): a specialized software system that attempts to automate the development of process plans.

computer-integrated manufacturing (CIM): the total integration of design, manufacture, and delivery of a product through the use of computer technology.

continuous process: the production of a very high-volume commodity product with highly automated equipment.

decision support system (DSS): an information system with which a manager interacts in order to reach a decision through an iterative process.

DNC machines: several NC machines under direct or distributed numerical control of a single computer.

expert system: a computer system that uses an expert knowledge base to solve a problem.

flexible manufacturing system: a versatile system that results from the physical connection of programmable machine tools with an automated material handling system.

group technology (GT): the grouping of parts into families based on similar shapes or processing requirements.

management information system (MIS): a system specifically designed to channel large quantities and numerous types of information through an organization.

mass production: the high-volume production of a standard product for a mass market.

numerically controlled (NC) machines: machines whose motion is numerically controlled by instructions contained on a punched tape.

operations process chart: a document that shows the series of operations necessary to make each item listed on the assembly chart.

process flowchart: a document that uses standardized symbols to chart the productive and nonproductive flow of activities involved in a process; it may be used to document current processes or as a vehicle for process improvement.

process planning: the conversion of designs into workable instructions for manufacture, along with associated decisions on component purchase or fabrication and process and equipment selection.

process strategy: an organization's overall approach for physically producing goods and services.

project: the one-of-a-kind production of a product to customer order that requires a long time to complete and a large investment of funds and resources.

reengineering: the total redesign of a process.

robots: manipulators that can be programmed to move workpieces or tools along a specified path.

virtual reality: a visual form of communication in which the user experiences animation as an active participant.

Solved Problem

Texloy Manufacturing Company must select a process for its new product, TX142, from among three different alternatives. The following cost data have been gathered:

	Process A	Process B	Process C
Fixed cost	$10,000	$20,000	$50,000
Variable cost	$5/unit	$4/unit	$2/unit

For what volume of demand would each process be desirable?

Solution:

If v represents the number of TX142s demanded (and, we assume, produced), then

$$\text{Total cost for process A} = \$10,000 + \$5v$$
$$\text{Total cost for process B} = \$20,000 + \$4v$$
$$\text{Total cost for process C} = \$50,000 + \$2v$$

Next, we calculate the points of indifference between the processes by equating their total costs and solving for demand volume, v. Note that in this problem there are three processes to consider, but we can compare only two at a time.

Comparison 1: Process A versus process B

$$\begin{array}{cc} \text{Process A} & \text{Process B} \\ \$10{,}000 + \$5v = & \$20{,}000 + \$4v \\ v = & 10{,}000 \text{ units} \end{array}$$

If the demand for units is 10,000 units, we can choose either process A or process B. But if demand is less than 10,000, we should choose the alternative with the lowest fixed cost, process A. Conversely, if demand is greater than 10,000, we should choose the alternative with the lowest variable cost, process B.

Comparison 2: Process B versus process C

$$\begin{array}{cc} \text{Process B} & \text{Process C} \\ \$20{,}000 + \$4v = & \$50{,}000 + \$2v \\ 2v = & 30{,}000 \\ v = & 15{,}000 \text{ units} \end{array}$$

If demand is 15,000 units, we are indifferent between process B and process C. If demand is greater than 15,000 units, we should choose process C. If demand is less than 15,000 but greater than 10,000 (see comparison 1), we should choose process B.

Comparison 3: Process A versus process C

$$\begin{array}{cc} \text{Process A} & \text{Process C} \\ \$10{,}000 + \$5v = & \$50{,}000 + \$2v \\ 3v = & 40{,}000 \\ v = & 13{,}333 \text{ units} \end{array}$$

We have already concluded that process B should be selected between 10,000 and 15,000 units. Therefore, this point of indifference can be ignored.

The graph of the problem is shown here.

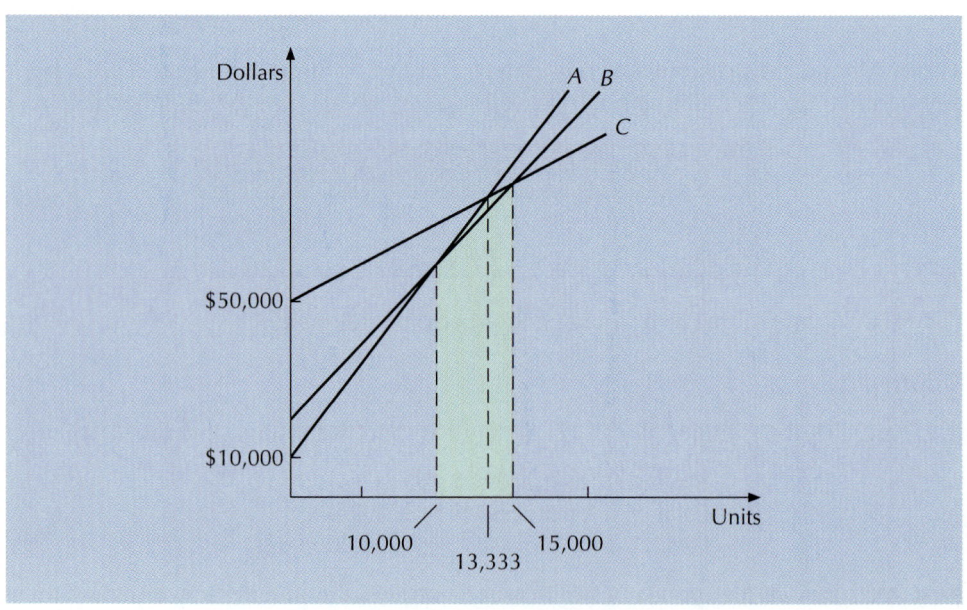

To summarize, from the graph and our decision rules, we can recommend the following process selection.

- Below 10,000 units, choose process A.
- Between 10,000 and 15,000 units, choose process B.
- Above 15,000 units, choose process C.

Questions

6-1. Discuss the types of decisions that are involved in creating a process strategy.

6-2. Describe the four basic types of production processes. What are the advantages and disadvantages of each? When should each be used?

6-3. How is break-even analysis used for process selection?

6-4. List and explain six factors that affect the make-or-buy decision.

6-5. List several factors that are often overlooked in a financial analysis of equipment purchases.

6-6. What kind of information do the following documents communicate?
   a. Assembly chart
   b. Operations process chart
   c. Process flowchart

6-7. Describe the output of process planning. How does process planning differ by type of process?

6-8. What is CAPP? How is it used?

6-9. What is reengineering? Explain the reengineering process.

6-10. Differentiate between a management information system, a decision support system, and an expert system.

6-11. Describe several approaches to artificial intelligence.

6-12. Describe several levels of automation for machine tools. How does the role of the operator change?

6-13. Give an example of an automated material handling system.

6-14. Define *flexible manufacturing system*. What are the advantages of an FMS?

6-15. What are robots? How are they most commonly used?

6-16. Briefly discuss the components of CIM.

6-17. What are the major impediments to CIM today?

6-18. List and explain four factors that should be considered in the adoption of technology.

Problems

6-1. Construct a process flowchart of a process with which you are familiar. Identify bottlenecks, potential failure points, and opportunities for improvement.

6-2. Create an operations process chart for making pancakes.

6-3. Mikey W. Smitty, an emerging rapper, is getting ready to cut his first CD, called "Western Rap." The cost of recording the CD is $5,000, but copies are $5 apiece. If the CDs can be sold for $15 each, how many CDs must be sold to break even? What is the break-even point in dollars?

6-4. Mikey W. Smitty is confident that demand for his "Western Rap" CD will substantially exceed the break-even point computed in Problem 6-3. So, Mikey is contemplating having his CD cut at a classier (and pricier) studio. The cost to record the CD would rise to $9,000. However, since this new studio works with very high volume, production costs would fall to $2 per CD.

a. What is the break-even point for this new process?

b. Compare this process to the process proposed in the previous problem. For what volume of demand should Mikey choose the classier studio?

6-5. Patricia Zell, a dollmaker from Olney, Maryland, is interested in the mass marketing and production of a ceramic doll of her own design called Tiny Trisha. The initial investment required for plant and equipment is estimated at $25,000. Labor and material costs are approximately $10 per doll. If the dolls can be sold for $50 each, what volume of demand is necessary for the Tiny Trisha doll to break even?

6-6. Although it will fulfill her lifelong dream, Patricia is not confident that demand for her Tiny Trisha doll will exceed the break-even point computed in Problem 6-5. If she chooses a less appealing site and does more of the work by hand, her initial investment cost can be reduced to $5,000, but her per-unit cost of manufacture will rise to $15 per doll.

a. What is the break-even point for this new process?

b. Compare this process to the process proposed in the previous problem. For what volume of demand should Patricia choose this process?

6-7. David Austin recently purchased a chain of dry cleaners in northern Wisconsin. Although the business is making a modest profit now, David suspects that if he invests in a new press, he could recognize a substantial increase in profits. The new press costs $15,400 to purchase and install and can press 40 shirts an hour (or 320 per day). David estimates that with the new press, it will cost $0.25 to launder and press each shirt. Customers are charged $1.10 per shirt.

a. How many shirts will David have to press to break even?

b. So far, David's workload has varied from 50 to 200 shirts a day. How long would it take to break even on the new press at the low-demand estimate? At the high-demand estimate?

c. If David cuts his price to $0.99 a shirt, he expects to be able to stabilize his customer base at 250 shirts per week. How long would it take to break even at the reduced price of $0.99? Should David cut his price and buy the new press?

6-8. The school cafeteria can make pizza for approximately $0.30 a slice. The cost of kitchen use and cafeteria staff runs about $200 per day. The Pizza Den nearby will deliver whole pizzas for $9.00 per pizza. The cafeteria staff cuts the pizza into 8 pieces and serves them in the usual cafeteria line. With no cooking duties, the staff can be reduced by half, for a fixed cost of $75 per day. Should the school cafeteria make or buy its pizzas?

6-9. ComputerEase supply store sells computer diskettes. Diskettes are purchased for $17.00 a box and sold for $19.70. To remain competitive, ComputerEase must constantly reevaluate its suppliers. A survey of new supplier sources yields the following options:

■ Supplier 1   Fixed order of 100 boxes/month of diskettes, $1,700 plus $15/box for every box over 100

■ Supplier 2   Fixed order of 100 boxes/month of diskettes, $2,000 plus $10/box for every box over 100

Should ComputerEase try supplier 1, try supplier 2, or stick with its current supplier? How does the monthly demand for diskettes affect your recommendation?

6-10. The office administrator of a large public accounting firm is calculating the cost of word processing a client's financial statements. The alternatives are to have the work done by the accounting firm's data-processing staff, which precludes the need for final review by an accountant (process A); have the client perform his or her own word processing, which requires extensive review by an accountant (process B); or contract out the work to a professional service, which requires some review by an accountant (process C). The cost of each alternative is outlined next.

	Process A	*Process B*	*Process C*
Word processing	$3,000	$2,300	$2,500
Accountant review	$0 per page	$10 per page	$5 per page

The office administrator has asked you to prepare a chart for the firm's clients that outlines the various word-processing costs and makes recommendations based on differing page lengths.

6-11. Alma McCoy has decided to purchase a cellular phone for her car, but she is confused about which rate plan to choose. The "occasional-user" plan is $0.50/minute, regardless of how many minutes of air time are used. The "frequent-user" plan charges a flat rate of $55/month for 70 minutes of air time plus $0.33/minute for any time over 70 minutes. The "executive" plan charges a flat fee of $75 per month for 100 minutes of air time plus $0.25/minute over 100 minutes. In the interest of simplicity, Alma has decided to go with the occasional-user plan to start with and then upgrade as she sees fit at a later date.

   a. How much air time per month would Alma need to use before she upgrades from the occasional-user plan to the frequent-user plan?

   b. At what usage rate should she switch from the frequent-user plan to the executive plan?

6-12. Merrimac Manufacturing Company has always purchased a certain component part from a supplier on the East Coast for $50 per part. The supplier is reliable and has maintained the same price structure for years. Recently, improvements in operations and reduced product demand have cleared up some capacity in Merrimac's own plant for producing component parts. The particular part in question could be produced at $40 per part, with an annual fixed investment of $25,000. Currently, Merrimac needs 300 of these parts per year.

   a. Should Merrimac make or buy the component part?

   b. As another alternative, a new supplier located nearby is offering volume discounts for new customers of $50 per part for the first 100 parts ordered and $45 per part for each additional unit ordered. Should Merrimac make the component in-house, buy it from the new supplier, or stick with the old supplier?

   c. Would your decision change if Merrimac's demand increased to 2,000 parts per month? Increased to 5,000 per month?

   d. Develop a set of rules that Merrimac can use to decide when to make this component, when to buy it from the old supplier, or when to buy it from the new supplier.

6-13. Prydain Pharmaceuticals is reviewing its employee health-care program. Currently, the company pays a fixed fee of $300 per month for each employee, regardless of the number or dollar amount of medical claims filed. Another health-care provider has offered to charge the company $100 per month per employee and $30 per claim filed. A third insurer charges $200 per month per employee and $10 per claim filed. Which health-care program should Prydain join? How would the average number of claims filed per employee per month affect your decision?

6-14. Gemstone Quarry is trying to decide whether or not to invest in a new material handling system. The current system (which is old and completely paid for) has an annual maintenance cost of $10,000 and costs approximately $25 to transport each load of material. The two new systems that are being considered vary both in sophistication and cost. System 1 has a fixed cost of $40,000 and a cost per load estimated at $10. System 2 has a fixed cost of $100,000 but a per-load cost of $5. At what volume of demand (i.e., number of loads) should Gemstone purchase System 1? System 2?

6-15. Tribal Systems, Inc., is opening a new plant and has yet to decide on the type of process to employ. A labor-intensive process would cost $10,000 for tools and equipment and $14 for labor and materials per item produced. A more automated process costs $50,000 in plant and equipment but has a labor/material cost of $8 per item produced. A fully automated process costs $300,000 for plant and equipment and $2 per item produced. If process selection were based solely on lowest cost, for what range of production would each process be chosen?

6-16. Lydia and Jon order their holiday gifts through the mail. They have spent many evenings at home comparison-shopping through gift catalogs and have found all the things they need from three mail-order houses, B. B. Lean, Spoogle's, and Sea's End. The purchase price for their selections from each catalog is given here. The shipping and handling charge per item is also given. If Lydia and Jon want to order all their gifts from the same source, which catalog should they choose? How does the number of items ordered affect your recommendation?

	B. B. Lean	Spoogle's	Sea's End
Purchase price	$400	$500	$460
Shipping/handling per item	$6	$3	$4

CASE PROBLEM

Herding the Patient

Bayside General Hospital is trying to streamline its operations. A problem-solving group consisting of a nurse, a technician, a doctor, an administrator, and a patient is examining outpatient procedures in an effort to speed up the process and make it more cost-effective. Listed here are the steps that a typical patient follows for diagnostic imaging:

- Patient enters main hospital entrance.
- Patient registers at central reception.
- Patient taken to diagnostic imaging department.
- Patient registers at diagnostic imaging reception.

- Patient sits in department waiting area until dressing area clear.
- Patient changes in dressing area.
- Patient waits in dressing area.
- Patient taken to exam room.
- Exam performed.
- Patient taken to dressing area.
- Patient dresses.
- Patient leaves.

Create a process flowchart of the procedure and identify opportunities for improvement.

CASE PROBLEM

Putting It All Together

Newman & Sons assembles bedroom furniture for a major manufacturer. Like many small businesses, the manner in which work is performed is more a matter of convenience than careful planning.

Consider the process of assembling drawers. Three drawer-clamp machines put the drawer together by pressing the dovetails in the drawer sides into the slots in the drawer fronts and backs. The drawer subassembly is then placed on a roller line and transported to a stop, where it waits to be placed on a motorized conveyor line. On the conveyor line, the bottom of the drawer is stapled on, drawer guides are installed, and glue blocks are added. The drawers encounter another stop until one of two sander operators removes them. The dovetail joints are then sanded on a belt sander and loaded onto a hanger conveyor. The hanger conveyor transports the drawer through a spray booth, where the finish is applied. The finished drawer then winds its way to the chest assembly area downstairs, by which time the finish has dried.

Construct an assembly chart for a drawer, as described here. Map out the flow of the process in a process flowchart. Do you have any suggestions for improving the process flow?

Streamlining the Refinancing Process

First National Bank has been swamped with refinancing requests this year. To handle the increased volume, it divided the process into five distinct stages and created departments for each stage.

The process begins with a customer completing a loan application for a *loan agent*. The loan agent discusses the refinancing options with the customer and performs quick calculations based on customer-reported data to see if the customer qualifies for loan approval. If the numbers work, the customer signs a few papers to allow a credit check and goes home to wait for notification of the loan's approval.

The customer's file is then passed on to a *loan processor*, who requests a credit check, verification of loans or mortgages from other financial institutions, an appraisal of the property, and employment verification. If any problems are encountered, the loan processor goes to the loan agent for advice. If items appear on the credit report that are not on the application or if other agencies have requested the credit report, the customer is required to explain the discrepancies in writing. If the explanation is acceptable, the letter is placed in the customer's file and the file is sent to the loan agent (and sometimes the bank's board) for final approval.

The customer receives a letter of loan approval and is asked to call the *closing agent* to schedule a closing date and to lock in a loan rate if the customer has not already done so.

The closing agent requests the name of the customer's attorney to forward the loan packet. The attorney is responsible for arranging a termite inspection, a survey, a title search, and insurance and for preparing the closing papers. The attorney and the closing agent correspond back and forth to verify fees, payment schedules, and payoff amounts.

The *loan-servicing specialist* makes sure the previous loan is paid off and the new loan is set up properly. After the closing takes place, the bank's *loan-payment specialist* takes care of issuing payment books or setting up the automatic drafting of mortgage fees and calculating the exact monthly payments, including escrow amounts. The loan-payment specialist also monitors late payment of mortgages.

It is difficult to evaluate the success or failure of the reengineered process, since the volume of refinancing requests is so much greater than it has ever been before. However, customer comments solicited by the loan-servicing specialist have been disturbing to management.

Customer Comments:

■ I refinanced with the same bank that held my original loan, thinking erroneously that I could save time and money. You took two months longer processing my loan than the other bank would have and the money I saved on closing costs was more than eaten up by the extra month's higher mortgage payments.

■ I just got a call from someone at your bank claiming my mortgage payment was overdue. How can it be overdue when you draft it automatically from my checking account?

■ How come you do everything in writing and through the mail? If you would just call and ask me these questions instead of sending forms for me to fill out, things would go much quicker.

■ If I haven't made any additions to my house or property in the past year, you appraised it last year, and you have access to my tax assessment, why bother with another appraisal? You guys just like to pass around the business.

■ I never know who to call for what. You have so many people working on my file. I know I've repeated the same thing to a dozen different people.

■ It took so long to get my loan approved that my credit report, appraisal report, and termite inspection ran out. You should pay for the new reports, not me.

■ I drove down to your office in person today to deliver the attorney's papers, and I hoped to re-

(Continued)

turn them with your signature and whatever else you add to the closing packet. The loan specialist said that the closing agent wouldn't get to my file until the morning of the scheduled closing and that if she hit a snag, the closing could be postponed! I'm taking off half a day from work to attend the closing and "rescheduling" is not convenient. I know you have lots of business, but I don't like being treated this way.

■ I received a letter from one of your loan-payment specialists today, along with a stack of forms to complete specifying how I want to set up my mortgage payments. I signed all these at closing—don't you read your own work? I'm worried that if I fill them out again you'll withdraw the payment twice from my account!

In the context of these customer comments, evaluate First National's refinancing process and recommend improvements. What additional information would be helpful in your analysis?

References

Bedworth, D., M. Henderson, and P. Wolfe. *Computer-Integrated Design and Manufacturing*. New York: McGraw-Hill, 1991.

Foston, L. *Fundamentals of Computer Integrated Manufacturing*. Englewood Cliffs, N.J.: Prentice Hall, 1991.

Goetsch, D. *Advanced Manufacturing Technology*. Albany, N.Y.: Delmar Publishers, 1990.

Gold, B. "CAM Sets New Rules for Production." *Harvard Business Review* (November–December 1982): 88–94.

Groover, M. "Fundamental Operations." *IEEE Spectrum* 20, no. 5 (May 1983): 65–69.

Haas, E. "Breakthrough Manufacturing." *Harvard Business Review* (March–April 1987): 75–81.

Hammer, Michael, and James Champy. *Reengineering the Corporation*. New York: HarperCollins, 1993.

Hammer, Michael, and Steven Stanton. *The Reengineering Revolution*. New York: HarperCollins, 1995.

Maus, R., and R. Allsup. *Robotics: A Manager's Guide*. New York: John Wiley, 1986.

Nevens, J., D. Whitney, T. DeFazio, A. Edsall, R. Gustavson, R. Metzinger, and W. Dvorak. *Concurrent Design of Products and Processes: A Strategy for the Next Generation in Manufacturing*. New York: McGraw-Hill, 1989.

Noori, H. *Managing the Dynamics of New Technology*. Englewood Cliffs, N.J.: Prentice Hall, 1990.

Office of Technology Assessment. *Computerized Manufacturing Automation: Employment, Education, and the Workplace*. Washington, D.C.: Government Printing Office, 1984.

Robot Institute of America. *Worldwide Robotics Survey and Directory*. 1991.

Saporito, B. "IBM's No-Hands Assembly Line." *Fortune* (September 15, 1986).

Schroeder, R. *Operations Management: Decision Making in the Operations Function*. New York: McGraw-Hill, 1989.

Skinner, W. *Manufacturing: The Formidable Competitive Weapon*. New York: John Wiley, 1985.

Valery, N. "Factory of the Future." *The Economist* (May 30, 1987): 3–18.

7

Facility Layout

Pittsburgh International: An Efficient Layout

Pittsburgh International Airport is the first airport to be constructed from scratch since airline deregulation. It is designed to mesh with the "hub-and-spokes" system, in which passengers from a variety of cities come to a central hub and then transfer to other flights en route to their destinations. Hub airports must be able to handle large volumes of passengers and flights with increased speed and efficiency. At Pittsburgh, moving walkways and shuttle trains transport passengers to distant gates in eleven minutes or less. Gates are more spacious, too, to handle the larger crowds. Baggage is bar-coded and channeled by computerized laser scanners along six miles of conveyor belts from flight to flight. The terminal itself is X-shaped to allow planes to approach from any direction. Dual taxiways run in opposite directions around the terminal to reduce queuing time on takeoffs. USAir estimates that the runway layout alone saves the airline more than $12 million in fuel costs each year.[1]

Good layouts can increase revenues, as well as save operating expenses. Pittsburgh Airport's innovative X-design allows planes to approach the airport from any direction, significantly increasing the airspace capacity of the airport.

Facility layout is the arrangement of areas within a facility.

Layout decisions impact quality and competitiveness.

Facility layout refers to the arrangement of machines, departments, workstations, storage areas, aisles, and common areas within an existing or proposed facility. Layouts have far-reaching implications for the quality, productivity, and competitiveness of a firm. Layout decisions significantly affect how efficiently workers can do their jobs, how fast goods can be produced, how difficult it is to automate a system, and

[1] Edwin McDowell, "For Pittsburgh, a Model Airport at an Immodest Price," *New York Times* November 8, 1992.

how responsive the system can be to changes in product or service design, product mix, and demand volume.

The basic objective of the layout decision is to ensure a smooth flow of work, material, people, and information through the system. Effective layouts also:

- Minimize material handling costs;
- Utilize space efficiently;
- Utilize labor efficiently;
- Eliminate bottlenecks;
- Facilitate communication and interaction between workers, between workers and their supervisors, or between workers and customers;
- Reduce manufacturing cycle time or customer service time;
- Eliminate wasted or redundant movement;
- Facilitate the entry, exit, and placement of material, products, or people;
- Incorporate safety and security measures;
- Promote product and service quality;
- Encourage proper maintenance activities;
- Provide a visual control of operations or activities;
- Provide flexibility to adapt to changing conditions.

> Facility layout decisions involve multiple objectives.

Basic Layouts

There are three basic types of layouts:

- process,
- product, and
- fixed-position

and three hybrid layouts:

- cellular layouts,
- flexible manufacturing systems, and
- mixed-model assembly lines.

We discuss basic layouts in this section and hybrid layouts later in the chapter.

Process Layouts

Process layouts, also known as *functional layouts*, group similar activities together in departments or work centers according to the process or function they perform. For example, all drills would be located in one work center, lathes in another work center, and milling machines in still another work center. All painting operations, of course, would be performed in the painting department. A department store is organized in this way, with women's clothes, men's clothes, children's clothes, cosmetics, and shoes in separate departments. A process layout is characteristic of intermittent operations, job shops, or batch production, which serve different customers with different needs. The volume of each customer's order is low, and the sequence of operations required to complete a customer's order can vary considerably.

The equipment in a process layout is general purpose, and the workers are skilled at operating the equipment in their particular department. The advantage of this layout is flexibility. The disadvantage is inefficiency. Jobs do not flow through the system

> **Process layouts** group similar activities together according to the process they perform.

www.prenhall.com/russell

Women's lingerie	Shoes	Housewares
Women's dresses	Cosmetics and jewelry	Children's department
Women's sportswear	Entry and display area	Men's department

FIGURE 7.1(a)   **A process layout in services**

in an orderly manner, backtracking is common, movement from department to department can take a considerable amount of time, and queues tend to develop. In addition, each new job arrival to a work center may require that the machine be set up differently for its particular processing requirements. Although workers can operate a number of machines in a single department, their workload often fluctuates—from queues of jobs waiting to be processed to idle time between jobs. Figure 7.1 (a) and (b) shows a schematic diagram of process layouts in services and manufacturing.

Material storage and movement are directly affected by the type of layout. Storage space in a process layout is large to accommodate the large amount of in-process inventory. The factory may look like a warehouse, with work centers strewn between storage aisles. In-process inventory is high because material moves from work center to work

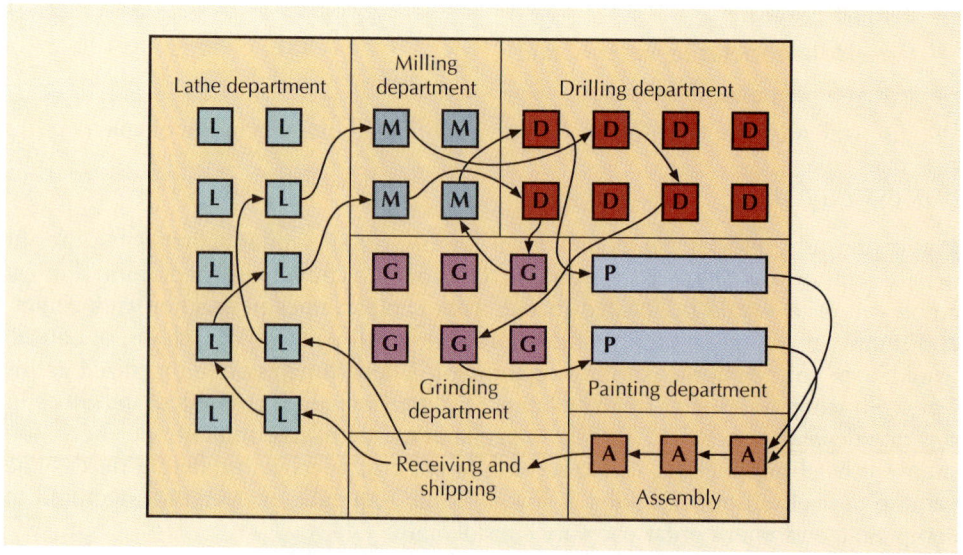

FIGURE 7.1(b)   **A process layout in manufacturing**

center in batches waiting to be processed. Finished goods inventory, on the other hand, is low because the goods are being made for a particular customer and are shipped out to that customer upon completion.

Process layouts require flexible <u>material handling</u> equipment (such as forklifts) that can follow multiple paths, move in any direction, and carry large loads of in-process goods. A *forklift* moving pallets of material from work center to work center needs wide aisles to accommodate heavy loads and two-way movement. Scheduling of forklifts is typically controlled by radio dispatch and varies from day to day and hour to hour. Routes have to be determined and priorities given to different loads competing for pickup.

The major layout concern for a process layout is where to locate the machine centers (i.e., groupings of similar machines) in relation to each other. Although each job potentially has a different route through the shop, some paths between machines will be more common than others. Past information on customer orders and projections of customer orders can be used to develop patterns of flow through the shop.

Product Layouts

Product layouts, better known as *assembly lines*, arrange activities in a line according to the sequence of operations that need to be performed to assemble a particular product. Each product has its own "line" specifically designed to meet its requirements. The flow of work is orderly and efficient, moving from one workstation to another down the assembly line until a finished product comes off the end of the line. Since the line is set up for one type of product, special machines can be purchased to match a product's specific processing requirements. <u>Product layouts</u> are suitable for mass production or repetitive operations in which demand is stable and volume is high. The product is a standard one made for a general market, not for a particular customer. Because of the high level of demand, product layouts are more automated than process layouts, and the role of the worker is different. Workers perform narrowly defined assembly tasks that do not demand as high a wage rate as those of the more versatile workers in a process layout.

The advantage of the product layout is its efficiency and ease of use. The disadvantage is its inflexibility. Significant changes in product design may require that a new assembly line be built and new equipment be purchased. This is what happened to U.S. automakers in the 1970s when demand shifted to smaller cars. The factories that could efficiently produce six-cylinder engines could not be adapted to produce four-cylinder engines. A similar inflexibility occurs when demand volume slows. The fixed costs of a product layout (mostly for equipment) allocated over fewer units can send the price of a product soaring.

The major concern in a product layout is balancing the assembly line so that no one workstation becomes a bottleneck and holds up the flow of work through the line. Figure 7.2 shows the product flow in a product layout. Contrast this with the flow of products through the process layout shown in Figure 7.1(b).

A product layout needs material moved in one direction along the assembly line and always in the same pattern. Conveyors are the most common material handling equipment for product layouts. Conveyors can be paced (automatically set to control the speed of work) or unpaced (stopped and started by the workers according to their pace). Assembly work can be performed on line (i.e., on the conveyor) or offline (at a workstation serviced by the conveyor). Aisles can be narrow because material is moved only one way, it is not moved very far, and the conveyor is an integral part of the as-

www.prenhall.com/russell

Product layouts arrange activities in a line according to the sequence of operations for a particular product.

www.prenhall.com/russell

Process layouts are flexible; product layouts are efficient.

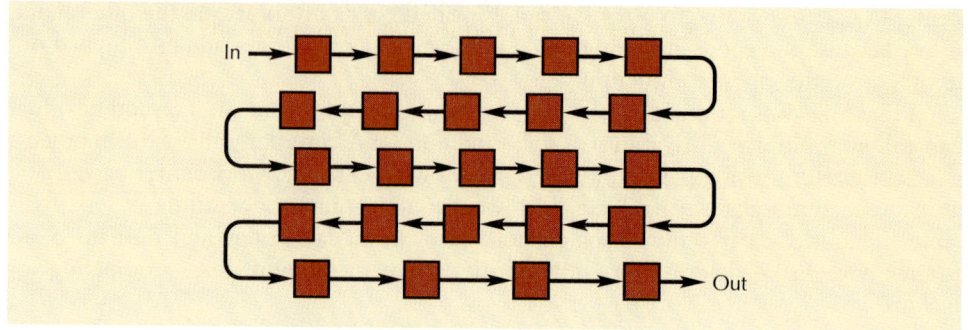

FIGURE 7.2   A Product Layout

sembly process, usually with workstations on either side. Scheduling of the conveyors, once they are installed, is simple—the only variable is how fast it should operate.

Storage space along an assembly line is quite small because in-process inventory is consumed in the assembly of the product as it moves down the assembly line. Finished

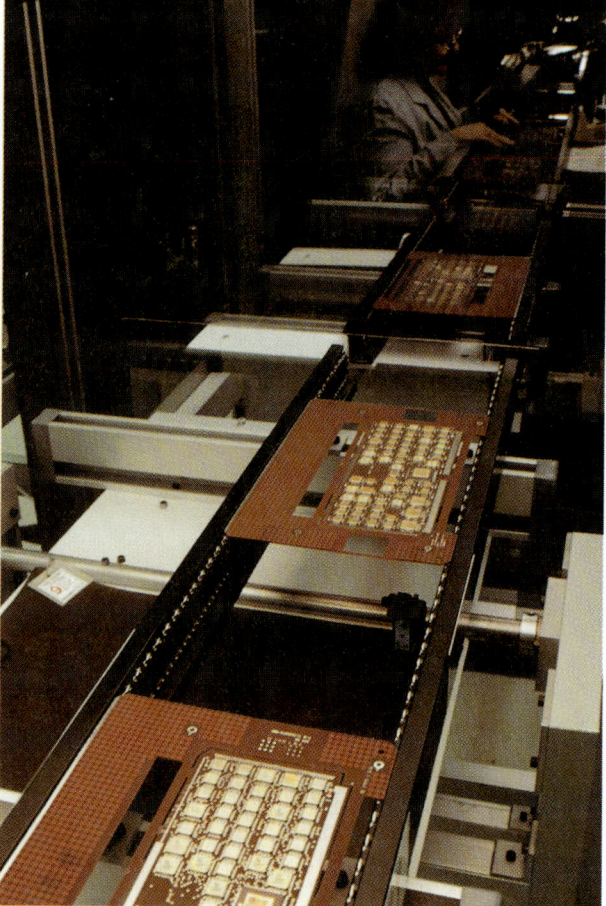

The photo on the left shows a process layout example: a forklift moves pallets of material from department to department in a stamping factory that makes automotive molding. The photo on the right shows a product layout example: partially completed units move by conveyor from one workstation to the next on an electronics assembly line.

TABLE 7.1   A Comparison of Product and Process Layouts

	Product Layout	Process Layout
1. Description	Sequential arrangement of activities	Functional grouping of activities
2. Type of process	Continuous, mass production, mainly assembly	Intermittent, job shop, batch production, mainly fabrication
3. Product	Standardized, made to stock	Varied, made to order
4. Demand	Stable	Fluctuating
5. Volume	High	Low
6. Equipment	Special purpose	General purpose
7. Workers	Limited skills	Varied skills
8. Inventory	Low in-process, high finished goods	High in-process, low finished goods
9. Storage space	Small	Large
10. Material handling	Fixed path (conveyor)	Variable path (forklift)
11. Aisles	Narrow	Wide
12. Scheduling	Part of balancing	Dynamic
13. Layout decision	Line balancing	Machine location
14. Goal	Equalize work at each station	Minimize material handling cost
15. Advantage	Efficiency	Flexibility

goods, however, may require a separate warehouse for storage before they are shipped to dealers or stores to be sold.

Product and process layouts look different, use different material handling methods, and have different layout concerns. Table 7.1 summarizes the differences between product and process layouts.

Fixed-Position Layouts

Fixed-position layouts are typical of projects in which the product produced is too fragile, bulky, or heavy to move. Ships, houses, and aircraft are examples. In this layout, the product remains stationary for the entire manufacturing cycle. Equipment, workers, materials, and other resources are brought to the production site. Equipment utilization is low because it is often less costly to leave equipment idle at a location where it will be needed again in a few days, than to move it back and forth. Frequently, the equipment is leased or subcontracted, because it is used for limited periods of time. The workers called to the work site are highly skilled at performing the special tasks they are requested to do. For instance, pipefitters may be needed at one stage of production, and electricians or plumbers at another. The wage rate for these workers is much higher than minimum wage. Thus, if we were to look at the cost breakdown for fixed-position layouts, the fixed cost would be relatively low (equipment may not be owned by the company), whereas the variable costs would be high (due to high labor rates and the cost of leasing and moving equipment).

Because the fixed-position layout is specialized, we concentrate on the product and process layouts and their variations for the remainder of this chapter. In the sections that follow, we examine some quantitative approaches for designing product and process layouts.

Fixed-position layouts are used in projects where the product cannot be moved.

www.prenhall.com/russell

The size and complexity of aircraft production requires a fixed-position layout. Construction takes place in stages at fixed locations. Rather than move the aircraft itself, crews of workers gather around each unit with their tools and equipment and move from site to site to complete their tasks. Notice the modular offices, and the various carts and bins with wheels for easy movement.

Designing Process Layouts

Process layout objective: Minimize material handling costs.

In designing a process layout, we want to minimize material handling cost, which is a function of the amount of material moved times the distance it is moved. This implies that departments that incur the most interdepartment movement should be located closest to each other, and those that do not interact should be located further away. The techniques used to design process layouts are based on logic and the visual representation of data.

Block Diagramming

We begin with data on historical or predicted movement of material between departments in the existing or proposed facility. This information is typically provided in the form of a from/to chart, or *load summary chart.* The chart gives the average number of **unit loads** transported between the departments over a given period of time. A unit load can be a single unit, a pallet of material, a bin of material, or a crate of material—however material is normally moved from location to location. In automobile manufacturing, a single car represents a unit load. For a ball-bearing producer, a unit load might consist of a bin of 100 or 1,000 ball bearings, depending on their size.

A **unit load** is the quantity in which material is normally moved.

The next step in designing the layout is to calculate the *composite movements* between departments and rank them from most movement to least movement. Composite movement, represented by a two-headed arrow, refers to the back-and-forth movement between each pair of departments.

Finally, trial layouts are placed on a grid that graphically represents the relative distances between departments in the form of uniform blocks. The objective is to assign each department to a block on the grid so that *nonadjacent loads* are minimized. The term *nonadjacent* is defined as a distance farther than the next block, either horizontally, vertically, or diagonally. The trial layouts are scored on the basis of the number of nonadjacent loads. Ideally, the optimum layout would have zero nonadjacent loads. In practice, this is rarely possible, and the process of trying different layout configurations to reduce the number of nonadjacent loads continues until an acceptable layout is found.

> Block diagramming tries to minimize non-adjacent loads.

· use when quantitative data is available ie. # of loads moving between work centres.

> **EXAMPLE 7.1**
>
> *Process Layout*

Barko, Inc. makes *bark scalpers*, processing equipment that strips the bark off of trees and turns it into nuggets or mulch for gardens. The facility that makes bark scalpers is a small job shop that employs 50 workers and is arranged into five departments: bar stock cutting, sheet metal, machining, painting, and assembly. The average number of loads transported between the five departments per month is given in the accompanying load summary chart. The current layout of the facility is shown schematically on the 2 × 3 grid. Notice that there is quite a bit of flexibility in the facility, as indicated by the six possible locations (i.e., intersections) available for five departments. In addition, the forklift used in the facility is very flexible, allowing horizontal, vertical, and diagonal movement of material.

Load Summary Chart

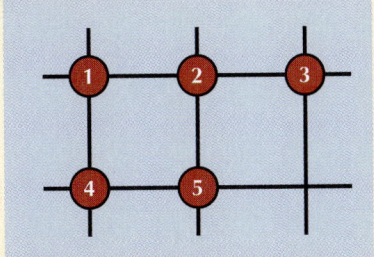

From \ To DEPARTMENT	DEPARTMENT 1	2	3	4	5
1	—	100	50		
2		—	200	50	
3	60		—	40	50
4		100		—	60
5		50			—

Barko management anticipates that a new bark scalper plant will soon be necessary and would like to know if a similar layout should be used or if a better layout can be designed. You are asked to do the following:

a. Evaluate the current layout in terms of nonadjacent loads.

b. If needed, propose a new layout on a 2 × 3 grid that will minimize the number of nonadjacent loads.

SOLUTION:

a. In order to evaluate the current layout, we need to calculate the composite, or back-and-forth, movements between departments. For example, the composite movement between department 1 and department 3 is the sum of 50 loads moved from 1 to 3 plus 60 loads moved from 3 to 1, or 110 loads of material. If we continue to calculate composite movements and rank them from highest to lowest, the following list results.

(Continued)

Composite Movements

$2 \leftrightarrow 3$	200 loads
$2 \leftrightarrow 4$	150 loads
$1 \leftrightarrow 3$	110 loads
$1 \leftrightarrow 2$	100 loads
$4 \leftrightarrow 5$	60 loads
$3 \leftrightarrow 5$	50 loads
$2 \leftrightarrow 5$	50 loads
$3 \leftrightarrow 4$	40 loads
$1 \leftrightarrow 4$	0 loads
$1 \leftrightarrow 5$	0 loads

Next, we evaluate the "goodness" of the layout by scoring it in terms of nonadjacent loads. The results are shown visually in grid 1.

Nonadjacent Loads

$1 \leftrightarrow 3$	110
$3 \leftrightarrow 4$	40
	150

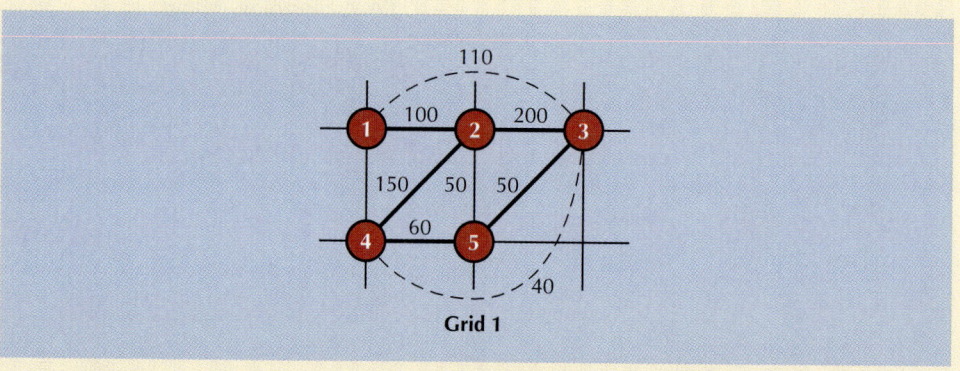

Grid 1

Following our composite movement list, $1 \leftrightarrow 2$ is an adjacent move, but $1 \leftrightarrow 3$ is not. The adjacent moves are marked with a solid line and the nonadjacent moves are shown with a curved dashed line to highlight the fact that material is required to move farther than we would like. Our nonadjacent score starts with 110 loads of material from $1 \leftrightarrow 3$. Continuing down our list, $2 \leftrightarrow 3$ and $2 \leftrightarrow 4$ are adjacent and are marked with solid lines. Movement $3 \leftrightarrow 4$ is nonadjacent, so we designate it as such and add 40 loads to our nonadjacent score. The remaining movements are adjacent. Thus, our score for this layout is $110 + 40 = 150$ nonadjacent loads.

b. To improve on this layout, we can look at our rankings of composite movements and conclude that departments 3 and 4 should be located adjacent to department 2 and that departments 4 and 5 may be located away from department 1 without adding to the score of nonadjacent loads. Let's put departments 4 and 5 on one end of the grid and department 1 on the other and then fill in departments 2 and 3 in the middle. The revised solution is shown in grid 2. The only nonadjacent moves are between departments 1 and 4, and 1 and 5. Since no loads of material are moved along those paths, the score for this layout is zero. It should be noted that there are multiple optimum solutions to this problem, and it may take several iterations before zero nonadjacent loads can be achieved.

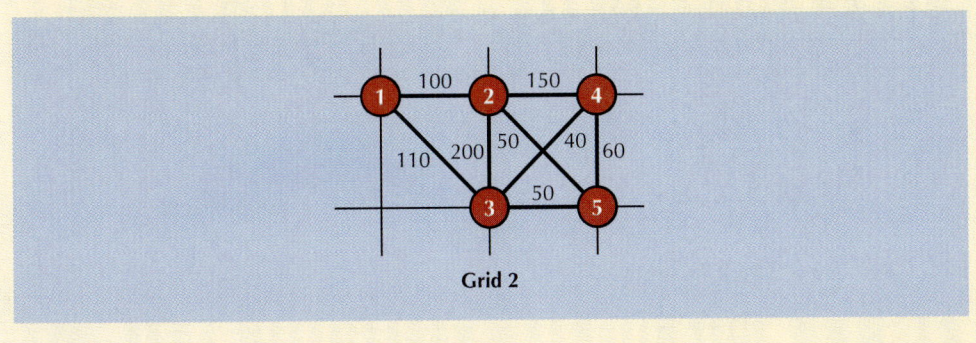

Grid 2

The layout solution in grid 2 represents the relative position of each department. The next step in the layout design is to add information about the space required for each department. Recommendations for workspace around machines can be requested from equipment vendors or found in safety regulations or operating manuals. In some cases, vendors provide templates of equipment layouts, with work areas included. Workspace allocations for workers can be specified as part of job design, recommended by professional groups, or agreed upon through union negotiations. A **block diagram** can be created by blocking in the work areas around the departments on the grid. The *final block diagram* adjusts the block diagram for the desired or proposed shape of the building. Standard building shapes include rectangles, L shapes, T shapes, and U shapes. Most manufacturing facilities and retail establishments are single-level facilities. Offices, hospitals, and banks tend to be multilevel. Multilevel buildings present special layout problems.

> A **block diagram** is a type of schematic layout diagram that includes space requirements.

Figure 7.3(a) shows an initial block diagram for Example 7.1, and Figure 7.3(b) shows a final block diagram. Notice that the space requirements vary considerably from department to department, but the relative location of departments has been retained from the grid.

Relationship Diagramming

The preceding solution procedure is appropriate for designing process layouts when quantitative data are available. However, in situations for which quantitative data are difficult to obtain or do not adequately address the layout problem, the load summary chart can be replaced with subjective input from analysts or managers. Richard Muther developed a format for displaying manager preferences for departmental locations, known as **Muther's grid**.[2] The preference information is coded into six categories associated with the five vowels, A, E, I, O, and U, plus the letter X. As shown in Figure 7.4, the vowels match the first letter of the closeness rating for locating two departments next to each other. The diamond-shaped grid is read similar to mileage charts on a road map. For example, reading down the highlighted row in Figure 7.4, it is *okay* if the of-

> **Muther's grid** is a format for displaying manager's preferences for department locations.

[2] R. Muther, *Systematic Layout Planning* (Boston: Industrial Education Institute, 1961).

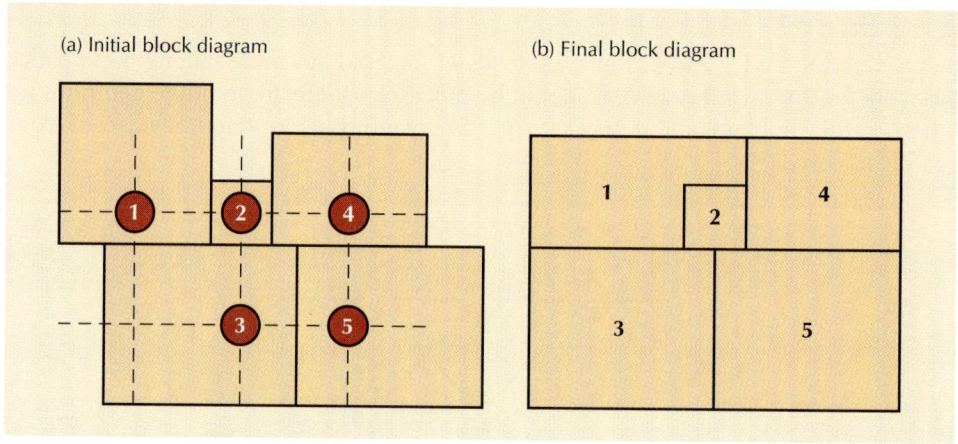

FIGURE 7.3 **Block Diagrams**

A **relationship diagram** is a schematic diagram that uses weighted lines to denote location preference.

fices are located next to production, *absolutely necessary* that the stockroom be located next to production, *important* that shipping and receiving be located next to production, and *absolutely necessary* that the toolroom be located next to production.

The information from Muther's grid can be used to construct a **relationship diagram** that evaluates existing or proposed layouts. Consider the relationship diagram shown in Figure 7.5(a). A schematic diagram of the six departments from Figure 7.5 is given in a 2 × 3 grid. Lines of different thicknesses are drawn from department to department. The thickest lines (three, four, or five strands) identify the closeness ratings with the highest priority—that is, for which departments it is *important, especially important*, or *absolutely necessary* that they be located next to each other. The priority diminishes with line thickness. *Undesirable* closeness ratings are marked with a zigzagged line. Visually, the best solution would show short heavy lines and no zigzagged lines (undesirable locations are noted only if they are adjacent). Thin lines (one or two strands, representing *unimportant* or *okay*) can be of any length and for that reason are sometimes eliminated from the analysis. An alternate form of relationship diagramming uses colors instead of line thickness to visualize closeness ratings.

Manager preferences for department locations are displayed as A, E, I, O, U, or X.

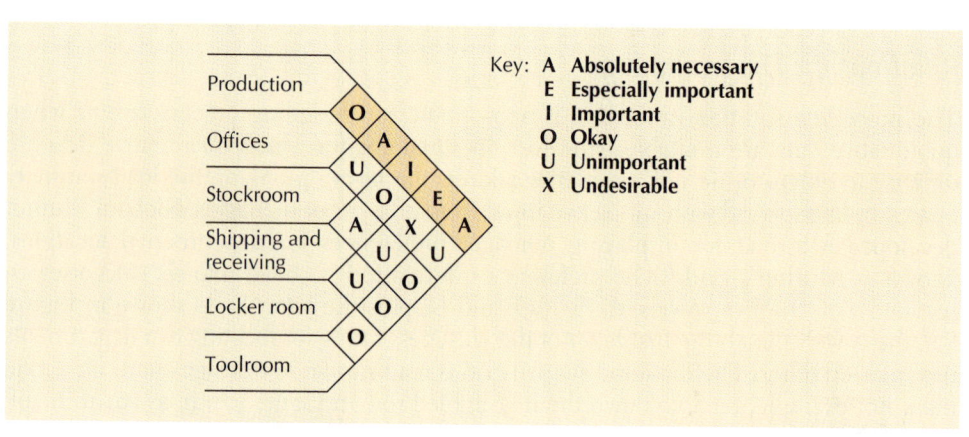

FIGURE 7.4 **Muther's Grid**

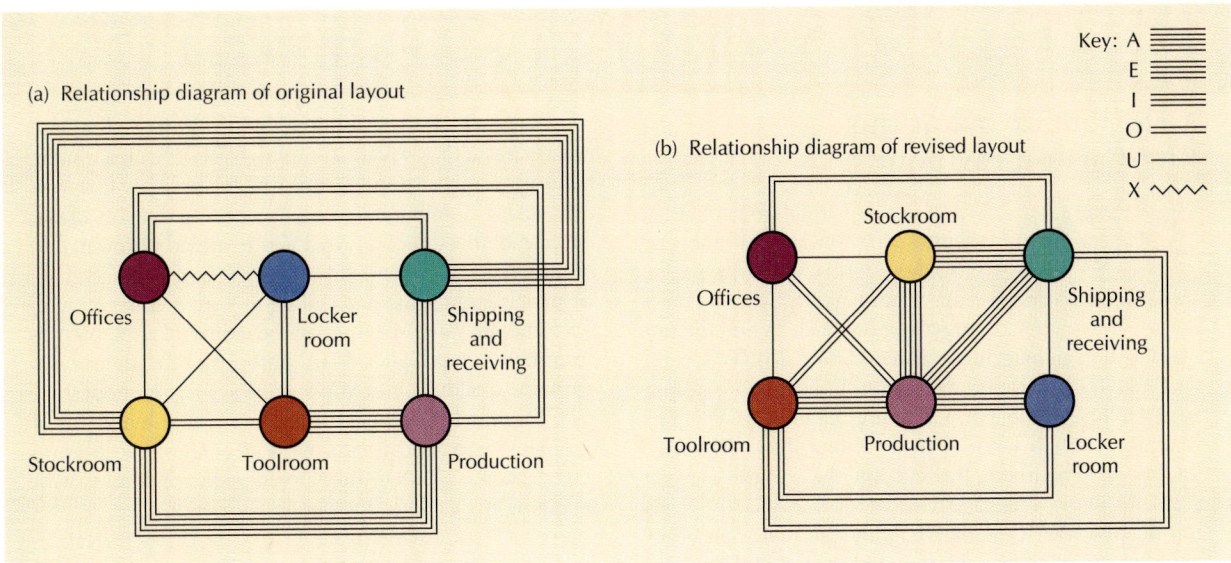

FIGURE 7.5   **Relationship Diagrams**

From Figure 7.5(a), it is obvious that production and shipping and receiving are located too far from the stockroom and that the offices and locker room are located too close to one another. Figure 7.5(b) shows a revised layout, and evaluates the layout with a relationship diagram. The revised layout appears to satisfy the preferences expressed in Muther's grid. The heavy lines are short and within the perimeter of the grid. The lengthy lines are thin, and there are no zigzagged lines.

Computerized Layout Solution

The diagrams just discussed help formulate ideas for the arrangement of departments in a process layout, but they can be cumbersome for large problems. Fortunately, several computer packages are available for designing process layouts. The best known is CRAFT (Computerized Relative Allocation of Facilities Technique). CRAFT takes a load summary chart and block diagram as input and then makes pairwise exchanges of departments until no improvements in cost or nonadjacency score can be found. The output is a revised block diagram after each iteration for a rectangular-shaped building, which may or may not be optimal. CRAFT is sensitive to the initial block diagram used; that is, different block diagrams as input will result in different layouts as outputs. For this reason, CRAFT is often used to improve upon existing layouts or to enhance the best manual attempts at designing a layout.

PREP (Plant Relayout and Evaluation Package) is similar to CRAFT, except it can handle more departments (ninety-nine instead of forty), a multistory facility, and different material handling equipment. ALDEP (Automated Layout Design Program) and CORELAP (Computerized Relationship Layout Planning) use nonquantitative input and relationship diagramming to produce a feasible layout. ALDEP can handle sixty-three departments and a multistory facility. It begins with an initial random layout and seeks to improve upon the values in Muther's grid that are not satisfied. CORELAP can process forty-five departments and take into account different building shapes. It attempts to create an acceptable layout from the beginning by locating department pairs

www.prenhall.com/russell

THE COMPETITIVE EDGE

A Flexible Layout at the Ritz-Carlton Pavilion

www.prenhall.com/russell

Ritz-Carlton Hotels listen to their customers. When customers in Naples, Florida, wanted a less formal place to gather, the hotel put up a tent out back. When the tent was too hot, management air conditioned it. When the tent was too small, they decided to build a more permanent facility, a shell of a building called the Pavilion. Looking through his files to determine how customers had used the ballroom, the tent, and the grounds over the years, the general manager concluded that what the Pavilion needed was "extreme flexibility," so that each group could create whatever environment it wanted. Flexibility was provided—right down to the basic structure.

The Pavilion's flexibility is built into its ceiling and walls. The ceiling is painted midnight black with a unique lighting system of hundreds of tiny white lights that look like stars. Computer-operated, the ceiling consists of different motorized sections that can be raised or lowered to create a tiered effect and different degrees of formality. Fabric panels hang across the ceiling to form a visual curtain.

The lighting system can be adjusted and preprogrammed to highlight certain portions of the room or to pinpoint specific tables and speakers. At a moment's notice, the hotel's AV department can create templates of company logos and theme party decorations to be projected on the painted, unpapered walls. Spotlights with changing hues add to the variety of moods.

SOURCE: Based on Grace Wagner "Customer-Driven Construction," *Lodging Hospitality* (November 1993): 23.

---

with *A* ratings first, then those with *E* ratings, and so on. All these computer packages are basically trial-and-error approaches to layout design that provide good—but not necessarily optimal—process layouts.

Service Layouts

www.prenhall.com/russell

Service layouts may have different objectives than manufacturing layouts.

Most service organizations use process layouts. This makes sense because of the variability in customer requests for service. Service layouts are designed in much the same way as process layouts in manufacturing firms, but the objectives may differ. For example, instead of minimizing the flow of materials through the system, services may seek to minimize the flow of customers or the flow of paperwork. In retail establishments, the objective is usually related to maximizing profit per unit of display space. If sales vary directly with customer exposure, then an effective layout would expose the customer to as many goods as possible. This means instead of minimizing a customer's flow, it would be more beneficial to maximize it (to a certain point). Grocery stores take this approach when they locate milk on one end of the store and bread on the other, forcing the customer to travel through aisles of merchandise that might prompt additional purchases.

Another aspect of service layout is the allocation of shelf space to various products. Industry-specific recommendations are available for layout and display decisions. Computerized versions, such as SLIM (Store Labor and Inventory Management) and COSMOS (Computerized Optimization and Simulation Modeling for Operating Supermarkets), consider shelf space, demand rates, profitability, and stockout probabilities in layout design. Finally, service layouts are often visible to the customer so they must be aesthetically pleasing as well as functional.

Designing Product Layouts

A product layout arranges machines or workers in a line according to the operations that need to be performed to assemble a particular product. From this description,

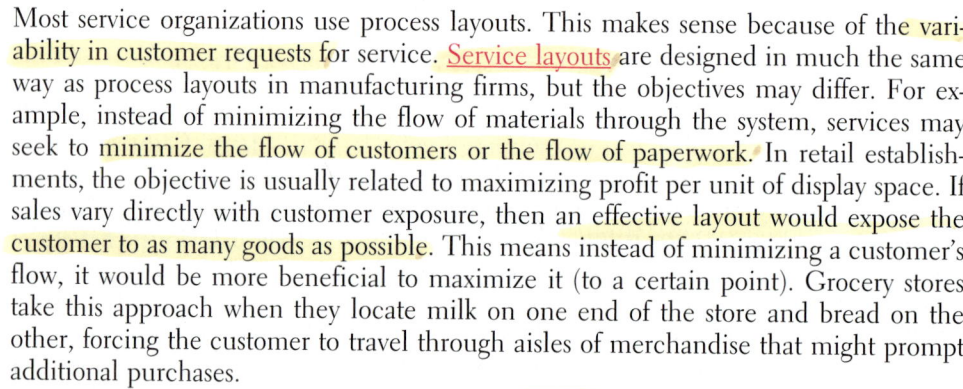

[Handwritten margin notes:]
Designing Product Layouts
- Product layout or assembly lines
- Develop precedence diagram of tasks
- jobs divided into work elements
- assign work elements to work stations
- try to balance the amt of work at each work station.

Service layouts must be attractive as well as functional. In the photo on the left, modular office units without permanent walls allow maximum flexibility, save space, and encourage communication. In the photo on the right, Fuddruckers restaurant creates an atmosphere of quality and freshness by allowing customers to prepare their own salads and hamburger fixings at spacious salad bars overflowing with extras. Customers get exactly what they want faster than if a waiter had processed the order. Who makes the best hamburgers? Fuddruckers and you!

it would seem the layout could be determined simply by following the order of assembly as contained in the bill of material for the product. To some extent, this is true. Precedence requirements specifying which operations must precede others, which can be done concurrently and which must wait until later, are an important input to the product layout decision. But there are other factors that make the decision more complicated.

Product layouts or assembly lines are used for high-volume production. One objective in this regard is to attain the required output rate as efficiently as possible. To do this, the jobs that must be performed are broken down into their smallest indivisible portions, called *work elements*. Work elements are so small that they cannot be performed by more than one worker or at more than one workstation. But it is common for one worker to perform several work elements as the product passes through his or her workstation. Part of the layout decision is concerned with grouping these work elements into workstations so products flow through the assembly line smoothly. A *workstation* is any area along the assembly line that requires at least one worker or one machine. If each workstation on the assembly line takes the same amount of time to perform the work elements that have been assigned, then products will move successively from workstation to workstation with no need for a product to wait or a worker to be idle. The process of equalizing the amount of work at each workstation is called **line balancing.**

> Product layout objective: Balance the assembly line.

> **Line balancing** tries to equalize the amount of work at each workstation.

Line Balancing

Assembly line balancing operates under two constraints, precedence requirements and cycle time restrictions.

Precedence requirements are physical restrictions on the *order* in which operations are performed on the assembly line. For example, we would not ask a worker to package a product before all the components were attached, even if he or she had the time to do so before passing the product to the next worker on the line. To facilitate line balancing, precedence requirements are often expressed in the form of a precedence diagram. The *precedence diagram* is a network, with work elements represented by circles or nodes and precedence relationships represented by directed line segments connecting the nodes.

> **Precedence requirements** are physical restrictions on the order in which operations are performed.

EXAMPLE
7.2

Precedence
Diagramming

Given the following information on work elements and time and precedence requirements, draw and label a precedence diagram for the assembly of fruit strip snacks.

	Work Element	Precedence	Time (min)
A	Press out sheet of fruit	—	0.1
B	Cut into strips	A	0.2
C	Outline fun shapes	A	0.4
D	Roll up and package	B, C	0.3

SOLUTION:

Element A has no elements preceding it, so node A can be placed anywhere. Element A precedes element B, so the line segment that begins at node A must end at node B.

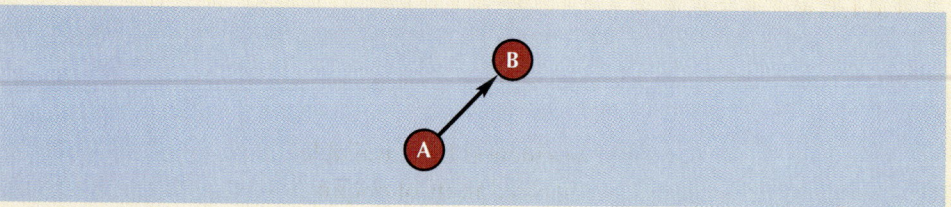

Element A precedes element C. Again, a line segment from node A must end at node C.

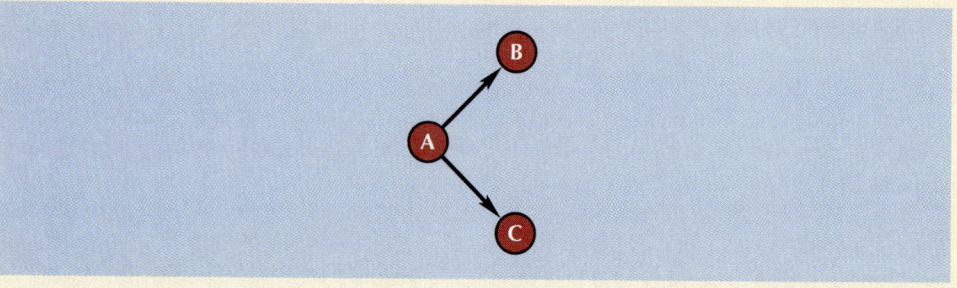

Elements B and C precede element D, so the line segments extending from nodes B and C must end at node D.

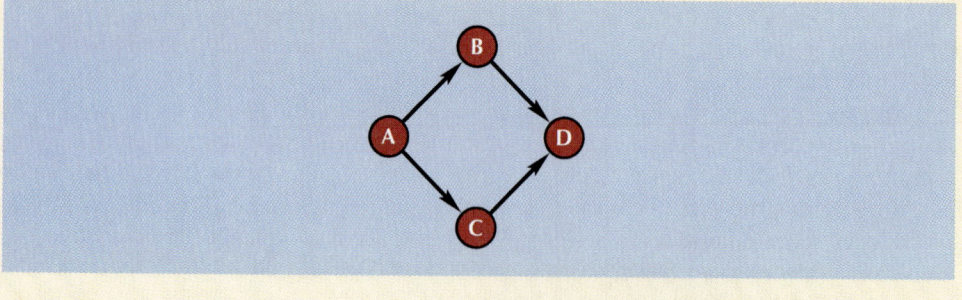

The precedence diagram is completed by adding the time requirements beside each node.

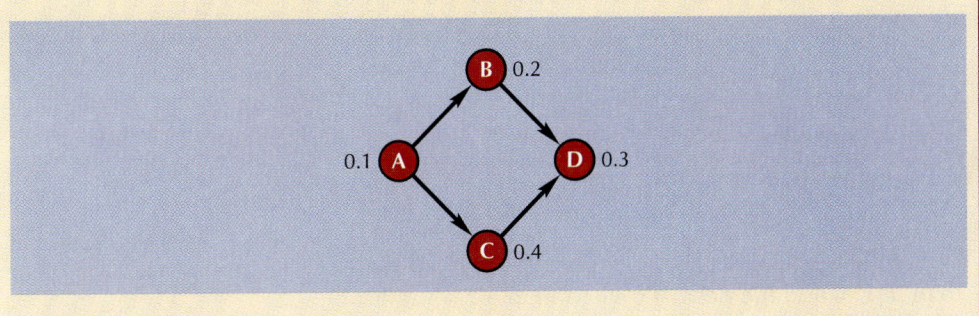

Cycle time, the other restriction on line balancing, refers to the maximum amount of time the product is allowed to spend at each workstation if the targeted production rate is to be reached. Cycle time is calculated by dividing the time available for production by the number of units scheduled to be produced:

$$C = \frac{\text{production time available}}{\text{desired units of output}}$$

C – is governed by the desired production rate

Suppose a company wanted to produce 120 units in an 8-hour day. The cycle time necessary to achieve that production quota is

$$C = \frac{(8 \text{ hours} \times 60 \text{ minutes/hour})}{(120 \text{ units})}$$

$$= \frac{480}{120} = 4 \text{ minutes}$$

Flow time = time to complete all stations

Cycle time = max. time spent at any station

Cycle time can also be viewed as the time between completed items rolling off the assembly line. Consider the three-station assembly line shown here.

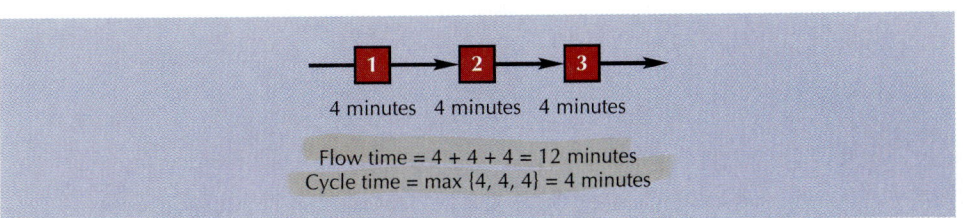

It takes 12 minutes (i.e., 4 + 4 + 4) for each item to pass completely through all three stations of the assembly line. The time required to complete an item is referred to as its *flow time*, or *lead time*. However, the assembly line does not work on only one item at a time. When fully operational, the line will be processing three items at a time, one at each workstation, in various stages of assembly. Every 4 minutes a new item enters the line at workstation 1, an item is passed from workstation 1 to workstation 2, another item is passed from workstation 2 to workstation 3, and a completed item leaves the assembly line. Thus, a completed item rolls off the assembly line every 4 minutes. This 4-minute interval is the cycle time of the line.

EXAMPLE
7.3

*Line-Balancing
Constraints*

Suppose the assembly process diagrammed in Example 7.2 requires the production of 6,000 fruit strips every 40-hour week. Group the elements into the fewest number of workstations that will achieve the production quota without violating precedence constraints.

SOLUTION:

First, we calculate desired cycle time:

$$C = \frac{40 \text{ hours} \times 60 \text{ minutes/hour}}{6,000 \text{ units}} = \frac{2,400}{6,000} = 0.4 \text{ minutes}$$

We must group elements into workstations so that the sum of the element times is less than or equal to the desired cycle time of 0.4 minutes.

Examining the precedence diagram, let's begin with A since it is the only element that does not have a precedence. We assign A to workstation 1. B and C are now available for assignment. Cycle time is exceeded with A and C in the same workstation, so we assign B to workstation 1 and place C in a second workstation. No other element can be added to workstation 2, due to cycle time constraints. That leaves D for assignment to a third workstation. Elements grouped into workstations are circled on the precedence diagram.

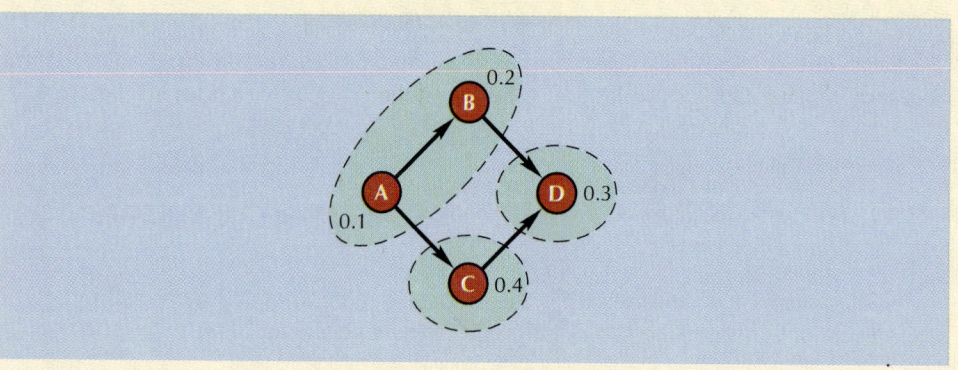

Our assembly line consists of three workstations, arranged as follows:

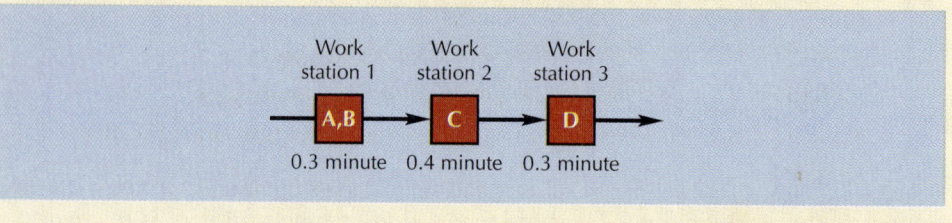

Calculate line *effi-
ciency* and the *theoretical minimum number
of workstations.*

The approach we used in Example 7.3 is basically trial and error. We tried different combinations of work elements, recognizing time and precedence constraints. The problem was simple enough to evaluate all feasible groupings of elements. For a more complicated problem, we may need some guidance as to when to stop trying different workstation configurations. The *efficiency* of the line can provide one type of guideline;

the *theoretical minimum number of workstations* provides another. The formulas for efficiency and minimum number of workstations are:

$$\text{Efficiency} = \frac{\sum_{i=1}^{j} t_i}{nC}$$

[handwritten: Total work done / work paid for (time)]

$$\text{Theoretical minimum number of workstations} = \frac{\sum_{i=1}^{j} t_i}{C}$$

where

t_i = completion time for element i

j = number of work elements

n = actual number of workstations

C = cycle time

The assembly line in Example 7.3 has an efficiency of

$$\text{Efficiency} = \frac{0.1 + 0.2 + 0.3 + 0.4}{3(0.4)}$$

$$= \frac{1.0}{1.2} = 0.833 = 83.3 \text{ percent}$$

The total idle time of the line, called **balance delay,** is calculated as $(1 - \text{efficiency})$, or for this example, 0.167, or 16.7 percent. Efficiency and balance delay are usually expressed as percentages.

Balance delay is the total idle time of the line.

The theoretical minimum number of workstations for Example 7.3 is

$$\frac{0.1 + 0.2 + 0.3 + 0.4}{0.4} = \frac{1.0}{0.4} = 2.5 \text{ workstations}$$

Since we cannot have half a workstation (or any portion of a workstation), we round up the theoretical number to 3 workstations. Recall that our assembly line solution also consisted of three workstations, so we know we have balanced the line as efficiently as possible.

[handwritten: Theoretical minimum # not usually achievable b/o: • "lumpiness" of work elements • precedence requirements]

The trial-and-error method of line balancing can be summarized as follows:

1. Draw and label a precedence diagram.
2. Calculate the desired cycle time required for the line. *[handwritten: based on desired production rate]*
3. Calculate the theoretical minimum number of workstations. *[handwritten: — round up]*
4. Group elements into workstations, recognizing cycle time and precedence constraints.
5. Calculate the efficiency of the line.
6. Determine if the theoretical minimum number of workstations or an acceptable efficiency level has been reached. If not, go back to step 4.

Line balancing groups elements into workstations.

It should be noted that using the theoretical minimum number of workstations as a guideline can lead to groupings of elements that violate precedence constraints. In practice, it may be difficult to attain the theoretical number of workstations or 100 percent efficiency. Cycle time based on production quotas can also be misleading. Sometimes the production quota cannot be achieved because the time required for one work

*[handwritten: * maximum number that can be assembled is the total time divided by the longest element work time]*

[Handwritten margin notes:
Computerized line Balancing
• Use heuristics to assign tasks to work stations
— longest operation time
— shortest operation time
— most # of following tasks
— least # of following tasks]

element is too large. To correct the situation, the quota can be revised downward or parallel stations can be set up for the bottleneck element. At other times, the production quota may not match the maximum output attainable by the system, in which case the desired cycle time and actual cycle time will be different. The actual cycle time is the maximum workstation time on the line. When calculating efficiency, the *actual cycle time* should be used.

Computerized Line Balancing

[Margin note: Line-balancing heuristics specify the order in which work elements are allocated to workstations.]

Line balancing by hand becomes unwieldy as the problems grow in size. Fortunately, there are software packages that will balance large lines quickly. IBM's COMSOAL (Computer Method for Sequencing Operations for Assembly Lines) and GE's ASYBL (Assembly Line Configuration Program) can assign hundreds of work elements to workstations on an assembly line. These programs, and most that are commercially available, do not guarantee optimal solutions. They use various *heuristics*, or rules, to balance the line at an acceptable level of efficiency. The POM for Windows software lets the user select from five different heuristics: ranked positional weight, longest operation time, shortest operation time, most number of following tasks, and least number of following tasks. These heuristics specify the *order* in which work elements are considered for allocation to workstations. Elements are assigned to workstations in the order given until the cycle time is reached or until all tasks have been assigned.

[Handwritten margin note: Heuristic = rule of thumb]

Hybrid Layouts

Hybrid layouts modify and/or combine some aspects of product and process layouts. We discuss three hybrid layouts: cellular layouts, flexible manufacturing systems, and mixed-model assembly lines.

THE COMPETITIVE EDGE

VW's Super Efficient Factory

www.prenhall.com/russell

Volkswagen built a $250 million truck and bus plant in Resende, Brazil, that is likely to become the model for new-car factories around the world. Seven suppliers, each responsible for a single module, make components in the plant using their own equipment and attach the components to trucks and buses on the final assembly line. German manufacturer VDO Kienzle, for example, is in charge of the truck cab. Marked off from other suppliers' workspaces by yellow lines on the floor, VDO workers install everything from cab seats to instrument panels. Then they attach the completed cab to the final chassis as it moves down the assembly line through VDO's section of the factory. Inventory costs are down because parts are made only an hour or so before they are needed and schedules are tightly coordinated.

In traditional automotive plants, suppliers deliver parts, assemblies, and modules to the final assembly line, but they never assemble them themselves. In pilot runs, improvements by suppliers in final assembly have cut work hours by 12%. On-site supplier suggestions for improved designs are also expected to yield lower costs and improved quality.

The plant is run by a daily roundtable discussion between VW and its *partners.* "VW has to be part of the table, not its owner," says the plant manager. That's one big advantage of the new system—VW and its suppliers are all in it together. Individual capital investment is dramatically lowered with VW providing the building and assembly line conveyors, and the suppliers putting in their own tools and fixtures, and hiring their own workers. Only 200 of the 1,400 workers are VW employees. If sales of trucks and buses do not meet predictions, everyone takes a hit, not just VW.

SOURCE: David Woodruff, "VW's Factory of the Future," *Business Week* (October 7, 1996): 52–56.

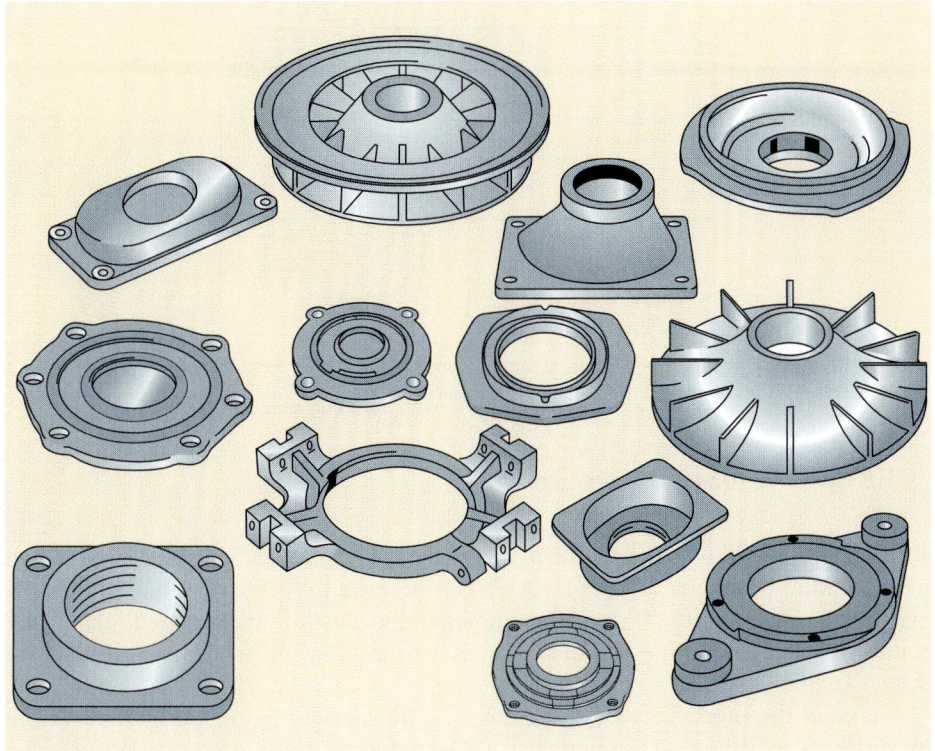

FIGURE 7.6 A Family of Similar Parts
SOURCE: Adapted from Mikell P. Groover, *Automation, Production Systems, and Computer-Aided Manufacturing* © 1980, p. 540. Reprinted by permission of Prentice Hall, Inc., Englewood Cliffs, New Jersey.

Cellular Layouts

Cellular layouts attempt to improve the efficiency of process layouts while maintaining their flexibility. Based on the concept of group technology (GT), dissimilar machines are grouped into work centers, called *cells*, that process parts with similar shapes or processing requirements. Figure 7.6 shows a family of parts with similar shapes.

Manufacturing cells are viewed as more efficient alternatives to the functional departments of the process layout. The concept of manufacturing cells was first proposed in 1925 by an American engineer but did not gain prominence until the 1980s when the Japanese perfected its application. A cellular layout is developed in four steps:

1. Identify families of parts that follow similar flow paths.
2. Regroup machines (from the process layout departments) into manufacturing cells according to the processing requirements of each part family.
3. Arrange the manufacturing cells in relation to each other so that material movement is minimized.
4. Locate large machines that cannot be split among cells near to the cells that use them, that is, at their *point of use*.

A cellular layout contains elements of both product and process layouts. The layout of machines *within* each manufacturing cell resembles a small assembly line. Thus, line-balancing procedures, with some adjustment, can be used to arrange the machines

> **Cellular layouts** group dissimilar machines into work centers (called cells) that process families of parts with similar shapes or processing requirements.

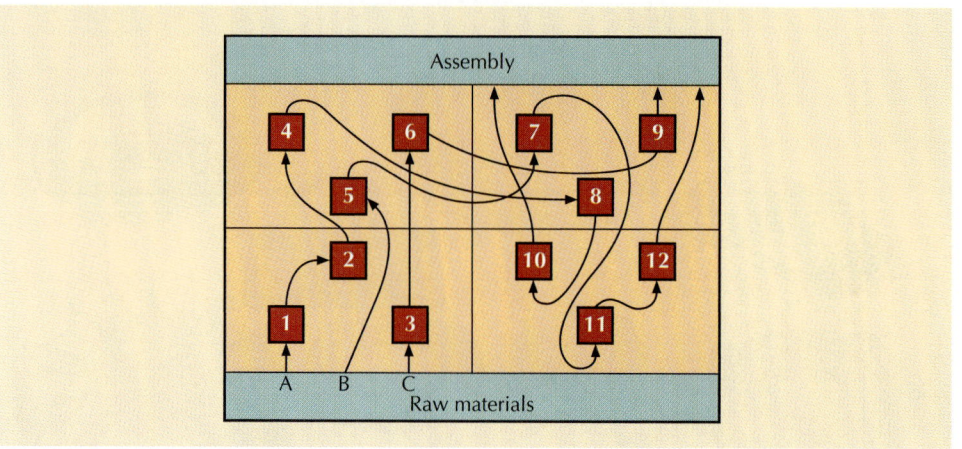

FIGURE 7.7   Original Process Layouts

within each cell. The layout *between* manufacturing cells is a process layout. Therefore, computer programs such as CRAFT can be used to locate cells and any leftover equipment in the facility. If group technology is successfully applied, cellular layouts should be able to combine the flexibility of a process layout with the efficiency of a product layout.

Consider the process layout in Figure 7.7. Machines are grouped by function into four distinct departments. Component parts manufactured in the process layout section of the factory are later assembled into a finished product on the assembly line. The parts follow different flow paths through the shop. Three representative routings, for parts A, B, and C, are shown in the figure. Notice the distance that each part must travel before completion and the irregularity of the part routings. A considerable amount of "paperwork" is needed to direct the flow of each individual part and to confirm that the right operation has been performed. Workers are skilled at operating the types of machines within a single department and typically can operate more than one machine at a time.

Figure 7.8 gives the complete part routing matrix for the eight parts processed through the facility. In its current form, there is no apparent pattern to the routings. **Production flow analysis (PFA)** is a group technology technique that reorders part routing matrices to identify families of parts with similar processing requirements. The re-

Production flow analysis reorders part routing matrices to identify families of parts with similar processing requirements.

Parts	Machines											
	1	2	3	4	5	6	7	8	9	10	11	12
A	×	×		×				×		×		
B				×		×					×	×
C			×			×			×			
D	×	×		×				×		×		
E					×	×						×
F	×			×				×				
G			×			×			×			×
H								×			×	×

FIGURE 7.8   Part Routing Matrix

Parts	1	2	4	8	10	3	6	9	5	7	11	12
A	×	×	×	×	×							
D	×	×	×	×	×							
F	×		×	×								
C						×	×	×				
G						×	×	×				×
B									×	×	×	×
H										×	×	×
E							×		×			×

(Machines)

Cell 1: Parts A, D, F
Machines 1, 2, 4, 8, 10

Cell 2: Parts C, G
Machines 3, 6, 9

Cell 3: Parts B, H, E
Machines 5, 7, 11, 12

FIGURE 7.9 Part Routing Matrix Reordered to Highlight Cells

ordering process can be as simple as listing which parts have four machines in common, then which have three in common, two in common, and the like, or as sophisticated as pattern-recognition algorithms from the field of artificial intelligence. Figure 7.9 shows the results of reordering Figure 7.8. Now the part families and cell formations are clear. Cell 1, consisting of machines 1, 2, 4, 8, and 10, will process parts A, D, and F; Cell 2, consisting of machines 3, 6, and 9, will process products C and G; and Cell 3, consisting of machines 5, 7, 11, and 12, will process parts B, H, and E. A complete cellular layout showing the three cells feeding a final assembly line is given in Figure 7.10. The representative part flows for parts A, B, and C are much more direct than those in the process layout. There is no backtracking or crisscrossing of routes, and the parts travel a shorter distance to be processed. Notice that parts G and E cannot be completely processed within cells 2 and 3, to which they have been assigned.

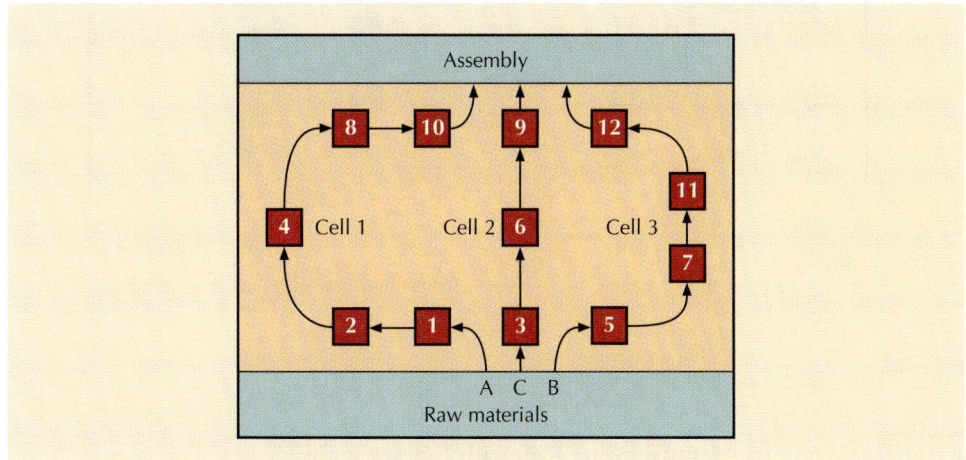

FIGURE 7.10 Revised Layout with Three Cells

However, the two cells are located in such a fashion that the transfer of parts between the cells does not involve much extra movement.

The U shape of cells 1 and 3 is a popular arrangement for manufacturing cells because it facilitates the rotation of workers among several machines. Workers in a cellular layout typically operate more than one machine, as was true of the process layout. However, workers who are assigned to each cell must now be multifunctional—that is, skilled at operating many different kinds of machines, not just one type, as in the process layout. In addition, workers are assigned a *path* to follow among the machines that they

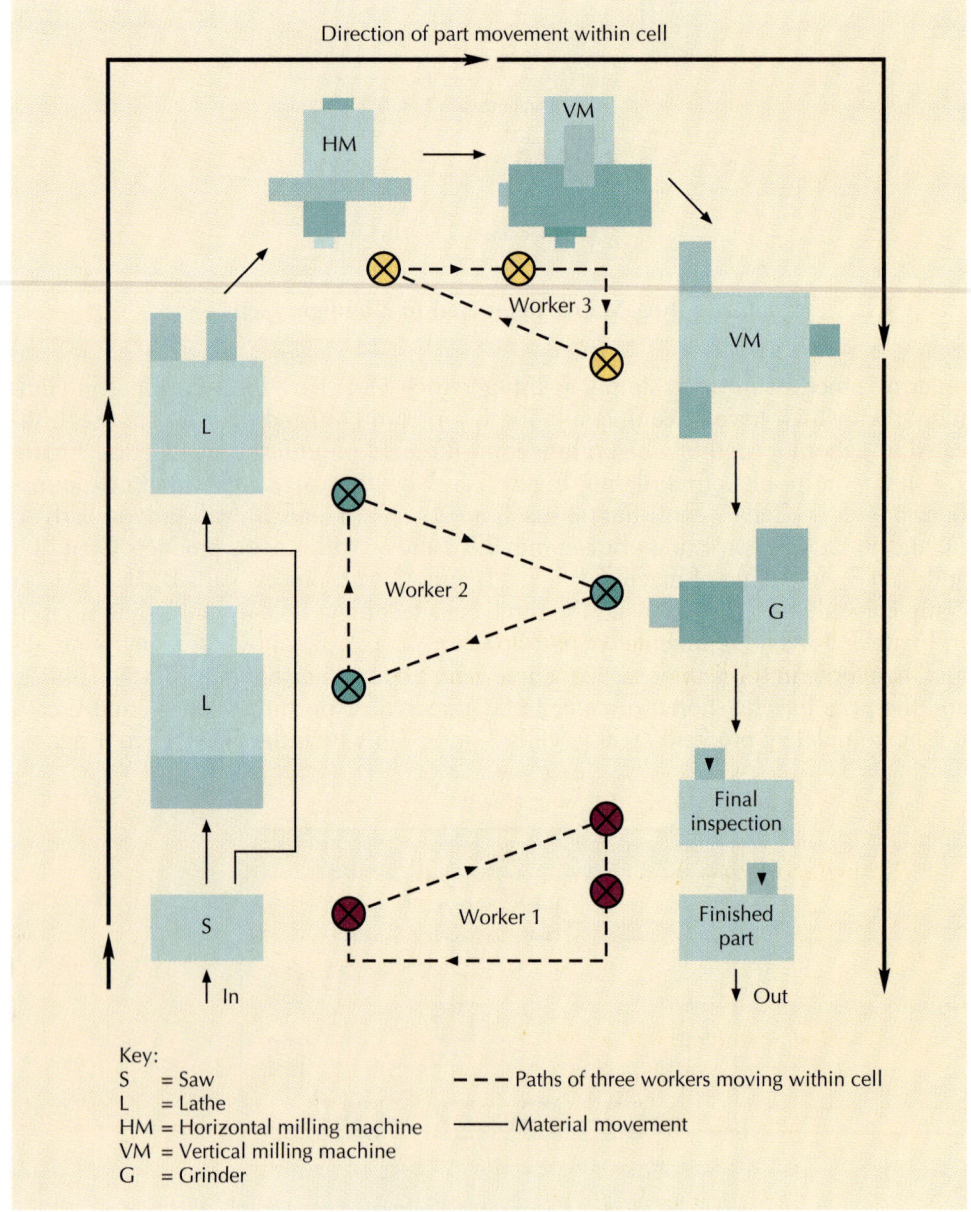

FIGURE 7.11   A Manufacturing Cell with Worker Paths

SOURCE: J. T. Black, "Cellular Manufacturing Systems Reduce Setup Time, Make Small Lot Production Economical," *Industrial Engineering* (November 1983). Copyright 1983 Institute of Industrial Engineers.

THE COMPETITIVE EDGE

Cells Make Furniture Customers Happy

Research shows that customers hate buying upholstered furniture. That's not good news when sofas and chairs are your main products. Customers want a wider selection than any showroom can house, and they don't want to wait months for a special order. Rowe Furniture Corporation responded by creating a computer network on which customers could match fabrics and styles. And they promised speedy delivery with no increase in price. It was an effective marketing solution—orders surged for the 1995 fall season—but could manufacturing deliver?

www.prenhall.com/russell

That was plant manager Charlene Pedrolie's job, and there was no doubt in her mind about the right approach. She annihilated the assembly line and brought sewers, gluers, staplers, and stuffers together into cells of 35 workers. Instead of doing one job on every piece of furniture, workers were cross-trained to do every job related to making a sofa. When someone got behind, others in the cell could help out.

Power tools that used to lay along the assembly line hung overhead in clusters. Squeezed together, workers were forced to communicate. Accustomed to having material brought to them, they were now getting their own raw materials and transporting their own parts, bumping into each other along the way. Productivity fell as staplers learned to glue and gluers learned to staple.

But before long the cells began to work as teams. Workers could solve problems as they occurred and organize their own work in the cell. Productivity recovered, then surpassed previous levels. Incentive payments grew and worker ideas for improvements were put into action. One group recommended larger truck trailers, another found a better way to stuff cushions. Still another suggested selling excess kiln capacity to local lumber-drying operations.

Today workers, managers and customers are happy. And Ms. Pedrolie? She's begun reorganizing the *office* into cells—cross-training credit approvers, order takers, and customer service representatives to respond as a team to dealer needs.

SOURCE: Thomas Petzinger, Jr., "Charlene Pedrolie Rearranged Furniture and Lifted a Business," *Wall Street Journal*, September 13, 1996.

---

operate, which may or may not coincide with the path the product follows through the cell. Figure 7.11 shows a U-shaped manufacturing cell including worker paths.

The advantages of cellular layouts are:

- *Reduced material handling and transit time.* Material movement is more direct. Less distance is traveled between operations. Material does not accumulate or wait long periods of time to be moved. Within a cell, the worker is more likely to carry a partially finished item from machine to machine than wait for material handling equipment, as is characteristic of process layouts, where larger loads must be moved farther distances.

- *Reduced setup time.* Since similar parts are processed together, the adjustments required to set up a machine should not be that different from item to item. If it doesn't take that long to change over from one item to another, then the changeover can occur more frequently, and items can be produced and transferred in very small batches or lot sizes.

Cellular layouts reduce transit time, setup time, and in-process inventory.

- *Reduced work-in-process inventory.* In a work cell, as with assembly lines, the flow of work is balanced so that no bottlenecks or significant buildup of material occurs between stations or machines. Less space is required for storage of in-process inventory between machines, and machines can be moved closer together, thereby saving transit time and increasing communication.

- *Better use of human resources.* Typically, a cell contains a small number of workers responsible for producing a completed part or product. The workers act as a self-managed team, in most cases more satisfied with the work that they do and more particular about the quality of their work. Labor in cellular manufacturing is a flex-

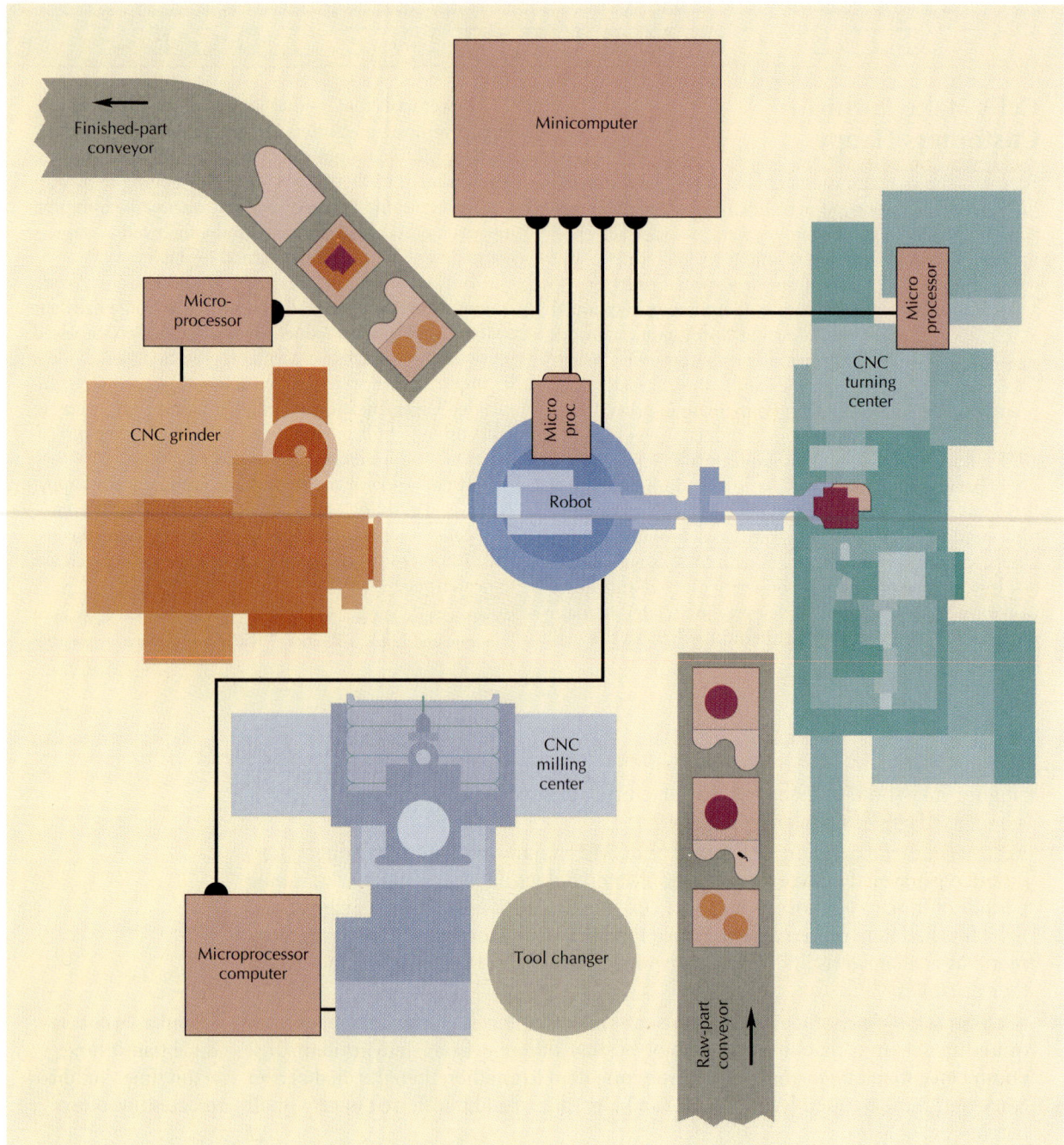

FIGURE 7.12   An Automated Manufacturing Cell

SOURCE: J. T. Black, "Cellular Manufacturing Systems Reduce Setup Time, Make Small Lot Production Economical," *Industrial Engineering* (November 1983). Copyright 1983 Institute of Industrial Engineers.

ible resource. Workers in each cell are multifunctional and can be assigned to different routes within a cell or between cells as demand volume changes.

■ *Easier to control.* Items in the same part family are processed in a similar manner through the work cell. There is a significant reduction in the paperwork necessary to document material travel, such as where an item should be routed next, if the right operation has been performed, and the current status of a job. With fewer jobs processed through a cell, smaller batch sizes, and less distance to travel between operations, the progress of a job can be verified *visually* rather than by mounds of paperwork.

■ *Easier to automate.* Automation is expensive. Rarely can a company afford to automate an entire factory all at once. Cellular layouts can be automated one cell at a time. Figure 7.12 shows an automated cell with one robot in the center to load and unload material from several CNC machines and an incoming and outgoing conveyor. Automating a few workstations on an assembly line will make it difficult to balance the line and achieve the increases in productivity expected. Introducing automated equipment in a job shop has similar results, because the "islands of automation" speed up only certain processes and are not integrated into the complete processing of a part or product.

Several disadvantages of cellular layouts must also be considered:

■ *Inadequate part families.* There must be enough similarity in the types of items processed to form distinct part families. Cellular manufacturing is appropriate for medium levels of product variety and volume. The formation of part families and the allocation of machines to cells is not always an easy task. Part families identified for design purposes may not be appropriate for manufacturing purposes.

■ *Poorly balanced cells.* It is more difficult to balance the flow of work through a cell than a single-product assembly line, because items may follow different sequences through the cell that require different machines or processing times. The sequence in which parts enter the cell can thus affect the length of time a worker or machine spends at a certain stage of processing. Poorly balanced cells can be very inefficient. It is also important to balance the workload among cells in the system, so that one cell is not overloaded while others are idle. This may be taken care of in the initial cellular layout, only to become a problem as changes occur in product designs or product mix. Several imbalances may require the reformation of cells around different part families, and the cost and disruption that implies.

> Cellular layouts require distinct part families, careful balances, expanded worker training, and increased capital investment.

■ *Expanded training and scheduling of workers.* Training workers to do different tasks is expensive and time-consuming and requires the workers' consent. Initial union reaction to multifunctional workers was not positive. Today, many unions have agreed to participate in the flexible assignment of workers in exchange for greater job security. Although flexibility in worker assignment is one of the advantages of

When Lantech, Inc. of Louisville, Kentucky, reorganized its production facility into manufacturing cells, defects went down by half and customer orders were completed in 12 hours instead of five weeks. As shown in this photo, the cells are small (they are labeled X13, X18, etc.) and are located close together. That's so workers can move between cells if necessary, share information, and "see everything."

Cells Keep Compaq Nimble

Computer makers are in a tough business. Technology turnover makes products obsolete within six months. That means computer factories must have the flexibility to constantly build new and improved models. Compaq says the answer is *cellular manufacturing*.

www.prenhall.com/russell

Compaq tried replacing a traditional assembly line with 48 cells. Each cell has three workers who, together, can build, test, and ship different computer models every day, if necessary. The cells have increased employee out-

put by 23% and product quality by 25%. But they cost more, too. "Cellularizing" a $2.5 million assembly line costs $10 million or more because each cell requires a full set of tools, and cell workers are better trained and paid than assembly line workers.

So Compaq uses both cells and assembly lines— assembly lines for the first few months of a new product's life when demand is strong, and cells when orders begin to taper off.

SOURCE: Dan McGraw, "Staying Loose in a Tense Tech Market," *U.S. News & World Report* (July 8, 1996).

cellular layouts, the task of determining and adjusting worker paths within or between cells can be quite complex.

■ *Increased capital investment.* In cellular manufacturing, multiple smaller machines are preferable to single large machines. Implementing a cellular layout can be economical if new machines are being purchased for a new facility, but it can be quite expensive and disruptive in existing production facilities where new layouts are required. Existing equipment may be too large to fit into cells or may be underutilized when placed in a single cell. Additional machines of the same type may have to be purchased for different cells. The cost and downtime required to move machines can also be high.

Cellular layouts have become popular in the past decade as the backbone of modern factories. Cells can differ considerably in size, in automation, and in the variety of parts processed. There is a definite trend towards smaller, interconnected layout units called cells. Cells are even becoming popular in service layouts.

Saturn Uses Flexible Machining Cells

www.prenhall.com/russell

General Motor's Saturn plant is one of the first U.S. automakers to use high-flexibility, high-volume machining cells. The five-cell system utilizes two operators per cell, fifty-nine pallets, and ten setup stations. Two of the cells machine front engine covers for two- and four-valve engines. Three additional cells machine transmission parts: upper and lower valve bodies, oil-pump housings, and rear covers. Each cell contains four machining centers serviced by a rail-guided automatic guided vehicle (AGV).

The flexible setup allows a number of different items

to be processed and also accommodates changes in production volume. More machines can easily be added as needed, retooling is simplified, and operators can be shared across cells. Currently, the cells run constantly except for scheduled preventive maintenance. Operators are used only to load the system (the cells can run unattended), so that a small number of operators can be assigned to each cell rather than to individual machines.

With flexible machine cells, Saturn was able to make more than 200 design revisions within a model year with only slight changes in CNC programs and no capital investment.

Source: Based on "Saturn Gets High Volume and Flexibility from LeBlond Makino Cells," *Industrial Engineering* (October, 1992): 18.

Flexible Manufacturing Systems (FMS)

The idea of a **flexible manufacturing system** was proposed in England in the 1960s with System 24 that could operate without human operators 24 hours a day under computer control. The emphasis from the beginning was on automation rather than the reorganization of work flow. Early FMSs were large and complex, consisting of dozens of CNC machines and sophisticated material handling systems. The systems were very automated, very expensive, and controlled by incredibly complex software. The FMS control computer operated the material handling system, maintained the library of CNC programs and downloaded them to the machines, scheduled the FMS, kept track of tool use and maintenance, and reported on the performance of the system.

There are not many industries that can afford the investment required for a traditional FMS as described. Fewer than 400 FMSs are in operation around the world today. Currently, the trend in flexible manufacturing is toward smaller versions of the traditional FMS, sometimes called *flexible manufacturing cells*. It is not unusual in today's terminology for two or more CNC machines to be considered a flexible cell and two or more cells, an FMS.

FMS layouts differ based on the variety of parts that the system can process, the size of the parts processed, and the average processing time required for part completion. Figures 7.13 and 7.14 show four basic types of FMS layouts:

A **flexible manufacturing system** can produce an enormous variety of items.

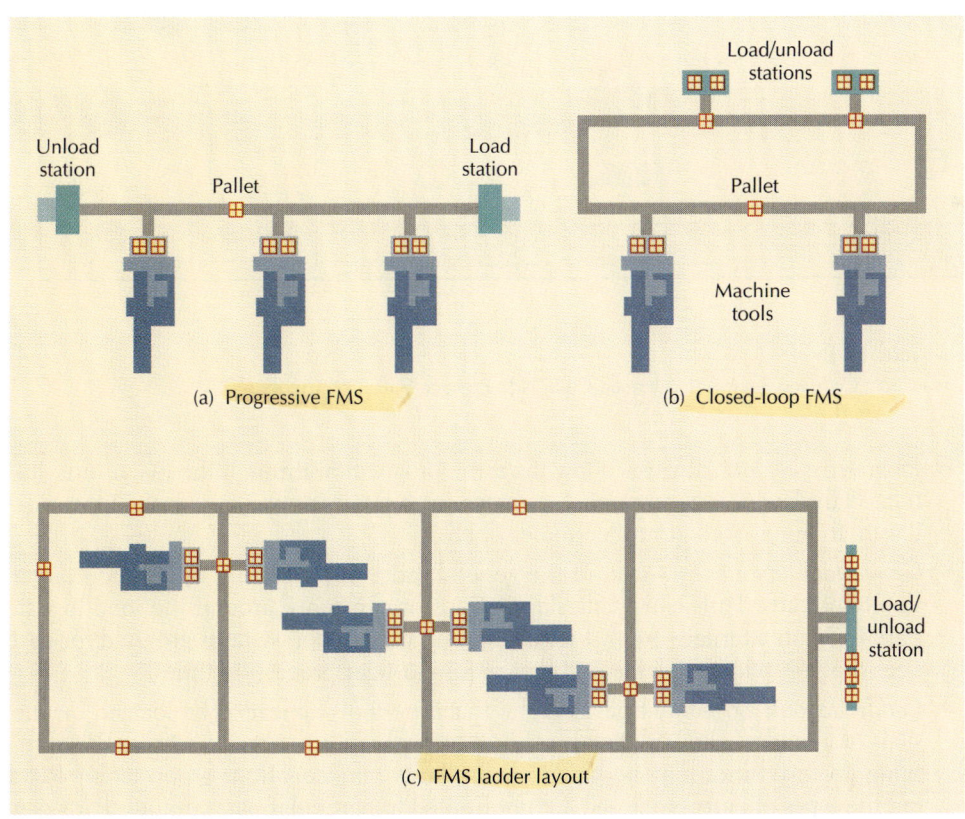

FIGURE 7.13 **Alternative FMS Layouts**

SOURCE: W. Luggen, *Flexible Manufacturing Cells and Systems* (Englewood Cliffs, N.J.: Prentice Hall, 1991), pp. 90–92.

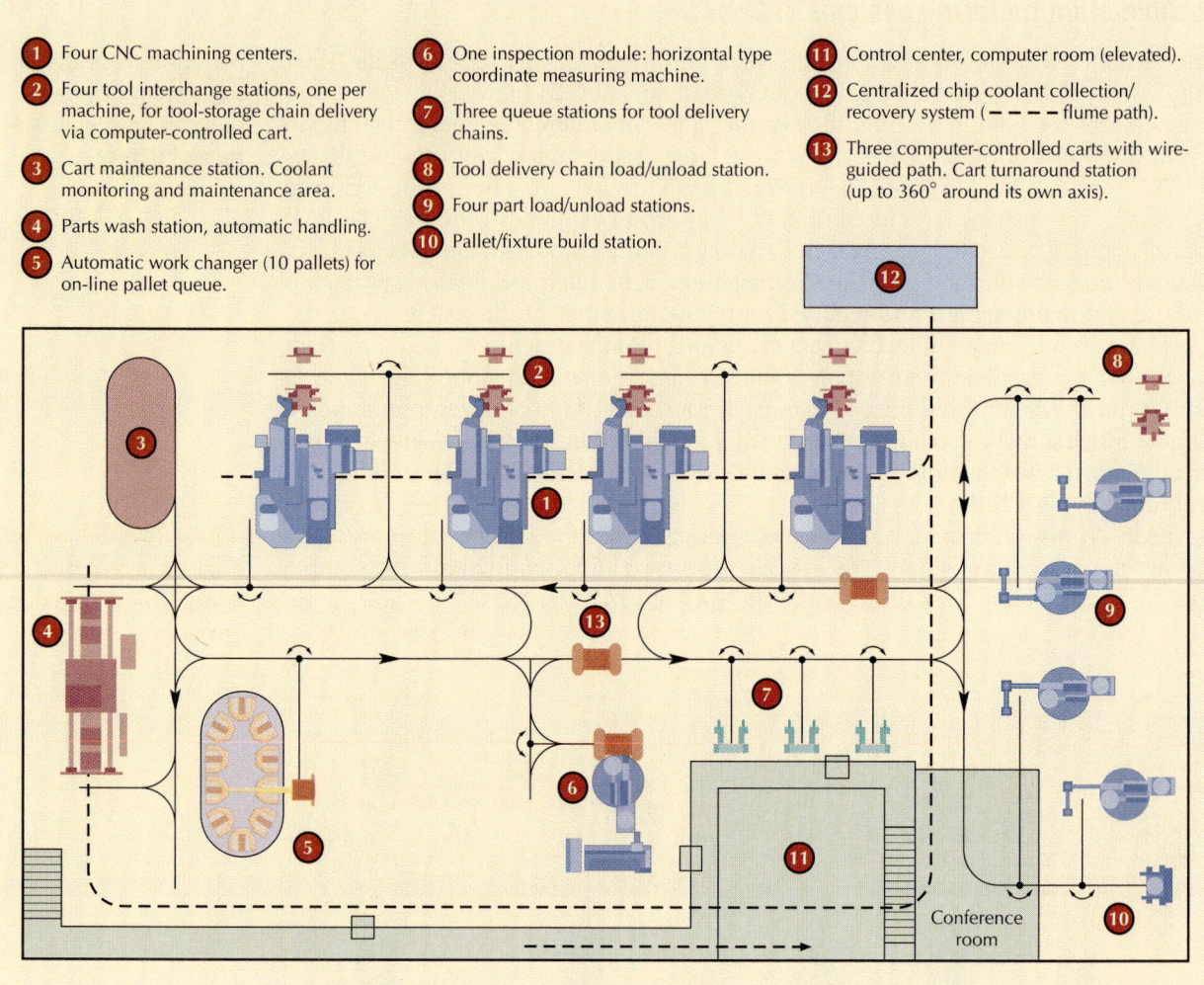

1. Four CNC machining centers.

2. Four tool interchange stations, one per machine, for tool-storage chain delivery via computer-controlled cart.

3. Cart maintenance station. Coolant monitoring and maintenance area.

4. Parts wash station, automatic handling.

5. Automatic work changer (10 pallets) for on-line pallet queue.

6. One inspection module: horizontal type coordinate measuring machine.

7. Three queue stations for tool delivery chains.

8. Tool delivery chain load/unload station.

9. Four part load/unload stations.

10. Pallet/fixture build station.

11. Control center, computer room (elevated).

12. Centralized chip coolant collection/recovery system (– – – – flume path).

13. Three computer-controlled carts with wire-guided path. Cart turnaround station (up to 360° around its own axis).

Conference room

FIGURE 7.14   An Open-Field FMS
Source: W. Luggen, *Flexible Manufacturing Cells and Systems* (Englewood Cliffs, N.J.: Prentice Hall, 1991), p. 93.

- *Progressive layout:* All parts follow the same progression through the machining stations. This layout is appropriate for processing a family of parts and is the most similar to an automated group technology cell.

- *Closed-loop layout:* Arranged in the general order of processing for a much larger variety of parts. Parts can easily skip stations or can move around the loop to visit stations in an alternate order. Progressive and closed-loop systems are used for part sizes that are relatively large and that require longer processing times.

- *Ladder layout:* So named because the machine tools appear to be located on the steps of a ladder, allowing two machines to work on one item at a time. Programming the machines may be based on similarity concepts from group technology, but the types of parts processed are not limited to particular part families. Parts can be routed to any machine in any sequence.

- *Open-field layout:* The most complex and flexible FMS layout. It allows material to move among the machine centers in any order and typically includes several support stations such as tool interchange stations, pallet or fixture build stations, inspection stations, and chip/coolant collection systems.

Mixed-Model Assembly Lines

Traditional assembly lines, designed to process a single model or type of product, can be used to process more than one type of product, but not efficiently. Models of the same type are produced in long production runs, sometimes lasting for months, and then the line is shut down and changed over for the next model. The next model is also run for an extended time, producing perhaps half a year to a year's supply; then the line is shut down again and changed over for yet another model, and so on. The problem with this arrangement is the difficulty in responding to changes in customer demand. If a certain model is selling well and customers want more of it, they have to wait until the next batch of that model is scheduled to be produced. On the other hand, if demand is disappointing for models that have already been produced, the manufacturer is stuck with high stocks of unwanted inventory.

Recognizing that this mismatch of production and demand is a problem, some manufacturers concentrated on devising more sophisticated forecasting techniques. Others changed the manner in which the assembly line was laid out and operated so that it really became a **mixed-model assembly line.** First, they reduced the time needed to change over the line to produce different models. Then they trained their workers to

Single-model and mixed-model assembly lines differ in layout and operation.

A **mixed-model assembly line** processes more than one product model.

The only manual operations in LTV's FMS are performed at the load/unload stations in the center of the photograph. Blank stock to be machined is shown in the foreground. The items rotating on the carousel are different fixturing devices that the workers build up and tear down to hold the various blanks in place for machining. Automated guided vehicles transport items to and from machining centers and the load/unload stations. Notice the computers (in blue) at each machining center and the main control room in the rear. Nearly 1,200 CNC part programs and 900 verification programs for part geometry are contained in the system.

www.prenhall.com/russell

perform a variety of tasks and allowed them to work at more than one workstation on the line, as needed. Finally, they changed the way in which the line was arranged and scheduled.

The following factors are important in the design and operation of mixed-model assembly lines:

■ *Line balancing:* In a mixed-model line, the time to complete a task can vary from model to model. Instead of using the completion times from one model to balance the line, a distribution of possible completion times from the array of models must be considered. In most cases, the expected value, or average, times are used in the balancing procedure. Otherwise, mixed-model lines are balanced in much the same way as single-model lines.

■ *U-shaped lines.* To compensate for the different work requirements of assembling different models, it is necessary to have a flexible work force and to arrange the line so that workers can assist one another as needed. Figure 7.15 shows how the efficiency of an assembly line can be improved when a U-shaped line is used.

■ *Flexible work force.* Although worker paths are predetermined to fit within a set cycle time, the use of average time values in mixed-model lines will produce variations in worker performance. Hence, the lines are not run at a set speed. Items move through the line at the pace of the slowest operation. This is not to say that production quotas are not important. If the cycle time (maximum time allowed if quota is to be met) is exceeded at any station on the line, other workers are notified by flashing lights or sounding alarms so that they can come to the aid of the

[handwritten margin notes: · Helps reduce finished product inventory - matches production rate to demand rate]

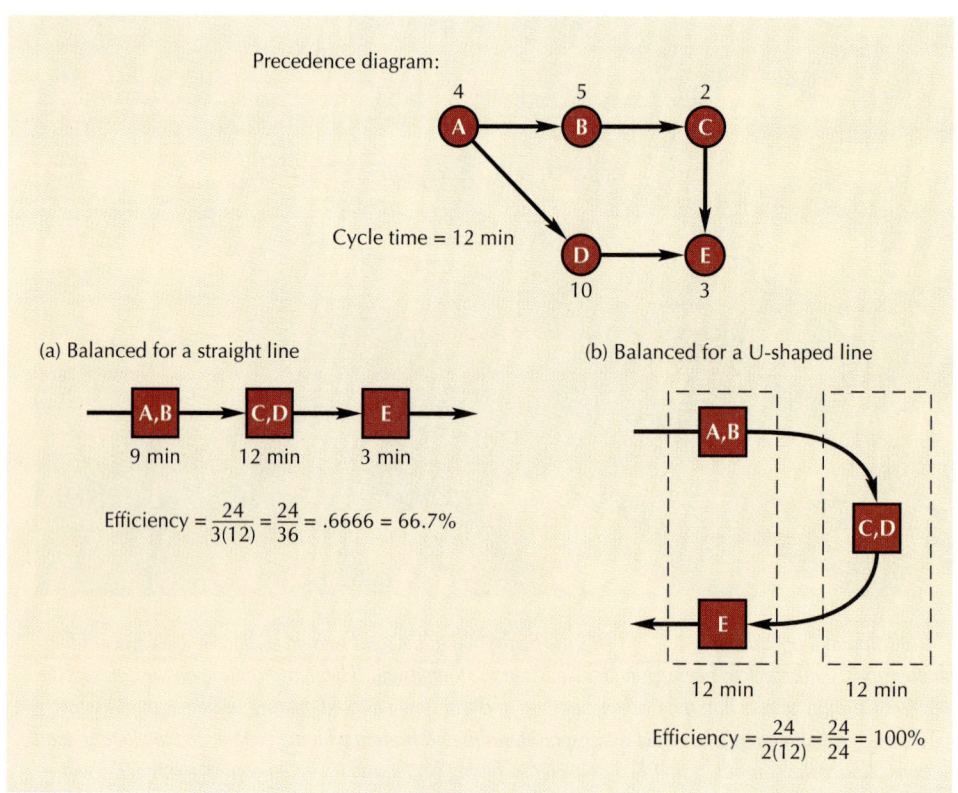

FIGURE 7.15   Balancing U-Shaped Lines

troubled station. The assembly line is slowed or stopped until the work at the errant workstation is completed. This flexibility of workers helping other workers makes a tremendous difference in the ability of the line to adapt to the varied length of tasks inherent in a mixed-model line.

■ *Model sequencing.* Since different models are produced on the same line, mixed-model scheduling involves an additional decision—the order, or sequence, of models to be run through the line. From a logical standpoint, it would be unwise to sequence two models back-to-back that require extra long processing times. It would make more sense to mix the assembling of models so that a short model (requiring less than the average time) followed a long one (requiring more than the average time). With this pattern, workers could "catch up" from one model to the next.

Another objective in model sequencing is to spread out the production of different models as evenly as possible throughout the time period scheduled. This will be discussed in Chapter 15 on "Just-in-Time Systems."

Summary

Facility layout decisions are an important part of operations strategy. An effective layout reflects a firm's competitive priorities and enables the firm to reach its strategic objectives. Batch production, which emphasizes flexibility, is most often organized into a *process layout* whereas mass production uses a *product layout* for maximum efficiency. Because of their size and scope, projects tend to use *fixed-position layouts. Service layouts* may try to process customers through the system as quickly as possible, or maximize customer exposure to products and services.

In the current manufacturing environment of new product introductions, rapidly changing technologies, and intense competition, the ability of a manufacturing system to adapt is essential. Thus, several hybrid layouts have emerged that combine flexibility and efficiency. Reductions in setup times have made *mixed-model assembly lines* feasible. The newest *flexible manufacturing systems (FMS)* can process any item that fits the dimensions of the pallet on which it is transported. *Manufacturing cells* that resemble small assembly lines are designed to process families of items. Some companies are placing wheels and casters on their machines so that the cells can be adjusted as needed. Others are experimenting with modular conveyor systems that allow assembly lines to be rearranged while workers are on their lunch break.

As important as flexibility is, the cost of moving material is still a primary consideration in layout design. Today, as in the past, layout decisions are concerned with minimizing material flow. However, with the trend toward reduced inventory levels, there has been a shift in emphasis from minimizing the *number* of loads moved to minimizing the *distance* they are moved. Instead of accumulating larger loads of material and moving them less often, machines are being shoved closer together to allow the frequent movement of smaller loads. Planners who used to devote a considerable amount of time to designing the location of storage areas and the movement of material into and out of storage areas are now also concerned with the rapid movement of material to and from the facility itself. Facility location and the logistics of material transportation are discussed in Chapter 9, "Supply Chain Management."

Summary of Key Formulas

Cycle Time $\quad C = \dfrac{\text{production time available}}{\text{desired units of output}}$

Theoretical Minimum Number of Workstations $\quad N = \dfrac{\sum_{i=1}^{j} t_i}{C}$

Efficiency $\quad E = \dfrac{\sum_{i=1}^{j} t_i}{nC}$

Balance Delay $\quad 1 -$ efficiency

Summary of Key Terms

balance delay: the total idle time of the line.

block diagram: a schematic layout diagram that includes the size of each work area.

cellular layout: a layout that groups dissimilar machines into cells that process parts with similar shapes or processing requirements.

cycle time: the maximum amount of time an item is allowed to spend at each workstation if the targeted production rate is to be achieved; also, the time between successive product completions.

facility layout: the arrangement of machines, departments, workstations, and other areas within a facility.

fixed-position layout: a layout in which the product remains at a stationary site for the entire manufacturing cycle.

flexible manufacturing system (FMS): programmable equipment connected by an automated material handling system and controlled by a central computer.

line balancing: a layout technique that attempts to equalize the amount of work assigned to each workstation on an assembly line.

mixed-model assembly line: an assembly line that processes more than one product model.

Muther's grid: a format for displaying manager preferences for department locations.

precedence requirements: physical restrictions on the order in which operations are performed.

process layout: a layout that groups similar activities together into work centers according to the process or function they perform.

product layout: a layout that arranges activities in a line according to the sequence of operations that are needed to assemble a particular product.

production flow analysis (PFA): a group technology technique that reorders part routing matrices to identify families of parts with similar processing requirements.

relationship diagram: a schematic diagram that denotes location preference with different line thicknesses.

unit load: the quantity in which material is normally moved; it could represent a single unit, pallet, or bin of material.

Solved Problems

1. Process Layout

Mohawk Valley Furniture Warehouse has purchased a retail outlet with six departments, as shown in grid 1. The anticipated number of customers that move between the departments each week is given in the load summary chart.

    a.   Calculate the nonadjacent loads for the layout shown in grid 1.

b. Revise Mohawk's layout such that nonadjacent loads are minimized.

Load Summary

From \ To	DEPARTMENT					
DEPARTMENT	A	B	C	D	E	F
A		70				50
B					100	
C		70				
D			80			
E	40					30
F		60			100	

Grid 1

Solution:

Composite movements ranked from highest to lowest are as follows:

E ↔ F	130
B ↔ E	100
C ↔ D	80
A ↔ B	70
B ↔ C	70
B ↔ F	60
A ↔ F	50
A ↔ E	40

a. Nonadjacent loads = 130.

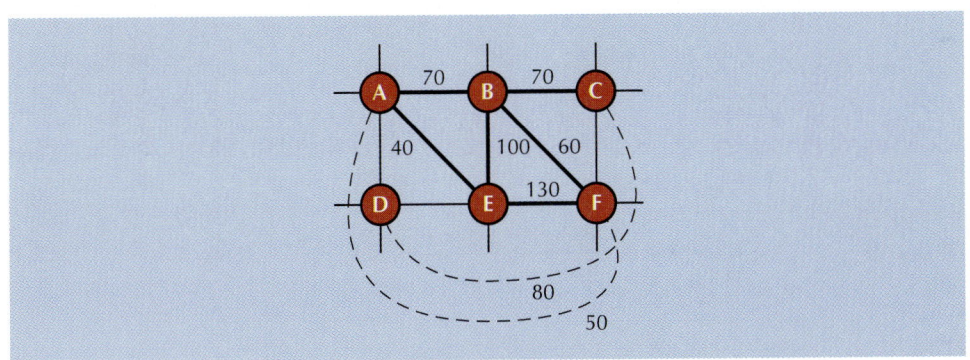

b. To reduce the number of nonadjacent loads, try switching the location of D and F.

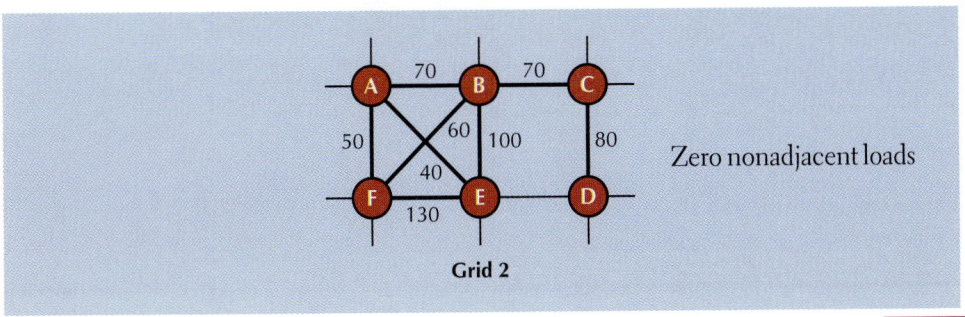

Zero nonadjacent loads

Grid 2

2. *Product Layout*

The Basic Block Company needs to produce 4,000 boxes of blocks per 40-hour week to meet upcoming holiday demand. The process of making blocks can be broken down into six work elements. The precedence and time requirements for each element are as follows. Draw and label a precedence diagram for the production process. Set up a balanced assembly line and calculate the efficiency of the line.

Work Element	Predecessor	Performance Time (min)
A	—	0.10
B	A	0.40
C	A	0.50
D	—	0.20
E	C, D	0.60
F	B, E	0.40

Solution:

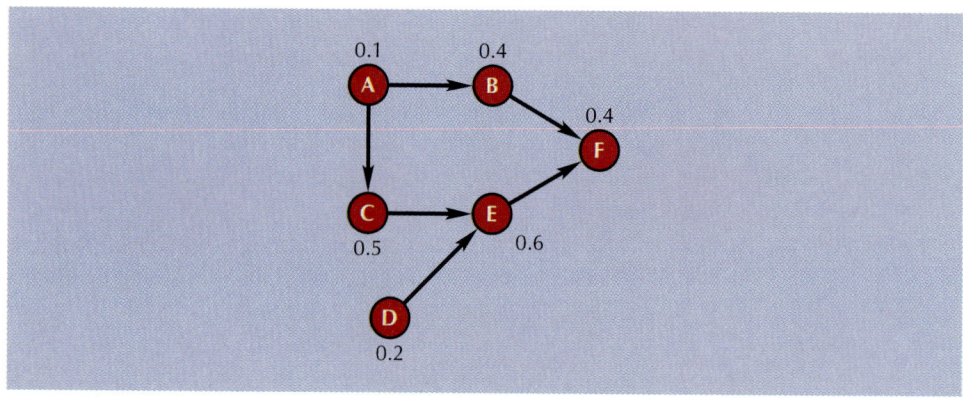

$$\text{Cycle time} = \frac{\text{time}}{\text{units}} = \frac{40 \times 60}{4,000} = \frac{2,400}{4,000} = 0.60$$

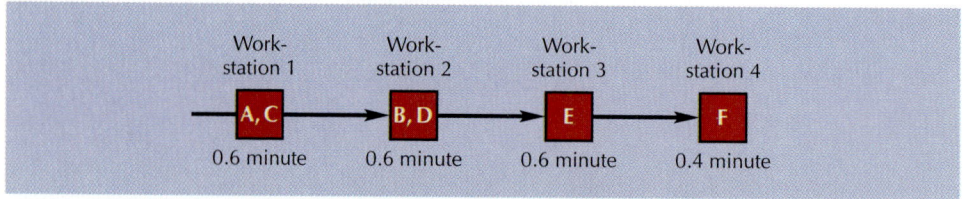

$$\text{Efficiency} = \frac{\sum t}{nC} = \frac{0.60 + 0.60 + 0.60 + 0.40}{4(0.60)} = \frac{2.2}{2.4}$$

$$= 91.67 \text{ percent}$$

Questions

7-1. List five or more objectives of facility layout. How does layout affect efficiency?

7-2. Distinguish between a process and product layout.

7-3. Give an example of a fixed-position layout for producing a product and providing a service.

7-4. What type of layout(s) would be appropriate for each?
   a. A grocery store
   b. Home construction
   c. Electronics assembly
   d. A university

7-5. How can layout promote product or service quality?

7-6. What are the fixed and variable cost trade-offs among product, process, and fixed-position layouts? Draw a cost/volume graph to illustrate your answer.

7-7. What is the difference between block diagramming and relationship diagramming?

7-8. How do service layouts differ from manufacturing layouts?

7-9. What are the objectives of line balancing?

7-10. Describe several heuristic approaches to line balancing.

7-11. What is group technology and how does it relate to cellular layouts?

7-12. How are manufacturing cells formed? How does the role of the worker differ in cellular manufacturing?

7-13. How does a cellular layout combine a product and process layout?

7-14. Discuss the advantages and disadvantages of cellular layouts.

7-15. Describe a flexible manufacturing system. How does it differ from a cellular layout?

7-16. How do mixed-model assembly lines differ from traditional assembly lines? What additional decisions are required?

7-17. Visit a local McDonald's, Burger King, and Taco Bell (or similar establishments). How do their layouts differ? Which appears to be most efficient? Why?

Problems

7-1. Spiffy Dry Cleaners recently underwent a change in management, and the new owners want to revise the current layout. The store performs four main services: laundry, dry cleaning, pressing, alterations and delivery. Each is located in a separate department, as shown here. The load summary chart gives the current level of interaction between the departments. Calculate the number of nonadjacent loads for the current layout. Design an alternate layout to minimize the number of nonadjacent loads.

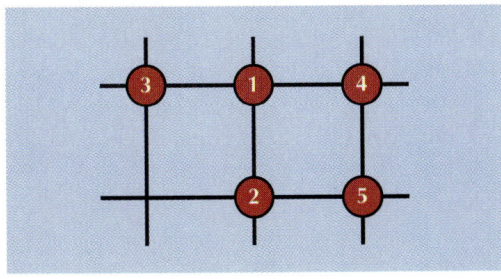

Load Summary

	1	*2*	*3*	*4*	*5*
1	—	0	125	40	0
2	0	—	45	75	0
3	0	0	—	20	235
4	60	30	10	—	85

7-2. Spiffy's has decided to add seasonal storage to its service offerings. A revised load summary chart is given next. Where should this sixth department be located? Calculate the number of nonadjacent loads for the new layout.

Load Summary Chart

	1	2	3	4	5	6
1	—	0	125	40	0	0
2	0	—	45	75	0	0
3	0	0	—	20	235	200
4	60	30	10	—	85	50
5	0	0	0	0	—	10
6	0	0	40	30	150	—

7-3. Given the following load summary chart, design a layout on a 2 × 3 grid that will minimize nonadjacent loads.

[handwritten margin note: Majority of lines should be between adjacent departments — if not, try to move to be adjacent.]

Load Summary Chart

From	To					
WORK CENTER	WORK CENTER					
	1	2	3	4	5	6
1		70		50		30
2	20		10			60
3		100			70	
4	25					50
5		40	10			
6	10		20		40	

7-4. Design a layout on a 2 × 3 grid that satisfies the preferences listed here.

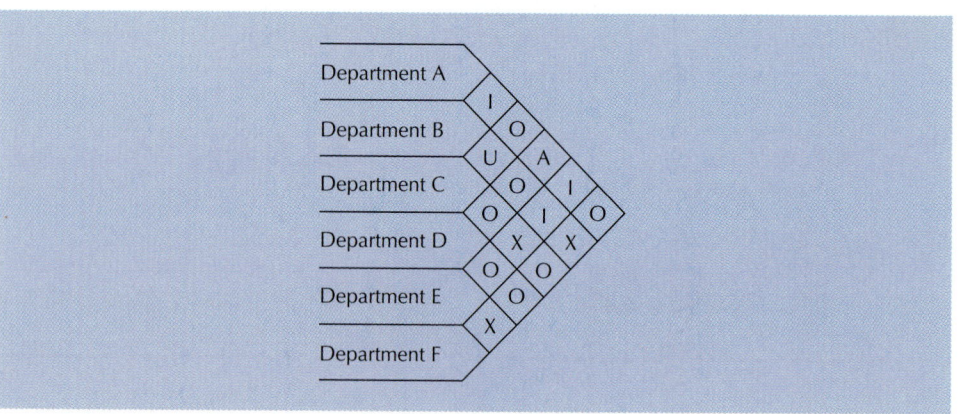

7-5. Pratt's Department Store is opening a new store in The Center's Mall. Customer movement tracked in its existing stores shows the following pattern:

Number of Customers

From \ To	Women's	Men's	Boys'	Girls'	Infants	Housewares	Accessories
Women's		20	50	50	50	70	60
Men's			20	10	5	20	30
Boys'		20		20			
Girl's	30		50		30		
Infants	30						
Housewares	40						30
Accessories	30					20	

a. Design a layout for Pratt's new store on a 3 × 3 grid that will minimize nonadjacent customer movement.

b. If you eliminate the squares of the grid where there are no departments, what is the shape of your building?

7-6. Avalanche, Inc. is a manufacturer of premium snow skis. The work is a combination of precision machining and skilled craftsmanship. Before completion, skis are processed back and forth between six different departments: (1) molding, (2) cutting, (3) fiberglass weaving, (4) gluing, (5) finishing, and (6) waxing. Avalanche is opening a new production facility and wants to lay it out as efficiently as possible. The number of loads of material moved from department to department at existing operations in other plants is shown below. Arrange the departments for Avalanche's new plant in a 2 × 3 grid so that nonadjacent loads are minimized.

Load Summary Chart

From \ To	1	2	3	4	5	6
1		100	75		100	60
2	10			45	60	
3	30				85	
4	100	50			70	35
5	25	70	30	40		65
6	65				35	

7-7. Design a layout on a 2 × 3 grid that satisfies these preferences:

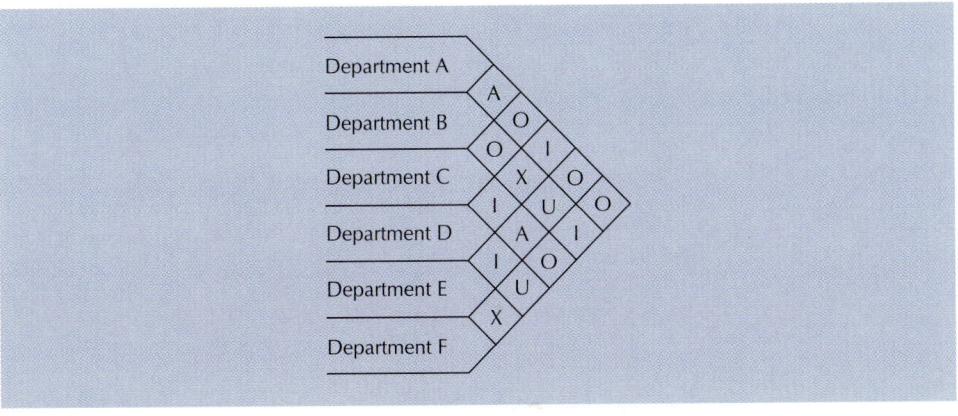

7-8. Professional Image Briefcases is an exclusive producer of handcrafted, stylish cases. Priding itself on its earlier reputation, the company assembles each case with care and attention to detail. This laborious process requires the completion of six primary work elements, which are listed here.

Work Element	Precedence	Time (min)
A Tan leather	—	30
B Dye leather	A	15
C Shape case	B	10
D Mold hinges and fixtures	—	5
E Install hinges and fixtures	C, D	10
F Assemble case	E	10

a. Construct a precedence diagram for the manufacture of briefcases.
b. If the demand is 50 cases per 40-hour week, compute the cycle time for the process.
c. Compute the lead time required for assembling one briefcase.
d. How would you balance this assembly line?
e. Compute the line's efficiency and balance delay.
f. Calculate the theoretical minimum number of workstations. Can a better arrangement be determined?

7-9. Referring to Problem 7-8, suppose the demand for briefcases increases to 80 cases per week.
a. Calculate a new cycle time and rebalance the line
b. Calculate the efficiency and balance delay of the manufacturing process.
c. Calculate the theoretical minimum number of workstations. Can a better arrangement be determined?

7-10. The TLB Yogurt Company has set a production quota of 600 party cakes per 40-hour workweek. Use the following information.
a. Draw and label a precedence diagram.
b. Compute cycle time.
c. Compute the theoretical minimum number of workstations.
d. Balance the assembly line by the trial-and-error technique.
e. Calculate the efficiency and balance delay of the assembly line.

Work Element	Predecessor	Performance Time (min)
A	—	1
B	A	2
C	B	2
D	A, E	4
E	—	3
F	C, D	4

7-11. The Speedy Pizza Palace is revamping its order processing and pizza-making procedures. In order to deliver fresh pizza fast, six elements must be completed.

Work Element	Precedence	Time (min)
A Receive order	—	2
B Shape dough	A	1
C Prepare toppings	A	2
D Assemble pizza	B, C	3
E Bake pizza	D	3
F Deliver pizza	E	3

a. Construct a precedence diagram.
b. If the demand is 120 pizzas per night (5:00 P.M. to 1:00 A.M.), compute the cycle time for the process.
c. Compute the lead time for the process.
d. How would you balance this line?
e. Compute the efficiency and balance delay of the line.
f. Calculate the theoretical minimum number of workstations. Is there a better way to arrange the line?

7-12. Referring to Problem 7-11, suppose demand increases to 160 pizzas per night.
a. How should the elements be arranged in order to balance the line?
b. Calculate the efficiency and balance delay of the process.
c. Calculate the theoretical minimum number of workstations. Can a better arrangement be determined?

7-13. EyeCare, Inc., is a full-service optical supplier that sells eyeglasses, contact lenses, and protective eye apparel to opticians. Almonzo's job is to assemble custom-ordered lenses into eyeglasses for customers. Sales have been good lately, and Almonzo has been assembling 100 glasses a day. The manager of EyeCare asked Almonzo to write down the precedence requirements and approximate assembly times for each step in the assembly process. The data are shown here.

Element	Description	Precedence	Time (min)
A	Inspect right and left lens for scratches and proper match	—	1
B	Pop lens into frame	A	1
C	Position right side piece and attach to frame	B	0.4
D	Position left side piece and attach to frame	B	0.4
E	Package	C, D	2

a. Assuming an 8-hour workday, how long does it take Almonzo to assemble one pair of glasses? If two workers were to work at Almonzo's pace, how many pairs of glasses could they assemble in one day?
b. EyeCare anticipates a surge in demand with the opening of its own retail outlets. If the assembly process is set up as an assembly line, what is the maximum number of eyeglasses that can be assembled in one day, regardless of the number of workers hired? What is the efficiency of the line? How many workers are needed?
c. The manager can afford to hire only one additional assembler. Set up the assembly process as an assembly line with two workers. Balance the line to produce as many units as it can. Calculate the efficiency of the line. How many pairs of eyeglasses can be assembled by two workers using an assembly line process?
d. Comment on the results of this problem. — Assembly line not efficient

7-14. Professor Garcia has assigned 15 cases in his POM Seminar class to be completed in a 15-week semester. The students, of course, are moaning and groaning that the caseload cannot possibly be completed in the time allotted. Professor Garcia sympathetically suggests that the students work in groups and learn to organize their work efficiently. Knowing when a situation is hopeless, the students make a list of the tasks that have to be completed in preparing a case. These tasks are listed here, along with precedence requirements and estimated time in days. Assuming students will work 5 days a week on this assignment, how many students should be assigned to each group, and what is the most efficient allocation of tasks? Can 15 cases be completed in a semester? Explain your answer.

Element	Description	Precedence	Time (days)
a	Read case	—	1
b	Gather data	a	4
c	Search literature	a	3
d	Load in data	b	1
e	Run computer analysis	d	4
f	Write/type case	c, e	4

7-15. The precedence diagram and task times (in minutes) for assembling McCauley's Mystifier are shown here. Set up an assembly line to produce 125 mystifiers in a 40-hour week. Balance the line by trial and error, and calculate the efficiency of the line.

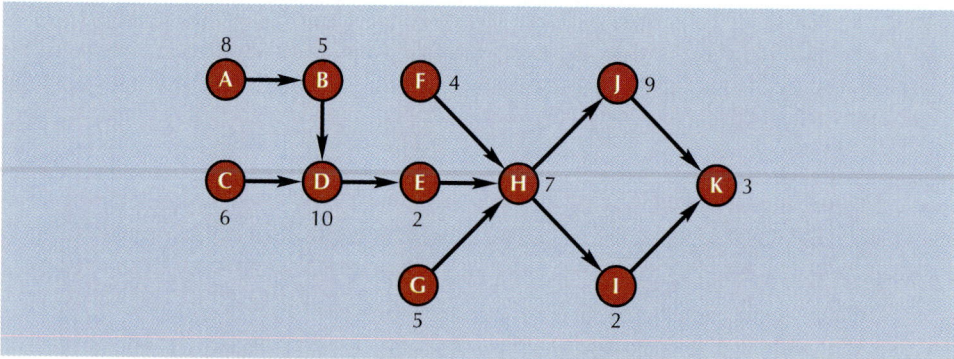

7-16. The work elements, precedence requirements, and time requirements to assemble a picture frame are shown here.
   a. Construct a precedence diagram of the process and label task times.
   b. Set up an assembly line capable of producing 1,600 frames per 40-hour week.
   c. Calculate the efficiency and balance delay of the line.

Element	Description	Precedence	Time (min)
A	Attach left frame side to top of frame	—	0.35
B	Attach right frame wide to bottom of frame	—	0.35
C	Attach left and right frame subassemblies	A, B	0.70
D	Cut 8-inch × 10-inch glass	—	0.50
E	Cut 8-inch × 10-inch cardboard	—	0.50
F	Place glass into frame	C, D	0.20
G	Place cardboard into frame	E, F	0.20
H	Secure cardboard and glass	F, G	0.50
I	Apply descriptive label to glass	D	0.10

7-17. Refer to Problem 7-16.
   a. Calculate the maximum number of frames that can be assembled each week.
   b. Rebalance the line for maximum production. Assuming one worker per workstation, how many workers would be required?

c. Assume the company can sell as many frames as can be produced. If workers are paid $8 an hour and the profit per frame is $5, should the production quota be set to maximum?

7-18. The precedence diagram and task times for assembling modular furniture are shown below. Set up an assembly line to assemble 1,000 sets of modular furniture in a 40-hour week. Balance the line by trial and error, and calculate the efficiency of the line.

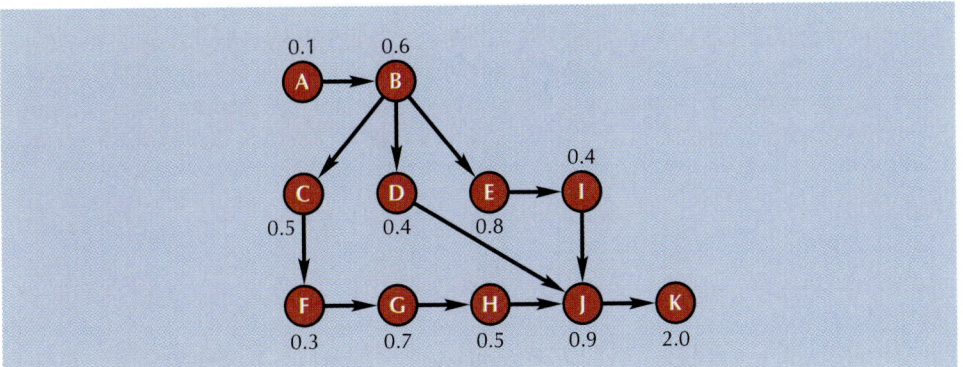

7-19. The Costplus Corporation has set a processing quota of 80 insurance claims per 8-hour day. The claims process consists of five elements, which are detailed below. Costplus has decided to use an assembly line arrangement to process the forms and would like to make sure they have set up the line in the most efficient fashion.

a. Construct a precedence diagram for the claims process and calculate the cycle time required to meet the processing quota.
b. Balance the assembly line and show your arrangement of workstations.
c. Determine how many claims can actually be processed on your line.
d. Calculate the efficiency of the line.

Element	Predecessor	Performance Time (min)
A	—	4
B	A	5
C	B	2
D	A	1
E	C, D	3

CASE PROBLEM

Arranging Darian's Gymnastics Center

Darian and Anita Rice looked around the office nervously as they waited for the architect to arrive. Building his own gymnastics center had been a dream of Darian's ever since childhood, now so close to becoming a reality.

"Hello, folks. Sorry I'm late," Tom Armstead, the architect, said apologetically as he entered the room. "Now tell me all about this gym of yours."

"It's not a gym, it's a gymnastics center," smiled Darian. "We want a full-service gymnastics center to train children who enjoy gymnastics as a recreational activity as well as those who wish to compete. We need a facility that is flexible and inexpensive."

(Continued)

"Don't we all. What kind of equipment will you need?" asked Tom.

Anita handed him a prepared list: "A 40-foot by 40-foot floor-exercise mat, four or five balance beams, a set of even parallel bars, a set of uneven parallel bars, a large trampoline, a foam pit, a power strip or two, a vault, a pommel horse, a climbing rope, stall bars, a mushroom, a horizontal bar, and rings."

"And what size building do you think you'll need for the gymnastics center?"

"About 7,500 square feet, just a shell of a building really. We expect to train around 500 youngsters per session and hold meets in which 50 or so team members are in competition. We'll need a small space for an office—really just a counter would do. Other than that, the entire building should be one open floor area for gymnastics."

"It sounds like you've put a lot of thought into this project. What exactly do you want me to do?"

"Well, we want this facility to be well planned. We want to have a basic layout before the building is designed. From a financial viewpoint, we want to get the most use out of our space; the space must be functional. We're tired of haphazard arrangements that endanger the gymnasts and disrupt classes."

"Sounds fair. If you will explain to me some of your preferences on where each piece of equipment should be located in relation to another, then I can draw up a relationship diagram that will satisfy your needs. After that we can worry about the size and shape of the building."

"Do you need dimensions or space requirements for the equipment?"

"Not yet. We're going to determine the *relative* location of the equipment first. Let me get out a new pad and pencil. . . . Okay, go to it."

Darian and Anita spoke rapidly, the ideas flying back and forth between them.

"The floor exercise area is for running and tumbling. It should not be located near any swinging apparatus, such as the rope or rings."

"Falls for the trampoline are potentially dangerous, so the trampoline should not be located where climbing or swinging activities take place."

"Sometimes the vault is used as a dismount aid, though."

"That's true . . . it's important the vault be near the trampoline. Speaking of the vault, we have to have a power strip for the vault and for the pit, too. But we should keep the balance beams and uneven bars away from the power strip."

"The pit?"

"Yes, the pit. The pit is an 8-foot-deep concrete hole in the floor filled with big pieces of foam rubber. It's great for learning tumbling skills, and a pit fight is the kids' favorite activity."

"We need the horizontal bars next to the pit. It would be nice if the uneven bars and stall bars were located near there, too.

"And the climbing rope should be somewhere nearby—the kids love to swing on it and drop into the pit."

"I like to have a class working on different pieces of equipment at the same time. It would be helpful if related equipment were grouped together."

"Yes, like uneven parallel bars and balance beams for the girls."

"And pommel horse, mushroom, even bars, and rings for the boys."

"We'll want the office/reception desk near the front door. We also want to keep the trampoline, pit, and anything that involves chalk dust away from the office/reception area."

"Well, that's enough to get me started. Make an appointment for next week and I'll show you what I've come up with."

1. Put Darian and Anita's preferences for equipment location into a Muther's grid.

2. Create a 3 × 5 layout in which you try to satisfy preferences. Draw a relationship diagram of the layout and look for opportunities for improvement.

C A S E P R O B L E M

Everyone Needs a Hokie Passport

Tech is modernizing its college ID system. Beginning this term, all faculty, staff, and students will be required to carry a "smart" identification card, called *Hokie passport*. What makes it smart is a magnetic strip with information on club memberships, library usage, class schedules (for taking exams), restrictions (such as no alcohol), medical insurance, emergency contacts, and medical conditions. If desired, it can also be set up as a debit card to pay fines or purchase items from the bookstore, vending machines, cash machines, copy machines, and several local retailers.

University administrators are excited about the revenue potential and increased control of the Hokie passport, but they are not looking forward to the process of issuing approximately 60,000 new cards. If applicants could be processed at the rate of 60 an hour, the entire university could be issued passports in a month's time (with a little overtime).

The steps in the process and approximate times follow. Steps 1 and 2 must be completed before step 3 can begin. Steps 3 and 4 must precede step 5, and step 5 must be completed before step 6.

Steps in Process	Approximate Time
1. Review application for correctness	10 seconds
2. Verify information and check for outstanding debt	60 seconds
3. Process and record payment	30 seconds
4. Take photo	20 seconds
5. Attach photo and laminate	10 seconds
6. Magnetize and issue passport	10 seconds

a. Is it possible to process one applicant every minute? Explain.

b. How would you assign tasks to workers in order to process 60 applicants an hour?

c. How many workers are required? How efficient is your line?

References

Black, J. T. *The Design of the Factory with a Future.* New York: McGraw-Hill, 1991.

Flanders, R. E. "Design, Manufacture and Production Control of a Standard Machine." *Transactions of ASME* 46 (1925).

Goetsch, D. *Advanced Manufacturing Technology.* Albany, N.Y.: Delmar, 1990.

Jablonowski, J. "Reexamining FMSs." *American Machinist,* Special Report 774 (March 1985).

Luggen, W. *Flexible Manufacturing Cells and Systems.* Englewood Cliffs, N.J.: Prentice Hall, 1991.

Monden, Y. *Toyota Production System,* 2d ed. Atlanta, Ga.: IIE Press, 1993.

Muther, R. *Systematic Layout Planning.* Boston: Industrial Education Institute, 1961.

Russell, R. S., P. Y. Huang, and Y. Y. Leu. "A Study of Labor Allocation in Cellular Manufacturing." *Decision Sciences* 22, no. 3 (1991): 594–611.

Sumichrast, R. T., R. S. Russell, and B. W. Taylor. "A Comparative Analysis of Sequencing Procedures for Mixed-Model Assembly Lines in a Just-In-Time Production System." *International Journal of Production Research* 30, no. 1 (1992): 199–214.

Towards a New Era in Manufacturing Studies Board. Washington D.C.: National Academy Press, 1986.

8

Human Resources in Operations Management

Employee Satisfaction at Federal Express

www.prenhall.com/russell

www.prenhall.com/russell

Federal Express, a $7 billion corporation with 85,000 employees, ships an average of 1.5 million packages daily. A key corporate goal is to achieve 100 percent customer satisfaction and service. The company believes employee satisfaction is a prerequisite to customer satisfaction. Federal Express hires highly motivated people and creates an environment for them that encourages and expects outstanding performance. The corporate philosophy, expressed as "People, Service, Profit (P-S-P)," reflects Federal Express's belief that if it puts its employees' welfare first, they will provide excellent service and profits will follow. In effect, Federal Express treats its employees as customers.

Employee-related programs and processes are designed to respond to three basic concerns of employees: What do you expect of me? What's in it for me? Where do I go with a problem? The answer to "What do you expect from me?" focuses on orientation and training, assuming that most employees want to do a good job and will, if shown how. The company has developed a wide variety of interactive video training programs. Every six months, couriers, customer service agents, and pilots are tested via interactive video, and their performance is appraised by their managers. Employees are also provided with the latest technology and trained in its use. Feedback is encouraged during the training process as well as during normal work, in the belief that the person closest to the job knows how to do it best.

Although Federal Express provides excellent wages, benefits, and profit-sharing opportunities, it also answers the question "What is in it for me?" through a number of recognition programs and awards designed to reward extra effort. The reward system includes extensive promotion from within. More than 75 percent of all positions are filled internally.

In response to "Where do I go with a problem?" Federal Express has developed three programs: Guaranteed Fair Treatment, Survey Feedback Action, and Open Door. The first program is a process for employees to appeal any perceived wrongs up through the highest level of the organization. (This process is also used as a means for reviewing and revising employee-related policies). The Survey Feedback Action program is an annual employee attitude survey about the work environment (with anonymous responses). Results are distributed to managers, who are required to participate in feedback sessions with their immediate employees to seek corrective action for problems identified in the survey. The third program, Open Door, enables employees to question any company policy or procedure in writing with-

Federal Express with its high pay scale, positive working environment, and philosophy of treating its employees like customers, is a much sought-after employer. As a result, it attracts and retains highly motivated, hard-working employees.

out fear of reprisal or intimidation. Questions are forwarded to the most appropriate respondent, including the CEO, who must answer within 10 days.

These programs are aimed at creating an environment of open, candid, and trusting communication. To facilitate communication Federal Express operates one of the world's largest private television networks, FXTV, to conduct training programs and provide up-to-date information and answers to employees.[1]

*E*mployees—the people who work in an organization—are "resources," as important as other company resources, such as natural resources and technology. In fact, it is the one resource that all companies have available to them. A company in Taiwan, Japan, or Denmark may have different and few natural resources, certainly fewer than U.S. companies have, but they all have people. With the same or superior technologies as their competitors, and with good people, foreign companies can compete and thrive. Increasingly, *skilled* human resources are the difference between successfully competing or failing.

The traditional view of employees or labor was not so much as a valuable resource, but as a replaceable part of the productive process that must be closely directed and controlled. The trend toward quality management, more than anything else, changed this perspective. W. E. Deming, the international quality expert, emphasized that good employees who are always improving are the key to successful quality management and a company's ultimate survival. Over half of Deming's fourteen points for quality improvement relate to employees. His point is that if a company is to attain its goals for quality improvement and customer service, its employees must be involved and committed. However, to get employees "with the program," the company must regard them and manage them as a valuable resource. Moreover, the company must treat employees as part of its family—a cultural perspective more common to Europe and Japan than to the United States.

Another thing that has changed the way companies regard employees and work is the shift in the U.S. economy toward the service sector and away from manufacturing. Since services tend to be more people intensive than capital intensive, human resources are becoming a more important competitive factor for service companies. The advances in information technologies have also changed the working environment, especially in service companies. Because they rely heavily on information technology, services need employees who are skilled with computers, software, and networks. They also need flexible employees who can apply their computing skills to a variety of tasks, and who are continuously trained to keep up with rapid advances in information technology.

Increasing technological advances in equipment and machinery have also resulted in manufacturing work that is more technically sophisticated. Employees are required to be better educated, have greater skill levels, have greater technical expertise, and are expected to take on greater responsibility. Certain industries that did not change for fifty or sixty years now change on a continuing basis. This fluctuating work environment is a result of changing technologies and international market conditions, global competition that emphasizes diverse products, and an emphasis on product and service quality.

In this chapter we first discuss employees' role in a company's overall strategic design. Next we provide a perspective on how work has developed and changed in the United States and then look at some of the current trends in human resources. We will

---

[1] F. W. Smith, "Our Human Side of Quality," *Quality Progress*, 23, no. 10 (1990): 19–21; N. Karabatsos, "Absolutely, Positively Quality," *Quality Progress* 23, no. 5 (1990): 24–28.

also discuss some of the traditional aspects of work and job design including work measurement. Work measurement is the act of determining the time required to do a job in order to generate a unit of output. It has historically been used to establish incentive wage rates. Work measurement has fallen into some disfavor because it is viewed as being detrimental to quality improvement efforts since it focuses on routine, repetitive tasks and individual incentives (rather than teamwork). However, many companies still use work measurement methods, and it has found new popularity with service companies because they are so labor intensive. The time required for service and manufacturing jobs is an essential part of a company's ability to determine labor needs, schedule work, estimate labor costs, and plan output.

Human Resources in the Strategic Planning Process

Most successful quality-oriented firms today recognize the importance of their employees when developing a competitive strategy. Since quality management is such an integral part of most companies' strategic design, and the role of employees is such an important aspect of TQM, it is only simple logic to recognize the crucial role of human resources in a company's strategic planning process. To change management's traditional control-oriented relationship with employees to one of cooperation, mutual trust, teamwork, and goal orientation necessary in a TQM-focused company generally requires a long-term commitment as a key part of a company's strategic plan.

In the traditional managerial-employee relationship, employees are given precise directions to achieve narrowly defined individual objectives. They are rewarded with merit pay based on individual performance in competition with their coworkers. Often individual excellence is rewarded while other employees look on in envy. In a successful TQM program employees are given broad latitude in their jobs, they are encouraged to improvise, and they have the power to use their own initiative to correct and prevent problems. Strategic goals are for quality and customer service instead of maximizing profit or minimizing cost, and rewards are based on group achievement. Instead of limited training for specific, narrowly defined jobs, employees are trained in a broad range of skills so they know more about the entire productive process, and they are flexible in where they can work.

www.prenhall.com/russell

To manage human resources from this perspective, a company must focus on employees as a key, even central, component in their strategic design. Federal Express's strategic philosophy, "People, Service, Profit," starts with people, reflecting the firm's belief that its people are its most important resource. The focus of Cadillac's "people strategy" plan is its employees. People strategy teams work to support employees by constantly researching and improving Cadillac's people processes.

www.prenhall.com/russell

Companies that successfully integrate this kind of "employees first" philosophy into their strategic design share several common characteristics. Employee training and education are recognized as necessary long-term investments. Strategic planning for product and technological innovation is tied to the development of employee skills, not only to help in the product development process but also to carry out innovations as they come to fruition. Motorola has a goal of providing employees with 160 hours of training annually by the year 2000 to keep up with technological changes and to learn how to understand and compete in newly emerging global markets.

Another characteristic of companies with a strategic design that focuses on quality is that employees have the power to make decisions that will improve quality and customer service. At AT&T employees can stop a production line if they detect a quality problem, and an employee at Ritz-Carlton can spend up to $2,000 to satisfy a guest, on his or her own initiative.

To make sure their strategic design for human resources is working, companies regularly monitor employee satisfaction using surveys and make changes when problems are identified. Ritz-Carlton and Texas Instruments conduct annual employee surveys, and AT&T conducts surveys every two years, to access employee satisfaction and make improvements. A safe, healthy working environment is a basic necessity to keep employees satisfied. Successful companies provide special services like recreational activities, day care, flexible work hours, cultural events, picnics, and fitness centers. Notice that these are services that treat employees like customers, an acknowledgment that there is not a lot of difference between employee satisfaction and customer satisfaction.

Strategic goals for quality and customer satisfaction require teamwork and group participation. Motorola lets employees pick their own team members and the problems they address, and then they compete in a Worldwide Total Customer Satisfaction Team Competition. Texas Instruments has as a goal that all employees be a member of at least one team to locate and solve quality-related problems. Team members and individuals are encouraged to make suggestions to improve group performance. The motivation for such suggestions is viewed as that of a concerned family member, not as a complaintant or as "sticking one's nose in." Cadillac shows its respect for employees' ideas by responding to all employee suggestions within twenty-four hours.

It is important that employees understand what the strategic goals of the company are, and that they feel like they can participate in achieving these goals. Employees need to believe they make a difference to be committed to goals and have pride in their work. Employee commitment and participation in the strategic plan can be enhanced if employees are involved in the planning process, especially at the local level. As the strategic plan passes down through the organization to the employee level, employees can participate in the development of local plans to achieve overall corporate goals.

www.prenhall.com/russell

The Changing Nature of Human Resources Management

The principles of *scientific management* developed by F. W. Taylor in the 1880s and 1890s dominated operations management during the first part of the twentieth century.

Before the turn of the century, the machine shop was the basic factory. Skilled machinists were subcontracted by owners and provided with tools, resources, materials, and a workplace, and semiskilled laborers were hired by the machinists. These machinists planned and supervised the work, which they also performed, and controlled the production process. The shop owner had little real control over the work area, which was mostly left to the skilled artisans/machinists.

This system was effective for small, provincial markets and limited technologies. As markets grew and owners invested greater sums of money in more sophisticated, heavier machinery and larger factories, they became more cost-conscious and eager to expand production to make more profit.

In this changing environment F. W. Taylor began his development of *scientific management.* Taylor's approach was to break jobs down into their most elemental activities and to simplify job designs so that only limited skills were required to learn a job, thus minimizing the time required for learning. This approach divided the jobs requiring less skill from the work required to set up machinery and maintain it, which required greater skill. In Taylor's system, a **job** is the set of all the tasks performed by a worker, **tasks** are individual activities consisting of *elements*, which encompass several **job motions,** or basic physical movements. As an example, sewing machine operators who make baseball-style caps sew together the individual wedges of material forming

www.prenhall.com/russell

Scientific management involves breaking down jobs into elemental activities and simplifying job design.

Jobs comprise a set of **tasks**, *elements*, and **job motions** (*basic physical movements*).

Competing at Lands' End

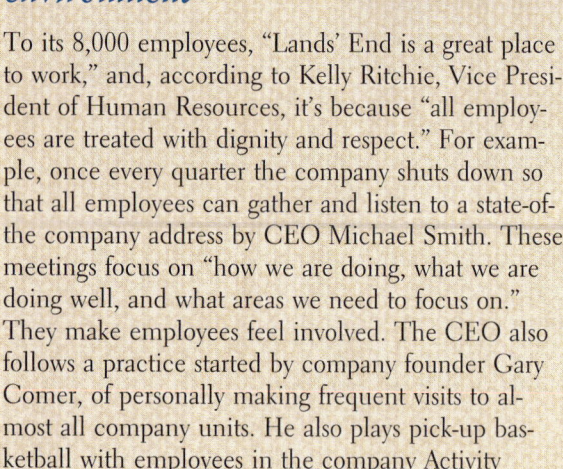

Establishing and maintaining a much envied work environment

To its 8,000 employees, "Lands' End is a great place to work," and, according to Kelly Ritchie, Vice President of Human Resources, it's because "all employees are treated with dignity and respect." For example, once every quarter the company shuts down so that all employees can gather and listen to a state-of-the-company address by CEO Michael Smith. These meetings focus on "how we are doing, what we are doing well, and what areas we need to focus on." They make employees feel involved. The CEO also follows a practice started by company founder Gary Comer, of personally making frequent visits to almost all company units. He also plays pick-up basketball with employees in the company Activity Center.

This $8 million, 80,000 square foot facility for employees includes an Olympic-size swimming pool, a full-size gymnasium, an indoor walking and jogging track, a cafeteria, an aerobics room, exercise and weightlifting equipment, handball courts, a wellness lab, a locker area, showers, a dressing room, and overnight laundry service for athletic wear. There is a view of the outdoors from almost any location in the building. Outdoor facilities include a soccer field that doubles as an ice-skating rink in the winter, tennis courts, a softball field, a golf driving range, an outdoor walking and jogging track, and bike paths (with equipment loaned free-of-charge in the Activity Center). Almost 80 percent of the Lands' End population will use the facility during the year. It also provides activities for employees' involvement including classes on cooking, parenting, swimming, and yoga.

Employees also receive discounts on Lands' End products. The work facilities are clean, modern, and aesthetically pleasing and employees have no dress code. Lands' End focuses on work performance and making employees comfortable at work.

Lands' End has also shown its commitment to employees by establishing the Comer Foundation Scholarship Fund. It assists the children of Lands' End employees pursue post-high school education, funded scholarships for Dodgeville, WI High School, and provided a computer lab.

Another way Lands' End improves its working environment and makes it comfortable for its employees is to provide them with lots of training. Before catalog phone operators take their first call they have received 80 hours of training on products, services, and computers.

Guidelines for every type of situation are explained, and training continues throughout the employee's career. Kelly Ritchie notes that, "in every employee at every level, we try to instill the idea that they must do whatever is needed to meet the customers' needs. What happens if they aren't sure what to do and make a mistake? They're told in advance not to worry about it." Lands' End has discovered (unlike other companies) that by spending money up front (on training and employee preparation), they have much happier employees, they don't have to spend nearly as much money on the backend on quality checks, and they have satisfied customers.

A guiding principle of Lands' End founder Gary Comer (that is still enacted) is that if you do what's best for the customer, you won't have to worry about the company—it'll take care of itself—and customers are both external and internal.

the crown, attach the cap bill, and stitch the cap logo. An element of a task might be positioning and sewing two wedges of material together or threading the sewing machine. The individual motions that make up the element are reaching for a wedge of material, grasping the material, positioning it, and releasing it.

Scientific management broke down a job into its simplest elements and motions, eliminated unnecessary motions, and then divided the tasks among several workers so that each would require only minimal skill. This system enabled the owner to hire large numbers of cheap, unskilled laborers, who were basically interchangeable and easily replaced. If a worker was fired or quit, another could easily be placed on the job with virtually no training expense. In this system, the timing of job elements (by stopwatch) enabled management to develop *standard times* for producing one unit of output. Workers were paid according to their total output in a *piece-rate system*. A worker was paid "extra" wages according to the amount he or she exceeded the "standard" daily output. Such a wage system is based on the premise that the single motivating factor for a worker to increase output is monetary reward.

> Traditionally, time has been a measure of job efficiency.

> In a *piece-rate wage system*, pay is based on output.

F. W. Taylor's work was not immediately accepted or implemented. This system required high volumes of output to make the large number of workers needed for the expanded number of jobs cost-effective. The principles of scientific management and mass production were brought together by Henry Ford and the assembly line production of automobiles.

The Assembly Line

Between 1908 and 1929 Ford Motor Company created and maintained a mass market for the Model-T automobile, over 15 million of which were eventually produced. During this period, Ford expanded production output by combining standardized parts and product design, continuous-flow production, and Taylor's scientific management. These elements were encompassed in the assembly line production process.

> The adoption of scientific management at Ford was the catalyst for its subsequent widespread acceptance.

On an assembly line, workers no longer moved from place to place to perform tasks, as they had in the factory/shop. Instead they remained at a single workplace and the work was conveyed to them along the assembly line. Technology had advanced from the general-purpose machinery available at the turn of the century, which required the abilities of a skilled machinist, to highly specialized, semiautomatic machine tools, which required less skill to feed parts into or perform repetitive tasks. Fifteen thousand of these machines were installed at Ford's Highland Park plant. The pace of work was established mechanically by the line and not by the worker or management. The jobs along the line were broken down into highly repetitive, simple tasks.

> Assembly line production meshed with the principles of scientific management.

The assembly line at Ford was enormously successful. The amount of labor time required to assemble a Model-T chassis was reduced from more than 12 hours in 1908 to a little less than 3 hours by 1913. By 1914 the average time for some tasks was as low as $1^1/_2$ minutes. The basic assembly line structure and many job designs that existed in 1914 remained virtually unchanged for the next fifty years.

Numerous U.S. firms imitated Ford's assembly line system in hopes of emulating Ford's success. Between the two World Wars, the assembly line system was exported overseas as Ford opened plants in Great Britain, Germany, and other European countries. Westinghouse provided several German electrical companies with technical expertise on assembly line manufacturing.

> After WWI, scientific management spread to Europe.

It is interesting that Taylor's principles were not popular in Japan and other Far Eastern nations. Industrialization occurred much more rapidly in Japan and essentially bypassed the skilled industrial artisan phase that engendered Taylor's work. Factory work teams were a tradition in Japanese industry, and job flexibility—as opposed to rigidity

> Scientific management was not adopted in Japan.

and specialization—was the cultural norm. Mitsubishi Electric of Japan attempted to adopt Westinghouse assembly line production concepts; Ford opened a plant in Yokohama in 1925, and General Motors opened another in Osaka in 1926. However, these efforts were largely unsuccessful, and U.S. tariff barriers caused both automobile plants to close by 1939. Ironically, many of the employees from these plants later formed the nucleus of the initial Toyota Company work force.

Limitations of Scientific Management

Advantages of task specialization include high output, low costs, and minimal training.

Scientific management had obvious advantages. It resulted in increased output and lower labor costs. Workers could easily be replaced and trained at low cost, taking advantage of a large pool of cheap unskilled labor shifting from farms to industry. Because of low-cost mass production, the U.S. standard of living was increased enormously and became the envy of the rest of the world. It also allowed unskilled, uneducated workers to gain employment based almost solely on their willingness to work hard physically at jobs that were mentally undemanding.

Disadvantages of task specialization include boredom, lack of motivation, and mental fatigue.

However, scientific management also proved to have serious disadvantages. Workers frequently became bored and dissatisfied with the numbing repetition of simple job tasks that required little thought, ingenuity, or responsibility.

F. W. Taylor thought that wages were the primary motivation for work, but behavioral scientists proved that the psychological content of work can be a more powerful motivating force for increasing productivity than pay. The skill level required in repetitive, specialized tasks is so low that workers do not have the opportunity to prove their worth or abilities for advancement. Repetitive tasks requiring the same monotonous physical motions can result in unnatural physical and mental fatigue.

There is minimal opportunity for workers to interact with other workers. These negative factors lead to tardiness, turnover, absenteeism, and a feeling of dissatisfaction.

Behavioral Influences on Job Design

Quality of Work Life: Program introduced at GM.

New approaches to human resources management appeared during the late 1960s and early 1970s, typified by the "Quality of Work Life" program popularized at General Motors and tried by several other companies. These programs promoted "good" job design. They generally included the following precepts.

Horizontal job enlargement involves expanding the scope of a job to include more tasks.

1. The scope of a job should include all the tasks necessary to complete a product or process, providing the worker with a sense of closure and achievement. This is referred to as **horizontal job enlargement.** It makes a job more interesting because of the greater variety of tasks and provides the worker with a sense that he or she has actually made something.

Vertical job enlargement allows workers more responsibility.

2. Control over their own work and some of the supervisory responsibilities for a job are transferred to the worker from management. This is **vertical job enlargement,** also called *job enrichment*, and provides a greater sense of job satisfaction.

Worker responsibility for quality

3. Workers should individually be responsible for job reliability and quality, a responsibility previously held solely by management.

Job rotation involves the capability of workers to move to different jobs.

4. Workers should be trained for a variety of jobs so that they develop greater skill levels, have a more complete understanding of the overall production process, and are capable of performing different jobs, also known as **job rotation,** or flexibility. By enhancing the skill level of workers, it provides them with a greater sense of self-worth and enhances their opportunities for advancement.

Communication between workers

5. The company should enable and promote interaction and communication among workers and between workers and management. This encourages workers to improve their own jobs and share this knowledge with their colleagues.

THE COMPETITIVE EDGE

Worker Training in the German Trumpf Company

Trumpf, a German manufacturer of precision machine tools, is internationally recognized for producing high-quality products. Trumpf's machines are highly sophisticated systems, are programmed by computer, and are usually customized to meet specific customer needs. Two thirds of its sales are abroad. Trumpf is a very innovative company, with 10 percent of its annual budget invested in research and development and with 60 percent of its annual sales coming from products not sold three years ago.

A primary reason for Trumpf's success is its highly skilled workers. Each Trumpf worker goes through a $3^1/_2$-year apprentice program. An apprentice spends four days each week at the Trumpf plant and one day at a state-run industrial school. A similar program is employed by manufacturing companies throughout Germany. This dual state-industry educational program ensures that German industry will have a large, skilled, flexible work force.

At Trumpf an apprentice spends the first six months of the program doing nothing but filing steel by hand. Trumpf believes that mastery of manual skills is a necessity for learning basic machine work. This emphasis on manual skills also teaches self-discipline and instills self-confidence, which will result in a high level of artisanship and quality. Workers are perceived as artisans and enjoy a high social status in Germany and throughout Western Europe. In the United States, industry historically has not developed extensive training programs on a national scale to the extent that Germany has. Further, the social status of manual workers in the United States has historically been lower than in Germany and Europe, making it a less attractive occupation. The result for U.S. manufacturing companies in recent years has often been a shortage of skilled workers that would allow them to compete effectively in international markets with European companies.

Trumpf has a U.S. plant, which produces the same high-quality work as its German plants, indicating that Trumpf quality and artisanship can be replicated with properly trained U.S. workers. Most of Trumpf's Japanese sales come from products it makes in America.

SOURCE: Based on Tom Peters, (narrator), "Germany's Quality Obsession." Video co-produced by The Tom Peters Group, KERA, and Video Publishing House, Inc., copyright Video Publishing House, Inc., and Excell, A California partnership, 1991.

Although these principles were widely praised and encouraged and some isolated cases of success resulted, they were not widely adopted. However, a turning point in the approach to human resources management was rapidly approaching.

Contemporary Trends in Human Resources Management

During the 1980s and 1990s the competitive advantage gained by many Japanese companies in international markets, and especially in the automobile industry, caused U.S. firms to reevaluate their management practices vis-à-vis those of the Japanese. Human resources management is one area where there was a striking difference between Japanese and U.S. approaches and results. For example, one Japanese automobile company was able to assemble a car with half the blue-collar labor as a comparable U.S. auto company—about 14 hours in Japan, compared to 25 hours in the United States. Japan did not adopt the traditional Western approaches to work. Instead Japanese work allowed for more individual worker responsibility and less supervision, group work and interaction, higher worker skill levels, and training across a variety of tasks and jobs. These characteristics are recognizable as the behavioral precepts included in the quality of work life programs from the mid-1970s. There is a tendency among Americans to think that these characteristics are unique to the Japanese culture. However, the successes of U.S. companies such as Ford and Motorola in implementing quality management programs as well as successful Japanese companies operating in America, such

Japanese successes are due less to cultural factors than to management practices.

as Nissan and Honda, show that cultural factors are less important than management practices.

Job Flexibility

Japanese train workers to do a variety of jobs and tasks.

Flexible employees resulting from extensive cross training creates a more skilled and integrated work force. It enables workers to move across different jobs. This versatility is especially important given the changing nature of product markets. Companies have to respond to changing consumer tastes that are diverse, fragmented, and concerned with quality. Mass, standardized production has been supplanted by the production of smaller production batches to reflect the consumer's desire for product variety. Advances in technology, machinery, and equipment also occur at a more rapid pace. Companies must be able to react quickly to these changes to remain competitive. The traditional approach of clearly defined, simple, repetitive tasks so that workers can be treated as replaceable parts is effective in a mass production system but is too rigid for the dynamics of international competition.

The flexibility to move workers between jobs as the need arises is well suited to the dynamics of new markets, product diversity, and new technologies. It is also necessary to maintain low work-in-progress inventories, as typified by the just-in-time (JIT) system. Buffer inventories are normally kept in stock at stages of the production process to offset irregularities and problems in the system and keep production moving smoothly. However, JIT companies seek to eliminate these buffer inventories completely by having the workers identify the causes of process problems and solve them. At Toyota, for example, as production problems are corrected, managers respond by progressively reducing the in-process buffer inventories, constantly seeking to drive them to zero. If irregularities threaten to stop production, workers are expected to work harder to avoid stoppages. Further, other workers are expected to fill in where needed to maintain the normal work level. Some companies also use warning lights to signify problems in assembly lines. When no lights are on, it is a signal to management that the work force can be reduced further. These management practices are feasible only if there is a high degree of job flexibility and workers are capable of moving from one job to another.

Responsibility and Empowerment

In the traditional U.S. approach, quality is management's responsibility, whereas Japanese approach says quality is the responsibility of the worker.

Empowerment is giving workers the authority to alert management to problems.

Workers have not traditionally felt responsibility for product quality. Quality is perceived as a management responsibility and prerogative not shared with workers.

For companies committed to TQM, the relationship of quality and the worker is completely different. Part of a worker's job responsibility is product quality and quality improvement. Achieving product quality at the job level—*quality at the source*—is fundamental to quality management. An important aspect of this approach is the concept of **empowerment,** wherein the worker has the authority and responsibility to alert management to quality problems and to act individually to correct problems without fear of reprisal. The authority of TQM company workers to halt an entire production operation or line on their own initiative if they discover a quality problem, is well documented at companies like AT&T.

Empowerment gives employees the authority to make decisions and more direct control over their work so that they can more easily achieve the company's goals for quality improvement and customer service. (However, employees are generally more conservative than their supervisors or managers in taking extraordinary actions.) Empowering employees is a key element in the success of a TQM program. Five of W. E. Deming's fourteen points for quality improvement relate to employee empowerment.

THE COMPETITIVE EDGE

Worker Empowerment at Harley-Davidson

www.prenhall.com/russell

In 1981 Harley-Davidson Company, the only U.S. manufacturer of motorcycles, was facing bankruptcy. Over a decade later the company is so successful that it cannot make motorcycles fast enough, and there is a waiting list of customers. One factor in Harley-Davidson's turnaround was the increased job responsibility for machining centers on the shop floor. Machinists, besides operating their complex, computerized, machining centers, also bargain directly with vendors and suppliers, set up their own workplace, set their budgets, and monitor quality. The workers essentially have responsibility for designing the work process. In so doing they have raised the quality of Harley-Davidson motorcycles to a level that provides the company with an international competitive edge.

SOURCE: Based on CNN *Work in Progress*, video documentary produced by CNN, hosted by Bernard Shaw, and narrated by Stephen Frazier.

A Motorola sales representative has the authority to replace a customer's defective product up to six years after its purchase. GM plant employees can call in suppliers to help them solve problems. Federal Express employees are empowered to do whatever it takes to ensure 100 percent customer satisfaction.

Increased Skill and Ability Levels

In order to perform in a variety of jobs, to monitor product quality, and to operate more sophisticated machinery and equipment, greater job skills, training, and ability are required than has been the case for workers in U.S. companies. The U.S. approach to work in the past has been to design jobs that require minimal skills so workers could easily and cheaply be replaced and trained.

In companies with a commitment to quality, job training is extensive and varied. Expectations for performance and advancement from both the employee and management tend to be high. Numerous courses are typically available for training in different jobs and functions. Job training is considered part of a structured career-development system that includes job rotation. This system of training and job rotation enhances the flexibility of the production process we mentioned earlier. It creates talent reserves that can be used as the need arises when products or processes change or the work force is reduced.

Extensive job training and job rotation are characteristic of Japanese system.

Companies successful with TQM programs invest heavily in training and education. Two of W. E. Deming's fourteen points refer to employee education and training. Most large TQM companies have extensive training staffs with state-of-the-art facilities. Federal Express has a television network that broadcasts over 2,000 different training course titles to employees. The typical Federal Express employee is a part-time college student, but each receives more training that most skilled factory workers in the United States. Motorola with an annual training budget of $120 million, employs 300 teachers of its own and 600 more consultant teachers to train all its employees at all levels. Baldrige Quality Award winners Milliken, Texas Instruments, Eastman Chemical, and Xerox provide training on quality to all of their employees.

www.prenhall.com/russell

Two other Baldrige Award winners, IBM Rochester and Wainwright Industries, invest the equivalent of 5 percent and 7 percent, respectively, of their payroll in training—seven times the national average. Cadillac spent $1 million to send over 1,400 of

www.prenhall.com/russell

its employees to a four-day Deming seminar. Ames Rubber, another Baldrige Award recipient, working with a community college, developed a training program that resulted in high school equivalency diplomas for 20 percent of its work force. Ames credits this training combined with its employee teamwork for reducing the number of defective parts it supplied to its largest customer, Xerox, from 30,000 per million to 11 per million.[2]

Employee Involvement

Quality circles: group problem solving.

Employee involvement is realized through groups or teams. The most well-known example is the *quality circle*, in which a group of eight to ten workers plus their supervisor address and solve problems in their immediate work area. These groups have a formal structure and methodology for selecting and solving problems. Quality circles are discussed in Chapter 3, "Quality Management.")

Quality circles solve problems in all areas of production process.

Work groups such as quality circles solve problems and attempt to improve productivity and efficiency in all areas, not just quality (although efforts for improvement in one area invariably lead to quality improvement as well). Quality circles are especially effective in job redesign and improvement and in job training. In many instances, the solution to a quality problem is discovered by the work group to be a problem in job design. However, the quality circle is not a democratic group that supersedes supervisory authority; involvement does not mean authority. In fact, the ratio of supervisors to workers is generally greater in Japan where quality circles are very popular than America, and supervisors there are at least as authoritative, if not more.

Successful quality-oriented companies share a commitment to employee involvement through teamwork. Motorola has over 4,500 quality council and quality circle

---

THE COMPETITIVE EDGE

Employee Training at Quad Graphics, Inc.

Quad Graphics, Inc., near Milwaukee, is a $500,000-a-year company that prints most of the magazines found on newsstands in the United States. Employees work either three 12-hour days or four 10-hour days per week. They come back to work one day per week without pay to learn or teach about refinements in the company's state-of-the-art presses. Everyone in the company must learn and everyone must instruct. No one is promoted unless he or she has trained a successor. The employees experiment with equipment to redesign and refine jobs. During the past decade 6,000 new jobs were created at the company; however, the jobs are not easy nor routine. The employees must use their one day of learning to keep up with job changes.

A similar commitment to worker training is characteristic of other companies that have achieved success

with TQM programs. For example, Baldrige Award winner AT&T Universal Card Services provides 84 hours of employee training annually. Another Baldrige Award winner, the Ritz Carlton Hotel, provides 136 hours of training annually, and the Granite Rock Company, also a Baldrige Award winner, spends three times the industry average on employee training. At all these companies and at Quad Graphics, the employers want a work force capable of being retrained again and again as jobs evolve and change.

SOURCE: Based on CNN *Work in Progress*, video documentary produced by CNN, hosted by Bernard Shaw, and narrated by Stephen Frazier; 1993. *Malcolm Baldrige Awards, Quest for Excellence* V, video presented by U.S. Department of Commerce, the Technology Administration, the National Institute of Standards and Technology, and the American Society for Quality Control, produced by Image Associates.

---

[2] R. A. Nadkarni, "A Not-So-Secret Recipe for Successful TQM" *Quality Progress* 28, no 11 (November 1995): 91–96.

THE COMPETITIVE EDGE

Employee Involvement at Xerox

www.prenhall.com/russell

In the 1980s, Xerox Corporation's revenue share of the copier business declined from 90 to 43 percent as a result of increased competition from Ricoh, Sharp, and Canon in Japan and Kodak and IBM in the United States. To reduce costs, Xerox developed plans to subcontract component parts to other companies. One such plan at the components' manufacturing operations (CMO) plant in Webster, New York, would save $3.2 million and eliminate one whole department and its 180 employees. However, the local chapter of the Amalgamated Clothing and Textile Workers Union (ACTWU) asked management to establish a joint labor-management *study action team*, to study the problem and see if solutions could be discovered that would reduce costs by $3.2 million without employee layoffs.

The team of eight employees, relieved of their normal work duties, studied the problem for six months. At the end of this period they had developed a set of recommendations that would save $3.7 million and the 180 jobs.

As a result of this success, other study action teams were developed to address problems at Xerox. These successes altered the labor-management relationship at Xerox and led to other changes in the work environment and employee involvement. Groups meet biweekly to set work schedules, identify customer needs, review area performance, and identify problems. At the Webster CMO plant 36 groups were established, each with 15 to 40 members, responsible for planning, scheduling, making changes, and solving problems in the work area.

SOURCE: Based on P. Lazes, L. Rumpeltes, A. Hoffner, L. Pace, and A. Costanza, "Xerox and the ACTWU: Using Labor-Management Teams to Remain Competitive," *National Productivity Review* 10, no. 3 (1991): 339–49.

---

teams. At Eastman Chemical (a Baldrige Award winner), every employee serves on at least one team and most serve on two or more. Texas Instruments Defense Systems and Electronics Group (another Baldrige winner) has over 1,900 teams operating at every level of its company.

Companies that promote employee involvement also encourage employees to make suggestions for improvement. For example, Baldrige Award winner Milliken has received over 260,000 ideas for improvement—19 per employee—in a single year. Each idea is acknowledged by management within 24 hours and acted upon within 72 hours. There are no monetary rewards for these ideas, but Milliken recognizes employee contributions at ceremonies and with awards. At Westinghouse, 80 percent of employee suggestions are accepted for use. At Wainwright Industries (a Baldrige Award winner) each employee averaged more than one implemented improvement suggestion per week in 1993.

www.prenhall.com/russell

Employee Compensation

Traditionally pay was believed to be the primary motivating force for workers. Although behavioralists later showed that wages are not the *sole* impetus for work and employee satisfaction, they are still a very important aspect of work.

The two basic forms of employee payment are the hourly wage and the individual incentive, or piece-rate, wage, both of which are tied to time. The hourly wage is self-explanatory; the longer someone works, the more he or she is paid. In a piece-rate system, employees are paid for the number of units they produce during the workday. The faster the employee performs, the more output generated and the greater the pay. These two forms of payment are also frequently combined with a guaranteed base hourly wage and additional incentive piece-rate payments based on the number of units produced above a standard hourly rate of output. Other basic forms of compensation include straight salary, the most common form of payment for management, and commissions, a payment system usually applied to sales and salespeople.

Traditional forms of worker payment are hourly wages and incentive pay systems.

THE COMPETITIVE EDGE

An Incentive Compensation Program at Viking Freight

www.prenhall.com/russell

All employees at Viking Freight Systems, Inc., participate in an incentive compensation program that financially rewards them for their combined contributions to the achievement of corporate objectives. Employees are divided into groups with shared job characteristics and objectives. For example, workers at each of the company's 47 terminal sites are considered groups, as well as all truck drivers, salespeople, maintenance personnel, and so on. A group's performance is measured every four weeks according to specific criteria. The primary criterion (common to all groups) is that the company's operating ratio (operating expenses divided by revenues) must be less than 95 percent for the month. Other criteria are group-specific. For example, the criteria for the forty-seven terminal groups are revenue attainment, percent of performance, on-time service, and claims ratio. Specific objectives are set by engineering for each criterion—for example, at least 98 percent on-time service—and, to receive incentive payments, the terminal groups must reach these targets. Payments are made by separate check in group meetings, and the frequency of the payments (every four weeks) continually maintains focus on the program. When the program was started in 1986, employees achieved 84.8 percent of company performance goals, and by 1991 performance against standards was 103.1 percent. In 1991 employees earned incentive payments in twelve of thirteen 4-week periods, averaging 5.5 percent of their gross pay, or approximately $125 to $200 per period.

SOURCE: Based on T. Stambaugh, "An Incentive Pay Success Story," *Personnel Journal* 71, no. 7 (1992): 48–54.

Piece-rate systems can be detrimental to quality.

An individual piece-rate system provides incentive to increase output, but it does not ensure high quality. It can do just the opposite! In an effort to produce as much as possible, the worker will become sloppy, take shortcuts, and pay less attention to detail. As a result, TQM companies have tried to move away from individual wage incentive systems based on output and time. There has been a trend toward other measures of performance, such as quality, productivity, cost reduction, and the achievement of organizational goals. These systems usually combine an hourly base payment or even a salary with some form of incentive payment. However, incentives are typically not individual but are tied to group or company performance.

www.prenhall.com/russell

Progressive, quality-oriented companies try to reward employees in ways not related to direct compensation. Disney has low entry-level pay of $4.85 per hour (about $10,000 annually), but its employee turnover rate is one-third lower than the service sector's national average. It accomplishes this seemingly contradictory result with a fast internal advancement system in which Disney promotes liberally from within. This cost-effective system allows Disney to reward employees who perform well without rewarding those who do not. However, Disney hardly ever fires anyone since it views every person as a potential customer. Disney also gives a $100 bonus to employees who bring in new employees because Disney discovered that its best potential employees are friends of current employees.

An alternative to individual compensation is the trend to indirect nonmonetary rewards. Individual and team awards to acknowledge exemplary job performance have become popular. This kind of visible public acknowledgment in front of an employee's peers is often a more powerful motivating force and provides more lasting satisfaction to employees than private monetary compensation. It is also good "publicity" for a company's quality and customer service goals among its employees. IBM and Xerox have formal recognition programs with individual and team awards. Westinghouse has a "Wall of Fame" to acknowledge exceptional employees at each of its sites. Texas Instruments gives a Site Quality Award to the top 2 percent of its employees nominated by their peers. At the IRS employees are recognized with awards that are publicized in a service newsletter. Domino's Pizza holds a national Olympics where regional teams compete in events based on job categories. The competition is broadcast live to Domino's employees around the country on their own network.[3]

Companies with TQM programs evaluate employees based on team and group achievement in addition to individual performance. Traditional performance appraisal is based on an individual's ability to achieve established objectives for a specified time period. However, this form of evaluation fails to recognize that an employee's performance is tied to coworkers' performance and other factors the employee has little or no control over. For example, a salesperson's performance evaluation and pay are often based on a sales quota. However, sales depend not only on how good a salesperson the individual is but also on how good the product is, product quality, the competition, customer satisfaction with the company, and the economy, among other things. Thus, it is more equitable to evaluate teams or groups of employees based on how well they achieve company objectives.

Many companies provide employees with special services such as day-care centers and fitness centers as an alternative to direct financial compensation. Solectron Corporation, a Baldrige Award winner and global corporation with a mostly Asian work force, offers free second language training in English and communication skills to its employees.

At one of its plants, Motorola has experimented with a system in which teams vote on members' performance to determine 20 percent of annual pay for outstanding employees. In general, peers are tougher evaluators of performance than managers.

Profit-sharing plans, in which employees receive a portion of company profits, are becoming increasingly popular in the United States. Other plans provide bonuses or incentive payments on top of hourly wages based on formulas that include cost reduction, the percentage of defective items or good-quality items, and/or productivity. However, such compensation plans base bonuses or incentive payments on group activity rather than individual effort; that is, a department's or plant's performance triggers incentive payments. An alternative to profit-sharing plans are plans based on sharing savings from improvements. An example is Xerox's "gainsharing" where employees share savings equally. At Monsanto Chemical Company, plants give employees bonuses based on unit or departmental cost savings.

In *profit sharing*, employees receive a share of company profits.

In Japan the reward system is often based on lifelong job security provided by many companies. This results in a high degree of employee loyalty to the company, which heightens the worker's willingness to accept job rotation, responsibility for job improvement, and the constant pressure of providing extra effort. These and other unique features of the Japanese management system require the "sacrifice of self" for the good for the organizational whole. This is different from the U.S. system, in which jobs are sometimes designed in such a way that the occupants are perceived as replaceable parts.

Job security is a key factor in Japanese reward system.

Technology and Automation

The worker-machine interface is possibly the most crucial aspect of job design, both in manufacturing industries and in service companies where workers interface with computers. New technologies has increased the educational requirements and need for training for employees. The development of computer technology and systems has heightened the need for workers with better skills and more job training.

Technology has broadened the scope of job design in the United States and overseas.

During the 1990s there has been substantial investment in new plants and equip-

[3] J. R. Evans and W. Lindsay, *The Management and Control of Quality*, 3d ed. (St. Paul, Minn.: West, 1996).

Robots do not necessarily perform a job faster than humans, but they can tolerate hostile environments, work longer hours, and do a job more consistently. Robots are used for a wide range of manufacturing jobs including material handling, machining, assembly and inspection. For example, at Ford over 98 percent of the welding for the Taurus is performed by robots; at General Dynamics holes are drilled for F-16 fighter planes with robots, and disk drives are installed in the manufacture of IBM personal computers with robots. The use of robotics in the United States has been limited primarily to larger industries, with the automobile industry accounting for over half the robots used in this country.

ment in the United States to compete globally. Companies developed and installed a new generation of automated equipment and robotics that enhanced their abilities to achieve higher output and lower costs. This new equipment also reduced the manual labor necessary to perform jobs and improve safety. Computer systems provided workers with an expanded array of information that increased their ability to identify and locate problems in the production process and monitor product quality. New job designs and redesigns of existing jobs were required that reflected these new technologies.

Temporary Employees

A trend among service companies especially, is the use of temporary, or *contingent*, employees. Part-time employees have accounted for over 40 percent of job growth in the retail industry during the past decade. By the year 2000 nearly 40 percent of all employees will be interim or part-time according to some predictions. Fast-food and restaurant chains, retail companies, and financial firms tend to use a large number of temporary employees. Companies that have seasonal demand make extensive use of temporary employees. L. L. Bean needs a lot more telephone service operators in the months before Christmas. Sometimes a company will undertake a project requiring technical expertise its permanent employees do not have. Instead of reassigning or retraining their employees, they will bring in temporary employees having the necessary expertise. There has been a growing market for firms that *lease* people for jobs, espe-

www.prenhall.com/russell

cially for computer services. As companies downsize to cut costs, they turn to temporary employees to fill temporary needs without adding to their long-term cost base. People with computer skills able to work from home have also increased the pool of available temporary workers.

Unfortunately temporary employees do not usually have the commitment to goals for quality and service that a company might want. Companies dependent on temporary employees not only suffer the inconsistent levels of their work ethic and skills, they also sacrifice productivity for lower costs. To offset this inconsistency and to protect product and service quality, firms try to hire temporary employees only into isolated work areas away from their core businesses that most directly affect quality.

Job Satisfaction

The cumulative effect of these new trends in human resources management has been a greater level of worker satisfaction with jobs in TQM companies in the United States. Jobs with these characteristics are more challenging, varied, and interesting, require more skill, and include more individual responsibility. Employees take greater pride in their jobs and have a clearer perspective of the contribution their job makes to the success of the organization. The reward system is more effective; as a result, employee loyalty is greater. Because of the team approach, there is greater interaction with supervisory management, which reduces potential employee-management conflict.

U.S. Adaptation of Trends in Human Resources Management

U.S. companies that have a strong commitment to a total quality management program, have had success with the new trends in human resources management. Jobs have been designed to include employee-involvement programs, more individual responsibility, and worker empowerment. The increased use of automated equipment and robotics by American manufacturing firms has forced them to redesign jobs to reflect the greater skill levels this new technology requires. The movement away from mass production to smaller batch production to meet changing consumer preferences has forced American companies to redesign work to create more flexibility to broaden the scopes of jobs, and to reduce the degree of task specialization. Many American companies have also come to realize that work-job satisfaction and pride can have an impact on both quality and productivity.

Although the dominant principles and approaches have come from the manufacturing sector, most of the recent trends in human resources management are just as applicable to service industries. It is ironic to note that the greatest degree of routine work and task specialization now appears to be in services and especially in clerical jobs. For example, fast-food operations have adopted many of the job-design and task-specialization principles of assembly lines to produce hamburgers. Such jobs tend to be low-paying and repetitive, and workers are easily replaced—familiar characteristics of traditional job-design principles.

Contemporary service jobs often exhibit characteristics of scientific management.

The traditional approaches and the current trends in job design and the differences between them are depicted in Figure 8.1.

The Elements of Job Design

In this section we focus on designing jobs and the factors that must be considered.

The elements of job design fall into three categories: an analysis of the tasks included in the job, employee requirements, and the environment in which the job takes place. These categories address the questions of how the job is performed, who does it, and

Elements of job design: analysis of tasks, worker requirements, and job environment.

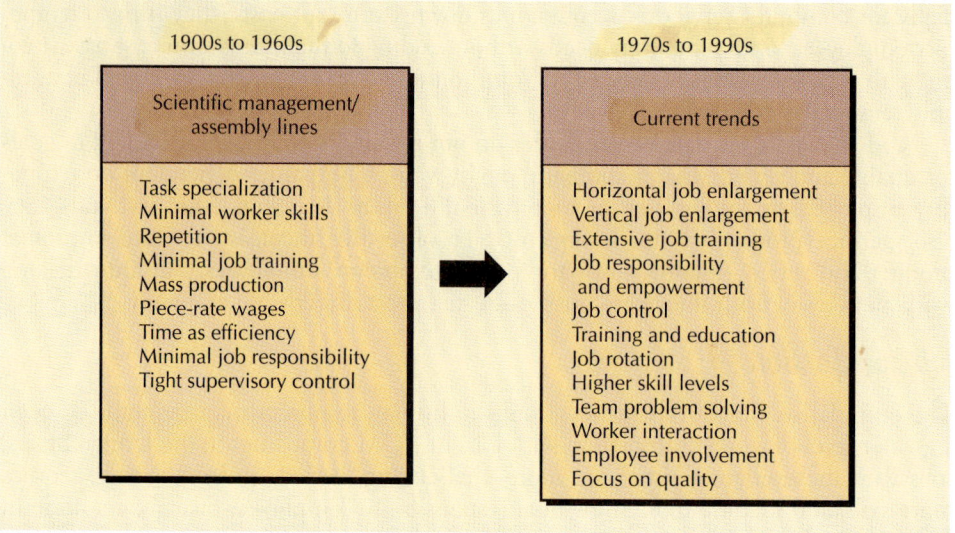

FIGURE 8.1 The Evolution of Job Design

where it is done. Table 8.1 summarizes a selection of individual elements that would generally be considered in the job design process.

Task Analysis

Task analysis: how tasks fit together to form a job.

Task analysis determines how to do each task and how all the tasks fit together to form a job. It includes defining and describing the individual tasks, determining their most efficient sequence, their duration, their relationship with other tasks, and their frequency. Task analysis should be sufficiently detailed so that it results in a step-by-step procedure for the job. The sequence of tasks in some jobs is a logical ordering; for example, the wedges of material used in making a baseball cap must be cut before they can be sewn together, and they must all be sewn together before the cap bill can be at-

TABLE 8.1 Elements of Job Design

Task Analysis	*Worker Analysis*	*Environmental Analysis*
■ Description of tasks to be performed	■ Capability requirements	■ Workplace location
■ Task sequence	■ Performance requirements	■ Process location
■ Function of tasks	■ Evaluation	■ Temperature and humidity
■ Frequency of tasks	■ Skill level	■ Lighting
■ Criticality of tasks	■ Job training	■ Ventilation
■ Relationship with other jobs/tasks	■ Physical requirements	■ Safety
■ Performance requirements	■ Mental stress	■ Logistics
■ Information requirements	■ Boredom	■ Space requirements
■ Control requirements	■ Motivation	■ Noise
■ Error possibilities	■ Number of workers	■ Vibration
■ Task duration(s)	■ Level of responsibility	
■ Equipment requirements	■ Monitoring level	
	■ Quality responsibility	
	■ Empowerment level	

tached. The *performance requirements of a task* can be the time required to complete the task, the accuracy in performing the task to specifications, the output level or productivity yield, or quality performance. The performance of some tasks require information such as a measurement (cutting furniture pieces), temperature (food processing), weight (filling bags of fertilizer), or a litmus test (for a chemical process).

Performance require-ments of a task: time, accuracy, productivity, quality.

Worker Analysis

Worker analysis determines the characteristics the worker must possess to meet the job requirements, the responsibilities the worker will have in the job, and how the worker will be rewarded. Some jobs require manual labor and physical strength, whereas others require none. Physical requirements are assessed not only to make sure the right worker is placed in a job but also to determine if the physical requirements are excessive, necessitating redesign. The same type of design questions must be addressed for mental stress.

Determining worker capabilities and re-sponsibilities for a job

Environmental Analysis

Environmental analysis refers to the physical location of the job in the production or service facility and the environmental conditions that must exist. These conditions include such things as proper temperature, lighting, ventilation, and noise. The production of microchips requires an extremely clean, climatically controlled, enclosed environment. Detail work, such as engraving or sewing, requires proper lighting; some jobs that create dust levels, such as lint in textile operations, require proper ventilation. Some jobs require a large amount of space around the immediate job area.

Job environment: the physical characteristics and location of a job.

Job Analysis

Part of job design is to study the *methods* used in the work included in the job to see how it should be done. This has traditionally been referred to as *methods analysis,* or simply *work methods.*

Methods analysis used to redesign or improve existing jobs. An analyst will study an existing job to see how the work is done to determine if it is being done in the most efficient manner possible; if all the present tasks are necessary; or if new tasks should be added. The analyst might also want to see how the job fits in with other jobs—that is, how well a job is integrated into the overall production process or a sequence of jobs. The development and installation of new machinery or equipment, new products or product changes, and changes in quality standards can all require that a job be analyzed for redesign.

Methods analysis is also used to develop new jobs. In this case the analyst must work with a description or outline of a proposed job and attempt to develop a mental picture of how the job will be performed.

The primary tools of methods analysis are a variety of charts that illustrate in different ways how a job or a work process is done. These charts allow supervisors, managers, and workers to see how a job is accomplished and to get their input and feedback on the design or redesign process. Two of the more popular charts are the *process flowchart* and the *worker-machine chart.*

Work methods: study-ing how a job is done.

Process Flowchart

A **process flowchart** is used to analyze how the steps of a job or how a set of jobs fit together into the overall flow of the production process. Examples might include the flow

A **process flowchart** is a graph of the steps of a job.

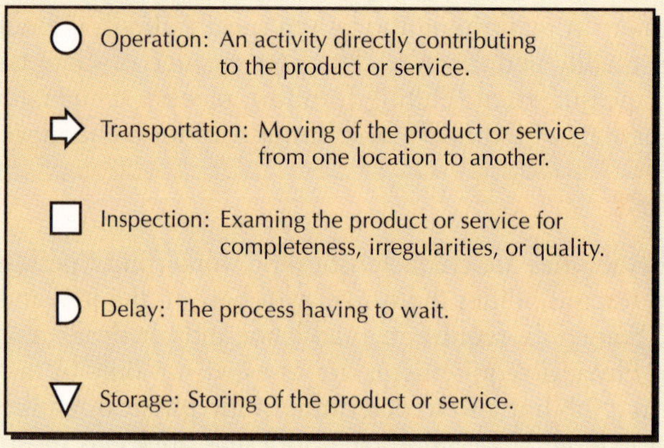

○ Operation: An activity directly contributing
to the product or service.

▷ Transportation: Moving of the product or service
from one location to another.

□ Inspection: Examing the product or service for
completeness, irregularities, or quality.

D Delay: The process having to wait.

▽ Storage: Storing of the product or service.

FIGURE 8.2   **Symbols for a Process Flowchart**

of a product through a manufacturing assembly process, the making of a pizza, the activities of a surgical team in an operating room, or the processing of a catalog mail or telephone order.

A process flowchart uses some basic symbols shown in Figure 8.2 to describe the tasks or steps in a job or a series of jobs. The symbols are connected by lines on the chart to show the flow of the process.

<table>
<tr><td>

EXAMPLE
8.1

*Developing a Job
Process Flowchart*

</td><td>

The QuikCopy Store does copying jobs for walk-in customers. When a customer comes in with a copy job, a desk operator fills out a work order (name, number of copies, quality of paper, etc.) and places it in a box. An operator subsequently picks up the job, makes the copies, and returns the completed job to the cashier, where the job transaction is completed. The store would like a job process flowchart that describes this sequence of tasks.

SOLUTION:

The process flowchart for the steps in this copying job are shown in Figure 8.3. Although the process encompasses several operators and jobs, it focuses primarily on the tasks of the copy machine operator, who actually makes the copies.

</td></tr>
</table>

Often a process flowchart is used in combination with other types of methods analysis charts and a written job description to form a comprehensive and detailed picture of a job. Essentially, the methods analyst is a "job detective," who wants to get as much evidence as possible about a job from as many perspectives as possible in order to improve the job.

Worker-Machine Chart

A worker-machine
chart determines if
worker and machine
time are used efficiently.

A **worker-machine chart** illustrates the amount of time a worker and a machine are working or idle in a job. This type of chart is occasionally used in conjunction with a process flowchart when the job process includes equipment or machinery. The worker-machine chart shows if the worker's time and the machine time are being used efficiently—that is, if the worker or machine is idle an excessive amount of time.

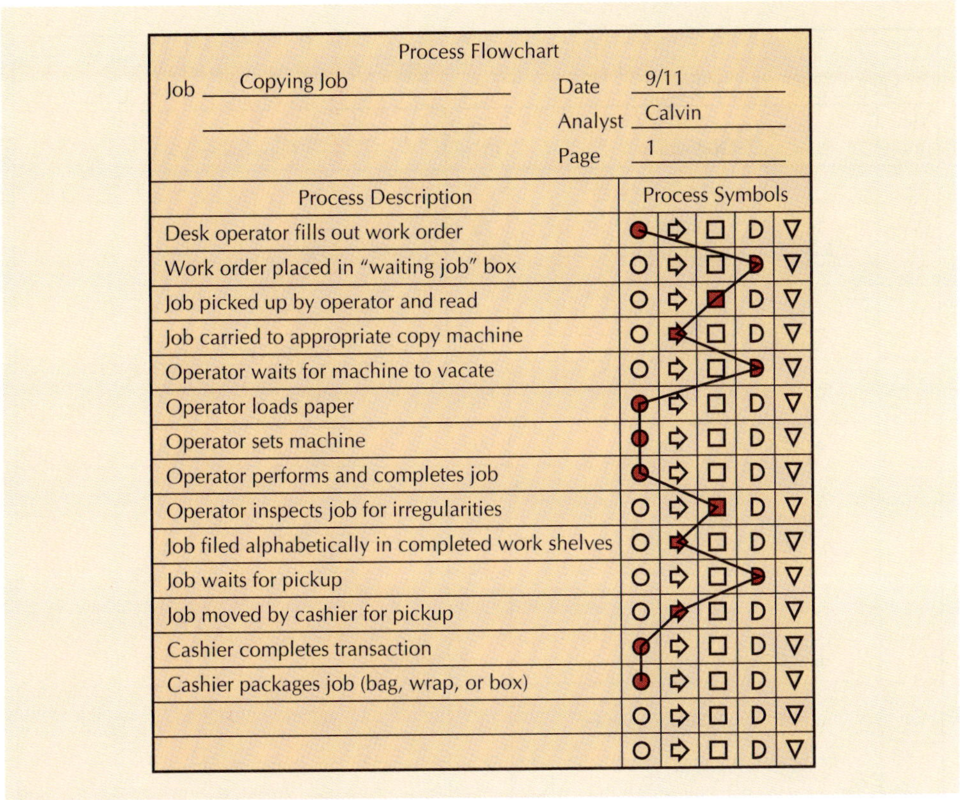

Process Flowchart						
Job _Copying Job_			Date	_9/11_		
			Analyst	_Calvin_		
			Page	_1_		
Process Description			**Process Symbols**			
Desk operator fills out work order	O	⇨	□	D	▽	
Work order placed in "waiting job" box	O	⇨	□	D	▽	
Job picked up by operator and read	O	⇨	■	D	▽	
Job carried to appropriate copy machine	O	⇨	□	D	▽	
Operator waits for machine to vacate	O	⇨	□	D	▽	
Operator loads paper	O	⇨	□	D	▽	
Operator sets machine	O	⇨	□	D	▽	
Operator performs and completes job	O	⇨	□	D	▽	
Operator inspects job for irregularities	O	⇨	■	D	▽	
Job filed alphabetically in completed work shelves	O	⇨	□	D	▽	
Job waits for pickup	O	⇨	□	D	▽	
Job moved by cashier for pickup	O	⇨	□	D	▽	
Cashier completes transaction	O	⇨	□	D	▽	
Cashier packages job (bag, wrap, or box)	O	⇨	□	D	▽	
	O	⇨	□	D	▽	
	O	⇨	□	D	▽	

FIGURE 8.3   Process Flowchart of Copying Job

EXAMPLE
8.2

*Developing a Worker-
Machine Chart*

The QuikCopy Store described in Example 8.1 also makes photo ID cards. An operator types in data about the customer on a card, submits this to the photo machine, positions the customer for the photo, and takes the photograph. The machine processes the photo ID card. The store would like to develop a worker-machine chart for this job.

SOLUTION:

Figure 8.4 on page 338 shows the worker-machine chart for the job of making photo ID cards.

The time scale along the left side of the chart provides a visual perspective of the amount of work and idle time in the job process. For this job, the summary at the bottom of Figure 8.4 indicates that the operator and machine were both working and idle approximately the same amount of time.

Another type of worker-machine chart is the *gang process chart*, which illustrates a job in which a team of workers are interacting with a piece of equipment or a machine. Examples include workers at a coal furnace in a steel mill or a military gunnery team on a battleship. A gang chart is constructed the same way as the chart in Figure 8.4, except there are columns for each of the different operators. The purpose of a gang process chart is to determine if the interaction between the workers is efficient and coordinated.

Worker-Machine Chart				
Job ___Photo-ID Cards___				Date ___10/14___
Time (min)	Operator	Time (min)		Photo Machine
1 — 2	Key in customer data on card	2.6		Idle
3	Feed data card in	0.4		Accept card
	Position customer for photo	1.0		Idle
4	Take picture	0.6		Begin photo process
5 — 6 — 7 — 8	Idle	3.4		Photo/card processed
8 — 9	Inspect card and trim edges	1.2		Idle
10				

Summary				
	Operator Time	%	Photo Machine Time	%
Work	5.8	63	4.8	52
Idle	3.4	37	4.4	48
Total	9.2 min	100%	9.2 min	100%

FIGURE 8.4 **Worker-Machine Chart**

Motion Study

Motion study is used to ensure efficiency of motion in a job.

The most detailed form of job analysis is **motion study,** the study of the individual human motions used in a task. The purpose of motion study is to make sure that a job task does not include any unnecessary motion by the worker and to select the sequence of motions that ensure that the task is being performed in the most efficient way.

Frank and Lillian Gilbreth developed motion study.

Motion study originated with Frank Gilbreth, a colleague of F. W. Taylor's at the turn of the century. F. W. Taylor's approach to the study of work methods was to select the best worker among a group of workers and use that worker's methods as the standard by which other workers were trained. Alternatively, Gilbreth studied many workers and from among them picked the best way to perform each activity. Then he combined these elements to form the "one best way" to perform a task.

Gilbreth and his wife, Lillian, used movies to study individual work motions in slow motion and frame by frame, called *micromotion analysis*. Using motion pictures the

Gilbreths carefully categorized the basic physical elements of motion used in work. They called these basic elements of motion **therbligs,** which is *Gilbreth* spelled backwards with the *t* and *h* reversed. Examples of therbligs (i.e., basic elemental motions) include *search* (look or feel for an item), *select* (choose from a group of items), *grasp* (enclose an item), *hold* (retain item after grasping), *position* (move an item), and *release* (let go of the item).

Therbligs are basic physical elements of motion.

The Gilbreths' research eventually evolved into a set of widely adopted *principles of motion study*, which companies have used as guidelines for the efficient design of work. These principles are categorized according to the efficient use of the *human body*, the efficient arrangement of the *workplace*, and the efficient use of *equipment and machinery*. The principles of motion study include about twenty-five rules for conserving motion. These rules can be grouped in the three categories shown in Table 8.2.

Principles of motion study: guidelines for work design.

Motion study and scientific management complemented each other. Motion study was effective for designing the repetitive, simplified, assembly line-type jobs characteristic of manufacturing operations. Frank Gilbreth's first subject was a bricklayer; through his study of this worker's motions, he was able to improve the bricklayer's productivity threefold. However, in Gilbreth's day, bricklayers were paid on the basis of how many bricks they could lay in an hour in a piece-rate wage system. Who would be able to find a bricklayer today paid according to such a system!

There has been a movement away from task specialization and simple, repetitive jobs in lieu of greater job responsibility and a broader range of tasks, which has reduced the use of motion study. Nevertheless, motion study is still employed for repetitive jobs, especially in service industries, such as postal workers in mailrooms, who process and route thousands of pieces of mail.

The Gilbreths, together with F. W. Taylor and Henry Gantt, are considered pioneers in operations management. The Gilbreths' use of motion pictures is still popular

Pioneers in the field of industrial engineering

TABLE 8.2   Summary of General Guidelines for Motion Study

Guiding Principles

Efficient Use of the Human Body
■ Work should be simplified, rhythmic, and symmetric.
■ Hand/arm motions should be coordinated and simultaneous.
■ The full extent of physical capabilities should be employed; all parts of the body should perform; the hand should never be idle.
■ Energy should be conserved by letting machines perform tasks when possible, minimizing the distance of movements, and physical momentum should be in favor of the worker.
■ Tasks should be simple, requiring minimal eye contact and minimal muscular effort, with no unnecessary motions, delays, or idleness.

Efficient Arrangement of the Workplace
■ All tools, materials, and equipment should have a designated, easily accessible location that minimizes the motions required to get them.
■ Seating and the general work environment should be comfortable and healthy.

Efficient Use of Equipment
■ Equipment and mechanized tools enhance worker abilities.
■ The use of foot-operated mechanized equipment that relieves the hand/arms of work should be maximized.
■ Equipment should be constructed and arranged to fit worker use.

today. Computer-generated images are used to analyze an athlete's movements to enhance performance, and video cameras are widely used to study everything from surgical procedures in the operating room to telephone operators.

Work Measurement

Work measurement is determining how long it takes to do a job. Managing human resources requires managers to know how much work employees can do during a specific period. Otherwise they cannot plan production schedules or output. Without a good idea of how long it takes to do a job, a company will not know if it can meet customer expectations for delivery or service time. Despite the unpopularity of wage-incentive systems among some TQM proponents, they are still widely used in the United States, and work measurement is required to set the output standards on which incentive rates are based. These wage rates determine the cost of a product or service.

Work measurement has also seen a revival within the ever-growing service sector. Services tend to be labor intensive and service jobs, especially clerical ones, are often repetitive. For example, sorting mail in the postal service, processing income tax returns in the IRS, making hamburgers at McDonald's, inputting data from insurance forms in a computer at Prudential, are all repetitive service jobs that can be measured, and standards can be set for output and wages. As a result work measurement is still an important aspect of operations management for many companies.

The traditional means for determining an estimate of the time to do a job has been the time study, in which a stopwatch is used to time the individual elements of a job. These elemental times are summed to get a time estimate for a job and then adjusted by a performance rating of the worker and an allowance factor for unavoidable delays, resulting in a **standard time.** The standard time is the time required by an "average" worker to perform a job once under normal circumstances and conditions.

Standard time is the time required by an average worker to perform a job once.

Work measurement and time study were introduced by Frederick W. Taylor in the late 1880s and 1890s. One of his objectives was to determine a "fair" method of job performance evaluation and payment, which at that time was frequently a matter of contention between management and labor. The basic form of wage payment was an incentive piece-rate system, in which workers were paid a wage rate per unit of output instead of an hourly wage rate; the more workers produced, the more they earned. The problem with this system at the time was that there was no way to determine a "normal," or "fair," rate of output. Management wanted the normal rate high, labor wanted it low. Since management made pay decisions, the piece rate was usually "tight," making it hard for the worker to make the expected, or fair, output rate. Thus, workers earned less. This was the scenario in which Taylor introduced his time study approach to develop an equitable piece-rate wage system based on fair standard job times.

Incentive piece-rate wage system based on time study

The stopwatch time study approach for work measurement was popular and widespread into the 1970s. Many union contracts in the automotive, textile, and other manufacturing industries for virtually every production job in a company were based almost entirely on standard times developed from time studies. However, the basic principle underlying an incentive wage system is that pay is the sole motivation for work. We have pointed out earlier in this chapter that this principle has been disproved. In fact, in recent years incentive wage systems have been shown to inhibit quality improvement.

Stopwatch time study used for work measurement

However, performance evaluation represents only one use for time study and work measurement. It is still widely used for planning purposes in order to predict the level of output a company might achieve in the future.

This person is performing a time study of an employee doing a manual task at a Hewlett-Packard plant. Although time studies are no longer as popular for establishing performance-based wage rates as they once were, they are still an effective means for studying jobs in order to improve them. Many jobs in manufacturing and especially in service businesses include simple, repetitive tasks, such as making a hamburger and wrapping it at McDonald's, checking in a rental car at Avis, or making a bed at a Ritz-Carlton. Reducing the time required to perform these tasks, while still making sure that they are done conscientiously and correctly by the employee, can result in quicker and more efficient customer-service and improved quality. However, speed and quickness only translates to good quality if they result in customer satisfaction.

Stopwatch Time Study

The result of a time study is a *standard time* for performing a repetitious job once. Time study is a statistical technique that is accurate for jobs that are highly repetitive.

The basic steps in a time study are:

1. *Establish the standard job method.* The job should be analyzed using methods analysis to make sure the best method is being used. *make sure worker knows how to do the* [Steps of a stopwatch time study] *job in this way.*

2. *Break down the job into elements.* The job is broken down into short, elemental tasks with obvious "break points" between them. The more detailed the elements, the easier it is to eliminate elemental times that are not normally included in each job cycle and might abnormally affect the standard time.

3. *Study the job.* Time studies have traditionally been conducted using a stopwatch attached to a clipboard, although hand-held electronic time-study machines (similar to an electronic calculator) are now available that store elemental times in a memory that can be transferred to a computer for processing. To conduct a time study with a stopwatch, the industrial engineer or technician takes a position near the worker and records each elemental time on an observation sheet. In recent years, videocameras

have been used to videotape jobs, with the time study conducted outside of the workplace at a later time.

4. *Rate the worker's performance.* As the time study is being conducted, the worker's performance is also rated by the person doing the study. The objective of the study is to determine a "normal," or average time for the job, so the engineer/technician must adjust the elemental times up or down with a rating factor. A performance rating factor of 100 percent reflects normal work performance, below 100 percent represents a below-average performance, and above 100 percent indicates performance better than normal. Rating factors usually range between 80 percent and 120 percent.

The observer conducting the study must, in effect, "judge" the difficulty of the job and mentally assess what normal performance is, primarily in terms of *speed.* Effort, or physical exertion, can also be a characteristic of performance; however, it must be viewed with caution, since a poor worker might exhibit a lot of exertion, whereas a good worker might exhibit little exertion in doing the same job.

The performance rating factor is a crucial component of the time study, but it is also subjective. The person conducting the study must be very familiar with the job in order to rate accurately the worker's performance. Films and videos are available that show different levels of performance, effort, and speed for a variety of motions, tasks, and jobs. Even then it is often difficult to evaluate performance during an actual study.

Workers are not always cooperative, and they sometimes resent time studies, especially if they know they are being used to set wages. They will purposely slow or speed up their normal work rate, make frequent mistakes, or alter the normal work methods, all designed to disrupt the work study.

It is easy to understand why quality consultants and teachers perceive incentive wage systems and work measurement to be detrimental to quality improvement.

5. *Compute the average time.* Once a sufficient number of job cycles have been observed, an average time for each work element is calculated. We talk more about the appropriate number of cycles to include in the study a little later.

6. *Compute the normal time.* The **normal time** is calculated by multiplying the elemental average time by the performance rating factor:

$$\text{Normal time} = (\text{elemental average time})(\text{rating factor})$$

or

$$Nt = (\bar{t})(RF)$$

The normal cycle time (NT) is computed by summing the elemental normal times,

$$NT = \Sigma Nt$$

7. *Compute the standard time.* The standard time is computed by adjusting the normal cycle time by an allowance factor for unavoidable work delays (such as a machine breakdown), personal delays (such as using the rest room), and normal mental or physical fatigue. The allowance factor is a percentage increase in the normal cycle time. The standard time is calculated as:

$$\text{Standard time} = (\text{normal cycle time})(1 + \text{allowance factor})$$

or

$$ST = (NT)(1 + AF)$$

RF

Determining the average time for a job

Judging job performance

Normal time is the elemental average time multiplied by a performance rating.

Allowing for abnormal factors

Allowance factor = personal+rest + delay

EXAMPLE
8.3

*Performing a Time
Study and Developing
a Standard Time*

The Metro Food Services Company delivers fresh sandwiches each morning to vending machines throughout the city. Workers work through the night to prepare the sandwiches for morning delivery. A worker normally makes several kinds of sandwiches. A time study for a worker making ham and cheese sandwiches is shown in Figure 8.5. Notice that each element has two readings. Row t includes the individual elemental times, whereas the R row contains a cumulative (running) clock reading recorded going down the column. In this case the individual elemental times are determined by subtracting the cumulative times between sequential readings.

RF below 1 means worker measured is slower than average.

Time Study Observation Sheet

Identification of operation		Sandwich Assembly										Date	5/17		

		Operator Smith				Approval Jones						Observer Russell			

		Cycles										Summary			
		1	2	3	4	5	6	7	8	9	10	Σt	$\bar{t}$	RF	Nt
1	Grasp and lay out bread slices	t 0.04	0.05	0.05	0.04	0.06	0.05	0.06	0.06	0.07	0.05	0.53	0.053	1.05	0.056
		R 0.04	0.38	0.72	1.05	1.40	1.76	2.13	2.50	2.89	3.29				
2	Spread mayonnaise on both slices	t 0.07	0.06	0.07	0.08	0.07	0.07	0.08	0.10	0.09	0.08	0.77	0.077	1.00	0.077
		R 0.11	0.44	0.79	1.13	1.47	1.83	2.21	2.60	2.98	3.37				
3	Place ham, cheese, and lettuce on bread	t 0.12	0.11	0.14	0.12	0.13	0.13	0.13	0.12	0.14	0.14	1.28	0.128	1.10	0.141
		R 0.23	0.55	0.93	1.25	1.60	1.96	2.34	2.72	3.12	3.51				
4	Place top on sandwich, slice, and stack	t 0.10	0.12	0.08	0.09	0.11	0.11	0.10	0.10	0.12	0.10	1.03	0.103	1.10	0.113
		R 0.33	0.67	1.01	1.34	1.71	2.07	2.44	2.82	3.24	3.61				
5		t													
		R													
6		t													
		R													
7		t													
		R													
8		t													
		R													
9		t													
		R													
10		t													
		R													

Normal cycle time ___0.387___ + Allowance ___15%___ = Std. time ___0.445 min.___

FIGURE 8.5 Time Study Observation Sheet

SOLUTION:

In Figure 8.5 the average element times are first computed as

$$\bar{t} = \frac{\Sigma t}{10}$$

For element 1 the average time is

$$\bar{t} = \frac{0.53}{10} = 0.053$$

The normal elemental times are computed by adjusting the average time, $\bar{t}$, by the performance rating factor, RF. For element 1 the normal time is

$$Nt = (\bar{t})(RF)$$
$$= (0.053)(1.05)$$
$$= 0.056$$

The normal cycle time, NT, is computed by summing the normal times for all elements, which for this example is 0.387. The standard time is computed by adjusting the normal cycle time by an allowance factor,

$$ST = (NT)(1 + AF)$$
$$= (0.387)(1 + 0.15)$$
$$= 0.445 \text{ min}$$

If, for example, the company wants to know how many ham and cheese sandwiches can be produced in a 2-hour period, they could simply divide the standard time into 120 minutes:

$$\frac{120 \text{ min}}{0.445 \text{ min/sandwich}} = 269.7 \text{ or } 270 \text{ sandwiches}$$

EXAMPLE 8.4

An Incentive Piece-Rate System

If the Metro Food Services Company pays workers a piece rate of $0.04 per sandwich, what would an average worker be paid per hour, and what would the subject of the time study in Example 8.3 expect to be paid?

SOLUTION:

The average worker would produce the following number of sandwiches in an hour:

$$\frac{60 \text{ min}}{0.445 \text{ min/sandwich}} = 134.8 \text{ or } 135 \text{ sandwiches}$$

The hourly wage rate would thus average

$$(135)(0.04) = \$5.40$$

Alternatively, the worker from Example 8.3 would produce at the average cycle time not adjusted by the rating factor, or 0.361 minutes. Adjusting this time by the allowance time results in a time of

$$(0.361)(1 + 0.15) = 0.415 \text{ min}$$

This worker could be expected to produce the following number of sandwiches per hour:

$$\frac{60 \text{ min}}{0.415 \text{ min/sandwich}} = 144.6 \text{ or } 145 \text{ sandwiches}$$

The average hourly wage rate for this worker would be

$$(145)(0.04) = \$5.80$$

or $0.40 more per hour.

An Excel spreadsheet of the time study observation sheet shown in Figure 8.5 is shown below in Exhibit 8.1.

Example 8.3. Performing a Time Study

Time Study Observation Sheet

Identification of Operation:		Sandwich Assembly											Date	5/17	
		Operator: Smith				Approval: Jones						Observer: Tillar			
		Cycles										Summary			
		1	2	3	4	5	6	7	8	9	10	Sum t	t	RF	Nt
1. Grasp and lay out	t	0	0.05	0.1	0.04	0.06	0.1	0.06	0.1	0.1	0.05	0.53	0.05	1.05	0.056
bread slices	R	0	0.38	0.7	1.05	1.40	1.8	2.13	2.50	2.9	3.29				
2. Spread mayonaise	t	0.1	0.06	0.1	0.08	0.07	0.1	0.08	0.10	0.1	0.08	0.77	0.08	1.00	0.077
on both slices	R	0.1	0.44	0.8	1.13	1.47	1.8	2.21	2.60	3	3.37				
3. Place ham,cheese	t	0.1	0.11	0.1	0.12	0.13	0.1	0.13	0.1	0.1	0.14	1.28	0.13	1.10	0.141
and lettuce on bread	R	0.2	0.55	0.9	1.25	1.60	2	2.34	2.7	3.1	3.51				
4. Place top, slice	t	0.10	0.12	0.1	0.09	0.11	0.1	0.10	0.10	0.1	0.10	1.03	0.1	1.10	0.113
and stack	R	0.3	0.67	1	1.34	1.71	2.1	2.44	2.8	3.2	3.61				

Normal cycle time = _0.387_ + Allowance _15%_ = Standard time _0.445 min._

EXHIBIT 8.1

Number of Cycles

In Example 8.3 the time study was conducted for ten cycles. However, was this sufficient for us to have confidence that the standard time was accurate? The time study is actually a statistical sample distribution, where the number of cycles is the sample size.

Assuming that this distribution of sample times is normally distributed (a traditional assumption for time study), we can use the following formula to determine the sample size, n, for a time study:

Determining the statistically appropriate number of job cycles to study

$$n = \left(\frac{zs}{e\overline{T}}\right)^2$$

where

z = the number of standard deviations from the mean in a normal distribution reflecting a level of statistical confidence

$s = \sqrt{\dfrac{\Sigma(x_i - \bar{x})^2}{n - 1}}$ = sample standard deviation from the sample time study

$\bar{T}$ = the average job cycle time from the sample time study

e = the degree of error from the true mean of the distribution

---

EXAMPLE 8.5

Determining the Number of Cycles for a Time Study

In Example 8.3 the Metro Food Services Company conducted a time study for 10 cycles of a job assembling ham and cheese sandwiches, which we will consider to be a sample. The average cycle time, $\bar{T}$, for the job was 0.361 minutes, computed by dividing the total time for 10 cycles of the job, 3.61, by the number of cycles, 10. The standard deviation of the sample was 0.03 minutes. The company wants to determine the number of cycles for a time study such that it can be 95 percent confident that the average time computed from the time study is within 5 percent of the true average cycle time.

SOLUTION:

The sample size is computed using $Z = 1.96$ for a probability of 0.95, as follows

$$n = \left(\frac{zs}{e\bar{T}}\right)^2$$

$$= \left[\frac{(1.96)(0.03)}{(0.05)(0.361)}\right]^2$$

$$= 10.61, \text{ or } 11$$

The time study should include 11 cycles to be 95 percent confident that the time-study average job cycle time is within 5 percent of the true average job cycle time. The 10 cycles that were used in our time study were just about right.

Elemental Time Files

Workers often do not like to be the subject of a time study and will not cooperate, and rating workers can be a difficult, subjective task. Time studies can also be time-consuming and costly. As an alternative, many companies have accumulated large files of time study data over time for elements common to many jobs throughout their organization. Instead of conducting an actual time study, these **elemental standard time files** can be accessed to derive the standard time, or the elemental times in the files can be used in conjunction with current time study data, reducing the time and cost required for the study.

Elemental standard time files are predetermined job element times.

However, it can be difficult to put together a standard time without the benefit of a time study. The engineer/technician is left wondering if anything was left out or if the environment or job conditions have changed enough since the data were collected to alter the original elemental times. Also, the individuals developing the current standard time must have a great deal of confidence in their predecessor's abilities and competence.

Predetermined Motion Times

The use of elemental standard times from company files is one way to construct a standard time without a time study, or before a task or job is even in effect yet. Another approach for developing time standards without a time study is to use a system of **predetermined motion times**. A predetermined motion time system provides normal times for basic, generic micromotions, such as reach, grasp, move, position, and release, that are common to many jobs. These basic motion times have been developed in a laboratory-type environment from studies of workers across a variety of industries and, in some cases, from motion pictures of workers.

Predetermined motion times are predetermined times for basic micromotions.

To develop a standard time using predetermined motion times, a job must be broken down into its basic micromotions. Then the appropriate motion time is selected from a set of tables (or a computerized database), taking into account job conditions such as the weight of an object moved and the distance it might be moved. The standard time is determined by summing all the motion times. As might be suspected, even a very short job can have many motions; a job of only 1 minute can have more than 100 basic motions.

Several systems of predetermined motion times exist, the two most well known being methods time measurement (MTM) and basic motion time study (BMT). Table 8.3 provides an example of an MTM table for the motion *move*. The motion times are measured in *time measurement units*, or *TMUs*, where one TMU equals 0.0006 minutes and 100,000 TMUs equal one hour.

TABLE 8.3   MTM Table for MOVE

Distance Moved (inches)	Time (TMU)				Weight Allowance			Case and Description
	A	B	C	Hand in motion B	Weight (lb) up to:	Dynamic factor	Static constant TMU	
$^3/_4$ or less	2.0	2.0	2.0	1.7				
1	2.5	2.9	3.4	2.3	2.5	1.00	0	
2	3.6	4.6	5.2	2.9				A. Move object
3	4.9	5.7	6.7	3.6	7.5	1.06	2.2	to other
4	6.1	6.9	8.0	4.3				hand or
5	7.3	8.0	9.2	5.0	12.5	1.11	3.9	against stop.
6	8.1	8.9	10.3	5.7				
7	8.9	9.7	11.1	6.5	17.5	1.17	5.6	
8	9.7	10.6	11.8	7.2				
9	10.5	11.5	12.7	7.9	22.5	1.22	7.4	B. Move object
10	11.3	12.2	13.5	8.6				to approximate
12	12.9	13.4	15.2	10.0	27.5	1.28	9.1	or indefinite
14	14.4	14.6	16.9	11.4				location.
16	16.0	15.8	18.7	12.8	32.5	1.33	10.8	
18	17.6	17.0	20.4	14.2				
20	19.2	18.2	22.1	15.6	37.5	1.39	12.5	
22	20.8	19.4	23.8	17.0				
24	22.4	20.6	25.5	18.4	42.5	1.44	14.3	C. Move object
26	24.0	21.8	27.3	19.8				to exact
28	25.5	23.1	29.0	21.2	47.5	1.50	16.0	location.
30	27.1	24.3	30.7	22.7				
Additional	0.8	0.6	0.85		TMU per inch over 30 in.			

SOURCE: MTM Association for Standards and Research.

There are several advantages of using a predetermined motion time system. It enables a standard time to be developed for a new job before the job is even part of the production process. Worker cooperation and compliance are not required, and the workplace is not disrupted. Performance ratings are included in the motion times, eliminating this subjective part of developing standard times.

There are also disadvantages with a predetermined motion time system. It ignores the job context within which a single motion takes place—that is, where each motion is considered independently of all others. What the hand comes from doing when it reaches for an object may effect the motion time as well as the overall sequence of motion. Also, although predetermined motion times are generally determined from a broad sample of workers across several industries, they may not reflect the skill level, training, or abilities of workers in a specific company.

Work Sampling

Work sampling is a technique for determining the proportion of time a worker or machine spends on various activities. The procedure for work sampling is to make brief, random observations of a worker or machine over a period of time and record the activity in which they are involved. An estimate of the proportion of time that is being spent on an activity is determined by dividing the number of observations recorded for that activity by the total number of observations. A work sample can indicate the proportion of time a worker is busy or idle or performing a task or how frequently a machine is idle or in use. A secretary's work can be sampled to determine what portion of the day is spent wordprocessing, answering the telephone, filing, and so on. It also can be used to determine the allowance factor that was used to calculate the standard time for a time study. (Recall that the allowance factor was a percentage of time reflecting worker delays and idle time for machine breakdowns, personal needs, etc.)

The primary uses of work sampling are to determine *ratio delay*, which is the percentage of time a worker or machine is delayed or idle, and to analyze jobs that have *nonrepetitive tasks*—for example, a secretary, a nurse, or a police officer. The information from a work sample in the form of the percentage of time spent on each job activity or task can be useful in designing or redesigning jobs, developing job descriptions, and determining the level of work output that can be expected from a worker for use in planning.

The steps in work sampling are summarized as follows.

1. *Define the job activities.* The activities that are to be observed must be complete so that any time an observation is made, an activity is clearly indicated. For example, if the activities of interest are "worker idle" and "worker not idle," this clearly defines all possible activities for the work sample.

2. *Determine the number of observations in the work sample.* The purpose of the work sample is to calculate a proportion of time that a worker is performing a specific job activity. The degree of accuracy of the work sample depends on the number of observations, or sample size. The larger the sample size, the more accurate the proportion estimate will be. The accuracy of the proportion, p, is usually expressed in terms of an allowable degree of error, e (for example, 3 or 4 percent), with a degree of confidence of, for example, 95 to 98 percent. Using these parameters and assuming the sample is approximately normally distributed, the sample size can be determined using the following formula:

$$n = \left(\frac{z}{e}\right)^2 p(1 - p)$$

where

> n = the sample size (number of sample observations)
>
> z = the number of standard deviations from the mean for the desired level of confidence
>
> e = the degree of allowable error in the sample estimate
>
> p = the proportion of time spent on a work activity estimated prior to calculating the work sample

3. *Determine the length of the sampling period.* The length of the work sampling study must be sufficient to record the number of observations for the work activity determined in step 2. The schedule of observations must be random. (If workers knew an observation would be taken every half hour, they might alter their normal work activity.) The most direct way to achieve randomness is to tie the observation schedule to a table or computer program of random numbers. For example, if a table of three-digit random numbers is used, the first one or two random numbers in the digit could specify the time in minutes between observations.

4. *Conduct the work sampling study and record the observations.* In the final step the observations are tallied and the proportion, p, is computed by dividing the number of activity observations by the total number of observations.

5. *Periodically recompute the number of observations.* Recall from step 2 that p is an estimate of the proportion of time spent on a work activity made prior to the sample. As the work sample is conducted it may be discovered that the actual proportion is different than what was originally estimated. Therefore, it is beneficial periodically to recompute the sample size, n, based on preliminary values of p to see if more or fewer observations are needed than first determined.

EXAMPLE 8.6

Conducting a Work Sampling Study

for 95% confidence

$Z = 1.96$

The Northern Lights Company is a retail catalog operation specializing in outdoor clothing. The company has a pool of 28 telephone operators to take catalog orders during the business hours of 9:00 A.M. to 5:00 P.M. (The company uses a smaller pool of operators for the remaining 16 off-peak hours.) The company has recently been experiencing a larger number of lost calls because operators are busy and suspects it is because the operators are spending around 30 percent of their time describing products to customers. The company believes that if operators knew more about the products instead of having to pull up a description screen on the computer each time a customer asked a question about a product, they could save a lot of operator time, so it is thinking about instituting a product awareness training program. However, first the company wants to perform a work sampling study to determine the proportion of time operators are answering product-related questions. The company wants the proportion of this activity to be accurate within ±2 percent, with a 95 percent degree of confidence.

SOLUTION:

First determine the number of observations to take, as follows:

$$n = \left(\frac{z}{e}\right)^2 p(1 - p)$$

$$= \left(\frac{1.96}{0.02}\right)^2 (0.3)(0.7)$$

$$= 2{,}016.84, \text{ or } 2{,}017$$

(Continued)

This is a large number of observations, however; since there are 28 operators, only 2,017/28, or 72, visits to observe the operators need to be taken. Actually, the observations could be made by picking up a one-way phone line to listen in on the operator-customer conversation. The "conversation" schedule was set up using a two-digit random number table (similar to Table S12.2). The random numbers are the minutes between each observation, and since the random numbers ranged from 00 to 99, the average time between observations is about 50 minutes. The study was expected to take about 8 days (with slightly over 9 observations per day).

In fact, after 10 observation trips and a total of 280 observations, the portion of time the operators spent answering the customers' product-related questions was 38 percent, so the random sample size was recomputed,

$$n = \left(\frac{1.96}{0.02}\right)^2 (0.38)(0.62)$$
$$= 2{,}263$$

This number of observations is 246 more than originally computed, or almost 9 additional observation trips, resulting in a total of 81. (As noted previously, it is beneficial periodically to recompute the sample size based on preliminary results in order to ensure that the final result will reflect the degree of accuracy and confidence originally specified.)

Work sampling is a cheaper, easier approach to work measurement.

Work sampling is an easier, cheaper, and quicker approach to work measurement than time study. It tends to be less disruptive of the workplace and less annoying to workers, because it requires much less time to sample than time study. Also, the "symbolic" stopwatch is absent. A disadvantage is the large number of observations needed to obtain an accurate sample estimate, sometimes requiring the study to span several days or weeks.

Learning Curves

www.prenhall.com/russell

A learning curve illustrates the improvement rate of workers as a job is repeated.

As workers produce more items, they become better at their job.

The processing time per unit decreases by a constant percentage each time output doubles.

A learning curve, or *improvement curve*, is a graph that reflects the fact that as workers repeat their tasks, they will improve performance. The learning curve effect was introduced in 1936 in an article in the *Journal of Aeronautical Sciences* by T. P. Wright, who described how the direct labor cost for producing airplanes decreased as the number of planes produced increased. This observation and the rate of improvement were found to be strikingly consistent across a number of airplane manufacturers. The premise of the learning curve is that improvement occurs because workers learn how to do a job better as they produce more and more units. However, it is generally recognized that other production-related factors also improve performance over time, such as methods analysis and improvement, job redesign, retooling, and worker motivation.

Figure 8.6 illustrates the general relationship defined by the learning curve; as the number of cumulative units produced increases, the labor time per unit decreases. Specifically, the learning curve reflects the fact that each time the number of units produced doubles, the processing time per unit decreases by a constant percentage.

The decrease in processing time per unit as production doubles will normally range from 10 to 20 percent. The convention is to describe a learning curve in terms of 1, or 100 percent, minus the percentage rate of improvement. For example, an 80 percent

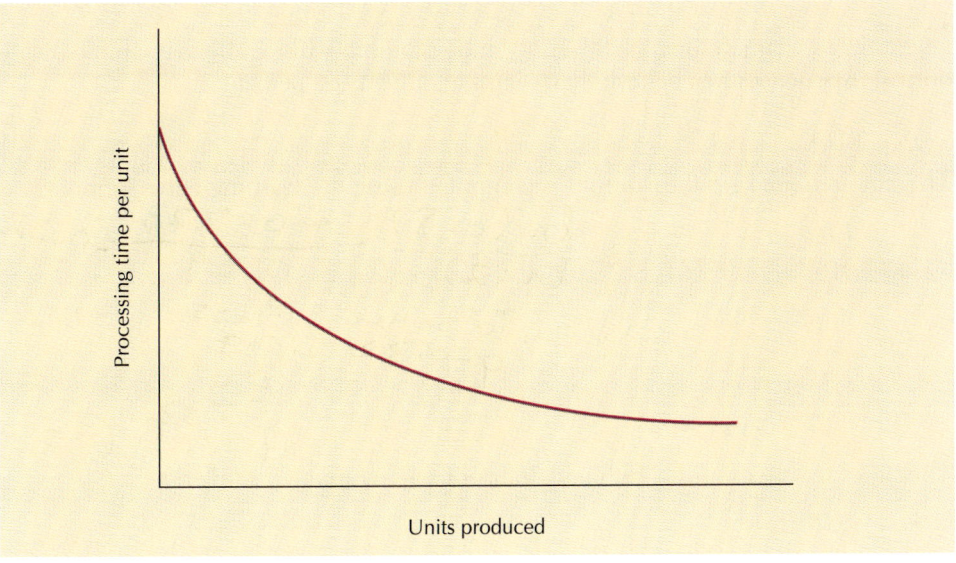

FIGURE 8.6   Learning Curve

learning curve describes an improvement rate of 20 percent each time production doubles, a 90 percent learning curve indicates a 10 percent improvement rate, and so forth.

The learning curve in Figure 8.6 is similar to an exponential distribution. The corresponding learning curve formula for computing the time required for the *n*th unit produced is

$$t_n = t_1 n^b$$

where

t_n = the time required for the *n*th unit produced
t_1 = the time required for the first unit produced
n = the cumulative number of units produced
$b = \ln r / \ln 2$, where *r* is the learning curve percentage (coefficient)

The lower 'r' - the faster you are learning.

EXAMPLE
8.7

Determining the Learning Curve Effect

Paulette Taylor and Maureen Becker, two undergraduates at State University, produce customized personal computer systems at night in their apartment (hence the name of their enterprise, PM Computer Services). They shop around and purchase cheap components and then put together generic personal computers, which have various special features, for faculty, students, and local businesses. Each time they get an order, it takes them a while to assemble the first unit, but they learn as they go, and they reduce the assembly time as they produce more units. They have recently received their biggest order to date from the statistics department at State for 36 customized personal computers. It is near the end of the university's fiscal year, and the computers are needed quickly to charge them on this year's budget. Paulette and Maureen assembled the first unit as a trial and found that it took them 18 hours of direct labor. To determine if they can fill the order in the time allotted, they want to apply the learning curve effect to

(Continued)

determine how much time the 9th, 18th, and 36th units will require to assemble. Based on past experience they believe their learning curve is 80 percent.

SOLUTION:

The time required for the 9th unit is computed using the learning curve formula:

$$t_n = t_1 n_b$$

$$t_9 = (18)(9)^{\ln(0.8)/\ln 2}$$

$$\frac{\ln(0.8)}{\ln(2)} = \frac{-0.223}{0.69} = 0.32$$

$$= (18)(9)^{-0.322} = \frac{18}{(9)} 0.322$$

To solve   Press:

$$9^{-0.32}$$

① 9 $\times$
② y^x
③ .32
④ $+/-$ ⑤ $=$

$$= (18)(0.493)$$

$$= 8.874 \text{ hours}$$

The times required for the 18th and 36th units are computed similarly:

$$t_{18} = (18)(18)^{\ln(0.8)/\ln 2}$$

$$= (18)(0.394)$$

$$= 7.092 \text{ hours}$$

and

$$t_{36} = (18)(36)^{\ln(0.8)/\ln 2}$$

$$= (18)(0.315)$$

$$= 5.67 \text{ hours}$$

Learning curves are not effective for mass production jobs.

Learning curves are useful for measuring work improvement for nonrepetitive, complex jobs requiring a long time to complete, such as building airplanes. For short, repetitive, and routine jobs, there may be little relative improvement, and it may occur in a brief time span during the first (of many) job repetitions. For that reason, learning curves can have limited use for mass production and assembly line–type jobs. A learning curve for this type of operation sometimes achieves any improvement early in the process and then flattens out and shows virtually no improvement, as reflected in Figure 8.7.

Advantages of learning curves: planning labor, budget, and scheduling requirements.

Learning curves help managers project labor and budgeting requirements in order to develop production scheduling plans. Knowing how many production labor hours will be required over time can enable managers to determine the number of workers to hire. Also, knowing how many labor hours will eventually be required for a product can help managers make overall product cost estimates to use in bidding for jobs and later for determining the product selling price. However, product or other changes during the production process can negate the learning curve effect.

Limitations of learning curves: product modifications negate lc effect, improvement can derive from sources besides learning, industry-derived lc rates may be inappropriate.

Determining Learning Curves with Excel

Learning curves can be calculated using Excel. The Excel spreadsheet for Example 8.7 is shown on page 354 in Exhibit 8.2. Notice that cell C8 is highlighted and the learning curve formula for computing the time required for the 9th unit is shown on the toolbar at the top of the screen. This formula includes the learning curve coefficient in cell D4, the time required for the first unit produced in cell D3, and the target unit in B8.

POM for Windows, used elsewhere in this text, also has a module for learning curves that will provide a learning curve graph.

Aircraft manufacturers like Boeing shown here have long relied on learning curves for production planning. Learning curves were first recognized in the aircraft industry in 1936 by T. P. Wright. Aircraft production at that time required a large amount of direct labor for assembly work, thus any marked increases in productivity were clearly recognizable. Based on empirical analysis, Wright discovered that on average when output doubled in the aircraft industry, labor requirements decreased by approximately 20 percent; that is, an 80 percent learning curve. During World War II when aircraft manufacturing proliferated, the learning curve became a tool for planning and an integral part of military aircraft contracts. Studies during these years demonstrated the existence of the learning curve in other industries as well. For example, studies of historical production figures at Ford Motor Company from 1909 to 1926 showed productivity improved for the Model T according to an 86 percent learning curve. The learning curve effect was subsequently shown to exist not only in labor-intensive manufacturing but also in capital-intensive manufacturing industries such as petroleum refining, steel, paper, construction, electronics and apparel, as well as in clerical operations.

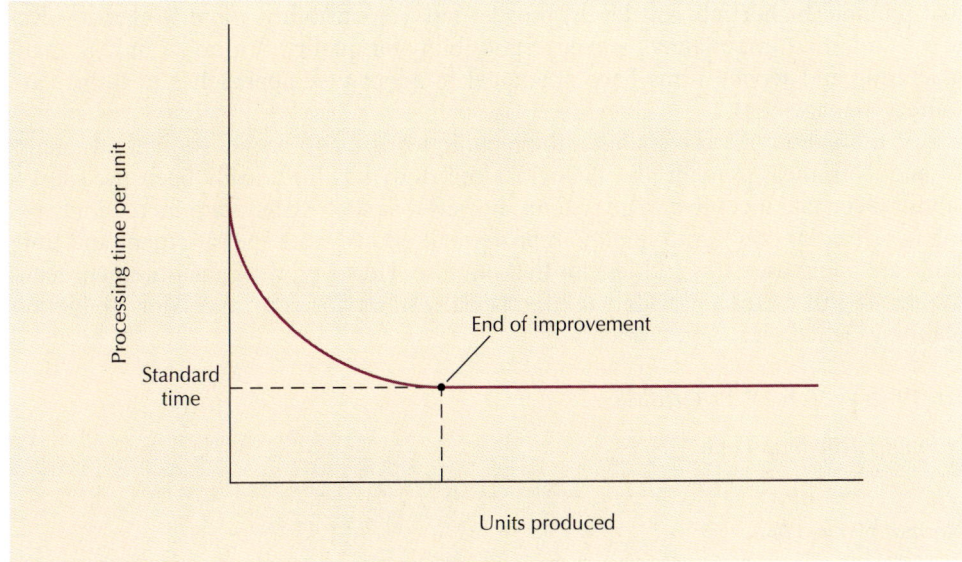

FIGURE 8.7   **Learning Curve for Mass Production Job**

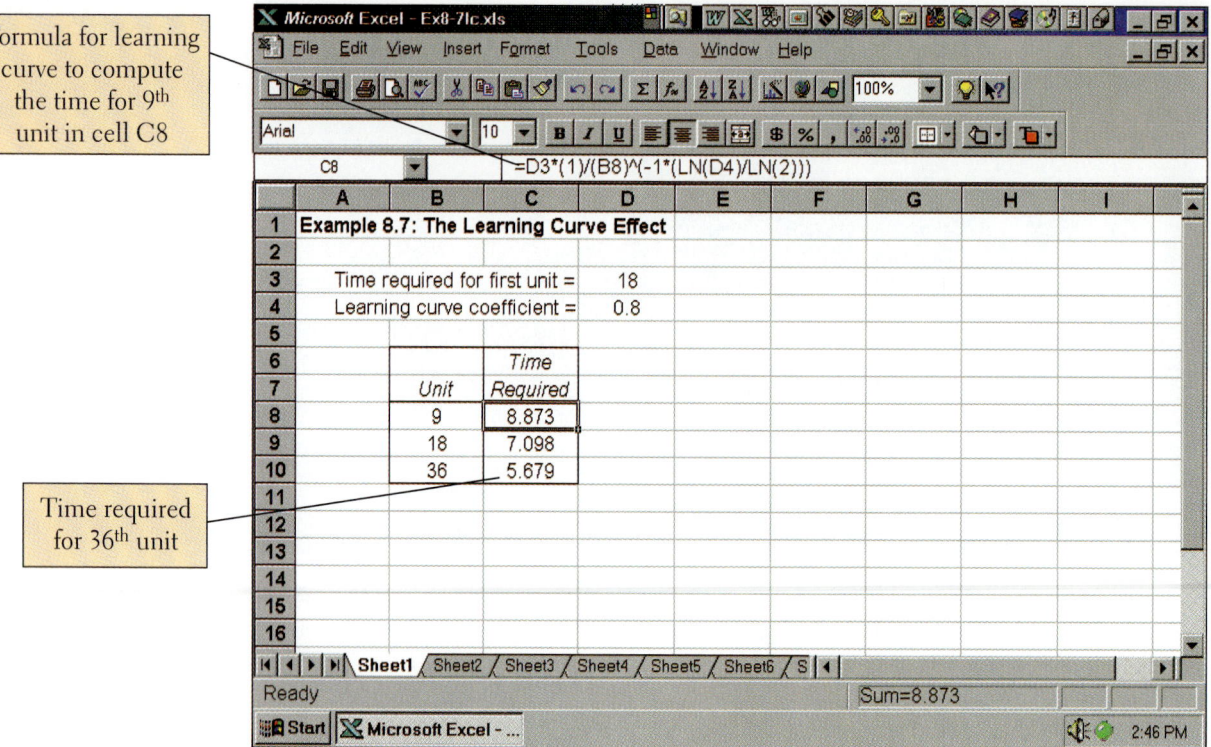

Formula for learning curve to compute the time for 9th unit in cell C8

Time required for 36th unit

EXHIBIT 8.2

Summary

As with many other areas in production and operations management, the quality movement and increased international competition have had a dramatic impact on human resources. Traditional approaches to work in the United States that once focused on task specialization, simplification, and repetition are being supplanted by approaches that promote higher job skill levels, broader task responsibility, more worker involvement, and, most importantly, worker responsibility for quality. A number of U.S. manufacturing and service firms have attempted to adopt new approaches to human resources management.

As the nature of work changes, the techniques and approaches to methods analysis and work measurement also change. Time study has historically been used to establish piece-rate incentive wage systems; however, as such systems are increasingly being perceived as counter to quality improvement efforts, work measurement and time study are being used less and less for that purpose. However, work measurement techniques are still useful and widely used, especially in service companies, for production planning, scheduling, and cost control.

Summary of Key Formulas

Normal Elemental Time

$$Nt = (\bar{t})(RF)$$

Normal Cycle Time

$$NT = \Sigma Nt$$

Standard Job Time
$$ST = (NT)(1 + AF)$$

Time Study Sample Size
$$n = \left(\frac{zs}{e\overline{T}} \right)^2$$

Work Sampling Sample Size
$$n = \left(\frac{z}{e} \right)^2 p(1 - p)$$

Learning Curve Formula
$$t_n = t_1 n^{\ln r / \ln 2}$$

Summary of Key Terms

elemental standard time files: company files containing historical data of elemental time studies that can be used to develop a standard time.

empowerment: the authority and responsibility of the workers to alert management about job-related problems.

horizontal job enlargement: the scope of a job that includes all tasks necessary to complete a product or process.

job: a defined set of tasks that comprise the work performed by employees that contributes to the production of a product or delivery of a service.

job motions: basic physical movements that comprise a job element.

job rotation: the capability of workers to move to different jobs.

learning curve: a graph that reflects the improvement rate of workers as a job is repeated and more units are produced.

motion study: the study of the individual human motions used in a task.

normal time: in a time study, the elemental average time multiplied by a performance rating.

predetermined motion times: normal times for basic, generic micromotions developed by an outside organization in a laboratory-type environment.

process flowchart: a flowchart that illustrates, with symbols, the steps for a job or how several jobs fit together within the flow of the production process.

standard time: the time required by an "average" worker to perform a job once under normal circumstances and conditions.

tasks: individual, defined job activities that consist of one or more elements.

therbligs: a term for the basic physical elements of motion.

vertical job enlargement: the degree of self-determination and control allowed workers over their own work; also referred to as job enrichment.

work sampling: a technique for determining the proportion of time a worker or machine spends on job activities.

worker-machine chart: a chart that illustrates on a time scale the amount of time an operator and a machine are working or are idle in a job.

Solved Problems

1. Standard Job Time

A manufacturing company has conducted a time study for ten cycles of a job. The job has five elements and the total elemental times (minutes) for each element and performance rating factors are as follows.

Element	Σt (min)	RF
1	3.61	1.05
2	4.84	0.90
3	2.93	1.00
4	4.91	1.10
5	1.78	0.95

Compute the standard time using an allowance factor of 18 percent.

Solution:

Step 1. Determine the normal elemental times by multiplying the average elemental times by the rating factors.

Element	Σt	$\bar{t}$	RF	$N\bar{t}$
1	3.61	0.361	1.05	0.379
2	4.84	0.484	0.90	0.436
3	2.93	0.293	1.00	0.293
4	4.91	0.491	1.10	0.542
5	1.78	0.178	0.95	0.169

Step 2. Compute the normal cycle time.

$$NT = \Sigma Nt$$
$$= 1.819 \text{ min}$$

Step 3. Compute the standard time.

$$ST = NT\,(1 + AF)$$
$$= 1.819(1 + 0.18)$$
$$= 2.146 \text{ min}$$

2. Time Study Sample Size

For the previous problem, determine the sample size, n, for a time study so there is 98 percent confidence that the average time computed from the time study is within 4 percent of the actual average cycle time. The sample standard deviation is 0.23.

Solution:

Step 1. Determine the value of z for a probability of 0.98 from the normal table in Appendix A and $\bar{t}$.

$$\overline{T} = \Sigma t = 1.807 \text{ min}$$
$$z = 2.33$$

Step 2. Compute the sample size.

$$n = \left(\frac{zs}{e\overline{T}}\right)^2$$
$$= \left[\frac{(2.33)(0.23)}{(0.04)(1.807)}\right]^2$$
$$= 54.97, \text{ or } 55 \text{ cycles}$$

3. Work Sampling

A technician is conducting a work sampling study of a machine maintenance worker to determine the portion of the time the worker spends in one particular department. Management has indicated that they believe that repairs in this department consume 50 percent of the maintenance worker's time, and they want the estimate to be within ±5 percent of the true proportion, with 95 percent confidence.

Solution:

Determine the number of observations in the sample.

$$n = \left(\frac{z}{e}\right)^2 p(1 - p)$$
$$= \left(\frac{1.96}{0.05}\right)^2 (0.5)(0.5)$$
$$= 384.16, \text{ or } 385 \text{ observations}$$

4. Learning Curve

A military contractor is manufacturing an electronic component for a weapons system. It is estimated from the production of a prototype unit that 176 hours of direct labor will be required to produce the first unit. The industrial standard learning curve for this type of component is 90 percent. The contractor wants to know the labor hours that will be required for the 144th (and last) unit produced.

Solution:

Determine the time for the 144th unit.

$$t_n = t_1 n^b$$
$$t_{144} = (176)(144)^{\ln(0.9)/\ln 2}$$
$$= (176)(4.69)$$
$$= 82.69 \text{ hours}$$

Questions

8-1. Discuss how human resources affects a company's strategic planning process.

8-2. Why has the name "human resources" become popular in recent years?

8-3. Describe the characteristics of job design according to the scientific management approach.

8-4. Describe the contributions of F. W. Taylor and the Gilbreths to job design and analysis, and work measurement.

8-5. Explain the difference between horizontal and vertical job enlargement.

8-6. What is the difference between tasks, elements, and motions in a basic job structure?

8-7. How did the development of the assembly line production process at Ford Motor Company popularize the scientific management approach to job design?

8-8. Why were the principles of scientific management not adopted in Japan during the first half of the twentieth century as they were in the United States and other Western nations?

8-9. Contrast the traditional U.S. approaches to job design with current trends.

8-10. What are the advantages of the scientific management approach to job design (specifically, task specialization, simplicity, and repetition) to both management and the worker?

8-11. Describe the primary characteristics of the behavioral approach to job design.

8-12. How has the increased emphasis on quality improvement affected human resources management in the United States?

8-13. How successful have companies in the United States been in adapting new trends in job design that mostly have originated in Japan?

8-14. Describe the three major categories of the elements of job design.

8-15. Describe the differences between a process flowchart and a worker-machine chart and what they are designed to achieve.

8-16. Compare the use of predetermined motion times for developing time standards instead of using time study methods and discuss the advantages and disadvantages.

8-17. Describe the steps involved in conducting a time study, and discuss any difficulties you might envision at various steps.

8-18. What are some of the criticisms of work measurement, in general, and time study, specifically, that have caused its popularity to wane in recent years?

8-19. A traditional performance rating benchmark (or guideline) for "normal" effort, or speed, is dealing 52 cards into four piles, forming a square with each pile 1 foot apart, in 0.50 minute. Conduct an experiment with one or more fellow students, where one deals the cards and the others rate the dealer's performance, and then compare these subjective ratings with the actual time of the dealer.

8-20. When conducting a work sampling study, how can the number of observations required by the study be reduced?

8-21. When is work sampling a more appropriate work measurement technique than time study?

8-22. Describe the steps involved in conducting a work sample.

8-23. Select a job that you are conveniently able to observe, such as a secretary, store clerk, or custodian, and design a work sampling study for a specific job activity. Indicate how the initial estimate of the proportion of time for the activity would be determined and how the observation schedule would be developed. (However, do not conduct the actual study.)

8-24. For what type of jobs are learning curves most useful?

8-25. What does a learning curve specifically measure?

8-26. Discuss some of the uses and limitations of learning curves.

Problems

8-1. A time study technician at the Southern Textile Company has conducted a time study of a spinning machine operator that spins rough cotton yarn into a finer yarn on bobbins for use in a weaving operation. The time study was requested as the result of a union grievance. The average cycle time for the operator to replace all the full bobbins on the machine with empty bobbins was 3.62 minutes. The technician assigned an overall performance rating for the job of 100 percent, and the allowance factor specified by the union contract is 15 percent. Compute the standard time for this job.

8-2. A sewing operator at the Gameday Sportswear Company assembles baseball-style caps with a team logo from precut wedges of material that form the crown, a precut bill, and additional precut pieces of material for the headband and reinforcing. The job encompasses seven basic elements. A time technician for the company has conducted a time study of the job for 20 cycles and accumulated the following elemental times and assigned performance ratings.

Element	Σt	RF
1	3.15	1.10
2	8.67	1.05
3	14.25	1.10
4	11.53	1.00
5	6.91	0.95
6	5.72	1.05
7	5.38	1.05

Determine the standard time for this job using an allowance factor of 12 percent.

8-3. The Braykup China Company makes an assortment of gift and commemorative items with team and college logos, such as plates, bowls, and mugs. One popular item is a commemorative stein. The steins are all physically identical, with the only style change being the team colors, name, and logo. The stein parts include a porcelain mug, a hinged pewter top that is opened up when someone drinks from the mug, and a bracket that attaches the top to the mug handle. The bracket is soldered together from two matching parts; on one end, the bracket encircles the handle and the other end attaches to the lid mechanism. The stein is assembled from these parts in one job. A time study chart for this job with the elements of the job and the time observations obtained from a stopwatch time study are as follows.

Time Study Observation Sheet															
Identification of operation			*Stein assembly*								Date	7/15			
		Operator Smith				Approval Jones					Observer Russell				
		Cycles										Summary			
		1	2	3	4	5	6	7	8	9	10	Σt	t̄	RF	Nt
1 Place mug in vice/ holder upside down	t														
	R	0.12	2.05	4.04	5.92	7.86	9.80	11.73	13.65	15.64	17.59			1.05	
2 Press both bracket sides around handle	t														
	R	0.19	2.12	4.09	6.01	7.94	9.88	11.81	13.72	15.7	17.66			1.00	
3 Solder bracket seam on inside of handle	t														
	R	1.05	3.01	4.91	6.87	8.81	10.71	12.66	14.56	16.52	18.50			1.10	
4 Turn stein right side up	t														
	R	1.13	3.08	4.98	6.93	8.90	10.79	12.74	14.66	16.63	18.59			1.10	
5 Solder lid top to bracket	t														
	R	1.75	3.76	5.65	7.60	9.56	11.45	13.36	15.34	17.31	19.28			1.05	
6 Remove stein from holder and place in box	t														
	R	1.91	3.90	5.79	7.75	9.70	11.61	13.53	15.49	17.46	19.44			1.00	
	t														

a. Using an allowance factor of 15 percent, determine the standard time for this job.
b. If the company pays workers a piece rate of $0.18 per stein, what wage would an average worker make per hour and what would the subject of this time study make per hour?

8-4. Puff'n Stuff Services is a small company that assembles mailings for clients in the Atlanta area. Different-size envelopes are stuffed with various items such as coupons, advertisements, political messages, and so on, by a staff of workers, who are paid on a piece-rate basis. A time study of a job has been conducted by an engineering consulting firm using a subject stuffing manila envelopes. The observations from the time study for ten cycles of the five-element job and the performance rating for each element are given next.

ELEMENTAL TIMES (MIN)											
ELEMENT	1	2	3	4	5	6	7	8	9	10	RF
1	0.09	0.10	0.12	0.09	0.08	0.07	0.09	0.06	0.10	0.09	1.10
2	0.08	0.09	0.08	0.07	0.10	0.10	0.08	0.06	0.11	0.09	0.95
3	0.15	0.13	0.14	0.16	0.12	0.15	0.16	0.15	0.15	0.14	0.90
4	0.10	0.09	0.09	0.08	0.11	0.08	0.09	0.10	0.10	0.09	1.00
5	0.06	0.05	0.09	0.06	0.07	0.05	0.08	0.05	0.09	0.07	0.95

a. Using an allowance factor of 10 percent, compute the standard time for this job.
b. If the firm pays workers a piece rate of $0.03 per envelope for this job, what would the average worker make per hour, and what would the subject of the study make per hour?

8-5. The Konishi Electronics Company manufactures computer microchips. A particular job that has been under analysis as part of a quality improvement program was the subject of a time study. The time study encompassed twenty job cycles, and the results include the following cumulative times and performance rating factors for each element.

Element	Σt (min)	RF
1	10.52	1.15
2	18.61	1.10
3	26.20	1.10
4	16.46	1.05

a. Compute the standard time for this job using an allowance factor of 15 percent.
b. Using a sample standard deviation of 0.51 minutes, determine the number of cycles for this time study such that the company would be 95 percent confident that the average time from the time study is within 5 percent of the true average cycle time.

8-6. Data Products, Inc., packages and distributes a variety of personal computer–related products. A time study has been conducted for a job packaging 3.5-inch personal computer diskettes for shipment to customers. The job requires a packager to place 20 diskettes in a rectangular plastic bag, close the bag with a twist tie, and place the filled bag into a bin, which is replaced by another worker when it is filled. The job can be broken into four basic elements. The following elemental times (in minutes) were obtained from the time study for 10 job cycles.

	ELEMENTAL TIMES										
ELEMENT	1	2	3	4	5	6	7	8	9	10	RF
1	0.36	0.31	0.42	0.35	0.38	0.30	0.41	0.42	0.35	0.35	1.05
2	0.81	0.95	0.76	0.85	1.01	1.02	0.95	0.90	0.87	0.88	0.90
3	0.56	0.38	0.42	0.45	0.51	0.48	0.50	0.52	0.39	0.46	1.00
4	0.19	0.12	0.16	0.21	0.15	0.16	0.18	0.19	0.19	0.15	1.05

a. Using an allowance factor of 16 percent, determine the standard time for this job.
b. Determine the number of cycles for this time study such that the company would be 95 percent confident that the average time from the time study is within ±4 percent of the true average cycle time.

8-7. In Problem 8-2, a time study was conducted for the job of sewing baseball-style caps. Using a sample standard deviation of 0.25, determine the number of cycles for the time study such that the company would be 98 percent confident that the average cycle time for the job is within 6 percent of the actual average cycle time.

8-8. Determine the sample size for the time study of the stein assembly operation described in Problem 8-3. The Braykup China Company wants to be 95 percent confident that the average cycle time from the study is within 2 percent of the true average.

8-9. Sonichi Electronics manufactures small electronic consumer items such as portable clocks, calculators, and radios. The company is concerned about the high cost of its product-inspection operation. As a result it had its industrial engineering department conduct a time study of an inspector who inspects portable radios. The operation consists of seven elements, as follows: (1) The package is opened and the radio is removed; (2) the battery casing cover is removed; (3) two AA batteries are inserted; (4) the radio is turned on, and the inspector turns the station-selector dial and listens briefly to at least two stations; (5) the radio is turned off and the batteries are removed; (6) the battery cover is replaced; and (7) the radio is repackaged. The time study observations (in minutes) for ten cycles are shown in the following table.

ELEMENT	ELEMENTAL TIMES										
	1	2	3	4	5	6	7	8	9	10	RF
1	0.23	0.20	0.19	0.20	0.18	0.18	0.24	0.25	0.17	0.20	1.05
2	0.12	0.10	0.08	0.09	0.10	0.10	0.13	0.14	0.10	0.11	1.00
3	0.16	0.18	0.17	0.17	0.17	0.20	0.16	0.15	0.18	0.18	1.05
4	0.26	0.28	0.32	0.19	0.35	0.33	0.22	0.28	0.28	0.27	0.95
5	0.10	0.08	0.09	0.10	0.11	0.11	0.09	0.12	0.12	0.12	1.00
6	0.06	0.08	0.08	0.08	0.07	0.06	0.10	0.08	0.09	0.11	1.05
7	0.20	0.28	0.25	0.36	0.17	0.22	0.33	0.19	0.20	0.16	1.05

a. The allowance factor for this job is 15 percent. Determine the standard time.
b. If management wants the estimate of the average cycle time to be within ±0.03 minute with a 95 percent level of confidence, how many job cycles should be observed?
c. Management is considering putting inspectors on a piece-rate wage system in order to provide them with greater incentive to inspect more items. What affect might this have on the quality inspection function?

8-10. Baker Street Stereo is a catalog ordering operation. The company maintains an ordering staff of 30 telephone operators, who take orders from customers. Management wants to determine the proportion of time that operators are idle. A work sampling study was conducted at random over a 4-day period, and the following random observations were recorded.

Observation		Operators Idle	Observation		Operators Idle
10/15:	1	6		11	4
	2	5	10/17:	12	7
	3	4		13	3
	4	7		14	3
	5	5		15	6
	6	2		16	5
10/16:	7	4		17	7
	8	3		18	4
	9	5	10/19:	19	5
	10	6		20	6

If management wants the proportion of time from the work sampling study to be ±2 percent accurate with a confidence level of 98 percent, how many additional sample observations should be taken?

8-11. The associate dean of the college of business at Tech has succumbed to faculty pressure to purchase a new fax machine, although she has always contended that the machine would have minimal use. She has estimated that the machine will be used only 20 percent of the time. Now that the machine has been installed, she has asked the students in the introductory POM course to conduct a work sampling study to see what proportion of time the new fax machine is used. She wants the estimate to be within 3 percent of the actual proportion, with a confidence level of 95 percent. Determine the sample size for the work sample.

8-12. The Rowntown Cab Company has 26 cabs. The local manager wants to conduct a work sampling study to determine what proportion of the time a cab driver is sitting idle, which he estimates is about 30 percent. The cabs were observed at random during a 5-day period by the dispatcher, who simply called each cab and checked on its status. The manager wants the estimate to be within ±3 percent of the actual proportion, with a 95 percent level of confidence.

a. Determine the sample size for this work sampling study.
b. The results of the first 20 observations of the work sampling study are shown as follows.

Observation	Idle Cabs	Observation	Idle Cabs
1	4	11	6
2	3	12	4
3	5	13	3
4	8	14	5
5	7	15	2
6	5	16	0
7	3	17	3
8	6	18	4
9	4	19	5
10	3	20	4

What is the revised estimate of the sample size based on these initial results?

8-13. The head of the department of management at State University has noticed that the four secretaries in the departmental office seem to spend a lot of time answering questions from students that could better be answered by the college advising office, by faculty advisors, or simply from the available literature; that is, course schedules, catalogs, the student handbook, and so on. As a result the department head is considering remodeling the office with cubicles so students do not have easy access to the secretaries. However, before investing in this project the head has decided to conduct a work sampling study to determine the proportion of time the secretaries spend assisting students. The head arranged for a graduate assistant to make observations for the work sample, but the graduate student's schedule enabled her to make only 300 random observations in the time allotted for the study. The results of the work sampling study showed that the secretaries assisted students 12 percent of the time, somewhat less than the head anticipated.

a. Given the number of observations that were included in the work sampling study, how confident can the department head be that the sample result is within 3 percent of the actual proportion?

b. How many fewer or additional observations would be required for the department head to be 95 percent confident in the work sampling results?

8-14. In Problem 8-11, the POM students have completed 100 observations of the work sampling study and have a preliminary result showing the fax machine is in use 31 percent of the time. How many additional observations are required based on this result?

8-15. Northwoods Backpackers is a mail-order operation specializing in outdoor camping and hiking equipment and clothing. In addition to its normal pool of telephone operators to take customer orders, the company has a group of customer service operators to respond to customer complaints and product-related inquiries. The time required for customer service operators to handle customer calls differs, based on an operator's ability to think fast and quickly recall from memory product information (without using product description screens on the computer). The company wants to determine the standard time required for a customer service operator to complete a call without having to resort to a time study. Instead, management had a work sampling study of an operator conducted during an 8-hour workday that included 160 observations. The study showed the operator was talking to customers only 78 percent of the time, and call records indicated that the operator handled 120 customer calls during the day. The customer service manager has indicated that the particular operator that was studied performs at about 110 percent compared to a normal operator. Company policy allows 15 percent personal time on the job for lunch, breaks, and so on. Determine the standard time per customer call.

8-16. In Problem 8-15 how confident can Northwoods Backpackers be in the standard time it computed if it assumed that the proportion of time that an operator is busy determined from the work sampling study is accurate within ±4 percent? How many additional observations might be needed for Northwoods to be 95 percent confident in the standard time per customer call?

8-17. The manager of the order distribution center for Northwoods Backpackers has a company directive to downsize his operation. He has decided to conduct work sampling studies of employees in the order processing department, the warehouse area, and the packaging area. In the warehouse area he has 17 employees who locate items, pull them, and put them on conveyors to the packaging area. A work sampling study was conducted over a 5-day period to determine the proportion of time warehouse employees were idle, and out of the 50 random observations, 400 employees were idle.

a. How many observations should be taken if the manager wants to be 90 percent confident the estimate is within ±5 percent of the actual proportion of time a warehouse employee is idle?

b. The manager also conducted a work sampling study of the packaging area and discovered that the 28 employees were idle approximately 37 percent of the time. How might the manager redesign his operation to downsize and be more efficient?

8-18. The manager of the Burger Doodle restaurant believes the time to fill orders at the drive-through window is too long. She suspects that the window cashier spends too much time making change, and she is considering using even pricing for most menu items to reduce the window time. She has decided to conduct a work sampling study to determine the proportion of time the cashier is making change. During a 3-day period the manager checked the cashier 150 times and recorded 84 observations where the cashier was making change.

a. How many more observations should be taken if the manager wants to be 99 percent confident that her estimate is with ± 1 percent of the actual proportion of time the cashier is making change?

b. Based on the time required to take the first 150 observations, how many days will be required to conduct this study?

c. How could the manager reduce the number of days required to conduct in part (b)?

8-19. The National Bank of Hamilton has opened up two new drive-through teller windows outside its main office building in downtown Hamilton. The bank is not sure that it needs both windows open all day so it has decided to conduct a work sampling study to determine the proportion of time the two tellers are idle between the hours of 10:00 A.M. to 11:30 A.M. and 1:00 P.M. to 3:00 P.M. The work sampling study was conducted at random over a 5-day period and the following observations were recorded.

Observation	Tellers Idle	Observation	Tellers Idle	Observation	Tellers Idle
1	1	11	1	21	2
2	1	12	1	22	2
3	0	13	2	23	2
4	0	14	2	24	0
5	0	15	0	25	1
6	2	16	1	26	1
7	1	17	2	27	0
8	2	18	2	28	2
9	2	19	0	29	0
10	1	20	1	30	2

a. Bank management wants the study to be ±5 percent accurate with a 95 percent confidence level. How many additional sample observations should be taken?

b. If the bank does not want to conduct a study of more than 100 observations, what level of confidence could it expect?

8-20. The United Mutual and Accident Insurance Company has a large pool of clerical employees who process insurance application forms on networked computers. When the company hires a new clerical employee, it takes that person about 48 minutes to process a form. The learning curve for this job is 90 percent, but no additional learning will take place after about the 100th form is processed. United Mutual has recently acquired a smaller competitor that will add 800 new forms per week to its clerical pool. If an employee works six hours per day (excluding breaks, meals, etc.) per 5-day week, how many employees would be hired to absorb the extra workload?

8-21. Professor Cook teaches operations management at State University. She is scheduled to give her class of 35 students a final exam on the last day of exam week, and she is leaving town the same day. She is concerned about her ability to finish grading her exams. She estimates that with everything else she has to do she has only 5 hours to grade the exams. From past experience she knows the first exam will take her about 12 minutes to grade. She estimates her learning curve to be about 90 percent and it will be fully realized after about 10 exams. Will she get the exams graded on time?

8-22. Nite-Site, Inc., manufactures image intensification devices used in products such as night-vision goggles and aviator's night-vision imaging systems. The primary customer for these products is the U.S. military. The military requires that learning curves be employed in the bid process for awarding military contracts. The company is planning to make a bid for 120 image intensifiers to be used in a military vehicle. The company estimates the first unit will require 86 hours of direct labor to produce. The industry learning curve for this particular type of product is 85 percent. Determine how many hours will be required to produce the 60th and 120th units.

8-23. Jericho Vehicles manufactures special-purpose all-terrain vehicles primarily for the military and government agencies in the United States and for foreign governments. The company is planning to bid on a new all-terrain vehicle specially equipped for desert military action. The company has experienced an 80 percent learning curve in the past for producing similar vehicles. Based on a prototype model, it estimates the first vehicle produced will require 1,600 hours of direct labor. The order is for 60 all-terrain vehicles. Determine the time that will be required for the 30th and 60th units.

8-24. Jericho Vehicles is considering making a bid for a mobile rocket-launching system for the U.S. military. However, the company has almost no experience in producing this type of vehicle. In an effort to develop a learning curve for the production of this new mobile weapon system, management has called contacts from several former competitors who went bankrupt. Although management could not obtain direct learning curve rates, they did learn from one contact that for a system with similar features, the first unit required 2,200 hours of direct labor to produce and the 30th and final unit required 810 hours to produce. Determine the learning curve rate for this vehicle.

8-25. PM Computer Services (described in Example 8.7) has received an order for 120 specially configured personal computers for a local business. Paulette and Maureen have so many orders that they can no longer perform the work themselves, and they must hire extra labor to assemble the units for this new order. They have hired 8 students from the university to work part time, 20 hours per week, to assemble the computers. Paulette and Maureen assembled a prototype unit and it required 26 hours of direct labor; from experience they know their computer assembly operation has an 84 percent learning curve. Approximately when will PM Computer Services be able to deliver the completed order?

Measuring Faculty Work Activity at State University

At several recent meetings of the faculty senate at State University there has been discussion of media reports that college faculty are more concerned about their research than about teaching and, specifically, that faculty don't spend enough time working with students, which should be their main task. These media reports imply that faculty work only during the time they are in class, which for most faculty is between six and twelve hours per week. The faculty believes this information is misleading and dangerous to higher education in general. The faculty representatives on the senate claim that the time they spend in class is only a small portion of their actual workload, and although they spend some time on their research, they also dedicate a large portion of their time outside of class to class preparation and meeting with students. Unfortunately, few people outside of the faculty appear to believe this, including the students, parents, certain legislators, and, recently, several highly placed university administrators.

In an attempt to educate the students more about what faculty actually do with their time, the senate invited several student leaders to one of its meetings, where they discussed the issue. Among the students invited to this meeting was Mary Shipley, editor of *The Daily State*, the student newspaper. Subsequently Mary wrote an editorial in the paper about how faculty members spent their time.

Mary was a student in the college of business at State; coincidentally, the topic currently under discussion in her production and operations management class was "Job Design and Work Measurement." The day after her editorial appeared, she was asked the following question in her class by a fellow student, Art Cohen.

"Mary, it looks like to me that all you did in your editorial was repeat what you had been told by the faculty at the faculty senate meeting. I don't really believe you have any idea about what faculty do, anymore than the rest of us!"

Before Mary could respond, another student, Angela Watts, broke in, "Well, it shouldn't be too hard to check out. That's what we're studying in class right now—how to measure work. Why don't we check out how much time the faculty work at different tasks?"

At this point their teacher, Dr. Larry Moore, broke in. "That's a good idea, Angela. It sounds to me you just resolved our problem of a class project for this term. I'm going to break you all into teams and let each team monitor a specific faculty member, using work sampling to determine the amount of time the faculty member spends with students outside the classroom."

"That's not really going to provide any relevant information," interrupted Bobby Jenkins. "That will just provide us with a percentage of time faculty work with students. If professors spend 90 percent of their time working with students, that sounds great, but if they are only in their offices two hours a day, 90 percent of two hours is not very much."

"I see what you mean," Dr. Moore replied. "That's a good point. Somehow we need to determine how many hours a day a faculty member devotes to his or her job to have a frame of reference."

"The way it looks to me, a professor works only about three or four hours a day," said Rodney Jefferson. This drew laughter from the class and Dr. Moore.

"I don't think that's really true," responded Mary Shipley. "One of the things the faculty pointed out to me and I indicated in my editorial was that even though faculty members may not be in their offices all the time, they may still be working, either at home or in the library. And a lot of times they have committee work at various locations around campus." A lot of the class seemed to be in general agreement with this. "Anyway," Mary continued, "I don't think the issue is how much a professor works. I believe we all agree they put in a full seven- or eight-hour day like almost anyone else. The point as I see it is, what do they do with that time? Do they spend it all on their own research and writing or are they working with students?"

"Okay then," said Dr. Moore. "If we can all

agree that the number of hours of work is a moot point, then let's set up our work sampling experiment. We'll break down the activities outside of classroom teaching as 'working with students,' or 'not working with students,' which could include anything else the faculty member is working on, such as research, making out tests, preparing for class, and so on. That should be all-inclusive. What proportion of time do you think a faculty member spends with students outside the classroom, to use a starting point? Ten percent? Twenty percent?"

The class seemed to mull this over for a few minutes and someone shouted, "20 percent." Someone else said 30 percent, and after a few seconds people were simply talking back and forth.

"Okay, okay," said Dr. Moore, "everyone calm down. Let's say 20 percent. That sounds like a reasonable number to me, and you can always adjust it in the course of your experiment. Let's allow for an error of 3 percent and use a confidence level of 95 percent. Does this sound okay to everybody?" He waited a few moments for any negative reaction, but there seemed to be general agreement. "Good, I'll post teams on my office door by tomorrow, and I'll let each team select the faculty member they want to study. Let me know by the end of the week and I'll alert the faculty members so they will know what to expect. Also, it's possible someone might not want to participate, and I'll let you know that too so you can select someone else. Please be as unobtrusive as possible and try not to bother anybody. Okay, if there are no other questions, that's it. Get busy."

Describe how you would set up this work sampling experiment at your school, and, if your teacher is agreeable, carry out this project. Also, describe how you might alter the work sample to analyze other faculty work activities.

References

Barnes, R. M. *Motion and Time Study: Design and Measurement of Work*, 8th ed. New York: John Wiley, 1980.

Belkaoui, A. *The Learning Curve*. Westport, Conn.: Quorum Books, 1986.

Emerson, H. P., and D. C. E. Maehring. *Origins of Industrial Engineering*. Atlanta, Ga.: Institute of Industrial Engineers, 1988.

Evans, J. R., and W. M. Lindsay. *The Management and Control of Quality*, 3d ed. St. Paul, Minn.: West, 1996.

Gilbreth, F. *Motion Study*. New York: D. Van Nostrand Co., 1911.

Knights, D., H. Willmott, and D. Collinson, eds. *Job Redesign: Critical Perspectives on the Labor Process*. Hants, England: Gower, 1985.

Mundel, M. E. *Motion and Time Study: Improving Productivity*, 6th ed. Englewood Cliffs, N.J.: Prentice Hall, 1985.

Smith, G. L., Jr. *Work Measurement: A Systems Approach*. Columbus, Ohio: Grid Publishing, 1978.

Taylor, F. W. *The Principles of Scientific Management*. New York: Harper and Brothers, 1911.

Wood, S., ed. *The Transformation of Work*. London: Unwin Hyman, 1989.

9

Supply Chain Management

Supply Chain Management at The Moscow McDonald's

www.prenhall.com/russell

Around the world, McDonald's operates more than 11,000 restaurants in 51 countries, 4,000 outside the United States. One of the most unique is the 700-seat McDonald's in Moscow. McDonald's insists that a Big Mac must taste the same in Moscow as it does in New York, Paris, or Sydney, yet all food products used to supply its restaurant in Russia must be secured locally. McDonald's prepared for this challenge by planning the supply chain for the Moscow restaurant six years in advance, when McDonald's experts began to work with Russians to upgrade their production standards to supply the desired quality of meat, wheat, potatoes, milk, and other necessary basic ingredients.

Supplier location is an important part of the supply chain at McDonald's, and past experience has shown that what works best is to combine a number of independently owned food-processing plants dedicated solely to supplying McDonald's restaurants. This type of centralized system, called a *food town*, reduces both transportation and material handling costs. A $60 million food town was established in Russia that combines a bakery, meat plant, chicken plant, lettuce plant, fish plant, and distribution center. Each of these processing facilities is independently managed, but all share cooling and freezing facilities with the distribution center. Locating dedicated processing facilities together is the only way McDonald's could ensure the standards of quality and customer service required in its Moscow restaurant. The system also reduces capital setup costs, inventory and material handling costs, and distribution costs.[1]

McDonald's in Pushkin Square in Moscow, adheres to founder Ray Kroc's creed of QSC&V (quality, service, cleanliness, and value) as any other McDonald's in the United States or around the world does. To achieve its expected level of quality and service in Moscow, McDonald's developed an entire supply chain for growing, processing, and distributing food, part of which is the $60 million food plant shown here. This follows McDonald's overall approach to supply chain management, which is to construct a strong logistical chain from suppliers to customers with no weak links, especially among suppliers. McDonald's makes sure everyone along the supply chain understands its expectations for performance and closely monitors this performance.

---

[1] P. Ritchie, "McDonald's: A Winner Through Logistics," *International Journal of Physical Distribution and Logistics Management* 20, no. 3 (1990): 21–24.

A **supply chain** encompasses all the facilities, functions, and activities involved in producing and delivering a product or service, from suppliers (and their suppliers) to customers (and their customers). It includes planning and managing supply and demand; acquiring materials; producing and scheduling the product or service; warehousing, inventory control, and distribution; and delivery and customer service. Supply chain management coordinates all these activities so that customers can be provided with prompt and reliable service of high-quality products at the least cost. Successful supply chain management in turn can provide the company with a competitive advantage.

Facilities along the supply chain include plants, warehouses, distribution centers, service centers, and retail operations. Products and services can be distributed by rail, truck, water, air, pipeline, computer, mail, telephone, or in person. Functions within the supply chain include forecasting of product or service demand, selecting suppliers (sourcing) and ordering materials (procurement), inventory control, scheduling production, shipping and delivery, information management, quality management, and customer service. Most of the topics in this text fall somewhere within the supply chain. Managing the supply chain is tantamount to coordinating all the operations of a company with the operations of its suppliers and customers.

The delivery of a product or service to a customer is a complex process encompassing many different interrelated facilities, functions, and activities. First, demand for a product or service is forecast, and plans and schedules are made to meet demand within a time frame. The product or service can require multiple suppliers (who have their own suppliers) who prepare and then ship parts and materials to manufacturing or service sites. One of the largest producers, General Motors, has over 2,500 suppliers that serve its 120 parts plants and 30 auto and truck assembly plants. Parts and materials are transformed through complex processes into final products or services. Finally, these products are shipped to external or internal customers. However, this may not be the final step at all as these customers may transform the product or service further and ship it on to their customers. All of this is part of the supply chain; that is, the flow of goods or services from the materials stage to the end user.

What makes this process so complicated, and the management of the supply chain so complex, is the uncertainty all along the supply chain at every stage. Uncertainty in the form of wrong forecasts, late deliveries, poor-quality materials or parts, machine breakdowns in the manufacturing process, canceled orders, erroneous information, transportation breakdowns, and the like cause "breaks" in the supply chain that can result in poor customer service; that is, not having the product or service available to customers when and where they want it. Companies cope with this uncertainty with their own form of "insurance," *inventory.* All companies carry inventory to minimize the negative effects of uncertainty and to keep the productive process flowing smoothly from suppliers to the customer. However, inventory is very costly so companies—both suppliers and their customers—would like to minimize it. Thus, one important objective of supply chain management is to coordinate all the different activities, or "links" of the chain, so that goods can move smoothly and on time from suppliers to customers to distribution to suppliers to customers, while keeping inventories low and costs down.

Unfortunately, the different companies that depend on each other to produce a product or service don't always work together and that is a dilemma of supply chain management. Customers don't want to have to keep large, costly inventories so they demand that their suppliers keep them instead so their service won't suffer, and these suppliers pressure their suppliers to do the same, and so on, all the way down the supply chain.

www.prenhall.com/russell

3 main functions
of supply chain
•Purchasing
of components
•Scheduling
of production
•Distribution

www.prenhall.com/russell

Inventory is used to cope with uncertainty along the supply chain.

Keys to effective supply chain management are information, communication, cooperation, and trust.

Effective supply chain management requires that suppliers and customers work together in a coordinated manner by sharing and communicating information by talking to one another. It is the rapid flow of information among customers, suppliers, distribution centers, and transportation systems that has enabled some companies to develop very efficient supply chains. Suppliers and customers must also have the same goals; that is, that they be on the same page. Suppliers and customers need to be able to trust each other: Customers need to be able to count on the "quality" of the products and services of their suppliers. Further, suppliers and customers must participate together in the design of the supply chain to achieve their shared goals and to facilitate communication and the flow of information.

Some companies attempt to gain control of their supply chains by *vertically integrating*—by owning and controlling all the different components along the supply chain from materials and parts procurement to delivery of the final product and customer service—like the McDonald's in Moscow described at the beginning of this chapter. However, even with this type of organizational structure, the different functions and operating units can be uncoordinated. For example, at a computer manufacturer one facility producing chips responded to demand pressure from another company facility producing motherboards by increasing capacity at considerable cost, only to learn later that the chips were never a source of delay in the delivery of motherboards farther up the supply chain. No matter what type of organizational structure exists within a company, it still must focus on coordinating its different activities to achieve overall company goals.

As this brief discussion illustrates, supply chain management encompasses so many different interrelated topics that it is not possible to cover all of them in a single chapter. Thus, we must devote separate chapters to some of them including forecasting, production and scheduling, inventory control and quality. In this chapter we will focus on several key elements of the supply chain including the supplier-customer relationship and purchasing (also known as sourcing and procurement), type and location of facilities, transportation, and distribution.

Supply Chain Design: *A Strategic Issue*

Supply chain management and quality management share similar characteristics.

Since a company's supply chain encompasses virtually all of its operating functions and facilities, its design is necessarily an integral part of its strategic planning process. For most companies the goals of their strategic plan are often the same as the objective of supply chain management—the prompt and reliable delivery of high-quality products and services at the least cost. To accomplish this requires strategic design decisions that effectively coordinate all of the supply chain functions. It is not surprising that many of the same strategic design considerations for a quality management program can be applied to supply chain design.

Benchmarking is measuring current performance against where a company wants performance to be.

The central component of the strategic planning process is a goal or set of goals. In supply chain management before goals can be established, it is necessary to know what current performance is and what is possible after improvement or reengineering. In total quality management (TQM), this is referred to as **benchmarking,** measuring where the company (and/or a competitor) is now and using that as a guideline as to where the company wants to be in the future. However, a company must measure performance and set goals in terms of the supply chain as a whole, not just itself. A company may set high goals for itself for minimizing inventory, but if the inventory levels of its suppliers are required to be excessively high just so the company can achieve its own local goals without regard to the suppliers' costs, then the cost of the high inventory will eventually be passed on to the company as higher delivery material and parts costs anyway. If a company achieves its own quality goals and ignores the quality programs of its suppliers, then its quality will be adversely affected. Thus, the supply chain must be designed to minimize inventory and achieve high quality among both suppliers and customers.

This level of interdependence and goal sharing makes the selection of suppliers, also called **sourcing,** and the purchasing process, also called **procurement,** important strategic decisions for a company. Suppliers must be reliable in terms of quantity, timeliness, and quality. McDonald's expects delivery of its food ingredients from suppliers within two days of placing an order—always. Changing suppliers frequently can lead to interruption and delays in the flow of materials to the production process; too many suppliers can be difficult to coordinate and control; and too few suppliers can be risky, if they are not reliable, and can cut down on competition and the incentive to keep prices low. Suppliers must be perceived as a virtual extension of the customer, operating with the same goals and quality expectations.

For a company to achieve its strategic goals, it must control the bane of supply chain management we mentioned earlier—uncertainty. This requires identifying and understanding the causes of the uncertainty, determining how it affects other activities up and down the supply chain, and then formulating ways to reduce or eliminate it. An effective means for identifying and reducing uncertainty is to strategically apply the principles of TQM, including statistical process control all along the supply chain. This means that suppliers use TQM to insure quality products are delivered on time to customers; distribution centers employ TQM to make sure that products are packaged, handled, and shipped on time with no damage or processing errors; and shippers deliver products undamaged to the right place on time.

Another important aspect of supply chain design is communication and information flow. Advances in computer technology have made it possible for suppliers, customers, distribution centers, and shippers to communicate almost instantaneously, thus enhancing the ability to coordinate these different supply chain functions. Computerized point-of-sale information can be transmitted instantaneously via communication networks to distribution centers and shippers enabling quick delivery to customers and quick replenishment of warehouse stocks by suppliers. If everyone along the supply chain has access to the same information at the same time, it enables them all to coordinate so closely and thus reduce uncertainty, which in turn allows them to reduce inventory levels.

The types and number of facilities to construct (or acquire) and where to locate them are strategic design issues since transportation and distribution costs can be a significant part of supply chain costs. Facility and location decisions are costly, long-term commitments. They also dictate other design decisions including which suppliers to use, modes of transportation, distribution centers, and customer markets. For example, 75 percent of Honda's suppliers are within 150 miles of its Marysville, Ohio, plant, and it uses locally based trucking companies to ships its parts and materials.

Wal-Mart is an example of a company that has incorporated these various design characteristics into an effective and successful supply chain. Wal-Mart's competitive strategy is to provide quality goods to its customers when and where they want them at a competitive price. The key to achieving these strategic goals has been a feature of its supply chain design known as "cross-docking." In its cross-docking system, products are delivered to Wal-Mart's warehouses on a continual basis where they are sorted, repackaged, and distributed to stores without sitting in inventory. Goods "cross" from one loading dock to another in forty-eight hours or less. This system allows Wal-Mart to purchase full truckloads of goods while avoiding the inventory and handling costs, in the process re-

Sourcing is selection of suppliers.

Procurement is purchasing parts, materials, and service.

www.prenhall.com/russell

ducing its cost of sales to 2 to 3 percent less than the industry average. Wal-Mart then passes these cost savings on to its customers as lower prices. Low prices enable them to forego frequent discount promotions which stabilizes prices, which in turn make sales more predictable, thus reducing stockouts and the need for excess inventory.

Retailers don't all use cross-docking because it's difficult to coordinate and manage. To make it work Wal-Mart has invested heavily in an integrated support system that provides continuous contact between all of Wal-Mart's suppliers, distribution centers, and every *point-of-sale* in every store via its own satellite communication system. This information system sends out point-of-sale (bar code) data directly to Wal-Mart's 4,000 suppliers. In addition, Wal-Mart owns 2,000 trucks to service its 19 distribution

Point-of-sale is a computer record of a sale at the retail site.

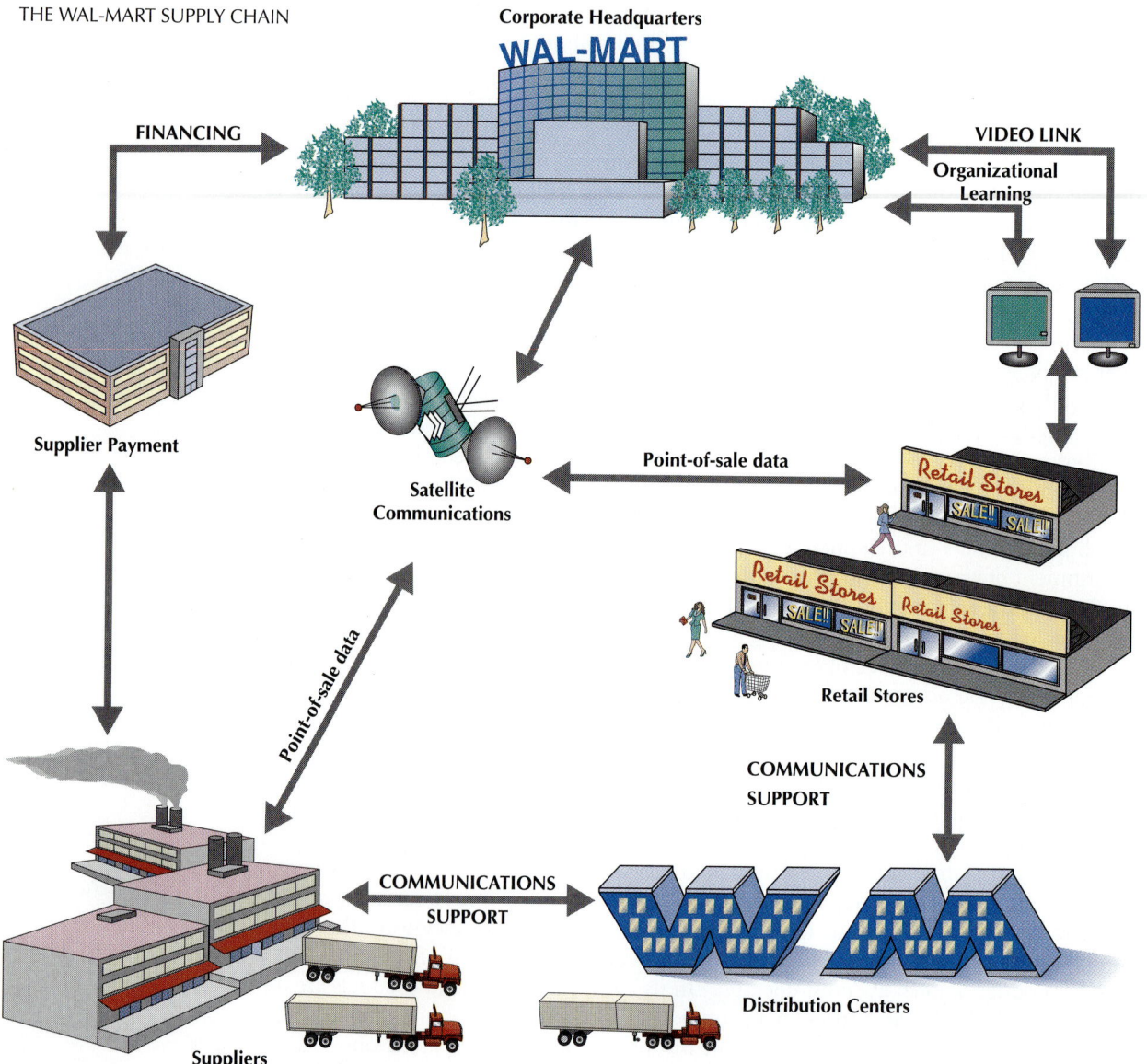

THE WAL-MART SUPPLY CHAIN

FIGURE 9.1   **The Relationship Between Facilities and Functions Along the Wal-Mart Supply Chain**
SOURCE: Adapted from Garrison Wieland for "Wal-Mart's Supply Chain," *Harvard Business Review*, vol. 70, no. 2, (March–April 1992) p. 60–61.

THE COMPETITIVE EDGE

Chrysler Excels at Outsourcing

www.prenhall.com/russell

Two thirds of the components used to make Chrysler cars—over 60,000 different items—come from outside sources. Chrysler shares its 150 major suppliers with Ford and GM. Being the smallest of the U.S. automakers, and thus lacking as much clout, it is surprising that Chrysler is the recognized pro at supplier relations. "None of the other car companies we work with are as accessible or as willing to take advice from suppliers," says Alcoa. Chrysler involves suppliers early in the design process and solicits their ideas on cost savings and technological innovation.

Most companies do not understand the full extent of their supply chains. In mapping out its supply chains, Chrysler discovered that even a simple $3 engine part can involve 35 separate suppliers. To coordinate supplier activities, Chrysler assigns a particular supplier to act as a team leader. Its job is to oversee other suppliers in the design and manufacture of a component such as an engine or a seat. The Plymouth Prowler, the first U.S. car with an all-aluminum body, was built with cutting-edge supply chain management techniques—so say AT&T, Harley Davidson, and the Department of Energy, who have all benchmarked Chrysler's outsourcing practices.

SOURCE: Justin Martin, "Are You as Good as You Think You Are?" *Fortune* (September 30, 1996): 145–46.

centers; this allows the company to ship goods from warehouses to stores within 48 hours and restock store shelves an average of twice a week, compared to the industry average of once every two weeks. Cross-docking also requires close management cooperation at all levels. Store managers are connected to each other and to corporate headquarters via a video link that allows for frequent information exchanges about products, pricing, sales, and promotions.[2] Figure 9.1 illustrates the relationship between facilities and functions along the Wal-Mart supply chain.

In one instance Wal-Mart found it to be more cost-effective to bypass distribution centers and warehouses altogether. Wal-Mart used to hold inventories of Pampers diapers in its warehouse before shipping them to stores. However, after looking at its whole supply chain, Wal-Mart realized that Pampers take up so much space and have such a low profit margin that the company was losing about 20 cents per case just handling the inventory. It found it was more profitable to have diapers shipped directly from the supplier to the store more frequently even though the cost of transportation and store labor would both be higher. By looking at the relationship between components of the supply chain (including inventory, warehousing, transportation and the retail operation) instead of just inventory, Wal-Mart was able to reduce supply chain costs.

The Global Supply Chain

International trade barriers are falling, and global markets are changing so that the supply chain of many companies extends around the world. The dissolution of communism opened up new markets in Middle and Eastern Europe, and the creation of the European Community (EC) in 1992 resulted in the world's largest potential economic market of nearly 400 million people. Europe with a total population of 850 million is the largest, best-educated, and wealthiest economic group in the world. Asia has experienced dramatic growth in its export-driven economies since trade barriers began falling in the late 1980s and 1990s.

Customs Union = a bloc of traders

---

[2] G. Stalk, P. Evans, and L. E. Shulman, "Competing on Capabilities: The New Rules of Corporate Strategy," *Harvard Business Review* 70, no. 2 (March–April 1992): 57–69.

For many U.S. companies eager to enter growing global markets, extending their supply chains to foreign countries represents a strategic challenge. Trading in foreign countries is not "business as usual." Transportation and distribution systems vary significantly among countries in availability, capability, and quality. Few countries have the transportation choices that are available in the United States. Governments frequently play a significant role in international trade by establishing duties or tariffs, import quotas to protect their local businesses, and regulations unique to their own country. Foreign markets are not homogeneous and often require customized service in terms of packaging and labeling. These factors and others only increase the amount of uncertainty involved in the flow of goods through the supply chain and result in the need for even higher inventory levels to protect against breaks in the supply chain than might be required domestically. In this section we will discuss some of the opportunities and problems along the global supply chain

www.prenhall.com/russell

Free Trade and Global Opportunities

Nation groups are nations joined together into trading groups.

Tariffs (duties) are taxes on imported goods.

The proliferation of trade agreements has changed global markets and has accelerated global trade activity. Nations have joined together to form trading groups, or **nation groups,** and within these groups products move freely with no import tax, called **tariffs** or **duties,** charged on member products. The members of a group charge uniform import duties to nations outside their group, thus removing tariff trade barriers within the group and raising barriers for outsiders. The group adopts rules and regulations for freely transporting goods across borders that, combined with reduced tariffs, gives member nations a competitive advantage over nonmembers. These trade advantages among member nations lower supply chain costs and reduce cycle time; that is, the time required for products to move through the supply chain.

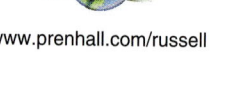

www.prenhall.com/russell

Figure 9.2 shows the various international trade groups the United States trades with. NAFTA in the United States is the North American Free Trade Agreement, and EU is the European Community trade group, which includes many of the countries of Western Europe. NAFTA has given U.S. auto parts suppliers, for example, an advantage over Japanese competitors with Canadian and Mexican automakers. Kodak has moved some of its production back to North America from Europe to accommodate increased demand for film exports as a result of NAFTA-driven market changes. Caterpillar has indicated that if Chile joins MERCOSUR, the South American trade group, it will shift some of its U.S. production to Brazil to serve customers in Chile. Global trade agreements have also given U.S. companies opportunities in markets previously unaccustomed to cross-border trade. From 1992 to 1994 U.S. exports to most of the emerging market regions (in Middle and Eastern Europe and Asia) participating in free trade agreements increased by more than 20 percent.[3]

Global Supply Chain Problems and Solutions

While new markets and lowered trade barriers have provided U.S. companies with opportunities around the world, they have also created challenges to supply chain management. Trade agreements that benefit member nations create obstacles for nonmembers. Import duties that typically average 5 to 10 percent of product value plus various transport and product regulations can significantly increase supply chain costs and transit times, inhibiting customer service.

[3] J. F. Zubrod, Jr., and M. B. Barron, "Trade Pacts Fuel a Transformation in the Rules of Global Logistics," *Transportation and Distribution* 37, no. 4 (April 1996): 60–67.

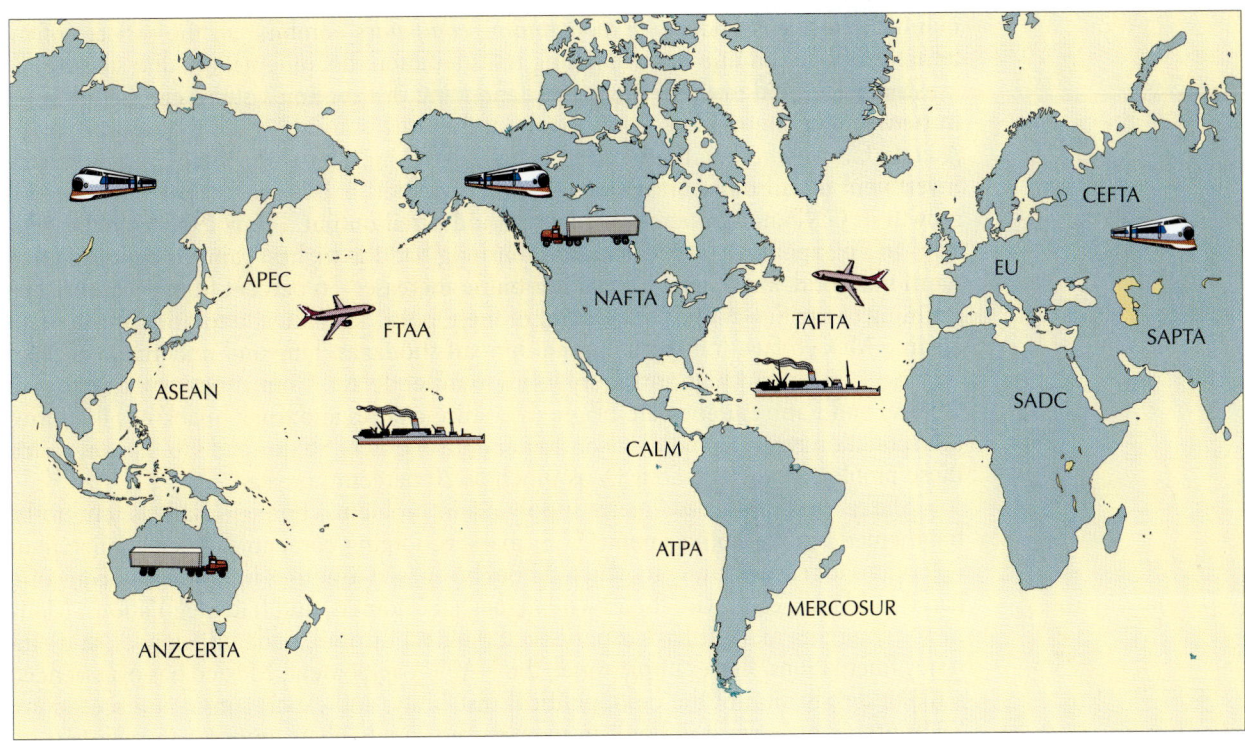

FIGURE 9.2 **Global Trading Groups** (See Fig. 1.5, page 14 for an explanation of these trade group abbreviations.)

To avoid or "drawback" (e.g., get back) duties, many companies have duty specialists, something akin to an international tax lawyer. These specialists advise how duties affect supply chain decisions and how to avoid duties. Digital Equipment Corporation in Europe imports LCD displays from Taiwan to use in the assembly of laptop PCs that it exports back to Taiwan. The import duty on LCDs is 4.9 percent; however, it can be avoided because of a trade regulation that allows a firm to import a product, add value to it, and then reexport it in a different condition.[4] This and similar duty drawbacks can reduce supply chain costs significantly. However, duty specialists do not always communicate their advice early enough in the process of designing the supply chain so that the company can take advantage of duty drawbacks.

Besides duty specialists, companies often use other international **trade specialists** to help manage transportation and distribution operations in foreign countries. For example, *international freight forwarders* handle the details of air and ship freight shipments and obtain the legal documents necessary for goods to cross foreign borders. This includes booking space on carriers, preparing export declarations, obtaining consular documents (that give permission for goods to enter a country and are used to determine duties), arranging for insurance, and preparing shipping notices that coordinate the physical movement of goods with their payment. *Customs house brokers* manage the movement of imported goods through a country's customs procedures. *Export packers* perform customized packaging and labeling. *Export management companies* handle overseas sales for companies and help them identify foreign companies that can be licensed to

Trade specialists are international freight forwarders, customs house brokers, export packers, export management and export trading companies.

---

[4] B. C. Arntzen, G. G. Brown, T. P. Harrison, and L. L. Trafton, "Global Supply Chain Management at Digital Equipment Corporation," *Interfaces* 25, no. 1 (January–February 1995): 69–93.

manufacture their products. *Export trading companies* combine all the services of international trade in one firm, handling transportation, documentation, and sales.

Inefficient and undersized transportation and distribution systems can be obstacles in newly emerging markets. Ports, roads, and railroads are stretched to the limit across Asia. In China where rail is the most common and inexpensive mode of transportation, investment in rail transport increased only 3 percent in 1993 compared to 13 percent growth in GNP and 23 percent growth in industrial output. From 1992 to 1993 Asian ports in Singapore, Hong Kong, and Kaohsiung had the highest gains in container traffic in the world, and China's container traffic increased 36 percent from 1993 to 1994, straining capacities to their limit in all of these ports.[5] Suppliers importing raw materials into Mexico face transportation equipment shortages, long and uncertain overland shipment times, and high inventory levels to offset delays. Companies exporting out of Central and Latin America are plagued by ship seizures and truck hijackings that drive transportation costs up and delay customer delivery. Levi Strauss and Co. has suggested these problems can raise costs by as much as 20 percent per year.[6]

www.prenhall.com/russell

Market instability also creates supply chain problems. Foreign markets tend to be fragmented, unlike homogeneous U.S. markets, forcing companies to customize their operations for each country in which it does business. Countries in Asia have been compared to islands, each with their own language, customers, and trade regulations. Many newly emerging markets have experienced political turmoil, trade imbalances, and currency fluctuations. For example, since the NAFTA agreement, Mexico has experienced a major devaluation of the peso, political instability, and export surges and recessions. Such problems make it difficult to manage the supply chain in order to maintain inventory levels and delivery times to satisfy customers and minimize costs.

Despite problems the economic opportunities are great among newly emerging global markets. U.S. companies must be innovative and strategically perceptive in their design and management of global supply chains. They must carefully research potential problems and develop strategic plans. Supply chain management must be flexible enough to react to sudden market changes or changes in the transportation and distribution systems and to provide effective customer service anywhere in the world. Companies need to take advantage of new information systems and technologies to help them manage and coordinate the movement of parts and products between countries.

Some companies have addressed their supply problems by vertically integrating; for example, investing in their own trucking fleets and distribution systems to control their own product delivery. Companies have also banded together to form consortiums for consolidating shipping, warehousing, and distribution, although problems inevitably arise when competing products travel through the same distribution channels.

Countries are also making infrastructure improvements to sustain and accelerate market growth. The Mexican government is privatizing its railroads and container terminals and is paving its major roads. Foreign investors are actively developing port and container facilities in China. Foreign trucking carriers are being invited to countries to establish transport systems and provide expertise for improving existing ones. Western models for retail distribution with large outlets instead of traditionally small stores are being implemented. Such improvements among the South American countries of MERCOSUR resulted in an increase in U.S. imports in excess of 40 percent from 1992 to 1994.

---

[5] J. F. Zubrod, R. Tasiaux, and A. Beebo, "The Challenges of Logistics Within Asia," *Transportation and Distribution* 37, no. 3 (March 1996): 83–86.

[6] Zubrod and Barron, "Trade Pacts Fuel a Transformation in the Rules of Global Logistics."

THE COMPETITIVE EDGE

Global Supply Chain Management at Digital Equipment Corporation

www.prenhall.com/russell

Digital Equipment Corporation is one of the world's largest computer manufacturers with customers in the United States and 81 countries. In the 1970s and 1980s, Digital focused on minicomputers and mainframes, producing most of its own components at 33 plants in 13 different countries. It distributed components, products, and service through 30 distribution and repair centers.

From 1987 to 1991 poor economic conditions plus changes in the computer market brought about by rapid advances in computer technology decreased the demand for large computers and increased demand for networks of smaller, less expensive computers. Faced with the need to produce and distribute many more PCs, which required less space and resources, Digital redesigned its supply chain, including its logistics systems and distribution practices, to deliver a huge number of desktop PCs and workstations instead of a smaller number of large com-

puter systems. Digital's strategy for restructuring was contained in its Global Supply Chain Model (GSCM), which recommends a worldwide production, distribution, and supplier network to determine the fastest, least-cost delivery system. The GSCM was applied to several large sectors within Digital. Digital reduced its plants from 33 to 12 located in three self-contained major customer regions in the Pacific Rim, the Americas, and Europe. Manufacturing costs decreased by $500 million and logistics costs decreased by over $300 million even though the number of units manufactured and shipped increased dramatically. Digital reduced its service facilities from 34 to 17 with associated annual cost reductions of over $80 million. In addition, physical assets were reduced by $34 million, and inventory was reduced by $74 million. Since 1991 Digital has reduced related costs by $1 billion and assets by $400 million while increasing unit production by 500 percent and increasing company revenues.

SOURCE: B. C. Arntzen, G. G. Brown, T. P. Harrison, and L. L. Trafton, "Global Supply Chain Management at Digital Equipment Corporation," *Interfaces* 25, no. 1 (January–February 1995): 69–93.

Purchasing and Suppliers

Purchased materials have historically accounted for about half of U.S. manufacturing costs, and many manufacturers purchase more than half of their parts. The purchasing or procurement function plays a crucial role in supply chain management. Purchasing must make sure that the parts and materials required by the product specifications are of the desired quality and are delivered on time. If poor-quality parts and materials are used, the final product will be poor quality. If deliveries are late from suppliers, final products will likely be late to the customer.

Purchasing must select suppliers that share the company's commitment to quality and scheduling and that maintain their own quality assurance program for providing good-quality materials and parts. A partnership exists between the supplier and the company. In this partnership the company expects and demands that the supplier monitor its own quality so that it is unnecessary for the company to inspect incoming parts and materials or worry that they will be delivered on time. The supplier, in effect, is an integral part of the company's quality management program and supply chain, and is subject to the same goals and responsibilities as other functional areas. More and more suppliers are recognizing they must adopt TQM to do business with companies that have become quality conscious. In a very competitive global economy, this means that American suppliers often must adopt TQM principles and practices to do business with countries around the world.

Single-Sourcing

In the past many manufacturing companies purposefully purchased a part or material from different suppliers, and it was not unusual for a company to limit its purchases of a part from any single supplier to a maximum percentage (for example, 10 or 15 percent) so the company would not be dependent on the uncertain performance of any one supplier. If a supplier was unable to meet delivery schedules, delivered a poor-quality batch, or even went out of business, the effect on the customer would be dampened by the other suppliers. However, TQM practices have resulted in a new approach called **single-sourcing.**

Single-sourcing limits suppliers to gain more control over quality and delivery.

With single-sourcing, a company purchases a part or material from very few suppliers, sometimes only one. With single-sourcing, a company has more direct influence and control over the quality and delivery performance of a supplier if the company has a major portion of that supplier's volume of business. The company and supplier enter into a partnership, referred to as *partnering*, where the supplier agrees to meet the quality standards of the customer in terms of parts, materials, service, and delivery. Suppliers become part of the supply chain of the customer. In return, the company enters into a long-term purchasing agreement with the supplier that includes a stable order and delivery schedule. Every part except the engine block in General Motor's Quad 4 engine (its first new engine in several decades) is single-sourced, resulting in only 69 total suppliers, which is half the normal number for a production engine. In return for the suppliers' assurance of top quality and low cost, GM guaranteed the suppliers their jobs for the life of the engine. In the development of its LH cars, the Chrysler Concorde, the Dodge Intrepid, and the Eagle Vision, Chrysler trimmed its supplier base from 3,000 to a few more than 750.[7] Single-sourcing obviously creates an intensely competitive environment among suppliers, with quality and service being factors in the selection process.

In *partnering*, the supplier becomes part of the customer's supply chain.

An additional aspect of the partnering relationship is the involvement of the supplier in the product design process. In many cases the supplier is given the responsibility of designing a new part or component to meet the quality standards and features outlined by the company. When Guardian Industries of Northville, Michigan, developed an oversized solar glass windshield for Chrysler's LH cars, its engineers met on an almost daily basis with the Chrysler design team to make sure the quality, features, and cost of the windshield met Chrysler standards. To produce the windshields, Guardian opened a new $35 million plant in Ligonier, Indiana.[8]

The Supplier-Customer Relationship

Acquiring quality parts and materials is a fundamental principle of TQM and is essential in supply chain management. However, the quality of parts and materials does not completely define the supplier-customer relationship. Another important aspect of this relationship is customer service, which to the customer often means prompt, on-time delivery. Customers insist not only that quality items be supplied but also that they be provided on time and in the right amount. As a result, location and transportation can be important parts of the supply chain.

www.prenhall.com/russell

On-demand requires the supplier to deliver goods when demanded by the customer.

The impact of the supplier-customer relationship on location is pronounced for those companies who require **on-demand** (also known as **direct-response**) shipments, or use the just-in-time (JIT) inventory system. For the supplier, JIT means contracting to deliver small quantities of items to their customers "just in time" for production. This can result in deliveries on a daily basis or even several deliveries per day. For example, every part used on the production line at the Honda Marysville, Ohio, plant is deliv-

---

[7] E. Raia, "The Extended Enterprise," *Purchasing* 114, no. 3 (March 4, 1993), 48–51.

[8] E. Raia, "The LH Story," *Purchasing* 114, no. 2 (February 18, 1993): 55–57.

THE COMPETITIVE EDGE

Supplier Quality and Reliability

Perdue Farms exercises a demanding set of controls over supplier operating procedures, which it closely monitors. As an example, approximately 2,000 farmers receive about 5,000 one-day-old chicks into 5,000 Perdue-built chicken houses. To make sure the Perdue quality process is implemented properly, a team of 100 service agents visits the chicken flocks daily.

In Monsanto Chemical Company's supplier quality-upgrading program called Total Quality/Total Partnership, suppliers are rated according to specific sites, products, and, services. In this program, suppliers climb four quality rating levels in the following order: supplier, approved, preferred, and, at the top, partner. Suppliers at the bottom level either move up or out.

Bethlehem Steel Corporation's Supplier excellence certification process evaluated and certified more than 1,250 suppliers and carriers. The certification process includes an evaluation of the supplier's quality system with levels of certification, qualified and preferred, depending on the numerical rating attained from the evaluation and a positive merit assessment. Suppliers must be certified or risk losing Bethlehem's business.

Union Camp Corporation looks favorably on suppliers who achieve ISO 9000 registration, a "third-party" quality certification process administered by the International Organization of Standards. An outside firm evaluates a supplier's quality management program using international standards.

Honda America's quality and purchasing departments work together to ensure supplier quality. The quality department reviews every supplier of Honda parts and suppliers are certified. Teams of three purchasing engineers are sent to Honda suppliers selected for their Best Position program and work with a three-person team from the supplier to brainstorm on new ways to improve product quality and productivity.

SOURCE: Based on J. P. Morgan and S. Cayer, "Quality: Up and Running," *Purchasing* 112, no. 1 (1992): 69–83.

---

ered on a daily basis.[9] When deliveries must be made this frequently and on-time delivery is so crucial to the customer's production process, a supplier's proximity to its customer can be a critical factor. Location of the supplier is one of the most important criteria used by JIT companies for selecting and evaluating suppliers.[10,11,12] Another criterion is on-time delivery performance. Local suppliers are usually preferred, and if that is not possible, suppliers that are close are often given preference.

Cost savings can also be obtained with **continuous replenishment.** Continuous replenishment is the continuous updating of data shared between suppliers and customers such that replenishment, as managed by the supplier, may occur daily or even less. The customer pays a premium for regular daily deliveries instead of weekly deliveries; however, continuous replenishment reduces the need for warehouse space and inventories, thus saving costs. Express courier service for daily deliveries may increase transportation costs for a company by $20 million, but it may reduce working capital requirements for warehousing and inventory by $200 million, thereby reducing overall supply chain costs significantly. However, a successful continuous replenishment system requires accurate product demand forecasting and an information system that includes up-to-date warehouse withdrawal data, shipping data, and point-of-sale data (i.e., computer record of a sale at the retail site) so that the inventory and distribution process can be managed with pinpoint control.

Continuous replenishment sets a predetermined schedule for small, frequent deliveries, thereby reducing customer inventory.

---

[9] E. Raia, "JIT in Detroit," *Purchasing* (1988): 68–77.

[10] A. Ansari and B. Modarress, *Just-In-Time Purchasing* (New York: Free Press, 1990).

[11] R. J. Schonberger and J. P. Gilbert, "Just-In-Time Purchasing: A Challenge for U.S. Industry," *California Management Review* (1983): 58.

[12] S. Dowst, "Quality Suppliers: The Search Goes On," *Purchasing* (September 15, 1988): 94A4–94A12.

Companies often suggest that potential suppliers relocate nearby if they want to be considered for business. Some larger manufacturing companies, such as in the automobile industry, have informed their suppliers that if they wish to continue supplying the company, they must relocate closer to provide the quality delivery performance and customer service expected. For example, more than 75 percent of the U.S. suppliers for Honda are within a 150-mile radius of their Marysville, Ohio, assembly plant. All the suppliers for Buick City in Flint, Michigan, are within 300 miles or 8 hours. Similarly, 75 percent of the suppliers for Ford's Lincoln Continental plant in Wixom, Michigan, are within this same radius. Most suppliers of seats are within 20 miles of the automobile plants they serve. Kasle Steel built a new mill within the gates of Buick City.[13]

In many cases, the supplier is an internal part of the company, and quality customer service means meeting the demands of the overall production process. For example, the box on McDonald's Australian distribution system describes a situation where the location of a food-distribution warehouse was determined by quality standards rather than operational costs. The most cost-effective location in Sydney was too far from the western Australian McDonald's to meet quality delivery standards. These standards include delivering food products to restaurants twice a week within two days after order placement and within fifteen minutes of a specified time. Decisions like this that are not cost-effective in the short run are made to achieve long-term strategic goals for supply chain management and quality improvement.

Types of Facilities

The type of facility is a major determinant of its location. The factors that are important for determining the location of a manufacturing plant are usually different from those that are important in locating a service facility or a warehouse. In this section we discuss the major categories of facilities and the different factors that are important in the location decision.

Heavy Manufacturing

Heavy-manufacturing facilities are large, require a lot of space, and are expensive.

Heavy-manufacturing facilities are plants that are large, require a lot of space, and are expensive to construct, such as automobile plants, steel mills, and oil refineries. The cost of Chrysler's new truck transmission plant in Kokomo, Indiana, is $1 billion, and its engine plant expansion in Detroit will cost $750 million. The cost of Nucor Corporation's new steel mill in Berkeley County, South Carolina, is $500 million. Ford's transaxle plant in Sterling Heights, Michigan, encompasses 2.7 million square feet of floor space.

Factors in the location decision for plants include construction costs, land costs, modes of transportation for shipping heavy manufactured items and receiving bulk shipments of raw materials, proximity to raw materials, utilities, means of waste disposal, and labor availability. Sites for manufacturing plants are normally selected where construction and land costs can be kept at a minimum and raw material sources are nearby in order to reduce transportation costs. Access to railroads is frequently a factor in locating a plant. Environmental issues have increasingly become a factor in plant location decisions. Plants can create pollution, including raw material wastes, burning and air pollution, noise pollution, and traffic pollution. These plants must be located where the harm to the environment is minimized. Although proximity to customers is a factor for some facility types, it is less so for manufacturing plants.

---

[13] Raia, "JIT in Detroit."

THE COMPETITIVE EDGE

Competing with Supply Chain Management at McDonald's in Australia

In 1971 the first McDonald's opened in Australia in Sydney, and by 1992 there were over 300. In most areas of operation, the Australia McDonald's function the same as their U.S. counterparts, except for supply and distribution. The unique geography of Australia—with large unpopulated expanses and relatively small population concentrations—has forced the location of restaurants in different patterns from the United States and has resulted in different logistical challenges.

Most of the Australia McDonald's are operated independently with McDonald's having corporate responsibility for purchasing food and arranging delivery to the restaurants. The first McDonald's restaurants in Sydney, Melbourne, and Brisbane were supplied directly by suppliers, selected and approved by McDonald's. However, in 1974 a central distribution system was established, with F. J. Walker Foods as the primary distributor. By 1990 Walker Foods distributed all food, paper, and supplies for all McDonald's across Australia, although McDonald's still selects all suppliers and negotiates food prices. When the centralized distribution system was started, Walker Foods supplied interstate restaurants in Victoria, Queensland, and South Australia directly from Sydney. As the number of restaurants grew in each market, distribution center warehouses were opened in these markets to serve local restaurants. This logistics system encompasses three functions: the procurement and shipment of 2,000 different ingredients, or raw materials, from 48 food and packaging plants to suppliers, the shipment of more than 200 types of finished products from suppliers to the interstate distribution centers, the ordering of products by the restaurants, and delivery. F. J. Walker Foods annually delivers approximately 6 million cases of food and paper products plus 500 different operating supply items to restaurants across Australia.

An exception to the system was the simultaneous opening of a western Australia restaurant and a serving warehouse in this market. Although it would have been more cost-efficient to make deliveries from the central distribution facility in Sydney to Perth (in western Australia), the 4,000-kilometer distance would have made it impossible to meet McDonald's expected standards of customer service. These standards include delivering frozen, dry, and chilled food products twice a week to each restaurant 98 percent of the time within 15 minutes of a specified time and delivery of complete orders 99.8 percent of the time within 2 days of the order being placed. Although McDonald's concentrates on minimizing inventory stock levels at distribution warehouses, it has not gone to a just-in-time system because of its standards for delivery and quality customer service. Stockouts are absolutely prohibited at distribution centers, and no expense is spared to ensure that every menu item is always available at every restaurant.

SOURCE: Based on P. Ritchie, "McDonald's: A Winner Through Logistics," *International Journal of Physical Distribution and Logistics Management* 20, no. 3 (1990): 21–24.

Light Industry

Light-industry facilities are perceived as cleaner plants that produce electronic equipment and components, computer products, assembled products like TVs, or breweries, or pharmaceutical firms.

Light-industry facilities are smaller, cleaner plants and are usually less costly.

Some of the largest and most expensive new plants in the United States are being constructed for manufacturing semiconductors and computer chips. Motorola's new $3 billion semiconductor facility in Goochland County, Virginia, will include fifteen to twenty campus-like buildings and Intel is constructing a new $2.2 billion semiconductor plant in Hillsboro, Oregon. Land and construction costs tend to be high for these facilities because they make use of the most advanced technology and equipment, and must provide a clean and climate-controlled manufacturing environment. They also depend on a skilled work force so they need to be located in attractive, easily accessible geographic areas with good education and training capabilities. Although close proximity to raw materials is not a requirement for light industry, a good transportation system for supply and distribution is required. The environment tends to be a less impor-

www.prenhall.com/russell

A key objective of Honda's corporate philosophy is to manufacture products in markets in which they are sold. Following this objective Honda opened its Marysville, Ohio plant in 1982, the first Japanese auto plant in America. The clean and bright 3.1 million square feet Marysville plant builds 380,000 Honda Accords annually for the U.S. market and for export. The Marysville plant has 5,200 employees, called associates, some of which are shown here eating lunch in the plant cafeteria. All plant employees including managers eat together in the plant cafeteria so that they can "brainstorm" problems together. In 1989 Honda built a plant in nearby East Liberty, Ohio to manufacture Civics and their engine and transmission plant is located in Anna, Ohio, just north of Dayton. Parts and materials for these plants are purchased from suppliers in 33 states. Five out of every seven Hondas sold in the U.S. are built here. A virtual tour of the Marysville, Ohio Honda plant can be accessed from the Honda home page on the internet at http://www.honda.com.

tant factor in light industry since burning raw materials is not part of the production process nor are there large quantities of toxic or hazardous waste.

Warehouses and Distribution Centers

Warehouses are buildings used to receive, handle, store, and ship products or materials.

Warehouses are an intermediate point in the supply chain where products are held for distribution. Normally a warehouse is a building that is used to receive, handle, store, and then ship products; however, some of the largest business facilities in the United States are warehouse/distribution centers. Light assembly and packaging may sometimes be done in a warehouse, and some warehouse operators will provide sales support and personnel.

Retail companies that have begun to operate on the Internet sometimes function almost exclusively out of a warehouse-type environment. For example, Amazon.com Books sells trade books online out of a group of offices furnished with desks and computers on the fourth floor of an old building in Seattle, supplemented by a 46,000 square-foot warehouse. The company went on-line in 1995 and in 1996 its annual sales revenue was estimated to be $17 million.

Distribution centers for The Gap in Gallatin, Tennessee, Target in Augusta City, Virginia, and Home Depot in Savannah, Georgia, each encompass more than 1.4 million square feet of space—about 30 times bigger than the area of a football field! The UPS Worldwide Logistics warehouse in Louisville, Kentucky, includes 1.3 million square feet of floor space. These centers generally require moderate environmental conditions, although some specialized warehouses require a controlled environment, such as refrigeration or security. Because of their role as intermediate points in the supply chain, transportation costs are often an important factor in the location decision for warehouses. The proximity to markets is also a consideration, depending on the delivery requirements, including frequency of delivery required by the customer. Con-

www.prenhall.com/russell

struction and land costs, labor availability, little proximity to raw materials, and waste disposal are less important.

Retail and Service

Retail and service operations usually require the smallest and least costly facilities. Examples include retail facilities like groceries and department stores, among many others, and such service facilities as restaurants, banks, hotels, cleaners, clinics, and law offices. However, there are always exceptions, and some service facilities like a hospital, a company headquarters, a resort hotel, or a university academic building can be large and expensive. One of the most important factors for locating a service or retail facility is proximity to customers. It is often critical that a service facility be near the customers it serves, and a retail facility must be near the customers who buy from it. Construction costs tend to be less important although land or leasing costs can be high. For retail operations, for which the saying "location is everything" is meaningful, site costs can be very high. Factors like zoning, utilities, transportation, environmental constraints, and labor tend to be less important for service operations, and closeness to suppliers is not usually as important as it is to manufacturing firms that must be close to materials and parts suppliers.

> Service facilities are usually the smallest and least costly.

Site Selection: Where to Locate

When we see in the news that a company has selected a site for a new plant, or a new store is opening, the announcement can appear trivial. Usually it is reported that a particular site was selected from among two or three alternatives, and a few reasons are provided, such as good community, heavy customer traffic, or available land. However, such media reports do not reveal the long, detailed process for selecting a site for a business facility. It usually culminates a selection process that can take several years and the evaluation of dozens or hundreds of potential sites.

Decisions regarding where to locate a business facility or plant are not made often but they tend to be crucial in terms of a firm's profitability and long-term survival. A mistake in location is not easily overcome. Business success often is being "in the right place at the right time." For a service operation such as a restaurant, hotel, or retail store, being in the right place usually means in a location that is convenient and easily accessible to customers.

Location decisions for services tend to be an important part of the overall market strategy for the delivery of their products or services to customers. However, a business cannot simply survey the demographic characteristics of a geographic area and build a facility at the location with the greatest potential for customer traffic; other factors, particularly financial considerations, must be part of the location decision. Obviously, a site on Fifth Avenue in New York City would be attractive for a McDonald's restaurant, but can enough hamburgers and French fries be sold to pay the rent? In this case, the answer is yes.

Location decisions are usually made more frequently for service operations than manufacturing facilities. Facilities for service-related businesses tend to be smaller and less costly, although a hospital can require a huge investment and be very large. Services depend upon a certain degree of market saturation; the location is actually part of their product. Where to locate a manufacturing facility is also important, but for different reasons, not the least of which is the very high expense of building a plant or factory. Although the primary location criteria for a service-related business is usually access to customers, a different set of criteria is important for a manufacturing facility.

These include the nature of the labor force, and labor costs, proximity to suppliers and markets, distribution and transportation costs, energy availability and cost, the community infrastructure of roads, sewers, and utilities, quality of life in a community, and government regulations and taxes.

When the site selection process is initiated, the pool of potential locations for a manufacturing or service facility is, literally, global. In today's international marketplace, countries around the world become potential sites. The site selection process is one of gradually and methodically narrowing down the pool of alternatives until the final location is determined. In the following discussion, we identify some of the factors that companies consider when determining the country, region, community, and site at which to locate a facility.

Global Location Factors

Until the last decade companies tended to locate within their national borders. This has changed in recent years as companies have begun to locate in foreign countries to be closer to newly emerging markets and to take advantage of lower labor costs. New trade agreements between countries have knocked down trade barriers around the world and created new markets like the European Community (EC). The fall of communism has opened up new markets in Eastern Europe and Asia. The trendy retail clothing store, The Gap, has opened over fifty-five stores in the United Kingdom and over seventy in Europe in recent years.

Foreign firms have also begun to locate in the United States to be closer to their customers. Mercedes Benz, BMW, and Honda have all located new facilities in the United States. For both U.S. and foreign companies, the motivation is the same—to reduce supply chain costs and better serve their customers. Relatively slow overseas transportation requires multinational companies to maintain large, costly inventories to serve their foreign customers in a timely manner. This drives up supply chain costs and makes it economical for companies to relocate closer to their markets. In a survey of corporate executives conducted by the International Development Research Council in 1995, one fourth said more than half of their company's revenue came from international operations. Half of the companies surveyed said their growth in the future would come from Asia, and 20 percent said their growth would come from Latin America or Europe.[14]

While foreign markets offer great opportunities, the problems with locating in a foreign country can be substantial, making site location a very important part of supply chain design. For example, while China offers an extremely attractive potential market because of its huge population, growing economy, and cheap labor force, it has probably the most inefficient transportation and distribution systems in Asia, and a morass of government regulations. Nevertheless, U.S. companies' investments in China grew by 500 percent from 1990 to 1994, and total direct foreign investment in China in 1995 totaled $37 billion, second in the world only to the United States. General Motors in a partnership with Shanghai Automotive Industry is building a new $1 billion auto plant in Shanghai; Motorola is constructing a new $700 million semiconductor plant in Tianjin; Intel is building a new microchip plant in Shanghai; and Avon Products is building a new cosmetics plant in Conghua.[15]

Quebec, an attractive market for U.S. companies with a population of 7.3 million and a $125 billion (US) economy, is the ninth largest trading partner of the United

---

[14] A. Pennington, "Global Facilities Go Gangbusters," *Site Selection* 41, no. 1 (February 1996): 156–60.

[15] Ibid.

States. However, Quebec's separatist movement makes it a questionable location for some foreign companies. An independent Quebec would have to reapply to join the North American Free Trade Agreement (NAFTA), and if it were unsuccessful it could be at a disadvantage as a location site. Despite the possibility of separatism, Bristol-Myers, Squibb, Goodyear, Hyundai, IBM, and Kraft Foods have all announced multi-million-dollar expansions in the last few years.[16]

Some of the factors that multinational firms must consider when locating in a foreign country include,

- Government stability
- Government regulations
- Political and economic systems
- Economic stability and growth
- Exchange rates
- Culture
- Climate
- Export and import regulations, duties and tariffs

- Raw material availability
- Number and proximity of suppliers
- Transportation and distribution systems
- Labor force cost and education
- Available technology
- Commercial travel
- Technical expertise
- Cross-border trade regulations
- Group trade agreements

Regional and Community Location Factors in the United States

Manufacturing facilities in the United States were historically located in the Midwest, especially in the Great Lakes region. Industry migrated to the sunbelt areas, the Southeast and Southwest, during the 1960s and 1970s, where labor was cheaper (and not unionized), the climate was better, and the economy was growing. However, in the late 1980s and 1990s, there has been a perceptible shift in new plants and plant expansion back to the nation's agricultural heartland.

From 1993 to 1995 the North Central region, consisting of Illinois, Indiana, Michigan, Ohio, and Wisconsin, attracted more than 4,300 new and expanded facilities—more than any other region in the country. The South Atlantic region was second during this period with just over 4,000 facilities. Ohio was the top state for new and expanded business facilities with almost 2,500; Texas was second with approximately 1,600. Ohio was also the top state in attracting foreign firms.

The most growth in manufacturing facilities is in the Midwest.

Certain states are successful in attracting new manufacturing facilities for a variety of reasons. Ohio, for example, is well located to serve the auto industry along the Interstate-75 corridor, and it is within one-day truck delivery of 60 percent of the U.S. population and two thirds of its purchasing power. It has a good base of skilled and educated labor, a large mass of industry which spawns other businesses, and it has established good incentive programs to attract new businesses. Ohio also benefits from a number of towns and cities with populations less than 50,000 that have a rich agricultural heritage. The residents of these communities have a strong work ethic and are self-reliant and neighborly. These communities typically have quality health services, low crime rates; solid infrastructures of roads, water and sewer systems; open spaces to expand; and quality education.[17]

Ohio attracts manufacturing facilities because of good transportation, skilled labor with a strong work ethic, incentive programs, and quality social services.

---

[16] J. Lyne, "What Next, Quebec?" *Site Selection* 41, no. 1 (February 1996): 58–62.

[17] T. Venable, "Triple Crown, Ohio Gallops to Third Straight Win in U.S. Business Location Race," *Site Selection* 41, no. 1 (February 1996): 124–40; and "Ohio Hometown: The Case for the Micropolitan Community," *Site Selection* 41, no. 1 (February 1996): 2–5.

Labor—cost, availability, work ethic, conflict, and skill—is important in a company's location decision.

Labor is one of the most important factors in a location decision, including the cost of labor, availability, work ethic, the presence of organized labor and labor conflict, and skill and educational level. Traditionally labor costs have been lower and organized labor less visible across the South and Southwest. While labor conflict is anathema to many companies, in some cases labor unions have assisted in attracting new plants or in keeping existing plants from relocating by making attractive concessions.

Closeness to customers can be a factor in providing quality service.

The proximity of suppliers and markets are important location factors. Manufacturing companies need to be close to materials, and service companies like fast-food restaurants, retail stores, groceries, and service stations need to be close to customers and distribution centers. Transportation costs can be significant if frequent deliveries over long distances are required. The closeness of suppliers can determine the amount of inventory a company must keep on hand and how quickly it can serve its own customers. Uncertainty in delivery schedules from suppliers can require excessive inventories.

Service facilities generally require high customer-traffic volume.

It is important for service-related businesses to be located near their customers. Many businesses simply look for a high volume of customer traffic as the main determinant of location, regardless of the competition. An interstate highway exit onto a major thoroughfare always has a number of competing service stations and fast-food restau-

Fashion Island Mall in Newport Beach, California is one of the approximately 38,000 shopping centers that operated in the United States during the first part of this decade. These shopping centers accounted for over $717 billion in annual sales and over 4$\frac{1}{2}$ billion square feet, or 19 square feet for every person in the United States. Three hundred and sixty-five of these centers encompassed over a million square feet each and included an average of 155 stores and businesses, which is more stores than many small towns and communities have. In fact, some of these mega-malls seem like small cities. Shopping centers and malls attract a mass of customers that will support a multitude of different stores and businesses, that on their own could not attract a sufficiently profitable number of customers to a single location. Many retail business chains now locate almost exclusively in shopping centers and malls, thus their location decision becomes one of center selection and where within a center they want to be located. Demographic and geographic considerations are left to the center developers.

rants. Shopping malls are an example of a location in which a critical mass of customer traffic is sought to support a variety of similar and dissimilar businesses. For example, a shopping mall typically has numerous restaurants (sometimes grouped into food courts), several large department stores, and a variety of small specialty stores that sell similar products. In fact, a large department store in a mall will stock almost every product (not brand) that every one of the smaller stores around it also stocks. Instead of seeking a location away from large competitors, these small retail stores cluster together to feed off the customer traffic created by the larger anchor stores. Businesses that rely on a steady customer clientele, such as doctors, dentists, lawyers, barber shops and hair salons, and health clubs often tend to seek locations with limited competition.

Although it is important to be located where customers are in order to make sales, it is also important to be near enough to customers to provide a high level of customer service. This is especially true given the current emphasis and expectations regarding quality service. As international markets have opened up, a number of major manufacturing companies have located plants overseas to minimize transportation costs and be closer to their customers.

Environmental regulations are a factor in many companies' site selection process. An incentive to attract new businesses has been a recent trend to liberalize regulations in many localities. Despite this trend, companies must carefully consider environmental regulations when making their location decision. For example, a new warehouse, considered to be an environmentally "clean" type of facility, may have no difficulty qualifying as an industrial park occupant even under stringent environmental covenants. However, it may later discover it cannot obtain a permit to store products classified as toxic or hazardous. Companies should do their environmental homework before selecting a site.

A company moving into an existing facility should learn about the activities of the previous occupants, or neighbors. They may have left hazardous materials or created conditions which adversely affected the soil or groundwater which the new occupant would have to clean up at considerable expense. Companies should also avoid the following sites: those near landfill areas; sites with underground storage tanks; buildings with asbestos; sites with inadequate sewage treatment, toxic waste discharges by prior occupants, oil and grease leaks from railroads, ships, or highways, runoffs of chemicals (e.g., fertilizers and pesticides) from golf courses and farms; and sites with inadequate storm water drainage.

Another important factor, **infrastructure,** is the collection of physical support systems of a location including the roads, water and sewer, and utilities. If a community does not have a good infrastructure, it must make improvements if it hopes to attract new business facilities. From a company's perspective an inadequate infrastructure will add to its supply chain costs and inhibit its customer service.

Infrastructure is the roads, water, and sewer, and utilities at a location.

www.prenhall.com/russell

As an example of an inadequate infrastructure, consider Martha's Vineyard, an island off the Massachusetts coast. Tourism is virtually the island's sole industry, and in recent years it has been successful in attracting increasing numbers of tourists. Its products are lodging, sightseeing, and food services, and its supply chain includes the road system and ferry that brings tourists to the island. However, visitors have increased so much in recent years that the road system can no longer accommodate the traffic. On the Fourth of July 1995, traffic lined up for three miles on the two-lane road leading to the ferry, angering residents and visitors. The solution was to require ferry reservations sixteen days in advance. However, all ferry space for 1996 was booked by February, leaving many residents without reservations to get on and off the island. Lodging reservations dropped significantly in some parts of the island because visitors were not sure they could make it onto the island.

Factors that are considered when selecting the part of the country and community for a facility are summarized as follows:

- Labor (availability, education, cost, and unions)
- Proximity of customers
- Number of customers
- Construction/leasing costs
- Land cost
- Modes and quality of transportation
- Transportation costs
- Community government
- Local business regulations
- Government services (Chamber of Commerce, etc.)
- Business climate
- Community services
- Incentive packages

- Government regulations
- Environmental regulations
- Raw material availability
- Commercial travel
- Climate
- Infrastructure (roads, water, sewers)
- Quality of life
- Taxes
- Availability of sites
- Financial services

- Community inducements
- Proximity of suppliers
- Education system

Site Location Factors

When locating at a new site, a business can either purchase or lease an existing building, or select a parcel of land and construct a new facility. Service-related businesses often rent or purchase existing facilities, for example, in shopping malls or office buildings. It is usually more difficult for manufacturing operations to find a building suitable for their specific needs, so construction is required.

If a new facility is built, the factors to consider include the size of the space, potential for expansion, soil stability and content, neighborhood, drainage, direct access to roads, sewer and water connections, utilities, and cost. When evaluating a site for lease or purchase, other considerations (that would be built into a new facility) include structural integrity of the facility, the ability to make alterations to the structure, existing parking and the potential for additional parking, neighborhood, loading-dock facilities, storage, maintenance and utility expenses, the lease rate (or purchase cost), and, if leasing, the length of the lease.

A recent trend in site locations has been industrial and office parks, in which many of the special needs of businesses have been planned for. Industrial parks usually have a combination of available parcels of land and structures that cater to service operations or vendors with storage requirements and light manufacturing. Office parks typically have buildings and office suites that are attractive to white-collar service operations such as insurance companies, lawyers, doctors, real estate, and financial institutions.

Location Incentives

Location incentives include tax credits, relaxed government regulations, job training, infrastructure improvements, and money.

Besides physical and societal characteristics, local incentives have increasingly become a major important factor in attracting companies to specific locations. Incentive packages typically include job tax credits, relaxed government regulations, job training, road and sewage infrastructure improvements, and sometimes just plain cash. These incentives plus the advantages of a superior location can significantly reduce a company's supply chain costs while helping it achieve its strategic goal for customer service.

Toyota selected Princeton, Indiana, a small town 20 miles north of Evansville, as the site for a new $700 million factory to manufacture its T100 midsize pickup trucks.

www.prenhall.com/russell

THE COMPETITIVE EDGE

Competing with Attractive, Small-Town Facility Location Sites in Ohio

www.prenhall.com/russell

From 1993 to 1995 Ohio was selected by Site Selection magazine as the top state in the United States for new and expanded business location sites. Ohio is an attractive location because of its large number of "micropolitan" communities, cities, and towns with a population of less than 50,000, that are economically, politically, and socially self-sustaining. Such small towns in the heartland of America are a favorite location site of industry.

A Ohio micropolitan community that has been successful in attracting new businesses is Bowling Green. Strategically located 20 miles from Toledo on I-75, it is the home of Bowling Green State University, itself an attractive asset to companies. The port of Toledo, one of the top three on Lake Erie, and Toledo Express Airport, hub for two international air freight carriers, are only 30 minutes away, and Detroit is 85 miles away. Bowling Green has inexpensive electricity with a reliable power system; the terrain is flat and inexpensive to develop, and the university provides a versatile student work force.

Another Ohio community that has been successful in attracting businesses is Marysville. Marysville, about 30 miles west of Columbus with a population of 10,000, gained international exposure in the 1980s when it was selected as the site for Honda's first manufacturing facility in America. Honda installed its TQM program, the "Honda Way," at Marysville, which was instrumental in changing American automaking, and Honda was the first Japanese automaker to supply world markets from the United States at Marysville. The city is also the home of the corporate headquarters of the Scotts Co., the world's foremost producer of home lawn-care products, the Nestlé R&D center, and a Goodyear plant. Marysville exhibits many of the attractive location features found in other Ohio small towns including ample development sites, flat terrain, close proximity to transportation and distribution centers, a strong area work ethic, good quality of life, few government restrictions, low cost of living, and little crime.

SOURCES: "Ohio Hometown: The Case for the Micropolitan Community," *Site Selection* 41, no. 1 (February 1996): 2–5; "Bowling Green: Endowed with Education, Rural Work Ethic," *Site Selection* 41, no. 1 (February 1996): 6–7; "Marysville: International Home Town," *Site Selection* 41, no. 1 (February 1996): 18–19.

The factory will employ 1,300 and produce about 100,000 trucks per year when it begins production in 1998. State and local government officials provided a $72 million incentive package that included $12 million to construct a new interchange and other improvements on US-41, $2.8 million to help train workers, and a maximum of $15 million in job tax credits for workers hired at the plant. However, this package was small compared to some offered by other states to attract automakers. Alabama offered an incentive package worth approximately $252 million to attract a Mercedes plant in 1993, and South Carolina provided BMW with a $130 million package for a plant in 1992.[18]

North Carolina also has an attractive incentive program administered through its Industrial Recruitment Competitive Fund. Inducements available to companies include cash incentives and a strong worker training program through the statewide community college system. Its Job Creation Tax Credit program provides new or expanding businesses a tax credit of $2,800 per new job created, for a minimum of nine new jobs. An Industrial Development Fund provides up to $2,400 for each new job created up to a maximum of $250,000. Also available are industrial development bonds. Locally communities will prepare sites, make infrastructure improvements, and extend rails and utilities to plant sites.[19]

States and communities cannot afford not to offer incentives if they hope to attract new companies and jobs. However, they must make sure that the amount of their invest-

Excessive incentives can overburden a community.

[18] T. Venable, "Toyota Turns into Indiana with $700 Million Truck Plant," *Site Selection* 41, no. 1 (February 1996): 46–52.

[19] L. Liston, "North Carolina's Eastern Eden," *Site Selection* 41, no. 1 (February 1996): 2–12.

THE COMPETITIVE EDGE

Using a Site Specialist at Motorola to Locate a New Semiconductor Plant

When Motorola selected Goochland County, Virginia, near Richmond for its new $3 billion semiconductor manufacturing plant, it ended a two-year search process that started with a list of 300 potential areas around the country. Motorola's first step was to hire a site search specialist from Park One, a real estate and facilities consulting firm in Virginia Beach.

The search specialist first reduced the list of sites to 30, primarily in the Southeast where right-to-work laws prohibit employees from being required to join unions. In May 1994 the specialist met with key representatives from organizations in the Richmond area, including the Greater Richmond Partnership, the Virginia Department of Economic Development, Virginia Power, the engineering school at Virginia Commonwealth University, Richmond International Airport, and other companies in the area such as AT&T. In August 1994 Motorola's vice

president for construction was given a tour of the three finalist sites near Raleigh and Durham, North Carolina, Austin, Texas, and in Goochland County, Virginia. The 370-acre site in Goochland County, with wooded seclusion, rolling topography, and good roads and utilities was the best the VP had ever seen for a semiconductor operation. From that point Motorola engaged in serious dialogue with state and local officials about labor force, taxes, utilities, the environment, and education. State officials presented an incentive package to Motorola, and in late November and early December 1994 the president of Motorola's semiconductor products division visited Richmond and the Goochland County site and met with key local leaders and officials. The process ended in April 1995 when Motorola purchased the Goochland site with plans to build a 15- to 20-building facility that could create 5,000 jobs in the area.

SOURCE: M. Martz, "Motorola Plant Site Sold Itself," *Richmond Times-Dispatch*, April 16, 1995, pp. A1, A12.

ment in incentive packages and the costs they incur for infrastructure improvements are balanced against the number of new jobs developed and the expansion of the economy the new plant will provide. Incentives are a good public investment unless they bankrupt the locality. A $150 million incentive package that Kentucky used to attract Toyota in the 1980s is estimated to have cost $50,000 per job created.[20] While some small communities are successful in attracting new businesses, they are left with little remaining tax base to pay for the infrastructure improvements needed to support the increased population drawn by job demand. Thus, states and communities, much like businesses, need a strategy for economic development that weighs the costs versus the benefits of attracting companies.

Location Analysis Techniques

We will discuss three techniques to help make a location decision—the location rating factor, the center-of-gravity technique, and the load-distance technique. The location factor rating mathematically evaluates location factors, such as those identified in the previous section. The center-of-gravity and load-distance techniques are quantitative models that centrally locates a proposed facility among existing facilities.

Location Factor Rating

The decision where to locate is based on many different types of information and inputs. There is no single model or technique that will select "the best" site from a group. However, techniques are available that help to organize site information and that can be used as a starting point for comparing different locations.

---

[20] J. A. Finkle, "Location Incentives Are Unfair and Poorly Justified," *Site Selection* 41, no. 1 (February 1996): 54–55.

In the **location factor rating** system, factors that are important in the location decision are identified. Each factor is weighted from 0 to 1.00 to prioritize the factor and reflect its importance. A subjective score is assigned (usually between 0 and 100) to each factor based on its attractiveness compared to other locations, and the weighted scores are summed. Decisions typically will not be made based solely on these ratings, but they provide a good way to organize and rank factors.

Location factor rating is a method for identifying and weighting important location factors.

The Dynaco Manufacturing Company is going to build a new plant to manufacture ring bearings (used in automobiles and trucks). The site selection team is evaluating three sites, and they have scored the important factors for each as follows. They want to use these ratings to compare the locations.

		SCORES (0 to 100)		
LOCATION FACTOR	Weight	Site 1	Site 2	Site 3
Labor pool and climate	0.30	80	65	90
Proximity to suppliers	0.20	100	91	75
Wage rates	0.15	60	95	72
Community environment	0.15	75	80	80
Proximity to customers	0.10	65	90	95
Shipping modes	0.05	85	92	65
Air service	0.05	50	65	90

(handwritten note: — ideal for group decision making)

SOLUTION:

The weighted scores for each site are computed by multiplying the factor weights by the score for that factor. For example the weighted score for "labor pool and climate" for site 1 is

(0.30) (80) = 24 points

The weighted scores for each factor for each site and the total scores are summarized as follows.

	WEIGHTED SCORES		
LOCATION FACTOR	Site 1	Site 2	Site 3
Labor pool and climate	24.00	19.50	27.00
Proximity to suppliers	20.00	18.20	15.00
Wage rates	9.00	14.25	10.80
Community environment	11.25	12.00	12.00
Proximity to customers	6.50	9.00	9.50
Shipping modes	4.25	4.60	3.25
Air service	2.50	3.25	4.50
Total score	77.50	80.80	82.05

Site 3 has the best factor rating compared to the other locations; however, this evaluation would have to be used with other information, particularly a cost analysis, before making a decision.

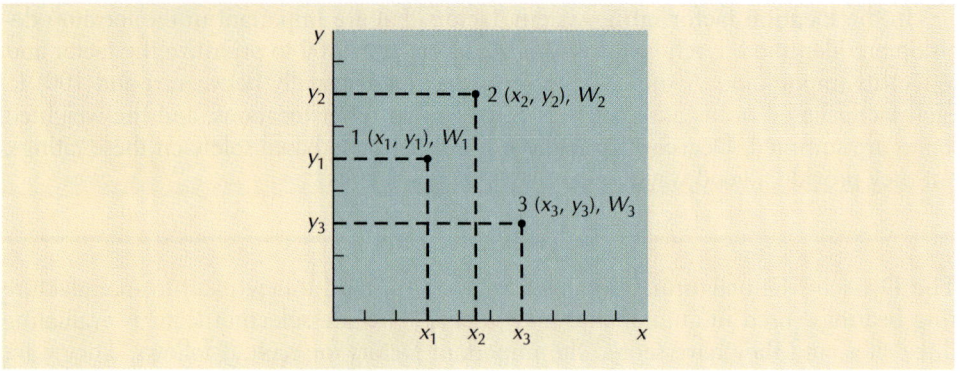

FIGURE 9.3   Grid Map Coordinates

Center-of-Gravity Technique

The **center of gravity** is the center of movement in a geographic area based on transport weight and distance.

In general, transportation costs are a function of distance, weight, and time. The **center-of-gravity,** or *weight center,* technique is a quantitative method for locating a facility such as a warehouse at the center of movement in a geographic area based on weight and distance. This method identifies a set of coordinates designating a central location on a map relative to all other locations.

The starting point for this method is a grid map set up on a Cartesian plane, as shown in Figure 9.3. There are three locations, 1, 2, and 3, each at a set of coordinates (x_i, y_i) identifying its location in the grid. The value W_i is the annual weight shipped from that location. The objective is to determine a central location for a new facility.

The coordinates for the location of the new facility are computed using the following formulas:

$$x = \frac{\sum_{i=1}^{n} x_i W_i}{\sum_{i=1}^{n} W_i}, \qquad y = \frac{\sum_{i=1}^{n} y_i W_i}{\sum_{i=1}^{n} W_i}$$

where

x, y = coordinates of the new facility at center of gravity

x_i, y_i = coordinates of existing facility i

W_i = annual weight shipped from facility i

**EXAMPLE
9.2**

*The Center-of-Gravity
Technique*

The Burger Doodle restaurant chain purchases ingredients from four different food suppliers. The company wants to construct a new central distribution center to process and package the ingredients before shipping them to their various restaurants. The suppliers transport ingredient items in 40-foot truck trailers, each with a capacity of 38,000 pounds. The locations of the four suppliers, A, B, C, and D, and the annual number of trailer loads that will be transported to the distribution center are shown in the following figure.

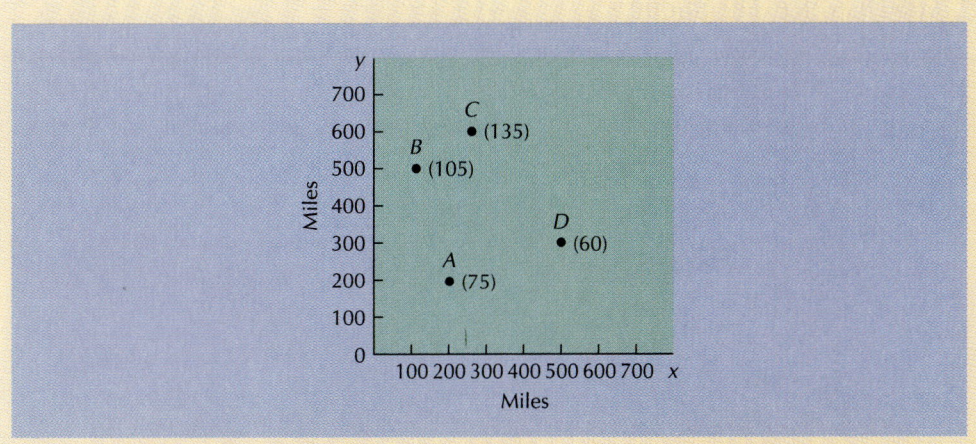

Using the center-of-gravity method, determine a possible location for the distribution center.

SOLUTION:

A	B	C	D
$x_A = 200$	$x_B = 100$	$x_C = 250$	$x_D = 500$
$y_A = 200$	$y_B = 500$	$y_C = 600$	$y_D = 300$
$W_A = 75$	$W_B = 105$	$W_C = 135$	$W_D = 60$

$$x = \frac{\sum\limits_{i=A}^{D} x_i W_i}{\sum\limits_{i=A}^{D} W_i}$$

$$= \frac{(200)(75) + (100)(105) + (250)(135) + (500)(60)}{75 + 105 + 135 + 60}$$

$$= 238$$

$$y = \frac{\sum\limits_{i=A}^{D} y_i W_i}{\sum\limits_{i=A}^{D} W_i}$$

$$= \frac{(200)(75) + (500)(105) + (600)(135) + (300)(60)}{75 + 105 + 135 + 60}$$

$$= 444$$

Thus, the suggested coordinates for the new distribution center location are $x = 238$ and $y = 444$. However, it should be kept in mind that these coordinates are based on straight-line distances, and in a real situation actual roads might follow more circuitous routes.

Load-Distance Technique

Load-distance technique is a method of evaluating different locations based on the load being transported and the distance.

A variation of the center-of-gravity method for determining the coordinates of a facility location is the **load-distance technique.** In this method, a single set of location coordinates is not identified. Instead, various locations are evaluated using a load-distance value that is a measure of weight and distance. For a single potential location, a load-distance value is computed as follows:

$$LD = \sum_{i=1}^{n} l_i d_i$$

where

LD = the load-distance value

l_i = the load expressed as a weight, number of trips, or units being shipped from the proposed site to location i

d_i = the distance between the proposed site and location i

The distance d_i in this formula can be the travel distance, if that value is known, or can be determined from a map. It can also be computed using the following formula for the straight-line distance between two points, which is also the hypotenuse of a right triangle.

$$d_i = \sqrt{(x_i - x)^2 + (y_i - y)^2}$$

where

(x,y) = coordinates of proposed site

(x_i, y_i) = coordinates of existing facility

The load-distance technique is applied by computing a load-distance value for each potential facility location. The implication is that the location with the lowest value would result in the minimum transportation cost and thus would be preferable.

[handwritten annotation: $d_i = \sqrt{(existing\ x_i - proposed\ x)^2 + (existing\ y_i - proposed\ y)^2}$]

EXAMPLE 9.3	

The Load-Distance Technique

Burger Doodle wants to evaluate three different sites it has identified for its new distribution center relative to the four suppliers identified in Example 9.2. The coordinates of the three sites under consideration are as follows:

Site 1: $x_1 = 360, y_1 = 180$

Site 2: $x_2 = 420, y_2 = 450$

Site 3: $x_3 = 250, y_3 = 400$

SOLUTION:

First, the distances between the proposed sites (1, 2, and 3) and each existing facility (A, B, C, and D), are computed using the straight-line formula for d_i:

Site 1: $d_A = \sqrt{(x_A - x_1)^2 + (y_A - y_1)^2}$

$= \sqrt{(200 - 360)^2 + (200 - 180)^2}$

$= 161.2$

$$d_B = \sqrt{(x_B - x_1)^2 + (y_B - y_1)^2}$$
$$= \sqrt{(100 - 360)^2 + (500 - 180)^2}$$
$$= 412.3$$

$$d_C = \sqrt{(x_C - x_1)^2 + (y_C - y_1)^2}$$
$$= \sqrt{(250 - 360)^2 + (600 - 180)^2}$$
$$= 434.2$$

$$d_D = \sqrt{(x_D - x_1)^2 + (y_D - y_1)^2}$$
$$= \sqrt{(500 - 360)^2 + (300 - 180)^2}$$
$$= 184.4$$

Site 2: $d_A = 333$, $d_B = 323.9$, $d_C = 226.7$, $d_D = 170$
Site 3: $d_A = 206.2$, $d_B = 180.3$, $d_C = 200$, $d_D = 269.3$

Next, the formula for load distance is computed for each proposed site.

$$\text{LD (site 1)} = \sum_{i=1}^{D} l_i d_i$$
$$= (75)(161.2) + (105)(412.3) + (135)(434.2) + (60)(184.4)$$
$$= 125{,}063$$

$$\text{LD (site 2)} = (75)(333) + (105)(323.9) + (135)(226.7) + (60)(170)$$
$$= 99{,}789$$

$$\text{LD (site 3)} = (75)(206.2) + (105)(180.3) + (135)(200) + (60)(269.3)$$
$$= 77{,}555$$

Since site 3 has the lowest load-distance value, it would be assumed that this location would also minimize transportation costs. Notice that site 3 is very close to the location determined using the center-of-gravity method in Example 9.2.

Computerized Location Analysis with Excel and POM for Windows

Location factor ratings can be done with Microsoft Excel. Exhibit 9.1 shows the Excel spreadsheet for Example 9.1. Notice that the active cell is E12 with the formula (shown on the formula bar at the top of the spreadsheet) for computing the weighted score for site 1.

POM for Windows also has a module for computing location factor ratings as well as the center-of-gravity technique. The solution screen for the application of the center-of-gravity technique in Example 9.2 is shown in Exhibit 9.2.

Transportation and Distribution Systems

Transportation is a key element in successful supply chain management. For some manufacturing firms, transportation costs can be as much as 20 percent of total production costs. For service companies involved in the distribution of retail items such as

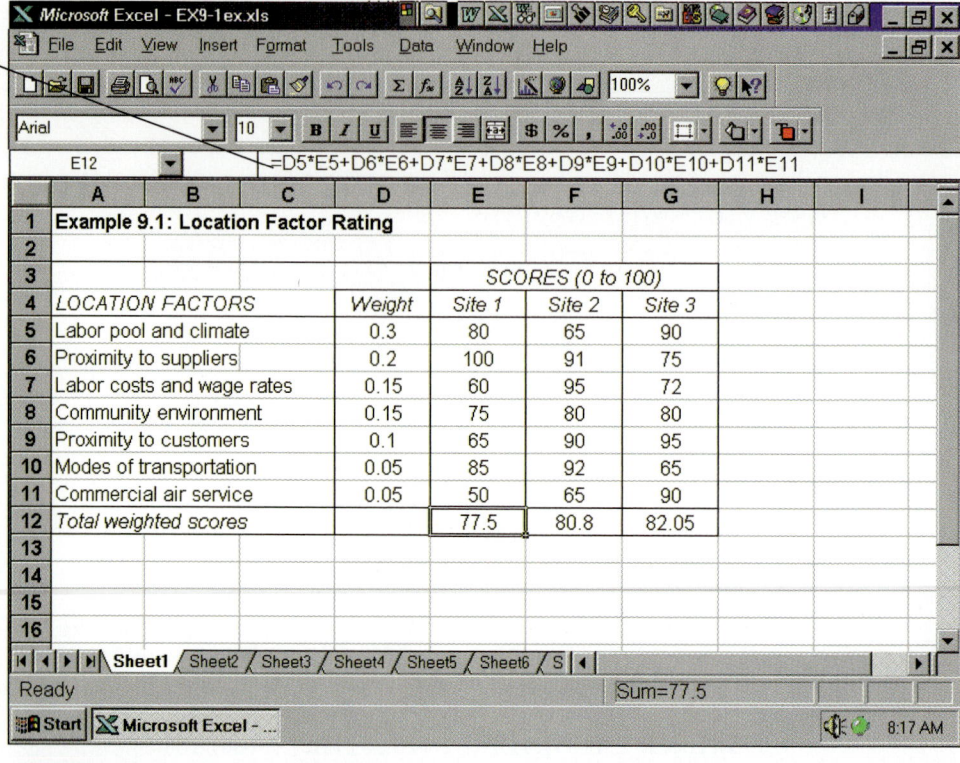

Formula for computing weighted score for site 1

EXHIBIT 9.1

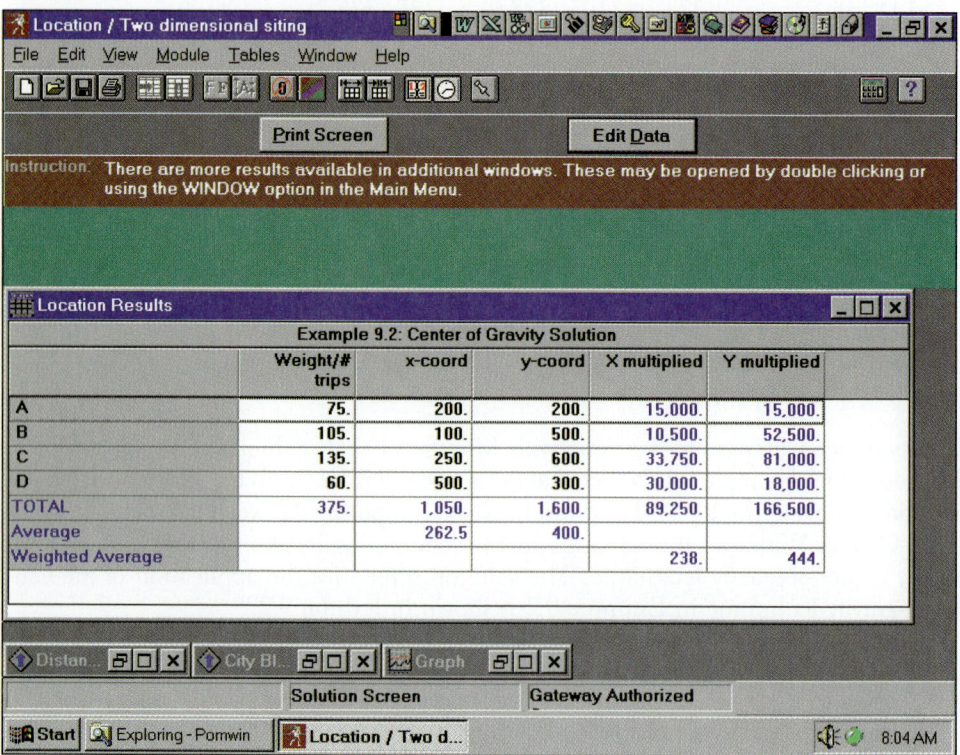

EXHIBIT 9.2

catalog sales, it can be even higher. In one year L. L. Bean ships approximately 11 million packages, 650,000 in a week, which is about 19 tractor-trailer loads. During the Christmas season, it will fill a 40-foot UPS trailer every 20 minutes.

Transportation costs depend largely on where a company is located relative to its suppliers, warehouses, distribution centers, and customers. The level of customer service—speed and frequency of delivery—required by a company's customers can determine the mode of transportation and costs. Inventory levels within a company's supply chain are affected by the mode of transportation used and how close it is to the company's physical facilities. The transportation mode selected by a company can dictate the type of material handling, packaging, loading, and order processing systems used.

The five principal modes of transportation within the United States and between countries are railroads, highways (trucking), water, air, and pipelines. In the United States the greatest volume of freight is shipped by railroads (approximately one third of the total), followed by trucking, pipeline, and inland waterways. By far the smallest volume is carried by air. The cheapest modes of transportation are pipelines and water, each averaging less than 2 cents per ton-mile (one ton of freight carried one mile), with rail costs slightly higher at 3 cents per ton-mile. Truck costs are a little less than 40 cents per ton-mile and air freight over twice as high as trucking at about 90 cents per ton-mile. Air is obviously the fastest form of transportation, and water and pipeline are the slowest. Trucks are faster than railroads for short distances, and they are about even over longer distances. However, because of different shipping requirements and the availability of different modes of transportation as goods move between regions of the country and between countries around the world, different modes of transportation are often combined. This is referred to as *intermodal transportation*.

Railroads

There are more than 150,000 miles of railroad lines in the United States, most concentrated in the East and Midwest. Railroads are particularly good for transporting low-value, high-density, bulk products such as raw materials over long distances between major distribution centers. Such products generally require little sorting or classification. Of the total annual rail freight tonnage, a little more than half comprises coal, minerals, and ores, with coal accounting for over 40 percent. In fact, 90 percent of all coal transport is by train.

In general, railroads have not been as economical for shipping small loads over short distances because of the high cost of terminal handling and the inflexibility of rail lines. Railroads also operate on less flexible schedules than trucks, and they usually cannot go directly from one business location or plant to another as trucks can; trains operate from railyard to railyard. Rail transportation is also usually slower than trucking, since shipments spend some amount of time being put together as trains at terminals. Rail freight service has the worst record of quality performance of all modes of freight transport—almost ten times more late deliveries than trucking.[21]

Railroads have made several innovations to help overcome some of these disadvantages and to compete more effectively with trucking for smaller loads. *Intermodal rail service* hauls truck trailers or containers on railroad flatcars or specially designed "well cars" which feature a well-like lower section in which the trailer or container rides.

www.prenhall.com/russell

The five major modes of transportation are railroads, trucking, water, air, and pipelines.

Intermodal transportation combines two or more modes of transportation.

www.prenhall.com/russell
Rails: low-cost, high-volume transport.

Rail quality is the worst of all major freight-transport modes.

---

[21] P. Bradley, "Carriers Pursue Great Leaps Along Road to Better Service," *Purchasing* (January 4, 1993): 83–87.

In one form of intermodal transportation, goods are loaded into truck trailers or containers, driven to a rail intermodal yard, and loaded on rail cars, such as the double stack cars shown here. The railway hauls the cars to other terminals or ports, where the trailers or containers may be transferred to ships or be delivered by truck to their final destinations. This combines the flexibility of trucking for pickup and delivery with the low cost of long haul rail service. Through the 1980's and into the 1990's over four million intermodal trailer loads were moved annually in the United States. Norfolk Southern uses cars (such as the double stack cars shown here) extensively to meet JIT manufacturing demands of automotive industry customers in the Detroit area. On the west coast the Southern Pacific Railroad originates thirty-five eastbound double stack trains per week from Southern California alone.

They combine the low-cost, long-distance travel of trains with the flexible delivery and pickup capabilities of trucking.

Double- and triple-stacking stacks containers on top of each other on a railcar.

Double-stacking, stacking one container on top of another on a railcar, as pioneered by American President Lines (APL) in 1984, can be as much as 40 percent cheaper than long-haul trucking. APL operates a long-haul container network of fifty-nine terminals in the United States, Mexico, and Canada. Triple-stacking was introduced by Mark VII, an intermodal carrier, in 1994.

Another recent innovation is the Road-Railer—a truck trailer with steel wheels for rail travel and rubber tires for road travel. These trailers can swiftly change from highway to rails and back again, allowing for more scheduling flexibility, faster deliveries, and smaller loads.

Intermodal shipping that combines rails and trucking grew faster than any other segment of the freight shipping industry from 1993 to 1995, averaging 5.7 percent compound annual growth since 1988. By 1997 intermodal transportation is expected to carry 35 percent of all freight shipments of 500 miles or more. Procter and Gamble ships between 7 and 10 percent of its freight intermodally, about 50,000 to 60,000 containers per year. However, P&G still adds a safety stock to loads to offset late rail deliveries. For example, if the Chicago to Los Angeles transit time is three days, Proctor and Gamble allows four days to make sure of on-time delivery to their customers.[22] However, these forms of intermodal shipping have demonstrated a much higher level of quality performance than traditional rail freight service, comparing more favorably with trucking.

[22] H. L. Richardson, "Partnerships for Intermodal Excellence," *Transportation and Distribution* 37, no. 3 (March 1996): 34–38.

Trucking

Trucking is the most used mode of freight transportation in the United States. Trucks provide flexible point-to-point service, delivering small loads over short to long distances over widely dispersed geographic areas. The trucking system is extensive, with thousands of firms in the United States, and service is typically fast, reliable, and less damage-prone than rail shipping. However, although the ability to handle small loads efficiently is an advantage, the inability to carry large loads economically is trucking's most serious disadvantage. Trucks also lose their cost advantage over railroads over long distances when terminal handling costs are proportionally less of the total transport bill and labor costs are proportionally more.

Companies that have adopted TQM programs and JIT systems or require on-demand delivery have put increased pressure on truck carriers to improve performance. This means picking up and delivering orders complete and free from damage, on time, with the paperwork in order, at a low cost. Carriers are now being looked at as a critical part of the supply chain from the supplier to the purchaser/processor to the eventual customer. An effective relationship between suppliers and their customers/purchasers can be disrupted by a carrier that is unable to meet tight delivery schedules and damages loads during transit. As a result many companies have reduced the number of truck carriers they employed to a select few, or single-sourcing their transportation needs.

Single-sourcing in transportation means reducing the number of transportation carriers to relatively few, although not usually one. From 1993 to 1996 Du Pont reduced its truck carrier base from twenty to about five. Over a five-year period, Monsanto cut its carriers from ten to several.[23] For the shipper and the carrier the advantages of single-sourcing include economies of scale, more volume per carrier, and the shipper becomes a more important customer. Single-sourcing results in a stronger relationship between shippers and carriers such that they become more dependent on each other and more willing to help each other. Some companies, as part of the strategic design of their supply chain, are selling their private carrier fleets and single-sourcing their transportation needs to focus more closely on their core businesses. Other companies use only one carrier, but allow that carrier to outsource to other carriers from a group acceptable to the shipper. In this type of relationship the carrier is usually obligated to take 100 percent of a customer's loads; it cannot turn down anything. Others like Wal-Mart have their own private truck fleet in order to gain more direct control over their supply chain.

Single-sourcing is also becoming a factor in rail transportation, but not necessarily by design from the shipper's perspective. Railroads have been consolidating through mergers leaving many shippers with only one rail source. These may leave some U.S. locations in a noncompetitive situation for rail transport, which may ultimately result in shippers seeking alternatives with truck carriers. This will be especially true if the trend toward smaller, more frequent deliveries with less inventory continues.

Airfreight

In recent years there have been a proliferation of airfreight carriers that carry relatively small packages, including UPS, DHL, Federal Express, and Puralator, domestically and overseas. However, the majority of this type of air cargo moves on passenger flights. Even though air transport is the least utilized of all shipping modes, it is the fastest grow-

www.prenhall.com/russell
Trucking: flexible, small loads, good quality.

Trucking has become part of the supply chain supplier-customer relationship.

---

[23] H. Richardson, "Bulk Shipping: Single Source Wise Favor," *Transportation and Distribution* 37, no. 4 (April 1996): 40–44.

ing. In 1995 total domestic and internal airfreight emanating from the United States grew by 4.5 percent while total international airfreight increased by almost 8 percent.

The type of products shipped by airfreight tend to be lightweight or small, such as electronic components, medical supplies, perishable products such as flowers or fruit, or emergency items where quick delivery outweighs cost. However, chartered aircraft are sometimes used for large all-freight shipments as well. For example, livestock are sometimes transported by chartered aircraft instead of ships because a short flight of less than a day is much less harmful to animals and quicker than transoceanic ship transport lasting twenty days or longer. Large aircraft like the Boeing 747 and the Airbus can be configured to carry freight containers only or a combination of passengers on an upper deck and containers or pallets beneath the passenger compartment in a lower deck.

The advantages of airfreight are quickness and reliability. It is an efficient and economical means of transport for high-value, lightweight products that need to be shipped over long distances. It can be advantageous for overseas transit, where the alternative is slower water transport. However, air transport is so much more expensive than other transport systems that it is cost-prohibitive for most types of products. In addition, airfreight is part of a terminal-to-terminal logistics system that requires handling, loading, and unloading at the origin and destination, combined with truck pickup and delivery. Airfreight companies have become very adept at combining air and trucking systems, resulting in reliable and rapid delivery in diverse geographic areas and over short distances. However, it is still very costly, and for short distances of less than 500 miles, or a single day's road travel, it may not be much quicker than a point-to-point truck carrier.

Air transport is quick but expensive.

www.prenhall.com/russell

The Federal Express Superhub in Memphis, Tennessee, is the headquarters of Federal Express. Federal Express, the industry leader in overnight mail service, began to see its market share and profitability erode during the mid-1980s from fierce competition, a burgeoning fax business, and electronic mail. In reaction Federal Express strategically shifted its focus from overnight letter service to the higher margin package delivery business. Federal Express has always been a leader in the use of technology. Hand-held Cosmos trackers and computer terminals in their vans allow drivers to track customer packages and quickly access customer data. Federal Express is using the same technology to manage customer inventories for high-priced goods in warehouses at its hubs. With an expanded truck fleet and second-day package delivery, Federal Express has become a just-in-time deliverer for companies like IBM who want to get out of warehousing.

THE COMPETITIVE EDGE

The Federal Express Superhub

The central component in Federal Express's global air-freight system is the terminal it constructed in Memphis, Tennessee. Called the *superhub*, this facility is the nerve center of Federal Express's vast distribution network. Packages from around the world are routed to the super-hub to be sorted and sent on to their destinations. The support network includes sorting operations in Los Angeles, Oakland, Chicago, Indianapolis, Newark, London, Brussels, and the Far East. Each night, in less than three hours, the superhub sorts and transfers more than a million packages between connecting flights encompassing more than 100 planes. The superhub, pioneered by Federal Express, has been copied by all other airfreight express services.

SOURCE: Based on *The Allyn and Bacon Plant Tour Video*, Program 1: "Federal Express: Setting the Pace for the 90s," copyright 1988 by Federal Express, distributed by Allyn and Bacon.

Water

Shipping by water is one of the oldest means of freight transport in the United States, beginning with the construction of the Erie Canal between 1817 and 1825. Over the years an intricate system of waterways, canals, and lock systems has been developed in the United States and abroad. Water transport is still a significant means for transporting certain types of products between specific locations, although it is less visible and publicized than other transport modes. The three primary water transport systems for the United States are inland waterways, consisting of river systems, canals, and the Great Lakes, the nation's coastlines, and the oceans that connect the United States with the rest of the world.

Water transport is a very low-cost form of shipping; however, it is also slow. It is tied to a fixed system of river and coastal ports that serve as terminals and distribution points. It is limited to heavy, bulk items such as raw materials, minerals, ores, grains, chemicals, and petroleum products. If delivery speed is not a factor, water transport is cost competitive with railroads for shipping these kinds of bulk products.

Water transport is the only means of international shipping between countries separated by oceans for most products, since air transport is limited to a very narrow range of freight items. Transoceanic shipping companies have been effective in developing intermodal transport systems. They combine trucks, railroads, and ships to connect markets, customers, and suppliers around the world. The most successful and visible example is container systems and container ships. Standardized containers that fit on rail flat cars and can be reloaded onto truck trailers are an effective and economical means of transporting products across long distances that encompass land and water.

www.prenhall.com/russell

Water transport: low-cost, high-volume, slow.

Pipelines

In the United States, pipelines are used primarily for transporting crude oil from oil fields to refineries and petroleum products such as gasoline from refineries to tank farms. There are about 150,000 miles of crude oil pipelines in the United States. Pipelines called slurry lines carry other products that have been pulverized and transformed into liquid form like coal and kaolin. Once the product arrives at its destination, water is removed leaving the solid material. Although pipelines require a high initial capital investment to construct, they are economical because they can carry materials over terrain that would be difficult for trucks or trains to travel across, for example, the Trans-Alaska pipeline. Once in place pipelines have a long life and are low-cost in terms of operation, maintenance, and labor.

www.prenhall.com/russell

Pipelines are used to transport petroleum products and other products in liquid form over terrain that is difficult for trucks.

More than eighty percent of the seaborne cargo handled by the Port of Singapore Authority is containerized. The Port of Singapore handles over 10 million TEU's (twenty-foot container equivalent units) annually at three container terminals. The Brani terminal shown here has 9 berths, 31 Quay cranes, and a capacity of 5.5 million TEUs. Since its first container ship in 1972, the Port of Singapore has grown from 130,000 TEUs annually to over 10 million TEUs annually and has been the world's busiest port in terms of shipping tonnage since 1986.

Distribution

A major goal of a distribution operation is speed—to reduce the time to get products to customers as much as possible. A key factor in reducing delivery time is location. Many companies, especially in the retail service industries, are building regional distribution centers within next-day or second-day truck delivery. This makes distribution more compatible with quick-response or on-demand delivery requirements of customers. The trend is to locate distribution centers in outlying areas of large markets where construction and other costs are lower. For example, distribution centers on Long Island

[handwritten margin note: Distribution centers → economies in transportation]

THE COMPETITIVE EDGE

Direct-Response Catalog Shipping at Donnelley Logistics Services and Mailfast

When direct marketers and retailers mail seasonal catalogs, delivery timing affects the entire supply chain. Additional telephone customer service representatives must be hired, inventories of merchandise must be available in warehouses, and employees to fill and package orders must be on hand. If a catalog reaches a customer too soon, it puts pressure on an unprepared supply chain; if it arrives too late the resources sit idle.

Donnelley Logistics Services serves direct marketers by transporting catalogs to the post office. Donnelley is the second largest user of the U.S. Postal Service. It delivers approximately 3.5 billion pounds of printed material to over 230 sectional post office centers each year. It is able to lower supply chain costs for customers in two ways. First, Donnelley penetrates the postal service as far into the mail stream as possible, thus reducing postal rates. Second, it delivers within the narrow time frame specified by direct-marketing customers, usually a range of one or two days. Donnelley is a service company whose own supply chain is almost completely vertically integrated, including antonomous divisions for printing all the way through to its own distribution centers.

Mailfast, part of TNT Express Worldwide, was established to provide global mail, distribution, and delivery services. Approximately 30 percent of its business is with direct-marketing firms. Mailfast helps direct-marketing companies who are expanding internationally to develop their own supply chains. For example, a U.S. direct marketer might want to have catalogs delivered in the United Kingdom. Mailfast would advise the company as to what data in what form is needed to assist with customs clearance and delivery systems in the United Kingdom before picking up the catalog packages. Careful research in advance results in on-time delivery at the end.

Source: R. Morton, "Direct Response Shipping," *Transportation and Distribution* 37, no. 4 (April 1996): 32–36.

serve the New York area; Springfield, Massachusetts is strategically located to serve New England; Indianapolis and Dayton can serve the Midwest; Raleigh is a popular site in the South Atlantic; Tulsa, Shreveport, and Fort Worth are becoming distribution centers in the southwest; and Orange County and Medford are popular locations in the Pacific region.

Companies are also making full use of information technology to speed distribution. Many companies use electronic data interchange (EDI) combined with bar codes to provide quick response to customers. EDI is a specialized network (sometimes on the Internet) that companies use to exchange orders and status with their suppliers and customers. This system allows companies to conduct secure business transactions with customers on the Internet. Levi Strauss uses EDI and regionalized distribution centers to deliver its jeans and related products within seventy-two hours. Levi Strauss's goal is a system of weekly store orders based on sales patterns that come directly from point-of-sale information captured at the store. Sales pass directly from the store register up the supply chain via EDI to Levi Strauss, and new shipping notices come quickly back down to the store. Manufacturing and distribution also receive this information, and they configure production and delivery processing and schedules accordingly. Distribution does not just include sending jeans on their way to the store. Some retailers may want jeans folded once, ready for the shelf, while another retailer may want jeans double-folded for shelving, or a store may require hanging jeans on their own hanger.[24] This type of electronic-based distribution reduces inventories and replenishes store stock quickly, which enables stores to have a better selection of products with the same space, accomplishing the strategic goal of quality customer service.

Global distribution presents companies in the international marketplace with special problems. It is not easy for a U.S. company to select a distribution site and construct a facility in another country since areas are unfamiliar, building codes and con-

www.prenhall.com/russell

EDI is the electronic transmission of data between businesses; including suppliers and customers.

EDI –
computer
to computer
data flow
– no human
intervention

THE COMPETITIVE EDGE

Quick and Secure Deliveries of the Beatles at UPS

When EMI-Capitol Music Group North American produced the Beatles *Anthology* I CD and cassette sets in November 1995, it insisted on simultaneous delivery of over 2 million copies to more than 18,000 retail stores and distributor outlets in the United States with tight security. The distribution of the recordings was timed to coincide with Capitol Music's promotional activities including the TV showing of the *Beatles Anthology* on ABC. The release of the CD on a weekend compounded the distribution difficulties. Cema Distribution, a division of EMI-Capitol, contracted with UPS to distribute the recording across the continental United States, Alaska, Hawaii, and Puerto Rico. UPS's concerns were timely de-

livery and security. There could be no "lost" copies that might air on the radio or be pirated prior to the release to stores and outlets. Security measures included continuous computer tracking of all packaging, screening all personnel processing the packages for copies of the recording, and security escort vehicles for all trailers carrying the packages. Project success was not possible if even one copy was delivered too early or too late. Packages were picked up on Sunday and carried by 43 trailers from the Cema warehouse in Illinois to UPS distribution hubs. All trucks and aircraft arrived on schedule late Sunday and early Monday for regular Monday processing and deliveries.

SOURCE: J. H. Fisher, "A Hard Day's Night at EMI," *Transportation and Distribution*, 37, no. 3 (March 1996): 78–82.

---

[24] P. A. Trunick, "Build for Speed," *Transportation and Distribution* 37, no. 3 (March 1996): 67–70.

struction methods are different, and methods of distribution can be unique to countries. One way to deal with these problems is for companies to outsource their distribution process; that is, let an international distribution specialist handle distribution. An example is Roadway Logistics Services (ROLS) which took over 3M's 300,000-square-foot distribution facility in Breda, the Netherlands, and brought in other clients to fill up unused space. This lowered 3M's supply chain costs. As other products flowed through the facility, transportation efficiency improved as well, further reducing costs.[25]

Summary

Supply chain management is one of the most important, strategic aspects of operations management since it encompasses so many related functions. Whom to buy materials from, where to locate facilities, how to transport goods and services, and how to distribute them in the most cost-effective, timely manner includes much of an organization's strategic planning. Contracting with the wrong supplier can result in poor-quality materials and late deliveries. A location decision is not easily reversed if it is a bad one. For a service operation, the wrong location can mean not enough customers to be profitable, whereas for a manufacturing operation, a wrong location can mean excessive costs, especially for transportation and distribution. Selecting the wrong mode of transportation or carrier can mean late customer deliveries that will require high, costly inventories to offset. All of these critical functional supply chain decisions are complicated by the fact that they often occur in a global environment within cultures and markets at a distance and much different from those in the United States.

Summary of Key Formulas

Center-of-Gravity Coordinates

$$x = \frac{\sum_{i=1}^{n} x_i W_i}{\sum_{i=1}^{n} W_i}, \qquad y = \frac{\sum_{i=1}^{n} y_i W_i}{\sum_{i=1}^{n} W_i}$$

Load-Distance Technique

$$LD = \sum_{i=1}^{n} l_i d_i$$

$$d_i = \sqrt{(x_i - x)^2 + (y_i - y)^2}$$

Summary of Key Terms

benchmarking: measuring current performance against where a company wants performance to be or against a competitor's performance.

center-of-gravity techniques: a quantitative method for locating a facility at the center of movement in a geographic area based on weight and distance.

---

[25] T. Andel, "Forge a New Role in the Supply Chain," *Transportation and Distribution* 37, no. 3 (March 1996): 107–12.

continuous replenishment: supplying orders in a short period of time according to a predetermined schedule.

infrastructure: the physical support structures in a community including roads, water and sewage systems, and utilities.

load-distance technique: a quantitative method for evaluating various facility locations using a value that is a measure of weight and distance.

location factor rating: a system for weighting the importance of different factors in the location decision, scoring the individual factors, and then developing an overall location score that enables a comparison of different location sites.

nation groups: nations joined together to form trading groups or partners.

on-demand (direct-response) delivery: requires the supplier to deliver goods when demanded by the customer.

procurement: purchasing parts, materials, and service.

single-sourcing: limiting suppliers or transportation carriers for a company to a relative few.

sourcing: the selection of suppliers.

supply chain: the facilities, functions, and activities involved in producing and delivering a product or service, from suppliers (and their suppliers) to customers (and their customers).

tariffs (duties): taxes on imported goods.

trade specialists: specialists who help manage transportation and distribution operations in foreign countries.

Solved Problem

Center-of-Gravity Technique

A company is going to construct a new warehouse served by suppliers A, B, and C. The locations of the three suppliers and the annual number of truck carriers that will serve the warehouse are shown in the following figure.

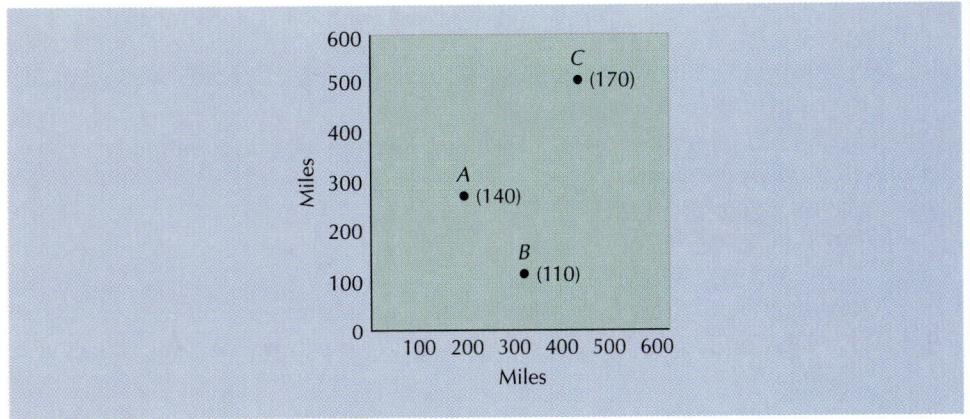

Determine the best site for the warehouse using the center-of-gravity technique.

Solution:

	A	B	C
	$x_A = 150$	$x_B = 300$	$x_C = 400$
	$y_A = 250$	$y_B = 100$	$y_C = 500$
	$w_A = 140$	$w_B = 110$	$w_C = 170$

$$x = \frac{\sum_{i=A}^{C} x_i W_i}{\sum_{i=A}^{C} W_i} = \frac{(150)(140) + (300)(110) + (400)(170)}{140 + 110 + 170}$$

$$= 290.5$$

$$y = \frac{\sum_{i=A}^{C} y_i W_i}{\sum_{i=A}^{C} W_i} = \frac{(250)(140) + (100)(110) + (500)(170)}{140 + 110 + 170}$$

$$= 311.9$$

The suggested coordinates for the new warehouse are $x = 290.5$ and $y = 311.9$.

Questions

9-1. How are the location decisions for service operations and manufacturing operations similar and how are they different?

9-2. Indicate what you perceive to be general location trends for service operations and manufacturing operations.

9-3. What factors make the southern region of the United States an attractive location for service and manufacturing businesses?

9-4. Describe the positive and negative factors for a company contemplating locating in a foreign country.

9-5. What would be the important location factors that McDonald's might consider before opening up a new restaurant?

9-6. The following businesses are considering locating in your community:
a. A pizza delivery service
b. A sporting goods store
c. A small brewery
d. A plant making aluminum cans
Describe the positive and negative location factors for each of these businesses.

9-7. What location factors make small cities and towns in the Midwest attractive to companies?

9-8. Describe the supply chain, in general terms, for McDonald's and for Ford.

9-9. Discuss why single-sourcing has become attractive to companies.

9-10. Define the strategic goals of supply chain management, and indicate how each element of a supply chain (purchasing, facility selection, location, production, inventory, and transportation and distribution) impacts on these goals.

9-11. Select a major (light or heavy) manufacturing facility in your community or immediate geographic area (within a radius of 100 miles), and identify the factors that make it a good or poor site, in your opinion.

9-12. Assume that you are going to open a fast-food restaurant in your community. Select three sites. Perform a location factor analysis for each and select the best site.

9-13. Identify five businesses in your community and determine what mode of transportation is used to supply them.

9-14. Suppose your college or university were planning to develop a new student center and athletic complex with a bookstore, theaters, meeting areas, pool, gymnasium, and weight and exercise rooms. Identify three potential sites on your campus for this facility and rank them according to location factors you can identify.

9-15. Discuss the negative aspects of each of the five major modes of transportation: rails, truck, air, water, and pipeline.

Problems

9-1. Sweats and Sweaters is a small chain of stores specializing in casual cotton clothing. The company currently has five stores in Georgia, South Carolina, and North Carolina, and it wants to open an new store in one of four new mall locations in the Southeast. A consulting firm has been hired to help the company decide where to locate its new store. The company has indicated five factors that are important to its decision, including proximity of a college, community median income, mall vehicle traffic flow and parking, quality and number of stores in the mall, and proximity of other malls or shopping areas. The consulting firm had the company weight the importance of each factor. The consultants visited each potential location and rated them according to each factor, as follows.

LOCATION FACTOR	WEIGHT	SCORES (0 to 100)			
		Mall 1	Mall 2	Mall 3	Mall 4
College proximity	0.30	40	60	90	60
Median income	0.25	75	80	65	90
Vehicle traffic	0.25	60	90	79	85
Mall quality and size	0.10	90	100	80	90
Proximity of other shopping	0.10	80	30	50	70

Given that all sites have basically the same leasing costs and labor and operating costs, recommend a location based on the rating factors.

9-2. Exotech Computers manufactures computer components such as chips, circuit boards, motherboards, keyboards, LCD panels, and the like and sells them around the world. It wants to construct a new warehouse/distribution center in Asia to serve emerging Asian markets. It has identified sites in Shanghai, Hong Kong, and Singapore and has rated the important location factors for each site as follows.

Location Factors	Weight	Scores (0 to 100)		
		Shanghai	Hong Kong	Singapore
Political stability	0.25	50	60	90
Economic growth	0.18	90	70	75
Port facilities	0.15	60	95	90
Container support	0.10	50	80	90
Land and construction cost	0.08	90	20	30
Transportation/distribution	0.08	50	80	70
Duties and tariffs	0.07	70	90	90
Trade regulations	0.05	70	95	95
Airline service	0.02	60	80	70
Area roads	0.02	60	70	80

Recommend a site based on these location factors and ratings.

9-3. State University is going to construct a new student center and athletic complex that will include a bookstore, post office, theaters, market, mini-mall, meeting rooms, swimming pool, and weight and exercise rooms. The university administration has hired a site selection specialist to identify the best potential sites on campus for the new facility. The site specialist has identified four sites on campus and has rated the important location factors for each site as follows.

Location Factors	Weight	Scores (0 to 100)			
		South	West A	West B	East
Proximity to housing	0.27	70	90	65	85
Student traffic	0.22	75	80	60	85
Parking availability	0.16	90	60	80	70
Plot size, terrain	0.12	80	70	90	75
Infrastructure	0.10	50	60	40	60
Off-campus accessibility	0.06	90	70	70	70
Proximity to dining facilities	0.05	60	80	70	90
Visitor traffic	0.04	70	80	65	55
Landscape/aesthetics	0.02	50	40	60	70

Recommend a site based on these location factors and ratings.

9-4. Arsenal Electronics is going to construct a new $1.2 billion semiconductor plant and has selected four small towns in the Midwest as potential sites. The important location factors and ratings for each town are as follows.

Location Factors	Weight	Scores (0 to 100)			
		Abbeton	Bayside	Cane Creek	Dunnville
Work ethic	0.18	80	90	70	75
Quality of life	0.16	75	85	95	90
Labor laws/unionization	0.12	90	90	60	70
Infrastructure	0.10	60	50	60	70
Education	0.08	80	90	85	95
Labor skill and education	0.07	75	65	70	80

(Continued)

Location Factors	Weight	Scores (0 to 100)			
		Abbeton	Bayside	Cane Creek	Dunnville
Cost of living	0.06	70	80	85	75
Taxes	0.05	65	70	55	60
Incentive package	0.05	90	95	70	80
Government regulations	0.03	40	50	65	55
Environmental regulations	0.03	65	60	70	80
Transportation	0.03	90	80	95	80
Space for expansion	0.02	90	95	90	90
Urban proximity	0.02	60	90	70	80

Recommend a site based on these location factors and ratings.

9-5. The Federal Parcel Service wants to build a new distribution center in Charlotte, North Carolina. The center needs to be in the vicinity of uncongested Interstate-77 and Interstate-85 interchanges, and the Charlotte-Douglas International Airport. The coordinates of these three sites and the number of weekly packages that flow to each are as follows.

I-77	I-85	Airport
x = 17	x = 20	x = 30
y = 30	y = 8	y = 14
w = 17,000	w = 12,000	w = 9,000

Determine the best site using the center-of-gravity technique.

9-6. The Burger Doodle restaurant chain uses a distribution center to prepare the food ingredients it provides its individual restaurants. The company is attempting to determine the location for a new distribution center that will service five restaurants. The grid-map coordinates of the five restaurants and the annual number of 40-foot trailer trucks transported to each restaurant are shown.

RESTAURANT	COORDINATES		Annual Truck Shipments
	x	y	
1	100	300	30
2	210	180	25
3	250	400	15
4	300	150	20
5	400	200	18

a. Determine the least cost location using the center-of-gravity method.
b. Plot the five restaurants and the proposed new distribution center on a grid map.

9-7. The Burger Doodle restaurant chain in Problem 9-6 is considering three potential sites, with the following grid-map coordinates, for its new distribution center; A(350, 300), B(150, 250), and C(250, 300). Determine the best location using the load-distance formula, and plot this location on a grid map with the five restaurants. How does this location compare with the location determined in Problem 9-6?

9-8. A development company is attempting to determine the location for a new outlet mall. The region where the outlet mall will be constructed includes four towns, which together have a sizable population base. The grid map coordinates of the four towns and the population of each are given.

| | COORDINATES | | Population |
TOWN	x	y	(10,000s)
Four Corners	30	60	6.5
Whitesburg	50	40	4.2
Russellville	10	70	5.9
Whistle Stop	40	30	3.5

a. Determine the best location for the outlet mall using the center-of-gravity method.

b. Plot the four towns and the location of the new mall on a grid map.

9-9. State University in Problem 9-3 is attempting to locate the best site for a new student center and athletic complex. The university administration would like to know what the best location is relative to the four main concentrations of student housing and classroom activity on campus. These coordinates of these housing and classroom areas (in yards) and daily student populations are as follows.

Campus Student Concentrations			
Anderson Dorm Complex	Ball Housing Complex	Carter Classroom Complex	Derring Classroom Complex
$x_A = 1,000$	$x_B = 1,500$	$x_C = 2,000$	$x_D = 2,200$
$y_A = 1,250$	$y_B = 2,700$	$y_C = 700$	$y_D = 2,000$
$w_A = 7,000$	$w_B = 9,000$	$w_C = 11,500$	$w_D = 4,300$

Determine the best site using the center-of-gravity method.

9-10. Mega-Mart, a discount store chain, wants to build a new superstore in an area in Southwest Virginia near five small towns with populations between 8,000 and 42,000. The coordinates (in miles) of these five towns and the market population in each are as follows.

Whitesburg	Altonville	Campburg	Milligan
$x = 12$	$x = 18$	$x = 30$	$x = 32$
$y = 20$	$y = 18$	$y = 7$	$y = 25$
$w = 26,000$	$w = 14,000$	$w = 9,500$	$w = 12,000$

Determine the best site using the center-of-gravity technique.

9-11. Home-Base, a home improvement/building supply chain, is going to build a new warehouse facility to serve its stores in six North Carolina cities—Charlotte, Winston-Salem, Greensboro, Durham, Raleigh, and Wilmington. The coordinates of these cities (in miles), using Columbia, South Carolina, as the origin (0,0) of a set of coordinates, and the annual truckloads that supply each city are shown as follows.

Charlotte	Winston-Salem	Greensboro	Durham	Raleigh	Wilmington
$x = 15$	$x = 42$	$x = 88$	$x = 125$	$x = 135$	$x = 180$
$y = 85$	$y = 145$	$y = 145$	$y = 140$	$y = 125$	$y = 18$
$w = 160$	$w = 90$	$w = 105$	$w = 35$	$w = 60$	$w = 75$

a. Determine the best site using the center-of-gravity technique.
b. Look at a map of North Carolina, and identify the closest town to the grid coordinates developed in Part (a). Looking at the map, can you suggest a better location in the vicinity? Explain your answer.

9-12. In Problem 9-11, Home-Base has two parcels of land in Fayetteville and Statesville, North Carolina. Use the load-distance technique to determine which would be the best.

CASE PROBLEM

Selecting a European Distribution Center Site for American International Automotive Industries

American International Automotive Industries (AIAI) manufactures auto and truck engine, transmission, and chassis parts for manufacturers and repair companies in the United States, South America, Canada, Mexico, Asia and Europe. The company transports to its foreign markets by container ships. To serve its customers in South America and Asia, AIAI has large warehouse/distribution centers. In Europe it ships into Hamburg and Gdansk where it has contracted with independent distribution companies to deliver its products to customers throughout Europe. However, AIAI has been displeased with a recent history of late deliveries and rough handling of its products. For a time AIAI was not overly concerned since its European market wasn't too big and its European customers didn't complain. Plus, it had more pressing supply chain problems elsewhere. In the last three years, since trade barriers have fallen in Europe, and Eastern European markets have opened up, its European business has expanded, as has new competition, and its customers have become more demanding and quality conscious. As a result, AIAI has initiated the process to select a site for a new European warehouse/distribution center. Although it provides parts to a number of smaller truck and auto maintenance and service centers in Europe, it has seven major customers—auto and truck manufacturers in Vienna, Leipzig, Budapest, Prague, Krakow, Munich, and Frankfurt. Its customers in Vienna and Budapest have adopted manufacturing processes requiring continuous replenishment of parts and materials.

AIAI's European headquarters is in Hamburg. The vice-president for construction and development in Dayton, Ohio, has asked the Hamburg office to do a preliminary site search based on location, geography, transportation, proximity to customers, and costs. The Hamburg office has identified five potential sites in Dresden, Lodz, Hamburg, Gdansk, and Frankfurt. The Hamburg office has forwarded information about each of these sites to corporate headquarters, including forecasts of the number of containers shipped annually to each customer as follows: Vienna, 160; Leipzig, 100; Budapest, 180; Prague, 210; Krakow, 90; Munich, 120; and, Frankfurt, 50. When the vice-president of construction in Dayton received this information, he pulled out his map of Europe and began to study the sites.

Assist AIAI with its site selection process in Europe. Recommend a site from the five possibilities, and indicate what other location factors you might consider in the selection process.

References

Bowersox, D. J. *Logistics Management*, 2d ed. New York: Macmillan, 1978.

Francis, R. L., and J. A. White. *Facilities Layout and Location: An Analytical Approach*. Englewood Cliffs, N.J.: Prentice Hall, 1987.

Fulton, M. "New Factors in Plant Location." *Harvard Business Review* (May–June 1971): 4–17, 166–68.

Hitchcock, F. L. "The Distribution of a Product from Several Sources to Numerous Localities." *Journal of Mathematics and Physics* 20 (1941): 224, 230.

Johnson, J. C., and D. F. Wood. *Contemporary Logistics*, 6th ed. Upper Saddle River, N.J.: Prentice Hall, 1996.

Moore, Laurence, J., Sang M. Lee, and Bernard W. Taylor. *Management Science*, 4th ed. Boston: Allyn and Bacon, 1993.

Schmenner, R. W. *Making Business Location Decisions*. Englewood Cliffs, N.J.: Prentice Hall, 1982.

Taylor, B. W. *Introduction to Management Science*, 5th ed. Upper Saddle River, N.J.: Prentice Hall, 1996.

9

Operational Decision-Making Tools: The Transportation Method

The Transportation Problem

An important factor in logistics management is determining the lowest-cost transportation provider from among several alternatives. In many cases it is possible to transport items from a plant or warehouse to a retail outlet or distributor via truck, rail, or air. Sometimes the modes of transportation may be the same, but the company must decide among different transportation providers; for example, different trucking firms. A quantitative technique that is used for determining the least cost means of transporting goods or services is the *transportation method.*

A **transportation problem** is formulated for a class of problems with the following characteristics: (1) A product is *transported* from a number of sources to a number of destinations at the minimum possible cost, and (2) each source is able to supply a fixed number of units of the product and each destination has a fixed demand for the product. The following example demonstrates the formulation of the transportation model.

A **transportation problem** involves transporting items from sources with fixed supply to destinations with fixed demand at lowest cost.

EXAMPLE S9.1

A Transportation Problem

Grain is harvested in the Midwest and stored in grain elevators in Kansas City, Omaha, and Des Moines. These grain elevators supply three mills, operated by the Heartland Bread and Cereal Company, located in Chicago, St. Louis, and Cincinnati. Grain is shipped to the mills in railroad cars. Each grain elevator is able to supply the following tons of grain to the mills on a monthly basis.

Grain Elevator	Supply
1. Kansas City	150
2. Omaha	175
3. Des Moines	275
	600 tons

Each mill demands the following tons of wheat per month.

Mill	Demand
A. Chicago	200
B. St. Louis	100
C. Cincinnati	300
	600 tons

The cost of transporting one ton of wheat from each grain elevator (source) to each mill (destination) differs according to the distance and rail system. These costs are shown next. For example, the cost of shipping 1 ton of wheat from the grain elevator at Omaha to the mill at Chicago is $7.

GRAIN ELEVATOR	MILL		
	Chicago A	St. Louis B	Cincinnati C
Kansas City	$6	$8	$10
Omaha	7	11	11
Des Moines	4	5	12

The problem is to determine how many tons of wheat to transport from each grain elevator to each mill on a monthly basis to minimize the total cost of transportation. A diagram of the different transportation routes with supply, demand, and cost figures is given in Figure S9.1.

Transportation models are solved within the context of a **transportation tableau**, which for our example model is shown in the following table. Each cell in the tableau represents the amount transported from one source to one destination. The smaller box within each cell contains the unit transportation cost for that route. For example, in cell 1A the value $6 is the cost of transporting 1 ton of wheat from Kansas City to Chicago. Along the outer rim of the tableau are the supply and demand constraint quantity values, referred to as **rim requirements.**

The Transportation Tableau

From \ To	Chicago	St. Louis	Cincinnati	SUPPLY
Kansas City	6	8	10	150
Omaha	7	11	11	175
Des Moines	4	5	12	275
DEMAND	200	100	300	600

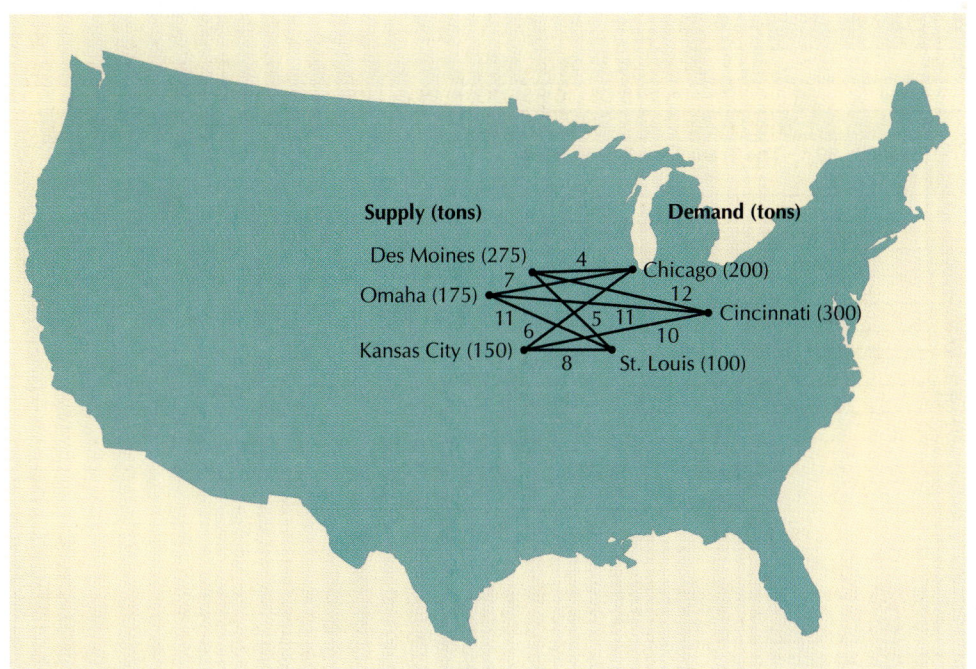

FIGURE S9.1 Network of Transportation Routes

There are several methods for solving transportation models manually, including the *stepping-stone method* and the *modified distribution method.* These methods require a number of computational steps and are very time-consuming if done by hand. We will not present the detailed solution procedure for these methods here. We will focus on computer solution of the transportation model using Excel.

Transportation Model Solution with Excel

Transportation models can also be solved using spreadsheets like Microsoft Excel. Exhibit S9.1 shows the initial Excel screen for Example S9.1.

Notice in this screen that the formula for the total transportation cost is embedded in cell C10 shown on the formula bar across the top of the screen. Total cost is computed by multiplying each cell cost by each cell value (currently 0) and summing these products.

Formulas must also be developed for the supply and demand rim requirements. Each grain elevator can supply only the amount it has available, and the amount shipped to each mill must not exceed what it demands. For example, the amount shipped from Kansas City is the sum of the shipments to Chicago, St. Louis, and Cincinnati. This sum, "C5 + D5 + E5," is embedded in cell G5 and shown on the formula bar at the top of the screen in Exhibit S9.2.

Similar summation formulas for the other grain elevators and each mill are also developed. If you click on cells G6, G7, C9, D9, and E9 you will see these formulas on the formula bar. Since this is a balanced transportation problem, where total supply equals total demand (i.e., 600 tons), then each amount shipped from each elevator

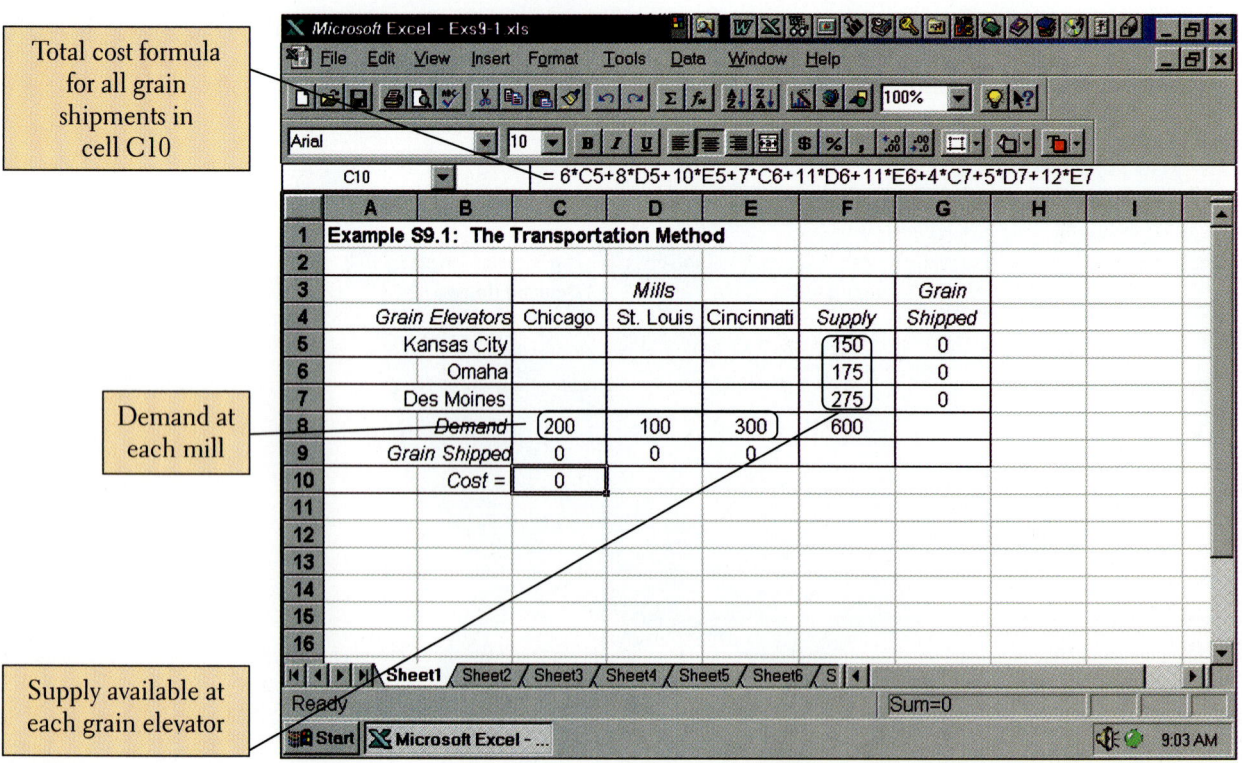

EXHIBIT S9.1

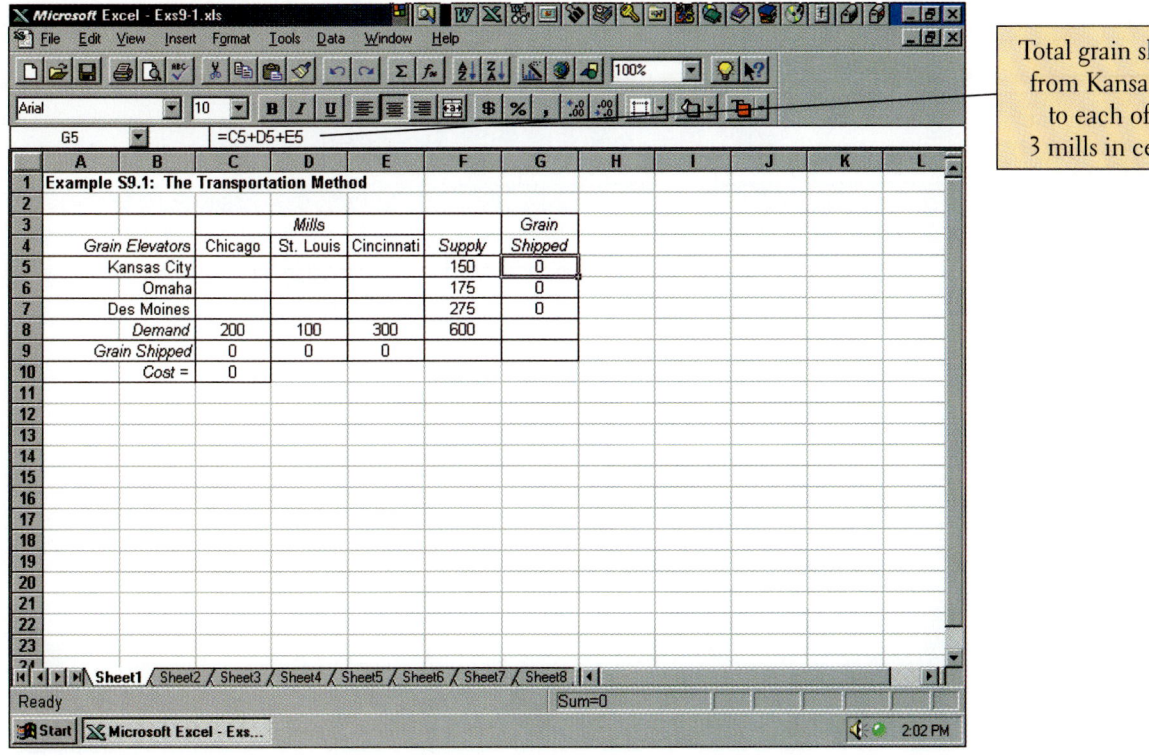

EXHIBIT S9.2

equals the available supply, and each amount shipped to each mill equals the amount demanded. These mathematical relationships are included in the "Solver" screen (shown in Exhibit S9.3) accessed from the "Tools" menu on the toolbar.

The "target" cell containing total cost is C10, and it is set equal to "min" since our objective is to minimize cost. The "variables" in our problem representing individual

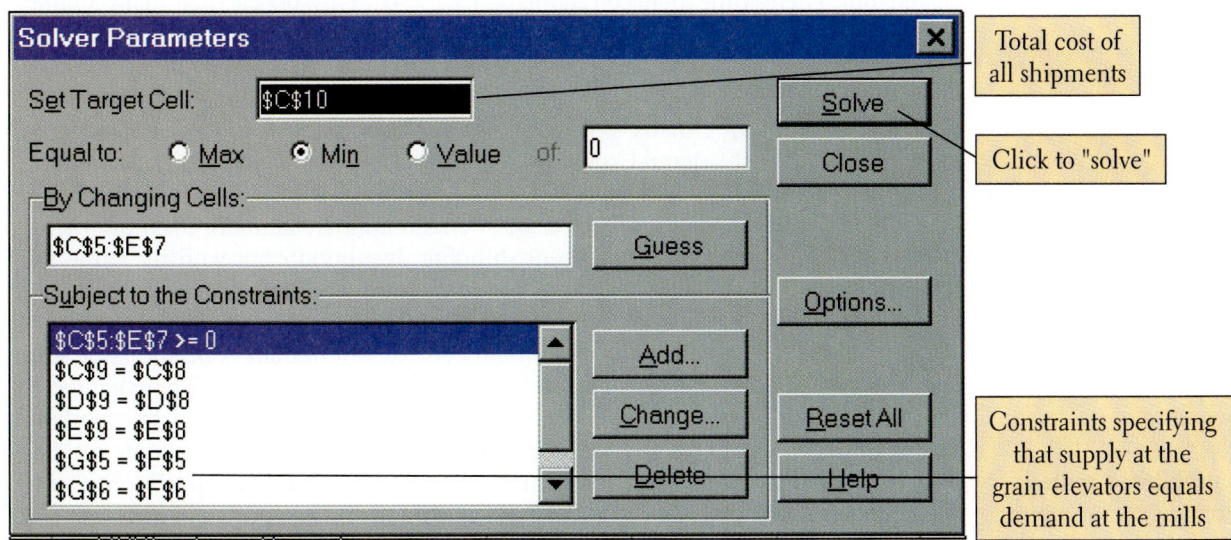

EXHIBIT S9.3

Formula for total cost computed in cell C10

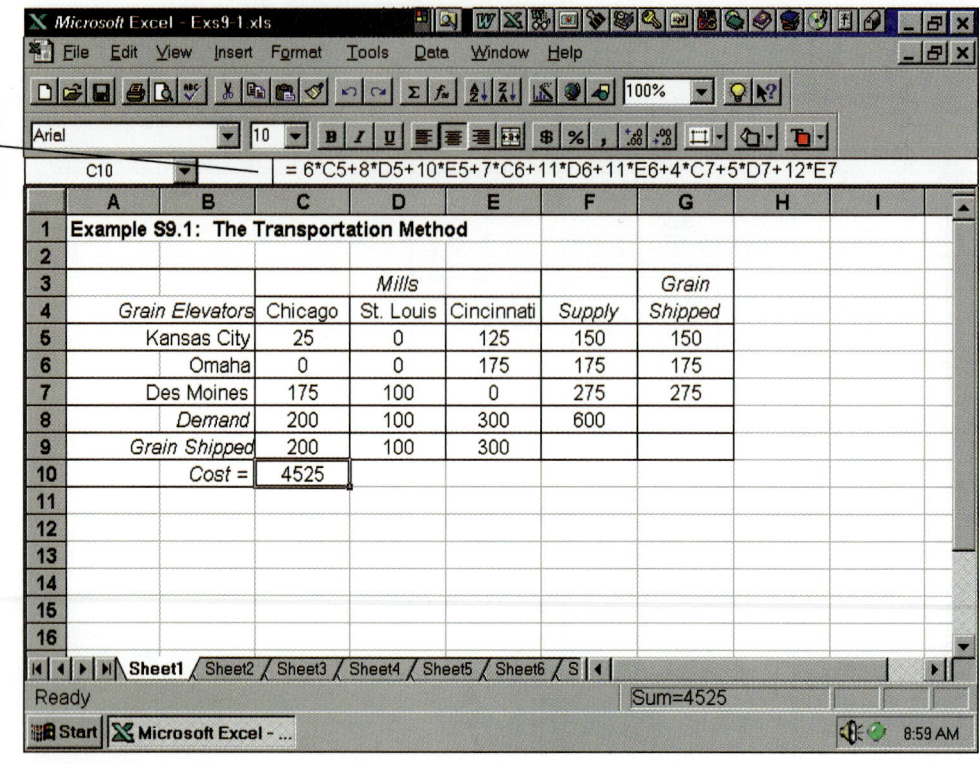

EXHIBIT S9.4

shipments from each elevator to each mill are cells C5 to E7 inclusive. This is designated as "C5:E7." (Excel adds the $s). The constraints mathematically specify that the amount shipped equals the amount available or demanded. For example, "C9 = C8" means that the sum of all shipments to Chicago from all three elevators, which is embedded in C9, equals the demand contained in C8. There are six constraints, one for each grain elevator and mill. There is one more constraint, "C5:E7 ≥ 0." This specifies that all the amounts shipped must be zero or positive. Once all the model parameters have been entered into the solver, click on "Solve." The solution is shown on the Excel screen in Exhibit S9.4.

Interpreting this solution, 125 tons are shipped from Kansas City to Cincinnati, 175 tons are shipped from Omaha to the mill at Cincinnati, and so on. The total shipping cost is $4,525. The Heartland Company could use these results to make decisions about how to ship wheat and to negotiate new rate agreements with railway shippers.

In this computer solution there is an alternate optimal solution, meaning there is a second solution reflecting a different shipping distribution but with the same total cost of $4,525. Manual solution is required to identify this alternate; however, it could provide a different shipping pattern that the company might view as advantageous.

In Example S9.1 the unique condition occurred where there were the same number of sources as destinations, three, and the supply at all three sources equaled the demand at all three destinations, 600 tons. This is the simplest form of transportation model; however, solution is not restricted to these conditions. Sources and destinations can be unequal, and total supply does not have to equal total demand, which is called an *unbalanced* problem. A model with these characteristics is provided in Example S9.2, along with a **prohibited route**. If a route is prohibited, units cannot be transported from a particular source to a particular destination.

In a *unbalanced transportation problem*, supply exceeds demand or vice versa.

A **prohibited route** is a transportation route over which goods cannot be transported.

EXAMPLE
S9.2

An Unbalanced
Transportation Model
with a Prohibited
Route

Tobacco purchased by Cooperative Tobacco Farmers, Inc., is stored in warehouses in four cities at the end of each growing season.

Location	Capacity (tons)
A. Charlotte	90
B. Raleigh	50
C. Lexington	80
D. Danville	60
	280

These warehouses supply the following amounts of tobacco to companies in three cities.

Plant	Demand (tons)
1. Richmond	120
2. Winston-Salem	100
3. Durham	110
	330

The railroad shipping costs per ton are shown below.

	To		
From	1	2	3
A	$ 70	$100	$ 50
B	120	90	40
C	70	30	110
D	90	50	70

Because of railroad construction, shipments are presently prohibited from Charlotte to Richmond.

SOLUTION:

The transportation solution tableau for this problem is as follows:

To From	Richmond	Winston-Salem	Durham	SUPPLY
Charlotte	500	100	90 ⌐50	90
Raleigh	30 ⌐120	90	20 ⌐40	50
Lexington	70	80 ⌐30	110	80
Danville	40 ⌐90	20 ⌐50	70	60
DEMAND	120	100	110	

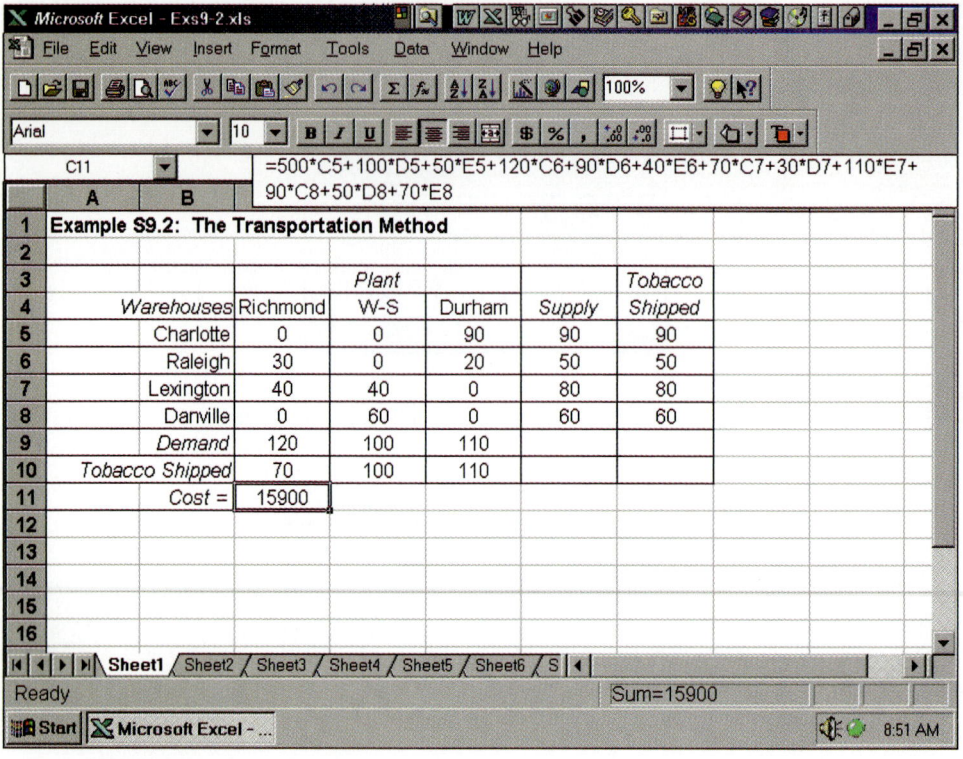

EXHIBIT S9.5

The Excel solution of Example S9.2, shown in Exhibits S9.5 and S9.6, is a little different than the previous example problem solution because it's an unbalanced problem and there is a prohibited route. In this example, since the amount demanded, 330 tons, exceeds the available supply, 280 tons, we have to formulate our constraints in the solver differently. Instead of equations (=) we have inequalities (≤) for the demand constraints.

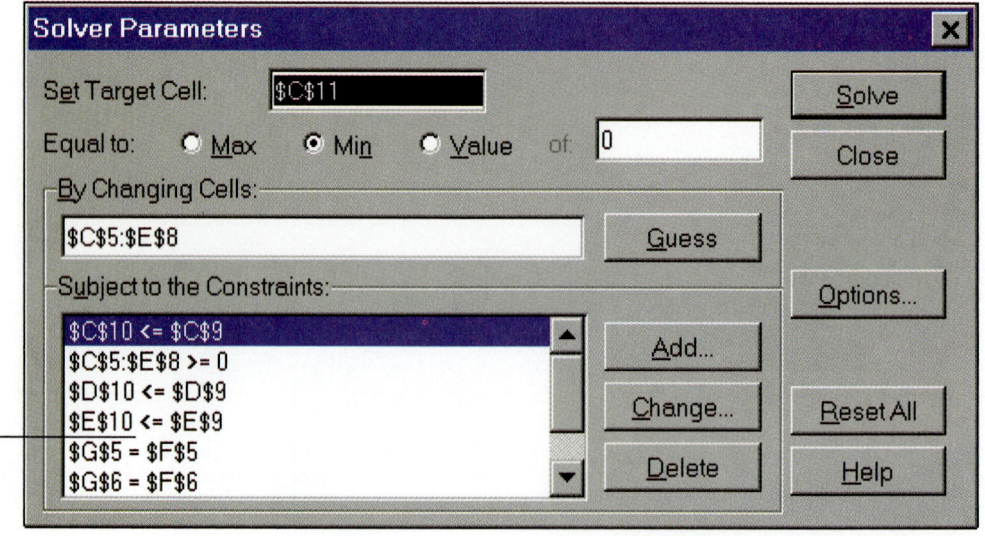

Constraint equations showing that the amount available is less than the grain demanded

EXHIBIT S9.6

Thus, the constraints "C10 ≤ C9, D10 ≤ D9, and E10 ≤ E9" mean that for at least one of the plants, demand will not be met. The solution screen shows the total cost formula on the toolbar, and a value of 500 for cell C5, indicating the prohibited route.

This is the basic formulation of a transportation model as a linear programming model. In fact, Excel is solving this problem as if it were a linear programming problem.

Modules to solve transportation models are generally available in most quantitative software packages. The transportation problem can be solved using the transportation module of POM for Windows. The program input requires that the number of sources and destinations be indicated, which establishes the basic dimensions of the model. The remaining inputs are the supply and demand values and the individual costs for each potential route. The "solved problem" Exhibit S9.7 shows the solution of an example problem using POM for Windows.

Summary

In this supplement we have described and demonstrated the transportation problem. We have relied solely on computer solution using Excel. Students interested in manual solution methods should consult the references at the end of this supplement. Transportation problems are also a form of linear programming problems and can be solved using linear programming solution techniques. Students interested in linear programming should consult the (Chapter 11) supplement.

Summary of Key Terms

prohibited route: a transportation route along which shipments cannot be transported.

rim requirements: the available supply at each source and the demand at each destination in a transportation tableau.

transportation problem: a class of problems in which items are transported from a number of sources that have a fixed supply, to a number of destinations with a fixed demand in order to achieve an objective such as minimum time or cost.

transportation tableau: a table which organizes the parameters and data of a transportation problem.

Solved Problem

Transportation Model

A manufacturing firm ships its finished products from three plants to three distribution warehouses. The supply capacities of the plants, the demand requirements at the warehouses, and the transportation costs per ton are shown as follows.

| PLANT | WAREHOUSES | | | |
	A	B	C	SUPPLY (units)
1	$ 8	5	6	120
2	15	10	12	80
3	3	9	10	80
DEMAND (units)	150	70	60	280

Solve this problem using POM for Windows.

Solution:

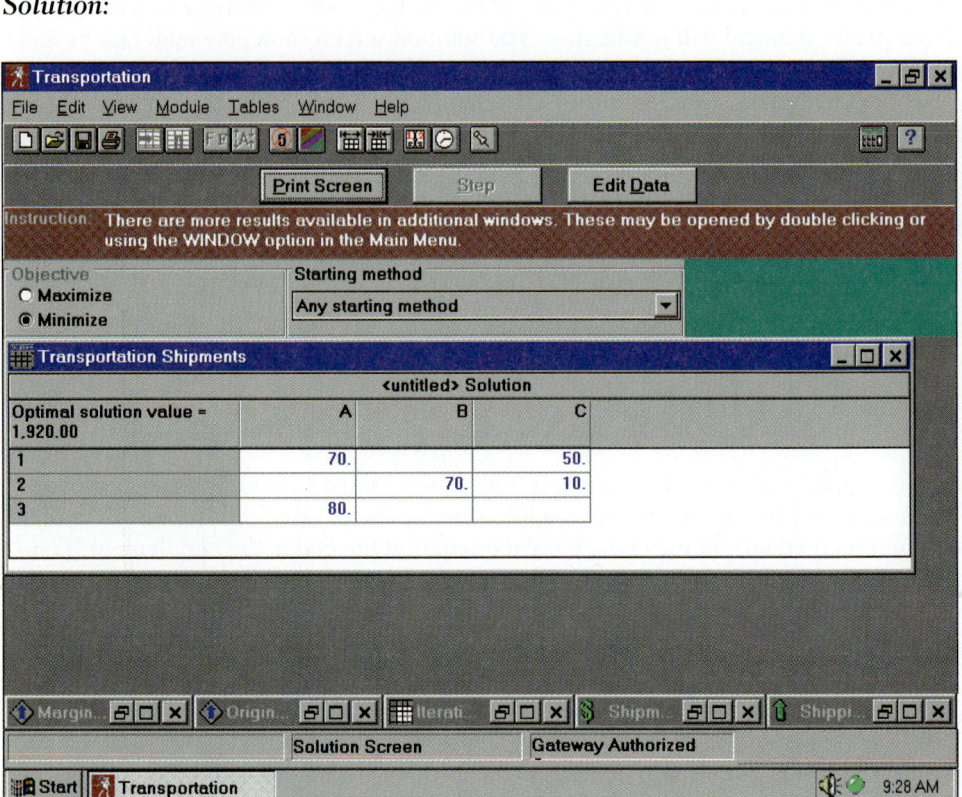

EXHIBIT S9.7

Questions

S9-1. The transportation model is thought of as a technique for logistics management. Describe how it might be used to help make facility location decisions.

S9-2. Explain the difference between a balanced and unbalanced transportation problem.

S9-3. Describe an example of a business you are familiar with that might make use of the transportation model to determine transport routes.

S9-4. A class of transportation problems are *transshipment* problems. Research transshipment problems and explain how they differ from normal transportation problems.

Problems

S9-1. Steel mills in three cities produce the following amounts of steel.

Location	Weekly Production (tons)
A. Bethlehem	150
B. Birmingham	210
C. Gary	320
	680

These mills supply steel to four cities, where manufacturing plants have the following demand.

Location	Weekly Demand (tons)
1. Detroit	130
2. St. Louis	70
3. Chicago	180
4. Norfolk	240
	620

Shipping costs per ton of steel are as follows.

	To			
From	1	2	3	4
A	$140	$ 90	$160	$180
B	110	80	70	160
C	160	120	100	220

Because of a truckers' strike, shipments are prohibited from Birmingham to Chicago. Solve this problem using a computer.

S9-2. In Problem S9-1, what would be the effect of a reduction in production capacity at the Gary location from 320 tons to 290 tons per week?

S9-3. Oranges are grown, picked, and then processed and packaged at distribution centers in Tampa, Miami, and Fresno. These centers supply oranges to markets in New York, Philadelphia, Chicago, and Boston. The following table shows the shipping costs per truckload ($100s), supply, and demand.

	To				
From	New York	Philadelphia	Chicago	Boston	SUPPLY
Tampa	$ 9	$14	$12	$17	200
Miami	11	10	6	10	200
Fresno	12	8	15	7	200
DEMAND	130	170	100	150	

Because of an agreement between distributors, shipments are prohibited from Miami to Chicago. Solve this problem using a computer.

S9-4. In Example S9-2, shipments are prohibited from Charlotte to Richmond because of railroad construction. Once the rail construction is completed, what will be the effect on the optimal shipping routes?

S9-5. A manufacturing firm produces diesel engines in four cities—Phoenix, Seattle, St. Louis, and Detroit. The company is able to produce the following numbers of engines per month:

Plant	Production
1. Phoenix	5
2. Seattle	25
3. St. Louis	20
4. Detroit	25

Three trucking firms purchase the following numbers of engines for their plants in three cities:

Firm	Demand
A. Greensboro	10
B. Charlotte	20
C. Louisville	15

The transportation costs per engine ($100s) from sources to destinations are as shown.

	To		
From	A	B	C
1	$ 7	$ 8	$ 5
2	6	10	6
3	10	4	5
4	3	9	11

However, the Charlotte firm will not accept engines made in Seattle, and the Louisville firm will not accept engines from Detroit; therefore, these routes are prohibited. Solve this problem.

S9-6. The Interstate Truck Rental firm has accumulated extra trucks at three of its truck leasing outlets, as shown.

Leasing Outlet	Extra Trucks
1. Atlanta	70
2. St. Louis	115
3. Greensboro	60
	245

The firm also has four outlets with shortages of rental trucks, as follows.

Leasing Outlet	Truck Shortage
A. New Orleans	80
B. Cincinnati	50
C. Louisville	90
D. Pittsburgh	25
	245

The firm wants to transfer trucks from those outlets with extras to those with shortages at the minimum total cost. The following costs of transporting these trucks from city to city have been determined.

	To			
From	*A*	*B*	*C*	*D*
1	$ 70	$80	$45	$90
2	120	40	30	75
3	110	60	70	80

Solve this problem.

S9-7. In Problem S9-6, what would be the effect on the optimal solution if there were no shortage of rental trucks at the New Orleans outlet?

S9-8. The Shotz Beer Company has breweries in three cities; the breweries can supply the following numbers of barrels of draft beer to the company's distributors each month.

Brewery	*Monthly Supply (barrels)*
A. Tampa	3,500
B. St. Louis	5,000
C. Milwaukee	2,500
	11,000

The distributors, spread throughout six states, have the following total monthly demand:

Distributor	*Monthly Demand (barrels)*
1. Tennessee	1,600
2. Georgia	1,800
3. North Carolina	1,500
4. South Carolina	950
5. Kentucky	2,250
6. Virginia	1,400
	9,500

The company must pay the following shipping costs per barrel:

	To					
From	*1*	*2*	*3*	*4*	*5*	*6*
A	$0.50	$0.35	$0.60	$0.45	$0.80	$0.75
B	0.25	0.65	0.40	0.55	0.20	0.65
C	0.40	0.70	0.55	0.50	0.35	0.50

Determine the minimum cost shipping routes for the company.

S9-9. In Problem S9-8, the Shotz Beer Company management has negotiated a new shipping contract with a trucking firm between its Tampa brewery and its distributor in Kentucky that reduces the shipping cost per barrel from $0.80 per barrel to $0.65 per barrel. How will this cost change affect the optimal solution?

S9-10. Computers Unlimited sells microcomputers to universities and colleges on the East Coast and ships them from three distribution warehouses. The firm is able to supply the following numbers of microcomputers to the universities by the beginning of the academic year.

Distribution Warehouse	Supply (microcomputers)
1. Richmond	420
2. Atlanta	610
3. Washington, D.C.	340
	1,370

Four universities have ordered microcomputers that must be delivered and installed by the beginning of the academic year:

University	Demand (microcomputers)
A. Tech	520
B. A and M	250
C. State	400
D. Central	380
	1,500

The shipping and installation costs per microcomputer from each distributor to each university are as follows:

	To			
From	A	B	C	D
1	$22	17	30	18
2	15	35	20	25
3	28	21	16	14

Solve this problem.

S9-11. In Problem S9-10, Computers Unlimited wants to meet demand more effectively at the four universities it supplies. It is considering two alternatives: (1) expand its warehouse at Richmond to a capacity of 600 at a cost equivalent to an additional $6 in handling and shipping per unit; or (2) purchase a new warehouse in Charlotte that can supply 300 units with shipping costs of $19 to Tech, $26 to A and M, $22 to State, and $16 to Central. Which alternative should management select based solely on transportation costs (i.e., no capital costs)?

S9-12. A large manufacturing company is closing three of its existing plants and intends to transfer some of its more skilled employees to three plants that will remain open. The number of employees available for transfer from each closing plant is as follows:

Closing Plant	Transferable Employees
1	60
2	105
3	70
	235

The following number of employees can be accommodated at the three plants remaining open:

Open Plants	Employees Demanded
A	45
B	90
C	35
	170

Each transferred employee will increase product output per day at each plant as follows:

	TO		
FROM	A	B	C
1	5	8	6
2	10	9	12
3	7	6	8

Determine the best way to transfer employees in order to ensure the maximum increase in product output.

S9-13. The Sav-Us Rental Car Agency has six lots in Nashville, and it wants to have a certain number of cars available at each lot at the beginning of each day for local rental. The agency would like a model it could quickly solve at the end of each day that would tell how to redistribute the cars among the six lots at the minimum total mileage. The distances between the six lots are as follows:

	TO (MILES)					
FROM	1	2	3	4	5	6
1	—	12	17	18	10	20
2	14	—	10	19	16	15
3	14	10	—	12	8	9
4	8	16	14	—	12	15
5	11	21	16	18	—	10
6	24	12	9	17	15	—

The agency would like the following number of cars at each lot at the end of the day. Also shown is the number of available cars at each lot at the end of a particular day.

Lot	1	2	3	4	5	6
Available	37	20	14	26	40	28
Desire	30	25	20	40	30	20

Determine the optimal reallocation of rental cars that will minimize the total mileage.

S9-14. The Roadnet Transport Company has expanded its shipping capacity by purchasing 90 trailer trucks from a competitor that went bankrupt. The company subsequently located 30 of the purchased trucks at each of its shipping warehouses in Charlotte, Memphis, and Louisville. The company makes shipments from each of these warehouses to terminals in St. Louis, Atlanta, and New York. Each truck is capable of making one shipment per week. The terminal managers have each indicated their capacity for extra shipments. The manager at St. Louis can accommodate 40 additional trucks per week, the manager at Atlanta can accommodate 40 additional trucks, and the manager at New York can accommodate 50 additional trucks. The company makes the following profit per truckload shipment from each warehouse to each terminal. The profits differ as a result of differences in products shipped, shipping costs, and transport rates.

	TERMINAL		
WAREHOUSE	St. Louis	Atlanta	New York
Charlotte	$1,800	$2,100	$1,600
Memphis	1,000	700	900
Louisville	1,400	800	2,200

Determine how many trucks to assign to each route (i.e., warehouse to terminal) to maximize profit.

S9-15. The Vanguard Publishing Company hires eight college students as salespeople to sell encyclopedias during the summer. The company desires to distribute them to three sales territories. Territory 1 requires three salespeople, and territories 2 and 3 require two salespeople each. It is estimated that each salesperson will be able to generate the following amounts of dollar sales per day in each of the three territories:

	TERRITORY		
SALESPERSON	1	2	3
A	$110	$150	$130
B	90	120	80
C	205	160	175
D	125	100	115
E	140	105	150
F	100	140	120
G	180	210	160
H	110	120	70

Determine which salespeople to allocate to the three territories so that sales will be maximized.

S9-16. The Southeastern Athletic Conference has six basketball officials who must be assigned to three conference games, two to each game. The conference office wants to assign the officials so that the time they travel the total distances will be minimized. The hours each official would have to travel to each game is given in the following table.

	GAME		
OFFICIAL	Athens	Columbia	Knoxville
1	2.0	4.5	1.0
2	4.0	9.0	7.0
3	6.0	7.0	3.0
4	3.0	6.0	4.0
5	7.0	1.5	5.0
6	8.0	2.5	3.5

Determine the optimal game assignments that will minimize the total time traveled by the officials.

S9-17. Bayville has built a new elementary school so that the town now has a total of four schools—Addison, Beeks, Canfield, and Daley. Each has a capacity of 400 students. The school wants to assign children to schools so that their travel time by bus is as short as possible. The school has partitioned the town into five districts conforming to population density—north, south, east, west, and central. The average bus travel time from each district to each school is shown as follows.

DISTRICT	TRAVEL TIME (MIN)				STUDENT POPULATION
	Addison	*Beeks*	*Canfield*	*Daley*	
North	12	23	35	17	250
South	26	15	21	27	340
East	18	20	22	31	310
West	29	24	35	10	210
Central	15	10	23	16	290

Determine the number of children that should be assigned from each district to each school in order to minimize total student travel time.

S9-18. In Problem S9-17, the school board has determined that it does not want any of the schools to be overly crowded compared with the other schools. It would like to assign students from each district to each school so that enrollments are evenly balanced between the four schools. However, the school board is concerned that this might significantly increase travel time. Determine the number of students to be assigned from each district to each school such that school enrollments are evenly balanced. Does this new solution appear to significantly increase travel time per student?

S9-19. The Easy Time Grocery chain operates in major metropolitan areas on the eastern seaboard. The stores have a "no-frills" approach, with low overhead and high volume. They generally buy their stock in volume at low prices. However, in some cases they actually buy stock at stores in other areas and ship it in. They can do this because of high prices in the cities they operate in compared with costs in other locations. One example is baby food. Easy Time purchases baby food at stores in Albany, Binghamton, Claremont, Dover, and Edison, and then trucks it to six stores in and around New York City. The stores in the outlying areas know what Easy Time is up to, so they limit the number of cases of baby food Easy Time can purchase. The following table shows the profit Easy Time makes per case of baby food based on where the chain purchases it and which store it's sold at, plus the available baby food per week at purchase locations and the shelf space available at each Easy Time store per week.

Purchase Location	Easy Time Store						Supply
	1	*2*	*3*	*4*	*5*	*6*	
Albany	9	8	11	12	7	8	26
Binghamton	10	10	8	6	9	7	40
Claremont	8	6	6	5	7	4	20
Dover	4	6	9	5	8	10	40
Edison	12	10	8	9	6	7	45
Demand	25	15	30	18	27	35	

Determine where Easy Time should purchase baby food and how the food should be distributed in order to maximize profit.

S9-20. Suppose that in Problem S9-19 Easy Time could purchase all the baby food it needs from a New York City distributor at a price that would result in a profit of $9 per case at stores 1, 3, and 4, $8 per case at stores 2 and 6, and $7 per case at store 5. Should Easy Time purchase all, none, or some of its baby food from the distributor rather than purchasing it at other stores and trucking it in?

S9-21. During the Gulf War, Operation Desert Storm required large amounts of military matériel and supplies to be shipped daily from supply depots in the United States to bases in the Middle East. The critical factor in the movement of these supplies was speed. The following table shows the number of planeloads of supplies available each day from each of six supply depots and the number of daily loads demanded at each of five bases. (Each planeload is approximately equal in tonnage.) Also included in the table are the transport hours per plane (where transport hours include loading and fueling time, actual flight time, and unloading and refueling times).

Supply Depot	Military Base					Supply
	A	B	C	D	E	
1	36	40	32	43	29	7
2	28	27	29	40	38	10
3	34	35	41	29	31	8
4	41	42	35	27	36	8
5	25	28	40	34	38	9
6	31	30	43	38	40	6
Demand	9	6	12	8	10	

Determine the optimal daily flight schedule that will minimize total transport time.

C A S E P R O B L E M

Stateline Shipping and Transport Company

Rachel Sundusky is the manager of the South-Atlantic office of the Stateline Shipping and Transport Company. She is in the process of negotiating a new shipping contract with Polychem, a company that manufactures chemicals for industrial use. Polychem wants Stateline to pick up and transport waste products from its six plants to four waste disposal sites. Rachel is very concerned about this proposed arrangement. The chemical wastes that will be hauled can be hazardous to humans and the environment if they leak. In addition, a number of towns and communities in the region where the plants are located prohibit hazardous materials from being shipped through their municipal limits. Thus, not only will the shipments have to be handled carefully and transported at reduced speeds, they will also have to traverse circuitous routes in many cases.

Rachel has estimated the cost of shipping a barrel of waste from each of the six plants to each of the three waste disposal sites as shown in Table S9.1.

Table S9.1

| Plants | Waste Disposal Sites | | |
	Whitewater	Los Canos	Duras
Kingsport	$12	$15	$17
Danville	14	9	10
Macon	13	20	11
Selma	17	16	19
Columbus	7	14	12
Allentown	22	16	18

Each week the plants generate amounts of waste as shown in Table S9.2.

Table S9.2

Plant	Waste per Week (bbl)
Kingsport	35
Danville	26
Macon	42
Selma	53
Columbus	29
Allentown	38

The three waste disposal sites at Whitewater, Los Canos, and Duras can accommodate a maximum of 65, 80, and 105 barrels per week, respectively.

In addition to shipping directly from each of the six plants to one of the three waste disposal sites, Rachel is also considering using each of the plants and waste disposal sites as intermediate shipping points. Trucks would be able to drop a load at a plant or disposal site to be picked up and carried on to the final destination by another truck, and vice versa. Stateline would not incur any handling costs since Polychem has agreed to take care of all local handling of the waste materials at the plants and the waste disposal sites. In other words, the only cost Stateline incurs is the actual transportation cost. So Rachel wants to be able to consider the possibility that it may be cheaper to drop and pick up loads at intermediate points rather than shipping them directly.

Table S9.3 shows how much Rachel estimates the shipping costs per barrel between each of the six plants to be.

The estimated shipping cost per barrel between each of the three waste disposal sites is shown in Table S9.4.

Table S9.4

Waste Disposal Site	Whitewater	Los Canos	Duras
Whitewater	$—	$12	$10
Los Canos	12	—	15
Duras	10	15	—

Rachel wants to determine the shipping routes that will minimize Stateline's total cost in order to develop a contract proposal to submit to Polychem for waste disposal. She particularly wants to know if it is cheaper to ship direct from the plants to the waste sites or if she should drop and pick up some loads at the various plants and waste sites. Develop a model to assist Rachel and solve the model to determine the optimal routes.

Table S9.3

Plants	Kingsport	Danville	Macon	Selma	Columbus	Allentown
Kingsport	$—	6	$4	$9	$7	$8
Danville	6	—	11	10	12	7
Macon	5	11	—	3	7	15
Selma	9	10	3	—	3	16
Columbus	7	12	7	3	—	14
Allentown	8	7	15	16	14	—

References

Hitchcock, F. L. "The Distribution of a Product from Several Sources to Numerous Localities." *Journal of Mathematics and Physics* 20 (1941): 224, 230.

Moore, Laurence J., Sang M. Lee, and Bernard W. Taylor. *Management Science*, 4th ed. Boston: Allyn and Bacon, 1993.

Taylor, B. W. *Introduction to Management Science*, 5th ed. Upper Saddle River, N.J.: Prentice Hall, 1996.

10

Forecasting

Forecasting Along the Supply Chain at American Airlines

Forecasting is an important part of supply chain management at American Airlines. At one end of the supply chain American Airlines must maintain an extensive inventory of expendable and repairable (rotatable) parts to support the operations of more than 400 aircraft. Expendable parts are of low value and are discarded when replaced. Rotatable parts are of much higher value, averaging $5,000; thus, maintaining an adequate inventory is costly. American Airlines has an inventory of more than 5,000 different types of rotatable parts, including such items as landing gear, wing flaps, altimeters, and coffee makers. Rotatable parts are allocated to different airports based upon anticipated demand. The airline developed the rotatables allocation and planning system (RAPS) to manage the inventory of rotatable parts. Critical components of RAPS are forecasts of expected demand for total parts across all airports and for demand at each individual airport. The forecast for total system demand is calculated using linear regression, which establishes the relationship between monthly parts usage and monthly flying hours. Each month the system updates an eighteen-month history of parts usage and flying hours using the most recent month's data. The process of generating the forecast using linear regression is completely automated, requiring only a few hours. It is estimated that RAPS has provided a one-time savings of $7 million and a recurring annual savings of almost $1 million.[1]

American Airlines jets at the airline's Dallas/Fort Worth hub. American Airlines forecasts everything along its supply chain from airplane parts to passengers. An accepted airline practice is overbooking on flights; that is, setting reservation levels higher than aircraft capacity in order to compensate for passenger cancellations and no-shows. Overbooking allows airlines to significantly reduce the number of empty seats on its flights it might experience otherwise. A key factor in setting the correct number of overbookings so that passengers will not have to be bumped because there are no seats, is an accurate forecast of passenger demand.

---

[1] M. J. Tedone, "Repairable Part Management," *Interfaces* 19, no. 4 (July–August 1989): 61–68.

At the other end of its supply chain, forecasting is a critical part of American's yield management program, booking passengers so there are as few empty seats as possible. Yield management consists of three major functions: *overbooking*—the practice of intentionally selling more seats than are available for a flight, to fly with as few empty seats as possible; *traffic management*—the coordination of passenger demand at different terminals to provide the mix of reservations and flights that will maximize revenues; and *discount allocation*—the determination of the number of discount fares to offer on a flight. Discount allocation is an especially important problem. Too few discount fares will leave a flight with empty seats; too many will limit the number of flights to schedule to different markets in order to maximize revenues. The process of determining the allocation of discount fares for a flight is based on a forecasting model for discount fare demand to determine the probability of selling a full fare seat when a discount fare is rejected by a customer due to restrictions. The demand forecasts for discount fares are computed using exponential smoothing.[2]

A forecast is a prediction of what will occur in the future. Meteorologists forecast the weather, sportscasters and gamblers predict the winners of football games, and companies attempt to predict how much of their product will be sold in the future. A forecast of product demand is the basis for most important planning decisions. Planning decisions regarding scheduling, inventory, production, facility layout and design, work force, distribution, purchasing, and so on, are functions of customer demand. Long-range, strategic plans by top management are based on forecasts of the type of products consumers will demand in the future and the size and location of product markets.

Forecasting is an uncertain process. It is not possible to predict consistently what the future will be, even with the help of a crystal ball and a deck of tarot cards. Management generally hopes to forecast demand with as much accuracy as possible, which is becoming increasingly difficult to do. In the current international business environment, consumers have more product choices and more information on which to base choices. They also demand and receive greater product diversity, made possible by rapid technological advances. This makes forecasting products and product demand more difficult. Consumers and markets have never been stationary targets, but they are moving more rapidly now than they ever have before.

Management sometimes uses **qualitative** methods based on judgment, opinion, past experience, or best guesses, to make forecasts. A number of **quantitative** forecasting methods are also available to aid management in making planning decisions. In this chapter we discuss two of the traditional types of mathematical forecasting methods, time series analysis and regression, as well as several nonmathematical, qualitative approaches to forecasting. Although no technique will result in a totally accurate forecast, these methods can provide reliable guidelines in making decisions.

www.prenhall.com/russell

Quantitative forecast methods are based on mathematical formulas; **qualitative forecast methods** are subjective methods.

The Strategic Role of Forecasting in Supply Chain Management and TQM

In today's global business environment, strategic planning and design tend to focus on supply chain management and total quality management (TQM).

[2] B. C. Smith, J. F. Leimkuhler, and R. M. Darrow, "Yield Management at American Airlines," *Interfaces* 22, no. 1 (January–February 1992): 8–31.

Supply Chain Management

A company's supply chain encompasses all of the facilities, functions, and activities involved in producing a product or service from suppliers (and their suppliers) to customers (and their customers). Supply chain functions include purchasing, inventory, production, scheduling, facility location, transportation, and distribution. All these functions are affected in the short run by product demand and in the long run by new products and processes, technology advances, and changing markets.

Forecasts of product demand determine how much inventory is needed, how much product to make, and how much material to purchase from suppliers to meet forecasted customer needs. This in turn determines the kind of transportation that will be needed and where plants, warehouses, and distribution centers will be located so that products and services can be delivered on time. Without accurate forecasts large stocks of costly inventory must be kept at each stage of the supply chain to compensate for the uncertainties of customer demand. If there are insufficient inventories, customer service suffers because of late deliveries and stockouts. This is especially hurtful in today's competitive global business environment where customer service and on-time delivery are critical factors.

Long-run forecasts of technology advances, new products, and changing markets are especially critical for the strategic design of a company's supply chain in the future. In today's global market if companies cannot effectively forecast what products will be demanded in the future and the products their competitors are likely to introduce, they will be unable to develop the production and service systems in time to compete. If companies do not forecast where newly emerging markets will be located and do not have the production and distribution system available to enter these markets, they will lose to competitors who have been able to forecast accurately.

A recent trend in supply chain design is *continuous replenishment* wherein continuous updating of data is shared between suppliers and customers. In this system customers are continuously being replenished, daily or even less, by their suppliers based on actual sales. Continuous replenishment, typically managed by the supplier, reduces inventory for the company and speeds customer delivery. Variations of continuous replenishment include quick response, JIT, VMI (vendor-managed inventory), and stockless inventory. Such systems rely heavily on extremely accurate short-term forecasts, usually on a weekly basis, of end-use sales to the ultimate customer. The supplier at one end of a company's supply chain must forecast the company's customer demand at the other end of the supply chain in order to maintain continuous replenishment. The forecast also has to be able to respond to sudden, quick changes in demand. Longer forecasts based on historical sales data for six to twelve months into the future are also generally required to help make weekly forecasts and suggest trend changes.

Levi Strauss employs a supply chain with regional clusters of suppliers, manufacturers, and distribution centers linked together, thereby reducing inventory and improving customer service. The goal of this supply chain design is to have inventory close to customers so that products can be delivered within seventy-two hours. Levi Strauss arranges weekly store orders based on actual sales patterns received electronically from stores through EDI (electronic data interchange). It uses weekly forecasts of demand that extend out sixty weeks into the future. The forecast determines weekly inventory levels and weekly replenishment to customers. Suppliers also use this forecast and store sales patterns to manage and schedule their deliveries to customers.[3]

Accurate forecasting determines how much inventory a company must keep at various points along its supply chain.

In continuous replenishment the supplier and customer share continuously updated data.

---

[3] P. A. Trunick, "Build for Speed," *Transportation and Distribution* 37, no. 3 (March 1996): 67–70.

Total Quality Management

Forecasting is crucial in a total quality management (TQM) environment. More and more, customers perceive good-quality service to mean having a product when they demand it. This holds true for manufacturing and service companies. When customers walk into a McDonald's to order a meal, they do not expect to wait long to place orders. They expect McDonald's to have the item they want, and they expect to receive their orders within a short period of time. An accurate forecast of customer traffic flow and product demand enables McDonald's to schedule enough servers, to stock enough food, and to schedule food production to provide high-quality service. An inaccurate forecast causes service to break down, resulting in poor quality. For manufacturing operations, especially for suppliers, customers expect parts to be provided when demanded. Accurately forecasting customer demand is a crucial part of providing the high-quality service.

Continuous replenishment and JIT complement TQM. JIT is an inventory system wherein parts or materials are not provided at a stage in the production process until they are needed. This eliminates the need for buffer inventory, which, in turn, reduces both waste and inventory costs, a primary goal of TQM. For JIT to work, there must be a smooth, uninterrupted process flow with no defective items. Traditionally inventory was held at in-process stages to compensate for defects, but with TQM the goal is to eliminate defects, thus obviating the need for inventory. Accurate forecasting is critical for a company that adopts both JIT and TQM. It is especially important for suppliers, who are expected to provide materials as needed. Failure to meet expectations violates the principles of TQM and is perceived as poor-quality service. TQM requires a finely tuned, efficient production process, with no defects, minimal inventory, and no waste. In this way costs are reduced. Accurate forecasting is essential for maintaining this type of process.

> Forecasting customer demand is a key to providing good-quality service.

> JIT requires accurate forecasting to be successful.

Strategic Planning

There can be no strategic planning without forecasting. The ultimate objective of strategic planning is to determine what the company should be in the future—what markets to compete in, with what products, to be successful and grow. To answer these questions the company needs to know what new products its customers will want, how much of these products customers will want, and the level of quality and other features that will be expected in these products. Forecasting answers these questions and is a key to a company's long-term competitiveness and success. The determination of future new products and their design subsequently determines process design, the kinds of new equipment and technologies that will be needed, and the design of the supply chain, including the facilities, transportation, and distribution systems that will be required. These elements are ultimately based on the company's forecast of the long-run future.

> Successful strategic planning requires accurate forecasts of future products and markets.

> The type of forecasting method depends on time frame, demand behavior, and causes of behavior.

Components of Forecasting Demand

The type of forecasting method to use depends on several factors including the time frame of the forecast (i.e., how far in the future is being forecasted), the *behavior* of demand, and the possible existence of patterns (trends, seasonality, etc.), and the *causes* of demand behavior.

> The **time frame** indicates how far into the future is forecast.

Time Frame

Forecasts are either short- to mid-range, or long-range. **Short-range (to mid-range) forecasts** are typically for daily, weekly, or monthly sales demand for up to approximately two years into the future, depending on the company and the type of industry. They

> A **short- to mid-range forecast** typically encompasses the immediate future—daily up to two years.

THE COMPETITIVE EDGE

Competing with Supply Chain Forecasting at CIBA-GEIGY

The supply chain of a textile company runs from converting fiber into yarn into fabric into apparel and then distribution to retail stores. Large safety stocks are built into all stages of the textile supply chain because of volatile consumer demand, which can result in huge losses when the wrong item is in stock. The whims of consumer fashion dictate the production scheduling process and all other related functions down the supply chain.

A critical part of the textile supply chain is color selection and dyeing. CIBA-GEIGY is one of the world's largest suppliers of color dyes for the apparel industry. The challenge at CIBA-GEIGY is to develop accurate color dye forecasts that will enable the company to minimize inventory while providing quick customer delivery. A dye manufacturer like CIGA-GEIGY normally is required to provide a selection of approximately 250 dyes to meet the different color requirements of the textile industry. Shading across color variations makes forecasting even more difficult. Dark colors require 10 times more dye than pale shades. Even if the manufacturer knows that reds will be "in" this season, it is difficult to know how many pounds of red dyes to produce to meet the different shades of red needed. Because of quick changes in consumer tastes, textile companies expect same-day shipment for any dye they order, in any quantity.

www.prenhall.com/russell

Traditionally, forecasts for color dye demand at CIBA-GEIGY were based on the experience and best guesses of inventory specialists. This resulted in "high"

demand forecasts to avoid stockouts and satisfy the sales force and customers. CIBA-GEIGY eventually changed to quantitative forecasting methods that reduced its forecast error from 30 percent to 10 percent in a short period of time. The improvement in forecast accuracy enabled CIBA-GEIGY to increase shipping date reliability from 88 percent to over 96 percent and to reduce inventory from a 4.5 month supply to 2 month supply.

The demand forecast is normally for a two-month duration; that is, inventory in stock at any time is based on a forecast conducted two months in the past. Thus, market changes in color trends are hidden from CIBA-GEIGY for two to three months. Textile companies do not want to share their color forecasts with the dye manufacturer since it is a competitive factor in the fashion apparel industry. If CIBA-GEIGY could develop "partnering" relationships with fabric producers, forecasts could be improved, which in turn would lead to quicker customer service. Forecast accuracy would also be improved if CIBA-GEIGY could receive color fabric and apparel sales information directly from major retailers, such as Wal-Mart. Its forecasts could then be based on current day-to-day actual sales instead of data two or three months old. Currently, Wal-Mart electronically transmits point-of-sale information to fiber and fabric producers nightly, but not to CIBA-GEIGY. However, only a small percentage of retailers and producers use this type of interconnected supply chain information. These difficulties point out that information flow along the supply chain is just as critical as product flow.

SOURCE: A. Dransfield, "Forecasting Color Demand at CIBA-GEIGY," *The Journal of Business Forecasting* 13, no. 1 (Spring 1994): 9–12.

www.prenhall.com/russell

A long-range forecast usually encompasses a period of time longer than two years.

are primarily used to determine production and delivery schedules and to establish inventory levels. At Unisys Corporation, an $8 billion producer of computer systems, monthly demand forecasts are prepared going out one year into the future. At Hewlett-Packard monthly forecasts for ink-jet printers are constructed from twelve to eighteen months into the future, while at Levi Strauss weekly forecasts are prepared for five years into the future.

A **long-range forecast** is usually for a period longer than two years into the future. A long-range forecast is normally used for strategic planning—to establish long-term goals, plan new products for changing markets, enter new markets, develop new facilities, develop technology, design the supply chain, and implement strategic programs such as TQM. At Unisys long-range strategic forecasts project three years into the future; Hewlett-Packard's long-term forecasts are developed for years two through six; and at Fiat, the Italian automaker, strategic plans for new and continuing products go ten years into the future.

These classifications are generalizations. The line between short- and long-range forecasts is not always distinct. For some companies a short-range forecast can be several years, and for other firms a long-range forecast can be in terms of months. The length of a forecast depends a lot on how rapidly the product market changes and how susceptible the market is to technological changes.

Demand Behavior

Demand sometimes behaves in a random, irregular way. At other times it exhibits predictable behavior, with trends or repetitive patterns which the forecast may reflect. The three types of demand behavior are *trends*, *cycles*, and *seasonal patterns*.

A **trend** is a gradual, long-term up or down movement of demand. For example, the demand for personal computers has followed an upward trend during the last few decades, without any sustained downward movement in the market. Trends are the easiest patterns of demand behavior to detect and are often the starting points for developing forecasts. Figure 10.1(a) illustrates a demand trend in which there is a general upward movement, or increase. Notice that Figure 10.1(a) also includes several random movements up and down. **Random variations** are movements that are not predictable and follow no pattern (and thus are virtually unpredictable).

A **cycle** is an up-and-down movement in demand that repeats itself over a lengthy time span (i.e., more than a year). For example, new housing starts and, thus, construction-related products tend to follow cycles in the economy. Automobile sales also tend to follow cycles. The demand for winter sports equipment increases every four

A **trend** is a gradual, long-term up or down movement of demand.

Random variations are movements in demand that do not follow a pattern.

A **cycle** is an up-and-down repetitive movement in demand.

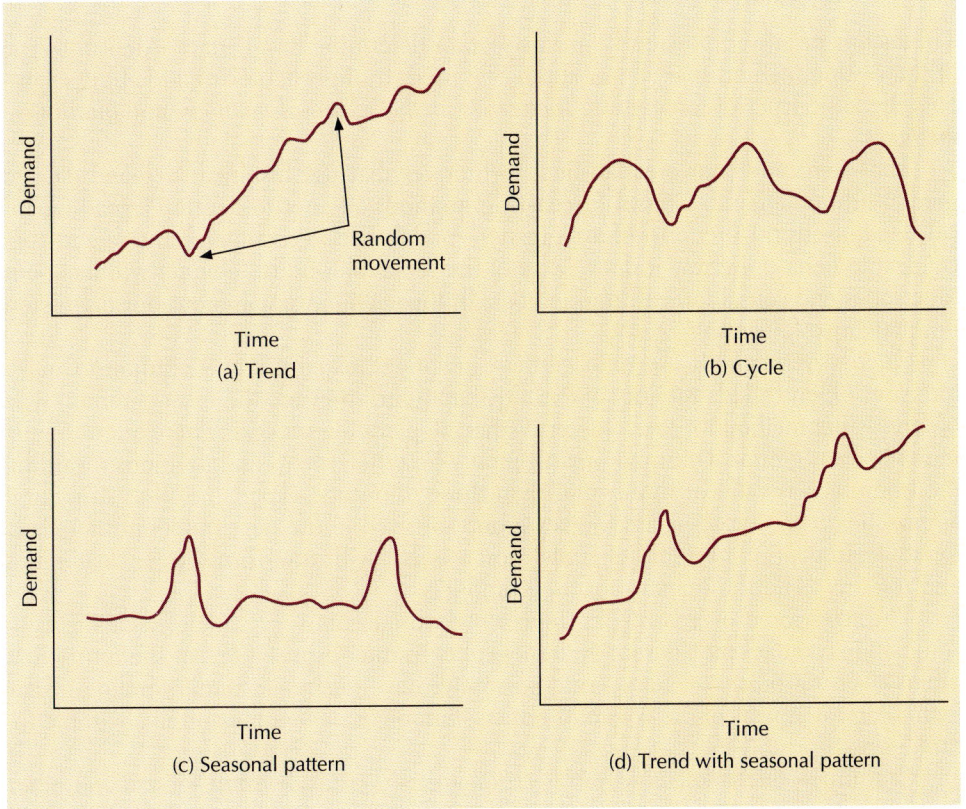

FIGURE 10.1 Forms of Forecast Movement

years before and after the Winter Olympics. Figure 10.1(b) shows the behavior of a demand cycle.

A **seasonal pattern** is an oscillating movement in demand that occurs periodically (in the short run) and is repetitive. Seasonality is often weather related. For example, every winter the demand for snowblowers and skis increases, and retail sales in general increase during the holiday season. However, a seasonal pattern can occur on a daily or weekly basis. For example, some restaurants are busier at lunch than at dinner, and shopping mall stores and theaters tend to have higher demand on weekends. Figure 10.1(c) illustrates a seasonal pattern in which the same demand behavior is repeated each year at the same time.

> A **seasonal pattern** is an up-and-down repetitive movement in demand occurring periodically.

Demand behavior frequently displays several of these characteristics simultaneously. Although housing starts display cyclical behavior, there has been an upward trend in new house construction over the years. Demand for skis is seasonal; however, there has been an upward trend in the demand for winter sports equipment during the past two decades. Figure 10.1(d) displays the combination of two demand patterns, a trend with a seasonal pattern.

Instances when demand behavior exhibits no pattern are referred to as *irregular movements*, or variations. For example, a local flood might cause a momentary increase in carpet demand, or a competitor's promotional campaign might cause a company's product demand to drop for a period of time. Although this behavior has a cause and, thus, is not totally random, it still does not follow a pattern that can be reflected in a forecast.

Forecasting Methods

> Types of methods: time series, causal, and qualitative.

The factors discussed previously in this section determine to a certain extent the type of forecasting method that can or should be used. In this chapter we are going to discuss the basic types of forecasting: *time series methods*, *causal methods*, and *qualitative methods*.

> **Causal forecasting methods** relate demand to other factors that cause demand behavior.
>
> Management, marketing and purchasing, and engineering are sources for internal qualitative forecasts.

Time series methods are statistical techniques that use historical demand data to predict future demand. **Causal forecasting methods** attempt to develop a mathematical relationship (in the form of a regression model) between demand and factors that cause it to behave the way it does. Most of the remainder of this chapter will be about time series and causal forecasting methods. In this section we will focus our discussion on qualitative forecasting.

Qualitative methods use management judgment, expertise, and opinion to make forecasts. Often called "the jury of executive opinion," they are the most common type of forecasting method for the long-term strategic planning process. There are normally individuals or groups within an organization whose judgments and opinions regarding the future are as valid or more valid than those of outside experts or other structured approaches. Top managers are the key group involved in the development of forecasts for strategic plans. They are generally most familiar with their firms' own capabilities and resources and the markets for their products.

The sales force of a company represents a direct point of contact with the consumer. This contact provides an awareness of consumer expectations in the future that others may not possess. Engineering personnel have an innate understanding of the technological aspects of the type of products that might be feasible and likely in the future.

Consumer, or market, research is an organized approach using surveys and other research techniques to determine what products and services customers want and will purchase, and to identify new markets and sources of customers. Consumer and market research is normally conducted by the marketing department within an organization, by industry organizations and groups, and by private marketing or consulting firms. Although market research can provide accurate and useful forecasts of product demand, it must be skillfully and correctly conducted, and it can be expensive.

The **Delphi method** is a procedure for acquiring informed judgments and opinions from knowledgeable individuals using a series of questionnaires to develop a consensus forecast about what will occur in the future. It was developed at the Rand Corporation shortly after World War II to forecast the impact of a hypothetical nuclear attack on the United States. Although the Delphi method has been used for a variety of applications, forecasting has been one of its primary uses. It has been especially useful for forecasting technological change and advances.

Technological forecasting has become increasingly crucial to compete in the modern international business environment. New enhanced computer technology, new production methods, and advanced machinery and equipment are constantly being made available to companies. These advances enable them to introduce more new products into the marketplace faster than ever before. The companies that succeed manage to get a "technological" jump on their competitors by accurately predicting what technology will be available in the future and how it can be exploited. What new products and services will be technologically feasible, when they be can introduced, and what their demand will be, are questions about the future for which answers cannot be predicted from historical data. Instead, the informed opinion and judgment of experts are necessary to make these types of single, long-term forecasts.

> The **Delphi method** involves soliciting forecasts about technological advances from experts.

Forecasting Process

Forecasting is not simply identifying and using a method to compute a numerical estimate of what demand will be in the future. It is a continuing process that requires constant monitoring and adjustment illustrated by the steps in Figure 10.2.

In the next few sections we present several different forecasting methods applicable for different patterns of demand behavior. Thus, one of the first steps in the forecasting process is to plot the available historical demand data and, by visually looking at them, attempt to determine the forecasting method that best seems to fit the patterns the data exhibit. Historical demand is usually past sales or orders data. There are several measures for comparing historical demand with the forecast to see how accurate the forecast is. Following our discussion of the forecasting methods, we present several measures of forecast accuracy. If the forecast does not seem to be accurate, another method can be tried until an accurate forecast method is identified. After the forecast is made over the desired planning horizon, it may be possible to use judgment, experience, knowledge of the market, or even intuition to adjust the forecast to enhance its accuracy. Finally, as demand actually occurs over the planning period, it must be monitored and compared with the forecast in order to assess the performance of the forecast method. If the forecast is accurate, then it is appropriate to continue using the forecast method. If it is not accurate, a new model or adjusting the existing one should be considered.

> Forecasting is a process that is continuous.

Time Series Methods

Time series methods are statistical techniques that make use of historical data accumulated over a period of time. Time series methods assume that what has occurred in the past will continue to occur in the future. As the name *time series* suggests, these methods relate the forecast to only one factor—time. They include the moving aver-

> **Time series methods** use historical demand data over a period of time to predict future demand.

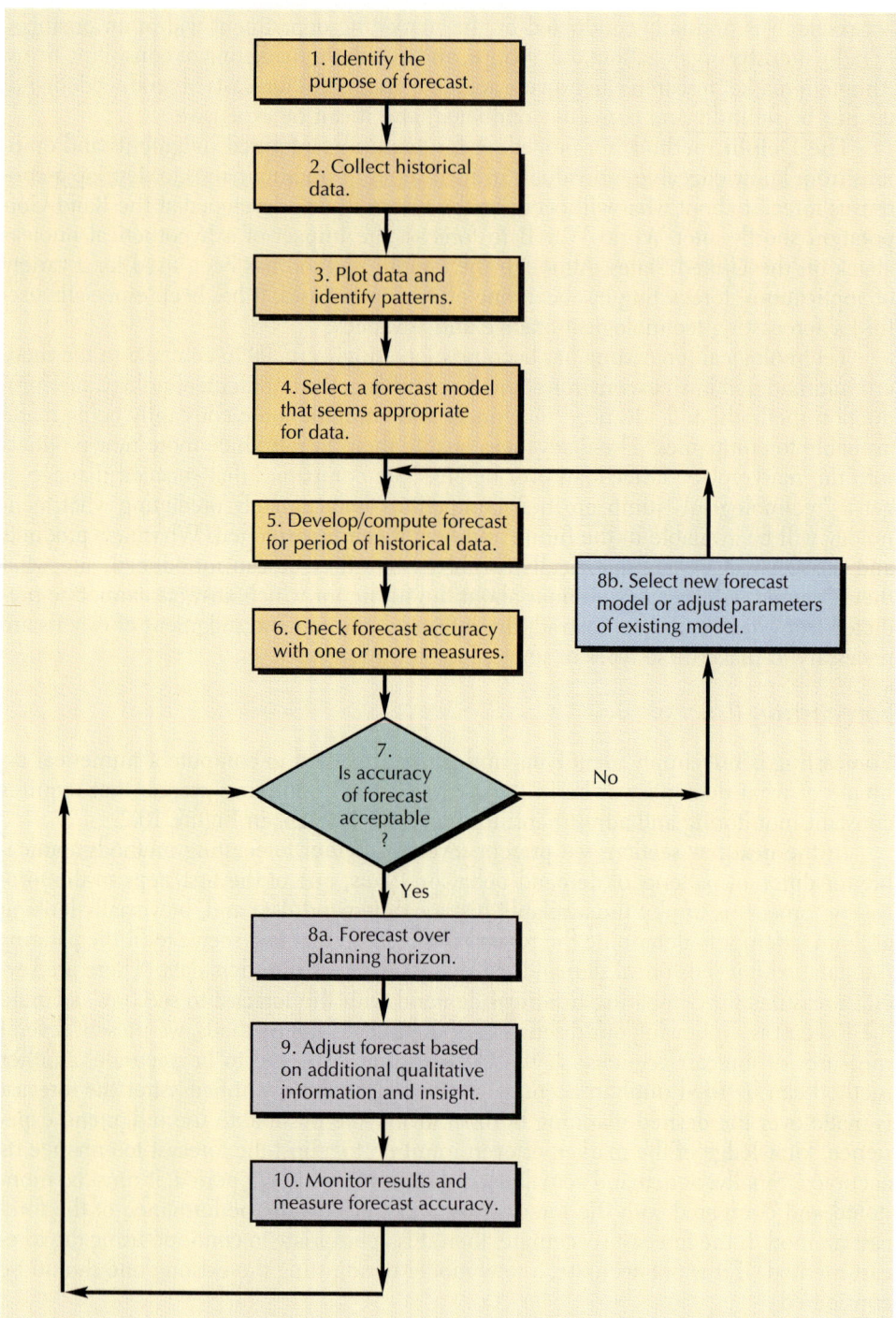

FIGURE 10.2   Steps of the Forecasting Process

age, exponential smoothing, and linear trend line; and they are among the most popular methods for short-range forecasting among service and manufacturing companies. These methods assume that identifiable historical patterns or trends for demand over time will repeat themselves.

Moving Average

A time series forecast can be as simple as using demand in the current period to predict demand in the next period. This is sometimes called a *naive* or *intuitive* forecast.[4] For example, if demand is 100 units this week, the forecast for next week's demand is 100 units; if demand turns out to be 90 units instead, then the following week's demand is 90 units, and so on. This type of forecasting method does not take into account historical demand *behavior*; it relies only on demand in the current period. It reacts directly to the normal, random movements in demand.

> In a *naive* forecast demand in the last period is used as the next period's forecast.

The simple **moving average** method uses several demand values during the recent past to develop a forecast. This tends to *dampen*, or *smooth out*, the random increases and decreases of a forecast that uses only one period. The simple moving average is useful for forecasting demand that is stable and does not display any pronounced demand behavior, such as a trend or seasonal pattern.

> The **moving average** method uses average demand for a fixed sequence of periods.

Moving averages are computed for specific periods, such as three months or five months, depending on how much the forecaster desires to "smooth" the demand data. The longer the moving average period, the smoother it will be. The formula for computing the simple moving average is

> Moving average is good for stable demand with no pronounced behavioral patterns.

$$MA_n = \frac{\sum_{i=1}^{n} D_i}{n}$$

where

n = number of periods in the moving average

D_i = demand in period i

EXAMPLE
10.1

Computing a Simple Moving Average

The Instant Paper Clip Office Supply Company sells and delivers office supplies to companies, schools, and agencies within a 50-mile radius of its warehouse. The office supply business is competitive, and the ability to deliver orders promptly is a factor in getting new customers and keeping old ones. (Offices typically order not when they run low on supplies, but when they completely run out. As a result, they need their orders immediately.) The manager of the company wants to be certain enough drivers and vehicles are available to deliver orders promptly and they have adequate inventory in stock. Therefore, the manager wants to be able to forecast the number of orders that will occur during the next month (i.e., to forecast the demand for deliveries).

From records of delivery orders, management has accumulated the following data for the past 10 months, from which it wants to compute 3- and 5-month moving averages.

(Continued)

---

[4] K. B. Kahn and J. T. Mentzer, "Forecasting in Consumer and Industrial Markets," *The Journal of Business Forecasting* 14, no. 2 (Summer 1995): 21–28.

Month	Orders
January	120
February	90
March	100
April	75
May	110
June	50
July	75
August	130
September	110
October	90

SOLUTION:

Let us assume that it is the end of October. The forecast resulting from either the 3- or the 5-month moving average is typically for the next month in the sequence, which in this case is November. The moving average is computed from the demand for orders for the prior 3 months in the sequence according to the following formula:

$$MA_3 = \frac{\sum_{i=1}^{3} D_i}{3}$$

$$= \frac{90 + 110 + 130}{3}$$

$$= 110 \text{ orders for November}$$

The 5-month moving average is computed from the prior 5 months of demand data as follows:

$$MA_5 = \frac{\sum_{i=1}^{5} D_i}{5}$$

$$= \frac{90 + 110 + 130 + 75 + 50}{5}$$

$$= 91 \text{ orders for November}$$

The 3- and 5-month moving average forecasts for all the months of demand data are shown in the table below. Actually, only the forecast for November based on the most recent monthly demand would be used by the manager. However, the earlier forecasts for prior months allow us to compare the forecasting with actual demand to see how accurate the forecasting method is—that is, how well it does.

Three- and Five-Month Averages

Month	Orders per Month	Three-Month Moving Average	Five-Month Moving Average
January	120	—	—
February	90	—	—

(Continued)

Month	Orders per Month	Three-Month Moving Average	Five-Month Moving Average
March	100	—	—
April	75	103.3	—
May	110	88.3	—
June	50	95.0	99.0
July	75	78.3	85.0
August	130	78.3	82.0
September	110	85.0	88.0
October	90	105.0	95.0
November	—	110.0	91.0

Both moving average forecasts in table above tend to smooth out the variability occurring in the actual data. This smoothing effect can be observed in the following figure in which the 3-month and 5-month averages have been superimposed on a graph of the original data.

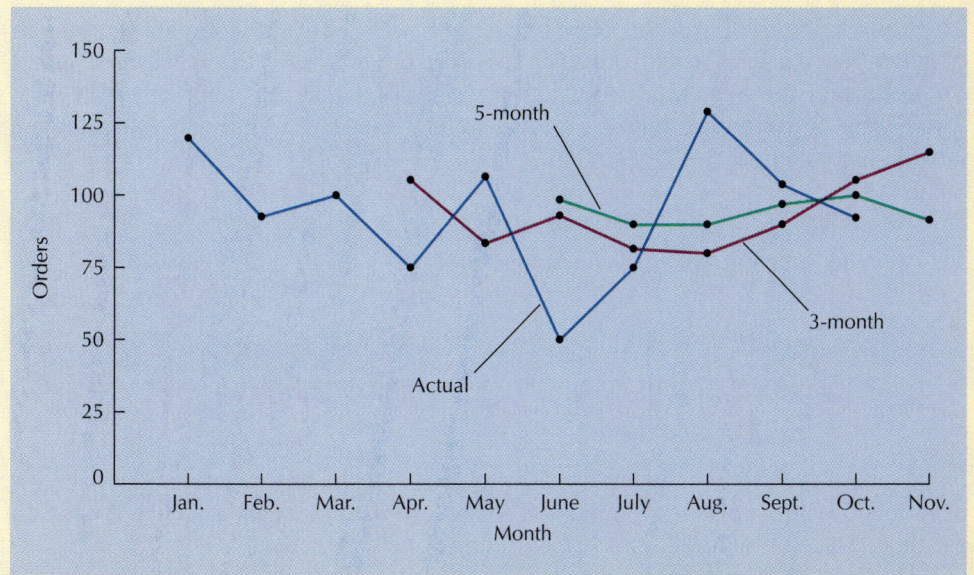

The 5-month moving average in the previous figure smooths out fluctuations to a greater extent than the 3-month moving average. However, the 3-month average more closely reflects the most recent data available to the office supply manager. In general, forecasts using the longer-period moving average are slower to react to recent changes in demand than would those made using shorter-period moving averages. The extra periods of data dampen the speed with which the forecast responds. Establishing the appropriate number of periods to use in a moving average forecast often requires some amount of trial-and-error experimentation.

Longer-period moving averages react more slowly to recent demand changes than shorter-period moving averages.

The disadvantage of the moving average method is that it does not react to variations that occur for a reason, such as cycles and seasonal effects. Factors that cause changes are generally ignored. It is basically a "mechanical" method, which reflects historical data in a consistent way. However, the moving average method does have the advantage of being easy to use, quick, and relatively inexpensive. In general, this method can provide a good forecast for the short run, but it should not be pushed too far into the future.

Weighted Moving Average

In the **weighted moving average**, weights are assigned to the most recent data.

The moving average method can be adjusted to more closely reflect fluctuations in the data. In the **weighted moving average** method, weights are assigned to the most recent data according to the following formula:

$$WMA_n = \sum_{i=1}^{n} W_i D_i$$

where

W_i = the weight for period i, between 0 and 100 percent.

$\Sigma W_i = 1.00$

The Instant Paper Clip Company in Example 10.1 wants to compute a 3-month weighted moving average with a weight of 50 percent for the October data, a weight of 33 percent for the September data, and a weight of 17 percent for the August data. These weights reflect the company's desire to have the most recent data influence the forecast most strongly.

SOLUTION:

The weighted moving average is computed as

$$WMA_3 = \sum_{i=1}^{3} W_i D_i$$

$$= (0.50)(90) + (0.33)(110) + (0.17)(130)$$

$$= 103.4 \text{ orders}$$

Notice that the forecast includes a fractional part, 0.4. In general, the fractional parts need to be included in the computation to achieve mathematical accuracy, but when the final forecast is achieved, it must be rounded up or down.

This forecast is slightly lower than our previously computed 3-month average forecast of 110 orders, reflecting the lower number of orders in October (the most recent month in the sequence).

Determining the precise weights to use for each period of data usually requires some trial-and-error experimentation, as does determining the number of periods to include in the moving average. If the most recent periods are weighted too heavily, the forecast might overreact to a random fluctuation in demand. If they are weighted too lightly, the forecast might underreact to actual changes in demand behavior.

Exponential smoothing is an averaging method that reacts more strongly to recent changes in demand.

Exponential Smoothing

Exponential smoothing is also an averaging method that weights the most recent data more strongly. As such, the forecast will react more to recent changes in demand. This is useful if the recent changes in the data result from a change such as a seasonal pattern instead of just random fluctuations (for which a simple moving average forecast would suffice).

Exponential smoothing is one of the more popular and frequently used forecasting techniques, for a variety of reasons. Exponential smoothing requires minimal data. Only the forecast for the current period, the actual demand for the current period, and a weighting factor called a smoothing constant are necessary. The mathematics of the technique are easy to understand by management. Virtually all POM and forecasting computer software packages include modules for exponential smoothing. Most importantly, exponential smoothing has a good track record of success. It has been employed over the years by many companies that have found it to be an accurate method of forecasting.

The exponential smoothing forecast is computed using the formula

$$F_{t+1} = \alpha D_t + (1 - \alpha)F_t$$

where

F_{t+1} = the forecast for the next period

D_t = actual demand in the present period

F_t = the previously determined forecast for the present period

α = a weighting factor referred to as the **smoothing constant**

> A **smoothing constant** is the weighting factor given to the most recent data in exponential smoothing forecasts.

The smoothing constant, α, is between 0.0 and 1.0. It reflects the weight given to the most recent demand data. For example, if $\alpha = 0.20$,

$$F_{t+1} = 0.20D_t + 0.80F_t$$

which means that our forecast for the next period is based on 20 percent of recent demand (D_t) and 80 percent of past demand (in the form of the forecast F_t, since F_t is derived from previous demands and forecasts). If we go to one extreme and let $\alpha = 0.0$, then

$$F_{t+1} = 0D_t + 1F_t$$
$$= F_t$$

and the forecast for the next period is the same as the forecast for this period. In other words, *the forecast does not reflect the most recent demand at all.*

On the other hand, if $\alpha = 1.0$, then

$$F_{t+1} = 1D_t + 0F_t$$
$$= 1D_t$$

and we have considered only the most recent data (demand in the present period) and nothing else. Thus, the higher α is, the more sensitive the forecast will be to changes in recent demand, and the smoothing will be less. The closer α is to zero, the greater will be the dampening, or smoothing, effect. As α approaches zero, the forecast will react and adjust more slowly to differences between the actual demand and the forecasted demand. The most commonly used values of α are in the range 0.01 to 0.50. However, the determination of α is usually judgmental and subjective and is often based on trial-and-error experimentation. An inaccurate estimate of α can limit the usefulness of this forecasting technique.

> The closer α is to 1.0, the greater the reaction to the most recent demand.

EXAMPLE
10.3

Computing an
Exponentially
Smoothed Forecast

PM Computer Services assembles customized personal computers from generic parts. Formed and operated by part-time State University students, Paulette Tyler and Maureen Becker, the company has had steady growth since it started. The company assembles computers mostly at night, using part-time students. Paulette and Maureen purchase generic computer parts in volume at discount from a variety of sources whenever they see a good deal. Thus, they need a good forecast of demand for their computers so that they will know how many computer component parts to purchase and stock.

The company has accumulated the demand data shown in the accompanying table for its computers for the past twelve months, from which it wants to consider exponential smoothing forecasts using smoothing constants (α) equal to 0.30 and 0.50.

Demand for Personal Computers

Period	Month	Demand
1	January	37
2	February	40
3	March	41
4	April	37
5	May	45
6	June	50
7	July	43
8	August	47
9	September	56
10	October	52
11	November	55
12	December	54

SOLUTION:

To develop the series of forecasts for the data in this table, we will start with period 1 (January) and compute the forecast for period 2 (February) using $\alpha = 0.30$. The formula for exponential smoothing also requires a forecast for period 1, which we do not have, so we will use the demand for period 1 as both *demand* and *forecast* for period 1. Other ways to determine a starting forecast include averaging the first three or four periods or making a subjective estimate. Thus, the forecast for February is

$$F_2 = \alpha D_1 + (1 - \alpha)F_1$$
$$= (0.30)(37) + (0.70)(37)$$
$$= 37 \text{ units}$$

The forecast for period 3 is computed similarly:

$$F_3 = \alpha D_2 + (1 - \alpha)F_2$$
$$= (0.30)(40) + (0.70)(37)$$
$$= 37.9 \text{ units}$$

The remainder of the monthly forecasts are shown in the following table. The final forecast is for period 13, January, and is the forecast of interest to PM Computer Services:

$$F_{13} = \alpha D_{12} + (1 - \alpha)F_{12}$$
$$= (0.30)(54) + (0.70)(50.84)$$
$$= 51.79 \text{ units}$$

Exponential Smoothing Forecasts, α = .30 and α = .50

Period	Month	Demand	Forecast, F_{t+1} $\alpha = 0.30$	$\alpha = 0.50$
1	January	37	—	—
2	February	40	37.00	37.00
3	March	41	37.90	38.50
4	April	37	38.83	39.75
5	May	45	38.28	38.37
6	June	50	40.29	41.68
7	July	43	43.20	45.84
8	August	47	43.14	44.42
9	September	56	44.30	45.71
10	October	52	47.81	50.85
11	November	55	49.06	51.42
12	December	54	50.84	53.21
13	January	—	51.79	53.61

This table also includes the forecast values using α = 0.50. Both exponential smoothing forecasts are shown in Figure 10.3 together with the actual data.

In Figure 10.3, the forecast using the higher smoothing constant, α = 0.50, reacts more strongly to changes in demand than does the forecast with α = 0.30, although both smooth out the random fluctuations in the forecast. Notice that both forecasts lag behind the actual demand. For example, a pronounced downward change in demand in July is not reflected in the forecast until August. If these changes mark a change in trend (i.e., a long-term upward or downward movement) rather

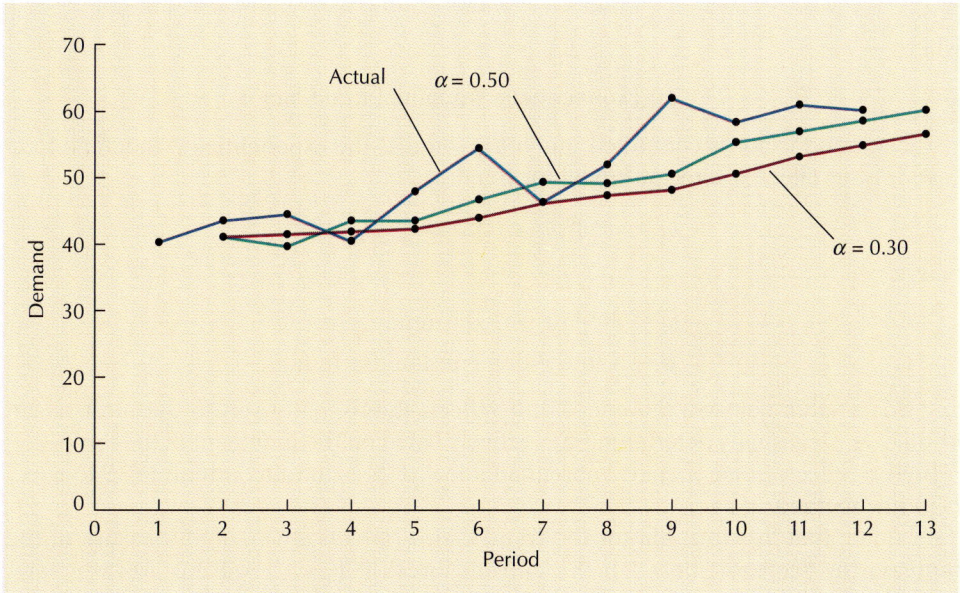

FIGURE 10.3   Exponential Smoothing Forecasts

than just a random fluctuation, then the forecast will always lag behind this trend. We can see a general upward trend in delivered orders throughout the year. Both forecasts tend to be consistently lower than the actual demand; that is, the forecasts lag the trend.

Based on simple observation of the two forecasts in Figure 10.3, $\alpha = 0.50$ seems to be the more accurate of the two in the sense that it seems to follow the actual data more closely. (Later in this chapter we discuss several quantitative methods for determining forecast accuracy.) When demand is relatively stable without any trend, a small value for α is more appropriate to simply smooth out the forecast. When actual demand displays an increasing (or decreasing) trend, as is the case in the figure, a larger value of α is better. It will react more quickly to more recent upward or downward movements in the actual data. In some approaches to exponential smoothing, the accuracy of the forecast is monitored in terms of the difference between the actual values and the forecasted values. If these differences become larger, then α is changed (higher or lower) in an attempt to adapt the forecast to the actual data. However, the exponential smoothing forecast can also be adjusted for the effects of a trend.

In Example 10.3, the final forecast computed was for one month, January. A forecast for two or three months could have been computed by grouping the demand data into the required number of periods and then using these values in the exponential smoothing computations. For example, if a three-month forecast were needed, demand for January, February, and March could be summed and used to compute the forecast for the next three-month period, and so on, until a final three-month forecast results. Alternatively, if a trend is present the final period forecast can be used for an extended forecast by adjusting it by a trend factor.

Adjusted Exponential Smoothing

An adjusted exponential smoothing forecast is an exponential smoothing forecast with an adjustment for a trend added to it.

The **adjusted exponential smoothing** forecast consists of the exponential smoothing forecast with a trend adjustment factor added to it,

$$AF_{t+1} = F_{t+1} + T_{t+1}$$

where

$$T = \text{an exponentially smoothed trend factor}$$

The trend factor is computed much the same as the exponentially smoothed forecast. It is, in effect, a forecast model for trend.

$$T_{t+1} = \beta(F_{t+1} - F_t) + (1 - \beta)T_t$$

where

$$T_t = \text{the last period's trend factor}$$
$$\beta = \text{a smoothing constant for trend}$$

The closer β is to 1.0, the stronger a trend is reflected.

β is a value between 0.0 and 1.0. It reflects the weight given to the most recent trend data. β is usually determined subjectively based on the judgment of the forecaster. A high β reflects trend changes more than a low β. It is not uncommon for β to equal α in this method.

Notice that this formula for the trend factor reflects a weighted measure of the increase (or decrease) between the current forecast, F_{t+1}, and the previous forecast, F_t.

EXAMPLE
10.4

*Computing an
Adjusted Exponentially
Smoothed Forecast*

PM Computer Services now wants to develop an adjusted exponentially smoothed forecast using the same twelve months of demand shown in the table for Example 10.3. It will use the exponentially smoothed forecast with $\alpha = 0.5$ computed in Example 10.3 with a smoothing constant for trend, β, of 0.30.

SOLUTION:

The formula for the adjusted exponential smoothing forecast requires an initial value for T_t to start the computational process. This initial trend factor is often an estimate determined subjectively or based on past data by the forecaster. In this case, since we have a long sequence of demand data (i.e., 12 months) we will start with the trend, T_t, equal to zero. By the time the forecast value of interest, F_{13}, is computed, we should have a relatively good value for the trend factor.

The adjusted forecast for February, AF_2, is the same as the exponentially smoothed forecast, since the trend computing factor will be zero (i.e., F_1 and F_2 are the same and $T_2 = 0$). Thus, we compute the adjusted forecast for March, AF_3, as follows, starting with the determination of the trend factor, T_3:

$$T_3 = \beta(F_3 - F_2) + (1 - \beta)T_2$$
$$= (0.30)(38.5 - 37.0) + (0.70)(0)$$
$$= 0.45$$

and

$$AF_3 = F_3 + T_3$$
$$= 38.5 + 0.45$$
$$= 38.95 \text{ units}$$

This adjusted forecast value for period 3 is shown in the accompanying table, with all other adjusted forecast values for the 12-month period plus the forecast for period 13, computed as follows.

$$T_{13} = \beta(F_{13} - F_{12}) + (1 - \beta)T_{12}$$
$$= (0.30)(53.61 - 53.21) + (0.70)(1.77)$$
$$= 1.36$$

and

$$AF_{13} = F_{13} + T_{13}$$
$$= 53.61 + 1.36$$
$$= 54.96 \text{ units}$$

Adjusted Exponential Smoothing Forecast Values

Period	Month	Demand	Forecast F_{t+1}	Trend T_{t+1}	Adjusted Forecast AF_{t+1}
1	January	37	37.00	—	—
2	February	40	37.00	0.00	37.00

(Continued)

Period	Month	Demand	Forecast F_{t+1}	Trend T_{t+1}	Adjusted Forecast AF_{t+1}
3	March	41	38.50	0.45	38.95
4	April	37	39.75	0.69	40.44
5	May	45	38.37	0.07	38.44
6	June	50	41.68	1.04	42.73
7	July	43	45.84	1.97	47.82
8	August	47	44.42	0.95	45.37
9	September	56	45.71	1.05	46.76
10	October	52	50.85	2.28	53.13
11	November	55	51.42	1.76	53.19
12	December	54	53.21	1.77	54.98
13	January	—	53.61	1.36	54.96

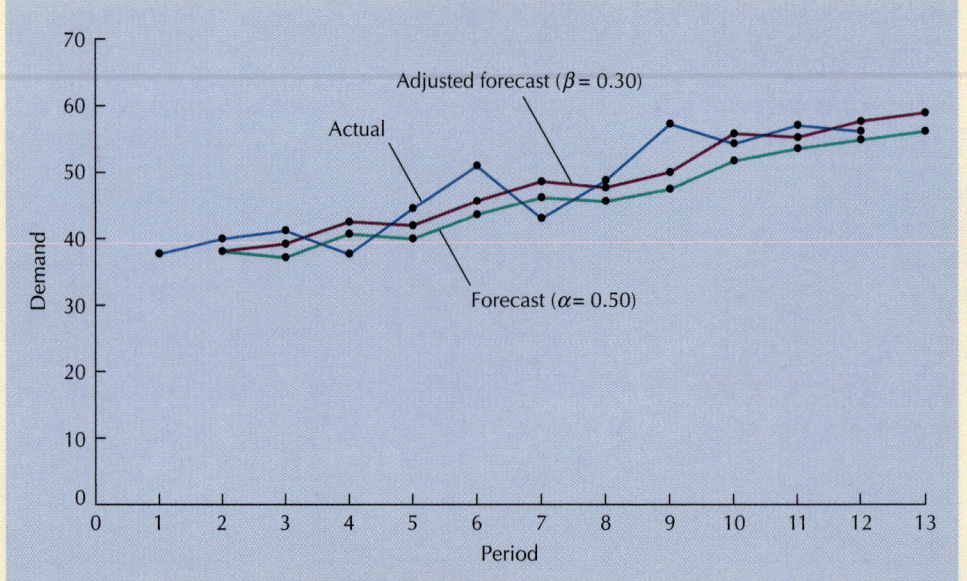

The adjusted exponentially smoothed forecast values shown in the table are compared with the exponentially smoothed forecast values and the actual data in the figure above. Notice that the adjusted forecast is consistently higher than the exponentially smoothed forecast and is thus more reflective of the generally increasing trend of the actual data. However, in general, the pattern, or degree of smoothing, is very similar for both forecasts.

Linear Trend Line

A linear trend line is a linear regression model relating demand to time.

Linear regression is a causal method of forecasting in which a mathematical relationship is developed between demand and some other factor that causes demand behavior. However, when demand displays an obvious trend over time, a least squares regression line, or **linear trend line**, can be used to forecast demand.

A linear trend line relates a dependent variable, which for our purposes is demand, to one independent variable, time, in form of a linear equation:

$$y = a + bx$$

where

a = intercept (at period 0)
b = slope of the line
x = the time period
y = forecast for demand for period x

These parameters of the linear trend line can be calculated using the least squares formulas for linear regression,

$$b = \frac{\Sigma xy - n\bar{x}\bar{y}}{\Sigma x^2 - n\bar{x}^2}$$

$$a = \bar{y} - b\bar{x}$$

where

n = number of periods

$\bar{x} = \dfrac{\Sigma x}{n}$ = the mean of the x values

$\bar{y} = \dfrac{\Sigma y}{n}$ = the mean of the y values

EXAMPLE
10.5

*Computing a Linear
Trend Line*

The demand data for PM Computer Services (shown in the table for Example 10.3) appears to follow an increasing linear trend. The company wants to compute a linear trend line to see if it is more accurate than the exponential smoothing and adjusted exponential smoothing forecasts developed in Examples 10.3 and 10.4.

SOLUTION:

The values required for the least squares calculations are:

Least Squares Calculations

x (period)	y (demand)	xy	x^2
1	37	37	1
2	40	80	4
3	41	123	9
4	37	148	16
5	45	225	25
6	50	300	36
7	43	301	49
8	47	376	64
9	56	504	81
10	52	520	100
11	55	605	121
12	54	648	144
78	557	3,867	650

(Continued)

Using these values, the parameters for the linear trend line are computed as follows,

$$\bar{x} = \frac{78}{12} = 6.5$$

$$\bar{y} = \frac{557}{12} = 46.42$$

$$b = \frac{\Sigma xy - n\bar{x}\bar{y}}{\Sigma x^2 - n\bar{x}^2}$$

$$= \frac{3{,}867 - (12)(6.5)(46.42)}{650 - 12(6.5)^2}$$

$$= 1.72$$

$$a = \bar{y} - b\bar{x}$$

$$= 46.42 - (1.72)(6.5)$$

$$= 35.2$$

Therefore, the linear trend line equation is

$$y = 35.2 + 1.72x$$

To calculate a forecast for period 13, let $x = 13$ in the linear trend line:

$$y = 35.2 + 1.72(13)$$

$$= 57.56 \text{ units}$$

The following graph shows the linear trend line compared to the actual data. The trend line appears to reflect closely the actual data—that is, to be a "good fit"—and would thus be a good forecast model for this problem. However, a disadvantage of the linear trend line is that it will not adjust to a change in the trend, as the exponential smoothing forecast methods will; that is, it is assumed that all future forecasts will follow a straight line. This limits the use of this method to a shorter time frame in which you can be relatively certain that the trend will not change.

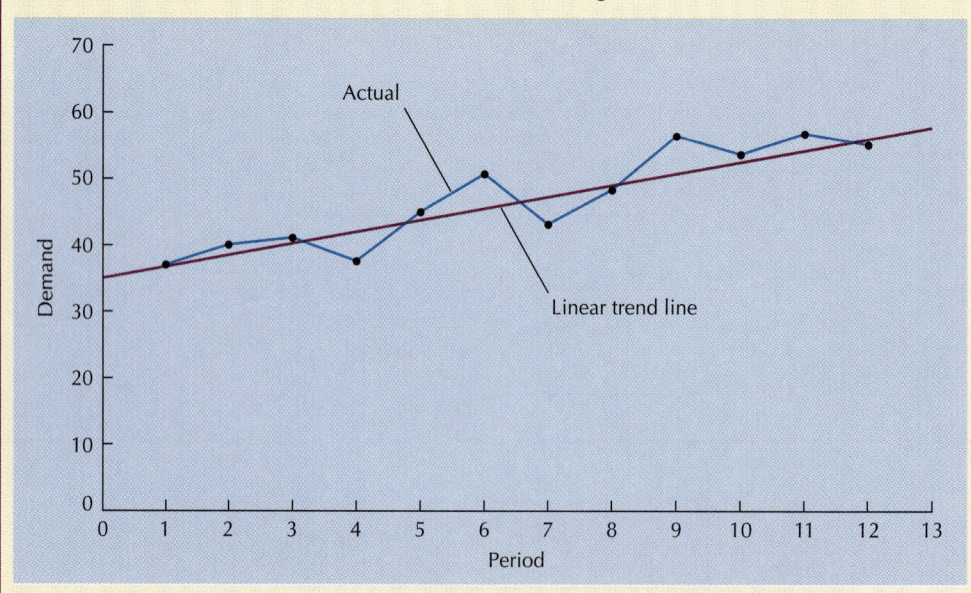

Seasonal Adjustments

A seasonal pattern is a repetitive increase and decrease in demand. Many demand items exhibit seasonal behavior. Clothing sales follow annual seasonal patterns, with demand for warm clothes increasing in the fall and winter and declining in the spring and summer as the demand for cooler clothing increases. Demand for many retail items, including toys, sports equipment, clothing, electronic appliances, hams, turkeys, wine, and fruit, increase during the holiday season. Greeting card demand increases in conjunction with special days such as Valentine's Day and Mother's Day. Seasonal patterns can also occur on a monthly, a weekly, or even a daily basis. Some restaurants have higher demand in the evening than at lunch or on weekends as opposed to weekdays. Traffic—hence sales—at shopping malls picks up on Friday and Saturday.

There are several methods for reflecting seasonal patterns in a time series forecast. We will describe one of the simpler methods using a *seasonal factor*. A **seasonal factor** is a numerical value that is multiplied by the normal forecast to get a seasonally adjusted forecast.

One method for developing a demand for seasonal factors is to divide the actual demand for each seasonal period by total annual demand, according to the following formula:

$$S_i = \frac{D_i}{\Sigma D}$$

The resulting seasonal factors between 0 and 1.0 are, in effect, the portion of total annual demand assigned to each season. These seasonal factors are multiplied by the annual forecasted demand to yield adjusted forecasts for each season.

Adjust for seasonality by multiplying the normal forecast by a **seasonal factor**.

Snow skiing is an industry that exhibits several different patterns of demand behavior. It is primarily a seasonal (i.e., winter) industry; thus, any forecasts of the demand for skiing-related products and services should include a seasonal adjustment. Over a long period of time the snow skiing industry has exhibited a generally increasing growth trend. The technique used to forecast demand for skiing products and services should also include an adjustment for trend, as well as a seasonal adjustment. Other, more random factors, can cause variations, or abrupt peaks and valleys, in demand. For example, demand for skiing products showed a pronounced increase after the 1994 Winter Olympics in Lilliehammer, Norway. Conversely, warm weather and a lack of snow in some regions of the United States during several winters in the late 1980s and early 1990s depressed the skiing industry, resulting in decreased demand.

EXAMPLE
10.6

*Computing a Forecast
with Seasonal
Adjustments*

Wishbone Farms grows turkeys to sell to a meat-processing company throughout the year. However, its peak season is obviously during the fourth quarter of the year, from October to December. Wishbone Farms has experienced the demand for turkeys for the past three years shown in the accompanying table.

Demand for Turkeys at Wishbone Farms

| Year | DEMAND (1,000s) PER QUARTER | | | | |
	1	2	3	4	Total
1995	12.6	8.6	6.3	17.5	45.0
1996	14.1	10.3	7.5	18.2	50.1
1997	15.3	10.6	8.1	19.6	53.6
Total	42.0	29.5	21.9	55.3	148.7

SOLUTION:

Because we have three years of demand data, we can compute the seasonal factors by dividing total quarterly demand for the three years by total demand across all three years.

$$S_1 = \frac{D_1}{\Sigma D} = \frac{42.0}{148.7} = 0.28$$

$$S_2 = \frac{D_2}{\Sigma D} = \frac{29.5}{148.7} = 0.20$$

$$S_3 = \frac{D_3}{\Sigma D} = \frac{21.9}{148.7} = 0.15$$

$$S_4 = \frac{D_4}{\Sigma D} = \frac{55.3}{148.7} = 0.37$$

Next, we want to multiply the forecasted demand for the next year, 1998, by each of the seasonal factors to get the forecasted demand for each quarter. To accomplish this, we need a demand forecast for 1998. In this case, since the demand data in the table seem to exhibit a generally increasing trend, we compute a linear trend line for the three years of data in the table to get a rough forecast estimate.

$$\begin{aligned} y &= 40.97 + 4.30x \\ &= 40.97 + 4.30(4) \\ &= 58.17 \end{aligned}$$

Thus, the forecast for 1998 is 58.17, or 58,170 turkeys.

Using this annual forecast of demand, the seasonally adjusted forecasts, SF_i, for 1998 are

$$SF_1 = (S_1)\,(F_5) = (0.28)(58.17) = 16.28$$
$$SF_2 = (S_2)\,(F_5) = (0.20)(58.17) = 11.63$$
$$SF_3 = (S_3)\,(F_5) = (0.15)(58.17) = 8.73$$
$$SF_4 = (S_4)\,(F_5) = (0.37)(58.17) = 21.53$$

Comparing these quarterly forecasts with the actual demand values in the table, they would seem to be relatively good forecast estimates, reflecting both the seasonal variations in the data and the general upward trend.

Forecast Accuracy

A forecast is never completely accurate; forecasts will always deviate from the actual demand. This difference between the forecast and the actual is the **forecast error.** Although forecast error is inevitable, the objective of forecasting is that it be as slight as possible. A large degree of error may indicate that either the forecasting technique is the wrong one or it needs to be adjusted by changing its parameters (for example, α in the exponential smoothing forecast).

There are different measures of forecast error. We will discuss several of the more popular ones: mean absolute deviation (MAD), mean absolute percent deviation (MAPD), cumulative error, and average error ($\overline{E}$) or bias ($\overline{E}$).

Forecast error is the difference between the forecast and actual demand.

Turkeys are an example of a product with a long-term trend for increasing demand with a seasonal pattern. Turkey sales have increased annually during the past decade. In 1996 almost 300 million turkeys valued at over $2.5 billion went to market in the U.S. Annual turkey production and sales are also more uniform during the year now than they were a decade ago because of changing (healthier) dietary habits in the U.S. Turkey has become a component of many food products including luncheon meats, sausage, hot dogs, and hamburgers in order to reduce fat content. However, turkey sales still show a distinct seasonal pattern by increasing markedly during the Thanksgiving holiday season. For example, turkey sales are lowest from January to May with about 19 to 23 million turkeys going to market each month. However, sales begin to rise to around 25 million turkeys in June and July up to a peak of about 26 to 28 million turkeys to market in August when distributors begin to build up their inventory of frozen turkeys for increased sales in November. Sales remain high at 25 to 27 million turkeys for September, October, and November and then begin to decline in December and January to around 19 to 20 million.

Mean Absolute Deviation

MAD is the average, absolute difference between the forecast and demand.

The **mean absolute deviation,** or **MAD,** is one of the most popular and simplest to use measures of forecast error. MAD is an average of the difference between the forecast and actual demand, as computed by the following formula:

$$\text{MAD} = \frac{\Sigma |D_t - F_t|}{n}$$

where

t = the period number
D_t = demand in period t
F_t = the forecast for period t
n = the total number of periods
$|\ \ |$ = absolute value

EXAMPLE
10.7

Measuring Forecast Accuracy with MAD

In Examples 10.3, 10.4, and 10.5, forecasts were developed using exponential smoothing, ($\alpha = 0.30$ and $\alpha = 0.50$), adjusted exponential smoothing ($\alpha = 0.50$, $\beta = 0.30$), and a linear trend line, respectively, for the demand data for PM Computer Services. The company wants to compare the accuracy of these different forecasts using MAD.

SOLUTION:

We will compute MAD for all four forecasts; however, we will present the computational detail for the exponential smoothing forecast only with $\alpha = 0.30$. The accompanying table shows the values necessary to compute MAD for the exponential smoothing forecast.

Computational Values for MAD

Period	Demand, D_t	Forecast $F_t(\alpha = 0.30)$	Error $(D_t - F_t)$	$\|D_t - F_t\|$
1	37	37.00	—	—
2	40	37.00	3.00	3.00
3	41	37.90	3.10	3.10
4	37	38.83	−1.83	1.83
5	45	38.28	6.72	6.72
6	50	40.29	9.69	9.69
7	43	43.20	−0.20	0.20
8	47	43.14	3.86	3.86
9	56	44.30	11.70	11.70
10	52	47.81	4.19	4.19
11	55	49.06	5.94	5.94
12	54	50.84	3.15	3.15
	557		49.31	53.39[a]

[a] The computation of MAD will be based on eleven periods, periods 2 through 12, excluding the initial demand and forecast values for period 1 since they both equal 37.

Using the data in the table, MAD is computed as

$$MAD = \frac{\Sigma|D_t - F_t|}{n}$$

$$= \frac{53.39}{11}$$

$$= 4.85$$

The smaller the value of MAD, the more accurate the forecast, although viewed alone, MAD is difficult to access. In this example, the data values were relatively small and the MAD value of 4.85 should be judged accordingly. Overall it would seem to be a "low" value; that is, the forecast appears to be relatively accurate. However, if the magnitude of the data values were in the thousands or millions, then a MAD value of a similar magnitude might not be bad either. The point is, you cannot compare a MAD value of 4.85 with a MAD value of 485 and say the former is good and the latter is bad; they depend to a certain extent on the relative magnitude of the data.

The lower the value of MAD, relative to the magnitude of the data, the more accurate the forecast.

One benefit of MAD is to compare the accuracy of several different forecasting techniques, as we are doing in this example. The MAD values for the remaining forecasts are as follows.

Exponential smoothing ($\alpha = 0.50$): MAD = 4.04
Adjusted exponential smoothing ($\alpha = 0.50$, $\beta = 0.30$): MAD = 3.81
Linear trend line: MAD = 2.29

Since the linear trend line has the lowest MAD value of 2.29, it would seem to be the most accurate, although it does not appear to be significantly better than the adjusted exponential smoothing forecast. Further, we can deduce from these MAD values that increasing α from 0.30 to 0.50 enhanced the accuracy of the exponentially smoothed forecast. The adjusted forecast is even more accurate.

The **mean absolute percent deviation (MAPD)** measures the absolute error as a percentage of demand rather than per period. As a result, it eliminates the problem of interpreting the measure of accuracy relative to the magnitude of the demand and forecast values, as MAD does. The mean percent deviation is computed according to the following formula:

MAPD is the absolute error as a percentage of demand.

$$MAPD = \frac{\Sigma|D_t - F_t|}{\Sigma D_t}$$

Using the data from the table in Example 10.7 for the exponential smoothing forecast ($\alpha = 0.30$) for PM Computer Services,

$$MAPD = \frac{53.39}{520}$$

$$= 0.096 \text{ or } 9.6 \text{ percent}$$

A lower percent deviation implies a more accurate forecast. The MAPD values for our other three forecasts are

Exponential smoothing ($\alpha = 0.50$): MAPD = 8.5 percent
Adjusted exponential smoothing ($\alpha = 0.50$, $\beta = 0.30$): MAPD = 8.1 percent
Linear trend line: MAPD = 4.9 percent

Cumulative Error

Cumulative error is the sum of the forecast errors.

Cumulative error is computed simply by summing the forecast errors, as shown in the following formula.

$$E = \Sigma e_t$$

Large $+E$ indicates forecast is biased low; large $-E$, forecast is biased high.

A large positive value indicates that the forecast is probably consistently lower than the actual demand, or is biased low. A large negative value implies the forecast is consistently higher than actual demand, or is biased high. Also, when the errors for each period are scrutinized, a preponderance of positive values shows the forecast is consistently less than the actual value and vice versa.

The cumulative error for the exponential smoothing forecast ($\alpha = 0.30$) for PM Computer Services can be read directly from the table in Example 10.7; it is simply the sum of the values in the "Error" column:

$$E = \Sigma e_t$$
$$= 49.31$$

This large positive error for cumulative error, plus the fact that the individual errors for each period in the table are positive, indicates that this forecast is consistently below the actual demand. A quick glance back at the plot of the exponential smoothing ($\alpha = 0.30$) forecast in Figure 10.3 visually verifies this result.

The cumulative error for the other forecasts are

Exponential smoothing ($\alpha = 0.50$): $E = 33.21$

Adjusted exponential smoothing ($\alpha = 0.50$, $\beta = 0.30$): $E = 21.14$

We did not show the cumulative error for the linear trend line. E will always equal zero for the linear trend line.

Average error is the per-period average of cumulative error.

A measure closely related to cumulative error is the **average error,** or *bias.* It is computed by averaging the cumulative error over the number of time periods,

$$\overline{E} = \frac{\Sigma e_t}{n}$$

For example, the average error for the exponential smoothing forecast ($\alpha = 0.30$) is computed as follows. (Notice a value of 11 was used for n, since we used actual demand for the first-period forecast, resulting in no error, that is, $D_1 = F_1 = 37$.)

$$\overline{E} = \frac{49.31}{11} = 4.48$$

The average error is interpreted similarly to the cumulative error. A positive value indicates low bias and a negative value indicates high bias. A value close to zero implies a lack of bias.

Table 10.1 summarizes the measures of forecast accuracy we have discussed in this section for the four example forecasts we developed in Examples 10.3, 10.4, and 10.5 for PM Computer Services. The results are consistent for all four forecasts, indicating that for the PM Computer Services example data, a larger value of α is preferable for the exponential smoothing forecast. The adjusted forecast is more accurate than the exponential smoothing forecasts, and the linear trend is more accurate than all the others. Although these results are for specific examples, they do not indicate how the different forecast measures for accuracy can be used to adjust a forecasting method or select the best method.

TABLE 10.1   Comparison of Forecasts for PM Computer Services

Forecast	MAD	MAPD	E	$\overline{E}$
Exponential smoothing ($\alpha = 0.30$)	4.85	9.6%	49.31	4.48
Exponential smoothing ($\alpha = 0.50$)	4.04	8.5%	33.21	3.02
Adjusted exponential smoothing ($\alpha = 0.50$, $\beta = 0.30$)	3.81	8.1%	21.14	1.92
Linear trend line	2.29	4.9%	—	—

Forecast Control

There are several ways to monitor forecast error over time to make sure that the forecast is performing correctly—that is, the forecast is in control. Forecasts can go "out of control" and start providing inaccurate forecasts for several reasons, including a change in trend, the unanticipated appearance of a cycle, or an irregular variation such as unseasonable weather, a promotional campaign, new competition, or a political event that distracts consumers.

A **tracking signal** indicates if the forecast is consistently biased high or low. It is computed by dividing the cumulative error by MAD, according to the formula

A **tracking signal** monitors the forecast to see if it is biased high or low.

$$\text{Tracking signal} = \frac{\Sigma(D_t - F_t)}{\text{MAD}} = \frac{E}{\text{MAD}}$$

The tracking signal is recomputed each period, with updated, "running" values of cumulative error and MAD. The movement of the tracking signal is compared to *control limits*; as long as the tracking signal is within these limits, the forecast is in control.

Forecast errors are typically normally distributed, which results in the following relationship between MAD and the standard deviation of the distribution of error, σ:

$$\text{MAD} \cong 0.8\sigma$$

This enables us to establish statistical control limits for the tracking signal that corresponds to the more familiar normal distribution. For example, statistical control limits of ± 3 standard deviations, corresponding to 99.7 percent of the errors, would translate to ± 3.75 MADs; that is, $3\sigma \div 0.8 = 3.75$ MADs. Control limits of ± 2 to ± 5 MADs are used most frequently.

EXAMPLE
10.8

Developing a Tracking Signal

In Example 10.7, the mean absolute deviation was computed for the exponential smoothing forecast ($\alpha = 0.30$) for PM Computer Services. Using a tracking signal, monitor the forecast accuracy using control limits of ± 3 MADs.

SOLUTION:

To use the tracking signal, we must recompute MAD each period as the cumulative error is computed.

Using MAD = 3.00, the tracking signal for period 2 is

$$\text{TS}_2 = \frac{E}{\text{MAD}} = \frac{3.00}{3.00} = 1.00$$

(Continued)

The tracking signal for period 3 is

$$TS_3 = \frac{6.10}{3.05} = 2.00$$

The remaining tracking signal values are shown in the accompanying table.

Tracking Signal Values

Period	Demand, D_t	Forecast, F_t	Error, $D_t - F_t$	$\Sigma E = \Sigma(D_t - F_t)$	MAD	Tracking Signal
1	37	37.00	—	—	—	—
2	40	37.00	3.00	3.00	3.00	1.00
3	41	37.90	3.10	6.10	3.05	2.00
4	37	38.83	−1.83	4.27	2.64	1.62
5	45	38.28	6.72	10.99	3.66	3.00
6	50	40.29	9.69	20.68	4.87	4.25
7	43	43.20	−0.20	20.48	4.09	5.01
8	47	43.14	3.86	24.34	4.06	6.00
9	56	44.30	11.70	36.04	5.01	7.19
10	52	47.81	4.19	40.23	4.92	8.18
11	55	49.06	5.94	46.17	5.02	9.20
12	54	50.84	3.15	49.32	4.85	10.17

The tracking signal values in the table above move outside ±3 MAD control limits (i.e., ±3.00) in period 5 *and* continue increasing. This suggests that the forecast is not performing accurately or, more precisely, is consistently biased low (i.e., actual demand consistently exceeds the forecast). This is illustrated in the graph below. Notice that the

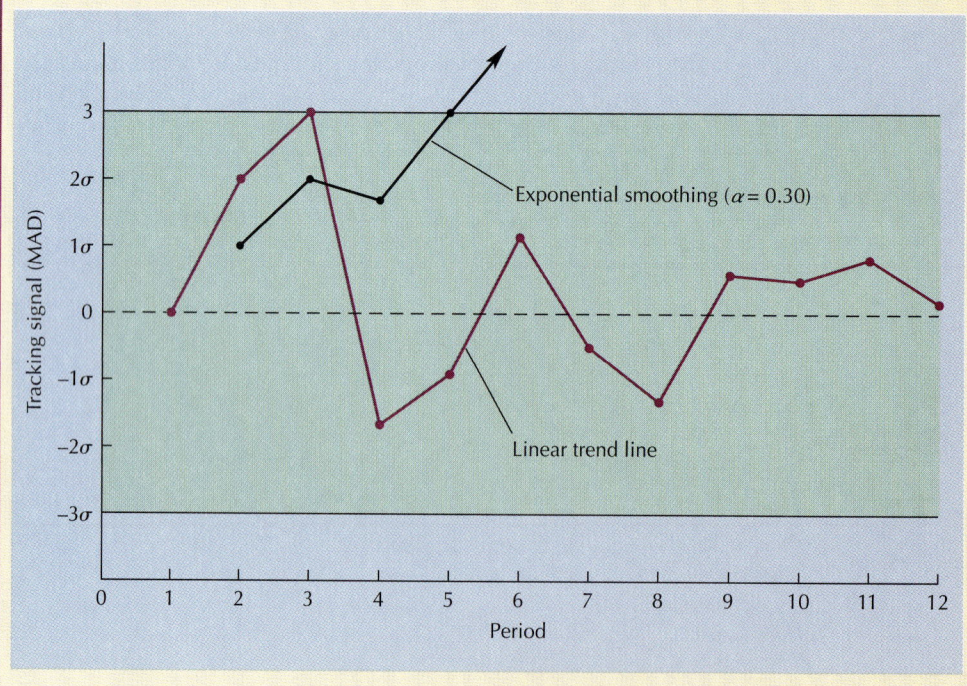

tracking signal moves beyond the upper limit of 3 following period 6 and continues to rise. For the sake of comparison, the tracking signal for the linear trend line forecast computed in Example 10.5 is also plotted on this graph. Notice that it remains within the limits (touching the upper limit in period 3), indicating a lack of consistent bias.

Another method for monitoring forecast error is statistical control charts. For example, $\pm 3\sigma$ control limits would reflect 99.7 percent of the forecast errors (assuming they are normally distributed). The sample standard deviation, σ, is computed as

$$\sigma = \sqrt{\frac{\Sigma (D_t - F_t)^2}{n - 1}}$$

This formula without the square root is known as the **mean squared error (MSE)**, and it is sometimes used as a measure of forecast error. It reacts to forecast error much like MAD does.

MSE is the average of the squared forecast errors.

Using the same example for the exponential smoothing forecast ($\alpha = 0.30$) for PM Computer Services, the standard deviation is computed as

$$\sigma = \sqrt{\frac{375.68}{10}} = 6.12$$

Using this value of σ we can compute statistical control limits for forecast errors for our exponential smoothing forecast ($\alpha = 0.30$) example for PM Computer Services. Plus or minus 3σ control limits, reflecting 99.7 percent of the forecast errors, gives $\pm 3(6.12)$, or ± 18.39. Although it can be observed from the table in Example 10.8 that all the er-

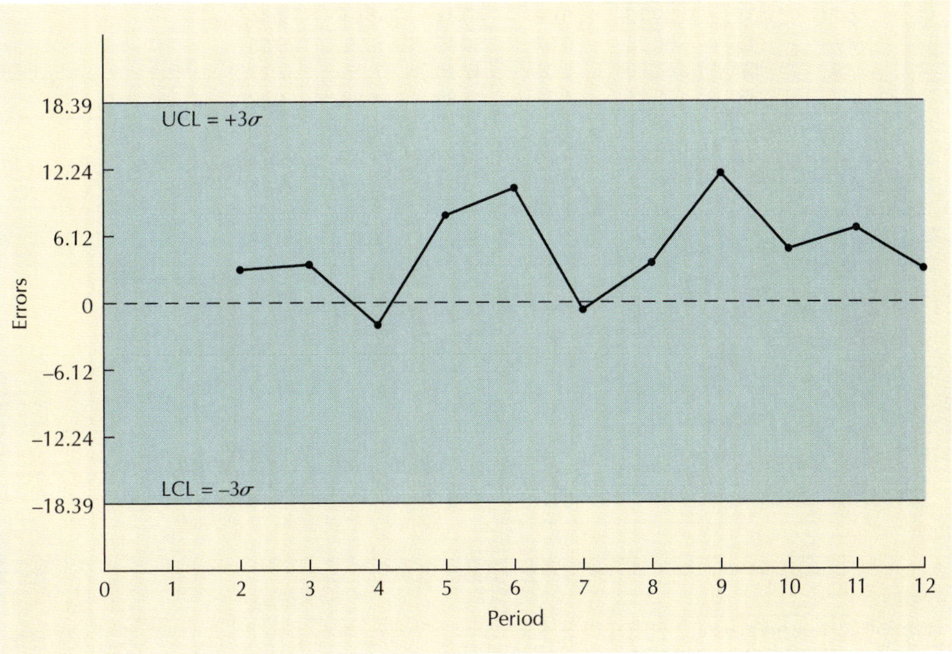

FIGURE 10.4 **Control Chart for Forecast Error**

ror values are within the control limits, we can still detect that most of the errors are positive, indicating a low bias in the forecast estimates. This is illustrated in a graph of the control chart in Figure 10.4 with the errors plotted on it.

Time Series Forecasting Using Excel and POM for Windows

Excel can be used to develop forecasts using the moving average, exponential smoothing, adjusted exponential smoothing, and linear trend line techniques. First we will demonstrate how to determine exponentially smoothed and adjusted exponentially smoothed forecasts using Excel as shown in Exhibit 10.1. We will demonstrate Excel

The exponentially smoothed forecast for March in cell C11

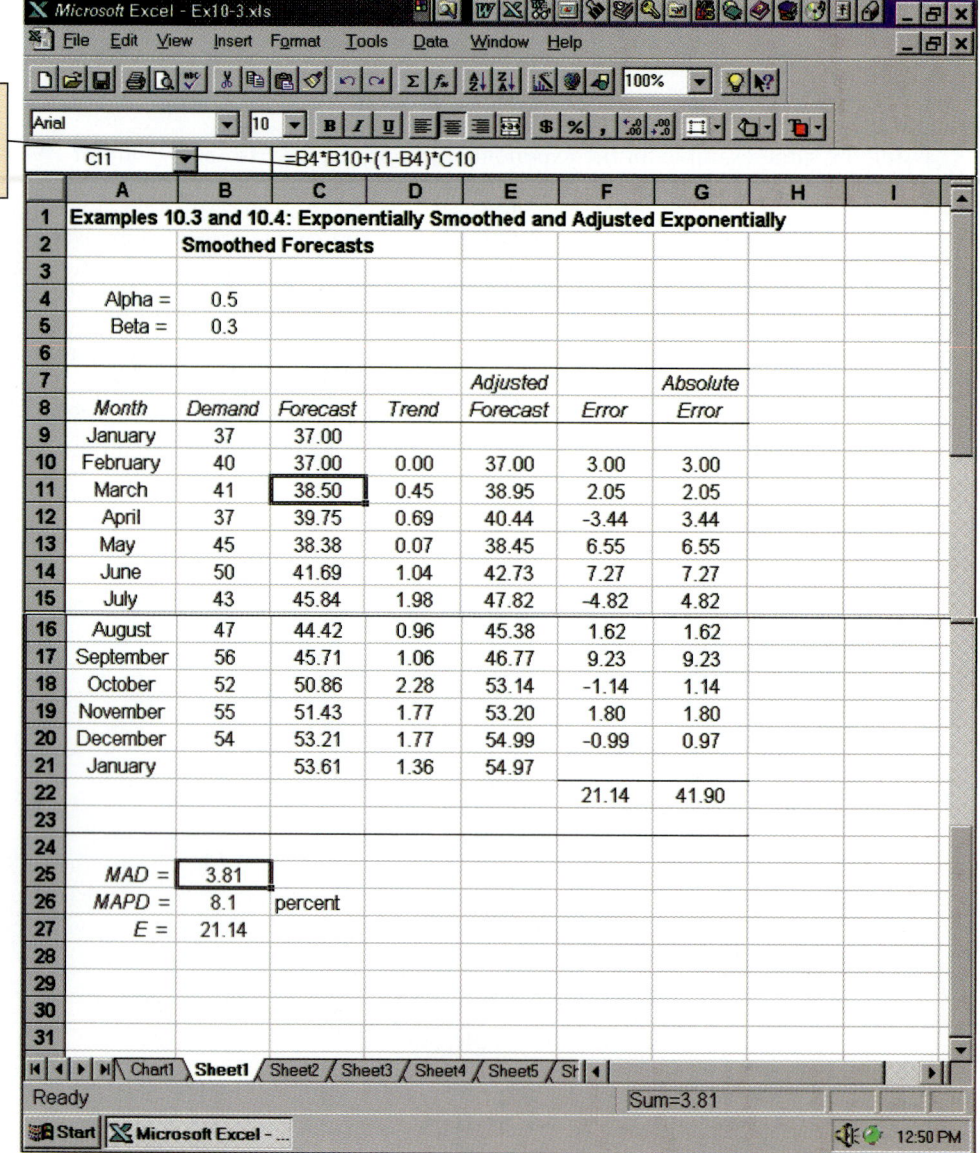

EXHIBIT 10.1

using Examples 10.3 and 10.4 for forecasting demand at PM Computer Services, including the Excel spreadsheets showing the exponentially smoothed forecast with $\alpha = 0.5$ and the adjusted exponentially smoothed forecast with $\beta = 0.3$. We have also computed the values for MAD, MAPD, and E.

Notice that the formula in Exhibit 10.1 for computing the exponentially smoothed forecast for March is embedded in cell C11 and shown on the formula bar at the top of the screen. The same formula is used to compute all the other forecast values in column C. For example, the formula for computing the trend value for March is =B5*(C11−C10)+(1−B5)*D10, and the formula for the adjusted forecast for March is =C11+D11. The error is computed for the adjusted forecast, and the formula for computing the error for March is =E11−B11, while the formula for absolute error for March is =ABS(F11).

A graph of the forecast can also be developed with Excel. To plot the exponentially smoothed forecast in column C and demand in column B, cover all cells from A8 to C21 with the mouse and click on "Insert" on the toolbar at the top of the worksheet. Next click on "Chart," which will invoke a window for constructing a chart. After verifying that the range of cells to include is correct, click on "Next." This will provide a menu of different chart types. Select a line chart and go to the next window where you can select a chart format that connects the data points with a line. Go to the next window which shows a chart. The next window allows you to label the axes and then clicking on "Finish" brings up a full-screen version of the graph. To clean it up you can double click on the lines and data points. The resulting graph for demand and the exponentially smoothed forecast for our example is shown in Exhibit 10.2. An exponentially smoothed forecast can also be computed in Excel by selecting 'Data Analysis' from the 'Tools' menu at the top of the spreadsheet, and then selecting the 'exponential smoothing' menu item.

Excel can also be used to develop more customized forecast models, like seasonal

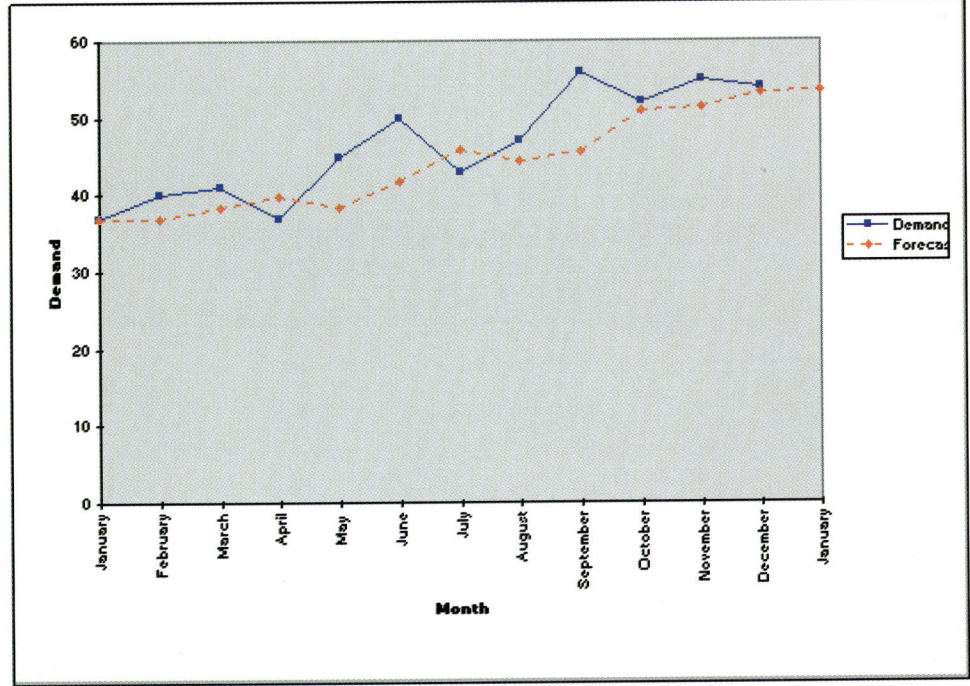

EXHIBIT 10.2

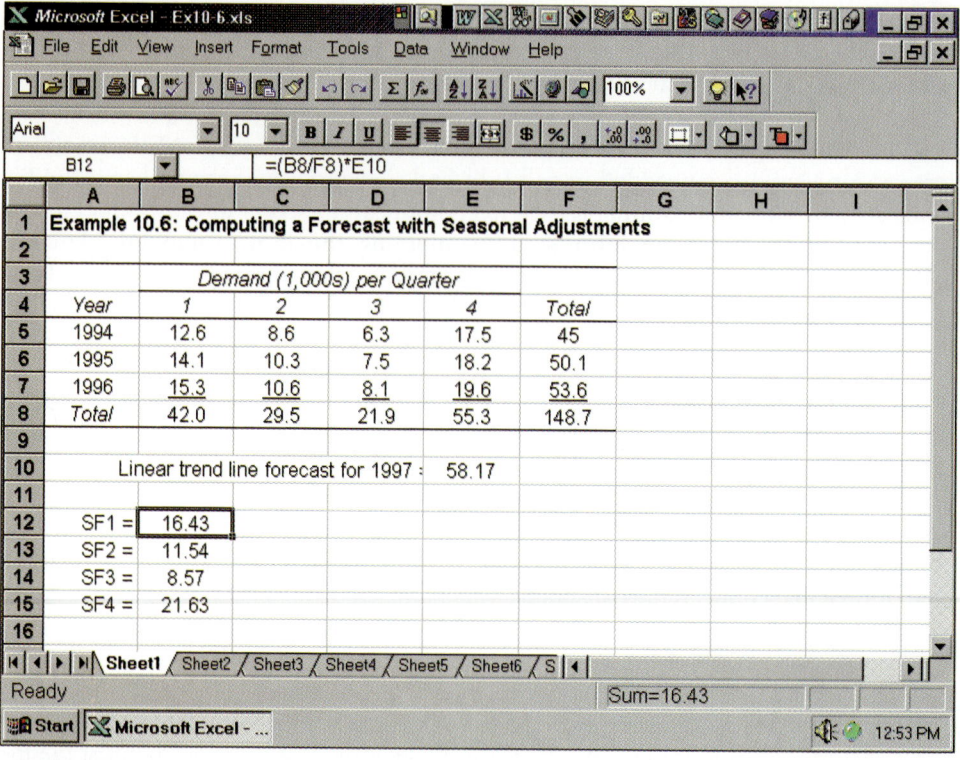

EXHIBIT 10.3

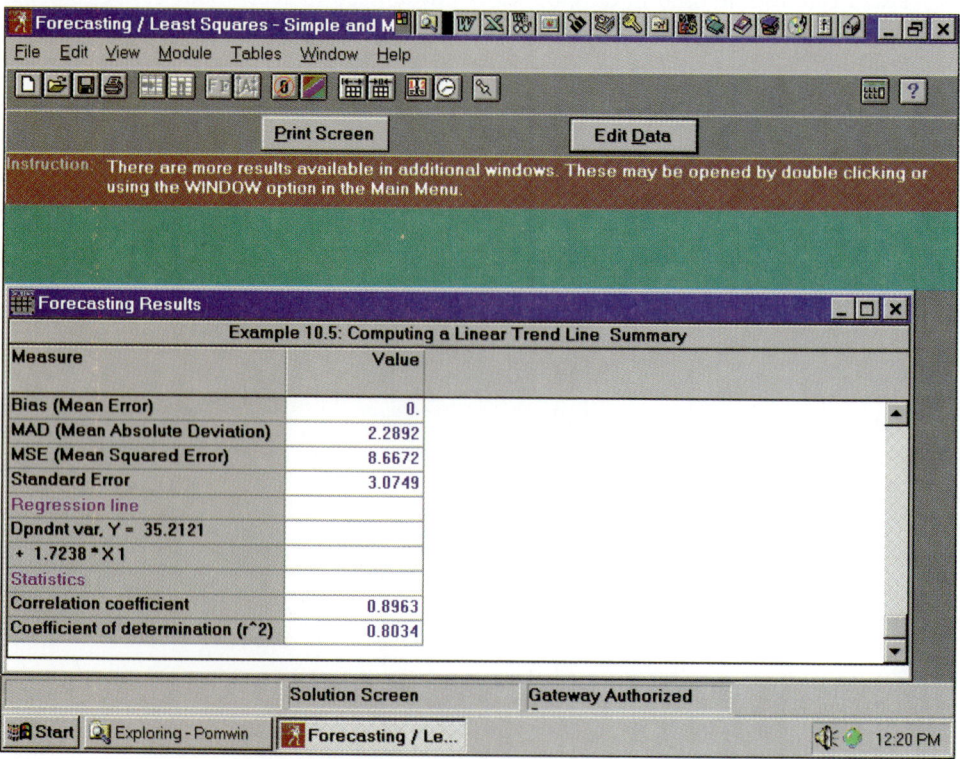

EXHIBIT 10.4

forecast models. Exhibit 10.3 shows an Excel screen for the seasonal forecast model developed in Example 10.6. Notice that the computation of the seasonal forecast for the first quarter (SF1) in cell B12 is computed using the formula shown on the formula bar at the top of the screen. The forecast value for SF1 is slightly different than the value in Example 10.6 because of rounding.

POM for Windows also has the capability to perform time series forecasting including exponential smoothing and adjusted exponential smoothing models. Exhibit 10.4 shows the solution screen for the linear trend line forecast we developed in Example 10.5.

Regression Methods

Regression is used for forecasting by attempting to establish a mathematical relationship between two or more variables. We are interested in identifying relationships between variables and demand. If we know that something has caused demand to behave in a certain way in the past, we would like to identify that relationship so if the same thing happens again in the future, we can predict what demand will be. For example, there is a relationship between increased demand in new housing and lower

THE COMPETITIVE EDGE

Global Forecasts for Inkjet Printers at Hewlett-Packard

Hewlett-Packard, the world's leading supplier of inkjet printers for PCs, has DeskJet brand product divisions in Barcelona, Spain, in Oregon, California, Singapore, and Vancouver. Forecasting global demand for inkjet printers is not easy—the printer market changes rapidly because of technological advances and the fact that prices drop frequently; large numbers of home PC users have begun to purchase printers when they purchase computers; and new competitors have begun to enter the inkjet printer market. These factors contribute to unstable demand data, which limit the effectiveness of time series models and result in poor forecast accuracy.

The Vancouver division consolidates forecasts of factory orders for inkjet printers from all of its global marketing regions and creates an overall divisional forecast. The regional forecasts are developed monthly using input from salespeople in the countries that make up the regions and from major customers. The duration of these regional forecasts are for 12 to 18 months. The marketing center in each region subjectively modifies this forecast by considering such factors as past performance of similar products, competition, distribution, promotional pricing, and advertising. At the same time the division develops a forecast with input from product managers including historical data and trend projections. A consensus forecast is developed from the regional and divisional

forecasts covering 12 months. This long-term forecast is used to determine factory production for printers for the coming year.

Each year the division reevaluates these forecasts for years 2 through 6, or when there is a change in future product strategies, the long-term market, or in the competition. The long-term forecast is integrated with the short-term forecast to create a consistent forecast for the 6-year planning horizon. The forecast is used to determine factory capacity and to make funding decisions. The long-term forecast has an error of ±35 percent. This degree of variability can have supply chain repercussions causing some products to be in short supply and some to have excessive supply for long periods, thereby making long-range factory planning difficult. However, despite this variability and the problems it causes, H-P believes the forecasting process it uses is right for the volatile global market it is in.

H-P has also developed some regression models for short-term forecasting. The basic model forecasts customer sales as a function of historical sales, advertising expenditures, new product distribution, price, and product features. With this model H-P is able to explore up to 90 percent of the variance for historical sales. The model is also useful for "what if?" analysis.

SOURCE: J. Bryant and K. Jensen, "Forecasting Inkjet Printers at Hewlett-Packard Company," *The Journal of Business Forecasting* 13, no. 2 (summer 1994): 27–28.

interest rates. Correspondingly, a whole myriad of building products and services display increased demand if new housing starts increase. The rapid increase in sales of VCRs has resulted in an increase in demand for video movies.

The simplest form of regression is linear regression, which we used previously to develop a linear trend line for forecasting. Now we will show how to develop a regression model for variables related to demand other than time.

Linear Regression

Linear regression is a mathematical technique that relates a dependent variable to an independent variable in the form of a linear equation.

Linear regression is a mathematical technique that relates one variable, called an *independent variable*, to another, the *dependent variable*, in the form of an equation for a straight line. A linear equation has the following general form:

$$y = a + bx$$

where

$$y = \text{the dependent variable}$$
$$a = \text{the intercept}$$

Intercollegiate athletics has become a big business at many schools like Notre Dame and Penn State, the opposing teams in this football game at South Bend. Notre Dame's television contract with NBC pays them millions of dollars and some of the major New Year's Day football games pay as much as $5 million apiece to the participants; the Rose Bowl pays over $6 million each. Revenues from athletics are generated not only from ticket sales, but also from private donations, television and radio fees, and an assortment of school- and team-related publications, clothing and paraphernalia. These revenues are dependent upon a number of critical variables and like any business, athletic departments would like to be able to forecast demand for their products based on these variables. For example, ticket sales to athletic events, television fees, and clothing sales are all dependent on how well the athletic teams perform, the quality of the opponents, marketing and advertising, and even the weather, among other things.

$$b = \text{the slope of the line}$$
$$x = \text{the independent variable}$$

Because we want to use linear regression as a forecasting model for demand, the dependent variable, y, represents demand, and x is an independent variable that causes demand to behave in a linear manner.

To develop the linear equation, the slope, b, and the intercept, a, must first be computed using the following least squares formulas:

$$a = \bar{y} - b\bar{x}$$

$$b = \frac{\Sigma xy - n\bar{x}\bar{y}}{\Sigma x^2 - n\bar{x}^2}$$

where

$$\bar{x} = \frac{\Sigma x}{n} = \text{mean of the } x \text{ data}$$

$$\bar{y} = \frac{\Sigma y}{n} = \text{mean of the } y \text{ data}$$

Linear regression relates demand (dependent variable) to an independent variable.

EXAMPLE 10.9

Developing a Linear Regression Forecast

The State University athletic department wants to develop its budget for the coming year using a forecast for football attendance. Football attendance accounts for the largest portion of its revenues, and the athletic director believes attendance is directly related to the number of wins by the team. The business manager has accumulated total annual attendance figures for the past eight years.

WINS	ATTENDANCE
4	36,300
6	40,100
6	41,200
8	53,000
6	44,000
7	45,600
5	39,000
7	47,500

Given the number of returning starters and the strength of the schedule, the athletic director believes the team will win at least seven games next year. Develop a simple regression equation for this data to forecast attendance for this level of success.

SOLUTION:

The computations necessary to compute a and b using the least squares formulas are summarized in the accompanying table. (Note that y is given in 1,000s to make manual computation easier.)

(Continued)

Least Squares Computations

x (wins)	y (attendance, 1,000s)	xy	x²
4	36.3	145.2	16
6	40.1	240.6	36
6	41.2	247.2	36
8	53.0	424.0	64
6	44.0	264.0	36
7	45.6	319.2	49
5	39.0	195.0	25
7	47.5	332.5	49
49	346.9	2,167.7	311

$$\bar{x} = \frac{49}{8} = 6.125$$

$$\bar{y} = \frac{346.9}{8} = 43.36$$

$$b = \frac{\Sigma xy - n\bar{x}\bar{y}}{\Sigma x^2 - n\bar{x}^2}$$

$$= \frac{(2,167.7) - (8)(6.125)(43.36)}{(311) - (8)(6.125)^2}$$

$$= 4.06$$

$$a = \bar{y} - b\bar{x}$$

$$= 43.36 - (4.06)(6.125)$$

$$= 18.46$$

Substituting these values for a and b into the linear equation line, we have

$$y = 18.46 + 4.06x$$

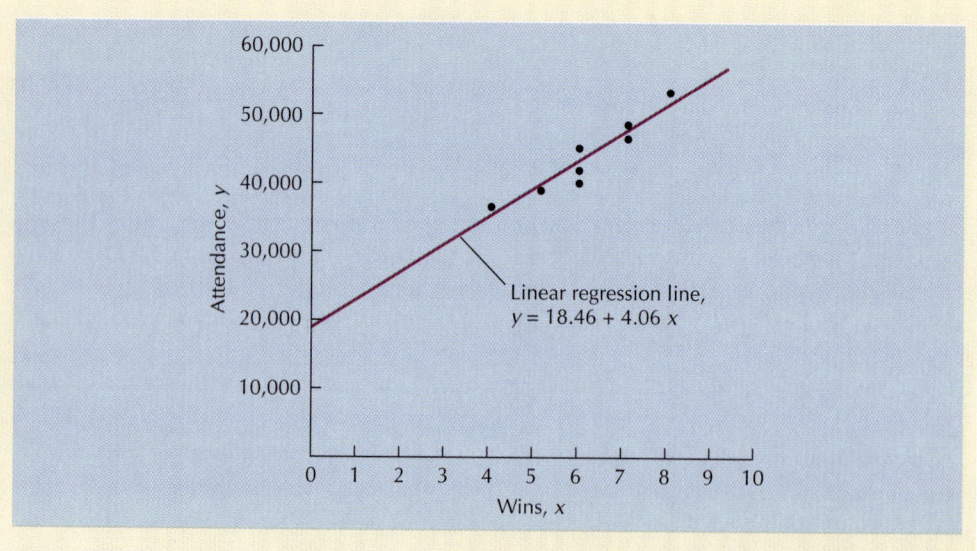

Thus, for $x = 7$ (wins), the forecast for attendance is

$$y = 18.46 + 4.06(7)$$
$$= 46.88, \text{ or } 46,880$$

The data points with the regression line are shown in the figure. Observing the regression line relative to the data points, it would appear that the data follow a distinct upward linear trend, which would indicate that the forecast should be relatively accurate. In fact, the MAD value for this forecasting model is 1.41, which suggests an accurate forecast.

Correlation

Correlation in a linear regression equation is a measure of the strength of the relationship between the independent and dependent variables. The formula for the correlation coefficient is

$$r = \frac{n\Sigma xy - \Sigma x \Sigma y}{\sqrt{[n\Sigma x^2 - (\Sigma x)^2][n\Sigma y^2 - (\Sigma y)^2]}}$$

Correlation is a measure of the strength of the relationship between independent and dependent variables.

The value of r varies between -1.00 and $+1.00$, with a value of $+1.00$ indicating a strong linear relationship between the variables. If $r = 1.00$, then an increase in the independent variable will result in a corresponding linear increase in the dependent variable. If $r = -1.00$, an increase in the dependent variable will result in a linear decrease in the dependent variable. A value of r near zero implies that there is little or no linear relationship between variables.

We can determine the correlation coefficient for the linear regression equation determined in Example 10.9 by substituting most of the terms calculated for the least squares formula (except for Σy^2) into the formula for r:

$$r = \frac{(8)(2,167.7) - (49)(346.9)}{\sqrt{[(8)(311) - (49)^2][(8)(15,224.7) - (346.9)^2]}}$$
$$= 0.947$$

This value for the correlation coefficient is very close to 1.00, indicating a strong linear relationship between the number of wins and home attendance.

Another measure of the strength of the relationship between the variables in a linear regression equation is the **coefficient of determination.** It is computed by squaring the value of r. It indicates the percentage of the variation in the dependent variable that is a result of the behavior of the independent variable. For our example, $r = 0.947$; thus, the coefficient of determination is

$$r^2 = (0.947)^2$$
$$= 0.897$$

The **coefficient of determination** is the percentage of the variation in the dependent variable that results from the independent variable.

This value for the coefficient of determination means that 89.7 percent of the amount of variation in attendance can be attributed to the number of wins by the team (with the remaining 10.3 percent due to other unexplained factors, such as weather, a good or poor start, or publicity). A value of 1.00 (or 100 percent) would indicate that attendance depends totally on wins. However, since 10.3 percent of the variation is a result of other factors, some amount of forecast error can be expected.

Multiple Regression

Multiple regression is a relationship of demand to two or more independent variables.

Another causal method of forecasting is **multiple regression**, a more powerful extension of linear regression. Linear regression relates demand to one other independent variable, whereas multiple regression reflects the relationship between a dependent variable and two or more independent variables. A multiple regression model has the following general form:

$$y = \beta_0 + \beta_1 x_1 + \beta_2 x_2 + \ldots + \beta_k x_k$$

where

$\beta_0 = $ the intercept

$\beta_1, \ldots, \beta_k = $ parameters representing the contribution of the independent variables

$x_1, \ldots, x_k = $ independent variables

For example, the demand for new housing (y) in a region might be a function of several independent variables, including interest rates, population, housing prices, and personal income. Development and computation of the multiple regression equation, including the compilation of data, is more complex than linear regression. The only means for forecasting using multiple regression is with a computer.

Regression Analysis with Excel

The development of the simple linear regression equation and the correlation coefficient for our example was not too difficult because the amount of data was relatively small. However, manual computation of the components of simple linear regression

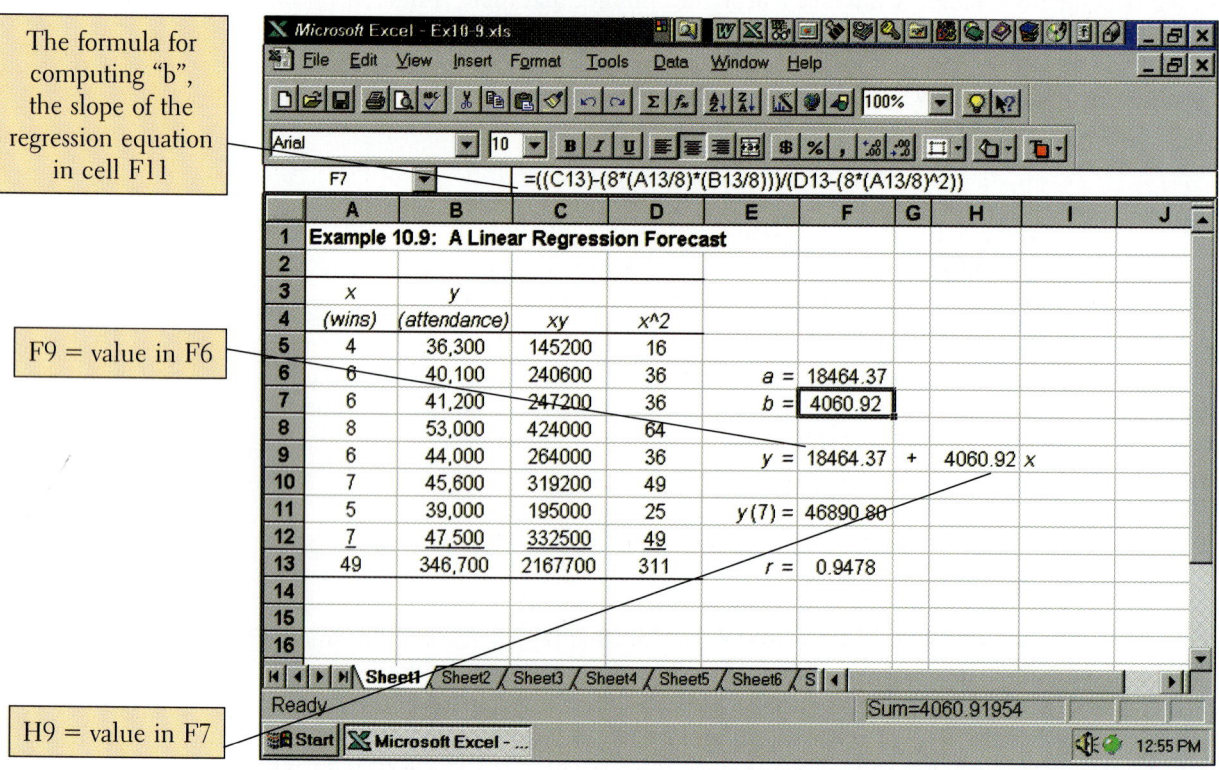

The formula for computing "b", the slope of the regression equation in cell F11

F9 = value in F6

H9 = value in F7

EXHIBIT 10.5

THE COMPETITIVE EDGE

Competing with Accurate Daily Demand Forecasts at Vermont Gas Systems

Vermont Gas Systems is a natural gas utility serving approximately 26,000 business, industrial, and residential customers in 13 towns and cities in northwestern Vermont. Demand forecasts are a critical part of Vermont Gas Systems' supply chain that stretches across Canada. Gas is transported from suppliers in western Canada to storage facilities along the Trans-Canada pipeline to Vermont Gas Systems' pipeline. Gas orders must be specified to suppliers at least 24 hours in advance. Enough gas must be ordered to meet customer needs, especially in the winter, but too much will needlessly and expensively tax Trans-Canada Pipelines' facilities. Vermont Gas Systems has storage capacity available for a buffer inventory of only one hour of gas use so an accurate daily forecast of gas demand is essential.

Vermont Gas Systems uses regression to forecast daily gas demand. In its forecast models, gas demand is the dependent variable and factors such as weather information, industrial customer demand, and changing end-use consumer demand are independent variables. During the winter customers use more gas for heat, making an accurate weather forecast a very important factor.

Detailed three-day weather forecasts are provided to Vermont Gas Systems five times per day from a weather forecasting service. Individual regression forecasts are developed for 24 large-use industrial and municipal customers such as factories, hospitals, and schools. End-use demand is the total potential capacity of all natural gas appliances in the system. It changes daily as new customers move into a new house, apartment, or business adding new appliances or equipment to the system. Another factor related to end-use demand is water temperature, which will decrease by as much as 25 degrees Fahrenheit within the city water system during the winter. End-use demand and water temperature changes have minimal affect on a daily basis, but their impact is significant over several weeks. To compensate for these factors, the utility uses only the most recent 30 days of demand data in developing its forecast models and updates the models on a weekly basis. The results of the forecast model are interpreted by Vermont Gas Systems and supplemented with its individual knowledge of the supply chain distribution system and customer usage to develop an overall, accurate daily forecast of gas demand.

SOURCE: M. Flock, "Forecasting Winter Daily Gas Demand at Vermont Gas Systems," *The Journal of Business Forecasting* 13, no. 1 (spring 1994): 2

---

equations can become very time-consuming and cumbersome as the amount of data increases. Excel (as well as POM for Windows) has the capability of performing linear regression. To demonstrate we use Example 10.9.

The Excel spreadsheet for Example 10.9 is shown in Exhibit 10.5. Notice that the formula for computing the slope, *b*, in cell F7 is shown on the formula bar at the top of the screen. Similar formulas are developed for the intercept, *a*; the regression function, *y*; and the correlation coefficient, *r*. A regression equation can also be computed in Excel by selecting 'Data Analysis' from the 'Tools' menu at the top of the spreadsheet and then selecting the 'regression' menu item.

Summary

Forecasts of product demand are a necessity for almost all aspects of operational planning. Short-range demand forecasts determine the daily resource requirements needed for production, including labor and material, as well as for developing work schedules and shipping dates and controlling inventory levels. Long-range forecasts are needed to plan new products for development and changes in existing products and to acquire the plant, equipment, personnel, resources, and supply chain necessary for future operations.

We have presented several methods of forecasting useful for different time frames. These quantitative forecasting techniques are easy to understand, simple to use, and not especially costly unless the data requirements are substantial. They also have exhibited a good track record of performance for many companies that have used them. For these reasons, regression methods, and especially times series, are popular.

When managers and students are first introduced to forecasting methods, they are sometimes surprised and disappointed at the lack of exactness of the forecasts. However, they soon learn that forecasting is not easy, and exactness is not possible. However, companies that have the skill and experience to obtain more accurate forecasts than their competitors' will gain a competitive edge.

Summary of Key Formulas

Moving Average

$$MA_n = \frac{\sum_{i=1}^{n} D_i}{n}$$

Weighted Moving Average

$$WMA_n = \sum_{i=1}^{n} W_i D_i$$

Exponential Smoothing

$$F_{t+1} = \alpha D_t + (1 - \alpha)F_t$$

Adjusted Exponential Smoothing

$$AF_{t+1} = F_{t+1} + T_{t+1}$$

Trend Factor

$$T_{t+1} = \beta(F_{t+1} - F_t) + (1 - \beta)T_t$$

Linear Trend Line

$$y = a + bx$$

Least Squares

$$b = \frac{\Sigma xy - n\bar{x}\bar{y}}{\Sigma x^2 - n\bar{x}^2}$$

$$a = \bar{y} - b\bar{x}$$

Seasonal Factor

$$S_i = \frac{D_i}{\Sigma D}$$

Seasonally Adjusted Forecast

$$SF_i = (S_i)(F_t)$$

Mean Absolute Deviation

$$MAD = \frac{\Sigma |D_t - F_t|}{n}$$

Mean Absolute Percent Deviation

$$MAPD = \frac{\Sigma |D_t - F_t|}{D_t}$$

Cumulative Error

$$E = \Sigma e_t$$

Average Error (Bias)

$$\overline{E} = \frac{\Sigma e_t}{n}$$

Tracking Signal

$$TS = \frac{\Sigma(D_t - F_t)}{MAD} = \frac{E}{MAD}$$

Mean Squared Error

$$MSE = \frac{\Sigma(D_t - F_t)^2}{n - 1}$$

Linear Regression Equation

$$y = a + bx$$

Correlation Coefficient

$$r = \frac{n\Sigma xy - \Sigma x \Sigma y}{\sqrt{[n\Sigma x^2 - (\Sigma x)^2][n\Sigma y^2 - (\Sigma y)^2]}}$$

Coefficient of Determination

$$\text{Coefficient of determination} = r^2$$

Summary of Key Terms

adjusted exponential smoothing: an exponential smoothing forecast adjusted for trend.

average error: the cumulative error averaged over the number of time periods.

causal forecasting methods: a class of mathematical techniques that relate demand to factors that cause demand behavior.

coefficient of determination: the correlation coefficient squared; it measures the portion of the variation in the dependent variable that can be attributed to the independent variable.

correlation: a measure of the strength of the causal relationship between the independent and dependent variables in a linear regression equation.

cumulative error: a sum of the forecast errors; also known as bias.

cycle: an up-and-down movement in demand over time.

Delphi method: a procedure for acquiring informed judgments and opinions from knowledgeable individuals to use as a subjective forecast.

exponential smoothing: an averaging method that weights the most recent data more strongly than more distant data.

forecast error: the difference between actual and forecasted demand.

linear regression: a mathematical technique that relates a dependent variable to an independent variable in the form of a linear equation.

linear trend line: a forecast using the linear regression equation to relate demand to time.

long-range forecast: a forecast encompassing a period longer than two years into the future.

mean absolute deviation (MAD): the per-period average of the absolute difference between actual and forecasted demand.

mean absolute percent deviation (MAPD): the absolute forecast error measured as a percent of demand.

mean squared error (MSE): the average of the squared forecast errors.

moving average: average demand for a fixed sequence of periods including the most recent period.

multiple regression: a mathematical relationship that relates a dependent variable to two or more independent variables.

qualitative forecast methods: nonquantitative, subjective forecasts based on judgment, opinion, experience, and expert opinion.

quantitative forecast methods: forecasts derived from a mathematical formula.

random variations: movements in demand that are not predictable and follow no pattern.

seasonal factor: a numerical value that is multiplied by the normal forecast to get a seasonally adjusted forecast.

seasonal pattern: an oscillating movement in demand that occurs periodically in the short run and is repetitive.

short range (to mid-range) forecast: a forecast encompassing the immediate future, usually days or weeks, but up to two years.

smoothing constant: the weighting factor given to the most recent data in exponential smoothing forecasts.

time frame: how far into the future is forecast.

time series methods: a class of statistical methods that uses historical demand data over a period of time to predict future demand.

tracking signal: a measure computed by dividing the cumulative error by MAD; used for monitoring bias in a forecast.

trend: a gradual, long-term up or down movement of demand.

weighted moving average: a moving average with more recent demand values adjusted with weights.

Solved Problems

1. Moving Average

A manufacturing company has monthly demand for one of its products as follows,

Month	Demand
February	520
March	490
April	550
May	580
June	600
July	420
August	510
September	610

Develop a three-period average forecast and a three-period weighted moving average forecast with weights of 0.50, 0.30, and 0.20 for the most recent demand values, in that order. Calculate MAD for each forecast, and indicate which would seem to be most accurate.

Solution:

Step 1. Compute the 3-month moving average using the formula

$$MA_3 = \sum_{i=1}^{3} \frac{D_i}{3}$$

For May, the moving average forecast is

$$MA_3 = \frac{520 + 490 + 550}{3} = 520$$

Step 2. Compute the 3-month weighted moving average using the formula

$$WMA_3 = \Sigma W_i D_i$$

For May, the weighted average forecast is

$$WMA_3 = (0.50)(520) = (0.30)(490) + (0.20)(550)$$
$$= 526.00$$

The values for both moving averages forecasts are shown in the following table.

Month	Demand	MA₃	WMA₃
February	520	—	—
March	490	—	—
April	550	—	—
May	580	520.00	526.00
June	600	540.00	553.00
July	420	576.67	584.00
August	510	533.33	506.00
September	610	510.00	501.00
October	—	513.33	542.00

Step 3. Compute the MAD value for both forecasts:

$$MAD = \frac{\Sigma |D_t - F_t|}{n}$$

The MAD value for the 3-month moving average is 80.0, and the MAD value for the 3-month weighted moving average is 75.6, indicating there is not much difference in accuracy between the two forecasts, although the weighted moving average is slightly better.

2. *Exponential Smoothing*

A computer software firm has experienced the following demand for its "Personal Finance" software package.

Period	Units
1	56
2	61
3	55
4	70
5	66
6	65
7	72
8	75

Develop an exponential smoothing forecast using $\alpha = 0.40$ and an adjusted exponential smoothing forecast using $\alpha = 0.40$ and $\beta = 0.20$. Compare the accuracy of the two forecasts using MAD and cumulative error.

Solution:

Step 1. Compute the exponential smoothing forecast with $\alpha = 0.40$ using the following formula:

$$F_{t+1} = \alpha D_t + (1 - \alpha)F_t$$

For period 2, the forecast (assuming $F_1 = 56$) is

$$
\begin{aligned}
F_2 &= \alpha D_1 + (1 - \alpha)F_1 \\
&= (0.40)(56) + (0.60)(56) \\
&= 56
\end{aligned}
$$

For period 3, the forecast is

$$
\begin{aligned}
F_3 &= (0.40)(61) + (0.60)(56) \\
&= 58
\end{aligned}
$$

The remaining forecasts are computed similarly and are shown in the accompanying table.

Step 2. Compute the adjusted exponential smoothing forecast with $\alpha = 0.40$ and $\beta = 0.20$ using the formula

$$AF_{t+1} = F_{t+1} + T_{t+1}$$
$$T_{t+1} = \beta(F_{t+1} - F_t) + (1 - \beta)T_t$$

Starting with the forecast for period 3 (since $F_1 = F_2$, and we will assume $T_2 = 0$),

$$
\begin{aligned}
T_3 &= \beta(F_3 - F_2) + (1 - \beta)T_2 \\
&= (0.20)(58 - 56) + (0.80)(0) \\
&= 0.40 \\
AF_3 &= F_3 + T_3 \\
&= 58 + 0.40 \\
&= 58.40
\end{aligned}
$$

The remaining adjusted forecasts are computed similarly and are shown in the following table.

Period	D_t	F_t	AF_t	$D_t - F_t$	$D_t - AF_t$
1	56	—	—	—	—
2	61	56.00	56.00	5.00	5.00
3	55	58.00	58.40	−3.00	−3.40
4	70	56.80	56.88	13.20	13.12
5	66	62.08	63.20	3.92	2.80
6	65	63.65	64.86	1.35	0.14
7	72	64.18	65.26	7.81	6.73
8	75	67.31	68.80	7.68	6.20
9	—	70.39	72.19		
				35.97	30.60

Step 3. Compute the MAD value for each forecast.

$$\text{MAD}(F_t) = \frac{\Sigma |D_t - F_t|}{n}$$

$$= \frac{41.97}{7}$$

$$= 5.99$$

$$\text{MAD}(AF_t) = \frac{37.39}{7}$$

$$= 5.34$$

Step 4. Compute the cumulative error for each forecast:

$$E(F_t) = 35.97$$
$$E(AF_t) = 30.60$$

Because both MAD and the cumulative error are less for the adjusted forecast, it would appear to be the most accurate.

3. Linear Regression

A local building products store has accumulated sales data for 2×4 lumber (in board feet) and the number of building permits in its area for the past ten quarters.

Quarter	Building permits x	Lumber sales (1,000s of board feet) y
1	8	12.6
2	12	16.3
3	7	9.3
4	9	11.5
5	15	18.1
6	6	7.6
7	5	6.2
8	8	14.2
9	10	15.0
10	12	17.8

Develop a linear regression model for these data and determine the strength of the linear relationship using correlation. If the model appears to be relatively strong, determine the forecast for lumber given ten building permits in the next quarter.

Solution:

Step 1. Compute the components of the linear regression equation, $y = a + bx$, using the least squares formulas,

$$\bar{x} = \frac{92}{10} = 9.2$$

$$\bar{y} = \frac{128.6}{10} = 12.86$$

$$b = \frac{\Sigma xy - n\bar{x}\bar{y}}{\Sigma x^2 - n\bar{x}^2}$$

$$= \frac{(1,170.3) - (10)(9.2)(12.86)}{(932) - (10)(9.2)^2}$$

$$b = 1.25$$

$$a = \bar{y} - b\bar{x}$$

$$= 12.86 - (1.25)(9.2)$$

$$a = 1.36$$

Step 2. Develop the linear regression equation.

$$y = a + bx$$

$$y = 1.36 + 1.25x$$

Step 3. Compute the correlation coefficient.

$$r = \frac{n\Sigma xy - \Sigma x\Sigma y}{\sqrt{[n\Sigma x^2 - (\Sigma x)^2][n\Sigma y^2 - (\Sigma y)^2]}}$$

$$= \frac{(10)(1,170.3) - (92)(128.6)}{\sqrt{[(10)(932) - (92)^2][(10)(1,810.48) - (128.6)^2]}}$$

$$= 0.925$$

Thus, there appears to be a strong linear relationship.

Step 4. Calculate the forecast for $x = 10$ permits.

$$y = a + bx$$

$$= 1.36 + 1.25(10)$$

$$= 13.86, \text{ or } 13,860 \text{ board feet}$$

Questions

10-1. List some of the operations and functions in a company that are dependent on a forecast for product demand.

10-2. What is the difference between quantitative forecast methods and qualitative forecast methods?

10-3. Describe the difference between short- and long-range forecasts.

10-4. Discuss the role of forecasting in supply chain management.

10-5. Why is accurate forecasting so important to companies who use a continuous replenishment inventory system?

10-6. Discuss the relationship between forecasting and TQM.

10-7. What kinds of forecasting methods are used for long-range strategic planning?

10-8. Describe the Delphi method for forecasting.

10-9. What is the difference between a trend and a cycle and a seasonal pattern?

10-10. How is the moving average method similar to exponential smoothing?

10-11. In the chapter examples for time series methods, the starting forecast was always assumed to be the same as actual demand in the first period. Suggest other ways that the starting forecast might be derived in actual use.

10-12. What effect on the exponential smoothing model will increasing the smoothing constant have?

10-13. How does adjusted exponential smoothing differ from exponential smoothing?

10-14. What determines the choice of the smoothing constant for trend in an adjusted exponential smoothing model?

10-15. How does the linear trend line forecasting model differ from a linear regression model for forecasting?

10-16. Of the time series models presented in this chapter, including the moving average and weighted moving average, exponential smoothing and adjusted exponential smoothing, and linear trend line, which one do you consider the best? Why?

10-17. What advantages does adjusted exponential smoothing have over a linear trend line for forecasted demand that exhibits a trend?

10-18. Describe how a forecast is monitored to detect bias.

10-19. Explain the relationship between the use of a tracking signal and statistical control limits for forecast control.

10-20. Selecting from MAD, MAPD, MSE, E, and $\overline{E}$, which measure of forecast accuracy do you consider superior? Why?

10-21. What is the difference between linear and multiple regression?

10-22. Define the different components (y, x, a, and b) of a linear regression equation.

10-23. A company that produces video equipment, including VCRs, video cameras, and televisions, is attempting to forecast what new products and product innovations might be technologically feasible and that customers might demand ten years into the future. Speculate on what type of qualitative methods it might use to develop this type of forecast.

Problems

10-1. The Saki motorcycle dealer in the Minneapolis–St. Paul area wants to be able to forecast accurately the demand for the Saki Super TX II motorcycle during the next month. Because the manufacturer is in Japan, it is difficult to send motorcycles back or reorder if the proper number is not ordered a month ahead. From sales records, the dealer has accumulated the following data for the past year.

Month	Motorcycle Sales
January	9
February	7
March	10
April	8
May	7
June	12
July	10
August	11
September	12
October	10
November	14
December	16

   a. Compute a 3-month moving average forecast of demand for April through January (of the next year).
   b. Compute a 5-month moving average forecast for June through January.
   c. Compare the two forecasts computed in parts (a) and (b) using MAD. Which one should the dealer use for January of the next year?

10-2. The manager of the Carpet City outlet needs to be able to forecast accurately the demand for Soft Shag carpet (its biggest seller). If the manager does not order enough carpet from the carpet mill, customers will buy their carpets from one of Carpet City's many competitors. The manager has collected the following demand data for the past eight months.

Month	Demand for Soft Shag Carpet (1,000 yd)
1	8
2	12
3	7
4	9
5	15
6	11
7	10
8	12

   a. Compute a 3-month moving average forecast for months 4 through 9.
   b. Compute a weighted 3-month moving average forecast for months 4 through 9. Assign weights of 0.55, 0.33, and 0.12 to the months in sequence, starting with the most recent month.
   c. Compare the two forecasts using MAD. Which forecast appears to be more accurate?

10-3. The Fastgro Fertilizer Company distributes fertilizer to various lawn and garden shops. The company must base its quarterly production schedule on a forecast of how many tons of fertilizer will be demanded from it. The company has gathered the following data for the past three years from its sales records.

Year	Quarter	Demand for Fertilizer (ton)
1	1	105
	2	150
	3	93
	4	121

(Continued)

Year	Quarter	Demand for Fertilizer (ton)
2	5	140
	6	170
	7	105
	8	150
3	9	150
	10	170
	11	110
	12	130

a. Compute a 3-quarter moving average forecast for quarters 4 through 13 and compute the forecast error for each quarter.
b. Compute a 5-quarter moving average forecast for quarters 6 through 13 and compute the forecast error for each quarter.
c. Compute a weighted 3-quarter moving average forecast using weights of 0.50, 0.33, and 0.17 for the most recent, next recent, and most distant data, respectively, and compute the forecast error for each quarter.
d. Compare the forecasts developed in parts (a), (b), and (c) using cumulative error. Which forecast appears to be most accurate? Do any exhibit any bias?

10-4. Graph the demand data in Problem 10-3. Can you identify any trends, cycles, and/or seasonal patterns?

10-5. The chairperson of the department of management at State University wants to forecast the number of students who will enroll in production and operations management next semester in order to determine how many sections to schedule. The chair has accumulated the following enrollment data for the past eight semesters.

Semester	Students Enrolled in POM
1	400
2	450
3	350
4	420
5	500
6	575
7	490
8	650

a. Compute a 3-semester moving average forecast for semesters 4 through 9.
b. Compute the exponentially smoothed forecast ($\alpha = 0.20$) for the enrollment data.
c. Compare the two forecasts using MAD and indicate the most accurate.

10-6. The manager of the Petroco Service Station wants to forecast the demand for unleaded gasoline next month so that the proper number of gallons can be ordered from the distributor. The owner has accumulated the following data on demand for unleaded gasoline from sales during the past ten months.

Month	Gasoline Demanded (gal)
October	800
November	725
December	630
January	500

(Continued)

Month	Gasoline Demanded (gal)
February	645
March	690
April	730
May	810
June	1,200
July	980

a. Compute an exponentially smoothed forecast using an α value of 0.30.
b. Compute an adjusted exponentially smoothed forecast ($\alpha = 0.30$ and $\beta = 0.20$).
c. Compare the two forecasts using MAPD and indicate which seems to be the most accurate.

10-7. The Victory Plus Mutual Fund of growth stocks has had the following average monthly price for the past ten months.

Month	Fund Price
1	62.7
2	63.9
3	68.0
4	66.4
5	67.2
6	65.8
7	68.2
8	69.3
9	67.2
10	70.1

Compute the exponentially smoothed forecast with $\alpha = 0.40$, the adjusted exponentially smoothed forecast with $\alpha = 0.40$ and $\beta = 0.30$, and the linear trend line forecast. Compare the accuracy of the three forecasts using cumulative error and MAD, and indicate which forecast appears to be most accurate.

10-8. The Bayside Fountain Hotel is adjacent to County Coliseum, a 24,000-seat arena that is home to the city's professional basketball and ice hockey teams and that hosts a variety of concerts, trade shows, and conventions throughout the year. The hotel has experienced the following occupancy rates for the nine years since the coliseum opened.

Year	Occupancy Rate
1989	83%
1990	78
1991	75
1992	81
1993	86
1994	85
1995	89
1996	90
1997	86

Compute an exponential smoothing forecast with $\alpha = 0.20$, an adjusted exponential smoothing forecast with $\alpha = 0.20$ and $\beta = 0.20$, and a linear trend line forecast. Compare the three forecasts using MAD and average error ($\overline{E}$), and indicate which forecast seems to be most accurate.

10-9. The Whistle Stop Café in Weems, Georgia, is well known for its popular homemade ice cream, which it makes in a small plant in back of the cafe. People drive all the way from Atlanta and Macon to buy the ice cream. The two ladies who own the café want to develop a forecasting model so they can plan their ice cream production operation and determine the number of employees they need to sell ice cream in the cafe. They have accumulated the following sales records for their ice cream for the past twelve quarters.

Year/Quarter		Ice Cream Sales (gal)
1994:	1	350
	2	510
	3	750
	4	420
1995:	5	370
	6	480
	7	860
	8	500
1996:	9	450
	10	550
	11	820
	12	570

Develop an adjusted exponential smoothing model with $\alpha = 0.50$ and $\beta = 0.50$ to forecast demand, and assess its accuracy using cumulative error (E) and average error $(\overline{E})$. Does there appear to be any bias in the forecast?

10-10. For the demand data in Problem 10-9, develop a seasonally adjusted forecast for 1998. (Use a linear trend line model to develop a forecast estimate for 1998.) Which forecast model do you perceive to be the most accurate, the adjusted exponential smoothing model from Problem 10-9 or the seasonally adjusted forecast?

10-11. Develop a seasonally adjusted forecast for the demand data for fertilizer in Problem 10-3. Use a linear trend line model to compute a forecast estimate for demand in year 4.

10-12. Monaghan's Pizza delivery service has randomly selected eight weekdays during the past month and recorded orders for pizza at four different time periods per day, as follows.

	DAYS							
TIME PERIOD	*1*	*2*	*3*	*4*	*5*	*6*	*7*	*8*
10:00 A.M.–3:00 P.M.	62	49	53	35	43	48	56	43
3:00 P.M.–7:00 P.M.	73	55	81	77	60	66	85	70
7:00 P.M.–11:00 P.M.	42	38	45	50	29	37	35	44
11:00 P.M.–2:00 A.M.	35	40	36	39	26	25	36	31

Develop a seasonally adjusted forecasting model for daily pizza demand and forecast demand for each of the time periods for a single upcoming day.

10-13. The Cat Creek Mining Company mines and ships coal. It has experienced the following demand for coal during the past eight years.

Year	Coal sales (tons)
1990	4,260
1991	4,510
1992	4,050
1993	3,720
1994	3,900
1995	3,470
1996	2,890
1997	3,100

Develop an adjusted exponential smoothing model ($\alpha = 0.30$, $\beta = 0.20$) and a linear trend line model, and compare the forecast accuracy of the two using MAD. Indicate which forecast seems to be most accurate.

10-14. The Northwoods Outdoor Company is a catalog sales operation that specializes in outdoor recreational clothing. Demand for its items is very seasonal, peaking during the holiday season and during the spring. It has accumulated the following data for order per "season" (quarter) during the past five years.

	ORDERS (1,000s)				
QUARTER	1993	1994	1995	1996	1997
January–March	18.6	18.1	22.4	23.2	24.5
April–June	23.5	24.7	28.8	27.6	31.0
July–September	20.4	19.5	21.0	24.4	23.7
October–December	41.9	46.3	45.5	47.1	52.8

a. Develop a seasonally adjusted forecast model for these order data. Forecast demand for each quarter for 1998 (using a linear trend line forecast estimate for orders in 1998).
b. Develop a separate linear trend line forecast for each of the four seasons and forecast each season for 1998.
c. Which of the two approaches used in parts (a) and (b) appear to be the most accurate? Use MAD to verify your selection.

10-15. Aztec Industries has developed a forecasting model that was used to forecast during a ten-month period. The forecasts and actual demand are shown as follows.

Month	Actual Demand	Forecast Demand
1	160	170
2	150	165
3	175	157
4	200	166
5	190	183
6	220	186
7	205	203
8	210	204
9	200	207
10	220	203

Measure the accuracy of the forecast using MAD, MAPD, and cumulative error. Does the forecast method appear to be accurate?

10-16. Monitor the forecast in Problem 10-15 for bias using a tracking signal and a control chart with ± 3 MAD. Does there appear to be any bias in the forecast?

10-17. Develop a statistical control chart for the forecast error in Problem 10-9 using $\pm 3\sigma$ control limits, and indicate if the forecast seems to be biased.

10-18. Monitor the adjusted exponential smoothing forecast in Problem 10-13 for bias using a tracking signal and a control chart with ± 3 MAD.

10-19. RAP Computers assembles minicomputers from generic parts it purchases at discount and sells the units via phone orders it receives from customers responding to their ads in trade journals. The business has developed an exponential smoothing forecast model to forecast future computer demand. Actual demand for their computers for the past eight months is as follows.

Month	Demand	Forecast
March	120	—
April	110	120.0
May	150	116.0
June	130	129.6
July	160	129.7
August	165	141.8
September	140	151.1
October	155	146.7
November	—	150.0

a. Using the measure of forecast accuracy of your choice, ascertain if the forecast appears to be accurate.

b. Determine if a 3-month moving average would provide a better forecast.

c. Use a tracking signal to monitor the forecast in part (a) for bias.

10-20. Develop an exponential smoothing forecast with $\alpha = 0.20$ for the demand data in Problem 10-1. Compare this forecast with the 3-month moving average computed in 10-1(a) using MAD and indicate which forecast seems to be most accurate.

10-21. The Jersey Dairy Products Company produces cheese which it sells to supermarkets and food processing companies. Because of concerns about cholesterol and fat in cheese, the company has seen demand for its products decline during the past decade. It is now considering introducing some alternative lowfat dairy products and wants to determine how much available plant capacity it will have next year. The company has developed an exponential smoothing forecast with $\alpha = 0.40$ to forecast cheese. The actual demand and the forecasts from its model are shown as follows.

YEAR	DEMAND (1,000 lb)	Forecast
1	16.8	—
2	14.1	16.8
3	15.3	15.7
4	12.7	15.5
5	11.9	14.4
6	12.3	13.4
7	11.5	12.9
8	10.8	12.4

Assess the accuracy of the forecast model using MAD and cumulative error, and determine if the forecast error reflects bias using a tracking signal and ± 3 MAD control limits. If the exponential smoothing forecast model is biased, determine if a linear trend model would provide a more accurate forecast.

10-22. The manager of the Ramona Inn Hotel near Cloverleaf Stadium believes that how well the local Blue Sox professional baseball team is playing has an impact on the occupancy rate at the hotel during the summer months. Following are the number of victories for the Blue Sox (in a 162-game schedule) for the past eight years and the hotel occupancy rates.

Year	Number of Blue Sox Wins	Occupancy Rate
1	75	83%
2	70	78
3	85	86
4	91	85
5	87	89
6	90	93
7	87	92
8	67	91

Develop a linear regression model for these data, and forecast the occupancy rate for next year if the Blue Sox win 88 games.

10-23. Carpet City wants to develop a means to forecast its carpet sales. The store manager believes that the store's sales are directly related to the number of new housing starts in town. The manager has gathered data from county records of monthly house construction permits and from store records on monthly sales. These data are as follows.

Monthly Carpet Sales (1,000 yd)	Monthly Construction Permits
5	21
10	35
4	10
3	12
8	16
2	9
12	41
11	15
9	18
14	26

a. Develop a linear regression model for this data and forecast carpet sales if 30 construction permits for new homes are filed.

b. Determine the strength of the causal relationship between monthly sales and new home construction using correlation.

10-24. The manager of Gilley's Ice Cream Parlor needs an accurate forecast of the demand for ice cream. The store orders ice cream from a distributor a week ahead, and if too little is ordered the store loses business. If it orders too much, it must be thrown away. The manager believes that a major determinant of ice cream sales is temperature; that is, the hotter it is, the more ice cream people buy. Using an almanac, the manager has determined the average daytime temperature for ten weeks selected at random and then, from store records, has determined the ice cream consumption for the same ten weeks. The data are summarized as follows.

Week	Temperature	(Gallons Sold)
1	73°	110
2	65	95
3	81	135
4	90	160
5	75	97
6	77	105
7	82	120
8	93	175
9	86	140
10	79	121

a. Develop a linear regression model for this data and forecast the ice cream consumption if the average weekly daytime temperature is expected to be 85°.

b. Determine the strength of the linear relationship between temperature and ice cream consumption using correlation.

10-25. Compute the coefficient of determination for the data in Problem 10-24 and explain its meaning.

10-26. Administrators at State University believe that decreases in the number of freshmen applications that they have experienced are directly related to tuition increases. They have collected the following enrollment and tuition data for the last decade.

Year	Freshman Applications	Annual Tuition ($)
1	6,050	3,600
2	4,060	3,600
3	5,200	4,000
4	4,410	4,400
5	4,380	4,500
6	4,160	5,700
7	3,560	6,000
8	2,970	6,000
9	3,280	7,500
10	3,430	8,000

a. Develop a linear regression model for these data and forecast the number of applications for State University if tuition increases to $9,000 per year and if tuition is lowered to $7,000 per year.

b. Determine the strength of the linear relationship between freshmen applications and tuition using correlation.

c. Describe the various planning decisions for State University that would be impacted by the forecast for freshmen applications.

10-27. Develop a linear trend line model for the freshmen applications data at State University in Problem 10-26.

a. Does this forecast appear to be more or less accurate than the linear regression forecast developed in Problem 10-26? Justify your answer.

b. Compute the correlation coefficient for the linear trend line forecast and explain its meaning.

10-28. Explain what the numerical value of the slope of the linear regression equation in Problem 10-24 means.

10-29. Infoworks is a large computer discount store that sells computers and ancillary equipment and software in the town where State University is located. It has collected historical data on computer sales and printer sales for the past ten years as follows.

Year	Personal Computer Sales	Printers Sold
1	1,045	326
2	1,610	510
3	860	296
4	1,211	478
5	975	305
6	1,117	506
7	1,066	612
8	1,310	560
9	1,517	590
10	1,246	676

a. Develop a linear trend line forecast to forecast printer demand in year 11.
b. Develop a linear regression model relating printer sales to computer sales to forecast printer demand in year 11 if 1,300 computers are sold.
c. Compare the forecasts developed in parts (a) and (b) and indicate which one appears to be the best.

10-30. Develop an exponential smoothing model with $\alpha = 0.30$ for the data in Problem 10-29 to forecast printer demand in year 11, and compare its accuracy to the linear trend line forecast developed in 10-29(a).

10-31. Arrow Air is a regional East Coast airline. It has collected data for the percentage of available seats occupied on its flights for four quarters—(1) January–March, (2) April–June, (3) July–September, and (4) October–December—for the past five years. The company also has collected data for the average percentage fare discount for each of these quarters as follows.

Year	Quarter	% Seat Occupancy	% Average Fare Discount	Year	Quarter	% Seat Occupancy	% Average Fare Discount
1	1	63	21		3	78	30
	2	75	34		4	69	35
	3	76	18	4	1	59	20
	4	58	26		2	61	35
2	1	59	18		3	83	26
	2	62	40		4	71	30
	3	81	25	5	1	60	25
	4	76	30		2	66	37
3	1	65	23		3	86	25
	2	70	28		4	74	30

a. Develop a seasonally adjusted forecast model for seat occupancy. Forecast seat occupancy for year 6 (using a linear trend line forecast estimate for seat occupancy in year (6).
b. Develop linear regression models relating seat occupancy to discount fares to forecast seat occupancy for each quarter in year 6. Assume a fare discount of 20 percent for quarter 1, 36 percent for quarter 2, 25 percent for quarter 3, and 30 percent for quarter 4.
c. Compare the forecasts developed in parts (a) and (b) and indicate which one appears to be the best.

10-32. Develop an adjusted exponential smoothing forecast model ($\alpha = 0.40$ and $\beta = 0.40$) for the data in Problem 10-31 to forecast seat occupancy, and compare its accuracy to the seasonally adjusted model developed in 10-31(a).

10-33. The consumer loan department at Central Union Bank and Trust wants to develop a forecasting model to help determine its potential loan application volume for the coming year. Since adjustable-rate home mortgages are based on government long-term treasury note rates, the bank has collected the following data for three- to five-year Treasury note interest rates for the past twenty-four years.

Year	Rate	Year	Rate	Year	Rate
1	5.77	9	9.71	17	7.68
2	5.85	10	11.55	18	8.26
3	6.92	11	14.44	19	8.55
4	7.82	12	12.92	20	8.26
5	7.49	13	10.45	21	6.80
6	6.67	14	11.89	22	6.12
7	6.69	15	9.64	23	5.48
8	8.29	16	7.06	24	6.09

Develop an appropriate forecast model for the bank to use to forecast Treasury note rates in the future, and indicate how accurate it appears to be compared to historical data.

10-34. Some members of management of the Fairface Cosmetics Firm believe that demand for its products is related to the promotional activities of local department stores where its cosmetics are sold. However, others in management believe that other factors, such as local demographics, are stronger determinants of demand behavior. The following data for local annual promotional expenditures for Fairface products and local annual unit sales for Fairface lip gloss have been collected from twenty stores selected at random from different localities.

Store	Annual Unit Sales ($1,000)	Annual Promotional Expenditures ($1,000)
1	3.5	12.6
2	7.2	15.5
3	3.1	10.8
4	1.6	8.7
5	8.9	20.3
6	5.7	21.9
7	6.3	25.6
8	9.1	14.3
9	10.2	15.1
10	7.3	18.7
11	2.5	9.6
12	4.6	12.7
13	8.1	16.3
14	2.5	8.1
15	3.0	7.5
16	4.8	12.4
17	10.2	17.3
18	5.1	11.2
19	11.3	18.5
20	10.4	16.7

Based on these data, does it appear that the strength of the relationship between sales and promotional expenditures is sufficient to warrant using a linear regression forecasting model? Explain your response. (Computer solution is suggested.)

10-35. The Gametime Hat company manufactures baseball-style caps with various team logos. The caps come in an assortment of designs and colors. The company has had monthly sales for the past twenty-four months as follows.

Month	Demand (1,000)	Month	Demand (1,000)
1	8.2	13	10.3
2	7.5	14	10.5
3	8.1	15	11.7
4	9.3	16	9.8
5	9.1	17	10.8
6	9.5	18	11.3
7	10.4	19	12.6
8	9.7	20	11.5
9	10.2	21	10.8
10	10.6	22	11.7
11	8.2	23	12.5
12	9.9	24	12.8

Develop a forecast model using the method you believe best, and justify your selection using a measure (or measures) of forecast accuracy. (Computer solution recommended.)

C A S E   P R O B L E M

Forecasting at State University

During the last few years the legislature has severely reduced funding for State University. In reaction, the administration at State has significantly raised tuition each year for the past five years. A bargain five years ago, State is now considered an expensive state-supported university. Some parents and students now question the value of a State education, and applications for admission have declined. Since a portion of state educational funding is based on a formula tied to enrollments, State has maintained its enrollment levels by going deeper into its applicant pool and accepting less qualified students.

On top of these problems, an increase in the college-age population is expected in the next decade, resulting from a "baby boom" in the early 1980s. Key members of the state legislature have told the university administration that State will be expected to absorb additional students during the next decade. However, because of the economic outlook and the budget situation, State should not expect any funding increases for additional facilities, classrooms, dormitory rooms, or faculty. The university already has a classroom deficit in excess of 25 percent, and class sizes are above the average of their peer institutions.

The president of the university, Tanisha Lindsey, established several task forces consisting of faculty and administrators to address these problems. These groups made a number of recommendations, including the implementation of total quality management (TQM) practices and more in-depth, focused planning.

Discuss in general terms how forecasting might be used for planning to address these specific problems and the role of forecasting in initiating a TQM approach. Include in your discussion the types of forecasting methods that might be used.

CASE PROBLEM

The University Bookstore Student Computer Purchase Program

The University Bookstore is owned and operated by State University through an independent corporation with its own board of directors. The bookstore has three locations on or near the State University campus. It stocks a range of items including textbooks, trade books, logo apparel, drawing and educational supplies, and computers and related products including printers, modems, and software. The bookstore has a program to sell personal computers to incoming freshman and other students at a substantial educational discount partly passed on from computer manufacturers. This means that the bookstore just covers computer costs with a very small profit margin remaining.

Each summer all incoming freshmen and their parents come to the State campus for a three-day orientation program. The students come in groups of 100 throughout the summer. During their visit the students and their parents are given details about the bookstore's computer purchase program. Some students place their computer orders for the fall semester at this time, while others wait until later in the summer. The bookstore also receives orders from returning students throughout the summer. This program presents a challenging supply chain management problem for the bookstore.

Orders come in throughout the summer, many only a few weeks before school starts in the fall, and the computer suppliers require at least six weeks for delivery. Thus, the bookstore must forecast computer demand to build up inventory to meet student demand in the fall. The student computer program and the forecast of computer demand has repercussions all along the bookstore supply chain. The bookstore has a warehouse near campus where it must store all computers since it has no storage space at its retail locations. Ordering too many computers

not only ties up the bookstore's cash reserves, but also takes up limited storage space and limits inventories for other bookstore products during the bookstore's busiest sales period. Since the bookstore has such a low profit margin on computers, its bottom line depends on these other products. As competition for good students has increased, the university has become very quality-conscious and insists that all university facilities provide exemplary student service, which for the bookstore means meeting all student demands for computers when the fall semester starts. The number of computers ordered also affects the number of temporary warehouse and bookstore workers that must be hired for handling and assisting with PC installations. The number of truck trips from the warehouse to the bookstore each day of fall registration is also affected by computer sales.

The bookstore student computer purchase program has been in place for fourteen years. Although the student population has remained stable during this period, computer sales have been somewhat volatile. Following is the historical sales data for computers during the first month of fall registration.

Year	Computers Sold	Year	Computers Sold
1	518	8	792
2	651	9	877
3	708	10	693
4	921	11	841
5	775	12	1,009
6	810	13	902
7	856	14	1,103

Develop an appropriate forecast model for bookstore management to use to forecast computer demand for the next fall semester and indicate how accurate it appears to be. What other forecasts might be useful to the bookstore in managing its supply chain?

References

Box, G. E. P., and G. M. Jenkins. *Time Series Analysis: Forecasting and Control*, 2d ed. Oakland, Calif.: Holden-Day, 1976.

Brown, R. G. *Statistical Forecasting for Inventory Control*. New York: McGraw-Hill, 1959.

Chambers, J. C., K. M. Satinder, and D. D. Smith. "How to Choose the Right Forecasting Technique." *Harvard Business Review* (July–August 1971): 45–74.

Gardner, E. S. "Exponential Smoothing: The State of the Art." *Journal of Forecasting* 4, no. 1 (1985).

Gardner, E. S., and D. G. Dannenbring. "Forecasting with Exponential Smoothing: Some Guidelines for Model Selection." *Decision Sciences* 11, no. 2 (1980): 370–83.

Makridakis, S., S. C. Wheelwright, and V. E. McGee. *Forecasting: Methods and Applications*, 2d ed. New York: John Wiley, 1983.

Tersine, R. J., and W. Riggs. "The Delphi Technique: A Long-Range Planning Tool." *Business Horizons* 19, no. 2 (1976).

11

Capacity Planning and Aggregate Production Planning

Planning Hospital Needs

The Henry Ford Health System in southeast Michigan consists of a 900-bed hospital and research facility, 35 ambulatory care centers, a 400,000-member HMO, and 920 salaried physicians. The hospital houses 30 different nursing units, ranging from an 8-bed neurosurgical intensive care unit to a 44-bed general medicine unit. As more complex medical procedures are performed on an outpatient basis, the overall demand for hospital beds has declined, and many communities have set about to reduce their excess capacity. Combining facilities, closing down facilities, or building new facilities are long-term capacity decisions.

Intermediate-term attempts to control health-care costs have centered on reducing nursing staff requirements, which account for 40 percent of personnel costs.

Henry Ford Hospital (HFH) exhibits many of the characteristics that make capacity planning a difficult process:

www.prenhall.com/russell

■ *Rapid demand changes.* Average turnover is 100 beds per day. A different mix of patients requires different resources, so even if overall demand is steady, the specific resources required by patient demand can be diverse. Demand is also sporadic. The number of occupied beds can vary by 150 in a two-week period.

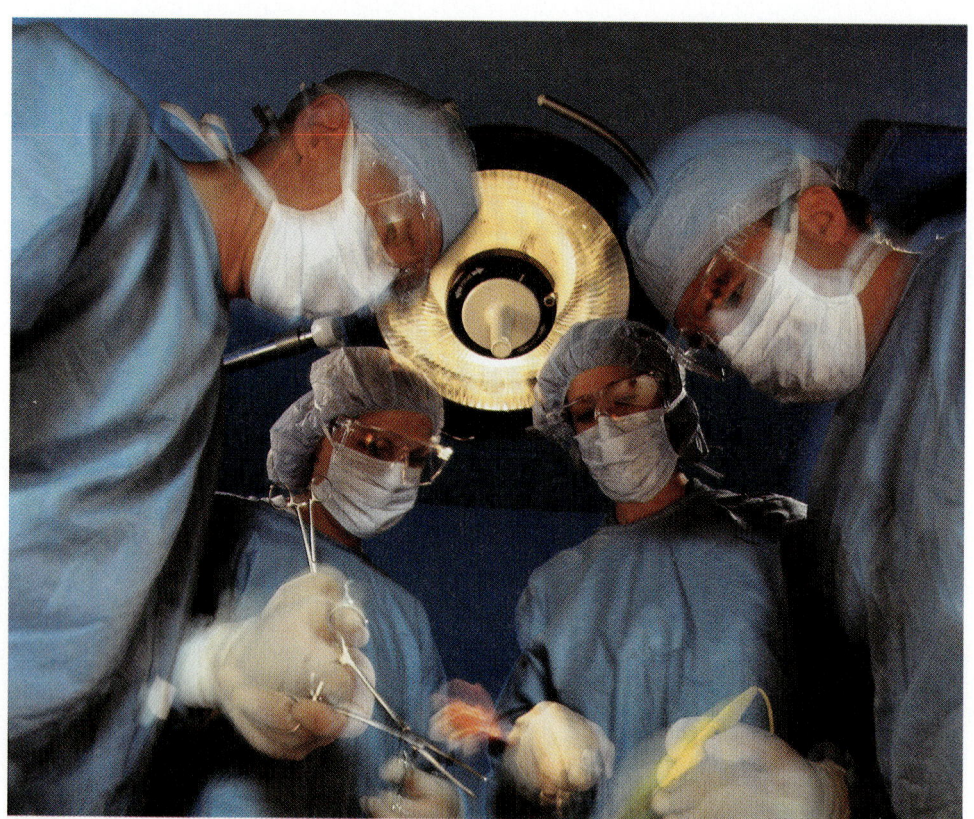

Every organization must determine their capacity needs and set resource levels. In many firms, demand for products and services is forecasted and resources are gathered to meet demand. If the forecast is in error, either resources go unused or customer demand unmet. In health care, planning resource levels is difficult because of uncertain or emergency demand, pressures for cost containment, and the potentially severe consequences of insufficient capacity.

■ *High penalty costs.* If a patient is not admitted to the hospital due to lack of space, the HFH system is doubly penalized. It loses the revenue it would have received from the patient, but also, as an HMO, it must pay another hospital to provide the required care. If the care is unsatisfactory, the potential for malpractice can be expensive.

■ *Limited resources.* The labor market for RNs is tight. It can take from three to four months to recruit and train a new RN and cost $7,600 per nurse.

■ *High carrying costs.* The cost of staffing an unoccupied patient module (defined as an eight-bed unit) is in excess of $35,000 per month.

The problems of matching resources to demand became apparent when HFH made a decision to reduce the nursing staff by several positions, only to reopen those positions and recruit more staff a short time later. To avoid a recurrence of such short-sighted decision making, HFH formulated the following policies on resource usage:

■ Although an average change in demand of fifty patients may affect the revenue of the hospital as a whole, when it is spread across twelve different medical units, the change in terms of resources required is negligible.

■ Organizing nurses into "pods" of two to four nursing units that require similar nursing skills uses resources more effectively. Nurses can float or be temporarily reassigned to any of the nursing units in their pod without retraining or reduction in performance.

■ Permanent staff reduction should not be considered for fewer than fifteen positions at a time. An overstaffed situation cannot be corrected in less than four weeks. The estimated cost of operating overstaffed is $14,600 per week.

■ Increases in permanent staff should not be considered until at least five extra personnel are needed. The cost of using overtime and temporary agency staff is approximately $6,300 per week.

■ Resources should not be reduced if the demand during the last 60 days in any unit or pod exceeded 90 percent of capacity in any one day.

These types of decision rules help HFH better manage its resources and more effectively respond to demand. Currently, the hospital is considering ways to improve its planning process by finding a forecasting method that can reasonably predict demand six to eight weeks into the future, and establishing procedures for rapidly opening beds for sudden surges in demand.[1]

Capacity Planning

Capacity planning is a long-term strategic decision that establishes a firm's overall level of resources. It extends over a time horizon long enough to obtain those resources—usually a year or more for building new facilities or acquiring new businesses. Capacity decisions affect product lead times, customer responsiveness, operating costs, and a firm's ability to compete. Inadequate capacity can lose customers and limit growth. Excess capacity can drain a company's resources and prevent investments in more lucrative ventures. *When* to increase capacity and *how much* to increase capacity are critical decisions.

Capacity planning establishes the overall level of productive resources for a firm.

---

[1] William R. Schramm and Louis E. Freund, "Application of Economic Control Charts by a Nursing Modeling Team," *Industrial Engineering* (April 1993): 27–31.

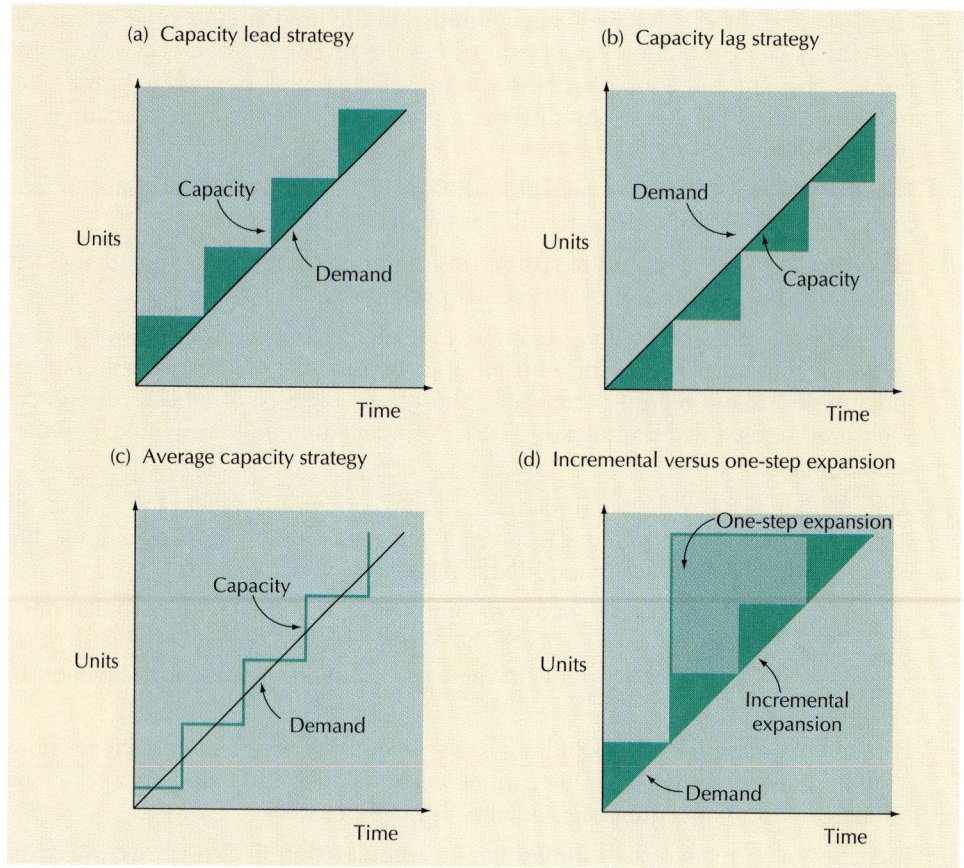

FIGURE 11.1   Capacity Expansion Strategies

Figure 11.1(a), (b), and (c) show three basic strategies for the timing of capacity expansion in relation to a steady growth in demand.

As demand grows, a *lead, lag,* or *average* capacity strategy can be applied.

- *Capacity lead strategy.* Capacity is expanded in anticipation of demand growth. This aggressive strategy is used to lure customers from competitors who are capacity constrained or to gain a foothold in a rapidly expanding market.

- *Capacity lag strategy.* Capacity is increased after an increase in demand has been documented. This conservative strategy produces a higher return on investment but may lose customers in the process. It is used in industries with standard products and cost-based or weak competition. The strategy assumes that lost customers will return from competitors after capacity has expanded.

- *Average capacity strategy.* Capacity is expanded to coincide with average expected demand. This is a moderate strategy in which managers are certain they will be able to sell at least some portion of the additional output.

Consider higher education's strategy in preparing for a tripling of the state's college-bound population in the next decade. An established university, guaranteed applicants even in lean years, may follow a capacity lag strategy. A young university might lead capacity expansion in hopes of capturing those students not admitted to the more established universities. A community college may choose the average capacity strategy to fulfill its mission of educating the state's youth but with little risk.

How much to increase capacity depends on (1) the volume and certainty of anticipated *demand*; (2) *strategic objectives* in terms of growth, customer service, and competition; and (3) the *costs* of expansion and operation.

Capacity can be increased incrementally or in one large step as shown in Figure 11.1(d). Incremental expansion is less risky but more costly. An attractive alternative to expanding capacity is *outsourcing*, in which suppliers absorb the risk of demand uncertainty.

The **best operating level** for a facility is the percent of capacity utilization that minimizes average unit cost. Rarely is the best operating level at 100 percent of capacity—at higher levels of utilization, productivity slows and things start to go wrong. Average capacity utilization differs by industry. An industry with an 80 percent average utilization would have a 20 percent **capacity cushion** for unexpected surges in demand or temporary work stoppages. Large capacity cushions are common in industries where demand is highly variable, resource flexibility is low, and customer service is important. Utilities, for example, maintain a 20 percent capacity cushion. Capital-intensive industries with less flexibility and higher costs maintain cushions under 10 percent. Airlines maintain a negative cushion—overbooking is a common practice!

Figure 11.2 shows the best operating level—in this case, the optimal occupancy rate—for three different size hotels. Of the three alternatives, the 500 room hotel has the lowest average unit cost. This is the point where the *economies of scale* have reached their peak and the *diseconomies of scale* have not yet begun.

High levels of output tend to cost less per unit. Called **economies of scale,** this holds true when:

■ Fixed costs can be spread over a larger number of units,

■ Construction costs do not increase linearly with output levels,

Capacity can be increased incrementally or in large steps.

The **best operating level** is the percent of capacity utilization that minimizes unit costs.

A **capacity cushion** is the percent of capacity held in reserve for unexpected occurrences.

Economies of scale occur when it costs less per unit to produce high levels of output.

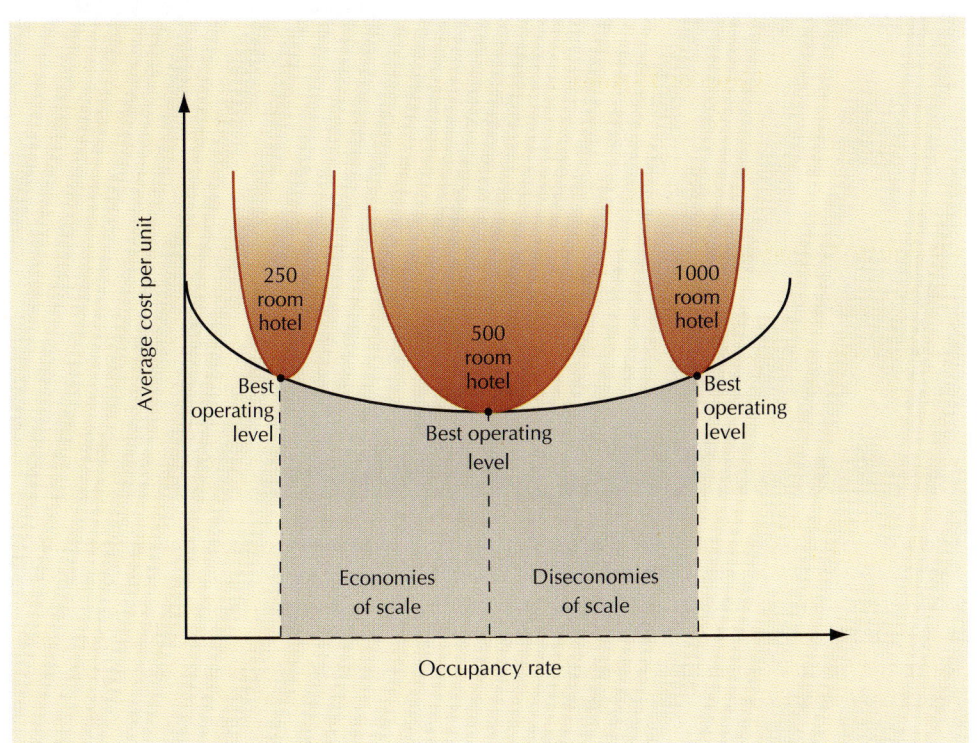

FIGURE 11.2   **Best Operating Levels with Economies and Diseconomies of Scale**

■ Quantity discounts are available for material purchases, and

■ Production efficiency increases as workers gain experience.

The electronics industry provides a good case example of economies of scale. The average cost per chip placement for printed circuit-board assembly is 32 cents in factories with a volume of 25 million placements, 15 cents in factories with 200 million placements, and only 10 cents in factories with 800 million placements.[2]

Above a certain level of output, diceconomies of scale can occur.

Economies of scale do not continue indefinitely. Above a certain level of output, **diseconomies of scale** can occur. Overtaxed machines and material handling equipment break down, service time slows, quality suffers requiring more rework, labor costs increase with overtime, and coordination and management activities become difficult. In addition, if customer preferences suddenly change, high-volume production can leave a firm with unusable inventory and excess capacity.

Long-term capacity decisions concerning the number of facilities and facility size provide the framework for making more intermediate-term capacity decisions—such as inventory policies, production rates, and staffing levels. These decisions are collectively known as *aggregate production planning* or just plain *aggregate planning*.

Aggregate Production Planning

Aggregate production planning determines the resource capacity needed to meet demand over an intermediate time horizon.

Aggregate production planning (APP) determines the resource capacity a firm will need to meet its demand over an intermediate time horizon—six to twelve months in the future. Within this time frame, it is usually not feasible to increase capacity by building new facilities or purchasing new equipment; however, it *is* feasible to hire or

Producers of pulp, paper, lumber, and other wood products have an interesting capacity planning problem—they must plan for the renewable resource of trees. Capacity planning starts with a mathematical simulation model of tree growth that determines the maximum sustainable flow of wood fiber from each acreage. Decisions are made as to which trees to harvest now; which ones to leave until later; where to plant new trees; and the type, amount, and location of new timberland that should be purchased. The planning horizon is the biological lead time to grow trees—over 80 years!

---

[2] "High Volumes Yield Greater Profits for High-Tech Factories," *IIE Solutions* (April 1996): 8.

T H E   C O M P E T I T I V E   E D G E

How Much Capacity Is Enough?

Determining capacity needs is critical to effective operations. *Mars, Inc.*, a privately held $13 billion candy producer, is known for its obsessive drive to minimize cost and maximize asset utilization. But attempts to squeeze more and more M&Ms and Snickers out of its production plants, while routinely allowing its salespersons to sell beyond what can be produced, has cost the company—in customers. In one year, tardy and incomplete product shipments lowered Mars' market share by 3% and earned it a bad reputation among retailers. Stores don't like to allocate shelf space to products that arrive late. And few customers will forego their purchase of candy until a new shipment arrives—they'll choose another brand instead. Look for a more customer-oriented capacity strategy from Mars in the future.

Mazda also has a severe capacity problem—too *much* capacity! With overseas sales hit hard by the value of the yen, Mazda made and sold only 800,000 vehicles in 1996, compared to its normal production of

www.prenhall.com/russell

1.4 million vehicles—that's excess capacity of over half a million cars. It probably should close one of its two huge assembly plants, but which one?

In 1992, Mazda built a $550 million highly automated assembly plant in Hofu, Japan. The Hofu plant is new and efficient, but inflexible. Designed to produce upscale passenger cars, it can't be modified to make sport utility wagons and vans that are now more popular with customers. Currently, the plant is operating at 35 percent of capacity. The other assembly plant in Ujina, Japan, is 30 years old, with aging equipment and workers. Closing that plant would trigger an intense backlash from Japanese leaders and consumers.

Ford's controlling interest in Mazda may provide a solution. Production of Ford cars in U.S. plants could be switched to Mazda's Japanese plants. Now what would the United Auto Workers think of that?

SOURCES: Based on B. Shapiro, "The Eclipse of Mars," *Fortune* (November 28, 1994): 82–92; and Edith Updike and Keith Naughton, "Ford Has a Long Haul at Mazda," *Business Week* (October 7, 1996): 108–14.

lay off workers, increase or reduce the work week, add an extra shift, subcontract out work, use overtime, or build up and deplete inventory levels.

We use the term *aggregate* because the plans are developed for product lines or product families, rather than individual products. An aggregate production plan might specify how many bicycles are to be produced but would not identify them by color, size, tires, or type of brakes. Resource capacity is also expressed in aggregate terms, typically as labor or machine hours. Labor hours would not be specified by type of labor, nor machine hours by type of machine. And they may be given only for critical work centers.

For services, capacity is often limited by *space*—number of airline seats, number of hotel rooms, number of beds in a correctional facility. *Time* can also affect capacity. The number of customers who can be served lunch in a restaurant is limited by the number of seats, as well as the number of hours lunch is served. In overcrowded schools, lunch begins at 10:00 A.M. so that all students can be served by 2:00 P.M.!

There are two objectives to aggregate planning:

- To establish a company-wide game plan for allocating resources, and
- To develop an economic strategy for meeting demand.

The first objective refers to the long-standing battle between the marketing and production functions within a firm. Marketing personnel—who are evaluated solely on sales volume—have the tendency to make unrealistic sales commitments (either in terms of quantity or timing) that production is expected to meet, sometimes at an exorbitant price. Production personnel—who are evaluated on keeping manufacturing costs down—may refuse to accept orders that require additional financial re-

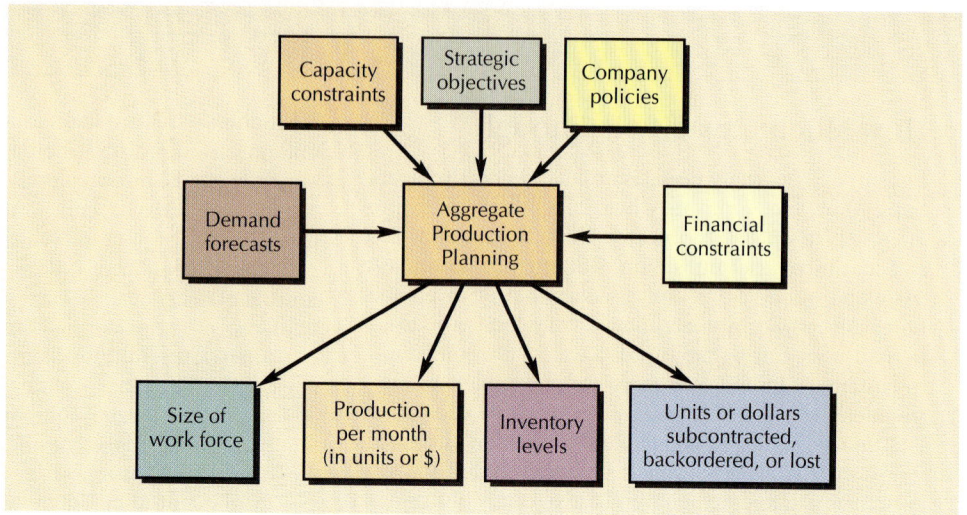

FIGURE 11.3 Inputs to and Outputs from Aggregate Production Planning

A company *game plan:* Don't promise what you can't deliver.

APP evaluates alternative capacity sources to find an economic strategy for satisfying demand.

sources (such as overtime wage rates) or hard-to-meet completion dates. The job of production planning is to match forecasted demand with available capacity. If capacity is inadequate, it can usually be expanded, but at a cost. The company needs to determine if the extra cost is worth the increased revenue from the sale, and if the sale is consistent with the strategy of the firm. Thus, the aggregate production plan should not be determined by manufacturing personnel alone; rather, it should be agreed upon by top management from all the functional areas of the firm—manufacturing, marketing, and finance. Furthermore, it should reflect company policy (such as avoiding layoffs, limiting inventory levels, or maintaining a specified customer service level) and strategic objectives (such as capturing a certain share of the market or achieving targeted levels of quality or profit). Because of the various factors and viewpoints that are considered, the production plan is often referred to as the company's *game plan* for the coming year, and deviations from the plan are carefully monitored.

The rest of this chapter covers the second objective—developing an economic strategy for meeting demand. Demand can be met by *adjusting capacity* or *managing demand*. First, we'll discuss several quantitative techniques for choosing the most cost-effective method of adjusting capacity. Then, we'll discuss some alternatives for managing demand.

Figure 11.3 shows the inputs to and outputs from aggregate production planning. The inputs are demand forecasts, capacity constraints, strategic objectives, company policies, and financial constraints. The outputs include size of the work force, production expressed as either units or sales dollars, inventory levels that support the production plan, and the number of units or dollars subcontracted, backordered, or lost.

Strategies for Meeting Demand

If demand for a company's products or services are stable over time or its resources are unlimited, then aggregate planning is trivial. Demand forecasts are converted to resource requirements, the resources necessary to meet demand are acquired and maintained over the time horizon of the plan, and minor variations in demand are handled with overtime or undertime. Aggregate production planning becomes a challenge when demand fluctuates over the planning horizon. For example, seasonal demand patterns can be met by:

1. Producing at a constant rate and using inventory to absorb fluctuations in demand (*level production*)
2. Hiring and firing workers to match demand (*chase demand*)
3. Maintaining resources for high-demand levels
4. Increasing or decreasing working hours (*overtime* and *undertime*)
5. Subcontracting work to other firms
6. Using part-time workers
7. Providing the service or product at a later time period (*backordering*)

When one of these is selected, a company is said to have a **pure strategy** for meeting demand. When two or more are selected, a company has a **mixed strategy.**

The **level production** strategy, shown in Figure 11.4(a), sets production at a fixed rate (usually to meet average demand) and uses inventory to absorb variations in demand. During periods of low demand, overproduction is stored as inventory, to be depleted in periods of high demand. The cost of this strategy is the cost of holding inventory, including the cost of obsolete or perishable items that may have to be discarded.

The **chase demand** strategy, shown in Figure 11.4(b), matches the production plan to the demand pattern and absorbs variations in demand by hiring and firing workers. During periods of low demand, production is cut back and workers are laid off. During periods of high demand, production is increased and additional workers are hired. The cost of this strategy is the cost of hiring and firing workers. This approach would not work for industries in which worker skills are scarce or competition for labor is intense, but it can be quite cost-effective during periods of high unemployment or for industries with low-skilled workers.

Maintaining resources for high-demand levels ensures high levels of customer service but can be very costly in terms of the investment in extra workers and machines that remain idle during low-demand periods. This strategy is used when superior customer service is important (such as Nordstrom's department store) or when customers are willing to pay extra for the availability of critical staff or equipment. Professional services trying to generate more demand may keep staff levels high, defense contractors may be paid to keep extra capacity "available," child-care facilities may elect to maintain staff levels

Meeting demand is a challenge when it fluctuates.

A pure strategy involves only one capacity factor.

A mixed strategy involves more than one.

Level production involves producing at a constant rate and using inventory as needed to meet demand.

Chase demand involves changing workforce levels so that production matches demand.

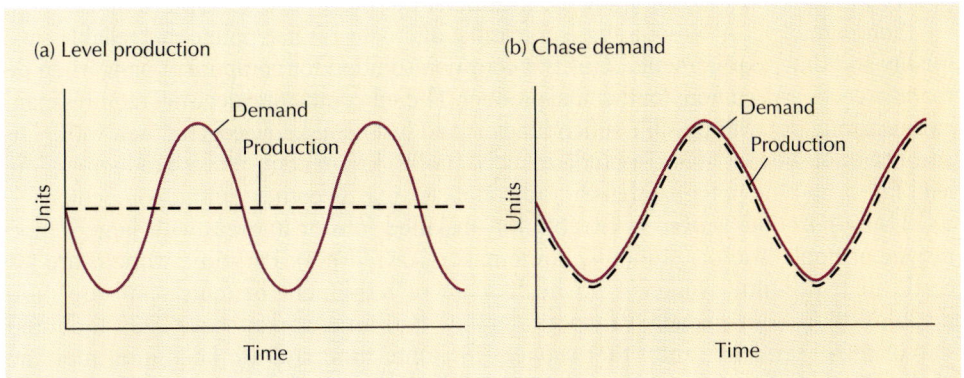

FIGURE 11.4   **Pure Strategies for Meeting Demand**

Retailers do almost 50 percent of their annual business in the holiday season. Manufacturers of holiday items, such as wrapping paper, have an even more skewed demand pattern. Sixty-eight percent of the annual demand for wrapping paper takes place during the months of November and December, 25 percent in the two weeks prior to Christmas. Producing early in the year and building up inventory is not cost effective because of the bulkiness of the product and the humidity requirements for storage. Heightened production levels mean hiring more workers and using overtime in late summer and fall—that's plenty of time for workers to save up their extra pay for purchasing holiday items!

Mixed strategies: a combination of overtime/undertime, subcontracting, hiring/firing, part-time workers, inventory, and backordering.

for continuity when attendance is low, and full-service hospitals may invest in specialized equipment that is rarely used but is critical for the care of a small number of patients.

Overtime and undertime are common strategies when demand fluctuations are not extreme. A competent staff is maintained, hiring and firing costs are avoided, and demand is met temporarily without investing in permanent resources. Disadvantages include the premium paid for overtime work, a tired and potentially less efficient work force, and the possibility that overtime alone may be insufficient to meet peak demand periods.

Subcontracting or outsourcing is a feasible alternative if a supplier can reliably meet quality and time requirements. This is a common solution for component parts when demand exceeds expectations for the final product. The subcontracting decision requires maintaining strong ties with possible subcontractors and first-hand knowledge of their work. Disadvantages of subcontracting include reduced profits, loss of control over production, long lead times, and the potential that the subcontractor may become a future competitor.

Using *part-time workers* is feasible for unskilled jobs or in areas with large temporary labor pools (such as students, homemakers, or retirees). Part-time workers are less costly than full-time workers—no health-care or retirement benefits—and are more flexible—their hours usually vary considerably. Part-time workers have been the mainstay of retail, fast-food, and other services for some time and are becoming more accepted in manufacturing and government jobs. Japanese manufacturers traditionally use a large percentage of part-time or temporary workers. IBM staffs its entire third shift at Research Triangle Park, North Carolina, with temporary workers (college students).

Part-time and temporary workers now account for about one third of our nation's work force. The temp agency Manpower, Inc. is the largest private employer in the world. Problems with part-time workers include high turnover, accelerated training requirements, less commitment, and scheduling difficulties.

Backordering is a viable alternative only if the customer is willing to wait for the product or service. For some restaurants you may be willing to wait an hour for a table, for others you may not.

One aggregate planning strategy is not always preferable to another. The most effective strategy depends on the demand distribution, competitive position, and cost structure of a firm or product line. Several quantitative techniques are available to help with the aggregate planning decision. We will discuss pure and mixed strategies using *trial and error*, the *transportation method*, and other quantitative techniques.

www.prenhall.com/russell

APP by Trial and Error

Using trial-and-error to solve aggregate production planning problems involves formulating several strategies for meeting demand, constructing production plans from those strategies, determining the cost and feasibility of each plan, and selecting the lowest cost plan

---

THE COMPETITIVE EDGE

Meeting Peak Holiday Demand at Neiman Marcus

www.prenhall.com/russell

Neiman Marcus operates a 377,000-square-foot mail-order distribution center in Irving, Texas. Forty percent of its business is accounted for by the 2.8 million "Christmas Book" catalogs mailed out in mid-September. A flurry of orders is received immediately after the catalogs are mailed; then volume drops off and levels out until early November. The sales volume then begins a steep ascent that peaks early in December. September demand represents 52 percent of peak shipments, and October represents 91 percent of peak shipments. Demand in November and December is in excess of 100,000 shipments per week. The peak demand volume of 28,000 orders per day is more than double normal sales. Despite these numbers, Neiman Marcus ships 90 percent of holiday orders within 1 day and 99 percent within 2 days, with 99.4 percent accuracy. How does it achieve such performance levels?

The company plans in advance. Although it's hard to predict which items will be hot sellers each year, close relations with suppliers and an early analysis of September's demand pattern (within 10 days of the catalog mailing) can make back ordering large volumes feasible. Fast-moving items are moved to a prominent place in the warehouse, and work flow is prioritized so that customer back orders receive immediate attention. A new conveyor system sports color-coded conveyors that identify flow patterns from different sources to shipping (from apparel to shipping, for example, versus toys or small gifts). It also uses bar codes extensively to route cartons to special areas for gift wrapping, Federal Express shipment, or special attention. Customers are given options for when their order is shipped. They can order now for shipment at a later date or receive Federal Express second-day service on any item in the catalog at no extra cost.

Another key to success is dedicated people with a great attitude. Neiman Marcus hires 300 extra people in their distribution center during the holiday season. Twenty percent of these workers return each year. To allow sufficient time for training, the company begins hiring temporaries when the catalogs are mailed out in September and gradually builds up their numbers over the next two months. Permanent staff personnel train the new hires, and the system of work is purposely designed to be simple and easy to learn.

Incentive pay, based on productivity and quality and reinforced with prizes and awards, adds fun and excitement to the work environment. With Neiman Marcus, as with many other retailers, making people happy during the holiday season ensures that the year will be a profitable one.

SOURCE: Based on Karen Auguston, "Neiman Marcus Plans Picking to Meet Peak Holiday Demands," *Modern Material Handling* (December 1992): 44–48.

from among the feasible alternatives. The effectiveness of trial and error is directly related to management's understanding of the cost variables involved and the reasonableness of the scenarios tested. Example 11.1 compares the cost of two pure strategies. Example 11.2 uses Excel to compare pure and mixed strategies for a more extensive problem.

EXAMPLE
11.1

Aggregate Production Planning Using Pure Strategies

The Good and Rich Candy Company makes a variety of candies in three factories worldwide. Its line of chocolate candies exhibits a highly seasonal demand pattern, with peaks during the winter months (for the holiday season and Valentine's Day) and valleys during the summer months (when chocolate tends to melt and customers are watching their weight). Given the following costs and quarterly sales forecasts, determine whether a level production or chase demand production strategy would more economically meet the demand for chocolate candies.

Quarter	Sales Forecast (lb)
Spring	80,000
Summer	50,000
Fall	120,000
Winter	150,000

$$\text{Hiring cost} = \$100 \text{ per worker}$$
$$\text{Firing cost} = \$500 \text{ per worker}$$
$$\text{Inventory carrying cost} = \$0.50 \text{ per pound per quarter}$$
$$\text{Production per employee} = 1,000 \text{ pounds per quarter}$$
$$\text{Beginning work force} = 100 \text{ workers}$$

SOLUTION:

For the level production strategy, we first need to calculate average quarterly demand.

$$\frac{(50,000 + 120,000 + 150,000 + 80,000)}{4} = \frac{400,000}{4} = 100,000 \text{ pounds}$$

This becomes our planned production for each quarter. Since each worker can produce 1,000 pounds a quarter, 100 workers will be needed each quarter to meet the production requirements of 100,000 pounds. Production in excess of demand is stored in inventory, where it remains until it is used to meet demand in a later period. Demand in excess of production is met by using inventory from the previous quarter. The production plan and resulting inventory costs are given in Exhibit 11.1.

For the chase demand strategy, production each quarter matches demand. To accomplish this, workers are hired and fired at a cost of $100 for each one hired and $500 for each one fired. Since each worker can produce 1,000 pounds per quarter, we divide the quarterly sales forecast by 1,000 to determine the required work-force size each quarter. We begin with 100 workers and hire and fire as needed. The production plan and resulting hiring and firing costs are given in Exhibit 11.2.

Comparing the cost of level production with chase demand, chase demand is the best strategy for the Good and Rich line of chocolate candies.

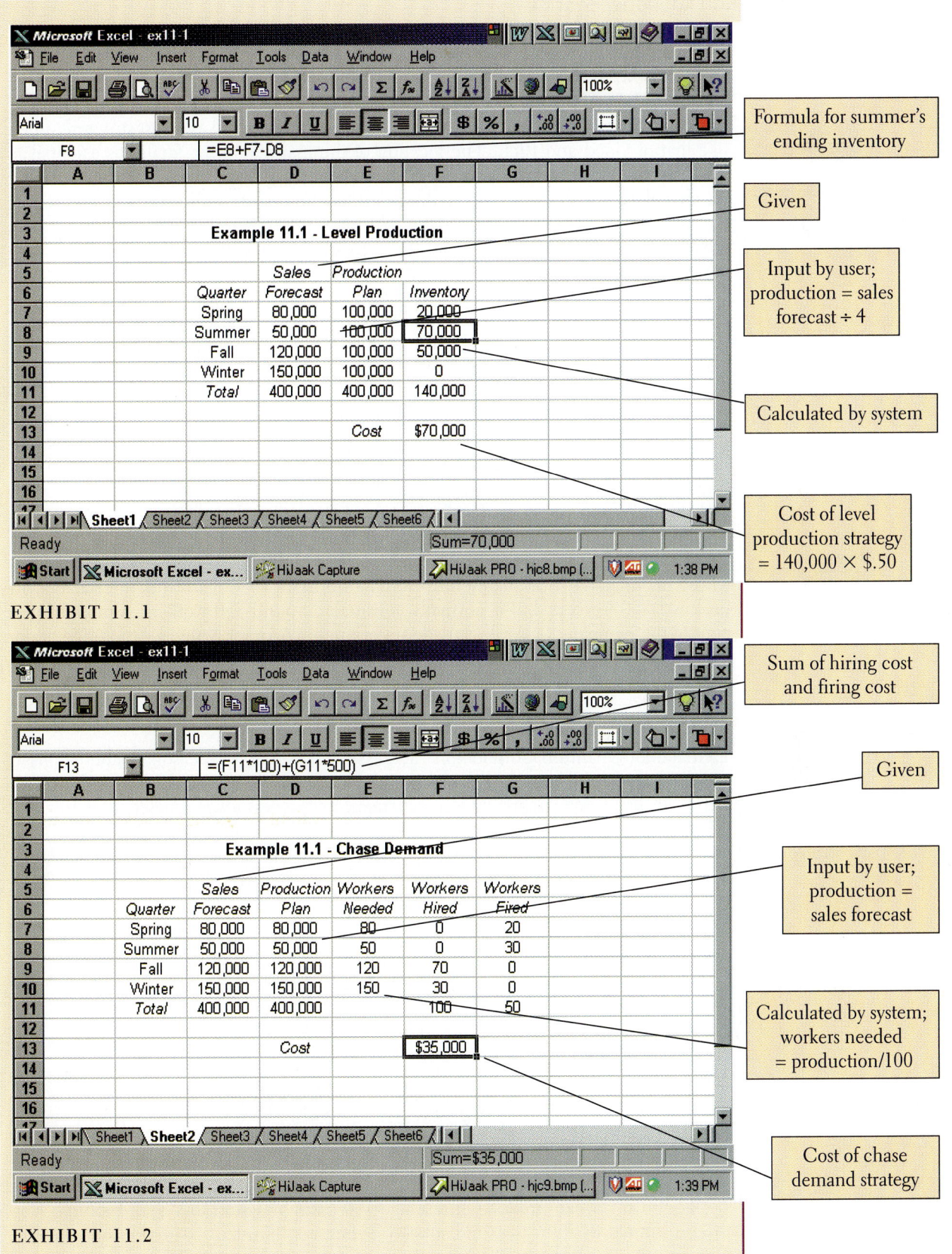

EXHIBIT 11.1

EXHIBIT 11.2

Exhibit 11.1 annotations:
- Formula for summer's ending inventory
- Given
- Input by user; production = sales forecast ÷ 4
- Calculated by system
- Cost of level production strategy = 140,000 × $.50

Exhibit 11.1 spreadsheet:
F8 = =E8+F7-D8

Example 11.1 - Level Production

Quarter	Sales Forecast	Production Plan	Inventory
Spring	80,000	100,000	20,000
Summer	50,000	100,000	70,000
Fall	120,000	100,000	50,000
Winter	150,000	100,000	0
Total	400,000	400,000	140,000
		Cost	$70,000

Sum=70,000

Exhibit 11.2 annotations:
- Sum of hiring cost and firing cost
- Given
- Input by user; production = sales forecast
- Calculated by system; workers needed = production/100
- Cost of chase demand strategy

Exhibit 11.2 spreadsheet:
F13 = =(F11*100)+(G11*500)

Example 11.1 - Chase Demand

Quarter	Sales Forecast	Production Plan	Workers Needed	Workers Hired	Workers Fired
Spring	80,000	80,000	80	0	20
Summer	50,000	50,000	50	0	30
Fall	120,000	120,000	120	70	0
Winter	150,000	150,000	150	30	0
Total	400,000	400,000		100	50
		Cost	$35,000		

Sum=$35,000

www.prenhall.com/russell

Although chase demand is the better strategy for Good and Rich from an economic point of view, it may seem unduly harsh on the company's work force. An example of a good "fit" between a company's chase demand strategy and the needs of the work force is Hershey's located in rural Pennsylvania with a demand and cost structure much like that of Good and Rich. The location of the manufacturing facility is essential to the effectiveness of the company's production plan. During the winter, when demand for chocolate is high, the company hires farmers from surrounding areas, who are idle that time of year. The farmers are let go during the spring and summer, when they are anxious to return to their fields and the demand for chocolate falls. The plan is cost-effective, and the extra help is content with the sporadic hiring and firing practices of the company.

The most common APP approach is trial and error using spreadsheets.

Probably the most common approach to production planning is trial and error using mixed strategies and spreadsheets to evaluate different options quickly. Mixed strategies can incorporate management policies, such as "no more than *x* percent of the work force can be laid off in one quarter" or "inventory levels cannot exceed *x* dollars." They can also be adapted to the quirks of a company or industry. For example, many industries that experience a slowdown during part of the year may simply shut down manufacturing during the low-demand season and schedule everyone's vacation during that time. Furniture manufacturers typically close down for the month of July each year, and shipbuilders close down for the month of December.

www.prenhall.com/russell

For some industries, the production planning task revolves around the supply of raw materials, not the demand pattern. Consider Motts, the applesauce manufacturer whose raw material is available only 40 days during a year. The work-force size at its peak is 1,500 workers, but it normally consists of around 350 workers. Almost 10 percent of the company's payroll is made up of unemployment benefits—the price of doing business in that particular industry.

EXAMPLE 11.2

Aggregate Production Planning Using Pure and Mixed Strategies

Demand for Quantum Corporation's action toy series follows a seasonal pattern—growing through the fall months and culminating in December, with smaller peaks in January (for after-season markdowns, exchanges, and accessory purchases) and July (for Christmas-in-July specials).

Month	Demand (cases)
January	1,000
February	200
March	200
April	400
May	400
June	500
July	900
August	400
September	1,000
October	1,500
November	2,500
December	3,000

Each worker can produce on average 100 cases of action toys each month. Overtime is limited to 300 cases, and subcontracting is unlimited. No action toys are currently in inventory. The wage rate is $10 per case for regular production, $15 for overtime production, and $25 for subcontracting. No stockouts are allowed. Holding cost is $1 per case per month. Increasing the work force costs approximately $1,000 per worker. Decreasing the work force costs $500 per worker.

Management wishes to test the following scenarios for planning production:

a. Level production over the twelve months. Do not allow overtime or subcontracting.

b. Produce to meet demand each month. Absorb variations in demand by changing the size of the work force. Do not allow overtime, subcontracting, or inventory.

c. Increase or decrease the work force in five-worker increments. Use overtime and subcontracting as necessary.

SOLUTION:

Excel was used to evaluate the three planning scenarios. The solution printouts are shown in Exhibits 11.3, 11.4, and 11.5, respectively. From the scenarios tested, level production is the best strategy.

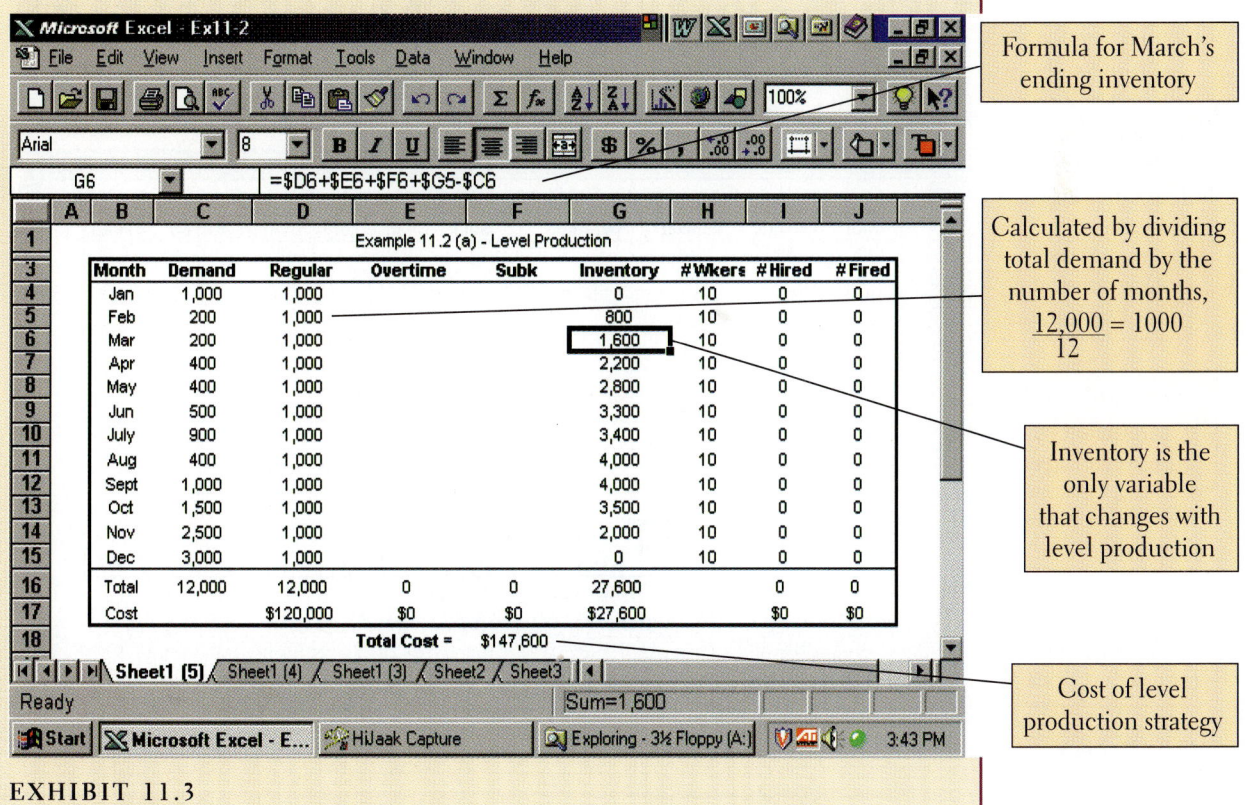

Formula for March's ending inventory

Calculated by dividing total demand by the number of months, $\frac{12,000}{12} = 1000$

Inventory is the only variable that changes with level production

Cost of level production strategy

EXHIBIT 11.3

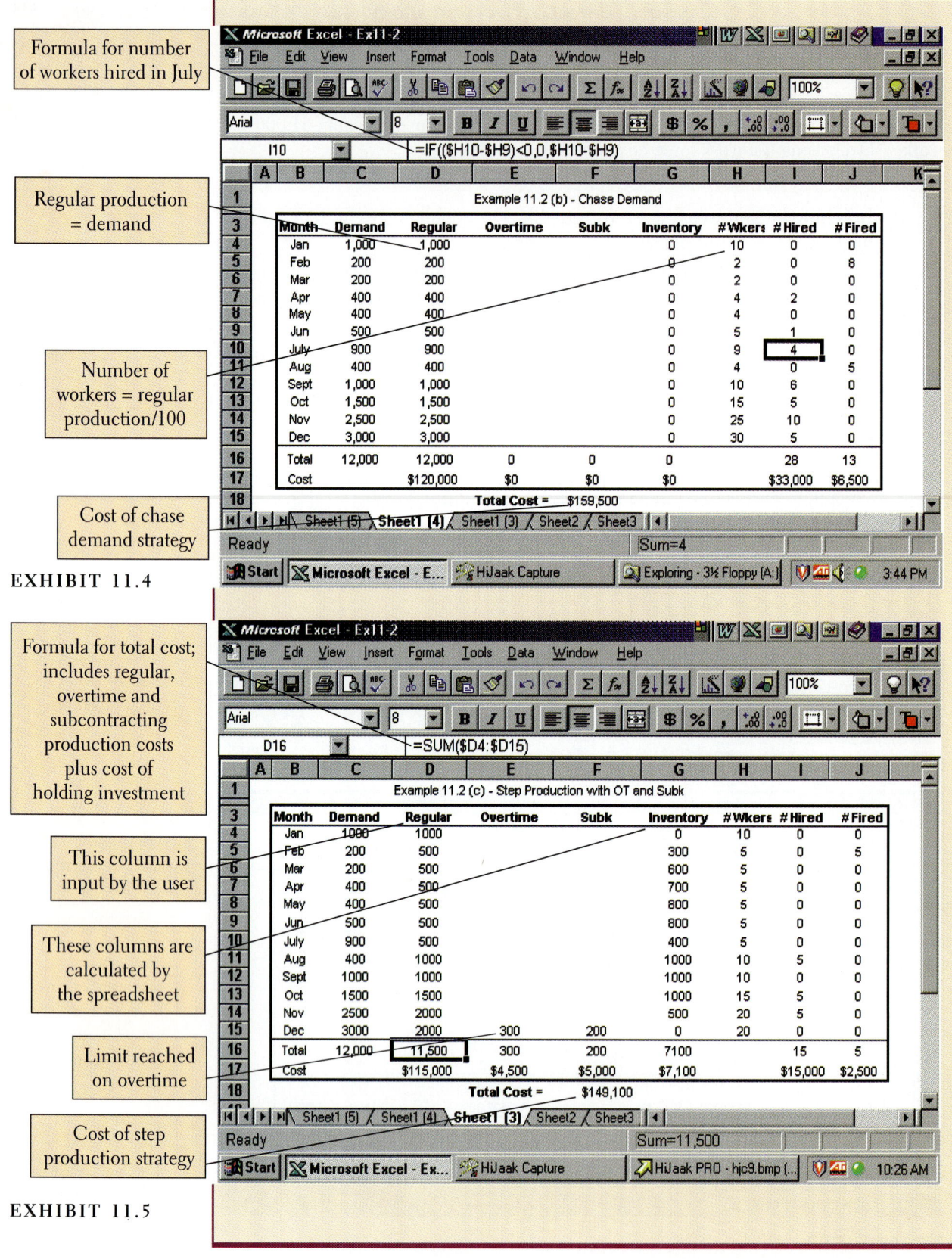

Formula for number of workers hired in July

Regular production = demand

Number of workers = regular production/100

Cost of chase demand strategy

EXHIBIT 11.4

Month	Demand	Regular	Overtime	Subk	Inventory	#Wkers	#Hired	#Fired
Jan	1,000	1,000			0	10	0	0
Feb	200	200			0	2	0	8
Mar	200	200			0	2	0	0
Apr	400	400			0	4	2	0
May	400	400			0	4	0	0
Jun	500	500			0	5	1	0
July	900	900			0	9	4	0
Aug	400	400			0	4	0	5
Sept	1,000	1,000			0	10	6	0
Oct	1,500	1,500			0	15	5	0
Nov	2,500	2,500			0	25	10	0
Dec	3,000	3,000			0	30	5	0
Total	12,000	12,000	0	0	0		28	13
Cost		$120,000	$0	$0	$0		$33,000	$6,500

Example 11.2 (b) - Chase Demand

=IF(($H10-$H9)<0,0,$H10-$H9)

Total Cost = $159,500

Formula for total cost; includes regular, overtime and subcontracting production costs plus cost of holding investment

This column is input by the user

These columns are calculated by the spreadsheet

Limit reached on overtime

Cost of step production strategy

EXHIBIT 11.5

=SUM($D4:$D15)

Month	Demand	Regular	Overtime	Subk	Inventory	#Wkers	#Hired	#Fired
Jan	1000	1000			0	10	0	0
Feb	200	500			300	5	0	5
Mar	200	500			600	5	0	0
Apr	400	500			700	5	0	0
May	400	500			800	5	0	0
Jun	500	500			800	5	0	0
July	900	500			400	5	0	0
Aug	400	1000			1000	10	5	0
Sept	1000	1000			1000	10	0	0
Oct	1500	1500			1000	15	5	0
Nov	2500	2000			500	20	5	0
Dec	3000	2000	300	200	0	20	0	0
Total	12,000	11,500	300	200	7100		15	5
Cost		$115,000	$4,500	$5,000	$7,100		$15,000	$2,500

Example 11.2 (c) - Step Production with OT and Subk

Total Cost = $149,100

General Linear Programming Model

Pure and mixed strategies for production planning are easy to evaluate, but they do not necessarily provide an optimum solution. Consider the Good and Rich Company of Example 11.1. The *optimum* production plan is probably some combination of inventory and work force adjustment. We could simply try different combinations and compare the costs (i.e., the trial-and-error approach), or we could find the optimum solution by using *linear programming*.[3] Example 11.3 develops an optimum aggregate production plan for Good and Rich chocolate candies using linear programming.

Linear programming gives an optimum solution, but demand and costs must be linear.

EXAMPLE 11.3

Aggregate Production Planning using Linear Programming

Formulate a linear programming model for Example 11.1 that will satisfy demand for Good and Rich chocolate candies at minimum cost. Solve the model with available linear programming software.

SOLUTION:

Model formulation:

$$\text{Minimize } Z = \$100(H_1 + H_2 + H_3 + H_4)$$
$$+ \$500(F_1 + F_2 + F_3 + F_4)$$
$$+ \$0.50(I_1 + I_2 + I_3 + I_4)$$

subject to

Demand constraints
$$P_1 - I_1 = 80,000 \quad (1)$$
$$I_1 + P_2 - I_2 = 50,000 \quad (2)$$
$$I_2 + P_3 - I_3 = 120,000 \quad (3)$$
$$I_3 + P_4 - I_4 = 150,000 \quad (4)$$

Production constraints
$$P_1 - 1,000W_1 = 0 \quad (5)$$
$$P_2 - 1,000W_2 = 0 \quad (6)$$
$$P_3 - 1,000W_3 = 0 \quad (7)$$
$$P_4 - 1,000W_4 = 0 \quad (8)$$

Work force constraints
$$W_1 - H_1 + F_1 = 100 \quad (9)$$
$$W_2 - W_1 - H_2 + F_2 = 0 \quad (10)$$
$$W_3 - W_2 - H_3 + F_3 = 0 \quad (11)$$
$$W_4 - W_3 - H_4 + F_4 = 0 \quad (12)$$

where
H_t = number of workers hired for period t
F_t = number of workers fired for period t
I_t = units in inventory at the end of period t

(Continued)

---

[3] Students unfamiliar with linear programming are referred to the chapter supplement for review.

P_t = units produced in period t

W_t = workforce size for period t

- *Objective function:* The objective function seeks to minimize the cost of hiring workers, firing workers, and holding inventory. Cost values are provided in the problem statement for Example 11.1. The number of workers hired and fired each quarter and the amount of inventory held are variables whose values are determined by solving the linear programming (LP) problem.

- *Demand constraints:* The first set of constraints ensure that demand is met each quarter. Demand can be met from production in the current period and inventory from the previous period. Units produced in excess of demand remain in inventory at the end of the period. In general form, the demand equations are constructed as

$$I_{t-1} + P_t = D_t + I_t$$

where D_t is the demand in period t, as specified in the problem.

To express the equation in standard LP format, the value on the right-hand side must be a constant. Leaving demand on the right-hand side, we have

$$I_{t-1} + P_t - I_t = D_t$$

There are four demand constraints, one for each quarter. Since there is no beginning inventory, $I_0 = 0$, and it can be dropped from the first demand constraint.

- *Production constraints:* The four production constraints convert the work force size to the number of units that can be produced. Each worker can produce 1,000 units a quarter, so the production each quarter is 1,000 times the number of workers employed, or

$$P_t = 1,000W_t$$

In standard LP format, the equation becomes:

$$P_t - 1,000W_t = 0$$

- *Work force constraints:* The work force constraints limit the work force size in each period to the previous period's work force plus the number of workers hired in the current period minus the number of workers fired.

$$W_t = W_{t-1} + H_t - F_t$$

Bringing all the variables to the left-hand side, the equation becomes

$$W_t - W_{t-1} - H_t + F_t = 0$$

Notice the first work force constraint appears slightly different. Since the beginning work force size of 100 is known, it remains on the right-hand side of the equation.

- *Additional constraints:* Additional constraints can be added to the LP formulation as needed to limit such options as subcontracting or overtime. The cost of those options is then added to the objective function.

The LP formulation is solved using POM for Windows to yield the solution in Exhibit 11.6. The cost of the optimum solution is $32,000, an improvement of $3,000 over the chase demand strategy and $38,000 over the level production strategy. This reduced cost figure was achieved by doing the following:

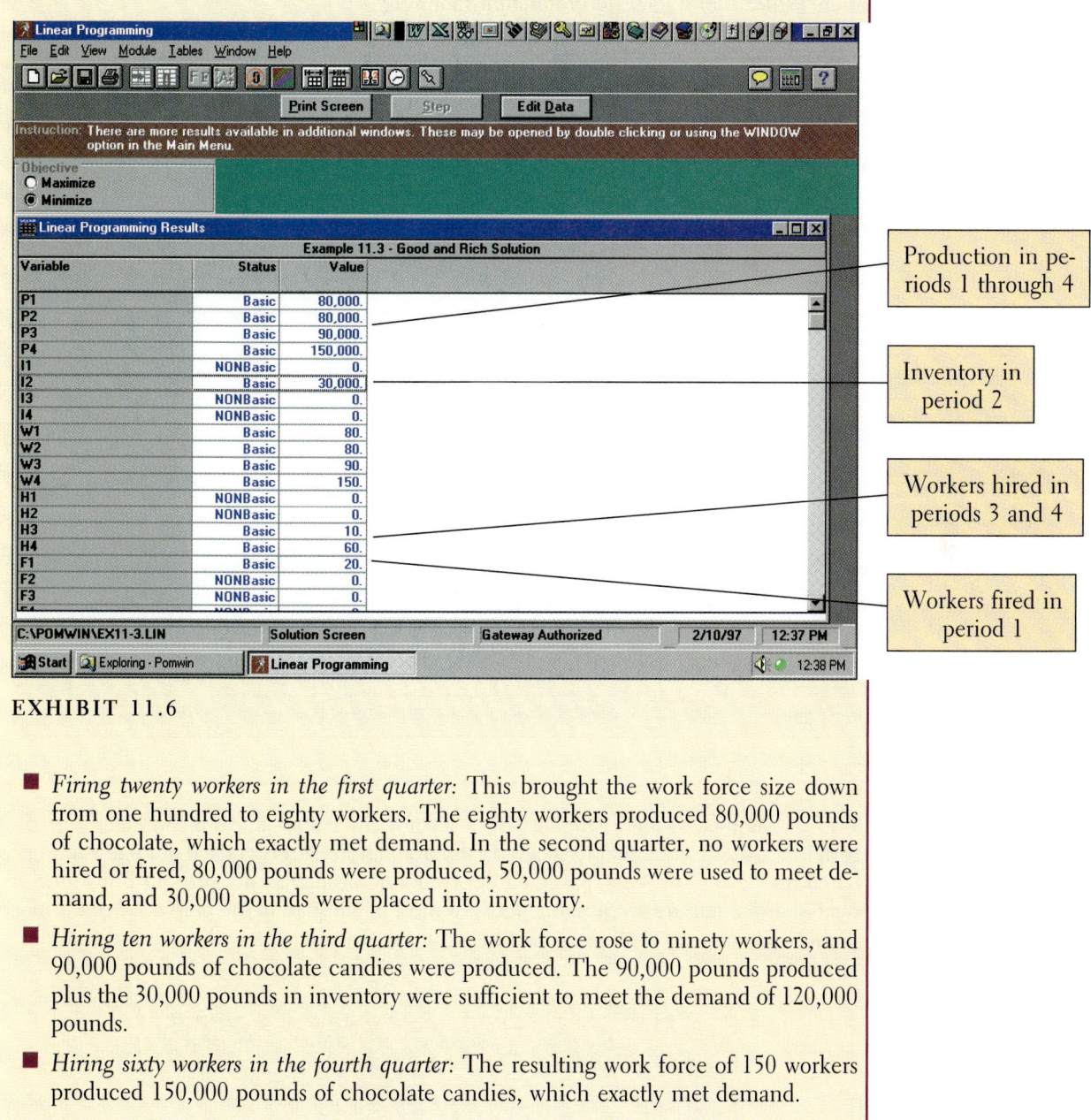

EXHIBIT 11.6

- *Firing twenty workers in the first quarter:* This brought the work force size down from one hundred to eighty workers. The eighty workers produced 80,000 pounds of chocolate, which exactly met demand. In the second quarter, no workers were hired or fired, 80,000 pounds were produced, 50,000 pounds were used to meet demand, and 30,000 pounds were placed into inventory.

- *Hiring ten workers in the third quarter:* The work force rose to ninety workers, and 90,000 pounds of chocolate candies were produced. The 90,000 pounds produced plus the 30,000 pounds in inventory were sufficient to meet the demand of 120,000 pounds.

- *Hiring sixty workers in the fourth quarter:* The resulting work force of 150 workers produced 150,000 pounds of chocolate candies, which exactly met demand.

APP by the Transportation Method

For those cases in which the decision to change the size of the work force has already been made or is prohibited, the transportation method of linear programming can be used to develop an aggregate production plan. The transportation method gathers all the cost information into one matrix and plans production based on the lowest-cost alternatives. Example 11.4 illustrates the procedure. Table 11.1 shows a blank transportation tableau for aggregate planning.

Use the transportation method when hiring and firing is not an option.

TABLE 11.1   Transportation Tableau for Aggregate Production Planning

			PERIOD OF USE				
PERIOD OF PRODUCTION		1	2	3	4	Unused Capacity	Capacity
1	Beginning Inventory						
	Regular						
	Overtime						
	Subcontract						
2	Regular						
	Overtime						
	Subcontract						
3	Regular						
	Overtime						
	Subcontract						
4	Regular						
	Overtime						
	Subcontract						
	Demand						

EXAMPLE 11.4

APP by the Transportation Method of Linear Programming

Burruss Manufacturing Company uses overtime, inventory, and subcontracting to absorb fluctuations in demand. An aggregate production plan is devised annually and updated quarterly. Cost data, expected demand, and available capacities in units for the next four quarters are given here. Demand must be satisfied in the period it occurs; that is, no backordering is allowed. Design a production plan that will satisfy demand at minimum cost.

Quarter	Expected Demand	Regular Capacity	Overtime Capacity	Subcontract Capacity
1	900	1000	100	500
2	1500	1200	150	500
3	1600	1300	200	500
4	3000	1300	200	500

Regular production cost per unit	$20
Overtime production cost per unit	$25
Subcontracting cost per unit	$28
Inventory holding cost per unit per period	$ 3
Beginning inventory	300 units

SOLUTION:

The problem is solved using the transportation tableau shown below. The tableau is a worksheet that is completed as follows:

■ To set up the tableau, demand requirements for each quarter are listed on the bottom row and capacity constraints for each type of production (i.e., regular, overtime, or subcontracting) are placed in the far right column.

■ Next, cost figures are entered into the small square at the corner of each cell. Reading across the first row, inventory on hand in period 1 that is used in period 1 incurs zero cost. Inventory on hand in period 1 that is not used until period 2 incurs $3 holding cost. If the inventory is held until period 3, the cost is $3 more, or $6. Similarly, if the inventory is held until period 4, the cost is an additional $3, or $9.

■ Interpreting the cost entries in the second row, if a unit is produced under regular production in period 1 and used in period 1, it costs $20. If a unit is produced under regular production in period 1 but is not used until period 2, it incurs a production cost of $20 plus an inventory cost of $3, or $23. If the unit is held until period 3, it will cost $3 more, or $26. If it is held until period 4, it will cost $29. The cost calculations continue in a similar fashion for overtime and subcontracting, beginning with production costs of $25 and $28, respectively.

PERIOD OF PRODUCTION		PERIOD OF USE				Unused Capacity	Capacity
		1	2	3	4		
	Beginning Inventory	300 [0]	— [3]	— [6]	— [9]	[0]	300
1	Regular	600 [20]	300 [23]	100 [26]	— [29]	[0]	1,000
	Overtime	[25]	[28]	[31]	100 [34]	[0]	100
	Subcontract	[28]	[31]	[34]	[37]	[0]	500
2	Regular		1,200 [20]	— [23]	— [26]	[0]	1,200
	Overtime		[25]	[28]	150 [31]	[0]	150
	Subcontract		[28]	[31]	250 [34]	250 [0]	500
3	Regular			1,300 [20]	— [23]	[0]	1,300
	Overtime			200 [25]	— [28]	[0]	200
	Subcontract			[28]	500 [31]	[0]	500
4	Regular				1,300 [20]	[0]	1,300
	Overtime				200 [25]	[0]	200
	Subcontract				500 [28]	[0]	500
	Demand	900	1,500	1,600	3,000	250	

(Continued)

- The costs for production in periods 2, 3, and 4 are determined in a similar fashion, with one exception. Half of the remaining transportation tableau is blocked out as infeasible. This occurs because no backordering is allowed for this problem, and production cannot take place in one period to satisfy demand that occurs in previous periods.

- Now that the tableau is set up, we can begin to allocate units to the cells and develop our production plan. The procedure is to assign units to the lowest-cost cells in a column so that demand requirements for the column are met, yet capacity constraints of each row are not exceeded. Beginning with the first demand column for period 1, we have 300 units of beginning inventory available to us at no cost. If we use all 300 units in period 1, there is no inventory left for use in later periods. We indicate this fact by putting a dash in the remaining cells of the beginning inventory row. We can satisfy the remaining 600 units of demand for period 1 with regular production at a cost of $20 per unit.

- In period 2, the lowest-cost alternative is regular production in period 2. We assign 1,200 units to that cell and, in the process, use up all the capacity for that row. Dashes are placed in the remaining cells of the row to indicate that they are no longer feasible choices. The remaining units needed to meet demand in period 2 are taken from regular production in period 1 that is inventoried until period 2, at a cost of $23 per unit. We assign 300 units to that cell.

- Continuing to the third period's demand of 1,600 units, we fully utilize the 1,300 units available from regular production in the same period and 200 units of overtime production. The remaining 100 units are produced with regular production in period 1 and held until period 3, at a cost of $26 per unit. As noted by the dashed line, period 1's regular production has reached its capacity and is no longer an alternative source of production.

- Of the fourth period's demand of 3,000 units, 1,300 come from regular production, 200 from overtime, and 500 from subcontracting in the same period. 150 more units can be provided at a cost of $31 per unit from overtime production in period 2 and 500 from subcontracting in period 3. The next-lowest alternative is $34 from overtime in period 1 or subcontracting in period 2. At this point, we can make a judgment call as to whether our workers want overtime or whether it would be easier to subcontract out the entire amount. As shown in Table 11.2, we decide to use overtime to its full capacity of 100 units and fill the remaining demand of 250 from subcontracting.

- The unused capacity column is filled in last. All cell costs are zero. In period 2, 250 units of subcontracting capacity are available, but unused. This information is valuable because it tells us the flexibility the company has to accept additional orders.

The optimum production plan, derived from the transportation tableau, is given in the following table.[4] The values in the production plan are taken from the transportation

---

[4] For this example, our initial solution to the aggregate production problem happens to be optimal. In other cases, it may be necessary to iterate to additional transportation tableaux before an optimum solution is reached. Students unfamiliar with the transportation method should review the supplement to Chapter 9.

Period	Demand	PRODUCTION PLAN			Ending Inventory
		Regular Production	*Overtime*	*Subcontract*	
1	900	1,000	100	0	500
2	1,500	1,200	150	250	600
3	1,600	1,300	200	500	1,000
4	3,000	1,300	200	500	0
Total	7,000	4,800	650	1,250	2,100

tableau one row at a time. For example, the 1,000 units of regular production for period 1 is the sum of 600 + 300 + 100 from the second row of the transportation tableau. Ending inventory is calculated by summing beginning inventory and all forms of production for that period and then subtracting demand. For example, the ending inventory for period 1 is

$$(300 + 1,000 + 100) - 900 = 500$$

The cost of the production plan can be determined directly from the transportation tableau by multiplying the units in each cell times the cost in the corner of the cell and summing them. Alternatively, the cost can be determined from the production plan by multiplying the total units produced in each production category or held in inventory by their respective costs and summing them, as follows:

$$(4,800 \times \$20) + (650 \times \$25) + (1,250 \times \$28) + (2,100 \times \$3) = \$153,550$$

Although linear programming models will yield an optimum solution to the aggregate planning problem, there are some limitations. The relationships among variables must be linear, the model is deterministic, and only one objective is allowed (usually minimizing cost).

Other Quantitative Techniques

The **linear decision rule (LDR)** is an optimizing technique originally developed for aggregate planning in a paint factory. It solves a set of four quadratic equations that describe the major capacity-related costs in the factory: payroll costs, hiring and firing, overtime and undertime, and inventory costs. The results yield the optimal work-force level and production rate.

The **search decision rule (SDR)** is a pattern search algorithm that tries to find the minimum cost combination of various work-force levels and production rates. Any type of cost function can be used. The search is performed by computer and may involve the evaluation of thousands of possible solutions, but an optimum solution is not guaranteed. The **management coefficients model** uses regression analysis to improve the consistency of planning decisions. Techniques like SDR and management coefficients are often embedded in commercial decision support systems or expert systems for aggregate planning.

The **linear decision rule**, **search decision rule**, and **management coefficients model** use different types of cost functions to solve aggregate planning problems.

THE COMPETITIVE EDGE

What-if? Planning at John Deere & Co.

www.prenhall.com/russell

The WaterLoo, Iowa, tractor works of John Deere & Co. employs 5,000 workers in a 7.5 million-square-foot facility. More than 60,000 parts are consumed daily in the production of farm tractors. Deere uses an interactive advanced planning system analysis to level demand and fine-tune labor requirements, evaluate inventory requirements for varying customer response times, and adjust its production plan when crises occur. Through what-if analysis Deere has:

1. Found a cost-saving balance between overtime and inventory for a period of gradually increasing demand;
2. Reduced the lead time required to restock its dealers from 12 weeks to 5 weeks; and
3. Kept production going, while shipping priority items on time, during a labor strike at a parts supplier.

SOURCE: Based on "System Helps Deere & Co. Weather Market Fluctuations," *Industrial Engineering* (June 1992): 16–17.

Strategies for Managing Demand

Aggregate planning can actively *manage demand* by:

Aggregate planning can be used to "manage" demand, too.

- Shifting demand into other time periods with incentives, sales promotions, and advertising campaigns; and
- Offering product or services with countercyclical demand patterns.

Shift demand into other periods.

www.prenhall.com/russell

Winter coat specials in July, bathing-suit sales in January, early-bird discounts on dinner, lower long-distance rates in the evenings, and getaway weekends at hotels during the off-season are all attempts to shift demand into different time periods. Electric utilities are especially skilled at off-peak pricing. Promotions can also be used to extend high demand into low-demand seasons. Holiday gift buying is encouraged earlier each year, and beach resorts plan festivals in September and October to extend the season. Frito-Lay, which normally experiences a dip in sales in October, recently teamed up with Hershey to display its potato chips alongside traditional Halloween candy. The coveted display space, plus special individual-sized bags with ghoulish characters, brought October chip sales in line with the rest of the year.

The second approach to managing demand involves examining the idleness of resources and creating a demand for those resources. McDonald's offers breakfast to keep its kitchens busy during the prelunch hours, pancake restaurants serve lunch and dinner, and heating firms also sell air conditioners.

Create demand for idle resources.

An example of a firm that has done an especially good job of finding countercyclical products to smooth the load on its manufacturing facility is a small U.S. manufacturer of peanut-harvesting equipment. The company is a job shop that has general-purpose equipment, fifty highly skilled workers, and a talented engineering staff. With these flexible resources, the company can make anything its engineers can design. Inventories of finished goods are frowned upon because they represent a significant investment in funds and because the product is so large that it takes up too much storage space. Peanut-harvesting equipment is generally purchased on an as-needed basis from August to October, so during the spring and early summer, the company makes bark-scalping equipment for processing mulch and pine nuggets used by landscaping services. Demand for peanut-harvesting equipment is also affected by the weather each growing season, so during years of extensive drought, the company produces and sells irrigation equipment. The company also decided to market its products internationally with a special eye to-

A carefully planned product mix can smooth out resource requirements. Existing products or services with cyclical demand patterns may be coupled with new products or services that exhibit countercyclical patterns in demand. One common example is a company that keeps its employment levels steady by removing snow in the wintertime and maintaining lawns during the summer.

ward countries whose growing seasons are opposite to that of the United States. Thus, many of its sales are made in China and India during the very months when demand in the United States is low.

Hierarchical Planning Process

By determining a strategy for meeting and managing demand, aggregate planning provides a framework within which shorter-term production and capacity decisions

---

THE COMPETITIVE EDGE

Smoothing Out Boeing's Punishing Business Cycle

www.prenhall.com/russell

After three years of declining revenue and six years of falling employment, orders for new aircraft are rolling in faster than Boeing can deliver. New employees are being hired at the rate of more than 1,000 a month, workers have been assigned a mandatory six weeks of overtime, and the annual two-week shutdown in August has been canceled. The boom in aircraft sales can be attributed to Boeing's expertise in large-scale system integration, its innovative designs (especially the computer-designed 777 widebody), and an emerging Asian market. But the boom will go bust if Boeing can't deliver—and that depends on Boeing workers.

Boeing's ups and downs are especially rough on workers, so Boeing management is trying to improve employee relations by smoothing out its business cycle with alternative work opportunities. That's one reason Boeing bought Rockwell's aerospace assets. Space stations, satellites, and reusable rockets will likely provide a steady business when aircraft sales moderate. Boeing is also considering diversifying into information services where it holds particular expertise, such as air traffic control and reservations systems.

SOURCE: Andy Reinhardt and Seanna Browder, "Booming Boeing," *Business Week* (September 30, 1996): 119–25.

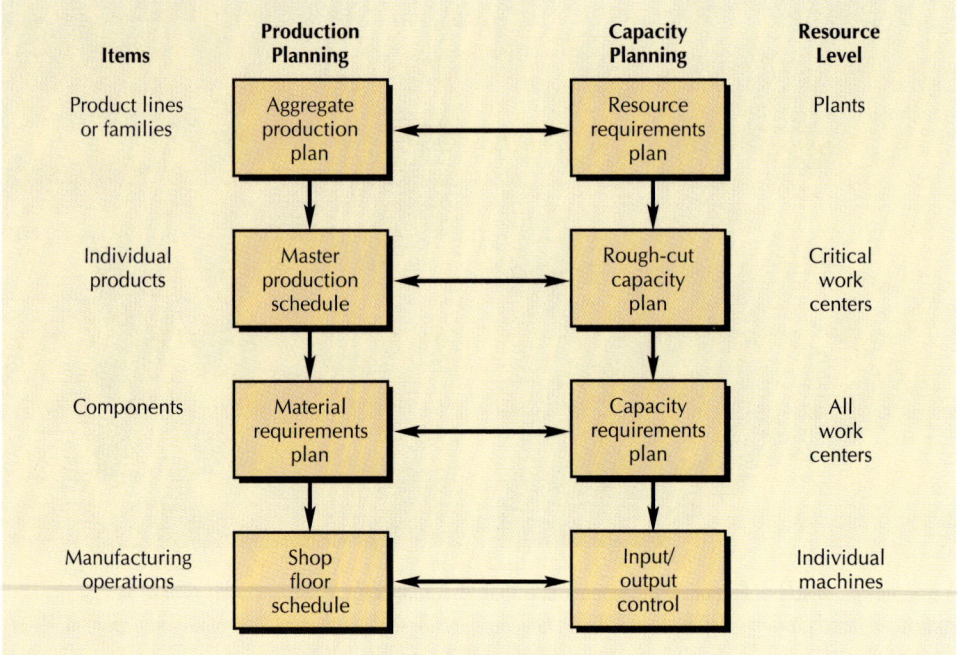

Items	Production Planning	Capacity Planning	Resource Level
Product lines or families	Aggregate production plan	Resource requirements plan	Plants
Individual products	Master production schedule	Rough-cut capacity plan	Critical work centers
Components	Material requirements plan	Capacity requirements plan	All work centers
Manufacturing operations	Shop floor schedule	Input/output control	Individual machines

FIGURE 11.5   Levels of Production and Capacity Planning

can be made. In production planning, the next level of detail is a *master production schedule,* in which weekly (not monthly or quarterly) production plans are specified by individual final product (not product line). At another level of detail, *material requirements planning* plans the production of the components that go into the final products. *Shop floor scheduling* schedules the manufacturing operations required to make each component.

In capacity planning, we might develop a *resource requirements plan,* to verify that an aggregate production plan is doable, and a *rough-cut capacity plan* as a quick check to see if the master production schedule is feasible. One level down, we would develop a much more detailed *capacity requirements plan* that matches the factory's machine and labor resources to the material requirements plan. Finally, we would use *input/output control* to monitor the production that takes place at individual machines or work centers. At each level, decisions are made within the parameters set by the higher-level decisions. The process of moving from the aggregate plan to the next level down is called **disaggregation.** Each level of production and capacity planning is shown in Figure 11.5. We discuss them more thoroughly in the Chapter 13.

> **Disaggregation** is the process of breaking an aggregate plan into more-detailed plans.

Aggregate Planning for Services

The aggregate planning process is different for services in the following ways:

1. *Most services can't be inventoried.* It is impossible to store an airline seat, hotel room, or hair appointment for use later when demand may be higher. When the goods that accompany a service can be inventoried, they typically have a very short life. Newspapers are good for only a day, flowers, at most a week, and cooked hamburgers, only ten minutes.

> Characteristics of aggregate planning for services

2. *Demand for services is difficult to predict.* Demand variations occur frequently and are often severe. The exponential distribution is commonly used to simulate the

erratic demand for services—high-demand peaks over short periods of time with long periods of low demand in between. *Customer service levels* established by management express the percentage of demand that must be met and, sometimes, how quickly demand must be met. This is an important input to aggregate planning for services.

3. *Capacity is also difficult to predict.* The variety of services offered and the individualized nature of services make capacity difficult to predict. The "capacity" of a bank teller depends on the number and type of transactions requested by the customer. Units of capacity can also vary. Should a hospital define capacity in terms of number of beds, number of patients, size of the nursing or medical staff, or number of patient hours?

4. *Service capacity must be provided at the appropriate place and time.* Many services have branches or outlets widely dispersed over a geographic region. Determining the range of services and staff levels at each location is part of aggregate planning.

5. *Labor is usually the most constraining resource for services.* This is an advantage in aggregate planning because labor is very flexible. Variations in demand can be handled by hiring temporary workers, using part-time workers, or using overtime. Summer recreation programs and theme parks hire teenagers out of school for the summer. Federal Express staffs its peak hours of midnight to 2 A.M. with area college students. McDonald's, Wal-Mart, and other retail establishments woo senior citizens as reliable part-time workers.

Workers can also be cross-trained to perform a variety of jobs and can be called upon as needed. A common example is the sales clerk who also stocks inventory. Less common are the police officers in a suburb of Detroit who are cross-trained as firefighters and paramedics.

There are several services that have unique aggregate planning problems. Doctors, lawyers, and other professionals have emergency or priority calls for their service that must be meshed with regular appointments. Hotels and airlines routinely *overbook* their capacity in anticipation of customers who do not show up. The pricing structure for different classes of customers adds an extra factor to the aggregate planning decision. Pricing structures for airlines are especially complex. As part of the aggregate planning process, planners must determine the percentage of seats or rooms to be allocated to different fare classes in order to maximize profit or yield. This process is called <u>yield management</u>

www.prenhall.com/russell
Yield management is a process for determining the percentage of seats or rooms to be allocated to different fare classes.

Summary

Capacity planning is the process of establishing the overall level of productive resources for a firm. It involves long-term strategic activities, such as the acquisition of new facilities, technologies, or businesses, that take a year or more to complete.

Capacity expansion can *lead* demand, *lag* behind demand, or meet *average* demand. The *best operating level* for a facility often includes a *capacity cushion* for unexpected occurrences. The tendency of high levels of output to cost less per unit is known as *economies of scale*. This normally holds true up to a certain level of output, at which point *diseconomies of scale* can take over.

Aggregate production planning does the following:

- Determines the resource capacity needed to meet demand
- Matches market demand to company resources
- Plans production six to twelve months in advance
- Expresses demand, resources, and capacity in general terms

■ Develops a strategy for economically meeting demand

■ Establishes a company-wide game plan for allocating resources

Aggregate planning is trivial in companies where demand is stable or resources are abundant, but it is critical for companies with seasonal demand patterns and for most services. Although there are several mathematical techniques for aggregate planning, practitioners prefer the trial-and-error approach using spreadsheets and what-if? analysis.

Production and capacity plans are developed at several levels of detail. The process of deriving more detailed production and capacity plans from the aggregate plan is called *disaggregation.*

Aggregate planning for services is somewhat different than for manufacturing because the variation in demand is usually more severe and occurs over shorter time frames. Fortunately, the constraining resource in most services is labor, which is quite flexible. Services use a lot of part-time workers, overtime, and undertime.

Summary of Key Terms

aggregate production planning (APP): the process of determining the quantity and timing of production over an intermediate time frame.

best operating level: the percent of capacity utilization at which unit costs are lowest.

capacity cushion: a percent of capacity held in reserve for unexpected occurrences.

capacity planning: a long-term strategic decision that establishes the overall level of productive resources for a firm.

chase demand: an aggregate planning strategy that schedules production to match demand and absorbs variations in demand by adjusting the size of the work force.

disaggregation: the process of breaking down the aggregate plan into more detailed plans.

diseconomies of scale: when higher levels of output cost more per unit to produce.

economies of scale: when higher levels of output cost less per unit to produce.

level production: an aggregate planning strategy that produces units at a constant rate and uses inventory to absorb variations in demand.

linear decision rule (LDR): a mathematical technique that solves a set of four quadratic equations to determine the optimal work-force size and production rate.

management coefficients model: an aggregate planning technique that uses regression analysis to improve the consistency of production planning decisions.

mixed strategy: an aggregate planning strategy that varies two or more capacity factors to determine a feasible production plan.

pure strategy: an aggregate planning strategy that varies only one capacity factor in determining a feasible production plan.

search decision rule (SDR): a pattern search algorithm for aggregate planning.

yield management: a term used in the airline and hotel industries to describe the process of determining the percentage of seats or rooms to be allocated to different fare classes.

Solved Problem

Vultex Fibers produces a line of sweatclothes that exhibits a varying demand pattern. Given the following demand forecasts, production costs, and constraints, design a production plan for Vultex using the transportation method of LP. Also, calculate the cost of the production plan.

Period	Demand
September	100
October	130
November	200
December	300

Maximum regular production	100 units/month
Maximum overtime production	50 units/month
Maximum subcontracting	50 units/month
Regular production costs	$10/unit
Overtime production costs	$25/unit
Subcontracting costs	$35/unit
Inventory holding costs	$5/unit/month
Beginning inventory	0

Solution:

PERIOD OF PRODUCTION		PERIOD OF USE				Unused Capacity	Capacity
		1	2	3	4		
	Beginning Inventory	[0] —	[5] —	[10] —	[15] —	[0]	0
1	Regular	100 [10]	— [15]	— [20]	— [25]	[0]	100
	Overtime	[25]	[30]	[35]	50 [40]	[0]	50
	Subcontract	[35]	[40]	[45]	[50]	50 [0]	50
2	Regular		100 [10]	— [15]	— [20]	[0]	100
	Overtime		30 [25]	20 [30]	— [35]	[0]	50
	Subcontract		[35]	[40]	30 [45]	20 [0]	50
3	Regular			100 [10]	— [15]	[0]	100
	Overtime			50 [25]	— [30]	[0]	50
	Subcontract			30 [35]	20 [40]	[0]	50
4	Regular				100 [10]	[0]	100
	Overtime				50 [25]	[0]	50
	Subcontract				50 [35]	[0]	50
	Demand	100	130	200	300		

| Period | Demand | PRODUCTION PLAN | | | Ending Inventory |
		Regular Production	Overtime	Subcontract	
Sept	100	100	50	0	50
Oct	130	100	50	30	100
Nov	200	100	50	50	100
Dec	300	100	50	50	0
Total	730	400	200	130	250

$$\text{Cost} = (400 \times \$10) + (200 \times \$25) + (130 \times \$35) + (250 \times \$5)$$
$$= 4{,}000 + 5{,}000 + 4{,}550 + 1{,}250$$
$$= \$14{,}800$$

Questions

11-1. Why is capacity planning strategically important?

11-2. Describe three strategies for expanding capacity.

11-3. What are the advantages and disadvantages of incremental versus one-step expansion?

11-4. Explain economies and diseconomies of scale. Give an example of each.

11-5. What is the purpose of aggregate production planning?

11-6. When is aggregate production planning most useful?

11-7. List several alternatives for adjusting capacity.

11-8. What is the difference between a pure and a mixed strategy?

11-9. Describe the output of aggregate production planning.

11-10. How do the following techniques differ in terms of the types of cost functions used and the type of solution produced?
   a. Linear programming
   b. Linear decision rule
   c. Search decision rule
   d. Management coefficients model

11-11. Identify several industries that have highly variable demand patterns. Explore how they adjust capacity.

11-12. What options are available for altering the capacity of each of the following?
   a. An elementary school
   b. A prison
   c. An airline

11-13. Discuss the advantages and disadvantages of the following strategies for meeting demand:
   a. Use part-time workers.
   b. Subcontract work.
   c. Build up and deplete inventory.

11-14. Discuss several strategies for managing demand. Give an example of those you personally have experienced.

11-15. Describe the levels of production and capacity planning in the disaggregation process.

11-16. How is the aggregate planning process different when used for services rather than for manufacturing?

11-17. Explore capacity planning at your university or place of business. How is capacity measured? What factors influence the acquisition and allocation of resources?

Problems

11-1. The Wetski Water Ski Company is the world's largest producer of water skis. As you might suspect, water skis exhibit a highly seasonal demand pattern, with peaks during the summer months and valleys during the winter months. Given the following costs and quarterly sales forecasts, use the transportation method to design a production plan that will economically meet demand. What is the cost of the plan?

Quarter	Sales Forecast
1	50,000
2	150,000
3	200,000
4	52,000

Inventory carrying cost	$3.00 per pair of skis per quarter
Production per employee	1,000 pairs of skis per quarter
Regular work force	50 workers
Overtime capacity	50,000 pairs of skis
Subcontracting capacity	40,000 pairs of skis
Cost of regular production	$50 per pair of skis
Cost of overtime production	$75 per pair of skis
Cost of subcontracting	$85 per pair of skis

11-2. The CEO of Wetski Water Ski from the previous problem, has decided to forego the company's policy of guaranteed employment. Assume the cost of hiring and firing workers is $100 per worker hired and $400 per worker fired. Try level production and chase demand production strategies. If necessary, allow backordering at $10 per pair of skis per quarter. Which production plan more economically meets demand?

11-3. Rowley Apparel, manufacturer of the famous "Race-A-Rama" swimwear line, needs help planning production for next year. Demand for swimwear follows a seasonal pattern, as shown here. Given the following costs and demand forecasts, test these three strategies for meeting demand: (a) level production with overtime and subcontracting, (b) level production with backorders as needed, (c) chase demand, and (d) 3,000 units regular production from April through September and as much regular, overtime, and subcontracting production in the other months as needed to meet annual demand. Determine the cost of each strategy. Which strategy would you recommend?

Month	Demand Forecast
January	1,000
February	500
March	500
April	2,000
May	3,000
June	4,000
July	5,000
August	3,000
September	1,000
October	500
November	500
December	3,000

Beginning work force	8 workers
Subcontracting capacity	unlimited
Overtime capacity	3,000 units/month
Production rate per worker	250 units/period
Regular wage rate	$15 per unit
Overtime wage rate	$25 per unit
Subcontracting cost	$30 per unit
Hiring cost	$100 per worker
Firing cost	$200 per worker
Holding cost	$0.50 per unit/period
Backordering cost	$10 per unit/period
No beginning inventory	

11-4. In Problem 11-3, assume increasing the work force costs $2,000 per worker, decreasing the work force $3,000 per worker, and backordering is $25 per unit per period. Which strategy is the best now?

11-5. In Problem 11-3, suppose the market for Race-A-Rama swimwear has increased 2,000 units per month. Consider these three strategies: (a) level production at 3,000 units with overtime and subcontracting, (b) level production at 4,000 units with backorders, and (c) chase demand. Which strategy would you recommend?

11-6. College Press publishes textbooks for the college market. The demand for college textbooks is high during the beginning of each semester and then tapers off during the semester. The unavailability of books can cause a professor to switch adoptions, but the cost of storing books and their rapid obsolescence must also be considered. Given the demand and cost factors shown here, use the transportation method to design an aggregate production plan for College Press that will economically meet demand. What is the cost of the production plan?

Months	Demand Forecast
February–April	5,000
May–July	10,000
August–October	30,000
November–January	25,000

Regular capacity per quarter	10,000 books
Overtime capacity per quarter	5,000 books
Subcontracting capacity per qtr	10,000 books
Regular production rate	$20 per book
Overtime wage rate	$30 per book
Subcontracting cost	$35 per book
Holding cost	$2.00 per book
No beginning inventory	

11-7. Mama's Stuffin' is a popular food item during the fall and winter months, but it is marginal in the spring and summer. Use the following demand forecasts and costs to determine which of the following production planning strategies is best for Mama's Stuffin':
   a. Level production over the twelve months. Supplement with overtime as necessary.
   b. Produce to meet demand each month. Absorb variations in demand by changing the size of the work force.
   c. Keep the work force at its current level. Allow variations in demand to be absorbed by inventory, overtime, and subcontracting.

Month	Demand Forecast
March	2,000
April	1,000
May	1,000
June	1,000
July	1,000
August	1,500
September	2,500
October	3,000
November	9,000
December	7,000
January	4,000
February	3,000

No backordering	
Overtime capacity per month	regular production
Subcontracting capacity per month	unlimited
Regular production cost	$30 per pallet
Overtime production cost	$40 per pallet
Subcontracting cost	$50 per pallet
Holding cost	$2 per pallet
No beginning inventory	
Beginning work force	10 workers
Production rate	200 pallets per worker per month
Hiring cost	$5,000 per worker
Firing cost	$8,000 per worker

11-8. Quik-Fix Tax Service prepares taxes for customers year round. However, demand is heaviest during March, April, and May. Quik-Fix increases its work force several times over during those months and uses as much overtime (half of the regular time) as is available. In rare cases, Quik-Fix subcontracts out some work, but that practice really eats into profits. The average cost to prepare a customer's taxes is $50. Customers whose taxes are completed late pay $10 less per month late. Use the following data to help Quik-Fix design an economical service strategy.

Month	Demand Forecast
January	1,000
February	1,000
March	3,000
April	10,000
May	5,000
June	600
July	600
August	500
September	500
October	600
November	600
December	600

Regular preparation cost	$50 per customer
Overtime preparation cost	$75 per customer
Subcontracting cost	$100 per customer
Backordering cost	$10 per customer per month
No inventory allowed	
Hiring cost	$500 per worker
Firing cost	$500 per worker
Beginning work force	2 workers
Preparation rate	200 customers per worker per month

11-9. Marc Klein is a manufacturer of rock-climbing equipment in Bohn, Germany. Demand for each of Marc's four product lines has been steady in recent months; however, government caps on worker hours threaten to slow down production. Marc's data on forecasted demand, labor requirements, and profit for each product line is shown. Marc estimates that his twenty-seven workers will be able to work a maximum of 1,080 hours per week, or 4,320 hours per month.

Product Line	Monthly Demand	Labor Required per Unit	Profit per Unit
Safety rope	200 units	15 hours	$30
Safety harness	100 units	20 hours	$25
Gloves	400 units	2 hours	$ 5
Shoes	300 units	10 hours	$50

a. What is the maximum profit Marc can earn per month, assuming he has the capacity to meet the monthly demand?
b. How much profit per month does Marc expect to lose with the new regulations?
c. What product mix will maximize profit should the work-hour restrictions be put into effect?

11-10. Ollie Auto Company is a small manufacturer of cars, vans, and trucks in Eastern Europe. Demand for each of Ollie's three product lines has been healthy in recent months, but an impending labor strike threatens to slow down production. Ollie's data on forecasted demand, labor requirements, and profit for each product line are shown here. He estimates that even if the workers strike next month, the company can maintain a core of 19 workers, giving a maximum of 760 hours per week, or 3,040 hours per month. Ollie has been studying capitalism and has decided that if the strike occurs, he will absorb the reduced labor hours by decreasing production of those product lines that yield the least profit.

a. Generate a new production plan using Ollie's logic.
b. How much projected profit will be lost next month with Ollie's production plan if the strike materializes?
c. Given that Ollie cannot possibly sell more than the demand forecast, design a production plan that will maximize profits during the strike.

Product Line	Monthly Demand	Labor Required per Unit	Profit per Unit
Cars	500 units	6 hours	$1,000
Vans	100 units	4 hours	$ 500
Trucks	200 units	2 hours	$ 400

CASE PROBLEM

An Aggregate Plan for Darian's Gymnastics Center

Darian's Gymnastics Center has been extremely successful in its first two years of operation. During peak demand, 500 youngsters per week are taught gymnastics from fundamentals to level 8 competition. Initially, Darian and Anita (his wife and partner) concentrated on generating enough demand for classes to keep their investment solvent. Now, they find themselves bursting at the seams, but only during the last half of the day. Anita does all the hiring and scheduling of employees and classes. She describes her dilemma as follows:

■ Most of our students are school-age, so our classes are scheduled from 4:00 P.M. to 9:00 P.M. weekdays and 8:00 A.M. to 6:00 P.M. on Saturdays. The gym is crowded during those times and even though we maintain an 8 to 1 ratio of teachers to students, parents seem bothered by the current level of activity. I'd like to see no more than five classes using the gym at any one time.

■ Most of our instructors are college students who have top-notch skills and identify well with the children. However, because of their age and other responsibilities, turnover is high. This is not popular with parents. It's hard on me, too.

■ We currently have around twenty individuals in each of our three competitive programs: women's gymnastics team, men's gymnastics team, and preteam. The competitive programs are based on a ten-month contract, with charges of $200/month, $100/month, and $100/month, respectively. The preteam and men's team practice for five hours a week, and the women's team practices ten hours a week. These programs provide financial stability for the center and are the basis for our reputation and, thus, class enrollments. However, the center cannot survive on competitive programs alone. The recreational programs "feed" the competitive programs and generate a lot of excitement at the center and in the community. I'd like to maintain at least our current level of enrollment. Several "Romp and Run" facilities (basically indoor playsets) have recently opened up in the city that take customers away from us.

■ Students sign up for the recreational program

(Continued)

in six-week blocks of time. Each class meets for an hour once a week. The classes are broken up into beginners, intermediates, and advanced. Within each level, there are boys and girls classes, classes grouped by age, and accelerated classes. The fee per six-week class is $60. Our enrollment is steady throughout the year. The center is not air conditioned, so we teach few classes over the summer. We're basically closed down during July and August.

■ Full time is forty hours per week. Part-time employees generally work thirty hours a week, although some work as few as ten hours a week. I would like to staff the center with a core of full-time people and supplement with part-timers.

■ I need some ideas for utilizing the center better and generating more revenue. I really don't know how to evaluate the trade-offs between expanding the competitive program and expanding the recreational program. We could easily take twenty more students in each team category, but I'm not sure that would be wise.

1. Calculate the capacity of Darian's gymnastics Center in terms of student hours. How close is the center to capacity?

2. Should Anita accept more team members? Expand the number of recreational classes? Recommend avenues for increasing capacity and revenue.

3. What staffing pattern should Anita use?

References

Bowman, E. H. "Production Planning by the Transportation Method of Linear Programming." *Journal of Operations Research Society* (February 1956): 100–103.

Bowman, E. H. "Consistency and Optimality in Managerial Decision Making." *Management Science* (January 1963): 310–21.

Buffa, E. S., and J. G. Miller. *Production-Inventory Systems: Planning and Control,* 3d ed. Homewood, Ill.: Irwin, 1979.

Holt, C., F. Modigliani, J. Muth, and H. Simon. *Planning Production, Inventories and Work Force.* Englewood Cliffs, N.J.: Prentice Hall, 1960.

Murdick, R., B. Render, and R. Russell. *Service Operations Management.* Boston: Allyn and Bacon, 1990.

Taubert, W. "A Search Decision Rule for the Aggregate Scheduling Problem." *Management Science* (February 1968): B343–59.

Tersine, R. *Production/Operations Management: Concepts, Structure, and Analysis.* New York: Elsevier-North Holland, 1985.

Vollmann, T., W. Berry, and D. C. Whybark. *Manufacturing Planning and Control Systems,* 3d ed. Homewood, Ill.: Irwin, 1994.

11

Operational Decision-Making Tools: Linear Programming

*I*n a series of five-year surveys conducted by the Operations Research Society of America (ORSA), linear programming consistently ranked as the most useful of the quantitative techniques used by businesses and industry practitioners.[1] It has been used, for example, by virtually all major companies in the petroleum industry from the mid-1950s to the present for problems such as blending gasoline and scheduling refineries.[2]

Linear programming is used to determine a level of operational activity in order to achieve an objective, subject to restrictions. Many decisions faced by an operations manager are centered around the best way to achieve the objectives of the firm subject to the restrictions of the operating environment. These restrictions can be limited resources, such as time, labor, energy, materials, or money, or they can be restrictive guidelines, such as a recipe for making cereal, engineering specifications, or a blend for gasoline. The most frequent objective of business firms is to *maximize profit*—whereas the objective of individual operational units within a firm (such as a production or packaging department) is often to *minimize cost*.

A common linear programming problem is to determine the number of units to produce to maximize profit subject to resource constraints such as labor and materials. All these components of the decision situation—the decisions, objectives, and constraints—are expressed as mathematically linear relationships that together form a model.

> **Linear programming** is a model consisting of linear relationships representing a firm's objective and resource constraints.

Model Formulation

A linear programming model consists of decision variables, an objective function, and model constraints. **Decision variables** are mathematical symbols that represent levels of activity of an operation. For example, an electrical manufacturing firm wants to produce radios, toasters, and clocks. The number of each item to produce is represented by symbols, x_1, x_2, and x_3. Thus x_1 = the number of radios, x_2 = the number of toasters, and x_3 = the number of clocks. The final values of x_1, x_2, and x_3, as determined by the firm, constitute a *decision* (e.g., $x_1 = 10$ radios is a decision by the firm to produce 10 radios).

> **Decision variables** are mathematical symbols representing levels of activity of an operation.

The **objective function** is a linear mathematical relationship that describes the objective of an operation in terms of the decision variables. The objective function always either *maximizes* or *minimizes* some value (e.g., maximizing the profit or minimizing the cost of producing radios). For example, if the profit from a radio is $6, the profit from a toaster is $4, and the profit from a clock is $2, then the total profit, Z, is $Z = \$6x_1 + 4x_2 + 2x_3$.

> The **objective function** is a linear relationship reflecting the objective of an operation.

The model **constraints** are also linear relationships of the decision variables; they represent the restrictions placed on the decision situation by the operating environment. The restrictions can be in the form of limited resources or restrictive guidelines. For example, if it requires 2 hours of labor to produce a radio, 1 hour to produce a toaster, and 1.5 hours to produce a clock, and only 40 hours of labor are available, the constraint reflecting this is $2x_1 + 1x_2 + 1.5x_3 \leq 40$.

> A **constraint** is a linear relationship representing a restriction on decision making.

The general structure of a linear programming model is as follows:

$$\text{Maximize (or minimize) } Z = c_1x_1 + c_2x_2 + \cdots + c_nx_n$$

[1] M. S. Lane, A. H. Mansow, and J. L. Harpell, "Operations Research Techniques: A Longitudinal Update 1973–1988," *Interfaces* 23, no. 2 (March–April 1993): 63–68.

[2] C. E. Bodington and T. E. Baker, "A History of Mathematical Programming in the Petroleum Industry," *Interfaces* 20, no. 4 (July–August 1990): 117–27.

THE COMPETITIVE EDGE

Determining Gasoline Blends with Linear Programming at Texaco

The petroleum industry first began using linear programming to solve gasoline blending problems in the 1950s. A single grade of gasoline can be a blend of from three to ten different components. A typical refinery might have as many as 20 different components it blends into four or more grades of gasoline. Each grade of gasoline differs according to octane level, volatility, and area marketing requirements.

www.prenhall.com/russell

At Texaco, for example, the typical gasoline blends are Power and unleaded regular, Plus, and Power Premium. These different grades are blended from a variety of available stocks that are intermediate refinery products such as distilled gasoline, reformate gasoline, and catalytically cracked gasoline. Additives include, among other things, lead and other octane enhancers. As many as 15 stocks can be blended to yield up to eight different blends. The properties or attributes of a blend are determined by a combination of properties that exist in the gasoline stocks and those of any additives. Examples of stock properties (that originally emanated from crude oil) include to some extent vapor pressure, sulfur content, aromatic content, and octane value, among other items. A linear programming model determines the volume of each blend subject to constraints for stock availability, demand, and the property (or attribute) specifications for each blend. A single blend may have up to 14 different characteristics. In a typical blend analysis involving seven input stocks and four blends, the problem will include 40 variable and 71 constraints.

SOURCES: C. E. Bodington and T. E. Baker, "A History of Mathematical Programming in the Petroleum Industry," *Interfaces* 20, no. 4 (July–August 1990): 117–27; and C. W. DeWitt et al., "OMEGA: An Improved Gasoline Blending System for Texaco," *Interfaces* 19, no. 1 (January–February 1989): 85–101.

subject to

$$a_{11}x_1 + a_{12}x_2 + \cdots + a_{1n}x_n \ (\leq, =, \geq) \ b_1$$
$$a_{21}x_1 + a_{22}x_2 + \cdots + a_{2n}x_n \ (\leq, =, \geq) \ b_2$$
$$\vdots$$
$$a_{n1}x_1 + a_{n2}x_2 + \cdots + a_{nn}x_n \ (\leq, =, \geq) \ b_n$$
$$x_i \geq 0$$

where

$$x_i = \text{decision variables}$$
$$b_i = \text{constraint levels}$$
$$c_j = \text{objective function coefficients}$$
$$a_{ij} = \text{constraint coefficients}$$

EXAMPLE S11.1

Linear Programming Model Formulation

The Beaver Creek Pottery Company is a small craft operation run by a Native American tribal council. The company employs artisans to produce clay bowls and mugs with authentic Native American designs and colors. The two primary resources used by the company are special pottery clay and skilled labor. Given these limited resources, the company wants to know how many bowls and mugs to produce each day to maximize profit.

The two products have the following resource requirements for production and selling price per item produced (i.e., the model parameters).

(Continued)

PRODUCT	RESOURCE REQUIREMENTS		
	Labor *(h/unit)*	*Clay* *(lb/unit)*	*Revenue* *($/unit)*
Bowl	1	4	40
Mug	2	3	50

There are 40 hours of labor and 120 pounds of clay available each day. Formulate this problem as a liner programming model.

SOLUTION:

Management's decision is how many bowls and mugs to produce represented by the following decision variables.

x_1 = number of bowls to produce

x_2 = number of mugs to produce

The objective of the company is to maximize total revenue computed as the sum of the individual profits gained from each bowl and mug:

Maximize $Z = \$40x_1 + 50x_2$

The model contains the constraints for labor and clay which are

$x_1 + 2x_2 \le 40$ hr

$4x_1 + 3x_2 \le 120$ lb

The less than or equal to inequality ($\le$) is used instead of an equality ($=$) because 40 hours of labor is a maximum that *can be used*, not an amount that *must be used*. However, constraints can be equalities ($=$), greater than or equal to inequalities ($\ge$), or less than or equal to inequalities ($\le$).

The complete linear programming model for this problem can now be summarized as follows:

Maximize $Z = \$40x_1 + \$50x_2$

subject to

$1x_1 + 2x_2 \le 40$

$4x_1 + 3x_2 \le 120$

$x_1, x_2 \ge 0$

The solution of this model will result in numerical values for x_1 and x_2 that maximize total profit, Z, without violating the constraints. The solution that achieves this objective is $x_1 = 24$ bowls and $x_2 = 8$ mugs, with a corresponding revenue of $1,360. We will discuss how we determined these values next.

A picture of how a solution is obtained for a linear programming model

Graphical Solution Method

The linear programming model in the previous section has characteristics common to all linear programming models. The mathematical relationships are additive; the model parameters are assumed to be known with certainty; the variable values are continuous (not restricted to integers); and the relationships are linear. Because of linearity, models with two decision variables (corresponding to two dimensions) can be solved graphically. Although graphical solution is cumbersome, it is useful in that it provides a picture of how a solution is derived.

The basic steps in the **graphical solution method** are to plot the model constraints on a set of coordinates in a plane and identify the area on the graph that satisfies all the constraints simultaneously. The point on the boundary of this space that maximizes (or minimizes) the objective function is the solution. The following example illustrates these steps.

> The **graphical solution method** is a method for solving a linear programming problem using a graph.

EXAMPLE
S11.2

Graphical Solution

Determine the solution for Beaver Creek Pottery Company in Example S11.1:

Maximize $Z = \$40x_1 + \$50x_2$

subject to

$x_1 + 2x_2 \le 40$

$4x_1 + 3x_2 \le 120$

$x_1, x_2 \ge 0$

SOLUTION:

The graph of the model constraints are shown in the following figure of the feasible solution space. The graph is produced in the positive quadrant since both decision variables must be positive or zero, that is, $x_1, x_2 \ge 0$.

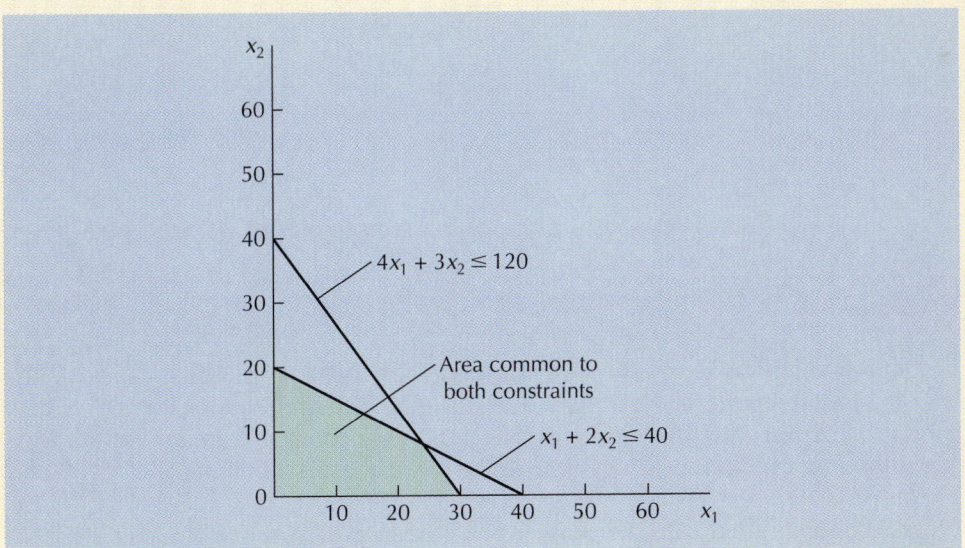

The first step is to plot the constraints on the graph. This is done by treating both constraints as equations (or straight lines) and plotting each line on the graph. A simple way to plot a line is to determine where it intersects the horizontal and vertical axes and draw a straight line connecting the points. The shaded area in the figure

(Continued)

above is the area that is common to both model constraints. Therefore, this is the only area on the graph that contains points (i.e., values for x_1 and x_2) that will satisfy both constraints simultaneously. This area is the **feasible solution space**, because it is the only area that contains values for the variables that are feasible, or do not violate the constraints.

The second step in the graphical solution method is to locate the point in the feasible solution area that represents the greatest total revenue. We will plot the objective function line for an *arbitrarily* selected level of revenue. For example, if revenue, Z, is $800, the objective function is

$$\$800 = 40x_1 + 50x_2$$

Plotting this line just as we plotted the constraint lines results in the graph showing the determination of the optimal point in the following figure. Every point on this line is in the feasible solution area and will result in a revenue of $800 (i.e., every combination of x_1 and x_2 on this line will give a Z value of $800). As the value of Z increases, the objective function line moves out through the feasible solution space away from the origin until it reaches the last feasible point on the boundary of the solution space and then leaves the solution space.

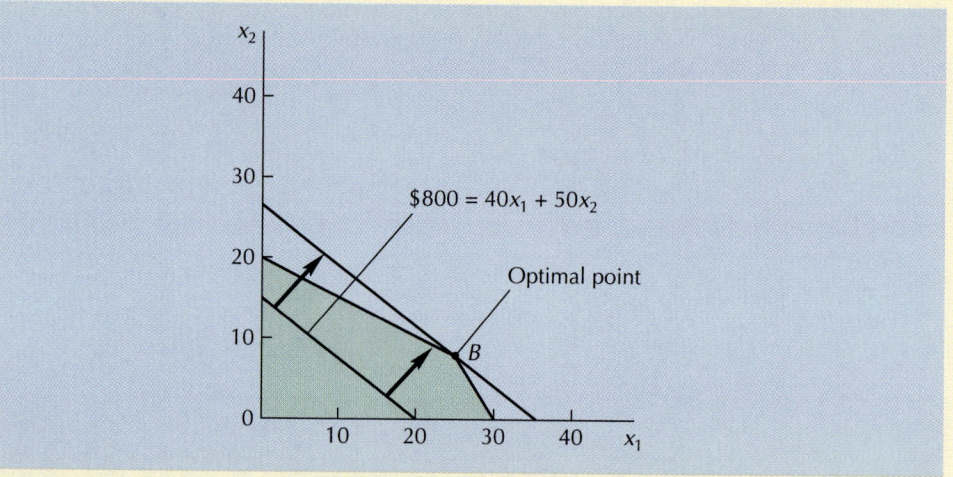

The solution point is always on this boundary, because the boundary contains the points farthest from the origin (i.e., the points corresponding to the greatest profit). Moreover, the solution point will not only be on the boundary of the feasible solution area, but it will be at one of the *corners* of the boundary where two constraint lines intersect. These corners (labeled A, B, and C in the following figure) are protrusions called **extreme points**. It has been proven mathematically that the optimal solution in a linear programming model will always occur at an extreme point. Therefore, in our example problem, the possible solution points are limited to the three extreme points, A, B, and C. The **optimal**, or "one best," **solution** point is B, since the objective function touches it last before it leaves the feasible solution area.

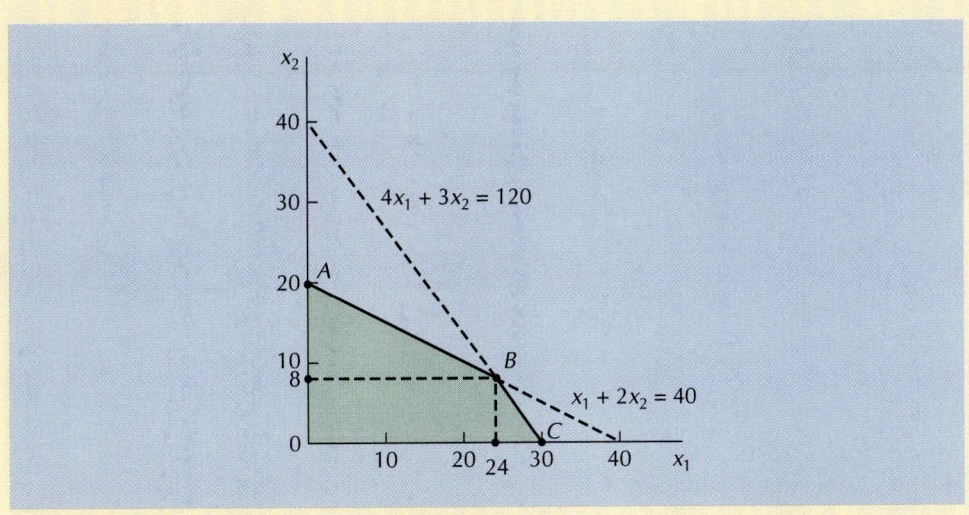

Because point *B* is formed by the intersection of two constraint lines, these two lines are *equal* at point *B*. Thus, the values of x_1 and x_2 at that intersection can be found by solving the two equations *simultaneously*:

$$x_1 + 2x_2 = 40$$
$$\underline{4x_1 + 3x_2 = 120}$$
$$4x_1 + 8x_2 = 160$$
$$\underline{-4x_1 - 3x_2 = -120}$$
$$5x_2 = 40$$
$$x_2 = 8$$

Thus

$$x_1 + 2(8) = 40$$
$$x_1 = 24$$

The optimal solution at point *B* in the figure above is $x_1 = 24$ bowls and $x_2 = 8$ mugs. Substituting these values into the objective function gives the maximum revenue,

$$Z = \$40(24) + \$50(8)$$
$$Z = \$1,360$$

Given that the optimal solution will be at one of the extreme corner points *A*, *B*, or *C*, you can find the solution by testing each of the three points to see which results in the greatest revenue rather than by graphing the objective function and seeing which point it last touches as it moves out of the feasible solution area. The figure below shows the solution values for all three points *A*, *B*, and *C* and the amount of revenue, *Z*, at each point.

(Continued)

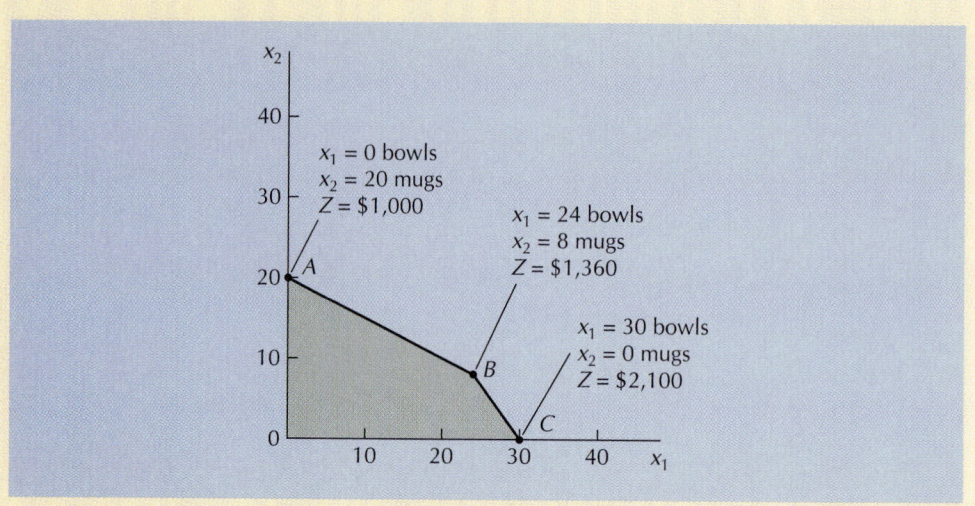

The objective function determines which extreme point is optimal, because the objective function designates the revenue that will accrue from each combination of x_1 and x_2 values at the extreme points. If the objective function had had different coefficients (i.e., different x_1 and x_2 profit values), one of the extreme points other than B might have been optimal.

Assume for a moment that the revenue for a bowl is $70 instead of $40 and the revenue for a mug is $20 instead of $50. These values result in a new objective function, $Z = \$70x_1 + 20x_2$. If the model constraints for labor or clay are not changed, the feasible solution area remains the same, as shown in the figure below. However, the location of the objective function in this figure is different from that of the original objective function in the previous figure because the new profit coefficients give the linear objective function a new *slope*. Point C becomes optimal, with $Z = \$2,100$. This demonstrates one of the useful functions of linear programming—and model analysis in general—called *sensitivity analysis*: the testing of changes in the model parameters reflecting different operating environments to analyze the impact on the solution.

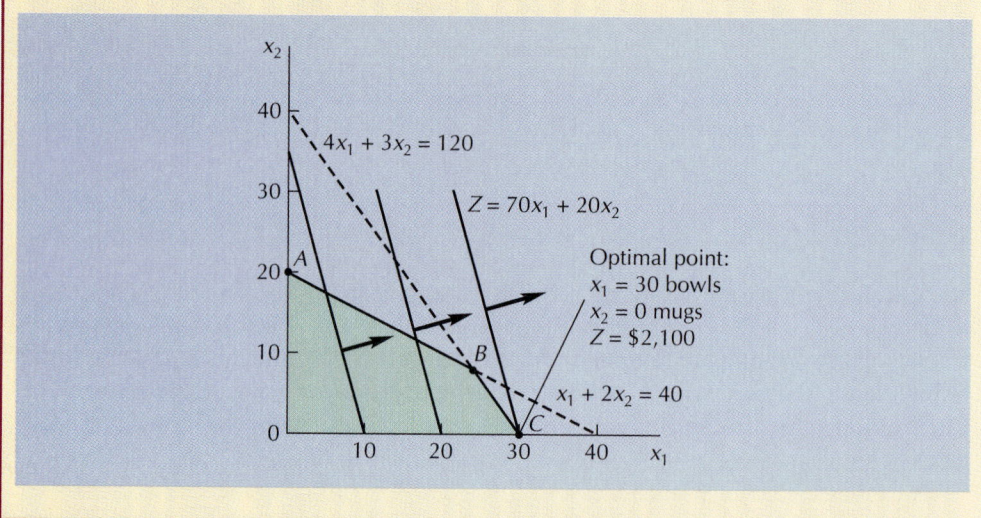

Format for Model Solution
The Simplex Method

Graphically determining the solution to a linear programming model can provide insight into how a solution is derived, but it is not generally effective or efficient. The traditional mathematical approach for solving a linear programming problem is a mathematical procedure called the **simplex method.** In the simplex method, the model is put into the form of a table, and then a number of mathematical steps are performed on the table. These mathematical steps are the same as moving from one extreme point on the solution boundary to another. However, unlike the graphical method, in which we simply searched through *all* the solution points to find the best one, the simplex method moves from one *better* solution to another until the best one is found.

The simplex method for solving linear programming problems is based, at least partially, on the solution of simultaneous equations and matrix algebra. In this supplement on linear programming we are not going to provide a detailed presentation of the simplex method. It is a mathematically cumbersome approach that is very time-consuming even for very small problems of two or three variables and a few constraints. It includes a number of mathematical steps and requires numerous arithmetic computations, which frequently result in simple arithmetic errors when done by hand. Instead, we will demonstrate how linear programming problems are solved on the computer. Depending on the software used, the computer solution to a linear programming problem may be in the same form as a simplex solution. As such, we will review the procedures for setting up a linear programming model in the simplex format for solution.

> The **simplex method** is a mathematical procedure for solving a linear programming problem according to a set of steps.

Converting Model Constraints

Recall that the solution to a linear programming problem occurs at an extreme point where constraint equation lines intersect with each other or with the axis. Thus, the model constraints must all be in the form of *equations* ($=$) rather than inequalities ($\geq$ or $\leq$).

The procedure for transforming $\leq$ inequality constraints into equations is by adding a new variable, called a **slack variable,** to each constraint. For the Beaver Creek Pottery Company, the addition of a unique slack variable (s_i) to each of the constraint inequalities results in the following equations:

$$x_1 + 2x_2 + s_1 = 40 \text{ hours of labor}$$
$$4x_1 + 3x_2 + s_2 = 120 \text{ lb of clay}$$

> A **slack variable** is a variable representing unused resources added to a $\leq$ constraint to make it an equality.

The slack variables, s_1 and s_2, will take on any value necessary to make the left-hand side of the equation equal to the right-hand side. If slack variables have a value in the solution, they generally represent unused resources. Since unused resources would contribute nothing to total revenue, they have a coefficient of zero in the objective function:

$$\text{Maximize } Z = \$40x_1 + 50x_2 + 0s_1 + 0s_2$$

The graph in Figure S11.1 shows all the solution points in our Beaver Creek Pottery Company example with the values for decision *and* slack variables. This example is a maximization problem with all $\leq$ constraints. A minimization problem with $\geq$ and $=$ constraints requires several different adjustments.

First, with a $\geq$ constraint, instead of adding a slack variable, we subtract a **surplus variable.** Whereas a slack variable is added and reflects unused resources, a surplus vari-

> A **surplus variable** is a variable representing an excess above a resource requirement that is subtracted from a $\geq$ constraint to make it an equality.

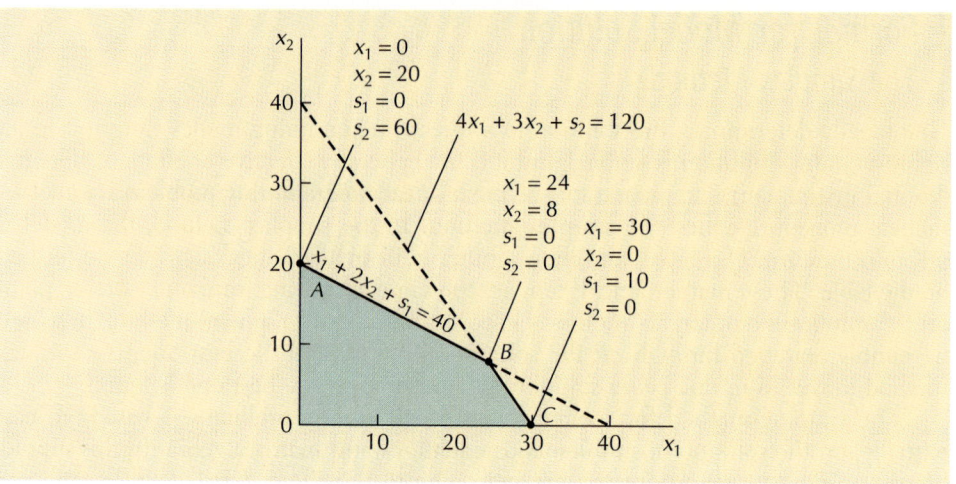

FIGURE S11.1   Solutions at Extreme Points

able is subtracted and reflects the excess above a minimum resource-requirement level. Like the slack variable, a surplus variable is represented symbolically by s_i and must be nonnegative. For example, consider the following constraint:

$$2x_1 + 4x_2 \geq 16$$

Subtracting a surplus variable results in

$$2x_1 + 4x_2 - s_1 = 16$$

However, the simplex method requires that the initial basic feasible solution be at the origin, where x_1 and $x_2 = 0$. Testing these solution values, we have

$$2x_1 + 4x_2 - s_1 = 16$$
$$2(0) + 4(0) - s_1 = 16$$
$$s_1 = -16$$

The idea of negative resources is illogical and violates the nonnegativity restriction of linear programming.

An *artificial variable* is a variable added to a constraint to give it a positive solution at the origin.

In order to alleviate this difficulty and get a solution at the origin, we add an *artificial variable* (A_i) to the constraint equation:

$$2x_1 + 4x_2 - s_1 + A_1 = 16$$

The artificial variable, A_1, does not have a meaning, as a slack variable or a surplus variable does. It is inserted into the equation simply to give a positive solution at the origin where all other values are zero.

$$2x_1 + 4x_2 - s_1 + A_1 = 16$$
$$2(0) + 4(0) - 0 + A_1 = 16$$
$$A_1 = 16$$

All variables in a linear programming model must be included in the objective function. Thus, whenever an artificial variable is added to a $\geq$ constraint, it must also be included in the model objective function. However, an artificial variable cannot be assigned a profit (or cost) value equal to zero, as would be the case with a slack or surplus variable. Assigning a value of 0 to an artificial variable in the objective function would not prohibit it from being in the final optimal solution. However, if the artificial variable appeared in the solution, it would render the final solution meaningless, since an artificial variable has no meaning. Therefore, we must ensure that an artificial variable is *not* in the final solution. We can prohibit a variable from being in the final solution by assigning it a large negative profit in a maximization problem or a large cost in a minimization problem. Rather than assigning a dollar cost or profit to an artificial variable, the convention is to assign a value of M, representing a very large cost for a minimization problem, or $-M$, representing a very large negative profit (i.e., loss) for a maximization problem.

Next consider the case where a constraint is already an equation, for example,

$$x_1 + x_2 = 30$$

Since this constraint is already an equation it is not necessary to add a slack or subtract a surplus; in fact neither would be possible since the sum of x_1 and x_2 must exactly equal 30. However, the initial solution at the origin $x_1 = 0$, and $x_2 = 0$, is not feasible, i.e., $0 + 0 \neq 30$. To rectify this difficulty we can add an artificial variable, just as we did with an $\geq$ constraint. Now at the origin, where $x_1 = 0$ and $x_2 = 0$, we would have,

$$x_1 + x_2 + A_1 = 30$$
$$0 + 0 + A_1 = 30$$
$$A_1 = 30$$

Any time a constraint is initially an equation, an artificial variable is added.

The following table summarizes the rules for transforming all three types of model constraints.

CONSTRAINT	ADJUSTMENT	OBJECTIVE FUNCTION COEFFICIENT	
		Maximization	*Minimization*
$\leq$	Add a slack variable	0	0
$=$	Add an artificial variable	$-M$	M
$\geq$	Subtract a surplus variable	0	0
	and add an artificial variable	$-M$	M

The following example illustrates a minimization model with $\geq$ constraints.

EXAMPLE S11.3

A Minimization Linear Programming Model

The Farmer's Hardware and Feed Store is preparing a fertilizer mix for a farmer who is preparing a field to plant a crop. The store will use two brands of fertilizer, Super-gro and Crop-quik, to make the proper mix for the farmer. Each brand yields a specific amount of nitrogen and phosphate, as follows.

BRAND	CHEMICAL CONTRIBUTION	
	Nitrogen (lb/bag)	*Phosphate (lb/bag)*
Super-gro	2	4
Crop-quik	4	3

(Continued)

The farmer's field requires at least 16 pounds of nitrogen and 24 pounds of phosphate. Super-gro costs $6 per bag, and Crop-quik costs $3. The store wants to know how many bags of each brand to purchase to minimize the total cost of fertilizing.

Formulate a linear programming model for this problem, and solve it using the graphical method.

SOLUTION:

This problem is formulated as follows:

Minimize $Z = \$6x_1 + 3x_2$

subject to

$2x_1 + 4x_2 \geq 16$ lb of nitrogen

$4x_1 + 3x_2 \geq 24$ lb of phosphate

$x_1, x_2 \geq 0$

The graphical solution of the problem is shown in the following figure. The conversion of the model constraints and objective function is as follows.

Minimize $Z = 6x_1 + 3x_2 + 0s_1 + 0s_2 + MA_1 + MA_2$

subject to

$2x_1 + 4x_2 - s_1 + A_1 = 16$

$4x_1 + 3x_2 - s_2 + A_2 = 24$

$x_1, x_2, s_1, s_2, A_1, A_2 \geq 0$

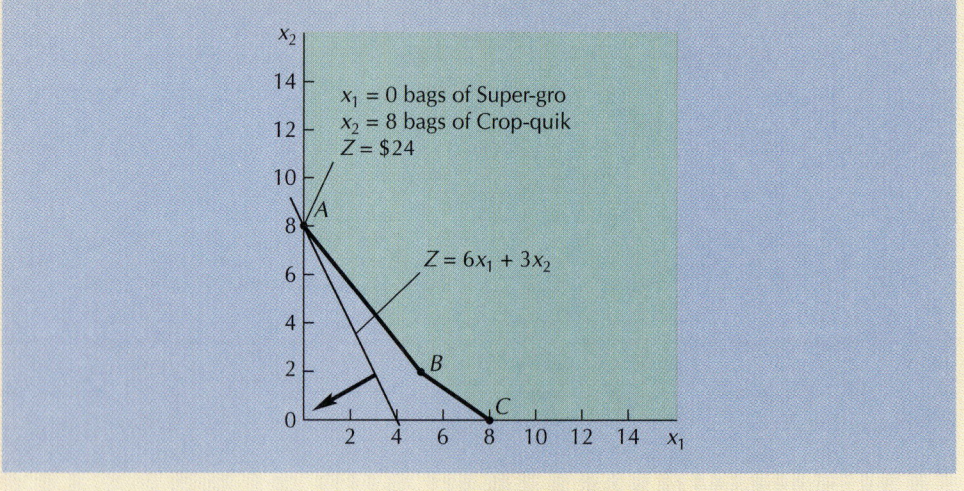

Solving Linear Programming Problems with POM for Windows and Excel

Solving linear programming problems by hand with the simplex method can become very tedious and cumbersome for a model with as few as three variables and four constraints, and most realistic problems are much larger than this. Fortunately, there are hundreds of linear programming and general-purpose quantitative methods software packages that can solve linear programming problems. In this section we will demonstrate how to use POM for Windows and Excel to solve our Beaver Creek Pottery Company model from Example S11.1

Exhibit S11.1 shows the POM for Windows solution output screen for Example S11.1. The graphical solution can also be generated with POM for Windows but it is not shown.

It is also possible to generate an output screen called "Ranging." The Ranging screen for our example is shown in Exhibit S11.2.

Notice the values 16 and 6 under the column labeled "Dual Value" for the rows labeled "Labor Constraint" and "Clay Constraint." These dual values are the *marginal values* of labor and clay in our problem. The marginal value is the amount the company would be willing to pay for one additional unit of a resource. For example, the dual value of 16 for the labor constraint means that if one additional hour of labor could be obtained by the company, it would increase total profit by $16. Likewise, if one additional pound of clay could be obtained, it would increase profit by $6. Sixteen dollars and $6 are the marginal values of labor and clay, respectively, for the company. The marginal value is not the original selling price of a resource; it is how much the company should pay to get more of the resource. The company should not be willing to pay more than $16 for an hour of labor because if it gets one more hour, profit will increase by only $16. The marginal value is helpful to the company in pricing resources and making decisions about securing additional resources.

The dual values do not hold for an unlimited supply of labor and clay. As the company increases (or reduces) the amount of labor or clay it has, the constraints change, which will eventually change the solution to a new point. Thus, the dual values are only

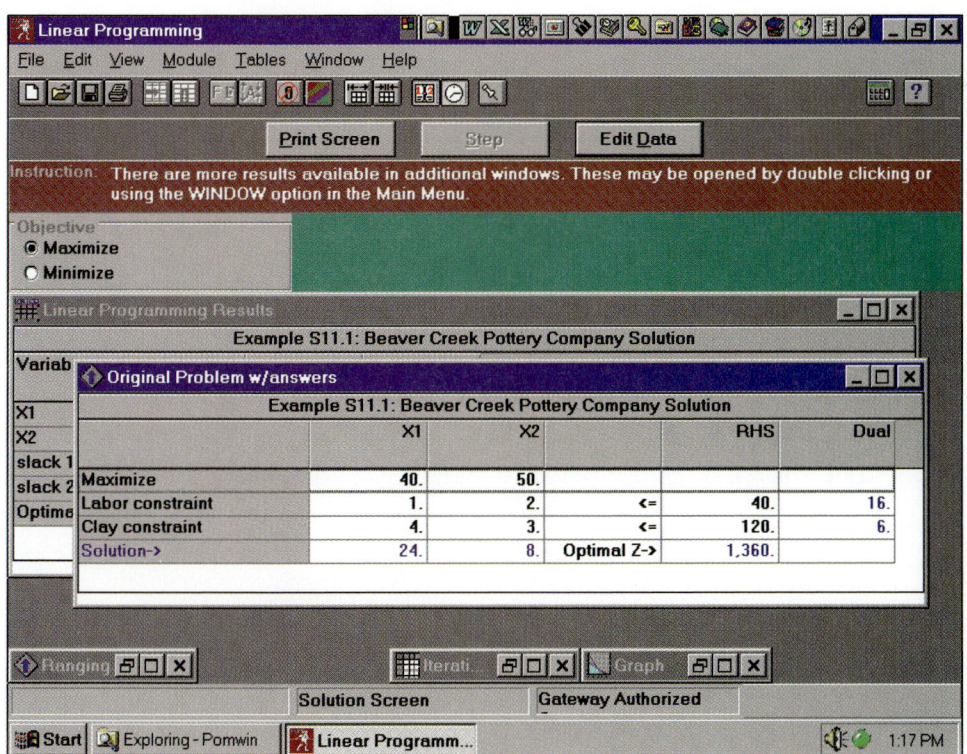

EXHIBIT S11.1

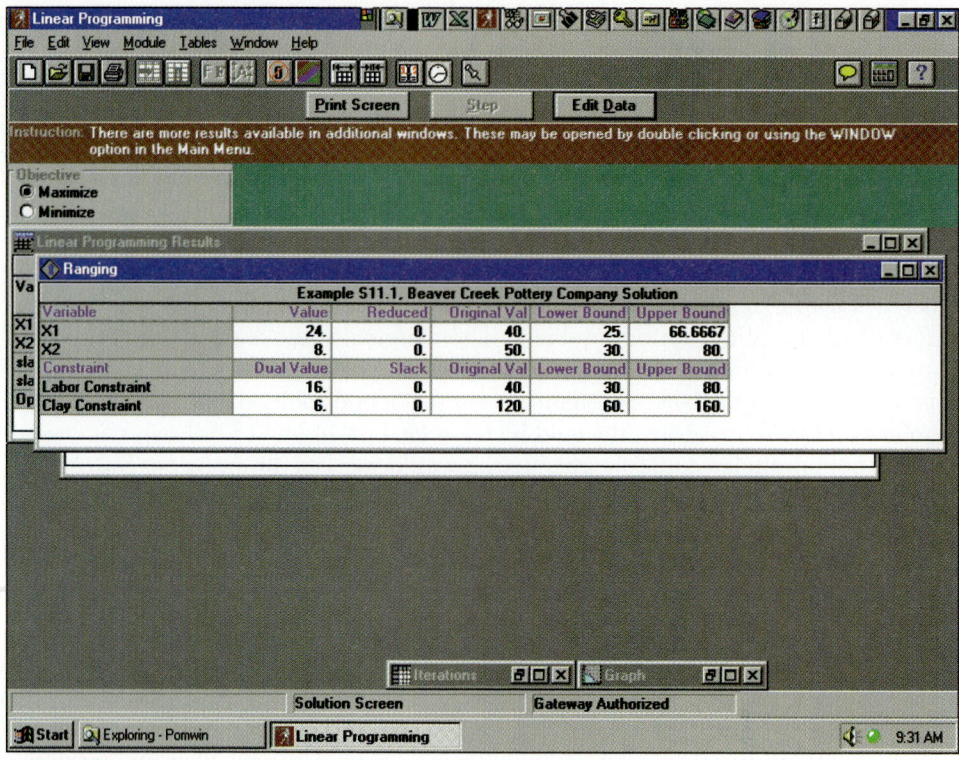

EXHIBIT S11.2

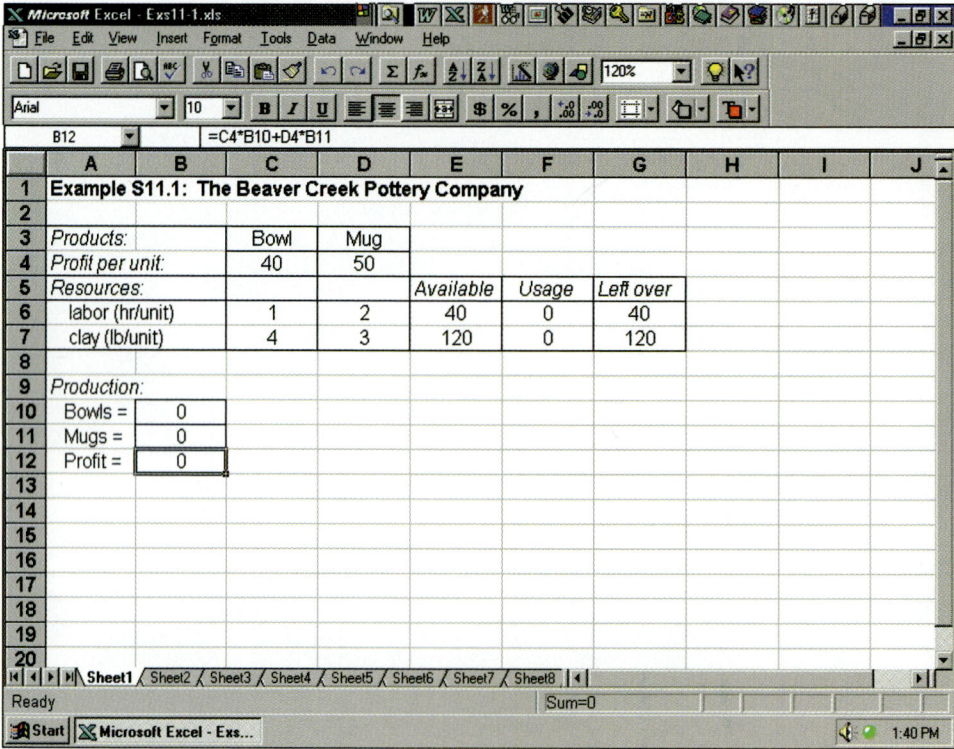

EXHIBIT S11.3

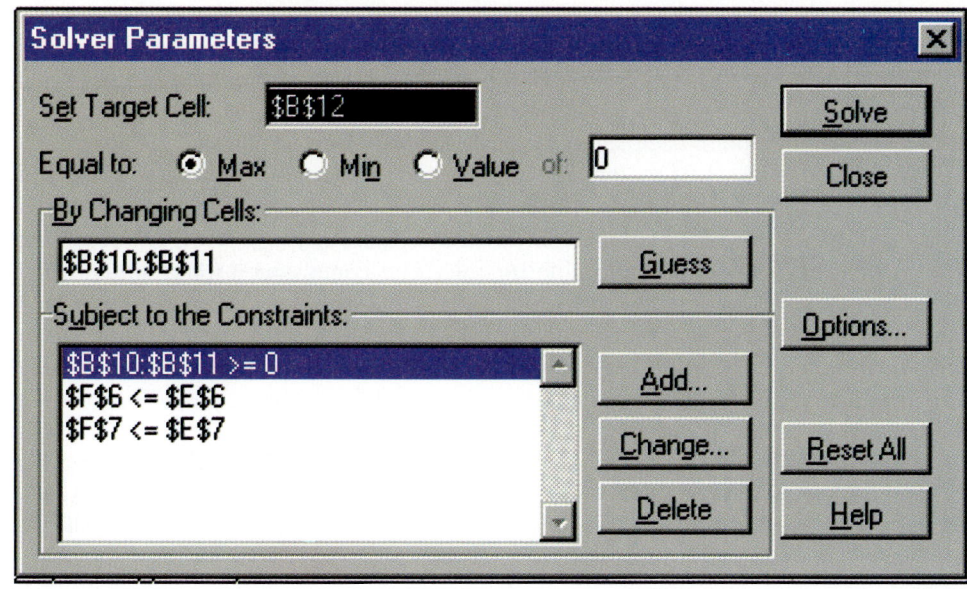

EXHIBIT S11.4

EXHIBIT S11.5

good within a range of constraint values. These ranges are given under the columns labeled "Lower Bound" and "Upper Bound" in Exhibit S11.2. For example, the original amount of labor available is 40 hours. The dual value of $16 for one hour of labor holds if the available labor is between 30 and 80 hours. If there are more than 80 hours of labor, then a new solution point occurs and the dual value of $16 is no longer valid. The problem would have to be solved again to see what the new solution is and the new dual value.

Excel can also be used to solve linear programming problems although the data input requirements are more tedious than with a software package like POM for Windows, which has a linear programming module. The Excel screen for Example S11.1 for Beaver Creek Pottery is shown in Exhibit S11.3. The values for bowls, mugs, and maximum profit are contained in cells B10, B11, and B12. They are currently empty since the problem has not yet been solved. The objective function for profit embedded in cell B12 is shown on the formula bar on the top of the screen. Similar formulas for the constraints for labor and clay are embedded in cells F6 and F7.

To solve this problem, first bring down the "Tools" window from the toolbar at the top of the screen and then select "Solver." The window for Solver (Exhibit S11.4) will appear and the model parameters are input, including the objective function cell, the cells representing the decision variables, and the cells associated with the constraints. Clicking on "Solve" will provide the model solution as shown in Exhibit S11.5.

Summary

Linear programming is one of several related quantitative techniques that are generally classified as mathematical programming models. Other quantitative techniques that fall into this general category include integer programming, nonlinear programming, goal, or multiobjective, programming, and dynamic programming. These modeling techniques are capable of addressing a large variety of complex operational decision-making problems, and they are used extensively to do so by businesses and companies around the world. Computer software packages are available to solve most of these types of models, which greatly promotes their use.

Summary of Key Terms

constraints: linear relationships of decision variables representing the restrictions placed on the decision situation by the operating environment.

decision variables: mathematical symbols that represent levels of activity of an operation.

extreme points: corner points, or protrusions, on the boundary of the feasible solution space in a linear programming model.

feasible solution space: an area that satisfies all constraints in a linear programming model simultaneously.

graphical solution method: a method for determining the solution of a linear programming problem using a two-dimensional graph of the model.

linear programming: a technique for general decision situations in which the decision is to determine a level of operational activity in order to achieve an objective, subject to restrictions.

objective function: a linear mathematical relationship that describes the objective of an operation in terms of decision variables.

optimal solution: the single best solution to a problem.

simplex method: a series of mathematical steps conducted within a tabular structure for solving a linear programming model.

slack variable: a variable added to a linear programming $\leq$ constraint to make it an equality.

surplus variable: a variable subtracted from a $\geq$ model constraint in a linear programming model in order to make it an equality.

Solved Problem

A leather shop makes custom-designed, hand-tooled briefcases and luggage. The shop makes a \$400 profit from each briefcase and a \$200 profit from each piece of luggage. (The profit for briefcases is higher because briefcases require more hand-tooling.) The shop has a contract to provide a store with exactly 30 items per month. A tannery supplies the shop with at least 80 square yards of leather per month. The shop must purchase at least this amount but can order more. Each briefcase requires 2 square yards of leather; each piece of luggage requires 8 square yards of leather. From past performance, the shop owners know they cannot make more than 20 briefcases per month. They want to know the number of briefcases and pieces of luggage to produce in order to maximize profit. Formulate a linear programming model for this problem and solve it graphically.

Solution:

Step 1. Model formulation

$$\text{Maximize } Z = \$400x_1 + 200x_2$$

subject to

$$x_1 + x_2 = 30 \text{ contracted items}$$
$$2x_1 + 8x_2 \geq 80 \text{ yd}^2 \text{ of leather}$$
$$x_1 \leq 20 \text{ briefcases}$$
$$x_1, x_2 \geq 0$$

where

$$x_1 = \text{briefcases}$$
$$x_2 = \text{pieces of luggage}$$

Step 2. Graphical solution

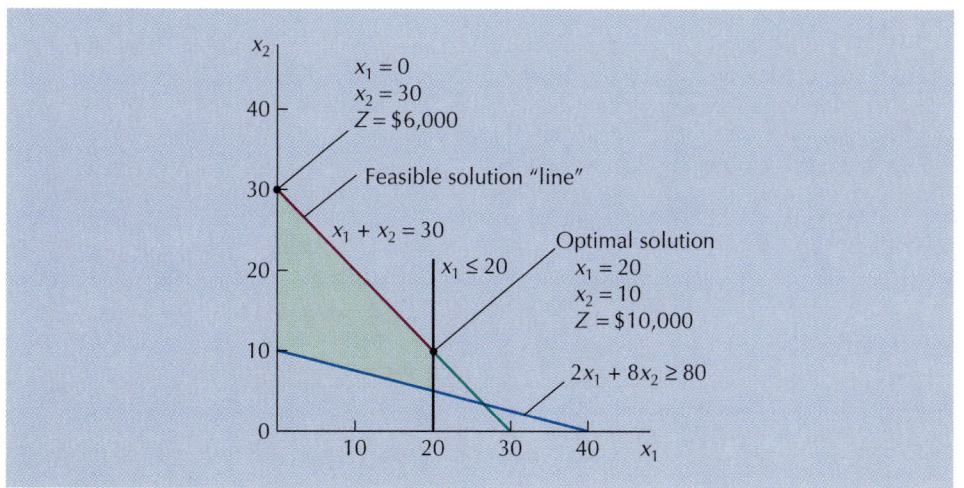

Step 3. Model solution format

The model in proper form for simplex solution is shown as follows.

$$\text{Maximize } Z = 400x_1 + 200x_2 + 0s_1 + 0s_2 - MA_1 - MA_2$$

subject to

$$x_1 + x_2 + A_1 = 30$$
$$2x_1 + 8x_2 - s_1 + A_2 = 80$$
$$x_1 + s_2 = 20$$
$$x_1, x_2, s_1, s_2, A_1, A_1, A_2 \geq 0$$

Questions

S11-1. Why is the term *linear* used in the name *linear programming?*

S11-2. Describe the steps one should follow in formulating a linear programming model.

S11-3. Summarize the steps for solving a linear programming model graphically.

S11-4. In the graphical analysis of a linear programming model, what occurs when the slope of the objective function is the same as the slope of one of the constraint equations?

S11-5. What are the benefits and limitations of the graphical method for solving linear programming problems?

S11-6. What constitutes the feasible solution area on the graph of a linear programming model?

S11-7. How is the optimal solution point identified on the graph of a linear programming model?

S11-8. Why does the coefficient of a slack variable equal zero in the objective function?

Problems

S11-1. Irwin Textile Mills produces two types of cotton cloth—denim and corduroy. Corduroy is a heavier grade of cotton cloth and, as such, requires 7.5 pounds of raw cotton per yard, whereas denim requires 5 pounds of raw cotton per yard. A yard of corduroy requires 3.2 hours of processing time; a yard of denim requires 3.0 hours. Although the demand for denim is practically unlimited, the maximum demand for corduroy is 510 yards per month. The manufacturer has 6,500 pounds of cotton and 3,000 hours of processing time available each month. The manufacturer makes a profit of $2.25 per yard of denim and $3.10 per yard of corduroy. The manufacturer wants to know how many yards of each type of cloth to produce the maximize profit.
  a. Formulate a linear programming model for this problem.
  b. Solve this model using the graphical method.
  c. Solve this problem using a computer.

S11-2. The Pyrotec Company produces three electrical products—clocks, radios, and toasters. These products have the following resource requirements.

| | RESOURCE REQUIREMENTS | |
PRODUCT	Cost/Unit	Labor Hours/Unit
Clock	$ 8	2
Radio	10	3
Toaster	5	2

The manufacturer has a daily production budget of $2,000 and a maximum of 660 hours of labor. Maximum daily customer demand is for 200 clocks, 300 radios, and 150 toasters. Clocks sell for $15, radios, for $20, and toasters, for $12. The company desires to know the optimal product mix that will maximize profit.
a. Formulate a linear programming model for this problem.
b. Solve the problem using a computer.

S11-3. The Roadnet Transport Company has expanded its shipping capacity by purchasing 90 trucks and trailers from a competitor that went bankrupt. The company subsequently located 30 of the purchased trucks at each of its shipping warehouses in Charlotte, Memphis, and Louisville. The company makes shipments from each of these warehouses to terminals in St. Louis, Atlanta, and New York. Each truck is capable of making one shipment per week. The terminal managers have each indicated their capacity for extra shipments. The manager at St. Louis can accommodate 40 additional trucks per week, the manager at Atlanta can accommodate 60 additional trucks, and the manager at New York can accommodate 50 additional trucks. The company makes the following profit per truckload shipment from each warehouse to each terminal. The profits differ as a result of differences in products shipped, shipping costs, and transport rates.

	TERMINAL		
WAREHOUSE	*St. Louis*	*Atlanta*	*New York*
Charlotte	$1,800	$2,100	$1,600
Memphis	1,000	700	900
Louisville	1,400	800	2,200

The company wants to know how many trucks to assign to each route (i.e., warehouse to terminal) to maximize profit. Formulate a linear programming model for this problem and solve using a computer.

S11-4. The Hickory Cabinet and Furniture Company produces sofas, tables, and chairs at its plant in Greensboro, North Carolina. The plant uses three main resources to make furniture—wood, upholstery, and labor. The resource requirements for each piece of furniture and the total resources available weekly are as follows.

	RESOURCE REQUIREMENTS		
FURNITURE PRODUCT	*Wood (lb)*	*Upholstery (yd)*	*Labor (hour)*
Sofa	7	12	6
Table	5	—	9
Chair	4	7	5
Total available resources	2,250	1,000	240

The furniture is produced on a weekly basis and stored in a warehouse until the end of the week, when it is shipped out. The warehouse has a total capacity of 650 pieces of furniture. Each sofa earns $400 in profit, each table, $275, and each chair, $190. The company wants to know how many pieces of each type of furniture to make per week in order to maximize profit.
a. Formulate a linear programming model for this problem.
b. Solve the problem using a computer.

S11-5. The Mill Mountain Coffee Shop blends coffee on the premises for its customers. It sells three basic blends in one-pound bags: Special, Mountain Dark, and Mill Regular. It uses four different types of coffee to produce the blends: Brazilian, mocha, Colombian, and mild. The shop used the following blend recipe requirements.

Blend	Mix Requirements	Selling Price/lb
Special	At least 40% Colombian, at least 30% mocha	$6.50
Dark	At least 60% Brazilian, no more than 10% mild	5.25
Regular	No more than 60% mild, at least 30% Brazilian	3.75

The cost of Brazilian coffee is $2.00 per pound, the cost of mocha is $2.75 per pound, the cost of Colombian is $2.90 per pound, and the cost of mild is $1.70 per pound. The shop has 110 pounds of Brazilian coffee, 70 pounds of mocha, 80 pounds of Colombian, and 150 pounds of mild coffee available per week. The shop wants to know the amount of each blend it should prepare each week in order to maximize profit.

a. Formulate a linear programming model for this problem.
b. Solve this model using a computer.

S11-6. A small metal-parts shop contains three machines—a drill press, a lathe, and a grinder— and has three operators, each certified to work on all three machines. However, each operator performs better on some machines than on others. The shop has contracted to do a big job that requires all three machines. The times required by the various operators to perform the required operations on each machine are summarized below.

Operator	Drill Press (min)	Lathe (min)	Grinder (min)
1	22	18	35
2	41	30	28
3	25	36	18

The shop manager wants to assign one operator to each machine so that the total operating time for all three operators is minimized. Formulate a linear programming model for this problem and solve using a computer.

S11-7. The Bluegrass Distillery produces custom-blended whiskey. A particular blend consists of rye and bourbon whiskey. The company has received an order for a minimum of 400 gallons of the custom blend. The customer specified that the order must contain at least 40 percent rye and not more than 250 gallons of bourbon. The customer also specified that the blend should be mixed in the ratio of two parts rye to one part bourbon. The distillery can produce 500 gallons per week, regardless of the blend. The production manager wants to complete the order in 1 week. The blend is sold for $12 per gallon. The distillery company's cost per gallon is $4 for rye and $2 for bourbon. The company wants to determine the blend mix that will meet customer requirements and maximize profits.

a. Formulate a linear programming model for this problem.
b. Solve the problem using the graphical method.

S11-8. A manufacturer of bathroom fixtures produces fiberglass bathtubs in an assembly operation consisting of three processes: molding, smoothing, and painting. The number of units that can be put through each process in an hour is as follows.

Process	Output (units/hr)
Molding	7
Smoothing	12
Painting	10

(*Note:* The three processes are continuous and sequential; thus, no more units can be smoothed or painted than have been molded.) The labor costs per hour are $8 for molding, $5 for smoothing, and $6.50 for painting. The company's labor budget is $3,000 per week. A total of 120 hours of labor is available for all three processes per week. Each completed bathtub requires 90 pounds of fiberglass, and the company has a total of 10,000 pounds of fiberglass available each week. Each bathtub earns a profit of $175. The manager of the company wants to know how many hours per week to run each process in order to maximize profit. Formulate a linear programming model for this problem and solve using a computer.

S11-9. A refinery blends four petroleum components into three grades of gasoline, regular, premium, and low-lead. The maximum quantities available of each component and the cost per barrel are as follows.

Component	Maximum Barrels Available/Day	Cost (barrel)
1	5,000	$ 9.00
2	2,400	7.00
3	4,000	12.00
4	1,500	6.00

To ensure that each gasoline grade retains certain essential characteristics, the refinery has put limits on the percentage of the components in each blend. The limits as well as the selling prices for the various grades are as follows.

Grade	Component Specifications	Selling Price (barrel)
Regular	Not less than 40% of 1 Not more than 20% of 2 Not less than 30% of 3	$12.00
Premium	Not less than 40% of 3	18.00
Low-lead	Not more than 50% of 2 Not less than 10% of 1	10.00

The refinery wants to produce at least 3,000 barrels of each grade of gasoline. Management wishes to determine the optimal mix of the four components that will maximize profit. Formulate a linear programming model for this problem and solve using a computer.

S11-10. The Cash and Carry Building Supply Company has received the following order for boards in three lengths.

Length	Order (quantity)
7 feet	700 boards
9 feet	1,200 boards
10 feet	300 boards

The company has 25-foot standard-length boards in stock. Therefore, the standard-length boards must be cut into the lengths necessary to meet order requirements. Naturally, the company wishes to minimize the number of standard-length boards used. The company must, therefore, determine how to cut up the 25-foot boards in order to meet the order requirements and minimize the number of standard-length boards used.

a. Formulate a linear programming model for this problem.
b. When a board is cut in a specific pattern, the amount of board left over is referred to as *trim loss*. Reformulate the linear programming model for this problem, assuming that the objective is to minimize trim loss rather than to minimize the total number of boards used.
c. Solve parts (a) and (b) using a computer.

S11-11. PM Computer Services assembles its own brand of personal computers from component parts it purchases overseas and domestically. PM sells most of its computers locally to different departments at State University as well as to individuals and businesses in the immediate geographic region.

PM has enough regular production capacity to produce 160 computers per week. It can produce an additional 50 computers with overtime. The cost of assembly, inspecting, and packaging a computer during regular time is $190. Overtime production of a computer costs $260. Further, it costs $10 per computer per week to hold a computer in inventory for future delivery. PM wants to be able to meet all customer orders with no shortages in order to provide quality service. PM's order schedule for the next six weeks is as follows.

Week	Computer Orders
1	105
2	170
3	230
4	180
5	150
6	250

PM Computers wants to determine a schedule that will indicate how much regular and overtime production it will need each week in order to meet its orders at the minimum cost. The company wants no inventory left over at the end of the six-week period. Formulate a linear programming model for this problem and solve using a computer.

S11-12. The manager of the Ewing and Barnes Department Store has four employees available to assign to three departments in the store: lamps, sporting goods, and linen. The manager wants each of these departments to have at least one employee but not more than two. Therefore, two departments will be assigned one employee and one department will be assigned two. Each employee has different areas of expertise, which are reflected in the following daily sales each employee is expected to generate in each department.

	DEPARTMENT		
EMPLOYEE	Lamps	Sporting Goods	Linen
1	$130	$150	$ 90
2	275	300	100
3	180	225	140
4	200	120	160

The manager wishes to know which employee(s) to assign to each department in order to maximize expected sales. Formulate a linear programming model for this problem and solve using a computer.

S11-13. Dr. Maureen Becker, the head administrator at Jefferson County Regional Hospital, must determine a schedule for nurses to make sure there are enough nurses on duty throughout the day. During the day, the demand for nurses varies. Maureen has broken the day into 12 two-hour periods. The slowest time of the day encompasses the three periods from 12:00 A.M. to 6:00 A.M., which, beginning at midnight, require a minimum of 30, 20, and 40, nurses, respectively. The demand for nurses steadily increases during the next four daytime periods. Beginning with the 6:00 A.M.–8:00 A.M. period, a minimum of 50, 60, 80, and 80 nurses are required for these four periods, respectively. After 2:00 P.M., the demand for nurses decreases during the afternoon and evening hours. For the five two-hour periods beginning at 2:00 P.M., and ending at midnight, 70, 70, 60, 50, and 50 nurses are required, respectively. A nurse reports for duty at the beginning of one of the two-hour periods and works eight consecutive hours (which is required in the nurses' contract). Dr. Becker wants to determine a nursing schedule that will meet the hospital's minimum requirements throughout the day while using the minimum number of nurses. Formulate a linear programming model for this problem and solve this model.

S11-14. A company that has a two-year contract to haul ore from an open-pit mine to load docks needs 200 additional trucks. The company can purchase trucks only at the beginning of the two-year period. Alternatively, the company can lease trucks for $80,000 per year (paid at the beginning of the year). Trucks cost $140,000 each to purchase and have a useful life of two years. They have no salvage value at the end of the two years. The mining company has $8 million cash available to lease and/or buy trucks at the beginning of year 1. In addition, the company can obtain a loan each year for as much as $20 million at 16 percent interest per year. The loan agreement requires that the company repay the borrowed amount plus interest at the end of the year. Each truck will earn $120,000 per year, which becomes part of the flow of cash available to the company for truck leasing and loan repayment. The company wants to minimize the total cost of expanding its fleet of trucks over a two-year period. Formulate a linear programming model for this problem and solve it using a computer.

S11-15. Lawns Unlimited is a lawn care and maintenance company. One of its services is to seed new lawns as well as bare areas or damaged areas in established lawns. The company uses three basic grass seed mixes it calls Home 1, Home 2, and Commercial 3. It uses three kinds of grass seed—tall fescue, mustang fescue, and bluegrass. The requirements for each grass mix are as follows.

Mix	Mix Requirements
Home 1	No more than 50% tall fescue
	At least 20% mustang fescue
Home 2	At least 30% bluegrass
	At least 30% mustang fescue
	No more than 20% tall fescue
Commercial 3	At least 50% but no more than 70% tall fescue
	At least 10% bluegrass

The company believes it needs to have at least 1,200 pounds of Home 1 mix, 900 pounds of Home 2 mix, and 2,400 pounds of Commercial 3 seed mix on hand. A pound of tall fescue costs the company $1.70, a pound of mustang fescue costs $2.80, and a pound of bluegrass costs $3.25. The company wants to know how many pounds of each type of grass seed to purchase in order to minimize cost. Formulate a linear programming model for this problem and solve using a computer.

S11-16. A metal works manufacturing company produces four products fabricated from sheet metal in a plant that consists of four operations—stamping, assembly, finishing, and packaging. The processing times per unit for each operation and total available hours per month are as follows.

Operation	Product (hour/unit)				Total Hours Available per Month
	1	2	3	4	
Stamping	0.07	0.20	0.10	0.15	700
Assembly	0.15	0.18	—	0.12	450
Finishing	0.08	0.21	0.06	0.10	600
Packaging	0.12	0.15	0.08	0.12	500

The sheet metal required for each product, the maximum demand per month, the minimum required contracted production, and the profit per product are as follows.

Product	Sheet Metal (ft^2)	Monthly Sales Demand		Profit ($)
		Minimum	Maximum	
1	2.1	300	3,000	9
2	1.5	200	1,400	10
3	2.8	400	4,200	8
4	3.1	300	1,800	12

The company has 5,200 square feet of fabricated metal available each month.
a. Formulate a linear programming model for this problem.
b. Solve the model using the computer.

S11-17. A jewelry store makes necklaces and bracelets from gold and platinum. The store has developed the following linear programming model for determining the number of necklaces and bracelets (x_1 and x_2) to make in order to maximize profit.

$$\text{Maximize } Z = 300x_1 + 400x_2 \text{ (profit, \$)}$$

subject to

$$3x_1 + 2x_2 \leq 18 \quad \text{(gold, oz)}$$
$$2x_1 + 4x_2 \leq 20 \quad \text{(platinum, oz)}$$
$$x_2 \leq 4 \quad \text{(demand, bracelets)}$$
$$x_1, x_2 \geq 0$$

a. Solve this model graphically.
b. The maximum demand for bracelets is 4. If the store produces the optimal number of bracelets and necklaces, will the maximum demand for bracelets be met? If not, by how much will it be missed?
c. What profit for a necklace would result in no bracelets being produced, and what would be the optimal solution for this problem?

S11-18. The Copperfield Mining Company owns two mines, which produce three grades of ore: high, medium, and low. The company has a contract to supply a smelting company with 12 tons of high-grade ore, 8 tons of medium-grade ore, and 24 tons of low-grade ore. Each mine produces a certain amount of each type of ore each hour it is in operation. The company has developed the following linear programming model to determine the number of hours to operate each mine (x_1 and x_2) so that contracted obligations can be met at the lowest cost.

$$\text{Minimize } Z = 200x_1 + 160x_2 \text{ (cost, \$)}$$

subject to

$$6x_1 + 2x_2 \geq 12 \quad \text{(high-grade ore, tons)}$$
$$2x_1 + 2x_2 \geq 8 \quad \text{(medium-grade ore, tons)}$$

$$4x_1 + 12x_2 \geq 24 \quad \text{(low-grade ore, tons)}$$
$$x_1, x_2 \geq 0$$

a. Solve this model graphically.
b. Solve the model using a computer.

S11-19. A manufacturing firm produces two products. Each product must go through an assembly process and a finishing process. The product is then transferred to the warehouse, which has space for only a limited number of items. The following linear programming model has been developed for determining the quantity of each product to produce in order to maximize profit.

$$\text{Maximize } Z = 30x_1 + 70x_2 \text{ (profit, \$)}$$

subject to

$$4x_1 + 10x_2 \leq 80 \quad \text{(assembly, hours)}$$
$$14x_1 + 8x_2 \leq 112 \quad \text{(finishing, hours)}$$
$$x_1 + x_2 \leq 10 \quad \text{(inventory, units)}$$
$$x_1, x_2 \geq 0$$

a. Solve this model graphically.
b. Assume that the objective function has been changed to $Z = 90x_1 + 70x_2$. Determine the slope of each objective function and discuss what effect these slopes have on the optimal solution.

S11-20. Breathtakers, a health and fitness center, operates a morning fitness program for senior citizens. The program includes aerobic exercise, either swimming or step exercise, followed by a healthy breakfast in its dining room. The dietitian of Breathtakers wants to develop a breakfast that will be high in calories, calcium, protein, and fiber, which are especially important to senior citizens, but low in fat and cholesterol. She also wants to minimize cost. She has selected the following possible food items, whose individual nutrient contributions and cost from which to develop a standard breakfast menu are shown below.

Breakfast Food	Calories	Fat (g)	Cholesterol (mg)	Iron (mg)	Calcium (mg)	Protein (g)	Fiber (g)	Cost ($)
1. Bran cereal (cup)	90	0	0	6	20	3	5	0.18
2. Dry cereal (cup)	110	2	0	4	48	4	2	0.22
3. Oatmeal (cup)	100	2	0	2	12	5	3	0.10
4. Oat bran (cup)	90	2	0	3	8	6	4	0.12
5. Egg	75	5	270	1	30	7	0	0.10
6. Bacon (slice)	35	3	8	0	0	2	0	0.09
7. Orange	65	0	0	1	52	1	1	0.40
8. Milk—2% (cup)	100	4	12	0	250	9	0	0.16
9. Orange juice (cup)	120	0	0	0	3	1	0	0.50
10. Wheat toast (slice)	65	1	0	1	26	3	3	0.07

The dietitian wants the breakfast to include at least 420 calories, 5 milligrams of iron, 400 milligrams of calcium, 20 grams of protein, and 12 grams of fiber. Further, she wants to limit fat to no more than 20 grams and cholesterol to 30 milligrams. Formulate the linear programming model for this problem and solve.

C A S E   P R O B L E M

Mossaic Tile Company

Gilbert Moss and Angela Pasaic spent several summers during their college years working at archaeological sites in the Southwest. While at these digs they learned how to make ceramic tiles from local artisans. After college they started a tile manufacturing firm called Mossaic Tiles, Ltd. They opened their plant in New Mexico, where they would have convenient access to a special clay to make a clay derivative for their tiles. Their manufacturing operation consists of a few simple but precarious steps, including molding the tiles, baking, and glazing.

Gilbert and Angela plan to produce two basic types of tile for use in home bathrooms, kitchens, sunrooms, and laundry rooms: a larger single-colored tile; and a smaller patterned tile. In the manufacturing process the color or pattern is added before a tile is glazed. Either a single color is sprayed over the top of a newly baked set of tiles or a stenciled pattern is sprayed on the top of a baked set of tiles.

The tiles are produced in batches of 100. The first step is to pour the clay derivative into specially constructed molds. It takes 18 minutes to mold a batch of 100 larger tiles and 15 minutes to prepare a mold for a batch of 100 smaller tiles. The company has 60 hours available each week for molding. After the tiles are molded they are baked in a kiln: 0.27 hour for a batch of 100 larger tiles and 0.58 hour for a batch of 100 smaller tiles. The company has 105 hours available each week for baking. After baking, the tiles are either colored or patterned and glazed. This process takes 0.16 hour for a batch of 100 larger tiles and 0.20 hour for a batch of 100 smaller tiles. Forty hours are available each week for the "glazing" process. Each batch of 100 large tiles requires 32.8 pounds of the clay derivative to produce, while each batch of smaller tiles requires 20 pounds. The company has 6,000 pounds of the clay derivative available each week.

Mossaic Tile earns a profit of $190 for each batch of 100 of the larger tiles and $240 for each batch of 100 smaller patterned tiles. Angela and Gilbert want to know how many batches of each type of tile to produce each week in order to maximize profit. They also have some questions about resource usage they would like to answer.

A. Formulate a linear programming model for the Mossaic Tile Company to determine the mix of the tiles it should manufacture each week.

B. Transform the model into standard form.

C. Solve the linear programming model graphically.

D. Determine the resources left over and not used at the optimal solution point.

E. For artistic reasons Gilbert and Angela like to produce the smaller patterned tiles best. They also believe in the long run the smaller tiles will be a more successful product. What must be the profit for the smaller tiles in order for the company to produce only the smaller tiles?

F. Solve the linear programming model using the computer.

G. Mossaic believes it may be able to reduce the time required for molding to 16 minutes for a batch of larger tiles and 12 minutes for a batch of the smaller tiles. How will this affect the solution?

H. The company that provides Mossaic with clay has indicated that it can deliver an additional 100 pounds of clay each week. Should Mossaic agree to this offer?

I. Mossaic is considering adding capacity to one of its kilns to provide 20 additional glazing hours per week at a cost of $90,000. Should it make the investment?

J. The kiln for glazing had to be shut down for three hours, reducing the available kiln hours from 40 to 37. What effect will this have on the solution?

CASE PROBLEM

Summer Sports Camp at State University

Mary Kelly is a scholarship soccer player at State University. During the summer she works at a youth all-sports camp that several of the university's coaches operate. The sports camp runs for eight weeks during July and August. Campers come for a one-week period, during which time they live in the State dormitories and use the State athletic fields and facilities. At the end of a week a new group of kids comes in. Mary primarily serves as one of the camp soccer instructors. However, she has also been placed in charge of arranging for sheets for the beds the campers will sleep on in the dormitories. Mary has been instructed to develop a plan for purchasing and cleaning sheets each week of camp at the lowest possible cost.

Clean sheets are needed at the beginning of each week, and the campers use the sheets all week. At the end of the week the campers strip their beds and place the sheets in large bins. Mary must arrange either to purchase new sheets or to clean old sheets. A set of new sheets costs $10. A local laundry has indicated that it will clean a set of sheets for $4. Also, a couple of Mary's friends have asked her to let them clean some of the sheets. They have told her they will charge only $2 for each set of sheets they clean. However, while the laundry will provide cleaned sheets in a week, Mary's friends can only deliver cleaned sheets in two weeks. They are going to summer school and plan to launder the sheets at night at a neighborhood laundromat.

The following number of campers have registered during each of the eight weeks the camp will operate.

Week	Registered Campers
1	115
2	210
3	250
4	230
5	260
6	300
7	250
8	190

Based on discussions with camp administrators from previous summers and on some old camp records and receipts, Mary estimates that each week about 20 percent of the cleaned sheets that are returned will have to be discarded and replaced. The campers spill food and drinks on the sheets, and sometimes the stains will not come out during cleaning. Also, the campers occasionally tear the sheets or the sheets can get torn at the cleaners. In either case, when the sheets come back from the cleaners and are put on the beds, 20 percent are taken off and thrown away.

At the beginning of the summer, the camp has no sheets available, so initially sheets must be purchased. Sheets are thrown away at the end of the summer.

Mary's major at State is operations management, and she wants to develop a plan for purchasing and cleaning sheets using linear programming. Help Mary formulate a linear programming model for this problem and solve it using the computer.

Spring Garden Tools

The Spring family has owned and operated a garden tool and implements manufacturing company since 1952. The company sells garden tools to distributors and also directly to hardware stores and home improvement discount chains. The Spring Company's four most popular small garden tools are a trowel, a hoe, a rake, and a shovel. Each of these tools is made from durable steel and has a wooden handle. The Spring family prides itself on its high-quality tools.

The manufacturing process encompasses two stages. The first stage includes two operations—stamping out the metal tool heads and drilling screw holes in them. The completed tool heads then flow to the second stage. The second stage includes an assembly operation where the handles are attached to the tool heads, a finishing step, and finally packaging. The processing times per tool for each operation are provided in the following table.

	Tool (hours/unit)				Total Hours Available per Month
Operation	Trowel	Hoe	Rake	Shovel	
Stamping	0.04	0.17	0.06	0.12	500
Drilling	0.05	0.14	—	0.14	400
Assembly	0.06	0.13	0.05	0.10	600
Finishing	0.05	0.21	0.02	0.10	550
Packaging	0.03	0.15	0.04	0.15	500

The steel the company uses is ordered from an iron and steel works in Japan. The company has 10,000 square feet of sheet steel available each month. The metal required for each tool and the monthly contracted production volume per tool are provided in the following table.

	Sheet Metal (ft²)	Monthly Contracted Sales
Trowel	1.2	1,800
Hoe	1.6	1,400
Rake	2.1	1,600
Shovel	2.4	1,800

The reasons the company has prospered are its ability to meet customer demand on time and its high quality. As a result, the Spring Company will produce on an overtime basis in order to meet its sales requirements, and it also has a long-standing arrangement with a local tool and die company to manufacture its tool heads. The Spring Company feels comfortable subcontracting the first-stage operations, since it is easier to detect defects prior to assembly and finishing. For the same reason, the company will not subcontract for the entire tool, since defects would be particularly hard to detect after the tool is finished and packaged. However, the company does have 100 hours of overtime available each month for each operation in both stages. The regular production and overtime costs per tool for both stages are provided in the following table.

	Stage 1		Stage 2	
	Regular Cost($)	Overtime Cost($)	Regular Cost($)	Overtime Cost($)
Trowel	6.00	6.20	3.00	3.10
Hoe	10.00	10.70	5.00	5.40
Rake	8.00	8.50	4.00	4.30
Shovel	10.00	10.70	5.00	5.40

The cost of subcontracting in stage 1 adds 20 percent to the regular production cost.

The Spring Company wants to establish a production schedule for regular and overtime production in each stage and for the number of tool heads subcontracted, at the minimum cost. Formulate a linear programming model for this problem and solve the model using a computer. Which resources appear to be most critical in the production process?

References

Charnes, A., and W. W. Cooper. *Management Models and Industrial Applications of Linear Programming.* New York: John Wiley, 1961.

Dantzig, G. B. *Linear Programming and Extensions.* Princeton, N.J.: Princeton University, 1963.

Gass, S. *Linear Programming,* 4th ed. New York: McGraw-Hill, 1975.

Moore, L. J., S. M. Lee, and B. W. Taylor. *Management Science,* 4th ed. Needham Heights, Mass.: Allyn and Bacon, 1993.

Taylor, B. W. *Introduction to Linear Programming,* 5th ed. Upper Saddle River, N.J.: Prentice Hall, 1995.

Wagner, A. M. *Principles of Operations Research,* 2d ed. Englewood Cliffs, N.J.: Prentice Hall, 1975.

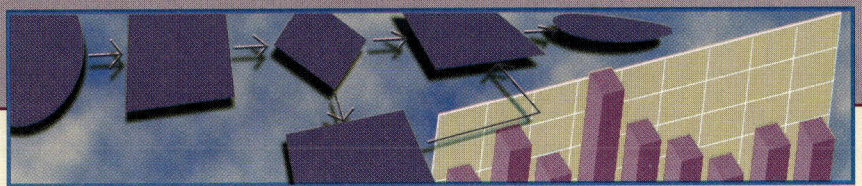

12

Inventory Management

Parts Inventory Management at IBM

The computer industry continues its explosive growth and rapidly advancing technology resulting in many new products. This trend has also led to the necessity of maintaining inventory service systems to support these products. For IBM the number and amount of machines and computing equipment has increased, and this has in turn created a need for more extensive service and more spare parts. Approximately 1,000 IBM products are currently in service, with installed units numbering in excess of tens of millions, and IBM has more than 200,000 part numbers to support these products. For IBM to compete effectively in the information processing industry, it is essential that it maintains a service parts inventory system to support the products it sells and installs.

IBM's National Service Division (NSD) has developed an extensive and sophisticated parts inventory management system (PIMS) to provide prompt and reliable customer service. This system manages a parts distribution network consisting of 2 central warehouses, 21 field distribution centers located in metropolitan areas, 64 parts stations, and 15,000 outside locations. NSD employs more than 15,000 customer engineers to repair and maintain its installed products. The parts inventory maintained in this system is valued in the billions of dollars. PIMS employed economic order quantity (EOQ) formulas to determine parts and replenishment batch sizes and to set service priority goals. Recently IBM made dramatic improvements to its parts inventory management system, embodied in a modeling framework called Optimizer. This system contained four basic modules: a forecasting system that estimates part failure rates; a system to provide inventory data;

This IBM employee is handling items for shipment at an IBM warehouse facility. Large companies like IBM maintain millions of dollars' worth of product and parts inventories, which represent a significant overall cost to the company. Companies ranging from IBM to the local grocery store continually attempt to reduce inventory levels in order to save money.

a decision model that determines a stock control policy at each location and for each part in the system and that minimizes the expected costs and satisfies service constraints; and a system that interfaces the output of the decision module and PIMS. The new system resulted in a reduction in inventory investment, improved service, greater flexibility in responding to changes in service requirements, better planning capabilities, and better understanding of the impact of parts operations on customer service. The Optimizer system recommended a reduction in the time-averaged value of inventory by approximately 25 percent—more than a half billion dollars in inventory investment. However, some of the proposed inventory reduction was reallocated to improve service levels, resulting in an annual total inventory reduction of a quarter of a billion dollars. Using the new system, IBM also made several strategic changes in its inventory network, including decreasing the number of field distribution centers, increasing parts stations, and increasing the replenishment rate at these stations. These changes resulted in a 10 percent improvement in parts availability and a $20 million annual savings in operating efficiency.[1]

T he objective of inventory management has been to keep enough inventory to meet customer demand and also be cost-effective. However, inventory has not always been perceived as an area to control cost. Companies maintained "generous" inventory levels to meet long-term customer demand because there were fewer competitors and products in a generally sheltered market environment. In the current international business environment with more competitors and highly diverse markets, in which new products and new product features are rapidly and continually introduced, the cost of inventory has increased due in part to quicker product obsolescence. At the same time, companies are continuously seeking to lower costs so they can provide a better product at a "lower" price. Inventory is an obvious candidate for cost reduction. It is estimated that the average cost of manufacturing goods inventory in the United States is approximately 30 percent of the total value of the inventory. That means if a company has $10 million worth of products in inventory, the cost of holding the inventory (including insurance, obsolescence, depreciation, interest, opportunity costs, storage costs, etc.) is approximately $3 million. If inventory could be reduced by half, to $5 million, then $1.5 million would be saved, a significant cost reduction.

www.prenhall.com/russell

The high cost of inventory has motivated companies to focus on efficient supply chain management and quality management. They believe that inventory can be significantly reduced by reducing uncertainty at various points along the supply chain. In many cases uncertainty is created by poor quality on the part of the company or its suppliers or both. This can be in the form of variations in delivery times, uncertain production schedules caused by late deliveries or large numbers of defects that require higher levels of production or service than what should be necessary, large fluctuations in customer demand, or poor forecasts of customer demand.

In a continuous replenishment system of inventory management, products or services are moved from one stage in the supply chain to the next according to a system of constant communication between customers and suppliers. Items are replaced as they are diminished without maintaining larger buffer stocks of inventory at each stage to compensate for late deliveries, inefficient service, poor quality, or uncertain demand. An

[1] Cohen, M. "Optimizer: IBM's Multi-Echelon Inventory System for Managing Service Logistics," *Interfaces* 20, no. 1 (January–February 1990): 65–82.

efficient, well-coordinated supply chain reduces or eliminates these types of uncertainty so that this type of system will work. In a JIT system, products are moved from one stage to the next in the production process as they are needed, with only minimal buffer inventories between stages. While some companies maintain in-process, buffer inventories between production stages to offset irregularities and problems and keep production flowing smoothly, quality-oriented companies consider large buffer inventories to be a costly crutch that masks problems and inefficiency primarily caused by poor quality.

Adherents of quality management believe that inventory should be minimized. However, this works primarily for a production or manufacturing process. For the retailer who sells finished goods directly to the consumer or the supplier who sells parts or materials to the manufacturer, inventory is a necessity. Few shoe stores, discount stores, or department stores can stay in business with only one or two items on their shelves or racks. For these operations the traditional inventory decisions of how much to order and when to order continue to be important. In addition, the traditional approaches to inventory management are still widely used by most companies.

In this chapter we review the basic elements of traditional inventory management and discuss several of the more popular models and techniques for making cost-effective inventory decisions. These decisions are basically *how much to order* and *when to order* to replenish inventory to an optimal level.

> Despite JIT influence, inventory stocks are still required for retailers and suppliers.

The Elements of Inventory Management

Inventory is a stock of items kept by an organization to meet internal or external customer demand. Virtually every type of organization maintains some form of inventory. Department stores carry inventories of all the retail items they sell; a nursery has inventories of different plants, trees, and flowers; a rental-car agency has inventories of cars; and a major league baseball team maintains an inventory of players on its minor league teams. Even a family household maintains inventories of items such as food, clothing, medical supplies, and personal hygiene products.

Most people think of inventory as a final product waiting to be sold to a retail customer—a new car or a can of tomatoes. This is certainly one of its most important uses. However, especially in a manufacturing firm, inventory can take on forms besides finished goods, including:

> **Inventory** is a stock of items kept to meet demand.

- Raw materials
- Purchased parts and supplies
- Labor
- In-process (partially completed) products
- Component parts
- Working capital
- Tools, machinery, and equipment
- Finished goods

> *Inventory management:* how much and when to order.

The purpose of *inventory management* is to determine the amount of inventory to keep in stock—how much to order and when to replenish, or order. In this chapter we describe several different inventory systems and techniques for making these determinations.

The Role of Inventory in Supply Chain Management

A company employs an <u>inventory strategy</u> for lots of reasons. The main one is holding inventories of finished goods to meet customer demand for a product, especially in a

www.prenhall.com/russell

retail operation. However, customer demand can also be a secretary going to a storage closet to get a printer cartridge or paper, or a carpenter getting a board or nail from a storage shed.

Since demand is usually not known with certainty, an additional amount of inventory, called safety, or buffer, stocks, is kept on hand to meet excess demand. Additional stocks of inventories are sometimes built up to meet demand that is seasonal or cyclical. Companies will continue to produce items when demand is low to meet high seasonal demand for which their production capacity is insufficient. For example, toy manufacturers produce large inventories during the summer and fall to meet anticipated demand during the holiday season. Doing so enables them to maintain a relatively smooth supply chain flow throughout the year. They would not normally have the production capacity or logistical support to produce enough to meet all of the holiday demand during that season. In the same way retailers might find it necessary to keep large stocks of inventory on their shelves to meet peak seasonal demand, or for display purposes to attract buyers.

At the other end of the supply chain from finished goods inventory, suppliers might keep large stocks of parts and material inventory to meet variations in customer demand. This is especially true of manufacturing suppliers who are under pressure to meet the exacting demands of continuous replenishment with frequent, on-time delivery of small lots. When JIT was introduced in the automobile industry, it was reported that suppliers created a boom in the warehousing business in Detroit, creating huge stocks of inventory to meet JIT schedules.[2]

A company will purchase large amounts of inventory to take advantage of price discounts, as a hedge against anticipated price increases in the future, or because it can get a lower price by purchasing in volume. Wal-Mart stores have been known to purchase an entire manufacturer's stock of soap powder or other retail item because they can get a very low price, which they subsequently pass on to their customers. Companies purchase large stocks of low-priced items when a supplier liquidates. In some cases large orders will be made simply because the cost of an order may be very high and it is more cost-effective to have higher inventories than to order frequently.

Many companies find it necessary to maintain **buffer inventories** at different stages of their supply chain to provide independence between stages and to avoid work stoppages or delays. Inventories of raw materials and purchased parts are kept on hand so that the production process will not be delayed as a result of missed or late deliveries or shortages from a supplier. Work-in-process inventories are kept between stages in the manufacturing process so that production can continue smoothly if there are temporary machine breakdowns or other work stoppages. Similarly, a stock of finished parts or products allows customer demand to be met in the event of a work stoppage or problem with transportation or distribution.

In-process (buffer) inventories are partially completed items kept between stages of a production process.

Demand

The starting point for the management of inventory is customer demand. Inventory exists to meet customer demand. Customers can be inside the organization, such as a machine operator waiting for a part or partially completed product to work on. Customers can also be outside the organization—for example, an individual purchasing groceries or a new VCR. In either case an essential determinant of effective inventory management is an accurate forecast of demand. For this reason the topics of forecasting (Chapter 10) and inventory management are directly interrelated.

---

[2] E. Raia, "JIT in Detroit," *Purchasing* (September 15, 1988): 68–77.

Tires like these stored at a Goodyear *plant are an example of a dependent demand item. The number of tires demanded by an automobile manufacturer like Ford is dependent upon the number of cars it produces. Other automotive products that reflect dependent demand include windshields, seats, steering wheels, and various engine parts. Cars are an example of independent demand, as are appliances, computers, and houses.*

Dependent demand items are used internally to produce a final product.

Independent demand items are final products demanded by external customers.

In general, the demand for items in inventory is either dependent or independent. **Dependent demand** items are typically component parts or materials used in the process of producing a final product. If an automobile company plans to produce 1,000 new cars, then it will need 5,000 wheels and tires (including spares). The demand for wheels is dependent on the production of cars—the demand for one item depends on demand for another item.

Cars are an example of an **independent demand** item. Independent demand items are final or finished products that are not a function of, or dependent upon, internal production activity. Independent demand is usually external and, thus, is beyond the direct control of the organization. In this chapter we focus on the management of inventory for independent demand items; Chapter 13 is devoted to inventory management for dependent demand items.

Inventory and Quality Management

Inventory must be sufficient to provide high-quality customer service in TQM.

A company maintains inventory to meet its own demand and its customers' demand for items. The ability to meet effectively internal organizational demand or external customer demand in a timely, efficient manner is referred to as the *level of customer service*. A primary objective of supply chain management is to provide as high a level of customer service in terms of on-time delivery as possible. This is especially important in today's highly competitive business environment, where quality is such an important product characteristic. Customers for finished goods usually perceive quality service as availability of goods they want when they want them. (This is equally true of internal customers, such as company departments or employees.) To provide this level of quality customer service, the tendency is to maintain large stocks of all types of items. However, there is a cost associated with carrying items in inventory, which creates a cost trade-off between the quality level of customer service and the cost of that service.

As the level of inventory increases to provide better customer service, inventory costs increase, whereas quality-related customer service costs, such as lost sales and loss of customers, decreases. The conventional approach to inventory management is to maintain a level of inventory that reflects a compromise between inventory costs and customer service. However, according to the contemporary "zero defects" philosophy of quality management, the long-term benefits of quality in terms of larger market share outweigh lower short-run production-related costs, such as inventory costs. Attempting to apply this philosophy to inventory management is not simple because one way of competing in today's diverse business environment is to reduce prices through reduced inventory costs. Nevertheless, it is an area where the traditional approach requires scrutiny in light of contemporary trends relative to TQM.

Inventory Costs

There are three basic costs associated with inventory: carrying, or holding, costs; ordering costs; and shortage costs.

Carrying costs are the costs of holding items in inventory. These costs vary with the level of inventory and occasionally with the length of time an item is held; that is, the greater the level of inventory over a period of time, the higher the carrying costs. Carrying costs can include the cost of losing the use of funds tied up in inventory; direct storage costs such as rent, heating, cooling, lighting, security, refrigeration, record keeping, and transportation; interest on loans used to purchase inventory; depreciation; obsolescence as markets for products in inventory diminish; product deterioration and spoilage; breakage; taxes; and pilferage.

Carrying costs are normally specified in one of two ways. The usual way is to assign total carrying costs, determined by summing all the individual costs just mentioned, on a per-unit basis per time period, such as a month or year. In this form, carrying costs are commonly expressed as a per-unit dollar amount on an annual basis; for example, $10 per unit per year. Alternatively, carrying costs are sometimes expressed as a percentage of the value of an item or as a percentage of average inventory value. It is generally estimated that carrying costs range from 10 to 40 percent of the value of a manufactured item.

Ordering costs are the costs associated with replenishing the stock of inventory being held. These are normally expressed as a dollar amount per order and are independent of the order size. Ordering costs vary with the number of orders made—as the number of orders increases, the ordering cost increases. Costs incurred each time an order is made can include requisition and purchase orders, transportation and shipping, receiving, inspection, handling and storage, and accounting and auditing costs.

Ordering costs generally react inversely to carrying costs. As the size of orders increases, fewer orders are required, reducing ordering costs. However, ordering larger amounts results in higher inventory levels and higher carrying costs. In general, as the order size increases, ordering costs decrease and carrying costs increase.

Shortage costs, also referred to as *stockout costs*, occur when customer demand cannot be met because of insufficient inventory. If these shortages result in a permanent loss of sales, shortage costs include the loss of profits. Shortages can also cause customer dissatisfaction and a loss of goodwill that can result in a permanent loss of customers

Inventory costs: carrying, ordering, and shortage costs.

Carrying costs are the costs of holding an item in inventory.

Ordering costs are the costs of replenishing inventory.

Shortage costs are temporary or permanent loss of sales when demand cannot be met.

and future sales. In some instances, the inability to meet customer demand or lateness in meeting demand results in penalties in the form of price discounts or rebates. When demand is internal, a shortage can cause work stoppages in the production process and create delays, resulting in downtime costs and the cost of lost production (including indirect and direct production costs).

Costs resulting from lost sales because demand cannot be met are more difficult to determine than carrying or ordering costs. Therefore, shortage costs are frequently subjective estimates and some times an educated guess.

Shortages occur because carrying inventory is costly. As a result, shortage costs have an inverse relationship to carrying costs—as the amount of inventory on hand increases, the carrying cost increases, whereas shortage costs decrease.

The objective of inventory management is to employ an inventory control system that will indicate how much should be ordered and when orders should take place so that the sum of the three inventory costs just described will be minimized.

Inventory Control Systems

An inventory system controls the level of inventory by determining how much to order (the level of replenishment), and when to order. There are two basic types of inventory systems: a *continuous* (or *fixed-order-quantity*) *system* and a *periodic* (or *fixed-time-period*) *system.* In a continuous system, an order is placed for the same constant amount whenever the inventory on hand decreases to a certain level, whereas in a periodic system, an order is placed for a variable amount after specific regular intervals.

Continuous Inventory Systems

In a **continuous in-ventory (or fixed-or-der-quantity) system,** a constant amount is ordered when inventory declines to a predetermined level.

In a **continuous inventory system** (also referred to as a *perpetual* system and a **fixed-order-quantity system**), a continual record of the inventory level for every item is maintained. Whenever the inventory on hand decreases to a predetermined level, referred to as the *reorder point*, a new order is placed to replenish the stock of inventory. The order that is placed is for a fixed amount that minimizes the total inventory costs. This amount, called the *economic order quantity*, is discussed in greater detail later.

A positive feature of a continuous system is that the inventory level is continuously monitored, so management always knows the inventory status. This is advantageous for critical items such as replacement parts or raw materials and supplies. However, maintaining a continual record of the amount of inventory on hand can also be costly.

A simple example of a continuous inventory system is a ledger-style checkbook that many of us use on a daily basis. Our checkbook comes with 300 checks; after the 200th check has been used (and there are 100 left), there is an order form for a new batch of checks. This form, when turned in at the bank, initiates an order for a new batch of 300 checks. Many office inventory systems use *reorder cards* that are placed within stacks of stationery or at the bottom of a case of pens or paper clips to signal when a new order should be placed. If you look behind the items on a hanging rack in a Kmart store, there will be a card indicating it is time to place an order for the item for an amount indicated on the card.

A more sophisticated example of a continuous inventory system is the computerized checkout system with a laser scanner used by many supermarkets and retail stores. The laser scanner reads the universal product code (UPC), or bar code, from the product package; the transaction is instantly recorded, and the inventory level updated. Such a system is not only quick and accurate, it also provides management with continuously updated information on the status of inventory levels. Many manufacturing companies'

Competing at Lands' End

Managing Inventory with Bar Codes and Computers at Lands' End

www.prenhall.com/russell

Efficient inventory management at Lands' End that enables the company to meet its promise of two-day service is achieved using bar codes and computers. The system begins in the receiving area where the night before an order is due to be trucked in, a bar code slip is printed for each box of items in the order. When the order arrives and is unloaded the bar code label is attached to each box. Operators unload each box and enter its contents into the computer, then compare the results with the original purchase order to make sure everything arrived. The bar code is then used to track the merchandise throughout the distribution center.

Based on current demand, the computer determines if a box will be sent to reserve storage, to active bins to meet that day's demand, to quality assurance, or straight to packing and shipping to meet back orders. Most merchandise goes to reserve storage, a warehouse area encompassing three large rooms, eight stories high, that can accommodate over 200,000 boxes. Using a special telescoping crane with a "fork-lift"-like apparatus on top, boxes are placed in storage wherever there's a vacant space, which is indicated by the computer. Thus, a box of men's green socks may be stacked on top of a box of lady's blue sweaters and next to a box of children's white shorts. The crane operator scans the bar code on the box and then the bar code on the shelf where the box is being put. These two numbers allow the computer to keep track of the precise location of each box. When items are needed to fill an order, the computer can quickly locate them in reserve storage using the matched set of shelf and box bar codes.

Arriving items and items pulled from storage that are needed to meet the immediate day's demand are routed to the correct aisle in the active-bin area by scanning bar codes. A stock keeper in each area puts merchandise into the correct active bins; when a bin gets low, the computer knows to send more of that item from reserve storage. Beginning at 7:30 a.m. order-fillers are given a stack of "pick" tickets that tell them what bins to pick items from to fill their orders. They have a one-hour period to fill their stack of orders. These order-fillers move rapidly up one aisle and down the next picking items from the bins to fill their stack of orders, never backtracking because the computer has given them their tickets in sequence. As each item is picked from a bin the order-filler places a pressure-sensitive ticket with a bar code onto the merchandise. When order-fillers' carts are filled, the merchandise is emptied onto a conveyor that takes it to packing.

As merchandise enters the packing department, operators place each item on a conveyorized tilting tray with the bar code up. As these conveyorized trays move toward the packing bin area a scanner (similar to a grocery-store scanner) reads the item bar code label on the pick ticket originally attached by the order-filler. When the tray arrives at the proper station to be joined with the rest of an order, the tray tips and the merchandise slides down into the proper bin with the other items that make up the order. The bar code on the pick ticket is actually the number of the packing bin and all items in an order have that same three-digit bar code. Packers then place items in mailing boxes or bags and check each item from the bin for accuracy against a packing list that also tells them the size box or bag to use. After the merchandise is packed, packages are placed on a conveyor and routed to shipping sorters where, once again, the computer scans the bar code on the address label and the conveyor tray tips to send the package down a chute for the appropriate shipper. The bar code on each package is scanned as it is loaded so that Lands' End always knows when an order left and what truck it went on.

To consumers the most familiar type of bar code scanners are used with cash registers at retail stores. These scanners not only register the price of the product but also keep a record of the sale for inventory purposes. The traditional bar code is a single line with 11 digits, the first six identifying a manufacturer and the last five assigned to a specific product by the manufacturer. This employee is using a portable hand-held bar code scanner to scan a two-dimensional bar code for inventory control. A two-dimensional bar code can store approximately 100 times more information (the equivalent of about two pages of text) than the traditional retail bar code and works just as fast. It contains as much information as a 20-foot strip of the familiar supermarket bar code. It is actually a stack of 90 one-dimensional bar codes that the scanner reads downward as well as across. In addition to identifying the product, it can indicate where a product came from, where it's supposed to go, and how the product should be handled in transit. It also can include emergency information for hazardous products and corrective information in case part of the code has been torn off or destroyed.

suppliers and distributors also use bar code systems and hand-held laser scanners to inventory materials, supplies, equipment, in-process parts, and finished goods.

Periodic Inventory Systems

In a **periodic inventory (or fixed-time-period) system,** an order is placed for a variable amount after a fixed passage of time.

In a **periodic inventory system** (also referred to as a **fixed-time-period system** or a *periodic review system*), the inventory on hand is counted at specific time intervals; for example, every week or at the end of each month. After the inventory in stock is determined, an order is placed for an amount that will bring inventory back up to a desired level. In this system the inventory level is not monitored at all during the time interval between orders, so it has the advantage of little or no required record keeping. The disadvantage is less direct control. This typically results in larger inventory levels for a periodic inventory system than in a continuous system to guard against unexpected stockouts early in the fixed period. Such a system also requires that a new order quantity be determined each time a periodic order is made.

An example of a periodic inventory system is a college or university bookstore. Textbooks are normally ordered according to a periodic system, wherein a count of textbooks in stock (for every course) is made after the first few weeks of a semester or quarter. An order for new textbooks for the next semester is then made according to estimated course enrollments for the next term (i.e., demand) and the amount remaining in stock. Smaller retail stores, drugstores, grocery stores, and offices sometimes use periodic systems—the stock level is checked every week or month, often by a vendor, to see how much should be ordered.

The ABC Classification System

The **ABC system** classifies inventory according to its dollar value to the firm. Typically thousands of independent demand items are held in inventory by a company, especially in manufacturing, but a small percentage is of such a high dollar value to warrant close inventory control. In general, about 5 to 15 percent of all inventory items account for 70 to 80 percent of the total dollar value of inventory. These are classified as *A*, or *Class A*, items. *B* items represent approximately 30 percent of total inventory units but only about 15 percent of total inventory dollar value. *C* items generally account for 50 to 60 percent of all inventory units but represent only 5 to 10 percent of total dollar value. For example, a discount store such as Wal-Mart normally stocks only a few television sets, a somewhat larger number of bicycles or sets of sheets, and hundreds of boxes of soap powder, bottles of shampoo, and AA batteries.

An **ABC system** is an inventory classification system in which a small percentage of (A) items account for most of the inventory value.

In ABC analysis each class of inventory requires different levels of inventory control—the higher the value of the inventory, the tighter the control. Class A items should experience tight inventory control; B and C require more relaxed (perhaps minimal) attention.

The first step in ABC analysis is to classify all inventory items as either A, B, or C. Each item is assigned a dollar value, which is computed by multiplying the dollar cost of one unit by the annual demand for that item. All items are then ranked according to their annual dollar value, with, for example, the top 10 percent classified as A items, the next 30 percent, as B items, and the last 60 percent, as C items. These classifications will not be exact, but they have been found to be close to the actual occurrence in firms with remarkable frequency.

A items require close inventory control because of their high value; B and C items less control.

The next step is to determine the level of inventory control for each classification. Class A items require tight inventory control because they represent such a large percentage of the total dollar value of inventory. These inventory levels should be as low as possible, and safety stocks minimized. This requires accurate demand forecasts and detailed record keeping. The appropriate inventory control system and inventory modeling procedure to determine order quantity should be applied. In addition, close attention should be given to purchasing policies and procedures if the inventory items are acquired from outside the firm. B and C items require less stringent inventory control. Since carrying costs are usually lower for C items, higher inventory levels can sometimes be maintained with larger safety stocks. It may not be necessary to control C items beyond simple observation. In general, A items frequently require a continuous control system, where the inventory level is continuously monitored; a periodic review system with less monitoring will suffice for C items.

EXAMPLE 12.1

ABC System Classification

The maintenance department for a small manufacturing firm has responsibility for maintaining an inventory of spare parts for the machinery it services. The parts inventory, unit cost, and annual usage are:

(Continued)

Part	Unit Cost	Annual Usage
1	$ 60	90
2	350	40
3	30	130
4	80	60
5	30	100
6	20	180
7	10	170
8	320	50
9	510	60
10	20	120

The department manager wants to classify the inventory parts according to the ABC system to determine which stocks of parts should most closely be monitored.

SOLUTION:

First rank the items according to their total value and also compute each item's percentage of total value and quantity.

Part	Total Value	% of Total Value	% of Total Quantity	% Cumulative
9	$30,600	35.9	6.0	6.0
8	16,000	18.7	5.0	11.0
2	14,000	16.4	4.0	15.0
1	5,400	6.3	9.0	24.0
4	4,800	5.6	6.0	30.0
3	3,900	4.6	10.0	40.0
6	3,600	4.2	18.0	58.0
5	3,000	3.5	13.0	71.0
10	2,400	2.8	12.0	83.0
7	1,700	2.0	17.0	100.0
	$85,400			

Based on simple observation, it appears that the first three items form a group with the highest value, the next three items form a second group, and the last four items constitute a group. Thus, the ABC classification for these items is as follows.

Class	Items	% of Total Value	% of Total Quantity
A	9, 8, 2	71.0	15.0
B	1, 4, 3	16.5	25.0
C	6, 5, 10, 7	12.5	60.0

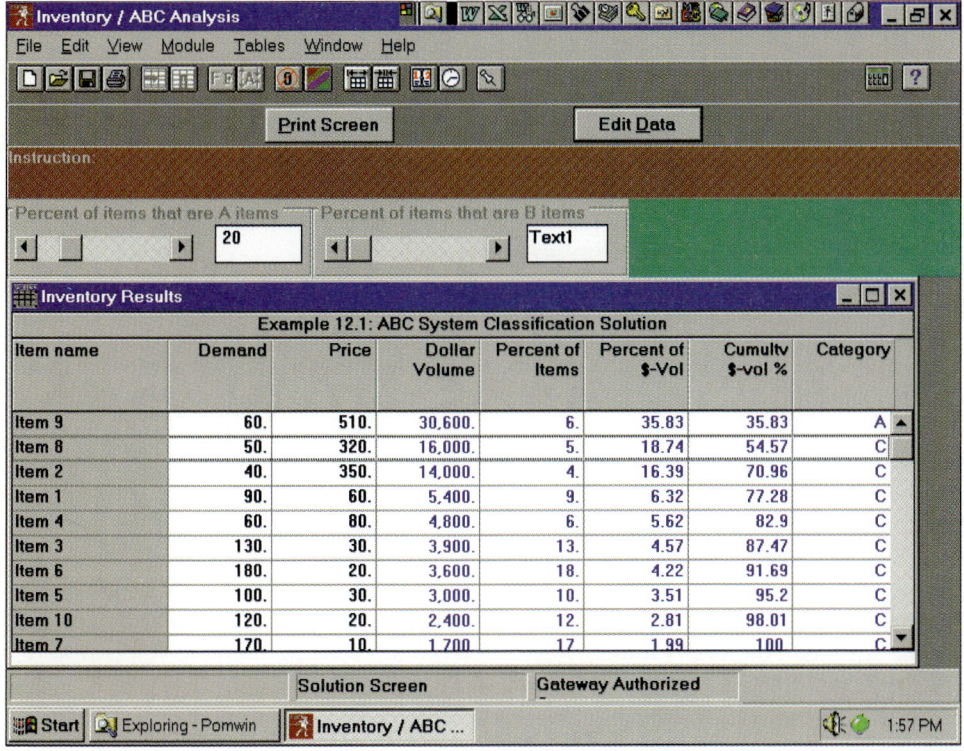

EXHIBIT 12.1

ABC Classification with POM for Windows

POM for Windows has a program for performing ABC classifications within its inventory module. The solution screen for the ABC classification in Example 12.1 is shown in Exhibit 12.1. Notice that this classification scheme is not the same as the one developed in Example 12.1, which can occur frequently in ABC classification since determination of the breakpoints between the three classification groups is often judgmental and based on observation.

Economic Order Quantity Models

In a continuous, or fixed-order-quantity, system when inventory reaches a specific level, referred to as the *reorder point*, a fixed amount is ordered. The most widely used and traditional means for determining how much to order in a continuous system is the **economic order quantity** (**EOQ**) model, also referred to as the economic lot-size model. The earliest published derivation of the basic EOQ model formula in 1915 is credited to Ford Harris, an employee at Westinghouse.

EOQ is the optimal order quantity that will minimize total inventory costs.

The function of the EOQ model is to determine the optimal order size that minimizes total inventory costs. There are several variations of the EOQ model, depending on the assumptions made about the inventory system. We will describe two model versions, including the basic EOQ model and the EOQ model with noninstantaneous receipt.

The Basic EOQ Model

The *basic EOQ model* is a formula for determining the optimal order size that minimizes the sum of carrying costs and ordering costs. The model formula is derived under a set of simplifying and restrictive assumptions, as follows:

Assumptions of EOQ model

- Demand is known with certainty and is relatively constant over time.
- No shortages are allowed.
- Lead time for the receipt of orders is constant.
- The order quantity is received all at once.

The **order cycle** is the time between receipt of orders in an inventory cycle.

EOQ is a continuous inventory system.

These basic model assumptions are reflected in Figure 12.1, which describes the continuous-inventory **order cycle** system inherent in the EOQ model. An order quantity, Q, is received and is used up over time at a constant rate. When the inventory level decreases to the reorder point, R, a new order is placed; a period of time, referred to as the *lead time*, is required for delivery. The order is received all at once just at the moment when demand depletes the entire stock of inventory—the inventory level reaches 0—so there will be no shortages. This cycle is repeated continuously for the same order quantity, reorder point, and lead time.

As we mentioned, the economic order quantity is the order size that minimizes the sum of carrying costs and ordering costs. These two costs react inversely to each other. As the order size increases, fewer orders are required, causing the ordering cost to decline, whereas the average amount of inventory on hand will increase, resulting in an increase in carrying costs. Thus, in effect, the optimal order quantity represents a compromise between these two inversely related costs.

The total annual ordering cost is computed by multiplying the cost per order, designated as C_o, times the number of orders per year. Since annual demand, D, is assumed to be known and to be constant, the number of orders will be D/Q, where Q is the order size and

$$\text{Annual ordering cost} = \frac{C_o D}{Q}$$

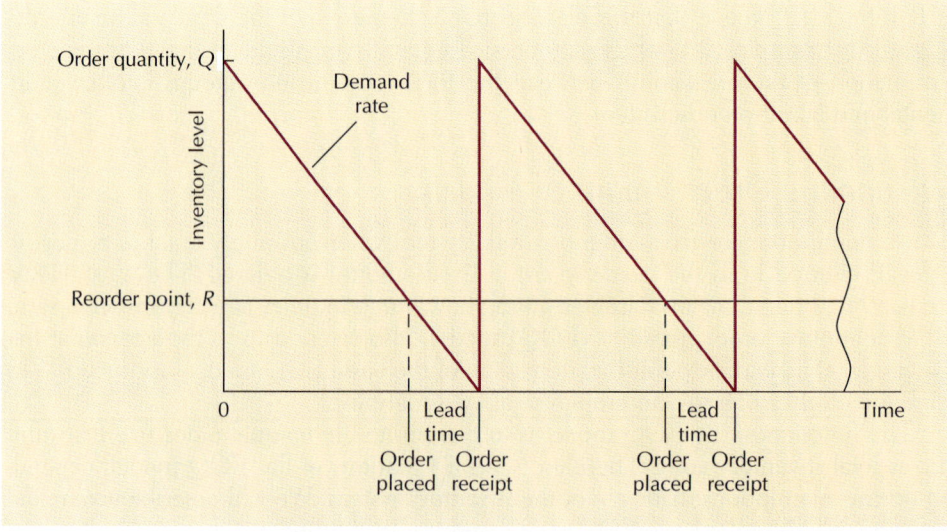

FIGURE 12.1   The Inventory Order Cycle

The only variable in this equation is Q; both C_o and D are constant parameters. Thus, the relative magnitude of the ordering cost is dependent upon the order size.

Total annual carrying cost is computed by multiplying the annual per-unit carrying cost, designated as C_c, times the average inventory level, determined by dividing the order size, Q, by 2: $Q/2$;

$$\text{Annual carrying cost} = \frac{C_c Q}{2}$$

The total annual inventory cost is the sum of the ordering and carrying costs:

$$TC = \frac{C_o D}{Q} + \frac{C_c Q}{2}$$

The graph in Figure 12.2 shows the inverse relationship between ordering cost and carrying cost, resulting in a convex total cost curve.

The optimal order quantity occurs at the point in Figure 12.2 where the total cost curve is at a minimum, which coincides exactly with the point where the carrying cost curve intersects the ordering cost curve. This enables us to determine the optimal value of Q by equating the two cost functions and solving for Q,

Optimal Q corresponds to the lowest point on the total cost curve.

$$\frac{C_o D}{Q} = \frac{C_c Q}{2}$$

$$Q^2 = \frac{2C_o D}{C_c}$$

$$Q_{opt} = \sqrt{\frac{2C_o D}{C_c}}$$

Alternatively, the optimal value of Q can be determined by differentiating the total cost curve with respect to Q, setting the resulting function equal to zero (the slope at the minimum point on the total cost curve), and solving for Q,

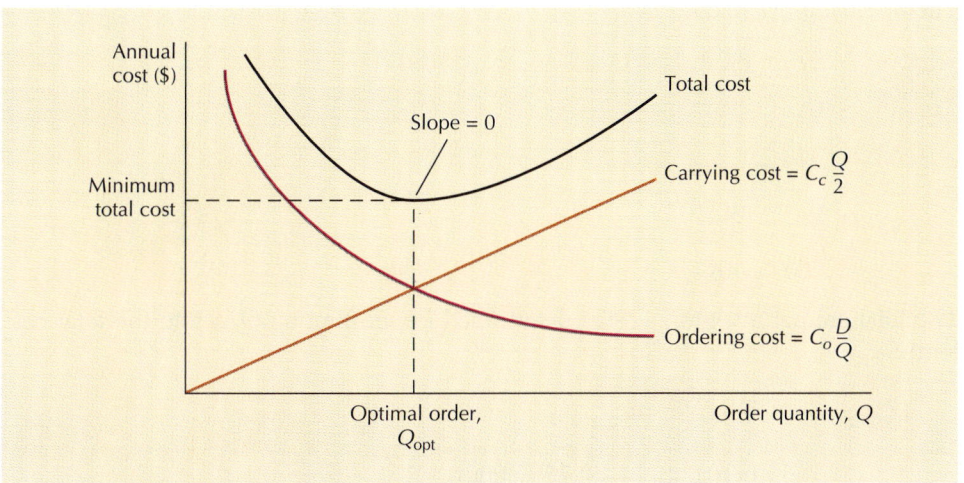

FIGURE 12.2 The EOQ Cost Model

$$TC = \frac{C_o D}{Q} + \frac{C_c Q}{2}$$

$$\frac{\partial TC}{\partial Q} = -\frac{C_o D}{Q^2} + \frac{C_c}{2}$$

$$0 = -\frac{C_o D}{Q^2} + \frac{C_c}{2}$$

$$Q_{opt} = \sqrt{\frac{2C_o D}{C_c}}$$

The total minimum cost is determined by substituting the value for the optimal order size, Q_{opt}, into the total cost equation,

$$TC_{min} = \frac{C_o D}{Q_{opt}} + \frac{C_c Q_{opt}}{2}$$

EXAMPLE 12.2

The Economic Order Quantity

The I-75 Carpet Discount Store in North Georgia stocks carpet in its warehouse and sells it through an adjoining showroom. The store keeps several brands and styles of carpet in stock; however, its biggest seller is Super Shag carpet. The store wants to determine the optimal order size and total inventory cost for this brand of carpet given an estimated annual demand of 10,000 yards of carpet, an annual carrying cost of $0.75 per yard, and an ordering cost of $150. The store would also like to know the number of orders that will be made annually and the time between orders (i.e., the order cycle) given that the store is open every day except Sunday, Thanksgiving Day, and Christmas Day (which is not on a Sunday).

SOLUTION:

C_c = $0.75 per yard
C_o = $150
D = 10,000 yards

The optimal order size is

$$Q_{opt} = \sqrt{\frac{2C_o D}{C_c}}$$

$$= \sqrt{\frac{2(150)(10,000)}{(0.75)}}$$

$$= 2,000 \text{ yards}$$

The total annual inventory cost is determined by substituting Q_{opt} into the total cost formula:

$$TC_{min} = \frac{C_o D}{Q_{opt}} + \frac{C_c Q_{opt}}{2}$$

$$= \frac{(150)(10,000)}{2,000} + \frac{(0.75)(2,000)}{2}$$

$$= \$750 + 750$$
$$= \$1,500$$

The number of orders per year is computed as follows.

$$\text{Number of orders per year} = \frac{D}{Q_{opt}}$$
$$= \frac{10,000}{2,000}$$
$$= 5 \text{ orders per year}$$

Given that the store is open 311 days annually (365 days minus 52 Sundays, Thanksgiving, and Christmas), the order cycle is

$$\text{Order cycle time} = \frac{311 \text{ days}}{D/Q_{opt}}$$
$$= \frac{311}{5}$$
$$= 62.2 \text{ store days}$$

The optimal order quantity, determined in this example, and in general, is an approximate value, since it is based on estimates of carrying and ordering costs as well as uncertain demand (although all of these parameters are treated as known, certain values in the EOQ model). In practice it is acceptable to round the Q values off to the nearest whole number. The precision of a decimal place is generally not necessary. In addition, because the optimal order quantity is computed from a square root, errors or variations in the cost parameters and demand tend to be dampened. For instance, in Example 12.2, if the order cost had actually been 30 percent higher, or $200, the resulting optimal order size would have varied only by a little under 10 percent (i.e., 2,190 yards instead of 2,000 yards). Variations in both inventory costs will tend to offset each other, since they have an inverse relationship. As a result, the EOQ model is relatively resilient to errors in the cost estimates and demand, or is *robust*, which has tended to enhance its popularity.

The EOQ Model with Noninstantaneous Receipt

A variation of the basic EOQ model is the **noninstantaneous receipt model,** also referred to as the *gradual usage* and *production lot-size model*. In this EOQ model the assumption that orders are received all at once is relaxed. The order quantity is received gradually over time, and the inventory level is depleted at the same time it is being replenished. This situation is most commonly found when the inventory user is also the producer, as in a manufacturing operation where a part is produced to use in a larger assembly. This situation also can occur when orders are delivered gradually over time or when the retailer is also the producer.

The noninstantaneous receipt model is shown graphically in Figure 12.3. The inventory level is gradually replenished as an order is received. In the basic EOQ model, average inventory was half the maximum inventory level, or $Q/2$, but in this model variation, the maximum inventory level is not simply Q; it is an amount somewhat lower than Q, adjusted for the fact the order quantity is depleted during the order receipt period.

The EOQ model is *robust*; because Q is a square root, errors in the estimation of D, C_c, and C_o are dampened.

The **noninstantaneous receipt model** is an inventory system in which an order is received gradually, as inventory is depleted.

Relaxing the assumption that Q is received all at once.

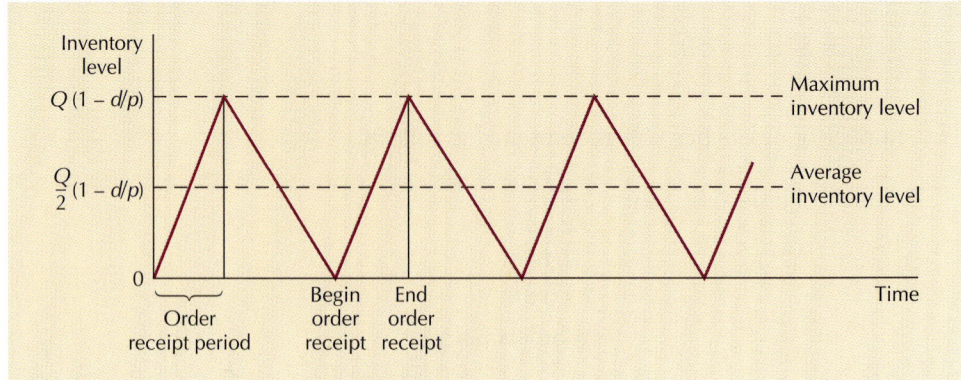

FIGURE 12.3   The EOQ Model with Noninstantaneous Order Receipt

In order to determine the average inventory level, we define the following parameters unique to this model.

p = daily rate at which the order is received over time, also known as the *production rate*

d = the daily rate at which inventory is demanded

The demand rate cannot exceed the production rate, since we are still assuming that no shortages are possible, and, if $d = p$, there is no order size, since items are used as fast as they are produced. For this model the production rate must exceed the demand rate, or $p > d$.

Observing Figure 12.3, the time required to receive an order is the order quantity divided by the rate at which the order is received, or Q/p. For example, if the order size is 100 units and the production rate, p, is 20 units per day, the order will be received in 5 days. The amount of inventory that will be depleted or used up during this time period is determined by multiplying by the demand rate: $(Q/p)d$. For example, if it takes 5 days to receive the order and during this time inventory is depleted at the rate of 2 units per day, then 10 units are used. As a result, the maximum amount of inventory on hand is the order size minus the amount depleted during the receipt period, computed as

$$\text{Maximum inventory level} = Q - \frac{Q}{p}d$$

$$= Q\left(1 - \frac{d}{p}\right)$$

Since this is the maximum inventory level, the average inventory level is determined by dividing this amount by 2:

$$\text{Average inventory level} = \frac{1}{2}\left[Q\left(1 - \frac{d}{p}\right)\right]$$

$$= \frac{Q}{2}\left(1 - \frac{d}{p}\right)$$

The total carrying cost using this function for average inventory is

$$\text{Total carrying cost} = \frac{C_c Q}{2}\left(1 - \frac{d}{p}\right)$$

Thus the total annual inventory cost is determined according to the following formula:

$$TC = \frac{C_oD}{Q} + \frac{C_cQ}{2}\left(1 - \frac{d}{p}\right)$$

Solving this function for the optimal value Q,

$$Q_{opt} = \sqrt{\frac{2C_oD}{C_c\left(1 - \frac{d}{p}\right)}}$$

EXAMPLE
12.3

*The EOQ Model with
Noninstantaneous
Receipt*

Assume that the I-75 Outlet Store has its own manufacturing facility in which it produces Super Shag carpet. The ordering cost, C_o, is the cost of setting up the production process to make Super Shag carpet. Recall $C_c = \$0.75$ per yard and $D = 10,000$ yards per year. The manufacturing facility operates the same days the store is open (i.e., 311 days) and produces 150 yards of the carpet per day. Determine the optimal order size, total inventory cost, the length of time to receive an order, the number of orders per year, and the maximum inventory level.

SOLUTION:

$C_o = \$150$

$C_c = \$0.75$ per yard

$D = 10,000$ yards

$d = \dfrac{10,000}{311} = 32.2$ yards per day

$p = 150$ yards per day

The optimal order size is determined as follows:

$$Q_{opt} = \sqrt{\frac{2C_oD}{C_c\left(1 - \frac{d}{p}\right)}}$$

$$= \sqrt{\frac{2(150)(10,000)}{0.75\left(1 - \frac{32.2}{150}\right)}}$$

$$= 2,256.8 \text{ yards}$$

This value is substituted into the following formula to determine total minimum annual inventory cost:

$$TC_{min} = \frac{C_oD}{Q} + \frac{C_cQ}{2}\left(1 - \frac{d}{p}\right)$$

$$= \frac{(150)(10,000)}{2,256.8} + \frac{(0.75)(2,256.8)}{2}\left(1 - \frac{32.2}{150}\right)$$

$$= \$1,329$$

(Continued)

The length of time to receive an order for this type of manufacturing operation is commonly called the length of the *production run*.

$$\text{Production run} = \frac{Q}{P}$$

$$= \frac{2{,}256.8}{150}$$

$$= 15.05 \text{ days per order}$$

The number of orders per year is actually the number of production runs that will be made:

$$\text{Number of production runs (from orders)} = \frac{D}{Q}$$

$$= \frac{10{,}000}{2{,}256.8}$$

$$= 4.43 \text{ runs per year}$$

Finally, the maximum inventory level is

$$\text{Maximum inventory level} = Q\left(1 - \frac{d}{p}\right)$$

$$= 2{,}256.8\left(1 - \frac{32.2}{150}\right)$$

$$= 1{,}772 \text{ yards}$$

Computer Solution of EOQ Models with Excel

EOQ analysis can be done with Excel (as well as with POM for Windows). The Excel screen for the noninstantaneous receipt model of Example 12.3 is shown in Exhibit 12.2. The formula for the optimal value of Q is contained in cell D10 as shown on the formula bar at the top of the screen.

Quantity Discounts

A quantity discount is given for specific higher order quantities.

A **quantity discount** is a price discount on an item if predetermined numbers of units are ordered. In the back of a magazine you might see an advertisement for a firm stating that it will produce a coffee mug (or hat) with a company or organizational logo on it, and the price will be $5 per mug if you purchase 100, $4 per mug if you purchase 200, or $3 per mug if you purchase 500 or more. Many manufacturing companies receive price discounts for ordering materials and supplies in high volume, and retail stores receive price discounts for ordering merchandise in large quantities.

Determining if an order size with a discount is more cost-effective than optimal Q.

The basic EOQ model can be used to determine the optimal order size with quantity discounts; however, the application of the model is slightly altered. The total inventory cost function must now include the purchase price of the item being ordered:

$$\text{TC} = \frac{C_o D}{Q} + \frac{C_c Q}{2} + PD$$

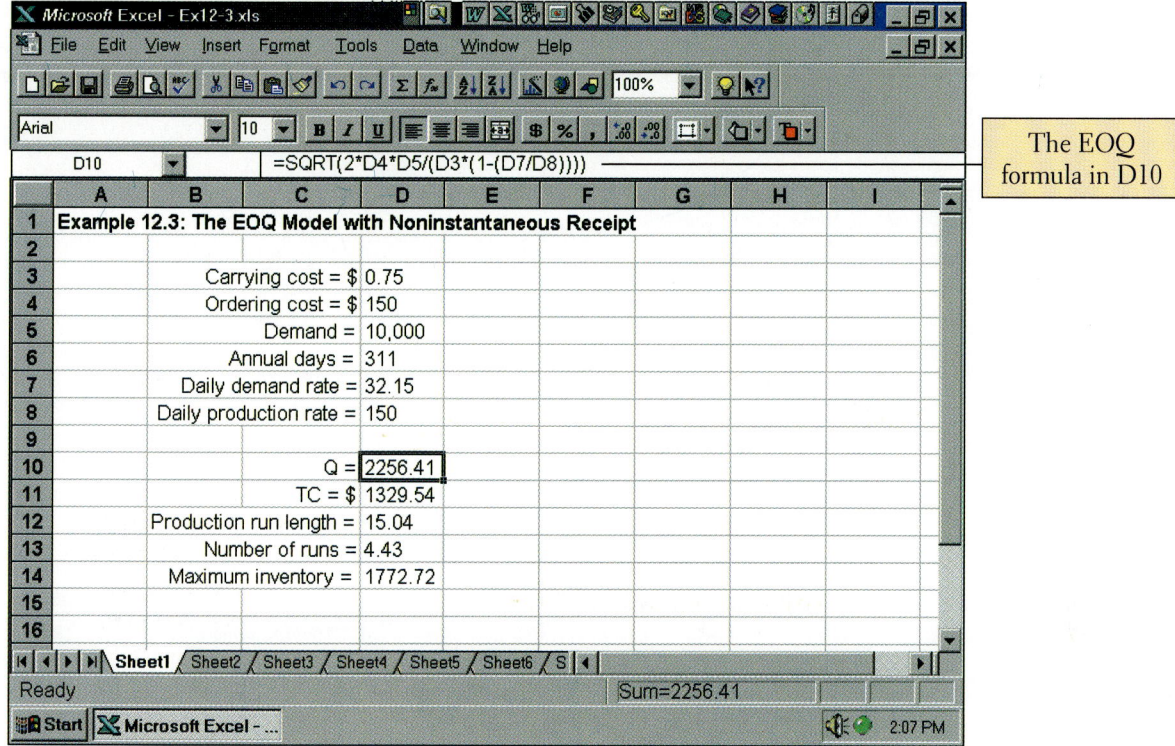

EXHIBIT 12.2

where

$$P = \text{per unit price of the item}$$
$$D = \text{annual demand}$$

Purchase price was not considered as part of our basic EOQ formulation earlier because it had no impact on the optimal order size. In the preceding formula PD is a constant value that would not alter the basic shape of the total cost curve; that is, the minimum point on the cost curve would still be at the same location, corresponding to the same value of Q. Thus, the optimal order size is the same no matter what the purchase price is. However, when a discount price is available, it is associated with a specific order size, which may be different from the optimal order size, and the customer must evaluate the trade-off between possibly higher carrying costs with the discount quantity versus EOQ cost. As a result, the purchase price does impact on the order-size decision when a discount is available.

Quantity Discounts with Constant Carrying Cost

The EOQ cost model with constant carrying costs for a pricing schedule with two discounts, d_1 and d_2, is illustrated in Figure 12.4 for the following discounts.

Order Size	Price
0–99	$10
100–199	8 (d_1)
200+	6 (d_2)

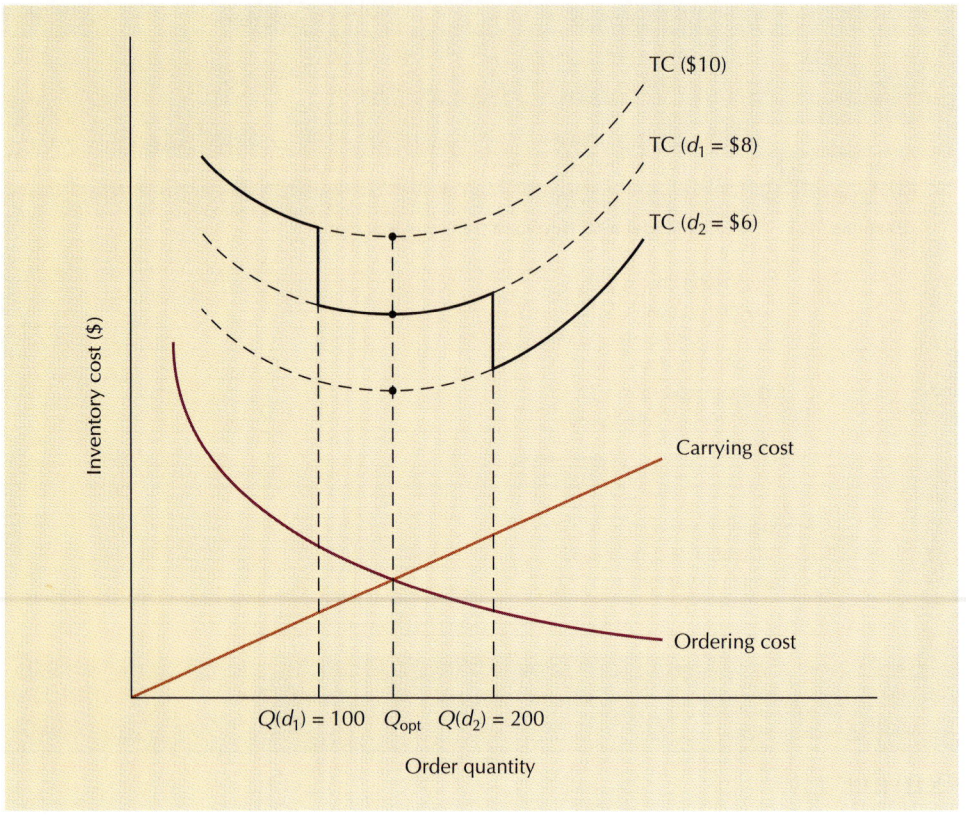

FIGURE 12.4   Quantity Discounts with Constant Carrying Cost

Notice in Figure 12.4 that the optimal order size, Q_{opt}, is the same regardless of the discount price. Although the total cost curve decreases with each discount in price (i.e., d_1 and d_2), since ordering and carrying cost are constant, the optimal order size, Q_{opt}, does not change.

The graph in Figure 12.4 reflects the composition of the total cost curve resulting from the discounts kicking in at two successively higher order quantities. The first segment of the total cost curve (with no discount) is valid only up to 99 units ordered. Beyond that quantity, the total cost curve (represented by the topmost dashed line) is meaningless because above 100 units there is a discount (d_1). Between 100 and 199 units the total cost drops down to the middle curve. This middle-level cost curve is valid only up to 199 units because at 200 units there is another, lower discount (d_2). So the total cost curve has two discrete steps, starting with the original total cost curve, dropping down to the next level cost curve for the first discount, and finally dropping to the third-level cost curve for the final discount.

Notice that the optimal order size, Q_{opt}, is feasible only for the middle level of the total cost curve, TC(d_1)—it does not coincide with the top level of the cost curve, TC, or the lowest level, TC(d_2). If the optimal EOQ order size had coincided with the lowest level of the total cost curve, it would have been the optimal order size for the entire discount price schedule. Since it does not coincide with the lowest level of the total cost curve, the total cost with Q_{opt} must be compared to the lower-level total cost using $Q(d_2)$ to see which results in the minimum total cost.

EXAMPLE
12.4

*A Quantity Discount
with Constant
Carrying Cost*

Comptek Computers wants to reduce a large stock of PCs it is discontinuing. It has offered the University Bookstore at Tech a quantity discount pricing schedule, as follows.

Quantity	Price
1–49	$1,400
50–89	1,100
90+	900

The annual carrying cost for the bookstore for a PC is $190, the ordering cost is $2,500, and annual demand for this particular model is estimated to be 200 units. The bookstore wants to determine if it should take advantage of this discount or order the basic EOQ order size.

SOLUTION:

First determine the optimal order size and total cost with the basic EOQ model.

$$C_o = \$2,500$$
$$C_c = \$190 \text{ per PC}$$
$$D = 200 \text{ PCs per year}$$

$$Q_{opt} = \sqrt{\frac{2C_oD}{C_c}}$$

$$= \sqrt{\frac{2(2,500)(200)}{190}}$$

$$= 72.5 \text{ PCs}$$

Although we will use $Q_{opt} = 72.5$ in the subsequent computations, realistically the order size would be 73 computers. This order size is eligible for the first discount of $1,100; therefore, this price is used to compute total cost,

$$TC = \frac{C_oD}{Q_{opt}} + \frac{C_cQ_{opt}}{2} + PD$$

$$= \frac{(2,500)(200)}{72.5} + \frac{(190)(72.5)}{2} + (1,100)(200)$$

$$TC_{min} = \$233,784$$

Since there is a discount for a larger order size than 50 units (i.e., there is a lower cost curve), this total cost of $233,784 must be compared with total cost with an order size of 90 and a discounted price of $900,

$$TC = \frac{C_oD}{Q} + \frac{C_cQ}{2} + PD$$

$$= \frac{(2,500)(200)}{90} + \frac{(190)(90)}{2} + (900)(200)$$

$$= \$194,105$$

(Continued)

Since this total cost is lower ($194,105 < $233,784), the maximum discount price should be taken, and 90 units should be ordered. We know that there is no order size larger than 90 that would result in a lower cost, since the minimum point on this total cost curve has already been determined to be 50.)

Quantity Discount Model Solution with POM for Windows

POM for Windows also has the capability to perform EOQ analysis with quantity discounts. Exhibit 12.3 shows the solution screen for Example 12.4. Exhibit 12.4 is a graph of the quantity discount model for this example generated by POM for Windows.

Reorder Point

In our description of the EOQ models in the previous sections, we addressed how much should be ordered. Now we will discuss the other aspect of inventory management, when to order. The determinant of when to order in a continuous inventory system is the **reorder point**, the inventory level at which a new order is placed.

The reorder point for our basic EOQ model with constant demand and a constant lead time to receive an order is equal to the amount demanded during the lead time,

$$R = dL$$

> The **reorder point** is the level of inventory at which a new order should be placed.

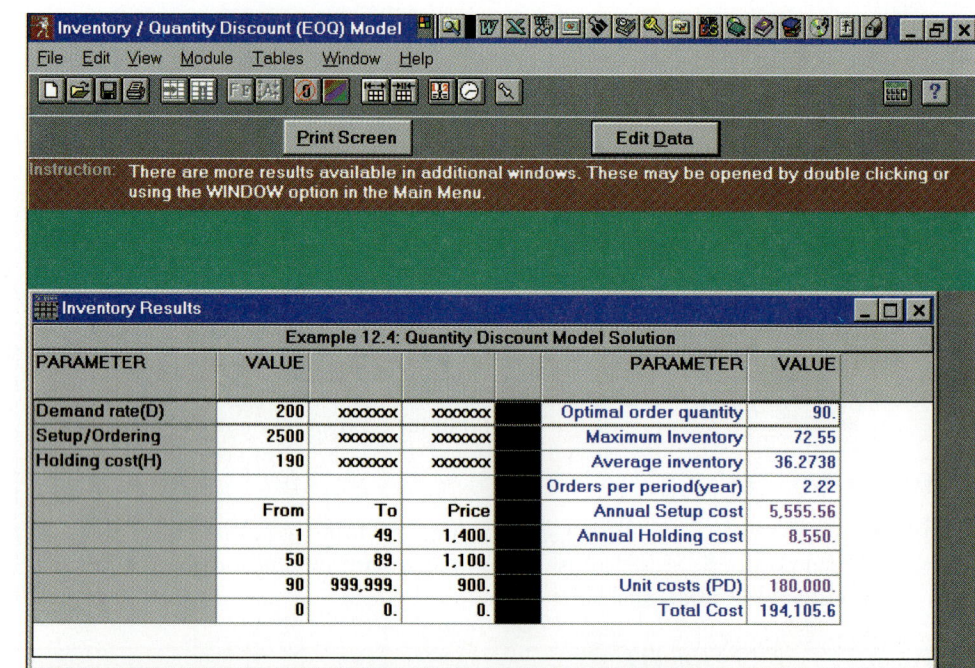

EXHIBIT 12.3

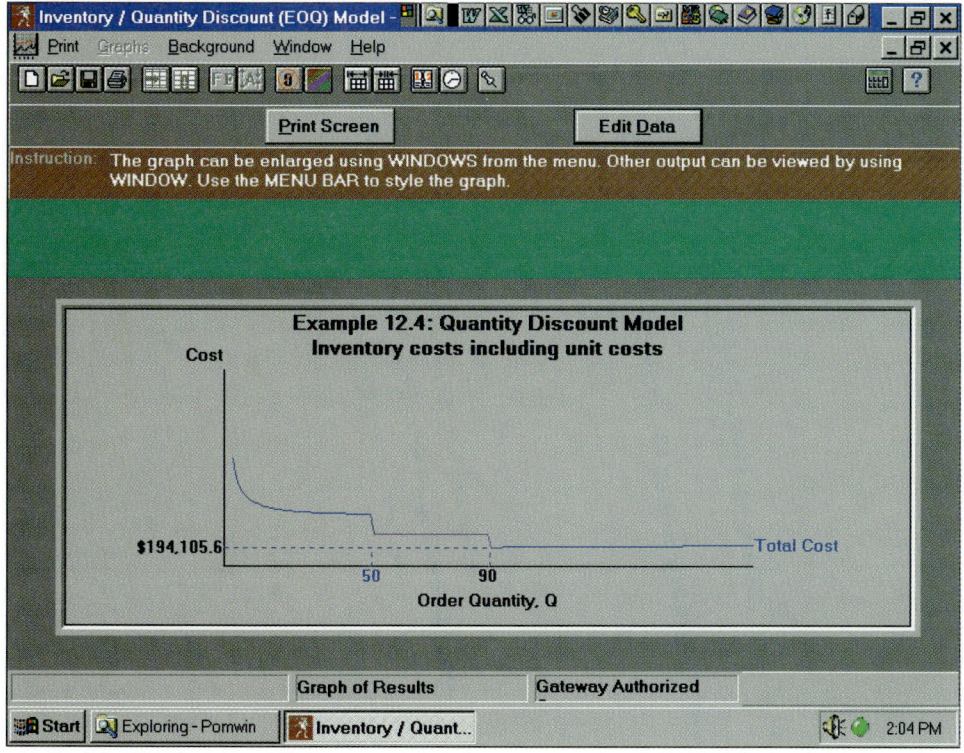

EXHIBIT 12.4

where

$$d = \text{demand rate per period (e.g., daily)}$$
$$L = \text{lead time}$$

EXAMPLE 12.5

Reorder Point for the Basic EOQ Model

The I-75 Discount Carpet Store in Example 12.2 is open 311 days per year. If annual demand is 10,000 yards of Super Shag carpet and the lead time to receive an order is 10 days, determine the reorder point for carpet.

SOLUTION:

$$R = dL$$
$$= \left(\frac{10,000}{311}\right)(10)$$
$$= 321.54 \text{ yards}$$

When the inventory level falls to approximately 321 yards of carpet, a new order is placed. Notice that the reorder point is not related to the optimal order quantity or any of the inventory costs.

Safety Stocks

In Example 12.5, an order is made when the inventory level reaches the reorder point. During the lead time, the remaining inventory in stock will be depleted at a constant demand rate, such that the new order quantity will arrive at exactly the same moment as the inventory level reaches zero. Realistically, demand—and, to a lesser extent lead time—are uncertain. The inventory level might be depleted at a slower or faster rate during lead time. This is depicted in Figure 12.5 for uncertain demand and a constant lead time.

A **stockout** is an inventory shortage.

Safety stock is a buffer added to the inventory on hand during lead time.

Notice in the second order cycle that a **stockout** occurs when demand exceeds the available inventory in stock. As a hedge against stockouts when demand is uncertain, a **safety** (or *buffer*) **stock** of inventory is frequently added to the expected demand during lead time. The addition of a safety stock to the stockout occurrence shown in Figure 12.5 is displayed in Figure 12.6.

Service Level

Service level is the probability that the inventory available during lead time will meet demand.

There are several ways to determine the amount of the safety stock. One popular method is to establish a safety stock that will meet a specified **service level.** The service level is the probability that the amount of inventory on hand during the lead time is sufficient to meet expected demand—that is, the probability that a stockout will not occur. The term *service* is used, since the higher the probability that inventory will be on hand, the more likely that customer demand will be met; that is, that the customer can be served. A service level of 90 percent means that there is a 0.90 probability that demand will be met during the lead time, and the probability that a stockout will occur is 10 percent. The service level is typically a policy decision based on a number of factors, including carrying costs for the extra safety stock and lost sales if customer demand cannot be met.

Reorder Point with Variable Demand

To compute the reorder point with a safety stock that will meet a specific service level, we will assume the demand during each day of lead time is uncertain, independent,

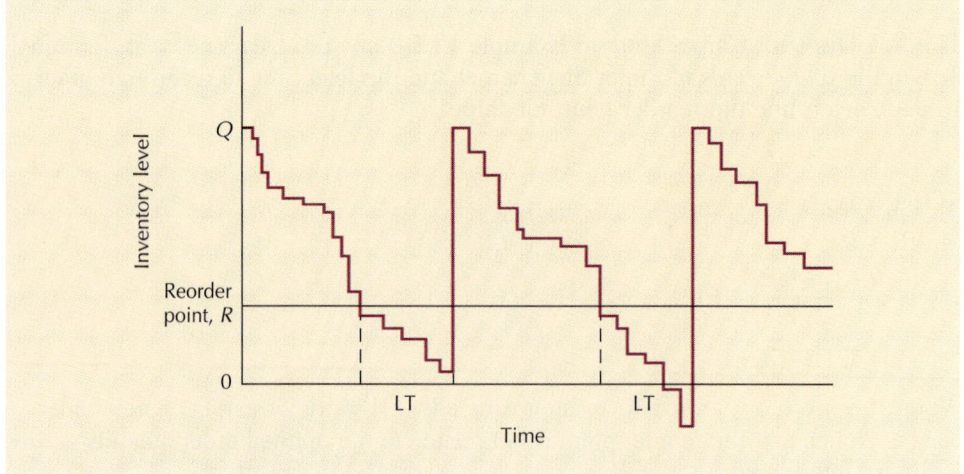

FIGURE 12.5   Variable Demand with a Reorder Point

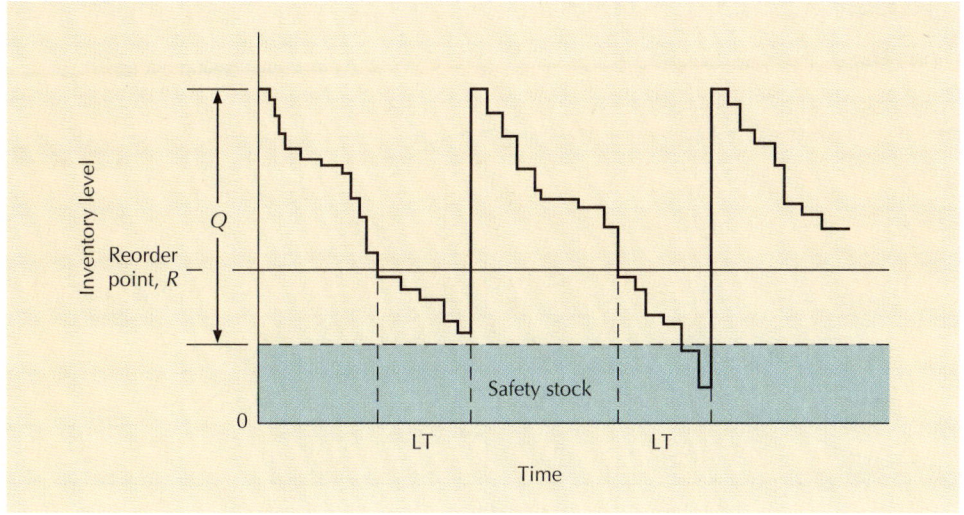

FIGURE 12.6 **Reorder Point with a Safety Stock**

and can be described by a normal distribution. The average demand for the lead time is the sum of the average daily demands for the days of the lead time, which is also the product of the average daily demands multiplied by the lead time. Likewise, the variance of the distribution is the sum of the daily variances for the number of days in the lead time. Using these parameters the reorder point to meet a specific service level can be computed as

$$R = \bar{d}L + z\sigma_d \sqrt{L}$$

where

$\quad\quad \bar{d}$ = average daily demand

$\quad\quad L$ = lead time

$\quad\quad \sigma_d$ = the standard deviation of daily demand

$\quad\quad z$ = number of standard deviations corresponding to the service level probability

$z\sigma_d \sqrt{L}$ = safety stock

The term $\sigma_d \sqrt{L}$ in this formula for the reorder point is the square root of the sum of the daily variances during lead time:

$$\text{Variance} = (\text{daily variance}) \times (\text{number of days of lead time})$$
$$= \sigma_d^2 L$$
$$\text{Standard deviation} = \sqrt{\sigma_d^2 L}$$
$$= \sigma_d \sqrt{L}$$

The reorder point relative to the service level is shown in Figure 12.7. The service level is the shaded area, or probability, to the left of the reorder point, R.

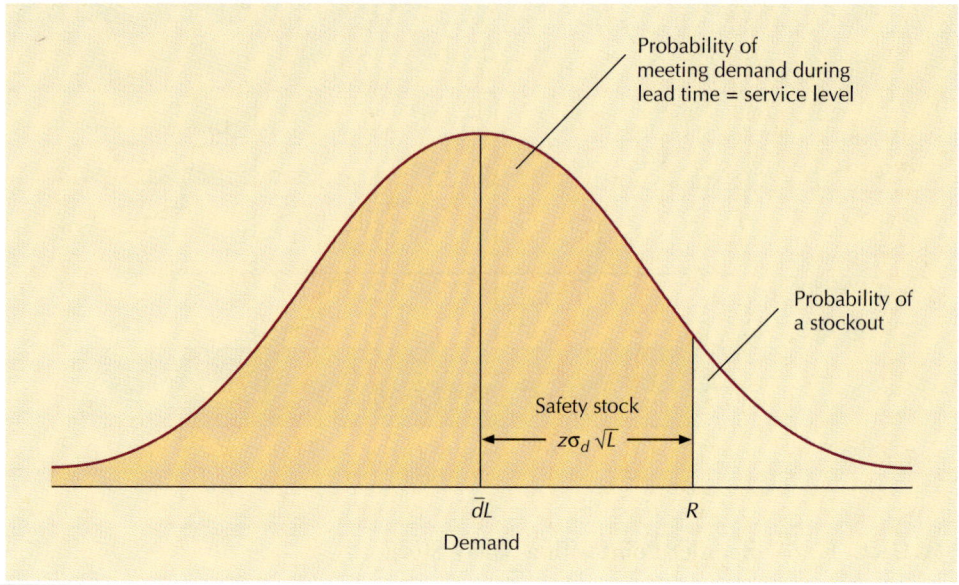

FIGURE 12.7   **Reorder Point for a Service Level**

<table>
<tr>
<td>

EXAMPLE
12.6

Reorder Point for
Variable Demand

</td>
<td>

For the I-75 Discount Carpet Store in Example 12.2, we will assume that daily demand for Super Shag carpet stocked by the store is normally distributed with an average daily demand of 30 yards and a standard deviation of 5 yards of carpet per day. The lead time for receiving a new order of carpet is 10 days. Determine the reorder point and safety stock if the store wants a service level of 95 percent with the probability of a stockout equal to 5 percent.

SOLUTION:

$$\bar{d} = 30 \text{ yards per day}$$
$$L = 10 \text{ days}$$
$$\sigma_d = 5 \text{ yards per day}$$

For a 95 percent service level, the value of z (from the Normal Table in Appendix A) is 1.65. The reorder point is computed as follows:

$$R = \bar{d}L + z\sigma_d \sqrt{L}$$
$$= 30(10) + (1.65)(5)(\sqrt{10})$$
$$= 300 + 26.1$$
$$= 326.1 \text{ yards}$$

The safety stock is the second term in the reorder point formula:

$$\text{Safety stock} = z\sigma_d \sqrt{L}$$
$$= (1.65)(5)(\sqrt{10})$$
$$= 26.1 \text{ yards}$$

</td>
</tr>
</table>

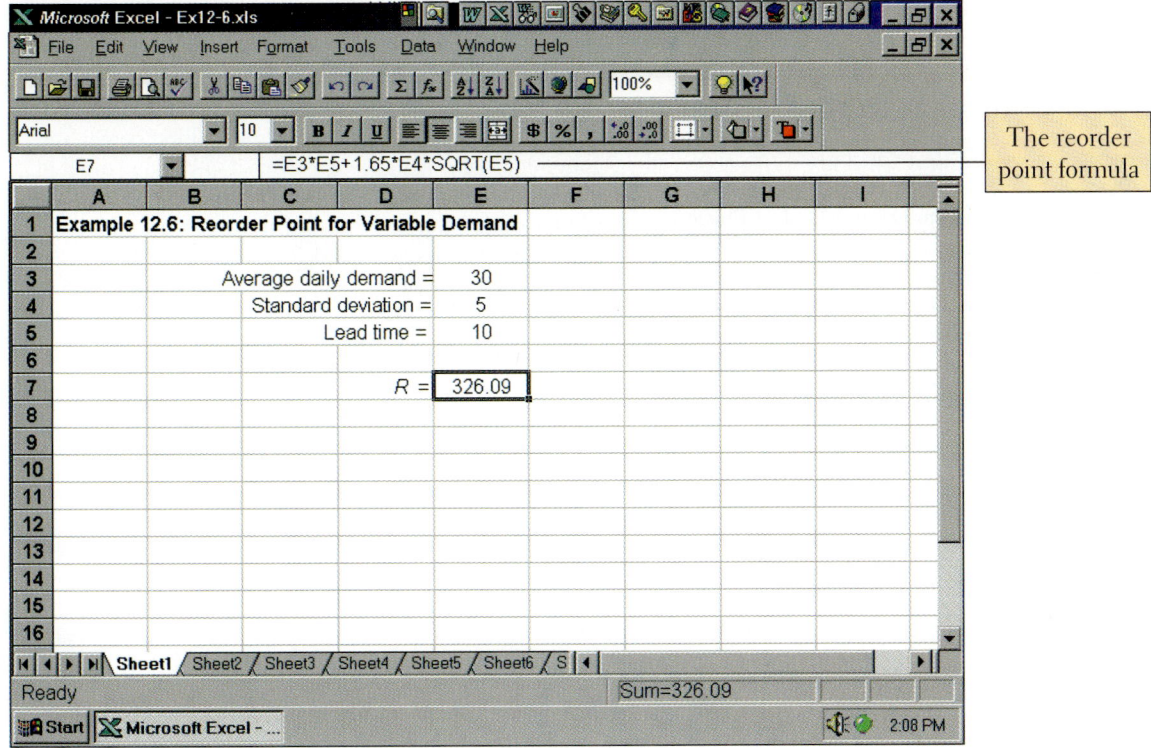

The reorder point formula

EXHIBIT 12.5

Determining the Reorder Point with Excel

Excel can be used to determine the reorder point for variable demand. Exhibit 12.5 shows the Excel screen for Example 12.6. Notice that the reorder point is computed using the formula in cell E7, which is shown on the formula bar at the top of the screen.

Order Quantity for a Periodic Inventory System

We defined a continuous, or fixed-order-quantity, inventory system as one which the order quantity was constant and the time between orders varied. So far this type of inventory system has been the focus of our discussion. The less common *periodic, or fixed-time-period, inventory system* is one in which the time between orders is constant and the order size varies. Drugstores are one example of a business that sometimes uses a fixed-period inventory system. Drugstores stock a number of personal hygiene- and health-related products such as shampoo, toothpaste, soap, bandages, cough medicine, and aspirin.

Normally, the vendors who provide these items to the store will make periodic visits—every few weeks or every month—and count the stock of inventory on hand for their product. If the inventory is exhausted or at some predetermined reorder point, a new order will be placed for an amount that will bring the inventory level back up to the desired level. The drugstore managers will generally not monitor the inventory level between vendor visits, but instead will rely on the vendor to take inventory.

Unfortunately, inventory might be exhausted early in the time period between visits, resulting in a stockout that will not be remedied until the next scheduled order. As

A periodic inventory system normally requires a larger safety stock.

THE COMPETITIVE EDGE

Inventory Control at Hewlett-Packard

www.prenhall.com/russell

The Vancouver division of Hewlett-Packard (HP) Company manufacturers Deskjet-Plus printers and ships them to distribution centers in North America, Europe, Asia, and the Pacific Rim. HP dealers like to carry very little inventory, but because of the highly competitive nature of the printer industry, they must supply printers to end users quickly. To accomplish a high customer service level, HP operates its distribution centers as inventory stocking points with large safety stocks to meet end-user demand. Because of uncertainties in material and parts acquisition and the manufacturing process at Vancouver, and customer demand, HP must maintain large safety stocks, especially at its European and Far East distribution centers where transit time (by sea) is approx-

imately one month. To minimize inventory levels, HP ships finished printers to its U.S. distribution center and generic printers without the power supply and manual to its overseas distribution centers. The overseas printers are subsequently "finished" at the distribution centers according to customer demand. The inventory system used at the HP distribution centers establishes a target inventory level based on the length and variability of lead time to replenish the stock from the factory and the length and variability of demand. The inventory safety stock level is expressed in terms of weeks of stock on hand. The inventory level (plus the amount on order) is reviewed each week; when the reorder point is reached, the quantity ordered is the actual production requirement at the factory.

SOURCE: H. Lee, C. Billington, and B. Carter, "Hewlett-Packard Gains Control of Inventory and Service Through Design for Localization," *Interfaces* 23, no. 4 (July–August 1993): 1–11.

a result of this drawback, a larger safety stock is normally required for the fixed-interval system.

Order Quantity with Variable Demand

If the demand rate and lead time are constant, then the fixed-period model will have a fixed-order quantity that will be made at specified time intervals, which is the same as the fixed-quantity (EOQ) model under similar conditions. However, as we have already explained, the fixed-period model reacts differently than the fixed-order model when demand is a variable.

The order size for a fixed-period model given variable daily demand that is normally distributed is determined by

$$Q = \bar{d}(t_b + L) + z\sigma_d \sqrt{t_b + L} - I$$

where

$$\bar{d} = \text{average demand rate}$$
$$t_b = \text{the fixed time between orders}$$
$$L = \text{lead time}$$
$$\sigma_d = \text{standard deviation of demand}$$
$$z\sigma_d \sqrt{t_b + L} = \text{safety stock}$$
$$I = \text{inventory in stock}$$

The first term in this formula, $\bar{d}(t_b + L)$, is the average demand during the order cycle time plus the lead time. It reflects the amount of inventory that will be needed to protect against the entire time from this order to the next and the lead time until the order is received. The second term, $z\sigma_d \sqrt{t_b + L}$, is the safety stock for a specific service level, determined in much the same way as previously described for a reorder point. The final term, I, is the amount of inventory on hand when the inventory level is checked and an order is made.

EXAMPLE
12.7

*Order Size for Fixed-
Period Model with
Variable Demand*

The Corner Drug Store stocks a popular brand of sunscreen. The average demand for the sunscreen is 6 bottles per day, with a standard deviation of 1.2 bottles. A vendor for the sunscreen producer checks the drugstore stock every 60 days. During one visit the drugstore had 8 bottles in stock. The lead time to receive an order is 5 days. Determine the order size for this order period that will enable the drugstore to maintain a 95 percent service level.

SOLUTION:

$\overline{d} = 6$ bottles per day

$\sigma_d = 1.2$ bottles

$t_b = 60$ days

$L = 5$ days

$I = 8$ bottles

$z = 1.65$ (for a 95 percent service level)

$$Q = \overline{d}(t_b + L) + z\sigma_d\sqrt{t_b + L} - I$$
$$= (6)(60 + 5) + (1.65)(1.2)\sqrt{60 + 5} - 8$$
$$= 397.96 \text{ bottles}$$

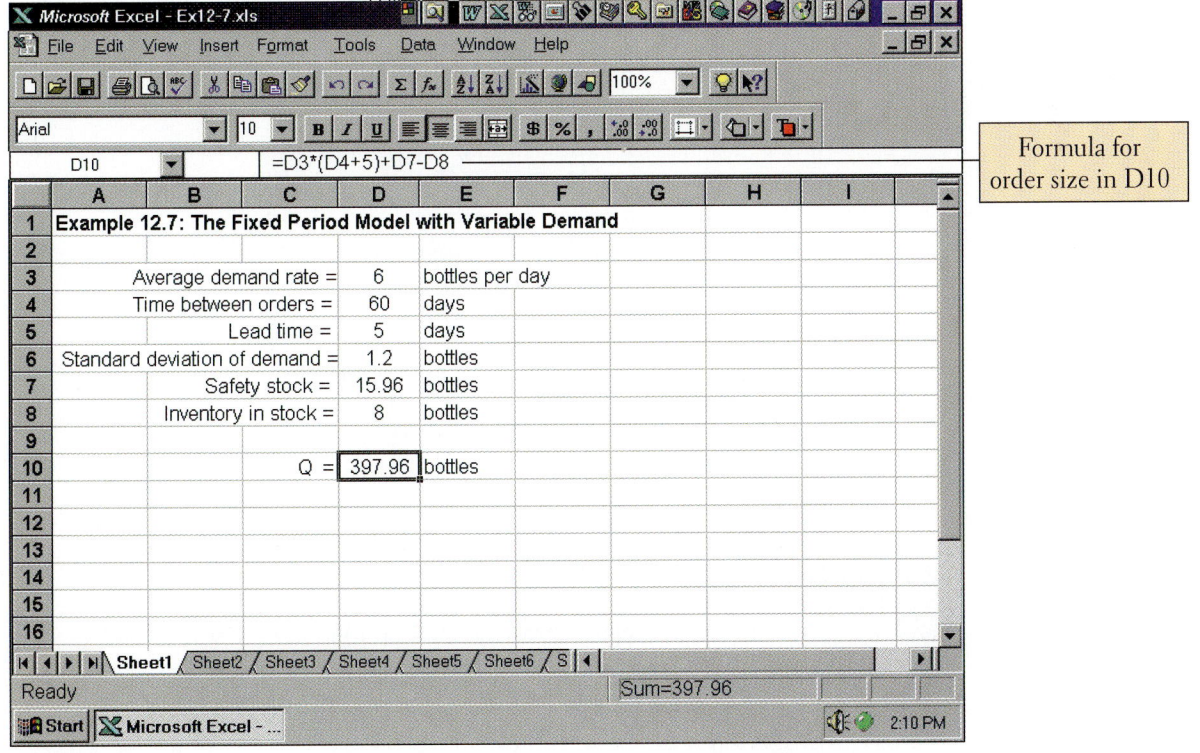

	A	B	C	D	E	F	G	H	I
1	Example 12.7: The Fixed Period Model with Variable Demand								
2									
3		Average demand rate =		6	bottles per day				
4		Time between orders =		60	days				
5		Lead time =		5	days				
6	Standard deviation of demand =			1.2	bottles				
7		Safety stock =		15.96	bottles				
8		Inventory in stock =		8	bottles				
9									
10		Q =		397.96	bottles				

D10 = =D3*(D4+5)+D7-D8

Formula for order size in D10

EXHIBIT 12.6

Determining the Order Quantity for the Fixed-Period Model with Excel

The order quantity for the fixed-period model with variable demand can be determined using Excel. The Excel screen for Example 12.7 is shown in Exhibit 12.6. Notice that the order quantity in cell D10 is computed with the formula shown on the formula bar at the top of the screen.

Summary

The two types of systems for managing inventory are continuous and periodic, and we presented several models for determining how much to order and when to order for each system. However, we focused our attention primarily on the more commonly used continuous, fixed-order-quantity systems with EOQ models for determining order size and reorder points for determining when to order.

The objective of these order quantity models is to determine the optimal trade-off between inventory carrying costs and ordering costs that would minimize total inventory cost. However, a drawback of approaching inventory management in this manner is that it can delude management into thinking that if they determine the minimum cost order quantity, they have achieved all they can in reducing inventory costs, which is not the case. Management should continually strive both to accurately assess and to reduce individual inventory costs. If management has accurately determined carrying and order costs, then they can seek ways to lower them that will reduce overall inventory costs regardless of the order size and reorder point.

Summary of Key Formulas

Basic EOQ Model

$$TC = \frac{C_oD}{Q} + \frac{C_cQ}{2}$$

$$Q_{opt} = \sqrt{\frac{2C_oD}{C_c}}$$

EOQ Model with Noninstantaneous Receipt

$$TC = \frac{C_oD}{Q} + \frac{C_cQ}{2}\left(1 - \frac{d}{p}\right)$$

$$Q_{opt} = \sqrt{\frac{2C_oD}{C_c\left(1 - \frac{d}{p}\right)}}$$

Inventory Cost for Quantity Discounts

$$TC = \frac{C_oD}{Q} + \frac{C_cQ}{2} + PD$$

Reorder Point with Constant Demand and Lead Time

$$R = dL$$

Reorder Point with Variable Demand

$$R = \bar{d}L + z\sigma_d\sqrt{L}$$

Fixed-Time-Period Order Quantity with Variable Demand

$$Q = \bar{d}(t_b + L) + z\sigma_d\sqrt{t_b + L} - I$$

Summary of Key Terms

ABC system: a method for classifying inventory items according to their dollar value to the firm based on the principle that only a few items account for the greatest dollar value of total inventory.

carrying costs: the cost of holding an item in inventory including lost opportunity costs, storage, rent, cooling, lighting, interest on loans, and so on.

continuous inventory system: a system in which the inventory level is continually monitored; when it decreases to a certain level, a fixed amount is ordered.

dependent demand: typically component parts or materials used in the process to produce a final product.

economic order quantity (EOQ): a fixed order quantity that minimizes total inventory costs.

fixed-order-quantity system: also known as a continuous system; an inventory system in which a fixed, predetermined amount is ordered whenever inventory in stock falls to a certain level called the reorder point.

fixed-time-period system: also known as a periodic system; an inventory system in which a variable amount is ordered after a predetermined, constant passage of time.

independent demand: final or finished products that are not a function of, or dependent upon, internal production activity.

inventory: a stock of items kept by an organization to meet internal or external customer demand.

in-process (buffer) inventory: stocks of partially completed items kept between stages of a production process.

noninstantaneous receipt model: also known as the production lot-size model; an inventory system in which an order is received gradually and the inventory level is depleted at the same time it is being replenished.

order cycle: the time between the receipt of orders in an inventory system.

ordering costs: the cost of replenishing the stock of inventory including requisition cost, transportation and shipping, receiving, inspection, handling, and so forth.

periodic inventory system: a system in which the inventory level is checked after a specific time period and a variable amount is ordered, depending on the inventory in stock.

quantity discount: a pricing schedule in which lower prices are provided for specific (higher) order quantities.

reorder point: a level of inventory in stock at which a new order is placed.

safety stock: an amount added to the expected amount demanded during the lead time (the reorder point level) as a hedge against a stockout.

service level: the probability that the amount of inventory on hand during the lead time is sufficient to meet expected demand.

shortage costs: temporary or permanent loss of sales that will result when customer demand cannot be met.

stockout: an inventory shortage occurring when demand exceeds the inventory in stock.

Solved Problems

1. Basic EOQ Model

Electronic Village stocks and sells a particular brand of personal computer. It costs the store $450 each time it places an order with the manufacturer for the personal computers. The annual cost of carrying the PCs in inventory is $170. The store manager estimates that annual demand for the PCs will be 1,200 units. Determine the optimal order quantity and the total minimum inventory cost.

Solution:

$$D = 1,200 \text{ personal computers}$$
$$C_c = \$170$$
$$C_o = \$450$$

$$Q_{opt} = \sqrt{\frac{2C_oD}{C_c}}$$

$$= \sqrt{\frac{2(450)(1,200)}{170}}$$

$$= 79.7 \text{ personal computers}$$

$$TC = \frac{C_oD}{Q_{opt}} + \frac{C_cQ_{opt}}{2}$$

$$= 450\left(\frac{1,200}{79.7}\right) + 170\left(\frac{79.7}{2}\right)$$

$$= \$13,549.91$$

2. Quantity Discount

A manufacturing firm has been offered a particular component part it uses according to the following discount pricing schedule provided by the supplier.

1–199	$65
200–599	59
600+	56

The manufacturing company uses 700 of the components annually, the annual carrying cost is $14 per unit, and the ordering cost is $275. Determine the amount the firm should order.

Solution:

First, determine the optimal order size and total cost with the basic EOQ model.

$$C_o = \$275$$

$$C_c = \$14$$
$$D = 700$$

$$Q_{opt} = \sqrt{\frac{2C_oD}{C_c}}$$

$$= \sqrt{\frac{2(275)(700)}{14}}$$

$$Q_{opt} = 165.83$$

$$TC = \frac{C_oD}{Q_{opt}} + \frac{C_cQ_{opt}}{2} + PD$$

$$= \frac{(275)(700)}{165.83} + \frac{(7)(165.83)}{2} + (\$65)(700)$$

$$= \$47,821$$

Next, compare the order size with the second-level quantity discount with an order size of 200 and a discount price of $59.

$$TC = \frac{(275)(700)}{200} + \frac{(14)(200)}{2} + (59)(700)$$

$$= \$43,662.50$$

This discount results in a lower cost.

Finally, compare the current discounted order size with the fixed-price discount for $Q = 600$.

$$TC = \frac{(275)(700)}{600} + \frac{(14)(600)}{2} + (56)(700)$$

$$= \$43,720.83$$

Since this total cost is higher, the optimal order size is 200 with a total cost of $43,662.50.

3. Reorder Point with Variable Demand

A computer products store stocks color graphics monitors, and the daily demand is normally distributed with a mean of 1.6 monitors and a standard deviation of 0.4 monitors. The lead time to receive an order from the manufacturer is 15 days. Determine the reorder point that will achieve a 98 percent service level.

Solution:

$$\bar{d} = 1.6 \text{ monitors per day}$$
$$L = 15 \text{ days}$$
$$\sigma_d = 0.4 \text{ monitors per day}$$
$$z = 2.05 \text{ (for a 98 percent service level)}$$
$$R = \bar{d}L + z\sigma_d\sqrt{L}$$
$$= (1.6)(15) + (2.05)(0.4)\sqrt{15}$$
$$= 24 + 3.18$$
$$= 27.18 = 28 \text{ monitors}$$

Questions

12-1. Describe the difference between independent and dependent demand and give an example of each for a pizza restaurant such as Domino's or Pizza Hut.

12-2. Distinguish between a fixed-order-quantity system and fixed-time-period system and give an example of each.

12-3. Discuss customer service level for an inventory system within the context of quality management.

12-4. Explain the ABC inventory classification system and indicate its advantages.

12-5. Identify the two basic decisions addressed by inventory management and discuss why the responses to these decisions differ for continuous and periodic inventory systems.

12-6. Describe the major cost categories used in inventory analysis and their functional relationship to each other.

12-7. Explain how the order quantity is determined using the basic EOQ model.

12-8. What are the assumptions of the basic EOQ model and to what extent do they limit the usefulness of the model?

12-9. How are the reorder point and lead time related in inventory analysis?

12-10. Describe how the noninstantaneous receipt model differs from the basic EOQ model.

12-11. How must the application of the basic EOQ model be altered in order to reflect quantity discounts?

12-12. Why do the basic EOQ model variations not include the price of an item?

12-13. In the noninstantaneous-receipt EOQ model, what would be the effect of the production rate becoming increasingly large as the demand rate became increasingly small, until the ratio d/p was negligible?

12-14. Explain in general terms how a safety stock level is determined using customer service level.

Problems

12-1. Hayes Electronics stocks and sells a particular brand of microcomputer. It costs the firm $450 each time it places an order with the manufacturer for the microcomputers. The cost of carrying one microcomputer in inventory for a year is $170. The store manager estimates that total annual demand for the computers will be 1,200 units, with a constant demand rate throughout the year. Orders are received within minutes after placement from a local warehouse maintained by the manufacturer. The store policy is never to have stockouts of the microcomputers. The store is open for business every day of the year except Christmas Day. Determine the following:
   a. Optimal order quantity per order
   b. Minimum total annual inventory costs
   c. The number of orders per year
   d. The time between orders (in working days)

12-2. Hayes Electronics (Problem 12-1) assumed with certainty that the ordering cost is $450/order and the inventory carrying cost is $170/unit/year. However, the inventory model parameters are frequently only estimates that are subject to some degree of uncertainty. Consider four cases of variation in the model parameters as follows: (a) Both ordering cost and carrying cost are 10 percent less than originally estimated; (b) both ordering cost and carrying cost are 10 percent higher than originally estimated; (c) ordering cost is 10 percent higher and carrying cost is 10 percent lower than originally estimated; and (d) ordering cost is 10 percent lower and carrying cost is 10 percent higher than originally estimated. Determine the optimal order quantity and total inventory cost for each of the four cases. Prepare a table with values from all four cases and compare the sensitivity of the model solution to changes in parameter values.

12-3. A firm is faced with the attractive situation in which it can obtain immediate delivery of an item it stocks for retail sale. The firm has therefore not bothered to order the item in any systematic way. However, recently profits have been squeezed due to increasing competitive pressures, and the firm has retained a management consultant to study its inventory management. The consultant has determined that the various costs associated with making an order for the item stocked are approximately $30 per order. She has also determined that the costs of carrying the item in inventory amount to approximately $20 per unit per year (primarily direct storage costs and foregone profit on investment in inventory). Demand for the item is reasonably constant over time, and the forecast is for 19,200 units per year. When an order is placed for the item, the entire order is immediately delivered to the firm by the supplier. The firm operates 6 days a week plus a few Sundays, or approximately 320 days per year. Determine the following:
   a. Optimal order quantity per order
   b. Total annual inventory costs
   c. Optimal number of orders to place per year
   d. Number of operating days between orders, based on the optimal ordering

12-4. The Western Jeans Company purchases denim from Cumberland Textile Mills. The Western Company uses 35,000 yards of denim per year to make jeans. The cost of ordering denim from the textile company is $500 per order. It costs Western $0.35 per yard annually to hold a yard of denim in inventory. Determine the optimal number of yards of denim the Western Company should order, the minimum total inventory cost, the optimal number of orders per year, and the optimal time between orders.

12-5. The Metropolitan Book Company purchases paper from the Atlantic Paper Company. Metropolitan produces magazines and paperbacks that require 1,215,000 yards of paper per year. The cost per order for the company is $1,200; the cost of holding 1 yard of paper in inventory is $0.08 per year. Determine the following:
   a. Economic order quantity
   b. Minimum total annual cost
   c. Optimal number of orders per year
   d. Optimal time between orders

12-6. The Simple Simon Bakery produces fruit pies for freezing and subsequent sale. The bakery, which operates 5 days a week, 52 weeks a year, can produce pies at the rate of 64 pies per day. The bakery sets up the pie-production operation and produces until a predetermined number (Q) have been produced. When not producing pies, the bakery uses its personnel and facilities for producing other bakery items. The setup cost for a production run of fruit pies is $500. The cost of holding frozen pies in storage is $5 per pie per year. The annual demand for frozen fruit pies, which is constant over time, is 5,000 pies. Determine the following:
   a. The optimum production run quantity (Q)
   b. Total annual inventory costs
   c. The optimum number of production runs per year
   d. The optimum cycle time (time between run starts)
   e. The run length in working days

12-7. The Pedal Pusher Bicycle Shop operates 364 days a year, closing only on Christmas Day. The shop pays $300 for a particular bicycle purchased from the manufacturer. The annual holding cost per bicycle is estimated to be 25 percent of the dollar value of inventory. The shop sells an average of 25 bikes per week. The ordering cost for each order is $100. Determine the optimal order quantity and the total minimum cost.

12-8. The Petroco Company uses a highly toxic chemical in one of its manufacturing processes. It must have the product delivered by special cargo trucks designed for safe shipment of chemicals. As such, ordering (and delivery) costs are relatively high, at $2,600 per order.

The chemical product is packaged in 1-gallon plastic containers. The cost of holding the chemical in storage is $50 per gallon per year. The annual demand for the chemical, which is constant over time, is 2,000 gallons per year. The lead time from time of order placement until receipt is 10 days. The company operates 310 workings days per year. Compute the optimal order quantity, total minimum inventory cost, and the reorder point.

12-9. The Big Buy Supermarket stocks Munchies Cereal. Demand for Munchies is 4,000 boxes per year (365 days). It costs the store $60 per order of Munchies, and it costs $0.80 per box per year to keep the cereal in stock. Once an order for Munchies is placed, it takes 4 days to receive the order from a food distributor. Determine the following:
   a. Optimal order size
   b. Minimum total annual inventory cost
   c. Reorder point

12-10. The Wood Valley Dairy makes cheese to supply to stores in its area. The dairy can make 250 pounds of cheese per day, and the demand at area stores is 180 pounds per day. Each time the dairy makes cheese, it costs $125 to set up the production process. The annual cost of carrying a pound of cheese in a refrigerated storage area is $12. Determine the optimal order size and the minimum total annual inventory cost.

12-11. The Rainwater Brewery produces Rainwater Light Beer, which it stores in barrels in its warehouse and supplies to its distributors on demand. The demand for Rainwater is 1,500 barrels of beer per day. The brewery can produce 2,000 barrels of rainwater per day. It costs $6,500 to set up a production run for Rainwater. Once it is brewed, the beer is stored in a refrigerated warehouse at an annual cost of $50 per barrel. Determine the economic order quantity and the minimum total annual inventory cost.

12-12. The purchasing manager for the Atlantic Steel Company must determine a policy for ordering coal to operate 12 converters. Each converter requires exactly 5 tons of coal per day to operate, and the firm operates 360 days per year. The purchasing manager has determined that the ordering cost is $80 per order, and the cost of holding coal is 20 percent of the average dollar value of inventory held. The purchasing manager has negotiated a contract to obtain the coal for $12 per ton for the coming year.
   a. Determine the optimal quantity of coal to receive in each order.
   b. Determine the total inventory-related costs associated with the optimal ordering policy (do not include the cost of the coal).
   c. If 5 days' lead time is required to receive an order of coal, how much coal should be on hand when an order is placed?

12-13. The Pacific Lumber Company and Mill processes 10,000 logs annually, operating 250 days per year. Immediately upon receiving an order, the logging company's supplier begins delivery to the lumber mill at the rate of 60 logs per day. The lumber mill has determined that the ordering cost is $1,600 per order, and the cost of carrying logs in inventory before they are processed is $15 per log on an annual basis. Determine the following:
   a. The optimal order size
   b. The total inventory cost associated with the optimal order quantity
   c. The number of operating days between orders
   d. The number of operating days required to receive an order

12-14. The Roadking Tire Company produces a brand of tire called the Roadrunner. The annual demand at its distribution center is 17,400 tires per year. The transport and handling costs are $2,600 each time a shipment of tires is ordered at the distribution center. The annual carrying cost is $3.75 per tire.
   a. Determine the optimal order quantity and the minimum total annual cost.
   b. The company is thinking about relocating its distribution center, which would reduce transport and handling costs to $1,900 per order but increase carrying costs to $4.50 per tire per year. Should the company relocate based on inventory costs?

12-15. The Spruce Creek Nursery produces its own natural organic fertilizer which it sells mostly to gardeners and homeowners. The annual demand for fertilizer is 270,000 pounds. The company is able to produce 305,000 pounds annually. The cost to transport the fertilizer from the plant to the nursery is $170 per load. The annual carrying cost is $0.12 per pound.

a. Compute the optimal order size, the maximum inventory level, and the total minimum cost.

b. If Spruce Creek can increase production capacity to 360,000 pounds per year, will it reduce total inventory cost?

12-16. The Uptown Kiln is an importer of ceramics from overseas. It has arranged to purchase a particular type of ceramic pottery from a Korean artisan. The artisan makes the pottery in 120-unit batches and will ship only that exact amount. The transportation and handling cost of a shipment is $7,600 (not including the unit cost). The Uptown Kiln estimates its annual demand to be 900 units. What storage and handling cost per unit does it need to achieve in order to minimize its inventory cost?

12-17. The I-75 Carpet Discount Store has annual demand of 10,000 yards of Super Shag carpet. The annual carrying cost for a yard of this carpet is $0.75, and the ordering cost is $150. The carpet manufacturer normally charges the store $8 per yard for the carpet. However, the manufacturer has offered a discount price of $6.50 per yard if the store will order 5,000 yards. How much should the store order, and what will be the total annual inventory cost for that order quantity?

12-18. The Fifth Quarter Bar Buys Old World draft beer by the barrel from a local distributor. The bar has an annual demand of 900 barrels, which it purchases at a price of $205 per barrel. The annual carrying cost is $24.60, and the cost per order is $160. The distributor has offered the bar a reduced price of $190 per barrel if it will order a minimum of 300 barrels. Should the bar take the discount?

12-19. The bookstore at State University purchases sweatshirts emblazoned with the school name and logo from a vendor. The vendor sells the sweatshirts to the store for $38 apiece. The cost to the bookstore for placing an order is $120, and the annual carrying cost is 25 percent of the cost of a sweatshirt. The bookstore manager estimates that 1,700 sweatshirts will be sold during the year. The vendor has offered the bookstore the following volume discount schedule.

Order Size	Discount
1–299	0%
300–499	2%
500–799	4%
800+	5%

The bookstore manager wants to determine the bookstore's optimal order quantity, given this quantity discount information.

12-20. Determine the optimal order quantity of sweatshirts and total annual cost in Problem 12-19 if the carrying cost is a constant $8 per shirt per year.

12-21. The office manager for the Gotham Life Insurance Company orders letterhead stationery from an office products firm in boxes of 500 sheets. The company uses 6,500 boxes per year. Annual carrying costs are $3 per box, and ordering costs are $28. The following discount price schedule is provided by the office supply company.

Order Quantity (boxes)	Price per Box
200–999	$16
1,000–2,999	14
3,000–5,999	13
6,000+	12

Determine the optimal order quantity and the total annual inventory cost.

12-22. Determine the optimal order quantity and total annual inventory cost for boxes of stationary in Problem 12-21 if the carrying cost is 20 percent of the price of a box of stationery.

12-23. The 23,000-seat City Coliseum houses the local professional ice hockey, basketball, indoor soccer, and arena football teams as well as various trade shows, wrestling and boxing matches, tractor pulls, and circuses. Coliseum vending annually sells large quantities of soft drinks and beer in plastic cups with the name of the coliseum and the various team logos on them. The local container cup manufacturer that supplies the cups in boxes of 100 has offered coliseum management the following discount price schedule for cups.

Order Quantity (boxes)	Price per Box
2,000–6,999	$47
7,000–11,999	43
12,000–19,999	41
20,000+	38

The annual demand for cups is 2.3 million, the annual carrying cost per box of cups is $1.90, and ordering cost is $320. Determine the optimal order quantity and total annual inventory cost.

12-24. Determine the optimal order quantity and total annual inventory cost for cups in Problem 12-23 if the carrying cost is 5 percent of the price of a box of cups.

12-25. The amount of denim used daily by The Western Jeans Company in its manufacturing process to make jeans is normally distributed with an average of 3,000 yards of denim and a standard deviation of 600 yards. The lead time required to receive an order of denim from the textile mill is a constant 6 days. Determine the safety stock and reorder point if The Western Jeans Company wants to limit the probability of a stockout and work stoppage to 5 percent.

12-26. In Problem 12-25, what level of service would a safety stock of 2,000 yards provide?

12-27. The Atlantic Paper company produces paper from wood pulp ordered from a lumber products firm. The paper company's daily demand for wood pulp is normally distributed with a mean of 8,000 pounds and a standard deviation of 1,900 pounds. Lead time is 7 days. Determine the reorder point if the paper company wants to limit the probability of a stockout and work stoppage to 2 percent.

12-28. The Uptown Bar and Grill serves Rainwater draft beer to its customers. The daily demand for beer is normally distributed with an average of 18 gallons and a standard deviation of 4 gallons. The lead time required to receive an order of beer from the local distributor is 3 days. Determine the safety stock and reorder point if the restaurant wants to maintain a 90 percent service level. What would be the increase in the safety stock if a 95 percent service level were desired?

12-29. The daily demand for Sunlight paint at the Rainbow Paint Store in East Ridge is normally distributed with a mean of 26 gallons and a standard deviation of 10 gallons. The lead time for receiving an order of paint from the Sunlight distributor is 9 days. Since this is the only paint store in East Ridge, the manager is interested in maintaining only a 75 percent service level. What reorder point should be used to meet this service level? The manager subsequently learned that a new paint store would open soon in East Ridge, which has prompted her to increase the service level to 95 percent. What reorder point will maintain this service level?

12-30. PM Computers assembles microcomputers from generic components. It purchases its color monitors from a manufacturer in Taiwan; thus, there is a long lead time of 25 days. Daily demand is normally distributed with a mean of 2.5 monitors and a standard deviation of 1.2 monitors. Determine the safety stock and reorder point corresponding to a 90 percent service level.

12-31. PM Computers (Problem 12-30) is considering purchasing monitors from a U.S. manufacturer that would guarantee a lead time of 8 days, instead of from the Taiwanese company. Determine the new reorder point given this lead time and identify the factors that would enter into the decision to change manufacturers.

12-32. The Corner Drug Store fills prescriptions for a popular children's antibiotic, Amoxycilin. The daily demand for Amoxycilin is normally distributed with a mean of 200 ounces and a standard deviation of 80 ounces. The vendor for the pharmaceutical firm that supplies the drug calls the drugstore's pharmacist every 30 days and checks the inventory of Amoxycilin. During a call the druggist indicated the store had 60 ounces of the antibiotic in stock. The lead time to receive an order is 4 days. Determine the order size that will enable the drugstore to maintain a 95 percent service level.

12-33. The Fast Service Food Mart stocks frozen pizzas in a refrigerated display case. The average daily demand for the pizzas is normally distributed with a mean of 8 pizzas and a standard deviation of 2.5 pizzas. A vendor for a packaged food distributor checks the market's inventory of frozen foods every 10 days; during a particular visit there were no pizzas in stock. The lead time to receive an order is 3 days. Determine the order size for this order period that will result in a 99 percent service level. During the vendor's following visit there were 5 frozen pizzas in stock. What is the order size for the next order period?

12-34. The Impanema Restaurant stocks a red Brazilian table wine it purchases from a wine merchant in a nearby city. The daily demand for the wine at the restaurant is normally distributed with a mean of 18 bottles and a standard deviation of 4 bottles. The wine merchant sends a representative to check the restaurant's wine cellar every 30 days, and during a recent visit there were 25 bottles in stock. The lead time to receive an order is 2 days. The restaurant manager has requested an order size that will enable him to limit the probability of a stockout to 2 percent.

12-35. The Dynaco Company stocks a variety of parts and materials it uses in its manufacturing processes. Recently, as demand for its finished goods has increased, management has had difficulty managing parts inventory; they frequently run out of some crucial parts and seem to have an endless supply of others. In an effort to control inventory more effectively, they would like to classify their inventory of parts according to the ABC approach. Following is a list of selected parts and the annual usage and unit value for each.

Item Number	Annual Usage	Unit Cost	Item Number	Annual Usage	Unit Cost
1	36	$ 350	16	60	$ 610
2	510	30	17	120	20
3	50	23	18	270	15
4	300	45	19	45	50
5	18	1,900	20	19	3,200
6	500	8	21	910	3
7	710	4	22	12	4,750
8	80	26	23	30	2,710
9	344	28	24	24	1,800
10	67	440	25	870	105
11	510	2	26	244	30
12	682	35	27	750	15
13	95	50	28	45	110
14	10	3	29	46	160
15	820	1	30	165	25

Classify the inventory items according to the ABC approach using dollar value of annual demand.

12-36. The Spoke and Wheel Bicycle Shop stocks bikes; helmets; clothing; a variety of bike parts including chains, gears, tires, wheels; and biking accessories. The shop is in a storefront location on a busy street and it has very limited storage space for inventory. It often runs out of items and is unable to serve customers. To help manage its inventory the shop would like to classify the stock using the ABC system. Following is a list of items the shop stocks and the annual demand and unit value for each.

Item Number	Annual Demand	Unit Cost	Item Number	Annual Demand	Unit Cost
1	10	$ 8	17	110	$ 23
2	18	16	18	74	18
3	36	30	19	8	610
4	9	1,230	20	10	935
5	4	760	21	7	270
6	3	810	22	5	1,400
7	19	420	23	5	900
8	56	35	24	46	67
9	105	17	25	32	160
10	27	350	26	101	45
11	19	36	27	83	12
12	12	115	28	54	16
13	7	2,300	29	14	42
14	10	245	30	9	705
15	6	665	31	7	37
16	18	28	32	16	26

Classify the inventory items according to the ABC approach using dollar value of annual demand.

CASE PROBLEM

The A to Z Office Supply Company

Christine Yamaguchi is the manager of the A to Z Office Supply Company in Charlotte. The company attempts to gain an advantage over its competitors by providing quality customer service, which includes prompt delivery of orders by truck or van and always being able to meet customer demand from its stock. In order to achieve this degree of customer service, A to Z must stock a large volume of items on a daily basis at a central warehouse and at three retail stores in the city and suburbs. Christine maintains these inventory levels by borrowing cash on a daily basis from the First Piedmont Bank. She estimates that for the coming fiscal year the company's demand for cash to pay for inventory will be $17,000 per day for 305 working days. Any money she borrows during the year must be repaid with interest by the end of the year. The annual interest rate currently charged by the bank is 9 per-

cent. Any time Christine takes out a loan to purchase inventory, the bank charges the company a loan origination fee of $1,200 plus $2^{1}/_{4}$ points (2.25 percent of the amount borrowed).

Christine often uses EOQ analysis to determine optimal amounts of inventory to order for different office supplies. Now she is wondering if she can use the same type of analysis to determine an optimal borrowing policy. Determine the amount of the loan Christine should borrow from the bank, the total annual cost of the company's borrowing policy, and the number of loans the company should obtain during the year. Also determine the level of cash on hand at which the company should apply for a new loan given that it takes fifteen days for a loan to be processed by the bank.

Suppose the bank offers Christine a discount as follows. On any loan amount equal to or greater than $500,000, the bank will lower the number of points charged on the loan origination fee from 2.25 percent to 2.00 percent. What would be the company's optimal amount borrowed?

CASE PROBLEM

The Texans Stadium Store

The Fort Worth Texans won the Super Bowl last year. As a result, sportswear such as hats, sweatshirts, sweatpants, and jackets with the Texans' logo are popular. The Texans operate a stadium store outside the football stadium. It is near a busy highway, so the store has heavy customer traffic throughout the year, not just on game days. In addition, the stadium has high school or college football and soccer games almost every week in the fall, and baseball games in the spring and summer. The most popular single item the stadium store sells is a blue and silver baseball-style cap with the Texans' logo on it. The cap has an elastic headband inside it, which conforms to different head sizes. However, the store has had a difficult time keeping the cap in stock especially during the time between the placement and receipt of an order. Often customers come to the store just for the hat; when it is not in stock, customers are upset, and the store management believes they tend to go to other competing stores to purchase their Texans' clothing. To rectify this problem, the store manager, Jenny Jones, would like to develop an inventory control policy that would ensure that customers would be able to purchase the cap 99 percent of the time they asked for it. Jenny has accumulated the following demand data for the cap for a thirty-week period. (Demand includes ac-

tual sales plus a record of the times a cap has been requested but not available and an estimate of the number of times a customer wanted a cap when it was not available but did not ask for it.)

Week	Demand	Week	Demand	Week	Demand
1	38	11	28	21	52
2	51	12	41	22	38
3	25	13	37	23	49
4	60	14	44	24	46
5	35	15	45	25	47
6	42	16	56	26	41
7	29	17	62	27	39
8	46	18	53	28	50
9	55	19	46	29	28
10	19	20	41	30	34

The store purchases the hats from a small manufacturing company in Jamaica. The shipments from Jamaica are erratic, with a lead time of twenty days.

In the past, Ms. Jones has placed an order whenever the stock got down to 150 caps. What level of service does this reorder point correspond to? What would the reorder point and safety stock need to be to achieve the desired service level? Discuss how Jenny Jones might determine the order size of caps and what additional, if any, information would be needed to determine the order size.

References

Brown, R. G. *Decision Rules for Inventory Management.* New York: Holt, Rinehart and Winston, 1967.

Buchan, J., and E. Koenigsberg. *Scientific Inventory Management.* Englewood Cliffs, N.J.: Prentice Hall, 1963.

Buffa, E. S., and Jefferey Miller. *Production-Inventory Systems: Planning and Control,* rev. ed. Homewood, Ill.: Irwin, 1979.

Churchman, C.W., R. L. Ackoff, and E. L. Arnoff. *Introduction to Operations Research.* New York: John Wiley, 1957.

Fetter, R. B., and W. C. Dalleck. *Decision Models for Inventory Management.* Homewood, Ill.: Irwin, 1961.

Greene, J. H. *Production and Inventory Control.* Homewood, Ill.: Irwin, 1974.

Hadley, G., and T. M. Whitin. *Analysis of Inventory Systems.* Englewood Cliffs, N.J.: Prentice Hall, 1963.

McGee, J. F., and D. M. Boodman. *Production Planning and Inventory Control,* 2d ed. New York: McGraw-Hill, 1967.

Monden, Y. *Toyota Production System.* Norcross, Ga.: Industrial Engineering and Management Press, 1983.

Starr, M. K., and D. W. Miller. *Inventory Control: Theory and Practice.* Englewood Cliffs, N.J.: Prentice Hall, 1962.

Wagner, H. M. *Statistical Management of Inventory Systems.* New York: John Wiley, 1962.

Whitin, T. M. *The Theory of Inventory Management.* Princeton, N.J.: Princeton University Press, 1957.

12

Operational Decision-Making Tools: Simulation

Simulation is a mathematical and computer modeling technique for replicating real-world problem situations.

Simulation is popular because it can be applied to virtually any type of problem. It can frequently be used when there is no other applicable quantitative method; it is the technique of last resort for many problems. It is a modeling approach primarily used to analyze probabilistic problems. It does not normally provide a solution; instead it provides information that is used to make a decision.

Much of the experimentation in astronaut-controlled space flight was conducted using physical simulation that re-created the conditions of space. Conditions of weightlessness were simulated using rooms filled with water. Other examples include wind tunnels that simulate the conditions of flight and treadmills that simulate automobile tire wear in a laboratory instead of on the road.

This supplement is concerned with another type of simulation, *computerized mathematical simulation*. In this form of simulation, systems are replicated with mathematical models, which are analyzed with a computer. This type of simulation is very popular and has been applied to a wide variety of operational problems.

Monte Carlo Simulation

Some problems are difficult to solve analytically because they consist of random variables represented by probability distributions. Thus, a large proportion of the applications of simulations are for probabilistic models.

The **Monte Carlo technique** is a method for selecting numbers randomly from a probability distribution for use in a simulation.

The term *Monte Carlo* has become synonymous with probabilistic simulation in recent years. However, the **Monte Carlo technique** can be more narrowly defined as a technique for selecting numbers *randomly* from a probability distribution (i.e., sampling) for use in a *trial* (computer) run of a simulation. As such, the Monte Carlo technique is not a type of simulation model but rather a mathematical process used within a simulation.

The name *Monte Carlo* is appropriate, since the basic principle behind the process is the same as in the operation of a gambling casino in Monaco. In Monaco devices like roulette wheels, dice, and playing cards produce numbered results at random from well-defined populations. For example, a 7 resulting from thrown dice is a random value from a population of eleven possible numbers (i.e., 2 through 12). This same process is employed, in principle, in the Monte Carlo process used in simulation models.

The Monte Carlo process of selecting random numbers according to a probability distribution is demonstrated using the following example. The manager of a supermarket must decide how many cases of milk to order each week, which is a random variable (which we will define as x) that ranges from 14 to 18 every week. From past records, the manager has determined the frequency of demand for cases of milk for the past 100 weeks. From this frequency distribution, a probability distribution of demand can be developed, as shown in Table S12.1.

TABLE S12.1   Probability Distribution of Demand

Cases Demanded per Week, x	Frequency of Demand	Probability of Demand P(x)
14	20	0.20
15	40	0.40
16	20	0.20
17	10	0.10
18	10	0.10
	100	1.00

The purpose of the Monte Carlo process is to generate the random variable, demand, by "sampling" from the probability distribution, $P(x)$. The demand per week could be randomly generated according to the probability distribution by spinning a roulette wheel that is partitioned into segments corresponding to the probabilities, as shown in Figure S12.1.

There are 100 numbers from 0 to 99 on the outer rim of the wheel, and they have been partitioned according to the probability of each demand value. For example, 20 numbers from 0 to 19 (i.e., 20 percent of the total 100 numbers) correspond to a demand of 14 cases of milk. Now we can determine the value of demand by the number the wheel stops at and the segment of the wheel.

When the manager spins this new wheel, the demand for cases of milk will be determined by a number. For example, if the number 71 comes up on a spin, the demand is 16 cases per week; the number 30 indicates a demand of 15. Since the manager does not know which number will come up prior to the spin and there is an equal chance of any of the 100 numbers occurring, the numbers occur at random. That is, they are **random numbers.**

It is not generally practical to predict weekly demand for milk by spinning a wheel. Alternatively, the process of spinning a wheel can be replicated using random numbers alone.

Random numbers each have an equal likelihood of being selected at random.

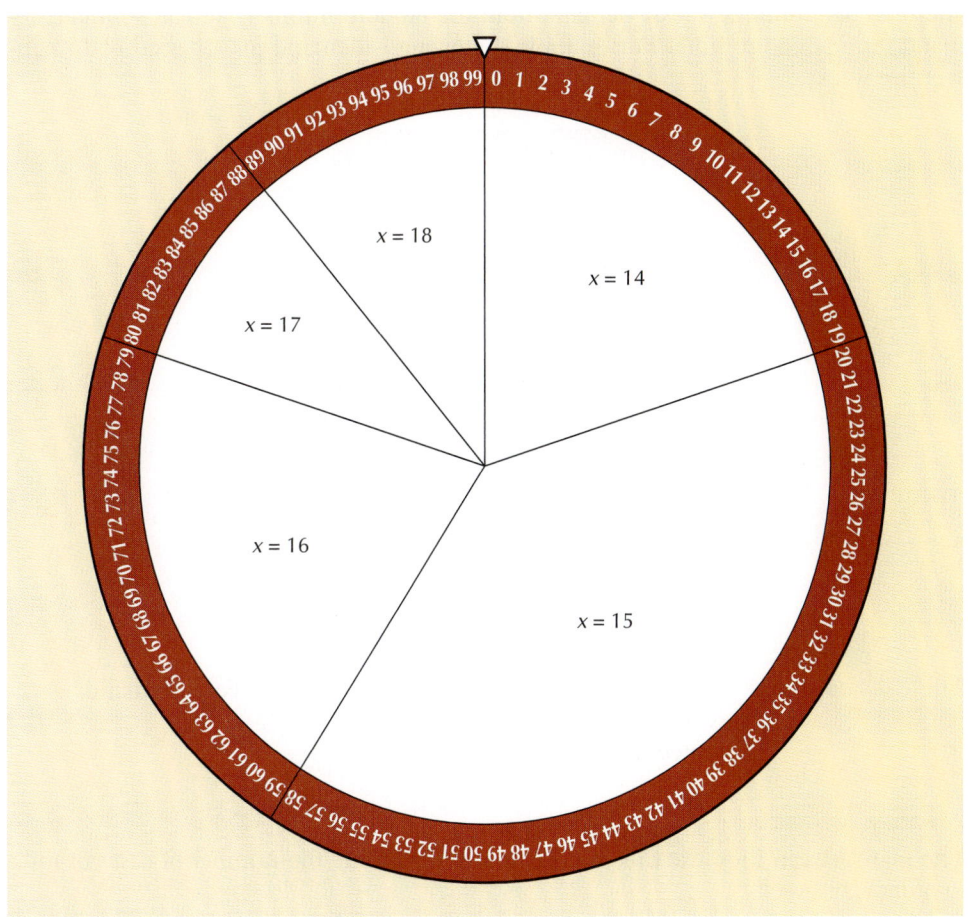

FIGURE S12.1 **A Roulette Wheel of Demand**

First, we will transfer the ranges of random numbers for each demand value from the roulette wheel to a table, as in Table S12.2. Next, instead of spinning the wheel to get a random number, we will select a random number from Table S12.3, which is referred to as a *random number table*. (These random numbers have been generated by computer so that they are *equally likely to occur*, just as if we had spun a wheel.) As an example, let us select the number 39 in Table S12.3. Looking again at Table S12.2, we can see that the random number 39 falls in the range 20–59, which corresponds to a weekly demand of 15 cases of milk.

TABLE S12.2   Generating Demand from Random Numbers

Demand x	Ranges of Random Numbers r	
14	0–19	
15	20–59	r = 39
16	60–79	
17	80–89	
18	90–99	

By repeating this process of selecting random numbers from Table S12.3 (starting anywhere in the table and moving in any direction but not repeating the same sequence) and then determining weekly demand from the random number, we can simulate demand for a period of time. For example, following is demand for a period of 15 consecutive weeks.

Week	r	Demand (x)
1	39	15
2	73	16
3	72	16
4	75	16
5	37	15
6	02	14
7	87	17
8	98	18
9	10	14
10	47	15
11	93	18
12	21	15
13	95	18
14	97	18
15	69	16
		$\Sigma = 241$

These data can now be used to compute the estimated average weekly demand.

$$\text{Estimated average demand} = \frac{241}{15}$$

$$= 16.1 \text{ cases per week}$$

The manager can then use this information to determine the number of cases of milk to order each week.

Although this example is convenient for illustrating how simulation works, the average demand could have been more appropriately calculated *analytically* using the

TABLE S12.3 **Random Number Table**

39 65 76 45 45	19 90 69 64 61	20 26 36 31 62	58 24 97 14 97	95 06 70 99 00
73 71 23 70 90	65 97 60 12 11	31 56 34 19 19	47 83 75 51 33	30 62 38 20 46
72 18 47 33 84	51 67 47 97 19	98 40 07 17 66	23 05 09 51 80	59 78 11 52 49
75 12 25 69 17	17 95 21 78 58	24 33 45 77 48	69 81 84 09 29	93 22 70 45 80
37 17 79 88 74	63 52 06 34 30	01 31 60 10 27	35 07 79 71 53	28 99 52 01 41
02 48 08 16 94	85 53 83 29 95	56 27 09 24 43	21 78 55 09 82	72 61 88 73 61
87 89 15 70 07	37 79 49 12 38	48 13 93 55 96	41 92 45 71 51	09 18 25 58 94
98 18 71 70 15	89 09 39 59 24	00 06 41 41 20	14 36 59 25 47	54 45 17 24 89
10 83 58 07 04	76 62 16 48 68	58 76 17 14 86	59 53 11 52 21	66 04 18 72 87
47 08 56 37 31	71 82 13 50 41	27 55 10 24 92	28 04 67 53 44	95 23 00 84 47
93 90 31 03 07	34 18 04 52 35	74 13 39 35 22	68 95 23 92 35	36 63 70 35 33
21 05 11 47 99	11 20 99 45 18	76 51 94 84 86	13 79 93 37 55	98 16 04 41 67
95 89 94 06 97	27 37 83 28 71	79 57 95 13 91	09 61 87 25 21	56 20 11 32 44
97 18 31 55 73	10 65 81 92 59	77 31 61 95 46	20 44 90 32 64	26 99 76 75 63
69 08 88 86 13	59 71 74 17 32	48 38 75 93 29	73 37 32 04 05	60 82 29 20 25
41 26 10 25 03	87 63 93 95 17	81 83 83 04 49	77 45 85 50 51	79 88 01 97 30
91 47 14 63 62	08 61 74 51 69	92 79 43 89 79	29 18 94 51 23	14 85 11 47 23
80 94 54 18 47	08 52 85 08 40	48 40 35 94 22	72 65 71 08 86	50 03 42 99 36
67 06 77 63 99	89 85 84 46 06	64 71 06 21 66	89 37 20 70 01	61 65 70 22 12
59 72 24 13 75	42 29 72 23 19	06 94 76 10 08	81 30 15 39 14	81 33 17 16 33
63 62 06 34 41	79 53 36 02 95	94 61 09 43 62	20 21 14 68 86	84 95 48 46 45
78 47 23 53 90	79 93 96 38 63	34 85 52 05 09	85 43 01 72 73	14 93 87 81 40
87 68 62 15 43	97 48 72 66 48	53 16 71 13 81	59 97 50 99 52	24 62 20 42 31
47 60 92 10 77	26 97 05 73 51	88 46 38 03 58	72 68 49 29 31	75 70 16 08 24
56 88 87 59 41	06 87 37 78 48	65 88 69 58 39	88 02 84 27 83	85 81 56 39 38
22 17 68 65 84	87 02 22 57 51	68 69 80 95 44	11 29 01 95 80	49 34 35 36 47
19 36 27 59 46	39 77 32 77 09	79 57 92 36 59	89 74 39 82 15	08 58 94 34 74
16 77 23 02 77	28 06 24 25 93	22 45 44 84 11	87 80 61 65 31	09 71 91 74 25
78 43 76 71 61	97 67 63 99 61	30 45 67 93 82	59 73 19 85 23	53 33 65 97 21
03 28 28 26 08	69 30 16 09 05	53 58 47 70 93	66 56 45 65 79	45 56 20 19 47
04 31 17 21 56	33 73 99 19 87	26 72 39 27 67	53 77 57 68 93	60 61 97 22 61
61 06 98 03 91	87 14 77 43 96	43 00 65 98 50	45 60 33 01 07	98 99 46 50 47
23 68 35 26 00	99 53 93 61 28	52 70 05 48 34	56 65 05 61 86	90 92 10 70 80
15 39 25 70 99	93 86 52 77 65	15 33 59 05 28	22 87 26 07 47	86 96 98 29 06
58 71 96 30 24	18 46 23 34 27	85 13 99 24 44	49 18 09 79 49	74 16 32 23 02
93 22 53 64 39	07 10 63 76 35	87 03 04 79 88	08 13 13 85 51	55 34 57 72 69
78 76 58 54 74	92 38 70 96 92	52 06 79 79 45	82 63 18 27 44	69 66 92 19 09
61 81 31 96 82	00 57 25 60 59	46 72 60 18 77	55 66 12 62 11	08 99 55 64 57
42 88 07 10 05	24 98 65 63 21	47 21 61 88 32	27 80 30 21 60	10 92 35 36 12
77 94 30 05 39	28 10 99 00 27	12 73 73 99 12	49 99 57 94 82	96 88 57 17 91

formula for expected value. The *expected value*, or average, for weekly demand can be computed analytically from the probability distribution, $P(x)$, as follows.

$$E(x) = (0.20)(14) + (0.40)(15) + (0.20)(16) + (0.10)(17) + (0.10)(18)$$
$$= 15.5 \text{ cases per week}$$

The analytical result of 15.5 cases is close to the simulated result of 16.1 cases. The difference (0.6 case) between the simulated value and the analytical value is a result of the number of periods over which the simulation was conducted. The results of any simulation study are subject to the number of times the simulation occurred (i.e., the number of *trials*). Thus, the more periods for which the simulation is conducted, the more accurate the result. For example, if demand were simulated for 1,000 weeks, in all likelihood an average value exactly equal to the analytical value (15.5 cases of milk per week) would result.

Once a simulation has been repeated enough times, it reaches an average result that remains constant, called a **steady-state result.** For this example, 15.5 cases is the long-run average or steady-state result, but we have seen that the simulation would have to be repeated more than 15 times (i.e., weeks) before this result was reached.

The simulation we performed manually for the milk-demand example was not too difficult. However, if we had performed the simulation for 1,000 weeks, it would have taken several hours. On the other hand, this simulation could be done on the computer in several seconds. Also, our simulation example was not very complex. As simulation models get progressively more complex, it becomes virtually impossible to perform them manually, making the computer a necessity.

The following example of a simulation model is slightly more complex but still not too difficult to analyze manually.

Steady-state result is an average result that remains constant after enough trials.

**EXAMPLE
S12.1**

*Simulation of an
Inventory System with
Uncertain Demand
and Lead Time*

The Videotech Store has the following probability distribution of weekly VCR demand.

Demand for VCRs	Probability
0	0.10
1	0.15
2	0.30
3	0.25
4	0.20
	1.00

The time it takes for the store to receive an order of VCRs from its distributor (i.e., the lead time) is defined by the following distribution.

Lead Time (weeks)	Probability
1	0.35
2	0.45
3	0.20
	1.00

When the number of VCRs in stock falls to a certain level (called the reorder point), the store manager orders from the distributor. (The reorder point is considered to be the number of units in stock plus the number on order.) The store manager wants to simulate this inventory system for ten weeks using an order size of five and a reorder point of three VCRs to see how many units of lost sales (i.e., VCRs demanded but not in stock) will result and the average number of units in stock.

SOLUTION:

The first step is to develop a range of random number values of each probability distribution as follows.

Demand	Probability	Random number (RN) Range
0	0.10	1–10
1	0.15	11–25
2	0.30	26–55
3	0.25	56–80
4	0.20	81–99, 00

Lead time	Probability	Random Number (RN) Range
1	0.35	1–35
2	0.45	36–80
3	0.20	81–99, 00

Next the inventory system is simulated for ten weeks, as shown in the following table.

Simulation for Inventory System

Time Period	Beginning Inventory	RN	Demand	Sold	Ending Inventory	Lost Sales	Place Order?	RN	Lead Time
1	5	44	2	2	3	0	Yes	17	1
2	3	92	4	3	0	1	No	—	0
3	5	02	0	0	5	0	No	—	0
4	5	12	1	1	4	0	No	—	0
5	4	25	1	1	3	0	Yes	53	2
6	3	93	4	3	0	1	No	—	0
7	0	46	2	0	0	2	No	—	0
8	5	34	2	2	3	0	Yes	21	1
9	3	22	1	1	2	0	No	—	0
10	7	79	3	3	4	0	No	—	0

The simulation works as follows.

1. The simulation is started with 5 units in stock, selected arbitrarily.

2. A random number is selected, 44, which results in demand of 2 units. Since 2 units are available, they are sold.

3. The amount sold is subtracted from the beginning inventory, which results in an ending inventory of 3 units. Since all items demanded were sold there were no lost sales.

4. Since the ending inventory level is at the reorder point of 3 units, a new order is placed.

5. A random number is selected, 17, which results in a lead time of 1 week. This means that a new order will arrive in week 3.

This same process is repeated for week 2. Notice that demand, 4, exceeds the inventory stock, 3, so there is one lost sale. An order is not placed during week 2 because the amount on order, 5, plus the ending inventory, 0, exceeds the reorder point (of 3).

For the 10-week simulation the following statistics are determined.

(Continued)

$$\text{Average lost sales} = \frac{4}{10} = 0.4 \text{ units per week}$$

$$\text{Average ending inventory} = \frac{24}{10} = 2.4 \text{ units per week}$$

The simulation was not conducted for enough time periods to generate steady-state statistics. However, this brief simulation does illustrate how a simulation model is constructed. For a more complex inventory problem of this type, where the demand might vary between 1 and 100 units and the lead times might vary between 1 and 10 weeks, computer simulation is the only means of analysis.

Areas of Simulation Application

Simulation can be used to address many types of operational problems.

Simulation is one of the most popular of all quantitative techniques because it can be applied to operational problems that are too difficult to model and solve analytically. Some analysts feel that complex systems should be studied via simulation whether or not they can be analyzed analytically, because it provides an easy vehicle for experimenting on the system. Surveys indicate that a large majority of major corporations use simulation in such functional areas as production, planning, engineering, financial analysis, research and development, information systems, and personnel. Following are descriptions of some of the more common applications of simulation.

THE COMPETITIVE EDGE

Simulating the Dispatching of Freight Carriers at Reynolds Metals Company

Reynolds Metals is decentralized into twelve operating divisions encompassing sixty domestic manufacturing facilities. The company incurs more than $80 million annually in truck freight expenses for approximately 75,000 truck shipments across its network of plants, warehouses, suppliers, and customers. Consistent with its decentralized operating philosophy, each of the company's divisions and plants has historically been responsible for managing its own freight operation, including the selection of independent carriers and their dispatchment for shipments. However, because of high costs and concern about service quality, in 1987 Reynolds Metals created a central dispatch system in Richmond, Virginia, to centralize the management and operation of its interstate truck shipping. A key component in the development of this system was a simulation model for carrier selection and deployment at central dispatch. Because of the uncertainty in the number and timing of daily shipments, it was not possible to use an optimization technique. The model

simulated daily freight operations and truck movements over time and was specifically used to finalize the number of carriers, select a group of "core" carriers (to be used exclusively by the company), assign carriers to locations, establish the carriers' fixed and variable truck commitments at each location, communicate expected shipping volumes and equipment commitment to carriers, and estimate costs and savings. The simulation basically replicates the daily central dispatching activity at a plant, warehouse, or supplier, which includes the identification of shipments, dispatching trucks, and shipping. The central dispatch system allowed Reynolds Metals to reduce its number of carriers from more than 200 to 14 and resulted in annual freight cost savings of more than $7 million. In addition, service was improved from 80 percent on-time deliveries to 95 percent, resulting in the attraction of new customers.

SOURCE: Based on E. W. Moore, Jr., "The Indispensable Role of Management Science in Centralizing Freight Operations at Reynolds Metals Company," *Interfaces* 21, no. 1 (January–February 1991): 107–29.

Waiting Lines/Service

A major application of simulation has been in the analysis of waiting line, or queuing, systems. For complex queuing systems, it is not possible to develop analytical formulas, and simulation is often the only means of analysis. For example, for a busy supermarket with multiple waiting lines, some for express service and some for regular service, simulation may be the only form of analysis to determine how many registers and servers are needed to meet customer demand.

Inventory Management

Product demand is an essential component in determining the amount of inventory a commercial enterprise should keep. Many of the traditional mathematical formulas used to analyze inventory systems make the assumption that this demand is certain (i.e., not a random variable). In practice, however, demand is rarely known with certainty. Simulation is one of the best means for analyzing inventory systems in which demand is a random variable. Simulation has been used to experiment with innovative inventory systems such as just-in-time (JIT). Companies use simulation to see how effective and costly a JIT system would be in their own manufacturing environment without having to implement the system physically.

Production and Manufacturing Systems

Simulation is often applied to production problems, such as production scheduling, production sequencing, assembly line balancing (of in-process inventory), plant layout, and plant location analysis. Many production processes can be viewed as queuing systems that can be analyzed only by using simulation. Since machine breakdowns typically occur according to some probability distributions, maintenance problems are also frequently analyzed using simulation. In the past few years, several software packages for the personal computer have been developed to simulate all aspects of manufacturing operations.

Capital Investment and Budgeting

Capital budgeting problems require estimates of cash flows, often resulting from many random variables. Simulation has been used to generate values of the various contributing factors to derive estimates of cash flows. Simulation has also been used to determine the inputs into rate-of-return calculations, where the inputs are random variables such as market size, selling price, growth rate, and market share.

Logistics

Logistics problems typically include numerous random variables, such as distance, different modes of transport, shipping rates, and schedules. Simulation can be used to analyze different distribution channels to determine the most efficient logistics system.

Service Operations

The operations of police departments, fire departments, post offices, hospitals, court systems, airports, and other public service systems have been analyzed using simulation. Typically, such operations are so complex and contain so many random variables that no technique except simulation can be employed for analysis.

THE COMPETITIVE EDGE

Simulating a Queuing Problem at a Security Gate

The Westinghouse Hanford Company is a secured work facility, which vehicles enter in the morning on a four-lane road and leave in the afternoon on a two-lane road. An average of 7 buses and approximately 285 private vehicles and vanpools entered in the morning at a gate where normally two security guards checked vehicles, drivers, and passengers. The vehicles formed a single line at the gate that extended past the available queue space of 40 vehicles and out onto the highway, which resulted in a major safety hazard. Buses formed a separate line. The situation was not only a safety hazard, but the waiting time was excessive. In the afternoon the vehicles exited in one lane and buses in the other, but vanpools picked up passengers in the bus lane, causing delays for the buses while they waited for the vanpools to merge into the vehicle lane. The objective in the morning was to minimize the queue length while also minimizing the number of security guards, and the afternoon goal was to move the buses through the gate as early as possible while also minimizing the number of security guards. An analytical queuing model did not fit this particular queuing scenario, so a simulation model was used instead. The first objective was to validate that the simulation model was

used instead. The first objective was to validate that the simulation model replicated the actual system. This was accomplished by comparing the simulation results to actual results for a three-day period. Next, two morning scenarios were tested, with the simulation model first increasing the number of guards to three while maintaining the single lane of traffic and then forming two traffic lines, each with a security guard.

The second scenario proved to be an excellent solution at no additional cost. It was implemented, and for most of the time fewer than five vehicles waited in line. The maximum number at any time was 21 vehicles for both lines combined. For the afternoon exiting problem, several scenarios were also tested, with the best assigning one security guard to each of the two lanes and having the vanpools remain in the bus lane and not changing lanes after passenger pickup. With this solution buses exited five to seven minutes earlier than in the original system, and the safety problem of passengers crossing traffic lanes to get to vanpools was eliminated. In both the morning and afternoon cases, effective no-cost solutions were achieved.

SOURCE: Based on E. Landaver and L. Becker, "Reducing Waiting Time at Security Checkpoints," *Interfaces* 19, no. 5 (September–October 1989): 57–65.

Environmental and Resource Analysis

Some of the more recent innovative applications of simulation have been directed at problems in the environment. Simulation models have been developed to ascertain the impact of projects such as manufacturing plants, waste-disposal facilities, and nuclear power plants. In many cases, these models include measures to analyze the financial feasibility of such projects. Other models have been developed to simulate waste and population conditions. In the area of resource analysis, numerous simulation models have been developed in recent years to simulate energy systems and the feasibility of alternative energy sources.

Summary

Simulation has become an increasingly important quantitative technique for solving problems in operations. Surveys have shown simulation to be one of the techniques most widely applied to real-world problems. Evidence of this popularity is the number of specialized simulation languages that have been developed by the computer industry and academia to deal with complex problem areas.

The popularity of simulation is due in large part to the flexibility it allows in analyzing systems, compared to more confining analytical techniques. In other words, the problem does not have to fit the model (or technique)—the simulation model can be constructed to fit the problem. Simulation is popular also because it is an excellent experimental technique, enabling systems and problems to be tested within a laboratory setting.

However, in spite of its versatility, simulation has limitations and must be used with caution. One limitation is that simulation models are typically unstructured and must be developed for a system or problem that is also unstructured. Unlike some of the structured techniques presented in this text, the models cannot simply be applied to a specific type of problem. As a result, developing simulation models often requires a certain amount of imagination and intuitiveness that is not required by some of the more straightforward solution techniques we have presented. In addition, the validation of simulation models is an area of serious concern. It is often impossible to validate simulation results realistically or to know if they accurately reflect the system under analysis. This problem has become an area of such concern that *output analysis* of simulation results is a field of study in its own right. Another limiting factor in simulation is the cost in terms of money and time of model building. Because simulation models are developed for unstructured systems, they often take large amounts of staff, computer time, and money to develop and run. For many business companies, these costs can be prohibitive.

The computer programming aspects of simulation can also be quite difficult. Fortunately, generalized simulation languages have been developed to perform many of the functions of a simulation study. Each of these languages requires at least some knowledge of a scientific or business-oriented programming language.

Summary of Key Terms

Monte Carlo technique: a technique for selecting numbers randomly from a probability distribution for use in a simulation model.

random numbers: numbers in a table, each of which has an equal likelihood of being selected at random.

simulation: an approach to operational problem solving in which a real-world problem situation is replicated within a mathematical model.

steady-state result: an average model result that approaches constancy after a sufficient passage of time or enough repetitions or trends.

Solved Problem

Simulation

Members of the Willow Creek Emergency Rescue Squad know from past experience that they will receive between zero and six emergency calls each night, according to the following discrete probability distribution.

Calls	Probability
0	0.05
1	0.12
2	0.15
3	0.25
4	0.22
5	0.15
6	0.06
	1.00

The rescue squad classifies each emergency call into one of three categories: minor, regular, or major emergency. The probability that a particular call will be each type of emergency is as follows.

Emergency Type	Probability
Minor	0.30
Regular	0.56
Major	0.14
	1.00

The type of emergency call determines the size of the crew sent in response. A minor emergency requires a two-person crew, a regular call requires a three-person crew, and a major emergency requires a five-person crew.

Simulate the emergency calls received by the rescue squad for ten nights, compute the average number of each type of emergency call each night, and determine the maximum number of crew members that might be needed on any given night.

Solution:

Step 1. Develop random number ranges for the probability distributions.

Calls	Probability	Cumulative Probability	Random Number Range, r_1
0	0.05	0.05	1–5
1	0.12	0.17	6–17
2	0.15	0.32	18–32
3	0.25	0.57	33–57
4	0.22	0.79	58–79
5	0.15	0.94	80–94
6	0.06	1.00	95–99, 00
	1.00		

Emergency Types	Probability	Cumulative Probability	Random Number Range, r_2
Minor	0.30	0.30	1–30
Regular	0.56	0.86	31–86
Major	0.14	1.00	87–99, 00
	1.00		

Step 2. Set up a tabular simulation. Use the second column of random numbers in Table S12.3.

Night	r_1	Number of Calls	r_2	Emergency Type	Crew Size	Total per Night
1	65	4	71	Regular	3	
			18	Minor	2	
			12	Minor	2	
			17	Minor	2	9
2	48	3	89	Major	5	
			18	Minor	2	
			83	Regular	3	10
3	08	1	90	Regular	3	3
4	05	0	—	—	—	—
5	89	5	18	Minor	2	
			08	Minor	2	
			26	Minor	2	
			47	Regular	3	
			94	Major	5	14
6	06	1	72	Regular	3	3
7	62	4	47	Regular	3	
			68	Regular	3	
			60	Regular	3	
			88	Major	5	14
8	17	1	36	Regular	3	3
9	77	4	43	Regular	3	
			28	Minor	2	
			31	Regular	3	
			06	Minor	2	10
10	68	4	39	Regular	3	
			71	Regular	3	
			22	Minor	2	
			76	Regular	3	11

Step 3. Compute the results.

$$\text{Average number of minor emergency calls per night} = \frac{10}{10} = 1.0$$

$$\text{Average number of regular emergency calls per night} = \frac{14}{10} = 1.4$$

$$\text{Average number of major emergency calls per night} = \frac{3}{10} = 0.30$$

If all the calls came in at the same time, the maximum number of squad members required during any one night would be 14.

Questions

S12-1. Explain what the Monte Carlo technique is and how random numbers are used in a Monte Carlo process.

S12-2. How are steady-state results achieved in a simulation?

S12-3. What type of information for decision making does simulation typically provide?

Problems

S12-1. The Hoylake Rescue Squad receives an emergency call every 1, 2, 3, 4, 5, or 6 hours, according to the following probability distribution.

Time Between Emergency Calls (hours)	Probability
1	0.05
2	0.10
3	0.30
4	0.30
5	0.20
6	0.05
	1.00

The squad is on duty 24 hours per day, 7 days per week.

a. Simulate the emergency calls for 3 days (note that this will require a "running," or cumulative, hourly clock) using the random number table.

b. Compute the average time between calls and compare this value with the expected value of the time between calls from the probabilistic distribution. Why are the results different?

c. How many calls were made during the 3-day period? Can you logically assume that this is an average number of calls per 3-day period? If not, how could you simulate to determine such an average?

S12-2. The Dynaco Manufacturing Company produces a product in a process consisting of operations of five machines. The probability distribution of the number of machines that will break down in a week is as follows.

Machine Breakdowns per Week	Probability
0	0.10
1	0.10
2	0.20
3	0.25
4	0.30
5	0.05
	1.00

Every time a machine breaks down at the Dynaco Manufacturing Company, either one, two, or three hours are required to fix it, according to the following probability distribution.

Repair Time (hours)	Probability
1	0.30
2	0.50
3	0.20
	1.00

a. Simulate the repair time for 20 weeks and compute the average weekly repair time.

b. If the random numbers that are used to simulate breakdowns per week are also used to simulate repair time per breakdown, will the results be affected in any way? Explain.

c. If it costs $50 per hour to repair a machine when it breaks down (including lost productivity), determine the average weekly breakdown cost.

d. The Dynaco Company is considering a preventive maintenance program that would alter probabilities of machine breakdowns per week as follows.

Machine Breakdowns per Week	Probability
0	0.20
1	0.30
2	0.20
3	0.15
4	0.10
5	0.05
	1.00

The weekly cost of the preventive maintenance program is $150. Using simulation, determine whether the company should institute the preventive maintenance program.

S12-3. The Stereo Warehouse in Georgetown sells stereo sets, which it orders from Fuji Electronics in Japan. Because of shipping and handling costs, each order must be for five stereos. Because of the time it takes to receive an order, the warehouse outlet places an order every time the present stock drops to five stereos. It costs $100 to place an order. It costs the warehouse $400 in lost sales when a customer asks for a stereo and the warehouse is out of stock. It costs $40 to keep each stereo stored in the warehouse. If a customer cannot purchase a stereo when it is requested, the customer will not wait until one comes in but will go to a competitor. The following probability distribution for demand for stereos has been determined.

Demand per Month	Probability
0	0.04
1	0.08
2	0.28
3	0.40
4	0.16
5	0.02
6	0.02
	1.00

The time required to receive an order once it is placed has the following probability distribution.

Time to Receive and Order (months)	Probability
1	0.60
2	0.30
3	0.10
	1.00

The warehouse presently has five stereos in stock. Orders are always received at the beginning of the week. Simulate the Stereo Warehouse's ordering and sales policy for 20 months, using the first column of random numbers in Table S12.3. Compute the average monthly cost.

S12-4. A baseball game consists of plays that can be described as follows.

Play	Description
No advance	An out where no runners advance. This includes strikeouts, pop ups, short flies, and the like.
Groundout	All runners can advance one base.
Possible double play	Double play if there is a runner on first base and fewer than two outs. The lead runner can be forced out; runners not out advance one base. If there is no runner on first or there are two outs, this play is treated as a "no advance."
Long fly	A runner on third base can score.
Very long fly	Runners on second and third base advance one base.
Walk	Includes a hit batter.
Infield single	All runners advance one base.
Outfield single	A runner on first base advances one base, but a runner on second or third base scores.
Long single	All runners can advance a maximum of two bases.
Double	Runners can advance a maximum of two bases.
Long double	All runners score.
Triple	
Home run	

Note: Singles also include a factor for errors, allowing the batter to reach first base.

Distributions for these plays for two teams, the White Sox (visitors) and the Yankees (home), are as follows.

Team: White Sox

Play	Probability
No advance	0.03
Groundout	0.39
Possible double play	0.06
Long fly	0.09
Very long fly	0.08
Walk	0.06
Infield single	0.02
Outfield single	0.10
Long single	0.03
Double	0.04
Long double	0.05
Triple	0.02
Home run	0.03
	1.00

Team: Yankees

Play	Probability
No advance	0.04
Groundout	0.38
Possible double play	0.04
Long fly	0.10
Very long fly	0.06
Walk	0.07
Infield single	0.04

(Continued)

Play	Probability
Outfield single	0.10
Long single	0.04
Double	0.05
Long double	0.03
Triple	0.01
Home run	0.04
	1.00

Simulate a nine-inning baseball game using this information.[1]

S12-5. The Saki automobile dealer in the Minneapolis–St. Paul area orders the Saki sport compact, which gets fifty miles per gallon of gasoline, from the manufacturer in Japan. However, the dealer never knows for sure how many months it will take to receive an order once it is placed. It can take one, two, or three months with the following probabilities.

Months to Receive an Order	Probability
1	.50
2	.30
3	.20
	1.00

The demand per month is given by the following distribution.

Demand per Month (cars)	Probability
1	.10
2	.30
3	.40
4	.20
	1.00

The dealer orders when the number of cars on the lot gets down to a certain level. In order to determine the appropriate level of cars to use as an indicator of when to order, the dealer needs to know how many cars will be demanded during the time required to receive an order. Simulate the demand for 30 orders, and compute the average number of cars demanded during the time required to receive an order. At what level of cars in stock should the dealer place an order?

S12-6. The Paymor Rental Car Agency rents cars in a small town. It wants to determine how many rental cars it should maintain. Based on market projections and historical data, the manager has determined probability distributions for the number of rentals per day and rental duration (in days only) as shown in the following tables.

---

[1] This problem was adapted from R. E. Trueman, "A Computer Simulation Model of Baseball: With Particular Application to Strategy Analysis," in R. E. Machol, S. P. Ladany, and D. G. Morrison, eds., *Management Science in Sports* (New York: North Holland Publishing, Co., 1976), pp. 1–14.

Number of Customers/Day	Probability
0	.20
1	.20
2	.50
3	.10

Rental Duration (days)	Probability
1	.10
2	.30
3	.40
4	.10
5	.10

Design a simulation experiment for the car agency and simulate, using a fleet of four rental cars, for ten days. Compute the probability that the agency will not have a car available upon demand. Should the agency expand its fleet? Explain how a simulation experiment could be designed to determine the optimal fleet size for the Paymor Agency.

S12-7. The emergency room of the community hospital in Farmburg has a receptionist, one doctor, and one nurse. The emergency room opens at time zero, and patients begin to arrive sometime later. Patients arrive at the emergency room according to the following probability distribution.

Time Between Arrivals (min)	Probability
5	.06
10	.10
15	.23
20	.29
25	.18
30	.14

The attention needed by a patient who comes to the emergency room is defined by the following probability distribution.

Patient Needs to See	Probability
Doctor alone	.50
Nurse alone	.20
Both	.30

If a patient needs to see both the doctor and the nurse, he or she cannot see one before the other; that is, the patient must wait to see both together. The length of the patient's visit (in minutes) is defined by the following probability distributions.

Doctor	Probability	Nurse	Probability	Both	Probability
10	.22	5	.08	15	.07
15	.31	10	.24	20	.16
20	.25	15	.51	25	.21
25	.12	20	.17	30	.28
30	.10			35	.17
				40	.11

Simulate the arrival of 30 patients to the emergency room and compute the probability that a patient must wait and the average waiting time. Based on this one simulation, does it appear this system provides adequate patient care?

References

Banks, J., and J. S. Carson. *Discrete-Event System Simulation.* Englewood Cliffs, N.J.: Prentice Hall, 1984.

Christy, D., and H. Watson. "The Applications of Simulation: A Survey of Industry Practice." *Interfaces* 13, no. 5 (October 1983): 47–52.

Hammersly, J. M., and D. C. Handscomb. *Monte Carlo Methods.* New York: John Wiley, 1984.

Law, A. M., and W. D. Kelton. *Simulation Modeling and Analysis.* New York: McGraw-Hill, 1982.

Meier, R. C., W. T. Newell, and H. L. Pazer. *Simulation in Business and Economics.* Englewood Cliffs, N.J.: Prentice Hall, 1969.

Naylor, T. H., J. L. Balintfy, D. S. Burdinck, and K. Chu. *Computer Simulation Techniques.* New York: John Wiley, 1966.

Payne, J. A. *Introduction to Simulation.* New York: McGraw-Hill, 1982.

Pritsker, A. A. B., C. E. Sigal, and R. D. Hammesfahr. *SLAM II: Network Models for Decision Support.* Englewood Cliffs, N.J.: Prentice Hall, 1989.

Taha, H. A. *Simulation Modeling and Simen.* New York: McGraw-Hill, 1988.

Taylor, B. W. *Introduction to Management Science,* 5th ed. Englewood Cliffs, NJ: Prentice Hall, 1996.

13

Material Requirements Planning

Five Million Possibilities at Hubbell Lighting

www.prenhall.com/russell

In the industrial lighting business, good quality is assumed. Prompt delivery wins the orders. Hubbell Lighting, a manufacturer of industrial lighting products, has always had a reputation for good-quality products but has not always met the due dates promised to its customers. Hubbell's customers are a diverse group, including schools, shopping malls, amusement parks, football franchises, and even NASA. The work is specialized for each customer, involves little automation, and can generally be described as a "glorified job shop." Its complexity is derived from the sheer size of the manufacturing task—the hundreds of different products produced, the thousands of parts needed to make up a typical product, the tremendous number of scheduling decisions required on a day-to-day basis, and the vast amount of information that is necessary to support those decisions. For example, one of Hubbell's factories, which employs around 425 workers, develops an aggregate production plan for 63 product families and weekly schedules for the production of 3,200 end items. These end items consist of 15,000 components that may be assembled into 5 million possible final product configurations. The factory (and the company as a whole) uses a computerized inventory control and production planning system called *material requirements planning* (MRP) to help plan and coordinate the various stages of production. Without an MRP system, a factory of this type simply could not function. Prior to MRP, the factory completed less than 75 percent of its orders on time. After MRP, on-time delivery rose to 97 percent, with an additional 2 percent completed within one or two days of promised completion.

Many U.S. manufacturers use a computerized production planning and inventory control system called material requirements planning (MRP). MRP is especially useful in industries with complex products, varying due dates, and fluctuating demand.

Material requirements planning (MRP) was introduced in the 1970s as a computerized inventory control system that would calculate the demand for component items, keep track of when they are needed, and generate work orders and purchase orders that take into account the lead time required to make the items in-house or buy them from a supplier. Much of the credit for introducing MRP and educating industry about its benefits goes to three individuals, Joseph Orlicky, George Plossl, and Oliver Wight, and to a professional society they endorsed, known as the American Production and Inventory Control Society (APICS). Basically an information system, MRP was quite revolutionary in its early days, because it brought computers and systematic planning to the manufacturing function. Since its introduction, the system has undergone several revisions that reflect the increased power and accessibility of computers and the changing role of manufacturing. For example, MRP II for *manufacturing resource planning*, is much broader in scope than the original material planner, incorporating marketing and financial functions as well. In today's modern factories, MRP II is the standard for management information systems and an important component of computer-integrated manufacturing (CIM).

MRP is a computerized inventory control and production planning system.

www.prenhall.com/russell

Objectives and Applicability of MRP

The main objective of any inventory system is to ensure that material is available when needed—which can easily lead to a tremendous investment of funds in unnecessary inventory. One objective of MRP is to maintain the lowest possible level of inventory. MRP does this by determining *when* component items are needed and scheduling them to be ready at that time, no earlier and no later.

MRP was the first inventory system to recognize that inventories of raw materials, components, and finished goods may need to be handled differently. In the process of planning inventory levels for these various types of goods, the system also planned purchasing activities (for raw materials and purchased components), manufacturing activities (for component parts and assemblies), and delivery schedules (for finished products). Thus, the system was more than an inventory control system; it became a production scheduling system as well.

MRP schedules component items when they are needed—no earlier and no later.

One of the few certainties in a manufacturing environment is that things rarely go as planned—orders arrive late, machines break down, workers are absent, designs are changed, and so on. With its computerized database, MRP is able to keep track of the relationship of job orders so that if a delay in one aspect of production is unavoidable, other related activities can be rescheduled, too. MRP systems have the ability to keep schedules valid and up-to-date.

When to Use MRP

Managing component demand inventory is different from managing finished goods inventory. For one thing, the demand for component parts does not have to be forecasted; it can be derived from the demand for the finished product. For example, suppose demand for a table, consisting of four legs and a tabletop, is 100 units per week. Then, demand for tabletops would also be 100 per week and demand for table legs would be 400 per week. Demand for table legs is totally *dependent* on the demand for tables. The demand for tables may be forecasted, but the demand for table legs is calculated. The tables are an example of *independent demand*. The tabletop and table legs exhibit *dependent demand*.

MRP is useful for dependent and discrete demand items, complex products, job shop production, and assemble-to-order environments.

Another difference between finished products and component parts is the continuity of their demand. For the inventory control systems in the previous chapter, we assumed demand occurred at a constant rate. The inventory systems were designed to keep some inventory on hand at all times, enough, we hoped, to meet each day's demand. With component items, demand does not necessarily occur on a continuous basis. Let's assume in our table example that table legs are the last items to be assembled onto the tables before shipping. Also assume that it takes one week to make a batch of tables and that table legs are assembled onto the tabletops every Friday. If we were to graph the demand for table legs, as shown in Figure 13.1, it would be zero for Monday, Tuesday, Wednesday, and Thursday, but on Friday the demand for table legs would jump to 400. The same pattern would repeat the following week. With this scenario, we do not need to keep an inventory of table legs available on Monday through Thursday of any week. We need table legs only on Fridays. Looking at our graph, demand for table legs occurs in *lumps*; it is *discrete*, not continuous. Using an inventory system such as EOQ for component items would result in inventory being held that we know

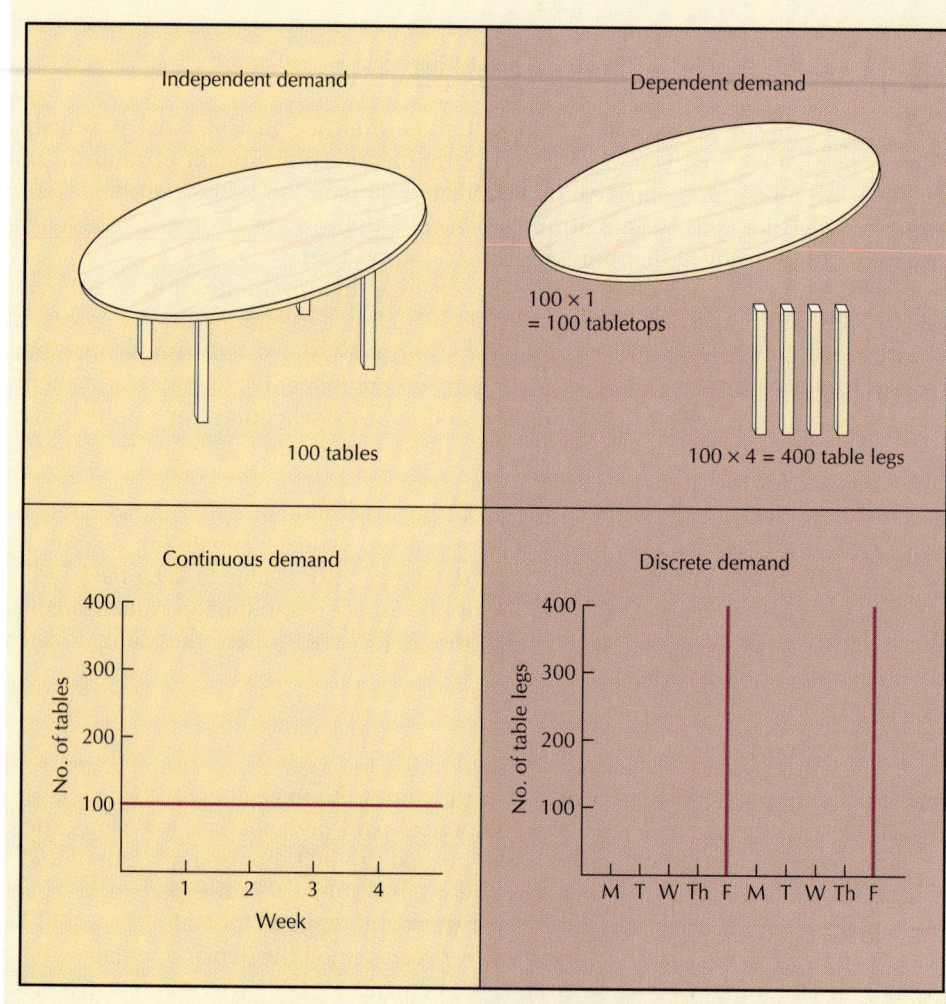

FIGURE 13.1   Demand Characteristics for Finished Products and Their Components

we won't need until a later date. The excess inventory takes up space, soaks up funds, and requires additional resources for counting, sorting, storing, and moving.

Industries that manufacture complex products, requiring the coordination of component production, find MRP especially useful. A complex product may have hundreds of component parts, dozens of assemblies, and several levels of assembly. MRP tries to ensure that multiple components of an assembly are ready at the same time so that they can be assembled together. Products with simple structures do not need MRP to plan production or monitor inventory levels.

The advantages of MRP are more evident when the manufacturing environment is complex and uncertain. Manufacturing environments in which customer orders are erratic, each job takes a different path through the system, lead time is uncertain, and due dates vary, need an information system such as MRP to keep track of the different jobs and coordinate their schedules. The type of environment we are describing is characteristic of *batch*, or *job shop*, processes.[1] Although MRP is currently available for continuous and repetitive manufacturing, it was designed primarily for systems that produce goods in batches.

Finally, MRP systems are very useful in industries where the customer is allowed to choose among many different options. These products have many common components and are inventoried in some form before the customer order is received. For example, customers of a well-known electronics firm routinely expect delivery in six weeks on goods that take twenty-eight weeks to manufacture. The manufacturer copes with this seemingly unrealistic demand by producing major assemblies and subassemblies in advance of the customer order and then completing the product upon receipt of the order. This type of operation is called **assemble-to-order.**

Assemble-to-order is a manufacturing environment in which previously completed subassemblies are configured to order.

MRP Inputs

As shown in Figure 13.2, there are three major inputs to the MRP process:

- The master production schedule
- The product structure file, and
- The inventory master file.

Master Production Schedule

The **master production schedule (MPS),** also called the *master schedule,* specifies which end items or finished products a firm is to produce, how many are needed, and when they are needed. Recall that aggregate production planning creates a similar schedule for product lines or families, given by months or quarters of a year. The master production schedule works within the constraints of the production plan but produces a more specific schedule by individual products. The time frame is more specific, too. An MPS is usually expressed in days or weeks and may extend over several months to cover the complete manufacture of the items contained in the MPS. The total length of time required to manufacture a product is called its **cumulative lead time.**

The **master production schedule** drives the MRP process with a schedule of finished products.

Table 13.1 shows a sample master production schedule consisting of four end items produced by a manufacturer of specialty writing accessories. Several comments should be made concerning the quantities contained in the MPS:

Cumulative lead time is the total length of time needed to manufacture a product.

---

[1]For a more thorough discussion of types of processes, see Chapter 6.

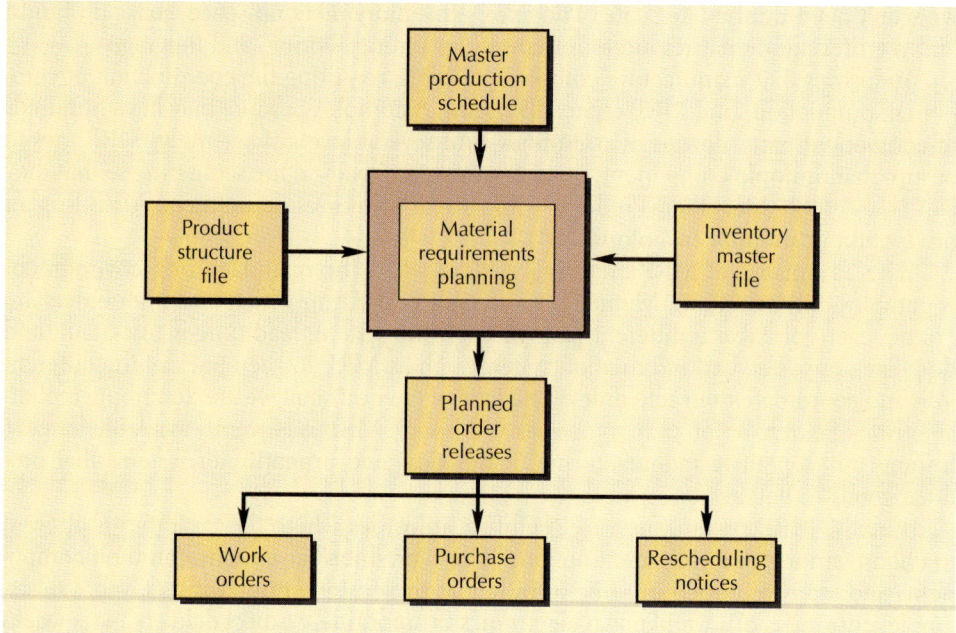

FIGURE 13.2   Material Requirements Planning

■ *The quantities represent production, not demand.* As we saw in the aggregate production planning chapter, production does not necessarily have to match demand. The strategy decisions made in the production planning stage filter down to the master production schedule. The steady production pattern of lapboards and pencil cases in Table 13.1 is probably the result of different production planning strategies.

■ *The quantities may consist of a combination of customer orders and demand forecasts.* Some figures in the MPS are confirmed, but others are predictions. As might be expected, the quantities in the more recent time periods are more firm, whereas the forecasted quantities further in the future may need to be revised several times before the schedule is completed. Some companies set a **time fence,** within which no more changes to the master schedule are allowed. This helps to stabilize the production environment.

A **time fence** is a management-specified date beyond which no changes in the master schedule are allowed.

The MPS for clipboards and lapboards shown in Table 13.1 illustrates two approaches to future scheduling. For clipboards, demand beyond period 3 is forecasted at an even 100 units per period. Projecting these requirements now based on past demand data helps in planning for the availability of resources. For lapdesks, demand beyond period 3 appears sparse, probably because it is based on actual customer orders

TABLE 13.1   Master Production Schedule

MPS Item	Period							
	1	*2*	*3*	*4*	*5*	*6*	*7*	*8*
Clipboard	86	93	119	100	100	100	100	100
Lapboard	0	50	0	50	0	50	0	50
Lap desk	75	120	47	20	17	10	0	0
Pencil case	125	125	125	125	125	125	125	125

received. We can expect those numbers to increase as the future time periods draw nearer. Evidently, a lengthy lead time is not necessary to gather the resources for producing lap desks.

■ *The quantities represent what needs to be produced, not what can be produced.* Because the MPS is derived from the production plan, its requirements are probably "doable," but until the MRP system considers the specific resource needs and the timing of those needs, the feasibility of the MPS cannot be guaranteed. Thus, the MRP system is often used to *simulate* production to verify that the MPS is feasible or to confirm that a particular order can be completed by a certain date before the quote is given to the customer.

The master production schedule drives the MRP process. The schedule of finished products provided by the master schedule is needed before the MRP system can do its job of generating production schedules for component items.

Product Structure File

Once the MPS is set, the MRP system accesses the **product structure file** to determine which component items need to be scheduled. The product structure file contains a **bill of material (BOM)** for every item produced. The bill of material for a product lists the items that go into the product, includes a brief description of each item, and specifies when and in what quantity each item is needed in the assembly process.

When each item is needed can best be described in the form of a product structure diagram, as shown in Figure 13.3 for a clipboard. An assembled item is sometimes referred to as a *parent*, and a component as a *child*. The number in parentheses beside each item is the quantity of a given component needed to make *one* parent. Thus, one clip assembly, two rivets, and one board are needed to make each clipboard. The clip assembly, rivets, and board appear at the same level of the product structure because they are to be assembled together.

A diagram can be converted to a computerized bill of material by labeling the levels in the product structure. The final product, or end item, at the top of the structure—

> The **product structure file** contains a **bill of material** for every item produced.

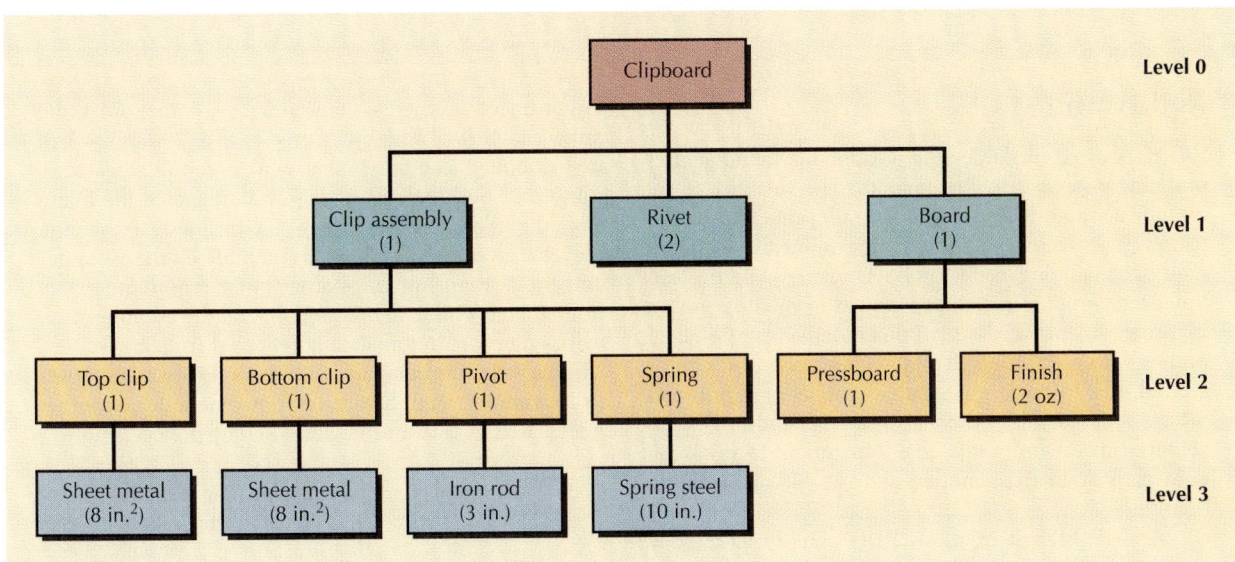

FIGURE 13.3 **Product Structure Diagram for a Clipboard**

TABLE 13.2   Multi-Level Indented Bill of Material

Level	Item	Unit of Measure	Quantity
0– – – –	Clipboard	ea	1
– 1 – – –	Clip assembly	ea	1
– – 2 – –	Top clip	ea	1
– – – 3 –	Sheet metal	in^2	8
– – 2 – –	Bottom clip	ea	1
– – – 3 –	Sheet metal	in^2	8
– – 2 – –	Pivot	ea	1
– – – 3 –	Iron rod	in	3
– – 2 – –	Spring	ea	1
– – – 3 –	Spring steel	in	10
– 1 – – –	Rivet	ea	2
– 1 – – –	Board	ea	1
– – 2 – –	Press board	ea	1
– – 2 – –	Finish	oz	2

in this case, the clipboard—is labeled level 0. The level number increases as we move down the product structure. The clipboard has three levels of assembly. The bill of material for the clipboard, listed in Table 13.2, shows some levels indented underneath others. This specifies which components belong to which parents and can easily be matched to the product structure diagram.

Several specialized bills of material have been designed to simplify information requirements, clarify relationships, and reduce computer processing time. They include phantom bills, K-bills, and modular bills.

Phantom bills, K-bills, and modular bills simplify planning.

■ *Phantom bills* are used for transient subassemblies that never see a stockroom because they are immediately consumed in the next stage of manufacture. These items have a lead time of zero and a special code so that no orders for them will be released. Phantom bills are becoming more common as companies adopt just-in-time and cel-

THE COMPETITIVE EDGE

Agility and MRP

REDA, located in Bartlesville, Oklahoma, manufactures pumping systems for oil companies. The volatility of the oil industry and the emergence of independent oil companies have made the industry more competitive with customers demanding better products faster. Lengthy lead times for pumping systems, measured in months, are no longer acceptable. Today's customers demand customized pumps within 48 hours. To guarantee such quick turnaround, REDA stocks major subassemblies of motors and pumps and assembles them to customer order. But inventory can eat up profits, so it's important to stock the right parts and subassemblies, and be able to configure them quickly.

An MRP II system allows REDA engineers to copy an existing bill of material and modify it to meet specific customer requirements. Translating a customer order into a manufacturing work order used to take 24 hours—half of the allotted lead time! Now, work orders are created in minutes. The MRP system has also integrated the financial and manufacturing sides of the business, so that employees can see how their job directly affects the customer and the bottom line. Customer order requirements are immediately visible to production, and the completion of work orders are automatically reflected in labor records. This provides the company with more timely control over its operations and better responsiveness to customer needs. REDA calls its new found competence "agility."

www.prenhall.com/russell

SOURCE: Based on "BPR Cuts Pump Manufacturer's MRP Run Time in Half," *IIE Solutions* (September 1996): 53.

lular manufacturing concepts that speed products through the manufacturing and assembly process.

■ Kit numbers, or *K-bills*, group small, loose parts such as fasteners, nuts, and bolts together under one pseudoitem number. In this way, requirements for the items are processed only once (for the group), rather than for each individual item. K-bills reduce the paperwork, processing time, and file space required in generating orders for small, inexpensive items that are usually ordered infrequently in large quantities.

■ **Modular bills of material** are appropriate when the product is manufactured in major subassemblies or modules that are later assembled into the final product with customer-designated options. With this approach, the end item in the master production schedule is not the finished product, but a major option or module. This reduces the number of bills of material that need to be input, maintained, and processed by the MRP system.

> **Modular bills of material** are used to plan the production of products with many optimal features.

Consider the options available on the X10 automobile, partially diagrammed in Figure 13.4. The customer has a choice between three engine types, eight exterior colors, three interiors, eight interior colors, and four car bodies. Thus, there are $3 \times 8 \times 3 \times 8 \times 4 = 2,304$ possible model configurations—and the same number of bills of material—unless modular bills are used. By establishing a bill of material for each option rather than each combination of options, the entire range of options can be accounted for by $3 + 8 + 3 + 8 + 4 = 26$ modular bills of material.

Modular bills of material also simplify forecasting and planning. The quantity per assembly for an option is given as a decimal figure, interpreted as a percentage of the requirements for the parent item. For example, from Figure 13.4, in preparation for an anticipated demand of 1,000 X10 automobiles, 1,000 engines are needed. Of those 1,000 engines, the master production schedule would generate requirements for 40 percent, or 400, four-cylinder engines, 50 percent, or 500, six-cylinder engines, and 10 percent, or 100, eight-cylinder engines.

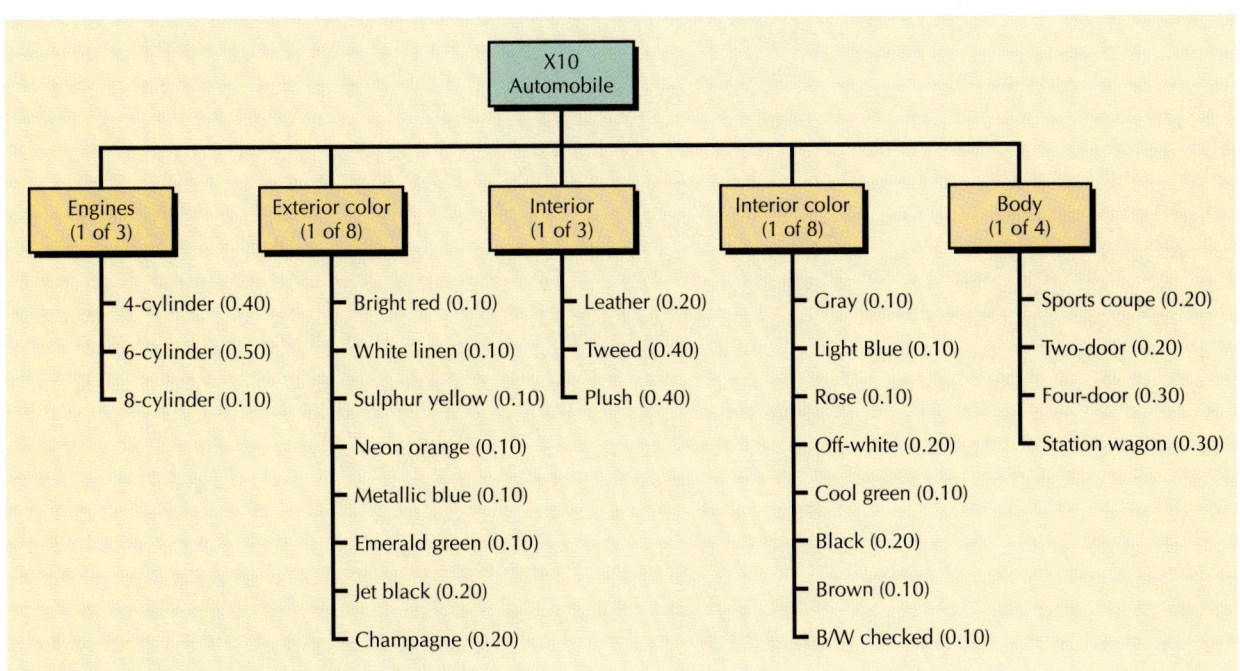

FIGURE 13.4   Modular Bills of Material

The creation of a product structure file can take a considerable amount of time. Accurate bills of material are essential to an effective MRP system. The bill of material must specify how a product is actually manufactured rather than how it was *designed* to be manufactured. Redundant or obsolete part numbers must be purged from the system. This may not seem like a big task, but in some companies every time a part is purchased from a different supplier, it is assigned a different part number. One firm in the process of implementing MRP was able to eliminate 6,000 extra part numbers from its database and dispose of thousands of dollars of obsolete inventory that had not previously been identified as such!

Inventory Master File

The **inventory master file** is a database of information on every item produced, ordered, or inventoried.

The **inventory master file** contains an extensive amount of information on every item that is produced, ordered, or inventoried in the system. It includes such data as on-hand quantities, on-order quantities, lot sizes, safety stock, lead time, and past usage figures. Table 13.3 displays the inventory master file of the "board" assembly from the clipboard example. It provides a detailed description of the item, specifies the inventory policy, updates the physical inventory count, summarizes the item's year-to-date or month-to-date usage, and provides internal codes to link this file with other related information in the MRP database.

The inventory master file is updated whenever items are withdrawn from or added to inventory or whenever an order is released, revised, or completed. Accuracy of inventory transactions is essential to MRP's ability to keep inventory levels at a minimum. It is estimated that 95 percent inventory accuracy is a prerequisite for an effective MRP

TABLE 13.3   Inventory Master File

DESCRIPTION		INVENTORY POLICY	
Item	Board	Lead time	2
Item no.	7341	Annual demand	5,000
Item type	Manuf.	Holding cost	1
Product/sales class	Ass'y	Ordering/setup cost	50
Value class	B	Safety stock	25
Buyer/planner	RSR	Reorder point	39
Vendor/drawing	07142	EOQ	316
Phantom code	N	Minimum order qty.	100
Unit price/cost	1.25	Maximum order qty.	500
Pegging	Y	Multiple order qty	100
LLC	1	Policy code	3
PHYSICAL INVENTORY		**USAGE/SALES**	
On hand	100	YTD usage/sales	1,100
Location	W142	MTD usage/sales	75
On order	100	YTD receipts	1,200
Allocated	75	MTD receipts	0
Cycle	3	Last receipt	8/25
Last count	9/5	Last issue	10/5
Difference	−2		
		CODES	
		Cost acct.	00754
		Routing	00326
		Engr.	07142

Accurate inventory counts are essential to a successful MRP system. Access to stockrooms is limited so that the withdrawal of inventory can be carefully monitored. Cycle counting, in which inventory is counted continuously during the year on a specified cycle, can improve operations by reconciling differences as they occur instead of waiting for end-of-the-year physical inventories.

system. Although technologies such as bar codes, voice-activated systems, and automated "picking" equipment can improve inventory accuracy considerably, a general overhaul of inventory procedures is often needed. This involves:

1. Maintaining orderly stockrooms;
2. Controlling access to stockrooms;
3. Establishing and enforcing procedures for inventory withdrawal;
4. Ensuring prompt and accurate entry of inventory transactions;
5. Taking physical inventory count on a regular basis; and
6. Reconciling inventory discrepancies in a timely manner.

If you have taken part in an end-of-year inventory count, you can verify the wide discrepancies that are commonly found between what the records say is in inventory and what is physically there. Unfortunately, by the time the errors are discovered, it's too late to correct them or find out why they occurred. The slate is merely cleaned for next year's record, with the hope or promise that next time will be better.

Cycle counting is taking physical counts of at least some inventory items daily and reconciling differences as they occur. The system specifies which items are to be counted each day on a computer printout and may tie the frequency of the count to the frequency of orders for the item within the MRP system. Thus, items that are used more often are counted more often. The cycle counting system may also be related to the *ABC classification system* discussed in Chapter 12. *A* items would be counted more often than *B* items. *C* items may still be counted only once a year. Approved cycle counting systems are accepted by the accounting standards board as valid replacements for end-of-year physical inventories.

Cycle counting improves inventory accuracy.

THE COMPETITIVE EDGE

MRP Improves Customer Service

Courtaulds Performance Films makes coextruded oriented polypropylene, the plastic film that covers food prod-

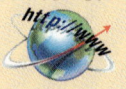

ucts in your supermarket. Courtaulds has two manufacturing plants, one in Swindon, England, and the other in Mantes, France.

www.prenhall.com/russell

The plants run 24 hours a day, 7 days a week. After the chemical process of making a film base, the film is extruded, gripped by a fast-moving chain, heated, and stretched lengthwise by 500 percent and sideways by 1,000 percent. That means the final product is five times longer and ten times wider than it was before the extruding process. Prior to MRP, Courtaulds met delivery promises only 75 percent of the time. The company had difficulty scheduling the 60 types of raw materials, 40 types of films, and 12,500 make-to-order end products. Courtaulds visited neighbor Formica, a Class A MRP user, to learn the secret of its 95 percent on-time deliveries.

Courtaulds implemented MRP and quickly became a class A user themselves.

The most beneficial aspect of MRP for Courtaulds is its master scheduling component. Courtaulds can instruct the system to keep 5 to 10 percent of the master schedule uncommitted until one week before production. This leaves space for "orders of opportunity." The system also reserves capacity in advance for major customers and treats all other customers on a first-come, first-served basis.

The *available-to-promise* (ATP) capability is especially useful in make-to-order environments. ATP displays the status of the four manufacturing lines in England and France and responds to inquiries about capacity that is available to promise to customers. With this information, Courtaulds can make better decisions on whether to accept new orders and can quote more realistic delivery dates for orders that are accepted.

SOURCE: Based on Walter Goddard, "Getting a Grip on Customer Service," *Modern Materials Handling* (September 1992): 41.

The MRP Process

The MRP system is responsible for scheduling the production of all items beneath the end item level. It recommends the release of work orders and purchase orders, and issues rescheduling notices when necessary.

The MRP process includes explosion, netting, and lead time offsetting.

The MRP process is best explained through an example. We will use a worksheet called the MRP matrix to record the calculations that are made. Table 13.4 shows the matrix and provides a brief description of the entries that are required. Example 13.1 follows.

TABLE 13.4   The MRP Matrix

Item: Lot Size:	LLC: LT:						PERIOD					
		PD	1	2	3	4	5	6	7	8	9	10
Gross requirements													
Scheduled receipts													
Projected on hand													
Net requirements													
Planned order receipts													
Planned order releases													

Item: the name or number that identifies the item being scheduled.
LLC: low-level code; the lowest level at which the item appears in a product structure.
Lot size: normally, an order will be placed in *multiples* of this quantity, but it can also represent a *minimum* or *maximum* order quantity or the type of lot-sizing technique.
LT: lead time; the time from when an order is placed until it is received.

PD: past-due time bucket. If an order appears in the PD time bucket, the schedule is infeasible and an error message will be generated. Projected on-hand entries in the PD column represent beginning inventory.

Gross requirements: the demand for an item by time period. For an end item, this quantity is obtained from the master production schedule. For a lower-level item, it is derived from the *planned order releases* of its parents.

Scheduled receipts: the quantity of material that is already ordered (from work orders or purchase orders) and when it is expected to arrive. Once a planned order is released, it becomes a scheduled receipt.

Projected on hand: the expected quantity in inventory at the end of a period that will be available for demand in subsequent periods. It is calculated by subtracting the *gross requirements* in the period from the sum of *scheduled receipts* for the same period, *projected on hand* from the previous period, and *planned order releases* from the $t - l$ period (where t represents the current period and l is the lead time).

Net requirements: the net number of items that must be provided and when they are needed. It is calculated by subtracting the *scheduled receipts* in the period plus the *projected on hand* in the previous period from *gross requirements*. It appears in the same time period as gross requirements.

Planned order receipts: the same as net requirements adjusted for lot sizing. If lot sizing is seldom used or lead time is negligible, this row can be deleted from the matrix.

Planned order releases: planned order receipts offset for lead times. It shows when an order should be placed (i.e., released) so that items are available when needed. *Planned order releases* at one level generate *gross requirements* at the next lower level.

EXAMPLE
13.1

*The Alpha Beta
Company*

The Alpha Beta Company produces two products, A and B, that are made from components C and D. Given the following product structures, master scheduling requirements, and inventory information, determine when orders should be released for A, B, C, and D and the size of those orders.

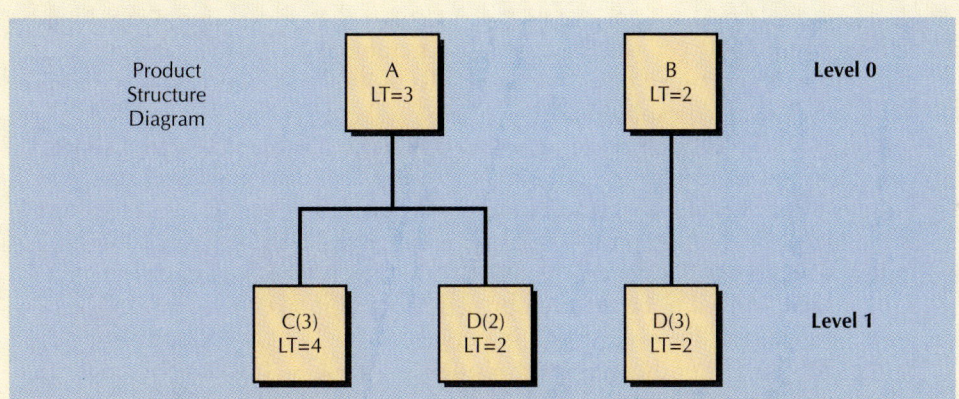

	On Hand	Scheduled Receipts	Lot Size (multiples)	MPS
A	10	0	1	100, period 8
B	5	0	1	200, period 6
C	140	0	150	—
D	200	250, period 2	250	—

SOLUTION:

Table 13.5, on page 644 shows a completed MRP matrix for each of the four items in the product structure diagram. The matrices were completed first for the level 0 items, A and B, then for the level 1 items, C and D.

■ *Item A:* First, we fill in the *gross requirements* for A, 100 units in period 8. Since A is an end item, we read this information from the master production schedule. In

(Continued)

Netting is the process of subtracting on-hand quantities from gross requirements to produce net requirements.

Lead time offsetting is the process of subtracting an item's lead time from its due date.

Explosion is the process of determining requirements for lower-level items.

the *projected on-hand row*, we begin with 10 units of A in inventory and continue with 10 units on hand until we need to use them. At the end of period 7, we have 10 units of A in inventory. We need 100 A's in period 8. We can use the 10 A's we have on hand and make 90 more. The subtraction of the on-hand quantity from the gross requirements is called **netting**. The net requirement of 90 A's is the gross requirement net of inventory. It appears in the same time period as the gross requirement. There are no lot-sizing requirements (A's are ordered in multiples of 1), so the planned order receipts are the same as the net requirements.

If we need to receive 90 A's by period 8 and it takes 3 periods to make A, we need to release an order for A in period 5. Thus, the quantity of 90 appears in period 5 of the planned order release row. This process of subtracting the lead time from the due date is called **lead time offsetting**, or *time phasing*, of requirements. The planned order release row is the result, or *output*, of the MRP calculations for item A. Only the entries in the final row of each matrix will be used in subsequent MRP calculations for component items.

■ *Item B:* Item B's matrix is completed in the same fashion as item A's. The gross requirement of 200 B's in period 6 is given in the master production schedule. Since there are 5 units of B on hand, the net requirement for B is 195 in period 5. There are no scheduled receipts for B and no lot-sizing requirements. If 195 B's are needed in period 5 and it takes 2 weeks to make B's, we need to release an order to begin production of B's in period 4.

■ *Item C:* For all level 1 items, we need to *calculate* the gross requirements by multiplying the quantity per assembly given in parentheses on the product structure diagram times the planned order release (POR) of the parent item. This multiplication process is called **explosion**.

An order for 90 A's is set to be released in period 5. Three C's are needed for every A, so we place a gross requirement for 270 C's in period 5. We have 140 C's in inventory. They remain in inventory until period 5, when we use them to satisfy partially the demand for C's. The net requirement for C is thus 130 units. But instead of ordering the net requirement of 130, we order the lot-size quantity of 150. If 130 C's need to be received by period 5 and it takes 4 weeks to make C's, we need to release the order for C in period 1. The 150 C's will arrive in period 5. We will use 130 of them to meet A's demand for C's. The remaining 20 units will be placed into inventory.

■ *Item D:* Item D has two parents, A and B. We need to gather all the gross requirements for D first before completing the rest of the matrix. Item A has a planned order release of 90 units in period 5. Two D's are required for every A, so $(90 \times 2) = 180$ D's need to be available by period 5. D's other parent, item B, has a planned order release of 195 units scheduled in period 4. Every B requires three D's, so $(195 \times 3) = 585$ D's are also needed by period 4.

We have 200 D's on hand at the end of period 1. An order of 250 D's is scheduled to be received in period 2. By the end of period 2, we project that $(200 + 250) = 450$ D's will be on hand. We plan to use those 450 D's to fill partially the first gross requirement entry, leaving a net requirement of $(585 - 450) = 135$ D's in period 4. Since D's are ordered in lots of 250, even though we need only 135 D's, we will place an order for 250. It takes 2 weeks to make D's. Since they are needed in period 4, we will plan to release the order in period 2. When the order arrives, 135 D's will go toward making B's, and the remaining $(250 - 135) = 115$ will be placed into inventory.

The 115 D's projected to be on hand by the end of period 4 can be used to satisfy partially the gross requirement for 180 D's in period 5, leaving a net requirement of $(180 - 115) = 65$ D's. Because of lot-sizing requirements, we will order 250 D's. Item D has a lead time of two periods. If we need to receive D's by period 5, we need to release an order for D in period 3. We plan the order release for 250 and project that $(250 - 65) = 185$ units will be left over and placed into inventory at the end of period 5.

■ We have now completed the MRP calculations. To summarize the results, we construct a *planned order report* from the planned order release row of each matrix, as follows:

Planned Order Report

Period	Item	Quantity
1	C	150
2	D	250
3	D	250
4	B	195
5	A	90

The MRP matrices are the worksheets that determine the planned orders for each inventory item. They are generally not printed out unless requested by the MRP planner. Looking at the MRP matrix for item D, it appears that the objective of maintaining the lowest possible level of inventory has been violated. This is due to the lot-sizing requirement that orders item D in multiples of 250 and the scheduled receipt for D that arrives before it is needed. The MRP system will issue an error message asking that the scheduled receipt be postponed until period 4, but it will not comment on the excess inventory due to lot sizing because the user has input those requirements. Unless there is some problem in obtaining the two orders for item D, the planner will probably never notice the excess inventory of item D either. This illustrates one of the problems with MRP systems. Users tend to input policies that undermine the basic objectives of the system, and the logic of the system is often hidden from the user.

If the MRP calculations seem tedious, remember that the system is computerized and no manual calculations are required. POM for Windows can be used to solve simple MRP problems.

MRP Outputs

The outputs of the MRP process are planned orders from the planned order release row of the MRP matrix. As shown in Figure 13.2, these can represent *work orders* to be released to the shop floor for in-house production or *purchase orders* to be sent to outside suppliers. MRP output can also recommend changes in previous plans or existing schedules. These *action notices*, or *rescheduling notices*, are issued for items that are no longer needed as soon as planned or for quantities that may have changed. One of the advantages of the MRP system is its ability to show the effect of a change in one part of the production process on the rest of the system. It simulates the ordering, receiving, and usage of raw materials, components, and assemblies into future time peri-

TABLE 13.5   MRP Matrices for Example 13.1

Item: A LLC: 0				*Period*					
Lot Size: 1 LT: 3	PD	1	2	3	4	5	6	7	8
Gross requirements									100
Scheduled receipts									
Projected on hand	10	10	10	10	10	10	10	10	0
Net requirements									90
Planned order receipts									90
Planned order releases						90			

ITEM: B LLC: 0				*Period*					
Lot Size: 1 LT: 2	PD	1	2	3	4	5	6	7	8
Gross requirements							200		
Scheduled receipts									
Projected on hand	5	5	5	5	5	5	0	0	0
Net requirements							195		
Planned order receipts							195		
Planned order releases					195				

$90 \times 3 = 270\}$

ITEM: C LLC: 1				*Period*					
Lot Size: 150 LT: 4	PD	1	2	3	4	5	6	7	8
Gross requirements						270			
Scheduled receipts									
Projected on hand	140	140	140	140	140	20	20	20	20
Net requirements						130			
Planned order receipts						150			
Planned order releases		150							

$195 \times 3 = 585\}$ $\{90 \times 2 = 180$

Item: D LLC:1				*Period*					
Lot Size: 250 LT: 2	PD	1	2	3	4	5	6	7	8
Gross requirements					585	180			
Scheduled receipts			250						
Projected on hand	200	200	450	450	115	185	185	185	185
Net requirements					135	65			
Planned order receipts					250	250			
Planned order releases			250	250					

ods and issues warnings to the MRP planner of impending stockouts or missed due dates.

Table 13.6 shows a monthly *planned order report* for an individual item, in this case, item #2740. The report maps out the material orders planned and released orders scheduled to be completed in anticipation of demand. Notice that safety stock is treated as a quantity not to be used and that a problem exists on 10-01, when projected on hand first goes negative. To correct this, the system suggests that the scheduled receipt of 200 units due on 10-08 be moved forward to 10-01. The MRP system will not generate a new order if a deficit can be solved by expediting existing orders. It is up to the MRP

MRP outputs include purchase orders, work orders, and various reports.

TABLE 13.6 Planned Order Report

Item	#2740			Date	9-25-98
On hand	100			Lead time	2 weeks
On order	200			Lot size	200
Allocated	50			Safety stock	50

Date	Order No.	Gross Reqs.	Scheduled Receipts	Projected On Hand	Action
				50	
9–26	AL 4416	25		25	
9–30	AL 4174	25		0	
10–01	GR 6470	50		−50	
10–08	SR 7542		200	150	Expedite SR 10–01
10–10	CO 4471	75		75	
10–15	GR 6471	50		25	
10–23	GR 6471	25		0	
10–27	GR 6473	50		−50	Release PO 10–13

Key: AL = allocated   WO = work order
CO = customer order   SR = scheduled receipt
PO = purchase order   GR = gross requirements

planner to assess the feasibility of expediting the scheduled receipt and to take appropriate action.

Table 13.7 shows an *MRP action report* for a family of items for which a particular MRP planner is responsible. It summarizes the action messages that have been compiled for individual items. On 10-01, we see the action message for item #2740 that appeared on the previous report. Notice the variety of action messages listed. Some suggest that planned orders be moved forward or backward. Others suggest that scheduled receipts be expedited or de-expedited.

It is the planner's job to respond to the actions contained in the action report. If a planner decides to **expedite** an order—that is, have it completed in less than its average lead time—he or she might call up a supplier or a shop supervisor and ask for priority treatment. Giving one job higher priority may involve reducing the priority of other jobs. This is possible if the MRP action report indicates that some jobs are not needed as early as anticipated. The process of moving some jobs *forward* in the schedule (expediting) and moving other jobs *backward* (de-expediting) allows the material planner, with the aid of the MRP system, to fine-tune the material plan. Temporary lead time adjustments through overtime or outside purchases of material can also fix a timing problem in the MRP plan, but at a cost. An MRP action report that is exceedingly long

To **expedite** an order is to speed it up so it is completed in less than its lead time.

TABLE 13.7 MRP Action Report

Current date: 9–25–98						

Item	Date	Order No.	Qty.	Action		
#2740	10–08	7542	200	Expedite	SR	10–01
#3616	10–09			Move forward	PO	10–07
#2412	10–10			Move forward	PO	10–05
#3427	10–15			Move backward	PO	10–25
#2516	10–20	7648	100	De-expedite	SR	10–30
#2740	10–27		200	Release	PO	10–13
#3666	10–31		50	Release	WO	10–24

or does not strike a balance between speeding up some orders and slowing down others can signify trouble. Action messages that recommend only the expediting of orders indicate an overloaded master schedule and an ineffective MRP system.

The MRP system, as the name implies, ensures that *material* requirements are met. However, material is not the only resource necessary to produce goods—a certain amount of labor and machine hours are also required. Thus, the next step in the planning process is to verify that the MRP plan is "feasible" by checking for the availability of labor and/or machine hours. This process is called *capacity requirements planning* and is similar to MRP.

Capacity Requirements Planning

CRP creates a load profile that identifies underloads and overloads.

Capacity requirements planning (CRP) is a computerized system that projects the load from a given material plan onto the capacity of a system and identifies underloads and overloads. It is then up to the MRP planner to *level the load*—smooth out the resource requirements so that capacity constraints are not violated. This can be accomplished by shifting requirements, reducing requirements, or temporarily expanding capacity.

There are three major inputs to CRP, as shown in Figure 13.5:

- The *planned order releases* from the MRP process;
- A *routing file*, which specifies which machines are required to complete an order from the MRP plan, in what order the operations are to be conducted, and the length of time each operation should take; and

A **load profile** compares released orders and planned orders with work center capacity.

- an *open orders file*, which contains information on the status of jobs that have already been released to the shop, but have not yet been completed.

With this information, CRP can produce a **load profile** for each machine or work center in the shop. The load profile compares released orders and planned orders with work center capacity.

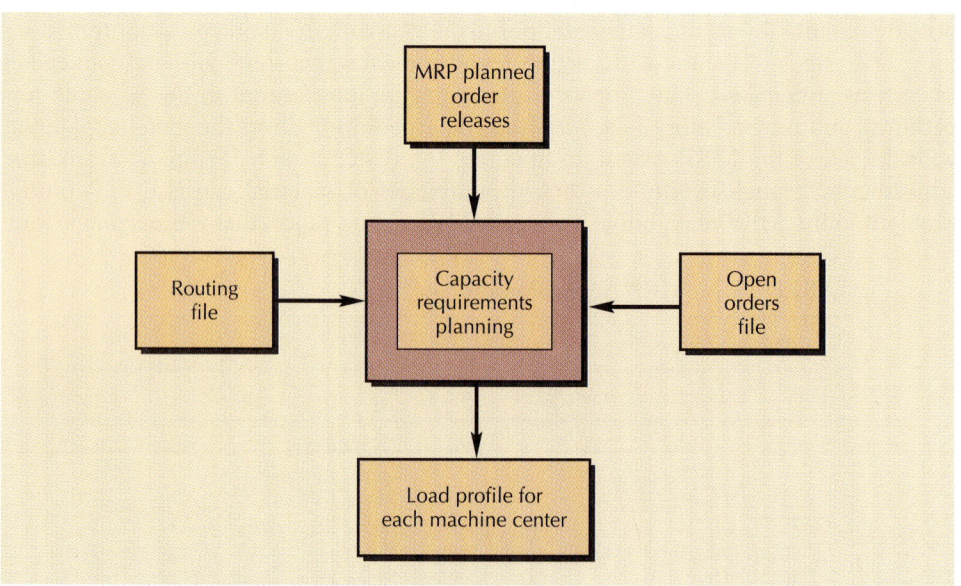

FIGURE 13.5   **Capacity Requirements Planning**

Capacity, usually expressed as standard machine hours or labor hours, is calculated as follows:

Capacity = (no. machines or workers) × (no. shifts) × (utilization) × (efficiency)

Utilization refers to the percentage of available working time that a worker actually works or a machine actually runs. Scheduled maintenance, lunch breaks, and setup time are examples of activities that reduce actual working time. **Efficiency** refers to how well a machine or worker performs compared to a standard output level. Standards can be based on past records of performance or can be developed from the work-measurement techniques discussed in Chapter 8. An efficiency of 100 percent is considered normal or standard performance, 125 percent is above normal, and 90 percent is below normal. Efficiency is also dependent on product mix. Some orders obviously will take longer than others to process, and some machines or workers may be better at processing certain types of orders.

Load is the standard hours of work (or equivalent units of production) assigned to a production facility. After load and capacity have been determined, a **load percent** can be calculated as

$$\text{Load percent} = \frac{\text{load}}{\text{capacity}} \times 100\%$$

Centers loaded above 100 percent will not be able to complete the scheduled work without some adjustment in capacity or reduction in load.

> **Capacity** is productive capability. Utilization and efficiency are used to calculate capacity.
>
> **Utilization** is the percentage of available working time that a worker spends working or a machine is running; **efficiency** is how well a machine or worker performs compared to a standard output level.
>
> **Load** refers to the standard hours of work assigned to a facility.
>
> **Load percent** is the ratio of load to capacity.

EXAMPLE 13.2

Determining Loads and Capacities

Copy Courier is a fledgling copy center in downtown Richmond run by two college students. Currently, the equipment consists of two high-speed copiers that can be operated by one operator. If the students work alone, it is conceivable that two shifts per day can be staffed. The students each work 8 hours a day, 5 days a week. They do not take breaks during the day, but they do allow themselves 30 minutes for lunch or dinner. In addition, they service the machines for about 30 minutes at the beginning of each shift. The time required to set up for each order varies by the type of paper, use of color, number of copies, and so on. Estimates of setup time are kept with each order. Since the machines are new, their efficiency is estimated at 100 percent.

Due to extensive advertising and new customer incentives, orders have been pouring in. The students need help determining the capacity of their operation and the current load on their facility. Use the following information to calculate the normal daily capacity of Copy Courier and to project next Monday's load profile and load percent.

Job No.	No. of Copies	Setup Time (min)	Run Time (min/unit)
10	500	5.2	0.08
20	1,000	10.6	0.10
30	5,000	3.4	0.12
40	10,000	11.2	0.14
50	2,000	15.3	0.10

(Continued)

SOLUTION:

The machines and/or operators at Copy Courier are out of service for 1 hour each shift for maintenance and lunch. Utilization is, thus, 7/8, or 87.5 percent. Daily copy shop capacity is

2 machines × 2 shifts × 8 hours/shift × 100% efficiency × 87.5% utilization
= 28 hours or 1,680 minutes

The projected load for Monday of next week is as follows.

Job No.	*Total Time*		
10	$5.2 + (500 \times 0.08)$	=	45.2
20	$10.6 + (1,000 \times 0.10)$	=	110.6
30	$3.4 + (5,000 \times 0.12)$	=	603.4
40	$11.2 + (10,000 \times 0.14)$	=	1,411.2
50	$15.3 + (2,000 \times 0.10)$	=	215.3
			2,385.7 minutes

$$\text{Load percent} = \frac{2,385.7}{1,680} = 1.42 \times 100\% = 142\%$$

Copy Courier is loaded 42 percent over capacity next Monday.

Increasing utilization (even to 100 percent) would not be sufficient to get the work done. To complete the customer orders on time, another shift could be added (i.e., another person hired). With this adjustment, the copy shop's daily capacity would increase to

2 machines × 3 shifts × 8 hours/shift × 100% efficiency × 87.5% utilization
= 42 hours or 2,520 minutes

The revised load percent is:

$$\frac{2,385.7}{2,520} = 0.9467 \times 100\% = 94.67\%$$

In the future, Copy Courier should determine if it has enough capacity to complete a job by the customer's requested due date *before* the job is accepted.

Load profiles can be displayed graphically, as shown in Figure 13.6. The normal capacity of machine 32A is 40 hours per week. We can see that the machine is *underloaded* in periods 1, 5, and 6, and *overloaded* in periods 2, 3, and 4.

Underloaded conditions can be leveled by:

1. Acquiring more work;
2. *Pulling work ahead* that is scheduled for later periods; or
3. Reducing normal capacity.

Remedies for underloads

Additional work can be acquired by transferring similar work from other machines in the same shop that are near or over capacity, by making components in-house that are normally purchased from outside suppliers, or by seeking work from outside sources. Pulling work ahead seems like a quick and easy alternative to alleviate both underloads

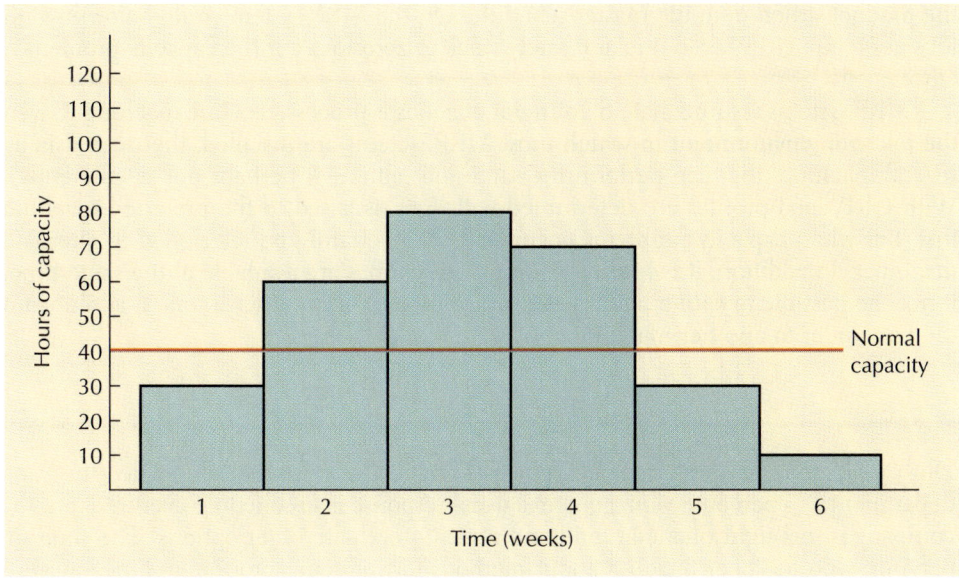

FIGURE 13.6 Initial Load Profile for Machine 32A

and overloads. However, we must remember that the MRP plan was devised based on an interrelated product structure, so the feasibility of scheduling work in an earlier time period is contingent on the availability of required materials or components. In addition, work completed prior to its due date must be stored in inventory and thus incurs a holding cost. When work is shifted to other time periods, the MRP plan should be rerun to check the feasibility of the proposed schedule.

If an underloaded condition continues for some time, reducing the size of the work force may be necessary. Smaller underloads can be handled by reducing the length of the working day or workweek, by scheduling idled workers for training sessions or vacations, or by transferring workers to other positions at machine centers or departments where overloads are occurring.

Overloaded conditions are the primary concern of the MRP planner because an overloaded schedule, left unchecked, cannot possibly be completed as planned. Overloads can be reduced by:

1. Eliminating unnecessary requirements;   Remedies for overloads
2. Rerouting jobs to alternative machines or work centers;
3. Splitting lots between two or more machines;
4. Increasing normal capacity;
5. Subcontracting;
6. Increasing the efficiency of the operation;
7. Pushing work back to later time periods; or
8. Revising the master schedule.

Some capacity problems are generated from an MRP plan that includes lot sizes, safety stock, or unsubstantiated requirements for service parts or forecasted demand. To verify that a capacity overload is caused by "real" need, the planner might examine the MRP matrices of the items processed through a machine center during an overloaded period as well as the matrices of the parents of those items processed, all the way up the product structure to the master schedule. Or, the MRP system could be rerun with lot sizes temporarily set to one and safety stock to zero to see if the capacity problem is eliminated.

MRP systems assume that an entire lot of goods is processed at one machine. Given the job shop environment in which most MRP systems are installed, there are usually several machines that can perform the same job (although perhaps not as efficiently). With CRP, load profiles are determined with jobs assigned to the preferred machine first, but when capacity problems occur, jobs can certainly be reassigned to alternate machines. In addition, if two or more similar machines are available at the same time, it may be possible to *split* a batch—that is, assign part of an order to one machine and the remainder to another machine.

EXAMPLE

13.3

Splitting Orders

Order splitting is the simultaneous processing of a single order in separate batches at several machines.

Duffy's Machine Shop has a shortage of lathes. Next week's schedule loaded the lathe department 125 percent. Management's usual response is to schedule overtime, but the company is in a tight financial bind and wants to evaluate other options. The shop supervisor, who has been reading about methods for reducing processing time, suggests something called **order splitting.**

It turns out that some of the lathe work can actually be performed on a milling machine, but it's rarely done that way because the process takes longer and the setup is more involved. Setup time for lathes averages 30 minutes, whereas setup for milling machines averages 45 minutes. Processing time per piece is 5 minutes on the lathe, compared to 10 minutes on the milling machine. Management is wondering what the effect would be of producing an entire order of 100 pieces on the lathe or splitting the order in half between the lathe and milling machine. Further, if the objective is to complete the order as soon as possible, is there an optimum split between the two types of machines?

SOLUTION:

If the order were processed on lathe alone, it would take

$30 + 5(100) = 530$ minutes to complete

If the order were equally split between lathe and milling machine, the processing time at each machine would be:

$30 + 5 (50) = 280$ minutes on lathe

$45 + 10 (50) = 545$ minutes on milling machine

Assuming that the lathe and milling machine are run simultaneously, the completion time for the entire order of 100 units is calculated by determining the completion time at each machine and taking the largest number, in this case, 545 minutes. Thus, if the order were equally split between the two machines, it would actually take longer to complete.

Determining the *optimal* split between machines requires algebra. We want the machines to finish processing at the same time, so we need to equate the processing-time equations for each machine and solve for the optimum number of units processed. If we let x represent the number of units processed on the lathe, then $(100 - x)$ is the number of units processed on the milling machine.

$$30 + 5x = 45 + 10(100 - x)$$
$$5x = 15 + 1,000 - 10x$$
$$15x = 1,015$$
$$x = 67.66, \text{ or } 68 \text{ units}$$
$$100 - x = 100 - 68 = 32 \text{ units}$$

Thus, the optimal split would process 68 units on the lathe and 32 units on the milling machine. Completion time for the optimal split is calculated as follows:

$$30 + 5(68) = 370 \text{ minutes}$$
$$45 + 10(32) = 365 \text{ minutes}$$

By splitting the order, it can be completed in 370 minutes, versus the 530 minutes on the lathe alone. That is a 39 percent reduction in processing time. Applied to the weekly demand, the 25 percent overload could be alleviated by splitting orders.

Normal capacity can be increased by adding extra hours to the workday, extra days to the workweek, or extra shifts. Temporary overloads are usually handled with overtime. More extensive overloads may require hiring additional workers. Work can also be subcontracted out.

Improving the efficiency of an operation increases its capacity. Assigning the most efficient workers to an overloaded machine, improving the operating procedures or tools, or decreasing the percentage of items that need to be reworked or scrapped increases efficiency and allows more items to be processed in the same amount of time. Because output increases with the same amount of input, *productivity* increases. This is especially useful for alleviating chronic overloads at bottleneck operations, but it does take time to put into effect.

If later time periods are underloaded, it may be possible to push work back to those periods, so that the work is completed but later than originally scheduled. There are two problems with this approach. First, postponing some jobs could throw the entire schedule off, meaning customers will not receive the goods when promised. This could involve a penalty for late delivery, loss of an order, or loss of a customer. Second, filling up the later time periods may preclude accepting new orders in those periods. It is normal for time periods further in the future to be underloaded. As these periods draw nearer, customer orders accelerate and begin taking up more of the system's capacity.

If all the preceding approaches to remedying overloads have been tried, but an overload still exists, the only option is to revise the master schedule. That means some customer will not receive goods as previously promised. The planner, in conjunction with someone from marketing, should determine which customer has the lowest priority and whether its order should be postponed or canceled.

There are cost consequences associated with each of these alternatives, but there is usually no attempt to derive an optimum solution. More than likely, the MRP planner will use the options that produce a feasible solution quickly. In many manufacturing environments, new customer orders arrive daily, and feasible MRP plans can become infeasible overnight.

Figure 13.7 shows one possible remedy for the overloads shown in Figure 13.6. Ten hours of work are pulled ahead from period 2 to period 1. Ten hours of overtime are

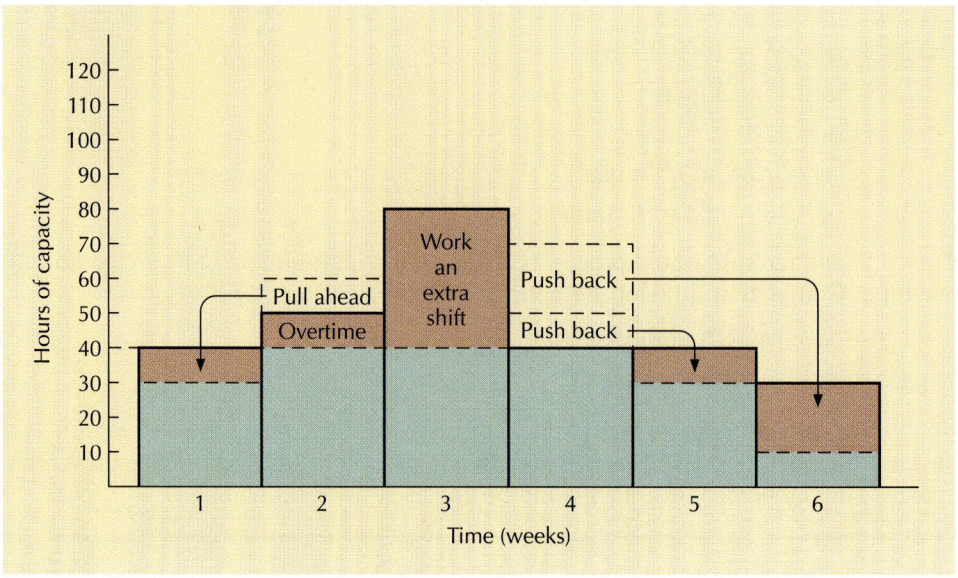

FIGURE 13.7   Adjusted Load Profile for Machine 32A

assigned in period 2. An entire 40-hour shift is added in period 3. Ten hours of work from period 4 are pushed back to period 5, and 20 hours are pushed back to period 6.

CRP *identifies* capacity problems, but the planner *solves* the problems. With experience, the task of shifting work and leveling loads is not as formidable as it appears. However, it is helpful if the initial load profile is as accurate as possible and if previous planning stages (i.e., aggregate production planning and master production scheduling) have considered capacity constraints. Some companies formalize capacity planning at each stage of production planning. *Resource requirements planning* is associated with an aggregate production plan, and *rough-cut capacity planning* is performed prior to the approval of a master schedule. Capacity requirements planning may still be performed on the material requirements plan, but its role is to fine-tune existing resources, rather than to find or develop new resources.

Once the feasibility of an MRP plan has been verified by CRP, the plan can be executed by releasing orders in the time periods indicated. Early MRP systems had no mechanism for monitoring the success of their plans. Today's MRP systems include elaborate capacity and reporting modules for scheduling and monitoring daily work requirements.

Manufacturing Resource Planning (MRP II)

The MRP systems on the market today are composed of many different modules that can be purchased separately. Typically, the modules include the following:

- Forecasting
- Customer order entry
- Production planning/master production scheduling
- Product structure/bill-of-material processor
- Inventory control
- Material requirements planning

MRP systems are usually implemented in modules.

- Capacity planning
- Shop floor control
- Purchasing
- Accounting
- Financial analysis

We can recognize some of these modules as inputs to or outputs from the basic <u>MRP</u> process. Others represent a broadened scope of MRP-related activities, beginning with forecasting demand and ending with a financial analysis of the firm.

Companies differ in their approach to implementing MRP, but seldom will a company purchase an entire MRP system at one time. Most firms opt for installing the product structure/bill-of-material processor first and then add the inventory module, followed by the MRP module. The BOM and inventory modules have large databases and serve as major inputs to the rest of the process.

Purchasing is also brought online early, usually shortly after the BOM module is installed. Assemble-to-order companies that tend to thrive on the *customer order entry* module will implement it as soon as possible.

It may be some time before the *master schedule* module or higher-level planning modules are added. How, you may wonder, does the MRP system run without a master schedule? Actually, a master production schedule is used, but it is not generated or maintained by the MRP system; it is input by hand.

The *capacity planning* module is important for a well-run MRP system, and its absence often separates the successful MRP user from the unsuccessful user.

Shop floor control is a difficult module to implement and is probably the most disappointing one in practice. Chapter 14 discusses shop floor control in more detail.

As MRP evolved and more modules and features were added in the areas of capacity planning, marketing, and finance, it became clear that the name *material requirements planning* was no longer adequate to describe the full range of activities this system could coordinate. In keeping with the MRP acronym, the new and improved MRP became known as **MRP II,** for **manufacturing resource planning.** Figure 13.8 shows how the various MRP II functions interact. The term *closed loop* has been used to describe the numerous feedback loops between plans for production and available capacity and between planned and actual occurrences.

MRP II, an extension of MRP, plans all the resources needed for running a business.

Manufacturing resource planning is a misnomer because MRP II software is also used in services, such as education, architecture, health care, distribution, and the like. Thus, systems such as SRP (service requirements planning), DRP (distribution requirements planning), and BRP (business requirements planning), are also available.

Advanced Planning and Control Systems

Advances in information technology have brought several new types of manufacturing control systems to market, each based on the MRP concept. **Enterprise resource planning** <u>(ERP)</u> updates MRP II with relational database management, graphical user interface (GUI), and client/server architecture. Except for very large implementations, most companies are migrating to PC-based information systems. Patchwork systems of PCs have evolved that need to be integrated into an overall network. *Client/server systems* use high-performance desktop computers and servers to move data, distribute processing, and transport information across the network to where it is most needed.

Advanced manufacturing control systems include enterprise resource planning, manufacturing execution systems, and customer-oriented manufacturing management systems.

Manufacturing execution systems <u>(MES)</u> forge a link between business planning and management control systems. The MES core is a relational database system ac-

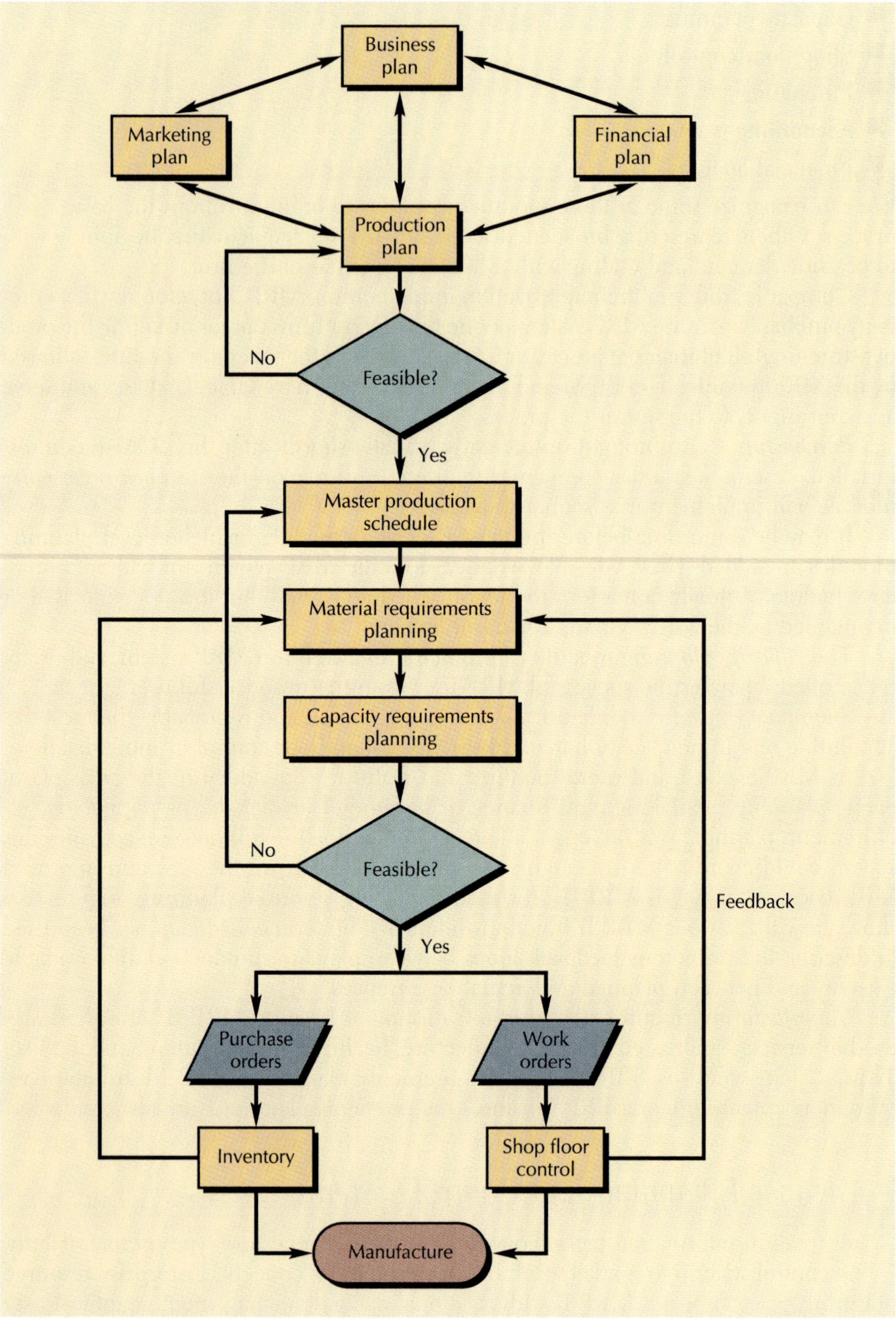

FIGURE 13.8 **Manufacturing Resource Planning (MRP II)**

cessible by any user from any station on a network without having to specify the node where the information resides. Most MES rely on MRP II for planning information.

Traditional MRP organizes information flow around finance and material requirements. **Customer-oriented manufacturing management systems (COMMS)** unite de-

MRP systems can be used for services, too. In renovating hotel rooms, Marriott develops a bill of material and a bill of labor for each room type, then "explodes" the bill throughout the facility to summarize its furniture and decorating needs. Menus in restaurants can be thought of as master schedules. Demand for menu items is forecasted, then multiplied by a bill of ingredients to ensure sufficient "material" is on hand for the chef to prepare what the customer orders. The bill of ingredients can also be used to accurately price menu items.

THE COMPETITIVE EDGE

Integration with ERP Drives Performance and Supports Corporate Strategy

Control Instruments manufactures a wide variety of industrial sensors, controllers, and monitors for the detection of hazardous gases and vapors. After a customer order is received, components are assembled to meet that customer's requirements, then inspected, calibrated, and tested before shipment. In recent years, a corporate growth strategy has taxed manufacturing operations to the limit, especially since the demand for control systems is so erratic. A customer order may consist of a single unit with a unique combination of components, or several thousand units representing several months' worth of production. The company decided to try an enterprise resource planning (ERP) system to improve operations.

www.prenhall.com/russell

End-of-the-month reports that previously took two weeks to prepare (and were thus outdated) were replaced by daily reports and weekly planning meetings between sales and operations. In the one- to two-hour meetings, managers examined ERP reports on sales forecasts and shipments against production plans; capacity by work center, work center performance; released capacity; performance to master schedule; purchased price and work order variances; and purchases, receipts, bookings, and shipments by product family. Sales and production staffs used this information to develop and maintain a master schedule that balanced production with forecasted and actual demand.

Production workers entered transactions into the ERP system, monitored the progress of jobs and customer orders, and received real-time measures of performance and quality. This knowledge gave them a better understanding of what was going on and how they contributed to the business. With the same data available to everyone, people began trusting one another across functions and levels. Sales began to trust manufacturing, and workers to trust management.

Within one year, productivity and inventory turns doubled while WIP and reject rates were cut in half. Engineering change orders dropped from 2500 a year to under 200. On-time deliveries improved from 70% to 90%, and completion time for "spike" orders fell from 6 months to 3 months. Control's adoption of ERP significantly improved both its customer service and business performance, enabling its strategy of increasing sales and expanding markets to become feasible once again.

SOURCE: Chris Schaeffer, "Performance Measurement Drives Enterprise Integration," *IIE Solutions* (March 1996): 20–27.

partments and suppliers around the customer. COMMS include multi-plant planning capabilities, support for multiple languages and currencies, and integrated logistics capabilities.

Problems and Prospects of MRP/MRP II

Companies that have carefully implemented MRP have seen dramatic improvements in performance and reductions in cost. Reports of 40 percent reductions in inventory levels, 33 percent improvements in customer service levels, and 20 percent reductions in production costs are common. Still, MRP has never fully achieved the successes that were promised in the early 1970s, when the concept was first introduced. Many of its problems have been associated with poor implementation strategies, lack of support by top management, and lack of commitment by other company personnel. Expectations for what MRP could accomplish were inflated by software vendors and consultants, who seemed to assure managers that the "problem" of manufacturing could be solved if they purchased certain hardware and software products. Money was thrown at the problem, in the form of MRP-related purchases, without an understanding of actual manufacturing needs. Automated systems, especially those dealing with large amounts of information, are only as good as the input provided to them. Inaccurate data can ruin an MRP system. Adding fancy options, such as lot sizing and safety stock, and unrealistic assessments of capacity are other common sources of problems.

Implementation problems have plagued MRP systems.

As a common database for the entire firm, MRP tends to be perceived initially by those in different functional areas as an intrusion into their turf. For example, with MRP, marketing can look at the production figures and determine whether manufacturing has scheduled enough production to meet demand, production can monitor the accuracy of marketing's demand forecasts by comparing planned against actual figures, and salespersons can access the status of customer orders themselves without relying on promises of service from production. Eventually, the common access to information improves managerial decision making, but there is an adjustment period while managers learn to work together.

MRP was the first computerized system used on the factory floor. And it was quite disruptive. Shop supervisors, whose jobs for the last twenty years had consisted of making daily schedules for their workers, were handed a computer printout on Monday mornings that laid out worker assignments for a week in advance. Workers accustomed to long queues of work waiting to be processed, instinctively slowed down their production rate as the results of tight MRP scheduling began to take effect and queues dwindled. These examples are representative of the behavioral problems that faced MRP in its early stages of development. As with many new technologies or concepts, the technical issues of MRP were solved far in advance of the behavioral issues. Fortunately, the passage of time and the educational efforts associated with a broadened MRP concept have helped to smooth the way for effective implementation of MRP II.

With implementation problems no longer at the forefront, practitioners and academicians alike began to search for the "real" problems inherent with MRP. They found that some aspects of the MRP concept do not match the realities of manufacturing. These mismatches include the following:

MRP causes problems by considering capacity last, using fixed lead times, and requiring excessive reporting.

■ *MRP plans for material requirements first; capacity is an afterthought.* The iterative procedure described in this chapter for leveling the load on a machine center and making an MRP schedule workable is not very efficient. Too many manual adjustments are required. Furthermore, in some industries, the approach is wrong. If there is a particular process that constrains the system or other capacity constraints that are difficult to relax, then they should drive the schedule rather than the availability of materials.

■ *Lead time in an MRP system is fixed.* This assumes that either lot sizes will continue unchanged or that they have no bearing on lead time. Under this assumption, the lead time necessary to process an order would remain the same whether that order consisted of one unit or one hundred units. In addition, the lead time figures used in MRP are typically averages of past practice, whether that practice produced good or bad manufacturing performance.

Fixed lead times ignore current shop loads. Lead times are as much a result of the scheduling system as an input to it. Consider two jobs whose processing time is five hours each. If these jobs require different resources and the resources are available, then the lead time will be five hours for each job. If, however, both jobs require the same resource (which is currently available), then one job will have a lead time of five hours, and the other will have a lead time of ten hours. Thus, lead time is a function of both capacity and priority. Most experts agree that the shop floor control problems experienced by MRP users are directly related to inaccurate lead times.

■ *The reporting requirements of MRP are excessive.* MRP tries to keep track of the status of all jobs in the system and reschedules jobs as problems occur. In a manufacturing environment of speed and small lot sizes, this is cumbersome. It might take as long to *record* the processing of an item at a workstation as it does to process the item. Bar code technology has helped alleviate this problem somewhat, but the issues still remain: How much processing detail is really needed in the common database? How much control is enough?

With these basic problems, what then, are the prospects for MRP/MRP II in the future? Actually, they are quite good, but in a modified form. Some industries, primarily companies that produce goods in standard batches, can successfully use MRP/MRP II as is. However, for most companies, the real benefits of MRP II are obtained from its

MRP II is an effective planning tool.

<u>John Deere</u> *runs a Class A MRP II system. Shown here are two workers putting the finishing touches on a combine attachment. A completed combine contains thousands of different parts, most of them made in-house. MRP II can coordinate the production and assembly of these components, and adjust schedules quickly to deal with unexpected occurrences. Customer-specific options can also be readily accommodated.*

www.prenhall.com/russell

ability to coordinate a company's strategy among different functional areas—that is, to "plan." The common database and simulation capabilities are very useful in responding quickly to what-if? questions at various levels of detail. BOM processors, purchasing modules, and customer order entry are standard requirements for manufacturing information systems. They are especially helpful in monitoring design quality, vendor quality, and customer service. The transparency of MRP-related decisions to different areas of the firm is invaluable in building trust, teamwork, and better decisions. The financial tie-ins can produce superior fine-tuning of cash flow planning and profit/cost projections.

MRP does a great job of planning and coordinating until it hits the shop floor. For execution, finite scheduling (discussed in Chapter 14) or JIT (discussed in Chapter 15) usually produce better results.

Summary

Material requirements planning (MRP) is a computerized inventory control and production planning system. It has enjoyed widespread use in U.S. industry, primarily for batch manufacturing, as an information system that improves manufacturing decision making. MRP began as a system for ensuring that sufficient *material* was available when needed. However, in application, it became clear that material was not the only resource in short supply. Planning capabilities for machine and labor resources were added to the system in the form of *capacity requirements planning* (CRP).

MRP requires input from other functional areas of a firm, such as marketing and finance. As these areas began to see the power of a common database system, they encouraged the expansion of MRP into areas such as demand forecasting, demand management, customer order entry, accounts payable, accounts receivable, budgets, and cash-flow analysis. Clearly, this enhanced version was more powerful than the original MRP systems that ordered material and scheduled production. It provided a common database that the entire company could use. Its what-if? capability proved invaluable in evaluating trade-offs, and the easy access to information encouraged more sophisticated planning. The "new" MRP, called MRP II, for manufacturing resource planning, has become a standard component for companies entering the age of computer-integrated manufacturing (CIM).

However, there are some drawbacks to MRP II. The system requires a lot of information, and the information must be accurate and timely. The reporting requirements are sometimes overwhelming, especially as manufacturers move toward more rapid production and shorter cycle times. Perhaps the biggest problem with MRP/MRP II has been its limited success in the execution of shop floor schedules at a time when just-in-time (JIT) has excelled in this endeavor. Manufacturing experts are now encouraging managers to take advantage of the planning capabilities of MRP II and the execution capabilities of finite scheduling or JIT. We explore those topics in the next two chapters.

Summary of Key Formulas

Capacity

$$\text{Capacity} = (\text{no. machines}) \times (\text{no. shifts}) \times (\text{utilization}) \times (\text{efficiency})$$

Utilization

$$\text{Utilization} = \frac{\text{time working}}{\text{total time available}}$$

Load percent

$$\text{Load percent} = \frac{\text{load}}{\text{capacity}} \times 100\%$$

Summary of Key Terms

assemble-to-order: a manufacturing environment in which major subassemblies are produced in advance of a customer's order and are then configured to order.

bill of material (BOM): a list of all the materials, parts, and assemblies that make up a product, including quantities, parent-component relationships, and order of assembly.

capacity: the productive capability of a worker, machine, work center, or system.

capacity requirements planning (CRP): a computerized system that projects the load from a given material plan onto the capacity of a system and identifies underloads and overloads.

cumulative lead time: the total length of time required to manufacture a product; also, the longest path through a product structure.

customer-oriented manufacturing management system (COMMS): a manufacturing control system that includes multi-plant planning capabilities, support for multiple languages and currencies, and integrated logistics capabilities.

cycle counting: a method for auditing inventory accuracy that counts inventory and reconciles errors on a cyclical schedule rather than once a year.

efficiency: how well a machine or worker performs compared to a standard output level.

enterprise resource planning (ERP): an updated MRP II system with relational database management, graphical user interface, and client/server architecture.

expediting: the process of speeding up orders so that they are completed in less than their average lead time.

explosion: the process of determining requirements for lower-level items by multiplying the planned orders for parent items by the quantity per assembly of component items.

inventory master file: a file that contains inventory status and descriptive information on every item in inventory.

lead time offsetting: the process of subtracting an item's lead time from its due date to determine when an order should be released; also called time phasing.

load: refers to the standard hours of work assigned to the facility.

load percent: the ratio of load to capacity.

load profile: a chart that compares released orders and planned orders with work center capacity.

manufacturing execution system (MES): a business planning and management control system that relies on MRP II for planning information.

manufacturing resource planning (MRP II): an extension of MRP that plans all the resources necessary for manufacturing; includes financial and marketing analysis, feedback loops, and an overall business plan.

master production schedule (MPS): a schedule for the production of end items (usually final products). It drives the MRP process that schedules the production of component parts.

material requirements planning (MRP): a computerized inventory control and production planning system for generating purchase orders and work orders of materials, components, and assemblies.

modular bill of material: a special bill of material used to plan the production of products with many optional features.

netting: the process of subtracting on-hand quantities from gross requirements to produce net requirements.

order splitting: the processing of a single order in separate batches at multiple machines simultaneously.

product structure file: a file that contains computerized bills of material for all products.

time fence: a date specified by management beyond which no changes in the master schedule are allowed.

utilization: the percentage of available working time that a worker spends working or a machine is running.

Solved Problem

Complete the following MRP matrix for item X.

Item: X LLC: 1 LT: 2 Lot Size: Min 50	PD	Period							
		1	2	3	4	5	6	7	8
Gross requirements		20	30	50	50	60	90	40	60
Scheduled receipts			50						
Projected on hand	40								
Net requirements									
Planned order receipts									
Planned order releases									

    a. In what periods should orders be released and what should be the size of those orders?

    b. How would the planned order releases change with no lot sizing?

    c. How would the planned order releases change with no lot sizing and a safety stock of 20?

Solution:

    a.

Item: X LLC: 1 Lot Size: Min 50 LT: 2	PD	Period							
		1	2	3	4	5	6	7	8
Gross requirements		20	30	50	50	60	90	40	60
Scheduled receipts			50						
Projected on hand	40	20	40	40	40	30	0	10	0
Net requirements				10	10	20	60	40	50
Planned order receipts				50	50	50	60	50	50
Planned order releases		50	50	50	60	50	50		

Orders should be released in periods 1, 2, 3, 4, 5, and 6 for quantities of 50, 50, 50, 60, 50, and 50, respectively.

b.

Item: X LLC: 1 Lot Size: 1 LT: 2	PD	Period							
		1	2	3	4	5	6	7	8
Gross requirements		20	30	50	50	60	90	40	60
Scheduled receipts			50						
Projected on hand	40	20	40	0	0	0	0	0	0
Net requirements				10	50	60	90	40	60
Planned order receipts				10	50	60	90	40	60
Planned order releases		10	50	60	90	40	60		

Orders would be released in periods 1 through 6 and for the quantities of 10, 50, 60, 90, 40, and 60 units, respectively.

c.

Item: X LLC: 1 Lot Size: 1 LT: 2	PD	Period							
		1	2	3	4	5	6	7	8
Gross requirements		20	30	50	50	60	90	40	60
Scheduled receipts			50						
Projected on hand	40	20	40	20	20	20	20	20	20
Net requirements				30	50	60	90	40	60
Planned order receipts				30	50	60	90	40	60
Planned order releases		30	50	60	90	40	60		

Orders would be placed in periods 1 through 6 in quantities of 30, 50, 60, 90, 40, and 60, respectively. The initial order quantity would be increased by 20 units to serve as safety stock, and that amount would remain in inventory throughout the planning horizon.

Questions

13-1. Describe a production environment in which MRP would be useful.

13-2. Explain with an example the difference between dependent and independent demand.

13-3. What are the objectives of an MRP system?

13-4. What are the three major inputs to MRP? What are the three forms of output?

13-5. How is a master production schedule created and how is it used?

13-6. What is the purpose of phantom bills, K-bills, and modular bills of material?

13-7. What type of information is included in the inventory master file?

13-8. Describe cycle counting. How does it improve inventory performance?

13-9. Describe the MRP process, including netting, explosion, and lead time offsetting.

13-10. How does a planned order report differ from an MRP action report?

13-11. What are the inputs to capacity requirements planning?

13-12. Discuss several alternatives for leveling the load on a facility.

13-13. How can capacity planning be incorporated at each stage of production planning?

13-14. What kinds of decisions does an MRP planner make?

13-15. List some typical modules available from MRP software vendors. Which modules are usually applied first? Last?

13-16. How does MRP II differ from MRP?

13-17. Why has MRP been difficult to implement?

13-18. What are the major benefits from MRP/MRP II?

13-19. What are the major drawbacks of MRP/MRP II?

13-20. Interview production managers at three plants in your area about their use of MRP/MRP II. How have their experiences been similar? What accounts for the similarities and differences?

13-21. Find out if there is a local APICS chapter in your area. Attend a meeting and write a summary of the speaker's comments.

Problems

13-1. Referring to the following product structure diagram, determine:
   a. how many K's are needed for each A.
   b. how many E's are needed for each A.
   c. the low-level code for item E.
   d. Construct a multi-level bill of material for product A.

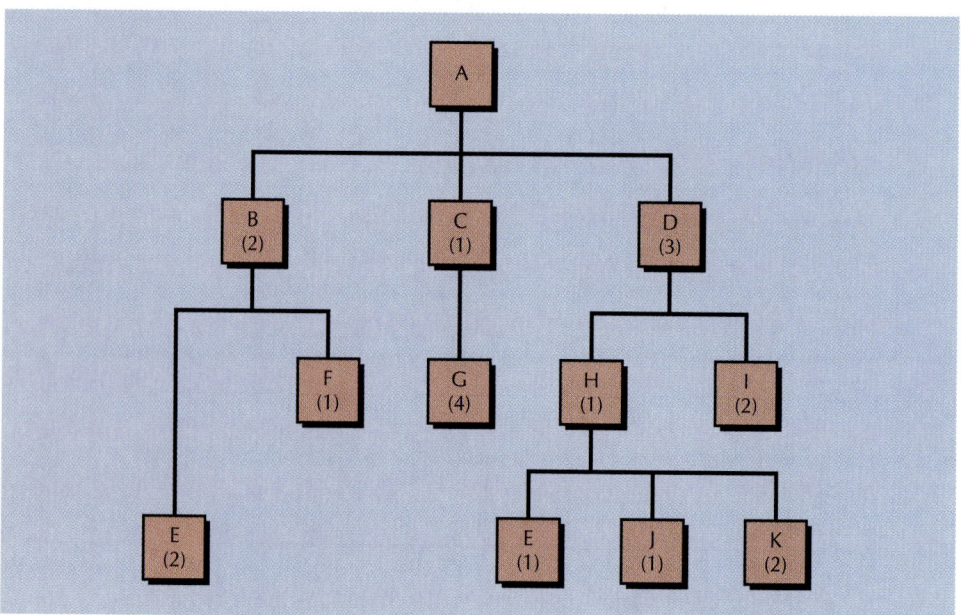

13-2. Construct a multi-level bill of material for product Z. How many U's are needed to make each Z? How many W's are needed to make each Z?

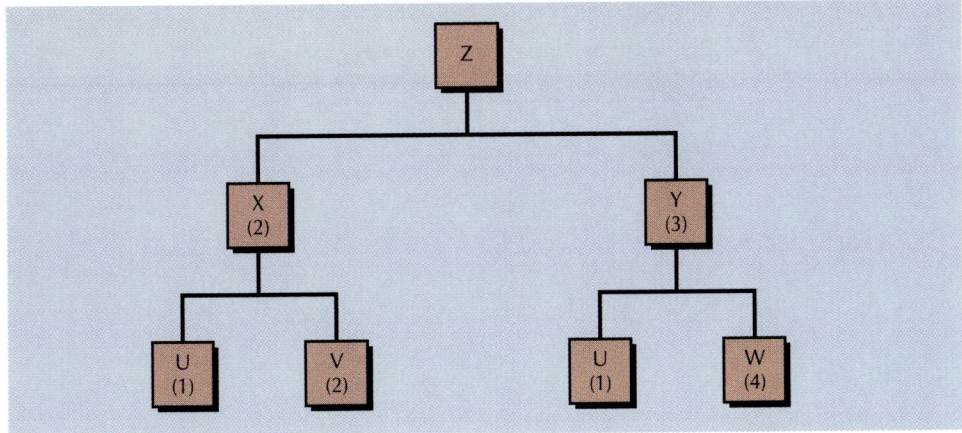

13-3. The classic One-Step step stool is assembled from a prefabricated seat, one bottom leg, one top leg, five nuts, and four leg tips. From the accompanying parts list and assembly instructions, construct a product structure diagram for the One-Step step stool.

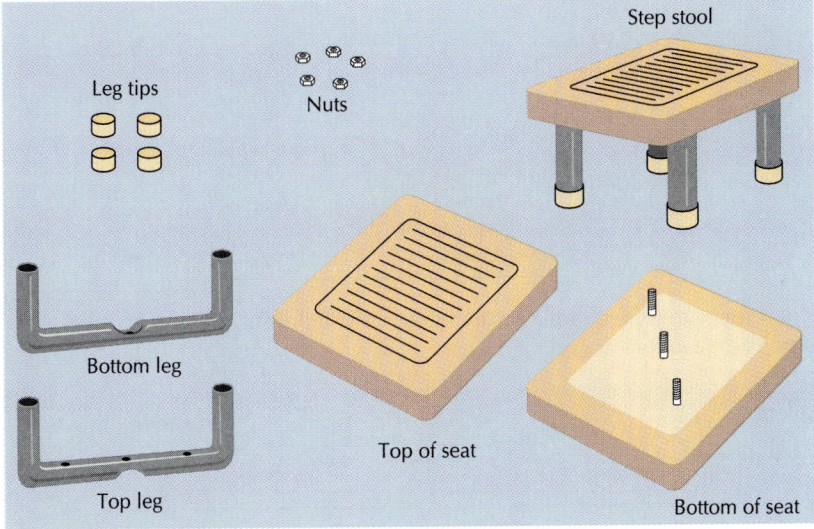

Assembly instructions:
Step 1. Push leg tips on legs.
Step 2. Position the bottom leg in the seat, as illustrated, so the bolt protrudes through hole A. Attach nuts to bolts indicated by A.
Step 3. Position the top leg in the seat, as illustrated, so bolts protrude through holes in leg. Attach nuts to bolts indicated by A, B and C.

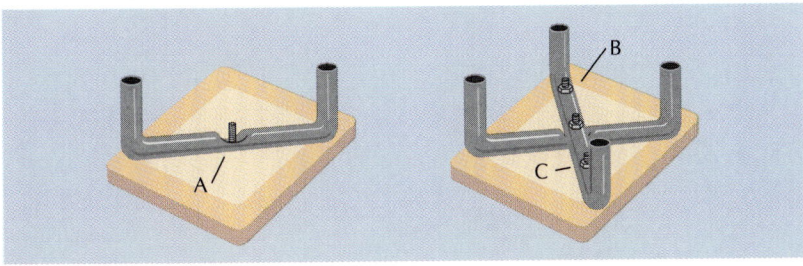

13-4. Draw a product structure diagram from this bill of material.

LEVEL	ITEM	QUANTITY
0	XYZ Assembly	1
− 1	X101	1
− − 2	Y110	1
− − 2	Y220	2
− 1	X201	3
− − 2	Y330	2
− 1	X301	4
− − 2	Y440	3
− − 2	Y550	1
− − − 3	Z111	2

13-5. Draw a product structure diagram from the following bill of material for a widget.

LEVEL	ITEM	QUANTITY
0	Widget	1
− 1	Widget casing	1
− − 2	Circuit card	1
− − 2	Control panel	1
− − − 3	Switches	2
− 1	Battery pack	1
− − 2	Housing	1
− − − 3	Batteries	4
− − 2	Clip	1
− 1	Antenna	1
− 1	Decals	2

13-6. Construct a multi-level bill of material from the following product structure diagram. Assume all quantities are one.

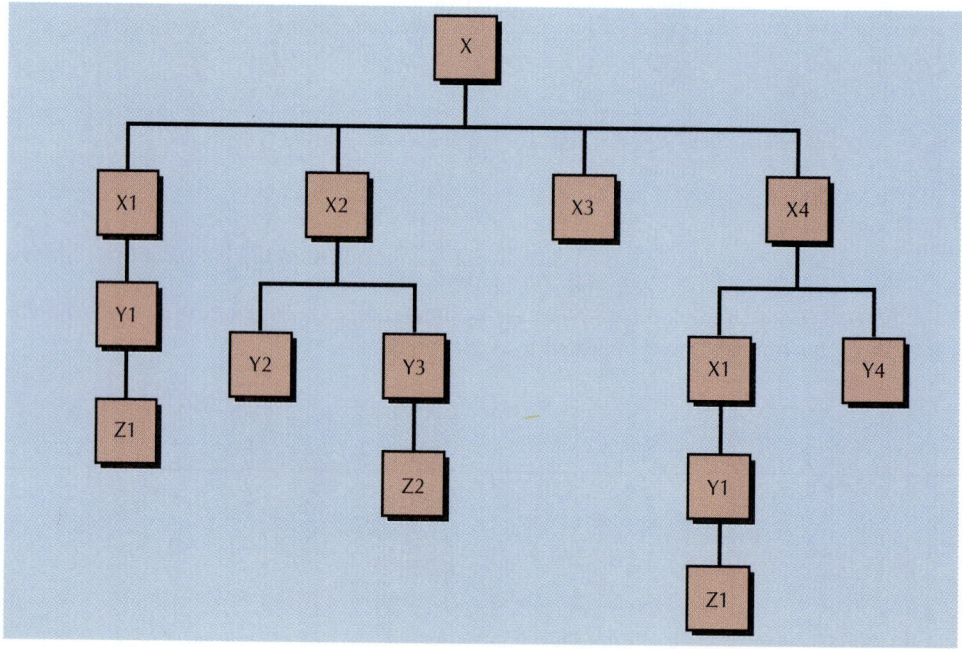

13-7. Construct a multi-level bill of materials from the following product structure diagram.

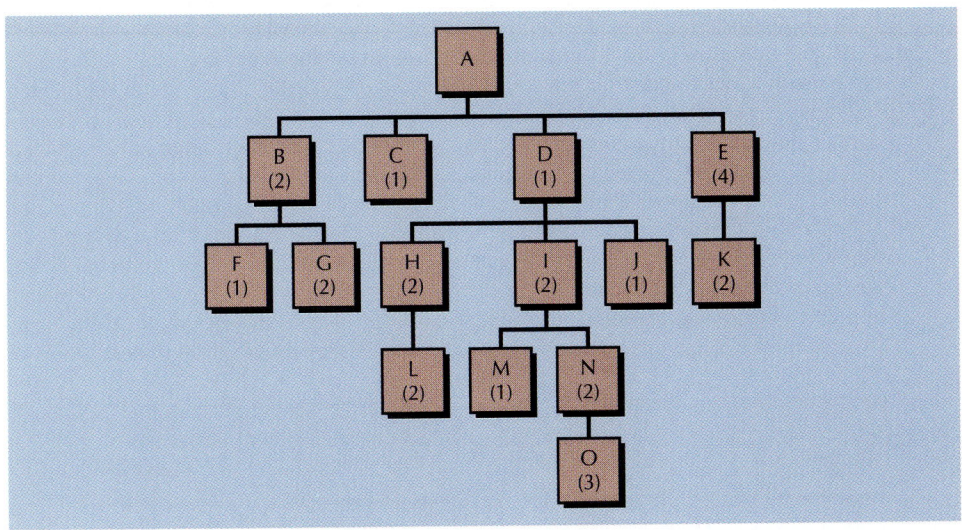

13-8. Kid's World sells outside play equipment for children. One of its most popular items is a 5-foot by 7-foot wooden sandbox. General assembly instructions, lead times, and lot-sizing information are given.

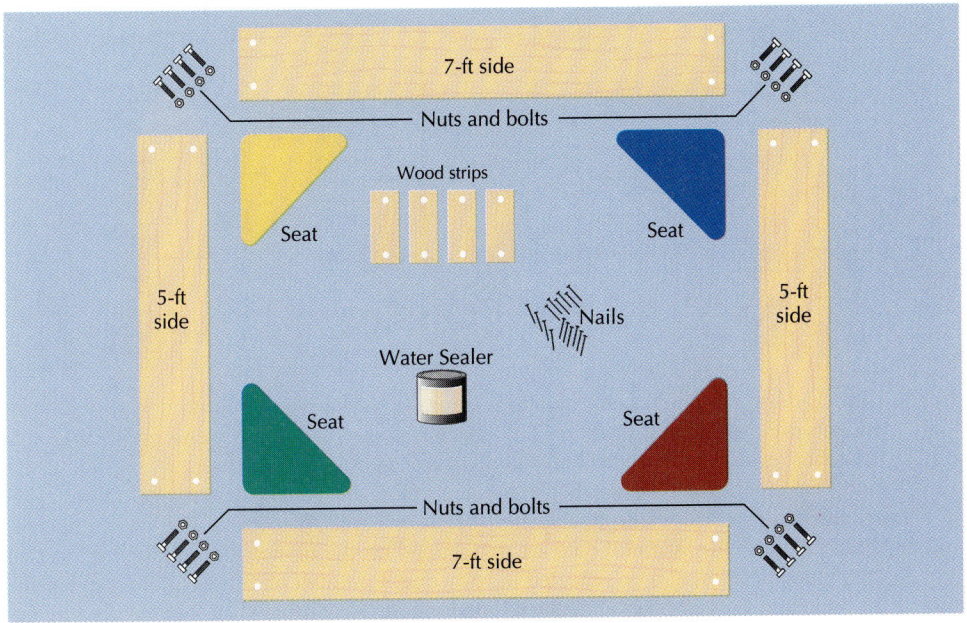

Assembly Instructions:
The wood pieces for the sandbox are ordered precut and treated. Kid's World sands the wood, drills several holes in each piece as required for assembly, and coats each piece with 2 ounces of water sealer. The sides are then assembled one corner at a time by attaching a 1-foot wood strip cater-corner between a 5-foot and 7-foot side. Four bolts are inserted through the predrilled holes and secured with nuts. After the left and right corners of the sandbox have been assembled, the two pieces are joined in a similar manner to form the box assembly. A triangular-shaped wooden seat is attached to each corner of the box assembly with four flat-headed nails for each seat. The sandbox is now complete.

The hardware and wood pieces are purchased from a local lumber yard and, in most cases, can be delivered with 3 days' notice. Nails are purchased in boxes of 200; nuts and bolts, by the dozen.

a. Prepare a multi-level bill of material for the 5-foot by 7-foot sandbox.

b. How many 1-foot wood strips are needed to make one sandbox? How many nails? How much water sealer?

13-9. Avery's Robotics manufactures small assembly robots to customer order. Avery's current policy of maintaining a separate bill of material for each possible combination of customer options has become unmanageable. Avery has heard of modular bills of material but is having difficulty understanding the concept. He has gathered some data on customer preference and knows that 60 percent of his customers choose controller A and 80 percent choose end effector 2. He is wondering whether or not to drop controller B and end effector 1 altogether. Explain the concept of modular BOMs to Avery by restructuring the following four individual bills into one modular bill of material.

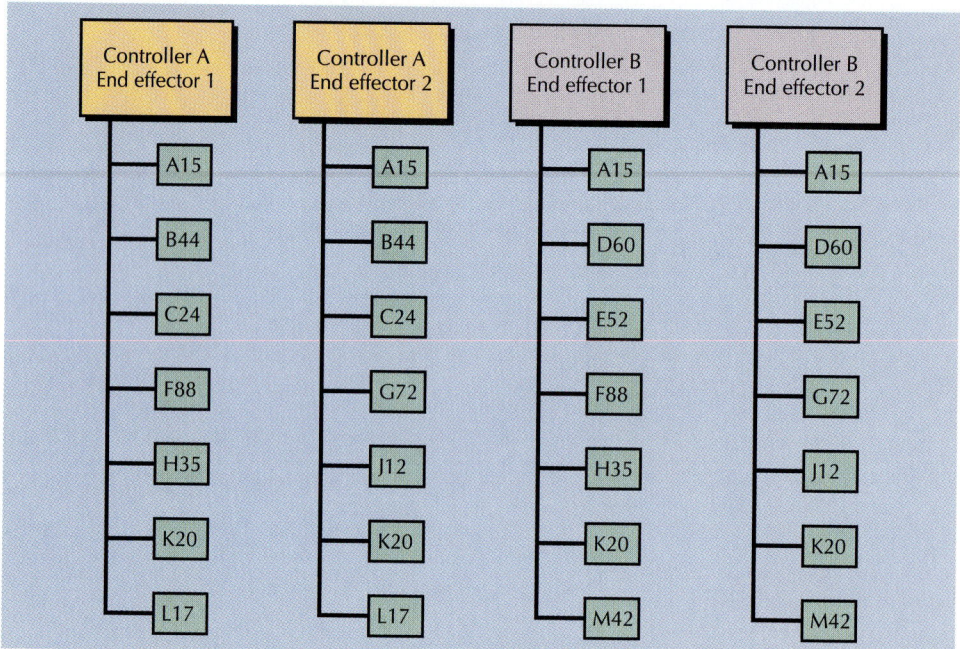

Hint: Determine which components are unique to the type of controller, which components are unique to the type of end effector, and which components are common to the robot regardless of controller or end effector option.

13-10. Tilco Toys makes the popular Battle Axe action figures. To maintain market share, Tilco has discovered it must introduce a new batch of Battle Axes (consisting of five figures) every three months. Careful data are maintained on the figures that sell the best so that their characteristics can be repeated in subsequent product offerings. In order to reduce the time and cost of development and production of each new batch of figures, the designers simply choose different combinations of options from the following list:

Group	*Force*	*Clothing*	*Weapons*	*Transportation*
Falcons (40%)	Knights (30%)	Armor (20%)	Sword (30%)	Horse (40%)
Hawks (40%)	Slayers (20%)	Cloth (40%)	Crossbow (20%)	Wagon (20%)
Woodsmen (20%)	Archers (30%)	Fur (10%)	Spear (10%)	Catapult (10%)
	Engineers (20%)	Leather (30%)	Longbow (10%)	Battering Ram (10%)
			Battle Axe (20%)	Dragon (10%)
			Throwing Star (10%)	Boat (10%)

Assuming the usage percentages shown above are an accurate reflection of the product offerings last year, and twenty new figures are introduced,

a. How many are Falcons? How many Knights? How many Dragons?

b. What is the probability that an armored Falcon engineer with a horse and sword was introduced?

c. Describe eight possible Falcon configurations.

13-11. Complete the following MRP matrix for item A:

| Item: A   LLC: 1 | | | | | *Period* | | | | |
LT: 2 Lot Size: Mult 25	PD	1	2	3	4	5	6	7	8
Gross requirements		10	15	50	75	60	85	45	60
Scheduled receipts			50						
Projected on hand	20								
Net requirements									
Planned order receipts									
Planned order releases									

13-12. Camp's Inc. produces two products, X and Z, with product structures as shown. An order for 200 units of X, and 350 units of Z has been received for period 8. An inquiry of available stock reveals 25 units of X on hand, 40 of Z, 30 of R, 100 of S, 90 of T, 120 of U, 150 of V, and 160 of W. Of the T's on order, 250 are due in by period 2; 75 S's should arrive in period 1. For economy reasons, U is never made in quantities under 500. Similarly, V and W have multiple order quantities of 900 and 1,500, respectively.

Determine when orders should be released for items V and W, and the size of those orders.

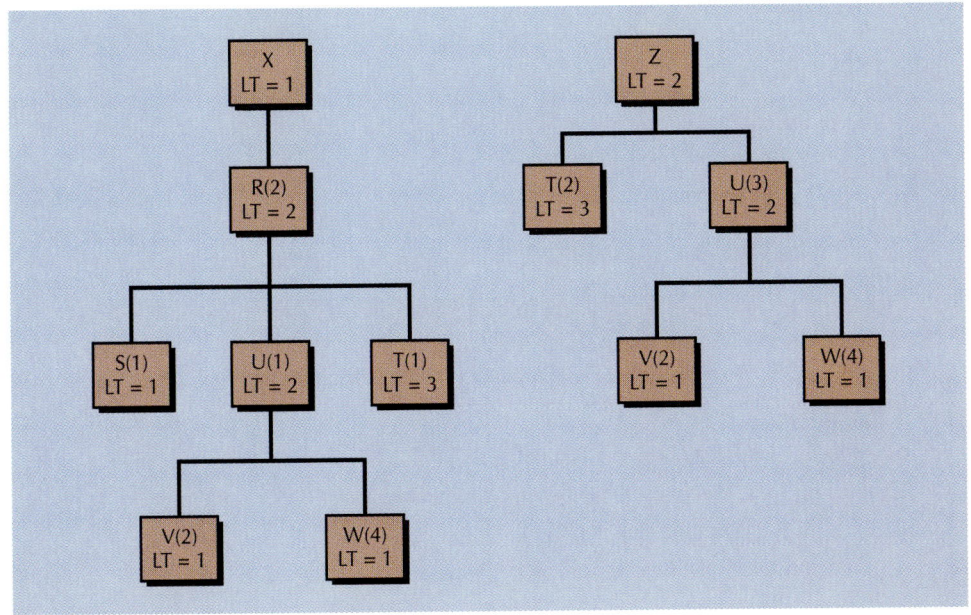

13-13. Spark, Short, & Fry, Inc. has been manufacturing electrical equipment since the early 1950s. The firm's most popular alternator, the famous "Zappo" model, has recently been restructured for assembly purposes. Because of favorable labor conditions, component parts are assembled in batch runs. At any given time each level of production has several partially assembled components. Given the following assembly and inventory information, construct a product structure diagram for the Zappo alternator, and plan the order releases necessary to assemble 400 alternators for period 10.

Description of the Production Process
Production of an alternator begins with the armature. The armature is placed and secured in a housing. Magnetic brushes are then installed on opposing sides of the armature housing. The rear armature cover is fitted on and held while the front cover is secured with longitudinal bolts. Next the pulley assembly is connected. Finally, contact wires are screwed on and the alternator is checked before shipping.

Inventory Master File

Item Description	Lead Time	On Order	Scheduled Receipt Date	On Hand	Lot Size (multiples)
Alternator	1	—	—	0	1
Contact wire	2	—	—	60	50
SA-410	1	—	—	80	1
Pulley assembly	3	100	Period 2	180	50
SA-310	1	—	—	20	1
Longitudinal bolt	3	—	—	210	100
Front cover	2	—	—	85	100
Rear cover	2	100	Period 1	0	100
SA-210	1	—	—	0	1
Magnetic brush	3	100	Period 1	180	100
SA-110	1	—	—	100	1
Armature	3	50	Period 2	75	50
Armature housing	4	50	Period 2	70	50

13-14. Files and More, Inc. (F & M), a manufacturer of office equipment, uses MRP to schedule its production. Due to the current recession and the need to cut costs, F & M has targeted inventory as a prime area of cost reduction. However, the company does not want to reduce its customer service level in the process. Demand and inventory data for a two-drawer file cabinet appear below. Complete an MRP matrix for the file cabinet using:
  a. no lot sizing,
  b. min 75, and
  c. mult 50 lot sizing.
    Which lot-sizing rule do you recommend?

Period	1	2	3	4	5
Demand	20	40	30	10	45

Ordering cost = $100 per order
Holding cost = $1 per cabinet per week
Lead time = 1 period
Beginning inventory = 25

13-15. Product A is assembled from one B and two C's. Each item requires one or more operations, as indicated by the circles in the product structure diagram. Assume lead time is negligible. From the information given:
   a. Develop a load profile chart for each of the three work centers.
   b. What would you recommend as normal capacity at each work center? How would you handle the overloads?

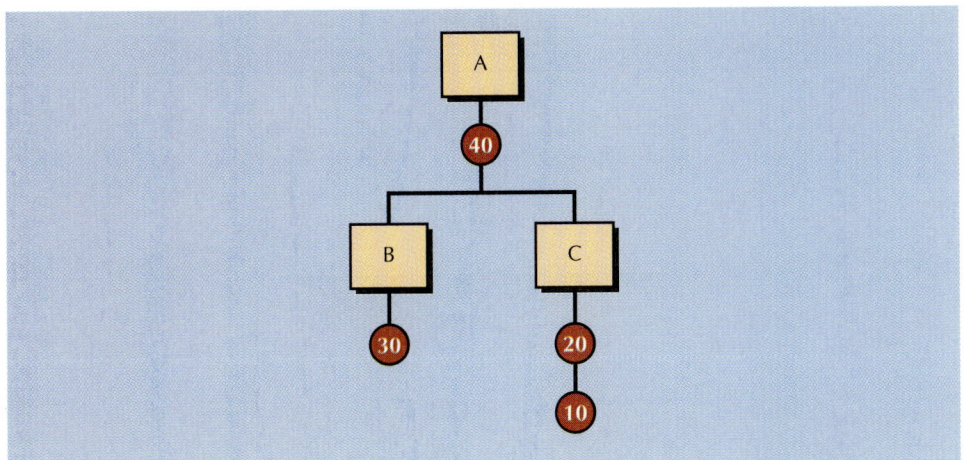

Master Production Schedule

Period	1	2	3	4	5	6
Product A	100	150	100	200	125	100

Routing and Work Standards File

Operation	Item	Work Center	Standard Time per Unit (hr)
10	C	Machining	0.50
20	C	Heat treat	2.00
30	B	Machining	1.00
40	A	Assembly	0.50

13-16. The Best Wheels Bicycle Company produces bicycles in different styles for boys and girls, in heights of 26 inches or 20 inches, and with ten speeds, three speeds, or one speed.
   a. How many different kinds of bicycles does Best Wheels make?
   b. Construct a modular bill of material for Best Wheels (one level). Assume that bike sales are equally split between boys and girls, 26-inch bikes are preferred two-to-one to 20-inch bikes, and three-speed bikes account for only 20 percent of sales. The remaining sales are divided equally between ten-speed and one-speed bikes.
   c. If bicycle sales are expected to reach 10,000 over the holiday shopping season, how many 26-inch bikes should Best Wheels plan to produce? How many ten-speed bikes?

13-17. The Best Wheels Bicycle Company has scheduled the production of the following bicycles this month.

	Model	Week			
		1	2	3	4
(B2610)	Boy's 26-inch 10-speed	50	100	200	150
(G2610)	Girl's 26-inch 10-speed	50	100	200	150
(B2003)	Boy's 20-inch 3-speed	15	30	60	45
(G2003)	Girl's 20-inch 3-speed	15	30	60	45
(B2001)	Boy's 20-inch 1-speed	20	40	80	60
(G2001)	Girl's 20-inch 1-speed	20	40	80	60

The two critical work centers for producing these bikes are welding and assembly. Welding has an efficiency of 95 percent and a utilization of 90 percent. Assembly has an efficiency of 90 percent and a utilization of 92 percent. The time required (in hours) by each bike in the two work centers is as follows:

	Welding	Assembly
B2610	0.20	0.18
G2610	0.22	0.18
B2003	0.15	0.15
G2003	0.17	0.15
B2001	0.07	0.10
G2001	0.09	0.10

    a. Assume 40 hours is available per week for each work center. Calculate the capacity and load percent per work center per week and construct a load profile chart for each work center.

    b. If any number of hours could be scheduled for each work center, how many hours should be scheduled so that the work center loads do not exceed 100 percent?

    c. If utilization and efficiency for both work centers can be increased to 99 percent, how many hours should be scheduled so that work center loads are still under 100 percent?

13-18. Jones' Dry Cleaning has just purchased a new machine that can press an entire shirt in 1 minute. The machine requires no setup beyond an initial warmup of 15 minutes at the beginning of a day. The old machine takes 4 minutes to press a shirt plus 1 minute to reposition the shirt during the process. If 250 shirts are waiting to be pressed, how long will it take to finish the day's work in each case?

    a. On the old machine alone

    b. On the new machine alone

    c. If the shirts are split evenly between the new machine and old machine

    d. If the optimal split between the old and new machine is used

C A S E   P R O B L E M

Overloaded at Kidstyle, International

Kidstyle, International makes furniture designed for children. Its most popular items are large and small toy boxes. Demand for toy boxes has overloaded its master production schedule, and the company doesn't know how it will meet demand. Something must be rescheduled, but what?

1. Given the following bills of material, master production schedule, and inventory master file, generate MRP matrices for each item and identify orders that are past due.

2. Use the MRP matrices, Kidstyle's scheduling notes and policies, and the pegging report[2] to identify several options in meeting the prospective shortages. What are the ramifications of each option? Which option would you recommend and why? Your report should include a copy of the MRP matrices as they would appear after your recommendations have been enacted.

---

[2] A report that identifies the source of requirements all the way back to the master schedule.

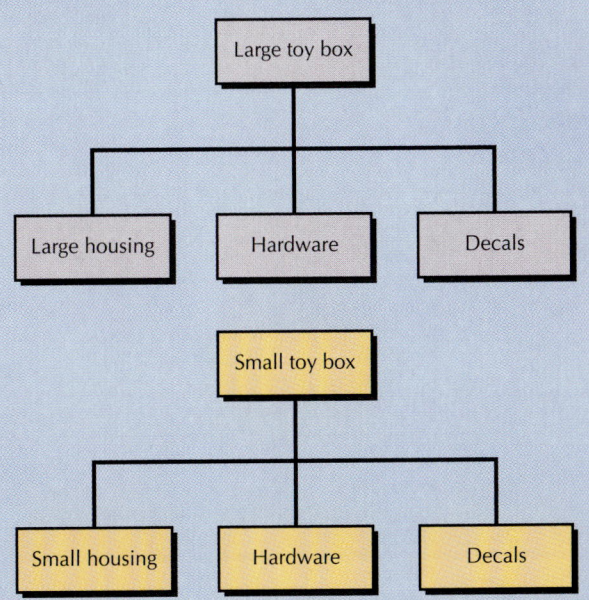

Master Production Schedule

Item	1	2	3	4	5	6	7	8
Large toy box		30		60		30		
Small toy box	25		45	60		30		

(Continued)

Item Master File

Item	On Hand	LT	Lot Size (multiples)	Scheduled Receipt Period	Scheduled Receipt Quantity	Unit Value
Large toy box	30	2	50	—	—	$50.00
Small toy box	25	2	1	—	—	30.00
Large housing	35	2	100	—	—	15.00
Small housing	45	2	75	—	—	10.00
Hardware	55	2	40	2	40	5.00
Decals	50	2	1	2	50	5.00

Kidstyle's Scheduling Notes and Policies

1. Monthly sales forecasts should be met within plus or minus 10 percent.

2. Delay of a customer's order costs 10 percent of the value of the order per week.

3. Customer orders may be delayed a maximum of two weeks.

4. It is possible to halve lead time, but the cost of producing or ordering the item increases by 50 percent (e.g., workers get paid time and a half for overtime.)

Pegging Report

Item	REQUIREMENTS Period	REQUIREMENTS Quantity	SOURCE Type	SOURCE Reference	SOURCE Period
Small toy box	1	25	MS-CO	B070002	1
	3	45	MS-CO	B070002	3
	4	30	MS-CO	B064444	4
		30	MS-FO	Z842009	
	6	30	MS-FO		6
Large toy box	2	30	MS-CO	A080100	2
	4	30	MS-CO	B064444	4
		30	MS-FO	Z900620	
	6	30	MS-FO		6

TYPE codes: MS-FO—forecasts from master schedule
MS-CO—customer order from master schedule
MS-SP—service parts from master schedule

Renovating the Grand Palms Hotel

The Grand Palms Hotel is an older, eight-floor hotel consisting of 36 efficiency rooms and 64 one-bedroom apartments. Its guests, mainly D.C. lobbyists, typically stay months at a time while Congress is in session. It is to be renovated during a two-month recess at the rate of one floor per week.

The renovation of each efficiency requires new pad and carpet (145 square feet), new draperies and sheers (50 yards of material), new window blinds (2 sets), a reupholstered sofa (12 yards of material), reupholstered dining chairs (4 chairs, 1 yard of material each), a new floor lamp, a new desk lamp, a new end table, new artwork (one still life), and a new evacuation plaque (in four languages).

Each one-bedroom apartment requires new pad and carpet (300 square feet), new draperies and sheers (78 yards of material), new window blinds (2 sets), a reupholstered sofa (22 yards of material), reupholstered dining chairs (5 chairs, 1 yard of mate-

rial each), a new floor lamp, a new desk lamp, a new end table, new artwork (two landscapes—coventry and reflections), and a new evacuation plaque (in four languages). The dining chairs are covered in a single solid color, while the sofa and bedspread are covered in the same material as the drapes.

Forty-two units will be decorated in pink/gray (floors 2, 5, and 8), and fifty-eight will be done in blue/green (floors 1, 3, 4, 6, and 7). Floor 1 has 10 units, floors 2 and 8 have 15 units, and the remaining floors each have 12 units. The efficiencies are located on the odd-numbered floors, and the one-bedroom apartments are on the even-numbered floors. Each floor has a different evacuation plaque.

1. How would an MRP system help in scheduling the renovation process?

2. Show how a bill of material could be constructed for renovation of the Grand Palms Hotel. (Choose one floor as an illustration.)

3. Assuming the work begins on the top floor and proceeds downward, determine the requirements for one week of the renovation.

Three Long Years

Bob Bryant looked at the reports in front of him and the five managers seated at the table. He wondered how his staff was going to explain this month's factory performance. Bob was the plant manager at Taylor Scientific Equipment, whose main customers were universities and the government. About three years ago, at the suggestion of the Department of Defense, the company had purchased an MRP II system to satisfy the government's record-keeping requirements. Bob had supported the move in hopes that the MRP system would solve the plant's efficiency problems as well. But things had not exactly turned out as planned. So far as he could tell, only

two of the system's ten modules were up and running—shipping and sales. It was time for some answers.

"John, let's go through the process again. Tell me what happens when an order is received."

"Since each customer order is unique, we sit down and develop a bill of material for the order."

"Sit down where—at the computer terminal?"

"No, we develop the bill by hand and then input it into the MRP system."

"But once the BOM is in the system, it generates routings and a schedule?"

"We wish. right now the routings are also developed manually and then input into the system, and the work standards, too."

(Continued)

"I suppose capacity planning is out of the question."

"We do that manually, but it's more like capacity control. We evaluate how well we've used the shop's capacity at the end of each week."

"And how are the lessons learned incorporated into next week's schedule?"

John squirmed, "I just remember them."

"I see. Fred, how is the inventory system coming along?"

"Great. We have this new bar-coded inventory information system that gives us more accurate information on what inventory is where. It's very fast and . . ."

"And it feeds this information directly into the MRP system?"

"Well, no. . . ."

"I know, WE DO THAT MANUALLY," chorused Bob in unison with Fred. His frustration was beginning to show.

"I have some good news to report," volunteered Donna from data processing. "In our preliminary test of the shop floor control module, Department 074 says the daily schedules we provide them with are the best thing we've done for them in years. In fact, they even came up with some suggestions for improving the report format to make it easier to use, which we took care of that very day. Right, Terry?"

"I hate to burst your bubble, Donna," spoke up Terry from 074, "but in all honesty, we asked you to triple-space the schedule so we could write our own one in beneath it. It saves us a lot of time having the work orders, machine centers, and workers listed on one page like you've done."

Bob threw up his hands in disgust. "Well, fellas, it looks like our company has invested $100,000 in a fancy report generator."

1. Why do you think Taylor Scientific is having so much difficulty implementing an MRP system?

2. What can Bob do, as plant manager, to remedy the situation?

References

Fox, R. E. "MRP, Kanban or OPT, What's Best?" *Inventories and Production* (January–February 1982).

Garwood, D. "Stop Before You Use the Bill Processor. . . ." *Production and Inventory Management* (Second Quarter, 1970): 73–75.

Kanet, J. J. "MRP 96: Time to Rethink Manufacturing Logistics." *Production and Inventory Management* (Second Quarter, 1988): 57–61.

Orlicky, J. *Material Requirements Planning.* New York: McGraw-Hill, 1975.

Tersine, R. J. *Production/Operations Management: Concepts, Structure, and Analysis.* New York: Elsevier North Holland, 1985.

Vollman, T. E., W. L. Berry, and D. C. Whybark. *Manufacturing Planning and Control Systems*, 3rd ed. Homewood, Ill.: Irwin, 1992.

Wallace, T. F. *MRP II: Making It Happen.* Essex Junction, Vt.: Oliver Wight Limited Publications, 1985.

Wight, O. *Production Planning and Inventory Control in the Computer Age.* Boston: Cahners Books International, 1974.

14

Scheduling

Hot, Warm, and Cold at TCONA

www.prenhall.com/russell

The TCONA (Truck Components Operations North American) Division of Eaton Corporation manufactures transmissions, axles, and brake components for medium to heavy trucks worldwide. The plant has 700 machine tools divided into five departments. More than 75 different parts can be processed in each department, and between 600 and 700 active part numbers are in production in any given month.

These days TCONA customers no longer accept lengthy lead times; they place their orders in smaller volumes more frequently. This makes the task of scheduling more critical. For example, machinists can find themselves tearing down and setting up new jobs of ten to fifteen parts several times a day. This is no problem for work centers that have been automated by CNC machines, but for older machines, it can significantly delay production. When this occurred at TCONA, Eaton quickly realized that it could not afford the capital investment required to automate operations completely. It's a good thing, because as it turns out, Eaton didn't need massive automation. What it needed was more effective scheduling.

Eaton chose FACTOR, a computerized scheduling system that allows the user to select from among eighteen different scheduling rules or create their own. Eaton created a priority sequencing rule that divides a thirty-day schedule into three categories: hot, warm, and cold. Customer orders due in less than ten days are placed in the "hot" category and processed according to earliest due date. Customer orders due in ten to twenty days are placed in the "warm" category and prioritized by minimum setup time, unless it causes the job to become "hot," in which case

Scheduling decisions involve a wide range of activities including worker and machine assignment, job sequencing, and the coordination of material handling and maintenance support. In this picture a material handler examines a computerized dispatch list and receives online information about pickups and deliveries.

it reverts to earliest due date. The remaining customer orders are classified as "cold" orders and are processed by minimum setup alone.

Within six months of using the new scheduling system, Eaton TCONA's shaft department had reduced setups and increased output by almost 30 percent. Late shipments to customers were entirely eliminated.[1]

Scheduling specifies *when* labor, equipment, and facilities are needed to produce a product or provide a service. It is the last stage of planning before production takes place.

Scheduling is the last stage of planning before production.

The scheduling function differs considerably based on the type of operation:

■ In *process industries*, such as chemicals and pharmaceuticals, scheduling might consist of determining the mix of ingredients that goes into a vat or when the system should stop producing one type of mixture, clean out the vat, and start producing another. Linear programming can find the lowest-cost mix of ingredients, and the economic order quantity with noninstantaneous replenishment can determine the optimum length of a production run. These techniques are described in detail in Chapter 11 Supplement and Chapter 12, respectively.

■ For *mass production*, the schedule of production is pretty much determined when the assembly line is laid out. Products simply flow down the assembly line from one station to the next in the same prescribed, nondeviating order every time. Day-to-day scheduling decisions consist of determining how fast to feed items into the line and how many hours per day to run the line. On a mixed-model assembly line, the *order* of products assembled also has to be determined. We discuss these issues in Chapters 7 and 15.

The scheduling function differs by type of process.

■ For *projects*, the scheduling decisions are so numerous and interrelated that specialized project-scheduling techniques such as PERT and CPM have been devised. Chapter 17 is devoted to these planning and control tools for project management.

■ For *batch* or *job shop production*, scheduling decisions can be quite complex. In previous chapters, we discussed *aggregate planning*, which plans for the production of product lines or families; *master scheduling*, which plans for the production of individual end items or finished goods; and *material requirements planning* (MRP) and *capacity requirements planning* (CRP), which plan for the production of components and assemblies. Scheduling determines to which machine a part will be routed for processing, which worker will operate a machine that produces a part, and the order in which the parts are to be processed. Scheduling also determines which patient to assign to an operating room, which doctors and nurses are to care for a patient during certain hours of the day, the order in which a doctor is to see patients, and when meals should be delivered or medications dispensed.

What makes scheduling so difficult in a job shop is the variety of jobs (or patients) that are processed, each with distinctive routing and processing requirements. In addition, although the volume of each customer order may be small, there are probably a great number of different orders in the shop at any one time. This necessitates planning for the production of each job as it arrives, scheduling its use of limited resources, and monitoring its progress through the system.

[1] Russell Credle, "Finite Scheduling Helps Eaton Cut Line Setups and Increase Line Throughput," *APICS—The Performance Advantage* (January 1993): 30–32.

This chapter concentrates on scheduling issues for job shop production. We also examine one of the most difficult scheduling problems for services—employee scheduling.

Objectives in Scheduling

There are many possible objectives in constructing a schedule, including

- Meeting customer due dates;
- Minimizing job lateness;
- Minimizing response time;
- Minimizing completion time;
- Minimizing time in the system;
- Minimizing overtime;
- Maximizing machine or labor utilization;
- Minimizing idle time; and
- Minimizing work-in-process inventory.

Handwritten annotations: minimize average # of days late; minimize # of days late; minimize # of jobs late

Managers have multiple, conflicting scheduling objectives.

Job shop scheduling is also known as **shop floor control (SFC)**, *production control*, and *production activity control* (PAC). Regardless of their primary scheduling objective, manufacturers typically have a **production control department** whose responsibilities consist of

1. **Loading**—*checking the availability of material, machines, and labor.* The MRP system plans for material availability. CRP converts the material plan into machine and labor requirements, and projects resource overloads and underloads. Production control assigns work to individual workers or machines, and then attempts to smooth out the load to make the MRP schedule "doable." Smoothing the load is called **load leveling.**

2. **Sequencing**—*releasing work orders to the shop and issuing dispatch lists for individual machines.* MRP recommends when orders should be released (hence the name, *planned* order releases). After verifying their feasibility, production control actually releases the orders. When several orders are released to one machine center, they must be prioritized so that the worker will know which ones to do first. The **dispatch list** contains the sequence in which jobs should be processed. This sequence is often based on certain *sequencing rules.*

3. **Monitoring**—*maintaining progress reports on each job until it is completed.* This is important because items may need to be rescheduled as changes occur in the system. In addition to timely data collection, it involves the use of Gantt charts and input/output control charts.

Shop floor control is the scheduling and monitoring of day-to-day production in a job shop. It is usually performed by the **production control department.**

Load leveling is the process of smoothing out the work assigned.

The dispatch list is a shop paper that specifies the sequence in which jobs should be processed.

Loading

Loading is the process of assigning work to limited resources.

Many times an operation can be performed by various persons, machines, or work centers but with varying efficiencies. If there is enough capacity, each worker should be assigned to the task that he or she performs best, and each job to the machine that can process it most efficiently. In effect, that is what happens when CRP generates a load profile for each machine center. The routing file used by CRP lists the machine that can perform the job most efficiently first. If no overloads appear in the load profile, then production control can proceed to the next task of sequencing the work at each center. However, when resource constraints produce overloads in the load profile, production control must examine the list of jobs initially assigned and decide which jobs to reassign elsewhere. The problem of determining how best to allocate jobs to machines or workers to tasks can be solved with the *assignment method* of linear programming.

The *assignment method* is a specialized linear programming solution procedure that is much simpler to apply than the method discussed in Chapter 11 Supplement. Given a table of jobs and machines, it develops an *opportunity cost matrix* for assigning particular jobs to particular machines. With this technique, only one job may be assigned to each machine. The procedure is as follows:

The *assignment method* of loading is a form of linear programming.

1. Perform *row reductions* by subtracting the minimum value in each row from all other row values.
2. Perform *column reductions* by subtracting the minimum value in each column from all other column values.
3. The resulting table is an *opportunity cost matrix*. Cross out all zeros in the matrix using the minimum number of horizontal or vertical lines.
4. If the number of lines equals the number of rows in the matrix, an optimum solution has been reached and assignments can be made where the zeros appear. Otherwise, *modify the matrix* by subtracting the minimum uncrossed value from all other uncrossed values and adding this same amount to all cells where two lines intersect. All other values in the matrix remain unchanged.
5. Repeat steps 3 and 4 until an optimum solution is reached.

EXAMPLE
14.1

The Assignment Method of Loading

Southern Cans packages processed food into cans for a variety of customers. The factory has four multipurpose cookers and canning lines that can pressure-cook, vacuum-pack, and apply labels to just about any type of food or size of can. The processing equipment was purchased some years apart and some of the cookers are faster and more efficient than others. Southern Cans has four orders that need to be run today for a particular customer: canned beans, canned peaches, canned tomatoes, and canned corn. The customer is operating under a just-in-time production system and needs the mixed order of canned food tomorrow. Southern Cans has estimated the number of hours required to pressure-cook, process, and can each type of food by type of cooker as follows:

FOOD	COOKER			
	1	2	3	4
Beans	10	5	6	10
Peaches	6	2	4	6
Tomatoes	7	6	5	6
Corn	9	5	4	10

Due to time constraints imposed by lengthy changeover procedures, only one job can be assigned to each cooker. How should the jobs be assigned to the cookers in order to process the food most efficiently (i.e., in the least amount of time)?

(Continued)

SOLUTION:

Row reduction:

5	0	1	5
4	0	2	4
2	1	0	1
5	1	0	6

Column reduction:

3	0	1	4
2	0	2	3
0	1	0	0
3	1	0	5

Cover all zeros:

3	0	1	4
2	0	2	3
—0—	1	—0—	—0—
3	1	0	5

Since the number of lines does not equal the number of rows, continue.

Modify the matrix:

1	0	1	2
0	0	2	1
0	3	2	0
1	1	0	3

Cover all zeros:

1	0	1	2
0	0	2	1
0	3	2	0
1	1	0	3

Since the number of lines equals the number of rows, we have reached the final solution.

Make assignments:

	COOKER			
FOOD	*1*	*2*	*3*	*4*
Beans	1	[0]	1	2
Peaches	[0]	0	2	1
Tomatoes	0	3	2	[0]
Corn	1	1	[0]	3

The first row has only one zero, so beans are assigned to cooker 2. The last row has only one zero, so corn is assigned to cooker 3. The second row has two zeros, but cooker 2 is already occupied, so peaches are assigned to cooker 1. That leaves cooker 4 for tomatoes. Referring back to our original matrix, beans will take 5 hours to cook, peaches will take 6 hours, tomatoes 6 hours, and corn 4 hours.

FOOD	COOKER			
	1	*2*	*3*	*4*
Beans	10	5	6	10
Peaches	6	2	4	6
Tomatoes	7	6	5	6
Corn	9	5	4	10

Given that the four cooker/canning lines can operate simultaneously, we can complete the customer's order in 6 hours.

Assignment models can be solved with POM for Windows. Solutions are given in terms of minimizing cost or maximizing profit, although the solution could represent minimized time, maximized quality levels, or other variables. The solution can be provided for minimizing the *sum* of assignment values or minimizing the worst value. The latter case, called the *bottleneck problem*, is useful in situations like Example 14.1 where machines may be operating simultaneously. In that case the completion time of a group of jobs is the *maximum* completion time of the individual jobs rather than the sum of completion times. The assignment method produces good, but not necessarily optimum, results when minimizing a maximum value.

Sequencing

When more than one job is assigned to a machine or activity, the operator needs to know the order in which to process the jobs. The process of prioritizing jobs is called **sequencing.** If no particular order is specified, the operator would probably process the job that arrived first. This default sequence is called *first-come, first-served* (FCFS). Or, if jobs are stacked upon arrival to a machine, it might be easier to process the job first that arrived last and is now on top of the stack. This is called *last-come, first-served* (LCFS) sequencing.

Sequencing prioritizes jobs that have been assigned to a resource.

Another common approach is to process the job first that is due the soonest or the job that has the highest customer priority. These are known as *earliest due date* (DDATE) and *highest customer priority* (CUSTPR) sequencing. Operators may also look through a stack of jobs to find one with a *similar setup* to the job that is currently being processed (SETUP). That would minimize the downtime of the machine and make the operator's job easier.

Variations on the DDATE rule include *minimum slack* (SLACK) and *smallest critical ratio* (CR). SLACK considers the work remaining to be performed on a job as well as the time remaining (until the due date) to perform that work. Jobs are processed first that have the least difference (or slack) between the two, as follows:

A sampling of heuristic sequencing rules

$$\text{SLACK} = (\text{due date} - \text{today's date}) - (\text{remaining processing time})$$

The critical ratio uses the same information as SLACK but arranges it in ratio form so that scheduling performance can be easily assessed. Mathematically, the CR is calculated as follows:

$$CR = \frac{\text{time remaining}}{\text{work remaining}} = \frac{\text{due date} - \text{today's date}}{\text{remaining processing time}}$$

If the work remaining is greater than the time remaining, the critical ratio will be less than 1. If the time remaining is greater than the work remaining, the critical ratio will be greater than 1. If time remaining equals work remaining, the critical ratio exactly equals 1. The critical ratio allows us to make the following statements about our schedule:

If CR > 1, then the job is *ahead of schedule.*

If CR < 1, then the job is *behind schedule.*

If CR = 1, then the job is exactly *on schedule.*

Other sequencing rules examine processing time at a particular operation and order the work either by shortest processing time (SPT) or longest processing time (LPT). LPT assumes long jobs are important jobs and is analogous to the strategy of doing larger tasks first to get them out of the way. SPT focuses instead on shorter jobs and is able to complete many more jobs earlier than LPT. With either rule, some jobs may be inordinately late because they are always put at the back of a queue.

All these "rules" for arranging jobs in a certain order for processing seem reasonable. We might wonder which methods are best or if it really matters which jobs are processed first anyway. Perhaps a few examples will help answer those questions.

Sequencing Jobs Through One Process

The simplest sequencing problem consists of a queue of jobs at one machine or process. No new jobs arrive to the machine during the analysis, processing times and due dates are fixed, and setup time is considered negligible. For this scenario, the *completion time* (also called **flow time**) of each job will differ depending on its place in the sequence, but the overall completion time for the set of jobs (called the **makespan**), will not change. **Tardiness** measures the difference between a job's due date and its completion time for those jobs completed after their due date. Even in this simple case, there is no sequencing rule that optimizes both processing efficiency and due date performance. Let's consider an example.

Flow time is the time it takes a job to flow through the system.

Makespan is the time it takes for a group of jobs to be completed.

Tardiness is the difference between the late job's due date and its completion time.

**EXAMPLE
14.2**

*Simple Sequencing
Rules*

Today is the morning of October 1. Because of the approaching holiday season, Joe Palotty is scheduled to work 7 days a week for the next 2 months. October's work for Joe consists of five jobs, A, B, C, D, and E. Job A takes 5 days to complete and is due October 10, job B takes 10 days to complete and is due October 15, job C takes 2 days to process and is due October 5, job D takes 8 days to process and is due October 12, and job E, which takes 6 days to process, is due October 8.

There are 120 possible sequences for the five jobs. Clearly, enumeration is impossible. Let's try some simple sequencing rules. Sequence the jobs by: (a) first-come, first-served (FCFS), (b) earliest due date (DDATE), (c) minimum slack (SLACK), (d) smallest critical ratio (CR), and (e) shortest processing time (SPT). Determine the completion time and tardiness of each job under each sequencing rule. Should Joe process his work as is—first-come, first-served? If not, what sequencing rule would you recommend to Joe?

SOLUTION:

Prepare a table for each sequencing rule. Start the first job at time 0 (since today is the *beginning* of October 1). Completion time is the sum of the start time and the processing time. The start time of the next job is the completion time of the previous job.

a. FCFS: Process the jobs in order of their arrival, A, B, C, D, E.

(Flowtime)

Sequence	Start Time	Processing Time	Completion Time	Due Date	Tardiness
A	0	5	5	10	0
B	5	10	15	15	0
C	15	2	17	5	12
D	17	8	25	12	13
E	25	6	31	8	23
Average			18.60		9.6

b. DDATE: Sequence the jobs by earliest due date.

Sequence	Start Time	Processing Time	Completion Time	Due Date	Tardiness
C	0	2	2	5	0
E	2	6	8	8	0
A	8	5	13	10	3
D	13	8	21	12	9
B	21	10	31	15	16
Average			15.00		5.6

c. SLACK: Sequence the jobs by minimum slack. The slack for each job is calculated as: (due date − today's date) − remaining processing time.

Job A $(10 - 1) - 5 = 4$

B $(15 - 1) - 10 = 4$

C $(5 - 1) - 2 = 2$

D $(12 - 1) - 8 = 3$

E $(8 - 1) - 6 = 1$

Sequence	Start Time	Processing Time	Completion Time	Due Date	Tardiness
E	0	6	6	8	0
C	6	2	8	5	3
D	8	8	16	12	4
A	16	5	21	10	11
B	21	10	31	15	16
Average			16.40		6.8

(Continued)

d.   CR: Sequence the jobs by smallest critical ratio, calculated as:

$$CR = \frac{\text{time remaining}}{\text{work remaining}}$$

Job   CR

A $\dfrac{(10-1)}{5} = 1.80$

B $\dfrac{(15-1)}{10} = 1.40$

C $\dfrac{(5-1)}{2} = 2.00$

D $\dfrac{(12-1)}{8} = 1.37$

E $\dfrac{(8-1)}{6} = 1.16$

Sequence	Start Time	Processing Time	Completion Time	Due Date	Tardiness
E	0	6	6	8	0
D	6	8	14	12	2
B	14	10	24	15	9
A	24	5	29	10	19
C	29	2	31	5	26
Average			20.8		11.2

e.   SPT: Sequence the jobs by smallest processing time.

Sequence	Start Time	Processing Time	Completion Time	Due Date	Tardiness
C	0	2	2	5	0
A	2	5	7	10	0
E	7	6	13	8	5
D	13	8	21	12	9
B	21	10	31	15	16
Average			14.80		6

Summary

Rule	Average Completion Time	Average Tardiness	No. of Jobs Tardy	Maximum Tardiness
FCFS	18.60	9.6	3*	23
DDATE	15.00	5.6*	3*	16*
SLACK	16.40	6.8	4	16*
CR	20.80	11.2	4	26
SPT	14.80*	6.0	3*	16*

*Best Value

All the sequencing rules complete the month's work by October 31, as planned. However, no sequencing rule is able to complete *all* jobs on time. The performance of FCFS is either met or exceeded by DDATE and SPT. Thus, Joe should take the time to sequence this month's work.

Whether Joe sequences his work by DDATE or SPT depends on the objectives of the company for whom he works. The particular jobs that are tardy may also make a difference.

Are the preceding results a function of this particular example, or are they indicative of the types of results we will get whenever these rules are applied? Analytically, we can prove that for a set number of jobs to be processed on *one* machine, the SPT sequencing rule will minimize mean job completion time (also known as *flowtime*) and minimize mean number of jobs in the system. On the other hand, the DDATE sequencing rule will minimize mean tardiness and maximum tardiness. No definitive statements can be made concerning the performance of the other sequencing rules.

> There is no one sequencing rule that optimizes both processing efficiency and due date performance.

Sequencing Jobs Through Two Serial Processes

Since few factories consist of just one process, we might wonder if techniques exist that will produce an optimal sequence for any number of jobs processed through more than one machine or process. **Johnson's rule** finds the fastest way to process a series of jobs through a two-machine system where every job follows the same sequence on the two machines. Based on a variation of the SPT rule, it requires that the sequence be "mapped out" to determine the final completion time, or *makespan*, for the set of jobs. The procedure is as follows:

> **Johnson's rule** gives an optimum sequence for jobs processed serially through two processes.

1. List the time required to process each job at each machine center. Set up a one-dimensional matrix to represent the desired sequence with the number of slots equal to the number of jobs.

2. Select the smallest processing time at either machine. If that time occurs at machine center 1, put the associated job as near to the *beginning* of the sequence as possible.

3. If the smallest time occurs at machine center 2, put the associated job as near to the *end* of the sequence as possible.

4. Remove the job from the list.

5. Repeat steps 2–4 until all slots in the matrix have been filled or all jobs have been sequenced.

Johnson's job shop has five jobs that must be sanded first at machine center 1 and then painted at machine center 2. Given the following processing times, determine the sequence that will allow the set of five jobs to be completed as soon as possible. Calculate the final completion time for the set of jobs and the idle time of each machine center.

> EXAMPLE
> 14·3

(Continued)

Job	Machine Center 1	Machine Center 2
A	6	8
B	11	6
C	7	3
D	9	7
E	5	10

SOLUTION:

The smallest processing time, 3 hours, occurs at machine center 2 for job C, so we place job C as near to the end of the sequence as possible. C is now eliminated from the job list.

The next smallest time is 5 hours. It occurs at machine center 1 for job E, so we place job E as near to the beginning of the sequence as possible. Job E is eliminated from the job list.

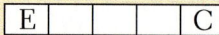

The next smallest time is 6 hours. It occurs at machine center 1 for job A and at machine center 2 for job B. Thus, we place job A as near to the beginning of the sequence as possible and job B as near to the end of the sequence as possible. Jobs A and B are eliminated from the job list.

```
| E | A |   | B | C |
```

The only job remaining is job D. It is placed in the only available slot, in the middle of the sequence.

```
| E | A | D | B | C |
```

This sequence will complete these jobs faster than any other sequence. The following bar charts (called *Gantt charts*) are used to determine the makespan or final completion time for the set of five jobs. Notice that the sequence of jobs (E, A, D, B, C) is the same for both machine centers and that a job cannot begin at machine center 2 until it has been completed at machine center 1. Also, a job cannot begin at machine center 2 if another job is currently in process. Time periods during which a job is being processed are labeled with the job's letter. The shaded areas represent idle time.

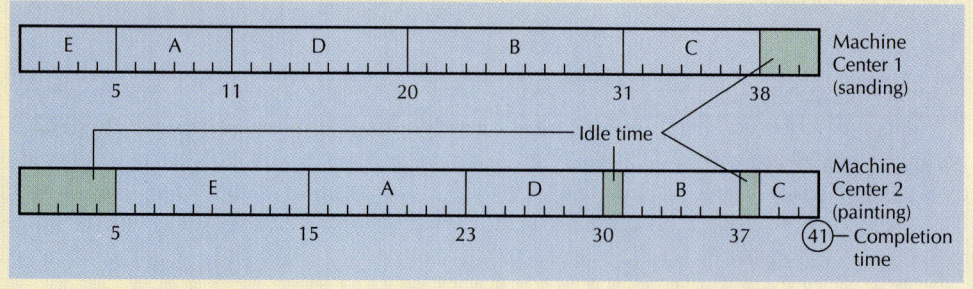

The completion time for the set of five jobs is 41 hours. Of those 41 hours, machine center 1 is idle 3 hours and machine center 2 is idle 7 hours. Note that although Johnson's rule minimizes makespan and idle time, it does not consider job due dates in constructing a sequence, so there is no attempt to minimize job tardiness.

As sequencing problems grow in size and complexity, they become difficult to solve by hand. POM for Windows performs FCFS, SPT, LPT, SLACK, and CR sequencing for one-machine problems and Johnson's rule sequencing for two-machine problems.

Sequencing Jobs Through Any Number of Processes in Any Order

In a real-world job shop, jobs follow different routes through a facility that consists of many different machine centers or departments. A small job shop may have three or four departments; a large job shop may have fifty or more. From several to several hundred jobs may be circulating the shop at any given time. New jobs are released into the shop daily and placed in competition with existing jobs for priority in processing. Queues form and dissipate as jobs move through the system. A dispatch list that shows the sequence in which jobs are to be processed at a particular machine may be valid at the beginning of a day or week but become outdated as new jobs arrive to the system. Some jobs may have to wait to be assembled with others before continuing to be processed. Delays in completing operations can cause due dates to be revised and schedules changed.

In this enlarged setting, the types of sequencing rules used can be expanded. We can still use simple sequencing rules such as SPT, FCFS, and DDATE, but we can also conceive of more complex, or *global*, rules. We may use FCFS to describe the arrival of jobs to a particular machine but *first-in-system, first-served* (FISFS) to differentiate the job's release into the system. Giving a job top priority at one machine only to have it endure a lengthy wait at the next machine seems fruitless, so we might consider looking ahead to the next operation and sequencing the jobs in the current queue by smallest *work-in-next-queue* (WINQ).

We can create new rules such as *fewest number of operations remaining* (NOPN) or *slack per remaining operation* (S/OPN), which require updating as jobs progress through the system. *Remaining work* (RWK) is a variation of SPT that processes jobs by the smallest total processing time for *all* remaining operations, not just the current operation. Any rule that has a remaining work component, such as SLACK or CR, needs to be updated as more operations of a job are completed. Thus, we need a mechanism for keeping track of and recording job progress. Recall that MRP systems can be used to change due dates, release orders, and, in general, coordinate production. Many of the rules described in this section are options in the shop floor module of standard MRP packages. Critical ratio is especially popular for use in conjunction with MRP.

The complexity and dynamic nature of the scheduling environment precludes the use of analytical solution techniques. The most popular form of analysis for these systems is *simulation*. Academia has especially enjoyed creating and testing sequencing rules in simulations of hypothetical job shops. One early simulation study alone examined ninety-two different sequencing rules. Although no optimum solutions have been identified in these simulation studies, they have produced some general guidelines for *when* certain sequencing rules may be appropriate. Here are a few of their suggestions:

More complicated production systems and more complicated sequencing rules are evaluated with simulation.

1. *SPT is most useful when the shop is highly congested.* SPT tends to minimize mean flow time, mean number of jobs in the system (and thus work-in-process inventory), and percent of jobs tardy. By completing more jobs quickly, it theoretically satisfies a greater number of customers than the other rules. However, with SPT some long jobs may be completed *very* late, resulting in a small number of very unsatisfied customers.

For this reason, when SPT is used in practice, it is usually truncated (or stopped), depending on the amount of time a job has been waiting or the nearness of its due date. For example, many mainframe computer systems process jobs by SPT. Jobs that are submitted are placed in several categories (A, B, or C) based on expected CPU time. The shorter jobs, or A jobs, are processed first, but every couple of hours the system stops processing A jobs and picks the first job from the B stack to run. After the B job is finished, the system returns to the A stack and continues processing. C jobs may be processed only once a day. Other systems that have access to due date information will keep a long job waiting until its SLACK is zero or its due date is within a certain range.

2. *Use SLACK or S/OPN for periods of normal activity.* When capacity is not severely restrained, a SLACK-oriented rule that takes into account both due date and processing time will produce good results.

Guidelines for selecting a sequencing rule

3. *Use DDATE when only small tardiness values can be tolerated.* DDATE tends to minimize mean tardiness and maximum tardiness. Although more jobs will be tardy under DDATE than SPT, the degree of tardiness will be much less.

4. *Use LPT if subcontracting is anticipated* so that larger jobs are completed in-house, and smaller jobs are sent out as their due date draws near.

5. *Use FCFS when operating at low-capacity levels.* FCFS allows the shop to operate essentially without sequencing jobs. When the workload at a facility is light, any sequencing rule will do, and FCFS is certainly the easiest to apply.

6. *Do not use SPT to sequence jobs that have to be assembled with other jobs at a later date.* For assembly jobs, a sequencing rule that gives a common priority to the processing of different components in an assembly, such as *assembly DDATE*, produces a more effective schedule.

Monitoring

In a job shop environment where jobs follow different paths through the shop, visit many different machine centers, and compete for similar resources, it is not always easy to keep track of the status of a job. When jobs are first released to the shop, it is relatively easy to observe the queue that they join and predict when their initial operations might be completed. As the job progresses, however, or the shop becomes more congested, it becomes increasingly difficult to follow the job through the system. Competition for resources (resulting in long queues), machine breakdowns, quality problems, and setup requirements are just a few of the things that can delay a job's progress.

A **work package** is shop paperwork that travels with a job.

Shop paperwork, sometimes called a **work package,** travels with a job to specify what work needs to be done at a particular work center and where the item should be routed next. Workers are usually required to sign off on a job, indicating the work they have performed either manually on the work package or electronically through a PC located on the shop floor. Bar code technology has made this task easier by eliminating much of the tedium and errors of entering the information by computer keyboard. In its simplest form, the bar code is attached to the work package, which the worker reads with a wand at the beginning and end of his or her work on the job. In other cases, the bar code is attached to the pallet or crate that carries the items from work center to work center. In this instance, the bar code is read automatically as it enters and leaves the work area. The time a worker spends on each job, the results of quality checks or inspections, and the utilization of resources can also be recorded in a similar fashion.

For the information gathered at each work center to be valuable, it must be up to date, accurate, and accessible to operations personnel. The monitoring function performed by production control takes this information and transforms it into various reports for workers and managers to use. Progress reports can be generated to show the status of individual jobs, the availability or utilization of certain resources, and the performance of individual workers or work centers. Exception reports may be generated to highlight deficiencies in certain areas, such as scrap, rework, shortages, anticipated delays, and unfilled orders. *Hot lists* show which jobs receive the highest priority and must be done immediately. A well-run facility will produce fewer *exception reports* and more *progress reports*. In the next two sections we describe two such progress reports, the Gantt chart and the input/output control chart.

Gantt Charts

Gantt charts, used to plan or map out work activities, can also be used to monitor a job's progress against the plan. As shown in Figure 14.1, Gantt charts can display both planned and completed activities against a time scale. In this figure, the arrow indicating today's date crosses over the schedules for job 12A, job 23C, and job 32B.

From the chart we can quickly see that job 12A is exactly on schedule because the

Gantt charts show both planned and completed activities against a time scale.

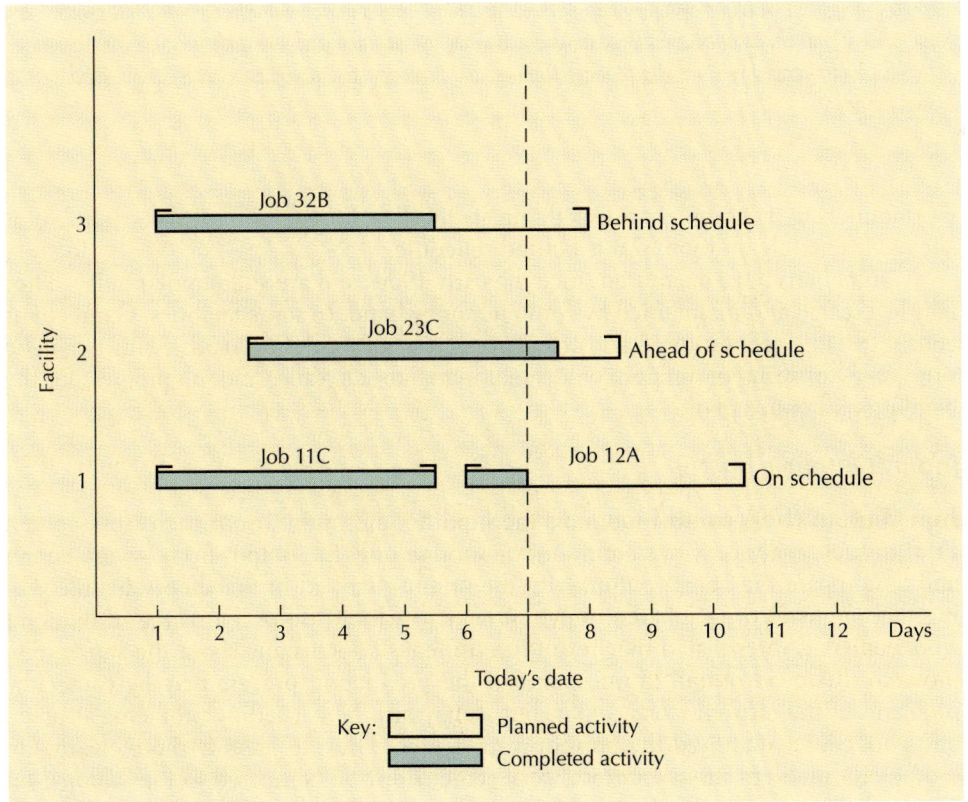

FIGURE 14.1 A Gantt Chart

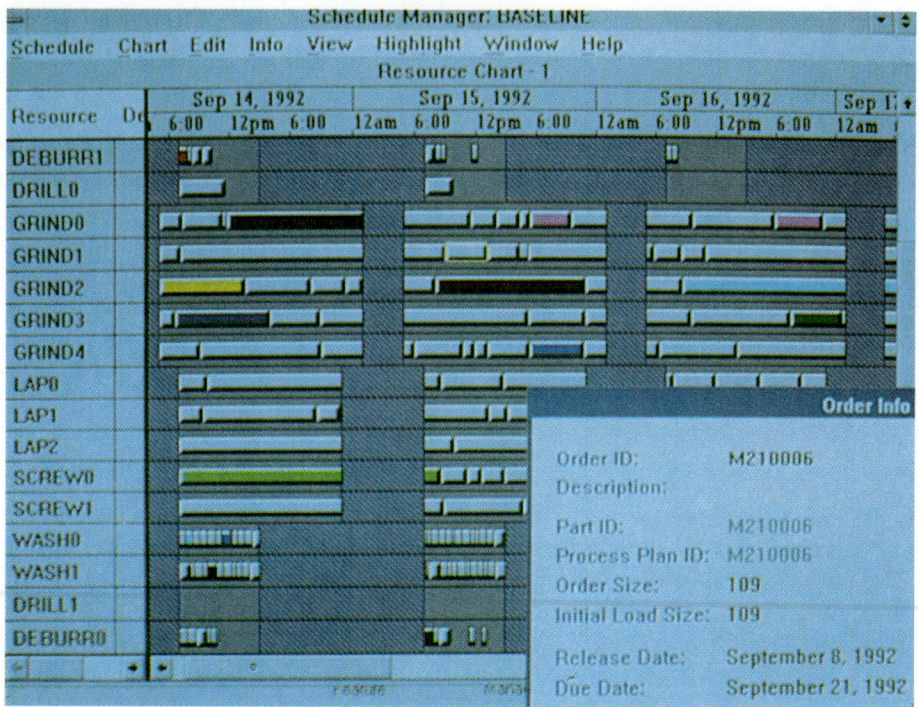

Gantt charts have been used for over 75 years to plan and monitor schedules. Today Gantt charts are more widely used than ever, often as part of the action plan from a quality-improvement team. In some factories, Gantt charts appear on large magnetic boards, displaying the plant's daily progress for everyone to see. Computerized versions chart time, resources, and precedence requirements in an easy-to-read visual format.

bar monitoring its completion exactly meets the line for the current date. Job 23C is ahead of schedule and job 32B is behind schedule.

Gantt charts have been used since the early 1900s and are still popular today. They may be created and maintained by computer or by hand. In some facilities, Gantt charts consist of large scheduling boards (the size of several bulletin boards) with magnetic strips, pegs, or string of different colors that mark job schedules and job progress for the benefit of an entire plant.

Input/Output Control

I/O control monitors the input and output from each work center.

Input/output (I/O) control monitors the input to and output from each work center. Prior to such analysis, it was common to examine only the output from a work center and to compare the actual output with the output planned in the shop schedule. Using that approach in a job shop environment in which the performance of different work centers is interrelated may result in erroneous conclusions about the source of a problem. Reduced output at one point in the production process may be caused by problems at the current work center, but it may also be caused by problems at previous work centers that *feed* the current work center. Thus, to identify more clearly the source of a problem, the *input* to a work center must be compared to the *planned input*, and the *output* must be compared to the *planned output*. Deviations between planned and actual values are calculated, and their cumulative effects are observed.

The resulting backlog or queue size is monitored to ensure that it stays within a manageable range.

The input rate to a work center can be controlled only for the initial operations of a job. These first work centers are often called *gateway* work centers, because the majority of jobs must pass through them before subsequent operations are performed. Input to later operations, performed at *downstream* work centers, is difficult to control because it is a function of how well the rest of the shop is operating—that is, where queues are forming and how smoothly jobs are progressing through the system. The deviation of planned to actual input for downstream work centers can be minimized by controlling the output rates of feeding work centers. The use of input/output reports can best be illustrated with an example.

EXAMPLE 14.4

Input/Output Control

The following information has been compiled in an input/output report for work center 5. Complete the report and interpret the results.

Input/Output Report

Period	1	2	3	4	Total
Planned input	60	65	70	75	
Actual input	60	60	65	65	
Deviation					
Planned output	75	75	75	75	
Actual output	70	70	65	65	
Deviation					
Backlog	30				

SOLUTION:

The input/output report has planned a level production of 75 units per period for work center 5. This is to be accomplished by working off the backlog of work and steadily increasing the input of work.

The report is completed by calculating the deviation of (actual–planned) for both inputs and outputs and then summing the values in the respective planned, actual, and deviation rows. The initial backlog (at the beginning of period 1) is 30 units. Subsequent backlogs are calculated by subtracting each period's actual output from the sum of its actual input and previous backlog.

Completed Input/Output Report

Period	1	2	3	4	Total
Planned input	60	65	70	75	270
Actual input	60	60	65	65	250
Deviation	0	−5	−5	−10	−20
Planned output	75	75	75	75	300
Actual output	70	70	65	65	270
Deviation	−5	−5	−10	−10	−30
Backlog 30	20	10	10	10	

(Continued)

> The completed input/output report shows that work center 5 did not process all the jobs that were available during the four periods; therefore, the desired output rate was not achieved. This can be attributed to a lower-than-expected input of work from feeding work centers. The I/O reports from those work centers need to be examined to locate the source of the problem.

Input/output control provides the information necessary to regulate the flow of work to and from a network of work centers. Increasing the capacity of a work center that is processing all the work available to it will not increase output. The source of the problem needs to be identified. Excessive queues, or *backlogs*, are one indication that *bottlenecks* exist. To alleviate bottleneck work centers, the problem causing the backlog can be worked on, the capacity of the work center can be adjusted, or input to the work center can be reduced. Increasing the input to a bottleneck work center will not increase the center's output. It will merely clog the system further and create longer queues of work-in-process.

Finite Scheduling

The process for scheduling that we have described thus far in this chapter, loading work into work centers, leveling the load, sequencing the work, and monitoring its progress, is called **infinite scheduling**. The term *infinite* is used because the initial loading process assumes infinite capacity. Leveling and sequencing decisions are made after overloads or underloads have been identified. This iterative process is time-consuming and not very efficient.

An alternative approach to scheduling called **finite scheduling** assumes a fixed maximum capacity and will not load the resource beyond its capacity. Loading and sequencing decisions are made at the same time, so that the first jobs loaded onto a work center are of highest priority. Any jobs remaining after the capacity of the work center or resource has been reached are of lower priority and are scheduled for later time periods. This approach is easier than the infinite scheduling approach, but it will be successful only if the criteria for choosing the work to be performed, as well as capacity limitations, can be expressed accurately and concisely.

Finite scheduling systems use a variety of methods to develop their schedules, including mathematical programming, network analysis, simulation, and expert systems or other forms of artificial intelligence. Because the scheduling system is making the decisions and not the human scheduler, companies may find it difficult to purchase a system off the shelf that can embody their specific manufacturing environment or can be readily updated as changes in the environment occur. Finite schedulers are becoming more popular as software systems become more adaptable and easier to use and as manufacturing environments are simplified and are better understood. There are several finite schedulers available. One of the oldest is IBM's CAPOSS (Capacity Planning and Operations Sequencing System). ISIS, developed at Carnegie-Mellon, was one of the first schedulers to use artificial intelligence. Another prominent finite scheduling system is synchronous manufacturing.

Synchronous Manufacturing

In the 1970s, an Israeli physicist named Eliyahu Goldratt responded to a friend's request for help in scheduling his chicken coop business. Lacking a background in man-

Infinite scheduling loads without regard to capacity, then levels the load and sequences the jobs.

Finite scheduling sequences jobs as part of the loading decision. Resources are never loaded beyond capacity.

www.prenhall.com/russell

ufacturing or production theory, Dr. Goldratt took a commonsense, intuitive approach to the scheduling problem. He developed a software system that used mathematical programming and simulation to create a schedule that realistically considered the constraints of the manufacturing system. The software produced good schedules quickly and was marketed in the early 1980s in the United States. After more than 100 firms had successfully used the scheduling system (called OPT), the creator sold the rights to the software and began marketing the theory behind the software instead. He called his approach to scheduling the theory of constraints. General Motors and other manufacturers call its application **synchronous manufacturing.**

Decision making in manufacturing is often difficult because of the size and complexity of the problems faced. Dr. Goldratt's first insight into the scheduling problem led him to simplify the number of variables considered. He learned early that manufacturing resources typically are not used evenly. Instead of trying to balance the capacity of the manufacturing system, he decided that most systems are inherently unbalanced and that he would try to balance the *flow* of work through the system instead. He identified resources as bottleneck or nonbottleneck and observed that the flow through the system is controlled by the bottleneck resources. These resources should always have material to work on, should spend as little time as possible on nonproductive activities (e.g., setups, waiting for work), should be fully staffed, and should be the focus of improvement or automation efforts. Goldratt pointed out that an hour's worth of production lost at a bottleneck reduces the output of the system by the same amount of time, whereas an hour lost at a nonbottleneck may have no effect on system output.

From this realization, Goldratt was able to simplify the scheduling problem signif-

www.prenhall.com/russell

Synchronous manufacturing, concentrates on scheduling the bottleneck resource.

— Same as the theory of constraints

THE COMPETITIVE EDGE

Constraint-Based Scheduling at Flow International

Flow International manufactures high-pressure waterjet systems for commercial customers in the paper, food, automotive, and aerospace industries. The systems are used to cut a variety of products from disposable diapers to titanium. Units can cost upward of $500,000, contain hundreds of parts, and require a special alloy with a six-month lead time. Because of their diverse applications, customization is routine and product designs change frequently.

Business is good for Flow—in two years, sales have grown from $42 million to $110 million. On-time delivery is important but, with peak demand, is increasingly harder to achieve. Customers demand a turnaround of just one day on spare parts and one week for complete systems. The company employs a highly skilled work force of 700 individuals organized into 80 work centers, 13 of which utilize CNC equipment. New equipment investment averages $2 million annually.

How do you schedule production to ship products on time when dealing with multiple resources, an exten-

sive bill of material, and changing and diverse products? Flow chose the *Theory of Constraints* to address these challenges. The production system is too large, interrelated, and dynamic to schedule optimally. It is even too complex to consider all products or all work centers. With the Theory of Constraints, only the *bottleneck* operations need to be considered because the most critical resources determine the overall capacity of a plant. Maximizing the throughput of bottlenecks will maximize the throughput of the entire plant.

Applying constraint-based scheduling, Flow reduced lot sizes, scheduled bottleneck work centers near to 100% capacity, and underscheduled nonbottleneck work centers to match the output of the bottleneck work centers. Work-in-process inventory decreased by 50% and finished goods inventory by 25%. Orders are completed faster, and new equipment purchases are targeted at relieving bottleneck resources. In addition, costs are down with more rational overtime and outsourcing decisions.

SOURCE: Michael Gadbois, "Shipments Flow Smoothly at Flow International," *IIE Solutions* (March 1996): 40–43.

icantly. He concentrated initially on scheduling production at bottleneck resources and then scheduled the nonbottleneck resources to support the bottleneck activities. Thus, production is synchronized, or "in sync," with the needs of the bottleneck and the system as a whole.

Goldratt's second insight into manufacturing concerned the concept of lot sizes or batch sizes. Goldratt saw no reason for fixed batch sizes. He differentiated between the quantity in which items are produced, called the *process batch,* and the quantity in which the items are transported, called the *transfer batch.* Ideally, items should be transferred in lot sizes of one. The process batch size for bottlenecks should be large, to eliminate the need for setups. The process batch size for nonbottlenecks can be small because time spent in setups for nonbottlenecks does not affect the rest of the system. The following example illustrates these concepts.

> Process batch sizes and transfer batch sizes do not have to match.

EXAMPLE 14·5

Synchronous Manufacturing

The following diagram contains the product structure, routing, and processing time information for product A. The process flows from the bottom of the diagram upward. Assume one unit of items B, C, and D are needed to make each A. The manufacture of each item requires three operations at machine centers 1, 2, or 3. Each machine center contains only one machine. A machine setup time of 60 minutes occurs whenever a machine is switched from one operation to another (within the same item or between items).

Design a schedule of production for each machine center that will produce 100 A's as quickly as possible. Show the schedule on a Gantt chart of each machine center. Use the following synchronous manufacturing concepts:

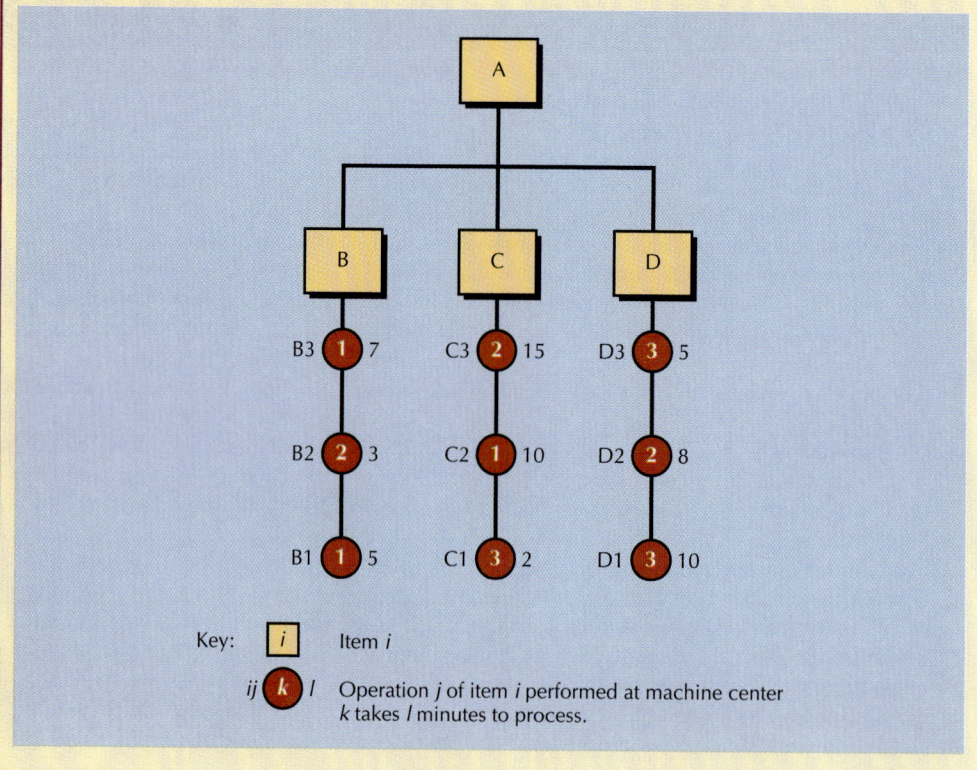

1. Identify the bottleneck machine.
2. To keep the bottleneck busy, schedule the item first whose lead time to the bottleneck is less than or equal to the bottleneck processing time.
3. Forward schedule the bottleneck machine.
4. Backward schedule the other machines to sustain the bottleneck schedule.
5. Remember that the transfer batch size does not have to match the process batch size.

SOLUTION:

■ The bottleneck machine is calculated by summing the processing times of all operations to be performed at a machine.

Machine 1		*Machine 2*		*Machine 3*	
B1	5	B2	3	C1	2
B3	7	C3	15	D3	5
C2	10	D2	8	D1	10
	22		26*		17

*Bottleneck

■ Machine 2 is identified as the bottleneck, so we schedule machine 2 first. From the product structure diagram, we see three operations that are performed at machine 2—B2, C3, and D2. If we schedule item B first, a B will reach machine 2 every 5 minutes (since B has to be processed through machine 1 first), but each B takes only 3 minutes to process at machine 2, so the bottleneck will be idle for 2 minutes of every 5 minutes. That's not keeping our bottlenecks busy. A similar result occurs if we schedule item D first on machine 2. The bottleneck will be idle for 2 minutes out of every 10 minutes until D has finished processing. The best alternative is to schedule item C first. The first C won't reach machine 2 until time 12, but after that a C will be waiting for the bottleneck machine, because it takes longer for C to be processed through machine 2 than through the first two machines in C's routing sequence combined.

■ We begin our Gantt charts by processing item C through the three machine centers. Before we continue, a few comments about the Gantt charts are needed. The charts will look different from our earlier Gantt charts because we will allow each item to be transferred to the next operation immediately after it is completed at the current operation (i.e., the transfer batch size is 1). We will process the items in batches of 100 to match our demand requirements. The diagonal lines represent idle time between operations due to setup time requirements or because a feeding operation has not yet been completed. Refer to the Gantt charts in Figure 14.2 on page 696 for the remainder of the discussion.

■ C3 is completed at machine center 2 at time 1512. After setup, it is ready for a new item at time 1572. We have a choice between B2 and D2, since both B1 and D1 can be completed by 1572. Completion time at machine center 2 will be the same regardless of whether B2 or D2 is processed first; however, the

(Continued)

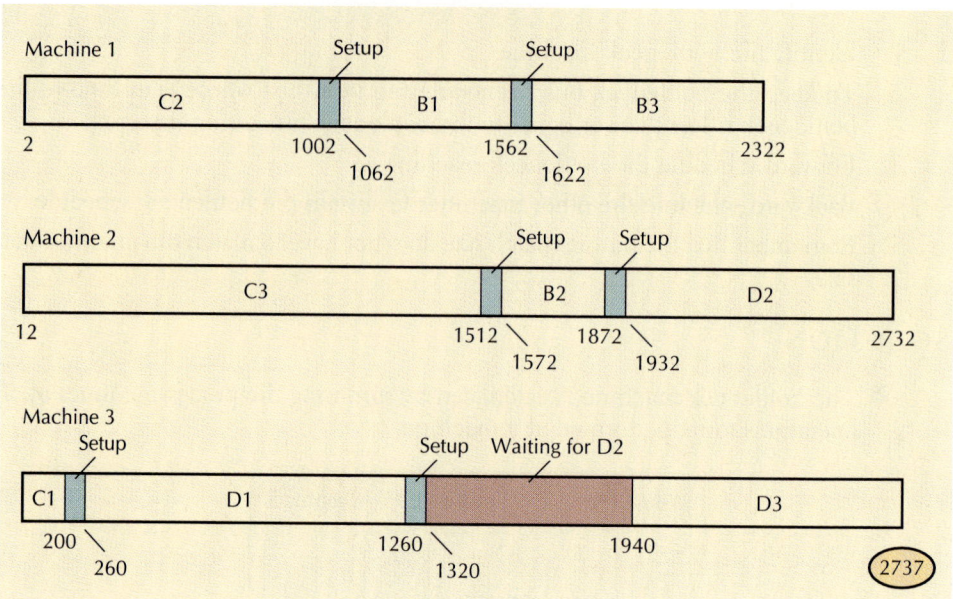

FIGURE 14.2   Gantt Chart Solution to Example 14.5

completion time at the other machine centers (and thus for product A) will be affected by the bottleneck sequence. From the product structure diagram, we note that B3 can be completed more quickly than D3 because D3 must wait 3 minutes for D2 to be completed, whereas B3 will always have a queue of items from B2 to work on. Thus, we schedule B2 and then D2 on machine center 2.

■ With the bottleneck sequence of C3, B2, D2 established, we can now schedule machine center 1 (C2, B1, B3) and machine center 3 (C1, D1, D3). The completion time for producing 100 A's is 2,737 minutes. The total idle time at the three machine centers is 980 minutes.

Employee Scheduling

Employee scheduling has lots of options because labor is a very flexible resource.

Labor is one of the most flexible resources. Workers can be hired and fired more easily than equipment can be purchased or sold. Labor-limited systems can expand capacity through overtime, expanded workweeks, extra shifts, or part-time workers. This flexibility is valuable but it tends to make scheduling difficult. Service firms especially spend an inordinate amount of time developing employee schedules. A supervisor might spend an entire week making up the next month's employee schedule. The task becomes even more daunting for facilities that operate on a twenty-four-hour basis with multiple shifts.

The assignment method of linear programming discussed earlier in this chapter can be used to assign workers with different performance ratings to available jobs. Large-scale linear programming is currently used by McDonald's to schedule its large part-time workforce. American Airlines uses a combination of integer linear programming and expert systems for scheduling ticket agents to coincide with peak and slack demand periods and for the complicated scheduling of flight crews. Although

www.prenhall.com/russell

Scheduling employees, especially part-time workers, can take considerable time and effort. Most employers develop weekly or monthly schedules by hand, trying to balance the needs of employees, supervisors, and customers. One way to avoid the headaches of employee scheduling and improve customer responsiveness is to automate. That's what the banking industry did with ATMs that operate 24 hours a day. Now maintenance activities must be scheduled to ensure that the facility is available to the customer as promised!

mathematical programming certainly has found application in employee scheduling, most scheduling problems are solved by heuristics (i.e., rules of thumb) that develop a repeating pattern of work assignments. Often heuristics are imbedded in a decision support system to facilitate their use and increase their flexibility. One such heuristic[2] used for scheduling full-time workers with two days off per week, is given next.

Employee Scheduling Heuristic:
1. Let N = no. of workers available

    D_i = demand for workers on day i

    X = day working

    O = day off
2. Assign the first $N - D_1$ workers day 1 off. Assign the next $N - D_2$ workers day 2 off. Continue in a similar manner until all days have been scheduled.
3. If the number of workdays for a full-time employee is less than 5, assign the remaining workdays so that consecutive days off are possible or where unmet demand is highest or arbitrarily.

---

[2] Kenneth R. Baker and Michael J. Magazine, "Workforce Scheduling with Cyclic Demands and Days-Off Constraints," *Management Science* 24, no. 2 (October 1977): 161–67.

4.   Assign any remaining work to part-time employees, subject to maximum hour restrictions.

5.   If consecutive days off are desired, consider switching schedules among days with the same demand requirements.

EXAMPLE 14.6
Employee Scheduling

Diet-Tech employs five workers to operate its weight-reduction facility. Demand for service each week (in terms of minimum number of workers required) is given in the following table. Create an employee schedule that will meet the demand requirements and guarantee each worker 2 days off per week.

Day of Week	M	T	W	Th	F	Sa	Su
Min. No. of Workers Required	3	3	4	3	4	5	3
Taylor							
Smith							
Simpson							
Allen							
Dickerson							

SOLUTION:

The completed employee schedule matrix is shown next.

Day of Week	M	T	W	Th	F	Sa	Su
Min. No. of Workers Required	3	3	4	3	4	5	3
Taylor	O	X	X	O	X	X	X
Smith	O	X	X	O	X	X	X
Simpson	X	O	X	X	O	X	X
Allen	X	O	X	X	X	X	O
Dickerson	X	X	O	X	X	X	O

Following the heuristic, the first $(5 - 3) = 2$ workers, Taylor and Smith, are assigned Monday off. The next $(5 - 3) = 2$ workers, Simpson and Allen, are assigned Tuesday off. The next $(5 - 4) = 1$ worker, Dickerson, is assigned Wednesday off. Returning to the top of the roster, the next $(5 - 3) = 2$ workers, Taylor and Smith, are assigned Thursday off. The next $(5 - 4) = 1$ worker, Simpson, is assigned Friday off. Everyone works on Saturday, and the next $(5 - 3) = 2$ workers, Allen and Dickerson, get Sunday off.

The resulting schedule meets demand and has every employee working 5 days a week with 2 days off. Unfortunately, none of the days off are consecutive. By switching the initial schedules for Tuesday and Thursday (both with a demand of 3) and the schedules for Wednesday and Friday (both with a demand of 4), the following schedule results:

Day of Week	M	T	W	Th	F	Sa	Su
Min. No. of Workers Required	3	3	4	3	4	5	3
Taylor	O	O	X	X	X	X	X
Smith	O	O	X	X	X	X	X
Simpson	X	X	O	O	X	X	X
Allen	X	X	X	O	X	X	O
Dickerson	X	X	X	X	O	X	O

In this revised schedule, the first three workers have consecutive days off. The last two workers have one weekend day off and one day off during the week.

THE COMPETITIVE EDGE

You Can Choose Your Own Hours at McDonald's

Employee scheduling is a headache with managers spending on average more than 8 hours a week manually preparing work schedules. Scheduling in fast-food restaurants has the following additional problems:

- *Sales volume and, thus, employee requirements, vary dramatically over the day.* Fast-food restaurants do 17% of their business during the noon hour. Worker requirements in the grill and counter areas can vary from one to eight or more employees.
- *There are no standard workdays or workweeks.* Shifts vary from three to eight hours. Legal restrictions on the length of the workday are watched carefully due to the number of teenage employees.
- *Employees differ in the times they are available to work.* This is especially true because most of the workers are part-timers.
- *Employee skills and performance levels vary considerably.* Workers qualified to work the drive-through are not necessarily the best workers behind the counter or at the grill.

A typical fast-food restaurant has 3 work areas, 150 employees, and 30 work shifts. This presents a very large scheduling problem. (If formulated as a linear programming model, it would contain approximately 100,000 variables and 3,000 constraints.) The system used by McDonald's generates employee schedules that

- Satisfy half-hourly personnel requirements with a minimum of surplus scheduled hours;
- Give each employee the same number of workdays and work hours;
- Assign employees to work areas where they perform the best;
- Schedule each employee during his or her preferred work times as much as possible;
- Schedule every employee to work around the same time each workday;
- Provide adequate skill coverage during each half-hour time period in each work area.

What-if? analysis can also be performed to handle adjustments in workforce size, modifications of sales and labor requirements, changes in desired work shifts, and changes in other operating parameters. The system has  standardized the scheduling process at McDonald's, reduced the time to prepare a schedule by 90 percent, and produced higher-quality schedules from the perspective of both management and labor.

www.prenhall.com/russell

SOURCE: Based on Robert Love, Jr., and James Hoey, "Management Science Improves Fast-Food Operations," *Interfaces* (March–April 1990): 21–29.

The heuristic just illustrated can be adapted to ensure the two days off per week are consecutive days. Other heuristics schedule workers two weeks at a time, with every other weekend off.

Decision support systems can enhance both the scheduling process and the quality of the resulting schedule. A typical DSS for scheduling might:

- Generate a scheduling pattern to be followed cyclically throughout the year;
- Determine whether a forty-hour or eighty-hour base for overtime is more cost-effective;
- Examine the effect of alternate-days-off patterns;
- Determine the appropriate breakdown of part-time versus full-time employees;
- Justify the use of additional staff;
- Assess the feasibility of vacation or other leave requests; and
- Determine the benefit of cross training employees in certain positions.

Decision support systems are popular for scheduling.

Summary

Scheduling in a job shop environment is difficult because jobs arrive at varying time intervals, require different resources and sequences of operations, and are due at different times. This lowest level of scheduling is referred to as *shop floor control* or *production control*. It involves assigning jobs to machines or workers (called loading), specifying the order in which operations are to be performed, and monitoring the work as it progresses. Techniques such as the assignment method are used for *loading*, various rules whose performance varies according to the scheduling objective are used for *sequencing*, and Gantt charts and input/output control charts are used for *monitoring*.

Realistic schedules must reflect capacity limitations. *Infinite scheduling* initially assumes infinite capacity and then manually "levels the load" of resources that have exceeded capacity. *Finite scheduling* loads jobs in priority order and delays those jobs for which current capacity is exceeded. *Synchronous manufacturing* is a finite scheduling approach that schedules bottleneck resources first and then schedules other resources to support the bottleneck schedule. It also allows items to be transferred between resources in lot sizes that differ from the lot size in which the item is produced.

Employee scheduling is often difficult because of the variety of options available and the special requirements for individual workers. Scheduling heuristics are typically used to develop patterns of worker assignment. Decision support systems for scheduling are becoming more commonplace.

Summary of Key Formulas

Minimum Slack

$$\text{SLACK} = (\text{due date} - \text{today's date}) - (\text{remaining processing time})$$

Critical Ratio

$$\text{CR} = \frac{\text{time remaining}}{\text{work remaining}} = \frac{\text{due date} - \text{today's date}}{\text{remaining processing time}}$$

Summary of Key Terms

dispatch list: a shop paper that specifies the sequence in which jobs should be processed; it is often derived from specific sequencing rules.

finite scheduling: an approach to scheduling that loads jobs in priority order and delays those jobs for which current capacity is exceeded.

flow time: the time that it takes for a job to "flow" through the system; that is, its completion time.

Gantt chart: a bar chart that shows a job's progress graphically or compares actual against planned performance.

infinite scheduling: an approach to scheduling that initially assumes infinite capacity and then manually "levels the load" of resources that have exceeded capacity.

input/output (I/O) control: a procedure for monitoring the input to and output from a work center to regulate the flow of work through a system.

Johnson's rule: an algorithm for sequencing any number of jobs through two serial operations to minimize makespan.

load leveling: the process of smoothing out the work assigned across time and the available resources.

loading: the process of assigning work to individual workers or machines.

makespan: the time that it takes for a group of jobs to be completed—that is, the completion time of the last job in a group.

production control department: a department within the manufacturing function responsible for loading, sequencing, and monitoring jobs.

scheduling: the determination of *when* labor, equipment, and facilities are needed to produce a product or provide a service.

sequencing: the process of assigning priorities to jobs so that they are processed in a particular order.

shop floor control (SFC): scheduling and monitoring day-to-day production in a job shop; also known as production control or production activity control.

synchronous manufacturing: a finite scheduling approach that differentiates between bottleneck and nonbottleneck resources and between transfer batches and process batches.

tardiness: the difference between a job's due date and its completion time for those jobs completed after their due date.

work package: shop paperwork that travels with a job to specify what work needs to be done at a particular machine center and where the item should be routed next.

Solved Problems

1. Assignment Problem

Wilkerson Printing has four jobs waiting to be run this morning. Fortunately, they have four printing presses available. However, the presses are of different vintage and operate at different speeds. The approximate times (in minutes) required to process each job on each press are given next. Assign jobs to presses so that the batch of jobs can be completed as soon as possible.

	PRESS			
JOB	1	2	3	4
A	20	90	40	10
B	40	45	50	35
C	30	70	35	25
D	60	45	70	40

Solution:

Row reduction:

10	80	30	0
5	10	15	0
5	45	10	0
20	5	30	0

Column reduction:

5	75	20	0
0	5	5	0
0	40	0	0
15	0	20	0

Cover all zeroes:

5	75	20	0
0	5	5	0
0	40	0	0
15 —	0 —	20 —	0

The number of lines equals the number of rows, so this is the final solution. Make assignments:

5	75	20	[0]
[0]	5	5	0
0	40	[0]	0
15	[0]	20	0

Assign job A to press 4, job B to press 1, job C to press 3, and job D to press 2. Refer to the original matrix for actual processing times. Since the jobs can be run concurrently, the entire batch will be completed by the maximum completion time of the individual jobs, or job D's time of 45 minutes. The total machining time required is (10 + 40 + 35 + 45) = 130 minutes.

2. Johnson's Rule

Clean and Shine Car Service has five cars waiting to be washed and waxed. The time required (in minutes) for each activity is given next. In what order should the cars be processed through the facility? When will the batch of cars be completed?

Car	Wash	Wax
1	5	10
2	7	2
3	10	5
4	8	6
5	3	5

Solution:

Use Johnson's rule to sequence the cars. The lowest processing time is 2 minutes for waxing car 2. Since waxing is the second operation, we place car 2 as near to the end of the sequence as possible, in last place. The next-lowest time is 3 minutes for washing car 5. Since washing is the first operation, we place car 5 as near to the front of the sequence as possible, in first place. The next-lowest time is 5 minutes for washing car 1 and waxing car 3. Car 1 is scheduled in second place, and car 3 is put in next-to-last place (i.e., fourth). That leaves car 4 for third place.

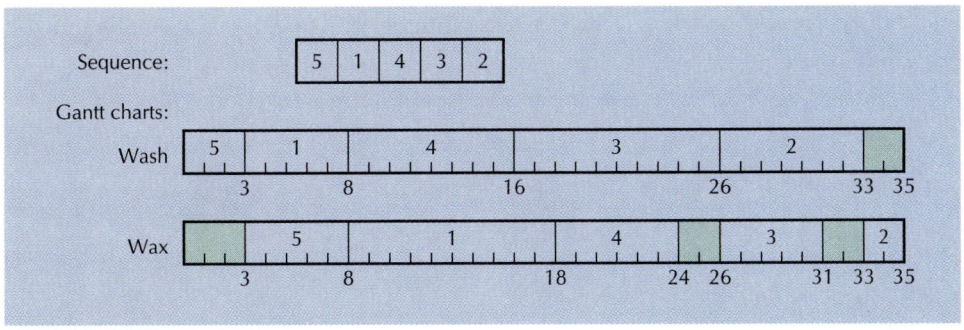

The completion time for washing and waxing the five cars is 35 minutes. The washing facility is idle for 2 minutes at the end of the cycle. The waxing facility is idle for 3 minutes at the beginning of the cycle and 4 minutes during the cycle.

Questions

14-1. How do scheduling activities differ for projects, mass production, and process industries?

14-2. Why is scheduling a job shop so difficult?

14-3. What three functions are typically performed by a production control department?

14-4. Give examples of four types of operations (manufacturing or service) and suggest which scheduling objectives might be appropriate for each.

14-5. How can the success of a scheduling system be measured?

14-6. Describe the process of loading and load leveling. What quantitative techniques are available to help in this process?

14-7. What is the purpose of dispatch lists? How are they usually constructed?

14-8. When should the following sequencing rules be used?

　a. SPT

　b. Johnson's rule

　c. DDATE

　d. FCFS

14-9. What is the difference between local and global sequencing rules? Give several examples of each.

14-10. What information is provided by the critical ratio sequencing rule? How does it differ from SLACK?

14-11. How are work packages, hot lists, and exception reports used in a job shop?

14-12. What are Gantt charts and why are they used so often?

14-13. Explain the concept behind input/output control.

14-14. Describe how gateway work centers, downstream work centers, and backlog affect shop performance.

14-15. Explain the difference between infinite and finite scheduling.

14-16. How does synchronized manufacturing differ from traditional scheduling?

14-17. How should bottleneck resources and nonbottleneck resources be scheduled?

14-18. Why should transfer batches and process batches be treated differently?

14-19. What are some typical issues involved in employee scheduling?

14-20. What quantitative techniques are available to help develop employee schedules?

Problems

14-1. At Valley Hospital, nurses beginning a new shift report to a central area to receive their primary patient assignments. Not every nurse is as efficient as another with particular kinds of patients. Given the following patient roster, care levels, and time estimates, assign nurses to patients to optimize efficiency. Also, determine how long it will take for the nurses to complete their routine tasks on this shift.

| | | TIME REQUIRED (HOURS) TO COMPLETE ROUTINE TASKS | | | |
PATIENT	CARE LEVEL	Nurse 1	Nurse 2	Nurse 3	Nurse 4
A. Jones	A2	3	5	4	3
B. Hathaway	B2	2	1	3	2
C. Bryant	B1	3	4	2	2
D. Sweeney	A1	4	3	3	4

14-2. Valley Hospital (from Problem 14-1) wants to focus on customer perceptions of quality, so it has asked its patients to evaluate the nursing staff and indicate preferences for assignment. Reassign the nursing staff to obtain the highest customer approval rating possible (a perfect score is 100).

	RATING			
PATIENT	Nurse 1	Nurse 2	Nurse 3	Nurse 4
A. Jones	89	95	83	84
B. Hathaway	88	80	96	85
C. Bryant	87	92	82	84
D. Sweeney	93	82	86	94

Compare the results with those from Problem 14-1. What is the average rating of the assignment? What other criteria could be used to assign nurses?

14-3. Fibrous Incorporated makes products from rough tree fibers. Its product line consists of five items processed through one of five machines. The machines are not identical, and some products are better suited to some machines. Given the following production time in minutes per unit, determine an optimal assignment of product to machine.

	MACHINE				
PRODUCT	A	B	C	D	E
1	17	10	15	16	20
2	12	9	16	9	14
3	11	16	14	15	12
4	14	10	10	18	17
5	13	12	9	15	11

14-4. Sunshine House received a contract this year as a supplier of Girl Scout cookies. Sunshine currently has five production lines, each of which will be dedicated to a particular kind of cookie. The production lines differ by sophistication of machines, site, and experience of personnel. Given the following estimates of processing times (in hours), assign cookies to lines so that the order can be completed as soon as possible.

	PRODUCTION LINE				
COOKIES	1	2	3	4	5
Chocolate Mint	30	18	26	17	15
Peanut Butter	23	22	32	25	30
Shortbread	17	31	24	22	29
Fudge Delight	28	19	13	18	23
Macaroons	23	14	16	20	27

14-5. Evan Schwartz has six jobs waiting to be processed through his machine. Today is November 1. Processing time (in days) and due date information for each job are given below.

Job	Processing Time	Due date
A	2	11-3
B	1	11-2
C	4	11-12
D	3	11-4
E	4	11-8
F	5	11-10

Sequence the jobs by FCFS, SPT, SLACK, and DDATE. Calculate the average completion time and average tardiness of the six jobs under each sequencing rule. Which rule would you recommend?

14-6. College students always have a lot of work to do, but this semester, Katie Lawrence is overwhelmed. Listed below are the assignments she faces, the estimated completion times (in days), and due dates.

Assignment	Estimated Completion Time	Due date
1. Management case	5	10-20
2. Marketing survey	10	11-3
3. Financial analysis	4	10-25
4. Term project	21	11-15
5. Computer program	14	11-2

a. Help Katie prioritize her work so that she completes as many assignments on time as possible. Today is October 1.

b. Would your sequence of assignments change if Katie were interested in minimizing the average tardiness of her assignments?

14-7. Today is day 4 of the planning cycle. Sequence the following jobs by FCFS, SPT, SLACK, CR, and DDATE. Calculate the mean completion time and mean tardiness for each sequencing rule. Which rule would you recommend?

Job	Processing Time (in days)	Due date
A	3	10
B	10	12
C	2	25
D	4	8
E	5	15
F	8	18
G	7	20

14-8. Alice's Alterations has eight jobs to be completed and only one sewing machine (and sewing machine operator). Given the processing times and due dates as shown here, prioritize the jobs by SPT, DDATE, SLACK, and CR. Today is day 5.

Task	Processing Time (in days)	Due Date
A	5	10
B	8	15
C	6	15
D	3	20
E	10	25
F	14	40
G	7	45
H	3	50

Calculate mean flow time, mean tardiness, maximum tardiness, and number of jobs tardy for each sequence. Which sequencing rule would you recommend? Why?

14-9. Tracy has six chapters on her desk that must be typed and proofed as soon as possible.

Tracy does the typing; the author does the proofing. Some chapters are easy to type but more difficult to proof. The estimated time (in minutes) for each activity is given here. In what order should Tracy type the chapters so that the entire batch can be finished as soon as possible? When can Tracy expect to be finished?

Chapter	Typing	Proofing
1	30	20
2	90	25
3	60	15
4	45	30
5	75	60
6	20	30

14-10. Claims received by Healthwise Insurance Company are reviewed at one station, adjudicated, and sent to another station for entry into the database. The processing time (in minutes) required for each general type of claim is shown here. Currently, Bill Frazier has ten claims to be reviewed. In what order should he process the claims so that the entire batch can get into the system as soon as possible? How long will it take to process completely the ten claims?

	PROCESSING TIME	
CLASSIFICATION	Review	Data Entry
1. Medicare I	8	5
2. Physician 24	15	10
3. Medicare II	6	5
4. Physician 4	5	10
5. HMO I	17	15
6. Physician 17	10	10
7. Emergency II	5	3
8. HMO II	4	15
9. Physician 37	12	10
10. Emergency I	20	3

14-11. Jobs processed through Percy's machine shop pass through three operations: milling, grinding, and turning. The hours required for each of these operations is shown below.

Job	Milling	Grinding	Turning
A	5	1	4
B	2	2	5
C	3	2	1
D	0	3	0
E	4	1	2

Sequence the jobs by (a) shortest processing time (SPT), and (b) least remaining work (RWK). Make a Gantt chart for each machine and each rule. Which sequencing rule would you recommend?

14-12. The following data have been compiled for an input/output report at work center 7. Complete the report and analyze the results.

Period	1	2	3	4	5	Total
Planned input	50	55	60	65	65	
Actual input	50	50	55	60	65	
Deviation						
Planned output	65	65	65	65	65	
Actual output	60	60	60	60	60	
Deviation						
Backlog	30					

14-13. The input/output report for work center 6 is as follows. Complete the report and comment on the results.

Period	1	2	3	4	5	Total
Planned input	50	55	60	65	65	
Actual input	40	50	55	60	65	
Deviation						
Planned output	50	55	60	65	65	
Actual output	50	50	55	60	65	
Deviation						
Backlog	10					

14-14. Kim Johnson, R.N., the charge nurse of the antepartum ward of City Hospital in Burtonsville, Maryland, needs help in scheduling the nurse workforce for next week.
   a. Create an employee schedule that will meet the demand requirements and guarantee each nurse two days off per week.
   b. Revise the schedule so that the two days off are consecutive.

Days of Week	M	T	W	Th	F	Sa	Su
Min. no of nurses	3	3	4	5	4	3	3
Kim Johnson							
Tom Swann							
Flo Coligny							
Shelly Betts							
Phuong Truong							

14-15. Rosemary Hanes needs help in scheduling the volunteers working at the local crisis pregnancy center. Create a work schedule that will meet the demand requirements, given that a volunteer will only work two days per week. Try to make the work days consecutive.

Days of Week	M	T	W	Th	F	Sa	Su
Min. no. of volunteers	4	3	2	3	6	4	2
Rosemary Hayhes							
Albert Taglieri							
Richard White							
Gail Cooke							
Shelly Black							
Karen Romero							
Jamie Dixson							
Susie Deyo							
Peter Bradley							
Rachel Hatcher							
C. J. Adams							
Sally Beck							

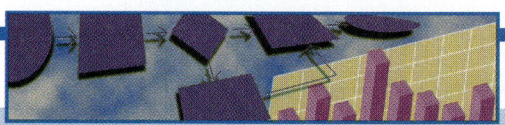

CASE PROBLEM

From a Different Perspective

"And do you have the answer to Problem 6, Pete?" asked Professor Grasso.

"Yes sir, I have the answer according to the textbook, but I'm not sure I get it," replied Pete.

"You don't understand how to get the solution?"

"Oh, I understand the numbers, but I don't know what they're good for. Where I work, nobody ever 'sequences' anything. You don't have time to calculate things like slack and critical ratio. You do what's next in line or on top of the stack, unless you see a red tag on something that needs to be rushed through. Or maybe you run what's most like what you've just finished working on so the machine doesn't have to be changed. Or you run what can get done the fastest because when you produce more you get paid more."

"Pete, it sounds to me like you *are* using sequencing rules—FCFS, highest priority, minimum setup, and SPT."

"Maybe you're right, but there's still something that bothers me. If you're going to go to all the trouble to rearrange a stack of jobs, you'd want more information than what we're working with."

"What do you mean?"

"I mean, there's no use rushing a job at one station to let it sit and wait at the next. It's like those maniacs who break their neck to pass you on the road, but they never get anywhere. A few minutes later you're right behind them at a stoplight."

"I see."

"You need some way of looking at the entire job, where it's going next, what resources it's going to use, if it has to be assembled with something else, things like that."

"You've got a point, Pete. Why don't you give us a 'real' example we can work with? You talk, I'll write it on the board."

(Continued)

Pete talked for about twenty more minutes, and when he was finished, Professor Grasso had the following diagram on the board:

"Okay, class, let's take this home and work on it. You have one of each machine type 1, 2, and 3. There's no inventory on hand and nothing on order. See how quickly you can produce 50 units of product X. Best schedule gets 5 extra points on the final exam."

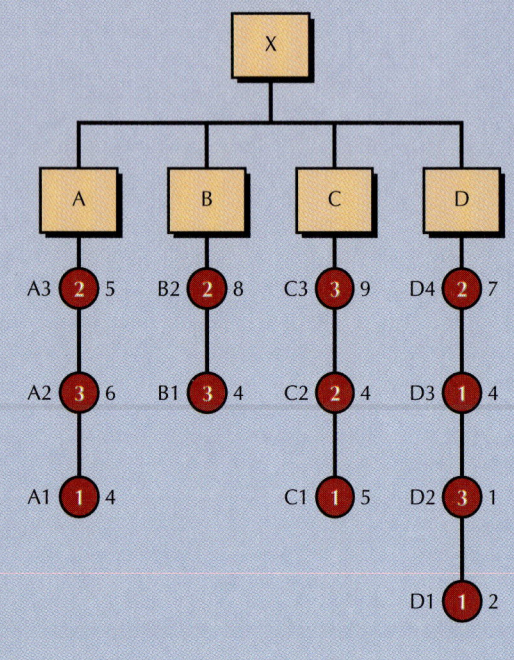

References

Baker, K., and M. Magazine. "Workforce Scheduling with Cyclic Demands and Days-Off Constraints." *Management Science* 24, no. 2 (October 1977): 161–67.

Conway, R., W. Maxwell, and L. Miller. *Theory of Scheduling.* Reading, Mass.: Addison-Wesley, 1967.

Goldratt, E. *What Is This Thing Called Theory of Constraints and How Should It Be Implemented?* Croton-on-Hudson, N.Y.: North River Press, 1990.

Goldratt, E., and J. Cox. *The Goal: Excellence in Manufacturing.* Croton-on-Hudson, N.Y.: North River Press, 1984.

Huang, P., L. Moore, and R. Russell. "Workload versus Scheduling Policies in a Dual-Resource Constrained Job Shop." *Computers and Operations Research* 11, no. 1 (1984): 37–47.

Russell, R., and B. W. Taylor. "An Evaluation of Sequencing Rules for an Assembly Shop." *Decision Sciences* 16, no. 2 (1985): 196–212.

Tersine, R. J. *Production/Operations Management: Concepts, Structure, and Analysis.* New York: Elsevier-North Holland, 1985.

Umble, M., and M. L. Srikanth. *Synchronous Manufacturing: Principles for World Class Excellence.* Cincinnati: South-Western Publishing Co., 1990.

Vollman, T., W. Berry, and D. C. Whybark. *Manufacturing Planning and Control Systems.* Homewood, Ill.: Irwin, 1992.

Xudong, H., R. Russell, and J. Dickey. "Workload Analysis Expert System and Optimizer." *Proceedings of the Seventh International Congress of Cybernetics and Systems,* Vol. 1, London (September 1987): 68–72.

15

Just-in-Time Systems

JIT Smooths the Flow

Ford's assembly plant in Avon Lake, Ohio, assembles vans and minivans, including Nissan's Quest. Inventory is limited to a few hours on some items, a few days for others. Sixty-five dock doors are strategically located around the building for delivery of material as close to its point of use as possible.

Tires and wheels, a major inventory and handling problem during automobile assembly, come already assembled. Bridgestone creates the assemblies (sometimes using General and Goodyear tires) and delivers them several times a day to the plant arranged in the sequence they will be used, at the proper height for installation. Every fifth tire is a spare.

Seats are manufactured by a local supplier located 25 miles away. Ford broadcasts the "build" sequence to the supplier, who assigns a sequence number to each delivery—no bar codes are needed. The driver delivers a trailer with enough seats for 22 vehicles, about one hour's worth of production. Seats are fed from the truck by conveyors to the assembly line in perfect style and color sequence, with no human intervention. A photo sensor determines when the last seat has been unloaded and when to begin loading empty pallets back onto the empty trailer.

Tires and seats are in constant use. Their only storage time is on the delivery truck. Smaller parts are stored along the assembly line in a mini-ASRS (automatic storage and retrieval system) to be "exposed" as the parts are needed for a particu-

Assembly lines traditionally were set up to process only one product model at a time. The machines and workers could then be specialized to the item produced. Production of another model would require the line to shut down and retool. With the advent of JIT, mixed models could be produced on the same assembly line at the same time. This required reductions in changeover times from one model to another and more flexible workers and machines. Notice the different color trucks coming off this mixed-model assembly line at Nissan's Smyrna, Tennessee, plant.

lar assembly at a particular workstation. The entire system supports the continuous flow of material through the plant—JIT style.[1]

Taiichi Ohno, a former shop manager and eventual vice president of <u>Toyota Motor Company</u>, is the individual most credited with the development of just-in-time. **Just-in-time (JIT)** is a U.S. term coined to describe the Toyota production system, widely recognized today as one of the most efficient manufacturing operations in the world. In its simplest form, JIT requires only necessary units be provided in necessary quantities at necessary times. Producing one unit extra is as bad as being one unit short. Completing production one day early is as bad as finishing one day late. Items are supplied only when needed, or "just in time."

JIT involves producing only what is needed, when it is needed.

This hardly seems the basis of a revolution in manufacturing, but the concept is deceptively simple. If you produce only what you need when you need it, then there is no room for error. For JIT to work, many fundamental elements must be in place—steady production, flexible resources, extremely high quality, no machine breakdowns, reliable suppliers, quick machine setups, and lots of discipline to maintain the other elements.

Just-in-time is both a philosophy and an integrated system for production management that evolved slowly through a trial-and-error process over a span of more than fifteen years. There was no master plan or blueprint for JIT. Ohno describes the development of JIT as follows:

JIT is a philosophy and an integrated management system.

> By actually trying, various problems became known. As such problems became gradually clear, they taught me the direction of the next move. I think that we can only understand how all of these pieces fit together in hindsight.[2]

In this chapter, we explore the pieces of JIT and try to discover how they came to be a part of Ohno's integrated management system, known as just-in-time. We also explore the benefits of JIT and JIT implementation. We conclude with a discussion of JIT in services.

Basic Elements of JIT

In the 1950s, the entire Japanese automobile industry produced 30,000 vehicles, fewer than a half day's production for U.S. automakers. With such low levels of demand, the principles of mass production that worked so well for U.S. manufacturers could not be applied in Japan. Further, the Japanese were short on capital and storage space. So it seems natural that efforts to improve performance (and stay solvent) would center on reducing that asset that soaks up both funds and space—inventory. What is significant is that a system originally designed to reduce inventory levels eventually became a system for continually improving all aspects of manufacturing operations. The stage was set for this evolution by the president of Toyota, Eiji Toyoda, who gave a mandate to his people to "eliminate waste." **Waste** was defined as "anything other than the minimum amount of equipment, materials, parts, space, and time which are absolutely essential to add value to the product."[3] Examples of waste in operations are shown in Figure 15.1.

JIT's mandate: Eliminate waste.

Waste is anything other than that which adds value to the product or service.

[1] Based on C. E. Witt, "Quality Manufacturing Drives New Minivan Plant," *Material Handling Engineering* (July 1992): 37–39.

[2] K. Suzaki, *The New Manufacturing Challenge* (New York: Free Press, 1985), p. 250.

[3] Ibid., pp. 8–9.

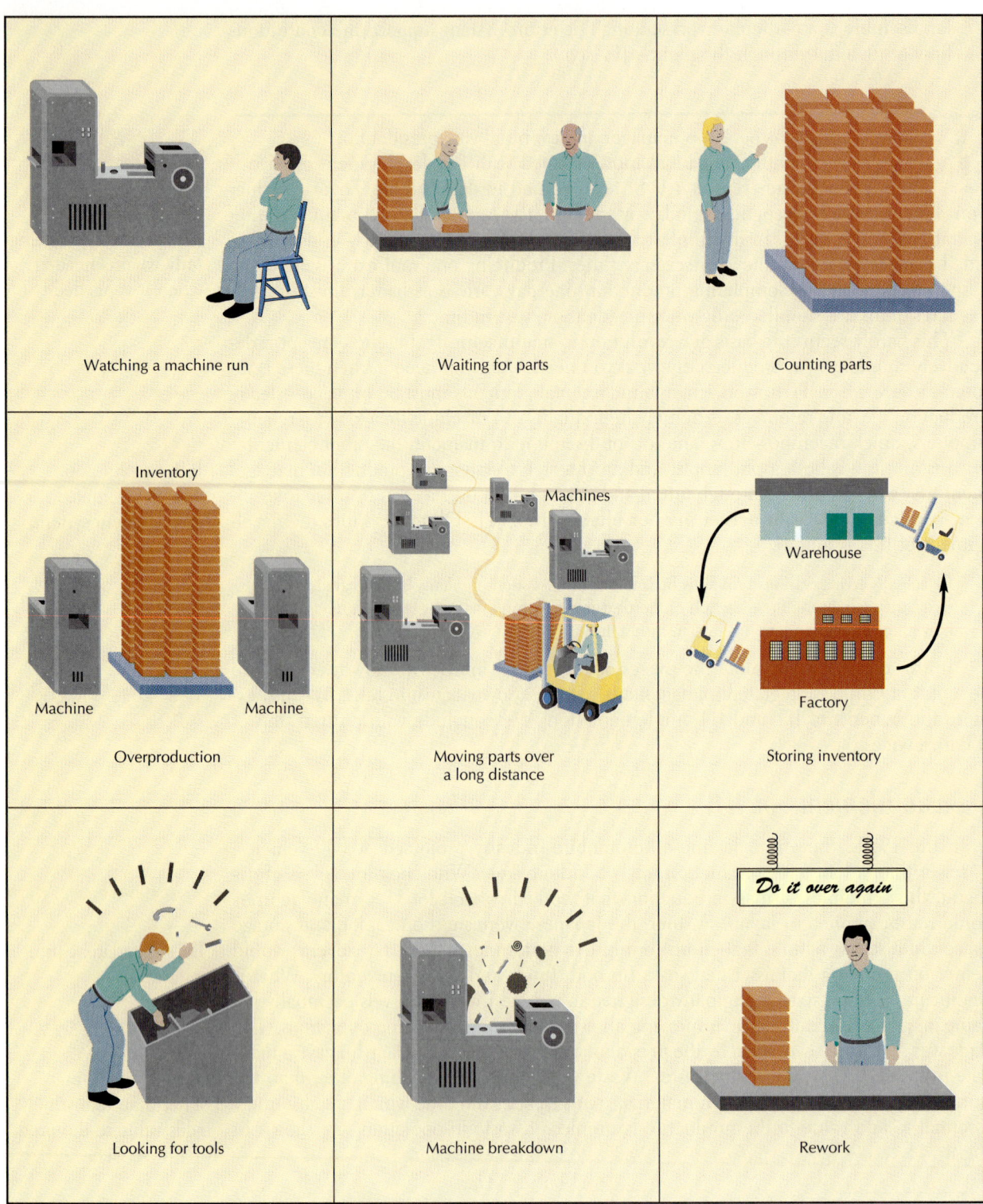

FIGURE 15.1   **Waste in Operations**

The JIT production system is the result of the mandate to eliminate waste. It is composed of the following elements:

1. Flexible resources
2. Cellular layouts
3. Pull production system
4. Kanban production control
5. Small-lot production
6. Quick setups
7. Uniform production levels
8. Quality at the source
9. Total productive maintenance
10. Supplier networks

Basic elements of JIT

Let's explore each of these elements and determine how they work in concert.[4]

Flexible Resources

The concept of flexible resources, in the form of **multifunctional workers** and **general-purpose machines,** is recognized as a key element of JIT, but most people do not realize that it was one of the first elements to fall into place. Taiichi Ohno had transferred to Toyota from Toyoda textile mills with no knowledge of (or preconceived notions about) automobile manufacturing. His first attempt to eliminate waste (not unlike U.S. managers) concentrated on worker productivity. Borrowing heavily from U.S. time and motion studies, he set out to analyze every job and every machine in his shop. He quickly noted a distinction between the operating time of a machine and the operating time of the worker. Initially, he asked each worker to operate two machines rather than one. To make this possible, he located the machines in parallel lines or in L-formations. After a time, he asked workers to operate three or four machines arranged in a U-shape. The machines were no longer of the same type (as in a job shop layout) but represented a series of processes common to a group of parts (i.e., a cellular layout).

The operation of different, multiple machines required additional training for workers and specific rotation schedules. Figure 15.2 shows a standard operating routine for an individual worker. The solid lines represent operator processing time (e.g., loading, unloading, or setting up a machine), the dashed lines represent machine processing time, and the squiggly lines represent walking time for the operator from machine to machine. The time required for the worker to complete one pass through the operations assigned is called the operator *cycle time.*

With single workers operating multiple machines, the machines themselves also required some adjustments. Limit switches were installed to turn off machines automatically after each operation was completed. Changes in jigs and fixtures allowed machines to hold a workpiece in place, rather than rely on the presence of an operator. Extra tools and fixtures were purchased and placed at their point of use so that operators didn't have to leave their stations to retrieve them when needed. By the time Ohno was finished with this phase of his improvement efforts, it was possible for one worker to operate as many as seventeen machines (the average was five to ten machines).

Multifunctional workers perform more than one job.

General-purpose machines perform several basic functions.

---

[4] Much of the material in these sections is adapted from Chapter 5 in Michael Cusomano's text, *The Japanese Automobile Industry* (Cambridge, Mass.: Howard University Press), 1985.

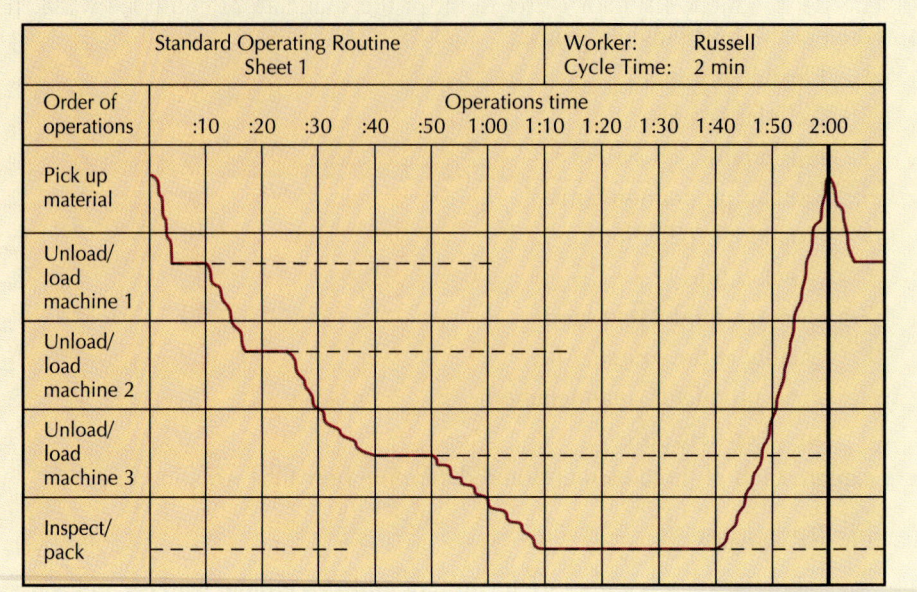

FIGURE 15.2 Standard Operating Routine for a Worker

The flexibility of labor brought about by Ohno's changes prompted a switch to more flexible machines. Thus, although other manufacturers were interested in purchasing more specialized automated equipment, Toyota preferred small, general-purpose machines. A general-purpose lathe, for example, might be used to bore holes in an engine block and then do other drilling, milling, and threading operations at the same station. The waste of movement to other machines, setting up other machines, and waiting at other machines was eliminated.

Cellular Layouts

Manufacturing cells are comprised of dissimilar machines brought together to manufacture a family of parts.

While it is true that Ohno first reorganized his shop into **manufacturing cells** to utilize labor more efficiently, the flexibility of the new layout proved to be fundamental to the effectiveness of JIT as a whole. The concept of cellular layouts did not originate with Ohno. It was first described by a U.S. engineer in the 1920s, but it was Ohno's inspired application of the idea that brought it to the attention of the world. We discussed cellular layouts (and the concept of group technology on which it is based) in Chapter 7. Let's review some of that material here.

Most cells are U-shaped.

Cells group dissimilar machines together to process a family of parts with similar shapes or processing requirements. The layout of machines within the cell resembles a small assembly line and is usually U-shaped. Work is moved within the cell, ideally one unit at a time, from one process to the next by a worker as he or she walks around the cell in a prescribed path. Figure 15.3 shows a typical manufacturing cell with worker routes.

Cycle time is adjusted by changing worker paths.

Work normally flows through the cell in one direction and experiences little waiting. In a one-person cell, the cycle time of the cell is determined by the time it takes for the worker to complete his or her path through the cell. This means that, although different items produced in the cell may take different amounts of time to complete, the time between successive items leaving the cell remains virtually the same because the worker's path remains the same. Thus, changes of product mix within the cell are easy to accommodate. Changes in volume can be handled by adding or subtracting

THE COMPETITIVE EDGE

Changes at Corning

www.prenhall.com/russell

Until recently, Corning held the patents for an important component of catalytic converters, a honeycombed ceramic part. Typical of many American firms, Corning could create innovative designs but could not manufacture them competitively. So, for years, production of the part had been licensed to a Japanese company, NGK Insulators. With the patient due to expire in the early 1990s, Corning decided it wanted to challenge NGK for the catalytic converter market. Corning reopened a mothballed plant in Blacksburg, Virginia, and used JIT principles to set up a new manufacturing system.

Because each automobile factory orders catalytic components of its own design, the volume of each order is not large. That means machines need to changeover quickly from one model to another, and workers on the assembly lines need to perform different tasks. This requirement for flexibility of both machines and labor led to radically different job structures for Corning workers and management.

Imagine a plant with no time clocks, one manager per 60 employees, and blanket authority for all employees to sign purchase orders up to $500. The workers, classified only as operations associates or maintenance engineers, work in self-managed teams. (This is in contrast to Corning's other plants, which have 50 or so job classifications.) They learn multiple skills, rotate through as many as 15 different jobs, and are paid based on the skills they have acquired, rather than their hourly production. They are also eligible for bonuses based on plant performance.

Corning decided to lean more on employee involvement than manufacturing technology. Says the plant manager, "There were places we could have robotized, but we decided against it, because we wanted humans to give us the critical feedback." For example, the extrusion process for ceramics uses computers and sensors to display crucial information but relies on workers to decide whether to change the kiln temperature or speed of flow.

The company is striving for a no-layoff policy and has contracted out such jobs as security and custodial care so those jobs can serve as a backup for production workers should sales fall. Job training includes statistical process control, machine maintenance, and shipping and receiving procedures. Workers who fail to complete the two-year training program face dismissal.

Corning pursued an aggressive strategy based on resource flexibility, and it paid off. The company currently supplies catalytic components to Japanese and U.S. automakers.

SOURCES: Based on "Beating Japan at Its Own Game," *New York Times*, July 16, 1989; Amal Kumar Naj, "Some Manufacturers Drop Efforts to Adopt Japanese Techniques," *Wall Street Journal*, May 7, 1993; and Mark Clothier, "It's not Just Corning Parts that are in Demand . . .," *The Roanoke Times*, May 4, 1997.

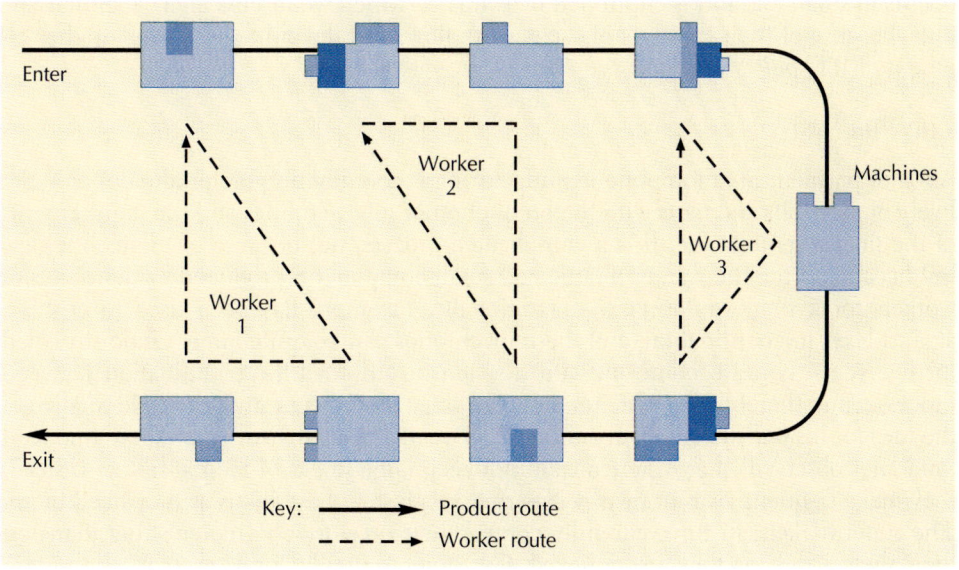

FIGURE 15.3 **Manufacturing Cell with Worker Routes**

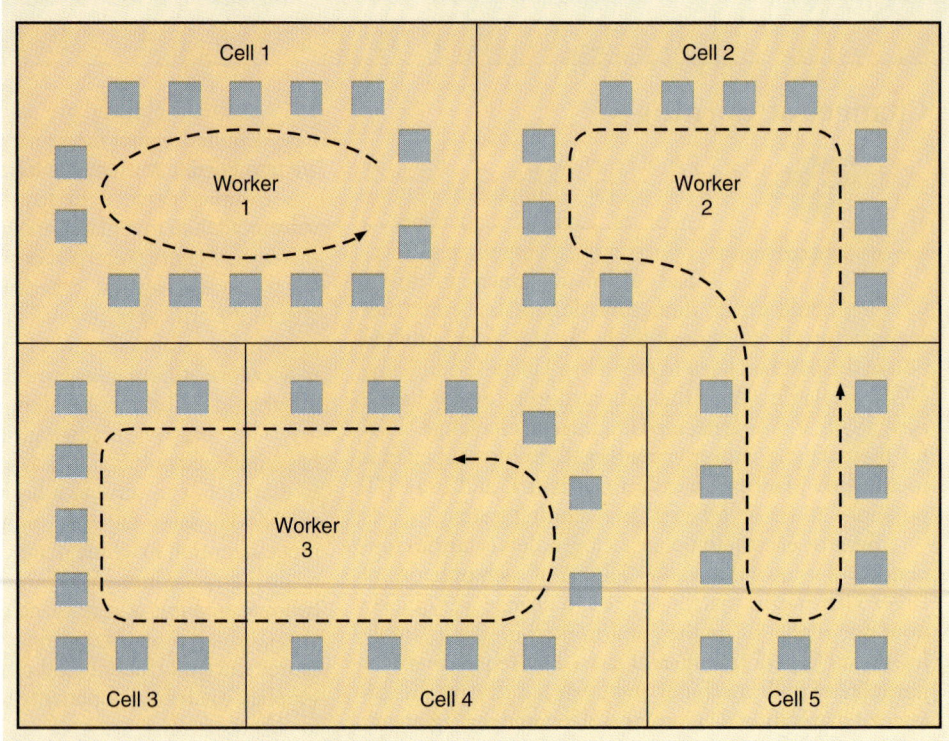

FIGURE 15.4 **Worker Routes Lengthened as Volume Decreases**

workers to the cell and adjusting their walking routes accordingly. Figure 15.4 shows how worker routes can be adjusted in a system of integrated cells.

Because cells produce similar items, setup time requirements are low and lot sizes can be reduced. Movement of output from the cells to subassembly or assembly lines occurs in small lots and is controlled by kanbans (which we discuss later). Cellular layouts, because of their manageable size, work flow, and flexibility, facilitate another element of JIT, *pull production*.

The Pull System

A major problem in automobile manufacturing is coordinating the production and delivery of materials and parts with the production of subassemblies and the requirements of the final assembly line. It is a complicated process, not because of the technology, but because of the thousands of large and small components produced by thousands of workers for a single automobile. Traditionally, inventory has been used to cushion against laxes in coordination, and these inventories can be quite large. Ohno struggled for five years trying to come up with a system to improve the coordination between processes and thereby eliminate the need for large amounts of inventory. He finally got the idea for his *pull* system from another American classic, the supermarket. Ohno read (and later observed) that Americans do not keep large stocks of food at home. Instead, they make frequent visits to nearby supermarkets to purchase items as they need them. The supermarkets, in turn, carefully control their inventory by replenishing items on their shelves only as they are removed. Customers actually "pull through" the system the items they need, and supermarkets do not order more items than can be sold.

Applying this concept to manufacturing requires a reversal of the normal process/information flow, called a *push* system. In a **push system,** a schedule is prepared in advance for a series of workstations, and each workstation pushes its completed work to the next station. With the **pull system,** workers go back to previous stations and take only those parts or materials they need and can process immediately. When their output has been taken, workers at the previous station know it is time to start producing more, and they replenish the exact quantity that the subsequent station just took away. If their output is not taken, workers at the previous station simply stop production; no excess is produced. This system forces operations to work in coordination with one another. It prevents overproduction and underproduction; only necessary quantities are produced. "Necessary" is not defined by a schedule that specifies what ought to be needed; rather, it is defined by the operation of the shop floor, complete with unanticipated occurrences and variations in performance.

Although the concept of pull production seems simple, it can be difficult to implement because it is so different from normal scheduling procedures. After several years of experimenting with the pull system, Ohno found it necessary to introduce *kanbans* to exercise more control over the pull process on the shop floor.

Push systems rely on a predetermined schedule.

Pull systems rely on customer requests.

Kanban Production Control System

Kanban is the Japanese word for card. In the pull system, each kanban corresponds to a standard quantity of production or size of container. A kanban contains basic information such as part number, brief description, type of container, unit load (i.e., quantity per container), preceding station (where it came from), and subsequent station (where it goes to). Sometimes the kanban is color-coded to indicate raw materials or other stages of manufacturing. The information on the kanban does not change during production. The same kanban can rotate back and forth between preceding and subsequent workstations.

Kanbans are closely associated with the fixed-quantity inventory system we discussed in Chapter 12. Recall that in the fixed-quantity system, a certain quantity, Q, is ordered whenever the stock on hand falls below a reorder point. The reorder point is determined so that demand can be met while an order for new material is being processed.

A **kanban** is a card that corresponds to a standard quantity of production (usually a container size).

This supplier Kanban attached to a container rotates between Purdenso Manufacturing and a Toyota assembly plant. The part number, description, and quantity per container appear in the center of the card, directly beneath the Kanban number. Notice the container holds four air flow meter assemblies. The store address in the upper left hand corner specifies where the full container is to be delivered. The line side address in the upper right hand corner specifies where the empty container is to be picked up. The lower left hand corner identifies the preceding process (the assemblies come from Purdenso) and the lower right hand corner identifies the subsequent process (N2). Barcoding the information on the card speeds processing and increases the accuracy of production and financial records.

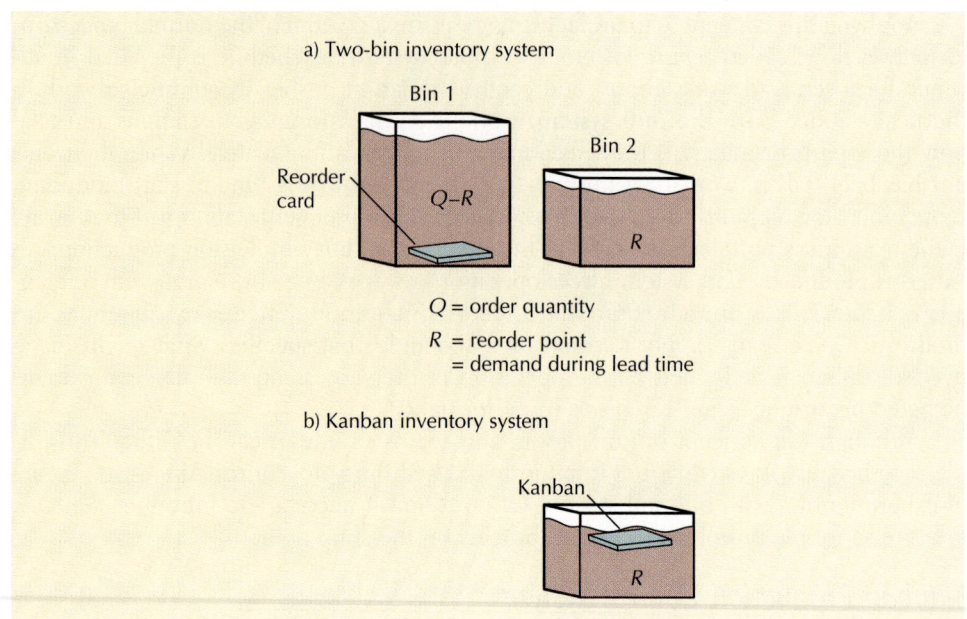

FIGURE 15.5   The Origin of Kanban

Thus, the reorder point corresponds to demand during lead time. A visual fixed-quantity system, called the *two-bin system*, illustrates the concept nicely. Referring to Figure 15.5(a), two bins are maintained for each item. The first (and usually larger bin) contains the order quantity minus the reorder point, the second bin contains the reorder point quantity. At the bottom of the first bin is an order card that describes the item and specifies the supplier and the quantity that is to be ordered. When the first bin is empty, the card is removed and sent to the purchasing department to order a new supply. While the order is being filled, the quantity in the second bin is used. If everything goes as planned, when the second bin is empty, the new order will arrive and both bins will be filled again.

Ohno looked at this system and liked its simplicity, but he could not understand the purpose of the first bin. As shown in Figure 15.5(b), by eliminating the first bin and placing the order card (which he called a *kanban*) at the top of the second bin, $Q - R$ inventory could be eliminated. In this system, an order is continually in transit. When the new order arrives, the supplier is reissued the same kanban to fill the order again. The only inventory that is maintained is the amount needed to cover usage until the next order can be processed. This concept is the basis for the kanban system.

Kanbans do not make the schedule of production; they maintain the discipline of pull production by authorizing the production and movement of materials. If there is no kanban, there is no production. If there is no kanban, there is no movement of material. There are many different types and variations of kanbans. The most sophisticated is probably the dual kanban system used by Toyota which uses two types of kanbans: *production kanbans* and *withdrawal kanbans*. As their names imply, a **production kanban** is a card authorizing production of goods, and a **withdrawal kanban** is a card authorizing the movement of goods. Each kanban is physically attached to a container. Let's follow the example in Figure 15.6(a) to see how they work.

1. Process B receives a production kanban. It must produce enough of the item requested to fill the empty container to which the production kanban is attached.

Margin notes:

Kanbans were derived from the *two-bin* inventory system.

Kanbans maintain the discipline of pull production.

A **production kanban** is a card authorizing production of goods.

A **withdrawal kanban** authorizes the movement of goods.

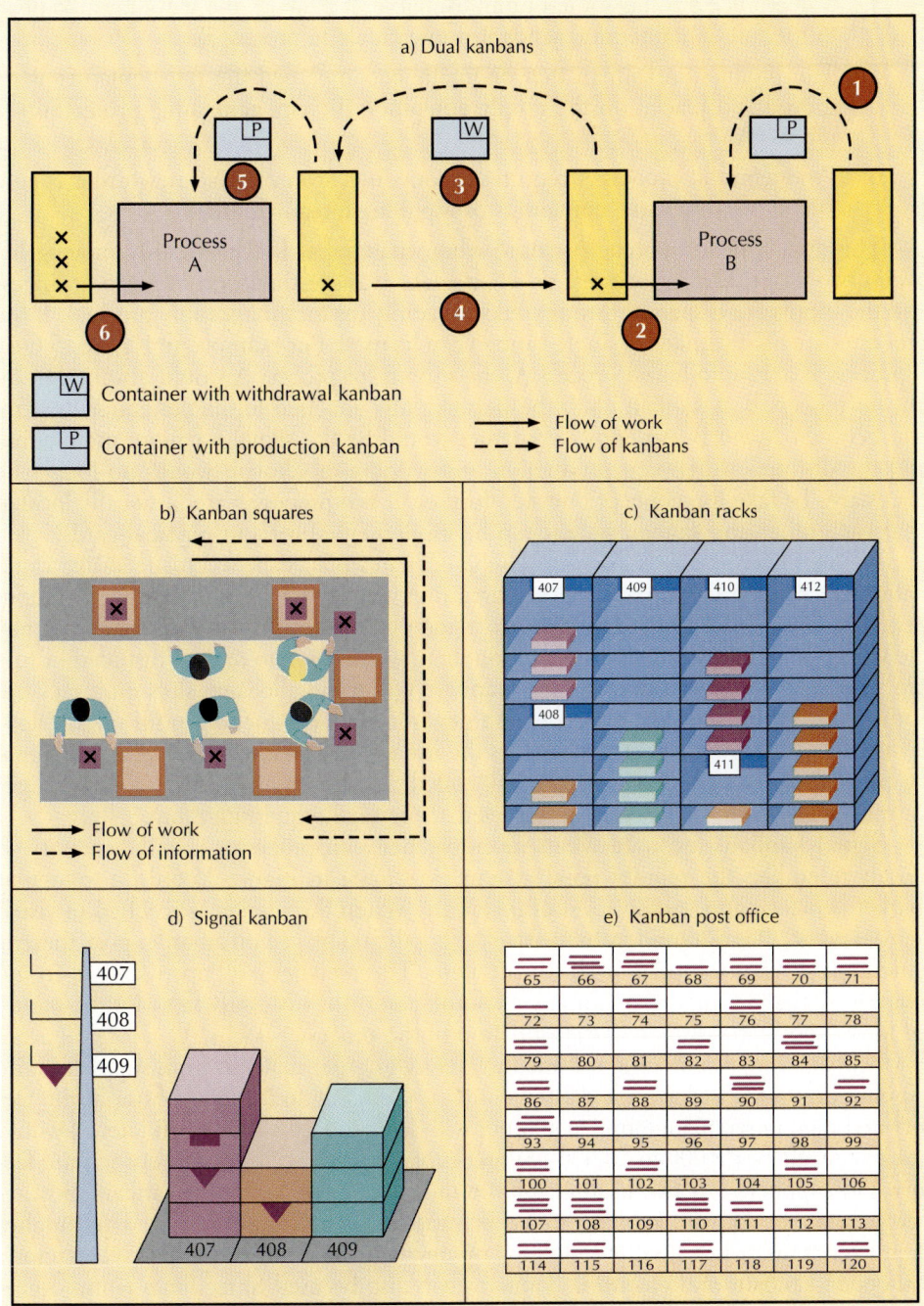

FIGURE 15.6 Types of Kanbans

2. To complete the requirements of production, process B uses a container of inputs and generates a request for more input from the preceding workstation, process A.

3. The request for more input items takes the form of a withdrawal kanban sent to process A.

4. Since process A has some output available, it attaches the withdrawal kanban to the full container and sends it immediately to process B.

5. The production kanban that originally accompanied the full container is removed and placed on the empty container, thereby generating production at process A.

6. Production at process A requires a container of inputs. No new order is generated because three containers of input are already on hand.

There are many variations of kanbans.

The dual kanban approach is used when material is not necessarily moving between two consecutive processes, or when there is more than one input to a process and the inputs are dispersed throughout the facility (as for an assembly process). If the processes are tightly linked, a single kanban can be used. For example, in Figure 15.6(a), if process B always followed process A, the output for process A would also be the input for process B. A kanban could be permanently attached to the containers that rotate between A and B. An empty container would be the signal for more production, and the distinction between production and withdrawal kanban would no longer be necessary. To take the concept one step further, if two processes are physically located near each other, the kanban system can be implemented *without* physical cards.

A **kanban square** is a marked area designated to hold items.

Figure 15.6(b) shows the use of kanban squares placed between successive workstations. A **kanban square** is a marked area that will hold a certain number of output items (usually one or two). If the kanban square following his or her process is empty, the worker knows it is time to begin production again. *Kanban racks*, illustrated in Figure 15.6(c), can be used in a similar manner. When the allocated slots on a rack are empty, workers know it is time to begin a new round of production to fill up the slots. If the distance between stations prohibits the use of kanban squares or racks, the signal for production can be a colored golf ball rolled down a tube, a flag on a post, a light flashing on a board, or an electronic or verbal message requesting more.

A **signal kanban** is a triangular kanban used to signal production at the previous workstation.

Signal kanbans are used when inventory between processes is still necessary. It closely resembles the reorder point system. As shown in Figure 15.6(d), a triangular marker is placed at a certain level of inventory. When the marker is reached (a visual reorder point), it is removed from the stack of goods and placed on an order post, thereby generating a replenishment order for the item. The rectangular-shaped kanban in the diagram is called a **material kanban.** In some cases it is necessary to order the *material* for a process in advance of the initiation of the process.

A **material kanban** is used to order material in advance of a process.

Supplier kanbans rotate between the factory and suppliers.

Kanbans can also be used outside the factory to order material from suppliers. The supplier brings the order (e.g., a filled container) directly to its point of use in the factory and then picks up an empty container with kanban to fill and return later. It would not be unusual for 5,000 to 10,000 of these *supplier kanbans* to rotate between the factory and suppliers. To handle this volume of transactions, a kind of kanban "post office" can be set up, with kanbans sorted by supplier, as in Figure 15.6(e). The supplier then checks his or her "mailbox" to pick up new orders before returning to the factory. Bar-coded kanbans and electronic kanbans can also be used to facilitate communication between customer and supplier.

It is easy to get caught up with the technical aspects of kanbans and lose sight of the objective of the pull system, which is to reduce inventory levels. The kanban system is actually very similar to the reorder point system. The difference is in application. The reorder point system attempts to create a permanent ordering policy, whereas the kanban system encourages the continual reduction of inventory. We can see how that occurs by examining the formula for determining the number of kanbans needed to control the production of a particular item.

$$\text{No. of kanbans} = \frac{\text{average demand during lead time} + \text{safety stock}}{\text{container size}}$$

$$N = \frac{dL + S}{C}$$

where

N = number of kanbans or containers

d = average number of units demanded over some time period

L = lead time; the time it takes to replenish an order (expressed in the same time terms as demand)

S = safety stock; usually given as a percentage of demand during lead time but can be based on service level and variance of demand during lead time (as in Chapter 12)

C = container size

The number of kanbans needed can be calculated from demand and lead time information.

To force the improvement process, the container size is usually much smaller than the demand during lead time. At Toyota, containers can hold at most 10 percent of a day's demand. This allows the number of kanbans (i.e., containers) to be reduced one at a time. The fewer number of kanbans (and corresponding lower level of inventory) causes problems in the system to become visible. Workers and managers then attempt to solve the problems that have been identified.

EXAMPLE
15.1

Determining the Number of Kanbans

Julie Hurling works in a cosmetic factory filling, capping, and labeling bottles. She is asked to process an average of 150 bottles per hour through her work cell. If one kanban is attached to every container, a container holds 25 bottles, it takes 30 minutes to receive new bottles from the previous workstation, and the factory uses a safety stock factor of 10 percent, how many kanbans are needed for the bottling process?

SOLUTION:

Given:

d = 150 bottles per hour

L = 30 minutes = 0.5 hour

S = 0.10 (150 × 0.5) = 7.5

C = 25 bottles

Then,

$$N = \frac{dL + S}{C} = \frac{(150 \times 0.5) + 7.5}{25}$$

$$= \frac{75 + 7.5}{25} = 3.3 \text{ kanbans or containers}$$

We can round either up or down (3 containers would force us to improve operations, and 4 would allow some slack).

Small-Lot Production

Small-lot production
provides many bene-
fits.

Small-lot production requires less space and capital investment than systems that incur large inventories. By producing small amounts at a time, processes can be physically moved closer together and transportation between stations can be simplified. In small-lot production, quality problems are easier to detect and workers show less tendency to let poor quality pass (as they might in a system that is producing huge amounts of an item anyway). Lower inventory levels make processes more dependent on each other. This is beneficial because it reveals errors and bottlenecks more quickly and gives workers an opportunity to solve them.

The analogy of water flowing over a bed or rocks is useful here. As shown in Figure 15.7, the inventory level is like the level of water. It hides problems but allows for smooth sailing. When the inventory level is reduced, the problems (or rocks) are exposed. After the exposed rocks are removed from the river, the boat can again progress, this time more quickly than before.

Although it is true that a company can produce in small lot sizes without using the pull system or kanbans, from experience we know that small-lot production in a push system is difficult to coordinate. Similarly, using large lot sizes with a pull system and kanbans would not be advisable. Let's look more closely at the relationship between small lot sizes, the pull system, and kanbans.

From the kanban formula, it becomes clear that a reduction in the number of kanbans (given a constant container size) requires a corresponding reduction in safety stock or in lead time itself. The need for safety stock can be reduced by making demand and supply more certain. Flexible resources allow the system to adapt more readily to unanticipated changes in demand. Demand fluctuations can also be controlled through closer contact with customers and better forecasting systems. Deficiencies in supply can be controlled through eliminating mistakes, producing only good units, and reducing or eliminating machine breakdowns.

Lead time is typically made up of four components:

- Processing time,
- Move time,
- Waiting time, and
- Setup time.

Processing time can be reduced by reducing the number of items processed and the efficiency or speed of the machine or worker. *Move time* can be decreased if machines are moved closer together, the method of movement is simplified, routings are standardized, or the need for movement is eliminated. *Waiting time* can be reduced through better scheduling of materials, workers, and machines and sufficient capacity. In many companies, however, lengthy *setup times* are the biggest bottleneck. Reduction of setup time is an important part of JIT.

Quick Setups

Several processes in automobile manufacturing defy production in small lots because of the enormous amount of time required to set up the machines. Stamping is a good example. First, a large roll of sheet steel is run through a blanking press to produce stacks of flat blanks slightly larger than the size of the desired parts. Then, the blanks are inserted into huge stamping presses that contain a matched set of upper and lower dies. When the dies are held together under thousands of pounds of pressure, a three-dimensional shape emerges, such as a car door or fender. Because the dies weigh sev-

a) Inventory hides problems.

Lengthy
setups

Poor
quality

Machine
breakdowns

Inefficient
layout

Bad
design

Unreliable
supplier

b) Lower levels of inventory expose problems.

Lengthy
setups

Poor
quality

Machine
breakdowns

Inefficient
layout

Bad
design

Unreliable
supplier

FIGURE 15.7 JIT Making Problems Visible

eral tons each and have to be aligned with exact precision, die changes typically take an entire day to complete.

Obviously, manufacturers are reluctant to change dies often. Ford, for example, might produce 500,000 right door panels and store them in inventory before switching dies to produce left door panels. Some Western manufacturers have found it easier to purchase several sets of presses and dedicate them to stamping out a specific part for months or years. Due to capital constraints, that was not an option for Toyota. Instead, Ohno began simplifying die-changing techniques. Convinced that major improvements could be made, a consultant, Shigeo Shingo, was hired to study die setup systemati-

www.prenhall.com/russell

cally, to reduce changeover times further, and to teach these techniques to production workers and Toyota suppliers.

Shingo proved to be a genius at the task. He reduced setup time on a 1,000-ton press from six hours to three minutes using a system he called *SMED* (single-minute exchange of dies). SMED is based on the following principles, which can be applied to any type of setup:

1. *Separate internal setup from external setup.* **Internal setup** has to be performed while the machine is stopped; it cannot take place until the machine has finished with the previous operation. **External setup,** on the other hand, can be performed in advance, while the machine is running. By the time a machine has finished processing its current operation, the worker should have completed the external setup and be ready to perform the internal setup for the next operation. Applying this concept alone can reduce setup time by 30 percent to 50 percent.

2. *Convert internal setup to external setup.* This process involves making sure that the operating conditions, such as gathering tools and fixtures, preheating an injection mold, centering a die, or standardizing die heights, are prepared in advance.

3. *Streamline all aspects of setup.* External setup activities can be reduced by organizing the workplace properly, locating tools and dies near their points of use, and keeping machines and fixtures in good repair. Internal setup activities can be reduced by simplifying or eliminating adjustments. Examples include precoding desired settings, using quick fasteners and locator pins, preventing misalignment, eliminating tools, and making movements easier. Figure 15.8 provides some common analogies for these improvements.

SMED delineates principles for quick setups.

Internal setup can be performed only when the machine is stopped; **external setup** can be done while the machine is operating.

In this photo, a worker sets up a drill press for the next job while the machine is stopped. This is known as an internal setup. In an external setup, the process is not interrupted by setup activities. Setup time can be significantly reduced by converting internal setups to external setups.

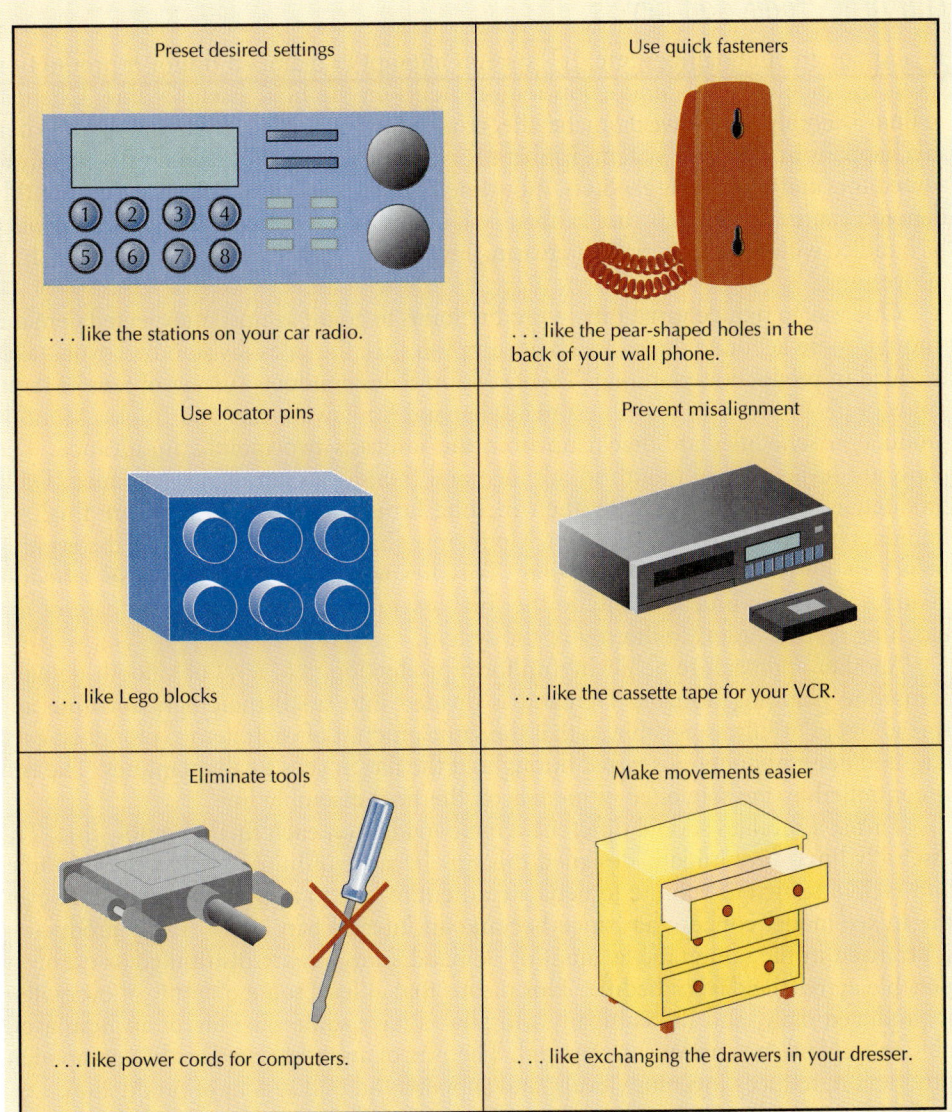

FIGURE 15.8   Some Common Techniques for Reducing Setup Time

4. *Perform setup activities in parallel or eliminate them entirely.* Adding an extra person to the setup team can reduce setup time considerably. In most cases, two people can perform a setup in less than half the time needed by a single person. In addition, standardizing components, parts, and raw materials can reduce and sometimes eliminate setup requirements.

In order to view the setup process objectively, it is useful to assign the task of setup-time reduction to a team of workers and engineers. Videotaping the setup in progress often helps the team generate ideas for improvement. Time and motion study principles (like those we discussed in Chapter 8) can be applied. After the new setup procedures have been agreed upon, they need to be practiced until they are perfected. One only has to view the pit crews at the Indy 500 to realize that quick changeovers have to be orchestrated and practiced.

Uniform Production Levels

Uniform production levels result from smoothing production requirements.

In addition to eliminating waste, JIT systems attempt to maintain **uniform production levels** by smoothing the production requirements on the final assembly line. Changes in final assembly often have dramatic effects on component production upstream. When this happens in a kanban system, kanbans for certain parts will circulate very quickly at some times and very slowly at others. Adjustments of plus or minus 10 percent in monthly demand can be absorbed by the kanban system, but wider demand fluctuations cannot be handled without substantially increasing inventory levels or scheduling large amounts of overtime.[5]

Reduce variability with more accurate forecasts.

One way to reduce variability in production is to guard against unexpected demand through more accurate forecasts. To accomplish this, the sales division of Toyota takes the lead in production planning. Toyota Motor Sales conducts surveys of tens of thousands of people twice a year to estimate demand for Toyota cars and trucks. Monthly production schedules are drawn up from the forecasts two months in advance. The plans are reviewed one month in advance and then again ten days in advance. Daily production schedules, which by then include firm orders from dealers, are finalized four days from the start of production. Model mix changes can still be made the evening before or the morning of production. This flexibility is possible because schedule changes are communicated only to the final assembly line. Kanbans take care of dispatching revised orders to the rest of the system.

Reduce variability by smoothing demand.

Another approach to achieving uniform production is to *level* or smooth demand across the planning horizon. Demand is divided into small increments of time and spread out as evenly as possible so that the same amount of each item is produced each day, and item production is *mixed* throughout the day in very small quantities. The mix is controlled by the sequence of models on the final assembly line.

Mixed-model assembly steadies component production.

Toyota assembles several different vehicle models on each final assembly line. The assembly lines were initially designed this way because of limited space and resources and lack of sufficient volume to dedicate an entire line to a specific model. However, the mixed-model concept has since become an integral part of JIT. Daily production is arranged in the same ratio as monthly demand, and jobs are distributed as evenly as possible across the day's schedule. This means that at least some quantity of every item is produced daily, and the company will always have some quantity of an item available to respond to variations in demand. The mix of assembly also steadies component production, reduces inventory levels, and supports the pull system of production. Let's look at an example of mixed-model sequencing.

EXAMPLE 15.2 *Mixed-Model Sequencing*	If Toyota receives a monthly demand estimate of 1,200 small cars (S), 2,400 midsize cars (M), and 2,400 luxury cars (L), how should the models be produced in order to smooth production as much as possible? (Assume 30 days in a month.) **SOLUTION:** Our first step is to convert monthly demand to a daily schedule by dividing by the number of days in a month. As a result, we need to produce 40, 80, and 80 of each model,

---

[5] P. Y. Huang, L. P. Rees, and B. W. Taylor, "A Simulation Analysis of the Just-in-Time Technique (with Kanbans) for a Multiline, Multistage Production System," *Decision Sciences* (July 1983).

respectively, per day. In mixing the production of models as much as possible throughout the day, we want to produce twice as many midsize and luxury cars as small cars. One possible final assembly sequence is L-M-S-M-L. This sequence would be repeated 40 times a day.

If the preceding example sounds extreme, it is not. Toyota assembles three models in 100 variations on a single assembly line at its Tahara plant, and the mix is jiggled daily with almost no warning.[6] The plant is highly automated, and each model carries with it a small yellow disc that transmits instructions to the next workstation. Cars roll off the final assembly line in what looks like unit production—a black Lexus sedan, a blue Camry, a red Lexus sports coupe, a white Camry with left-hand drive, and so on.

This is in sharp contrast to the large lots of similar items produced by mass production factories, in which 2,400 luxury cars might be produced the first week and a half of the month, 2,400 midsize cars, the second week and a half, and 1,200 small cars, the final week. Under this system, it would be difficult to change product mix midway through the month, and small-car customers would have to wait three to four weeks before their order would be available.

Quality at the Source

For a JIT system to work well, quality has to be extremely high. There is no extra inventory to buffer against defective units. Producing poor-quality items and then having to rework or reject them is a waste that should be eliminated. Quality improvement efforts at Toyota accelerated as processes were being streamlined and the JIT system was formulated. It soon became obvious that smaller lot sizes actually encouraged better quality. Workers can observe quality problems more easily; when problems are detected, they can be traced to their source and remedied without reworking too many units. Also, by inspecting the first and the last unit in a small batch or by having a worker make a part and then use the part, virtually 100 percent inspection can be achieved.

> Smaller lot sizes encourage quality.

Toyota's quality objective is zero defects (just as its inventory objective is zero inventory). In pursuit of zero defects the company seeks to identify quality problems at their source, to solve them, and *never* to pass on a defective item. To this end, Ohno was determined that the workers, not inspectors, should be responsible for product quality. To go along with this responsibility, he also gave workers the unprecedented authority of **jidoka**—the authority to stop the production line if quality problems were encountered.

> **Jidoka** is authority to stop the production line.

To encourage jidoka, each worker is given access to a switch that can be used to activate call lights or to halt production. The call lights, called **andons**, flash above the workstation and at several andon boards throughout the plant. Green lights indicate normal operation, yellow lights show a call for help, and red lights indicate a line stoppage. Supervisors, maintenance personnel, and engineers are summoned to troubled workstations quickly by flashing lights on the andon board. At Toyota, the assembly line is stopped for an average of twenty minutes a day because of jidoka. Each jidoka drill is recorded on easels kept at the work area. A block of time is reserved at the end of the day for workers to go over the list and work on solving the problems raised. For example, an eight-hour day might consist of seven hours of production and one hour of problem solving.

> **Andons** are call lights that signal quality problems.

---

[6] Fred Hiatt, "Japan Creating Mass-Produced Customization," *Washington Post*, March 25, 1990.

Undercapacity scheduling leaves time for planning, problem solving, and maintenance.

This concept of allocating extra time to a schedule for nonproductive tasks is called **undercapacity scheduling.** Another example of undercapacity scheduling is producing for two shifts each day and reserving the third shift for preventive maintenance activities. Making time to plan, train, solve problems, and maintain the work environment is an important part of JIT's success.

Visual control makes problems visible.

Quality improves when problems are made visible and workers have clear expectations of performance. Production systems designed with quality in mind include visible instructions for worker or machine action, and direct feedback on the results of that action. This is known as **visual control.** Examples include kanbans, standard operation sheets, andons, process control charts, and tool boards. A factory with visual control will look different than other factories. You may find machines or stockpoints in each section painted different colors, material handling routes marked clearly on the floor, demonstration stands and instructional photographs placed near machines, graphs of quality or performance data displayed at each workstation, and explanations and pictures of recent improvement efforts posted by work teams. Figure 15.9 shows several examples of visual control.

Poka-yokes prevent defects from occurring.

Visual control of quality often leads to what the Japanese call a **poka-yoke.** A poka-yoke is any foolproof device or mechanism that prevents defects from occurring. For example, a dial on which desired ranges are marked in different colors is an example of visual control. A dial that shuts off a machine whenever the instrument needle falls above or below the desired range is a poka-yoke. Machines set to stop after a certain amount of production are poka-yokes, as are sensors that prevent the addition of too many items into a package or the misalignment of components for an assembly.

www.prenhall.com/russell

Kaizen is a system of continuous improvement.

Finally, quality in JIT is based on **kaizen,** the Japanese term for *continuous improvement.* As a practical system for production created from trial-and-error experiences in eliminating waste and simplifying operations, JIT continually looks for ways to reduce inventory, quicken setups, improve quality, and react faster to customer demand. Continuous improvement is not something that can be delegated to a department or a staff of experts. It is a monumental undertaking that requires **total employee involvement (TEI)**—the participation of every employee at every level. The essence of JIT success is the willingness of workers to spot quality problems, halt production when necessary, generate ideas for improvement, analyze process, perform different functions, and adjust their working routines.

Total employee involvement is a system for encouraging participation by every employee at every level.

Total Productive Maintenance

Machines cannot operate continuously without some attention. Maintenance activities can be performed when a machine breaks down to restore the machine to its original operating condition, or at different times during regular operation of the machine in an attempt to prevent a breakdown from occurring. The first type of activity is referred to as **breakdown maintenance;** the second is called **preventive maintenance.**

Breakdown maintenance involves the repairs needed to make a failed machine operational.

Breakdowns seldom occur at convenient times. Lost production, poor quality, and missed deadlines from an inefficient or broken-down machine can represent a significant expense. In addition, the cost of breakdown maintenance is usually much greater than preventive maintenance. (Most of us know that to be true from our own experience at maintaining an automobile. Regular oil changes cost pennies compared to replacing a car engine.) For these reasons, most companies do not find it cost-effective to rely solely on breakdown maintenance. The question then becomes, how much preventive maintenance is necessary and when should it be performed?

Preventive maintenance is a system of periodic inspection and maintenance designed to keep a machine in operation.

With accurate records on the time between breakdowns, the frequency of breakdowns, and the cost of breakdown and preventive maintenance, we can mathematically

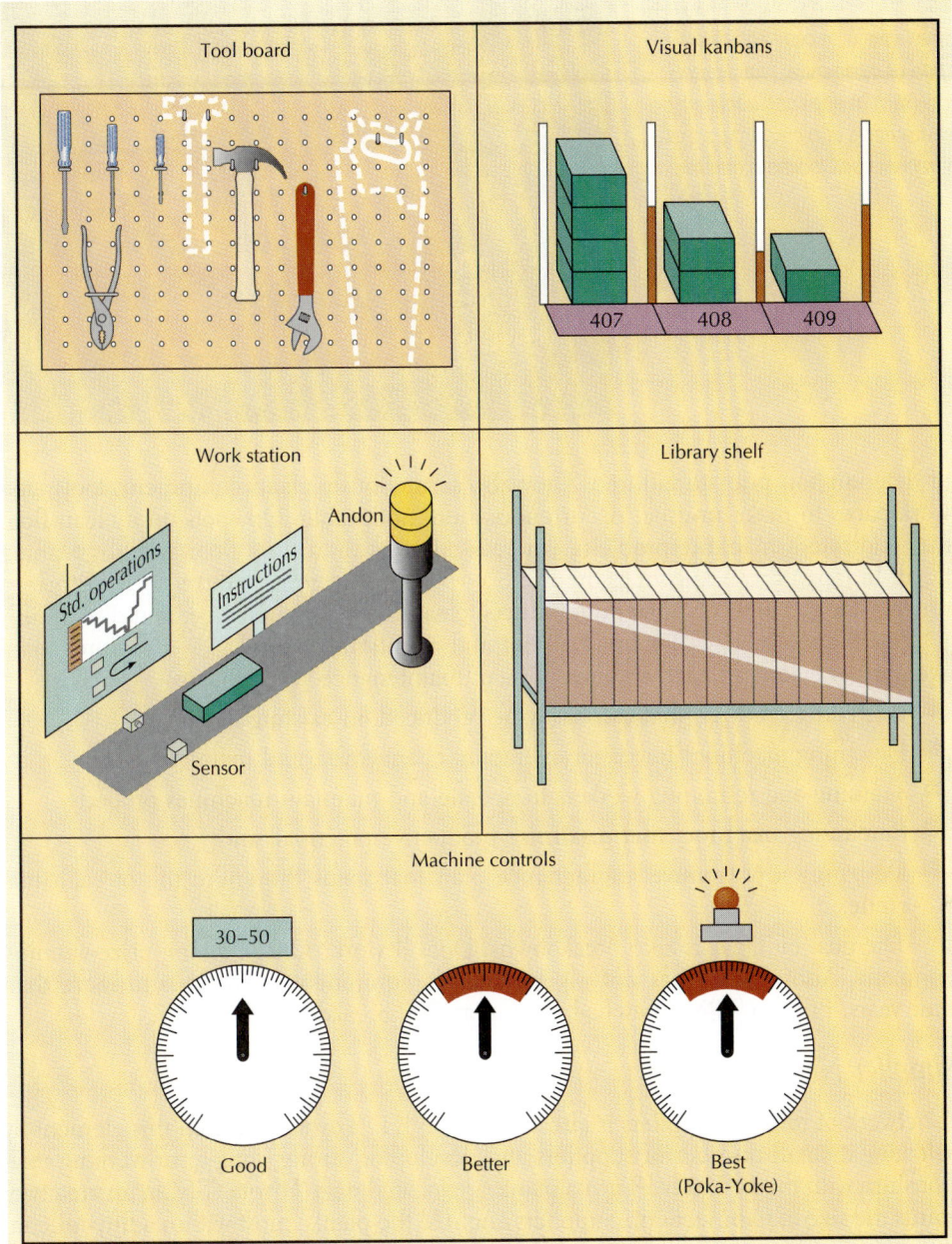

FIGURE 15.9 **Examples of Visual Control**

determine the best preventive maintenance schedule. But even with this degree of precision, breakdowns can still occur. JIT requires more than preventive maintenance—it requires *total productive maintenance*.

Total productive maintenance (TPM) combines the practice of preventive maintenance with the concepts of total quality—employee involvement, decisions based on data, zero defects, and a strategic focus. Machine operators maintain their own machines with daily care, periodic inspections, and preventive repair activities. They compile and interpret maintenance and operating data on their machines, identifying signs

Total productive maintenance combines the practice of preventive maintenance with the concepts of total quality.

Honda is known for innovation, quality, and—a spotless work environment. How does cleanliness affect quality or competitiveness? Keeping the work area shining is part of a preventive maintenance effort in which unusual occurrences (such as drips and abrasions) are detected quickly. An orderly environment also encourages workers to replace tools and materials in prescribed locations and to take more care in their work.

of deterioration prior to failure.[7] They also scrupulously clean equipment, tools, and workspaces to make unusual occurrences more noticeable. Oil spots on a clean floor may indicate a machine problem, whereas oil spots on a dirty floor would go unnoticed. In Japan this is known as the five S's—*seiri, seiton, seiso, seiketsu, and shitsuke*—roughly translated as organization, tidiness, cleanliness, maintenance, and discipline.

www.prenhall.com/russell

In addition to operator involvement and attention to detail, TPM requires management to take a broader, strategic view of maintenance. That means:

- Designing products that can easily be produced on existing machines;
- Designing machines for easier operation, changeover, and maintenance;
- Training and retraining workers to operate and maintain machines properly;
- Purchasing machines that maximize productive potential; and
- Designing a preventive maintenance plan that spans the entire life of each machine.

The goal of TPM is zero breakdowns. Does it work? One Deming prize-winning company, Aishin Seiki, has not experienced an equipment breakdown in more than four years. Prior to TPM, they had more than 700 breakdowns a month!

Supplier Networks

A network of reliable suppliers is also essential to JIT. Toyota mastered this element by selecting a small number of suppliers and developing strong, long-term working relationships with them. Twelve Toyota plants are located near Toyota City, in an area two-thirds the size of Connecticut. Suppliers encircle the plants, most within a fifty-mile radius. This enables parts to be delivered several times a day. Bulky parts, such as engines and transmissions, are delivered every fifteen to thirty minutes. Supplier kanbans and JIT at supplier plants are used to accomplish this feat.

Use fewer suppliers.

Toyota began working with its suppliers in 1962 to improve responsiveness and quality. By 1970, 60 percent of them were using kanbans and by 1982, 98 percent were. Suppliers who met stringent quality standards could forego inspection of incoming goods. This meant goods could be brought right to the assembly line or area of use without being counted, inspected, tagged, or stocked. Because of geography, manufac-

---

[7] Maintaining and repairing your own machine is called *autonomous maintenance*. Collecting data and designing maintenance remedies based on the data collected is referred to as *predictive maintenance*.

turers in the United States can probably never match the frequency of delivery enjoyed by Toyota, but they can reduce the number of suppliers, work more closely with them in the design of parts and the quality of parts, and expect prompt—even daily—deliveries.

One of the common misconceptions about JIT is that inventory is pushed back to the suppliers. That is true only if producers are not really using JIT or if suppliers try to meet JIT demand requirements without practicing JIT themselves. Otherwise, suppliers can benefit from the guaranteed demand, steadiness of demand, advanced notice of volume changes, minimal design changes, engineering and management assistance, and sharing of profits characteristic of the close vendor-producer partnerships of JIT. That said, JIT has certainly changed the manner in which suppliers are chosen and goods are supplied to producers. The following is a list of trends in supplier policies since the advent of JIT:

www.prenhall.com/russell

1. *Locate near to the customer.* Although this is not possible in all cases, it does occur, as evidenced by the circle of suppliers that surrounds the Tennessee valley where the Nissan and Saturn plants are located. Nissan receives deliveries of vehicle seats four times an hour and notifies the supplier two hours in advance the exact sequence (i.e., type and color) in which the seats are to be unloaded.

2. *Use small, side-loaded trucks and ship mixed loads.* These trucks are easier to load and can be loaded in the sequence that the customer will be using the items. Several suppliers may combine their loads on one truck that will tour the supplier plants to pick up items for delivery to the customer.

Supplier policies have changed with JIT.

3. *Consider establishing small warehouses near to the customer or consolidating warehouses with other suppliers.* The small warehouses could be used for frequently delivered items, and the consolidation warehouses could become *load-switching points* when geographic distances between supplier and customer prohibit daily deliveries. Yellow Freight has been very successful with this approach.

4. *Use standardized containers and make deliveries according to a precise delivery schedule.* Exchanging containers makes deliveries and replenishment move along quickly. Delivery windows are becoming very short, and penalties for missing them are high. Chrysler penalizes its trucking firm $32,000 for each hour a delivery is late.

www.prenhall.com/russell

5. *Become a certified supplier and accept payment at regular intervals rather than upon delivery.* This eliminates much of the paperwork and waiting time associated with traditional delivery. Certified suppliers are subjected to a limited amount of quality and quantity checks or may be exempt from them altogether.

Benefits of JIT

A study of the average benefits accrued to U.S. manufacturers over a five-year period from implementing JIT are impressive: 90 percent reductions in manufacturing cycle time, 70 percent reductions in inventory, 50 percent reductions in labor costs, and 80 percent reductions in space requirements.

While not every company can achieve results at this level, JIT does provide a wide range of benefits, including:

1. Reduced inventory
2. Improved quality
3. Lower costs
4. Reduced space requirements
5. Shorter lead time

JIT provides a wide range of benefits.

THE COMPETITIVE EDGE

JIT Suppliers Join the Partnership

The automotive industry increasingly relies on its suppliers as partners. Budd Co., a subsidiary of Germany's Thyssen AG, is a major supplier to the automotive industry, producing parts for over 50% of vehicles produced in North America. Twenty-five Budd factories around the world employ 9,000 workers to make automotive components from steel, aluminum, plastic, and iron. Budd has followed the automakers' lead in locating globally, improving quality, and using new materials.

One of Budd's newest plants, located in Shelbyville, Kentucky, is a JIT supplier of large stampings for Ford's Explorer and GM's Saturn. The stampings include fenders, doors, door frames, body sides, and deck lids. The plant is divided into five areas: the press shop, in-process rack storage, assembly, finished-goods rack storage, and shipping.

The press shop receives a one-day supply of steel coils daily. The coils, 72 inches wide and 25 tons in weight, are decoiled, cut into flat blanks, and stacked by size. The blanks are then stamped into various component parts and manually loaded into racks. Quick changeovers allow a variety of items to be stamped on each press. The rack serves the same purpose as a container in other factories—an empty rack is a signal or *kanban* to begin production.

The assembly area consists of several dedicated lines with automatic transfer between operations. In-process stampings are removed from the racks and placed on the appropriate assembly line with other component parts. Assembly operations include resistance welding, crimping, sealing, and restriking. Finished assemblies are placed in shipping racks and taken to the shipping area where they are loaded onto trucks and rail at the end of each day.

Production is orderly, work-in-process limited, demand steady, and quality high. Acceptable quality standards three years ago of 800 defective parts per million have given way to tougher standards of 25 defects per million. Workers are salaried and work in self-directed teams. Productivity bonuses are based on ten factory performance measures, including efficiency, scrap, rework, inventory, material usage, absenteeism, and safety. Although lifetime employment is not guaranteed, 15% of the workforce is temporary to allow position shifts when demand slows. Continuous improvement ideas from workers have involved redesigning parts containers, eliminating redundant part handling, and combining subassembly operations.

SOURCES: Kathryn Cooper VanGilder, "Auto Industry Trends," *IIE Solutions* (November 1995): 22–25; and Ziegfried Buschmann, "The Auto Industry in the 90's: Driving with Both Hands," speech to the German-American Chamber of Commerce, July 21, 1995.

6. Increased productivity
7. Greater flexibility
8. Better relations with suppliers
9. Simplified scheduling and control activities
10. Increased capacity
11. Better use of human resources
12. More product variety

JIT Implementation

www.prenhall.com/russell

Japanese industry embraced JIT in the mid-1970s, after manufacturers observed Toyota's superior ability to withstand the 1973 oil crisis. Many U.S. firms, in turn, adopted JIT in some form in the 1980s. Those firms that tried to implement JIT by slashing inventory and demanding that their suppliers make frequent deliveries missed the power of the system. Supplier deliveries and kanbans are some of the last elements of JIT to implement.

The firms that have been most successful in implementing JIT understood the breadth and interrelatedness of the concepts and adapted them to their own particular environment. This makes sense when you consider the essence of JIT—eliminate waste, speed up changeovers, work closely with suppliers, streamline the flow of work, use flexible resources, pay attention to quality, expose problems, and use worker teams to solve problems. None of these concepts or techniques are new or particularly revolutionary. How they are applied can differ considerably from company to company. What is unique and remarkable is how the pieces are tied together into a finely tuned operating system and how synchronized that system can be with both the external and internal business environments.

> Use JIT to finely tune an operating system.

Many firms have their own name for their version of just-in-time. JIT is called stockless production at Hewlett-Packard, material as needed (MAN) at Harley-Davidson, continuous-flow manufacturing (CFM) at IBM, zero inventory production system (ZIPS) at Omark Industries, and <u>lean production</u> in the landmark book *The Machine That Changed the World* by Womack, Jones, and Roos that chronicles the automobile industry.

> **Lean production** is a term used to describe JIT and the Toyota production system.

JIT applications on U.S. soil, whether in Japanese- or U.S.-run plants, differ somewhat from the original Japanese versions. U.S. JIT plants are typically larger, deliveries from suppliers are less frequent, more buffer inventory is held (because of the longer delivery lead times), and kanbans, if used at all, are very simple. Worker-designed feedback systems are different, too. Instead of alarms and flashing lights when things go

www.prenhall.com/russell

THE COMPETITIVE EDGE

JIT Keeps It Simple for Lantech

In 1989, Lantech Inc., a manufacturer of industrial packaging equipment, lost its patent for a key component of wrapping machines and, with it, its competitive edge. For five years, the company floundered, trying to increase productivity with automation, computers, and specialization. No amount of cost cutting, NC machining, or process optimization worked. Workers excelled at their individual jobs, but no one understood the full production process. VP of operations, Pat Lancaster, illustrates: ". . . as our business grew, it became easier to be talked out of our common sense. The computer system would tell us to cut costs by producing in EOQ quantities. But with the EOQ of one component part at 100, and another at 1,000, we were stuck with extra inventory that never went away."

Then, Lantech abandoned high tech for the simple life of JIT. Visual aids and manual procedures were used as much as possible. The flow of work was reorganized so that "everyone sees everything." Workers were given the skills and authority to make their own decisions. That's a far cry from the old system where no one was allowed to do anything unless the computer system told them it was okay. Said one worker, "[Before] . . . everything not mandatory was forbidden."

Now, there's so much space and light, the factory floor feels like a convention center. Handwritten diagrams of the assembly process on whiteboards replace computer-generated work orders. Kanban cards signal when to order new supplies, and strips of tape on the floor indicate the direction of production flow. Workers are organized into *microlines* or cells which contain all of the core processes: sawing, machining, fabrication, painting, electrical assembly, and final assembly. Instead of specializing in one task, workers are cross-trained as generalists. Machines and people are pushed together so that work is handed from one worker to the next and sophisticated material handling equipment is not needed. Piles of work-in-process inventory have been eliminated and work is processed faster.

The current operation of Lantech's plant approaches *lean production* or *one-piece flow*, in which components moving through any of the fourteen microlines correspond to a specific customer order. Customer orders are now completed within twelve hours, instead of five weeks, and production defects have been cut in half. Excess capacity is used to build pallets to its own specs for use in manufacturing, and Lantech is again competitive.

SOURCE: Fred Hapgood, "Keeping It Simple," *Inc. Technology* (March 19, 1996): 66–72.

wrong, workers at the Saturn plant hear a recording of "The Pink Panther." At the Nissan plant, workers are reminded to change workstations along an S-shaped assembly line by the changing tempo of piped-in music (from country to rock). Morning calisthenics are out for most U.S. plants, but the placement of ping-pong tables and basketball hoops alongside the assembly line for exercise during worker-designated breaks is popular.

JIT is still evolving.

As might be expected, JIT is still evolving. Toyota has learned from its U.S. plants that the stress of arbitrarily reducing inventory to reveal problems does not necessarily make workers more creative in improving the system.[8] To the contrary, creating an environment that is receptive to change, without forcing it, seems to work just as well. Shorter workdays and longer breaks during the day do not seriously impede productivity either. In Japan, Toyota's practice of clustering plants and suppliers in geographic proximity to one another has worked well for frequent deliveries and small-lot production, but it has also used up the available labor in the area. Toyota's new plants are more dispersed, like U.S. plants, and require more inventory. They are also more automated. The Tahara plant, for example, is almost entirely automated, with buffers of inventory between the seven major sections of the final assembly line.[9] Although this seems to be a divergence from the principles of JIT, it may merely reflect that JIT, like other management systems, must be adapted to the manufacturing environment.

JIT isn't for everyone!

We should note that JIT is not appropriate for every type of operation. For high-volume, repetitive items, mass production is still the best process to use. Even Toyota produces high-demand components (typically small items that require stamping and forging) in lots as large as 10,000 units, sending them to subsequent processes in small batches only when requested. Similarly, JIT is inappropriate for very low volume items or unique orders. For JIT to be successful, there must be some stability of demand. A true make-to-order shop would find it difficult to operate under JIT. Even in make-to-order businesses, however, there are usually some parts or processes that are common or repetitive and can benefit from JIT concepts. What we are finding is that there are more operations that can benefit from JIT than cannot.

JIT in Services

Most people who think of JIT as a system for reducing inventory do not consider the system to be applicable to services. However, you know from reading this chapter that JIT consists of more than low inventory levels. It eliminates waste, streamlines operations, promotes fast changeovers and close supplier relations, and adjusts quickly to changes in demand. As a result, products (or services) can be provided quickly, at less cost, and in more variety. Although it is rarely referred to as such, we can readily observe some of the basic elements of JIT in service operations. Think about:

Many services use JIT concepts.

- McDonald's, Domino's, and Federal Express, who compete on speed and still provide their products and services at low cost and with increasing variety;
- Construction firms that coordinate the arrival of material "just as it is needed" instead of stockpiling them at the site;
- Multifunctional workers in department stores that work the cash register, stock goods, arrange displays, and make sales;

---

[8] Jean Hilltop, "Just-In-Time Manufacturing: Implications for the Management of Human Resources," *European Management Journal* (March 1992): 49–54.

[9] Alex Taylor, "How Toyota Copes with Hard Times," *Fortune* (January 25, 1993): 78–81.

JIT in services? The basic concept for JIT began in a service operation—the supermarket! Japanese factories, trying to duplicate the ease with which goods are replenished in American supermarkets, decided to forego huge inventory buildups and complex scheduling algorithms in favor of simply replacing items as they are used. This pull system is the basis for just-in-time production.

- Work cells at fast-food restaurants that allow workers to be added during peak times and reduced during slow times;
- "Dollar" stores that price everything the same and simply count the number of items purchased as the customer leaves;
- Process mapping that has streamlined operations and eliminated waste in many services (especially in terms of paper flow and information processing);
- Medical facilities that have the flexibility to fill prescriptions, perform tests, and treat patients without routing them from one end of the building to another;
- Just-in-time publishing that allows professors to choose material from a variety of sources and construct a custom-made book in the same amount of time off-the-shelf books can be ordered and at competitive prices;
- Lens providers, cleaners, and car-repair services that can turn around customer orders in an hour;
- Cleaning teams that follow standard operations routines in quickly performing their tasks; and
- Supermarkets that replenish their shelves according to what the customer withdraws.

In a broader sense, then, JIT concepts are flourishing in services.

Services have also been dramatically affected by JIT in manufacturing. Trucking firms, railroads, and delivery services have increased the speed at which their services are performed and increased their reliability in response to JIT. Retail stores can provide customers with more choices faster than ever before. Milliken promises custom-ordered carpets within two weeks, Benetton can create and ship new product lines within ten days of redesign, and Motorola can provide customized pagers overnight. With this type of rapid response, stores can order and receive goods faster from the manufacturer than they can retrieve them from their warehouses.

Finally, much of the emphasis of JIT comes from being close to the customer, close to the supplier, and close to the worker. Services have traditionally excelled in those areas.

www.prenhall.com/russell

Summary

Just-in-time (JIT) has truly changed the face of manufacturing and transformed the global economy. JIT originated at Toyota Motor Company as an effort to eliminate waste (particularly inventories), but it evolved into a system for the continuous improvement of all aspects of manufacturing operations. JIT is both a philosophy and a collection of management methods and techniques. The main advantage of the system is derived from the integration of the techniques into a focused, smooth-running management system.

In JIT systems, workers are multifunctional and are required to perform different tasks, as well as aid in the improvement process. Machines are also multi-functional and are arranged in small, U-shaped work cells that enable parts to be processed in a continuous flow through the cell. Workers produce parts one at a time within the cells and transport parts between cells in small lots as called for by subassembly lines, assembly lines, or other work cells. The work environment is kept clean, orderly, and free of waste so that unusual occurrences are visible.

Schedules are prepared only for the final assembly line, in which several different models are assembled on the same line. Requirements for component parts and subassemblies are then pulled through the system with kanbans. The principle of the pull system is not to make anything until requested to do so by the next station. The "pull" element of JIT will not work unless production is uniform, setups are quick, and lot sizes are low.

The pull system and kanbans are also used to order materials from outside suppliers. Suppliers are fewer in number and must be very reliable. They may be requested to make multiple deliveries of the same item in the same day, so their manufacturing system must be flexible, too. Deliveries are made directly to the factory floor, eliminating stockrooms and the waste of counting, inspecting, recording, storing, and transporting.

Just-in-time, as the name implies, does not produce in anticipation of need. It produces only necessary items in necessary quantities at necessary times. Inventory is viewed as a waste of resources and an obstacle to improvement. Because there is little buffer inventory between workstations, quality must be extremely high, and every effort is made to prevent machine breakdowns.

When all these elements are in place, JIT systems produce high-quality goods, quickly and at low cost. These systems also are able to respond to changes in customer demand. JIT systems are most effective in repetitive environments, but elements of JIT can be applied to almost any operation, including service operations.

Summary of Key Formulas

Determining the Number of Kanbans

$$N = \frac{dL + S}{C}$$

Summary of Key Terms

andons: call lights installed at workstations to notify management and other workers of a quality problem in production

breakdown maintenance: a maintenance activity that involves repairs needed to make a failed machine operational.

external setup: setup activities that can be performed in advance while the machine is operating.

general-purpose machines: machines that perform basic functions such as turning, drilling, and milling.

internal setup: setup activities that can be performed only when the machine is stopped.

jidoka: authority given to the workers to stop the assembly line when quality problems are encountered.

just-in-time (JIT): both a philosophy and an integrated system for production management that emphasizes the elimination of waste and the continuous improvement of operations.

kaizen: a Japanese term for a system of continuous improvement.

kanban: a card corresponding to a standard quantity of production (or size container) used in the pull system to authorize the production or withdrawal of goods.

kanban square: a marked area designated to hold a certain amount of items; an empty square is the signal to produce more items.

lean production: a term used to describe JIT and the Toyota production system.

manufacturing cell: a group of dissimilar machines brought together to manufacture a family of parts with similar shapes or processing requirements.

material kanban: a rectangular-shaped kanban used to order material in advance of a process.

multifunctional workers: workers who have been trained to perform more than one job or function.

poka-yoke: any foolproof device or mechanism that prevents defects from occurring.

preventive maintenance: a system of daily maintenance, periodic inspection, and preventive repairs designed to reduce the probability of machine breakdown.

production kanban: a card authorizing the production of a container of goods.

pull system: a production system in which items are manufactured only when called for by the users of those items.

push system: a production system in which items are manufactured according to a schedule prepared in advance.

signal kanban: a triangular kanban used as a reorder point to signal production at the previous workstation.

total employee involvement (TEI): a system that involves every employee at every level in continuous improvement efforts.

total productive maintenance (TPM): an approach to machine maintenance that combines the practice of preventive maintenance with the concepts of total quality and employer involvement.

undercapacity scheduling: the allocation of extra time in a schedule for nonproductive tasks such as problem solving or maintenance.

uniform production levels: the result of smoothing production requirements on the final assembly line.

visual control: procedures and mechanisms for making problems visible.

waste: anything other than the minimum amount of equipment, materials, parts, space, and time that are absolutely essential to add value to the product.

withdrawal kanban: a card authorizing the withdrawal and movement of a container of goods.

Questions

15-1. What is the purpose of JIT?

15-2. How did JIT evolve into a system of continuous improvement?

15-3. Why are flexible resources essential to JIT?

15-4. What does a cellular layout contribute to JIT?

15-5. Differentiate between a push and a pull production system.

15-6. How was the concept of kanban developed from the two-bin inventory system?

15-7. How are the kanban system and the reorder point system similar? How are they different?

15-8. Describe how the following kanbans operate:
   a. Production and withdrawal kanbans
   b. Kanban squares
   c. Signal kanbans
   d. Material kanbans
   e. Supplier kanbans

15-9. What are the advantages of small lot sizes?

15-10. Why do large lot sizes not work well with pull systems?

15-11. Why are small lot sizes not as effective in a push system?

15-12. Explain the principles of SMED. What does SMED try to achieve?

15-13. Why is uniform production important to JIT? How is it achieved?

15-14. What are the advantages of mixed-model sequencing?

15-15. How are JIT and TQC related? Which should be implemented first?

15-16. How can a balance be struck between the cost of breakdown maintenance and the cost of preventive maintenance?

15-17. Explain the concept of total productive maintenance (TPM).

15-18. What role does the equipment operator play in TPM?

15-19. Preventive maintenance can be viewed as the process of maintaining the "health" of a machine. Using health care as an analogy, explain the differences and trade-offs between breakdown maintenance, preventive maintenance, and total productive maintenance.

15-20. How are suppliers affected by JIT?

15-21. Suggest several ways that JIT requirements can be made easier for suppliers.

15-22. Give examples of visual control. How does visual control affect quality?

15-23. What is a poka-yoke? Give an example.

15-24. Why is worker involvement important to continuous improvement?

15-25. What are some typical benefits from implementing JIT?

15-26. Is JIT falling out of favor? How widely used is JIT?

15-27. Which elements of JIT do you think would be difficult for U.S. firms to implement?

15-28. Design a strategy for JIT implementation.

15-29. In what type of environment is JIT most successful?

15-30. Can JIT be applied to services? How?

Problems

15-1. Demand for the popular water toy Sudsy Soaker has far exceeded expectations. In order to increase the availability of different models of the toy, the manufacturer has decided to begin producing its most popular models as often as possible on its one assembly line. Given monthly requirements of 7,200, 3,600, and 3,600 units for Sudsy Soaker 50, Sudsy Soaker 100, and Sudsy Soaker 200, respectively, determine a model sequence for the final assembly line that will smooth out the production of each model. (Assume 30 working days per month and 8 working hours per day. Also assume that the time required to assemble each model is approximately the same.)

15-2. As local developers prepare for an increase in housing starts, they must anticipate their demand for various materials. One such material is tile. Used in bathrooms, kitchens, and for decoration, tiles come in many shapes, colors, and sizes. In order to accommodate the varying needs, the tile manufacturer must schedule its production efficiently. Each month developers order 30,000 boxes of quarry tile, 15,000 boxes of Italian mosaic tile, and 45,000 boxes of 4-inch bathroom tile. Determine a mixed-model sequence that will efficiently meet these needs. Assume 30 days per month.

15-3. An assembly station is asked to process 100 circuit boards per hour. It takes 20 minutes to receive the necessary components from the previous workstation. Completed circuit boards are placed in a rack that will hold 10 boards. The rack must be full before it is sent on to the next workstation. If the factor uses a safety factor of 10 percent, how many kanbans are needed for the circuit board assembly process?

15-4. Referring to Problem 15-3, how many kanbans would be needed in each case?
   a. Demand is increased to 200 circuit boards per hour.
   b. The lead time for components is increased to 30 minutes.
   c. The rack size is halved.
   d. The safety factor is increased to 20 percent.

15-5. It takes Aaron 15 minutes to produce 10 widgets to fill a container and 5 minutes to transport the container to the next station, where Maria works. Maria's process takes about 30 minutes. The factory uses a safety factor of 20 percent. Currently, 5 kanbans rotate between Aaron and Maria's stations. What is the approximate demand for widgets?

15-6. Stan Weakly can sort a bin of 100 letters in 10 minutes. He typically sorts 500 letters an hour. A truck arrives with more bins every 30 minutes. The office uses a safety factor of 10 percent. How many kanbans are needed for the letter-sorting process?

15-7. The office administrator wishes to decrease the number of kanbans in the letter-sorting process described in Problem 15-6. Which of the following alternatives has the greatest effect on reducing the number of kanbans?
   a. Eliminating the safety factor
   b. Receiving truck deliveries every 15 minutes
   c. Increasing the bin capacity to 200 letters
   What is the effect on inventory levels of decreasing the number of kanbans?

15-8. Sandy is asked to produce 250 squidgets an hour. It takes 30 minutes to receive the necessary material from the previous workstation. Each output container holds 25 squidgets. The factor currently works with a safety factor of 10 percent. How many kanbans should be circulating between Sandy's process and the previous process?

15-9. Referring to Problem 15-8, what happens to the number of kanbans and to inventory levels in each case?
   a. The time required to receive material is increased to 45 minutes.
   b. Output expectations decrease to 125 squidgets an hour.
   c. The size of the container is cut to 10 squidgets.

15-10. In a large microelectronics plant, the assembly cell for circuit boards has a demand for 200 units an hour. Two feeder cells supply parts A and B to the assembly cell (one A and one B for each board). Standard containers that look like divided trays are used. A container will hold 20 A's or 10 B's. It takes 10 minutes to fill up a container with A's and 20 minutes to fill up a container with B's. Transit time to the assembly cell is 5 minutes for both A and B. No safety factor is used. Set up a kanban control system for the assembly process.

CASE PROBLEM

JIT Woes

B&B Electronics, a supplier in the telecommunications industry, has a problem. Demand is down, but competitive pressures for better quality at a reduced price are up. Customers who used to order in large lots with plenty of lead time now want daily deliveries of small quantities. Contracts use terms such as "statistical evidence of quality" and "just-in-time delivery." More and more customers are requiring supplier certification with standards that B&B cannot meet. Plant manager John Walters has to take action.

"If JIT is good enough for our customers, it's good enough for us," he declared, and called in one of his managers, Kelly Thompson.

"Kelly, I can always rely on you to get us out of a jam, so don't let me down this time. I want you to implement JIT on the circuit board assembly line. Create a success story to show other employees how

great this JIT stuff is. You've got free rein . . . not much money, but free rein to change anything you want in the system. Oh, and I want some results by next month."

"Okay, boss," replied Kelly shakily. "What's your philosophy on JIT? I mean what do you consider its most important points?"

"My philosophy? JIT is cutting inventory, squeezing your suppliers, and using those kanban card things. My philosophy is just do it!"

"I get the picture," said Kelly as she retreated to her office cubby to study up on JIT.

1. What do you think of the plant manager's view of JIT?

2. If you were Kelly, how would you go about the task ahead of you? What parts of JIT would you try to implement first? Last? How would you gain worker support?

References

Black, J. T. *The Design of the Factory with a Future.* New York: McGraw-Hill, 1991.

Chase, R., and N. Aquilano. *Production and Operations Management.* Homewood, Ill.: Irwin 1992.

Cusomano, Michael. *The Japanese Automobile Industry.* Cambridge, Mass.: Harvard University Press, 1985.

Hall, Robert. *Zero Inventories.* Homewood, Ill.: Dow Jones-Irwin, 1983.

Heard, Julie. "JIT for White Collar Work—The Rest of the Story." Chapter 12 in *Strategic Manufacturing: Dynamic New Directions for the 1990's,* P. Moody, ed. Homewood, Ill.: Irwin, 1990.

Hilltop, Jean. "Just-In-Time Manufacturing: Implications for the Management of Human Resources." *European Management Journal* (March 1992): 49–54.

Hirano, H. *JIT Factory Revolution.* Cambridge, Mass: Productivity Press, 1988.

Huang, P. Y., L. P. Rees, and B. W. Taylor. "A Simulation Analysis of the Just-in-Time Technique (with Kanbans) for a Multiline, Multistage Production System." *Decision Sciences* (July 1983).

Monden, Yasuhiro, ed. *Applying Just-In-Time: The American/Japanese Experience.* Atlanta, Ga.: Industrial Engineering and Management Press, 1986.

Monden, Yasuhiro. *Toyota Production System,* 2d ed. Atlanta, Ga.: Industrial Engineering and Management Press, 1993.

Sepehri, M. *Just-in-Time, Not Just in Japan.* Falls Church, Va.: APICS, 1986.

Shingo, S. *Modern Approaches to Manufacturing Improvement.* Cambridge, Mass.: Productivity Press, 1990.

Suzaki, Kiyoshi. *The New Manufacturing Challenge.* New York: Free Press, 1985.

Womack, James, Daniel Jones, and Daniel Roos. *The Machine That Changed the World.* New York: Macmillan, 1990.

16

Waiting Line Models For Service Improvement

Providing Quality Telephone Order Service At L. L. Bean

www.prenhall.com/russell

Long-term decisions in <u>L. L. Bean's</u> telemarketing operation relate to the number of telephone (trunk) lines to install and the number of agent positions and support equipment needed; short-term decisions must be made on daily staff scheduling and the capacity needed to handle waiting calls. Intermediate decisions include the number of agents that are hired and trained. These decisions are normally routine, but not during the 3-week period prior to Christmas, when 20 percent of the annual phone-order volume occurs. At this time, management must make rapid, critical decisions about daily schedules, the number of agents on duty, the number of temporary agents to hire and train, the number of workstations, the number of telephone trunk lines, and other operational capacity considerations. At the other extreme, following this peak period, the system must gear down to reflect a reduction in call volume.

On sales of $580 million in 1988, the company estimated a loss of $10 million in profit due to the suboptimal allocation of resources and unacceptable customer

Annually over 13.6 billion catalogs are sent by 10,000 mail-order companies. Each year over 100 million customers, or 55 percent of the adult population in the United States, buys $50 billion worth of goods from these catalogs. During the 1980s and 1990s the catalog mail-order business grew three times faster than most traditional retail operations. Catalogs represent one third of the total volume of mail handled annually by the U.S. Postal Service and generate $7 billion in postal revenues. Mail-order business has increased due to the introduction of ZIP codes; the spread of credit cards; the evolution of computer systems; and toll-free telephone numbers. Most orders taken by mail-order companies like J. Crew, Eddie Bauer, L. L. Bean, Speigel, Inc., and Lands' End are by telephone. These telephone ordering systems are, in effect, large scale waiting line systems where telephone operators serve customers who "wait in line" over the phone for service. To the customer, quality service means knowledgeable, pleasant, and fast service. Fast service in a telephone ordering system is determined by the number of customer calls coming in, the length of the calls, and the number of operators available to answer the calls and take orders.

service. There were times when 80 percent of calls received a busy signal, and customers who connected might have waited 10 minutes for an agent. On busy days the total lost orders because of busy signals and caller abandonment while waiting for an agent approached $500,000.

To address this problem a decision-making model, called the economic optimization model (EOM), was developed using queuing analysis. The purpose of the model was to determine the optimal number of telephone trunks for incoming calls, the number of agents scheduled, and the queue capacity (the maximum number of customers who are put on hold to wait for an agent). The objective was to minimize expected cost rather than simply to achieve a specific service level. In general, the EOM balanced the cost of the resources (i.e., trunk lines and agents) against the sum of queuing costs and the cost of lost orders at a point where total costs are minimized. Queuing models were used to estimate operating characteristics for the trunk lines and agents, which were then used to determine the economic impact of busy signals, customer waiting time, and lost orders. The model was implemented in 1989; for the 3-week peak holiday season, the number of telephone agents was increased from 500 to 1,275, and the number of telephone trunk lines was increased from 150 to 576. Comparing this 3-week period in 1989 (with EOM) and the same period in 1988 (without EOM) showed a 24 percent increase in calls answered, a 16.7 percent increase in orders taken, an increase in revenues of 16.3 percent (approximately $15 million), an 81.3 percent reduction in the number of callers who abandoned, and a reduction in the average answer speed from 93 seconds to 15 seconds. Annual profits increased by approximately $10 million and the cost savings was estimated at approximately $1.6 million. The model also had the effect of improving agent morale and alleviating customer dissatisfaction due to long waits. The cost for this project was $40,000.[1]

A nyone who goes shopping or to a movie experiences the inconvenience of waiting in line. Not only do people spend time waiting in lines, but parts and products queue up prior to a manufacturing operation and wait to be worked on, machinery waits in line to be serviced or repaired, trucks line up to be loaded or unloaded at a shipping terminal, and planes wait to take off and land. Waiting takes place in virtually every productive process or service. Since the time spent by people and things waiting in line is a valuable resource, the reduction of waiting time is an important aspect of operations management.

Waiting time has also become more important because of the increased emphasis on quality, especially in service-related operations. When customers go into a bank to take out a loan, cash a check, or make a deposit, take their car into a dealer for service or repair, or shop at a grocery store, they equate quality service with quick service. Companies focus on reducing waiting time as a component of quality improvement. Companies are able to reduce waiting time and provide faster service by increasing their service capacity, which usually means adding more servers—that is, more tellers, more mechanics, or more checkout clerks. However, increasing service capacity has a monetary cost, and therein lies the basis of waiting line, or queuing, analysis, the trade-off between the cost of improved service and the cost of making customers wait.

Providing quick service is an important aspect of quality customer service and TQM.

---

[1] P. Quinn, et al., "Allocating Telecommunications Resources at L. L. Bean, Inc.," *Interfaces* 21, no. 1, (January–February 1991): 75–91.

Waiting lines are analyzed with a set of mathematical formulas which comprise a field of study called *queuing theory*. The origin of queuing theory is found in telephone-network congestion problems and the work of A. K. Erlang. Erlang (1878–1929), a Danish mathematician, was the scientific adviser for the Copenhagen Telephone Company. In 1917 he published a paper outlining the development of telephone traffic theory, in which he was able to determine the probability of different numbers of calls waiting and the waiting time when the system was in equilibrium. Erlang's work provided the stimulus and formed the basis for the subsequent development of queuing theory.

Different queuing models and mathematical formulas exist to deal with different types of waiting line systems. Although we discuss several of the most common types of queuing systems, we do not investigate the mathematical derivation of the queuing formulas. They are generally complex and not really pertinent to our understanding of the use of queuing theory to improve service.

Elements of Waiting Line Analysis

Waiting lines form because people or things arrive at the servicing function, or server, faster than they can be served. This does not mean that the service operation is understaffed or does not have the capacity to handle the influx of customers. Most businesses and organizations have sufficient serving capacity available to handle its customers *in the long run*. Waiting lines result because customers do not arrive at a constant, evenly paced rate, nor are they all served in an equal amount of time. Customers arrive at random times, and the time required to serve each individually is not the same. A waiting line is continually increasing and decreasing in length (and is sometimes empty) and in the long run approaches an average rate of customer arrivals and an average time to serve the customer. For example, the checkout counters at a grocery store may have enough clerks to serve an average of 100 customers in an hour, and in a particular hour only 60 customers might arrive. However, at specific points in time during the hour, waiting lines may form because more than an average number of customers arrive and they have larger than average purchases.

Decisions about waiting lines and the management of waiting lines are based on these averages for customer arrivals and service times. They are used in queuing formulas to compute **operating characteristics** such as the average number of customers waiting in line and the average time a customer must wait in line. Different sets of formulas are used, depending on the type of waiting line system being investigated. A bank drive-in teller window at which one bank clerk serves a single line of customers in cars is different than a single line of passengers at an airport ticket counter that are served by three or four airline agents. In this section we present the elements that make up waiting lines before looking at waiting line formulas in the following sections.

Elements of a Waiting Line

The basic elements of a waiting line, or **queue,** are arrivals, servers, and the waiting line. The relationship between these elements is shown in Figure 16.1 for the simplest type of *waiting line system*, a single server with a single queue. This is commonly referred to as a *single-channel* queuing system. Following is a brief description of each of these waiting line components.

The Calling Population

In our discussions of queuing, a customer is a person or thing that wants service from an operation. The **calling population** is the source of the customers to the queuing sys-

---

Operating characteristics are average values for characteristics that describe the performance of a waiting line system.

A **queue** is a single waiting line.

A *waiting line system* consists of arrivals, servers, and waiting line structure.

The **calling population** is the source of customers; *infinite* or *finite*.

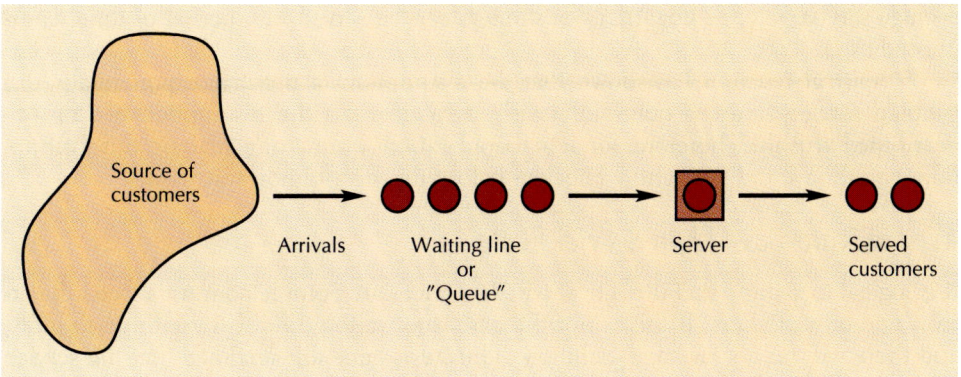

FIGURE 16.1   Components of a Queuing System

tem, and it can be either *infinite* or *finite*. An infinite calling population assumes such a large number of potential customers that it is always possible for one more customer to arrive to be served. For example, a grocery store, a bank, and a service station are assumed to have infinite calling populations; that is, the whole town or geographic area. A finite calling population has a specific, countable number of potential customers. It is possible for all the customers to be served or waiting in line at the same time; that is, it may occur that there is not one more customer to be served. Examples of a finite calling population are a repair facility in a shop, where there is a fixed number of machines available to be worked on, a trucking terminal that services a fleet of a specific number of trucks, or a nurse assigned to attend to a specific number of patients.

The Arrival Rate

The **arrival rate** is the rate at which customers arrive at the service facility during a specified period of time. This rate can be estimated from empirical data derived from studying the system or a similar system, or it can be an average of these empirical data. For example, if 100 customers arrive at a store checkout counter during a 10-hour day, we could say the arrival rate averages 10 customers per hour. However, although we might be able to determine a rate for arrivals by counting the number of customers during a specific time period, we would not know exactly when these customers would arrive. It might be that no customers would arrive during one hour and 20 customers would arrive during another hour. Arrivals are assumed to be independent of each other and to vary randomly over time.

The **arrival rate** is the frequency at which customers arrive at a waiting line according to a probability distribution.

We further assume that arrivals at a service facility conform to some probability distribution. Arrivals could be described by many distributions, but it has been determined (through years of research and the practical experience of people in the field of queuing) that the number of arrivals per unit of time at a service facility can frequently be defined by a *Poisson distribution*. In queuing the average arrival rate, or how many customers arrive during a period of time, is signified by λ.

Arrival rate (λ) is most frequently described by a Poisson distribution.

Service Times

The queuing theory arrivals are described in terms of a *rate* and service in terms of *time*. **Service times** in a queuing process may also be any one of a large number of different probability distributions. The distribution most commonly assumed for service times is the *negative exponential distribution*. Although this probability distribution is for service *times*, service must be expressed as a *rate* to be compatible with the arrival rate. The

Service time, the time required to serve a customer, is most frequently described by the negative exponential distribution.

average service rate, or how many customers can be served in a period of time, is expressed as μ.

Empirical research has shown that the assumption of negative exponentially distributed service times is not valid nearly as often as is the assumption of Poisson-distributed arrivals. Therefore, for actual applications of queuing analysis, this assumption would have to be carefully checked before this distribution was used.

Arrival Rate Less Than Service Rate

> Customers must be served faster than they arrive or an infinitely large queue will build up, $\lambda < \mu$.

It is logical to assume that the rate at which services are completed must exceed the arrival rate of customers. If this is not the case, the waiting line will continue to grow, and there will be no "average" solution. Thus, it is generally assumed that the service rate exceeds the arrival rate, $\lambda < \mu$.

Queue Discipline and Length

> **Queue discipline** is the order in which customers are served.
>
> The most common service rule is first come, first served.

The **queue discipline** is the order in which waiting customers are served. The most common type of queue discipline is *first come, first served*—the first person or item in line waiting is served first. Other disciplines are possible. For example, a machine operator might stack in-process parts beside a machine so that the last part is on top of the stack and will be selected first. This queue discipline is *last in, first out*. Or, the machine operator might reach into a box full of parts and select one at random. This queue discipline is *random*. Often customers are scheduled for service according to a predetermined appointment, such as patients at a dentist's office or diners at a restaurant where reservations are required. These customers are taken according to a prearranged schedule regardless of when they arrive at the facility. Another example of the many types of queue disciplines is when customers are processed alphabetically according to their last names, such as at school registration or at job interviews.

> An **infinite queue** can be of any length; the length of a **finite queue** is limited.

Queues can be of an infinite or finite size or length. An **infinite queue** can be of any size with no upper limit and is the most common queue structure. For example, it is assumed that the waiting line at a movie theater could stretch through the lobby and out the door if necessary. A **finite queue** is limited in size. An example is the driveway at a bank teller window that can accommodate only a limited number of cars.

Basic Waiting Line Structures

Waiting line processes are generally categorized into four basic structures, according to the nature of the service facilities: single-channel, single-phase; single-channel, multiple-phase; multiple-channel, single-phase; and multiple-channel, multiple-phase processes. These are illustrated graphically in Figure 16.2.

> **Channels** are the number of parallel servers; **phases** denote the number of sequential servers a customer must go through to receive service.

The number of **channels** in a queuing process is the number of parallel servers for servicing arriving customers. The number of **phases**, on the other hand, denotes the number of sequential servers each customer must go through to complete service. An example of a *single-channel, single-phase* queuing operation is a post office with only one postal clerk waiting on a single line of customers. A post office with several postal clerks waiting on a single line of customers is an example of a *multiple-channel, single-phase* operation.

When patients go to a doctor for treatment or check into a hospital, they wait in a reception room prior to entering the treatment facility. When they get to the treatment room, the patients receive an initial checkup or treatment from a nurse, followed by treatment from a doctor. This arrangement constitutes a *single-channel, multiple-phase* queuing process. If there are several doctors and nurses, the process is a *multiple-channel, multiple-phase* process.

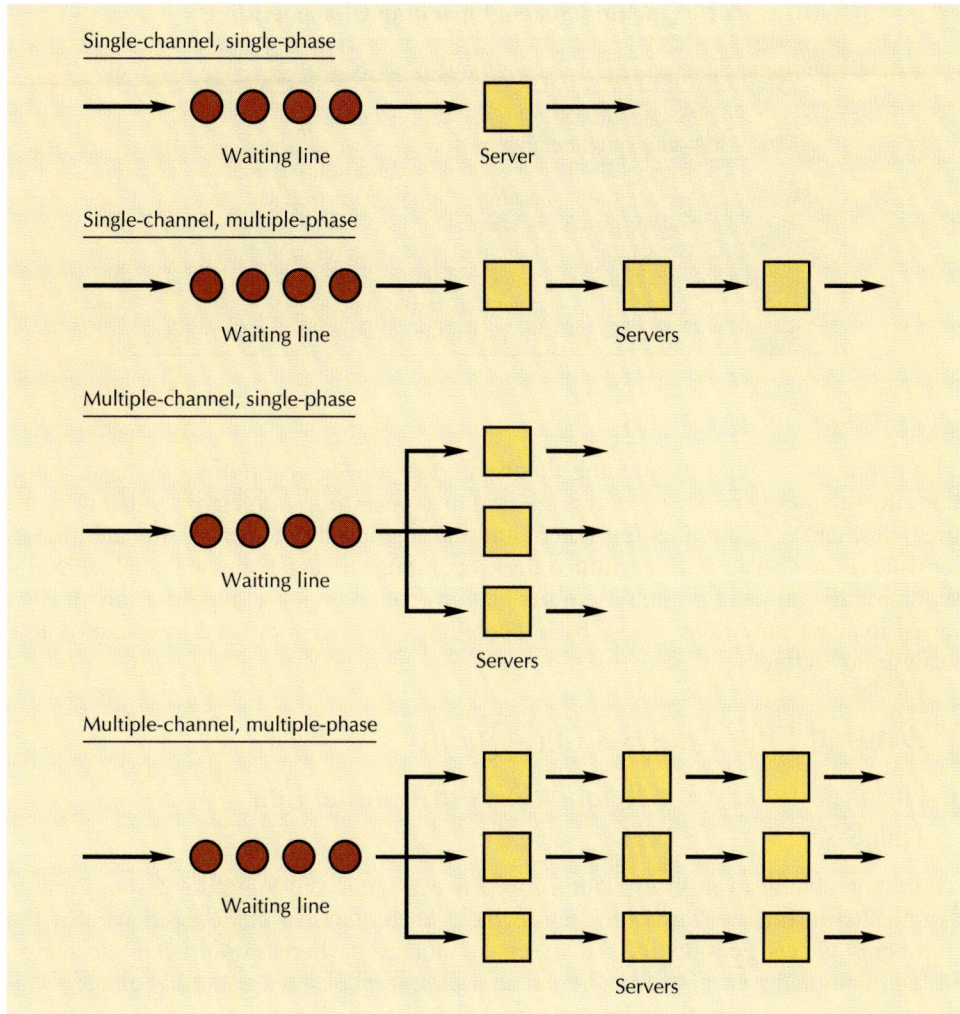

FIGURE 16.2 **Basic Waiting Line Structures**

An example of another multiple-phase system is a manufacturing assembly in which a product is worked on at several sequential machines or operators at a workstation. An example of a single-channel, multiple-phase system is a manufacturing assembly line type operation in which in-process product units are fed to several sequential machines or operators at workstations to be worked on. Two or more of these lines operating in tandem and being fed by a single line of product units are an example of a multi-channel, multi-phase system.

You may immediately visualize a familiar waiting situation that fits none of these categories of waiting line structures. The four categories of queuing processes presented are simply the four basic categories; there are many variations. For example, rather than a single queue preceding the multiple-channel, single-phase case, there might be a separate queue preceding each server. In the multiple-channel, multiple-phase case, items might switch back and forth from one channel to the other between each of the various service phases. Queuing models can become quite complex. However, the fundamentals of basic queuing theory are relevant to the analysis of all queuing problems, regardless of their complexity.

TABLE 16.1 Queuing System Operating Characteristics

Notation	Operating Characteristic
L	Average number of customers in the system (waiting and being served)
L_q	Average number of customers in the waiting line
W	Average time a customer spends in the system (waiting and being served)
W_q	Average time a customer spends waiting in line
P_0	Probability of no (zero) customers in the system
P_n	Probability of n customers in the system
ρ	Utilization rate; the proportion of time the system is in use

Operating Characteristics

The mathematics used in queuing theory do not provide an optimal, or "best," solution. Instead they generate measures referred to as *operating characteristics* that describe the performance of the queuing system and that management uses to evaluate the system and make decisions. It is assumed these operating characteristics will approach constant, average values after the system has been in operation for a long time, which is referred to as a *steady state*. These basic operating characteristics used in a waiting line analysis are defined in Table 16.1.

A steady state is a constant, average value for performance characteristics that the system will attain after a long time.

Waiting Line Analysis and Quality
The Traditional Cost Relationships in Waiting Line Analysis

There is generally an inverse relationship between service cost and the cost of waiting, as reflected in the cost curves in Figure 16.3. As the level of service, reflected by the number of servers, goes up, the cost of service increases, whereas waiting cost decreases. In the traditional view of waiting line analysis, the level of service should coincide with the minimum point on the total cost curve.

As the level of service improves, the cost of service increases.

Better service requires more servers.

The cost of providing the service is usually reflected in the cost of the servers, such as the cost of the tellers at a bank, postal workers at a post office counter, or the repair crew in a plant or shop. As the number of servers is increased to reduce waiting time, service cost goes up. Service cost is normally direct and easy to compute. The cost of waiting is not as easy to determine. The major determinant of waiting cost is the loss of business that might result because customers get tired of waiting and leave; then, they may purchase the product or service elsewhere. This business loss can be temporary (a single event) or permanent (the customer never comes back). The cost due to a loss of business is especially difficult to determine, since it is not part of normal accounting records, although some trade organizations for businesses and industries occasionally provide such data. Other types of waiting costs include the loss of production time and salary for employees waiting to use machinery or equipment, load or unload vehicles, and so forth.

Waiting Line Costs and Quality Service

The TQM approach is that absolute quality service will be the most cost-effective in the long run.

The modern approach to quality management is to assume that the traditional quality-cost relationship is a short-run perspective that understates the potential long-term loss of business from poor quality. In the long run, a higher level of quality will gain mar-

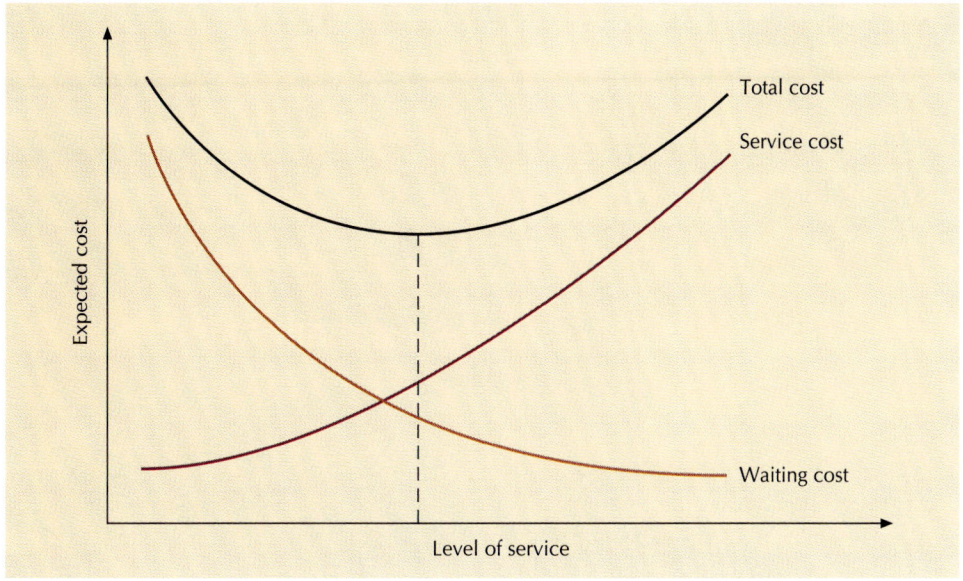

FIGURE 16.3 **The Cost Relationship in Waiting Line Analysis**

ket share and increase business and thus is more cost-effective. Further, as the company focuses on improving quality service, the cost of achieving good quality will be less because of the innovations in processes and work design that will result. This is the philosophy of "zero defects," which in waiting line analysis means no waiting. This level of better-quality, that is, quicker, service will, in the long run, increase business and be more cost-effective than the traditional view implies.

An alternative to improving service quality by reducing waiting time, is to make waiting more palatable by providing diversions. Waiting rooms, such as at a doctor's office, provide magazines and newspapers for customers to read while waiting. Televisions are occasionally available in auto repair waiting areas, in airport terminals, or in bars and lounges of restaurants where customers wait. At Disney World costumed characters entertain park visitors while they wait in line for rides. Mirrors are purposely located near elevators to distract people while they wait. Supermarkets locate magazines and other "impulse-purchase" items at the checkout counter, not only as a diversion while waiting but as potential purchases. All these tactics are designed to improve the quality of service that requires waiting without actually incurring the cost of reducing waiting time.

Single-Channel, Single-Phase Models

The simplest, most basic of the waiting line structures illustrated in Figure 16.2 is the single-channel, single-phase—or, simply, *single-server*—model. There are several variations of the single-server waiting line system, and in this chapter we present several of the following frequently used variations:

- Poisson arrival rate, exponential service times
- Poisson arrival rate, general (or unknown) distribution of service times
- Poisson arrival rate, constant service times
- Poisson arrival rate, exponential service times with a finite queue
- Poisson arrival rate, exponential service times with a finite calling population

Variations of the basic single-server model

"Good" operating characteristics for a waiting line system, and hence good service, are relative and must have some basis for comparison. For example, the waiting time at this <u>McDonald's</u> *in Pushkin Square in Moscow averages about 45 minutes. Americans would not accept this level of service. To Muscovites used to waiting in lines that often consume the better part of a day, the waiting time at this McDonald's is amazingly short. It represents good service.*

www.prenhall.com/russell

The Basic Single-Server Model

In the basic single-server model we assume the following:

Assumptions of the basic single-server model

- Poisson arrival rate
- Exponential service times
- First-come, first-served queue discipline
- Infinite queue length
- Infinite calling population

λ = mean arrival rate; μ = mean service rate.

The basic operating characteristics of this single-server model are computed using the following formulas, where λ = mean arrival rate, μ = mean service rate, and n = the number of customers in the waiting line system.

The probability that no customers are in the queuing system (either in the queue or being served) is

Basic single-server queuing formulas

$$P_0 = \left(1 - \frac{\lambda}{\mu}\right)$$

The probability of exactly n customers in the queuing system is

$$P_n = \left(\frac{\lambda}{\mu}\right)^n \cdot P_0$$

$$= \left(\frac{\lambda}{\mu}\right)^n \left(1 - \frac{\lambda}{\mu}\right)$$

The average number of customers in the queuing system (i.e., the customers being serviced and in the waiting line) is

$$L = \frac{\lambda}{\mu - \lambda}$$

The average number of customers in the waiting line is

$$L_q = \frac{\lambda^2}{\mu(\mu - \lambda)}$$

The average time a customer spends in the queuing system (i.e., waiting and being served) is

$$W = \frac{1}{\mu - \lambda}$$
$$= \frac{L}{\lambda}$$

The average time a customer spends waiting in line to be served is

$$W_q = \frac{\lambda}{\mu(\mu - \lambda)}$$

The probability that the server is busy and a customer has to wait, known as the utilization factor is

$$\rho = \frac{\lambda}{\mu}$$

The probability that the server is idle and a customer can be served is

$$I = 1 - \rho$$
$$= 1 - \frac{\lambda}{\mu} = P_0$$

EXAMPLE 16.1

A Single-Server Model

The Fast Shop Drive-In Market has one checkout counter where one employee operates the cash register. The combination of the cash register and the operator is the server (or service facility) in this queuing system; the customers who line up at the counter to pay for their selections form the waiting line.

Customers arrive at a rate of 24 per hour according to a Poisson distribution ($\lambda = 24$), and service times are exponentially distributed with a mean rate of 30 customers per hour ($\mu = 30$). The market manager wants to determine the operating characteristics for this waiting line system.

SOLUTION:

The operating characteristics are computed using the queuing formulas for the single-server model as follows:

$$P_0 = \left(1 - \frac{\lambda}{\mu}\right)$$
$$= \left(1 - \frac{24}{30}\right)$$

(Continued)

$$= 0.20 \text{ probability of no customers in the system}$$

$$L = \frac{\lambda}{\mu - \lambda}$$

$$= \frac{24}{30 - 24}$$

$$= 4 \text{ customers on the average in the queuing system}$$

$$L_q = \frac{\lambda^2}{\mu(\mu - \lambda)}$$

$$= \frac{(24)^2}{30(30 - 24)}$$

$$= 3.2 \text{ customers on the average in the waiting line}$$

$$W = \frac{1}{\mu - \lambda}$$

$$= \frac{1}{30 - 24}$$

$$= 0.167 \text{ hour (10 minutes) average time in the system per customer}$$

$$W_q = \frac{\lambda}{\mu(\mu - \lambda)}$$

$$= \frac{24}{30(30 - 24)}$$

$$= 0.133 \text{ hour (8 minutes) average time in the waiting line per customer}$$

$$\rho = \frac{\lambda}{\mu}$$

$$= \frac{24}{30}$$

$$= 0.80 \text{ probability that the server will be busy and the customer must wait}$$

$$I = 1 - \rho$$

$$= 1 - 0.80$$

$$= 0.20 \text{ probability that the server will be idle and a customer can be served}$$

Remember that these operating characteristics are averages that result over a period of time; they are not absolutes. In other words, customers who arrive at the Fast Shop Drive-In Market checkout counter will not find 3.2 customers in line. There could be no customers or 1, 2, 3, or 4 customers. The value 3.2 is simply an average over time, as are the other operating characteristics.

EXAMPLE 16.2

Waiting Line Cost Analysis

At the Fast Shop Drive-In Market in Example 16.1, the arrival rate of 24 customers per hour means that, on the average, a customer arrives about every 2.5 minutes (i.e., $^{1}/_{24} \times$ 60 minutes). This indicates the store is busy. Because of the nature of the store, customers purchase a few items and expect quick service. Customers expect to spend more time in a supermarket where they make larger purchases, but they shop at a drive-in market because it is quicker than a supermarket.

Given customers' expectations, the manager believes that it is unacceptable for a customer to wait 8 minutes and spend a total of 10 minutes in the queuing system (not including the actual shopping time). The manager wants to test several alternatives for reducing customer waiting time: (1) another employee to pack up the purchases; and (2) another checkout counter.

SOLUTION:

Alternative I: Add an Employee

An extra employee will cost the market manager $150 per week. With the help of the market's national office's marketing research group, the manager has determined that for each minute that customer waiting time is reduced, the store avoids a loss in sales of $75 per week. (The store loses money when customers leave prior to shopping because of the long line or when customers do not return.)

If an employee is hired, customers can be served in less time—the service rate, the number of customers served per time period, will increase. The service rate with one employee is

$\mu = 30$ customers served per hour

The service rate with two employees will be

$\mu = 40$ customers served per hour

We assume the arrival rate will remain the same ($\lambda = 24$ per hour), since the increased service rate will not increase arrivals but will minimize the loss of customers. (It is not illogical to assume an increase in service might eventually increase arrivals in the long run.)

Given the new λ and μ values, the operating characteristics can be recomputed as follows.

$P_0 = 0.40$ probability of no customers in the system

$L = 1.5$ customers on the average in the queuing system

$L_q = 0.90$ customer on the average in the waiting line

$W = 0.063$ hour (3.75 minutes) average time in the system per customer

$W_q = 0.038$ hour (2.25 minutes) average time in the waiting line per customer

$\rho = 0.60$ probability that the customer must wait

$I = 0.40$ probability that the server will be idle and a customer can be served

The average waiting time per customer has been reduced from 8 minutes to 2.25 minutes, a significant amount. The savings (that is, the decrease in lost sales) is computed as

8.00 minutes − 2.25 minutes = 5.75 minutes

5.75 minutes × $75/minute/week = $431.25 per week

Since the extra employee costs management $150 per week, the total savings will be

$431.25 − $150 = $281.25 per week

The market manager would probably welcome this savings and prefer two employees.

(Continued)

Alternative II: Add a Checkout Counter

The total cost of a new checkout counter would be $6,000, plus an extra $200 per week for an additional cashier.

The new checkout counter would be opposite the present counter (so that the servers would have their backs to each other in an enclosed counter area). There would be several display cases and racks between the two lines, so that customers waiting in line would not move back and forth between lines. (Such movement, called *jockeying*, would invalidate the queuing formulas for this model.) We will assume that the customers would divide themselves equally between both lines, so the arrival rate for each line would be half of the arrival rate for a single checkout counter, or

$\lambda = 12$ customers per hour

The service rate remains the same for each counter:

$\mu = 30$ customers served per hour

Substituting this new arrival rate and the service rate into our queuing formulas results in the following operating characteristics:

$P_0 = 0.60$ probability of no customers in the system

$L = 0.67$ customer in the queuing system

$L_q = 0.27$ customer in the waiting line

$W = 0.055$ hour (3.33 minutes) per customer in the system

$W_q = 0.022$ hour (1.33 minutes) per customer in the waiting line

$\rho = 0.40$ probability that a customer must wait

$I = 0.60$ probability that a server will be idle and a customer can be served

Using the same sales savings of $75 per week for each minute's reduction in waiting time, we find that the store would save

8.00 minutes − 1.33 minutes = 6.67 minutes

6.67 minutes × $75/minute = $500.00 per week

Next we subtract the $200 per week cost for the new cashier from this amount saved.

$500 − 200 = $300

Since the capital outlay of this project is $6,000, it would take about 20 weeks ($6,000/$300 = 20 weeks) to recoup the initial cost (ignoring the cost of interest on the $6,000). Once the cost has been recovered, the store would save $18.75 ($300.00 − 281.25) more per week by adding a new checkout counter rather than simply hiring an extra employee. However, we must not disregard the fact that during the 20-week cost recovery period, the $281.25 savings incurred by simply hiring a new employee would be lost.

For the market manager both of these alternatives seem preferable to the original conditions, which resulted in a waiting time of 8 minutes per customer. However, the manager might have a difficult time selecting between the two alternatives. It might be appropriate to consider other factors besides waiting time. For example, the portion of time the employee is idle is 40 percent with the first alternative and 60 percent with the second, a significant difference. An additional factor is the loss of space resulting from a new checkout counter.

The final decision must be based on the manager's own experience and perceived needs. As we said, the results of queuing analysis simply provide information for decision making.

These two alternatives illustrate the cost trade-offs associated with improved service. As the level of service increases, the corresponding cost of this service also increases. For example, when we added an extra employee in alternative I, the service was improved, but the cost of providing service also increased. But when the level of service was increased, the costs associated with customer waiting decreased.

Solution of the Single-Server Model with POM for Windows

The "waiting lines" module in POM for Windows can be used to solve all of the queuing models in this chapter. The solution screen for the single-server model for the Fast Shop Drive-In Market in Example 16.1 is shown in Exhibit 16.1, as follows.

Constant Service Times

The single-server model with Poisson arrivals and *constant service times* is a queuing variation that is of particular interest in operations management, since the most frequent occurrence of constant service times is with automated equipment and machinery. This type of queuing model has direct application for many manufacturing operations.

The constant service time model is actually a special case of a more general variation of the single-server model in which service times cannot be assumed to be expo-

Constant service times occur with machinery and automated equipment.

Constant service times are a special case of the single-server model with undefined service times.

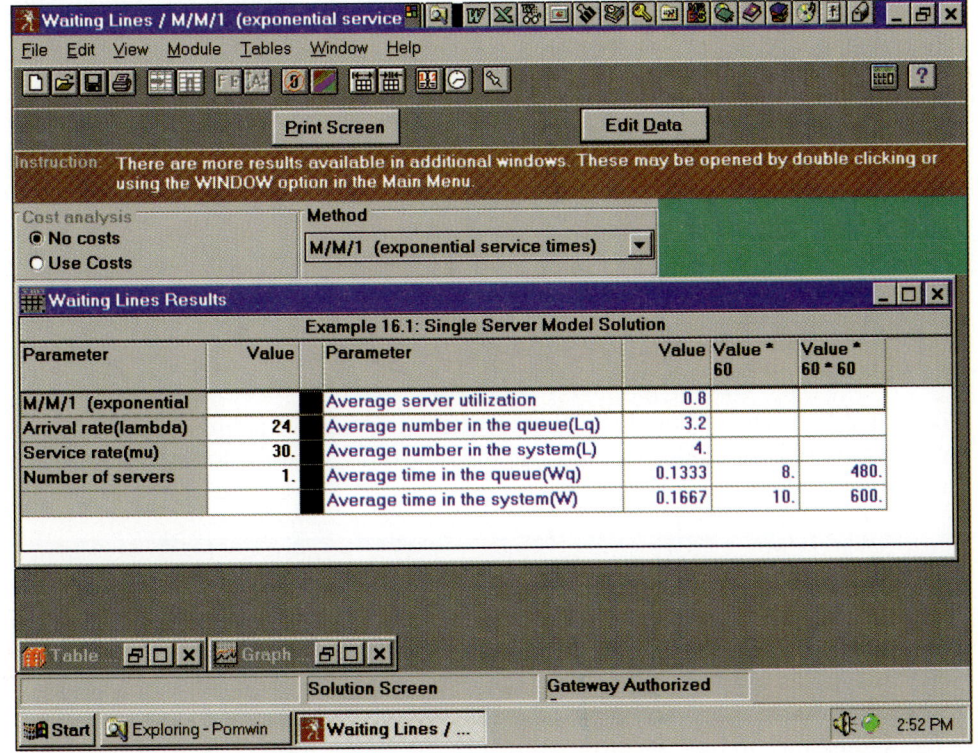

EXHIBIT 16.1

nentially distributed. Service times are said to be *general*, or *undefined*. The basic queuing formulas for the operating characteristics of the undefined service time model are as follows.

$$P_0 = 1 - \frac{\lambda}{\mu}$$

$$L_q = \frac{\lambda^2\sigma^2 + (\lambda/\mu)^2}{2(1 - \lambda/\mu)}$$

$$L = L_q + \frac{\lambda}{\mu}$$

$$W_q = \frac{L_q}{\lambda}$$

$$W = W_q = \frac{1}{\mu}$$

$$\rho = \frac{\lambda}{\mu}$$

The key formula for undefined service times is for L_q, the number of customers in the waiting line. In this formula μ and σ are the mean and standard deviation, respectively, for any general probability distribution with independent service times. If we let $\sigma = \mu$ in the formula for L_q for undefined service times, it becomes the same as our basic formula with exponential service times. In fact all the queuing formulas become the same as the basic single-server model.

In the case of constant service times, there is no variability in service times (i.e., service time is the same constant value for each customer); thus, $\sigma = 0$. Substituting $\sigma = 0$ into the undefined service time formula for L_q results in the following formula for constant service times.

$$\begin{aligned} L_q &= \frac{\lambda^2\sigma^2 + (\lambda/\mu)^2}{2(1 - \lambda/\mu)} \\ &= \frac{\lambda^2(0) + (\lambda/\mu)^2}{2(1 - \lambda/\mu)} \\ &= \frac{(\lambda/\mu)^2}{2(1 - \lambda/\mu)} \\ &= \frac{\lambda^2}{2\mu(\mu - \lambda)} \end{aligned}$$

Notice that this new formula for L_q for constant service times is simply the basic single-server formula for L_q divided by 2. All the remaining formulas for the single-server model are the same.

EXAMPLE
16.3

A Single-Server Model with Constant Service Times

The Petrolco Service Station has an automatic car wash, and cars purchasing gas at the station receive a discounted car wash, depending on the number of gallons of gas they buy. The car wash can accommodate one car at a time, and it requires a constant time of 4.5 minutes for a wash. Cars arrive at the car wash at an average rate of 10 per hour (Poisson distributed). The service station manager wants to determine the average length of the waiting line and the average waiting time at the car wash.

SOLUTION:

First determine λ and μ such that they are expressed as rates:

$\lambda = 10$ cars per hour

$\mu = \dfrac{60}{4.5} = 13.3$ cars per hour

Substituting λ and μ into the queuing formulas for constant service time gives

$$L_q = \frac{\lambda^2}{2\mu(\mu - \lambda)}$$

$$= \frac{(10)^2}{2(13.3)(13.3 - 10)}$$

$$= 1.14 \text{ cars waiting}$$

$$W_q = \frac{L_q}{\lambda}$$

$$= \frac{1.14}{10}$$

$$= 0.114 \text{ hour, or } 6.84 \text{ minutes, waiting in line}$$

The Excel screen for Example 16.3 is shown below.

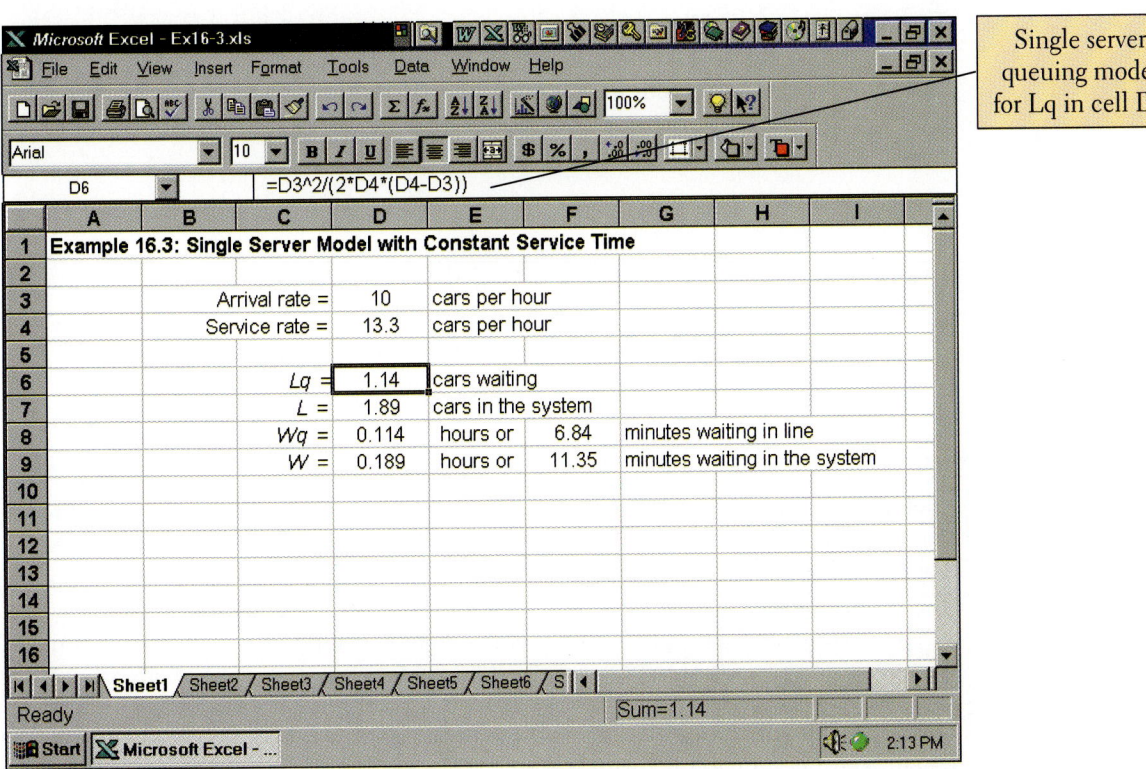

Single server queuing model for Lq in cell D6

EXHIBIT 16.2

Solution of the Constant Service Time Model with Excel

Several of the queuing models in this chapter can be solved with Excel including the single-server model with constant service times. The Excel screen for Example 16.3 is shown in Exhibit 16.2. Notice that the queuing formula for L_q in cell D6 is also shown on the formula bar at the top of the screen.

Finite Queue Length

For some waiting line systems, the length of the queue may be limited by the physical area in which the queue forms; space may permit only a limited number of customers to enter the queue. Such a waiting line is referred to as a *finite queue*; it results in another variation of the single-phase, single-channel queuing model.

The basic single-server model must be modified to consider the finite queuing system. For this case the service rate does not have to exceed the arrival rate $(\mu > \lambda)$ to obtain steady-state conditions. The resultant operating characteristics, where M is the maximum number in the system, are,

$$P_0 = \frac{1 - \lambda/\mu}{1 - (\lambda/\mu)^{M+1}}$$

$$P_n = (P_0) \left(\frac{\lambda}{\mu}\right)^n \text{ for } n \leq M$$

$$L = \frac{\lambda/\mu}{1 - \lambda/\mu} - \frac{(M + 1)(\lambda/\mu)^{M+1}}{1 - (\lambda/\mu)^{M+1}}$$

Since P_n is the probability of n units in the system, if we define M as the maximum number allowed in the system, then P_M (the value of P_n for $n = M$) is the probability that a customer will not join the system. The remaining equations are

$$L_q = L - \frac{\lambda(1 - P_M)}{\mu}$$

$$W = \frac{L}{\lambda(1 - P_M)}$$

$$W_q = W - \frac{1}{\mu}$$

EXAMPLE 16.4	

**EXAMPLE
16.4**

*A Single-Server Model
with Finite Queue*

Slick's Quick Lube is a one-bay service facility next to a busy highway. The facility has space for only one vehicle in service and three vehicles lined up to wait for service. There is no space for cars to line up on the busy adjacent highway, so if the waiting line is full (3 cars), prospective customers must drive on.

The mean time between arrivals for customers seeking lube service is 3 minutes. The mean time required to perform the lube operation is 2 minutes. Both the interarrival times and the service times are exponentially distributed. The maximum number of vehicles in the system is four. Determine the average waiting time, the average queue length, and the probability that a customer will have to drive on.

SOLUTION:

$\lambda = 20$

$\mu = 30$

$M = 4$ cars

First, we compute the probability that the system is full and the customer must drive on, P_M. However, this first requires the determination of P_0, as follows:

$$P_0 = \frac{1 - \lambda/\mu}{1 - (\lambda/\mu)^{M+1}}$$

$$= \frac{1 - 20/30}{1 - (20/30)^5}$$

$= 0.38$ probability of no cars in the system

$$P_M = (P_0)\left(\frac{\lambda}{\mu}\right)^{n=M}$$

$$= (0.38\left(\frac{20}{30}\right)^4$$

$= 0.076$ probability that 4 cars are in the system, it is full (and the customer must drive on)

Next, to compute the average queue length, L_q, the average number of cars in the system, L, must be computed as follows.

$$L = \frac{\lambda/\mu}{1 - \lambda/\mu} - \frac{(M + 1)(\lambda/\mu)^{M+1}}{1 - (\lambda/\mu)^{M+1}}$$

$$= \frac{20/30}{1 - 20/30} - \frac{(5)(20/30)^5}{1 - (20/30)^5}$$

$= 1.24$ cars in the system

$$L_q = L - \frac{\lambda(1 - P_M)}{\mu}$$

$$= 1.24 - \frac{20(1 - 0.076)}{30}$$

$= 0.62$ cars waiting

To compute the average waiting time W_q, the average time in the system, W, must be computed first.

$$W = \frac{L}{\lambda(1 - P_M)}$$

$$= \frac{1.24}{20(1 - 0.076)}$$

$= 0.067$ hour or 4.03 minutes in the system

$$W_q = W - \frac{1}{\mu}$$

$$= 0.067 - \frac{1}{30}$$

$= 0.033$ hour or 2.03 minutes waiting in line

Finite Calling Populations

The population of customers from which arrivals originate is limited, such as the number of police cars at a station to answer calls.

The single-server model with a Poisson arrival and exponential service times and a finite calling population has the following set of formulas for determining operating characteristics.

$$P_0 = \frac{1}{\displaystyle\sum_{n=0}^{N} \frac{N!}{(N-n)!}\left(\frac{\lambda}{\mu}\right)^n}, \quad \text{where } N = \text{population size}$$

$$P_n = \frac{N!}{(N-n)!}\left(\frac{\lambda}{\mu}\right)^n P_0, \text{ where } n = 1, 2, \ldots, N$$

$$L_q = N - \left(\frac{\lambda + \mu}{\lambda}\right)(1 - P_0)$$

$$L = L_q + (1 - P_0)$$

$$W_q = \frac{L_q}{(N - L)\lambda}$$

$$W = W_q + \frac{1}{\mu}$$

In this model λ is the arrival rate of each member of the population. The formulas for P_0 and P_n are both relatively complex and can be cumbersome to compute manually. POM for Windows has the capability of solving the finite calling population model.

EXAMPLE
16.5

A Single-Server Model with Finite Calling Population

The Wheelco Manufacturing Company operates a job shop that has 20 machines. Due to the type of work performed in the shop, there is a lot of wear and tear on the machines, and they require frequent repair. When a machine breaks down, it is tagged for repair, with the date of breakdown noted. The company has one senior repair person, with an assistant, who repairs the machines based on an oldest-date-of-breakdown rule (i.e., a FIFO queue discipline). Each machine operates an average of 200 hours before breaking down, and the mean repair time is 3.6 hours. The breakdown rate is Poisson distributed and the service times are exponentially distributed. The company would like an analysis performed of machine idle time due to breakdowns in order to determine if the present repair staff is sufficient.

SOLUTION:

$$\lambda = \frac{1}{200 \text{ hour}} = 0.005 \text{ per hour}$$

$$\mu = \frac{1}{3.6 \text{ hour}} = 0.2778 \text{ per hour}$$

$$N = 20 \text{ machines}$$

$$P_0 = \frac{1}{\displaystyle\sum_{n=0}^{N} \frac{N!}{(N-n)!}\left(\frac{\lambda}{\mu}\right)^n}$$

$$= \cfrac{1}{\displaystyle\sum_{n=0}^{20} \frac{20!}{(20-n)!} \left(\frac{0.005}{0.2778}\right)^n}$$

$$= .652$$

$$L_q = N - \left(\frac{\lambda + \mu}{\lambda}\right)(1 - P_0)$$

$$= 20 - \frac{0.005 + 0.2778}{0.005}(1 - 0.652)$$

$$= .169 \text{ machines waiting}$$

$$L = L_q + (1 - P_0)$$

$$= .169 + (1 - 0.652)$$

$$= .520 \text{ machines in the system}$$

$$W_q = \frac{L_q}{(N - L)\lambda}$$

$$= \frac{.169}{(20 - .520)(0.005)}$$

$$= 1.74 \text{ hours waiting for repair}$$

$$W = W_q + \frac{1}{\mu}$$

$$= 1.74 + \frac{1}{0.2778}$$

$$= 5.33 \text{ hours time in the system}$$

These results show that the repairperson and assistant are busy 35 percent of the time repairing machines. Of the 20 machines, an average of 0.52 or 2.6 percent, are broken down waiting for repair or under repair. Each broken-down machine is idle (broken down waiting for repair or under repair) an average of 5.33 hours. The system seems adequate.

Multiple-Channel, Single-Phase Models

A larger number of operational waiting line systems include multiple servers. These models can be very complex, so in this section we present only the most basic multiple-server (or channel) waiting line structure. This system includes a single waiting line and a service facility with several independent servers in parallel, as shown in Figure 16.2. An example of a multiple-server system is an airline ticket and check-in counter, where passengers line up in a roped-off single line waiting for one of several agents for service. The same waiting line structure is frequently found at the post office, where customers in a single line wait for service from several postal clerks.

The Basic Multiple-Server Model

The formulas for determining the operating characteristics for the *multiple-server model* are based on the same assumptions as the single-server model—Poisson arrival rate, exponential service times, infinite calling population and queue length, and FIFO queue

With multiple-server models, two or more independent servers in parallel serve a single waiting line.

These passengers waiting in line to purchase tickets or check baggage and get a boarding pass at the Orange County, California airport are part of a waiting line system with multiple servers. Passengers are cordoned into a single line to wait for one of several airline agents to serve them. The number of agents scheduled for duty at the check-in counter is determined by waiting line operating characteristics based on different passenger arrival rates during the day and for different days. On New Year's Day only one agent might be on duty, while on the Wednesday before Thanksgiving, one of the busiest airline travel days of the year, the maximum number of agents would be used.

$s\mu > \lambda$: The total number of servers must be able to serve customers faster than they arrive.

discipline. Also, recall that in the single-server model, $\mu > \lambda$; however, in the multiple-server model, $s\mu > \lambda$, where s is the number of servers. The operating characteristics formulas are as follows.

The probability that there are no customers in the system (all servers are idle) is

$$P_0 = \frac{1}{\left[\sum_{n=0}^{n=s-1} \frac{1}{n!}\left(\frac{\lambda}{\mu}\right)^n\right] + \frac{1}{s!}\left(\frac{\lambda}{\mu}\right)^s \left(\frac{s\mu}{s\mu - \lambda}\right)}$$

The probability of n customers in the queuing system is

$$P_n = \begin{cases} \dfrac{1}{s!s^{n-s}}\left(\dfrac{\lambda}{\mu}\right)^n P_0, & \text{for } n > s \\[3mm] \dfrac{1}{n!}\left(\dfrac{\lambda}{\mu}\right)^n P_0, & \text{for } n \leq s \end{cases}$$

The probability that a customer arriving in the system must wait for service (i.e., the probability that all the servers are busy) is

$$P_w = \frac{1}{s!}\left(\frac{\lambda}{\mu}\right)^s \frac{s\mu}{s\mu - \lambda} P_0$$

$$L = \frac{\lambda\mu(\lambda/\mu)^s}{(s-1)!(s\mu - \lambda)^2} P_0 + \frac{\lambda}{\mu}$$

$$W = \frac{L}{\lambda}$$

$$L_q = L - \frac{\lambda}{\mu}$$

$$W_q = W - \frac{1}{\mu}$$

$$= \frac{L_q}{\lambda}$$

$$\rho = \frac{\lambda}{s\mu}$$

The key formula in this set is for P_0, which can be time-consuming to compute manually. Table 16.2 provides values for P_0 for selected values of the server utilization factor, ρ, and the number of servers, s.

TABLE 16.2   Selected Values of P_0 for the Multiple-Server Model

$\rho = \lambda/s\mu$				Number of Channels: s						
ρ	2	3	4	5	6	7	8	9	10	15
0.02	0.96079	0.94177	0.92312	0.90484	0.88692	0.86936	0.85215	0.83527	0.81873	0.74082
0.04	0.92308	0.88692	0.85215	0.81873	0.78663	0.75578	0.72615	0.69768	0.67032	0.54881
0.06	0.88679	0.83526	0.78663	0.74082	0.69768	0.65705	0.61878	0.58275	0.54881	0.40657
0.08	0.85185	0.78659	0.72615	0.67032	0.61878	0.57121	0.52729	0.48675	0.44983	0.30119
0.10	0.81818	0.74074	0.67031	0.60653	0.54881	0.49659	0.44933	0.40657	0.36788	0.22313
0.12	0.78571	0.69753	0.61876	0.54881	0.48675	0.43171	0.38289	0.33960	0.30119	0.16530
0.14	0.75439	0.65679	0.57116	0.49657	0.43171	0.37531	0.72628	0.28365	0.24660	0.12246
0.16	0.72414	0.61838	0.52720	0.44931	0.38289	0.32628	0.27804	0.23693	0.20190	0.09072
0.18	0.69492	0.58214	0.48660	0.40653	0.33959	0.28365	0.23693	0.19790	0.16530	0.06721
0.20	0.66667	0.54795	0.44910	0.36782	0.30118	0.24659	0.20189	0.16530	0.13534	0.04979
0.22	0.63934	0.51567	0.41445	0.33277	0.26711	0.21437	0.17204	0.13807	0.11080	0.03688
0.24	0.61290	0.48519	0.38244	0.30105	0.23688	0.18636	0.14660	0.11532	0.09072	0.02732
0.26	0.58730	0.45640	0.35284	0.27233	0.21007	0.16200	0.12492	0.09632	0.07427	0.02024
0.28	0.56250	0.42918	0.32548	0.24633	0.18628	0.14082	0.10645	0.08045	0.06081	0.01500
0.30	0.53846	0.40346	0.30017	0.22277	0.16517	0.12241	0.09070	0.06720	0.04978	0.01111
0.32	0.51515	0.37913	0.27676	0.20144	0.14644	0.10639	0.07728	0.05612	0.04076	0.00823
0.34	0.49254	0.35610	0.25510	0.18211	0.12981	0.09247	0.06584	0.04687	0.03337	0.00610
0.36	0.47059	0.33431	0.23505	0.16460	0.11505	0.08035	0.05609	0.03915	0.02732	0.00452
0.38	0.44928	0.31367	0.21649	0.14872	0.10195	0.06981	0.04778	0.03269	0.02236	0.00335
0.40	0.42857	0.29412	0.19929	0.13433	0.09032	0.06065	0.04069	0.02729	0.01830	0.00248
0.42	0.40845	0.27559	0.18336	0.12128	0.07998	0.05627	0.03465	0.02279	0.01498	0.00184
0.44	0.38889	0.25802	0.16860	0.10944	0.07080	0.04573	0.02950	0.01902	0.01225	0.00136
0.46	0.36986	0.24135	0.15491	0.09870	0.0265	0.03968	0.02511	0.01587	0.01003	0.00101
0.48	0.35135	0.22554	0.14221	0.08895	0.05540	0.03442	0.02136	0.01324	0.00826	0.00075
0.50	0.3333	0.21053	0.13043	0.08010	0.04896	0.02984	0.01816	0.01104	0.00671	0.00055
0.52	0.31579	0.19627	0.11951	0.07207	0.04323	0.02586	0.01544	0.00920	0.00548	0.00041
0.54	0.29870	0.18273	0.10936	0.06477	0.03814	0.02239	0.01313	0.00767	0.00448	0.00030
0.56	0.28205	0.16986	0.09994	0.05814	0.03362	0.01936	0.01113	0.00638	0.00366	0.00022
0.58	0.26582	0.15762	0.09119	0.05212	0.02959	0.01673	0.00943	0.00531	0.00298	0.00017
0.60	0.25000	0.14599	0.08306	0.04665	0.02601	0.01443	0.00799	0.00441	0.00243	0.00012

(Continued)

$\rho = \lambda/s\mu$				Number of Channels: s						
ρ	2	3	4	5	6	7	8	9	10	15
0.62	0.23457	0.13491	0.07550	0.04167	0.02282	0.01243	0.00675	0.00366	0.00198	0.00009
0.64	0.21951	0.12438	0.06847	0.03715	0.01999	0.01069	0.00570	0.00303	0.00161	0.00007
0.66	0.20482	0.11435	0.06194	0.03304	0.01746	0.00918	0.00480	0.00251	0.00131	0.00005
0.68	0.19048	0.10479	0.05587	0.02930	0.01522	0.00786	0.00404	0.00207	0.00106	0.00004
0.70	0.17647	0.09569	0.05021	0.02590	0.01322	0.00670	0.00338	0.00170	0.00085	0.00003
0.72	0.16279	0.08702	0.04495	0.02280	0.01144	0.00570	0.00283	0.00140	0.00069	0.00002
0.74	0.14943	0.07875	0.04006	0.01999	0.00986	0.00483	0.00235	0.00114	0.00055	0.00001
0.76	0.13636	0.07087	0.03550	0.01743	0.00847	0.00407	0.00195	0.00093	0.00044	0.00001
0.78	0.12360	0.06335	0.03125	0.01510	0.00721	0.00341	0.00160	0.00075	0.00035	0.00001
0.80	0.11111	0.05618	0.02730	0.01299	0.00610	0.00284	0.00131	0.00060	0.00028	0.00001
0.82	0.09890	0.04933	0.02362	0.01106	0.00511	0.00234	0.00106	0.00048	0.00022	0.00000
0.84	0.08696	0.04280	0.02019	0.00931	0.00423	0.00190	0.00085	0.00038	0.00017	0.00000
0.86	0.07527	0.03656	0.01700	0.00772	0.00345	0.00153	0.00067	0.00029	0.00013	0.00000
0.88	0.06383	0.03060	0.01403	0.00627	0.00276	0.00120	0.00052	0.00022	0.00010	0.00000
0.90	0.05263	0.02491	0.01126	0.00496	0.00215	0.00092	0.00039	0.00017	0.00007	0.00000
0.92	0.04167	0.01947	0.00867	0.00377	0.00161	0.00068	0.00028	0.00012	0.00005	0.00000
0.94	0.03093	0.01427	0.00627	0.00268	0.00113	0.00047	0.00019	0.00008	0.00003	0.00000
0.96	0.02041	0.00930	0.00403	0.00170	0.00070	0.00029	0.00012	0.00005	0.00002	0.00000
0.98	0.01010	0.00454	0.00194	0.00081	0.00033	0.00013	0.00005	0.00002	0.00001	0.00000

EXAMPLE 16.6

A Multiple-Server Waiting Line System

The customer service department of the Biggs Department Store has a waiting room in which chairs are placed along a wall, forming a single waiting line. Customers come with questions or complaints or matters regarding credit-card bills. The customers are served by three store representatives, each located in a partitioned stall. Customers are treated on a first-come, first-served basis.

The store management wants to analyze this queuing system because excessive waiting times can make customers angry enough to shop at other stores. Typically, customers who come to this area have some problem and thus are impatient anyway. Waiting increases their impatience.

A study of the customer service department for a 6-month period shows that an average of 10 customers arrive per hour (according to a Poisson distribution), and an average of 4 customers can be served per hour by a customer service representative (Poisson distributed).

SOLUTION:

$\lambda = 10$ customers per hour

$\mu = 4$ customers per hour per service representative

$s = 3$ customer service representatives

$s\mu = (3)(4) = 12 \quad (> \lambda = 10)$

Using the multiple-server model formulas, we can compute the following operating characteristics for the service department.

$$P_0 = \frac{1}{\left[\sum_{n=0}^{n=s-1} \frac{1}{n!}\left(\frac{\lambda}{\mu}\right)^n\right] + \frac{1}{s!}\left(\frac{\lambda}{\mu}\right)^s \left(\frac{s\mu}{s\mu - \lambda}\right)}$$

$$= \frac{1}{\left[\frac{1}{0!}\left(\frac{10}{4}\right)^0 + \frac{1}{1!}\left(\frac{10}{4}\right)^1 + \frac{1}{2!}\left(\frac{10}{4}\right)^2\right] + \frac{1}{3!}\left(\frac{10}{4}\right)^3 \frac{3(4)}{3(4) - 10}}$$

$$= 0.045 \text{ probability that no customers are in the service department}$$

Notice that this value could have been estimated from Table 16.2 using $\rho = 0.833$ (i.e., $\rho = \lambda/s\mu = 10/12 = 0.833$) and $s = 3$. ρ is read from the left-hand column and s across the top.

$$L = \frac{\lambda\mu(\lambda/\mu)^s}{(s-1)!(s\mu - \lambda)^2} P_0 + \frac{\lambda}{\mu}$$

$$= \frac{(10)(4)(10/4)^3}{(3-1)![3(4) - 10]^2} (0.045) + \frac{10}{4}$$

$$= 6 \text{ customers in the service department}$$

$$W = \frac{L}{\lambda}$$

$$= \frac{6}{10}$$

$$= 0.60 \text{ hour or 36 minutes in the service department}$$

$$L_q = L - \frac{\lambda}{\mu}$$

$$= 6 - \frac{10}{4}$$

$$= 3.5 \text{ customers waiting to be served}$$

$$W_q = \frac{L_q}{\lambda}$$

$$= \frac{3.5}{10}$$

$$= 0.35 \text{ hour or 21 minutes waiting in line}$$

$$P_w = \frac{1}{s!}\left(\frac{\lambda}{\mu}\right)^s \frac{s\mu}{s\mu - \lambda} P_0$$

$$= \frac{1}{3!}\left(\frac{10}{4}\right)^3 \frac{3(4)}{3(4) - 10} (.045)$$

$= 0.703$ probability that a customer must wait for service (i.e., that there are three or more customers in the system)

(Continued)

The department store's management has observed that customers are frustrated by the waiting time of 21 minutes and the 0.703 probability of waiting. To try to improve matters, management is considering an extra service representative. The operating characteristics for this system must be recomputed with $s = 4$ service representatives.

Substituting $s = 4$ along with λ and μ in the queuing formulas results in the following operating characteristics:

$P_0 = 0.073$ probability that no customers are in the service department

$L = 3.0$ customers in the service department

$W = 0.30$ hour, or 18 minutes, in the service department

$L_q = 0.5$ customer waiting to be served

$W_q = 0.05$ hour, or 3 minutes, waiting in line

$P_w = 0.31$ probability that a customer must wait for service

These results are significantly better; waiting time is reduced from 21 minutes to 3 minutes. This improvement in the quality of the service would have to be compared to the cost of adding an extra service representative to make a decision.

Solution of the Multiple-Server Model with POM for Windows

The POM for Windows solution screen for the multiple-server model in Example 16.6 is shown in Exhibit 16.3. Although more complex multiple-server models with finite queue or finite calling population are not presented in this chapter, POM for Windows has the capability to solve these model variations.

THE COMPETITIVE EDGE

Competing With Local Area Network Service at Merrill Lynch

www.prenhall.com/russell

Merrill Lynch and Company is the largest retail stockbroker in the United States, with more than 450 branch offices and 10,000 brokers (or financial consultants). The company was using a communication and information network that provided brokers with information through terminals at the branch offices connected to remote mainframe and minicomputers. The company wanted to replace this terminal-based system with local area networks (LANs) at each branch, at a cost of tens of millions of dollars. Each branch LAN would access from local databases that were updated nightly via downloads from a remote mainframe, with one common database being updated continually during business hours. The data would reside locally on from one to four microcomputers acting as database servers. Several critical is-

sues were related to the planning of this new system, including the overall cost of installation (i.e., the economic feasibility of the system), and the capacity of the database servers to handle the volume of transaction/inquiries from the brokers during business hours. A general multiple-server queuing model approach was developed to evaluate potential server response time under different levels of user demand (Poisson distributed). The modeling analysis showed that at most two database servers would be needed at any Merrill Lynch branch office (regardless of the size of the office and number of brokers) to provide adequate response time to brokers using the LAN system. This allowed Merrill Lynch to determine a maximum required capital expenditure for the system that proved to be economically feasible and allowed the company to proceed with conversion to the new LAN system.

SOURCE: Based on L. Berman and R. Nigum, "Optimal Partitioning of Data Bases Across Multiple Servers in a LAN," *Interfaces* 22, no. 2 (March–April 1992): 18–27.

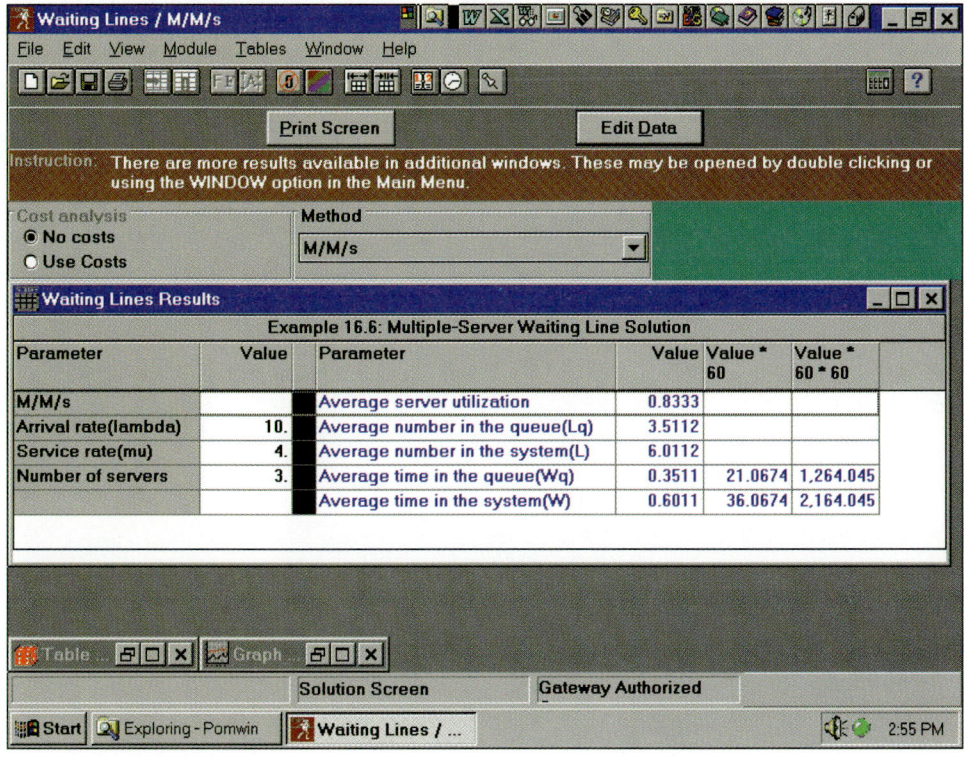

EXHIBIT 16.3

Summary

Since waiting is an integral part of many service-related operations, it is an important area of analysis, especially relative to achieving improved-quality service. The mathematical formulas for analyzing a variety of waiting line structures provide operating characteristics that are the basis for designing and improving waiting line systems.

However, although the queuing models presented in this chapter describe a wide variety of realistic waiting line systems, the number of conceivable waiting line structures is almost infinite, and many are so complex that no specific queuing model or formula is directly applicable. Examples of such complex queuing systems include a network of queues in which the leaving customers from several queuing systems provide the arrivals for succeeding queuing systems. A manufacturing system in which the in-process output from several production areas or production lines is the input to subsequent production areas or lines is an example of such a network. For such complex systems, a specific analytical model, such as those presented in this chapter, is not available, and simulation is the only alternative.

Summary of Key Formulas

Single-Server Model

$$P_0 = 1 - \frac{\lambda}{\mu} \qquad\qquad W = \frac{1}{\mu - \lambda}$$

$$P_n = \left(\frac{\lambda}{\mu}\right)^n \left(\frac{1 - \lambda}{\mu}\right) \qquad W_q = \frac{\lambda}{\mu(\mu - \lambda)}$$

$$L = \frac{\lambda}{\mu - \lambda} \qquad\qquad \rho = \frac{\lambda}{\mu}$$

$$L_q = \frac{\lambda^2}{\mu(\mu - \lambda)} \qquad\qquad I = 1 - \frac{\lambda}{\mu}$$

Single-Server Model with Undefined Service Times

$$P_0 = 1 - \frac{\lambda}{\mu} \qquad\qquad W_q = \frac{L_q}{\lambda}$$

$$L_q = \frac{\lambda^2\sigma^2 + (\lambda/\mu)^2}{2\,(1 - \lambda/\mu)} \qquad\qquad W = W_q + \frac{1}{\mu}$$

$$L = L_q + \frac{\lambda}{\mu} \qquad\qquad \rho = \frac{\lambda}{\mu}$$

Single-Server Model with Constant Service Times

$$P_0 = 1 - \frac{\lambda}{\mu} \qquad\qquad W_q = \frac{L_q}{\lambda}$$

$$L_q = \frac{\lambda^2}{2\mu(\mu - \lambda)} \qquad\qquad W = W_q + \frac{1}{\mu}$$

$$L = L_q + \frac{\lambda}{\mu} \qquad\qquad \rho = \frac{\lambda}{\mu}$$

Single-Server Model with Finite Queue

$$P_0 = \frac{1 - \lambda/\mu}{1 - (\lambda/\mu)^{M+1}} \qquad\qquad W = \frac{L}{\lambda(1 - P_M)}$$

$$P_n = (P_0)(\lambda/\mu)^n, \qquad n \le M \qquad\qquad W_q = W - \frac{1}{\mu}$$

$$L = \frac{\lambda/\mu}{1 - \lambda/\mu} - \frac{(M + 1)(\lambda/\mu)^{M+1}}{1 - (\lambda/\mu)^{M+1}}$$

$$L_q = L - \frac{\lambda(1 - P_M)}{\mu}$$

Single-Server Model with Finite Calling Population

$$P_0 = \frac{1}{\displaystyle\sum_{n=0}^{N} \frac{N!}{(N - n)!}\left(\frac{\lambda}{\mu}\right)^n} \qquad\qquad W_q = \frac{L_q}{(N - L)\lambda}$$

$$\frac{1}{\mu} \qquad\qquad P_n = \frac{N!}{(N - n)!}\left(\frac{\lambda}{\mu}\right)^n P_0 \qquad W = W_q =$$

$$L_q = N - \left(\frac{\lambda + \mu}{\lambda}\right)(1 - P_0)$$

$$L = L_q + (1 - P_0)$$

Multiple-Server Model

$$P_0 = \frac{1}{\left[\displaystyle\sum_{n=0}^{n=s-1} \frac{1}{n!}\left(\frac{\lambda}{\mu}\right)^n\right] + \frac{1}{s!}\left(\frac{\lambda}{\mu}\right)^s\left(\frac{s\mu}{s\mu - \lambda}\right)}$$

$$P_n = \begin{cases} \dfrac{1}{s!s^{n-s}}\left(\dfrac{\lambda}{\mu}\right)^n P_0, & \text{for } n > s \\[2ex] \dfrac{1}{n!}\left(\dfrac{\lambda}{\mu}\right)^n P_0, & \text{for } n \le s \end{cases}$$

$$P_w = \frac{1}{s!}\left(\frac{\lambda}{\mu}\right)^s \frac{s\mu}{s\mu - \lambda} P_0$$

$$L = \frac{\lambda\mu(\lambda/\mu)^s}{(s-1)!(s\mu - \lambda)^2} P_0 + \frac{\lambda}{\mu}$$

$$W = \frac{L}{\lambda}$$

$$L_q = L - \frac{\lambda}{\mu}$$

$$W_q = W - \frac{1}{\mu}$$

Summary of Key Terms

arrival rate: the rate at which customers arrive at a service facility during a specified period of time.

calling population: the source of customers to a waiting line.

channels: the number of parallel servers.

finite queue: a waiting line that has a limited capacity.

infinite queue: a waiting line that grows to any length.

operating characteristics: measures of waiting line performance expressed as averages.

phases: the number of sequential servers a customer must go through to receive service.

queue: a single waiting line that forms prior to a service facility.

queue discipline: the order in which customers are served.

service time: the time required to serve a customer.

Solved Problems

1. Single-Server Model

The new-accounts officer at the Citizens Northern Savings Bank enrolls all new customers in checking accounts. During the 3-week period in August encompassing the beginning of the new school year at State University, the bank opens a lot of new accounts for students. The bank estimates that the arrival rate during this period will be Poisson distributed with an average of 4 customers per hour. The service time is exponentially distributed with an average of 12 minutes per customer to set up a new account. The bank wants to determine the operating characteristics for this system to determine if the current person is sufficient to handle the increased traffic.

Solution:

Determine operating characteristics for the single-server system:

$$\lambda = 4 \text{ customers per hour arrive}$$
$$\mu = 5 \text{ customers per hour are served}$$

$$P_0 = \left(1 - \frac{\lambda}{\mu}\right) = \left(1 - \frac{4}{5}\right)$$

= 0.20 probability of no customers in the system

$$L = \frac{\lambda}{\mu - \lambda} = \frac{5}{5 - 4}$$

= 4 customers on average in the queuing system

$$L_q = \frac{\lambda^2}{\mu(\mu - \lambda)} = \frac{(4)^2}{5(5 - 4)}$$

= 3.2 customers on average waiting

$$W = \frac{1}{\mu - \lambda} = \frac{1}{5 - 4}$$

= 1 hour average time in the system

$$W_q = \frac{\lambda}{\mu(\mu - \lambda)} = \frac{5}{5(5 - 4)}$$

= 0.80 hour (48 minutes) average time waiting

$$P_w = \frac{\lambda}{\mu} = \frac{4}{5}$$

= 0.80 probability that the new-accounts officer will
be busy and that a customer must wait

The average waiting time of 48 minutes and the average time in the system are excessive, and the bank needs to add an extra employee during the busy period.

2. Multiple-Server Model

The Citizens Northern Bank wants to compute the operating characteristics if an extra employee was added to assist with new-accounts enrollments.

Solution:

Determine the operating characteristics for the multiple-server system:

$$\lambda = 4 \text{ customers per hour arrive}$$
$$\mu = 5 \text{ customers per hour are served}$$
$$s = 2 \text{ servers}$$

$$P_0 = \frac{1}{\left[\sum_{n=0}^{n=s-1} \frac{1}{n!} \left(\frac{\lambda}{\mu}\right)^n\right] + \frac{1}{s!} \left(\frac{\lambda}{\mu}\right)^s \left(\frac{s\mu}{s\mu - \lambda}\right)}$$

$$= \frac{1}{\left[\frac{1}{0!} \left(\frac{4}{5}\right)^0 + \frac{1}{1!} \left(\frac{4}{5}\right)^1\right] + \frac{1}{2!} \left(\frac{4}{5}\right)^2 \frac{(2)(5)}{(2)(5) - 4}}$$

= 0.429 probability that no customers are in the system

$$L = \frac{\lambda\mu(\lambda/\mu)^s}{(s-1)!(s\mu-\lambda)^2} P_0 + \frac{\lambda}{\mu}$$

$$= \frac{(4)(5)(4/5)^2}{1![(2)(5)-4]^2} (0.429) + \frac{4}{5}$$

$= 0.952$ customer on average in the system

$$L_q = L - \frac{\lambda}{\mu} = 0.952 - \frac{4}{5}$$

$= 0.152$ customer on average waiting to be served

$$W = \frac{L}{\lambda} = \frac{0.952}{4}$$

$= 0.238$ hour (14.3 minutes) average time in the system

$$W_q = \frac{L_q}{\lambda} = \frac{0.152}{4}$$

$= 0.038$ hour (2.3 minutes) average time spent waiting in line

$$P_w = \frac{1}{s!}\left(\frac{\lambda}{\mu}\right)^s \frac{s\mu}{s\mu-\lambda} P_0$$

$$= \frac{1}{2!}\left(\frac{4}{5}\right)^2 \frac{(2)(5)}{(2)(5)-4} (0.429)$$

$= 0.229$ probability that a customer must wait for service

The waiting time with the multiple-server model is 2.3 minutes, which is a significant improvement over the previous system; thus the bank should add the second new-accounts officer.

Questions

16-1. Identify ten real-life examples of queuing systems with which you are familiar.
16-2. Why must the utilization factor in a single-server model be less than 1?
16-3. Give five examples of real-world queuing systems with finite calling populations.
16-4. List the elements that define a queuing system.
16-5. How can the results of queuing analysis be used by a decision maker for making decisions?
16-6. What is the mean effective service rate in a multiple-server model, and what must be its relationship to the arrival rate?
16-7. For each of the following queuing systems, indicate if it is a single- or multiple-server model, the queue discipline, and if its calling population is infinite or finite.
a. Hair salon
b. Bank
c. Laundromat
d. Doctor's office
e. Adviser's office
f. Airport runway
g. Service station

h. Copy center
i. Team trainer
j. Mainframe computer

16-8. In Example 16.2 in this chapter, the second alternative was to add a new checkout counter at the market. This alternative was analyzed using the single-server model. Why was the multiple-server model not used?

16-9. Discuss briefly the relationship between waiting line analysis and quality improvement.

16-10. Define the four basic waiting line structures and give an example of each.

16-11. Describe the traditional cost relationship in waiting line analysis.

16-12. a. Is the following statement true or false? The single-phase, single-channel model with Poisson arrivals and undefined service times will always have larger (i.e., greater) operating characteristic values (i.e., W, W_q, L, L_q) than the same model with exponentially distributed service times. Explain your answer.
b. Is the following statement true or false? The single-phase, single-channel model with Poisson arrivals and constant service times will always have smaller (i.e., lower) operating characteristic values (i.e., W, W_q, L, L_q) than the same model with exponentially distributed service times. Explain your answer.

16-13. Under what conditions can the basic single-server and multiple-server models be used to analyze a multiple-phase waiting line system?

16-14. Why do waiting lines form at a service facility even though there may be more than enough service capacity to meet normal demand in the long run?

16-15. Provide an example of when a first-in, first-out (FIFO) rule for queue discipline would not be appropriate.

16-16. Under what conditions will the single-channel, single-phase queuing model with Poisson arrivals and undefined service times provide the same operating characteristics as the basic model with exponentially distributed service times?

16-17. What types of waiting line systems have constant service times?

Problems

16-1. McBurger's fast-food restaurant has a drive-through window with a single server who takes orders from an intercom and also is the cashier. The window operator is assisted by other employees who prepare the orders. Customers arrive at the ordering station prior to the drive-through window every 4.5 minutes (Poisson distributed) and the service time is 2.8 minutes. Determine the average length of the waiting line and the waiting time. Discuss the quality implications of your results. If you decide that the quality of the service could be improved, indicate what things you might do to improve quality.

16-2. The ticket booth on the Tech campus is operated by one person, who is selling tickets for the annual Tech versus State football game on Saturday. The ticket seller can serve an average of 12 customers per hour; on average, 10 customers arrive to purchase tickets each hour. Determine the average time a ticket buyer must wait and the portion of time the ticket seller is busy.

16-3. The Whistle Stop Market has one pump for gasoline, which can service 10 customers per hour. Cars arrive at the pump at a rate of 6 per hour.
a. Determine the average queue length, the average time a car is in the system, and the average time a car must wait.
b. If, during the period from 4:00 P.M. to 5:00 P.M., the arrival rate increases to 12 cars per hour, what will be the effect on the average queue length?

16-4. The Dynaco Manufacturing Company produces a particular product in an assembly line operation. One of the machines on the line is a drill press that has a single assembly line feeding into it. A partially completed unit arrives at the press to be worked on every 7.5 minutes, on average, according to an exponential distribution. The machine operator can process an average of 10 parts per hour (Poisson distributed). Determine the average number of parts waiting to be worked on, the percentage of time the operator is working, and the percentage of time the machine is idle.

16-5. The management of Dynaco Manufacturing Company (Problem 16-4) likes to have its operators working 90 percent of the time. What must the assembly line arrival rate be in order for the operators to be as busy as management would like?

16-6. The Peachtree Airport in Atlanta serves light aircraft. It has a single runway and one air traffic controller to land planes. It takes an airplane 12 minutes to land and clear the runway (exponentially distributed). Planes arrive at the airport at the rate of 4 per hour (Poisson distributed).

   a. Determine the average number of planes that will stack up waiting to land.

   b. Find the average time a plane must wait in line before it can land.

   c. Calculate the average time it takes a plane to clear the runway once it has notified the airport that it is in the vicinity and wants to land.

   d. The FAA has a rule that an air traffic controller can, on the average, land planes a maximum of 45 minutes out of every hour. There must be 15 minutes of idle time available to relieve the tension. Will this airport have to hire an extra air traffic controller?

16-7. The First American Bank of Rapid City presently has one outside drive-up teller. It takes the teller an average of 4 minutes (exponentially distributed) to serve a bank customer. Customers arrive at the drive-up window at the rate of 12 per hour (Poisson distributed). The bank operations officer is currently analyzing the possibility of adding a second drive-up window at an annual cost of $20,000. It is assumed that arriving cars would be equally divided between both windows. The operations officer estimates that each minute's reduction in customer waiting time would increase the bank's revenue by $2,000 annually. Should the second drive-up window be installed?

16-8. During registration at State University every quarter, students in the College of Business must have their courses approved by the college adviser. It takes the adviser an average of 2 minutes (exponentially distributed) to approve each schedule, and students arrive at the adviser's office at the rate of 28 per hour (Poisson distributed).

   a. Compute L, L_q, W, W_q, and ρ.

   b. The dean of the college has received a number of complaints from students about the length of time they must wait to have their schedules approved. The dean feels that waiting 10 minutes to get a schedule approved is not unreasonable. Each assistant the dean assigns to the adviser's office will reduce the average time required to approve a schedule by 0.25 minute, down to a minimum time of 1.0 minute to approve a schedule. How many assistants should the dean assign to the adviser?

16-9. All trucks traveling on Interstate 40 between Albuquerque and Amarillo are required to stop at a weigh station. Trucks arrive at the weigh station at a rate of 200 per 8-hour day (Poisson distributed), and the station can weigh, on the average, 220 trucks per day (Poisson distributed).

   a. Determine the average number of trucks waiting, the average time spent at the weigh station by each truck, and the average waiting time before being weighed for each truck.

   b. If the truck drivers find out they must remain at the weigh station longer than 15 minutes on the average, they will start taking a different route or traveling at night, thus depriving the state of taxes. The state of New Mexico estimates it loses $10,000 in taxes per year for each extra minute that trucks must remain at the weigh station. A new set of scales would have the same service capacity as the present set of scales, and it is assumed that arriving trucks would line up equally behind the two sets of scales. It would cost $50,000 per year to operate the new scales. Should the state install the new set of scales?

16-10. In Problem 16-9, suppose arriving truck drivers look to see how many trucks are waiting to be weighed at the weigh station. If they see four or more trucks in line, they will pass by the station and risk being caught and ticketed. What is the probability that a truck will pass by the station?

16-11. In Problem 16-8, the dean of the College of Business at State University is considering the addition of a second adviser in the college advising office to serve students waiting to have their schedules approved. This new adviser could serve the same number of students per hour as the present adviser. Determine L, L_q, W, and W_q for this altered advising system. As a student, would you recommend adding the adviser?

16-12. Maggie Smith is a nurse on the evening shift from 10:00 P.M. to 6:00 A.M. at Community Hospital. She is responsible for 15 patients in her area. She averages 2 calls from each of her patients every evening (Poisson distributed), and she must spend an average of 10 minutes (negative exponential distribution) with each patient who calls. Nurse Smith has indicated to her shift supervisor that although she has not kept records she believes her patients must wait about 10 minutes on average for her to respond and she has requested that her supervisor assign a second nurse to her area. The supervisor believes 10 minutes is too long to wait, but she does not want her nurses to be idle more than 40 percent of the time. Determine what the supervisor should do.

16-13. A to Z Publishers has a large number of employees who use the company's single fax machine. Employees arrive randomly to use the fax machine at an average rate of 20 per hour. This arrival process is approximated by a Poisson distribution. Employees spend an average of 2 minutes using the fax machine, either transmitting or receiving items. The time spent using the machine is distributed according to a negative exponential distribution. Employees line up in single file to use the machine, and they obtain access to it on a first-come, first-served basis. There is no defined limit to the number who can line up to use the machine.

Management has determined that by assigning an operator to the fax machine rather than allowing the employees to operate the machine themselves, it can reduce the average service time from the current 2 minutes to 1.5 minutes. However, the fax operator's salary is $8 per hour, which must be paid 8 hours per day even if there are no employees wishing to use the fax machine part of the time. Management has estimated the cost of employee time spent waiting in line and at the fax machine during service to be 17¢ per minute (based on an average salary of $10.20 per hour per employee). Should the firm assign an operator to the fax machine?

16-14. The Dynaco Manufacturing Company has an assembly line that feeds two drill presses. As partially completed products come off the line, they are lined up to be worked on as drill presses become available. The units arrive at the workstation (containing both presses) at the rate of 100 per hour (Poisson distributed). Each press operator can process an average of 60 units per hour (Poisson distributed). Compute L, L_q, W, and W_q.

16-15. The Escargot is a small French restaurant with 6 waiters and waitresses. The average service time at the restaurant for a table (of any size) is 85 minutes (Poisson distributed). The restaurant does not take reservations and parties arrive for dinner (and stay and wait) every 18 minutes (negative exponential distribution). The restaurant is concerned that a lengthy waiting time might hurt its business in the long run. What is the current waiting time and queue length for the restaurant? Discuss the quality implications of the current waiting time and any actions the restaurant might take.

16-16. Cakes baked by the Freshfood Bakery are transported from the ovens to be packaged by one of three wrappers. Each wrapper can wrap an average of 200 cakes per hour (Poisson distributed). The cakes are brought to the wrappers at the rate of 500 per hour (Poisson distributed). If a cake sits longer than 5 minutes before being wrapped, it will not be fresh enough to meet the bakery's quality control standards. Does the bakery need to hire another wrapper?

16-17. The Riverview Clinic has two general practitioners who see patients daily. An average of six patients arrive at the clinic per hour (Poisson distributed). Each doctor spends an average of 15 minutes (exponentially distributed) with a patient. The patients wait in a waiting area until one of the two doctors is able to see them. However, since patients typically do not feel well when they come to the clinic, the doctors do not believe it is good practice to have a patient wait longer than an average of 15 minutes. Should this clinic add a third doctor, and, if so, will this alleviate the waiting problem?

16-18. The Footrite Shoe Company is going to open a new branch at a mall, and company managers are attempting to determine how many salespeople to hire. Based on an analysis of mall traffic, the company estimates that customers will arrive at the store at the rate of 10 per hour (Poisson distributed), and from past experience at its other branches, the company knows that salespeople can serve an average of 6 customers per hour (Poisson distributed). How many salespeople should the company hire in order to maintain a company policy that on average a customer should have to wait for service no more than 30 percent of the time?

16-19. When customers arrive at Gilley's Ice Cream Shop, they take a number and wait to be called to purchase ice cream from one of the counter servers. From experience in past summers, the store's staff knows that customers arrive at the rate of 40 per hour (Poisson distributed) on summer days between 3:00 P.M. and 10:00 P.M. and a server can serve 15 customers per hour on average (Poisson distributed). Gilley's wants to make sure that customers wait no longer than 10 minutes for service. Gilley's is contemplating keeping 3 servers behind the ice cream counter during the peak summer hours. Will this number be adequate to meet the waiting time policy?

16-20. Moore's television-repair service receives an average of 6 TV sets per 8-hour day to be repaired. The service manager would like to be able to tell customers that they can expect their TV back in 4 days. What average repair time per set will the repair shop have to achieve to provide 4-day service on the average? (Assume that the arrival rate is Poisson distributed and repair times are exponentially distributed.)

16-21. Partially completed products arrive at a workstation in a manufacturing operation at a mean rate of 40 per hour (Poisson distributed). The processing time at the workstation averages 1.2 minutes per unit (exponentially distributed). The manufacturing company estimates that each unit of in-process inventory at the workstation costs $31 per day (on the average). However, the company can add extra employees and reduce the processing time to 0.90 minute per unit at a cost of $52 per day. Determine whether the company should continue the present operation or add extra employees.

16-22. The Atlantic Coast Shipping Company has a warehouse terminal in Spartanburg, South Carolina. The capacity of each terminal dock is three trucks. As trucks enter the terminal, the drivers receive numbers, and when one of the three dock spaces become available, the truck with the lowest number enters the vacant dock. Truck arrivals are Poisson distributed, and the unloading and loading times (service times) are exponentially distributed. The average arrival rate at the terminal is 5 trucks per hour, and the average service rate per dock is 2 trucks per hour (30 minutes per truck).

   a. Compute L, L_q, W, and W_q.

   b. The management of the shipping company is considering adding extra employees and equipment to improve the average service time per terminal dock to 25 minutes per truck. It would cost the company $18,000 per year to achieve this improved service. Management estimates that it will increase its profit by $750 per year for each minute it is able to reduce a truck's waiting time. Determine whether management should make the investment.

   c. Now suppose that the managers of the shipping company have decided that truck waiting time is excessive and they want to reduce the waiting time. They have determined that there are two alternatives available for reducing the waiting time. They can add a fourth dock, or they can add extra employees and equipment at the existing docks, which will reduce the average service time per location from the original 30 minutes per truck to 23 minutes per truck. The costs of these alternatives are approximately equal. Management desires to implement the alternative that reduces waiting time by the greatest amount. Which alternative should be selected?

16-23. Drivers who come to get their licenses at the department of motor vehicles have their photograph taken by an automated machine that develops the photograph onto the license card and laminates the complete license. The machine requires a constant time of 4.5 minutes to develop a completed license. If drivers arrive at the machine at the mean rate of 10 per hour (Poisson distributed), determine the average length of the waiting line and the average waiting time.

16-24. A vending machine at City Airport dispenses hot coffee, hot chocolate, or hot tea in a constant service time of 20 seconds. Customers arrive at the vending machine at a mean rate of 60 per hour, Poisson distributed. Determine the average length of the waiting line and the average time a customer must wait.

16-25. In Problem 16-20 suppose that Moore's television-repair service cannot accommodate more than 30 TV sets at a time. What is the probability that the number of TV sets on hand (under repair and waiting for service) will exceed the shop capacity?

16-26. Norfolk, Virginia, a major seaport on the East Coast, has a ship coal-loading facility. Coal trucks filled with coal presently arrive at the port facility at the mean rate of 149 per day (Poisson distributed). The facility operates 24 hours a day. The coal trucks are unloaded one at a time on a first-come, first-served basis by automated mechanical equipment that empties the trucks in a constant time of 8 minutes per truck, regardless of truck size. The port authority is negotiating with a coal company for an additional 30 trucks per day. However, the coal company will not use this port facility unless the port authority can assure them that their coal trucks will not have to wait to be unloaded at the port facility for more than 12 hours per truck on the average. Can the port authority provide this assurance?

16-27. The Waterfall Buffet in the lower level of the National Art Gallery serves food cafeteria-style daily to visitors and employees. The buffet is self-service. From 7:00 A.M. to 9:00 A.M. customers arrive at the buffet at a rate of 10 per minute; from 9:00 A.M. to noon, at 4 per minute; from noon to 2:00 , at 14 per minute; and from 2:00 P.M. to closing at 5:00 P.M., at 8 per minute (Poisson distributed). All the customers take about the same amount of time to serve themselves and proceed to the buffet. Once a customer goes through the buffet, it takes an average of 0.4 minute (exponentially distributed) to pay the cashier. The gallery does not want a customer to have to wait longer than 4 minutes to pay. How many cashiers should be working at each of the four times during the day?

16-28. The Clip Joint is a hair-styling salon at University Mall. Four stylists are always available to serve customers on a first-come, first-served basis. Customers arrive at an average rate of 5 per hour (Poisson distributed), and the stylists spend an average of 35 minutes (exponentially distributed) on each customer.

   a. Determine the average number of customers in the salon, the average time a customer must wait, and the average number waiting to be served.

   b. The salon manager is considering adding a fifth stylist. Would this have a significant impact on waiting time?

16-29. The Bay City Police Department has eight patrol cars that are on constant call 24 hours per day. A patrol car requires repairs every 20 days, on average, according to an exponential distribution. When a patrol car is in need of repair it is driven into the motor pool, which has a repairperson on duty at all times. The average time required to repair a patrol car is 18 hours (exponentially distributed). Determine the average time a patrol car is not available for use and the average number of patrol cars out of service at any one time, and indicate if the repair service seems adequate.

16-30. The Rowntown Cab Company has four cabs on duty during normal business hours. The cab company dispatcher receives requests for service every 8 minutes, on average, according to an exponential distribution. The average time to complete a trip is 20 minutes (exponentially distributed). Determine the average number of customers waiting for service and the average time a customer must wait for a cab.

16-31. A retail catalog operation employs a bank of six telephone operators, who process orders using computer terminals. When a terminal breaks down, it must be disconnected and taken to a nearby electronics repair shop, where it is repaired. The mean time between terminal breakdowns is 6 working days, and the mean time required to repair a terminal is 2 working days (both exponentially distributed). As a result of lost sales, it costs the mail-order operation an estimated $50 per day in lost profits each day a terminal is out for repair. The company pays the electronics repair shop $3,000 per year on a service agreement to repair the terminals. The company is considering the possibility of signing a new service agreement with another electronics repair shop that will provide substitute terminals while the broken ones are at the repair shop. However, the new service agreement would cost the mail-order operation $15,000 per year. Assuming that there are 250 working days in a year, determine what the mail-order operation should do.

16-32. The Riverton Post Office has four stations for service. Customers line up in single file for service on an FIFO basis. The mean arrival rate is 40 per hour, Poisson distributed, and the mean service time per server is 4 minutes, exponentially distributed. Compute the operating characteristics for this operation. Does the operation appear to be satisfactory in terms of: (a) postal workers' (servers') idle time; (b) customer waiting time and/or the number waiting for service; and (c) the percentage of the time a customer can walk in and get served without waiting at all?

CASE PROBLEM

The College of Business Copy Center

The copy center in the College of Business at State University has become an increasingly contentious item among the college administrators. The department heads have complained to the associate dean about the long lines and waiting times for their secretaries at the copy center. They claim that it is a waste of scarce resources for the secretaries to wait in line talking when they could be doing more productive work in the office. Hanford Burris, the associate dean, says the limited operating budget will not allow the college to purchase a new copier or copiers to relieve the problem. This standoff has been going on for several years.

To make her case for improved copying facilities, Lauren Moore, a teacher in Operations Management, assigned students in her class to gather some information about the copy center as a class project. The students were to record the arrivals at the center and the length of time it took to do a copy job once the secretary actually reached a copy machine. In addition, the students were to describe how the copy center system worked.

When the students completed the project, they turned in a report to Professor Moore. The report described the copy center as containing two machines. When secretaries arrive for a copy job, they join a queue, which looked more like milling around to the students, but they acknowledged that each secretary knew when it was his or her turn, and, in effect, the secretaries formed a single queue for the first available copy machine. Also, since copy

jobs are assigned tasks, secretaries always stayed to do the job no matter how long the line was or how long they had to wait. They never left the queue.

From the data the students gathered, Professor Moore was able to determine that secretaries arrived every 8 minutes for a copy job and that the arrival rate was Poisson distributed. Further, she was able to determine that the average time it takes to complete a job was 12 minutes, and this is exponentially distributed.

Using her department's personnel records and data from the university personnel office, Dr. Moore determined that a secretary's average salary is $8.50 per hour. From her academic calendar she added up the actual days in the year when the college and departmental offices were open and found there were 247. However, as she added up working days, it occurred to her that during the summer months the workload is much less, and the copy center would probably gets less traffic. The summer included about 70 days, during which she expected the copy center traffic would be about half of what it is during the normal year, but she speculated that the average time of a copying job would remain about the same.

Professor Moore next called a local office supply firm to check the prices on copiers. A new copier of the type in the copy center now would cost $36,000. It would also require $8,000 per year for maintenance and would have a normal useful life of 6 years.

Do you think Dr. Moore will be able to convince the associate dean that a new copy machine will be cost-effective?

Northwoods Backpackers

Bob and Carol Packer operate a successful outdoor-wear store in Vermont called Northwoods Backpackers. They stock mostly cold-weather outdoor items such as hiking and backpacking clothes, gear, and accessories. They established an excellent reputation throughout New England for quality products and service. Eventually, Bob and Carol noticed that more and more of their sales were from customers who did not live in the immediate vicinity but were calling in orders on the telephone. As a result, the Packers decided to distribute a catalog and establish a phone-order service. The order department consisted of five operators working eight hours per day from 10:00 A.M. to 6:00 P.M., Monday through Friday. For a few years the mail-order service was only moderately successful; the Packers just about broke even on their investment. However, during the holiday season of the third year of the catalog order service, they were overwhelmed with phone orders. Although they made a substantial profit, they were concerned about the large number of lost sales they estimated they incurred. Based on information provided by the telephone company regarding call volume and complaints from customers, the Packers estimated they lost sales of approximately $100,000. Also they felt they had lost a substantial number of old and potentially new customers because of the poor service of the catalog order department.

Prior to the next holiday season, the Packers explored several alternatives for improving the catalog order service. The current system includes the five original operators with computer terminals who work eight-hour days, five days per week. The Packers have hired a consultant to study this system, and she reported that the time for an operator to take a customer order is exponentially distributed with a mean of 3.6 minutes. Calls are expected to arrive at the telephone center during the six-week holiday season according to a Poisson distribution with a mean rate of 175 calls per hour. When all operators are busy, callers are put on hold, listening to music until an operator can answer. Waiting calls are an-

swered on a first-in, first-out basis. Based on her experience with other catalog telephone order operations and data from Northwoods Backpackers, the consultant has determined that if Northwoods Backpackers can reduce customer call waiting time to approximately one-half minute or less, the company will save $135,000 in lost sales during the coming holiday season.

Therefore, the Packers have adopted this level of call service as their goal. However, in addition to simply avoiding lost sales, the Packers believe it is important to reduce waiting time to maintain their reputation for good customer service. Thus, they would like about 70 percent of their callers to receive immediate service.

The Packers can maintain the same number of workstations/computer terminals they currently have and increase their service to sixteen hours per day with two operator shifts running from 8:00 A.M. to midnight. The Packers believe when customers become aware of their extended hours the calls will spread out uniformly, resulting in a new call average arrival rate of 87.5 calls per hour (still Poisson-distributed). This schedule change would cost Northwoods Backpackers approximately $11,500 for the six-week holiday season.

Another alternative for reducing customer waiting times is to offer weekend service. However, the Packers believe that if they do offer weekend service, it must coincide with whatever service they offer during the week. In other words, if they have phone order service eight hours per day during the week, they must have the same service during the weekend; the same is true with sixteen-hours-per-day service. They feel that if weekend hours differ from weekday hours it will confuse customers. If eight-hour service is offered seven days per week, the new call arrival rate will be reduced to 125 calls per hour at a cost of $3,600. If Northwoods offers sixteen-hour service, the mean call arrival rate will be reduced to 62.5 hours, at a cost of $7,300.

Still another possibility is to add more operator stations. Each station includes a desk, an operator, a phone, and a computer terminal. An additional station that is in operation five days per week, eight hours per day, will cost $2,900 for the holiday season. For a sixteen-hour day the cost per new station is $4,700. For seven-day service the cost of an additional station for eight-hour per-day service is $3,800; for sixteen-hour-per-day service the cost is $6,300.

The facility Northwoods Backpackers uses to house its operators can accommodate a maximum of ten stations. Additional operators in excess of ten would require the Packers to lease, remodel, and wire a new facility, which is a capital expenditure they do not want to undertake this holiday season. Alternatively, the Packers do not want to reduce their current number of operator stations.

Determine what order service configuration the Packers should use to achieve their goals, and explain your recommendation.

References

Cooper, R. B. *Introduction to Queuing Theory*, 2d ed. New York: North Holland, 1981.

Gross, D., and C. Harris. *Fundamentals of Queuing Theory*, 2d ed. New York: John Wiley, 1985.

Hillier, F. S., and O. S. Yu. *Queuing Tables and Graphics*. New York: North Holland, 1981.

Kleinrock, L. *Queuing Systems*, vols. 1 and 2. New York: John Wiley, 1975.

Lee, A. *Applied Queuing Theory*. New York: St. Martin's Press, 1966.

Morse, P. M. *Queues, Inventories, and Maintenance*. New York: John Wiley, 1958.

Saaty, T. L. *Elements of Queuing Theory with Applications*. New York: Dover, 1983.

Solomon, S. L. *Simulation of Waiting Line Systems*. Englewood Cliffs, N.J.: Prentice Hall, 1983.

White, J. A., J. W. Schmidt, and G. K. Bennett. *Analysis of Queuing Systems*. New York: Academic Press, 1975.

17

Project Management

Product Design Teams at Chrysler and Ford

www.prenhall.com/russell

www.prenhall.com/russell

In the late 1980s Chrysler created a product design team, called a *platform* group, to design its new LH cars including the Dodge Intrepid, Eagle Vision, and Chrysler Concorde. The design team evolved from a need to reduce the time to develop new cars. U.S. automakers took as long as five years to develop a new car. The best Japanese automakers developed new cars in three years. The design team concept was first used for the development of the Viper, Chrysler's $50,000 sports car. The project design team consisted of 80 members, and the company's goal was to develop the car in less than four years. Introduced in 1992, the Viper was put into production in only 36 months. The same design team approach was applied to the LH cars, and they reached production in 39 months.[1]

When the Ford Mustang was introduced in 1964, it was an immediate hit, with sales over 417,000 within 12 months. However, annual sales, which were around 500,000 through the 1960s, had dropped to only 86,000 by 1992. In 1989 Ford management almost decided to discontinue the Mustang when a study showed the cost for redesigning it would be $1 billion. However, a group of Ford employees

This group is part of the design team working on the LH project at the Chrysler Technology Center at Auburn Hills, Michigan. The overall design team is referred to as a platform group, where platform refers to one of four car classifications at Chrysler that is, small cars, large cars, jeeps and trucks, and minivans. The platform team is a self-contained entity consisting of buyers, suppliers, designers, and engineers that has total responsibility for the development of each car assigned to its platform. The platform group for LH cars (such as the Dodge Intrepid) at Chrysler included over 800 members. Chrysler embraced the team concept for car design and development in order to reduce project time and budget. For the LH project, the development time was only 39 months compared to the previous norm for a new car of 5 years.

---

[1] E. Raia, "LH Story," *Purchasing* (February 18, 1993): 55–57.

and Mustang loyalists persuaded the company to let them take on the redesign project, promising a lower cost. Operating with more independence than most project teams, the 400-member group brought the car online after three years in 1994 for $700 million, 25 percent faster and 30 percent cheaper than any other comparable design project at Ford.[2]

In other chapters we discussed the scheduling of repetitive operations and activities, such as work scheduling and job scheduling, as an important aspect of managing an operation. Operational schedules are established to keep the flow of products or services through the supply chain on time. However, not all operational activities are repetitive; some are unique, occurring only once within a specified time frame. Such unique, one-time activities are referred to as **projects.**

Project management is the management of the work to develop and implement an innovation or change in an existing operation. It encompasses planning the project and controlling the project activities, subject to resource and budget constraints, to keep the project on schedule. Examples of projects include constructing facilities and buildings, such as houses, factories, a shopping mall, an athletic stadium, or an arena; developing a military weapons system, a new aircraft, or a new ship; launching a satellite system; constructing an oil pipeline; developing and implementing a new computer system; planning a rock concert, football bowl game, or basketball tournament; and introducing new products into the market.

Projects have become increasingly pervasive in companies in recent years. This is a result of the diversity of new products and product markets and the shorter life span of products, combined with rapid technological changes. The nature of the international business environment is such that new machinery and equipment, as well as new production processes and computer support systems, are constantly evolving. This provides the capability of developing new products and services, which generates consumer demand for even greater product diversity. As a result a larger proportion of total organizational effort now goes toward project-oriented activities than in the past. Thus, the planning and management of projects has taken on a more crucial role in operations management.

In this chapter we focus on project management using CPM and PERT network scheduling techniques that are popular because they provide a graph or visual representation of the interrelationship and sequence of individual project activities, rather than simply a verbal or mathematical description. However, prior to our presentation of the CPM/PERT technique, we will discuss the elements of project management.

A **project** is a unique, one-time operational activity or effort.

www.prenhall.com/russell

The Elements of Project Management

Management is concerned with the planning, organization, and control of an ongoing process or activity such as the production of a product or delivery of a service. Project management is different in that it reflects a commitment of resources and people to an important activity for a relatively short time frame, after which the management effort is dissolved. The features and characteristics of project management tend to be unique. In this section, we will discuss the three primary elements of project management: the project team, project planning, and project control.

---

[2] J. Kennedy, "Pony Express," *Roanoke Times and World News*, October 15, 1993, pp. Extra 1, 4.

The Project Team

Project teams are made up of individuals from various areas and departments within a company.

The project team typically consists of a group of individuals selected from other areas in the organization or from outside the organization because of their special skills, expertise, and experience related to the project activities. Members of the engineering staff are often assigned to project work because of their technical skills, especially if the project is related to production processes or equipment. The project team may also include managers and staff personnel from specific areas related to the project. Workers can also be involved on the project team if their job is a function of the project activity. For example, a project team for the construction of a new loading dock facility might include truck drivers, forklift operators, dock workers, and staff personnel and managers from purchasing, shipping, receiving, and packaging, as well as engineers to assess vehicle flow, routes, and space considerations. A principle of TQM is that the employees who work in an area be part of the "problem-solving," or project, team in order to take advantage of their unique perspective and expertise.

Matrix organization is a team structure with members from functional areas, depending on the skills required.

The term **matrix organization** refers to a team approach to special projects. The team is developed from members of different functional areas or departments in the company. For example, team members might come from engineering, production, marketing, or personnel, depending on the specialized skills required by the project. The team members are, in effect, on loan from their home departments to work on a project. The term *matrix* is derived from the two-dimensional characteristics of this type of organizational structure. On one dimension, the vertical, is the company's normal organizational structure for performing jobs, whereas the horizontal dimension is the special functional structure (i.e., the functional team members) required by the project.

Projects related to product design require a team approach in TQM.

In recent years a team approach to problem solving has developed as part of many companies' commitment to total quality management. In a TQM environment the purpose of the team is to bring together different functional representatives and specialists from inside and outside the company that will successfully solve problems. An objective of the team approach is to get new products to the market before competitors. For example, a product design team might include members from marketing, engineering, purchasing, manufacturing, quality management, and suppliers.

Assignment to a project team is usually temporary which can have both positive and negative repercussions. The temporary loss of workers and staff from their permanent jobs can be disruptive for both the employee and the work area. The employee must sometimes "serve two masters," reporting to both the project manager and a regular supervisor. Since projects are usually exciting, they provide an opportunity to do work that is new and innovative, although the employee may be reluctant to report back to a more mundane, regular job after the project is completed.

The most important member of the project team is the *project manager*. Managing a project is subject to lots of uncertainty and the distinct possibility of failure. Since a project is unique and usually has not been attempted previously, the outcome is not as certain as the outcome of an ongoing process would be. A degree of security is attained in the supervision of a continuing process that is not present in project management. The project team members are often from diverse areas of the organization and possess different skills, which must be coordinated into a single, focused effort to complete the project successfully. The project is subject to time and budgetary constraints that are not the same as normal work schedules and resource consumption in an ongoing process.

The project manager is often under greater pressure.

There is usually more perceived and real pressure associated with project management than in a normal management position. However, there are potential opportunities, including demonstrating management abilities in a difficult situation, the challenge of working on a unique project, and the excitement of doing something new.

Project Planning

Planning a project requires that the objectives of the project be clearly defined so the manager and the team know what is expected. Sometimes this is in the form of a formal written description of what is to be accomplished, the work to be done, and the project time frame, called a **statement of work** (or project scope). All activities (or steps) in the project must be completely identified. This is not a simple task, since the work in the project is new, without a great deal of experiential references to draw on. An **activity** is the performance of an individual job or work effort that requires labor, resources, and time and that is subject to management control or supervision. Once the activities have been identified, their sequential relationship to each other, called a **precedence relationship,** must be determined; that is, it must be decided which activities come first, which follow, and so on. In the CPM/PERT technique we discuss later in the chapter, the precedence relationship is visually displayed in the form of a graph called a *network*. The following graph is a very simplified project network for constructing a new sidewalk.

A **statement of work** is a written description of the goals, work, and time frame of a project.

An **activity** requires labor, resources, and time.

A **precedence relationship** is the sequential relationship of activities in a project.

This network shows the precedence relationship between two project activities—"constructing the sidewalk forms," followed by "pouring concrete into the forms."

Once the activities of the project have been identified and their relationship to each other has been determined, the project activities must be scheduled. Scheduling is accomplished by determining estimates of the time required by each activity and then using these estimates to develop an overall project schedule and time to project completion. The estimated project time must be compared to the project objective; if the project time estimate is too long, then means must be sought to reduce project time. This is usually accomplished by assigning more resources or work effort to activities to reduce the time they require.

To summarize, the elements of the project planning process are

- Define project objective(s).
- Identify activities.
- Establish precedence relationships.
- Make time estimates.
- Determine project completion time.
- Compare project schedule objectives.
- Determine resource requirements to meet objectives.

Elements of project planning.

Project Control

Project management consists of two distinct phases, planning and control. Once the project planning process is completed, the project can physically be initiated—the activities can begin. At this point project management focuses on the control of the work involved in the project. Control includes making sure all activities are identified and included and making sure the activities are completed in the proper sequence. Resource needs must be identified as work is initiated and completed, and the schedule must be adjusted to reflect time changes and corrections. In most cases the primary focus of control is on maintaining the project schedule and making sure the project is completed on time.

WBS breaks down a project into components, subcomponents, activities, and tasks.

The **work breakdown structure (WBS)** is a method for project planning and control. In a WBS a project is broken down into its major components, referred to as modules. These components are then subdivided into detailed subcomponents, which are further broken down into activities and, finally, individual tasks. The end result is a project organizational structure made up of different levels, with the overall project at the top of the structure and the individual tasks for each activity at the bottom level. The WBS format is a good way to identify activities and to determine the individual task, module, and project workloads and resources required. Further, it helps to identify relationships between modules and activities. It also identifies unnecessary duplication of activities.

The Gantt Chart

A Gantt chart is a graph or bar chart with a bar for each project activity that shows the passage of time.

A **Gantt chart** is a traditional management technique for scheduling and planning small projects with relatively few activities and precedence relationships. The scheduling technique (also called a *bar chart*) was developed by Henry Gantt, a pioneer in the field of industrial engineering at the artillery ammunition shops of the Frankford

---

THE COMPETITIVE EDGE

Project Management Teams at IBM

www.prenhall.com/russell

Within the Commercial Data Processing Products Division at IBM, new computer-based systems are developed for internal operational and management information needs. The Information Systems Department within this division used its own experiences in project management while developing these systems to establish a training/project development program for project management teams.

A systems development project for creating an information system consists of five generic steps: project initiation (prioritize needs), system design, planning and scheduling, system development, system test, and system implementation and evaluation. When projects are first initiated, managers transferred from operations (such as manufacturing) to project management teams must be reoriented to the differing management styles, including the difference in time frames (i.e., daily operations versus six-month to two-year project planning). The project development program structure includes a five- (nonconsecutive) day workshop in which the project team develops the project schedule for actual ongoing projects. The starting point in the workshop for developing the project schedule plan is a *project phase structure chart*, a graphic display that divides the project into four basic phases (ini-

tiation, planning, development, and implementation) and describes the basic activities for each. Next, project milestones and completion criteria for each are developed. These are targets around which the project schedule is constructed. The project phases are then divided into *work breakdown structure outlines*, which show all activities for the project and include time estimates and resource requirements. This document is subsequently used to build the project network. The actual project network is constructed using "adhesive" notes for activities and laying out precedence relationships on a wall chart. The network development includes the following steps: build the initial network chart, input time estimates and print schedules, replan the critical path to meet the acceptable finish date, level person resources within the time constraint of the critical path, and develop a project control action plan. This last item is an effort to brainstorm the final schedule plan to expose possible risky critical and near-critical activities that might delay the project. Team members are assigned to investigate potential problem activities and develop an action plan to avoid the problem. This process is repeated at the completion of each project milestone.

SOURCE: Based on L. A. Rogers, "Project Team Training: A Proven Key to Organizational Teamwork and a Breakthrough in Planning Performances," *Project Management Journal* 21, no. 2 (June 1990): 9–18.

Arsenal in 1914. The Gantt chart has been a popular project scheduling tool since its inception and is still widely used today. It is the direct precursor of the CPM/PERT technique, which we will discuss later.

The Gantt chart is a graph with a bar representing time for each activity in the project being analyzed. Figure 17.1 illustrates a Gantt chart for a simplified project description for building a house. The project contains only seven general activities, such as designing the house, laying the foundation, ordering materials, and so forth. The first activity is "design house and obtain financing," and it requires three months to complete shown by the bar from left to right across the chart. After the first activity is finished, the next two activities, "lay foundation" and "order and receive materials,"

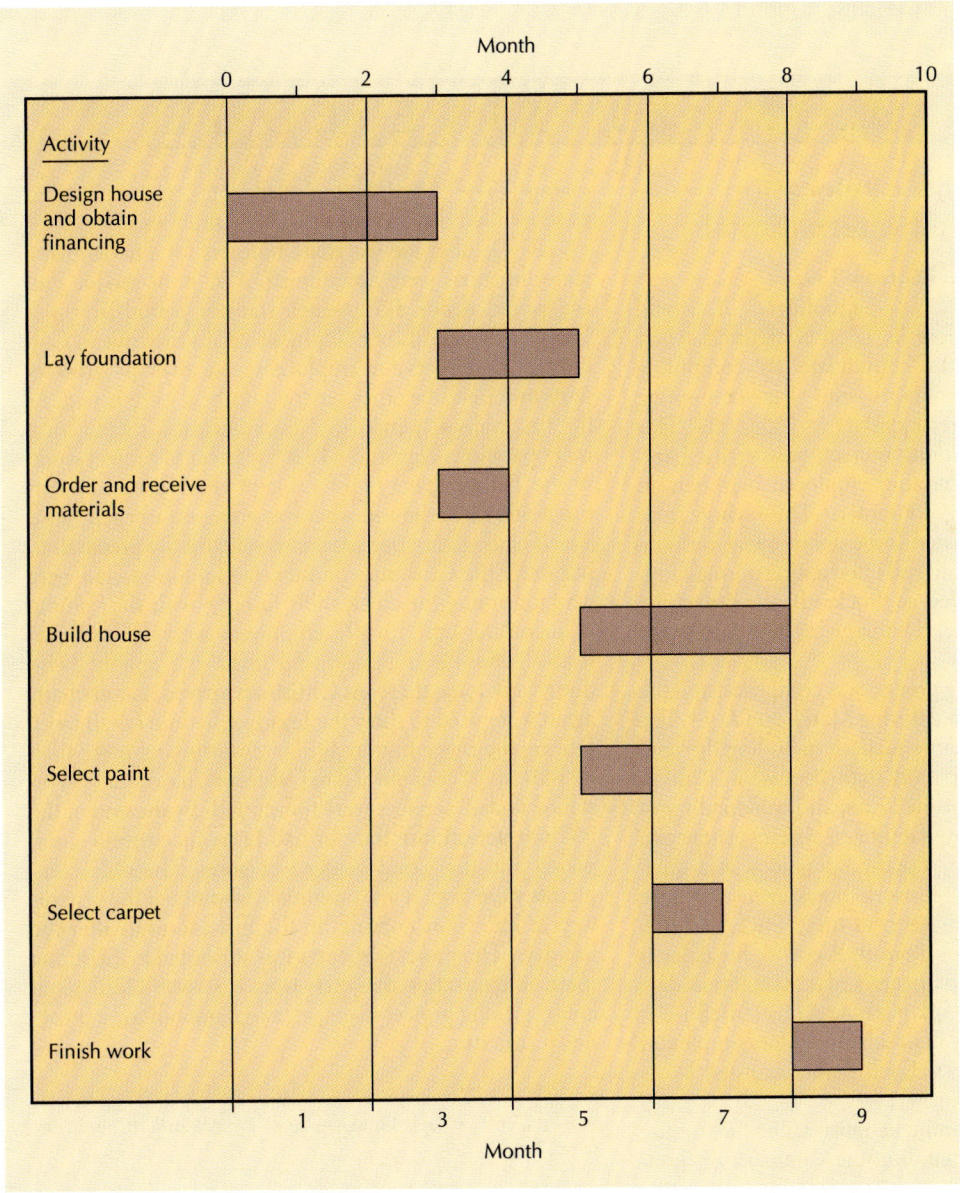

FIGURE 17.1 A Gantt Chart

can start simultaneously. This set of activities demonstrates how a precedence relationship works; the design of the house and the financing must precede the next two activities.

The activity "lay foundation" requires two months to complete, so it will be finished, at the earliest, at the end of month 5. "Order and receive materials" requires one month to complete, and it could be finished after month 4. However, observe that it is possible to delay the start of this activity one month until month 4. This delay would still enable the activity to be completed by the end of month 5, when the next activity, "build house," is scheduled to start. This extra time for the activity "order materials" is called *slack.* **Slack** is the amount by which an activity can be delayed without delaying any of the activities that follow it or the project as a whole. The remainder of the Gantt chart is constructed in a similar manner, and the project is scheduled to be completed at the end of month 9.

> **Slack** is the amount of time an activity can be delayed without delaying the project.

THE COMPETITIVE EDGE

A Computing Center Relocation Project at Rockwell International

www.prenhall.com/russell

In February 1992 Rockwell International announced it would close its Texas computing center and consolidate its computing functions into the computing center at its corporate headquarters in California. This would be a complex yearlong project, transferring hardware and software, downsizing employee members in Texas, and reconfiguring computers. The savings from the relocation was estimated to be about $48.4 million. However, the project would risk interrupting normal business and customer service so Rockwell scheduled the transfer to take place over Thanksgiving and Christmas of 1992.

The project planning process was completed and the project team was assembled during March and April. The project was broken into three sections including the consolidation of technical support staff (people) in California; transitional operations in Texas; and workload transfer including hardware, facilities, systems, network, vendor support, customer support, operations, and quality assurance functions. A work breakdown structure (WBS) was developed for each of these three sections. From May to August each item in the work breakdown structure was assigned a manager and a completion date schedule. Each week a work package status bulletin was published, updating each item scheduled for completion within the next two weeks. Each item was listed by its WBS and the project manager.

By September the complete transfer schedule for the project was published including the shipment of thousands of tapes, computers, and new mainframe configurations. (The schedule included dates where transfers were avoided due to Space Shuttle launches.)

By October the workload transfers for Thanksgiving and Christmas were announced. A 96-hour service outage would occur during each transfer period. By mid-October truckloads of equipment began to arrive in California. Customers and employees were given progress reports and new customer service numbers were issued. As the first transfer period in November drew nearer, normal operations began to take a back seat to project work. At the Thanksgiving transfer, Gantt charts sorted by start times and tasks showed what was going on in each hour. The Thanksgiving transfer went well and the preparation began for the Christmas transfer. In California, staff were working round-the-clock shifts to cope with the volume of incoming tapes, while employees were being flown from California to Texas to fill in for the rapidly dwindling work force there. As Christmas arrived, Gantt charts again were used to show the hourly schedule for all tasks. During the move hundreds of circuits linking more than 50 sites were reestablished in California, hardware was installed and all services were transferred. By the end of the 96-hour period, the transfer had been successfully completed and the Texas center was gone. The only complaints were from a few customers who noted the systems were a little slow coming up the first morning after the holidays. The project's success was attributed to the strong matrix organization that drew from Rockwell's functional areas, a strong project manager, and a smooth work breakdown structure.

SOURCE: A. L. Zambrano and E. H. Briones, "Data Center Relocation Project: The Rockwell Experience," *PM Network* 10, no. 1 (January 1996): 31–37.

The Gantt chart provides a visual display of the project schedule, indicating when activities are scheduled to start, when finished, and where extra time is available and activities can be delayed. The project manager can use the chart to monitor the progress of the activities and see which ones are ahead of schedule and which ones are behind schedule. The Gantt chart also indicates the precedence relationships between activities; however, these relationships are not always easily discernible. This problem is one of the disadvantages of the Gantt chart method, and it limits the chart's use to smaller projects with relatively few activities. The CPM/PERT network technique does not suffer this disadvantage.

CPM/PERT

In 1956 a research team at E. I. du Pont de Nemours & Company, Inc., led by a du Pont engineer, Morgan R. Walker, and a Remington-Rand computer specialist, James E. Kelley, Jr., initiated a project to develop a computerized system to improve the planning, scheduling, and reporting of the company's engineering programs (including plant maintenance and construction projects). The resulting network approach is known as the **critical path method (CPM)**. At the same time the U.S. Navy established a research team composed of members of the Navy Special Projects Office, Lockheed, and the consulting firm of Booz, Allen, and Hamilton, led by D. G. Malcolm. They developed a similar network approach for the design of a management control system for the development of the Polaris Missile Project (a ballistic missile-firing nuclear submarine). This network scheduling technique was named the **project evaluation and review technique,** or **PERT.** The Polaris project eventually included 23 PERT networks encompassing 3,000 activities.

> In **CPM** activities are shown as a network of precedence relationships using activity-on-node network construction.
>
> In **PERT** activities are shown as a network of precedence relationships using activity-on-arrow network construction.

Both CPM and PERT are derivatives of the Gantt chart and, as a result, are very similar. There were originally two primary differences between CPM and PERT. With CPM a single estimate for activity time was used that did not allow for any variation in activity times—activity times were treated as if they were known for certain, or "deterministic." With PERT, multiple time estimates were used for each activity that allowed for variation in activity times—activity times were treated as "probabilistic." The other difference was related to the mechanics of drawing the project network. In PERT activities were represented as arcs, or arrowed lines, between two nodes, or circles, whereas in CPM activities were represented as the nodes or circles. However, over time CPM and PERT have been effectively merged into a single technique conventionally referred to as CPM/PERT.

The advantage of CPM/PERT over the Gantt chart is in the use of a network to depict the precedence relationships between activities. The Gantt chart does not clearly show precedence relationships, which is a disadvantage that limited its use to small projects. The CPM/PERT is a more efficient and direct means of displaying precedence relationships. In other words, in a network it is visually easier to see the precedence relationships, which makes CPM/PERT popular with managers and other users, especially for large projects with many activities.

> CPM/PERT uses a network to depict the precedence relationships among activities.

The Project Network

A CPM/PERT network consists of *branches* and *nodes*, as shown in Figure 17.2. When CPM and PERT were first developed, they employed different conventions for constructing a network. With CPM the nodes, or circles in Figure 17.2, represented the project activities. The arrows in between the nodes indicated the precedence relationships between activities. For the network in Figure 17.2, activity 1, represented by node 1,

The Lafayette, the nuclear-powered ballistic missile submarine shown here, is a direct descendent of the Polaris, the first nuclear submarine of this type. In the late 1950s the Polaris Fleet Ballistic Missile Project was a massive undertaking that was a cornerstone of the United States' defense program. The project included over 250 prime contractors and 9,000 subcontractors. A failure by any of these subcontractors could have resulted in a significant delay in the project, which was considered a risk to national security. As such, a method was sought to coordinate the work of these subcontractors, anticipate and avoid bottlenecks, to forecast target completion dates, and in general to coordinate the work of hundreds of thousands of persons, into the finished weapon system. PERT, originally called the Program Evaluation Research Task and later changed to Program Evaluation and Review Technique, was the method developed to achieve this task. The Navy Department subsequently credited PERT with bringing the Polaris missile submarine to combat readiness approximately two years ahead of the originally scheduled completion date.

In **AON,** nodes represent activities and arrows show precedence relationships.

An **event** is the completion or beginning of an activity in a project.

In **AOA,** arrows represent activities and nodes are events for points in time.

precedes activity 2, and 2 precedes 3. This approach to network construction is called **activity-on-node (AON).** With PERT the opposite convention was taken. The branches represented the activities and the nodes in between them reflected **events,** or points in time such as the end of one activity and the beginning of another. In this approach, referred to as **activity-on-arrow (AOA),** the activities are normally identified by the node numbers at the start and end of an activity; for example, activity 1-2 precedes activity 2-3 in Figure 17.2. In this text we will employ the activity-on-arrow convention.

To demonstrate how these components are used to construct a network, we will use our example project of building a house used in the Gantt chart in Figure 17.1. The comparable CPM/PERT network for this project is shown in Figure 17.3. The precedence relationships are reflected in this network by the arrangement of the arrowed (or directed) branches in Figure 17.3. The first activity (1-2) in the project is to design the house and obtain financing. This activity must be completed before any subsequent activities can begin. Thus, activities 2-3, laying the foundation, and 2-4, ordering and receiving materials, can start only when node 2 is *realized,* indicating the event that activity 1-2 is finished. (Notice in Figure 17.3 that a time estimate of three

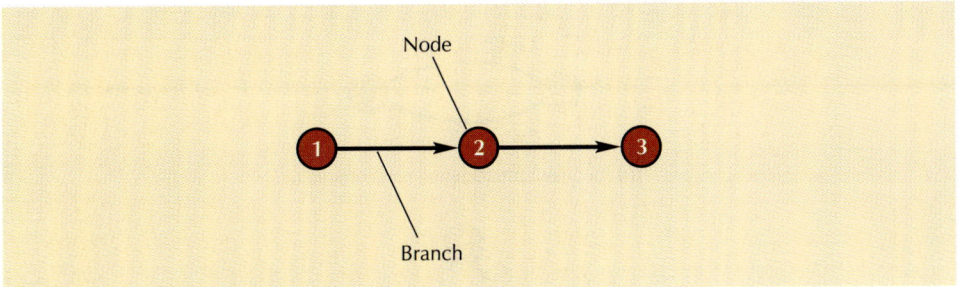

FIGURE 17.2 **Network Components**

months has been assigned for the completion of this activity). Activity 2-3 and activity 3-4 can occur concurrently; neither depends on the other and both depend only on the completion of activity 1-2.

When the activities of laying the foundation (2-3) and ordering and receiving materials (2-4) are completed, then activities 4-5 and 4-6 can begin simultaneously. However, before discussing these activities further, notice activity 3-4, referred to in the network as a dummy.

A **dummy** activity is inserted into the network to show a precedence relationships, but it does not represent any actual passage of time. Activities 2-3 and 2-4 have the precedence relationship shown in Figure 17.4(a). However, in a CPM/PERT network, two or more activities are not allowed to share the same starting and ending nodes. (The reason will become apparent later when we develop a schedule for the network.) Instead, activity 3-4 is inserted to give two activities separate end nodes and, thus, two separate identities as shown in Figure 17.4(b). Notice, though, that a time of zero months has been assigned to activity 3-4. The dummy activity shows that activity 2-3 must be completed prior to any activities beginning at node 4, but it does not represent the passage of time.

> Two or more activities cannot share the same start and end nodes; **dummy** required.

Returning to the network in Figure 17.3, we see that two activities start at node 4. Activity 4-6 is the actual building of the house, and activity 4-5 is the search for and selection of the paint for the exterior and interior of the house. Activity 4-6 and activity 4-5 can begin simultaneously and take place concurrently. Following the selection of the paint (activity 4-5) and the realization of node 5, the carpet can be selected (since

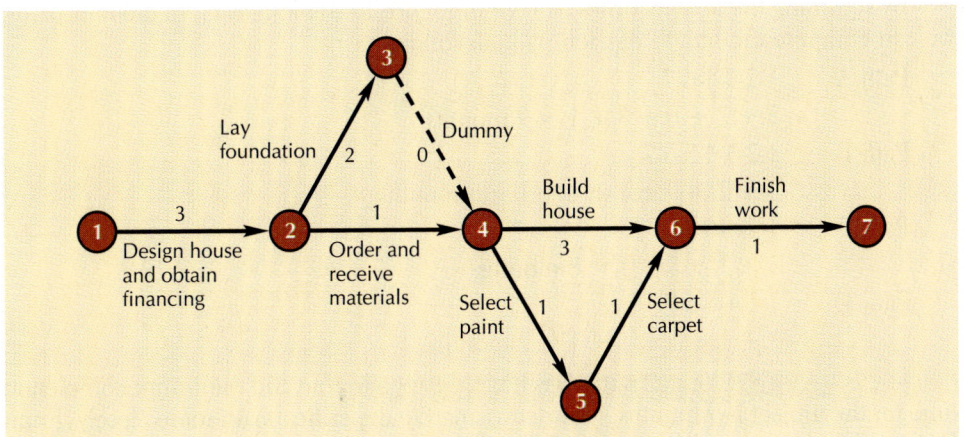

FIGURE 17.3 **The Project Network for Building a House**

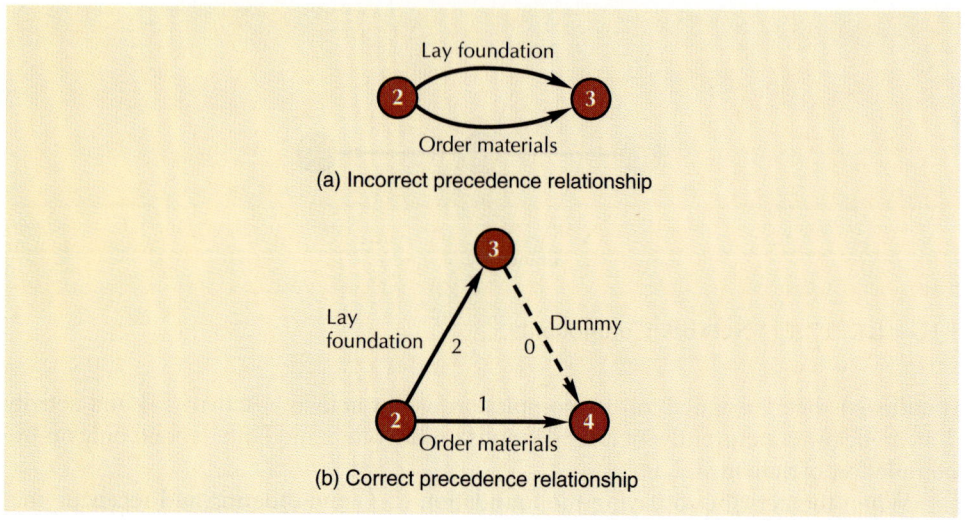

FIGURE 17.4   Concurrent Activities

the carpet color depends on the paint color). This activity can also occur concurrently with the building of the house (activity 4-6). When the building is completed and the paint and carpet are selected, the house can be finished (activity 6-7).

The Critical Path

A network path is a sequence of connected activities that runs from the start node to the end node in the network. The network in Figure 17.3 has several paths through it. In fact, close observations of this network show four paths, identified as A, B, C, and D:

A:	1-2-3-4-6-7
B:	1-2-3-4-5-6-7
C:	1-2-4-6-7
D:	1-2-4-5-6-7

The project cannot be completed (i.e., the house cannot be built) sooner than the time required by the longest path in the network, in terms of time. The path with the longest duration of time is referred to as the **critical path.**

By summing the activity times (shown in Figure 17.3) along each of the four paths, we can compute the length of each path, as follows:

Path A: 1-2-3-4-6-7
           $3 + 2 + 0 + 3 + 1 = 9$ months

Path B: 1-2-3-4-5-6-7
           $3 + 2 + 0 + 1 + 1 + 1 = 8$ months

Path C: 1-2-4-6-7
           $3 + 1 + 3 + 1 = 8$ months

Path D: 1-2-4-5-6-7
           $3 + 1 + 1 + 1 + 1 = 7$ months

Because path A is the longest path, it is the critical path; thus the minimum completion time for the project is 9 months. Now let us analyze the critical path more closely. From Figure 17.5 we can see that activities 2-3 and 2-4 cannot start until 3 months have passed. It is also easy to see that activity 3-4 will not start until 5 months have passed. The start

The **critical path** is the longest path through a network; it is the minimum project completion time.

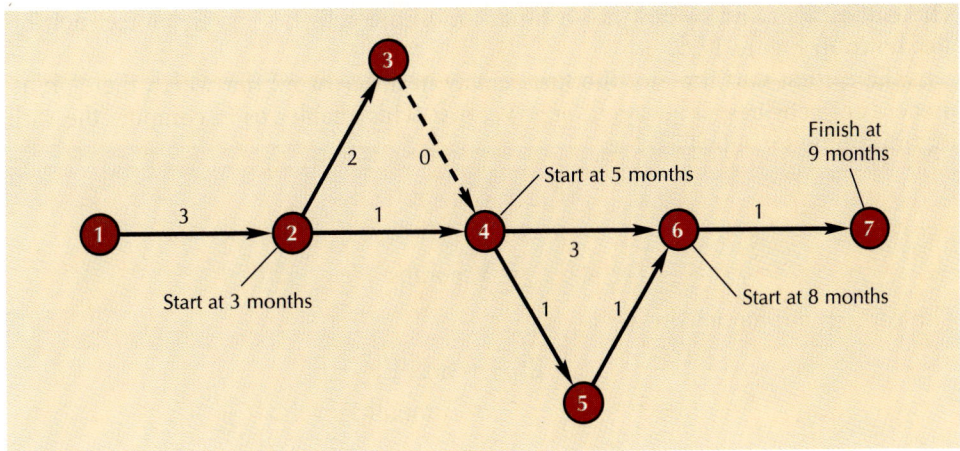

FIGURE 17.5 **Activity Start Times**

of activities 4-5 and 4-6 is dependent on two activities leading into node 4. Activity 3-4 is completed after 5 months (which we determine by adding the dummy activity time of zero to the time of 5 months until node 3 occurs), but activity 2-4 is completed at the end of 4 months. Thus, we have two possible start times for activities 4-5 and 4-6, 5 months and 4 months. However, since no activity starting at node 4 can occur until all preceding activities have been finished, the soonest node 4 can be realized is 5 months.

Now consider the activities leading from node 4. Using the same logic as before, activity 6-7 cannot start until after 8 months (5 months at node 4 plus the 3 months required by activity 4-6) or after 7 months (5 months at node 4 plus the 2 months required by activities 4-5 and 5-6). Because all activities ending at node 6 must be completed before activity 6-7 can start, the soonest they can occur is 8 months. Adding 1 month for activity 6-7 to the time at node 6 gives a project duration of 9 months. This is the time of the longest path in the network—the critical path.

This brief analysis demonstrates the concept of a critical path and the determination of the minimum completion time of a project. However, this was a cumbersome method for determining a critical path. Next, we discuss a mathematical approach to scheduling the project activities and determining the critical path.

Activity Scheduling

In our analysis of the critical path, we determined the soonest time that each activity could be finished. For example, we found that the earliest time activity 4-5 could start was 5 months. This time is referred to as the **earliest start time**, and it is expressed symbolically as **ES**.

To determine the earliest start time for every activity, we make a **forward pass** through the network. That is, we start at the first node and move forward through the network. The earliest time for an activity is the maximum time in which all preceding activities have been completed—the time when the activity start node is realized.

The **earliest finish time, EF,** for an activity is simply the earliest start time plus the activity time estimate. For example, if the earliest start time for activity 1-2 is at time 0, then the earliest finish time is 3 months. In general, the earliest start and finish times for an activity *i-j* are computed according to the following mathematical relationship (where $i < j$).

$$ES_{ij} = \text{maximum } (EF_i)$$
$$EF_{ij} = ES_{ij} + t_{ij}$$

ES is the earliest time an activity can start.

A **forward pass** starts at the beginning of a CPM/PERT network to determine the earliest activity times.

EF is the earliest start time plus the activity time.

The earliest start and earliest finish times for all the activities in our project network are shown in Figure 17.6.

The earliest start time for the first activity in the network (for which there are no predecessor activities) is always 0, or, $ES_{12} = 0$. This enables us to compute the earliest finish time for activity 1-2 as

$$EF_{12} = ES_{12} + t_{12}$$
$$= 0 + 3$$
$$= 3 \text{ months}$$

The earliest start for activity 2-3 is

$$ES_{23} = \max EF_2$$
$$= 3 \text{ months}$$

and the corresponding earliest finish time is

$$EF_{23} = ES_{23} + t_{23}$$
$$= 3 + 2$$
$$= 5 \text{ months}$$

For activity 3-4 the earliest start time (ES_{34}) is 5 months and the earliest finish time (EF_{34}) is 5 months, and for activity 2-4 the earliest start time (ES_{24}) is 3 months and the earliest finish time (EF_{24}) is 4 months.

Now consider activity 4-6, which has two predecessor activities. The earliest start time is

$$ES_{46} = \max EF_4$$
$$= \max (5, 4)$$
$$= 5 \text{ months}$$

and the earliest finish time is

$$EF_{46} = ES_{46} + t_{46}$$
$$= 5 + 3$$
$$= 8 \text{ months}$$

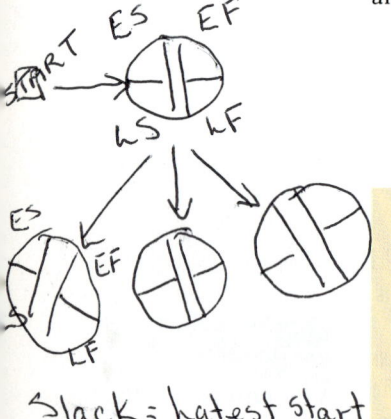

Slack = latest start minus earliest start

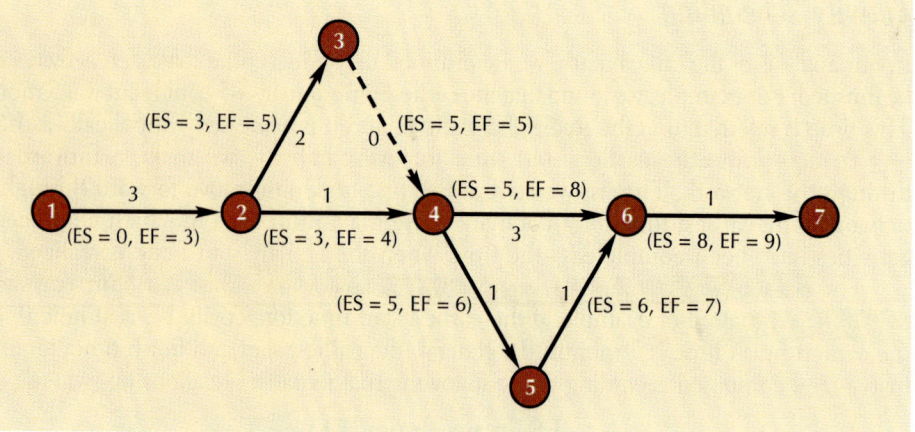

FIGURE 17.6   Earliest Activity Start and Finish Times

All the remaining earliest start and finish times are computed similarly. Notice in Figure 17.6 that the earliest finish time for activity 6-7, the last activity in the network, is 9 months, which is the total project duration, or critical path time.

Companions to the earliest start and finish are the **latest start** and **latest finish times, LS** and **LF.** The latest start time is the latest time an activity can start without delaying the completion of the project beyond the project critical path time. For our example, the project completion time (and earliest finish time) at node 7 is 9 months. Thus, the objective of determining latest times is to see how long each activity can be delayed without the project exceeding 9 months.

In general, the latest start and finish times for an activity *i-j* are computed according to the following formulas:

$$LS_{ij} = LF_{ij} - t_{ij}$$
$$LF_{ij} = min (LS_j)$$

The term min(LS_j) means the minimum latest start time for all activities leaving node *j*. Whereas a forward pass through the network is made to determine the earliest times, the latest times are computed using a **backward pass.** We start at the end of the network at node 7 and work backward, computing the latest times for each activity. Since we want to determine how long each activity in the network can be delayed without extending the project time, the latest finish time at node 7 cannot exceed the earliest finish time. Therefore, the latest finish time at node 7 is 9 months. This and all other latest times are shown in Figure 17.7.

Starting at the end of the network, the critical path time, which is also equal to the earliest finish time of activity 6-7, is 9 months. This automatically becomes the latest finish time for activity 6-7, or,

$$LF_{67} = 9 \text{ months}$$

Using this value, the latest start time for activity 6-7 is

$$LS_{67} = LF_{67} - t_{67}$$
$$= 9 - 1$$
$$= 8 \text{ months}$$

LS is the latest time an activity can start without delaying critical path time. **LF** is the latest time an activity can be completed and still maintain the project critical path time.

A **backward pass** determines latest activity times by starting at the end of a CPM/PERT network and working forward.

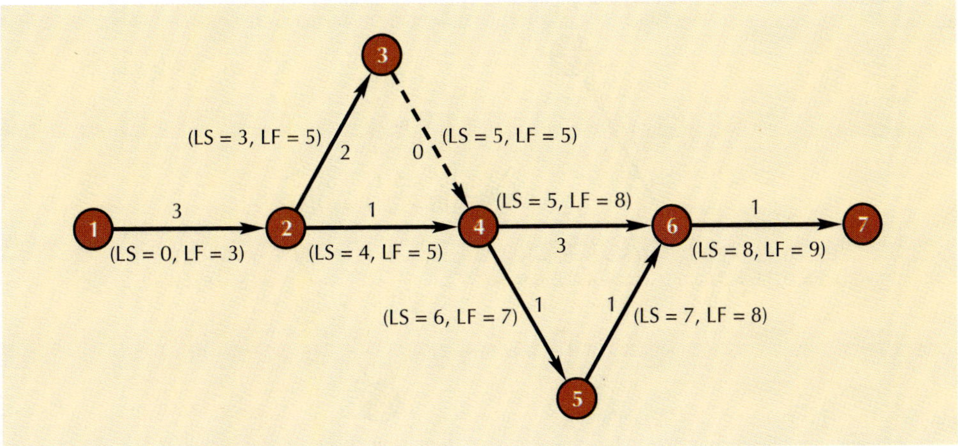

FIGURE 17.7 **Latest Activity Start and Finish Times**

The latest finish time for activity 5-6 is the minimum of the latest start times for the activities leaving node 6. Since activity 6-7 leaves node 6, the latest start time is

$$LF_{56} = \min(LS_6)$$
$$= 8 \text{ months}$$

The latest start time for activity 5-6 is

$$LS_{56} = LF_{56} - t_{56}$$
$$= 8 - 1$$
$$= 7 \text{ months}$$

For activity 4-6, the latest finish time (LF_{46}) is 8 months, and the latest start time (LS_{46}) is 5 months; for activity 4-5, the latest finish time (LF_{45}) is 7 months, and the latest start time (LS_{45}) is 6 months.

Now consider activity 2-4, which has two activities, 4-6 and 4-5, following it. The latest finish time is computed as

$$LF_{24} = \min(LF_4)$$
$$= \min(5,6)$$
$$= 5 \text{ months}$$

The latest start time is

$$LS_{24} = LF_{24} - t_{24}$$
$$= 5 - 1$$
$$= 4 \text{ months}$$

All the remaining latest start and latest finish times are computed similarly. Figure 17.8 includes the earliest and latest start times, and earliest and latest finish times for all activities.

Activity Slack

The project network in Figure 17.8, with all activity start and finish times, highlights the critical path (1-2-3-4-6-7) we determined earlier by inspection. Notice that for the activities on the critical path, the earliest start times and latest times are equal. This

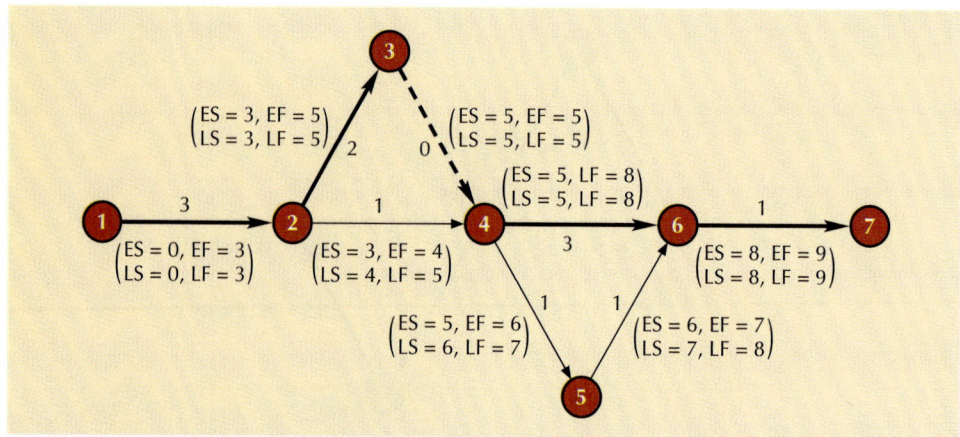

FIGURE 17.8   Earliest Activity Start and Finish Times

means that these activities on the critical path must start exactly on time and cannot be delayed at all. If the start of any activity on the critical path is delayed, then the overall project time will be increased. We now have an alternate way to determine the critical path besides simply inspecting the network. The activities on the critical path can be determined by seeing for which activities ES = LS or EF = LF. In Figure 17.8 the activities 1-2, 2-3, 3-4, 4-6 and 6-7 all have earliest start times and latest start times that are equal (and EF = LF); thus, they are on the critical path.

For activities not on the critical path for which the earliest and latest start times (or earliest and latest finish times) are not equal, *slack* time exists. We introduced slack with our discussion of the Gantt chart in Figure 17.1. Slack is the amount of time an activity can be delayed without affecting the overall project duration. In effect, it is extra time available for completing an activity.

Slack, S, is computed using either of the following formulas:

$$S_{ij} = LS_{ij} - ES_{ij}$$

or

$$S_{ij} = LF_{ij} - EF_{ij}$$

For example, the slack for activity 2-4 is

$$S_{24} = LS_{24} - ES_{24}$$
$$= 4 - 3$$
$$= 1 \text{ month}$$

If the start of activity 2-4 were delayed for 1 month, the activity could still be completed by month 5 without delaying the project completion time. The slack for each activity

THE COMPETITIVE EDGE

Highway Construction at the Minnesota Department of Transportation

Highway-related construction is a prominent area of use of project management techniques. As an example, the Minnesota Department of Transportation (MN/DOT) generally has approximately 1,100 ongoing construction projects under development at any time. These projects involve highway improvement, such as a new highway or freeway segment, a new bridge, or restoration of an existing facility, as well as projects involving airports, waterways, railroads, and so on. The highway department allows about 300 new project contracts each year.

This volume of project work requires an extensive project management organizational structure. Near the top of MN/DOT, the Office of Highway Programs Implementation coordinates project management teams located at the nine district offices in the system. Each district has between 5 and 15 project managers, each responsible for the design of several projects at one time.

An example of the use of critical path methods (CPM) at MN/DOT was for a $9.5 million flood-control project, which requires a road segment less than 1 mile in length to be raised with flood walls and new bridges to be constructed. It was critical that the project be completed prior to the winter of the second year of the project. All construction activities were networked, and a critical path was determined. Bar charts were also used as a supplement to assist visualization of critical activities. Project control and the schedule were maintained through weekly meetings of the contractors. The project was completed on time, and the use of CPM was deemed successful.

SOURCES: Based on R. Pearson, "Project Management in the Minnesota Department of Transportation, Delivering Products: The Preconstruction Phase," *The PM Network* 2, no. 5 (November 1988): 7–18; G. Dirlan, "A View of Construction in MN/DOT Management," *The PM Network* 2, no. 5 (November 1988): 19.

TABLE 17.1   Activity Slack

Activity	LS	ES	LF	EF	Slack S
*1–2	0	0	3	3	0
*2–3	3	3	5	5	0
2–4	4	3	5	4	1
*3–4	5	5	5	5	0
4–5	6	5	7	6	1
*4–6	5	5	8	8	0
5–6	7	6	8	7	1
*6–7	8	8	9	9	0

* = critical path.

in our example project network is shown in Table 17.1 and Figure 17.9. Table 17.1 shows there is no slack for the activities on the critical path (marked with an asterisk); activities not on the critical path have slack.

Notice in Figure 17.9 that *either* activity 4-5 can be delayed 1 month *or* activity 5-6 can be delayed 1 month, but they both cannot be delayed 1 month. If activity 4-5 starts at month 6 instead of 5, then it will be completed at month 7, which will not allow the start of activity 5-6 to be delayed. The opposite is also true. If 4-5 starts at month 5, activity 5-6 can be delayed 1 month. The slack on these two activities is called *shared slack*. This means that the sequence of activities 4-5-6 can be delayed 1 month jointly without delaying the project.

Slack is beneficial to the project manager since it enables resources to be temporarily diverted from activities with slack and used for other activities that might be delayed for various reasons or for which the time estimate has proved to be inaccurate.

The times for the network activities are simply estimates, for which there is usually not a lot of historical basis (since projects tend to be unique undertakings). As such, activity time estimates are subject to quite a bit of uncertainty. However, the uncertainty inherent in activity time estimates can be reflected to a certain extent by using probabilistic time estimates instead of the single, deterministic estimates we have used so far.

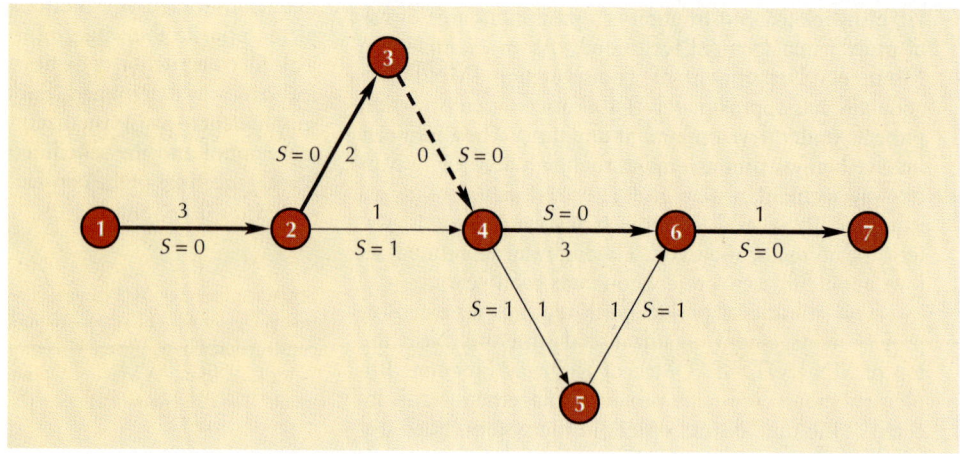

FIGURE 17.9   Activity Slack

Since its inception, a primary use of the CPM/PERT has been to plan, manage and control construction projects of all types. Federal and state agencies often require contractors to develop and submit CPM/PERT networks for the construction of roads, buildings and other public facilities. Project management techniques provide an effective means to avoid delays and budget overruns for projects that may include hundreds or even thousands of subcontractors, such as the construction of the Olympic Stadium for the 1996 Summer Olympic Games in Atlanta shown here. The Olympic Stadium took 3 years and $232 million to build. It required 10,000 tons of steel to construct, encompassed 1.7 million square feet and had a seating capacity of 85,000. Following the Olympic Games the stadium was converted to a 48,900 seat stadium for the Atlanta Braves.

Probabilistic Activity Times

In the project network for building a house in the previous section, all activity time estimates were single values. By using only a single activity time estimate, we are, in effect, assuming that activity times are known with certainty (i.e., they are deterministic). For example, in Figure 17.3, the time estimate for activity 2-3 (laying the foundation) is 2 months. Since only this one value is given, we must assume that the activity time does not vary (or varies very little) from 2 months. It is rare that activity time estimates can be made with certainty. Project activities are likely to be unique. There is little historical evidence that can be used as a basis to predict activity times. Recall that one of the primary differences between CPM and PERT is that PERT uses probabilistic activity times.

Probabilistic Time Estimates

In the PERT-type approach to estimating activity times, three time estimates for each activity are determined, which enables us to estimate the mean and variance of a **beta distribution** of the activity times.

Probabilistic time estimates reflect uncertainty of activity times.

We assume that the activity times can be described by a beta distribution for several reasons. The beta distribution mean and variance can be approximated with three time estimates. Also, the beta distribution is continuous, but it has no predetermined shape (such as the bell shape of the normal curve). It will take on the shape indicated— that is, be skewed—by the time estimates given. This is beneficial, since typically we have no prior knowledge of the shapes of the distributions of activity times in a unique project network. Although other types of distributions have been shown to be no more or less accurate than the beta, it has become traditional to use the beta distribution to estimate probabilistic activity times.

A **beta distribution** is a probability distribution traditionally used in CPM/PERT.

The three time estimates for each activity are the **most likely time (*m*),** the **optimistic time (*a*),** and the **pessimistic time (*b*).** The most likely time is a subjective estimate of the activity time that would most frequently occur if the activity were repeated many times. The optimistic time is the shortest possible time to complete the activity if everything went right. The pessimistic time is the longest possible time to complete the activity assuming everything went wrong. The person most familiar with an activity or the project manager makes these "subjective" estimates to the best of his or her knowledge and ability.

Time estimates for an activity are **optimistic (*a*), most likely (*m*),** and **pessimistic (*b*)** times.

THE COMPETITIVE EDGE

Repair Project Management at Sasol

www.prenhall.com/russell

Sasol is a leading South African company that converts coal to oil and chemicals. On March 8, 1994, a fire broke out in a regeneration column (e.g., chimney/smokestack) used to process hydrogen in the Benfield Unit at Sasol Three, one of Sasol's factories. The column is 70m (231 feet) high, and the fire caused it to buckle in the middle so that it tilted to one side. Without the column, a large section of the factory could not function, resulting in a substantial loss of income. It was imperative that the Benfield column be repaired as soon as possible, which required the damaged portion of the column shell to be cut out and replaced. A goal was immediately established to have the column back in service within 47 days.

Sustech, a subsidiary of Sasol's, was assigned the repair project. A project team was put together consisting of 27 members including 4 process engineers, 6 mechanical engineers, a pressure vessel specialist, a metallurgist, a welding engineer, a pipe stress engineer, a piping draftsman, a mechanical draftsman, a structural engineer and draftsman, 3 quality assurance inspectors, and commercial contract and procurement officers. Team members came not only from Sasol but also from the original column fabricators, Chicago Bridge and

Iron Works, and various equipment and material suppliers.

The scope statement was brief—repair the Benfield column as soon as possible. First a work breakdown structure was developed. This was accomplished at open "brainstorming" meetings with all interested parties and team members present. Each topic identified was written on a Post-it note and attached to a huge white board. A project schedule was established using Microsoft Project for Windows. Special attention was focused on critical path activities. Team members responsible for critical path activities received voluntary help from all other members of the team. Quality control was strictly enforced. Not only would this result in a safe and durable new column; it would negate the need to rework poor quality work that might delay the project.

The repair project was completed in just 25 days—15 days ahead of schedule. The initial project budget was $85.28 million and the final cost was $63.74 million, a savings of 25 percent of the total estimated project cost. Keys to project success were a simple plan with good communication and leadership, and a motivated work force. The Benfield column repair project was named the 1995 International Project of the Year by the Project Management Institute.

SOURCE: I. Boggon, "The Benfield Column Repair Project," *PM Network* 10, no. 2 (February 1996): 25–30.

These three time estimates are used to estimate the mean and variance of a beta distribution, as follows:

$$\text{Mean (expected time): } t = \frac{a + 4m + b}{6}$$

$$\text{Variance: } \sigma^2 = \left(\frac{b - a}{6}\right)^2$$

where

$$a = \text{optimistic time estimate}$$
$$m = \text{most likely time estimate}$$
$$b = \text{pessimistic time estimate}$$

These formulas provide a reasonable estimate of the mean and variance of the beta distribution, a distribution that is continuous and can take on various shapes, or exhibit skewness.

Figure 17.10 illustrates the general form of beta distributions for different relative values of *a*, *m*, and *b*.

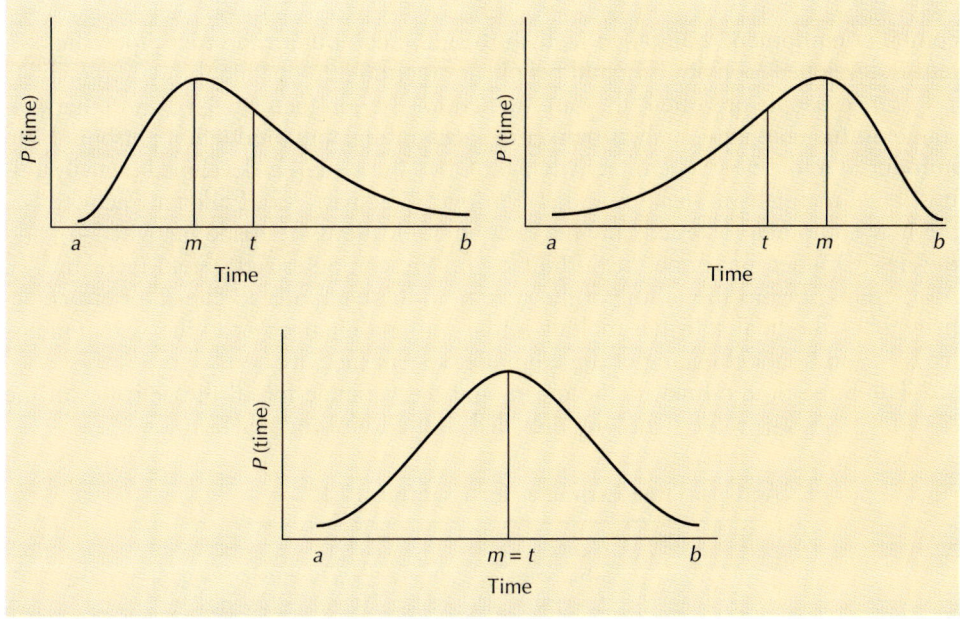

FIGURE 17.10   Examples of the Beta Distribution

EXAMPLE
17.1

*A Project Network
with Probabilistic
Time Estimates*

The Southern Textile Company has decided to install a new computerized order-processing system. In the past, orders were processed manually, which contributed to delays in delivery orders and resulted in lost sales. The new system will improve the quality of the service the company provides. The company wants to develop a project network for the installation of the new system.

The network for the installation of the new order-processing system is shown in the accompanying figure. The network begins with three concurrent activities: The new

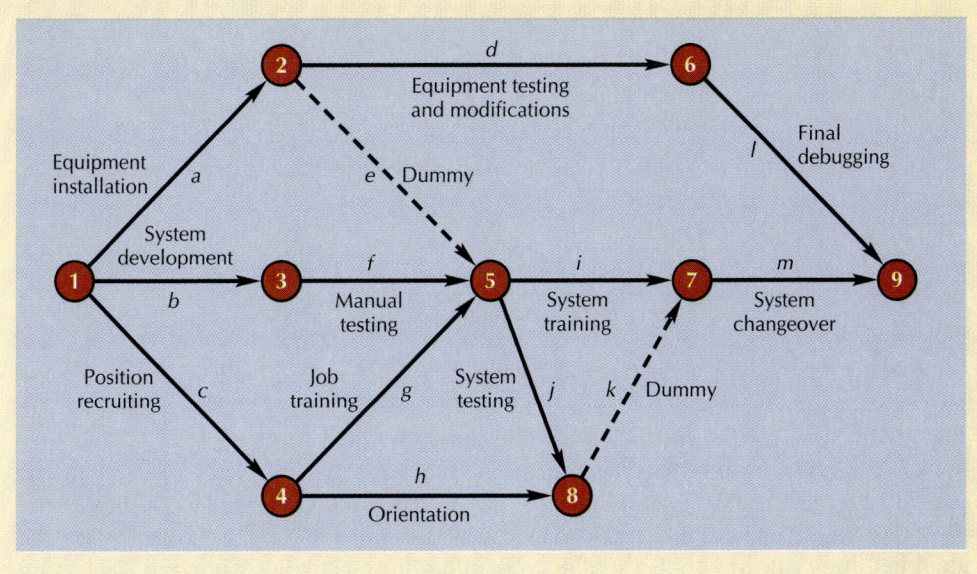

(Continued)

computer equipment is installed (activity 1-2); the computerized order-processing system is developed (activity 1-3); and people are recruited to operate the system (activity 1-4). Once people are hired, they are trained for the job (activity 4-5), and other personnel in the company, such as marketing, accounting, and production personnel, are introduced to the new system (activity 4-8). Once the system is developed (activity 1-3) it is tested manually to make sure that it is logical (activity 3-5). Following activity 1-2, the new equipment is tested, any necessary modifications are made (activity 2-6), and the newly trained personnel begin training on the computerized system (activity 5-7). Also, event 5 begins the testing of the system on the computer to check for errors (activity 5-8). The final activities include a trial run and changeover to the system (activity 7-9), and final debugging of the computer system (activity 6-9).

The three time estimates, the mean, and the variance for all the activities in the network as shown in the figure are provided in the following table.

Activity Time Estimates for Example 17.1

Activity	Time Estimates (weeks)			Mean Time	Variance
	a	m	b	t	σ^2
1-2	6	8	10	8	0.44
1-3	3	6	9	6	1.00
1-4	1	3	5	3	0.44
2-5	0	0	0	0	0.00
2-6	2	4	12	5	2.78
3-5	2	3	4	3	0.11
4-5	3	4	5	4	0.11
4-8	2	2	2	2	0.00
5-7	3	7	11	7	1.78
5-8	2	4	6	4	0.44
8-7	0	0	0	0	0.00
6-9	1	4	7	4	1.00
7-9	1	10	13	9	4.00

SOLUTION:

As an example of the computation of the individual activity mean times and variance, consider activity 1-2. The three time estimates ($a = 6$, $m = 8$, $b = 10$) are substituted in the formulas as follows:

$$t = \frac{a + 4m + b}{6} = \frac{6 + 4(8) + 10}{6} = 8 \text{ weeks}$$

$$\sigma^2 = \left(\frac{b - a}{6}\right)^2 = \left(\frac{10 - 6}{6}\right)^2 = \frac{4}{9} \text{ week}$$

The other values for the mean and variance are computed similarly.

Once the mean times have been computed for each activity, we can determine the critical path the same way we did in the deterministic time network, except that we use the expected activity times, t. Recall that in the home building project network, we identified the critical path as the one containing those activities with zero slack. This requires the determination of earliest and latest start and finish times for each activity, as shown in the accompanying table and figures.

Activity Earliest and Latest Times and Slack

Activity	t	σ^2	ES	EF	LS	LF	S
1-2	8	0.44	0	8	1	9	1
1-3	6	1.00	0	6	0	6	0
1-4	3	0.44	0	3	2	5	2
2-5	0	0.00	8	8	9	9	1
2-6	5	2.78	8	13	16	21	8
3-5	3	0.11	6	9	6	9	0
4-5	4	0.11	3	7	5	9	2
4-8	2	0.00	3	5	14	16	11
5-7	7	1.78	9	16	9	16	0
5-8	4	0.44	9	13	12	16	3
8-7	0	0.00	13	13	16	16	3
6-9	4	1.00	13	17	21	25	8
7-9	9	4.00	16	25	16	25	0

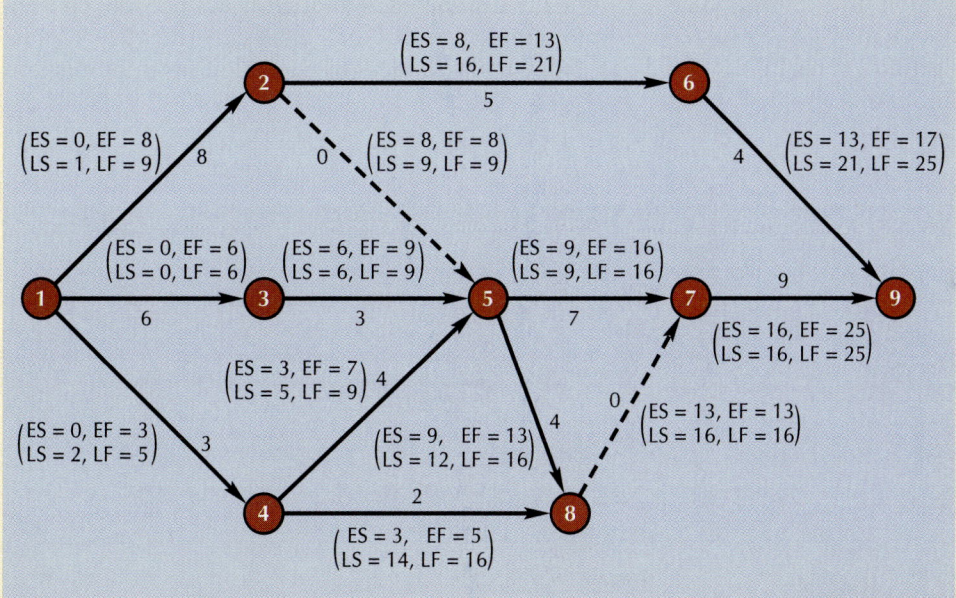

From the table, we can see that the critical path encompasses activities 1-3-5-7-9, since these activities have no available slack. We can also see that the expected project completion time (t_p) is the same as the earliest or latest finish for activity 7-9, or $t_p =$ 25 weeks. To determine the project variance, we *sum the variances for those activities on the critical path*. Using the variances shown in the table above for the critical path activities, the total project variance can be computed as follows:

$$\sigma^2 = \sigma_{13}^2 + \sigma_{35}^2 + \sigma_{57}^2 + \sigma_{79}^2$$
$$= 1.00 + 0.11 + 1.78 + 4.00$$
$$= 6.89 \text{ weeks}$$

Project variance is the sum of variances on the critical path.

CPM/PERT Network Analysis with POM for Windows

POM for Windows will provide the same scheduling analysis that we computed in Example 17.1. Following are the POM for Windows solution screens in Exhibits 17.1 and 17.2 for Example 17.1 with earliest start and latest finish times and slack for each activity. Notice that instead of activity variances the computer output provides activity standard deviations (i.e., σ instead of σ^2).

Probabilistic Network Analysis

The CPM/PERT method assumes that the activity times are statistically independent, which allows us to sum the individual expected activity times and variances to get an expected project time and variance. It is further assumed that the network mean and variance are normally distributed. This assumption is based on the central limit theorem of probability, which for CPM/PERT analysis and our purposes states that if the number of activities is large enough and the activities are statistically independent, then the sum of the means of the activities along the critical path will approach the mean of a normal distribution. For the small examples in this chapter, it is questionable whether there are sufficient activities to guarantee that the mean project completion time and variance are normally distributed. Although it has become conventional in CPM/PERT analysis to employ probability analysis using the normal distribution regardless of the network size, the prudent user should bear this limitation in mind.

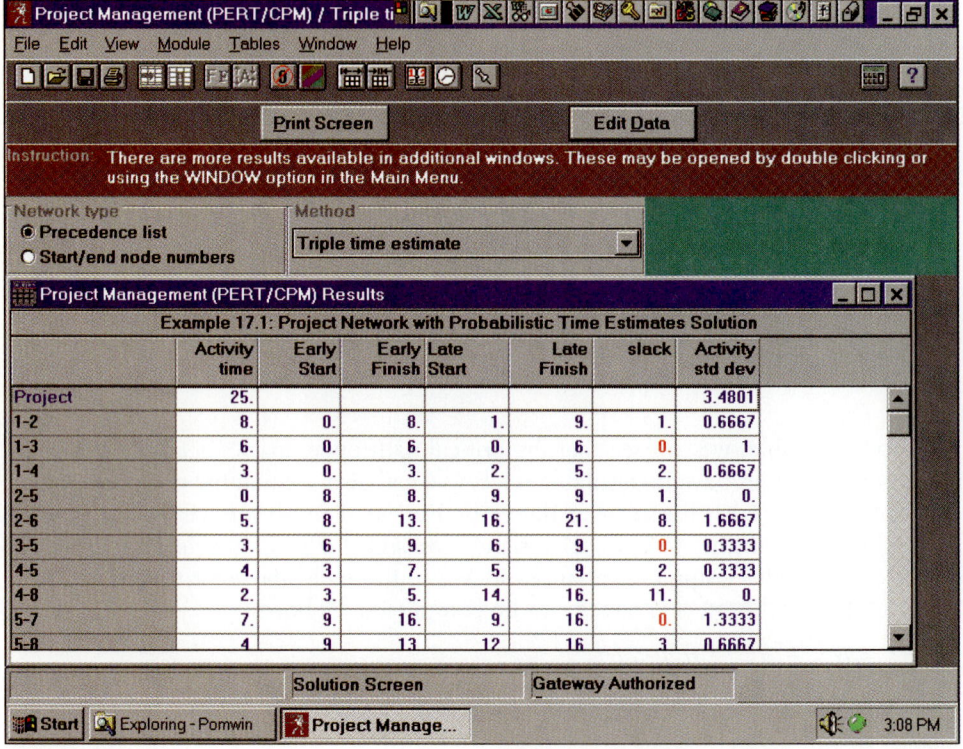

EXHIBIT 17.1

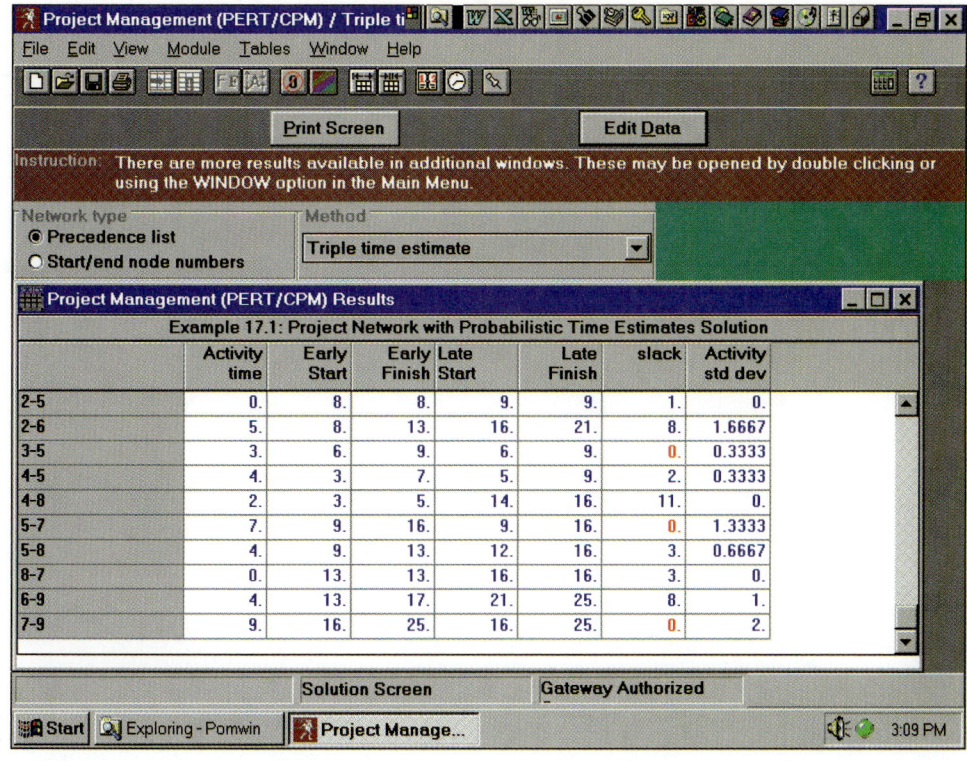

EXHIBIT 17.2

Probabilistic analysis of a CPM/PERT network is the determination of the probability that the project will be completed within a certain time period given the mean and variance of a normally distributed project completion time. This is illustrated in Figure 17.11. The value Z is computed using the following formula:

$$Z = \frac{x - \mu}{\sigma}$$

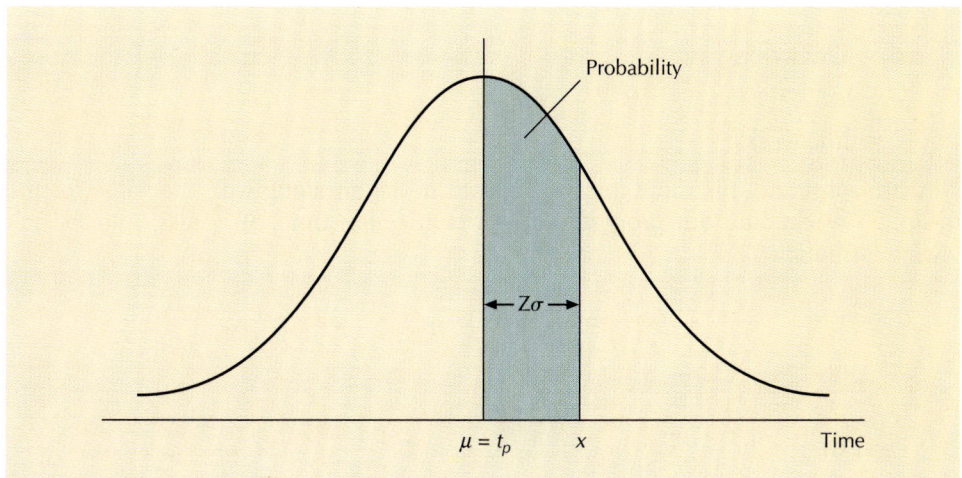

FIGURE 17.11   Normal Distribution of Project Time

where

$$\mu = t_p = \text{project mean time}$$
$$x = \text{the proposed project time}$$
$$Z = \text{number of standard deviations } x \text{ is from the mean}$$

This value of Z is then used to find the corresponding probability in Table A.1 (Appendix A).

The Southern Textile Company in Example 17.1 has told its customers that the new order-processing system will be operational in 30 weeks. What is the probability that the system will be ready by that time?

SOLUTION:

The probability that the project will be completed within 30 weeks is shown as the shaded area in the accompanying figure. To compute the Z value for a time of 30 weeks, we must first compute the standard deviation (σ) from the variance (σ^2).

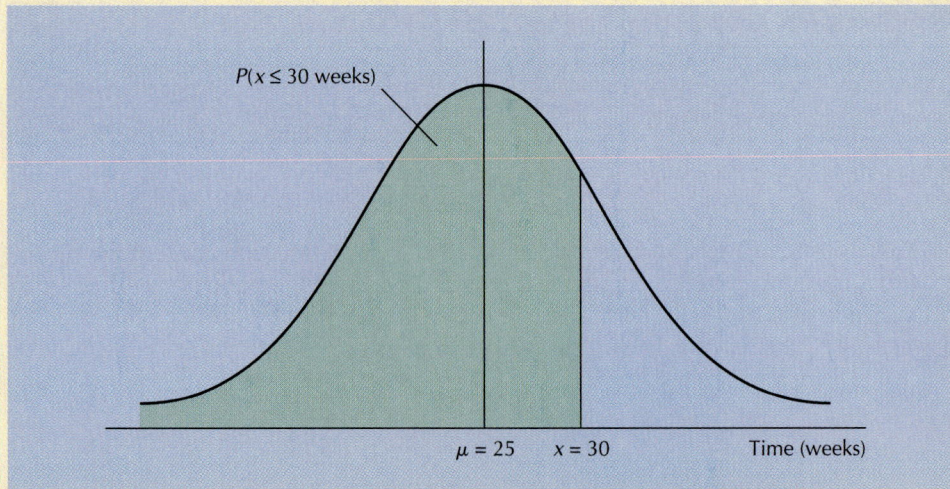

$$\sigma^2 = 6.89 \text{ weeks}$$
$$\sigma = \sqrt{6.89}$$
$$= 2.62 \text{ weeks}$$

Next we substitute this value for the standard deviation along with the value for the mean, 25 weeks, and our proposed project completion time, 30 weeks, into the following formula:

$$Z = \frac{x - \mu}{\sigma}$$
$$= \frac{30 - 25}{2.62}$$
$$= 1.91$$

A Z value of 1.91 corresponds to a probability of 0.4719 in Table A.1 in Appendix A. This means that there is a 0.9719 probability of completing the project in 30 weeks or less (adding the probability of the area to the left of $\mu = 25$, or .5000 to .4719).

EXAMPLE
17.3

*Probabilistic Analysis
of the Project Network*

A customer of the Southern Textile Company has become frustrated with delayed orders and told the company that if the new ordering system is not working within 22 weeks, it will not do any more business with the textile company. What is the probability the order-processing system will be operational within 22 weeks?

SOLUTION:

The probability that the project will be completed within 22 weeks is shown as the shaded area in the accompanying figure.

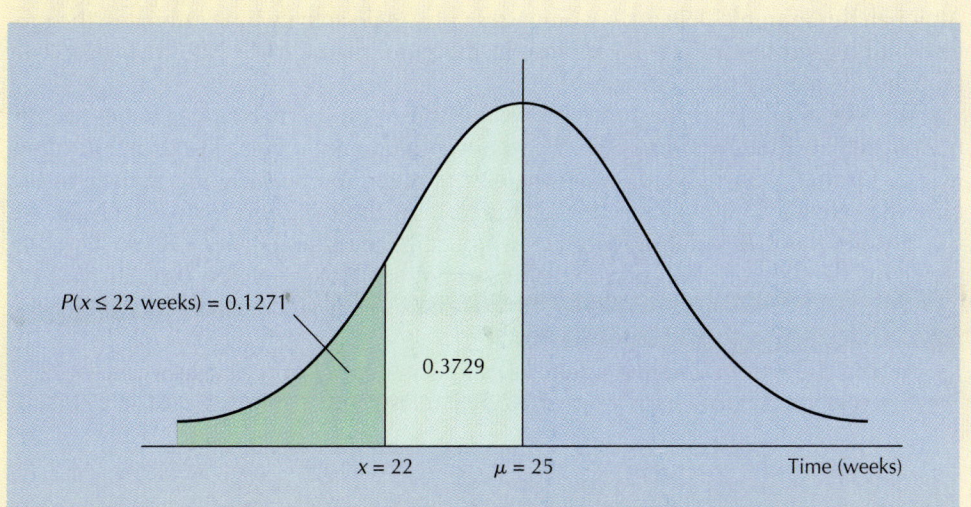

$P(x \le 22 \text{ weeks}) = 0.1271$

0.3729

$x = 22$ $\mu = 25$ Time (weeks)

The probability of the project's being completed within 22 weeks is computed as follows:

$$Z = \frac{22 - 25}{2.62}$$

$$= \frac{-3}{2.62}$$

$$= -1.14$$

A Z value of -1.14 corresponds to a probability of 0.3729 in the normal table in Appendix A. Thus, there is only a 0.1271 (i.e., $0.5000 - 0.3729$) probability that the system will be operational in 22 weeks.

Project Crashing and Time-Cost Trade-Off

The project manager is frequently confronted with having to reduce the scheduled completion time of a project to meet a deadline. In other words, the manager must finish the project sooner than indicated by the CPM/PERT network analysis. Project duration can often be reduced by assigning more labor to project activities, in the form of overtime, and by assigning more resources (material, equipment, etc.). However, additional labor and resources increase the project cost. Thus, the decision to reduce the project duration must be based on an analysis of the trade-off between time and cost. *Project crashing* is a method for shortening the project duration by reducing the time of one (or more) of the critical project activities to less than its normal activity time. This reduction in the normal activity time is referred to as **crashing.** Crashing is achieved by devoting more resources, usually measured in terms of dollars, to the activities to be crashed.

> **Crashing** is reducing project time by expending additional resources.

Project Crashing

To demonstrate how project crashing works, we will employ the CPM/PERT network for constructing a house in Figure 17.3. This network is repeated in Figure 17.12, except that the activity times previously shown as months have been converted to weeks. Although this example network encompasses only single-activity time estimates, the project crashing procedure can be applied in the same manner to PERT networks with probabilistic activity time estimates.

We will assume that the times (in weeks) shown on the network activities are the normal activity times. For example, 12 weeks are normally required to complete activity 1-2. Further, we will assume that the cost required to complete this activity in the time indicated is $3,000. This cost is referred to as the *normal activity cost*. Next, we will assume that the building contractor has estimated that activity 1-2 can be completed in 7 weeks, but it will cost $5,000 instead of $3,000 to complete the activity. This new estimated activity time is known as the **crash time,** and the cost to achieve the crash time is referred to as the **crash cost.**

> **Crash time** is an amount of time an activity is reduced; **crash cost** is the cost of reducing activity time.

Activity 1-2 can be crashed a total of 5 weeks (normal time − crash time = 12 − 7 = 5 weeks) at a total crash cost of $2,000 (crash cost − normal cost = $5,000 −

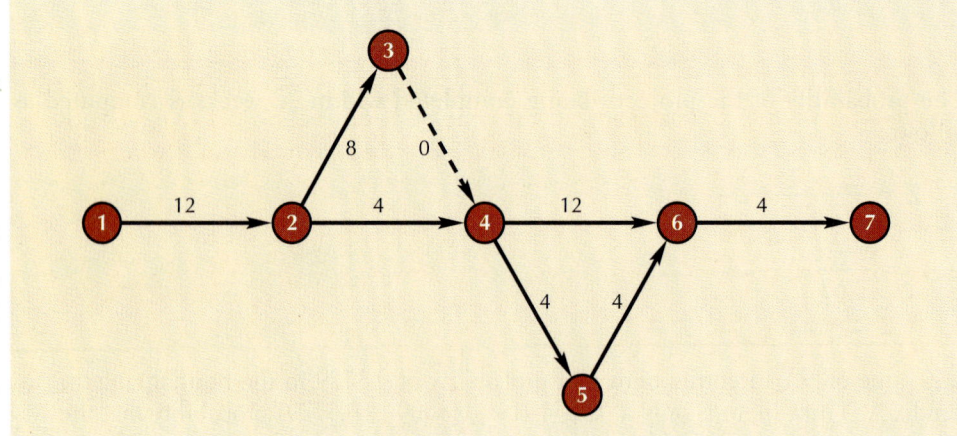

FIGURE 17.12   The Project Network for Building a House

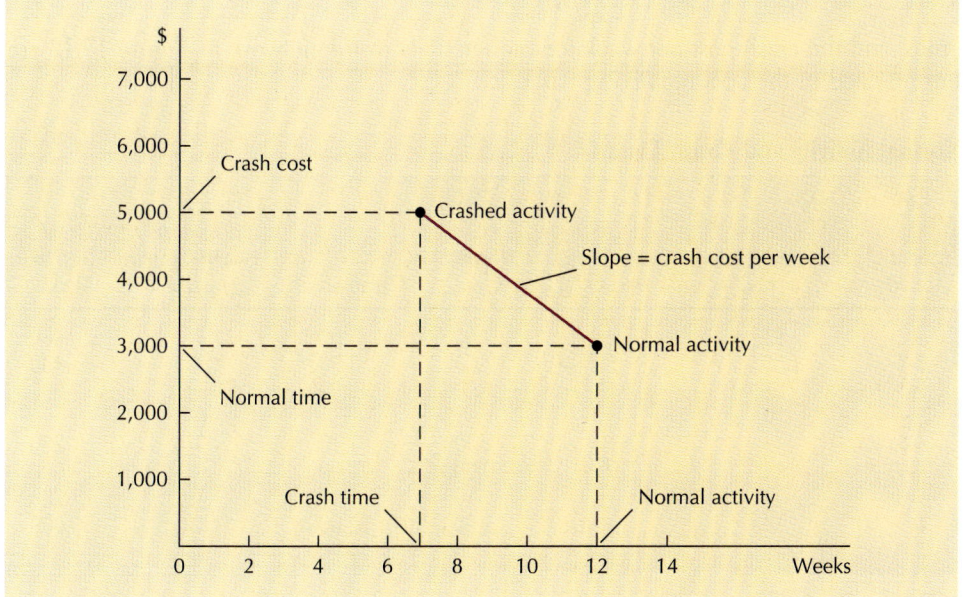

FIGURE 17.13   **The Relationship Between Normal Time and Cost, and Crash Time and Cost**

3,000 = $2,000). Dividing the total crash cost by the total allowable crash time yields the crash cost per week:

$$\frac{\text{Total crash cost}}{\text{Total crash time}} = \frac{\$2,000}{5} = \$400 \text{ per week}$$

If we assume that the relationship between crash cost and crash time is linear, then activity 1-2 can be crashed by any amount of time (not exceeding the maximum allowable crash time) at a rate of $400 per week. For example, if the contractor decided to crash activity 1-2 by only 2 weeks (reducing activity time to 10 weeks), the crash cost would be $800 ($400 per week × 2 weeks). The linear relationships between crash cost and crash time and between normal cost and normal time are illustrated in Figure 17.13.

The objective of project crashing is to reduce project duration while minimizing the cost of crashing. Since the project completion time can be shortened only by crashing activities on the critical path, it may turn out that not all activities have to be crashed. However, as activities are crashed, the critical path may change, requiring crashing of previously noncritical activities to reduce the project completion time even further.

> The goal of crashing is to reduce project duration at minimum cost.

EXAMPLE 17.4

Project Crashing

Recall that the critical path for the house building network in Figure 17.12 encompassed activities 1-2-3-4-6-7 and the project duration was 9 months, or 36 weeks. Suppose the home builder needed the house in 30 weeks and wanted to know how much extra cost would be incurred to complete the house by this time.

The normal times and costs, the crash times and costs, the total allowable crash

(Continued)

Handwritten margin notes:
Cost/weekly crashed
$$\frac{\text{Crash cost} - \text{normal cost}}{\text{normal time} - \text{crash time}}$$

times, and the crash cost per week for each activity in the network in Figure 17.12 are summarized in the accompanying table.

Normal Activity and Crash Data

Activity	Normal Time (weeks)	Crash Time (weeks)	Normal Cost	Crash Cost	Total Allowable Crash Time (weeks)	Crash Cost per Week
1-2	12	7	$ 3,000	$ 5,000	5	$ 400
2-3	8	5	2,000	3,500	3	500
2-4	4	3	4,000	7,000	1	3,000
3-4	0	0	0	0	0	0
4-5	4	1	500	1,100	3	200
4-6	12	9	50,000	71,000	3	7,000
5-6	4	1	500	1,100	3	200
6-7	4	3	15,000	22,000	1	7,000
			75,000	$110,700		

SOLUTION:

We start by looking at the critical path and seeing which activity has the minimum crash cost per week. Observing the table above and the figure below, we see activity 1-2 has the minimum crash cost of $400 (excluding the dummy activity 3-4, which cannot be reduced). Activity 1-2 will be reduced as much as possible. The table shows that the maximum allowable reduction for activity 1-2 is 5 weeks, but we can reduce activity 1-2 only to the point where another path becomes critical. When two paths simultaneously become critical, activities on both must be reduced by the same amount. If we reduce the activity time beyond the point where another path becomes critical, we may be incurring an unnecessary cost. This last stipulation means that we must keep up with all the network paths as we reduce individual activities, a condition that makes manual crashing very cumbersome. For that reason we will rely on the computer for project crashing; however, for the moment we pursue this example in order to demonstrate the logic of project crashing.

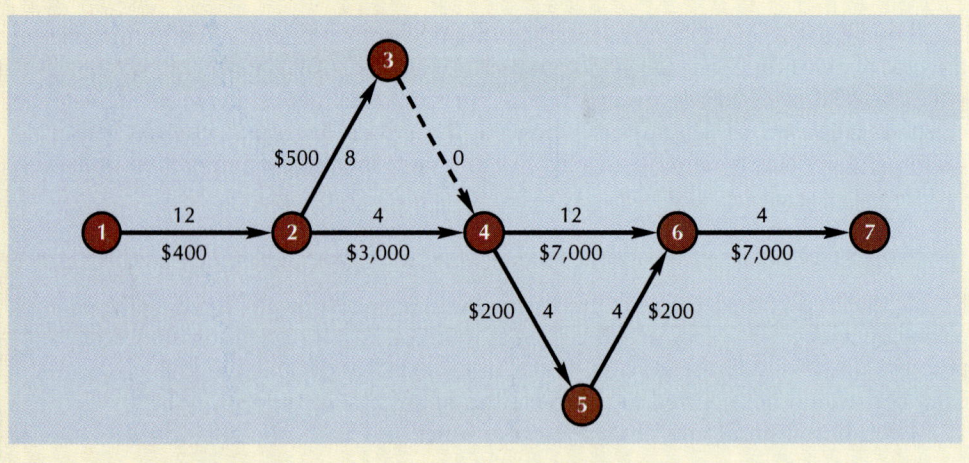

It turns out that activity 1-2 can be crashed by the total amount of 5 weeks without another path becoming critical, since activity 1-2 is included in all four paths in the network. Crashing this activity results in a revised project duration of 31 weeks at a crashing cost of $2,000. The revised network is shown in the following figure.

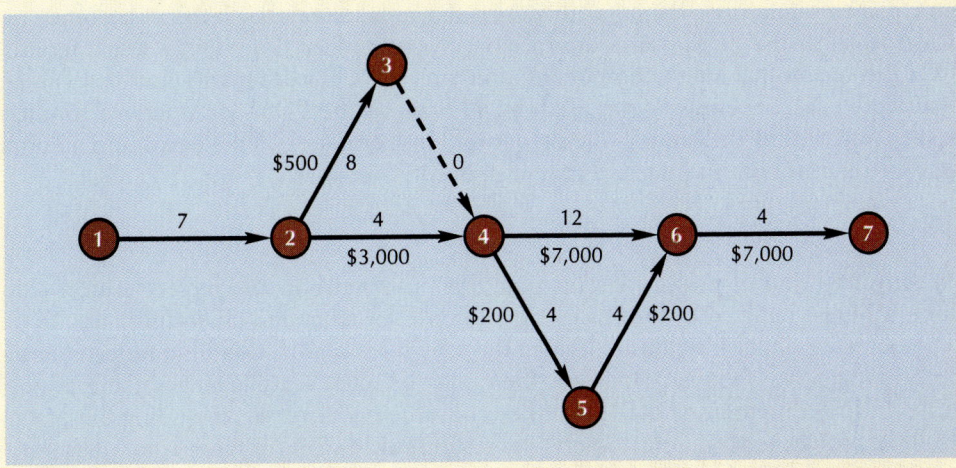

Since we have not reached our crashing goal of 30 weeks, we must continue and the process is repeated. The critical path in the figure above remains the same, and the minimum activity crash cost on the critical path is $500 for activity 2-3. Activity 2-3 can be crashed a total of 3 weeks, but since the contractor desires to crash the network only to 30 weeks, we need to crash activity 2-3 by only 1 week. Crashing activity 2-3 by 1 week does not result in any other path becoming critical, so we can safely make this reduction. Crashing activity 2-3 to 7 weeks (i.e., a 1-week reduction) costs $500 and reduces the project duration to 30 weeks.

The total cost of crashing the project to 30 weeks is $2,500. The contractor could inform the customer that an additional cost of only $2,500 would be incurred to finish the house in 30 weeks.

Suppose we wanted to continue to crash this network, reducing the project duration down to the minimum time possible; that is, crashing the network the maximum amount possible. We can determine how much the network can be crashed by crashing each activity the maximum amount possible and then determining the critical path of this completely crashed network. For example, activity 1-2 is 7 weeks, activity 2-3 is 5 weeks, 2-4 is 3 weeks, and so on. The critical path of this totally crashed network is 1-2-3-4-6-7 with a project duration of 24 weeks. This is the least amount of time the project can be completed in. If we crashed all the activities by their maximum amount, the total crashing cost is $35,700, computed by subtracting the total normal cost of $75,000 from the total crash cost of $110,700 in the table above. However, if we followed the crashing procedure outlined in this example, the network can be crashed to 24 weeks at a cost of $31,500, a savings of $4,000.

Project Crashing with POM for Windows

The manual procedure for crashing a network is cumbersome. It is basically a trial-and-error approach useful for demonstrating the logic of crashing. It quickly becomes unmanageable for larger networks. This approach would have become difficult if we had pursued even the house building example to a crash time greater than 30 weeks, with more than one path becoming critical.

When more than one path becomes critical, all critical paths must be reduced by an equal amount. Since the possibility exists that an additional path might become critical each time the network is reduced by even one unit of time (i.e., 1 week, month, etc.) this means that a reduction of one time unit is the maximum amount that can be considered at each crashing step. Exhibit 17.3 shows the POM for Windows solution screen for crashing the house building network in Example 17.4 the maximum amount possible to a minimum project duration of twenty-four weeks.

The General Relationship of Time and Cost

In our discussion of project crashing, we demonstrated how the project critical path time could be reduced by increasing expenditures for labor and other direct resources. The objective of crashing was to reduce the scheduled completion time to reap the results of the project sooner. However, there may be other reasons for reducing project time. As projects continue over time, they consume *indirect costs*, including the cost of facilities, equipment, and machinery, interest on investment, utilities, labor, personnel costs, and the loss of skills and labor from members of the project team who are not working at their regular jobs. There also may be direct financial penalties for not com-

Crashing costs increase as project time decreases; indirect costs increase as project time increases.

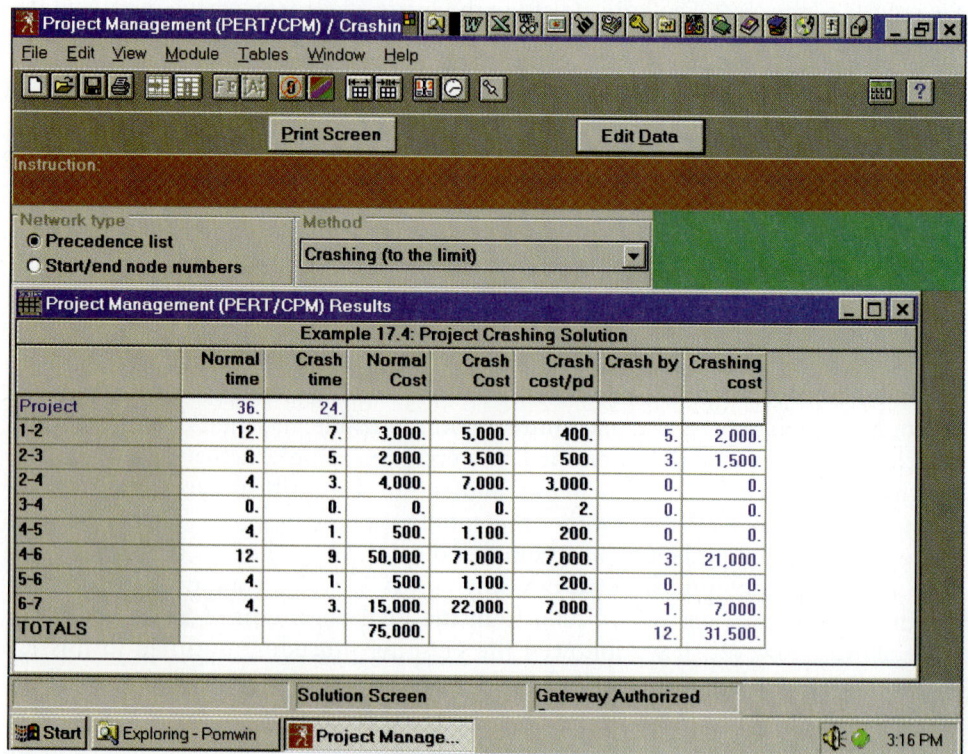

	Normal time	Crash time	Normal Cost	Crash Cost	Crash cost/pd	Crash by	Crashing cost
Project	36.	24.					
1-2	12.	7.	3,000.	5,000.	400.	5.	2,000.
2-3	8.	5.	2,000.	3,500.	500.	3.	1,500.
2-4	4.	3.	4,000.	7,000.	3,000.	0.	0.
3-4	0.	0.	0.	0.	2.	0.	0.
4-5	4.	1.	500.	1,100.	200.	0.	0.
4-6	12.	9.	50,000.	71,000.	7,000.	3.	21,000.
5-6	4.	1.	500.	1,100.	200.	0.	0.
6-7	4.	3.	15,000.	22,000.	7,000.	1.	7,000.
TOTALS			75,000.			12.	31,500.

EXHIBIT 17.3

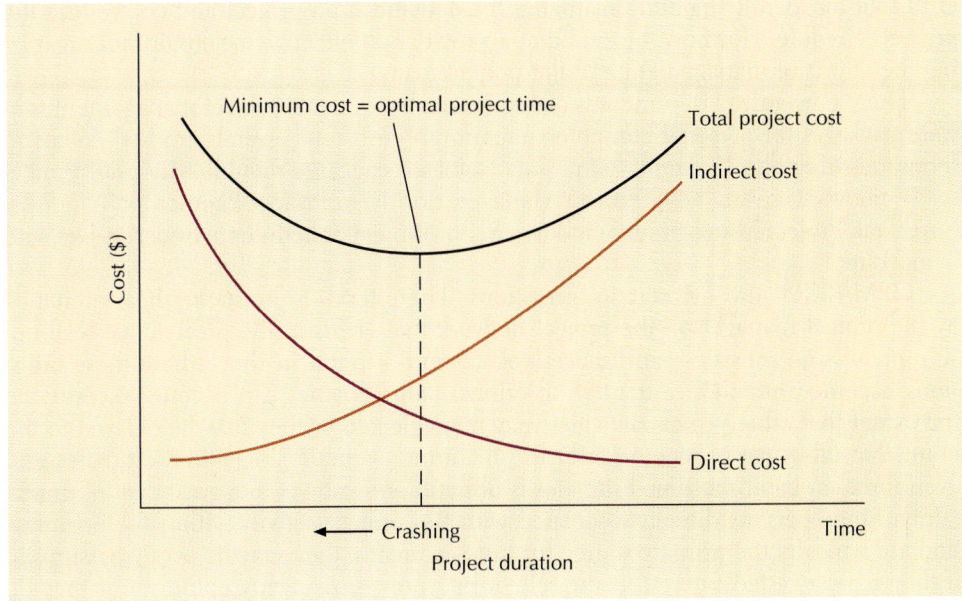

FIGURE 17.14 The Time-Cost Trade-off

pleting a project on time. For example, many construction contracts and government contracts have penalty clauses for exceeding the project completion date.

In general, project crashing costs and indirect costs have an inverse relationship; crashing costs are highest when the project is shortened, whereas indirect costs increase as the project duration increases. This time-cost relationship is illustrated in Figure 17.14. The best, or optimal, project time is at the minimum point on the total cost curve.

Summary

Since the development of CPM/PERT in the 1950s, it has been applied in a variety of government agencies concerned with project control, including military agencies, NASA, the Federal Aviation Agency (FAA), and the General Services Administration (GSA). These agencies are frequently involved in large-scale projects involving millions of dollars and many subcontractors. Examples of such governmental projects include the development of weapons systems, aircraft, and such NASA space-exploration projects as the space shuttle. It has become common for these agencies to require subcontractors to develop and use a CPM/PERT analysis to maintain management control of the myriad of project components and subprojects.

CPM/PERT has also been widely applied in the private sector. Two of the areas of application of CPM/PERT in the private sector have been research and development (R&D) and construction. CPM/PERT has been applied to R&D projects, such as developing new drugs, planning and introducing new products, and developing new and more powerful computer systems. CPM/PERT analysis has been particularly applicable to construction projects. Almost every type of construction project—from building a house, to constructing a major sports stadium, to building a ship, to constructing the Alaska oil pipeline—has been the subject of network analysis.

One reason for this popularity is that a network analysis provides a visual display of the project that is easy for managers and staff to understand and interpret. It is a powerful tool for identifying and organizing the activities in a project and controlling the project schedule. However, beyond that it provides an effective focal point for organizing the efforts of management and the project team.

There currently exist hundreds of commercially available project management software packages for personal computers ranging in cost from several hundred dollars to thousands of dollars. Examples of popular software packages include Microsoft Project for Windows, Harvard Total Project Manager, Primivera Project Planner for Windows, Sure Trak Project Manager for Windows, Scitor Project Scheduler 6, SuperProject, and Time Line.

CPM/PERT also has certain limitations. There tends to be such a heavy reliance by the project manager on the project network that errors in the precedence relationship or missing activities can be overlooked, until a point in time where these omissions become a problem. Attention to critical path activities can become excessive to the extent that other project activities may be neglected or they may be delayed to the point that other paths become critical. Obtaining accurate single-time estimates and even three probabilistic time estimates is difficult and subject to a great deal of uncertainty. Since persons directly associated with the project activity within the organization are typically the primary source for time estimates, they may be overly pessimistic if they have a vested interest in the scheduling process or overly optimistic if they do not. Personal interests aside, it is frequently difficult to define, within the context of an activity, what an optimistic or pessimistic time means. Nevertheless, such reservations have not diminished the popularity of CPM/PERT, because most people feel its usefulness far outweighs any speculative or theoretical drawbacks.

Summary of Key Formulas

Earliest Start and Finish Times

$$EF_{ij} = ES_{ij} + t_{ij}$$
$$ES_{ij} = \max (EF_i)$$

Latest Start and Finish Times

$$LS_{ij} = LF_{ij} - t_{ij}$$
$$LF_{ij} = \min (LS_j)$$

Activity Slack

$$S_{ij} = LS_{ij} - ES_{ij} = LF_{ij} - EF_{ij}$$

Mean Activity Time and Variance

$$t = \frac{a + 4m + b}{6}$$

$$\sigma^2 = \left(\frac{b - a}{6}\right)^2$$

Summary of Key Terms

activity: performance of an individual job or work effort that requires labor, resources, and time and is subject to management control.

activity-on-arrow (AOA): a convention for constructing a CPM/PERT network in which the branches between nodes represent project activities.

activity-on-node (AON): a convention for constructing a CPM/PERT network in which the nodes represent project activities.

backward pass: starting at the end of a CPM/PERT network, a procedure for determining latest activity times.

beta distribution: a probability distribution traditionally used in CPM/PERT for estimating the mean and variance of project activity times.

crash cost: the cost of reducing the normal activity time.

crash time: the amount of time an activity is reduced.

crashing: a method for shortening the project duration by reducing the time of one or more critical activities at a cost.

critical path: the longest path through a CPM/PERT network, indicating the minimum time in which a project can be completed.

critical path method (CPM): a project scheduling technique in which activities are shown as a network of precedence relationships, traditionally using single-activity time estimates and activity-on-node network construction.

dummy: an activity in a network that shows a precedence relationship but represents no passage of time.

earliest finish time (EF): the earliest time an activity can be completed.

earliest start time (ES): the earliest time an activity can begin subject to preceding activities.

event: the completion or beginning of an activity in a project.

forward pass: starting at the beginning of a CPM/PERT network, a procedure for determining earliest activity times.

Gantt chart: a graphical display using bars (or time lines) to show the duration of project activities and precedence relationships.

latest finish time (LF): the latest time an activity can be completed and still maintain the project critical path time.

latest start time (LS): the latest time an activity can begin and not delay subsequent activities.

matrix organization: an organizational structure of project teams that includes members from various functional areas in the company.

most likely time (m): the subjective estimate of the time that would occur most frequently if the activity were repeated many times.

optimistic time (a): the shortest possible time to complete the activity if everything went right.

pessimistic time (b): the longest possible time to complete the activity given that everything went wrong.

precedence relationship: the sequential relationship of project activities to each other.

project: a unique, one-time operational activity or effort.

project evaluation and review technique (PERT): a project scheduling technique in which activities are shown as a network of precedence relationships, traditionally using probabilistic time estimates and activity-on-arrow network construction.

slack: the amount by which a project activity can be delayed without delaying any of the activities that follow it or the project as a whole.

statement of work: a written description of the objectives of a project.

work breakdown structure (WBS): a methodology for subdividing a project into different hierarchical levels of components.

Solved Problem

CPM/PERT Network Analysis

Given the following network and activity time estimates, determine earliest and latest activity times, slack, the expected project completion time and variance, and the probability that the project will be completed in 28 days or less.

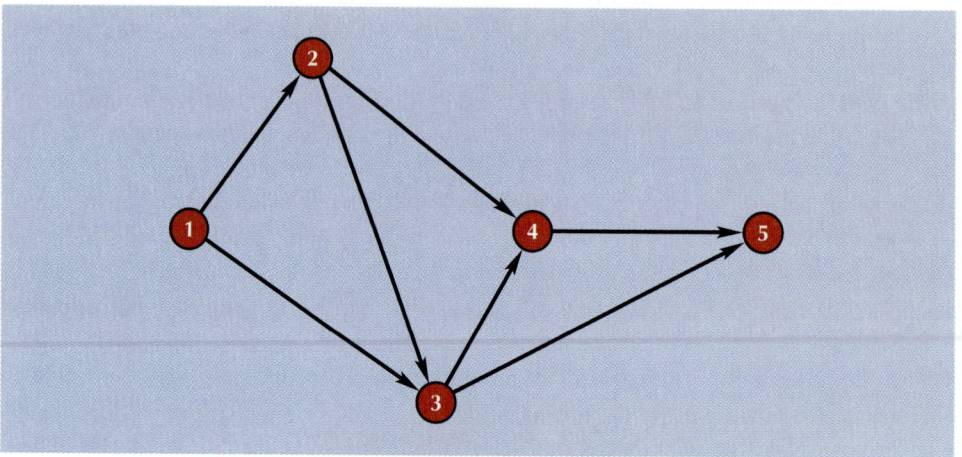

	Time Estimates (days)		
Activity	a	m	b
1-2	5	8	17
1-3	7	10	13
2-3	3	5	7
2-4	1	3	5
3-4	4	6	8
3-5	3	3	3
4-5	3	4	5

Solution:

Step 1. Compute the expected activity times and variances,

$$t = \frac{a + 4m + b}{6}$$

$$\sigma^2 = \left(\frac{b - a}{6}\right)^2$$

For example, the expected time and variance for activity 1-2 are

$$t = \frac{5 + 4(8) + 17}{6} = 9 \text{ days}$$

$$\sigma^2 = \left(\frac{17 - 5}{6}\right)^2 = 4 \text{ days}$$

These values and the remaining expected times and variances for each activity are shown in the following table.

Activity	t	σ^2
1-2	9	4
1-3	10	1
2-3	5	4/9
2-4	3	4/9
3-4	6	4/9
3-5	3	0
4-5	4	1/9

Step 2. Determine the earliest and latest activity times and activity slack.

Activity	t	ES	EF	LS	LF	S
1-2	9	0	9	0	9	0
1-3	10	0	10	4	14	4
2-3	5	9	14	9	14	0
2-4	3	9	12	17	20	8
3-4	6	14	20	14	20	0
3-5	3	14	17	21	24	7
4-5	4	20	24	20	24	0

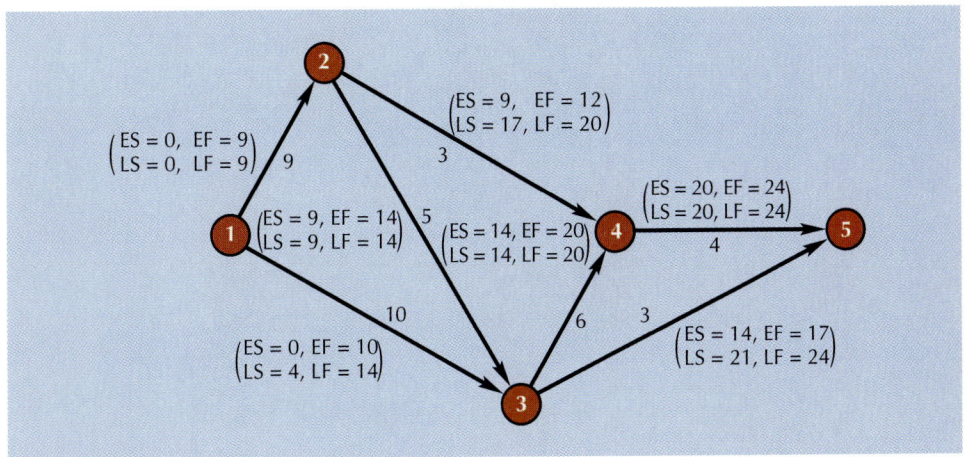

As an example, the earliest start and finish times for activity 1-2 are

$$ES_{ij} = \max(EF_i)$$
$$ES_{12} = \max(EF_1)$$
$$= 0$$
$$EF_{ij} = ES_{ij} + t_{ij}$$
$$EF_{12} = ES_{12} + t_{12}$$
$$= 0 + 9$$
$$= 9$$

The latest start and finish times for activity 4-5 are

$$LF_{ij} = \min\ (LS_j)$$
$$LF_{45} = \min\ (LS_5)$$
$$= 24$$
$$LS_{ij} = LF_{ij} - t_{ij}$$
$$LS_{45} = LF_{45} - t_{45}$$
$$= 24 - 4$$
$$= 20$$

Step 3. Identify the critical path and compute expected project completion time and variance. Observing the preceding table and those activities with no slack (i.e., $s = 0$), we can identify the critical path as 1-2-3-4-5. The expected project completion time (t_p) is 24 days. The variance is computed by summing the variances for the activities in the critical path:

$$\sigma^2 = 4 + \frac{4}{9} + \frac{4}{9} + \frac{1}{9}$$
$$= 5 \text{ days}$$

Step 4. Determine the probability that the project will be completed in 28 days or less. The following normal probability distribution describes the probability analysis.

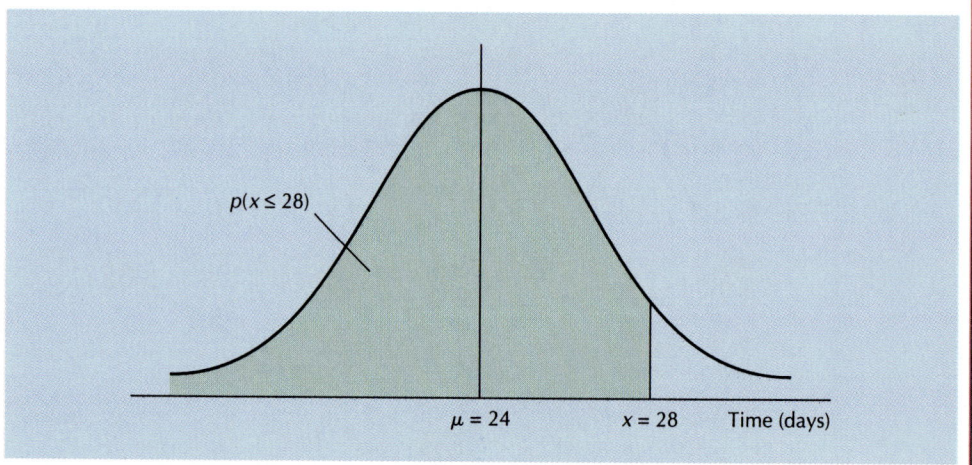

Compute Z using the following formula.

$$Z = \frac{x - \mu}{\sigma}$$
$$= \frac{28 - 24}{\sqrt{5}}$$
$$= 1.79$$

The corresponding probability from the normal table in Appendix A is 0.4633; thus,

$$P(x \le 28) = 0.9633$$

Questions

17-1. Why is CPM/PERT a popular and widely applied project scheduling technique?

17-2. What is the purpose of a CPM/PERT network?

17-3. Why are dummy activities used in a CPM/PERT network?

17-4. What is the critical path and what is its importance in project planning?

17-5. What is slack and how is it computed?

17-6. How are the mean activity times and activity variances computed in probabilistic CPM/PERT analysis?

17-7. How is total project variance determined in CPM/PERT analysis?

17-8. What is the purpose of project crashing analysis?

17-9. Describe the process of manually crashing a project network.

17-10. Which method for determining activity time estimates, deterministic or probabilistic, do you perceive to be preferable? Explain.

17-11. Explain how a Gantt chart differs from a CPM/PERT network and indicate the advantage of the latter.

17-12. Discuss the relationship of direct and indirect costs in project management.

17-13. Describe the limitations and disadvantages of CPM/PERT.

17-14. Describe the difference between activity-on-node and activity-on-arrow project networks.

17-15. Identify and briefly describe the major elements of project management.

Problems

17-1. Construct a Gantt chart for the project described by the following set of activities, and indicate the project completion time.

Activity	Time (weeks)
1-2	5
1-3	4
2-4	3
3-4	6

17-2. Construct a Gantt chart for the project described by the following set of activities, and indicate the project completion time and the available slack for each activity.

Activity	Time (weeks)
1-2	3
1-3	7
2-4	2
3-4	5
3-5	6
4-6	1
5-6	4

17-3. Use the project activities that follow to determine the following:
a. Construct a Gantt chart; indicate the project completion time and slack for each activity.

b. Construct the CPM/PERT network, compute the length of each path in the network, and indicate the critical path.

Activity	Time (weeks)
1-2	4
1-3	7
2-4	8
2-5	3
3-5	9
4-5	5
4-6	2
5-6	6
3-6	5

17-4. Identify all the paths in the following network, compute the length of each, and indicate the critical path. (Activity times are in weeks.)

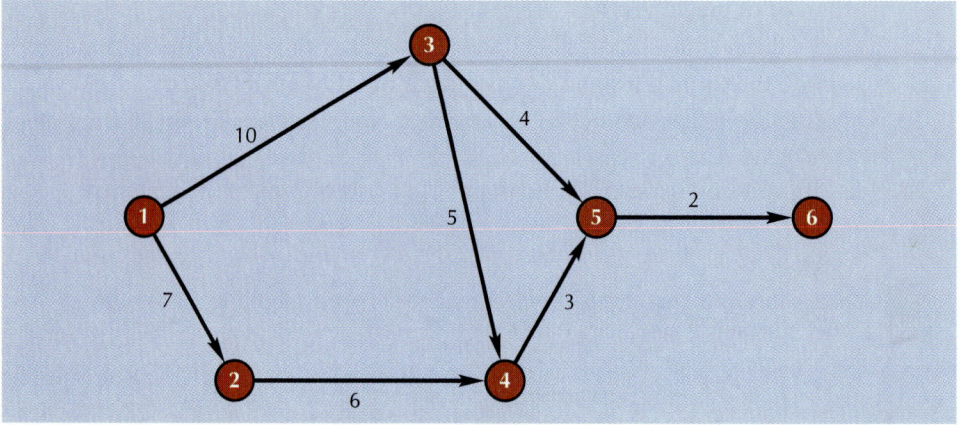

17-5. For the network in Problem 17-4, determine the earliest start and finish times, latest start and finish times, and slack for each activity. Indicate how the critical path would be determined from this information.

17-6. Given the following network with activity times in months, determine the earliest start and finish times, latest start and finish times, and slack for each activity. Indicate the critical path and the project duration.

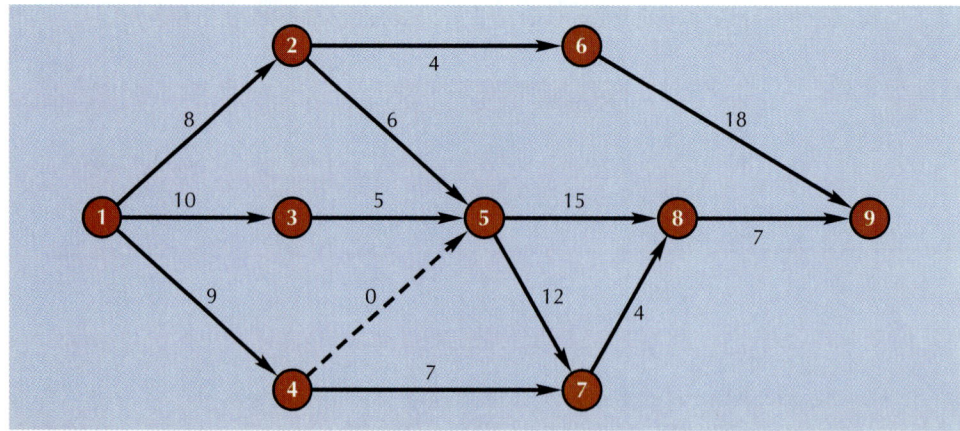

17-7. Given the following network with activity times in weeks, determine the earliest start and finish times, latest start and finish times, and slack for each activity. Indicate the critical path and the project duration.

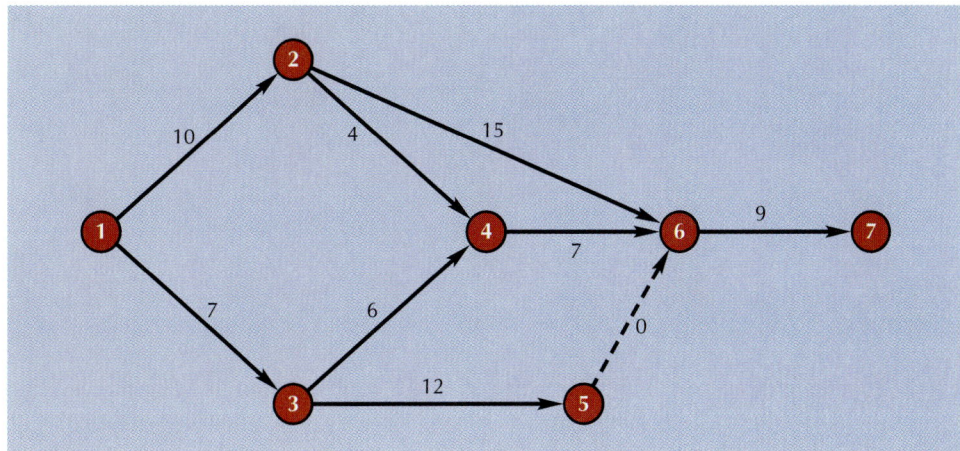

17-8. A marketing firm is planning to conduct a survey of a segment of the potential product audience for one of its customers. The planning process for preparing to conduct the survey consists of six activities with procedure relationships and activity time estimates as follows.

Activity	Description	Activity Predecessor	Time Estimates (days)
a	Determine survey objectives	—	3
b	Select and hire personnel	a	3
c	Design questionnaire	a	5
d	Train personnel	b,c	4
e	Select target audience	c	3
f	Make personnel assignments	d,e	2

a. Determine all paths through the network from node a to node f and the duration of each, and indicate the critical path.
b. Determine the earliest and latest activity start and finish times.
c. Determine the slack for each activity.

17-9. In one of the little-known battles of the Civil War, General Tecumseh Beauregard lost the Third Battle of Bull Run because his preparations were not complete when the enemy attacked. If the critical path method had been available, the general could have planned better. Suppose that the following project network with activity times in days had been available. Determine the earliest start and finish times, latest start and finish times, and activity slack for the network. Indicate the critical path and the time between the general's receipt of battle orders and the onset of battle.

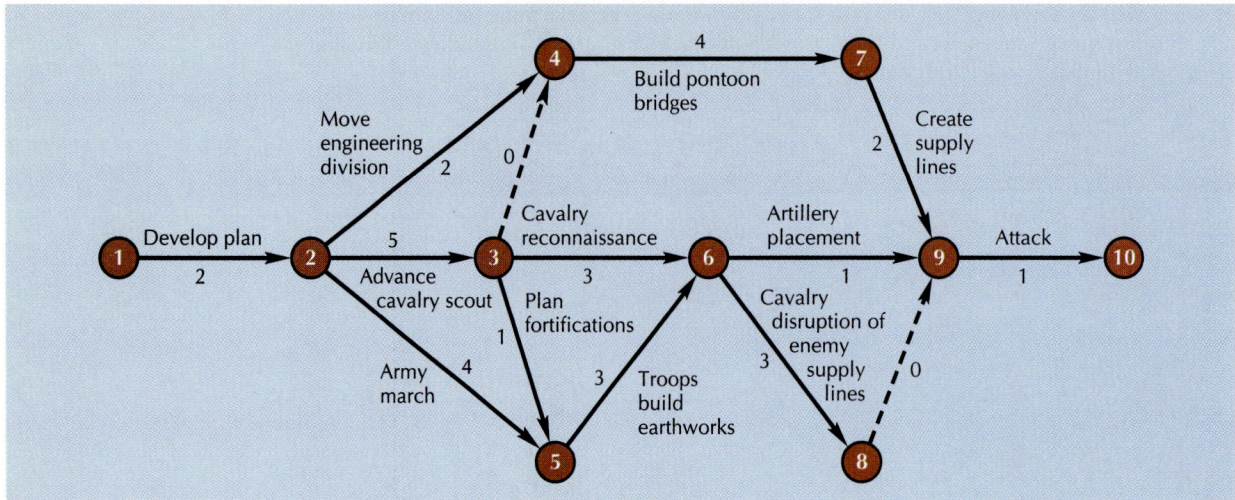

17-10. A group of developers is building a new shopping center. A consultant for the developers has constructed the following CPM/PERT network and assigned activity times in weeks. Determine the earliest start and finish times, latest start and finish times, activity slack, critical path, and duration for the project.

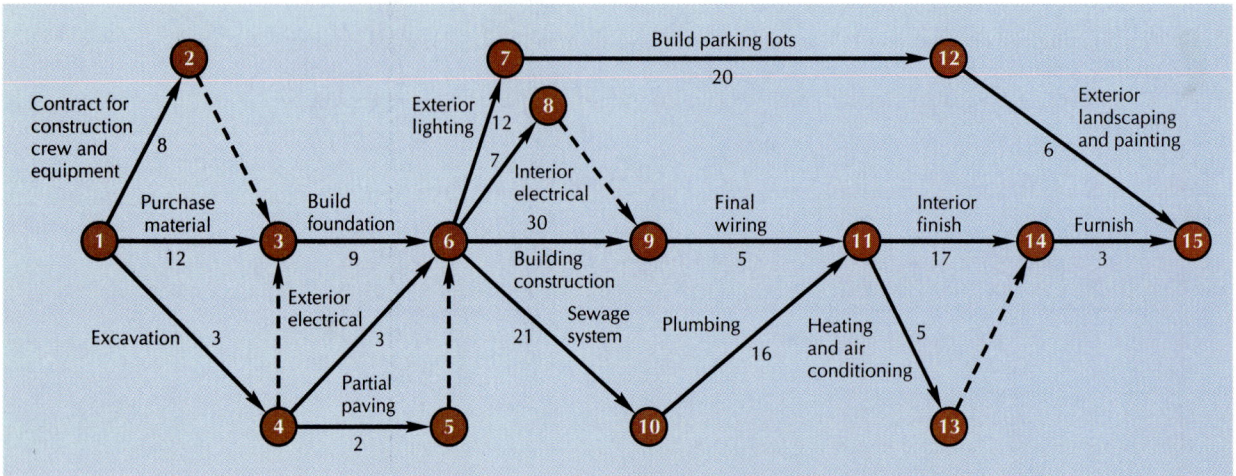

17-11. The management of a factory is going to erect a maintenance building with a connecting electrical generator and water tank. The activities, activity descriptions, and estimated durations are given in the following table. (Notice that the activities are defined not by node numbers, but by activity descriptions. This alternate form of expressing activities and precedence relationships is sometimes used in CPM/PERT.)

Activity	Activity Description	Activity Predecessor	Activity Duration (weeks)
a	Excavate	—	2
b	Erect building	a	6
c	Install generator	a	4

(Continued)

Activity	Activity Description	Activity Predecessor	Activity Duration (weeks)
d	Install tank	a	2
e	Install maintenance equipment	b	4
f	Connect generator and tank to building	b, c, d	5
g	Paint on a finish	b	3
h	Check out facility	e, f	2

Construct the network for this project, identify the critical path, and determine the project duration time.

17-12. Given the following network and probabilistic activity time estimates, determine the expected time and standard deviation for each activity and indicate the critical path.

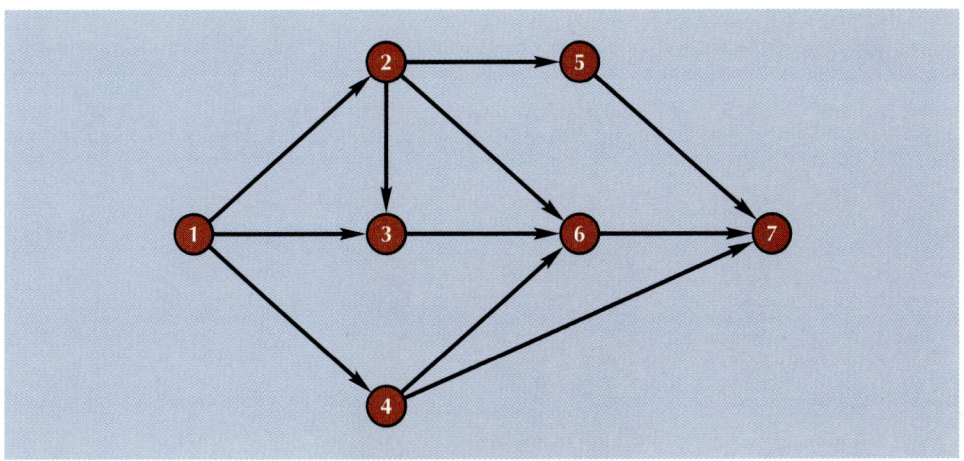

Activity	Time Estimates (weeks)		
	a	m	b
1-2	6	10	15
1-3	2	7	16
1-4	4	8	11
2-3	3	10	15
2-5	7	9	20
2-6	4	12	15
3-6	3	6	9
4-6	5	9	16
5-7	3	20	35
4-7	4	12	16
6-7	2	9	14

17-13. The Farmer's American Bank of Leesburg is planning to install a new computerized accounts system. Bank management has determined the activities required to complete the project, the precedence relationships of the activities, and activity time estimates as follows:

Activity	Description	Activity Predecessor	Time Estimates (weeks)		
			a	*m*	*b*
a	Position recruiting	—	5	8	17
b	System development	—	3	12	15
c	System training	a	4	7	10
d	Equipment training	a	5	8	23
e	Manual system test	b, c	1	1	1
f	Preliminary system changeover	b, c	1	4	13
g	Computer-personnel interface	d, e	3	6	9
h	Equipment modification	d, e	1	2.5	7
i	Equipment testing	h	1	1	1
j	System debugging and installation	f, g	2	2	2
k	Equipment changeover	g, i	5	8	11

Determine the earliest and latest activity times, the expected completion time and standard deviation, and the probability that the project will be completed in 40 weeks or less.

17-14. The following probabilistic activity time estimates are for the network in Problem 17-6.

Activity	Time Estimates (months)		
	a	*m*	*b*
1-2	4	8	12
1-3	6	10	15
1-4	2	10	14
2-5	3	6	9
2-6	1	4	13
3-5	3	6	18
4-5	0	0	0
4-7	2	8	12
5-8	9	15	22
5-7	5	12	21
7-8	5	6	12
6-9	7	20	25
8-9	3	8	20

Determine the following:
a. Expected activity times
b. Earliest start and finish times
c. Latest start and finish times
d. Activity slack
e. Critical path
f. Expected project duration and standard deviation

17-15. The following probabilistic activity time estimates are for the CPM/PERT network in Problem 17-9.

| | Time Estimates (months) | | |
Activity	*a*	*m*	*b*
1-2	1	2	6
2-4	1	3	5
2-3	3	5	10
2-5	3	6	14
3-4	0	0	0
3-5	1	1.5	2
3-6	2	3	7
4-7	2	4	9
5-6	1	3	5
7-9	1	2	3
6-9	1	1	5
6-8	2	4	9
8-9	0	0	0
9-10	1	1	1

Determine the following:
a. Expected activity times
b. Earliest start and finish times
c. Latest start and finish times
d. Activity slack
e. Critical path
f. Expected project duration and standard deviation

17-16. For the CPM/PERT network in Problem 17-14, determine the probability that the network duration will exceed 50 months.

17-17. The Stone River Textile Mill was inspected by OSHA and found to be in violation of a number of safety regulations. The OSHA inspectors ordered the mill to alter some existing machinery to make it safer (i.e., add safety guards, etc.); purchase some new machinery to replace older, dangerous machinery; and relocate some machinery to make safer passages and unobstructed entrances and exits. OSHA gave the mill only 35 weeks to make the changes; if the changes were not made by then, the mill would be fined $300,000.

The mill determined the activities in a PERT network that would have to be completed and then estimated the indicated activity times, as shown in the table. Construct the PERT network for this project and determine the following:

a. Expected activity times
b. Earliest and latest activity times and activity slack
c. Critical path
d. Expected project duration and variance
e. The probability that the mill will be fined $300,000

Activity	Description	Activity Predecessor	Time Estimates (weeks)		
			a	*m*	*b*
a	Order new machinery	—	1	2	3
b	Plan new physical layout	—	2	5	8
c	Determine safety changes in existing machinery	—	1	3	5

(Continued)

Activity	Description	Activity Predecessor	Time Estimates (weeks) a	m	b
d	Receive equipment	a	4	10	25
e	Hire new employees	a	3	7	12
f	Make plant alterations	b	10	15	25
g	Make changes in existing machinery	c	5	9	14
h	Train new employees	d, e	2	3	7
i	Install new machinery	d, e, f	1	4	6
j	Relocate old machinery	d, e, f, g	2	5	10
k	Conduct employee safety orientation	h, i, j	2	2	2

17-18. In the Third Battle of Bull Run, for which a CPM/PERT network was developed in Problem 17-15, General Beauregard would have won if his preparations had been completed in 15 days. What would the probability of General Beauregard's winning the battle have been?

17-19. On May 21, 1927, Charles Lindbergh landed at Le Bourget Field in Paris, completing his famous transatlantic solo flight. The preparation period prior to his flight was quite hectic and time was very critical, since several other famous pilots of the day were also planning transatlantic flights. Once Ryan Aircraft was contracted to build the *Spirit of St. Louis*, it took only a little over $2\frac{1}{2}$ months to construct the plane and fly it to New York for the takeoff. If CPM/PERT had been available to Charles Lindbergh, it no doubt would have been useful in helping him plan this project. Use your imagination and assume that a CPM/PERT network, as shown in the following figure, with the following estimated activity times, was developed for the flight.

Activity	Time Estimates (days) a	m	b
1-2	1	3	5
1-4	4	6	10
1-6	20	35	50
2-3	4	7	12
3-4	2	3	5
4-7	8	12	25
4-8	10	16	21
4-5	5	9	15
3-9	6	8	14
6-8	1	2	2
6-13	5	8	12
8-10	5	10	15
8-11	4	7	10
9-13	5	7	12
11-12	5	9	20
12-13	1	3	7

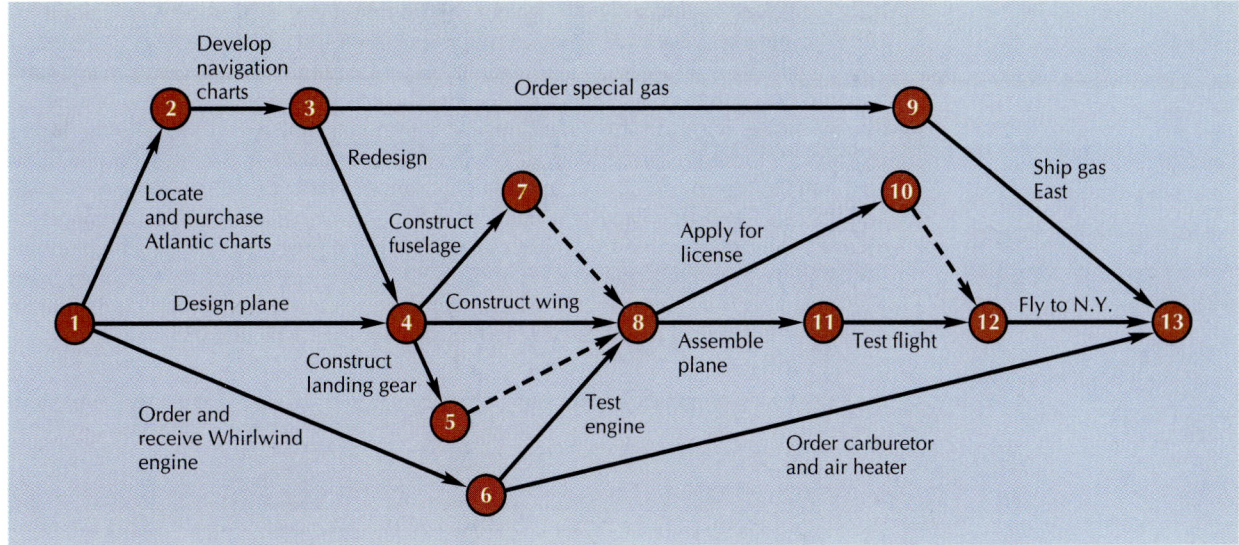

Determine the expected project duration and variance and the probability of completing the project in 67 days.

17-20. RusTech Tooling, Inc., is a large job shop operation that builds machine tools and dies to manufacture parts for specialized items. The company bids primarily on contracts for government-related activities to produce parts for such things as military aircraft, weapons systems, and the space program. The company is bidding on a contract to produce a component part for the fuselage assembly in a new space shuttle. A major criterion for selecting the winning bid besides low cost is the time required to produce the part. However, if the company is awarded the contract it will be held strictly to the completion date specified in the bid, and any delays will result in severe financial penalties. In order to determine the project completion time to put in its bid, the company has identified the project activities, precedence relationships, and activity times shown in the following table.

Activity	Activity Predecessor	Time Estimates (weeks)		
		a	m	b
a	—	3	5	9
b	a	2	5	8
c	a	1	4	6
d	a	4	6	10
e	b	2	8	11
f	b	5	9	16
g	c	4	12	20
h	c	6	9	13
i	d	3	7	14
j	d	8	14	22
k	f, g	9	12	20
l	h, i	6	11	15
m	e	4	7	12
n	j	3	8	16
o	n	5	10	8

If RusTech, Inc., wants to be 90 percent certain that it can deliver the part without incurring a penalty, what time frame should it specify in the bid?

17-21. PM Computers is an international manufacturer of computer equipment and software. It is going to introduce a number of new products in the coming year, and it wants to develop marketing programs to accompany the product introductions. The marketing program includes the preparation of printed materials distributed directly by the company and used by the company's marketing personnel, vendors, and representatives; print advertising in regular magazines, trade journals, and newspapers; and television commercials. The program also includes extensive training programs for marketing personnel, vendors, and representatives about the new products. A project management team with members from the marketing department and manufacturing areas has developed the following list of activities for the development of the marketing program.

Activity	Description	Predecessors	a	m	b
a	Preliminary budget and plan approval	—	10	15	20
b	Select marketing personnel for training	—	5	9	12
c	Develop overall media plan	a	15	25	30
d	Prepare separate media plans	c	12	20	25
e	Develop training plan	c	5	8	12
f	Design training course	e	6	14	20
g	Train marketing personnel	b, f	16	20	25
h	Plan TV commercials with agency	d	15	25	35
i	Draft in-house print materials	d	8	15	20
j	Develop print advertising layouts with agency	d	16	23	30
k	Review print advertising layouts	j	4	9	12
l	Review TV commercials	h	3	7	12
m	Review and print in-house materials	i	3	5	7
n	Release advertising to print media	g, i, k	2	4	8
o	Release TV commercials to networks	l	4	7	10
p	Final marketing personnel review	g, i, k	4	5	9
q	Run media advertising, mailings	m, n, o	15	20	30

Time Estimates (days) for columns a, m, b.

Construct the network for this project and determine the activity schedule. Identify the critical path and determine the expected project duration time and variance. What is the probability the program can be completed within four months?

17-22. The following table provides the information necessary to construct a project network and project crash data.

Activity	Normal	Crash	Normal	Crash
1-2	20	8	1,000	1,480
1-4	24	20	1,200	1,400
1-3	14	7	700	1,190
2-4	10	6	500	820
3-4	11	5	550	730

Activity Time (weeks): Normal, Crash. *Activity Cost ($)*: Normal, Crash.

a. Construct the project network.

b. Determine the maximum possible crash time for the network, and crash the network the maximum amount possible.

c. Compute the normal project cost and the cost of the crashed project.

17-23. The following table provides the information necessary to construct a project network and project crash data.

Activity	Predecessor	Activity Time (weeks) Normal	Crash	Activity Cost ($) Normal	Crash
a	—	16	8	2,000	4,400
b	—	14	9	1,000	1,800
c	a	8	6	500	700
d	a	5	4	600	1,300
e	b	4	2	1,500	3,000
f	b	6	4	800	1,600
g	c	10	7	3,000	4,500
h	d, e	15	10	5,000	8,000

Construct the project network, and crash the network the maximum amount possible.

17-24. For the Solved Problem at the end of this chapter, assume that the most likely times (m) are the normal activity times and the optimistic times (a) are the activity crash times. Further assume that the activities have the following normal and crash costs.

Activity	Costs (normal cost, crash cost)
1-2	($100, 400)
1-3	($250, 400)
2-3	($400, 800)
2-4	($200, 400)
3-4	($150, 300)
3-5	($100, 100)
4-5	($300, 500)

Crash the network the maximum amount possible and indicate the total crash cost.

17-25. The following table provides the crash data for the network project in Problem 17-13. The normal activity times are considered to be deterministic and not probabilistic.

Activity	Activity Time (weeks) Normal	Crash	Activity Cost ($) Normal	Crash
a	9	7	4,800	6,300
b	11	9	9,100	15,500
c	7	5	3,000	4,000
d	10	8	3,600	5,000
e	1	1	0	0
f	5	3	1,500	2,000
g	6	5	1,800	2,000
h	3	3	0	0
i	1	1	0	0
j	2	2	0	0
k	8	6	5,000	7,000

Crash the network the maximum amount, indicate how much it would cost the bank, and identify the new critical path(s).

17-26. The following table provides the project crash data for the network in Problem 17-6.

	Activity Time (weeks)		Activity Cost ($)	
Activity	Normal	Crash	Normal	Crash
1-2	8	5	700	1,200
1-3	10	9	1,600	2,000
1-4	9	7	900	1,500
2-5	6	3	500	900
2-6	4	2	500	700
3-5	5	4	500	800
4-5	0	0	0	0
4-7	7	5	700	1,000
5-7	12	10	1,800	2,300
5-8	15	12	1,400	2,000
6-9	18	14	1,400	3,200
7-8	4	3	500	800
8-9	7	6	800	1,400

Crash the network the maximum amount and indicate the new critical path activities and the cost of crashing the network.

CASE PROBLEM

The Bloodless Coup Concert

John Aaron had just called the meeting of the Programs and Arts Committee of the Student Government Association to order.

"Okay, okay, everybody, quiet down. I have an important announcement to make," he shouted above the noise. The room got quiet and John started again. "Well, you guys, we can have the Coup."

His audience looked puzzled and Randy Jones asked, "What coup have we scored this time John?"

"The Coup, the Coup! You know, the rock group, the Bloodless Coup!"

Everyone in the room cheered and started talking excitedly. John stood up, waved his arms, and shouted, "Hey, calm down, everybody, and listen up." The room quieted again and everyone focused on John. "The good news is that they can come." He paused a moment. "The bad news is that they will be here in eighteen days."

The students groaned and seemed to share Jim Hasting's feelings, "No way, man. It can't be done. Why can't we put it off for a couple of weeks?"

John answered, "They're just starting their new tour and are looking for some warm-up concerts. They will be traveling near here for their first concert date in D.C. and saw they had a letter from us, so they said they could come now—but that's it, now or never." He looked around the room at the solemn faces. "Look you guys, we can handle this. Let's think of what we have to do. Come on, perk up. Let's make a list of everything we have to do to get ready and figure out how long it will take. So somebody tell me what we have to do first!"

Anna Mendoza shouted from the back of the room, "We have to find a place; you know, get an auditorium somewhere. I've done that before, and it should take anywhere from 2 days up to 7 days, most likely about 4 days."

"Okay, that's great," John said as he wrote down

the activity "secure auditorium" on the blackboard with the times out to the side. "What's next?"

"We need to print tickets and quick," Tracey Shea blurted. "It could only take a day if the printer isn't busy but it could take up to 4 days if it is. It should probably take about 2 days."

"But we can't print tickets until we know where the concert will be because of the security arrangement," Andy Taylor noted.

"Right," said John. "Get the auditorium first then print the tickets. What else?"

"We need to make hotel and transportation arrangements for the Coup and their entourage while they are here," Jim Hastings said. "But we better not do that until we get the auditorium. If we can't find a place for the concert, everything falls through."

"How long do you think it will take to make the arrangements?" John asked.

"Oh, between 3 and 10 days, probably about 5, most likely," Jim answered.

"We also have to negotiate with the local union for concert employees, stagehands, and whomever else we need to hire," said Reggie Wilkes. "That could take a day or up to 8 days, but 3 days would be my best guess."

"We should probably also hold off on talking to the union until we get the auditorium," John added. "That will probably be a factor in the negotiations."

"After we work things out with the union we can hire some stagehands," Reggie continued. "That could take as few as 2 days but as long as 7. I imagine it'll take about 4 days. We should also be able to get some student ushers at the same time once we get union approval. That could take only a day, but it has taken 5 days in the past; 3 days is probably the most likely."

"We need to arrange a press conference," said Art Cohen, leaning against a wall. "This is a heavy group, big-time."

"But doesn't a press conference usually take place at the hotel?" John asked.

"Yeah, that's right," said Art. "We can't make arrangements for the press conference until we work things out with the hotel. When we do that it should take about 3 days to set up a press conference, 2 days if we're lucky and 4 at the most."

The room got quiet as everyone thought.

"What else?" John said.

"Hey, I know," said Annie Roark. "Once we hire the stagehands they have to set up the stage. I think that could be done in a couple of days, but it could take up to 6 days, with 3 most likely." She paused for a moment before adding, "And we can assign the ushers to their jobs once we hire them. That shouldn't take long, maybe only a day, 3 days worst. Probably 2 days would be a good time to put down."

"We also have to do some advertising and promotion if we want anyone to show for this thing," said Art nonchalantly. "I guess we need to wait until we print the tickets first so we'll have something to sell. That depends on the media, the paper, and radio stations. I've worked with this before. It could get done really quick, like 2 days, if we can make the right contacts, but it could take a lot longer, like 12 days if we hit any snags. We probably ought to count on 6 days as our best estimate."

"Hey, if we're going to promote this shouldn't we also have a preliminary act, some other group?" said Annie.

"Wow, I forgot all about that," said John. "Hiring another act will take me between 4 and 8 days; I can probably do it in 5. I can start on that right away at the same time you guys are arranging for an auditorium." He thought for a moment. "But we really can't begin to work on the promotion until I get the lead-in group. So what's left?"

"Sell the tickets," shouted several people at once.

"Right," said John, "we have to wait until they are printed; but I don't think we have to wait for the advertising and promotion to start do we?"

"No," said Jim, "but we should hire the preliminary act first so people will know what they're buying a ticket for."

"Agreed," said John. "The tickets could go quick; I suppose in the first day."

"Or," interrupted Mike Eggleston, "it could take longer. I remember two years ago it took 12 days to sell out for the Cosmic Modem."

"Okay, so it's between 1 and 12 days to sell the tickets," said John, "but I think about 5 days is more likely. Everybody agree?"

The group nodded in unison and they all turned at once to the list of activities and times John had written on the blackboard.

Use PERT analysis to determine the probability the concert preparations will be completed in time.

Moore Housing Contractors

Moore Housing Contractors is negotiating a deal with Countryside Realtors to build six houses in a new development. Countryside wants Moore Contractors to start in late winter or early spring when the weather begins to moderate and build through the summer into the fall. The summer months are a busy time for the realty company, and it believes it can sell the houses almost as soon as they are ready—sometimes before. The houses all have similar floor plans and are of approximately equal size; only the exteriors are noticeably different. The completion time is so critical for Countryside Realtors that it is insisting a project management network accompany the contractor's bid for the job with an estimate of the completion time for a house. The realtor also needs to be able to plan its offerings and marketing for the summer. The realtor wants each house to be completed within forty-five days after it is started. If a house is not completed within this time frame, the realtor wants to be able to charge the contractor a penalty. Mary and Sandy Moore, the president and vice president, of Moore Housing Contractors, are concerned about the prospect of a penalty. They want to be confident they can meet the deadline for a house before entering into any agreement with a penalty involved. (If there is a reasonable likelihood they cannot finish a house within forty-five days, they want to increase their bid to cover potential penalty charges.)

The Moores are experienced home builders, so it was not difficult for them to list the activities involved in building a house or to estimate activity times. However, they made their estimates conservatively and tended to increase their pessimistic estimates to compensate for the possibility of bad weather and variations in their work force. Following is a list of the activities for building a house and the activity time estimates.

Activity	Description	Predecessors	Time (days) a	m	b
a	Excavation, pour footers	—	3	4	6
b	Lay foundation	a	2	3	5
c	Frame and roof	b	2	4	5
d	Lay drain tiles	b	1	2	4
e	Sewer (floor) drains	b	1	2	3
f	Install insulation	c	2	4	5
g	Pour basement floor	e	2	3	5
h	Rough plumbing, pipes	e	2	4	7
i	Install windows	f	1	3	4
j	Rough electrical wiring	f	1	2	4
k	Install furnace, air conditioner	c, g	3	5	8
l	Exterior brickwork	i	5	6	10
m	Install plasterboard, mud, plaster	j, h, k	6	8	12
n	Roof shingles, flashing	l	2	3	6
o	Attach gutter, downspouts	n	1	2	5
p	Grading	d, o	2	3	7
q	Lay subflooring	m	3	4	6
r	Lay driveway, walks, landscape	p	4	6	10
s	Finish carpentry	q	3	5	12
t	Kitchen cabinetry, sink, and appliances	q	2	4	8
u	Bathroom cabinetry, fixtures	q	2	3	6
v	Painting (interior and exterior)	t, u	4	6	10
w	Finish wood floors, lay carpet	v, s	2	5	8
x	Final electrical, light fixtures	v	1	3	4

1. Develop a CPM/PERT network for Moore House Contractors and determine the probability that the contractors can complete a house within forty-five days. Does it appear that the Moores might need to increase their bid to compensate for potential penalties?

2. Indicate which project activities Moore Contractors should be particularly diligent to keep on schedule by making sure workers and materials are always available. Also indicate which activities the company might shift workers from as the need arises.

References

Burman, P. J. *Precedence Networks for Project Planning and Control.* New York: McGraw-Hill, 1972.

Cleland, D. I., and W. R. King. *Project Management Handbook.* New York: Van Nostrand Reinhold, 1983.

Levy, F., G. Thompson, and J. Wiest. "The ABC's of the Critical Path Method." *Harvard Business Review* 41, no. 5 (October 1963).

Moder, J., C. R. Phillips, and E. W. Davis. *Project Management with CPM and PERT and Precedence Diagramming,* 3d ed. New York: Van Nostrand Reinhold, 1983.

O'Brian, J. *CPM in Construction Management.* New York: McGraw-Hill, 1965.

Wiest, J. D., and F. K. Levy. A *Management Guide to PERT/CPM,* 2d ed. Englewood Cliffs, N.J.: Prentice Hall, 1977.

Epilogue: Change

The single most pervasive factor that has impacted the field of operations management—and business in general—during the past two decades is change. Although we have focused on the impact of quality management on all facets of operations and its effect on strategy and competitiveness, quality is just one manifestation of the rapid, mind-boggling changes that have occurred since the late 1970s. As the 1980s approached, we were keypunching cards for mainframe computers and the PC was only in the planning steps at IBM. When one thought of Honda it was in terms of motorcycles, or boxlike little cars that people jokingly said were run by lawnmower engines. VCRs were unimaginable to most people and televisions were made in America. JIT was the way they pronounced *jet* in Texas, not a revolutionary approach to inventory management; and strategic planning at many companies was nothing more than next year's "management by objectives (MBO)" plan. Robots were in science fiction movies, not on assembly lines, and good stereo speakers were only slightly smaller than a closet door. Quality was something most U.S. consumers thought they could not afford.

Although technology progressed at a steady pace, markets remained parochial and were certainly not international. The changes in products often tended to be cosmetic rather than substantiative. Cars looked different in 1970 than they did in 1940; but to our parents the only real difference was that they were higher-priced, came in colors other than black, broke down more frequently, and cost more to repair. They had the same basic features, traveled at the same speed, got the same gas mileage, and were about as comfortable. Basic operational principles and functions remained relatively consistent. Manufacturing was dominated by the assembly line, and workers and jobs conformed to norms that had gained credence at the turn of the 20th century. The field of operations management was static, sustaining the basic principles and techniques of scheduling, inventory control, purchasing, and job design throughout the half decade. There was no need for change, as consumer demands and tastes seemed to remain the same.

During the approximately half-century between the end of World War I and the late 1970s, the pace of change in manufacturing was slow and deliberate, almost creeping in comparison to the change of the last 15 years. A friend who worked at a textile mill that was a major manufacturer of denim in the early 1970s recounts that some of the machines in the plant dated back to just after the Civil War. Parts were replaced as they wore out, but the basic technology and products remained the same. Visiting the plant a decade later, he found it unrecognizable. It has undergone not only a technological metamorphosis, but it was clean and safe. Unable to compete with foreign competitors under the old ground rules, the textile company adapted to change.

When change came in the late 1970s, it seemed to start with a low rumble, recognizable to only a few seers and visionaries. Then it gained momentum, like a snowball, going downhill fast through the 1980s and hurtling into the 1990s. Change became both the diagnosis for the failure of hundreds of businesses and enterprises and the prescription for success for many others. Technological change, change in modes of transportation, changes in communication, and, most importantly, the development of computer technology and electronics resulted in a new and expanded international market environment and new products to drive it. Consumer tastes and expectations, once static, undemanding and parochial, suddenly became eclectic, diverse, and discriminating.

If there is one consistent theme that seems to run through all the success stories reported in the media and described in this text, it is recognition of the need to adapt to change. Companies that have survived in this changing environment—so far—point to their ability to adapt to changes as the key to their success. However, they are also quick to point out that their future depends on their ability to recognize changes in the future before they are overwhelmed by them and to react to them as rapidly as possible. Employers demand that employees be willing to accept change and to retrain and adapt or lose their jobs. Likewise, employees now look to companies for a commitment to invest in their training and education to help them withstand the onslaught of change in the future. There is a renewed commitment to research and new product development and to changing the way companies operate.

How has this affected the field of operations management and its teaching? Initially caught napping, OM educators and academicians are now riding the whirlwind and, like others, are reeducating themselves so they can teach a new generation of students the latest methods and techniques in OM. This text has attempted to reflect this era of change and provide a contemporary, up-to-date perspective on OM. This need explains why we have focused on quality and competitiveness in this text.

In our opinion quality is the most pervasive and important change in operations management in the last decade and strategy or strategic planning is the most important means for coping with change now and in the future, in order to remain competitive. Unfortunately, parts of this text will probably be outdated by the time it reaches students and teachers. The interval between the time we started revising this edition and the time when it was published was approximately two years, plenty of time for significant changes to occur. So we apologize in advance for our omissions and deficiencies and assure you that they did not result from a lack of trying.

Yet as we speak of change, we are also reminded of a popular song of the 1970s, "Everything Old is New Again." A number of the most important reactions to change have been the rediscovery of things that worked in the past. We have recounted how the basic principles of TQM, W. E. Deming's fourteen points, and statistical process control are not new but are simply rediscovered philosophies and tools from an earlier era. Worker empowerment, as described at Harley-Davidson in The Competitive Edge Box in Chapter 8 seems like a throwback to the era before F. W. Taylor at the turn of the century. It does not appear that Harley-Davidson's machinists, who control their own work centers, deal with vendors, and are responsible for product quality, are much different from the skilled craftspeople/machinists of the early 1900s. They, likewise, controlled their own workplaces and were not subject to supervisory management. We hear our grandparents reminisce about this era, products were made to last and workers took pride in what they made—not so much different than today's emerging "new" philosophy of the workplace. Adapting to change means not only trying the new, but also discovering the best of the old.

What change does the future hold? We are no more able to predict the changes of the next decade now than businesspeople and academicians were in the 1970s. However, it is certain that change will occur, and it is likely to be as rapid and powerful—even more so—than the changes we have just experienced. The lesson of the recent past is that to be successful in the future, companies must be ready, able, and willing to adapt to change. Likewise, to secure and retain jobs in the future, employees and students must be willing to retrain and educate themselves to adapt to change.

January, 1997
Roberta S. Russell
Bernard W. Taylor III

Appendix A: Normal Curve Areas

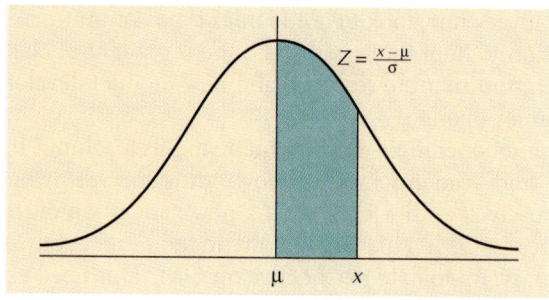

TABLE A.1 Normal Curve Areas

Z	0.00	0.01	0.02	0.03	0.04	0.05	0.06	0.07	0.08	0.09
0.0	0.0000	0.0040	0.0080	0.0120	0.0160	0.0199	0.0239	0.0279	0.0319	0.0359
0.1	0.0398	0.0438	0.0478	0.0517	0.0557	0.0596	0.0636	0.0675	0.0714	0.0753
0.2	0.0793	0.0832	0.0871	0.0910	0.0948	0.0987	0.1026	0.1064	0.1103	0.1141
0.3	0.1179	0.1217	0.1255	0.1293	0.1331	0.1368	0.1406	0.1443	0.1480	0.1517
0.4	0.1554	0.1591	0.1628	0.1664	0.1700	0.1736	0.1772	0.1808	0.1844	0.1879
0.5	0.1915	0.1950	0.1985	0.2019	0.2054	0.2088	0.2123	0.2157	0.2190	0.2224
0.6	0.2257	0.2291	0.2324	0.2357	0.2389	0.2422	0.2454	0.2486	0.2517	0.2549
0.7	0.2580	0.2611	0.2642	0.2673	0.2704	0.2734	0.2764	0.2794	0.2823	0.2852
0.8	0.2881	0.2910	0.2939	0.2967	0.2995	0.3023	0.3051	0.3078	0.3106	0.3133
0.9	0.3159	0.3186	0.3212	0.3238	0.3264	0.3289	0.3315	0.3340	0.3365	0.3389
1.0	0.3413	0.3438	0.3461	0.3485	0.3508	0.3531	0.3554	0.3577	0.3599	0.3621
1.1	0.3643	0.3665	0.3686	0.3708	0.3729	0.3749	0.3770	0.3790	0.3810	0.3830
1.2	0.3849	0.3869	0.3888	0.3907	0.3925	0.3944	0.3962	0.3980	0.3997	0.4015
1.3	0.4032	0.4049	0.4066	0.4082	0.4099	0.4115	0.4131	0.4147	0.4162	0.4177
1.4	0.4192	0.4207	0.4222	0.4236	0.4251	0.4265	0.4279	0.4292	0.4306	0.4319
1.5	0.4332	0.4345	0.4357	0.4370	0.4382	0.4394	0.4406	0.4418	0.4429	0.4441
1.6	0.4452	0.4463	0.4474	0.4484	0.4495	0.4505	0.4515	0.4525	0.4535	0.4545
1.7	0.4554	0.4564	0.4573	0.4582	0.4591	0.4599	0.4608	0.4616	0.4625	0.4633
1.8	0.4641	0.4649	0.4656	0.4664	0.4671	0.4678	0.4686	0.4693	0.4699	0.4706
1.9	0.4713	0.4719	0.4726	0.4732	0.4738	0.4744	0.4750	0.4756	0.4761	0.4767
2.0	0.4772	0.4778	0.4783	0.4788	0.4793	0.4798	0.4803	0.4808	0.4812	0.4817
2.1	0.4821	0.4826	0.4830	0.4834	0.4838	0.4842	0.4846	0.4850	0.4854	0.4857
2.2	0.4861	0.4864	0.4868	0.4871	0.4875	0.4878	0.4881	0.4884	0.4887	0.4890
2.3	0.4893	0.4896	0.4898	0.4901	0.4904	0.4906	0.4909	0.4911	0.4913	0.4916
2.4	0.4918	0.4920	0.4922	0.4925	0.4927	0.4929	0.4931	0.493	0.4934	0.4936
2.5	0.4938	0.4940	0.4941	0.4943	0.4945	0.4946	0.4948	0.4949	0.4951	0.4952
2.6	0.4953	0.4955	0.4956	0.4957	0.4959	0.4960	0.4961	0.4962	0.4963	0.4964
2.7	0.4965	0.4966	0.4967	0.4968	0.4969	0.4970	0.4971	0.4972	0.4973	0.4974
2.8	0.4974	0.4975	0.4976	0.4977	0.4977	0.4978	0.4979	0.4979	0.4980	0.4981
2.9	0.4981	0.4982	0.4982	0.4983	0.4984	0.4984	0.4985	0.4985	0.4986	0.4986
3.0	0.4987	0.4987	0.4987	0.4988	0.4988	0.4989	0.4989	0.4989	0.4990	0.4990

Solutions to Selected Odd-Numbered Problems

SUPPLEMENT 2

1. a. Mexico; b. China; c. Taiwan; d. Taiwan
3. a. risk fund; b. savings bonds or government fund; c. stock growth fund; d. bond fund; e. risk fund; f. bond fund
5. Widget, EV = $70,000
7. a. stock 28 boxes, $53.30; b. EV = $54.90, EVPI = $1.60
9. Widget, EV = $69,966, EVSI = 0

CHAPTER 3

1. a. 1992: 84.24%, 1993: 80.22%, 1994: 72.28%, 1995: 65.6%, 1996: 58.3%, decreasing trend; b. 1992: 1.71% and 14.04%, 1993: 5.3% and 14.48%, 1994: 13.32% and 14.4%, 1995: 21.97% and 12.43%, 1996: 29.96% and 11.74%; c. 1992: 6.93 and 44.48, 1993: 7.50 and 47.64, 1994: 7.85 and 50.04, 1995: 6.90 and 44.46, 1996: 5.79 and 38.32
3. a. 139.8; b. good = 91.6%
5. 1994: $10.54, 1995: $9.77, 1996: $9.41; 1994–95: −7.31%, 1995–96: −3.67%
7. a. alternative 2, 203; b. alternative 2
9. a. 5.11; b. 5.11; c. 5.66; d. 4.96
11. a. 56.38; b. $29,784

CHAPTER 4

1. $\bar{p} = 0.151$, UCL = 0.258, LCL = 0.044; in control
3. $\bar{p} = 0.053$, UCL = 0.101, LCL = 0.005; in control
5. a. $\bar{c} = 24.73$, UCL = 39.65, LCL = 9.81; b. out of control
7. $\bar{c} = 10.67$, UCL = 17.20, LCL = 4.14; in control
9. a. $\bar{R} = 0.57$, UCL = 1.21, LCL = 0; b. in control
11. a. $\bar{R} = 2$, UCL = 4.56, LCL = 0; b. out of control
13. $\bar{\bar{x}} = 39.7$, UCL = 43.32, LCL = 36.08; in control
15. no pattern
17. pattern may exist
19. patterns exist
21. $\bar{\bar{x}} = 3.25$, UCL = 5.48, LCL = 1.01; in control
23. $\bar{c} = 16.3$, UCL = 28.4, LCL = 4.19, in control
25. $\bar{p} = .22$, UCL = .45, LCL = 0, in control
27. $\bar{\bar{x}} = 3.17$, UCL = 5.04, LCL = 1.29, in control
29. $n = 155$, c = 10, $\alpha = .05$, $\beta = .09$

CHAPTER 5

5. 0.998
7. a. no; b. add backup equipment with a reliability of 95% for pieces 2 and 4

CHAPTER 6

3. 500; $7,500
5. 625

7. a. 18, 118; b. 363 days, 91 days; c. 84 days
9. < 100 boxes, choose current supplier; > 160 boxes, choose supplier 2; otherwise, choose supplier 1
11. a. > 187 min; b. > 226 min
13. > 10 claims, choose provider 1; < 5 claims, choose provider 2; otherwise, choose provider 3
15. < 6,666 units, choose labor intensive; > 41,666 units, choose fully automated; otherwise, choose automated

CHAPTER 7

1. 30 nonadjacent loads;

2	3	1
5	4	

3.

1	2	3
4	6	5

5. a.

H	A	
M	W	
B	G	I

b. L-shaped

7.

E	C	B
D	A	F

9. a. 30 min, $\boxed{A} \to \boxed{B, C, D} \to \boxed{E, F}$;
b. 88.9%, 11.1%; c. 3, no
11. b. 4 min; c. 14 min;
d. $\boxed{A, C} \to \boxed{B, D} \to \boxed{E} \to \boxed{F}$;
e. 87.5%, 12.5%; f. 4, no
13. a. 4.8 min, 200; b. 240, 80%, 3; c. $\boxed{A, B, C} \to \boxed{D, E}$, 100%, 200
15. $\boxed{A, B, C} \to \boxed{D, F, G} \to \boxed{E, H, J} \to \boxed{I, K}$, 79.4%
17. a. 3,428; b. 5 workers; c. yes
19. a. C = 6 mins; b. $\boxed{A, D} \to \boxed{B} \to \boxed{C, E}$;
c. 96 claims; d. 100%

CHAPTER 8

1. 4.163 min
3. a. 2.39 min; b. avg. = $4.52/hr, subject = $4.82/hr
5. a. 4.52 min; b. $n = 31$
7. $n = 12.2$

9. a. 1.383 min; b. $n = 7.7$; c. poorer quality
11. $n = 683$
13. a. 88.8%; b. 151 more observations
15. 3.946 min
17. a. $n = 271$
19. a. 347 additional observations; b. 69 percent
21. First 10 exams = 96 minutes, 204 minutes left; not in time
23. $t_{30} = 535.29$ hr., $t_{60} = 428.23$ hr.
25. 7.38 weeks

CHAPTER 9

1. Mall 1 = 62.75, mall 2 = 73.50, mall 3 = 76.00, mall 4 = 77.75; mall 4
3. South = 73.80, West A = 78.10, West B = 67.25, East = 76.75; East
5. $x = 21.03$, $y = 19.26$
7. LD(A) = 19,405.35, LD(B) = 15,325.2, LD(C) = 15,569.49; site B
9. $x = 1{,}665.4$, $y = 1{,}562.9$
11. a. $x = 78.8$, $y = 106.0$; Seagrove closest, Ashboro better

SUPPLEMENT 9

1. $A - 2 = 70$, $A - 4 = 80$, $B - 1 = 50$, $B - 4 = 160$, $C - 1 = 80$, $C - 3 = 180$; TC = \$82,600
3. $T - NY = 100$, $T - C = 100$, $M - NY = 30$, $M - P = 120$, $F - P = 50$, $F - B = 150$; TC = \$5,080
5. $1 - C = 5$, $2 - C = 10$, $3 - B = 20$, $4 - A = 10$; TC = \$19,500
7. $1 - C = 25$, $2 - B = 50$, $2 - C = 65$, $3 - D = 25$; TC = \$7,075
9. no change
11. alternative 1: TC = \$29,130; alternative 2: TC = \$24,930; Select 2
13. $1 - 1 = 30$, $1 - 2 = 5$, $1 - 4 = 2$, $2 - 2 = 20$, $3 - 3 = 14$, $4 - 4 = 26$, $5 - 4 = 10$, $5 - 5 = 30$, $6 - 4 = 2$, $6 - 6 = 20$; TM = 364
15. $A - 2 = 1$, $C - 1 = 1$, $D - 1 = 1$, $E - 3 = 1$, $F - 3 = 1$, $G - 2 = 1$, $H - 1 = 1$; TC = \$1,070
17. $N - A = 250$, $S - B = 300$, $S - C = 40$, $E - A = 150$, $E - C = 160$, $W - D = 210$, $C - B = 100$, $C - D = 190$; total time = 20,700 min
19. $A - 3 = 8$, $A - 4 = 18$, $B - 3 = 13$, $B - 5 = 27$, $D - 3 = 5$, $D - 6 = 35$, $E - 1 = 25$, $E - 2 = 15$, $E - 3 = 4$; TP = \$1,528
21. $1 - C = 2$, $1 - E = 5$, $2 - C = 10$, $3 - E = 5$, $4 - D = 8$, $5 - A = 9$, $6 - B = 6$; total time = 1,275

CHAPTER 10

1. a. Apr = 8.67, May = 8.33, Jun = 8.33, Jul = 9.00, Aug = 9.67, Sep = 11.0, Oct = 11.00, Nov = 11.00, Dec = 12.00, Jan = 13.33; b. Jun = 8.20, Jul = 8.80, Aug = 9.40, Sep = 9.60, Oct = 10.40, Nov = 11.00, Dec = 11.40, Jan = 12.60; c. MAD(3) = 1.89, MAD(5) = 2.43
3. a. $F_4 = 116.00$, $F_5 = 121.33$, $F_6 = 118.00$, $F_7 = 143.67$, $F_8 = 138.33$, $F_9 = 141.67$, $F_{10} = 135.00$, $F_{11} = 156.67$, $F_{12} = 143.33$, $F_{13} = 136.67$; b. $F_6 = 121.80$, $F_7 = 134.80$, $F_8 = 125.80$, $F_9 = 137.20$, $F_{10} = 143.00$, $F_{11} = 149.00$, $F_{12} = 137.00$, $F_{13} = 142.00$; c. $F_4 = 113.85$, $F_5 = 116.69$, $F_6 = 125.74$, $F_7 = 151.77$, $F_8 = 132.4$, $F_9 = 136.89$, $F_{10} = 142.35$, $F_{11} = 160.00$, $F_{12} = 136.69$, $F_{13} = 130.00$; d. $3 - $ qtr MA: $E = 32.0$, $5 - $ qtr MA: $E = 36.4$, weighted MA: $E = 28.09$

5. a. $F_4 = 400.00$, $F_5 = 406.67$, $F_6 = 423.33$, $F_7 = 498.33$, $F_8 = 521.67$, $F_9 = 571.67$; b. $F_2 = 400.00$, $F_3 = 410.00$, $F_4 = 398.00$, $F_5 = 402.40$, $F_6 = 421.92$, $F_7 = 452.53$, $F_8 = 460.00$, $F_9 = 498.02$; c. 3-sem MAD = 80.33, exp. smooth MAD = 87.16

7. F_{11} (exp. smooth) = 68.6, F_{11} (adjusted) = 69.17, F_{11} (linear trend) = 70.22; exp. smooth: $E = 14.75$, MAD = 1.89; adjusted: $E = 10.73$, MAD = 1.72; linear trend: MAD = 1.09

9. $F_{13} = 631.22$, $\overline{E} = 26.30$, $E = 289.33$, biased low

11. $F_1 = 155.6$, $F_2 = 192.9$, $F_3 = 118.2$, $F_4 = 155.6$

13. F_{98} (adjusted) = 3,313.19, F_{98} (linear trend) = 2,785.00; adjusted: MAD = 431.71, $E = -2,522$; linear trend: MAD = 166.25

15. $E = 86.00$, $\overline{E} = 8.60$, MAD = 15.00, MAPD = 0.08

17. UCL = 684.72, LCL = 684.72, no apparent bias

19. a. $\overline{E} = 10.73$, MAD = 16.76, MAPD = 0.37, $E = 75.10$; b. $\overline{E} = 8.00$, MAD = 12.67, MAPD = 0.24, $E = 39.99$; c. biased low

21. MAD = 1.78, $E = 12.36$, biased high; MAD (linear trend) = 0.688

23. $y = 2.36 + 0.267x$, y $(x = 30) = 10.40$; b. $R = 0.699$

25. 0.863

27. $y = 5582 - 260.36x$; a. MAD (linear regression) = 466.9, MAD (linear trend) = 372.1; b. -0.843

29. a. $y = 298.13 + 34.14$ x $(y = 673.67)$; b = $74.77 + .34$ x $(y = 516.77)$; a best

31. a. $SF_1 = 65.43$, $SF_2 = 75.69$, $SF_3 = 86.38$, $SF_4 = 74.41$; b. Q1 = 64.64, Q2 = 66.06, Q3 = 80.82, Q4 = 69.27

33. Exponential smoothing models appear to be most accurate

CHAPTER 11

1. Cost = $30,290,000

3. a. $448,000; b. $443,250; c. $366,600; d. $390,700; choose c

5. a. $846,900; b. $804,050; c. $726,200; choose c

7. a. $1,232,000; b. $1,360,000; c. $1,267,000; choose a

9. a. $25,500; b. depends on product mix; c. 34 ropes, 400 gloves, 300 shoes

SUPPLEMENT 11

1. a. Maximize $Z = \$2.25x_1 + 3.10x_2$; s.t. $5.0x_1 + 7.5x_2 \le 6,500$, $3.0x_1 + 3.2x_2 \le 3,000$, $x_2 \le 510$, $x_1 \ge 0$, $x_2 \ge 0$; b. and c. $x_1 = 456$, $x_2 = 510$, $Z = \$2,607$

3. Maximize $Z = 1,800x_{1a} + 2,100x_{1b} + 1,600x_{1c} + 1,000x_{2a} + 700x_{2b} + 900x_{2c} + 1,400x_{3a} + 800x_{3b} + 2,200x_{3c}$; s.t. $x_{1a} + x_{1b} + x_{1c} = 30$, $x_{2a} + x_{2b} + x_{2c} = 30$, $x_{3a} + x_{3b} + x_{3c} = 30$, $x_{1a} + x_{2a} + x_{3a} \le 40$, $x_{1b} + x_{2b} + x_{3b} \le 60$, $x_{1c} + x_{2c} + x_{3c} \le 50$, $x_{ij} \ge 0$; $x_{1b} = 30$, $x_{2a} = 30$, $x_{3c} = 30$, $Z = 159,000$

5. Maximize $Z = 0.7x_{cr} + 0.6x_{br} + 0.4x_{pr} + 0.85x_{ar} + 1.05x_{cb} + 0.95x_{bb} + 0.75x_{pb} + 1.20x_{ab} + 1.55x_{cm} + 1.45x_{bm} + 1.25x_{pm} + 1.70x_{am}$; s.t. $x_{cr} + x_{cb} + x_{cm} \le 200$, $x_{br} + x_{bb} + x_{bm} \le 300$, $x_{pr} + x_{pb} + x_{pm} \le 150$, $x_{ar} + x_{ab} + x_{am} \le 400$, $0.90x_{br} + 0.90x_{pr} - 0.10x_{cr} - 0.10x_{ar} \le 0$, $0.80x_{cr} + 0.20x_{br} - 0.20x_{pr} - 0.20x_{ar} \ge 0$, $0.25x_{bb} + 0.75x_{cb} - 0.75x_{pb} - 0.75x_{ab} \ge 0$, $x_{am} = 0$, $0.5x_{bm} + .5x_{pm} - 0.5x_{cm} - .5x_{am}$, $x_{ij} \ge 0$; $x_{cr} = 75$, $x_{ar} = 300$, $x_{bb} = 300$, $x_{ab} = 100$, $x_{cm} = 125$, $x_{pm} = 125$, $Z = 1,062.5$

7. a. Maximize $Z = 8x_1 + 10x_2$; s.t. $x_1 + x_2 \ge 400$, $x_1 \ge 0.4(x_1 + x_2)$, $x_2 \le 250$, $x_1 = 2x_2$, $x_1 + x_2 \le 500$, $x_i \ge 0$; b. $x_1 = 333.3$, $x_2 = 166.6$, $Z = 4,332.4$

9. Maximize $Z = 3x_{1R} + 5x_{2R} + 6x_{4R} + 9x_{1P} + 11x_{2P} + 6x_{3P} + 12x_{4P} + 1x_{1L} + 3x_{2L} + 4x_{4L} - 2x_{3L}$; s.t. $x_{1R} + x_{2R} + x_{3R} + x_{4R} \ge 3,000$, $x_{1P} + x_{2P} + x_{3P} + x_{4P} \ge$

$3,000, x_{1L} + x_{2L} + x_{3L} + x_{4L} \geq 3,000, x_{1R} + x_{1P} + x_{1L} \leq 5,000, x_{2R} + x_{2P} + x_{2L} \leq 2,400, x_{3R} + x_{3P} + x_{3L} \leq 4,000, x_{4R} + x_{4P} + x_{4L} \leq 1,500, 0.6x_{1R} - 0.4x_{2R} - 0.4x_{3R} - 0.4x_{4R} \geq 0, -0.2x_{1R} + 0.8x_{2R} - 0.2x_{3R} - 0.2x_{4R} \leq 0, -0.3x_{1R} - 0.3x_{2R} + 0.7x_{3R} - 0.3x_{4R} \geq 0, -0.4x_{1P} - 0.4x_{2P} + 0.6x_{3P} - 0.4x_{4P} \geq 0, -0.5x_{1L} + 0.5x_{2L} - 0.5x_{3L} - 0.5x_{4L} \leq 0, 0.9x_{1L} - 0.1x_{2L} - 0.1x_{3L} - 0.1x_{4L} \geq 0, x_{ij} \geq 0;$
$x_{1R} = 2,000, x_{2R} = 100, x_{3R} = 900, x_{2P} = 2,300, x_{3P} = 3,100, x_{4L} = 1,500, x_{1L} = 3,000, Z = 71,400$ (multiple optimal solutions)

11. Minimize $Z = 10(x_1 + x_2 + x_3 + x_4 + x_5) + 15(y_1 + y_2 + y_3 + y_4 + y_5) + 2(w_1 + w_2 + w_3 + w_4)$; s.t. $x_i \leq 2,000, y_i \leq 600, x_1 + y_1 - w_1 = 1,200, x_2 + y_2 + w_1 - w_2 = 2,100, x_3 + y_3 + w_2 - w_3 = 2,400, x_4 + y_4 + w_3 - w_4 = 3,000, x_5 + y_5 + w_4 = 4,000, x_i \geq 0, y_i \geq 0, w_i \geq 0; x_1 = x_2 = x_3 = x_4 = x_5 = 2,000, y_1 = 300, y_2 = y_3 = y_4 = y_5 = 600, w_1 = 1,100, w_2 = 1,600, w_3 = 1,800, w_4 = 1,400, Z = 152,300$

13. $x_1 = 12$ AM–2 AM $= 30, x_3 = 10, x_4 = 10, x_5 = 40, x_6 = 20, x_7 = 10, x_9 = 40, x_{10} = 10, Z = 170$

15. $x_{t1} = 600, x_{t2} = 180, x_{t3} = 1,680, x_{m1} = 240, x_{m2} = 660, x_{m3} = 480, x_{b1} = 360, x_{b2} = 60, x_{b3} = 240, Z = 10,191$

17. a. $x_1 = 4, x_2 = 3, Z = 2,400$; b. no, 1 bracelet; c. $600, x_1 = 60, x_2 = 0, Z = 3,600$

19. a. $x_1 = 3.3, x_2 = 6.7, Z = 568$; b. steeper, changes optimal point

CHAPTER 12

1. a. $Q = 79.7$; b. \$13,550; c. 15.05 orders; d. 24.18 days
3. a. $Q = 240$; b. \$4,800; c. 80 orders; d. 4 days
5. a. $Q = 190,918.8$ yd; b. \$15,273.51; c. 6.36 orders; d. 57.4 days
7. $Q = 58.8, TC = \$4,415.88$
9. a. $Q = 774.6$ boxes, $TC = \$619.68, R = 43.84$ boxes
11. $Q = 23.862, TC = \$298,276$
13. a. $Q = 2,529.8$ logs; b. $TC = \$12,649.11$; c. $T_b = 63.3$ days; d. 42.2 days
15. a. $Q = 155,928.59, TC = \$2,148.07$; b. $Q = 105,640.9, TC = \$3,169.23$
17. $Q = 5,000; TC = \$67,175$
19. $Q = 500$
21. $Q = 6,000; TC = \$87,030.33$
23. $Q = 20,000; TC \$893,368$
25. $R = 20,410.30$; safety stock $= 2,410.29$ yd
27. $R = 66,305,216$
29. $R = 254.4, R = 295.8$
31. $R = 24.38$
33. $Q = 125$; 120 pizzas

SUPPLEMENT 12

1. b. $\mu = 3.48, EV = 3.65$, not enough simulations; c. 21 calls, no, repeat simulation
3. $\mu = \$250$
5. reorder at 5-car level
7. avg. waiting time $= 22$ min

CHAPTER 13

1. a. 6; b. 7; c. 3
13. Release orders for 100 armature housings in period 1; 100 armatures in period 2; 400 magnetic brushes in period 3; 400 longitudinal bolts in period 4; 50 pully as-

semblies and 200 SA 110 is in period 5; 300 SA 310's, 300 front covers, 200 rear covers, and 300 SA 210's in period 6; 750 contact wires in period 7; 320 SA 410's in period 8; and 400 alternators in period 9.
15. b. normal capacity of 250 hours for machining, 500 hours for heat treat, and 60 hours for assembly. Overtime is also required for assembly.
17. a. Load percent: 84.8%, 170%, 295%, 254% at welding; 80%, 160%, 320%, 240% at assembly; b. 34, 68, 136, 102 hours at welding; 32, 64, 128, 96 hours at assembly; c. 30, 59, 118, 89 hours at welding; 27, 54, 108, 81 hours at assembly

CHAPTER 14

1. Jones to Nurse 1, Hathaway to Nurse 2, Sweeney to Nurse 3, Bryant to Nurse 4
3. Product 1 to machine B, product 2 to machine D, product 3 to machine A, product 4 to machine C, product 5 to machine E
5. DDATE or SPT
7. SPT
9. 6, 5, 4, 2, 1, 3; 5 hr 35 min
11. SPT
13. Backlog 0, 0, 0, 0, 0
15. One worker does not have two consecutive work days.

CHAPTER 15

1. A − B − A − C
3. 4
5. 126/hr
7. b; decreases
9. a. 9 Kanbans, inventory up by 25 units; b. 3 Kanbans, inventory halved; c. 14 Kanbans, no change in inventory

CHAPTER 16

1. $L_q = 1.02$, $W_q = 4.61$ min; not good service
3. a. $L_q = 0.9$, $W = 0.25$ hr, $W_q = 0.15$ hr; b. $\lambda > \mu$
5. $\lambda = 9$/hr
7. yes
9. a. $L_q = 9.09$ trucks, $W = 0.05$ days, $W_q = 0.045$ days; b. yes
11. $L = 1.19$, $L_q = 0.26$, $W = 0.043$ hr, $W_q = 0.009$ hr; yes
13. Yes, assign an operator
15. $P_o = .007$, $L = 6.545$, $L_q = 1.821$, $W_q = .547$, $W = 1.96$
17. Yes, hire a third doctor
19. 3 servers should be sufficient
21. Add additional employees; expected savings = $25.50/day
23. $L_q = 1.13$, $W_q = 0.112$ hr
25. $P_{n \geq 31} = 0.281$
27. 7:00 A.M. − 9:00 A.M. = 5, 9:00 A.M. − noon = 2, noon − 2:00 P.M. = 6, 2:00 P.M. − 5:00 P.M. = 4
29. $L = .3755$ cars out of service, $W = 23.6778$ hr
31. Select new service agreement, savings = $1,813.50

CHAPTER 17

1. Time = 10 weeks
3. a. 23 wks; $s_{12} = 0$, $s_{13} = 1$, $s_{24} = 0$, $s_{25} = 10$, $s_{35} = 1$, $s_{45} = 0$, $s_{46} = 9$, $s_{56} = 0$, $s_{36} = 11$; b. 1-2-4-5-6
5. 1-2: ES = 0, EF = 7, LS = 2, LF = 9, S = 2; 1-3: ES = 0, EF = 10, LS = 0, LF = 10, S = 0; 2-4: ES = 7, EF = 13, LS = 9, LF = 15, S = 2; 3-4: ES = 10, EF = 15, LS = 10, LF = 15, S = 0; 3-5: ES = 10, EF = 14, LS = 14, LF = 18, S = 4; 4-5: ES = 15, EF = 18, LS = 15, LF = 18, S = 0; 5-6: ES = 18, EF = 20, LS = 18, LF = 20, S = 0; CP = 1-3-4-5-6
7. 1-2: ES = 0, EF = 10, LS = 0, LF = 10, S = 0; 1-3: ES = 0, EF = 7, LS = 5, LF = 12, S = 5; 2-4: ES = 10, EF = 14, LS = 14, LF = 18, S = 4; 2-6: ES = 10, EF = 25, LS = 10, LF = 25, S = 0; 3-4: ES = 7, EF = 13, LS = 12, LF = 18, S = 5; 3-5: ES = 17, EF = 19, LS = 13; LF = 25, S = 6; 4-6: ES = 14, EF = 21, LS = 18, LF = 25, S = 4; 5-6: ES = 19, EF = 19, LS = 25, LF = 25, S = 6; 6-7: ES = 25, EF = 34, LS = 25, LF = 34, S = 0; CP = 1-2-6-7 = 34
9. CP = 1-2-3-5-6-8-9-10 = 15 days
11. CP = a-b-dummy-f-h = 15 wk
13. CP = a-d-g-dummy-k = 33 wk, $\sigma = 3.87$, $P(x \le 40) = .9649$
15. CP = 1-2-3-5-6-8-9-10 = 18 days
17. c. CP = b-f-dummy-j-k; d. 28.17 wk; e. 0.0113
19. 57.37 days; $P(x \le 67) = .9535$
21. CP = a-c-d-h-l-o-q = 118.67; $P(x \le 120) = .59$
23. crash cost = $25,300
25. CP = 1-2-4-5-8-9, crashing cost = $5,100

Index